D0772596

A SELECT LIBRARY

OF THE

NICENE AND POST-NICENE FATHERS

OF

THE CHRISTIAN CHURCH

EDITED BY

PHILIP SCHAFF, D.D., LL.D.,

PROFESSOR OF CHURCH HISTORY IN THE UNION THEOLOGICAL SEMINARY, NEW YORK

IN CONNECTION WITH A NUMBER OF PATRISTIC SCHOLARS OF EUROPE
AND AMERICA

VOLUME X

SAINT CHRYSOSTOM:

HOMILIES ON THE GOSPEL OF SAINT MATTHEW

WM. B. EERDMANS PUBLISHING COMPANY
GRAND RAPIDS   MICHIGAN

Reprinted, June 1975

ISBN 0-8028-8108-4

PHOTOLITHOPRINTED BY CUSHING - MALLOY, INC.
ANN ARBOR, MICHIGAN, UNITED STATES OF AMERICA

PREFACE TO THE AMERICAN EDITION.

THIS volume, according to the previous announcement of the publishers, contains a reprint of the Oxford edition of the Homilies of St. Chrysostom on the Gospel of St. Matthew.

The Homilies on this Gospel formed three volumes of the Oxford edition, published respectively in 1843, 1844 and 1851. The dedication appears in the third volume, as a memorial of Archbishop Howley, who died in 1848. The preface is from the pen of Charles Marriott of Oriel College.

As regards the present volume, it may be remarked that the archaic style of the English translation has been preserved without material alteration. Even when obscure and involved, the form seemed to be a fitting dress for the original. Occasionally an emendation, or rather suggestion, has been made in a foot-note by the American editor. The spelling has been altered throughout by the printer, to accord with the usage more common among us. Some obvious typographical errors have been corrected, and these have usually been indicated. Instead of the brackets, used in the Oxford edition, to mark words or phrases supplied by the translator, *Italics* have been substituted. The same remark applies to passages where the Greek text is in doubt. The editor has felt at liberty to indicate more fully than the translator the portions supplied by the latter. In a few cases an emphatic word is printed in Italics, but these instances can be readily distinguished from the passages above referred to.

The English translator of these Homilies was fortunate in having the Greek text of Mr. Frederick Field as the basis of his renderings. This text is also accessible in the edition of Migne, and has been compared throughout in the preparation of this volume. At the time when the Oxford edition appeared textual criticism had received but slight attention in England; hence the translator seems to have occasionally failed to estimate aright the value of the authorities for various readings. But in few patristic works do we have better security for the accuracy of the text than in the case of these Homilies on Matthew. The labor of the American editor has been, of course, supplementary. Attention has been called quite frequently to the Greek phrase used in the Homily, with a view to marking the usage in Ecclesiastical Greek. Many foot-notes have been added, to indicate the readings of the New Testament text appearing in the Homilies. The constant use of the Authorized

Version by the translator made this necessary. The Greek phrase has frequently been given; still more frequently the rendering (and reading) of the Revised version. Where these agree with the text of the Homily, they are cited, without comment, in brackets. Differences between readings are carefully indicated.

Occasionally the editor has noted his dissent from the renderings or annotations of the translator, but he has not felt warranted in expressing every difference of judgment. All additions made in this volume are enclosed in brackets, and except in the cases where the Revised Version is cited without comment, the letter R. has been appended.

Much time and care have been bestowed upon the Indexes.

M. B. R.

ALLEGHENY, PA., Sept. 24, 1888.

CONTENTS.

THE HOMILIES

OF

ST. JOHN CHRYSOSTOM,

ARCHBISHOP OF CONSTANTINOPLE,

ON THE

GOSPEL OF ST. MATTHEW.

TRANSLATED BY

REV. SIR GEORGE PREVOST, BARONET, M.A.,

OF ORIEL COLLEGE, OXFORD.

REVISED, WITH NOTES, BY

REV. M. B. RIDDLE, D.D.,

PROFESSOR OF NEW TESTAMENT EXEGESIS IN THE WESTERN THEOLOGICAL
SEMINARY AT ALLEGHENY, PA.

PREFACE TO THE OXFORD EDITION.

THE Homilies of St. Chrysostom on St. Matthew were undoubtedly delivered at Antioch (see Hom. vii. p. 43) and probably in the latter part of the time during which he preached as a Presbyter. Montfaucon considers his little mention of the sin of swearing a sign of his having accomplished some reformation on that point by his previous exertions. In the Homilies delivered from 386 to 388, it is a constant topic; and the Homilies known to belong to that date are so numerous, as scarcely to leave room for such a series as the present. These, however, contain very little to mark the period to which they belong. The argument from his reference to dissensions some time gone by, possibly those between St. Meletius and Paulinus and Evagrius, in commenting on St. Matt. xxiii. 6. is not very conclusive.

A modern reader must sometimes be struck with finding in St. Chrysostom a kind of criticism, which we are apt to think belongs only to later times. His main object, however, is moral, and he searches out with diligence both the meaning and the applications of particular passages, usually concluding with an eloquent exhortation to some special virtue. Some of the most remarkable of these exhortations are on the subject of Alms-giving, which he seems to have pressed with success at last. His calculation in Hom. lxvi. as to what might be done, is somewhat curious. In the end of Hom. lxxxviii. he demands a reformation as the condition of his entering on the controversy with Infidels. In the next Homily he discusses the evidence of the Resurrection with nearly the same arguments as would still be used against an objector.

The Theatres are the theme of his frequent reprobation, and the Monks of the mountains near Antioch of his praise. In Hom. lxix. and lxx. he describes their mode of life as an edifying example to all. He frequently attacks the Anomœan or extreme Arian Heresy, and sometimes also the Manichean. It is perhaps worth while to recollect the nearly contemporaneous prevalence of Manicheism in the West, as it appears in the early history of St. Augustine. In Hom. lxxxvi. there are some remarks on the device of Satan by which evil is introduced by little and little, which are worthy of consideration as applicable to the growth of erroneous doctrine and practice within the Church.

For all information with respect to the Text and Manuscripts of these Homilies, the learned reader is referred to the Greek Edition of Mr. Field, which has been of great service, as affording a safe basis for the Translation. The paucity of materials possessed by Savile, and the carelessness of the Benedictine Editor, had left much room for improvement by a judicious and faithful use of the existing copies. It may now at last be hoped, that we have a Text very closely approximating to the genuine work of the Author.

For the Translation, the Editors are indebted to the REV. SIR GEORGE PREVOST, M.A. of Oriel College, and for the Index to the Rev. J. E. TWEED, M.A. of Christ Church, Oxford. It will be their endeavour to complete the Commentaries of St. Chrysostom on the New Testament, by bringing out the remainder of the Homilies on the Acts of the Apostles, and those on the Epistle to the Hebrews, as soon as they are able. In both instances, however, the corrupt state of the Text has occasioned some difficulty and delay.

C. MARRIOTT.

Oxford, Advent, 1851.

CONTENTS OF THE HOMILIES.

INTRODUCTORY ESSAY.

ST. CHRYSOSTOM AS AN EXEGETE.

BY M. B. RIDDLE, D.D.

THE pre-eminence of Chrysostom as a preacher remains undisputed, despite the many reversals of judgment that have resulted from modern historical investigations; no voice has been raised against the popular verdict, repeated in every age, that awards to him the first place among pulpit orators in the Eastern Church.

Nor has there been any serious difference of opinion in regard to his personal character. His intense moral earnestness has always been recognized, and the man has been honored because it was distinctly felt that the man gave power to the oration. "Golden mouth" avails little, unless it belongs to a golden man. The rhetorical training of his earlier years doubtless contributed much to his skill as a preacher, but his exegetical method was perhaps a still more important factor.

I. THE PLACE OF CHRYSOSTOM IN THE HISTORY OF EXEGESIS.

The position held by Chrysostom in the history of exegesis is remarkable. Owing to a peculiar combination of circumstances he, more than any of the Fathers, was enabled to avoid the errors alike of the allegorizing and dogmatic tendencies. The former tendency was the prevalent one in the Christian Church in the Ante-Nicene period; the latter, especially in the West, became dominant during the Post-Nicene period, using for its own ends the earlier erroneous theory. Chrysostom represents the Antiochian reaction against the allegorizing method, while he ante-dates by a generation, at least, the time when the ecclesiastical or dogmatic theory became overpowering in its influence. This historical position must be recognized in estimating his character as an exegete, as well as in accounting for his eminence as an interpreter of Scripture. Modern scholarship with comparative unanimity accords to him this eminence. It is true that one is disposed to dissent from this judgment on first reading the Homilies of Chrysostom. Trained in our modern exegetical methods the reader may unconsciously compare the expositions of the Greek Father with those of Luther and Calvin, if not with those of Meyer and Weiss. Such a comparison is of course an anachronism. A study of other patristic exegetes must lead to an endorsement of the prevalent opinion as to the merits of Chrysostom as an expositor. An immense mass of homiletical literature of which he was the author has been preserved, and of course reveals very unequal results. Marks of carelessness, especially in citation, abound; the habits of the "practical preacher" often leads to long digressions, to elaboration of matters that at best hold only the relation of a tangent to the truth of the text. Yet less than most pulpit orators does Chrysostom warp the interpretation itself to suit his homiletical purpose. Occasionally vehement invective occurs when an exegetical difficulty is encountered, and it is easy to suppose that unconsciously the former has been used to cover up the latter. But there are few evidences of lack of candor in the treatment of such difficulties. It must be confessed that Chrysostom is not always true to his own principles of interpretation, yet these instances of inconsistency are usually due to a desire to enforce an ethical lesson pertinent to the occasion, even though the application was scarcely pertinent to the text. Owing to his ignorance of Hebrew, Chrysostom was not properly equipped for the work of expounding the Old Testament. He treats the LXX. as though it were of final authority, save in a few instances where the variations of other Greek versions have occasioned discussion. Frequently he makes use of verbal suggestions of the Greek that have no warrant in the Hebrew text. Yet, where he is not thus misled, his comments on the Old Testament present the same characteristics as those on the New.

The most marked peculiarity of Chrysostom as an exegete is his comparative freedom from the allegorizing tendency that prevailed in the early Christian centuries. In contending with the Jews, the Christian apologists, from Justin Martyr onward, had inevitably followed to some extent the methods of their opponents. The Jewish schools of interpreters, both at Alexandria and in Palestine, while somewhat antagonistic to each other, had in common this allegorizing habit. Argument about the meaning of the Old Testament necessarily fostered a similar tendency among Christian writers. Moreover, the Christian authors of the second and third centuries were not men of pre-eminent talent or acquirements. The victory won by the church was ethical rather than intellectual. Then, as now, profound piety, when not combined with accurate knowledge and mental acumen, delighted in mystical fancies. Types could be invented far more easily than texts could be investigated. At length this tendency found in Origen an advocate who had the ability to formulate its principles, and also the learning and industry necessary to illustrate the method by copious comments of his own. *Facile princeps* as a mystical interpreter, Origen's influence is still felt, and in his own age it was dominant in exegesis. It is true the dogmatic principle was already gaining the mastery, yet both the Orthodox and their opponents made use of allegory: the former combined the two tendencies, the latter placed them in antagonism. Curiously enough the doctrinal controversy that arose in consequence of some of Origen's views was made the occasion of an attack upon Chrysostom, and the kindness he showed to certain Egyptian monks, who were followers of Origen, became the pretext for those harsh measures which resulted in his banishment and death.[1] Yet Chrysostom, in his writings, shows no sympathy with the philosophic speculations of Origen, and his method as an exegete is far removed from that implied in the principles laid down by the latter. The great preacher never dishonors the literal, or historical, sense of Scripture, and though he occasionally refers to interpretations κατὰ ἀναγωγήν, using the phrase applied by Origen to the mystical sense of passages, these are never exalted above the plain meaning of the words of the text. No one living in the age of Chrysostom could be a diligent student of the Bible and ignore the labors of Origen. Despite his advocacy of the mystical theory and his excessive speculative tendency he had done more for exegetical theology than any of his predecessors. In these days we owe him too much to forget these services. The wonder is that Chrysostom, familiar with his writings, was so little influenced by the erroneous hermeneutical principles he advocated and exemplified. The earnest practical purpose of Chrysostom did much in preserving him from allegorizing, but his training of Antioch under Diodorus, afterwards bishop of Tarsus, was probably still more influential for good. Diodorus is reckoned the leader of the so-called Antiochian school of exegetes.

---

[1] See STEPHENS, *Life of St. Chrysostom*, pp. 286-326 ; SCHAFF, *History of the Christian Church*, vol. III., pp. 702 et seq.

He was the first to oppose directly the false methods of Origen. It is true "the three. Cappadocians," Basil the Great, his brother Gregory of Nyssa, and his friend Gregory Nazianzen, had but a qualified admiration for the exegetical results attained by Origen, though diligent in their use of his writings. The conflicts of the period interfered, however, with any decided hermeneutical advance; the dogmatic interest of the Arian controversy still overshadowing all other theological movements. Diodorus († 394) was president of a monastery in the vicinity of Antioch. Under his guidance Chrysostom and his friend Basil pursued a semi-monastic life of seclusion and study for nearly six years (ending in A. D. 381). Theodore, who was afterwards bishop of Mopsuestia, and the father of the Nestorian theology, was also his friend and fellow-student. While Diodorus was not free from rationalizing tendencies, he undoubtedly represents a healthy re-action toward the historico-exegetical theory of interpretation. His writings and his influence on his two most distinguished pupils, Chrysostom and Theodore, plainly prove this. " The practical element in Diodorus, his method of literal and common-sense interpretation of Holy Scripture, was inherited chiefly by Chrysostom; the intellectual vein, his conceptions of the relation between the Godhead and Manhood in Christ, his opinions respecting the final restoration of mankind, which were almost equivalent to a denial of eternal punishment, were reproduced mainly by Theodore." [1]

While the influence of the Antiochian school seems transient, it has achieved much in stating more clearly the correct principles of interpretation; it has achieved still more in preparing for his work the greatest preacher of the Greek church. Avoiding to a great extent the extremes of both Origen and Diodorus, Chrysostom as an interpreter is probably nearer to us than any Father of the Eastern Church. A careful study of his Homilies must lead to that conviction. " He set forth the verbal meaning with constant attention to the course of thought, and connected therewith, in harmony with the form which he had chosen, the religious and moral observations which were founded directly on the text. Dogmatic and polemic digressions were not necessarily excluded, but were never made the principal thing, and the more or less frequently inserted allegorical additions appear rather as rhetorical ornament and deference to custom than as something necessary to the expositor." [2]

The doctrinal views of Chrysostom were positive and usually well defined. He does not fail to oppose heretical opinions. So great a preacher could not be without a theology. Yet, as already intimated, the dogmatic principle of interpretation does not dominate his exegesis to any great extent.

It thus appears that, whatever may be defects in his expositions, however faulty his comments may seem to us, Chrysostom stands as the representative of more correct principles than any of the early Fathers. That his eminence as a preacher is due to this fact can scarcely be doubted. A new interest in his writings would serve to emphasize the importance of adherence to the historico-exegetical method of interpretation. Great pulpit orators do not need to indulge in mystical fancies, nor does their true power arise from dogmatic warping of the sense of Scripture.

II. Extent and Character of Chrysostom's Exegetical Labors.

1. The exegetical labors of Chrysostom are embodied in his Homilies, of which more than six hundred have been preserved. These are for the most part expository in their character, usually forming a continuous series upon some book of Scripture. The parts of

[1] STEPHENS St. Chrysostom, p. 31; comp. pp. 27-32, on Diodorus. On the Antiochian School, see SCHAFF, Church History, III. pp. 935-7; REUSS History of the New Testament, II., pp. 542-6, American edition.
[2] REUSS, History New Testament, p. 544, American edition.

the Bible thus treated are: in the Old Testament, Genesis and the Book of Psalms; in the New Testament, all the books except the gospels of Mark and Luke, the Catholic Epistles and Revelation. "Commentaries, properly so-called, he wrote only on the first eight chapters of Isaiah and on the Epistle to the Galatians" (Schaff[1]). Most of the Homilies were preserved by short-hand reports, but some were published by Chrysostom himself.[2] There are internal evidences that in many cases the spoken discourse had not been previously written, e. g., the rebuke of applause and of inattention on account of some distracting incident. Previous study is equally manifest in the expository portions; but the method of delivery as well as the method of preservation must modify our judgment of the preacher's exegetical accuracy. Probably many of the inconsistencies and inexact citations, noticeable in the Homilies, are due to one or the other of these causes.

From an exegetical point of view the Homilies on the Old Testament rank lowest, those on the Pauline Epistles highest. The reasons for this are easily discovered. For the exposition of the Old Testament Chrysostom did not have the necessary equipment, being ignorant of Hebrew. In explaining the Gospels he fails to discuss the historical questions with fullness. This was owing no doubt to his distinct homiletical purpose. For the same reason he passes over most of the harmonistic questions, or answers them indefinitely. But in expounding our Lord's longer discourses the same qualities as an interpreter which fitted him so well for explaining the Pauline Epistles enable him to rise to his full eminence.

2. In all the Homilies there is apparent a proper conception of the relation of the Old Testament and the New. Chrysostom's treatment of the two parts of revelation agrees in many respects with the methods now generally accepted in the subdivision of Exegetical Theology technically termed Biblical Theology. He recognizes the progressive movement; thus holding to the essential unity of Scripture, but also admitting the incompleteness of the Old Testament and the superiority of the New. The distinction between the two is never regarded as an antagonism. Indeed some of the severest utterances in the Homilies is in opposition to the error that denies the authority of the Old Testament as a revelation from the Father of our Lord Jesus Christ. But the unity of the two parts of Scripture are not maintained at the expense of the historical sense of the Old Testament. While Chrysostom finds in the older revelation a prophecy of Christ who was to come, " he fails not also to point out the moral aspect of prophecy as a system of teaching rather than prediction, as preparatory to the advent of Jesus Christ in the flesh, not only by informing men's minds, but disciplining their hearts to receive Him. "[3] Probably the absence of any polemical purpose against the Jews aided him in attaining a position more correct than most of some of the earlier Fathers. His view of the relation of Christ to the law is set forth in Homily XVI. on Matthew.[4] In his view of inspiration Chrysostom recognized the Divine-human character of the Scriptures. While he does not formally state his theory, the method he adopts implies the value of each and every part of the Bible, the importance of marking the sense of every word. But the mechanical theory is nowhere suggested: it is in fact opposed by his statements regarding the variations in the Gospels.[5] Indeed no one could be such an expositor as Chrysostom was without an acceptance alike of the Divine authority and human authorship of the Scriptures. These not in antithesis, but in synthesis. Denying the former, there could have been no such power in preaching; ignoring the latter, there would have been no such care in his comments. This view of the Bible was the result of his profound and constant study of it. The same study gave him the

---

[1] *History of the Christian Church*, III., p. 939.

[2] STEPHENS, *St. Chrysostom*, p. 427. He refers to TILLEMONT, *Memoires*, vol. xi., p. 37.

[3] STEPHENS, pp. 423-4.

[4] See pp. 103, etc., in this volume.

[5] See p. 3, in this volume.

wealth of Scriptural illustration and suggestion so noticeable in his Homilies. Knowledge of the whole Bible and love of the whole Bible are manifest everywhere.

3. In textual criticism Chrysostom does not afford us the help that might be expected from the extent of his labors. Origen is incomparably more useful to the textual critic. Even in citing the LXX. many inaccuracies occur, and the Hebrew text is ignored, except in a few cases where doctrinal discussion had arisen.[1]

As Westcott and Hort have shown,[2] the Syrian text of the New Testament had become dominant in the Eastern church about A. D. 350. It held in the time of Chrysostom very much the same position afterwards allowed to the received text during the seventeenth and eighteenth centuries. Accordingly we find few indications of any critical investigations of the text, and the variations from the Syrian text in the Homilies are neither numerous nor important. Yet the differences from the received text of our day are worth noticing.[3] In all such matters, however, there enter several elements of uncertainty, combining to subtract from the value of the Homilies for critical purposes.[4] In the case of Chrysostom we know that the Homilies were taken down by others. Hence we are not sure how accurately the preacher made his citations, how correctly they were reported, nor how much of change has been made by copyists in the interest of conformity to the text prevalent at the time of transcription. Quite frequently the same passage occurs in two forms within the limits of the same Homily. The labors of Mr. Field on the Greek text of Chrysostom show how much remains to be done before we can cite this Father as a trustworthy witness in regard to the minor variations of the New Testament text. Fortunately Tischendorf, who had access to a very ancient codex of the Homilies on Matthew,[5] has given the results of his collation in his painstaking way. As this codex was not included in the *apparatus criticus* of Mr. Field, the supplementary value of Tischendorf's citations is increased.

Some peculiar readings occur in the Homilies on Matthew; the most remarkable is, however, a reading of Luke ix. 31. In Homily LVI. 3 (p. 346 of this volume), Chrysostom expressly reads δόξαν for ἔξοδον, commenting upon the word. It seems altogether probable that there was no such reading prevalent in his day, but that the word δόξῃ, which stands immediately before in Luke ix. 31, was accidentally substituted for ἔξοδον. This might happen from a slip of the memory on the part of Chrysostom, or some scribe might have made the blunder in an isolated copy used by the preacher. In other respects Chrysostom is a witness for the prevalence of the Antiochian or Syrian text, from which our received text has descended. He ignores the pericope of the woman taken in adultery (John vii. 53, viii. 11), as do all the Greek Fathers before the eighth century.

The minor variations do not fully appear in the Oxford translation, owing to the habit of using the text of the Authorized Version, even when its differences from the text of Chrysostom were quite obvious. Accordingly the emendations of the Revised Version have been given, without comment, in the additional foot-notes to this volume, wherever that Version represents more accurately the readings in the Homilies.

4. As already intimated, Chrysostom's ignorance of Hebrew detracts from his trustworthiness as an Old Testament expositor. In the New Testament he is much superior. Yet even here he is open to criticism. Besides an occasional allegorizing comment, he shows much inaccuracy, sometimes inconsistency, in dealing with the historical questions that arise in connection with the Gospel History. He seems to have no taste for the dis-

---

[1] See, for example, on p. 32, where the pre-eminence of the LXX. version is asserted, in the discussion of Isa. viii. 3.

[2] WESTCOTT AND HORT, *Greek Testament*, vol. ii. pp. 135-143.

[3] In this volume most of the variations from the received text are indicated in the additional foot-notes.

[4] On the untrustworthiness of patristic citations, see SCRIVENER, *Introduction to Criticism of New Testament*, 3d ed., pp. 416-7. The labor bestowed on the present volume enables the editor to endorse, *con amore*, the judgment of Mr. Scrivener.

[5] The codex is of the sixth century (Wolfenbüttel), designated in Tischendorf's notes as Chr^gue. See SCRIVENER, *Introduction*, etc., p. 419.

cussion of such questions.   Augustin shows far more judgment in his treatment of these problems.   But the ethical purpose probably debarred Chrysostom from such investigations.   As regards the length of our Lord's ministry, the vexed question of our Lord's brethren, the identity of Mary Magdalene and the woman who was a sinner, etc., we derive little satisfaction from these Homilies.   Occasionally topographical and archæological topics are referred to in terms that are misleading or positively erroneous.   Hence the Homilies on the Gospels are usually estimated as less valuable than those on the Epistles.

But where the exegesis deals with the human heart, its motives, its weakness, or with the grace and love of Jesus Christ, there Chrysostom rises, and remains "the Master in Israel."   Few have made advances beyond him in commenting upon the parables, the miracles of healing, the great discourses of our Lord.   His sturdy common sense enabled him to expound the great eschatological discourse (Mat. xxiv., xxv.) in a manner so free from chiliastic extravagance, that to-day his exposition can be used with little alteration.

These characteristics of his exegesis fitted Chrysostom to excel in his exposition of the Epistles.   Here there is more of continuated and logical method than in the Homilies on the Gospels.   Each Epistle he is careful to consider "as a connected whole; and, in order to impress this on his hearers, he frequently recapitulates at the beginning of a Homily all the steps by which the part under consideration has been reached.   In his introduction to each letter he generally makes useful observations on the author, the time, place, and style of composition, the readers for whom it was intended, the general character and arrangement of its contents." [1]   The Pauline authorship of the Epistle to the Hebrews is accepted in all the references to that book which occur in the Homilies or other portions of Scripture.

The doctrinal positions of Chrysostom naturally influence his explanations of certain portions of the Epistle, but these are to be judged by the stage of development attained by the theology of the Eastern Church in the Post-Nicene period.

The minute attention necessary in editing this volume has compelled the writer to note the excellence of the great Greek Father as an exegete.   Beginning the task with some prejudice, mainly due to a knowledge of the inaccuracy of Chrysostom's citations, he now gladly pays his humble tribute to the genius of the author, hoping that students of the volume will be enabled to echo the praises that for so many centuries have been bestowed upon John of the Golden Mouth.

---

[1] STEPHENS, *St. Chrysostom*, p. 425.

HOMILIES OF ST. JOHN CHRYSOSTOM,

ARCHBISHOP OF CONSTANTINOPLE,

ON THE

GOSPEL ACCORDING TO ST. MATTHEW

HOMILY I.

It were indeed meet for us not at all to require [1] the aid of the written Word, but to exhibit a life so pure, that the grace of the Spirit should be instead of books to our souls, and that as these are inscribed with ink, even so should our hearts be with the Spirit. But, since we have utterly put away from us this grace, come, let us at any rate embrace the second best course.

For that the former was better, God hath made manifest,[2] both by His words, and by His doings. Since unto Noah, and unto Abraham, and unto his offspring, and unto Job, and unto Moses too, He discoursed not by writings, but Himself by Himself, finding their mind pure. But after the whole people of the Hebrews had fallen into the very pit of wickedness, then and thereafter was a written word, and tables, and the admonition which is given by these.

And this one may perceive was the case, not of the saints in the Old Testament only, but also of those in the New. For neither to the apostles did God give anything in writing, but instead of written words He promised that He would give them the grace of the Spirit: for "He," saith our Lord, "shall bring all things to your remembrance."[3] And that thou mayest learn that this was far bet-

ter, hear what He saith by the Prophet: "I will make a new covenant with you, putting my laws into their mind, and in their heart I will write them," and, "they shall be all taught of God."[4] And Paul too, pointing out the same superiority, said, that they had received a law "not in tables of stone, but in fleshy tables of the heart."[5]

But since in process of time they made shipwreck, some with regard to doctrines, others as to life and manners, there was again need that they should be put in remembrance by the written word.

2. Reflect then how great an evil it is for us, who ought to live so purely as not even to need written words, but to yield up our hearts, as books, to the Spirit; now that we have lost that honor, and are come to have need of these, to fail again in duly employing even this second remedy. For if it be a blame to stand in need of written words, and not to have brought down on ourselves the grace of the Spirit; consider how heavy the charge of not choosing to profit even after this assistance, but rather treating what is written with neglect, as if it were cast forth without purpose, and at random, and so bringing down upon ourselves our punishment with increase.[6]

But that no such effect may ensue, let us

---

1 [μηδὲ δεῖσθαι, " not even to need," as below in sec. 2.--R.]
2 [ἐδήλωσεν, " made evident, showed." The translator very frequently renders the aorist by the English perfect. Attention will be called to some instances, where the sense is affected by such renderings.—R.]
3 John xiv. 26.

4 Jerem. xxxi. 31-33 ; Is. liv. 13 ; Heb. viii. 8-11 ; John vi. 45.
5 2 Cor. iii. 3. [The text here agrees with the Rec., not with the oldest mss., followed in the R. V.—R.]
6 [Literally, " the punishment that is greater."—R.]

give strict heed unto the things that are written; and let us learn how the Old Law was given on the one hand, how on the other the New Covenant.

3. How then was that law given in time past, and when, and where? After the destruction of the Egyptians, in the wilderness, on Mount Sinai, when smoke and fire were rising up out of the mountain, a trumpet sounding, thunders and lightnings, and Moses entering into the very depth of the cloud.[1] But in the new covenant not so,—neither in a wilderness, nor in a mountain, nor with smoke and darkness and cloud and tempest; but at the beginning of the day, in a house, while all were sitting together, with great quietness, all took place. For to those, being more unreasonable, and hard to guide, there was need of outward pomp,[2] as of a wilderness, a mountain, a smoke, a sound of trumpet, and the other like things: but they who were of a higher character, and submissive, and who had risen above mere corporeal imaginations,[3] required none of these. And if even in their case there was a sound, it was not for the sake of the apostles, but for the Jews, who were present, on whose account also the tongues of fire appeared. For if, even after this, some said, "they are filled with new wine,"[4] much more would they have said so, had they seen none of these things.

And in the Old Testament, it was upon Moses' going up, that God came down; but here, when our nature hath been carried up into Heaven, or rather unto the royal throne, then the Spirit makes His descent.

Now had the Spirit been an inferior being,[5] the results would not have been greater and more wonderful. For indeed these tables are far better, and the achievements more illustrious. Since the apostles came not down from a mountain, as Moses, bearing monuments of stone in their hands, but carrying about the Spirit in their mind, and pouring forth a kind of treasure and fountain of doctrines and of gifts and of all things that are good, so they went everywhere around, and became, through that grace, living books and laws. Thus they won over "the three thousand," thus "the five thousand,"[6] thus the nations of the world; God, by their tongue, discoursing with all that approached them.

4. By whom Matthew also, being filled with the Spirit, wrote, what he did write:—Matthew the Publican, for I am not ashamed to name him by his trade, neither him nor the others. For this in a very special way indicates both the grace of the Spirit, and their virtue.

And He hath properly called His work by a name (which signifies) good tidings.[7] Yea, for it was removal of punishment, and remission of sins, and "righteousness, and sanctification, and redemption,"[8] and adoption, and an inheritance of Heaven, and a relationship unto the Son of God, which he came declaring unto all; to enemies, to the perverse, to them that were sitting in darkness. What then could ever be equal to these good tidings? God on earth, man in Heaven; and all became mingled together, angels joined the choirs of men, men had fellowship with the angels, and with the other powers above: and one might see the long war brought to an end, and reconciliation made between God and our nature,[9] the devil brought to shame, demons in flight, death destroyed, Paradise opened, the curse blotted out, sin put out of the way, error driven off, truth returning, the word of godliness everywhere sown, and flourishing in its growth, the polity of those above planted on the earth, those powers in secure intercourse with us, and on earth angels continually haunting, and hope abundant touching things to come.

Therefore he hath called the history good tidings, forasmuch as all other things surely are words only without substance; as, for instance, plenty of wealth, greatness of power, kingdoms, and glories, and honors, and whatever other things among men are accounted to be good: but those which are published by the fishermen would be legitimately and properly called good tidings: not only as being sure and immoveable blessings, and beyond our deserts, but also as being given to us with all facility.

For not by laboring and sweating, not by fatigue and suffering, but merely as being beloved of God, we received what we have received.

5. And why can it have been, that when there were so many disciples, two write only from among the apostles, and two from among their followers? (For one that was a disciple of Paul, and another of Peter, together with Matthew and John, wrote the Gospels.) It was because they did nothing for vainglory, but all things for use.

---

[1] [Literally, "the very cloud."—R.]
[2] σωματικῆς φαντασίας.   [3] τὴν τῶν σωμάτων ἔννοιαν.
[4] Acts ii. 13.
[5] Alluding to the blasphemy of the Macedonians, so often referred to by St. Chrysostom.
[6] Acts ii. 41; and iv. 4.

[7] [Literally, "And he properly called his work good tidings" (εὐαγγέλιον).—R.]
[8] [A reminiscence of 1 Cor. i. 30.—R.]
[9] [Literally, "reconciliations of God to our nature." The doctrinal point of view is Pauline: God is reconciled, His anger removed.—R.]

"What then? Was not one evangelist sufficient to tell all?" One indeed was sufficient; but if there be four that write, not at the same times, nor in the same places, neither after having met together, and conversed one with another, and then they speak all things as it were out of one mouth, this becomes a very great demonstration of the truth.[1]

6. "But the contrary," it may be said, "hath come to pass, for in many places they are convicted of discordance." Nay, this very thing is a very great evidence of their truth. For if they had agreed in all things exactly even to time, and place, and to the very words, none of our enemies would have believed but that they had met together, and had written what they wrote by some human compact; because such entire agreement as this cometh not of simplicity. But now even that discordance which seems to exist in little matters delivers them from all suspicion, and speaks clearly in behalf of the character of the writers.

But if there be anything touching times or places, which they have related differently, this nothing[2] injures the truth of what they have said. And these things too, so far as God shall enable us, we will endeavor, as we proceed, to point out; requiring you, together with what we have mentioned, to observe, that in the chief heads, those which constitute our life and furnish out[3] our doctrine, nowhere is any of them found to have disagreed, no not ever so little.

But what are these points? Such as follow: That God became man, that He wrought miracles, that He was crucified, that He was buried, that He rose again, that He ascended, that He will judge, that He hath given commandments tending to salvation, that He hath brought in a law not contrary to the Old Testament, that He is a Son, that He is only-begotten, that He is a true Son, that He is of the same substance with the Father, and as many things as are like these; for touching these we shall find that there is in them a full agreement.

And if amongst the miracles they have not all of them mentioned all, but one these, the other those, let not this trouble thee. For if on the one hand one had spoken of all, the number of the rest would have been superfluous; and if again all had written fresh things, and different one from another, the proof of

their agreement would not have been manifest. For this cause they have both treated of many in common, and each of them hath also received and declared something of his own; that, on the one hand, he might not seem superfluous, and cast on the heap[4] to no purpose; on the other, he might make our test of the truth of their affirmations perfect.[5]

7. Now Luke tells us also the cause wherefore he proceeds to write: "that thou mayest hold," saith he, "the certainty of the words wherein thou hast been instructed;"[6] that is, that being continually reminded thou mayest hold to the certainty,[7] and abide in certainty.

But as to John, he hath himself kept silence touching the cause; yet,[8] (as a tradition[9] saith, which hath come down to us from the first, even from the Fathers,) neither did he come to write without purpose; but forasmuch as it had been the care of the three to dwell upon the account of the dispensation,[10] and the doctrines of the Godhead were near being left in silence, he, moved by Christ, then and not till then set himself to compose his Gospel.[11] And this is manifest both from the history itself, and from the opening of his Gospel. For he doth not begin like the rest from beneath, but from above, from the same point, at which he was aiming, and it was with a view to this that[12] he composed the whole book. And not in the beginning only, but throughout all the Gospel, he is more lofty than the rest.

Of Matthew again it is said,[13] that when those who from amongst the Jews had believed came to him, and besought him to leave to them in writing those same things, which he had spoken to them by word, he also composed his Gospel in the language of the Hebrews. And Mark too, in Egypt,[14] is

---

4 προσερρίφθαι ἁπλῶς.   5 ["accurate."—R.]

6 Luke i. 4.

7 Ἀσφάλεια, "certainty," seems to be used here first *objectively*, as when we say, "a thing is certain," then *subjectively*, as "I am certain of it."

8 [The translator, with the Latin, follows the reading δέ; most MSS. have γάρ, which is the more difficult reading.—R.]

9 So St. Irenæus, iii. 11, 1. "John, the disciple of the Lord, purposing by the publication of a Gospel to take away the error which Cerinthus had sown among men, and long before him those who are called Nicolaitans . . . . thus began the instruction of his Gospel: *In the beginning, &c.*" See also St. Clem. of Alex. in Euseb. E. H. vi. 14; St. Jerome, Pref. to Com. on St. Matth.

10 οἰκονομία, *i.e.*, our Lord's assumption of the Manhood. The word is so used continually by the Fathers.

11 [This paraphrase fairly brings out the sense, but is a very free rendering of the text.—R.]

12 [καὶ διὰ τοῦτο.]

13 Euseb. E. H. iii. 24; St. Jer. de Vir. Ill. 3; Orig. in Matth. t. iii. 440; St. Iren. iii. 1 But St. Chrysostom seems to be quoting the words of some other writer besides these.

14 Or in Rome, before the death of St. Peter, who approved the Gospel. So St. Clem. Alex. in Euseb. E. H. ii. 15; St. Jer. de Vir. Illustr. c. 8. St. Iren. iii. 1, seems rather to agree with St. Chrysostom. Perhaps they may be reconciled by supposing St. Mark's Gospel written at Rome and approved by St. Peter, but not published until after his death, when St. Mark was in Egypt. See Massuet's note on the place in St. Irenæus; and Euseb. ii. 16.

---

1 [The independence of the Gospels is thus emphasized by the most competent exegete of the Nicene period. His treatment of the apparent discrepancies is suggestive.—R.]

2 [That is, "in nothing," in no respect.—R.]

3 συγκροτοῦσιν. [Literally, "weld together," used of organizing a body of soldiers.—R.]

said to have done this self-same thing at the entreaty of the disciples.

For this cause then Matthew, as writing to Hebrews, sought to shew nothing more, than that He was from Abraham, and David; but Luke, as discoursing to all in general, traces up the account higher, going on even to Adam. And the one begins with His generation, because nothing was so soothing to the Jew as to be told that Christ was the offspring of Abraham and David: the other doth not so, but mentions many other things, and then proceeds to the genealogy.

8. But the harmony between them we will establish, both by the whole world, which hath received their statements, and by the very enemies of the truth. For many sects have had birth, since their time, holding opinions opposed to their words; whereof some have received all that they have said, while some have cut off from the rest certain portions of their statements, and so retain them for themselves.[1] But if there were any hostility[2] in their statements, neither would the sects, who maintain the contrary part, have received all, but only so much as seemed to harmonize with themselves; nor would those, which have parted off a portion, be utterly refuted by that portion; so that the very fragments[3] cannot be hid, but declare aloud their connexion[3] with the whole body. And like as if thou shouldest take any part from the side of an animal, even in that part thou wouldest find all the things out of which the whole is composed;—nerves and veins, bones, arteries, and blood, and a sample, as one might say, of the whole lump;—so likewise with regard to the Scriptures; in each portion of what is there stated, one may see the connexion with the whole clearly appearing. Whereas, if they were in discord, neither could this have been pointed out, and the doctrine itself had long since been brought to nought: "for every kingdom," saith He, "divided against itself shall not stand."[4] But now even in this shines forth the might of the Spirit, namely, in that it prevailed on these men, engaged as they were in those things which are more necessary and very urgent, to take no hurt at all from these little matters.

Now, where each one was abiding, when he wrote, it is not right for us to affirm very positively.

But that they are not opposed to each other, this we will endeavor to prove, throughout the whole work. And thou, in accusing them of disagreement, art doing just the same as if thou wert to insist upon their using the same words and forms of speech.

9. And I do not yet say, that those likewise who glory greatly in rhetoric and philosophy, having many of them written many books touching the same matters, have not merely expressed themselves differently, but have even spoken in opposition to one another (for it is one thing to speak differently and another to speak at variance); none of these things do I say. Far be it from me to frame our defense from the frenzy of those men, neither am I willing out of falsehood to make recommendations for the truth.

But this I would be glad to inquire: how were the differing accounts believed? how did they prevail? how was it that, while saying opposite things, they were admired, were believed, were celebrated everywhere in the world?

And yet the witnesses of what they said were many, and many too were the adversaries and enemies thereof. For they did not write these things in one corner and bury them, but everywhere, by sea and by land, they unfolded them in the ears of all, and these things were read in the presence of enemies, even as they are now, and none of the things which they said offended any one. And very naturally. for it was a divine power that pervaded all, and made it to prosper with all men.

10. For if it had not been so, how could the publican, and the fisherman, and the unlearned, have attained to such philosophy?[5] For things, which they that are without have never been able to imagine, no not in a dream, are by these men with great certainty both published and made convincing, and not in their lives only, but even after death: neither to two men, nor twenty men, nor an hundred, nor a thousand, nor ten thousand, but to cities, nations, and people, both to land and sea, in the land both of Greeks and barbarians, both inhabited and desert; and all concerning things far beyond our nature. For leaving the earth, all their discourse is concerning the things in heaven, while they bring in unto us another principle of life, another

---

[1] The Arians, *e.g.* and kindred sects, received all the Scriptures; the Marcionites, besides rejecting the Old Testament received only the Gospel of St. Luke, and ten of St. Paul's epistles: out of which, Tertullian refutes them at large. The Manichæans rejected the Old Testament and the Acts of the Apostles in which latter the Montanists agreed with them. This was besides numerous interpolations which they all alleged in the books which they did receive. See St. Aug. Ep. 237.

[2] [μάχη, the technical term for "contradiction" when applied to statements. See *Sophocles' Greek Lexicon of the Roman and Byzantine periods; sub voce.*—R.]

[3] κόμματα, Gr.   [4] Matt. xii. 25; Mark iii. 24; Luke xi. 17.

[5] [Literally, "philosophize such things." Chrysostom, in common with other and earlier Fathers, uses the terms, φιλοσοφία and φιλοσοφεῖν, in a wide sense. As the translator varies his rendering of these words to suit the context, it seems proper to indicate when Chrysostom uses them.—R]

manner of living: both wealth and poverty, freedom and slavery, life and death, our world and our polity, all changed.

Not like Plato, who composed that ridiculous Republic,[1] or Zeno, or if there be any one else that hath written a polity, or hath framed laws. For indeed, touching all these, it hath been made manifest by themselves, that an evil spirit, and some cruel demon at war with our race, a foe to modesty, and an enemy to good order, oversetting all things, hath made his voice be heard in their soul. When, for example, they make their women common to all, and stripping virgins naked in the Palæstra, bring them into the gaze of men; and when they establish secret marriages, mingling all things together and confounding them, and overturning the limits of nature, what else is there to say? For that these their sayings are all inventions of devils, and contrary to nature, even nature herself would testify, not tolerating what we have mentioned; and this, though they write not amidst persecutions, nor dangers, nor fightings, but in all security and freedom, and deck it out with many ornaments from many sources. But these doctrines of the fishermen, chased as they were, scourged and in jeopardy, both learned and unlearned, both bond and free, both kings and private soldiers, both barbarians and Greeks, have received with all good will.

11. And thou canst not say, that it was because these things were trifling and low, that they were easily to be received by all men: nay, for these doctrines are far higher than those. For as to virginity, they never imagined even the name thereof so much as in a dream, nor yet of voluntary poverty, nor of fasting, nor of any other of those things that are high.

But they that are of our part not only exterminate lust, they chastise not only the act, but even an unchaste look, and insulting language, and disorderly laughter, and dress, and gait, and clamor, and they carry on their exactness even to the smallest things, and have filled the whole earth with the plant of virginity. And touching God too, and the things in heaven, they persuade men to be wise[2] with such knowledge as no one of those hath at any time been able so much as to conceive in his mind. For how could they, who made for gods images of beasts, and of mon-

sters that crawl on the earth, and of other things still more vile?

Yet these high doctrines were both accepted and believed, and they flourish every day and increase; but the others have passed away, and perished, having disappeared more easily than spiders' webs.

And very naturally, for they were demons that published these things; wherefore besides their uncleanness, their obscurity is great, and the labor they require greater. For what could be more ridiculous than that "republic,"[3] in which, besides what I have mentioned, the philosopher, when he hath spent lines without number, that he may be able to shew what justice is, hath over and above this prolixity filled his discourse with much indistinctness? This, even if it did contain anything profitable, must needs be very useless for the life of man. For if the husbandman and the smith, the builder and the pilot, and every one who subsists by the labor of his hands, is to leave his trade, and his honest toils, and is to spend such and such a number of years in order to learn what justice is; before he has learnt he will often times be absolutely destroyed by hunger, and perish because of this justice, not having learnt anything else useful to be known, and having ended his life by a cruel death.

12. But our lessons are not such; rather Christ hath taught[4] us what is just, and what is seemly, and what is expedient, and all virtue in general, comprising it in few and plain words: at one time saying that, "on two commandments hang the Law and the Prophets;[5] that is to say, on the love of God and on the love of our neighbor: at another time, "Whatsoever ye would that men should do to you, do ye also to them; for this is the Law and the Prophets.[6]

And these things even to a laborer, and to a servant, and to a widow woman, and to a very child, and to him that appeareth to be exceedingly slow of understanding, are all plain to comprehend and easy to learn. For the lessons of the truth are like this; and the actual result bears witness thereto. All at least have learned what things they are to do, and not learned only, but been emulous also of them; and not in the cities alone nor in the midst of the market places, but also in the summits of the mountains.

Yea, for there wilt thou see true wisdom[7] abounding, and choirs of angels shining forth in a human body, and the commonwealth[8] of Heaven manifested here on earth. For a

---

[1] [πολιτείαν, as in the latter part of the sentence. This term also is variously rendered by the translator, to suit the context. But in this Homily there is always a reference to Plato's Republic, when the word πολιτεία is used. Hence attention is called to the instances where it occurs.—R.]

[2] [φιλοσοφεῖν. Literally: "to philosophize what no one of them was at any time able even to," etc. The negatives are repeated in the original for greater emphasis.—R.]

[3] [πολιτείας.]　　[4] [ἐδίδαξεν.]　　[5] Matt. xxii. 40.
[6] Matt. vii. 12.　　[7] [φιλοσοφίαν = true wisdom.—R.]
[8] [πολιτεία, in its proper case.]

commonwealth¹ did these fishermen too write for us, not with commands that it should be embraced from childhood, like those others, nor making it a law that the virtuous man must be so many years old, but addressing their discourse generally to every age. For those lessons are children's toys, but these are the truth of things.

And as a place for this their commonwealth¹ they have assigned Heaven, and God they have brought in as the framer thereof, and as lawgiver of the statutes there set; as indeed was their duty. And the rewards in their commonwealth¹ are not leaves of bay nor olive, nor an allowance of meat in the public hall, nor statues of brass, these cold and ordinary things, but a life which hath no end, and to become children of God, to join the angels' choir, and to stand by the royal throne, and to be always with Christ. And the popular guides of this commonwealth¹ are publicans, and fishermen, and tent-makers, not such as have lived for a short time, but such as are now living for ever. Therefore even after their death they may possibly do the greatest good to the governed.

This republic¹ is at war not with men, but with devils, and those incorporeal powers. Wherefore also their captain is no one of men, nor of angels, but God Himself. And the armor too of these warriors suits the nature of the warfare, for it is not formed of hides and steel, but of truth and of righteousness, and faith, and all true love of wisdom.²

13. Since then the aforesaid republic¹ is both the subject on which this book was written, and it is now proposed for us to speak thereof, let us give careful heed to Matthew, discoursing plainly concerning this: for what he saith is not his own, but all Christ's, who hath made the laws of this city.¹ Let us give heed, I say, that we may be capable of enrolment therein, and of shining forth among those that have already become citizens thereof, and are awaiting those incorruptible crowns. To many, however, this discourse seems to be easy, while the prophetic writings are difficult. But this again is the view of men who know not the depth of the thoughts laid up therein. Wherefore I entreat you to follow us with much diligence, so as to enter into the very ocean of the things written, with Christ for our guide at this our entering in.

But in order that the word may be the more easy to learn, we pray and entreat you, as we have done also with respect to the other Scriptures, to take up beforehand that portion of the Scripture which we may be going to

explain, that your reading may prepare the way for your understanding (as also was the case with the eunuch³), and so may greatly facilitate our task.

14. And this because⁴ the questions are many and frequent. See, for instance, at once in the beginning of his Gospel, how many difficulties might be raised one after the other. As first, wherefore the genealogy of Joseph is traced, who was not father of Christ. Secondly, whence may it be made manifest that He derives His origin from David, while the forefathers of Mary, who bare Him, are not known, for the Virgin's genealogy is not traced? Thirdly, on what account Joseph's genealogy is traced, when he had nothing to do with the birth; while with regard to the Virgin, who was the very mother, it is not shown of what fathers, or grandfathers, or ancestors, she is sprung.

And along with these things, this is also worth inquiry, wherefore it can be, that, when tracing the genealogy through the men, he hath mentioned women also; and why since he determined upon doing this, he yet did not mention them all, but passing over the more eminent, such as Sarah, Rebecca, and as many as are like them, he hath brought forward only them that are famed for some bad thing; as, for instance, if any was a harlot, or an adulteress, or a mother by an unlawful marriage, if any was a stranger or barbarian. For he hath made mention of the wife of Uriah, and of Thamar, and of Rahab, and of Ruth, of whom one was of a strange race, another an harlot, another was defiled by her near kinsman, and with him not in the form of marriage, but by a stolen intercourse, when she had put on herself the mask of an harlot; and touching the wife of Uriah no one is ignorant, by reason of the notoriety of the crime. And yet the evangelist hath passed by all the rest, and inserted in the genealogy these alone. Whereas, if women were to be mentioned, all ought to be so; if not all but some, then those famed in the way of virtue, not for evil deeds.

See you how much care is required of us straightway in the first beginning? and yet the beginning seems to be plainer than the rest; to many perhaps even superfluous, as being a mere numbering of names.

After this, another point again is worth inquiry; wherefore he hath omitted three kings. For if, because they were exceeding ungodly, he therefore passed by their names in silence, neither should he have mentioned the others, that were like them.

---

¹ [πολιτεία, in its proper case.]   ² [φιλοσοφίας.]   ³ Acts viii. 28.   ⁴ [Καὶ γάρ.]

And this again [1] is another question; why, after having spoken of fourteen generations, he hath not in the third division maintained the number. [2]

And wherefore Luke hath made mention of other names, and not only not all of them the same, but also many more of them, while Matthew hath both fewer and different, though he too hath ended with Joseph, with whom Luke likewise concluded.

Ye see how much wakeful attention is needed on our part, not only for explanation, but even that we may learn what things we have to explain. For neither is this a little matter, to be able to find out the difficulties; there being also this other hard point, how Elizabeth, who was of the Levitical tribe, was kinswoman to Mary.

15. But that we may not overload your memory, by stringing many things together, here let us stay our discourse for a time. For it is enough for you in order that ye be thoroughly roused, that you learn [3] the questions only. But if ye long for [4] their solution also, this again depends on yourselves, before we speak. For if I see you thoroughly awakened, and longing to learn, I will endeavor to add the solution also; but if gaping and not attending, I will conceal both the difficulties, and their solution, in obedience to a divine law. For, saith He, "Give not the holy things to the dogs, neither cast ye your pearls before swine, lest they trample them under their feet." [5]

But who is he that tramples them under foot? He that doth not account these things precious, and venerable. And who, it may be asked, is so wretched as not to esteem these things venerable, and more precious than all? He who doth not bestow on them so much leisure as on the harlot women in the theatres of Satan. For there the multitude pass the whole day, and give up not a few of their domestic concerns for the sake of this unseasonable employment, and they retain with exactness whatever they have heard, and this though it be to the injury of their souls, that they keep it. But here, where God is speaking, they will not bear to tarry even a little time.

Therefore, let me warn you, we have nothing in common with Heaven, but our citizenship [6] goes no further than words. And yet because of this, God hath threatened even hell, not in order to cast us therein, but that

He might persuade us to flee this grievous tyranny. But we do the opposite, and run each day the way that leads thither, and while God is commanding us not only to hear, but also to do what He saith, we do not submit so much as to hearken.

When then, I pray thee, are we to do what is commanded, and to put our hand to the works, if we do not endure so much as to hear the words that relate to them, but are impatient and restless about the time we stay here, although it be exceedingly short?

16. And besides, when we are talking of indifferent matters, if we see those that are in company do not attend, we call what they do an insult; but do we consider that we are provoking God, if, while He is discoursing of such things as these, we despise what is said, and look another way?

Why, he that is grown old, and hath travelled over much country, reports to us with all exactness the number of stadia, and the situations of cities, their plans, and their harbors and markets; but we ourselves know not even how far we are from the city that is in Heaven. For surely we should have endeavored to shorten the space, had we known the distance. That city being not only as far from us as Heaven is from the earth, but even much farther, if we be negligent; like as, on the other hand, if we do our best, [7] even in one instant we shall come to the gates thereof. For not by local space, but by moral disposition, are these distances defined.

But thou knowest exactly the affairs of the world, as well new as old, and such too as are quite ancient; thou canst number the princes under whom thou hast served in time past, and the ruler of the games, and them that gained the prize, and the leaders of armies, matters that are of no concern to thee; but who hath become ruler in this city, the first or the second or the third, and for how long, each of them; and what each hath accomplished, and brought to pass, thou hast not imagined even as in a dream. And the laws that are set in this city thou wilt not endure to hear, nor attend to them, even when others tell thee of them. How then, I pray thee, dost thou expect to obtain the blessings that are promised, when thou dost not even attend to what is said?

17. But though never before, now, at any rate, let us do this. Yea, for we [8] are on the point of entering into a city (if God permit) of gold, and more precious than any gold.

Let us then mark her foundations, her

---

1 [Καὶ γὰρ καὶ τοῦτο.]
2 [See Homily iv., where this question is discussed.—R.]
3 [Literally, " and learn."—R.]　　　4 ἐρᾶτε.
5 Matt. vii. 6. [The citation is not, however, verbally accurate.—R.]
6 [πολιτεία.]

7 [σπουδάζωμεν; the verb is rendered " endeavor " in the preceding sentence.—R.]
8 [Καὶ γάρ.]

gates consisting of sapphires and pearls; for indeed we have in Matthew an excellent guide. For through his gate we shall now enter in, and much diligence is required on our part. For should He see any one not attentive, He casts him out of the city.

Yes, for the city is most kingly and glorious; not as the cities with us, divided into a market-place, and the royal courts; for there all is the court of the King. Let us open therefore the gates of our mind, let us open our ears, and with great trembling, when on the point of setting foot on the threshold, let us worship the King that is therein. For indeed the first approach hath power straightway to confound the beholder.

For the present we find the gates closed; but when we see them thrown open (for this is the solution of the difficulties), then we shall perceive the greatness of the splendor within. For there also, leading thee with the eyes of the Spirit, is one who offers to show thee all, even this Publican; where the King sitteth, and who of His host stand by Him; where are the angels, where the archangels; and what place is set apart for the new citizens in this city, and what kind of way it is that leads thither, and what manner of portion they have received, who first were citizens therein, and those next after them, and such as followed these. And how many are the orders of these tribes, how many those of the senate, how many the distinctions of dignity.

Let us not therefore with noise or tumult enter in, but with a mystical silence.

For if in a theatre, when a great silence hath been made, then the letters of the king are read, much more in this city must all be composed, and stand with soul and ear erect. For it is not the letters of any earthly master, but of the Lord of angels, which are on the point of being read.

If we would order ourselves on this wise, the grace itself of the Spirit will lead us in great perfection, and we shall arrive at the very royal throne, and attain to all the good things, by the grace and love towards man of our Lord Jesus Christ, to whom be glory and might, together with the Father and the Holy Ghost, now and always, even for ever and ever. Amen.

HOMILY II.

MATT. I. I.

" The book of the generation of Jesus Christ, the Son of David, the Son of Abraham."

Do ye indeed remember the charge, which we lately made you, entreating you to hearken unto all the things that are said with all silence, and mystical quietness? For [1] we are to-day to set foot within the holy vestibule, wherefore I have also put you in mind of the charge.

Since, if the Jews, when they were to approach " a mountain that burned, and fire, and blackness, and darkness, and tempest; " [2] —or rather when they were not so much as to approach, but both to see and to hear these things from afar;—were commanded for three days before to abstain from their wives, and to wash their garments, and were in trembling and fear, both themselves and Moses with them; much more we, when we are to hearken to such words, and are not to stand far from a smoking mountain, but to enter into Heaven itself, ought to show forth a greater self-denial; [3] not washing our garments, but wiping clean the robe of our soul, and ridding ourselves of all mixture with worldly things. For it is not blackness that ye shall see, nor smoke, nor tempest, but the King Himself sitting on the throne of that unspeakable glory, and angels, and archangels standing by Him, and the tribes of the saints, with those interminable myriads.

For such is the city of God, having " the Church of the first-born, the spirits of the just, the general assembly of the angels, the

---

1 [Καὶ γάρ ; but there is some variation in the readings.—R.]
2 Heb. xii. 18. [Here the Greek text agrees more closely with that of the received text in Hebrews than with that of the earliest MSS.—R.]

3 [φιλοσοφίαν.]

blood of sprinkling,"[1] whereby all are knit into one, and Heaven hath received the things of earth, and earth the things of Heaven, and that peace hath come which was of old longed for both by angels and by saints.

Herein standeth the trophy of the cross, glorious, and conspicuous, the spoils won by Christ, the first-fruits[2] of our nature, the booty of our King; all these, I say, we shall out of the Gospels know perfectly. If thou follow in becoming quietness, we shall be able to lead thee about everywhere, and to show where death is set forth crucified, and where sin is hanged up, and where are the many and wondrous offerings from this war, from this battle.

Thou shalt see likewise the tyrant here bound, and the multitude of the captives following, and the citadel from which that unholy demon overran all things in time past. Thou wilt see the hiding places, and the dens of the robber, broken up now, and laid open, for even there also was our King present.[3]

But be not thou weary, beloved, for if any one were describing a visible war, and trophies, and victories, wouldest thou feel no satiety at all; nay, thou wouldest not prefer either drink or meat to this history. But if that kind of narrative be welcome, much more this. For consider what a thing it is to hear, how on the one side God from Heaven, arising "out of the royal thrones, leaped down[4]" unto the earth, and even unto hell itself, and stood in the battle array; and how the devil on the other hand set himself in array against Him; or rather not against God unveiled, but God hidden in man's nature.

And what is marvellous, thou wilt see death destroyed by death, and curse extinguished by curse, and the dominion of the devil put down by those very things whereby he did prevail. Let us therefore rouse ourselves thoroughly, and let us not sleep, for lo, I see the gates opening to us; but let us enter in with all seemly order, and with trembling, setting foot straightway within the vestibule itself.

2. But what is this vestibule? "The book of the generation of Jesus Christ, Son of David, Son of Abraham."

"What sayest thou? Didst thou not promise to discourse of the Only-begotten Son of God, and dost thou make mention of David, a man born after a thousand generations, and say that he is both father and ancestor?" Stay, seek not to learn all at once, but gently and by little and little. Why, it is in the vestibule that thou art standing, by the very porch; why then dost thou hasten towards the inner shrine? As yet thou hast not well marked all without. For neither for a while do I declare unto thee that other generation: or rather not even this which cometh after, for it is unutterable, and unspeakable. And before me the Prophet Esaias hath told thee this; where[5] when proclaiming His passion, and His great care for the world, and admiring who He was, and what He became, and whither He descended, he cried out loud and clear, saying thus, "Who shall declare His generation?"[6]

It is not then of that we are now to speak, but of this beneath, this which took place on earth, which was amongst ten thousand witnesses. And concerning this again we will relate in such wise as it may be possible for us, having received the grace of the Spirit. For not even this may any one set forth altogether plainly, forasmuch as this too is most awful. Think not, therefore, it is of small things thou art hearing, when thou hearest of this birth, but rouse up thy mind, and straightway tremble, being told that God hath come upon earth. For so marvellous was this, and beyond expectation, that because of these things the very angels formed a choir, and in behalf of the world offered up their praise for them, and the prophets from the first were amazed at this, that "He was seen upon earth, and conversed with men[7]." Yea, for it is far beyond all thought to hear that God the Unspeakable,[8] the Unutterable, the Incomprehensible, and He that is equal to the Father, hath passed through a virgin's womb, and hath vouchsafed to be born of a woman, and to have Abraham and David for forefathers. But why do I say Abraham and David? For what is even more amazing, there are those women, whom we have lately mentioned.

3. Hearing these things, arise, and surmise nothing low: but even because of this very thing most of all shouldest thou marvel,[9] that being Son of the Unoriginate God, and His true Son, He suffered Himself to be called also Son of David, that He might make

[1] Heb xii 22, 23, 44. [The citation is free; but it is evident that Chrysostom accepts the view indicated in the R. V. margin: "the general assembly of angels."—R.]

[2] [τὰ ἀκροθίνια, "the chief spoils," see Heb. vii. 4.—R.]

[3] See 1 Pet. iii. 19, 20; iv. 6; St. Iren. iv. 45; iii. 23; iv. 39, 56, 66; v. 31; Orig. in Joan, t. ii. 30; contr. Cels. ii. 43; in Rom. lib. 5, l. t. iv. 551. B; Tert. de Anim. 7; St. Greg. Naz. Or. 42 p 693. Ed. Morell; and others cited by Cotelerius on St. Hermas, iii. 16.

[4] Wisd. xviii. 15.

[5] [Literally, "for."]

[6] Isaiah liii. 8. [Here γενεάν occurs; not the term used by Matthew, but in the phrase "that other generation," γέννησιν occurs.—R.]

[7] Baruch iii. 37.

[8] Or Unapproachable ἀπρόσιτος, according to some MSS. Savil.

[9] [Chrysostom uses the imperative: "Because of this very thing especially marvel," etc.—R.]

thee Son of God. He suffered a slave to be father to Him, that He might make the Lord Father to thee a slave.

Seest thou at once from the beginning of what nature are the Gospels? If thou doubt concerning the things that pertain to thee, from what belongs to Him believe these also. For it is far more difficult, judging by human reason, for God to become man, than for a man to be declared a Son of God. When therefore thou art told that the Son of God is Son of David and of Abraham, doubt not any more that thou too, the son of Adam, shalt be son of God. For not at random, nor in vain did He abase Himself so greatly, only He was minded to exalt us. Thus He was born after the flesh, that thou mightest be born after the Spirit; He was born of a woman, that thou mightest cease to be the son of a woman.

Wherefore the birth was twofold, both made like unto us, and also surpassing ours. For to be born of a woman indeed was our lot, but "to be born not of blood, nor of the will of flesh, nor of man," but of the Holy Ghost,[1] was to proclaim beforehand the birth surpassing us, the birth to come, which He was about freely to give us of the Spirit. And everything else too was like this. Thus His baptism also was of the same kind, for it partook of the old, and it partook also of the new. To be baptized by the prophet marked the old, but the coming down of the Spirit shadowed out the new. And like as though any one were to place himself in the space between any two persons that were standing apart, and stretching forth both his hands were to lay hold on either side, and tie them together; even so hath He done, joining the old covenant with the new, God's nature with man's, the things that are His with ours.

Seest thou the flashing brightness[2] of the city, with how great a splendor it hath dazzled thee from the very beginning? how it hath straightway shown the King in thine own form; as though in a camp? For neither there doth the king always appear bearing his proper dignity, but laying aside the purple and the diadem, he often disguises himself in the garb of a common soldier. But there it is, lest by being known he should draw the enemy upon himself; but here on the contrary, lest, if He were known, He should cause the enemy to fly from the conflict with Him, and lest He should confound all His own people: for His purpose was to save, not to dismay.

4. For this reason he hath also straightway called Him by this title, naming Him Jesus. For this name, Jesus, is not Greek, but in the Hebrew language it is thus called Jesus; which is, when interpreted into the Greek tongue, "A Saviour." And He is called a Saviour, from His saving His people.

Seest thou how he hath given wings to the hearer, at once speaking things familiar, and at the same time by these indicating to us things beyond all hope? I mean that[3] both these names were well known to the Jews. For, because the things that were to happen were beyond expectation, the types even of the names went before, in order that from the very first all the unsettling power of novelty might be taken away. Thus he is called Jesus, who after Moses brought the people into the land of promise. Hast thou seen the type? Behold the truth. That led into the land of promise, this into heaven, and to the good things in the heavens; that, after Moses was dead, this after the law had ceased; that as a leader, this as a King.

However, lest having heard the word Jesus, thou shouldest by reason of the identity of the name be perplexed, he hath added, "Jesus Christ, Son of David." But that other was not of David, but of another tribe.

5. But wherefore doth he call it a "book of the generation of Jesus Christ," while yet this book hath not the birth only, but the whole dispensation? Because this is the sum of the whole dispensation, and is made an origin and root of all our blessings. As then Moses calleth it the book of heaven and earth,[4] although he hath not discoursed of heaven and earth only, but also of all things that are in the midst thereof; so also this man hath named his book from that which is the sum of all the great things done. For that which teems with astonishment, and is beyond hope and all expectation, is that God should become man. But this having come to pass, all afterwards follows in reasonable consequence

6. But wherefore did he not say, "the Son of Abraham," and then "the Son of David?" It is not, as some suppose, that he means to proceed upward from the lower point, since then he would have done the same as Luke, but now he doth the contrary. Why then hath he made mention of David? The man was in the mouths of all, both from his distinction, and from the time, for he had not been so very long since dead, like Abraham. And though God made promises to both, yet the one, as old, was passed over in silence,

---

[1] John i. 13.
[2] ἀστραπήν. [Used of a flash of lightning, or dazzling brightness.—R.]

[3] [Καὶ γάρ.]   [4] Gen. ii. 4.

while the other, as fresh and recent, was repeated of all. Themselves, for instance, say, "Doth not Christ come of the seed of David, and out of Bethlehem, the town where David was?"[1] And no man called Him Son of Abraham, but all Son of David; and that because this last was more in the recollection of all, both on account of the time, as I have already said, and because of his royalty. On this principle again all the kings whom they had in honor after his time were named from him, both by the people themselves and by God. For both Ezekiel[2] and other prophets besides speak of David as coming and rising again; not meaning him that was dead, but them who were emulating his virtue. And to Hezekiah He saith, "I will defend this city, for mine own sake and for my servant David's sake."[3] And to Solomon too He said, that for David's sake He rent not the kingdom during his lifetime.[4] For great was the glory of the man, both with God and with men.

On account of this he makes the beginning at once from him who was more known, and then runs up to his father; accounting it superfluous, as far as regards the Jews, to carry the genealogy higher up. For these were principally the persons held in admiration; the one as a prophet and a king, the other as a patriarch and a prophet.

7. "But[5] whence is it manifest that He is of David?" one may say. For if He was not sprung of a man, but from a woman only, and the Virgin hath not her genealogy traced, how shall we know that He was of David's race? Thus, there are two things inquired; both why His mother's genealogy is not recited, and wherefore it can be that Joseph is mentioned by them, who hath no part in the birth: since the latter seems to be superfluous, and the former a defect.

Of which then is it necessary to speak first? How the Virgin is of David. How then shall we know that she is of David? Hearken unto God, telling Gabriel to go unto "a virgin betrothed to a man (whose name was Joseph), of the house and lineage of David."[6] What now wouldest thou have plainer than this, when thou hast heard that the Virgin was of the house and lineage of David?

Hence it is evident that Joseph also was of the same. Yes, for there was a law, which bade that it should not be lawful to take a wife from any other stock, but from the same

tribe. And the patriarch Jacob also foretold that He should arise out of the tribe of Judah, saying on this wise: "there shall not fail a ruler out of Judah, nor a governor out of his loins, until He come for whom it is appointed, and He is the expectation of the Gentiles."[7]

"Well; this prophecy doth indeed make it clear that He was of the tribe of Judah, but not also that He was of the family of David. Was there then in the tribe of Judah one family only, even that of David, or were there not also many others? And might it not happen for one to be of the tribe of Judah, but not also of the family of David?"

Nay, lest thou shouldest say this, the evangelist hath removed this suspicion of thine, by saying, that He was "of the house and lineage of David."

And if thou wish to learn this from another reason besides, neither shall we be at a loss for another proof. For not only was it not allowed to take a wife out of another tribe, but not even from another lineage, that is, from another kindred. So that if either we connect with the Virgin the words, "of the house and lineage of David," what hath been said stands good; or if with Joseph, by that fact this also is proved. For if Joseph was of the house and lineage of David, he would not have taken his wife from another than that whence he himself was sprung.

"What then," one may say, "if he transgressed the law?" Why, for this cause he hath by anticipation testified that Joseph was righteous, on purpose that thou mightest not say this, but having been told his virtue, mightest be sure also that he would not have transgressed the law. For he who was so benevolent, and free from passion, as not to wish, even when urged by suspicion, to attempt inflicting punishment on the Virgin, how should he have transgressed the law for lust? he that showed wisdom and self-restraint beyond the law (for to put her away, and that privily, was to act with self-restraint beyond the law), how should he have done anything contrary to the law; and this when there was no cause to urge him?[8]

8. Now that the Virgin was of the race of David is indeed from these things evident; but wherefore he gave not her genealogy, but Joseph's, requires explanation. For what cause was it then? It was not the law among the Jews that the genealogy of women should

[1] John vii. 42.
[2] Ezek. xxxiv. 23, 24; xxxvii. 24, 25; Jer. xxx. 9; Hos. iii. 5.
[3] 2 Kings xix. 34.   [4] 1 Kings ii. 11, 12, 13.   [5] [Καί.]
[6] Luke i. 27. [The words "and lineage" occur in some MSS. of the New Testament. But the citation here is probably made with freedom.—R.]

[7] Gen. xlix. 10, from LXX. Our translation preserving the Hebrew word renders it, "until Shiloh come." [Comp. the marginal renderings of the R. V. in loco.—R.]
[8] [The labored argument here suggests that Chrysostom was not sure of his exegetical position. In Luke i. 27, the phrase " of the house of David " is most naturally joined with " Joseph," and so Chrysostom himself implies.—R.]

be traced. In order then that he might keep the custom, and not seem to be making alterations[1] from the beginning, and yet might make the Virgin known to us, for this cause he hath passed over her ancestors in silence, and traced the genealogy of Joseph. For if he had done this with respect to the Virgin, he would have seemed to be introducing novelties; and if he had passed over Joseph in silence, we should not have known the Virgin's forefathers. In order therefore that we might learn, touching Mary, who she was, and of what origin, and that the laws might remain undisturbed, he hath traced the genealogy of her espoused husband, and shown him to be of the house of David. For when this hath been clearly proved, that other fact is demonstrated with it, namely, that the Virgin likewise is sprung from thence, by reason that this righteous man, even as I have already said, would not have endured to take a wife from another race.

There is also another reason, which one might mention, of a more mystical nature, because of which the Virgin's forefathers were passed over in silence; but this it were not seasonable now to declare, because so much has been already said.[2]

9. Wherefore let us stay at this point our discourse concerning the questions, and in the meanwhile let us retain with accuracy what hath been revealed to us; as, for instance, why he mentioned David first; wherefore he called the book, "a book of the generation;" on what account he said, "of Jesus Christ;" how the birth is common and not common; whence it was that Mary was shown to be from David; and wherefore Joseph's genealogy is traced, while her ancestors are passed over in silence.

For if ye retain these things, ye will the more encourage us with respect to what is to come; but if ye reject and cast them from your mind, we shall be the more backward as to the rest. Just as no husbandman would care to pay attention to a soil which had destroyed the former seed.

Wherefore I entreat you to revolve these things. For from taking thought concerning such matters, there springs in the soul some great good, tending unto salvation. For by these meditations we shall be able to please God Himself; and our mouths will be pure from insults, and filthy talking, and reviling, while they are exercising themselves in spiritual sayings; and we shall be formidable to the devils, while arming our tongue with such

words; and we shall draw unto ourselves God's grace the more, and it will render our eye more piercing. For indeed both eyes and mouth and hearing He set in us to this intent, that all our members may serve Him, that we may speak His words, and do His deeds, that we may sing unto Him continual hymns, that we may offer up sacrifices of thanksgiving,[3] and by these may thoroughly purify our consciences.

For as a body will be more in health when enjoying the benefits of a pure air, even so will a soul be more endued with practical wisdom[4] when nourished in such exercises as these. Seest thou not even the eyes of the body, that when they abide in smoke they are always weeping; but when they are in clear air, and in a meadow, and in fountains and gardens, they become more quicksighted and more healthy? Like this is the soul's eye also, for should it feed in the meadow of spiritual oracles, it will be clear and piercing, and quick of sight; but should it depart into the smoke of the things of this life, it will weep without end, and wail both now and hereafter. For indeed the things of this life are like smoke. On this account also one hath said, "My days have failed like smoke."[5] He indeed was referring to their shortness of duration, and to their unsubstantial nature, but I would say that we should take what is said, not in this sense alone, but also as to their turbid character.

For nothing doth so hurt and dim the eye of the soul as the crowd of worldly anxieties and the swarm of desires. For these are the wood that feedeth this smoke. And as fire, when it lays hold of any damp and saturated fuel, kindles much smoke; so likewise this desire, so vehement and burning, when it lays hold of a soul that is (so to speak) damp and dissolute, produces also in its way abundance of smoke. For this cause there is need of the dew of the Spirit, and of that air, that it may extinguish the fire, and scatter the smoke, and give wings to our thoughts. For it cannot, it cannot be that one weighed down with so great evils should soar up to heaven; it is well if being without impediment[6] we can cleave our way thither; or rather it is not possible even so, unless we obtain the wing of the Spirit.

Now if there be need both of an unencum-

[1] παραχαράττειν. [This word is the technical one for counterfeiting or forging.--R.]
[2] See Hom. iii. sec. 1.

[3] εὐχαριστίας.
[4] [φιλοσοφωτέρα is rendered, "more endued with practical wisdom."--R.]
[5] Ps. cii. 3, LXX. [R. V., "My days consume away like smoke." The LXX. has the aorist, hence, "have failed" is the rendering here adopted. Some editions of Chrysostom read the imperfect here. The Oxford edition has a second note, the meaning of which is not clear: "Rather have failed, LXX."--R.]
[6] [εὐζώνους, "well-girded," then figuratively, "unencumbered."--R.]

bered mind, and of spiritual grace, that we may mount up to that height: what if there be none of these things, but we draw to ourselves whatever is opposite to them, even a satanical weight? how shall we be able to soar upwards, when dragged down by so great a load? For indeed, should any one attempt to weigh our words as it were in just balances; in ten thousand talents of worldly talk he will scarcely find an hundred pence of spiritual words, or rather, I should say, not even ten farthings. Is it not then a disgrace, and an extreme mockery, that if we have a servant, we make use of him for the most part in things necessary, but being possessed of a tongue, we do not deal with our member so well even as with a slave, but on the contrary make use of it for things unprofitable, and mere makeweights?[1] And would it were only for makeweights:[1] but now it is for what are contrary and hurtful and in no respect advantageous to us. For if the things that we spoke were profitable to us, they would assuredly be also pleasing to God. But as it is, whatever the devil may suggest, we speak it all, now laughing, and now speaking wittily; now cursing and insulting, and now swearing, lying, and taking false oaths; now murmuring, and now making vain babblings, and talking trifles more than old wives; uttering all things that are of no concern to us.

For, tell me, who of you that stand here, if he were required, could repeat one Psalm, or any other portion of the divine Scriptures? There is not one.

And it is not this only that is the grievous thing, but that while ye are become so backward with respect to things spiritual, yet in regard of what belongs to Satan ye are more vehement than fire. Thus should any one be minded to ask of you songs of devils and impure effeminate melodies, he will find many that know these perfectly, and repeat them with much pleasure.

10. But what is the answer to these charges? "I am not," you will say, "one of the monks, but I have both a wife and children, and the care of a household." Why, this is what hath ruined all, your supposing that the reading of the divine Scriptures appertains to those only, when ye need it much more than they. For they that dwell in the world,[2] and each day receive wounds, these have most need of medicines. So that it is far worse than not reading, to account the thing even "superfluous:" for these are the words of diabolical invention. Hear ye not Paul saying, "that all these things are written for our admonition"?[3]

And thou, if thou hadst to take up a Gospel, wouldest not choose to do so with hands unwashed; but the things that are laid up within it, dost thou not think to be highly necessary? It is because of this, that all things are turned upside down.

For if thou wouldest learn how great is the profit of the Scriptures, examine thyself, what thou becomest by hearing Psalms, and what by listening to a song of Satan; and how thou art disposed when staying in a Church, and how when sitting in a theatre; and thou wilt see that great is the difference between this soul and that, although both be one. Therefore Paul said, "Evil communications corrupt good manners."[4] For this cause we have need continually of those songs, which serve as charms from the Spirit. Yes, for this it is whereby we excel the irrational creatures, since with respect to all other things, we are even exceedingly inferior to them.

This is a soul's food, this its ornament, this its security; even as not to hear is famine and wasting; for "I will give them," saith He, "not a famine of bread, nor a thirst of water, but a famine of hearing the word of the Lord."[5]

What then can be more wretched? when the very evil, which God threatens in the way of punishment, this thou art drawing upon thine head of thine own accord, bringing into thy soul a sort of grievous famine, and making it the feeblest thing in the world? For it is its nature both to be wasted and to be saved by words. Yea, this leads it on to anger; and the same kind of thing again makes it meek: a filthy expression is wont to kindle it to lust, and it is trained to temperance by speech full of gravity.

But if a word merely have such great power, tell me, how is it thou dost despise the Scriptures? And if an admonition can do such great things, far more when the admonitions are with the Spirit. Yes, for a word from the divine Scriptures, made to sound in the ear, doth more than fire soften the hardened soul, and renders it fit for all good things.

11. In this way too did Paul, when he had found the Corinthians puffed up and inflamed, compose them, and make them more considerate. For they were priding themselves on those very things, touching which they ought to have been ashamed, and to have hid their face. But after they had received the letter, hear the change in them, of which the Teacher himself hath borne witness for them, saying on this wise: for "this very thing,

1 [παρέλκοντα.]   2 [ἐν μέσῳ στρεφομένοις.]   3 1 Cor. x. 11.   4 1 Cor. xv. 33.   5 Amos viii. 11.

that ye sorrowed after a godly sort, what carefulness it wrought in you, yea, what clearing of yourselves, yea, what indignation, yea, what zeal, yea, what revenge."[1] In this way do we bring to order servants and children, wives, and friends, and make our enemies friends.

In this way the great men too, they that were dear to God, became better. David, for instance, after his sin, when he had had the benefit of certain words, then it was that he came unto that most excellent repentance; and the apostles also by this mean became what they did become, and drew after them the whole world.

"And what is the profit," one may say, "when any one hears, but doeth not what is said?" No little will the profit be even from hearing. For he will go on to condemn himself,[2] and to groan inwardly, and will come in time also to do the things that are spoken of. But he that doth not even know that he hath sinned, when will he cease from his negligence? when will he condemn himself?

Let us not therefore despise the hearing of the divine Scriptures. For this is of Satan's devising; not suffering us to see the treasure, lest we should gain the riches. Therefore he saith that the hearing the divine laws is nothing, lest he should see us from the hearing acquiring the practice also.

Knowing then this his evil art, let us fortify ourselves against him on all sides, that being fenced with this armor, we may both abide unconquered ourselves, and smite him on the head: and thus, having crowned ourselves with the glorious wreaths of victory, we may attain unto the good things to come, by the grace and love towards man of our Lord Jesus Christ, to whom be glory and might for ever and ever. Amen.

---

[1] [2 Cor. vii. 11 is here cited, but in abridged form. All the MSS. and editions of Chrysostom, except the Benedictine, give the briefer reading, but in Migne's edition, αλλὰ φόβον, αλλὰ ἐπιπόθησιν (" yea, *what* fear, yea, *what* vehement desire ") are supplied in brackets. In the New Testament passage there is no variation in text, so far as these phrases are concerned. Like most patristic authors, this great Homilist was quite free in his method of citing Scripture.—R.]

[2] [Literally, " will condemn himself."—R.]

HOMILY III.

MATT. I. 1.

" The book of the generation of Jesus Christ, the Son of David, the Son of Abraham."

BEHOLD a third discourse, and we have not yet made an end of the prefatory matter. It was not then for nought that I said, It is the nature of these thoughts to have a great depth.

Come, then, let us speak to-day what remains. What is it then that is now required? Why Joseph's genealogy is traced, who had no part in the birth. And one cause we have mentioned already; but it is necessary to mention likewise the other, that which is more mystical and secret than the first. What then is this? He would not that it should be manifest to the Jews, at the time of the birth, that Christ was born of a virgin.

Nay, be not troubled at the strangeness of the saying. For it is no statement of mine, but of our fathers, wonderful and illustrious men.[1] For if He disguised many things from the first, calling Himself Son of Man, and hath not everywhere clearly unfolded to us

---

ἐπράχθη. " Now the virginity of Mary, and her delivery, was kept in secret from the prince of this world, as was also the Lord's death ; three most notable mysteries, yet done in secret of God." [See *Ante-Nicene Fathers*, Vol. I., p. 57 The Greek given in this note is from the " briefer" form of the Ignatian Epistles. But the " longer" form differs very little, and the Syriac version, brief as it is, contains this sentence.—R.] And Origen, 6th Homily on St. Luke, says, " It has been well written in one of the epistles of a certain martyr, I mean Ignatius, the next Bishop of Antioch after the blessed Peter, him who fought with wild beasts in the persecution at Rome, ' Now the virginity of Mary was kept in secret from the prince of this world.' It was concealed because of Joseph, because of her espousals, because she was supposed to have a husband. For, had she had no spouse or supposed husband, it could not have been concealed from the prince of this world. For presently the thought would have silently occurred to the evil one, ' How is she with child, who knoweth not a man ? This conception must be divine, it must be something higher than human nature.' On the contrary, our Saviour had purposed that the devil should be ignorant of His (Economy and Incarnation ; for which cause He both in His birth concealed the same, and commanded His disciples afterwards that they should not make Him known. Also when tempted by the devil in person, He no where owned Himself Son of God." Origen then quotes 1 Cor. ii. 6-8, to the same effect. And in answer to the objection, How the devils which were from time to time cast out knew Him to be the Son of God, he suggests that it might be owing to their inferiority in malice and mischief ; according to the rule among men, that the worse they are, the less they can know of Christ. [The *Homilies* of Origen are not included in the *Ante-Nicene Fathers*.]

See also a supposed Homily of St. Basil's, *De Christi generatione*, Ed. Ben. ii. 598, c.; and St. Jerome on St. Matt. i. 18.

---

[1] St. Ignatius ad Ephes. xix. init. Καὶ ἔλαθεν τον ἄρχοντα τοῦ αἰῶνος τουτοῦ ἡ παρθενία Μαρίας, καὶ ὁ τοκετὸς αὐτῆς, ὁμοίως καὶ ὁ θάνατος τοῦ Κυρίου τρία μυστήρια κραυγῆς ἄτινα ἐν ἡσυχίᾳ Θεοῦ

even His equality with the Father; why dost thou wonder at His having for a time disguised this also, taking order as He was for a certain great and marvellous purpose?[1]

But what kind of marvel? it may be asked. That the Virgin should be preserved, and delivered from evil suspicion. For if this had been discovered by the Jews from the beginning, they would have stoned the Virgin, making the report a handle for mischief,[2] and would have condemned her for adultery. For if in regard to the other matters, for which they had frequent precedents likewise in the old dispensation, they were quite shameless in their obstinacy[3] (for so, because He had cast out devils, they called Him possessed; and because He healed on the Sabbath day, they supposed Him to be an adversary of God; and yet oftentimes even before this had the Sabbath been broken), what would they not have said, if this had been told them? Especially as[4] they had all time before this on their side, in that it never had produced any such thing. For if after so many miracles they still called Him son of Joseph, how before the miracles would they have believed that He was born of a virgin?

It is then for this reason that both Joseph has his genealogy traced, and the Virgin betrothed to him. For if even he, who was both a just and wondrous man, required many things, in order that he should receive that which had come to pass; an angel, and the vision in dreams, and the testimony from the prophets; how could the Jews, being both dull and depraved, and of so unfriendly spirit towards Him, have admitted this idea into their minds? For the strangeness and novelty thereof would be sure greatly to disturb them, and the fact that they had never so much as heard of such a thing having happened in the times of their forefathers. For as the man who was once persuaded that He is Son of God, would after that have no cause to doubt concerning this too; so he who was accounting Him to be a deceiver and an adversary of God, how could he but have been yet more offended by this, and have been led on unto the opposite[5] notion? For this cause neither do the apostles at the first directly say this, but while of His resurrection they discourse much and often (forasmuch as of this there were examples in the times before, although not such as this); that He was born of a virgin they do not say always: nay, not even His mother herself ventured to utter this. See, for instance, what saith the Virgin even to Himself: "Behold, Thy father and I have sought Thee."[6] For if this suspicion had been entertained, neither would He any longer have been accounted to be a Son of David, and this opinion not being held, many other evils besides would have arisen. For this cause neither do the angels say these things to all, but to Mary only, and Joseph; but when showing to the shepherds the glad tidings of that which was come to pass, they no longer added this.

2. But why is it, that having mentioned Abraham, and having said that "he begat Isaac, and Isaac, Jacob;" and not having made any mention of his brother; when he is come to Jacob, he remembers both "Judah, and his brethren"? Now there are some that say, it was because of the perverseness of Esau, and of the rest that came before. But I should not say this; for if it were so, how is it that he a little after mentions such women? It being out of contraries, in this place, that His glory is manifested; not by having great forefathers, but low and of little account. For to the lofty One it is a great glory to be able to abase Himself exceedingly. Wherefore then did He not mention them? Because Saracens, and Ishmaelites, and Arabians, and as many as are sprung from those ancestors, have nothing in common with the race of the Israelites. For this cause then he passes over those in silence, and hastens on to His forefathers, and those of the Jewish people. Wherefore he saith, "And Jacob begat Judas and his brethren." For at this point the race of the Jews begins to have its peculiar mark.

3. "And Judas begat Phares and Zara of Thamar."[7] "What doest thou, O man, putting us in remembrance of a history that contains an unlawful intercourse?" But why is this said?[8] Since, if we were recounting the race of a mere man, one might naturally have been silent touching these things; but if of God Incarnate, so far from being silent, one ought to make a glory of them, showing forth His tender care, and His power. Yea, it was for this cause He came, not to escape our disgraces, but to bear them away. Therefore as He is the more admired, in that He not only died, but was even crucified (though the thing be opprobrious, yet the more opprobrious the more doth it show Him full of love to man), so likewise may we speak touching His birth; it is not only because He took flesh upon Him, and became man, that we justly stand amazed at Him, but because He vouchsafed to have also such kinsfolk,

---

[1] [θαυμαστόν τι καὶ μέγα οἰκονομῶν.]   [2] κακουργοῦντες.
[3] [φανερῶς ἠναισχύντουν.]   [4] [Καὶ γάρ.]   [5] [ἐκείνην.]
[6] Luke ii. 48.   [7] Matt. i. 3.
[8] [More accurately, "But why is this? one may say."—R.]

being in no respect ashamed of our evils. And this He was proclaiming from the very beginnings of His birth, that He is ashamed of none of those things that belong to us; while He teaches us also hereby, never to hide our face at our forefathers' wickedness, but to seek after one thing alone, even virtue. For such a man, though he have an alien for his ancestor, though he have a mother who is a prostitute, or what you will, can take no hurt thereby. For if the whoremonger himself, being changed, is nothing disgraced by his former life, much more will the wickedness of his ancestry have no power to bring to shame him that is sprung of an harlot or an adulteress, if he be virtuous.

But he did these things not only to instruct us, but also to bring down the haughtiness of the Jews. For since they, negligent about virtue in their own souls, were parading the name of Abraham,[1] thinking they had for a plea their forefathers' virtue; he shows from the very beginning that it is not in these things men ought to glory, but in their own good deeds.

Besides this, he is establishing another point also, to show that all are under sin, even their forefathers themselves. At least their patriarch and namesake is shown to have committed no small sin, for Thamar stands against him, to accuse his whoredom. And David too had Solomon by the wife whom he corrupted. But if by the great ones the law was not fulfilled, much more by the less. And if it was not fulfilled, all have sinned, and Christ's coming is become necessary.

For this cause he made mention also of the twelve patriarchs, by this again bringing down their pride at the noble birth of their fathers. Because many of these also were born of women that were slaves; but nevertheless the difference of the parents did not make a difference in the children. For all were equally both patriarchs and heads of tribes. For this is the precedence of the Church, this the prerogative of the nobility that is among us, taking its type from the beginning. So that whether thou be bond or free, thou hast from thence nothing more nor less; but the question is all about one thing only, namely, the mind, and the disposition of the soul.

4. But besides what we have said, there is another cause also, wherefore he hath mentioned even this history; for to be sure, Zara's name was not cast at random on that of Phares. (For indeed it was irrelevant, and superfluous, when he had mentioned

Phares, from whom he was to trace Christ's genealogy, to mention Zara also.) Wherefore then did he mention him? When Thamar was on the point of giving birth to them, the pangs having come upon her, Zara put forth his hand first.[2] Then the midwife, when she saw this, in order that the first should be known, bound his hand with scarlet; but the child, when he was bound, drew in his hand, and when he had drawn it in, Phares came forth first, and then Zara. The midwife when she saw this said, "Why was the hedge broken up for thee?"[3]

Seest thou the dark expression of mysteries? For it was not without purpose that these things were recorded for us: since neither was it worth our study to learn, what it might be that the midwife said; nor worth a narrative to know, that he who came out second, put forth his hand first. What then is the mysterious lesson?[4] First, from the name of the child[5] we learn what is inquired, for Phares is "a division," and "a breach." And moreover from the thing itself, which took place; for it was not in the order of nature that, having thrust out his hand, he should draw it in again when bound; these thing neither belonged to a movement directed by reason, nor did they take place in the way of natural consequence. For after the hand had found its way out, that another child should come forth before was perhaps not unnatural; but that he should draw it back, and give a passage for another, was no longer after the manner of children at the birth, but the grace of God was present with the children, ordering these things, and sketching out for us by them a sort of image of the things that were to come.

What then? Some of those who have examined these things accurately say, that these children are a type of the two nations.[6]

---

[2] Gen. xxxviii. 27.

[3] Our marginal translation is, "Wherefore hast thou made this breach against thee?" Gen. xxxviii. 29. [R. V. text: "Wherefore hast thou made a breach for thyself," with the margin: "Or, How hast thou made a breach! A breach be upon thee!" The LXX. rendering, which Chrysostom cites, misses the suggestion of the original Hebrew.—R.]

[4] τὸ αἴνιγμα.

[5] [τῆς προσηγορίας τοῦ παιδίου. The terms seem to be chosen to suggest that the name of the child came from the greeting given it by the midwife.—R.]

[6] i.e., The Jewish and the Christian. Compare the 62d Homily on Genesis, t. i. 478, ed. Sav. "Zara, being interpreted. is 'the East.' And that these things did not take place at random, but were a type of what was to come, the facts themselves indicate. For that which happened was not in the order of nature. For how was it possible, when the hand had been bound with the scarlet thread, for it to be again drawn back to afford passage to him who came after, had there not been some divine power which before ordained these things, and as in a kind of shadow drew out this figure; that at first and from the beginning Zara (that is, the East, which is the type of the Church) began to increase, and after it had made a little progress and then retired, the observance of the Law, represented by Phares, came in: and after prevailing a long time, on a second advance of Zara, who had before retired, made room on the contrary for the Church; I mean, the whole Jewish polity did so.

"Perhaps, however, it is necessary now to state the matter

---

[1] [τὸν Ἀβραὰμ ἄνω καὶ κάτω παρέφερον.]

And so in order that thou mightest learn that the polity of the latter people shone forth previously to the origin of the former, the child that hath the hand stretched forth doth not show itself entire, but draws even it in again; and after his brother had glided forth whole, then he too appears entire. And this took place also with regard to the two nations. I mean, that after the polity of the Church had been manifested in the times of Abraham, and then had been withdrawn in the midst of its course, the Jewish people came, and the legal polity, and then the new people appeared entire with their own laws. Wherefore also the midwife saith, " Why was the hedge broken up for thee ? " because the law coming in had broken in upon the freedom of the polity. For indeed the Scripture is ever wont to call the law a hedge; as the prophet saith: " Thou hast broken down her hedge, so that all they which pass by the way do pluck off her grapes: "[1] and, " I have set a hedge about it: "[2] and Paul, " Having broken down the middle wall of the hedge."[3] But others say, that the saying, " Why was the hedge broken up for thee ? " was spoken touching the new people: for this at its coming put down the law.[4]

5. Seest thou that it was not for few nor small causes that he brought to our remembrance the whole history concerning Judah ? For this end he hath mentioned Ruth also and Rahab, the one an alien, the other an harlot, that thou mayest learn that He came to do away with all our ills. For He hath come as a Physician, not as a Judge. Therefore in like manner as those of old took harlots for wives, even so God too espoused unto Himself the nature which had played the har-

lot: and this also prophets[5] from the beginning declare to have taken place with respect to the Synagogue. But that spouse was ungrateful towards Him who had been an husband to her, whereas, the Church, when once delivered from the evils received from our fathers, continued to embrace the Bridegroom.

See, for instance, what befell Ruth, how like it is to the things which belong to us. For she was both of a strange race, and reduced to the utmost poverty, yet Boaz when he saw her neither despised her poverty nor abhorred her mean birth, as Christ having received the Church, being both an alien and in much poverty, took her to be partaker of the great blessings. But even as Ruth, if she had not before left her father, and renounced household and race, country and kindred, would not have attained unto this alliance; so the Church too, having forsaken the customs which men had received from their fathers, then, and not before,[6] became lovely to the Bridegroom. Of this therefore the prophet discourses unto her, and saith, " Forget thy people, and thy father's house, so shall the king have pleasure in thy beauty."[7] This Ruth did too, and because of this she became a mother of kings, even as the Church did likewise. For of her David himself sprung. So then to shame them by all these things, and to prevail on them not to be high-minded, he hath both composed the genealogy, and brought forward these women. Yes, for this last, through those who intervened, was parent to the great king, and of these David is not ashamed. For it cannot, nay, it cannot be that a man should be good or bad, obscure or glorious, either by the virtue or by the vice of his forefathers; but if one must say somewhat even paradoxical, he shines forth the more, who not being of worthy ancestors, has yet become excellent.

6. Let no one therefore be high-minded on account of these matters, but let him consider the forefathers of the Lord, and put away all his haughtiness, and let good actions be his pride; or rather, not even these. For thus it was that the Pharisee came to be inferior to the Publican. Thus, if thou wouldest show the good work to be great, have no high thought,[8] and thou hast proved it so much the greater. Make account that thou hast done nothing, and then thou hast done all. For if, being sinners, when we account ourselves to be what we are, we

more briefly and clearly. There was a beginning, like the putting forth of Zara's hand, in Abel, Enoch, Noah, Melchisedek, Abraham, making extreme account of what might please God. Afterwards, when they had grown into a multitude, and had heaped on themselves heavy burdens of sin, and needed the benefit of some slight consolation, the Law was given as a kind of shadow, not as taking away sins, but as declaring and making them manifest : that as imperfect children living on milk they might be capable of attaining full age. But when even thus they failed of profiting, yea, kept mingling themselves up again with their sins, all the while that the Law was pointing out the greatness of the same, He came who is our common Lord, and freely bestowed on mankind this present spiritual polity, full of all virtue, whereof Zara was to stand as a type. For this cause the evangelist also hath mentioned Thamar and her children, saying, ' Judas begat Pharez and Zarah of Thamar.' " Compare also St. Cyr. of Alex. 6 lib. in Gen. t. i. 201, ed. Aubert ; Theod. in Gen. qu. 96 ; St. Aug. in Ps. 61, t. iv. 442, D. [A good specimen of the allegorizing exegesis which even such 'an expositor as Chrysostom could indulge in. The detailed account of the birth of Pharez is justified by the importance attached to the position of first-born.—R.]

[1] Ps. lxxx. 12.

[2] Is. v. 2, where the marginal translation is, *He made a wall about it :* the word hedge occurs verse 5. [R. V. verse 2. " He made a trench about it," with margin, " Or, digged it." In the LXX. φραγμόν occurs, however.—R.]

[3] Eph. ii. 14, where this word is translated " partition." [Retained in the R. V.]

[4] [The entire paragraph is based on the LXX. rendering, which by introducing φραγμός suggests an idea foreign to the original Hebrew.—R.]

[5] Hos. i. 2 ; Jer. iii.; Ezek. xxiii. 4, 5, 11.

[6] [The Greek text has simply τότε, a term that is usually paraphrased by the translator.—R.]

[7] Ps. xlv. 11, 12,   [8] [That is, no proud thought.—R.]

become righteous, as indeed the Publican did; how much more, when being righteous we account ourselves to be sinners. Since if out of sinners men are made righteous by a lowly mind (although this were not to be lowly-minded but to be right-minded); if then to be right-minded avails so much in the case of sinners, consider what will not lowliness of mind do with respect to righteous men.

Do not then mar thy labors, nor cast away from thee the fruits of thy toils, neither run thou in vain, making frustrate all thy labor after the many courses thou hast run. Nay, for thy Lord knows thy good works better than thou dost. Though thou give but a cup of cold water, not even this doth He overlook; though thou contribute but a farthing, though thou shouldest utter a sigh only, He receives it all with great favor and is mindful thereof, and assigns for it great rewards.

But wherefore dost thou search out thine own doings, and bring them out before us continually? Knowest thou not, that if thou praise thyself, God will no more praise thee? even as if thou bewail *thyself*,[1] He will not cease proclaiming thee before all. For it is not at all His will that thy labors should be disparaged. Why do I say, disparaged? Nay, He is doing and contriving all things, so that even for little He may crown thee; and He goes about seeking excuses, whereby thou mayest be delivered from hell. For this cause, though thou shouldest work but the eleventh hour of the day, He gives thy wages entire; and though thou afford no ground of salvation, He saith, "I do it for mine own sake, that my name be not profaned:"[2] though thou shouldest sigh only, though thou shouldest only weep, all these things He quickly catches hold of, for an occasion of saving thee.

Let us not therefore lift up ourselves, but let us declare ourselves unprofitable, that we may become profitable. For if thou call thyself approved, thou art become unprofitable, though thou wert approved; but if useless, thou art become profitable, even though thou wert reprobate.

7. Wherefore it is necessary to forget our good actions. "Yet how is it possible," one may say, "not to know these things with which we are well acquainted?" How sayest thou? Offending thy Lord perpetually, thou livest delicately, and laughest, and dost not so much as know that thou hast sinned, but hast consigned all to oblivion; and of thy good actions canst thou not put away the memory? And yet fear is a stronger kind of

thing. But we do the very contrary; on the one hand, whilst each day we are offending, we do not so much as put it before our mind; on the other, if we give a little money to a poor person, this we are ever revolving. This kind of conduct comes of utter madness, and it is a very great loss to him who so makes his reckoning.[2] For the secure storehouse of good works is to forget our good works. And as with regard to raiment and gold, when we expose them in a market-place, we attract many ill-meaning persons; but if we put them by at home and hide them, we shall deposit them all in security: even so with respect to our good deeds; if we are continually keeping them in memory, we provoke the Lord, we arm the enemy, we invite him to steal them away; but if no one know of them, besides Him who alone ought to know, they will lie in safety.

Be not therefore for ever parading them, lest some one should take them away. As was the case with the Pharisee, for bearing them about upon his lips; whence also the devil caught them away. And yet it was with thanksgiving he made mention of them, and referred the whole to God. But not even did this suffice Him. For it is not thanksgiving to revile others, to be vainglorious before many, to exalt one's self against them that have offended. Rather, if thou art giving thanks to God, be content with Him only, and publish it not unto men, neither condemn thy neighbor; for this is not thanksgiving. Wouldest thou learn words of thanksgiving? hearken unto the Three Children, saying, "We have sinned, we have transgressed. Thou art righteous, O Lord, in all that thou hast done unto us, because thou hast brought all things upon us by a true judgment."[4] For to confess[5] one's own sins, this is to give thanks with confession[5] unto God: a kind of thing which implies one to be guilty of numberless offenses, yet not to have the due penalty exacted. This man most of all is the giver of thanks.

8. Let us beware therefore of saying anything about ourselves, for this renders us both odious with men and abominable to God. For this reason, the greater the good works we do, the less let us say of ourselves; this being the way to reap the greatest glory both with men and with God. Or rather, not only glory from God, but a reward, yea, a great recompense. Demand not therefore a reward that thou mayest receive a reward.

[1] ["Thyself" is supplied by the translator.—R.]
[2] Ezek. xxxvi. 22.
[3] τοῦ συλλέγοντος.
[4] Song of the Three Children, vers. 6, 8, 4.
[5] ὁμολογεῖν—ὁμολογοῦντα. There seems an allusion to the two meanings of *confiteor* and the kindred words.

Confess thyself to be saved by grace, that He may profess Himself a debtor to thee; and not for thy good works only, but also for such rightness of mind. For when we do good works, we have Him debtor for our good works only; but when we do not so much as think we have done any good work, then also for this disposition itself; and more for this, than for the other things: so that this is equivalent to our good works. For should this be absent, neither will they appear great. For in the same way, we too, when we have servants,[1] do then most approve them when, after having performed all their service with good will, they do not think they have done anything great. Wherefore, if thou wouldest make thy good deeds great, do not think them to be great, and then they will be great.

It was in this way that the centurion also said, "I am not fit that thou shouldest enter under my roof;" because of this, he became worthy, and was "marvelled at"[2] above all Jews. On this wise again Paul saith, "I am not meet to be called an apostle;"[3] because of this he became even first of all. So likewise John: "I am not meet to loose the latchet of His shoe;"[4] because of this he was the "friend of the Bridegroom," and the hand which he affirmed to be unworthy to touch His shoes, this did Christ draw unto His own head.[5] So Peter too said, "Depart from me, for I am a sinful man;"[6] because of this he became a foundation of the Church.

For nothing is so acceptable to God as to number one's self with the last. This is a first principle of all practical wisdom.[7] For he that is humbled, and bruised in heart, will not be vainglorious, will not be wrathful, will not envy his neighbor, will not harbor any other passion. For neither when a hand is bruised, though we strive ten thousand times, shall we be able to lift it up on high. If therefore we were thus to bruise our heart[8] likewise, though it were stirred by ten thousand swelling passions, it could not be lifted up, no, not ever so little. For if a man, by mourning for things pertaining to this life, drives out all the diseases of his soul, much more will he, who mourns for sins, enjoy the blessing of self-restraint.[9]

9. "But who," one may say, "will be able thus to bruise his own heart?" Listen to David, who became illustrious chiefly because of this, and see the contrition of his soul. How after ten thousand good works, and when he was on the point of being deprived of country, and home, and life itself, at the very season of his calamity, seeing a vile and outcast common soldier trample on the turn of his fortunes[10] and revile him; so far from reviling him again, he utterly forbad one of his captains, who was desirous to have slain him, saying, "Let him alone, for the Lord hath bidden him."[11] And again, when the priests desired to carry about the ark *of God*[12] with him, he did not permit it; but what doth he say?[13] "Let me set it down in the temple, and if God deliver me from the dangers that are before me, I shall see the beauty thereof; but if He say to me, I have no delight in thee, behold, here am I, let Him do to me as seemeth good unto Him." And that which was done with regard to Saul, again and again, even oftentimes, what excellence of self-restraint doth it not show? Yea, for he even surpassed the old law, and came near to the apostolic injunctions. For this cause he bore with contentedness all that came from the Lord's hands; not contending against what befell him, but aiming at one object alone, namely, in everything to obey, and follow the laws set by Him. And when after so many noble deeds on his part, he saw the tyrant, the parricide, the murderer of his own brother, that injurious, that frenzied one, possessing in his stead his own kingdom, not even so was he offended. But "if this please God," saith he, "that I should be chased, and wander, and flee, and that he should be in honor, I acquiesce, and accept it, and do thank God for His many afflictions." Not like many of the shameless and impudent ones, who when they have not done, no not the least part of his good works, yet if they see any in prosperity, and themselves enduring a little discouragement, ruin their own souls by ten thousand blasphemies. But David was not such an one; rather he showed forth all modesty.[14] Wherefore also God said, "I have found David, the son of Jesse, a man after mine own heart."[15]

Such a spirit as this let us too acquire, and whatever we may suffer we shall bear it easily, and before the Kingdom, we shall reap here the gain accruing from lowliness of

---

1 Luke xvii. 10.   2 Matt. viii. 8.

3 1 Cor. xv. 9.   4 Mark i. 7 ; Luke iii. 16 ; John i. 27, iii. 29

5 Alluding to Matthew iii. 14, 15 ; and to the custom of the ancient Church of adding imposition of hands for the gift of the strengthening Spirit immediately on baptism, if the bishop were present. See Bingham, xii. 1, 1, and the writers quoted by him, especially Tertullian, de Bapt. 7. "As soon as we are come out of the water, we are anointed with the consecrated oil. . . Then we receive imposition of hands, summoning and inviting the Holy Spirit in the way of solemn benediction." [*Ante-Nicene Fathers*, vol. iii. p. 672. The second sentence is the beginning of chap. 8 in Tertullian's treatise.—R.]

6 Luke v. 8.   7 [φιλοσοφίας.]

8 [ψυχήν.]   9 [τῆς φιλοσοφιας.]

10 ἐπεμβαίνοντα αὐτοῦ τῷ καιρῷ.   11 2 Sam. xvi. 10.

12 [The words " of God " are supplied by the translator.—R.]

13 Or, " Carry back the ark of God into the city, and put it in its place : if I shall find favor in the eyes of the Lord," &c. Benedict. and Savil. 2 Sam. xv. 25, 26.

14 ἐπιείκειαν.   15 Acts xiii. 22 ; 1 Sam. xiii. 14.

mind. Thus "learn," saith He, "of me, for I am meek and lowly in heart, and ye shall find rest unto your souls." [1] Therefore in order that we may enjoy rest both here and hereafter, let us with great diligence implant in our souls the mother of all things that are good, I mean humility. For thus we shall be enabled both to pass over the sea of this life without waves, and to end our voyage in that calm harbor; by the grace and love towards man of our Lord Jesus Christ, to whom be glory and might for ever and ever. Amen.

[1] Matt. xi. 29.

HOMILY IV.

MATT. I. 17.

"So all the generations from Abraham to David are fourteen generations, and from David until the carrying away into Babylon are fourteen generations, and from the carrying away into Babylon unto Christ are fourteen generations."

HE hath divided all the generations into three portions, to indicate that not even when their form of government was changed did they become better, but alike under an aristocracy, and under a king, and under an oligarchy, they were in the same evil ways, and whether popular leaders, or priests, or kings controlled them, it was no advantage to them in the way of virtue.

But wherefore hath he in the middle portion passed over three kings, and in the last, having set down twelve generations, affirmed them to be fourteen? The former question I leave for you to examine; [1] for neither is it needful for me to explain all things to you, lest ye should grow indolent: but the second we will explain. [2] To me then he seems in this place to be putting in the place of a generation, both the time of the captivity, and Christ Himself, by every means connecting Him with us. And full well doth he put us in mind of that captivity, making it manifest that not even when they went down thither, did they become more sober-minded; in order that from everything His coming may be shown to be necessary.

"Why then," one may say, "doth not Mark do this, nor trace Christ's genealogy, but utter everything briefly?" It seems to me that Matthew was before the rest in entering on the subject (wherefore he both sets down the genealogy with exactness, and stops at those things which require it): but that Mark came after him, which is why he took a short course, as putting his hand to what had been already spoken and made manifest. [3]

How is it then that Luke not only traces the genealogy, but doth it through a greater number? As was natural, Matthew having led the way, he seeks to teach us somewhat in addition to former statements. And each too in like manner imitated his master; the one Paul, who flows fuller than any river; the other Peter, who studies brevity.

2. And what may be the reason that Matthew said not at the beginning, in the same way as the prophet, "the vision which I saw," and "the word which came unto me"? Because he was writing unto men well disposed, and exceedingly attentive to him. For both the miracles that were done cried aloud, and they who received the word were exceeding faithful. But in the case of the prophets, there were neither so many miracles to proclaim them; and besides, the tribe of the false prophets, no small one, was riotously breaking in upon them: to whom the people of the Jews gave even more heed. This kind of opening therefore was necessary in their case.

And if ever miracles were done, they were done for the aliens' sake, to increase the number of the proselytes; and for manifestation of God's power, if haply their enemies having taken them captives, fancied they prevailed,

[1] See St. Jerome *in loc.*
[2] [See Augustin's *Harmony of the Gospels,* ii. 4; *Nicene Fathers,* vol. vi. pp. 105, 106, where the sum of the names (forty) is given a symbolical significance.—R.]

[3] [But see Homily I. 5, 6, where the independence of the evangelists is emphasized.—R.]

because their own gods were mighty: like as in Egypt, out of which no small "mixed multitude"[1] went up; and, after that, in Babylon, what befell touching the furnace and the dreams. And miracles were wrought also, when they were by themselves in the wilderness; as also in our case: for among us too, when we had just come out of error, many wonderful works were shown forth; but afterwards they stayed, when in all countries true religion had taken root.

And what took place at a later period[2] were few and at intervals; for example, when the sun stood still in its course, and started back in the opposite direction. And this one may see to have occurred in our case also. For so even in our generation, in the instance of him who surpassed all in ungodliness, I mean Julian, many strange things happened. Thus when the Jews were attempting to raise up again the temple at Jerusalem, fire burst out from the foundations, and utterly hindered them all; and when both his treasurer,[3] and his uncle and namesake, made the sacred vessels the subject of their open insolence, the one was "eaten with worms, and gave up the ghost,"[4] the other "burst asunder in the midst." Moreover, the fountains failing,[5] when sacrifices were made there, and the entrance of the famine into the cities together with the emperor himself, was a very great sign. For it is usual with God to do such things; when evils are multiplied, and He sees His own people afflicted, and their adversaries greatly intoxicated with their dominion over them, then to display His own power; which he did also in Persia with respect to the Jews.

3. Wherefore, that he was not acting without an object, or by chance, when he distributed Christ's forefathers into three portions, is plain from what hath been said. And mark, too, whence he begins, and where he ends. From Abraham to David; from David to the captivity of Babylon; from this unto Christ Himself. For both at the beginning he put the two in close succession, David and Abraham, and also in summing up he mentions both in the same way. And this, because, as I have already said, it was to them that the promises were made.

But why can it be, that as he mentioned the captivity of Babylon, he did not mention also the descent into Egypt? Because they had ceased to be any longer afraid of the Egyptians, but the Babylonians they dreaded still. And the one thing was ancient, but the other fresh, and had taken place of late. And to the one they were carried down for no sins, but to the other, transgressions were the cause of their being removed.

And also with regard to the very names, if any one were to attempt to translate their etymologies, even thence would he derive great matter of divine speculation,[6] and such as is of great importance with regard to the New Testament: as, for instance, from Abraham's name, from Jacob's, from Solomon's, from Zorobabel's. For it was not without purpose that these names were given them. But lest we should seem to be wearisome by running out a great length, let us pass these things by, and proceed to what is urgent.

4. Having then mentioned all His forefathers, and ending with Joseph, he did not stop at this, but added, "Joseph the husband of Mary;" intimating that it was for her sake he traced his genealogy also. Then, lest when thou hast heard of the "husband of Mary," thou shouldest suppose that Christ was born after the common law of nature, mark, how he sets it right by that which follows. "Thou hast heard," saith he, "of an husband, thou hast heard of a mother, thou hast heard a name assigned to the child, therefore hear the manner too of the birth. "The birth of Jesus Christ was on this wise."[7] "Of what kind of birth art thou telling me, I pray thee, since thou hast already mentioned His ancestors?" "I still wish to tell thee the manner also of His birth." Seest thou, how he wakens up the hearer? For as though he were about to speak of something unusual,[8] he promises to tell also the manner thereof.

And observe a most admirable order in the things he hath mentioned. For he did not proceed directly to the birth, but puts us in mind first, how many generations he was from Abraham, how many from David, and from the captivity of Babylon; and thus he

---

[1] Exod. xii. 38 ; Jer. l. 37.		[2] [Εἰ δὲ καὶ μετὰ ταῦτα γέγονεν.]
[3] "The tyrant commanded the sacred vessels to be delivered up to the imperial treasury. . . . Into the Temple of God then," at Antioch, "there entered, along with Julian the Prefect of the East, Felix the Steward of the Imperial Treasures. . . And they say that Julian grievously insulted the sacred table, and when Euzoius" (the Arian bishop) "endeavored to prevent him, he gave him a blow on the temple. . . . Julian, however, presently fell into a grievous disease, and had his bowels wasted with a kind of mortification . . . and so came to an end of his life. Felix also for his part being afflicted with a scourge from God, had to vomit blood night and day from his mouth . . . until he also wasted away." Theodoret. E. H. iii. 8, 9, ed. Schulze. See also Sozom. E. H. v. 8. St. Chrys. Orat. in Babylam. t. v. p. 246, *sub fin.* where he says that Felix "burst asunder."
[4] Acts xii. 23, i. 18.
[5] He mentions this miracle too with the former ones, Hom. in Ps. cx. t. 1, 738 ; and in his first Hom. on St. Paul, t. 8, 44. "The fountains among us, whose current is stronger than the rivers, shrank suddenly and started back (a thing which never had occurred to them before), upon the Emperor's attempting to defile the place with sacrifices and libations."

[6] θεωρίαν : the allegorical or mystical sense. See Suicer on the word ; and St. Just. Mart. Cohort. ad Græc. p. 29. A. Ed. Morell. See also in the Catena Aurea, from St. Jerome, the interpretation of the names in our Lord's genealogy.
[7] Matt. i. 18.				[8] [καινότερον.]

sets the careful hearer upon considering the times, to show that this is the Christ who was preached by the prophets. For when thou hast numbered the generations, and hast learnt by the time that this is He, thou wilt readily receive likewise the miracle which took place in His birth. Thus, being about to tell of a certain great thing, His birth of a virgin, he first shadows over the statement, until he hath numbered the generations, by speaking of "an husband of Mary;" or rather he doth even put in short space[1] the narration of the birth itself, and then proceeds to number also the years, reminding the hearer, that this is He, of whom the patriarch Jacob had said, He should then at length come, when the Jewish rulers had come to an end; of whom the prophet Daniel had proclaimed beforehand, that He should come after those many weeks. And if any one, counting the years spoken of to Daniel by the angel in a number of weeks, would trace down the time from the building of the city to His birth, by reckoning he will perceive the one to agree with the other.[2]

5. How then was He born, I pray thee? "When as His mother Mary was espoused:"[3] He saith not "virgin," but merely "mother;" so that his account is easy to be received. And so having beforehand prepared the hearer to look for some ordinary piece of information, and by this laying hold of him, after all he amazes him by adding the marvellous fact, saying, "Before they came together, she was found with child of the Holy Ghost." He saith not, "before she was brought to the bridegroom's house;" for indeed she was therein. It being the way of the ancients for the most part to keep their espoused wives in their house:[4] in those parts, at least, where one may see the same practised even now. Thus also Lot's sons-in-law were in his house with him. Mary then herself likewise was in the house with Joseph.

And wherefore did she not conceive before her espousal? It was, as I said at first, that what had been done might be concealed awhile, and that the Virgin might escape every evil suspicion. For when he, who had most right of all to feel jealousy, so far from making her a show, or degrading her, is found even receiving and cherishing her after her conception; it was quite clear that, unless he had fully persuaded himself that what was done was of the operation of the Holy Spirit,

he would not have kept her with him, and ministered to her in all other things. And most properly hath he said, that "she was 'found' with child," the sort of expression that is wont to be used with respect to things strange, and such as happen beyond all expectation, and are unlooked for.

Proceed therefore no further, neither require anything more than what hath been said; neither say thou, "But how was it that the Spirit wrought this of a virgin?" For if, when nature is at work, it is impossible to explain the manner of the formation; how, when the Spirit is working miracles, shall we be able to express these? And lest thou shouldest weary the evangelist, or disturb him by continually asking these things, he hath said who it was that wrought the miracle, and so withdrawn himself. "For I know," saith he, "nothing more, but that what was done was the work of the Holy Ghost."

6. Shame on them who busy themselves touching the generation on high. For if this birth, which hath witnesses without number, and had been proclaimed so long a time before, and was manifested and handled with hands, can by no man be explained; of what excess of madness do they come short who make themselves busy and curious touching that unutterable generation? For neither Gabriel nor Matthew was able to say anything more, but only that it was of the Spirit; but how, of the Spirit, or in what manner, neither of them hath explained; for neither was it possible.

Nor think that thou hast learnt all, by hearing "of the Spirit;" nay, for we are ignorant of many things, even when we have learnt this; as, for instance, how the Infinite is in a womb, how He that contains all things is carried, as unborn, by a woman; how the Virgin bears, and continues a virgin. How, I pray thee, did the Spirit frame that Temple? how did He take not all the flesh from the womb, but a part thereof, and increased it, and fashioned it? For that He did come forth of the Virgin's flesh, He hath declared by speaking of "that which was conceived in her;"[5] and Paul, by saying, "made of a woman;" whereby he stops the mouths of them[6] that say, Christ came among us as

[1] σύντεμνει.
[2] See the different opinions of the Fathers on these dates, in St. Jerome on Daniel ix.
[3] Matt. i. 18.   [4] Gen. xix. 8, 14.

[5] Gal. iv. 4.
  i. e., the Valentinians and some other Gnostics. Theodoret, Ep. 145. "Valentinus, and Basilides, and Bardesanes, and Harmonius, and those of their company, allow indeed the Virgin's conception and the birth, but affirm that God the Word took nothing of the Virgin, but in a manner made Himself a passage through her as through a conduit, and that in manifesting Himself to men He was employing a mere phantom, and only seeming to be a man ; as He appeared to Abraham and certain other of the ancients." S. Epiph. Hær. xxxi. 7. "They affirm that He brought down His body from Heaven, and that as water through

through some conduit. For, if this were so, what need of the womb? If this were so, He hath nothing in common with us, but that flesh is of some other kind, and not of the mass which belongs to us. How then was He of the root of Jesse? How was He a rod? how Son of man? how was Mary His mother? how was He of David's seed? how did he "take the form of a servant?"[1] how "was the Word made flesh?"[2] and how saith Paul to the Romans, "Of whom as concerning the flesh Christ came, who is God over all?"[3] Therefore that He was of us, and of our substance,[4] and of the Virgin's womb, is manifest from these things, and from others beside; but how, is not also manifest. Do not either thou then inquire; but receive what is revealed, and be not curious about what is kept secret.

7. "And Joseph her husband, being," saith he, "a just man, and not willing to make her a public example, was minded to put her away privily."[5]

Having said that it was of the Holy Ghost, and without cohabitation, he establishes his statement in another way again.[6] Lest any one should say, "Whence doth this appear? Who hath heard, who hath seen any such thing ever come to pass?"—or lest you should suspect the disciple as inventing these things to favor his Master;—he introduces Joseph as contributing, by what he underwent, to the proof of the things mentioned; and by his narrative all but says, "If thou doubt, me, and if thou suspect my testimony, believe her husband." For "Joseph," saith he, "her husband, being a just man." By "a just man" in this place he means him that is virtuous in all things. For both freedom from covetousness is justice, and universal virtue is also justice;[7] and it is mostly in this latter sense that the Scripture uses the name of justice; as when it saith, "a man that was just and true;"[8] and again, "they were both just."[9] Being then "just," that is good and considerate, "he was minded to put her away privily." For this intent he tells what took place before Joseph's being fully informed, that thou mightest not mistrust what was done after he knew.

However, such a one was not liable to be made a public example only, but that she should also be punished was the command of the law. Whereas Joseph remitted not only that greater punishment, but the less likewise, namely, the disgrace. For so far from punishing, he was not minded even to make an example of her. Seest thou a man under self-restraint, and freed from the most tyrannical of passions. For ye know how great a thing jealousy is: and therefore He said, to whom these things are clearly known, "For full of jealousy is the rage of a husband;"[10] "he will not spare in the day of vengeance:" and "jealousy is cruel as the grave."[11] And we too know of many that have chosen to give up their lives rather than fall under the suspicion of jealousy. But in this case it was not so little as suspicion, the burden of the womb entirely convicting her. But nevertheless he was so free from passion as to be unwilling to grieve the Virgin even in the least matters. Thus, whereas to keep her in his house seemed like a transgression of the law, but to expose and bring her to trial would constrain him to deliver her to die; he doth none of these things, but conducts himself now by a higher rule than the law. For grace being come, there must needs henceforth be many tokens of that exalted citizenship. For as the sun, though as yet he show not his beams, doth from afar by his light illumine more than half[12] the world; so likewise Christ, when about to rise from that womb, even before He came forth, shone over all the world. Wherefore, even before her travail, prophets danced for joy, and women foretold what was to come, and John, when he had not yet come forth from the belly, leaped from the very womb. Hence also this man exhibited great self-command, in that he neither accused nor upbraided, but only set about putting her away.

8. The matter then being in this state, and all at their wits' end,[13] the angel comes to solve all their difficulties. But it is worth inquiring, why the angel did not speak sooner, before the husband had such thoughts: but, "when he thought on it," not until then, he came; for it is said, "While he thought on these things, the angel" comes. And yet to her he declares the good tidings even before she conceived. And this again contains another difficulty; for even though the angel had not spoken, wherefore was the Virgin silent, who had been informed by the angel; and why, when she saw her betrothed husband in trouble, did she not put an end to his perplexity?

a conduit, so He passed through the Virgin Mary taking nothing of His mother's womb, but having His body from Heaven, as I said before." Comp. Massuet's 1st Dissert. prefixed to the Benedictine Irenæus, sec. 73. [Comp. the recovered work of Hippolytus (unknown when the Oxford translation was made), *Refutation of all Heresies,* Book VI., VII., *Ante-Nicene Fathers,* Vol. V. pp. 81 *et sqq.*—R.]

　[1] Phil. ii. 7.　　[2] John i. 14.　　[3] Rom. ix. 5.
[4] φυράματος.　[5] Matt. i. 19.
[6] [The punctuation of the translation has here been conformed to that of the Greek text.—R.]
　[7] See Arist. Eth. Nicom. v. 1, 2.　[8] Job i. 1.　[9] Luke i. 6.

[10] Prov. vi. 34.　　　　[11] Cant. viii. 6.
[12] [τὸ πλεον.]　　　[13] [πάντων ἐν ἀμηχανίᾳ καθεστώτων.]

Wherefore then did not the angel speak before Joseph became troubled. For we must needs explain the former difficulty first. For what reason then did he not speak? Lest Joseph should be unbelieving, and the same happen to him as to Zacharias. For when the thing was visible, belief was thenceforth easy; but when it had not yet a beginning, it was not equally easy to receive his saying. For this reason the angel spake not at the first, and through the same cause the Virgin too held her peace. For she did not think to obtain credit with her betrothed husband, in declaring to him a thing unheard of, but rather that she should provoke him the more, as though she were cloking a sin that had been committed. Since if she herself, who was to receive so great a favor, is affected somewhat after the manner of man, and saith, "How shall this be, seeing I know not a man?"[1] much more would he have doubted; and especially when hearing it from the woman who was under suspicion. Wherefore the Virgin saith nothing to him, but the angel, the time demanding it, presents himself to him.

9. Why then, it may be asked, did he not so in the Virgin's case also, and declare the good tidings to her after the conception? Lest she should be in agitation and great trouble. For it were likely that she, not knowing the certainty, might have even devised something amiss touching herself, and have gone on to strangle or to stab herself, not enduring the disgrace. For wondrous indeed was that Virgin, and Luke points out her excellency, saying, that when she heard the salutation, she did not straightway pour herself out,[2] neither did she accept the saying, but "was troubled," seeking "what manner of salutation this might be."[3] Now she who was of such perfect delicacy would even have been distracted with dismay at the thought of her shame, not expecting, by whatever she might say, to convince any one who should hear of it, but that what had happened was adultery. Therefore to prevent these things, the angel came before the conception. Besides that, it was meet that womb should be free from trouble which the Maker of all things entered; and the soul rid of all perturbation, which was thought worthy to become the minister of such mysteries. For these reasons He speaks to the Virgin before the conception, but to Joseph at the time of travail.

And this many of the simpler sort, not understanding, have said there is a discordance; because Luke saith it was Mary to whom he declared the good tidings, but Matthew, that it was Joseph; not knowing that both took place. And this sort of thing it is necessary to bear in mind throughout the whole history; for in this way we shall solve many seeming discordances.

10. The angel then comes, when Joseph is troubled. For in addition to the causes mentioned, with a view also to the manifestation of his self-command, he defers his coming. But when the thing was on the point of taking place, then at last he presents himself. "While he thought on these things, an angel appeareth to Joseph in a dream."[4]

Seest thou the mildness of the husband? So far from punishing, he did not even declare it to any one, no not even to her whom he suspected, but was thinking it over with himself, as aiming to conceal the cause even from the Virgin herself. For neither is it said that he was minded to "cast her out," but to "put her away," so very mild and gentle was the man. "But while he is thinking on these things, the angel appeareth in a dream."

And why not openly, as to the shepherds, and to Zacharias, and to the Virgin? The man was exceedingly full of faith, and needed not this vision. Whereas the Virgin, as having declared to her very exceeding good tidings, greater than to Zacharias, and this before the event, needed also a marvellous vision; and the shepherds, as being by disposition rather dull and clownish.[5] But this man, after the conception,[6] when his soul was actually possessed with that evil suspicion, and ready to exchange it for good hopes, if there appeared any one to guide that way, readily receives the revelation. Wherefore he hath the good tidings declared to him after his suspicion, that this selfsame thing might be to him a convincing proof of the things spoken. I mean, that the fact of his having mentioned it to no one, and his hearing the angel say the very things which he thought in his mind, this afforded him an unquestionable sign that one had come from God to say it. For to Him alone it belongs to know the secrets of the heart.

Mark only, what a number of results are here. The man's self-command is thoroughly shown; the word spoken in season contributes to his faith, and the history is freed from suspicion, in that it shows him to have felt what it was likely a husband would feel.

---

[1] Luke i. 34.
[2] [That is, did not give way to her feeling, with loud cry, whether of joy or grief.—R.]
[3] Luke i. 29.

[4] Matt. i. 20. [5] [ἀγροικικώτερον, "more boorish."—R.]
[6] τὸν τόκον.

11. How then doth the angel assure him? Hear and marvel at the wisdom of his words. For being come he saith, "Joseph, thou son of David, fear not to take unto thee Mary thy wife." He straightway puts him in mind of David, of whom the Christ was to spring, and he doth not suffer him to be greatly perturbed, by the title of his forefathers, reminding him of the promise made to the whole race. Else wherefore doth he call him "Son of David"?

"Fear not:" and yet in another case God doeth not so, but when one was devising about a certain woman what he ought not, He spake the word more in a way of rebuke, and with a threat.[1] And yet there too, the act was of ignorance, for not with knowledge did that person take Sarah; yet nevertheless He rebuked him: but here mildly. For exceeding great were the mysteries He was dispensing,[2] and wide the interval between the two men; wherefore neither was there need of rebuke.

But by saying, "fear not," he signifies him to have been afraid, lest he should give offense to God, as retaining an adulteress; since, if it had not been for this, he would not have even thought of casting her out. In all ways then he points out that the angel came from God, bringing forward and setting before him all, both what he thought to do, and what he felt in his mind.

Now having mentioned her name, he stayed not at this, but added also, "thy wife;" whereas he would not have called her so, if she had been corrupted. And here he calls her that is espoused "a wife;" as indeed the Scripture is wont to call betrothed husbands sons-in-law even before marriage.

But what means, "to take unto thee?" To retain her in his house, for in intention she had been now put away by him. "Her, being put away, do thou retain," saith he, "as committed unto thee by God, not by her parents. And He commits her not for marriage; but to dwell with thee; and by my voice doth He commit her." Much as Christ Himself afterwards committed her to His disciple, so even now unto Joseph.

12. Then having obscurely signified the matter in hand, he mentioned not the evil suspicion; but, in a manner more reverent and seemly, by telling the cause of travail he removed this also; implying that the very thing which had made him afraid, and for which he would have cast her out,—this very thing, I say, was a just cause why he should take her and retain her in his house. Thus more than entirely[3] doing away with his distress. "For she is not only free," saith he, "from unlawful intercourse, but even above all nature is her conception. Not only therefore put away thy fear, but even rejoice more exceedingly, 'for that which is conceived in her is of the Holy Ghost.'"

A strange thing it was which he spake of, surpassing man's reason, and above all the laws of nature. How then is he to believe, to whom such tidings are altogether new? "By the things that are past," saith he, "by the revelations." For with this intent he laid open all things that were in his mind, what he felt, what he feared, what he was resolved to do;—that by these he might assure himself of this point.

Or rather, not by things past only, but likewise by things to come, he wins him over. "And she shall bring forth," saith he, "a Son, and thou shall call His name JESUS."[4] "For do not thou, because He is of the Holy Ghost, imagine that thou art an alien to the ministry of this dispensation. Since although in the birth thou hast no part, but the Virgin abode untouched, nevertheless, what pertains to a father, not injuring the honor of virginity, that do I give thee, to set a Name on that which is born: for "thou shalt call Him." For though the offspring be not thine, yet shalt thou exhibit a father's care towards Him. Wherefore I do straightway, even from the giving of the name, connect thee with Him that is born."

Then lest on the other hand any one should from this suspect him to be the father, hear what follows, with what exact care he states it. "She shall bring forth," he saith, "a Son:" he doth not say, "bring forth to thee," but merely "she shall bring forth," putting it indefinitely:[5] since not to him did she bring forth, but to the whole world.

13. For this cause too the angel came bringing His name from Heaven, hereby again intimating that this is a wondrous birth: it being God Himself who sends the name from above by the angel to Joseph. For neither was this without an object, but a treasure of ten thousand blessings. Wherefore the angel also interprets it, and suggests good hopes, in this way again leading him to belief. For to these things we are wont to be more inclined, and therefore are also fonder of believing them.

So having established his faith by all, by the past things, by the future, by the present, by the honor given to himself, he rings in the prophet also in good time, to give his

---

[1] Gen. xx. 3.   [2] οἰκονομούμενα.

[3] [ἐκ περιουσίας, "superabundantly."—R.]
[4] Matt. i. 21.   [5] μετεωρον.

suffrage in support of all these. But before introducing him, he proclaims beforehand the good things which were to befall the world through Him. And what are these? Sins removed and done away.[1] "For He shall save His people from their sins."

Here again the thing is signified to be beyond all expectation. For not from visible wars, neither from barbarians, but what was far greater than these, from sins, he declares the glad tidings of deliverance; a work which had never been possible to any one before.

But wherefore, one may ask, did he say, "His people," and not add the Gentiles also? That he might not startle the hearer yet a while. For to him that listens with understanding he darkly signified the Gentiles too. For "His people" are not the Jews only, but also all that draw nigh and receive the knowledge that is from Him.

And mark how he hath by the way discovered to us also His dignity, by calling the Jewish nation "His people." For this is the word of one implying nought else, but that He who is born is God's child, and that the King of those on high is the subject of his discourse. As neither doth forgiving sins belong to any other power, but only to that single essence.

14. Forasmuch then as we have partaken of so great a gift, let us do everything not to dishonor such a benefit. For if even before this honor, what was done was worthy of punishment, much more now, after this unspeakable benefit. And this I say not now for no cause,[2] but because I see many after their baptism living more carelessly than the uninitiated, and having nothing peculiar to distinguish them in their way of life. It is, you see, for this cause, that neither in the market nor in the Church is it possible to know quickly who is a believer and who an unbeliever; unless one be present at the time of the mysteries, and see the one sort put out, the others remaining within. Whereas they ought to be distinguished not by their place, but by their way of life. For as men's outward[3] dignities are naturally to be discovered by the outward signs with which they are invested, so ours ought to be discernible by the soul. That is, the believer ought to be manifest not by the gift only, but also by the new life. The believer ought to be the light and salt of the world. But when thou dost not give light even to thyself, neither bind up thine own gangrene, what remains, whereby

we are to know thee? Because thou hast entered the holy waters? Nay, this to thee becomes a store[4] of punishment. For greatness of honor is, to them who do not choose to live worthy of the honor, an increase of vengeance. Yea, the believer ought to shine forth not only by what he hath received from God, but also by what he himself hath contributed; and should be discernible by everything, by his gait, by his look, by his garb, by his voice. And this I have said, not that display, but that the profit of beholders, may be the rule by which we frame ourselves.

15. But now, what things soever I might seek to recognize thee by, I find thee in all points distinguished by the contraries of the same. For whether by thy place I would fain discern thee, I see thee spending thy day in horse races, and theatres, and scenes of lawlessness, in the market places, and in companies of depraved men; or by the fashion of thy countenance, I see thee continually laughing to excess, and dissolute as a grinning[5] and abandoned harlot; or by thy clothes, I see thee in no better trim than the people on the stage; or by thy followers, thou art leading about parasites and flatterers; or by thy words, I hear thee say nothing wholesome, nothing necessary, nothing of moment to our life; or by thy table, yet heavier from thence will the charge against thee appear.

By what then, tell me, am I to recognize the believer[6] in thee, while all the things I have mentioned give the contrary sentence? And why do I say, the believer? since I can not clearly make out whether thou art a man. For when thou art like an ass, kicking, and like a bull, wantoning, and like a horse neighing after women; when thou dost play the glutton like the bear, and pamper thy flesh as the mule, and bear malice like the camel;[7] when thou dost raven as a wolf, art wrathful as a serpent, stingest like a scorpion, and art crafty as a fox, treasurest the poison of wickedness like an asp or a viper, and warrest against thy brethren like that evil demon;—how shall I be able to number thee with men, not seeing in thee the marks of man's nature. Why, whilst I am seeking the difference of catechumen and believer, I come near not to find even the difference between a man and a wild beast. For what shall I

---

[1] [More literally, "Removal and destruction of sins."—R.]
[2] [οὐχ ἁπλῶς, here in the sense, "not generally, not at random."—R.]
[3] ἔξωθεν. 1 Cor. v. 13.

[4] ἐφόδιον.   [5] σεσηρυῖαν.
[6] [πιστόν. The translator sometimes, as in this instance, rendered the word "Christian." For the sake of uniformity, "believer" has been substituted several times in this paragraph.—R.]
[7] The Hebrew name גָּמָל is borrowed according to Bochart from גָּמַל, retribuit, "because it is an animal retaining anger long, and returning evil for evil." Simon. Lex. in verb.

call thee? a wild beast? Nay, the wild beasts are possessed by some one of these defects, but thou heapest all together, and far surpassest their brutishness. Shall I then call thee a devil?[1] Nay, a devil is not a slave to the dominion of the belly, neither doth he set his love on riches. When therefore thou hast more faults than either wild beasts or devils, how, I pray thee, shall we call thee a man? And if thou art not to be styled a man, how shall we address thee as a believer?

16. And what is yet more grievous is this, that being in such evil case, we have no idea whatever of the deformity of our own soul, nor discern the hideousness thereof. And yet when thou art sitting at a hairdresser's, and having thine hair cut, thou takest the mirror, and dost examine with care the arrangement of thy locks, and askest them that stand by, and the haircutter himself, if he hath well disposed what is on the forehead; and being old, for so it often happens, art not ashamed of going wild with the fancies of youth: while of our own soul, not only deformed, but transformed into a wild beast, and made a sort of Scylla or Chimæra, according to the heathen fable, we have not even a slight perception. And yet in this case too there is a mirror, spiritual, and far more excellent, and more serviceable than that other one; for it not only shows our own deformity, but transforms it too, if we be willing, into surpassing beauty. This mirror is the memory of good men, and the history of their blessed lives; the reading of the Scriptures; the laws given by God. If thou be willing once only to look upon the portraitures of those holy men, thou will both see the foulness of thine own mind, and having seen this, wilt need nothing else to be set free from that deformity. Because the mirror is useful for this purpose also, and makes the change easy.

Let no man therefore continue in the form of the irrational creatures. For if the slave doth not enter into the father's house, how wilt thou, having become even a wild beast, be able to set thy foot within those vestibules? And why say I, a wild beast? Nay, such a one is more unmanageable than any wild beast. For they, although by nature savage, yet when they have had the advantage of man's art, oftentimes grow tame; but thou who hast changed their natural wildness into this unnatural gentleness, what sort of plea wilt thou have, when thou hast trained thine own natural meekness into the savageness that is contrary to nature? when that which

is wild by nature thou exhibitest in gentle mood, but presentest thyself, by nature so gentle, unnaturally savage? and the lion[2] thou tamest and makest tractable, but thine own wrath thou renderest wilder than any lion. And yet in that case there are two hindrances, first that the beast is deprived of reason, and then that it is the most wrathful of all things; nevertheless by the excellency of the wisdom given to thee of God, thou dost overcome even nature. Thou therefore, who in wild beasts art victorious over nature herself, how is it that in thine own case together with nature thou givest up thine admirable quality of free will[3] also?

Further, if I were bidding thee make another man gentle, not even so ought I to seem as one enjoining impossible things; however, thou mightest then object that thou hast not the control of another's disposition, and that it doth not altogether rest with thee. But now it is thine own wild beast, and a thing which absolutely depends on thee. What plea then hast thou? or what fair excuse wilt thou be able to put forth, turning as thou art a lion into a man, and regardless that thou thyself art of a man becoming a lion; upon the beast bestowing what is above nature, but for thyself not even preserving what is natural? Yea, while the wild beasts are by thine earnest endeavors advanced into our noble estate, thou art by thyself cast down from the throne of the kingdom, and thrust out into their madness. Thus, imagine, if thou wilt, thy wrath to be a kind of wild beast, and as much zeal as others have displayed about lions, so much do thou in regard of thyself, and cause that way of taking things[4] to become gentle and meek. Because this too hath grievous teeth and talons, and if thou tame it not, it will lay waste all things. For not even lion nor serpent hath such power to rend the vitals as wrath, with its iron talons continually doing so. Since it mars, we see, not the body only, but the very health likewise of the soul is corrupted by it, devouring, rending, tearing to pieces all its strength, and making it useless for everything. For if a man nourishing worms in his entrails, shall not be able so much as to breathe, his inward parts all wasting away; how shall we, having so large a serpent eating up all within us (it is wrath I mean), how, I say, shall we be able to produce anything noble?

17. How then are we to be freed from this

---

[1] [Greek, "demon," and so in the following sentences.—R.]

[2] This illustration about taming the lion might come with peculiar force to the people of Antioch, who were especially attached to the games of the circus. See Gibbon, c. 24.

[3] [προαιρέσεως, deliberate choice.—R.]

[4] τὸν τοιοῦτον λογισμόν.

pest? If we can drink a potion that is able to kill the worms within us and the serpents. "And of what nature," it will be asked, "may this potion be, that hath such power?" The precious Blood of Christ, if it be received with full assurance,[1] (for this will have power to extinguish every disease); and together with this the divine Scriptures carefully heard, and almsgiving added to our hearing; for by means of all these things we shall be enabled to mortify the affections that mar our soul. And then only shall we live; for now surely we are in no better state than the dead: forasmuch as it cannot be, that while those passions live, we should live too, but we must necessarily perish. And unless we first kill them here, they will be sure to kill us in the other life; or rather before that death they will exact of us, even here, the utmost penalty. Yes, for every such passion is both cruel and tyrannical and insatiable, and never ceases to devour us every day. For "their teeth are the teeth of a lion,"[2] or rather even far more fierce. For the lion, as soon as ever he is satisfied, is wont to leave the carcass that hath fallen in his way; but these passions neither are satisfied, nor do they leave the man whom they have seized, until they have set him nigh the devil. For so great is their power, that the very service which Paul showed forth to Christ,[3] despising both hell and the kingdom for His sake, even this same do they require of them whom they have seized. For whether it be with the love of women, or of riches, or of glory, that any one is entangled, he laughs at hell thenceforth, and despises the kingdom, that he may work the will of these. Let us not then doubt Paul when he saith that he so loved Christ. For when some are found so doing service to their passions, how should that other afterwards seem incredible? Yea, and this is the reason why our longing for Christ is feebler, because all our strength is consumed on this love, and we rob, and defraud, and are slaves to vainglory; than which what can be more worthless?

For though thou shouldest become infinitely conspicuous, thou wilt be nothing better than the base: rather for this selfsame cause thou wilt even be baser. For when they who are willing to give thee glory, and make thee illustrious, do for this very cause ridicule thee, that thou desirest the glory which comes of them, how can such instances fail to turn the contrary way in regard of thee. For indeed this thing is among those which attract censure. So that even as in the

case of one desiring to commit adultery or fornication, should any one praise or flatter him, by this very act he becomes an accuser, rather than a commender of the person indulging such desires: so with regard to him who is desirous of glory; when we all praise, it is accusation rather than praise which we bestow on those who wish to be made glorious.

18. Why then bring upon thyself that, from which the very opposite is wont to befall thee. Yea, if thou wilt be glorified, despise glory; so shalt thou be more illustrious than any. Why feel as Nebuchadnezzar felt? For he too set up an image, thinking from wood and from a senseless figure to procure to himself an increase of fame, and the living would fain appear more glorious by the help of that which hath no life. Seest thou the excess of his madness; how, thinking to do honor, he rather offered insult, to himself? For when it appears that he is relying rather on the lifeless thing, than on himself and the soul that lives in him, and when for this cause he advances the stock unto such high precedence, how can he be other than ridiculous, endeavoring as he doth to adorn himself, not by his way of living, but by planks of wood? Just as if a man should think proper to give himself airs, because of the pavement of his house, and his beautiful staircase, rather than because he is a man. Him do many too amongst us imitate now. For as he for his image, so some men claim to be admired for their clothes, others for their house; or for their mules and chariots, and for the columns in their house. For inasmuch as they have lost their being as men, they go about gathering to themselves from other quarters such glory as is full of exceeding ridicule.

But as to the noble and great servants of God, not by these means, but by such as best became them, even by such did they shine forth. For captives as they were, and slaves, and youths, and strangers, and stripped of all resources of their own, they proved at that time far more awful than he who was invested with all these things. And while Nebuchadnezzar found neither so great an image, nor satraps, nor captains of the host, nor endless legions, nor abundance of gold, nor other pomp, enough to meet his desire, and to show him great; to these, on the other hand, stripped of all this, their high self-restraint alone was sufficient, and showed him that wore the diadem and the purple, as much inferior in glory to those who had no such thing, as the sun is more glorious than a pearl.[4] For they were led forth in the midst of the whole world, being at once

---

[1] παῤῥησίας. ["Boldness" or "confidence" would better express the meaning.—R.]   [2] Joel i.6.   [3] Rom. viii. 38.

[4] μαργάρου.

youths, and captives, and slaves, and straightway on their appearance the king darted fire from his eyes, and captains, and deputies, and governors, and the whole amphitheatre of the devil, stood around; and a voice of pipes from all sides, and of trumpets, and of all music, borne up to Heaven, was sounding in their ears, and the furnace burned up to a boundless height, and the flame reached the very clouds, and all was full of terror and dismay. But none of these things dismayed them, but they laughed it all to scorn, as they would children mocking them, and exhibited their courage and meekness, and uttering a voice clearer than those trumpets, they said, " Be it known unto thee, O king."[1] For they did not wish to affront the king, no not so much as by a word, but to declare their religion[2] only. For which cause, neither did they extend their speech to any great length, but set forth all briefly; " For there is," say they, " a God in Heaven, who is able to deliver us,"[3] " why showest thou me the multitude? why the furnace? why the sharpened swords? why the terrible guards? our Lord is higher and more mighty than all these."

Then when they considered that it was possible that God might be willing even to permit them to be burnt; lest, if this should come to pass, they might seem to be speaking falsehoods; they add this also and say, " If this happen not, be it known unto thee, O king, that we serve not thy gods."[4] For had they said, " Sins are the cause of His not delivering us, should He fail to deliver," they would not have been believed. Wherefore in this place they are silent on that subject, though they speak of it in the furnace, again and again alleging their sins. But before the king they say no such thing; only, that though they were to be burnt, they would not give up their religion.

For it was not for rewards and recompenses that they did what they did, but out of love alone; and yet they were in captivity too, and in slavery, and had enjoyed no good thing. Yea, they had lost their country, and their freedom, and all their possessions. For tell me not of their honors in the king's courts, for holy and righteous as they were, they would have chosen ten thousand times rather to have been beggars at home, and to have been partakers of the blessings in the temple. " For I had rather," it is said, " be an outcast[5] in the house of my God,

than to dwell in the tents of sinners." And " one day in thy courts is better than thousands."[6] They would have chosen then ten thousand times rather to be outcasts at home, than kings in Babylon. And this is manifest, from what they declare even in the furnace, grieving at their continuance in that country. For although themselves enjoyed great honors, yet seeing the calamities of the rest they were exceedingly vexed; and this kind of thing is most especially characteristic of saints, that no glory, nor honor, nor anything else should be more precious to them than their neighbor's welfare. See, for example, how even when they were in a furnace, they made their supplication for all the people. But we not even when at large bear our brethren in mind. And again, when they were inquiring about the dreams,[7] they were looking " not to their own, but the common good,"[8] for that they despised death they showed by many things afterwards. But everywhere they put themselves forward, as wishing to prevail[9] with God by importunity. Next, as not accounting themselves either to be sufficient, they flee to the Fathers; but of themseves they said that they offer nothing more than " a contrite spirit."[10]

19. These men then let us also imitate. Because now too there is set up a golden image, even the tyranny of Mammon. But let us not give heed to the timbrels, nor to the flutes, nor to the harps, nor to the rest of the pomp of riches; yea, though we must needs fall into a furnace of poverty, let us choose it, rather than worship that idol, and there will be " in the midst a moist whistling wind."[11] Let us not then shudder at hearing of " a furnace of poverty." For so too at that time they that fell into the furnace were shewn the more glorious, but they that worshipped were destroyed. Only then all took place at once, but in this case some part will be accomplished here, some there, some both here and in the day that is to come. For they that have chosen poverty, in order that they might not worship mammon, will be more glorious both here and then, but they that have been rich unjustly here, shall then pay the utmost penalty.

From this furnace Lazarus too went forth, not less glorious than those children; but the rich man who was in the place of them that worshipped the image, was condemned to

---

[1] Dan. iii. 18.　　　　　　　　[2] [εὐσέβειαν.]
[3] Dan. iii. 17.　　　　　　　　[4] Dan. iii. 18.
[5] παραῤῥιπτεῖσθαι, i. e., be a worshipper outside the courts. Our marginal translation is, " I would choose rather to sit at the threshold." [The R. V. margin is, " I had rather stand at the threshold."—R.]

[6] Ps. lxxxiv. 10, LXX.　　[7] Dan. ii. 17, 18.
[8] Phil. ii. 4 ; 1 Cor. x. 33.　[9] δυσωπῆσαι.
[10] Song of the Three Children, v. 16.
[11] Song of the Three Children, v. 26. [The Greek phrase, δρόσος διασυρίζουσα, literally means, " a dew continually whistling." Chrysostom refers several times in what follows to the " dew," having this citation in mind.—R.]

hell.[1] For indeed what we have now mentioned was a type of this. Wherefore as in this instance they who fell into the furnace suffered no hurt, but they who sat without were laid hold of with great fierceness, so likewise shall it be then. The saints walking through the river of fire shall suffer no pain, nay they will even appear joyous; but they that have worshipped the image, shall see the fire rest upon them fiercer than any wild beast, and draw them in. So that if any one disbelieves hell, when he sees this furnace, let him from the things present believe things to come, and fear not the furnace of poverty, but the furnace of sin. For this is flame and torment, but that, dew[2] and refreshment; and by this stands the devil, by that, angels wafting aside the flame.

20. These things let them hear that are rich, that are kindling the furnace of poverty. For though they shall not hurt those others, "the dew"[2] coming to their aid; yet themselves they will render an easy prey to the flame, which they have kindled with their own hands.

Then, an angel went down with those children; now, let us go down with[3] them that are in the furnace of poverty, and by alms-deeds let us make a "dewy air,"[2] and waft the flame quite aside, that we may be partakers of their crowns also; that the flames of hell may likewise be scattered by the voice of Christ saying, "Ye saw me an hungered, and fed me."[4] For that voice shall then be with us instead of a "moist wind whistling"[2] through the midst of the flame. Let us then go down with alms-giving, unto the furnace of poverty; let us behold them that in self-restraint walk therein, and trample on the burning coals; let us behold the marvel, strange and beyond thought, a man singing praise in a furnace, a man giving thanks in fire, chained unto extreme poverty, yet offering much praise to Christ. Since they, who bear poverty with thankfulness, really become equal to those children. For no flame is so terrible as poverty, nor so apt to set us on fire. But those children were not set on fire; rather, on their giving thanks to the Lord, their bonds too were at once loosed. So likewise now, if when thou hast fallen into poverty, thou art thankful, both the bonds are loosened, and the flame extinguished; or though it be not extinguished (what is much more marvellous), it becomes a fountain instead of a flame: which then likewise came to pass, and in the midst of a furnace they enjoyed a pure dew. For the fire indeed it quenched not, but the burning of those cast in it altogether hindered. This one may see in their case also who live by the rules of wisdom,[5] for they, even in poverty, feel more secure than the rich.

Let us not therefore sit down without the furnace, feeling no pity towards the poor; lest the same befall us as then befell those executioners. For if thou shouldest go down to them, and take thy stand with the children, the fire will no longer work thee any harm; but if thou shouldest sit above and neglect them in the flame of their poverty, the flame will burn thee up. Go down therefore into the fire, that thou mayest not be burnt up by the fire; sit not down without the fire, lest the flame catch hold of thee. For if it should find thee amongst the poor, it will depart from thee; but if alienated from them, it will run upon thee quickly, and catch thee. Do not therefore stand off from them that are cast in, but when the devil gives command to cast them that have not worshipped gold into the furnace of poverty, be not thou of them that cast others in, but of them that are cast in; that thou mayest be of the number of the saved, and not of the burned. For indeed it is a most effectual *dew*, to be held in no subjection by desire of wealth, to be associate with poor persons. These are wealthier than all, who have trampled under foot the desire of riches. Forasmuch as those children too, by despising the king at that time, became more glorious than the king. And thou therefore, if thou despise the things of the world, shalt become more honorable than all the world; like those holy men, "of whom the world was not worthy."[6]

In order then to become worthy of the things in Heaven, I bid thee laugh to scorn things present. For in this way thou shalt both be more glorious here, and enjoy the good things to come, by the grace and love towards man of our Lord Jesus Christ; to whom be glory and might for ever and ever. Amen.

---

[1] Gehenna. [But in Luke xvi. 23, "Hades" occurs. The context in the Gospel, however, justifies the interpretation of the passage given here.—R.]
[2] [See note 11, (p. 29).—R.]　[3] συγκαταβῶμεν, "condescend."
[4] Matt. xxv. 35.

[5] [τῶν φιλοσοφούντων.]　　　　[6] Heb. xi. 38.

HOMILY V.

MATT. I. 22, 23.

"Now all this was done, that it might be fulfilled which was spoken of the Lord by the Prophet, saying, Behold, a Virgin shall be with child, and shall bring forth a Son, and they shall call His name Emmanuel."

I HEAR many say, "While we are here, and enjoying the privilege of hearing, we are awed, but when we are gone out, we become altered men again, and the flame of zeal is quenched." What then may be done, that this may not come to pass? Let us observe whence it arises. Whence then doth so great a change in us arise? From the unbecoming employment of our time, and from the company of evil men. For we ought not as soon as we retire from the Communion,[1] to plunge into business unsuited to the Communion, but as soon as ever we get home, to take our Bible into our hands, and call our wife and children to join us in putting together what we have heard, and then, not before, engage in the business of life.[2]

For if after the bath you would not choose to hurry into the market place, lest by the business in the market you should destroy the refreshment thence derived; much more ought we to act on this principle after the Communion. But as it is, we do the contrary, and in this very way throw away all. For while the profitable effect of what hath been said to us is not yet well fixed, the great force of the things that press upon us from without sweeps all entirely away.

That this then may not be the case, when you retire from the Communion, you must account nothing more necessary than that you should put together the things that have been said to you. Yes, for it were the utmost folly for us, while we give up five and even six days to the business of this life, not to bestow on things spiritual so much as one day, or rather not so much as a small part of one day. See ye not our own children, that whatever lessons are given them, those they study throughout the whole day? This then let us do likewise, since otherwise we shall derive no profit from coming here, drawing water daily into a vessel with holes, and not bestowing on the retaining of what we have heard even so much earnestness as we plainly show with respect to gold and silver. For any one who has received a few pence both puts them into a bag and sets a seal thereon; but we, having given us oracles more precious than either gold or costly stones, and receiving the treasures of the Spirit, do not put them away in the storehouses of our soul, but thoughtlessly and at random suffer them to escape from our minds. Who then will pity us after all this, plotting against our own interests, and casting ourselves into so deep poverty? Therefore, that this may not be so, let us write it down an unalterable law for ourselves, for our wives, and for our children, to give up this one day of the week entire to hearing, and to the recollection of the things we have heard. For thus with greater aptness for learning shall we approach what is next to be said; and to us the labor will be less, and to you the profit greater, when, bearing in memory what hath been lately spoken, ye hearken accordingly to what comes afterwards. For no little doth this also contribute towards the understanding of what is said, when ye know accurately the connexion of the thoughts, which we are busy in weaving together for you. For since it is not possible to set down all in one day, you must by continued remembrance make the things laid before you on many days into a kind of chain, and so wrap it about your soul: that the body of the Scriptures may appear entire.

Therefore let us not either to-day go on to the subjects set before us, without first recalling what was lately said to our memory.[3]

2. But what are the things set before us to-day? "Now all this was done, that it might be fulfilled which was spoken of the Lord by the prophet, saying." In a tone worthy of the wonder, with all his might he

---

[1] [τῆς συνάξεως, the technical term for a religious service among Christians. It does not of itself imply a Eucharistic service, as the above rendering seems to suggest. Indeed, the exordium of this Homily points directly to a service in which the sermon was prominent, making no allusion to the Lord's Supper. For a wider use, see the close of Homily LXXXVIII.—R.]

[2] Comp. Herbert's Country Parson, c. 10. "He himself, or his wife, takes account of sermons, and how every one profits, comparing this year with the last."

[3] ["Let us therefore remember again what was lately said, and thus go on to what is set before us to-day."—R.]

hath uttered his voice, saying, "Now all this was done." For when he saw the sea and the abyss of the love of God towards man, and that actually come to pass which never had been looked for, and nature's laws broken, and reconciliations made, Him who is above all come down to him that is lower than all, and "the middle walls of partition broken,"[1] and the impediments removed, and many more things than these done besides; in one word he hath put before us the miracle, saying, "Now all this was done that it might be fulfilled which was spoken of the Lord." For, "think not," saith he, "that these things are now determined upon; they were prefigured of old." Which same thing, Paul also everywhere labors to prove.

And the angel proceeds to refer Joseph to Isaiah; in order that even if he should, when awakened, forget his own words, as newly spoken, he might by being reminded of those of the prophet, with which he had been nourished up continually, retain likewise the substance of what he had said.[2] And to the woman he mentioned none of these things, as being a damsel and unskilled in them, but to the husband, as being a righteous man, and one who studied the prophets, from them he reasons. And before this he saith, "Mary, thy wife;" but now, when he hath brought the prophet before him, he then trusts him with the name of virginity; for Joseph would not have continued thus unshaken, when he heard from him of a virgin, unless[3] he had first heard it also from Isaiah. For indeed it was nothing novel that he was to hear out of the prophets,[4] but what was familiar to him, and had been for a long time the subject of his meditations. For this cause the angel, to make what he said easy to be received, brings in Isaiah. And neither here doth he stop, but connects the discourse with God. For he doth not call the saying Isaiah's, but that of the God of all things. For this cause he said not, "that it might be fulfilled which was spoken of Isaiah," but "which was spoken of the Lord." For the mouth indeed was Isaiah's, but the oracle was wafted from above.

3. What then saith this oracle? "Behold, a virgin shall be with child, and shall bring forth a son, and they shall call His name Emmanuel."

How was it then, one may say, that His name was not called Emmanuel, but Jesus Christ? Because he said not, "thou shalt call," but "they shall call," that is, the multitude, and the issue of events. For here he puts the event as a name: and this is customary in Scripture, to substitute the events that take place for names.

Therefore, to say, "they shall call" Him "Emmanuel," means nothing else than that they shall see God amongst men. For He hath indeed always been amongst men, but never so manifestly.

But if Jews are obstinate, we will ask them, when was the child called, "Make speed to the spoil, hasten the prey?" Why, they could not say. How is it then that the prophet said, "Call his name Maher-shalal-hash-baz?"[5] Because, when he was born, there was a taking and dividing of spoils, therefore the event that took place in his time is put as his name. And the city, too, it is said, shall be called "the city of righteousness, the faithful city Sion."[6] And yet we nowhere find that the city was called "righteousness," but it continued to be called Jerusalem. However, inasmuch as this came to pass in fact, when the city underwent a change for the better, on that account he saith it is so called. For when any event happens which marks out him who brings it to pass, or who is benefited by it, more clearly than his name, the Scripture[7] speaks of the truth of the event as being a name to him.

4. But if, when their mouths are stopped on this point, they should seek another, namely, what is said touching Mary's virginity, and should object to us other translators,[8] saying, that they used not the term "virgin," but "young woman;" in the first place we will say this, that the Seventy were justly entitled to confidence above all the others. For these made their translation after Christ's coming, continuing to be Jews, and may justly be suspected as having spoken rather in enmity, and as darkening the prophecies on purpose; but the Seventy, as having entered upon this work an hundred years or more before the coming of Christ, stand clear from all such suspicion, and on account

---

[1] Ephes. ii. 14.
[2] [The view here indicated, that this citation was part of the angelic message, is not generally held (but see J. A. Alexander *in loco*). It seems to me inconsistent with the last clause of verse 23: "which is, being interpreted," etc.—R.]
[3] ["Unless," is not found in the MSS., but inserted by the editors as necessary to the sense.—R.]
[4] ["Prophet" is the correct rendering; the plural in the Oxford version is probably due to a typographical error.—R.]

[5] Isa. viii. 3. [Chrysostom does not use the Hebrew name here, but simply repeats a part of the Greek phrase used to translate "Maher-shalal-hash-baz" in the LXX., which he had already given in the previous sentence: Ταχέως σκύλευσον, ὀξέως προνόμευσον. The R. V. *in loco* does not accept the imperative rendering, but gives this marginal explanation: "That is, *The spoil speedeth, the prey hasteth*."—R.]
[6] Isa. i. 26, 27.
[7] [Supplied by translator; literally, "it speaks."—R.]
[8] *i. e.,* Aquila who flourished A.D. 128, Theodotion, A.D. 175, Symmachus, A.D. 201: who were all of them Jews or Judaizing heretics. Cave, Hist. Lit. i. 32, 48, 64.

of the date, and of their number, and of their agreement,[1] would have a better right to be trusted.

But even if they bring in the testimony of those others, yet so the tokens of victory would be with us. Because the Scripture is wont to put the word "youth," for "virginity;" and this with respect not to women only, but also to men. For it is said, "young men and maidens, old men with younger ones."[2] And again, speaking of the damsel who is attacked, it saith, "if the young woman cry out,"[3] meaning the virgin.

And what goes before also establishes this interpretation. For he doth not merely say, "Behold, the Virgin shall be with child," but having first said, "Behold, the Lord Himself shall give you a sign," then he subjoins, "Behold, the Virgin shall be with child."[4] Whereas, if she that was to give birth was not a virgin, but this happened in the way of marriage, what sort of sign would the event be? For that which is a sign must of course be beyond the course of common events, it must be strange and extraordinary; else how could it be a sign?

5. "Then Joseph, being raised from sleep, did as the angel of the Lord had bidden him." Seest thou obedience, and a submissive mind? Seest thou a soul truly wakened, and in all things incorruptible? For neither when he suspected something painful or amiss could he endure to keep the Virgin with him; nor yet, after he was freed from this suspicion, could he bear to cast her out, but he rather keeps her with him, and ministers to the whole Dispensation.

"And took unto him Mary his wife." Seest thou how continually the evangelist uses this word, not willing that that mystery should be disclosed as yet, and annihilating that evil suspicion?

And when he had taken her, "he knew her not, till she had brought forth her first-born Son."[5] He hath here used the word "till," not that thou shouldest suspect that afterwards he did know her, but to inform thee that before the birth the Virgin was wholly untouched by man. But why then, it may be said, hath he used the word, "till"? Because it is usual in Scripture often to do this, and to use this expression without reference to limited times. For so with respect to the ark likewise, it is said, "The raven returned not till the earth was dried up."[6] And yet it did not return even after that time. And when discoursing also of God, the Scripture saith, "From age until age Thou art,"[7] not as fixing limits in this case. And again when it is preaching the Gospel beforehand, and saying, "In his days shall righteousness flourish, and abundance of peace, till the moon be taken away,"[8] it doth not set a limit to this fair part of creation. So then here likewise, it uses the word "till," to make certain what was before the birth, but as to what follows, it leaves thee to make the inference. Thus, what it was necessary for thee to learn of Him, this He Himself hath said; that the Virgin was untouched by man until the birth; but that which both was seen to be a consequence of the former statement, and was acknowledged, this in its turn he leaves for thee to perceive; namely, that not even after this, she having so become a mother, and having been counted worthy of a new sort of travail, and a child-bearing so strange, could that righteous man ever have endured to know her. For if he had known her, and had kept her in the place of a wife, how is it that our Lord[9] commits her, as unprotected, and having no one, to His disciple, and commands him to take her to his own home?

How then, one may say, are James and the others called His brethren? In the same kind of way as Joseph himself was supposed to be husband of Mary. For many were the veils provided, that the birth, being such as it was, might be for a time screened. Wherefore even John so called them, saying, "For neither did His brethren believe in Him."[10]

6. Nevertheless they, who did not believe at first, became afterwards admirable, and illustrious. At least when Paul and they that were of his company were come up to Jerusalem about decrees,[11] they went in straightway unto James. For he was so admired as even to be the first to be entrusted with the bishop's office. And they say he gave himself up to such great austerity, that even his members became all of them as dead, and that from his continual praying, and his perpetual intercourse with the ground, his forehead became so callous as to be in no better state than a camel's knees, simply by reason

---

[1] [This reference to the "agreement" of the LXX. seems to indicate an acceptance of the current tradition in regard to the supernatural exactness of that version.—R.]

[2] Ps. cxlviii. 12.

[3] Deut. xxii. 27. In our translation, "the betrothed damsel cried." This place is cited by St. Jerome on Matt. with reference to the same argument.

[4] Isa. vii. 14.

[5] [There is no indication here of any knowledge of the reading found in the oldest authorities of every class (uncials, cursives and versions): ἔτεκεν υἱόν, instead of ἔτεκεν τὸν υἱὸν αὐτῆς τὸν πρωτότοκον. The latter is the reading of all authorities in Luke ii. 7.—R.]

[6] Gen. viii. 7.

[7] Ps. xc. 2.

[8] Ps. lxxii. 7.

[9] John xix. 27.

[10] John vii. 5. [In regard to the "brethren of our Lord," there seems to be some confusion in the statements of Chrysostom: Comp. Hom. LXXXVIII., on chap. xxvii. 55, 56. The digression here to the character of James seems intended to divert from the historical discussion.—R.]

[11] Acts xv. 4, xvi. 4, xxi. 18.

3

of his striking it so against the earth.[1] This man gives directions to Paul himself, when he was after this come up again to Jerusalem, saying,[2] "Thou seest, brother, how many thousands there are of them that are come together." So great was his understanding and his zeal, or rather so great the power of Christ. For they that mock Him when living, after His death are so filled with awe, as even to die for Him with exceeding readiness. Such things most of all show the power of His resurrection. For this, you see, was the reason of the more glorious things being kept till afterwards, *viz.* that this proof might become indisputable. For seeing that even those who are admired amongst us in their life, when they are gone, are apt to be forgotten by us; how was it that they, who made light of this Man living, afterwards thought Him to be God, if He was but one of the many? How was it that they consented even to be slain for His sake, unless they received His resurrection on clear proof?

7. And these things we tell you, that ye may not hear only, but imitate also his manly severity,[3] his plainness of speech, his righteousness in all things; that no one may despair of himself, though hitherto he have been careless, that he may set his hopes on nothing else, after God's mercy, but on his own virtue. For if these were nothing the better for such a kindred, though they were of the same house and lineage with Christ, until they gave proof of virtue; what favor can we possibly receive, when we plead righteous kinsmen and brethren, unless we be exceeding dutiful,[4] and have lived in virtue? As the prophet too said, intimating the selfsame thing, "A brother redeemeth not, shall a man redeem?"[5] No, not although it were[6] Moses, Samuel, Jeremiah. Hear, for example, what God saith unto this last, "Pray not thou for this people, for I will not hear thee."[7] And why marvellest thou if I hear not thee? "Though Moses himself and Samuel stood before me,"[8] I would not receive their supplication for these men." Yea, if it be Ezekiel who entreats, he will be told, "Though Noah stand forth, and Job, and Daniel, they shall deliver neither sons nor daughters."[9] Though the patriarch Abraham be supplicating for them that are most incurably diseased, and change not, God will leave him and go His way,[10] that he

may not receive his cry in their behalf. Though again it be Samuel who is doing this, He saith unto him, "Mourn not thou for Saul."[11] Though for his own sister one entreat, when it is not fitting, he again shall have the same sort of answer as Moses, "If her father had but spit in her face."[12]

Let us not then be looking open-mouthed towards others. For it is true, the prayers of the saints have the greatest power; on condition however of our repentance and amendment. Since even Moses, who had rescued his own brother and six hundred thousand men from the wrath that was then coming upon them from God, had no power to deliver his sister;[13] and yet the sin was not equal; for whereas she had done despite but to Moses, in that other case it was plain impiety, what they ventured on. But this difficulty I leave for you; while that which is yet harder, I will try to explain.

For why should we speak of his sister? since he who stood forth the advocate of so great a people had not power to prevail for himself, but after his countless toils, and sufferings, and his assiduity for forty years, was prohibited from setting foot on that land, touching which there had been so many declarations and promises. What then was the cause? To grant this favor would not be profitable, but would, on the contrary, bring with it much harm, and would be sure to prove a stumbling-block to many of the Jews. For if when they were merely delivered from Egypt, they forsook God, and sought after Moses, and imputed all to him; had they seen him also lead them into the land of promise, to what extent of impiety might they not have been cast away? And for this reason also, let me add, neither was his tomb made known.

And Samuel again was not able to save Saul from the wrath from above, yet he oftentimes preserved the Israelites. And Jeremiah prevailed not for the Jews, but some one else he did haply cover from evil by his prophecy.[14] And Daniel saved the barbarians from slaughter,[15] but he did not deliver the Jews from their captivity.

And in the Gospels too we shall see both these events come to pass, not in the case of different persons, but of the same; and the same man now prevailing for himself and now given up. For he who owed the ten thousand talents, though he had delivered himself from the danger by entreaty, yet again he prevailed not,[16] and another on the contrary,

1 See Hegesippus in St. Jerome de Viris Illustr., c. 2.
2 Acts xxi. 20 ; see also verse 22.
3 [ἀνδρείαν, " manliness."—R.]   4 ἐπιεικεῖς.
5 Ps. xlix. 7. [This is the rendering of the LXX.—R.]
6 [κἂν ᾖ, " even if it were."—R.]   7 Jer. xi. 14.
8 Jer. xv. 1.   9 Ezek. xiv. 14, 16.   10 Gen. xviii. 33.

11 1 Sam. xvi. 1.   12 Num. xii. 14.   13 Ex. xxxii.; Num. xii.
14 Alluding, perhaps, to 2 Maccab. xv. 13-16.
15 Dan. ii. 24.   16 Matt. xviii. 26-34.

who had before thrown himself away, afterwards had power to help himself in the greatest degree.[1] But who is this? He that devoured his Father's substance.

So that on the one hand, if we be careless, we shall not be able to obtain salvation, no not even by the help of others; if, on the other hand, we be watchful, we shall be able to do this by ourselves, and by ourselves rather than by others. Yes; for God is more willing to give His grace to us, than to others for us; that we by endeavoring ourselves to do away His wrath, may both enjoy confidence towards Him, and become better men. Thus He had pity on the Canaanitish woman, thus He saved the harlot, thus the thief, when there was none to be mediator nor advocate.

8. And this I say, not that we ·may omit supplicating the saints, but to hinder our being careless, and entrusting our concerns to others only, while we fall back and slumber ourselves. For so when He said, "make to yourselves friends,"[2] he did not stop at this only, but He added, "of the unrighteous mammon;" that so again the good work may be thine own; for it is nothing else but almsgiving which He hath here signified. And, what is marvellous, neither doth He make a strict account with us, if we withdraw ourselves from injustice. For what He saith is like this: "Hast thou gained ill? spend well. Hast thou gathered by unrighteousness? scatter abroad in righteousness." And yet, what manner of virtue is this, to give out of such gains? God, however, being full of love to man, condescends even to this, and if we thus do, promises us many good things. But we are so past all feeling, as not to give even of our unjust gain, but while plundering without end, if we contribute the smallest part, we think we have fulfilled all. Hast thou not heard Paul saying, "He which soweth sparingly, shall reap also sparingly"?[3] Wherefore then dost thou spare? What, is the act an outlay? is it an expense? Nay, it is gain and good merchandise. Where there is merchandise, there is also increase; where there is sowing, there is also reaping. But thou, if thou hadst to till a rich and deep soil, and capable of receiving much seed, wouldest both spend what thou hadst, and wouldest borrow of other men, accounting parsimony in such cases to be loss; but, when it is Heaven which thou art to cultivate,

which is exposed to no variation of weather, and will surely repay thine outlay with abundant increase, thou art slow and backward, and considerest not that it is possible by sparing to lose, and by not sparing to gain.

9. Disperse therefore, that thou mayest not lose; keep not, that thou mayest keep; lay out, that thou mayest save; spend, that thou mayest gain. If thy treasures are to be hoarded, do not thou hoard them, for thou wilt surely cast them away; but entrust them to God, for thence no man makes spoil of them. Do not thou traffic, for thou knowest not at all how to gain; but lend unto Him who gives an interest greater than the principal. Lend, where is no envy, no accusation, nor evil design, nor fear. Lend unto Him who wants nothing, yet hath need for thy sake; who feeds all men, yet is an hungered, that thou mayest not suffer famine; who is poor, that thou mayest be rich. Lend there, where thy return cannot be death, but life instead of death. For this usury is the harbinger of a kingdom, that, of hell; the one coming of covetousness, the other of self-denial; the one of cruelty, the other of humanity. What excuse then will be ours, when having the power to receive more, and that with security, and in due season, and in great freedom, without either reproaches, or fears, or dangers, we let go these gains, and follow after that other sort, base and vile as they are, insecure and perishable, and greatly aggravating the furnace for us? For nothing, nothing is baser than the usury of this world, nothing more cruel. Why, other persons' calamities are such a man's traffic; he makes himself gain of the distress of another, and demands wages for kindness, as though he were afraid to seem merciful, and under the cloak of kindness he digs the pitfall deeper, by the act of help galling a man's poverty, and in the act of stretching out the hand thrusting him down, and when receiving him as in harbor, involving him in shipwreck, as on a rock, or shoal, or reef.

"But what dost thou require?" saith one; "that I should give another for his use that money which I have got together, and which is to me useful, and demand no recompense?" Far from it: I say not this: yea, I earnestly desire that thou shouldest have a recompense; not however a mean nor small one, but far greater; for in return for gold, I would that thou shouldest receive Heaven for usury. Why then shut thyself up in poverty, crawling about the earth, and demanding little for great? Nay, this is the part of one who knows not how to be rich. For when God in return for a little money is promising thee

---

[1] Luke xv. 13-20.
[2] Luke xvi. 9. It would seem from this that the saints whom we are to supplicate for their help are those on earth, whom we may assist by our alms. And the examples before tend to confirm this view.
[3] 2 Cor. xix. 6.

the good things that are in Heaven, and thou sayest, "Give me not Heaven, but instead of Heaven the gold that perisheth," this is for one who wishes to continue in poverty. Even as he surely who desires wealth and abundance will choose things abiding rather than things perishing; the inexhaustible, rather than such as waste away; much rather than little, the incorruptible rather than the corruptible. For so the other sort too will follow. For as he who seeks earth before Heaven, will surely lose earth also, so he that prefers Heaven to earth, shall enjoy both in great excellency. And that this may be the case with us, let us despise all things here, and choose the good things to come. For thus shall we obtain both the one and the other, by the grace and love towards man of our Lord Jesus Christ; to whom be glory and might for ever and ever. Amen.

HOMILY VI.

MATT. II. 1, 2.

" When Jesus was born in Bethlehem of Judæa in the days of Herod the king, behold, there came wise men from the east to Jerusalem, saying, Where is He that is born King of the Jews? for we have seen His star in the east, and are come to worship Him.'

WE have need of much wakefulness, and many prayers, that we may arrive at the interpretation of the passage now before us, and that we may learn who these wise men were, and whence they came, and how; and at whose persuasion, and what was the star. Or rather, if ye will, let us first bring forward what the enemies of the truth say. Because the devil hath blown upon them with so violent a blast, as even from this passage to try to arm them against the words of truth.

What then do they allege? " Behold," say they, " even when Christ was born a star appeared; which is a sign that astrology may be depended on." How then, if He had His birth according to that law, did He put down astrology, and take away fate, and stop the mouths of demons, and cast out error, and overthrow all such sorcery?

And what moreover do the wise men learn from the star of itself? That He was King of the Jews? And yet He was not king of this kingdom; even as He said also to Pilate, " My kingdom is not of this world." At any rate He made no display of this kind, for He had neither guards armed with spear or shield, nor horses, nor chariots of mules, nor any other such thing around Him; but He followed this life of meanness and poverty, carrying about with Him twelve men of mean estate.

And even if they knew Him to be a king, for what intent are they come? For surely this is not the business of astrology, to know from the stars who are born, but from the hour when men are born to predict what shall befall them: so it is said. But these were neither present with the mother in her pangs, nor did they know the time when He was born, neither did they, beginning at that moment, from the motion of the stars compute what was to happen: but conversely, having a long time before seen a star appear in their own country, they come to see Him that was born.

Which circumstance in itself would afford a still greater difficulty even than the former. For what reason induced them, or the hope of what benefits, to worship one who was king so far off? Why, had He been to reign over themselves, most assuredly not even so would the circumstance be capable of a reasonable account. To be sure, if He had been born in royal courts, and with His father, himself a king, present by Him, any one would naturally say, that they, from a wish to pay court to the father, had worshipped the child that was born, and in this way were laying up for themselves beforehand much ground of patronage. But now when they did not so much as expect Him to be their own king, but of a strange nation, far distant from their country, neither seeing Him as yet grown to manhood; wherefore do they set forth on so long a journey, and offer gifts, and this when dangers were sure to beset their whole proceeding? For both Herod, when he heard it, was exceedingly troubled, and the whole people was confounded on being told of these things by them.

"But these men did not foresee this." Nay, this is not reasonable. For let them have been ever so foolish, of this they could not be ignorant, that when they came to a city under a king, and proclaimed such things as these, and set forth another king besides him who then reigned, they must needs be bringing down on themselves a thousand deaths.

2. And why did they at all worship one who was in swaddling clothes? For if He had been a grown man, one might say, that in expectation of the succor they should receive from Him, they cast themselves into a danger which they foresaw; a thing however to the utmost degree unreasonable, that the Persian, the barbarian, and one that had nothing in common with the nation of the Jews, should be willing to depart from his home, to give up country, and kindred, and friends, and that they should subject themselves to another kingdom.

But if this be foolish, what follows is much more foolish. Of what nature then is this? That after they had entered on so long a journey, and worshipped, and thrown all into confusion, they went away immediately. And what sign at all of royalty did they behold, when they saw a shed, and a manger, and a child in swaddling clothes, and a poor mother? And to whom moreover did they offer their gifts, and for what intent? Was it then usual and customary, thus to pay court to the kings that were born in every place? and did they always keep going about the whole world, worshipping them who they knew should become kings out of a low and mean estate, before they ascended the royal throne? Nay, this no one can say.

And for what purpose did they worship Him at all? If for the sake of things present, then what did they expect to receive from an infant, and a mother of mean condition? If for things future, then whence did they know that the child whom they had worshipped in swaddling clothes would remember what was then done? But if His mother was to remind Him, not even so were they worthy of honor, but of punishment, as bringing Him into danger which they must have foreseen. Thence at any rate it was that Herod was troubled, and sought, and pried, and took in hand to slay Him. And indeed everywhere, he who makes known the future king, supposing him in his earliest age in a private condition, doth nothing else than betray him to slaughter, and kindle against him endless warfare.

Seest thou how manifold the absurdities appear, if we examine these transactions according to the course of human things and ordinary custom? For not these topics only, but more than these might be mentioned, containing more matter for questions than what we have spoken of. But lest, stringing questions upon questions, we should bewilder you, come let us now enter upon the solution of the matters inquired of, making a beginning of our solution with the star itself.

3. For if ye can learn what the star was, and of what kind, and whether it were one of the common stars, or new and unlike the rest, and whether it was a star by nature or a star in appearance only, we shall easily know the other things also. Whence then will these points be manifest? From the very things that are written. Thus, that this star was not of the common sort, or rather not a star at all, as it seems at least to me, but some invisible power transformed into this appearance, is in the first place evident from its very course. For there is not, there is not any star that moves by this way, but whether it be the sun you mention, or the moon, or all the other stars, we see them going from east to west; but this was wafted from north to south; for so is Palestine situated with respect to Persia.

In the second place, one may see this from the time also. For it appears not in the night, but in mid-day, while the sun is shining; and this is not within the power of a star, nay not of the moon; for the moon that so much surpasses all, when the beams of the sun appear, straightway hides herself, and vanishes away. But this by the excess of its own splendor overcame even the beams of the sun, appearing brighter than they, and in so much light shining out more illustriously.

In the third place, from its appearing, and hiding itself again. For on their way as far as Palestine it appeared leading them, but after they set foot within Jerusalem, it hid itself: then again, when they had left Herod, having told him on what account they came, and were on the point of departing, it shows itself; all which is not like the motion of a star, but of some power highly endued with reason. For it had not even any course at all of its own, but when they were to move, it moved; when to stand, it stood, dispensing[1] all as need required: in the same kind of way as the pillar of the cloud, now halting

---

[1] οἰκονομῶν.

and now rousing up the camp of the Jews, when it was needful.

In the fourth place, one may perceive this clearly, from its mode of pointing Him out. For it did not, remaining on high, point out the place; it not being possible for them so to ascertain it, but it came down and performed this office. For ye know that a spot of so small dimensions, being only as much as a shed would occupy, or rather as much as the body of a little infant would take up, could not possibly be marked out by a star. For by reason of its immense height, it could not sufficiently distinguish so confined a spot, and discover it to them that were desiring to see it. And this any one may see by the moon, which being so far superior to the stars, seems to all that dwell in the world, and are scattered over so great an extent of earth, —seems, I say, near to them every one. How then, tell me, did the star point out a spot so confined, just the space of a manger and shed, unless it left that height and came down, and stood over the very head of the young child? And at this the evangelist was hinting when he said, " Lo, the star went before them, till it came and stood over where the young Child was."

4. Seest thou, by what store of proofs this star is shown not to be one of the many, nor to have shown itself according to the order of the outward creation? And for what intent did it appear? To reprove the Jews for their insensibility, and to cut off from them all occasion of excuse for their willful ignorance. For, since He who came was to put an end to the ancient polity, and to call the world to the worship of Himself, and to be worshipped in all land and sea, straightway, from the beginning, He opens the door to the Gentiles, willing through strangers to admonish His own people. Thus, because the prophets were continually heard speaking of His advent, and they gave no great heed, He made even barbarians come from a far country, to seek after the king that was among them. And they learn from a Persian tongue first of all, what they would not submit to learn from the prophets; that, if on the one hand they were disposed to be candid, they might have the strongest motive for obedience; if, on the other hand, they were contentious, they might henceforth be deprived of all excuse. For what could they have to say, who did not receive Christ after so many prophets, when they saw that wise men, at the sight of a single star, had received this same, and had worshipped Him who was made manifest. Much in the same way then as He acted in the case of the Ninevites, when He sent Jonas, and as in the case of the Samaritan and the Canaanitish women; so He did likewise in the instance of the magi. For this cause He also said, " The men of Nineveh shall rise up, and shall condemn:" and, "the Queen of the South shall rise up, and shall condemn this generation:"[1] because these believed the lesser things, but the Jews not even the greater.

"And wherefore," one may say, " did He attract them by such a vision?" Why, how should He have done? Sent prophets? But the magi would not have submitted to prophets. Uttered a voice from above? Nay, they would not have attended. Sent an angel? But even him they would have hurried by. And so for this cause dismissing all those means, God calleth them by the things that are familiar, in exceeding condescension; and He shows a large and extraordinary star, so as to astonish them, both at the greatness and beauty of its appearance, and the manner of its course.

In imitation of this, Paul also reasons with the Greeks from an heathen altar, and brings forward testimonies from the poets.[2] And not without circumcision doth he harangue the Jews. Sacrifices he makes the beginning of his instruction to them that are living under the law. For, since to every one what is familiar is dear, both God, and the men that are sent by Him, manage things on this principle with a view to the salvation of the world. Think it not therefore unworthy of Him to have called them by a star; since by the same rule thou wilt find fault with all the Jewish rites also, the sacrifices, and the purifications, and the new moons, and the ark, and the temple too itself, For even these derived their origin from Gentile grossness.[3] Yet for all that, God, for the salvation of them that were in error, endured to be served by these things, whereby those without were used to serve devils; only He slightly altered them; that He might draw them off by degrees from their customs, and lead them towards the highest wisdom. Just so He did in the case of the wise men also, not disdaining to call them by sight of a star, that He might lift them higher ever after. There-fore after He hath brought them, leading them by the hand, and hath set them by the manger, it is no longer by a star, but by an angel that He now discourses unto them. Thus did they by little and little become better men.

---

[1] Matt. xii. 41, 42.
[2] Acts xvii. 23, 28 ; 1 Cor. xv. 33 ; Titus i. 12.
[3] See St. Iren. iv. 28, 29 ; Tertull. adv. Marc. i. 18, 22 ; St. Chrys. adv. Jud. Hom. i. t. 6, 318.

This did He also with respect to them of Ascalon, and of Gaza. For those five cities too (when at the coming of the ark they had been smitten with a deadly plague, and found no deliverance from the ills under which they lay)—the men of them called their prophets, and gathered an assembly, and sought to discover an escape from this divine scourge. Then, when their prophets said that they should yoke to the ark heifers untamed, and having their first calves, and let them go their way, with no man to guide them, for so it would be evident whether the plague was from God or whether it was any accident which brought the disease;—("for if," it is said, "they break the yoke in pieces for want of practice, or turn where their calves are lowing, 'it is a chance that hath happened;'[1] but if they go on right, and err not from the way, and neither the lowing of their young, nor their ignorance of the way, have any effect on them, it is quite plain that it is the hand of God that hath visited those cities:")—when, I say, on these words of their prophets the inhabitants of those cities obeyed and did as they were commanded, God also followed up the counsel of the prophets, showing condescension in that instance also, and counted it not unworthy of Himself to bring to effect the prediction of the prophets, and to make them seem trustworthy in what they had then said. For so the good achieved was greater, in that His very enemies themselves bore witness to the power of God; yea, their own teachers gave their voice concerning Him. And one may see many other such things brought about by God. For what took place with respect to the witch,[2] is again like this sort of dispensation; which circumstance also you will now be able to explain from what hath been said.

With respect to the star, we have said these things, and yet more perhaps may be said by you; for, it is said, "Give occasion to a wise man, and he will be yet wiser:"[3] but we must now come to the beginning of what hath been read.

5. And what is the beginning? "When Jesus was born in Bethlehem of Judæa, in the days of Herod the king, behold, there came wise men from the east to Jerusalem." While wise men followed under the auspices of a star, these believed not, with prophets even sounding in their ears. But wherefore doth he mention to us both the time and the place, saying, "in Bethlehem," and "in the days of Herod the king?" And for what reason doth he add his rank also? His

rank, because there was also another Herod, he who slew John: but that was a tetrarch, this a king. And the place likewise, and the time, he puts down, to bring to our remembrance ancient prophecies; whereof one was uttered by Micah, saying, "And thou, Bethlehem, in the land of Judah, art by no means the least among the princes of Judah;"[4] and the other by the patriarch Jacob, distinctly marking out to us the time, and setting forth the great sign of His coming. For, "A ruler," saith he, "shall not fail out of Judah, nor a leader out of his loins, until He come for whom it is appointed, and He is the expectation of the Gentiles."[5]

And this again is worth inquiry, whence it was that they came to entertain such a thought, and who it was that stirred them up to this. For it doth not seem to me to be the work of the star only, but also of God, who moved their soul; which same kind of thing He did also in the case of Cyrus, disposing him to let the Jews go. He did not however so do this as to destroy their free will, since even when He called Paul from above by a voice, He manifested both His own grace and Paul's obedience.

And wherefore, one may ask, did He not reveal this to all the wise men of the East? Because all would not have believed, but these were better prepared than the rest; since also there were countless nations that perished, but it was to the Ninevites only that the prophet was sent; and there were two thieves on the cross, but one only was saved. See at least the virtue of these men, not only by their coming, but also by their boldness of speech. For so that they may not seem to be a sort of impostors,[6] they tell who showed them the way, and the length of their journey; and being come, they had boldness of speech: "for we are come," that is their statement, "to worship Him:" and they were afraid neither of the people's anger, nor of the tyranny of the king. Whence to me at least they seem to have been at home also teachers of their countrymen.[7] For they who here did not shrink from saying this, much more would they speak boldly in their own country, as having received both the oracle from the angel, and the testimony from the prophet.

6. But "when Herod," saith the Scripture, "had heard, he was troubled, and all Jerusa-

---

[1] 1 Sam. vi. 9.   [2] 1 Sam. xxviii.   [3] Prov. ix. 9.

[4] Micah v. 2.   [5] Gen. xlix. 10.   [6] ὑποβολιμαῖοί τινες.
[7] So in Op. Imperf. in Matt. Hom. 2. "After their return, they continued serving God more than before, and instructed many by their preaching. And at last, when Thomas had gone into that province, they joined themselves to him and were baptized, and became doers of his word." This work has been attributed to St. Chrysostom, and seems certainly of the same date with him.

lem with him." Herod naturally, as being king, and afraid both for himself and for his children; but why Jerusalem? Surely the prophets had foretold Him a Saviour, and Benefactor, and a Deliverer from above. Wherefore then was Jerusalem[1] troubled? From the same feeling which caused them before also to turn away from God when pouring His benefits on them, and to be mindful of the flesh-pots of Egypt, while in the enjoyment of great freedom.

But mark, I pray thee, the accuracy of the prophets. For this selfsame thing also had the prophet foretold from the first,[2] saying, "They would be glad, if they had been burnt with fire; for unto us a Child is born, unto us a Son is given."[3]

But nevertheless, although troubled, they seek not to see what hath happened, neither do they follow the wise men, nor make any particular inquiry; to such a degree were they at once both contentious and careless above all men. For when they had reason rather to pride themselves that the king was born amongst them, and had attracted to Him the land of the Persians, and they were on the point of having all subject to them, as though their affairs had advanced towards improvement, and from the very outset His empire had become so glorious; nevertheless, they do not even for this become better. And yet they were but just delivered from their captivity there; and it was natural for them to think (even if they knew none of those things that are high and mysterious, but formed their judgment from what is present only), "If they thus tremble before our king at His birth, much more when grown up will they fear and obey Him, and our estate will be more glorious than that of the barbarians."

7. But none of these things thoroughly awakens them, so great was their dullness, and with this their envy also: both which we must with exact care root out of our mind; and he must be more fervent than fire who is to stand in such an array. Wherefore also Christ said, "I am come to send fire on earth, and I would it were already kindled."[4]

And the Spirit on this account appears in fire.

But we are grown more cold than a cinder, and more lifeless than the dead; and this, when we see Paul soaring above the Heaven, and the Heaven of Heaven, and more fervent than any flame, conquering and overpassing all things, the things beneath, and the things above; the things present, and the things to come; the things that are, and the things that are not.

But if that example be too great for thee, in the first place, this saying itself cometh of sloth; for what had Paul more than thou, that thou shouldest say emulation of him is to thee impossible? However, not to be contentious, let us leave Paul, and consider the first believers, who cast away both goods and gains, together with all worldly care and worldly leisure, and devoted themselves to God entire, every night and day giving attendance on the teaching of the word. For such is the fire of the Spirit, it suffers us not to have any desire for the things that are here, but removes us to another love. For this cause, he who hath set his love on such things as these, though what he hath must be given away, or luxury or glory laughed to scorn, or his very soul yielded up, he doeth all these things with perfect ease. For the warmth of that fire entering into the soul casts out all sluggishness, and makes him whom it hath seized more light than anything that soars; and thenceforth overlooking the things that are seen, such a one abides in continual compunction, pouring forth neverceasing fountains of tears, and thence reaping fruit of great delight. For nothing so binds and unites unto God as do such tears. Such a one, though he be dwelling in the midst of cities, spends his time as in a desert, and in mountains and woods; none of them that are present doth he see, neither feel any satiety of such lamentations; whether it be for himself, or for the negligences of others, that he is weeping. For this cause God blessed these above all the rest of men, saying, "Blessed are they that mourn."

8. And how saith Paul, "Rejoice in the Lord alway?"[5] The joy he is speaking of is what springs from those tears. For as men's joy for the world's sake hath a sorrow[6] in the same lot with it, even so godly tears are a germ of perpetual and unfading joy. In this way the very harlot became more honorable than virgins when seized by this fire. That is, being thoroughly warmed by repentance, she was thenceforth carried out

---

[1] [Literally, "were they."—R.]

[2] [ἄνωθεν, "from above." The word occurs in the previous paragraph, and is probably used here in the same sense. —R.]

[3] Is. ix. 5, 6, LXX. *i. e.* "They (the enemies of Christ) would rather have been burned, than for this to happen." The LXX., reading differently from the present Hebrew, seem to construe the passage thus. [The R. V. renders Is. ix. 5 thus: "For all the armor of the armed man in the tumult, and the garments rolled in blood, shall even be for burning, for fuel of fire." This opposes entirely the interpretation given above (and possibly implied in the LXX.). The rendering of the A. V. is quite obscure, in spite of its verbal splendor.—R.]

[4] ἤθελον for τί θέλω. Luke xii. 49. [The American appendix to the R.V. gives as a marginal rendering: "How I would that it were already kindled," thus accepting the interpretation given above. It seems on the whole the most natural view of this difficult passage.—R.]

[5] Phil. iv. 4. [6] συγκεκληρωμένην.

of herself by her longing desire toward Christ; loosing her hair, and drenching with her tears His holy feet, and wiping them with her own tresses, and exhausting the ointment.[1]   And all these were outward results, but those wrought in her mind were far more fervent than these; which things God Himself alone beheld.   And therefore, every one, when he hears, rejoices with her and takes delight in her good works, and acquits her of every blame.   But if we that are evil pass this judgment, consider what sentence she obtained from that God who is a lover of mankind; and how much, even before God's gifts, her repentance caused her to reap in the way of blessing.

For much as after a violent burst of rain, there is a clear open sky; so likewise when tears are pouring down, a calm arises, and serenity, and the darkness that ensues on our sins quite disappears.   And like as by water and the spirit, so by tears and confession are we cleansed the second time; unless we be acting thus for display and vanity: for as to a woman whose tears were of that sort, I should call her justly condemnable, more than if she decked herself out with[2] lines and coloring.   For I seek those tears which are shed not for display, but in compunction; those which trickle down secretly and in closets, and in sight of no man, softly and noiselessly; those which arise from a certain depth of mind, those shed in anguish and in sorrow, those which are for God alone; such as were Hannah's, for "her lips moved," it is said, "but her voice was not heard;"[3] however, her tears alone uttered a cry more clear than any trumpet.   And because of this, God also opened her womb, and made the hard rock a fruitful field.

If thou also weep thus, thou art become a follower of thy Lord.   Yea, for He also wept, both over Lazarus, and over the city; and touching Judas He was greatly troubled. And this indeed one may often see Him do, but nowhere laugh, nay, nor smile but a little; no one at least of the evangelists hath mentioned this.   Therefore also with regard to Paul, that he wept, that he did so three years night and day,[4] both he hath said of himself, and others say this of him; but that he laughed, neither hath he said himself any-

where, neither hath so much as one other of the saints, either concerning him, or any other like him; but this is said of Sarah only,[5] when she is blamed, and of the son of Noe, when for a freeman he became a slave.[6]

9. And these things I say, not to suppress [7] all laughter, but to take away dissipation of mind.   For wherefore, I pray thee, art thou luxurious and dissolute, while thou art still liable to such heavy charges, and are to stand at a fearful judgment-seat, and to give a strict account of all that hath been done here ?   Yes: for we are to give an account both of what we have sinned willingly, and what against our will:—for " whosoever shall deny me," saith He, " before men, him will I also deny before my Father:"[8]—and surely such a denial is against our will; but nevertheless it doth not escape punishment, but of it too we have to give account:—both of what we know, and of what we do not know; "For I know nothing by myself," saith one, " yet am I not hereby justified:"[9] —both for what we have done in ignorance, and what in knowledge; " For I bear them record," it is said, "that they have a zeal of God, but not according to knowledge;"[10] but yet this doth not suffice for an excuse for them.   And when writing to the Corinthians also he saith, " For I fear, lest by any means, as the serpent beguiled Eve through his subtlety, so your minds should be corrupted from the simplicity that is in Christ."[11]

The things then being so great, for which thou art to give account, dost thou sit laughing and talking wittily, and giving thyself up to luxury ? " Why," one may say, " if I did not so, but mourned, what would be the profit ?"   Very great indeed; even so great, as it is not possible so much as to set it forth by word.   For while, before the temporal tribunals, be thy weeping ever so abundant, thou canst not escape punishment after the sentence; here, on the contrary, shouldest thou only sigh, thou hast annulled the sentence, and hast obtained pardon.   Therefore it is that Christ discourses to us much of mourning, and blesses them that mourn, and pronounces them that laugh wretched.   For this is not the theatre for laughter, neither did we come together for this intent, that we may give way to immoderate mirth, but that we may groan, and by this groaning inherit a kingdom.   But thou, when standing by a

[1] [In Homily LXXX. the woman who was "a sinner" is identified with the woman who anointed our Lord at Bethany. The confusion of the persons is wide-spread, and the name of Mary Magdalene has been unwarrantably connected with one or both occasions.- R.]

[2] [The MSS. read καί, for which some editors substitute ἐν. The better supported reading must be rendered " with both lines and colorings."—R.]

[3] 1 Sam. i. 13. [The LXX., followed in the text, reads καί " and her voice," etc.—R.]

[4] Acts xx. 31 ; comp. v. 37.

[5] Gen. xviii. 12–15.   [6] Gen. ix. 25.   [7] ἐκκόπτων.
[8] Matt. x. 33.   [9] 1 Cor. iv. 4.   [10] Rom. x. 2.
[11] 2 Cor. xii. 3. [It is interesting to note that this citation has three readings, followed in the received text, but rejected by recent critics on the authority of the most ancient MSS. In one reading the order is that of the ancient MSS. against the received text. Still the text of these Homilies may have been edited to conform to the later Syrian N. T. text.—R.]

king, dost not endure so much as merely to smile; having then the Lord of the angels dwelling in thee, dost thou not stand with trembling, and all due self-restraint, but rather laughest, oftentimes when He is displeased? · And dost thou not consider that thou provokest Him in this way more than by thy sins? For God is not wont to turn Himself away so much from them that sin, as from those that are not awestruck after their sin.

But for all this, some are of so senseless a disposition, as even after these words to say, "Nay, far be it from me to weep at any time, but may God grant me to laugh and to play all my days." And what can be more childish than this mind? For it is not God that grants to play, but the devil. At least hear, what was the portion of them that played. "The people," it is said, "sat down to eat and drink, and rose up to play."[1] Such were they at Sodom, such were they at the time of the deluge. For touching them of Sodom likewise it is said, that "in pride, and in plenty, and in fullness of bread, they waxed wanton."[2] And they who were in Noah's time, seeing the ark a preparing for so many years, lived on in senseless mirth, forseeing nought of what was coming. For this cause also the flood came and swept them all away, and wrought in that instant the common shipwreck of the world.

Ask not then of God these things, which thou receivest of the devil. For it is God's part to give a contrite and humbled heart, sober, self-possessed, and awestruck, full of repentance and compunction. These are His gifts, forasmuch as it is also of these things that we are most in need. Yes, for a grievous conflict is at hand, and against the powers unseen is our wrestling; against "the spiritual wickednesses"[3] our fight, "against principalities, against powers" our warfare: and it is well for us, if when we are earnest and sober and thoroughly awakened, we can be able to sustain that savage phalanx. But if we are laughing and sporting, and always taking things easily, even before the conflict, we shall be overthrown by our own remissness.

10. It becometh not us then to be continually laughing, and to be dissolute, and luxurious, but it belongs to those upon the stage, the harlot women, the men that are trimmed for this intent, parasites, and flatterers; not them that are called unto heaven, not them that are enrolled into the city above, not them that bear spiritual arms, but them that are enlisted on the devil's side. For it is he, yea, it is he, that even made the thing an art, that he might weaken Christ's soldiers, and soften the nerves of their zeal. For this cause he also built theatres in the cities, and having trained those buffoons, by their pernicious influence he causes that kind of pestilence to light upon the whole city, persuading men to follow those things which Paul bade us flee, "foolish talking and jesting."[4] And what is yet more grievous than these things is the subject of the laughter. For when they that act those absurd things utter any word of blasphemy or filthiness, then many among the more thoughtless laugh and are pleased, applauding in them what they ought to stone them for; and drawing down on their own heads by this amusement the furnace of fire. For they who praise the utterers of such words, it is these above all who induce men so to speak: wherefore they must be more justly accountable for the penalty allotted to these things. For were there no one to be a spectator in such cases, neither would there be one to act; but when they see you forsaking your workshops, and your crafts, and your income from these, and in short everything, for the sake of continuing there, they derive hence a greater forwardness, and exert a greater diligence about these things.

And this I say, not freeing them from reproof, but that ye may learn that it is you chiefly who supply the principle and root of such lawlessness; ye who consume your whole day on these matters, and profanely exhibit the sacred things of marriage, and make an open mock of the great mystery. For not even he who acts these things is so much the offender, as thou art before him; thou who biddest him make a play on these things, or rather who not only biddest him, but art even zealous about it, taking delight, and laughing, and praising what is done, and in every way gaining strength for such workshops of the devil.

Tell me then, with what eyes wilt thou after this look upon thy wife at home, having seen her insulted there? Or how dost thou not blush being put in mind of the partner of thy home, when thou seest nature herself put to an open shame? Nay, tell me not, that what is done is acting; for this acting hath made many adulterers, and subverted many families. And it is for this most especially that I grieve, that what is done doth not so much as seem evil, but there is even applause and clamor, and much laughter, at

[1] 1 Cor. x. 7 ; Exod. xxxii. 6. [2] Ezek. xvi. 49.
[3] Eph. vi. 12.   [4] Eph. v. 4.

commission of so foul adultery. What say-est thou? that what is done is acting? Why, for this selfsame reason they must be worthy of ten thousand deaths, that what things all laws command men to flee, they have taken pains to imitate. For if the thing itself be bad, the imitation thereof also is bad. And I do not yet say how many adulterers they make who act these scenes of adultery, how they render the spectators of such things bold and shameless; for nothing is more full of whoredom and boldness than an eye that endures to look at such things.

And thou in a market-place wouldest not choose to see a woman stripped naked, or rather not even in a house, but callest such a thing an outrage. And goest thou up into the theatre, to insult the common nature of men and women, and disgrace thine own eyes? For say not this, that she that is stripped is an harlot; but that the nature is the same, and they are bodies alike, both that of the harlot, and that of the free-woman. For if this be nothing amiss, what is the cause that if thou were to see this done in a market place, thou wouldest both hasten away thyself, and drive thence her who was behaving herself unseemly? Or is it that when we are apart, then such a thing is outrageous, but when we are assembled and all sitting together, it is no longer equally shameful? Nay, this is absurdity and a disgrace, and words of the utmost madness; and it were better to besmear the eyes all over with mud and mire than to be a spectator of such a transgression. For surely mire is not so much an hurt to an eye, as an unchaste sight, and the spectacle of a woman stripped naked.

Hear, for example, what it was that caused nakedness at the beginning, and read the occasion of such disgrace. What then did cause nakedness? Our disobedience,[1] and the devil's counsel. Thus, from the first, even from the very beginning, this was his contrivance. Yet they were at least ashamed when they were naked, but ye take a pride in it; "having," according to that saying of the apostle, "your glory in your shame."[2]

How then will thy wife thenceforward look upon thee, when thou art returned from such wickedness? how receive thee? how speak to thee, after thou hast so publicly put to shame the common nature of woman, and art made by such a sight the harlots' captive and slave?[3]

Now if ye grieve at hearing these things, I thank you much, for "who is he that maketh me glad, but he which is made sorry by me?"[4] Do not then ever cease to grieve and be vexed for them, for the sorrow that comes of such things will be to you a beginning of a change for the better. For this cause I also have made my language the stronger, that by cutting deeper I might free you from the venom of them that intoxicate you; that I might bring you back to a pure health of soul; which God grant we may all enjoy by all means, and attain unto the rewards laid up for these good deeds; by the grace and love towards man of our Lord Jesus Christ, to whom be glory and dominion forever and ever. Amen.

---

[1] ['Η παρακοή, " the disobedience," recorded in Genesis.—R.]
[2] Phil. iii. 19.
[3] [It is a long step from the troubled mind of Jerusalem to the denunciation of libidinous play-acting. But the protest has not lost its force, since the modern theatre, and too often the modern novel, is open to the same severe criticism. See Homily VII. 7, 8, for another instance of the same method of application.—R.]
[4] 2 Cor. ii. 2.

HOMILY VII.

MATT. II. 4, 5.

"And when he had gathered all the chief priests and scribes of the people together, he demanded of them where Christ should be born. And they said unto him, In Bethlehem of Judæa."

SEEST thou how all things are done to convict the Jews? how, as long as He was out of their sight, the envy had not yet laid hold of them, and they rehearsed the testimonies *of Him* with truth; but when they saw the glory that arose from the miracles, a grudg-ing spirit possessed them, and thenceforth they betrayed the truth.

However, the truth was exalted by all things, and strength was the more gathered for it even by its enemies. See for example in this very case, how wonderful and beyond expectation are the results secretly provided for.[1] For both the barbarians and the Jews do the same time alike learn something more of one another, and teach one another. Thus the Jews, for their part, heard from the wise men, that a star also had proclaimed Him in the land of the Persians; the wise men, in their turn, were informed by the Jews that this Man, whom the star proclaimed, prophets also had made known from a long time of old. And the ground[2] of their inquiry was made to both an occasion of setting forth clearer and more perfect instruction; and the enemies of the truth are compelled even against their will to read the writings in favor of the truth, and to interpret the prophecy; although not all of it. For having spoken of Bethlehem, and how that out of it He shall come that should rule Israel, they proceed not afterwards to add what follows, out of flattery to the king. And what was this? That "His goings forth are from of old, from everlasting."

2. "But why," one may say, "if He was to come from thence, did He live in Nazareth after the birth, and obscure the prophecy?" Nay, He did not obscure it, but unfolded it the more. For the fact, that while His mother had her constant residence in the one place, He was born in the other, shows the thing to have been done by a Divine dispensation.[3]

And for this cause, let me add, neither did He remove from thence straightway after His birth, but abode forty days, giving opportunity to them that were disposed to be inquisitive to examine all things accurately. Because there were in truth many things to move them to such an inquiry, at least if they had been disposed to give heed to them. Thus at the coming of the wise men the whole city was in a flutter,[4] and together with the city the king, and the prophet was brought forward, and a court of high authority was summoned; and many other things too were done there, all which Luke relates minutely. Such were what concerns Anna, and Simeon, and Zacharias, and the angels, and the shepherds; all which things were to the attentive sufficient to give hints for ascertaining what had taken place. For if the wise men, who came from Persia, were not ignorant of the place, much more might they, whose abode it was, acquaint themselves with these things.

He manifested Himself then from the beginning by many miracles, but when they would not see, He hid Himself for a while, to be again revealed from another more glorious beginning. For it was no longer the wise men, nor the star, but the Father from above that proclaimed Him at the streams of Jordan; and the Spirit likewise came upon Him, guiding that voice to the head of Him just baptized; and John, with all plainness of speech, cried out everywhere in Judæa, till inhabited and waste country alike were filled with that kind of doctrine; and the witness too of the miracles, and earth, and sea, and the whole creation, uttered in His behalf a distinct voice. But at the time of the birth, just so many things happened as were fitted quietly to mark out Him that was come. Thus, in order that the Jews might not say, "We know not when He was born, nor whereabouts," both all these events in which the wise men were concerned were brought about by God's providence, and the rest of the things which we have mentioned; so that they would have no excuse to plead, for not having inquired into that which had come to pass.

But mark also the exactness of the prophecy. For it does not say, "He will *abide*" in Bethlehem," but "He will *come out*" thence." So that this too was a subject of prophecy, His being simply born there.

Some of them, however, being past shame, say that these things were spoken of Zerubbabel. But how can they be right? For surely "his goings forth" were not "from of old, from everlasting."[5] And how can that suit him which is said at the beginning, "Out of thee shall He come forth:" Zorobabel not having been born in Judæa, but in Babylon, whence also he was called Zorobabel,[6] because he had his origin there? And as many as know the Syrians' language know what I say.

And together with what hath been said, all the time also since these things is sufficient to establish the testimony. For what saith he? "Thou art not the least among the princes of Judah," and he adds the cause of the pre-eminence, saying, "out of thee shall He come." But no one else hath made that place illustrious or eminent, excepting Him alone. For example: since that birth, men come from the ends of the earth to see the manger, and the site of the shed. And this the prophet foretold aloud from the first, saying, "Thou art not the

---

[1] οἰκονομεῖται.
[2] *i. e.* Their assuming that the Christ should be born at that time.
[3] ἐξ οἰκονομίας.   [4] ἀνεπτέρωθη.

[5] Micah v. 2.
[6] St. Jerome, de Nom. Hebr. t. 3, 77, ed. Venet. 1767. "*Zorobabel,* '*princeps vel magister Babylonis*,' *sive* '*aliena translatio*,' *vel* '*ortus in Babylone*.'"

least among the princes of Judah;" that is, among the heads of tribes. By which expression he comprehended even Jerusalem.[1] But not even so have they given heed, although the advantage passes on to themselves. Yea, and because of this the prophets at the beginning discourse nowhere so much of His dignity, as touching the benefit which accrued to them by Him. For so, when the Virgin was bearing the child, he saith, "Thou shalt call His name Jesus;"[2] and he gives the reason saying, "for He shall save His people from their sins." And the wise men too said not, "Where is the Son of God?" but "He that is born King of the Jews." And here again it is not affirmed, "Out of thee shall come forth" the Son of God, but "a Governor, that shall feed my people Israel."[3] For it was needful to converse with them at first, setting out in a tone of very exceeding condescension, lest they should be offended; and to preach what related to their salvation in particular, that hereby they might be the rather won over. At any rate, all the testimonies that are first cited, and for which it was the season immediately at the time of the birth, say nothing great, nor lofty concerning Him, nor such as those subsequent to the manifestation of the miracles; for these discourse more distinctly concerning His dignity. For instance, when after many miracles children were singing hymns unto Him, hear what saith the prophet, "Out of the mouth of babes and sucklings Thou hast perfected praise."[4] And again, "I will consider the Heavens, the works of Thy fingers;" which signifies Him to be Maker of the universe. And the testimony too, which was produced after the ascension, manifests His equality with the Father; thus saying, "The Lord said unto my Lord, Sit Thou on my right hand."[5] And Isaiah too saith, "He that riseth up to rule over the Gentiles, in Him shall the Gentiles trust."[6]

But how saith he that Bethlehem is "not the least among the princes of Judah?" for not in Palestine alone, but in the whole world, the village hath become conspicuous. Why, so far he was speaking to Jews; wherefore also he added, "He shall feed my people Israel." And yet He fed the whole world; but as I have said, He is fain not to offend as yet, by revealing what He hath to say touching the Gentiles.

But how was it, one may say, that He did not feed the Jewish people? I answer, first, this too is accomplished: for by the term Israel in this place, he figuratively meant such as believed on Him from among the Jews. And Paul interpreting this, saith, "For they are not all Israel, which are of Israel,"[7] but as many as have been born by faith and promise. And if He did not feed them all, this is their own fault and blame. For when they ought to have worshipped with the wise men, and have glorified God that such a time was come, doing away all their sins (for not a word was spoken to them of judgments set, or of accounts to be given, but of a mild and meek Shepherd); they for their part do just the contrary, and are troubled, and make disturbance, and go on continually framing plots without end.

3. "Then Herod, when he had privily called the wise men, inquired of them diligently[8] what time the star appeared:"[9]

Attempting to slay that which was born, —an act of extreme idiotcy[10] not of madness only; since what had been said and done was enough to have withholden him from any such attempt. For those occurrences were not after the manner of man. A star, I mean, calling the wise men from on high; and barbarians making so long a pilgrimage, to worship Him that lay in swaddling clothes and a manger; and prophets too from of old, proclaiming beforehand all this;—these and all the rest were more than human events: but nevertheless, none of these things restrained him. For such a thing is wickedness. It falls foul of itself, and is ever attempting impossibilities. And mark his utter folly. If on the one hand he believed the prophecy, and accounted it to be unchangeable, it was quite clear that he was attempting impossibilities; if again he disbelieved, and did not expect that those sayings would come to pass, he need not have been in fear and alarm, nor have formed any plot on that behalf. So that in either way his craft was superfluous.

And this too came of the utmost folly, to think that the wise men would make more account of him than of the Child that was born, for the sake of which they had come so long a journey. For if, before they saw, they were so inflamed with longing for Him;

---

[1] i. e. He made Bethlehem so far greater than Jerusalem: because "not the least" seems here equivalent to "the greatest."
[2] Matt. i. 21.
[3] [The R. V. renders more accurately: "Which shall be shepherd of my people Israel."—R.]
[4] Matt. xxi. 16; Ps. viii. 2.   [5] Ps. cx. 1; Acts ii. 34.
[6] Isa. xi. 10; Rom. xv. 12. [The latter passage also follows the LXX. The word "trust" should be changed to "hope," as in R.V., Rom. xv. 12.—R.]

[7] Rom. ix. 6.
[8] [R. V., "learned of them carefully" (ἠκρίβωσεν παρ' αὐτῶν). "Diligently" is from the Vulgate.—R.]
[9] Matt. ii. 7.
[10] ἀνοίας. [Rendered "folly," "extreme folly," etc., below. —R.]

after they had seen with their eyes, and been confirmed by the prophecy, how hoped he to persuade them to betray the young Child to him?

Nevertheless, many as were the reasons to withhold him, he made the attempt; and having "privily called the wise men, he inquired of them."[1] Because he thought that Jews would be concerned in favor of the Child, and he never could expect that they would fall away unto such madness as to be willing to give up to His enemies their Protector and Saviour, and Him who was come for the deliverance of their nation. On account of this he both calls them privily, and seeks the time not of the Child, but of the star; thereby marking out the object of his chase so as to include far more than it.[2] For the star, I think, must have appeared a long time before. It was a long time which the wise men had to spend on their journey. In order, therefore, that they might present themselves just after His birth (it being meet for Him to be worshipped in His very swaddling clothes, that the marvellous and strange nature of the thing might appear), the star, a long time before, makes itself visible. Whereas if at the moment of His birth in Palestine, and not before, it had been seen by them in the East, they, consuming a long time in their journey, would not have seen Him in swaddling clothes on their arrival. As to his slaying the children "from two years old and under," let us not marvel; for his wrath and dread, for the sake of a fuller security, added very much to the time, so that not one might escape.

Having therefore called them, he saith, "Go and search diligently[3] for the young Child; and when ye have found Him, bring me word again, that I may come and worship Him also.'[4]

Seest thou his extreme folly? Why, if thou sayest these things in sincerity, wherefore dost thou inquire privily? But if intending to plot against Him, how is it thou dost not perceive, that from the fact of their being asked secretly the wise men will be able to perceive thy craft? But as I have already said, a soul taken captive by any wickedness becomes more utterly senseless than any thing.

And he said not, "go and learn concerning the King," but "concerning the young Child;" for he could not even endure to call Him by the name of His dominion.

4. But the wise men perceive nothing of this, by reason of their exceeding reverence (for they never could have expected that he could have gone on to so great wickedness, and would have attempted to form plots against a dispensation so marvellous): and they depart suspecting none of these things, but from what was in themselves auguring all that would be in the rest of mankind.

"And, lo! the star, which they saw in the east, went before them."[5]

For therefore only was it hidden, that having lost their guide, they might come to be obliged to make inquiry of the Jews, and so the matter might be made evident to all. Since after they have made inquiries, and have had His enemies[6] for informants, it appears to them again. And mark how excellent was the order; how in the first place after the star the people[7] of the Jews receives them, and the king, and these bring in the prophecy to explain what had appeared: how next, after the prophet, an angel again took them up and taught them all things; but for a time they journey from Jerusalem to Bethlehem by the guidance of the star, the star again journeying with them from that place also; that hence too thou mightest learn, that this was not one of the ordinary stars, for there is not so much as one star that hath this nature. And it not merely moved, but "went before them," drawing and guiding them on in mid-day.

"But what need of this star any more," one may ask, "when the place was ascertained?" In order that the Child also might be seen. For there was not anything to make Him manifest, since the house was not conspicuous, neither was His mother glorious, or distinguished. There was need then of the star, to set them by the place. Wherefore it re-appears on their coming out of Jerusalem, and stays not, before it hath reached the manger.

And marvel was linked on to marvel; for both were strange things, as well the magi worshipping, as the star going before them; and enough to attract even such as were made all of stone. For if the wise men had said, they had heard prophets say these things, or that angels had discoursed with them in private, they might have been disbelieved; but now, when the vision of the star appeared on

---

[1] [ἐπυνθάνετο παρ' αὐτῶν, a paraphrase of the New Testament passage, a trace of which appears in the A. V.—R.]

[2] ἐκ πολλῆς τῆς περιουσίας τιθεὶς τὸ θήραμα. Comp. Viger. de Idiotism. Græc. ix. 3, 3. ["Marking his prey out of great superfluity," is the more literal rendering. The sense seems to be, "including more than was necessary that he might certainly include his prey."—R.]

[3] ["Search out carefully," R. V. The Greek text of the New Testament is accurately cited.—R.]

[4] Matt. ii. 8.

[5] Matt. ii. 9.   [6] Some mss. read "the Jews."

[7] [δῆμος. The translation is somewhat obscure, throughout the entire sentence.—R.]

high, even they that were exceeding shameless had their mouths stopped.

Moreover, the star, when it stood over the young Child, stayed its course again: which thing itself also was of a greater power than belongs to a star, now to hide itself, now to appear, and having appeared to stand still. Hence they too received an increase of faith. For this cause they rejoiced also, that they had found what they were seeking, that they had proved messengers of truth, that not without fruit had they come so great a journey; so great a longing (so to speak) had they for Christ. For first it came and stood over His very head, showing that what is born is Divine; next standing there, it leads them to worship Him; being not simply barbarians, but the wiser sort amongst them.

Seest thou, with how great fitness the star appeared? Why; because even after the prophecy, and after the interpretation of the chief priests and scribes, they still had their minds turned towards it.

5. Shame upon Marcion, shame upon Paul of Samosata,[1] for refusing to see what those wise men saw, — the forefathers of the Church; for I am not ashamed so to call them. Let Marcion be ashamed, beholding God worshipped in the flesh. Let Paul be ashamed, beholding Him worshipped as not being merely a man. As to His being in the flesh, that first is signified by the swaddling clothes and the manger; as to their not worshipping Him as a mere man, they declare it, by offering Him, at that unripe age, such gifts as were meet to be offered to God. And together with them let the Jews also be ashamed, seeing themselves anticipated by barbarians and magi, whilst they submit not so much as to come after them. For indeed what happened then was a type of the things to come, and from the very beginning it was shown that the Gentiles would anticipate their nation.

"But how was it," one may ask, "that not at the beginning, but afterwards, He said, ' Go ye, and make disciples of all nations ' "? Because the occurrence was a type, as I said, of the future, and a sort of declaration of it beforehand. For the natural order was that Jews should come unto Him first; but forasmuch as they of their own choice gave up their proper benefit, the order of things was inverted. Since not even in this instance should the wise men have come before the Jews, nor should persons from so great a distance have anticipated those who were settled about the very city, nor should those who had

heard nothing have pre/ented[2] them that were nurtured in so many prophecies. But because they were exceedingly ignorant of their own blessings, those from Persia anticipate those at Jerusalem. And this indeed is what Paul also saith: " It was necessary that the word of the Lord should first have been spoken to you, but seeing ye have judged yourselves unworthy, lo, we turn to the Gentiles."[3] For even though before they did not obey, at any rate when they heard it from the wise men, they ought to have made all haste; but they would not. Therefore, while those are slumbering, these run before.

6. Let us then also follow the magi, let us separate ourselves from our barbarian customs, and make our distance therefrom great, that we may see Christ, since they too, had they not been far from their own country, would have missed seeing Him. Let us depart from the things of earth. For so the wise men, while they were in Persia, saw but the star, but after they had departed from Persia, they beheld the Sun of Righteousness. Or rather, they would not have seen so much as the star, unless they had readily risen up from thence. Let us then also rise up; though all men be troubled, let us run to the house of the young Child; though kings, though nations, though tyrants interrupt this our path, let not our desire pass away. For so shall we thoroughly repel all the dangers that beset us. Since these too, except they had seen the young Child, would not have escaped their danger from the king. Before seeing the young Child, fears and dangers and troubles pressed upon them from every side; but after the adoration, it is calm and security; and no longer a star but an angel receives them, having become priests from the act of adoration; for we see that they offered gifts also.

Do thou therefore likewise leave the Jewish people, the troubled city, the blood-thirsty tyrant, the pomp of the world, and hasten to Bethlehem, where is the[3] house of the spiritual Bread.[4] For though thou be a shepherd, and come hither, thou wilt behold the young Child in an inn: though thou be a king, and approach not here, thy purple robe will profit thee nothing; though thou be one of the wise men, this will be no hindrance to thee; only let thy coming be to honor and adore, not to spurn the Son of God; only do this with trembling and joy: for it is possible for both of these to concur in one.

---

[1] Because Marcion denied Christ's human nature, Paul His Divinity. See St. Epiph. Hær. 22 and 65.

[2] [That is, " preceded ;" comp. 1 Thess. iv. 15 (R. V.) where the same Greek word occurs, which is rendered " prevent " in the A. V.—R.]
[3] Acts xiii. 46.
[4] Bethlehem signifies, in Hebrew, " the house of bread."

But take heed that thou be not like Herod, and say, "that I may come and worship Him," and when thou art come, be minded to slay Him. For him do they resemble, who partake of the mysteries unworthily: being said, that such a one " shall be guilty of the Body and Blood of the Lord."¹ Yes; for they have in themselves the tyrant who is grieved at Christ's kingdom, him that is more wicked than Herod of old, even Mammon. For he would fain have the dominion, and sends them that are his own to worship in appearance, but slaying while they worship. Let us fear then, lest at any time, while we have the appearance of suppliants and worshippers, we should in deed show forth the contrary.

And let us cast everything out of our hands when we are to worship; though it be gold that we have, let us offer it unto him, and not bury it. For if those barbarians then offered it for honor, what will become of thee, not giving even to Him that hath need? If those men journeyed so far to see Him newly born, what sort of excuse wilt thou have, not going out of thy way one alley's length, that thou mayest visit Him sick or in bonds? And yet when they are sick or in bonds, even our enemies have our pity; thine is denied even to thy Benefactor and Lord. And they offered gold, thou hardly givest bread. They saw the star and were glad, thou, seeing Christ Himself a stranger and naked, art not moved.

For which of you, for Christ's sake, hath made so long a pilgrimage, you that have received countless benefits, as these barbarians, or rather, these wiser than the wisest philosophers? And why say I, so long a journey? Nay, many of our women are so delicate, that they go not over so much as one crossing of the streets to behold Him on the spiritual manger,² unless they can have mules to draw them. And others being able to walk, yet prefer to their attendance here, some a crowd of worldly business, some the theatres. Whereas the barbarians accomplished so great a journey for His sake, before seeing Him; thou not even after thou hast seen Him dost emulate them, but forsakest Him after seeing Him, and runnest to see the stage player. (For I touch again on the same subjects, as I did also of late.³) And seeing Christ lying in the manger, thou leavest Him, that thou mayest see women on the stage.

7. What thunderbolts do not these things deserve? For tell me, if any one were to

lead⁴ thee into a palace, and show thee the king on his throne, wouldest thou indeed choose to see the theatre instead of those things? And yet even in the palace there is nothing to gain; but here a spiritual well of fire gushes up out of this table. And thou leavest this, and runnest down to the theatre, to see women swimming, and nature put to open dishonor, leaving Christ sitting by the well? Yes: for now, as of old, He sits down by the well, not discoursing to a Samaritan woman, but to a whole city. Or perchance now too with a Samaritan woman only. For neither now is any one with Him; but some with their bodies only, and some not even with these. But nevertheless, He retires not, but remains, and asks of us to drink, not water, but holiness, for " His holy things He gives unto the holy."⁵ For it is not water that He gives us from this fountain, but living blood; and it is indeed a symbol of death, but it is become the cause of life.

But thou, leaving the fountain of blood, the awful cup, goest thy way unto the fountain of the devil, to see a harlot swim, and to suffer shipwreck of the soul. For that water is a sea of lasciviousness, not drowning bodies, but working shipwreck of souls. And whereas she swims with naked body, thou beholding, art sunk into the deep of lasciviousness. For such is the devil's net; it sinks, not them that go down into the water itself, but them that sit above more than such as wallow therein; and it chokes them more grievously than Pharaoh, who was of old sunk in the sea with his horses and his chariots. And if souls could but be seen, I could show you many floating on these waters, like the bodies of the Egyptians at that time. But what is still more grievous is this, that they even call such utter destruction a delight, and they term the sea of perdition a channel for a pleasure voyage.⁶ Yet surely one might easier pass over in safety the Ægean or the Tuscan sea, than this spectacle. For in the first place, through a whole night the devil preoccupies their souls with the expectation of it; then having shown them the expected object, he binds them at once, and makes them captives. For think not, because thou hast not been joined unto the harlot, thou art clean from the sin; for in the purpose of thine heart thou hast done it all. Since if thou be taken by lust, thou hast kindled the flame up higher; if thou feel nothing at what

---

¹ 1 Cor. xi. 27. ² Or, " Spiritual Table." Savile.
³ See Hom. vi. 10.

⁴ [εἰσαγαγεῖν ἐπηγγελλέτο, "were promising to introduce." —R.]
⁵ This expression, Τὰ ἅγια τοῖς ἁγίοις, " Holy Things for Holy Persons," is used in the liturgies of St. Clement, St. James, St. Mark, St. Chrysostom, the Ethiopian liturgy, and that of Severus.
⁶ ἡδονῆς εὔριπον.

thou seest, thou deservest a heavier charge, for being a scandal to others, by encouraging them in these spectacles, and for polluting thine own eye-sight, and together with thine eye-sight, thy soul.

However, not merely to find fault, come let us devise a mode of correction too. What then will the mode be? I would commit you to your own wives, that they may instruct you. It is true, according to Paul's law,[1] you ought to be the teachers. But since that order is reversed by sin, and the body has come to be above, and the head beneath, let us even take this way.

But if thou art ashamed to have a woman for thy teacher, fly from sin, and thou wilt quickly be able to mount up on the throne which God hath given thee. Since so long as thou sinnest the Scripture sends thee not to a woman only, but even to things irrational, and those of the viler sort; yea, it is not ashamed to send thee who art honored with reason, as a disciple to the ant.[2] Plainly this is no charge against the Scripture, but against them that so betray their own nobility of race. This then we will do likewise; and for the present we will commit thee to thy wife; but if thou despise her, we will send thee away to the school of the very brutes, and will point out to thee how many birds, fishes, four-footed beasts, and creeping things are found more honorable, and chaster than thou.

If now thou art ashamed, and dost blush at the comparison, mount up to thine own nobility, and fly the sea of hell, and the flood of fire, I mean the pool in the theatre. For this pool introduces to that sea, and kindles that abyss of flame. Since if "he that looketh on a woman to lust after her hath already committed adultery,"[3] he who is forced even to see her naked, how doth he not become ten thousandfold a captive? The flood in the days of Noah did not so utterly destroy the race of men as these swimming women drown all that are there with great disgrace. For as to that rain, though it wrought indeed a death of the body, yet did it repress the wickedness of the soul; but this hath the contrary effect; while the bodies remain, it destroys the soul. And ye, when there is a question of precedence, claim to take place of the whole world, forasmuch as our city first crowned itself with the name of Christian;[4] but in the competition of chastity, ye are not ashamed to be behind the rudest cities.

8. "Well," saith one, "and what dost thou require us to do? to occupy the mountains, and become monks?" Why it is this which makes me sigh, that ye think them alone to be properly concerned with decency and chastity; and yet assuredly Christ made His laws common to all. Thus, when He saith, "if any one look on a woman to lust after her," He speaks not to the solitary, but to him also that hath a wife; since in fact that mount was at that time filled with all kinds of persons of that description. Form then in thy mind an image of that amphitheatre, and hate thou this, which is the devil's. Neither do thou condemn the severity of my speech. For I neither "forbid to marry,"[5] nor hinder thy taking pleasure; but I would have this be done in chastity, not with shame, and reproach, and imputations without end. I do not make it a law that you are to occupy the mountains and the deserts, but to be good and considerate and chaste, dwelling in the midst of the city. For in fact all our laws are common to the monks also, except marriage; yea rather, even with respect to this, Paul commands us to put ourselves altogether on a level with them; saying, "For the fashion of this world passeth away:" that "they that have wives be as though they had none."[6]

"Wherefore" (so he speaks) "I do not bid you take possession of the summits of the mountains; it is true I could wish it, since the cities imitate the things that were done in Sodom; nevertheless, I do not enforce this. Abide, having house and children and wife; only do not insult thy wife, nor put thy children to shame, neither bring into thine house the infection from the theatre." Hearest thou not Paul saying, "The husband hath not power of his own body, but the wife,"[7] and setting down laws common to both? But thou, if thy wife be continually thrusting herself into a public assembly, art severe in blaming her; but thyself, spending whole days on public shows, thou dost not account worthy of blame. Yea, touching thy wife's modesty thou art so strict as even to go beyond necessity or measure, and not to allow her so much as indispensable absences; but to thyself thou deemest all things lawful. Yet Paul allows thee not, who gives the wife likewise the same authority, for thus he speaks: "Let the husband render unto the wife due honor."[8] What sort of

---

[1] 1 Cor. xiv. 34, 35.   [2] Prov. vi. 6.
[3] Matt. v. 28.
[4] Acts xi. 26. [More literally, "the name of the Christians," indicating more directly the reference to the passage in Acts.—R.]

[5] 1 Tim. iv. 2.   [6] 1 Cor. vii. 31, 29.   [7] 1 Cor. vii. 4.
[8] 1 Cor. vii. 3. In our copies of the Greek Testament, and in the MSS. of St. Chrysostom, here, it is, εὔνοιαν, not τιμήν. But Mr. Field writes τιμήν, 1, from internal evidence; 2, from comparison of St. Chrysostom's own Commentary on this place of St. Paul; and accounts for it by supposing that he quoted from mem-

honor then is this, when thou insultest her in the chiefest things, and givest up her body to harlots (for thy body is hers); when thou bringest tumults and wars into thine house, when thou doest in the market place such things, as being related by thyself to thy wife at home, overwhelm her with shame, and put to shame also thy daughter if present, and more than them, surely, thyself? For thou must necessarily either be silent, or behave thyself so unseemly, that it would be just for thy very servants to be scourged for it.

ory, as often, and confused the verse with, 1 Peter iii. 7. [The text in 1 Cor. vii. 3, according to most of the best Greek and Latin MSS., is τὴν ὀφειλήν (R. V., "her duo"). The text and argument of Chrysostom indicate careless citation. The translator's note was written before New Testament textual criticism had received any attention from more modern English divines.—R.]

What plea then wilt thou have, I pray thee, beholding, as thou dost, with great eagerness, things which even to name is disgraceful; preferring to all sights these, which even to recount is intolerable?

Now then for a season, in order not to be too burdensome, I will here bring my discourse to an end. But if ye continue in the same courses, I will make the knife sharper, and the cut deeper; and I will not cease, till I have scattered the theatre of the devil, and so purified the assembly of the Church. For in this way we shall both be delivered from the present disgrace, and shall reap the fruit of the life to come, by the grace and love towards man of our Lord Jesus Christ, to whom be glory and might for ever and ever. Amen.

HOMILY VIII.

Matt. II. 2.

"And when they were come into the house, they saw the young Child with Mary His mother."[1]

How then saith Luke, that He was lying in the manger? Because at the birth indeed she presently laid Him there (for, as was not unlikely, in that large assemblage for the taxing, they could find no house; which Luke also signifies, by saying, "Because there was no room, she laid Him" there); but afterwards she took Him up, and held Him on her knees. For no sooner was she arrived at Bethlehem than she brought her pangs to an end,[2] that thou mayest thence also learn the whole dispensation, and that these things were not done at random, or by chance, but that they all were in course of accomplishment, according to some Divine foreknowledge, and prophetic order.

But what was it that induced them to worship? For neither was the Virgin conspicuous, nor the house distinguished, nor was any other of the things which they saw apt to amaze or attract them. Yet they not only worship, but also "open their treasures," and "offer gifts;" and gifts, not as to a man, but as to God. For the frankin-

cense and the myrrh were a symbol of this. What then was their inducement? That which wrought upon them to set out from home and to come so long a journey; and this was both the star, and the illumination wrought of God in their mind, guiding them by little and little to the more perfect knowledge. For, surely, had it not been so, all that was in sight being ordinary, they would not have shown so great honor. Therefore none of the outward circumstances was great in that instance, but it was a manger, and a shed, and a mother in poor estate; to set before thine eyes, naked *and bare*, those wise men's love of wisdom,[3] and to prove to thee, that not as mere man they approached Him, but as a God, and Benefactor. Wherefore neither were they offended by ought of what they saw outwardly, but even worshipped, and brought gifts; gifts not only free from Judaical grossness, in that they sacrificed not sheep and calves, but also coming nigh to the self-devotion of the Church, for it was knowledge and obedience and love that they offered unto Him.

---

[1] [The entire verse is given in Field's Greek text; the Homily covers verses 11-15.—R.)

[2] ὠδῖνας ἔλυσεν. Comp. Acts ii. 24.

[3] φιλοσοφίαν.

"And being warned of God in a dream that they should not return unto Herod, they departed into their own country another way." [1]

See from this also their faith, how they were not offended, but are docile, and considerate; neither are they troubled, nor reason with themselves, saying, "And yet, if this Child be great, and hath any might, what need of flight, and of a clandestine retreat? and wherefore can it be, that when we have come openly and with boldness, and have stood against so great a people, and against a king's madness, the angel sends us out of the city as runaways and fugitives?" But none of these things did they either say or think. For this most especially belongs to faith, not to seek an account of what is enjoined, but merely to obey the commandments laid upon us.

2. "And when they were departed, behold, an angel appeareth to Joseph in a dream, saying, Arise, and take the young Child and His mother, and flee into Egypt." [2]

There is something here worth inquiring into, both touching the magi, and touching the Child; for if even they were not troubled, but received all with faith, it is worthy of examination on our part, why they and the young Child are not preserved, continuing there, but they as fugitives go into Persia, He with His mother into Egypt. But what? should He have fallen into the hands of Herod, and having fallen, not have been cut off? Nay, He would not have been thought to have taken flesh upon Him; the greatness of the Economy would not have been believed.

For if, while these things are taking place, and many circumstances are being ordered mysteriously after the manner of men, some have dared to say that His assumption of our flesh [3] is a fable; in what degree of impiety would they not have been wrecked, had He done all in a manner becoming His Godhead, and according to His own power?

As to the wise men, He sends them off quickly, at once both commissioning them as teachers to the land of the Persians, and at the same time intercepting the madness of the king, that he might learn that he was attempting things impossible, and might quench his wrath, and desist from this his vain labor. For not alone openly to subdue His enemies, but also to deceive them with ease, is worthy of His power. Thus, for example, He deceived the Egyptians also in the case of the Jews, and having power to transfer their wealth openly into the hands of the Hebrews, He bids them do this secretly and with craft; and this surely, not less than the other miracles, made Him an object of terror to His enemies. At least, they of Ascalon, and all the rest, when they had taken the ark, and being smitten, did after that devise their countrymen not to fight, nor to set themselves against Him, with the other miracles brought this also forward, saying, " Wherefore harden ye your hearts, as Egypt and Pharaoh hardened? when He had mocked them, did He not after that send forth His people, and they departed?" [4] Now this they said, as accounting this *fresh* one not inferior to those other signs that had been done openly, towards the demonstration of His power, and of His greatness. And the like ensued on this occasion too; a thing sufficient to astonish the tyrant. For consider what it was natural for Herod to feel, and how his very breath would be stopped, deceived as he was by the wise men, and thus laughed to scorn. For what, if he did not become better? It is not His fault, who marvellously ordered all this, but it is the excess of Herod's madness, not yielding even to those things which had virtue [5] to have persuaded him, and deterred him from his wickedness, but going on still further, to receive a yet sharper punishment for folly so great.

3. But wherefore, it may be said, is the young Child sent into Egypt? In the first place, the evangelist himself hath mentioned the cause, saying," That it might be fulfilled, Out of Egypt have I called my Son." And at the same time beginnings of fair hopes were thenceforth proclaimed before to the world. That is, since Babylon and Egypt, most in the whole earth, were burnt up with the flame of ungodliness, He, signifying from the first that He means to correct and amend both, and inducing men hereby to expect His bounties in regard of the whole world likewise, sent to the one the wise men, the other He Himself visited with His mother.

And besides what I have said, there is another lesson also, which we are hereby taught, tending not slightly to true self-command in us. Of what kind then is it? To look from the beginning for temptations and plots. See, for instance, how this was the case even at once from His swaddling clothes. Thus you see at His birth, first a tyrant raging, then flight ensuing, and departure beyond the border; and for no crime His mother is exiled into the land of the barbarians: that

[1] Matt. ii. 12.　　　[2] Matt. ii. 13.　　　[3] [τῆς σαρκός.]　　　[4] 1 Sam. vi. 6, LXX.　　　[5] [τοῖς δυναμένοις.]

thou, hearing these things (supposing thee thought worthy to minister to any spiritual matter, and then to see thyself suffering incurable ills, and enduring countless dangers), shouldest not be greatly troubled, nor say, "What can this be? yet surely I ought to be crowned and celebrated, and be glorious and illustrious for fulfilling the Lord's commandment:" but that having this example, thou mightest bear all things nobly, knowing that this especially is the order of all things spiritual, to have everywhere temptations in the same lot with them. See at least how this is the case not only with regard to the mother of the young Child, but also of those barbarians; since they for their part retire secretly in the condition of fugitives; and she again, who had never passed over the threshold of her house, is commanded to undergo so long a journey of affliction, on account of this wonderful birth, and her spiritual travail.

And behold a wonder again. Palestine plots, and Egypt receives and preserves Him that is the object of the plots. For, as it appears, not only in the instance of the sons of the patriarch[1] did types take place, but also in our Lord's own case. In many instances, we are sure, His doings at that time were prophetic declarations of what was to happen afterwards; as, for example, in the matter of the ass and the colt.[2]

4. Now the angel having thus appeared, talks not with Mary, but with Joseph; and what saith he? "Arise, and take the young Child and His mother." Here, he saith not any more, "thy wife," but "His mother." For after that the birth had taken place, and the suspicion was done away, and the husband appeased, thenceforth the angel talks openly, calling neither child nor wife his, but "take the young Child and His mother, and flee into Egypt;" and he mentions the cause of the flight: "For Herod," saith he, "will seek the young Child's life."

Joseph, when he had heard these things, was not offended, neither did he say, "The thing is hard to understand: Didst thou not

say just now, that He should 'save His people?' and now He saves not even Himself: but we must fly, and go far from home, and be a long time away: the facts are contrary to the promise." Nay, none of these things doth he say (for the man was faithful): neither is he curious about the time of his return; and this though the angel had put it indefinitely thus: "Be thou there until I tell thee." But nevertheless, not even at this did he shudder, but submits and obeys, undergoing all the trials with joy.

And this because God, who is full of love to man, did with these hardships mingle things pleasant also; which indeed is His way with regard to all the saints, making neither their dangers nor their refreshment continual, but weaving the life of all righteous men, out of both the one and the other. This very thing He did here also: for consider, Joseph saw the Virgin with child; this cast him into agitation and the utmost trouble, for he was suspecting the damsel of adultery. But straightway the angel was at hand to do away his suspicion, and remove his fears; and seeing the young child born, he reaped the greatest joy. Again, this joy no trifling danger succeeds, the city being troubled, and the king in his madness seeking after Him that was born. But this trouble was again succeeded by another joy; the star, and the adoration of the wise men. Again, after this pleasure, fear and danger; "For Herod," saith he, "is seeking the young Child's life," and He must needs fly and withdraw Himself as any mortal might: the working of miracles not being seasonable as yet. For if from His earliest infancy He had shown forth wonders, He would not have been accounted a Man.

Because of this, let me add, neither is a temple framed at once; but a regular conception takes place, and a time of nine months, and pangs, and a delivery, and giving suck, and silence for so long a space, and He awaits the age proper to manhood; that by all means acceptance might be won for the mystery of His Economy.

"But wherefore then," one may say, "were even these signs wrought at the beginning?" For His mother's sake; for the sake of Joseph and of Simeon, who was presently to depart; for the sake of the shepherds and of the wise men; for the sake of the Jews. Since they, had they been willing to mind diligently what was taking place, would from this event also have reaped no small advantage in regard of what was to come.

But if the prophets do not mention what

---

[1] i. e., of Jacob.

[2] The received mystical interpretation of our Lord's final entry into Jerusalem represented the ass as the type of the Jewish converts, and the colt, of the Gentile Church. See hereafter, Hom. LXVI., and comp. Origen on St. Matt. t. 16, 15; St. Amb. in Luc. lib. 9, 4–14; St. Just. Mart. Dial. cum. Tryph. c. 53. The interpretation to which St. Chrysostom points of the flight into Egypt, is probably the same with that of St. Hilary on this place. "Joseph is admonished by the angel to take the young child into Egypt: Egypt full of idols, and given to the worship of all kinds of portents for gods. Accordingly, after the persecution by the Jews, and the assent of that profane multitude to His murder, Christ passes over to the nations, sold as they were to the vainest superstitions. He leaves Jewry, and is carried into the world which knows Him not: while Bethlehem, i. e., Judæa, overflows with the blood of martyrs. As to Herod's rage and his murdering the infants, it is the type of the Jewish people raging against the Christians, under the notion that by the slaughter of the blessed martyrs they may blot out Christ's name from the faith and profession of all men." p. 613, ed. Ben. Paris, 1693.

relates to the wise men, be not troubled; for they neither foretold all things, nor were they silent touching all. For as without any warning to see those things coming to pass, would naturally occasion much astonishment and trouble; so also to have been informed of all would dispose the hearer to sleep, and would have left nothing for the evangelists to add.

5. And if the Jews should raise a question touching the prophecy, and say, that the words, "Out of Egypt have I called my Son," were uttered concerning themselves; we would tell them, This is a law of prophecy, that in many cases much that is spoken of one set of persons is fulfilled in another; of which kind is that which is said touching Simeon and Levi, "I will divide them," saith He, "in Jacob, and scatter them in Israel." [1] And yet not in themselves did this come to pass, but in their descendants; and Noah's saying again about Canaan, came to pass in the Gibeonites, Canaan's descendants. [2] And that concerning Jacob one may see to have so come to pass; for those blessings which say, "Be lord over thy brother, and let thy father's sons worship thee," [3] had no accomplishment in himself (how could they, he being in fear and trembling, and worshipping his brother over and over again? [4]), but in his offspring they had. The very same may be said in this case also. For which may be called the truer son of God, he that worships a calf, and is joined to Baalpeor, [5] and sacrifices his sons to devils? or He that is a Son by nature, and honors Him that begat Him? So that, except this man had come, the prophecy would not have received, its due fulfillment. It is worth observing, too, that the evangelist intimates the same by the phrase, "that it might be fulfilled;" implying that it would not have been fulfilled, unless He had come.

And this makes the Virgin also in no common degree glorious and distinguished; that the very thing which was the whole people's special endowment in the way of praise, she also might thenceforth have for her own. I mean, that whereas they were proud of their coming up from Egypt, and used to boast of it (which indeed the prophet also was hinting at, when he said, "Have I not brought up the strangers from Cappadocia, and the Assyrians from the pit" [6]), He makes this pre-eminence belong to the Virgin likewise.

Rather, however, both the people and the patriarch, going down thither, and coming up thence, were together completing the type of this *His* return. Thus, as they went down to avoid death by famine, so He death by conspiracy. But whereas they on their arrival were for the time delivered from the famine, this man, when He had gone down, sanctified the whole land, by setting His foot thereon.

At least it is observable how, in the midst of His humiliations, the tokens of His Godhead are disclosed. Thus, first of all, the angel saying, "Flee into Egypt," did not promise to journey with them, either in their descent or return; intimating that they have a great fellow-traveller, the Child that had been born; such an one as actually changed all things immediately on His appearing, and wrought so that His enemies should minister in many ways to this Economy. Thus magi and barbarians, leaving the superstition of their fathers, are come to worship: thus Augustus ministers to the birth at Bethlehem by the decree for the taxing; Egypt receives and preserves Him, driven from His home, and plotted against, and obtains a sort of first impulse towards her union unto Him; so that when in after-time she should hear Him preached by the apostles, she might have this at least to glory of, as having received Him first. And yet this privilege did belong unto Palestine alone; but the second proved more fervent than the first.

6. And now, shouldest thou come unto the desert of Egypt, thou wilt see this desert become better than any paradise, and ten thousand choirs of angels in human forms, and nations of martyrs, and companies of virgins, and all the devil's tyranny put down, while Christ's kingdom shines forth in its brightness. And the mother of poets, and wise men, and magicians, [7] the inventor of every kind of sorcery, and propagator thereof among all others, her thou wilt see now taking pride in the fishermen, and treating all those with contempt, but carrying about everywhere the publican, and the tentmaker, and protecting herself with the cross; and these good things not in the cities only, but also in the deserts more than in the cities; since in truth everywhere in that land may be seen the camp of Christ, and the royal flock, and the polity of the powers above. And these rules one may find in force, not among men only, but also in woman's nature. Yea, they, not less than men, practise that search

---

[1] Gen. xlix. 7.   [2] Gen. ix. 25; Josh. ix. 27; 2 Chron. viii. 7-9.
[3] Gen. xxvii. 29.   [4] Gen. xxxiii. 3.
[5] [The reference is to Numb. xxv. 3. But as usual, the LXX. form of the name is cited : βεελφεγώρ.—R.]
[6] Amos ix. 7. "The Philistines from Caphtor, and the Syrians from Kir," Heb. [The LXX. has τοὺς ἀλλοφύλους (here rendered "the strangers") the usual term for designating "the Philistines." Comp. 1 and 2 Samuel, *passim* (in LXX.).—R.]

[7] [σοφῶν καὶ μάγων. The translator has rendered μάγοι sometimes by "wise men," and sometimes by "magi." Probably the term here refers more exactly to "magicians."—R.]

of wisdom, not taking shield, and mounting horse, as the Grecians' grave lawgivers and philosophers direct, but another and far severer fight are they undertaking. For the war against the devil and his powers is common to them and to the men, and in no respect doth the delicacy of their nature become an impediment in such conflicts, for not by bodily constitution, but by mental choice, are these struggles decided. Wherefore women in many cases have actually been more forward in the contest than men, and have set up more brilliant trophies. Heaven is not so glorious with the varied choir of the stars, as the wilderness of Egypt, exhibiting to us all around the tents of the monks.

Whoever knows that ancient Egypt, her that fought against God in frenzy, her that was the slave of cats, that feared and dreaded onions; this man will know well the power of Christ. Or rather, we have no need of ancient histories; for even yet there remain relics of that senseless race, for a specimen of their former madness. Nevertheless, these who of old broke out all of them into so great madness, now seek to be wise touching heaven, and the things above heaven, and laugh to scorn the customs of their fathers, and acknowledge the wretchedness of their ancestors, and hold the philosophers in no estimation: having learnt by the real facts, that all that was theirs[1] were but inventions of sottish old women, but the real philosophy, and worthy of heaven, is this, which was declared unto them by the fishermen. And for this very cause, together with their so great exactness in doctrine, they exhibit also by their life that extreme seriousness. For when they have stripped themselves of all that they have, and are crucified to the whole world, they urge their course on again yet farther, using the labor of their body for the nourishment of them that be in need. For neither, because they fast and watch, do they think it meet to be idle by day; but their nights they spend in the holy hymns and in vigils, and their days in prayers, and at the same time in laboring with their own hands; imitating the zeal of the apostle. For if he, when the whole world was looking unto him, for the sake of nourishing them that were in need, both occupied a workshop, and practised a craft, and being thus employed did not so much as sleep by night; how much more, say they, is it meet that we, who have taken up our abode in the wilderness, and have nothing to do with the turmoils in the cities, should use the leisure of our quiet for spiritual labors !

Let us then be ashamed all of us, both they that are rich, and they that are poor, when those having nothing at all but a body only and hands, force their way on and strive eagerly to find thence a supply for the poor; while we, having endless stores within, touch not even our superfluities for these objects. What kind of plea shall we have then, I pray thee? and what sort of excuse?

Yet further consider, how of old these Egyptians were both avaricious, and gluttonous, together with their other vices. For there were the flesh-pots[3] which the Jews remember; there, the great tyranny of the belly. Nevertheless, having a willing mind, they changed: and having caught fire from Christ, they set off at once on their voyage towards heaven; and though more ardent than the rest of mankind, and more headstrong, both in anger, and in bodily pleasures, they imitate the incorporeal powers in meekness, and in the rest of that freedom from passions which pertains unto self-denial.

7. Now if any man hath been in the country, he knows what I say. But if he have never entered those tabernacles, let him call to mind him who even until now is in the mouths of all men,—him whom, after the apostles, Egypt brought forth,—the blessed and great Antony; and let him put it to himself, "This man, too, was born in the same country with Pharaoh; nevertheless he was not thereby damaged, but both had a divine vision vouchsafed him, and showed forth such a life as the laws of Christ require." And this any man shall know perfectly, when he hath read the book that contains the history of that man's life;[4] in which also he will perceive much prophecy. I allude to his prediction about those infected with the errors of Arius, and his statement of the mischief that would arise from them; God even then having shown them to him, and sketched out before his eyes all that was coming. A thing which most especially (among the rest) serves to demonstrate the truth, that no person, belonging to the heresies without, hath such a man to mention. But, not to depend on us for this information, look earnestly into what is written in that book, and ye will learn all exactly, and thence be instructed in much self-denial.

And this advice I give, that we not merely peruse what is written there, but that we also emulate it, and make neither place, nor education, nor forefathers' wickedness an excuse.

---

[1] [τὰ μὲν ἐκείνων, i. e., those things taught by the heathen philosophers of Egypt.—R.]
[2] Acts xx. 34; 1 Thess. ii. 9.

[3] Ex. xvi. 3.   [4] In the works of St. Athanasius.

For if we will take heed to ourselves, none of these things shall be an hindrance to us, since even Abraham had an ungodly father,[1] but he inherited not his wickedness; and Hezekiah, Ahaz: yet nevertheless he became dear to God. And Joseph too when in the midst of Egypt, adorned himself with the crowns of temperance; and the Three Children no less in the midst of Babylon, and of the palace, when a table like those at Sybaris was set before them, showed the highest self-denial; and Moses also in Egypt, and Paul in the whole world; but nothing was to any one of these an hindrance in the race of virtue.

Let us then, bearing in mind all these things, put out of the way these our superfluous pleas and excuses, and apply ourselves to those toils which the cause of virtue requires. For thus shall we both attract to ourselves more favor from God, and persuade Him to assist us in our struggles, and we shall obtain the eternal blessings; unto which God grant that we may all attain, by the grace and love towards man of our Lord Jesus Christ, to whom be glory and victory for ever and ever. Amen.

---

[1] Josh. xxiv. 2.

HOMILY IX.

Matt. II. 16.

" Then Herod, when he saw that he was mocked of the wise men, was exceeding wroth."

Yet surely it was a case not for anger, but for fear and awe: he ought to have perceived that he was attempting impossible things. But he is not refrained. For when a soul is insensible and incurable, it yields to none of the medicines given by God. See for example this man following up his former efforts,[1] and adding many murders to one, and hurried down the steep any whither. For driven wild by this anger, and envy, as by some demon, he takes account of nothing, but rages even against nature herself, and his anger against the wise men who had mocked him he vents upon the children that had done no wrong: venturing then in Palestine upon a deed akin to the things that had been done in Egypt. For he " sent forth," it is said, " and slew all the children that were in Bethlehem, and in all the coasts thereof, from two years old and under, according to the time which he had diligently inquired of the wise men."

Here attend to me carefully. Because many things are uttered by many very idly touching these children, and the course of events is charged with injustice, and some of these express their perplexity about it in a more moderate way, others with more of audaciousness and frenzy. In order then that we may free these of their madness and those of their perplexity, suffer us to discourse a little upon this topic. Plainly, then, if this be their charge, that the children were left to be slain, they should find fault likewise with the slaughter of the soldiers that kept Peter.[2] For as here, when the young Child had fled, other children are massacred in the place of Him who was sought; even so then, too, Peter having been delivered from his prison and chains by the angel, one of like name with this tyrant, and like temper too, when he had sought him, and found him not, slew instead of him the soldiers that kept him.

" But what is this ? " it may be said; " why this is not a solution, but an enhancement of our difficulty." I know it too, and for this intent I bring forward all such cases, that to all I may adduce one and the same solution. What then is the solution of these things ? or what fair account of them can we give ? That Christ was not the cause of their slaughter, but the king's cruelty; as indeed neither was Peter to those others, but the madness of Herod. For if he had seen the wall broken through, or the doors overthrown, he might, perhaps, have had ground to accuse the soldiers that kept the apostle, of neglect; but now when all things continued in due form,[3] and the doors were thrown wide open,

---

[1] τοῖς προτέροις ἐπαγωνιζόμενον. Comp. Jude 3. [2] Acts xii. 19. [3] ἐπὶ σχήματος.

and the chains fastened to the hands of them that kept him (for in fact they were bound unto him), he might have inferred from these things (that is, if he had been strictly doing a judge's office on the matters before him), that the event was not of human power or craft, but of some divine and wonder-working power; he might have adored the doer of these things, instead of waging war with the sentinels. For God had so done all that He did, that so far from exposing the keepers, He was by their means leading the king unto the truth. But if he proved senseless, what signifies to[1] the skillful Physician of Souls, managing all things to do good, the insubordination of him that is diseased?

And just this one may say in the present case likewise. For, wherefore art thou wroth, O Herod, at being mocked of the wise men? didst thou not know that the birth was divine? didst thou not summon the chief priests? didst thou not gather together the scribes? did not they, being called, bring the prophet also with them into thy court of judgment, proclaiming these things beforehand from of old? Didst thou not see how the old things agreed with the new? Didst thou not hear that a star also ministered to these men? Didst thou not reverence the zeal of the barbarians? Didst thou not marvel at their boldness? Wast thou not horror-struck at the truth of the prophet? Didst thou not from the former things perceive the very last also? Wherefore didst thou not reason with thyself from all these things, that this event was not of the craft of the wise men, but of a Divine Power, duly dispensing all things? And even if thou wert deceived by the wise men, what is that to[2] the young children, who have done no wrong?

2. "Yea," saith one, "Herod thou hast full well deprived of excuse, and proved him blood-thirsty; but thou hast not yet solved the question about the injustice of what took place. For if he did unjustly, wherefore did God permit it?" Now, what should we say to this? That which I do not cease to say continually, in church, in the market-place, and everywhere; that which I also wish you carefully to keep in mind, for it is a sort of rule for us, suited to every such perplexity. What then is our rule, and what our saying? That although there be many that injure, yet is there not so much as one that is injured. And in order that the riddle may not disturb you too much, I add the solution too with all speed. I mean, that what we may suffer unjustly from any one, it tells either to the

doing away of our sins, God so putting that wrong to our account; or unto the recompense of rewards. .

And that what I may say may be clearer, let us conduct our argument in the way of illustration. As thus: suppose a certain servant who owes much money to his master, and then that this servant has been despitefully used by unjust men, and robbed of some of his goods. If then the master, in whose power it was to stay the plunderer and wrong doer, should not indeed restore that same property, but should reckon what was taken away towards what was owed him by his servant, is the servant then injured? By no means. But what if he should repay him even more? Has he not then even gained more than he has lost? Every one, I suppose, perceives it.

Now this same reckoning we are to make in regard of our own sufferings. For as to the fact, that in consideration of what we may suffer wrongfully, we either have sins done away, or receive more glorious crowns, if the amount of our sins be not so great: hear what Paul says concerning him that had committed fornication, "Deliver ye such a one to Satan for the destruction of the flesh, that the spirit may be saved."[3] "But what is this?" you may say, "for the discourse was about them that were injured by others, not about them that are corrected by their teachers." I might answer, that there is no difference;[4] for the question was, whether to suffer evil be not an indignity to the sufferer. But, to bring my argument nearer the very point inquired of; remember David, how, when he saw Shimei at a certain time assailing him, and trampling on his affliction, and pouring on him revilings without end, his captains desiring to slay him, he utterly forbade them, saying, "Let him curse, that the Lord may look upon mine abasement, and that he may requite me good for this cursing this day."[5] And in the Psalms too in his chanting, he said, "Consider mine enemies, that they are multiplied, and they hate me with unjust hatred," and "forgive all my sins."[6] And Lazarus again for the same cause enjoyed remission, having in this life suffered innumerable evils. They therefore who are wronged, are not wronged if they bear nobly all that they suffer, yea, rather they gain even more abundantly, whether they be smitten of God, or scourged by the devil.

---

[1] [τι πρός, "what is that to," as in following paragraph.—R.]
[2] [τι πρός.]

[3] 1 Cor. v. 5.   [4] [Μάλιστα μὲν οὐδὲν τὸ μέσον.]
[5] 2 Sam. xvi. 11, 12. [The citation varies from the LXX., and the latter from the Hebrew: comp. R. V. in loco, where the LXX. is represented in the marginal note.—R.]
[6] Ps. xxv. 18, 17.

3. "But what kind of sin had these children," it may be said, "that they should do it away? for touching those who are of full age, and have been guilty of many negligences, one might with show of reason speak thus: but they who so underwent premature death, what sort of sins did they by their sufferings put away?" Didst thou not hear me say, that though there were no sins, there is a recompense of rewards hereafter for them that suffer ill here? Wherein then were the young children hurt in being slain for such a cause, and borne away speedily into that waveless harbor? "Because," sayest thou, "they would in many instances have achieved, had they lived, many and great deeds of goodness." Why, for this cause He lays up for them beforehand no small reward, the ending their lives for such a cause. Besides, if the children were to have been any great persons, He would not have suffered them to be snatched away beforehand. For if they that eventually will live in continual wickedness are endured by Him with so great long-sufferings, much more would He not have suffered these to be so taken off had He foreknown they would accomplish any great things.

And these are the reasons we have to give; yet these are not all; but there are also others more mysterious than these, which He knoweth perfectly, who Himself ordereth these things. Let us then give up unto Him the more perfect understanding of this matter, and apply ourselves to what follows, and in the calamities of others let us learn to bear all things nobly. Yea, for it was no little scene of woe, which then befell Bethlehem, the children were snatched from their mother's breast, and dragged unto this unjust slaughter.

And if thou art yet faint-hearted, and not equal to controlling thyself in these things, learn the end of him who dared all this, and recover thyself a little. For very quickly was he overtaken by punishment for these things; and he paid the due penalty of such an abominable act, ending his life by a grievous death, and more pitiable than that which he now dared inflict;[1] suffering also countless additional ills, which ye may know of by perusing Josephus' account of these events. But, lest we should make our discourse long, and interrupt its continuity, we have not thought it necessary to insert that account in what we are saying.

4. "Then was fulfilled that which was spoken by Jeremy the prophet,[2] saying, In Rama was there a voice heard, Rachel weeping for her children, and would not be comforted, because they are not."[3]

Thus having filled the hearer with horror by relating these things: the slaughter so violent and unjust, so extremely cruel and lawless; he comforts him again, by saying, Not from God's wanting power to prevent it did all this take place, nor from any ignorance of His, but when He both knew it, and foretold it,[4] and that loudly by His prophet. Be not troubled then, neither despond, looking unto His unspeakable providence, which one may most clearly see, alike by what He works, and by what He permits. And this He intimated in another place also, when discoursing to His disciples. I mean where, having forewarned them of the judgment seats, and executions, and of the wars of the world, and of the battle that knows no truce, to uphold their spirit and to comfort them He saith, "Are not two sparrows sold for a farthing? and one of them shall not fall on the ground without your Father which is in Heaven."[5] These things He said, signifying that nothing is done without His knowledge, but while He knows all, yet not in all doth He act. "Be not then troubled," He saith, "neither be disturbed." For if He know what ye suffer, and hath power to hinder it, it is quite clear that it is in His providence and care for you that He doth not hinder it. And this we ought to bear in mind in our own temptations also, and great will be the consolation we shall thence receive.

But what, it may be said, hath Rachel to do with Bethlehem? For it saith, "Rachel weeping for her children." And what hath Rama to do with Rachel? Rachel was the mother of Benjamin, and on his death, they buried her in the horse-course that was near this place.[6] The tomb then being near, and the portion pertaining unto Benjamin her infant (for Rama was of the tribe of Benjamin), from the head of the tribe first, and next from the place of her sepulture, He naturally denominates her young children who were massacred.[7] Then to show that the wound that befell her was incurable and cruel, He saith, "she would not be comforted because they are not."

Hence again we are taught this, which I mentioned before, never to be confounded when what is happening is contrary to the promise of God. Behold, for instance, when

---

[1] See Josephus, A. J. xvii. 6, 5.   [2] Jer. xxxi. 15.

[3] Matt. ii. 17, 18.
[4] [προαναϰηρύττοντος, "proclaiming beforehand," a technical term of ecclesiastical Greek.—R.]
[5] Matt. x. 29.   [6] Gen. xxxv. 19, LXX., and xlviii. 7.
[7] [" He calls the young children who were massacred hers," i. e., Rachel's. —R.]

He was come for the salvation of the people, or rather for the salvation of the world, of what kind were His beginnings. His mother, first, in flight; His birth-place is involved in irremediable calamities, and a murder is perpetrated of all murders the bitterest, and there is lamentation and great mourning, and wailings everywhere. But be not troubled; for He is wont ever to accomplish His own dispensations by their contraries, affording us from thence a very great demonstration of His power.

Thus did He lead on His own disciples also, and prepared them to do all their duty, bringing about things by their contraries, that the marvel might be greater. They, at any rate, being scourged and persecuted, and suffering terrors without end, did in this way get the better of them that were beating and persecuting them.

5. "But when Herod was dead, behold, an angel of the Lord appeareth in a dream to Joseph, saying, Arise, and take the young Child and His mother, and go into the land of Israel."[1]

He no more saith "fly," but "go." Seest thou again after the temptation refreshment? then after the refreshment danger again? in that he was freed indeed from his banishment, and came back again to his own country; and beheld the murderer of the children brought to the slaughter;[2] but when he hath set foot on his own country, he finds again a remnant of the former perils, the son of the tyrant living, and being king.

But how did Archelaus reign over Judæa, when Pontius Pilate was governor? Herod's death had recently taken place, and the kingdom had not yet been divided into many parts; but as he had only just ended his life, the son for a while kept possession of the kingdom "in the room of his father Herod;" his brother also bearing this name, which is the reason why the evangelist added, "in the room of *his father* Herod."

It may be said, however, "if he was afraid to settle in Judæa on account of Archelaus, he had cause to fear Galilee also on account of Herod." I answer, By his changing the place, the whole matter was thenceforward thrown into shade; for the whole assault was upon "Bethlehem and the coasts thereof." Therefore now that the slaughter had taken place, the youth Archelaus had no other thought, but that the whole was come to an end, and that amongst the many, He that was sought had been destroyed. And besides, his father having come to such an end

of his life before his eyes, he became for the future more cautious about farther proceedings, and about urging on that course of iniquity.

Joseph therefore comes to Nazareth, partly to avoid the danger, partly also delighting to abide in his native place. To give him the more courage, he receives also an oracle from the angel touching this matter. Luke, however, doth not say that he came there by Divine warning, but that when they had fulfilled all the purification, they returned to Nazareth.[3] What then may one say? That Luke is giving an account of the time before the going down to Egypt, when he saith these things. For He would not have brought them down thither before the purification, in order that nothing should be done contrary to the law, but he waited for her to be purified, and to go to Nazareth, and that then they should go down to Egypt. Then, after their return, He bids them go to Nazareth. But before this they were not warned of God to go thither, but yearning after their native place, they did so of their own accord. For since they had gone up for no other cause but on account of the taxing, and had not so much as a place where to stay, when they had fulfilled that for which they had come up, they went down to Nazareth.[4]

6. We see here the cause why the angel also, putting them at ease for the future, restores them to their home. And not even this simply, but he adds to it a prophecy, "That it might be fulfilled," saith he, "which was spoken by the prophets, He shall be called a Nazarene."[5]

And what manner of prophet said this? Be not curious, nor overbusy. For many of the prophetic writings have been lost; and this one may see from the history of the Chronicles.[6] For being negligent, and continually falling into ungodliness, some they suffered to perish, others they themselves burnt up[7] and cut to pieces. The latter fact Jeremiah relates;[8] the former, he who composed the fourth book of Kings, saying, that after[9] a long time the book of Deuteronomy was hardly found, buried somewhere and lost. But if, when there was no barbarian there, they so betrayed their books, much

---

[1] Matt. ii. 19, 20.
[2] σφαγιασθέντα. ["Massacred," a bold figure of speech.—R.]

[3] Luke ii. 39.
[4] [Of this there is no hint in the narrative; it is a harmonistic conjecture, with little to recommend it.—R.]
[5] Matt. ii. 23.
[6] See 2 Chron. ix. 29, where it is said that certain of the acts of Solomon were *written in the book of Nathan the prophet, and in the prophecy of Ahijah the Shilonite ; and in the visions of Iddo the Seer against Jeroboam the son of Nebat.* See also *ibid.* xii. 15, and xiii. 22. [The explanation given above is as bold as it is ingenious.—R.]
[7] [The Oxford edition reads "brought up ;" evidently a misprint for "burnt up" (κατέκαιον).—R.]
[8] Jer. xxxvi. 23.
[9] 2 Kings xxii. 8, etc.

more when the barbarians had overrun them. For as to the fact, that the prophet had foretold it, the apostles themselves in many places call Him a Nazarene.[1]

"Was not this then," one may say, "casting a shade over the prophecy touching Bethlehem?" By no means: rather this very fact was sure greatly to stir up men, and to awaken them to the search of what was said of Him. Thus, for example, Nathanael too enters on the inquiry concerning Him, saying, "Can there any good thing come out of Nazareth?"[2] For the place was of little esteem; or rather not that place only, but also the whole district of Galilee. Therefore the Pharisees said, "Search and look, for out of Galilee ariseth no prophet."[3] Nevertheless, He is not ashamed to be named even from thence, signifying that He needs not ought of the things of men; and His disciples also He choses out of Galilee; everywhere cutting off the pretexts of them who are disposed to be remiss, and giving tokens that we have no need of outward things, if we practise virtue. For this cause He doth not choose for Himself so much as a house; for "the Son of Man," saith He, "hath not where to lay His head;"[4] and when Herod is plotting against Him, He fleeth, and at His birth is laid in a manger, and abides in an inn, and takes a mother of low estate; teaching us to think no such thing a disgrace, and from the first outset trampling under foot the haughtiness of man, and bidding us give ourselves up to virtue only.

7. For why dost thou pride thyself on thy country, when I am commanding thee to be a stranger to the whole world? (so He speaks); when thou hast leave to become such as that all the universe shall not be worthy of thee? For these things are so utterly contemptible, that they are not thought worthy of any consideration even amongst the philosophers of the Greeks, but are called *Externals*, and occupy the lowest place.

"But yet Paul," one may say, "allows them, saying on this wise, 'As touching the election, they are beloved for the fathers' sake.'"[5] But tell me, when, and of what things was he discoursing, and to whom? Why, to those of Gentile origin, who were puffing themselves up on their faith, and exalting themselves against the Jews, and so breaking them off the more: to quell the swelling pride of the one, and to win over the others, and thoroughly excite them to the same emulation. For when he is speaking of those noble and great men, hear how he saith, "They that say these things, show plainly that they seek a country; and truly if they had been mindful of that from whence they came out, they might have had opportunity to have returned: but now they desire another, a better country."[6] And again, "These all died in faith, not having obtained the promises, but having seen them afar off, and embraced them."[7] And John too said unto those that were coming to him, "Think not to say, We have Abraham to our father."[8] And Paul again, "For they are not all Israel, which are of Israel; neither they, which are the children of the flesh, are they the children of God."[9] For what were the sons of Samuel advantaged, tell me, by their father's nobleness, when they were not heirs of their father's virtue? And what profit had Moses' sons, not having emulated his perfection?[10] Therefore neither did they inherit the dominion; but whilst they enrolled him as their father, the rule of the people passed away to another, to him who had become his son in the way of virtue. And what harm was it to Timothy, that he was of a Greek father? Or what on the other hand again was Noah's son profited by the virtue of his father, when he became a slave instead of free? Seest thou, how little the nobleness of a father avails his children in the way of advocacy?[11] For the wickedness of Ham's disposition overcame the laws of nature, and cast him not only out of the nobility which he had in respect of his father, but also out of his free estate. And what of Esau? Was he not son of Isaac, and had he not his father to stand his friend? Yea, his father too endeavored and desired that he should partake of the blessings, and he himself for the sake of this did all that was commanded him. Nevertheless, because he was untoward,[12] none of these things profited him; but although he was by birth first, and had his father on his side doing everything for this object, yet not having God with him, he lost all.

But why do I speak of men? The Jews were sons of God, and gained nothing by this their high birth. Now if a man, having become a son of God, but failing to show forth an excellency meet for this noble birth, is even punished the more abundantly; why

---

[1] See Acts iii. 22, iii. 6, iv. 10, vi. 14, etc.
[2] John i. 46.
[3] John vii. 52. [R. V. text: "Search, and see that out of Galilee ariseth no prophet."—R.]
[4] Matt viii 20.
[5] Rom. xi. 28. [The Oxford edition reads: "for the Father's sake;" a misprint, conveying an incorrect sense.—R.]

[6] Heb. xi. 14, 15.
[7] Heb. xi. 13. [R. V., more correctly: 'having seen them and greeted them from afar.'"—R.]
[8] Matt. iii. 9.   [9] Rom. ix. 6-8.
[10] [ἀκρίβειαν, "strictness."—R.]
[11] [προστασίαν, "advancement."—R.]   [12] σκαιός.

dost thou bring me forward the nobleness of ancestors remote or near? For not under the old covenant[1] only, but even under the new, one may find this rule to have been held. For "as many as received Him," it is said, "to them gave He power to become the sons of God."[2] And yet many of these children Paul hath affirmed to be nothing profited by their father; "For if ye be circumcised," saith he, "Christ shall profit you nothing."[3] And if Christ be no help to those who will not take heed to themselves, how shall a man stand up in their behalf?

8. Let us not therefore pride ourselves either on high birth, or on wealth, but rather despise them who are so minded: neither let us be dejected at poverty. But let us seek that wealth, which consists in good works; let us flee that poverty, which causes men to be in wickedness, by reason of which also that rich man was poor;[4] wherefore he had not at his command so much as a drop of water, and that, although he made much entreaty. Whereas, who can be so poor amongst us,[5] *as to want water enough even for comfort?* There is none such. For even they that are pining with extreme hunger, may have the comfort of a drop of water; and not of a drop only, but of refreshment too far more abundant. Not so that rich man, but he was poor even to this degree: and what was yet more grievous, he could not so much as soothe his poverty from any source. Why then do we gape after riches, since they bring us not into Heaven?

For tell me, if any king among those upon earth had said, It is impossible for him that is rich to be distinguished at court, or to enjoy any honor; would ye not have thrown away every one his riches with contempt? So then, if they cast us out from such honor as is in the palaces below, they shall be worthy of all contempt: but, when the King of Heaven is day by day crying aloud and saying, "It is hard with them, to set foot on that sacred threshold;" shall we not give up all, and withdraw from our possessions, that with boldness we may enter into the kingdom? And of what consideration are we worthy, who are at great pains to encompass ourselves with the things that obstruct our way thither; and to hide them not only in chests, but even in the earth, when we might entrust them to the guard of the very Heavens? Since now surely thou art doing

the same, as if any husbandman, having gotten wheat wherewith to sow a rich land, was to leave the land alone, and bury all the wheat in a pit, so as neither to enjoy it himself, nor for the wheat to come to ought, but decay and waste.

But what is their common plea, when we accuse them of these things? It gives no little comfort, say they, to know that all is laid up for us in safety at home. Nay, rather not to know of its being laid up is a comfort. For even if thou art not afraid of famine, yet other more grievous things, on account of this store, must needs be a terror to thee: deaths, wars, plots laid against thee. And if a famine should ever befall us, the people again, constrained by the belly, takes weapon in hand against thy house. Or rather, in so doing, thou art first of all bringing famine into our cities, and next thou art forming for thine own house this gulf, more grievous than famine. For by stress of famine I know not any who have come to a speedy end; there being in fact many means in many quarters which may be devised to assuage that evil: but for possessions and riches, and the pursuits connected with them, I can show many to have come by their ruin, some in secret, some openly. And with many such instances the highways abound, with many the courts of law, and the market-places, But why speak I of the highways, the courts of law and the market-places? Why, the very sea thou mayest behold filled with their blood. For not over the land only, as it seems, hath this tyranny prevailed, but over the ocean also hath walked in festal procession with great excess. And one makes a voyage for gold, another, again, is stabbed for the same; and the same tyrannical power hath made one a merchant, the other a murderer.

What then can be less trustworthy than Mammon, seeing that for his sake one travels, and ventures, and is slain? "But who," it is said, "will pity a charmer that is bitten with a serpent?"[6] For we ought, knowing its cruel tyranny, to flee that slavery, and destroy that grievous longing. "But how," saith one, "is this possible?" By introducing another longing, the longing for Heaven. Since he that desires the kingdom will laugh covetousness to scorn; he that is become Christ's slave is no slave of mammon, but rather his lord; for him that flieth from him, he is wont to follow, and to fly from him that pursues. He honors not so much his pursuer as his despiser; no one doth he so laugh to scorn, as them that desire him; nor

[1] [τῇ παλαιᾷ, without a substantive, the technical term in ecclesiastical Greek for the Old Testament.—R.]
[2] John i. 12. [3] Gal. v. 2. [4] Luke xvi. 24.
[5] The words in italics are omitted in several MSS. [In four MSS. and two versions the clause is wanting; see note at close of this Homily.—R.]
[6] Ecclus. xii. 13.

doth he only laugh them to scorn, but wraps round them also innumerable bonds.

Be it ours then, however late, to loose these grievous chains. Why bring thy reasonable soul into bondage to brute matter, to the mother of those untold evils? But, oh the absurdity! that while we are warring against it in words, it makes war with us by deeds, and leads and carries us everywhere about, insulting us as purchased with money, and meet for the lash; and what can be more disgraceful and dishonorable than this?

Again: if we do not get the better of senseless forms of matter, how shall we have the advantage of the incorporeal powers? If we despise not vile earth and abject stones, how shall we bring into subjection the principalities and authorities? How shall we practise temperance? I mean, if silver dazzle and overpower us, when shall we be able to hurry by a fair face? For, in fact, some are so sold under this tyranny, as be moved somehow even at the mere show of the gold, and in playfulness to say, that the very eyes are the better for a gold coin coming in sight. But make not such jests, whoever thou art;[1] for nothing so injures the eyes, both those of the body and those of the soul, as the lust of these things. For instance; it was this grievous longing that put out the lamps of those virgins, and cast them out of the bride-chamber. This sight, which (as thou saidst) "doeth good to the eyes," suffered not the

wretched Judas to hearken unto the Lord's voice, but led him even to the halter, made him burst asunder in the midst; and, after all that, conducted him on to hell.

What then can be more lawless than this? what more horrible? I do not mean the substance of riches, but the unseasonable and frantic desire of them? Why, it even drops human gore, and looks murder, and is fiercer than any wild beast, tearing in pieces them that fall in its way, and what is much worse, it suffers them not even to have any sense of being so mangled. For reason would that those who are so treated should stretch forth their hand to them that pass by, and call them to their assistance, but these are even thankful for such rendings of their flesh, than which what can be more wretched?

Let us then, bearing in mind all these things, flee the incurable disease; let us heal the wounds it hath made, and withdraw ourselves from such a pest: in order that both here we may live a secure and untroubled life, and attain to the future treasure; *unto which God grant that we may all attain,*[2] by the grace and love towards man of our Lord Jesus Christ, with whom unto the Father together with the Holy Ghost be glory, might, honor, now and ever, and world without end. Amen.

[1] [ἄνθρωπε.]

[2] Om. in one or two MSS. [The clause in brackets is wanting in four MSS. and in two versions; the identical authorities which omit the clause in sec. 8. The Oxford editor estimates the facts differently in the two instances, without any adequate reason.—R.]

HOMILY X.

MATT. III. 1, 2.

" In those days cometh John the Baptist, preaching in the wilderness of Judæa, and saying, Repent ye: for the kingdom of Heaven is at hand."

How "in those days"? For not then, surely, when He was a child, and came to Nazareth, but thirty years after, John cometh; as Luke also testifies. How then is it said, "in those days"? The Scripture is always wont to use this manner of speech, not only when it is mentioning what occurs in the time immediately after, but also of things which are to come to pass many years later.

Thus also, for example, when His disciples came unto Him as He sat on the Mount of Olives, and sought to learn about His coming, and the taking of Jerusalem:[1] and yet ye know how great is the interval between those several periods. I mean, that having spoken of the subversion of the mother city,

[1] Matt. xxiv. 3.

and completed His discourse on that subject, and being about to pass to that on the consummation, he inserted, "*Then* shall these things also come to pass;"[1] not bringing together the times by the word *then*, but indicating that time only in which these things were to happen. And this sort of thing he doth now also, saying, "In those days." For this is not put to signify the days that come immediately after, but those in which these things were to take place, which he was preparing to relate.

"But why was it after thirty years," it may be said, "that Jesus came unto His baptism"? After this baptism He was thenceforth to do away with the law: wherefore even until this age, which admits of all sins, He continues fulfilling it all; that no one might say, that because He Himself could not fulfill it, He did it away. For neither do all passions assail us at all times; but while in the first age of life there is much thoughtlessness and timidity, in that which comes after it, pleasure is more vehement, and after this again the desire of wealth. For this cause he awaits the fullness of His adult age, and throughout it all fulfills the law, and so comes to His baptism, adding it as something which follows upon the complete keeping of all the other commandments.

To prove that this was to Him the last good work of those enjoined by the law, hear His own words: "For thus it becometh us to fulfill all righteousness."[2] Now what He saith is like this: "We have performed all the duties of the law, we have not transgressed so much as one commandment. Since therefore this only remains, this too must be added, and so shall we "fulfill all righteousness." For He here calls by the name of "righteousness" the full performance of all the commandments.

2. Now that on this account Christ came to His baptism, is from this evident. But wherefore was this baptism devised for Him? For that not of himself did the son of Zacharias proceed to this, but of God who moved him,—this Luke also declares, when he saith, "The word of the Lord came unto him,"[3] that is, His commandment. And he himself too saith, "He that sent me to baptize with water, the same said to me, upon whom thou shalt see the Spirit descending like a dove, and remaining on Him, the same is He which baptizeth with the Holy Ghost."[4] Wherefore then was he sent to baptize? The Baptist again makes this also plain to us, saying, "I knew Him not, but that He should

be made manifest to Israel, therefore am I come baptizing with water."[5]

And if this was the only cause, how saith Luke, that "he came into the country about Jordan, preaching the baptism of repentance for the remission of sins?"[6] And yet it had not remission, but this gift pertained unto the baptism that was given afterwards; for in this "we are buried with Him,"[7] and our old man was then crucified with Him, and before the cross there doth not appear remission anywhere; for everywhere this is imputed to His blood. And Paul too saith, "But ye are washed, but ye are sanctified," not by the baptism of John, but "in the name of our Lord Jesus Christ, and by the Spirit of our God."[8] And elsewhere too he saith, "John verily preached a baptism of repentance," (he saith not "of remission,") "that they should believe on Him that should come after him."[9] For when the sacrifice was not yet offered, neither had the spirit yet come down, nor sin was put away, nor the enmity removed, nor the curse destroyed; how was remission to take place?

What means then, "for the remission of sins?"

The Jews were senseless, and had never any feeling of their own sins, but while they were justly accountable for the worst evils, they were justifying themselves in every respect; and this more than anything caused their destruction, and led them away from the faith. This, for example, Paul himself was laying to their charge, when he said, that "they being ignorant of God's righteousness, and going about[10] to establish their own, had not submitted themselves unto the righteousness of God."[11] And again: "What shall we say then? That the Gentiles, which followed not after righteousness, have attained[12] to righteousness; but Israel, which followed after the law of righteousness, hath not attained[13] unto the law of righteousness. Wherefore? Because they sought it not by faith, but as it were by works."[14]

Since therefore this was the cause of their evils, John cometh, doing nothing else but bringing them to a sense of their own sins. This, among other things, his very garb declared, being that of repentance and confession. This was indicated also by what he preached, for nothing else did he say, but

5 John i. 31.   6 Luke iii. 3.   7 Col. ii. 12; Rom. vi. 4.
8 1 Cor. vi. 11.   9 Acts xix. 4.
10 [ζητοῦντες, "seeking," R. V.]   11 Rom. x. 3.
12 κατέλαβε [R. V., "attained."]
13 ἔφθασε [R. V., "did not arrive."]
14 Rom. ix. 30 32. [See R. V. The text of Chrysostom follows one of the readings accepted by the Revisers, omitting νόμου at the close of the citation; but it inserts δικαιοσύνης (with Rec.) a second time in verse 31.—R.]

1 Matt. xxiv. 23.   2 Matt. iii. 15.
3 Luke iii. 2.   4 John i. 33.

"bring forth fruits meet for repentance."[1] Forasmuch then as their not condemning their own sins, as Paul also hath explained, made them start off from Christ, while their coming to a sense thereof would set them upon longing to seek after their Redeemer, and to desire remission; this John came to bring about, and to persuade them to repent, not in order that they might be punished, but that having become by repentance more humble, and condemning themselves, they might hasten to receive remission.

But let us see how exactly he hath expressed it; how, having said, that he "came preaching the baptism of repentance in the wilderness of Judæa," he adds, "for remission,"as though he said, For this end he exhorted them to confess and repent of their sins; not that they should be punished, but that they might more easily receive the subsequent remission. For had they not condemned themselves, they could not have sought after His grace; and not seeking, they could not have obtained remission.

Thus that baptism led the way for this; wherefore also he said, that "they should believe on Him which should come after him;"[2] together with that which hath been mentioned setting forth this other cause of His baptism. For neither would it have been as much for him to have gone about to their houses, and to have led Christ around, taking Him by the hand, and to have said, "Believe in This Man;" as for that blessed voice to be uttered, and all those other things performed in the presence and sight of all.

On account of this He cometh to the baptism. Since in fact both the credit of him that was baptizing, and the purport of the thing itself,[3] was attracting the whole city, and calling it unto Jordan; and it became a great spectacle.[4]

Therefore he humbles them also when they are come, and persuades them to have no high fancies about themselves; showing them liable to the utmost evils, unless they would repent, and leaving their forefathers, and all vaunting in them, would receive Him that was coming.

Because in fact the things concerning Christ had been up to that time veiled, and many thought He was dead, owing to the massacre which took place at Bethlehem. For though at twelve years old He discovered Himself, yet did He also quickly veil Himself again. And for this cause there was need of that splendid exordium and of a loftier beginning. Wherefore also then for the first time he with clear voice proclaims things which the Jews had never heard, neither from prophets, nor from any besides; making mention of Heaven, and of the kingdom there, and no longer saying anything touching the earth.

But by the kingdom in this place he means His former and His last advent.

3. "But what is this to the Jews?" one may say, "for they know not even what thou sayest." "Why, for this cause," saith he, "do I so speak, in order that being roused by the obscurity of my words, they may proceed to seek Him, whom I preach." In point of fact, he so excited them with good hopes when they came near, that even many publicans and soldiers inquired what they should do, and how they should direct their own life; which was a sign of being thenceforth set free from all worldly things, and of looking to other greater objects, and of foreboding[5] things to come. Yea, for all, both the sights and the words of that time, led them unto lofty thoughts.

Conceive, for example, how great a thing it was to see a man after thirty years coming down from the wilderness, being the son of a chief priest, who had never known the common wants of men, and was on every account venerable, and had Isaiah with him. For he too was present, proclaiming him, and saying, "This is he who I said should come crying, and preaching throughout the whole wilderness with a clear voice." For so great was the earnestness of the prophets touching these things, that not their own Lord only, but him also who was to minister unto Him, they proclaimed a long time beforehand, and they not only mentioned him, but the place too in which he was to abide, and the manner of the doctrine which he had to teach when he came, and the good effect that was produced by him.

See, at least, how both the prophet and the Baptist go upon the same ideas, although not upon the same words.

Thus the prophet saith that he shall come saying, "Prepare ye the way of the Lord, make his paths straight."[6] And he himself when he was come said, "Bring forth fruits meet for repentance,"[7] which corresponds with, "Prepare ye the way of the Lord." Seest thou that both by the words of the prophet, and by his own preaching, this one thing is manifested alone; that he was come, making a way and preparing beforehand, not bestowing the gift, which was the remission, but ordering in good time the souls of such as should receive the God of all?

---

[1] Matt. iii. 8.
[2] Acts xix. 4.
[3] ἡ τοῦ πράγματος ὑπόθεσις.
[4] θέατρον.
[5] ὀνειροπολεῖν.
[6] Is. xl. 3.
[7] Matt. iii. 8.

But Luke expresses somewhat further: not repeating the exordium, and so passing on, but setting down likewise all the prophecy. "For every valley," saith he, "shall be filled; and every mountain and hill shall be brought low; and the crooked shall be made straight, and the rough ways smooth; and all flesh shall see the salvation of God." [1] Dost thou perceive how the prophet hath anticipated all by his words; the concourse of the people, the change of things for the better, the easiness of that which was preached, the first cause of all that was occurring, even if he hath expressed it rather as in figure, it being in truth a prophecy which he was uttering? Thus, when he saith, "Every valley shall be filled, and every mountain and hill shall be brought low, and the rough ways shall be made smooth;" he is signifying the exaltation of the lowly, the humiliation of the self-willed, the hardness of the law changed into easiness of faith. For it is no longer toils and labors, saith he, but grace, and forgiveness of sins, affording great facility of salvation. Next he states the cause of these things, saying, "All flesh shall see the salvation of God;" no longer Jews and proselytes only, but also all earth and sea, and the whole race of men. Because by "the crooked things" he signified our whole corrupt life, publicans, harlots, robbers, magicians, as many as having been perverted before afterwards walked in the right way: much as He Himself likewise said, "publicans and harlots go into the kingdom of God before you," [2] because they believed. And in other words also again the prophet declared the self-same thing, thus saying, "Then wolves and lambs shall feed together." [3] For like as here by the hills and valleys, he meant that incongruities of character [4] are blended into one and the same evenness of self-restraint, so also there, by the characters of the brute animals indicating the different dispositions of men, he again spoke of their being linked in one and the same harmony of godliness. Here also, as before, stating the cause. That cause is, "There shall be He that riseth to reign over the Gentiles, in Him shall the Gentiles trust:" [5] much the same as here too he said, "All flesh shall see the salvation of God," everywhere declaring that the power and knowledge of these our Gospels would be poured out to the ends of the world, converting the human race, from a brutish disposi-

tion and a fierce temper to something very gentle and mild.

4. "And the same John had his raiment of camel's hair, and a leathern girdle about his loins." [6]

Observe, how the prophets foretold some things, others they left to the evangelists. Wherefore also Matthew both sets down the prophecies, and adds his own part, not accounting even this superfluous, to speak of the dress of the righteous man.

For indeed it was a marvellous and strange thing to behold so great austerity in a human frame: which thing also particularly attracted the Jews, seeing in him the great Elijah, and guided by what they then beheld, to the memory of that blessed man; or rather, even to a greater astonishment. For the one indeed was brought up in cities and in houses, the other dwelt entirely in the wilderness from his very swaddling clothes. For it became the forerunner of Him who was to put away all the ancient ills, the labor, for example, the curse, the sorrow, the sweat; himself also to have certain tokens of such a gift, and to come at once to be above that condemnation. Thus he neither ploughed land, nor opened furrow, he ate not his bread by the sweat of his face, but his table was hastily supplied, and his clothing more easily furnished than his table, and his lodging yet less troublesome than his clothing. For he needed neither roof, nor bed, nor table, nor any other of these things, but a kind of angel's life in this our flesh did he exhibit. For this cause his very garment was of hair, that by his dress he might instruct men to separate themselves from all things human, and to have nothing in common with the earth, but to hasten back to their earlier nobleness, wherein Adam was before he wanted garments or robe. Thus that garb bore tokens of *nothing less than* a kingdom, and of repentance.

And do not say to me, "Whence had he a garment of hair and a girdle, dwelling as he did in the wilderness?" For if thou art to make a difficulty of this, thou wilt also inquire into more things besides; how in the winters, and how in the heats of summer, he continued in the wilderness, and this with a delicate body, and at an immature age? how the nature of his infant flesh endured such great inconstancy of weather, and a diet so uncommon, and all the other hardships arising from the wilderness?

Where now are the philosophers of the Greeks, who at random and for nought emu-

---

1 Luke iii. 5, 6.   2 Matt. xxi. 31.
3 Isa. xi. 6.   4 τὸ ἀνώμαλον τοῦ ἤθους.
5 Isa. xi. 10; see also Rom. xv. 12. ["Hope" instead of "trust;" see foot-note on Hom. vii. 2, p. 45.—R.]

6 Matt. iii. 4.

lated the shamelessness of the Cynics (for what is the profit of being shut up in a tub, and afterwards running into such wantonness)? they who encompassed themselves with rings and cups, and men servants and maid servants, and with much pomp besides, falling into either extreme. But this man was not so; but he dwelt in the wilderness as in Heaven, showing forth all strictness of self-restraint. And from thence, like some angel from Heaven, he went down unto the cities, being a champion of godliness, and a crowned victor over the world, and a philosopher of that philosophy which is worthy of the heavens. And these things were, when sin was not yet put away, when the law had not yet ceased, when death was not yet bound, when the brazen gates were not yet broken up, but while the ancient polity still was in force.

Such is the nature of a noble and thoroughly vigilant soul, for it is everywhere springing forward, and passing beyond the limits set to it; as Paul[1] also did with respect to the new polity.

But why, it may be asked, did he use a girdle with his raiment? This was customary with them of old time, before men passed into this soft and loose kind of dress. Thus, for instance, both Peter[2] appears to have been "girded," and Paul; for it saith, "the man that owneth this girdle."[3] And Elijah[4] too was thus arrayed, and every one of the saints, because they were at work continually, laboring, and busying themselves either in journeyings, or about some other necessary matter; and not for this cause only, but also with a view of trampling under foot all ornaments, and practising all austerity. This very kind of thing accordingly Christ declares to be the greatest praise of virtue, thus saying, "What went ye out for to see? a man clothed in soft raiment? behold, they that wear soft clothing are in king's houses."[5]

But if he, who was so pure, and more glorious than the heaven, and above all prophets, than whom none greater was born, and who had such great boldness of speech, thus exercised himself in austerity, scorning so exceedingly all dissolute delicacy, and training himself to this hard life; what excuse shall we have, who after so great a benefit, and the unnumbered burdens of our sins, do not show forth so much as the least part of his penance,[6] but are drinking and surfeiting, and smelling of perfumes, and in no better

trim than the harlot women on the stage, and are by all means softening ourselves, and making ourselves an easy prey to the devil?[7]

5. "Then went out to him all Judea, and Jerusalem, and all the region round about Jordan, and were baptized of him, confessing their sins."[8]

Seest thou how great power was in the coming of the prophet? how he stirred up all the people; how he led them to a consideration of their own sins? For it was indeed worthy of wonder to behold him in human form showing forth such things and using so great freedom of speech, and rising up in condemnation of all as children, and having his great grace beaming out from his countenance. And, moreover, the appearance of a prophet after the great interval of time contributed to their amazement, because the gift had failed them, and returned to them after a long time. And the nature of his preaching too was strange and unusual. For they heard of none of those things to which they were accustomed; such as wars and battles and victories below, and famine and pestilence, and Babylonians and Persians, and the taking of the city, and the other things with which they were familiar, but of Heaven and of the kingdom there, and of the punishment in hell. And it was for this cause, let me add, that although they that committed revolt in the wilderness, those in the company of Judas, and of Theudas,[9] had been all of them slain no great while before, yet they were not the more backward to go out thither. For neither was it for the same objects that he summoned them, as for dominion, or revolt, or revolution; but in order to lead them by the hand to the kingdom on high. Wherefore neither did he keep them in the wilderness to take them about with him, but baptizing them, and teaching them the rules concerning self-denial, he dismissed them; by all means instructing them to scorn whatever things are on earth, and to raise themselves up to the things to come, and press on every day.

6. This man then let us also emulate, and forsaking luxury and drunkenness let us go over unto the life of restraint. For this surely is the time of confession both for the uninitiated and for the baptized; for the one, that upon their repentance they may partake of the sacred mysteries; for the others, that having washed away their stain after baptism, they may approach the table with a clean

---

[1] As in refusing to be supported (in several cases) by those to whom he preached the gospel. See his account of his views in so doing, 1 Cor. ix., especially towards the end of the chapter.
[2] John xxi. 7.   [3] Acts xxi. 11.   [4] 2 Kings i. 8.
[5] Matt. xi. 8.   [6] ἐξομολογήσεως.

[7] [τῷ διαβόλῳ. The Oxford edition has "the devils," but this is misleading, since it suggests a reference to "demons." Probably the plural is a misprint.—R.]
[8] Matt. iii. 5, 6.   [9] Acts v. 36, 37.

5

conscience. Let us then forsake this soft and effeminate way of living. For it is not, it is not possible at once both to do penance[1] and to live in luxury. And this let John teach you by his raiment, by his food, by his abode. What then? dost thou require us, you may say, to practise such self-restraint as this? I do not require it, but I advise and recommend it. But if this be not possible to you, let us at least, though in cities, show forth repentance, for the judgment is surely at our doors. But even if it were further off, we ought not even so to be emboldened, for the term of each man's life is the end of the world virtually to him that is summoned. But that it is even at the doors, hear Paul saying, "The night is far spent, the day is at hand;"[2] and again, "He that cometh will come, and will not tarry."[3]

For the signs too are now complete, which announce that day. For "this Gospel of the Kingdom," saith He, "shall be preached in all the world for a witness unto all nations; and then shall the end come."[4] Attend with care to what is said. He said not, "when it hath been believed by all men," but "when it hath been preached to[5] all." For this cause he also said, "for a witness to the nations," to show, that He doth not wait for all men to believe, and then for Him to come. Since the phrase, "for a witness," hath this meaning, "for accusation," "for reproof," "for condemnation of them that have not believed."

But we, while hearing these things and seeing them, slumber, and see dreams, sunk in a lethargy, as in some very deepest night.[6] For the things present are nothing better than dreams, whether they be prosperous, or whether they be painful. Wherefore I entreat you now at length to be awakened, and to look another way, unto the Sun of Righteousness. For no man while sleeping can see the sun, or delight his eyes with the beauty of its beams; but whatever he may see, he beholds all as in a dream. For this cause we need much penance, and many tears; both as being in a state of insensibility while we err, and because our sins are great, and beyond excuse. And that I lie not, the more part of them that hear me are witnesses. Nevertheless, although they be beyond excuse, let us repent, and we shall receive crowns.

7. But by repentance I mean, not only to forsake our former evil deeds, but also to show forth good deeds greater than those. For, "bring forth," saith he, "fruits meet for repentance."[7] But how shall we bring them forth? If we do the opposite things: as for instance, hast thou seized by violence the goods of others? henceforth give away even thine own. Hast thou been guilty of fornication for a long time? abstain even from thy wife for certain appointed days; exercise continence. Hast thou insulted and stricken such as were passing by? Henceforth bless them that insult thee, and do good to them that smite thee. For it sufficeth not for our health to have plucked out the dart only, but we must also apply remedies to the wound. Hast thou lived in self-indulgence, and been drunken in time past? Fast, and take care to drink water, in order to destroy the mischief that hath so grown up within thee. Hast thou beheld with unchaste eyes beauty that belonged to another? Henceforth do not so much as look upon a woman at all, that thou mayest stand in more safety. For it is said, "Depart from evil, and do good;"[8] and again, "Make thy tongue to cease from evil, and thy lips that they speak no guile."[9] "But tell me the good too." "Seek peace, and pursue it:" I mean not peace with man only, but also peace with God. And he hath well said, "pursue" her: for she is driven away, and cast out; she hath left the earth, and is gone to sojourn in Heaven. Yet shall we be able to bring her back again, if we will put away pride and boasting, and whatsoever things stand in her away, and will follow this temperate and frugal life.[10] For nothing is more grievous than wrath and fierce anger. This renders men both puffed up and servile, by the former making them ridiculous, by the other hateful; and bringing in opposite vices, pride and flattery, at the same time. But if we will cut off the greediness of this passion, we shall be both lowly with exactness, and exalted with safety. For in our bodies too all distempers arise from excess; and when the elements thereof leave their proper limits, and go on beyond moderation, then all these countless diseases are generated, and grievous kinds of death. Somewhat of the same kind one may see take place with respect to the soul likewise.

8. Let us therefore cut away excess, and drinking the salutary medicine of moderation,

---

[1] ἐξομολογεῖσθαι.   [2] Rom. xiii. 12.   [3] Heb. x. 37.
[4] Matt. xxiv. 14.] [" All the nations," so R. V., and comp. what follows here.—R.]
[5] [παρὰ πάντων ἀνθρώπων . . . παρὰ πᾶσι, is the explanation of Chrysostom, paraphrasing the New Testament passage.—R.]
[6] [ἐν βαθυτάτῃ νυκτί.]

[7] Matt. iii. 8. [R. V., more literally, "worthy of repentance," with margin, "Or, your repentance," the Greek being τῆς μετανοίας; so in the text of Chrysostom.—R.]
[8] Ps. xxxiv. 14.   [9] Ps. xxxiv. 13 [LXX.].
[10] [" If we desire (θελωμεν), by putting away, etc. . . . to pursue this temperate and frugal life."—R.]

let us abide in our proper temperament, and give careful heed to our prayers. Though we receive not, let us persevere that we may receive; and if we do receive, then because we have received. For it is not at all His wish to defer giving, but by such delay He is contriving for us to persevere. With this intent He doth also lengthen out [1] our supplication, and at times permits a temptation to come upon us, that we may continually flee for refuge unto Him, and where we have fled for refuge, may there abide. Thus also do affectionate fathers act, and mothers that love their children; when they see their little children forsake their society, and playing witn those of their own age, they cause their servants to enact many fearful things, that by such fear they may be constrained to flee for refuge to their mother's bosom. Even so doth God oftentimes hold out some kind of threat; not that He may bring it upon us, but that He may draw us unto Himself. At any rate, when we return, he doth away with our fear at once; since assuredly, if we were alike in temptations and at ease, there would have been no need of temptations.

But why do I speak of us? Since even to those saints of old great was the lesson of moderation hence derived. For this cause the prophet too saith, "It is good for me that Thou hast humbled me." [2] And He Himself likewise said to the apostles, "In the world ye shall have tribulation." [3] And Paul signifies this self-same thing, when he saith, "There was given to me a thorn in the flesh, the messenger of Satan to buffet me." [4] Wherefore also when he sought to be delivered from the temptation, he obtained it not, by reason of the great benefit thence ensuing. And if we should go over the whole life of David, we shall find him more glorious in his dangers; both himself and all the others that were like him. For so Job at that season shone forth the more abundantly, and Joseph too in this way became the more approved, and Jacob also, and his father likewise, and his father's father; and all as many as ever put on crowns of peculiar glory, it was by tribulations and temptations that they first won their crowns, then had their names recited.

Being conscious of all these things, according to the wise saying, let us "not make haste in time of trouble," [5] but let us teach ourselves one thing only, how to bear all nobly, and not to be curious or inquisitive about any of the things that are coming to pass. For to know when our tribulations should be done away, belongs to God who permits them to befall us; but to bear them, brought upon us, with all thankfulness, all that is the work of a good disposition on our part; and if this be so, then all our blessings will follow. In order therefore that these may follow, and that we may become better approved here, and more glorious in that world, let us submit to all, whatever may be brought upon us, for all thanking Him who knows [6] what is good for us better than we do, and loves us more ardently than those who gave us birth. And let both these considerations be a charm for us to chant to ourselves in every terror that occurs, that so we may quell our despondency, and in all things glorify Him, who on our behalf doeth and ordereth all, even God.

For so we shall both easily repulse all hostile devices, and attain unto the incorruptible crowns: by the grace and love towards man of our Lord Jesus Christ, with whom be unto the Father glory, might, and honor, together with the Holy Ghost, now, and always, even for ever and ever. Amen.

---

[1] ὑπερτίθεται, used as in the word ὑπέρθεσις, *superpositio*, whioh was a kind of technical word in the Church for the prolongation of a fast. See Routh, *Reliq. Sacr.* i. 397, &c.; St. Irenæus, St. Dionys. Alex., and St. Epiphanius, as quoted by him.
[2] Ps. cxix. 71.　　[3] John xvi. 33.　　[4] 2 Cor. xii. 7.
[5] Ecclus. ii. 2.　　[6] [χάριν εἰδότες ὑπὲρ πάντων τῷ εἰδότι.]

HOMILY XI.

MATT. III. 7.

" But when he saw many of the Pharisees and Sadducees come to his baptism, he said unto them, O generation of vipers, who hath warned you to flee from the wrath to come ? "

How then doth Christ say, that they did not believe John? [1] Because this was not believing, to decline receiving Him whom he preached. For so they thought they regarded their prophets and their lawgiver, nevertheless He said they had not regarded them, forasmuch as they received not Him, that was foretold by them. "For if ye had

---

[1] Luke xx. 5.

believed Moses," saith He, " ye would have believed Me." [1]   And after this again, being asked by Christ, " The baptism of John, whence is it?" [2] they said, " If we shall say, Of earth, we fear the people; if we shall say, From heaven, He will say unto us, How then did ye not believe him?"

So that from all these things it is manifest that they came indeed and were baptized, yet they did not abide in the belief of that which which was preached. For John also points out their wickedness, by their sending [3] unto the Baptist, and saying, "Art thou Elias? Art thou Christ?" wherefore he also added, "they which were sent were of the Pharisees." [4]

" What then? were not the multitudes also of this same mind"? one may say. Nay, the multitudes in simplicity of mind had this suspicion, but the Pharisees, wishing to lay hold of Him. For since it was acknowledged that Christ comes out of the village of David, and this man was of the tribe of Levi, they laid a snare by the question, in order that if he should say any such thing they might quickly come upon him. This at any rate he hath declared by what follows; for on his not acknowledging any of the things which they expected, even so they take hold of him, saying, " Why baptizest thou then, if thou be not the Christ?" [5]

And to convince thee that the Pharisees came with one mind, and the people with another, hear how the evangelist hath declared this too; saying of the people, " that they came and were baptized of him, confessing their sins;" [6] but concerning the Pharisees, no longer like that, but that " when he saw many of the Pharisees and Sadducees coming, he said, O generation of vipers, who hath warned you to flee from the wrath to come?" O greatness of mind! How doth he discourse unto men ever thirsting after the blood of the prophets, and in disposition no better than serpents! how doth he disparage both themselves and their progenitors with all plainness!

2. " Yea," saith one; " he speaks plainly enough, but the question is if there be any reason in this plainness. For he did not see them sinning, but in the act of change; wherefore they did not deserve blame, but rather praise and approbation, for having left city and houses, and making haste to hear his preaching."

What then shall we say? That he had not things present, and even now doing, in his view, but he knew the secrets of their mind, God having revealed this. Since then they were priding themselves on their forefathers, and this was like to prove the cause of their destruction, and was casting them into a state of carelessness, he cuts away the roots of their pride. For this cause Isaiah also calls them, " rulers of Sodom," and " people of Gomorrah;" [7] and another prophet saith, "Are ye not as children of the Ethiopians;" [8] and all withdraw them from this way of thinking, bringing down their pride, which had caused them unnumbered evils.

" But the prophets," you will say, " naturally did so; for they saw them sinning: but in this case, with what view and for what cause doeth he the same, seeing them obey him." To make them yet more tender-hearted.

But if one accurately mark his words, he hath also tempered his rebuke with commendation. For he spake these things, as marvelling at them, that they were become able, however late, to do what seemed almost an impossibility for them. His rebuke, you see, is rather that of one bringing them over, and working upon them to arouse themselves. For in that he appears amazed, he implies both their former wickedness to be great, and their conversion marvellous and beyond expectation. Thus, "what hath come to pass," saith he, " that being children of those men, and brought up so badly, they have repented? Whence hath come so great a change? Who hath softened down the harshness of their spirit? Who corrected that which was incurable?"

And see how straightway from the beginning he alarmed them, by laying first, for a foundation, his words concerning hell. For he spake not of the usual topics: " Who hath warned you to flee from wars, from the inroads of the barbarians, from captivities, from famines, from pestilences?" but concerning another sort of punishment, never before made manifest to them, he was striking the first preparatory note, saying thus, " Who hath warned you to flee from the wrath to come?"

And full well did he likewise call them, " generation of vipers." For that animal too is said to destroy the mother that is in travail with her, and eating through her belly, thus to come forth unto light; which kind of thing these men also did, being " murderers of fathers, and murderers of mothers," [9] and destroying their instructors with their own hands.

---

[1] John v. 46.   [2] Matt. xxi. 25, 26.
[3] [" When some of them were sending."—R.]
John i. 24.   [5] John i. 25.   [6] Matt. iii. 6.

[7] Is. i. 10.   [8] Amos ix. 7.   [9] 1 Tim. i. 9.

3. However, he stops not at the rebuke, but introduces advice also. For,

"Bring forth," says he, "fruits meet for repentance."[1]

For to flee from wickedness is not enough, but you must show forth also great virtue. For let me not have that contradictory yet ordinary[2] case, that[3] refraining yourselves for a little while, ye return unto the same wickedness. For we are not come for the same objects as the prophets before. Nay, the things that are now are changed, and are more exalted, forasmuch as the Judge henceforth is coming, His very self, the very Lord of the kingdom, leading unto greater self-restraint, calling us to heaven, and drawing us upward to those abodes. For this cause do I unfold the doctrine also touching hell, because both the good things and the painful are for ever. Do not therefore abide as ye are, neither bring forward the accustomed pleas, Abraham, Isaac, Jacob, the noble race of your ancestors."

And these things he said, not as forbidding them to say that they were sprung from those holy men, but as forbidding them to put confidence in this, while they were neglecting the virtue of the soul; at once bringing forward publicly what was in their minds, and foretelling things to come. Because after this they are found to say, "We have Abraham to our father, and were never in bondage to any man."[4] Since then it was this, which most of all lifted them up with pride and ruined them, he first puts it down.

And see how with his honor paid to the patriarch he combines his correction touching these things. Namely, having said, "Think not to say, We have Abraham to our father," he said not, "for the patriarch shall not be able to profit you anything," but somehow in a more gentle and acceptable manner he intimated the self-same thing, by saying,

"For God is able of these stones to raise up children to Abraham."[5]

Now some say, that concerning the Gentiles he saith these things, calling them *stones*, metaphorically; but I say, that the expression hath also another meaning. But of what kind is this? Think not, saith he, that if you should perish, you would make the patriarch childless. This is not, this is not so. For with God it is possible, both out of stones to give him men, and to bring them to that relationship; since at the beginning also it was so done. For it was like the birth of

men out of stones, when a child came forth from that hardened womb.

This accordingly the prophet also was intimating, when he said, "Look unto the hard rock, whence ye are hewn, and to the hole of the pit, whence ye are digged: look unto Abraham your father, and unto Sarah that bare you."[6] Now of this prophecy, you see, he reminds them, showing that if at the beginning he made him a father, as marvellously as if he had made him so out of stones, it was possible for this now also to come to pass. And see how he both alarms them, and cuts them off: in that he said not, "He had already raised up," lest they should despair of themselves, but that He "is able to raise up:" and he said not, "He is able out of stones to make men," but what was a much greater thing, "kinsmen and children of Abraham."

Seest thou how for the time he drew them off from their vain imagination about things of the body, and from their refuge in their forefathers; in order that they might rest the hope of their salvation in their own repentance and continence? Seest thou how by casting out their carnal relationship, he is bringing in that which is of faith?

4. Mark then how by what follows also he increases their alarm, and adds intensity to their agonizing fear.

For having said that "God is able of these stones to raise up children unto Abraham," he added, "And now also the axe is laid unto the root of the trees,"[7] by all means making his speech alarming. For as he from his way of life had much freedom of speech, so they needed his severe rebuke, having been left barren[8] now for a long time. For "why do I say" (such are his words) "that ye are on the point of falling away from your relationship to the patriarch, and of seeing others, even those that are of stones, brought in to your pre-eminence? Nay, not to this point only will your penalty reach, but your punishment will proceed further. "For now," saith he, "the axe is laid unto the root of the trees." There is nothing more terrible than this turn of his discourse. For it is no longer "a flying sickle,"[9] nor "the taking down of a hedge," nor "the treading under foot of the vineyard;"[10] but an axe exceeding sharp, and what is worse, it is even at the doors. For inasmuch as they continually disbelieved the prophets, and used to say, "Where is the day of the Lord:"[11] and "let

---

[1] [R. V., "worthy of repentance," marg., "your repentance."]
[2] [συνήθη.]
[3] [The correct reading seems to be ὅτε, "when," not ὅτι, "that."—R.]
[4] John viii. 33.   [5] Matt. iii. 9.

[6] Is. li. 1, 2.
[7] Matt. iii. 10. [R. V., "And even now is the axe laid," etc. —R.]
[8] χερσωθέντες.   [9] Zech. v. 1, LXX.   [10] Is. v. 5.
[11] See Amos v. 18; Jer. xvii. 15; Ezek. xii. 22, 27.

the counsel of the Holy One of Israel come, that we may know it,"[1] by reason that it was many years before what they said came to pass; to lead them off from this encouragement also, he sets the terrors close to them And this he declared by saying "now," and by his putting it to "the root." "For the space between is nothing now," saith he, "but it is laid to the very root." And he said not, "to the branches," nor "to the fruits," but "to the root." Signifying, that if they were negligent, they would have incurable horrors to endure, and not have so much as a hope of remedy. It being no servant who is now come, as those before Him were, but the very Lord of all, bringing on them His fierce and most effectual vengeance.

Yet, although he hath terrified them again, he suffers them not to fall into despair; but as before he said not "He hath raised up," but "He is able to raise up children to Abraham" (at once both alarming and comforting them); even so here also he did not say that "it hath touched the root," but "it is laid to the root, and is now hard by it, and shows signs of no delay." However, even though He hath brought it so near, He makes its cutting depend upon you. For if ye change and become better men, this axe will depart without doing anything; but if ye continue in the same ways, He will tear up the tree by the roots. And therefore, observe, it is neither removed from the root, nor applied as it is doth it cut at all: the one, that ye may not grow supine, the other to let you know that it is possible even in a short time to be changed and saved. Wherefore he doth also from all topics heighten their fear, thoroughly awakening and pressing them on to repentance. Thus first their falling away from their forefathers; next, others being introduced instead; lastly, those terrors being at their doors, the certainty of suffering incurable evils (both which he declared by the root and the axe), was sufficient to rouse thoroughly those even that were very supine, and to make them full of anxiety. I may add, that Paul too was setting forth the same, when he said, "A short word[2] will the Lord make upon the whole world."[3]

But be not afraid; or rather, be afraid, but despair not. For thou hast yet a hope of change; the sentence is not quite absolute,[4] neither did the axe come to cut (else what hindered it from cutting, close as it was to the root?); but on purpose by this fear to make thee a better man, and to prepare thee to bring forth fruit. For this cause he added, "Therefore every tree, which bringeth not forth good fruit, is hewn down, and cast into the fire."[5] Now by the word "every," he rejects again the privilege which they had from their noble descent; "Why, if thou be Abraham's own descendant," saith he, "if thou have thousands of patriarchs to enumerate, thou wilt but undergo a double punishment, abiding unfruitful."

By these words he alarmed even publicans, the soldiers' mind was startled by him, not casting them into despair, yet ridding them of all security. For along with the terror, there is also much encouragement in what he saith; since by the expression, "which bringeth not forth good fruit," he signified that what bears fruit is delivered from all vengeance.

5. "And how," saith one, "shall we be able to bring forth fruit, when the edge is being applied, and the time so strait, and the appointed season cut short." "Thou wilt be able," saith he, "for this fruit is not of the same kind as that of common trees, waiting a long time, and in bondage to the necessities[6] of seasons, and requiring much other management; but it is enough to be willing, and the tree at once hath put forth its fruit. For not the nature of the root only, but also the skill of the husbandman contributes the most to that kind of fruit-bearing."

For (let me add) on account of this,—lest they should say, "Thou art alarming and pressing, and constraining us, applying an axe, and threatening us with being cut down, yet requiring produce in time of punishment,"—he hath added, to signify the ease of bearing that fruit, "I indeed baptize you with water, but He that cometh after me is mightier than I, the latchet of whose shoe I am not worthy to unloose; He shall baptize you with the Holy Ghost and with fire:"[7] implying hereby that consideration[8] only is needed and faith, not labors and toils; and as it is easy to be baptized, so is it easy to be converted, and to become better men. So having stirred their mind by the fear of *God's* judgment, and the expectation of *His* punishment, and by the mention of the axe, and by the loss of their ancestors, and by the bringing in of those other children, and by the double vengeance of cutting off and burning, and having by all means softened their hardness, and brought them to desire deliverance from so great evils; then he brings in what

---

[1] Is. v. 19.   [2] λόγον.   [3] Rom. ix. 28.
[4] αὐτοτελής, *self-executed.*

[5] Matt. iii. 10.   [6] ἀναγκαίς.
[7] Matt. iii. 11. Comp. Luke iii. 16. [In neither passage is the preposition repeated in the Greek text. Chrysostom (see sec. 6) interprets "fire" as part of the blessing promised. So many modern commentators.—R.]
[8] [γνώμης.]

he hath to say touching Christ; and not simply, but with a declaration of His great superiority. Then in setting forth the difference between himself and Him, lest he should seem to say this out of favor, he establishes the fact by comparison of the gifts bestowed by each of them. For he did not at once say, "I am not worthy to unloose the latchet of His shoe;" but when he had first set forth the little value of his own baptism, and had shown that it hath nothing more than to lead them to repentance (for he did not say with water of remission, but of repentance), he sets forth Christ's also, which is full of the unspeakable gift. Thus he seems to say, "Lest, on being told that He cometh after me, thou shouldest despise Him as having come later; learn thou the virtue[1] of His gift, and thou wilt clearly know that I uttered nothing worthy nor great, when I said, "I am not worthy to unloose the latchet of His shoe." So too when thou art told, "He is mightier than I," do not think I said this in the way of making a comparison. For I am not worthy to be ranked so much as among His servants, no, not even the lowest of His servants, nor to receive the least honored portion of His ministry." Therefore He did not merely say, "His shoes," but not even "the latchet," which kind of office was counted the last of all. Then to hinder thy attributing what he had said to humility, he adds also the proof from the facts: "For He shall baptize you," saith he, "with the Holy Ghost and with fire."

6. Seest thou how great is the wisdom of the Baptist? how, when He Himself is preaching, He saith everything to alarm, and fill them with anxiety; but when He is sending men to Him, whatever was mild and apt to recover them: not bringing forward the axe, nor the tree that is cut down and burnt, and cast into the fire, nor the wrath to come, but remission of sins, and removing of punishment, and righteousness, and sanctification, and redemption, and adoption, and brotherhood, and a partaking of the inheritance, and an abundant supply of the Holy Ghost. For all these things he obscurely denoted, when he said, "He shall baptize you with the Holy Ghost;" at once, by the very figure of speech, declaring the abundance of the grace (for he said not, "He will give you the Holy Ghost," but "He will baptize you with the Holy Ghost"); and by the specification of fire on the other hand indicating the vehement and uncontrollable quality of His grace.

Imagine only what sort of men it was meet for the hearers to become, when they considered that they were at once to be like the prophets, and like those great ones. For it was on this account, you see, that he made mention at all of fire; that he might lead them to reflect on the memory of those men. Because, of all the visions that appeared unto them, I had almost said, the more part appeared in fire; thus God discoursed with Moses in the bush, thus with all the people in the mount Sinai, thus with Ezekiel on the cherubim.[2]

And mark again how he rouses the hearer, by putting that first which was to take place after all. For the Lamb was to be slain, and sin to be blotted out, and the enmity to be destroyed, and the burial to take place, and the resurrection, and then the Spirit to come. But none of these things doth he mention as yet, but that first which was last, and for the sake of which all the former were done, and which was fittest to proclaim His dignity; so that when the hearer should be told that he was to receive so great a Spirit, he might search with himself, how and in what manner this shall be, while sin so prevails; that finding him full of thought and prepared for that lesson, he might thereupon introduce what he had to say touching the Passion, no man being any more offended, under the expectation of such a gift.

Wherefore he again cried out, saying, "Behold the Lamb of God, which beareth the sin of the world."[3] He did not say, "which remitteth," but, that which implies a more guardian care, "which beareth it." For it is not all one, simply to remit, and to take it upon Himself.[4] For the one was to be done without peril, the other with death.

And again, he said, "He is Son of God."[5] But not even this declared His rank openly to the hearers (for they did not so much as know yet how to conceive of Him as a true Son): but by so great a gift of the Spirit that also was established. Therefore the Father also in sending John gave him, *as you know*, this as a first token of the dignity of Him that was come, saying, "Upon whom thou shalt see the Spirit descending and remaining, the same is He which baptizeth with the Holy Ghost."[6] Wherefore himself too

---

[2] Ezek. i. 27.
[3] John i. 29 ; Engl. Vers. *in marg.* [So R. V. marg. The Greek phrase is ὁ αἴρων, " he that taketh up."--R.]
[4] [αὐτὸν ἀναλαβεῖν is the better supported reading, but various conjectural emendations occur. " Himself to assume *it*," is the most literal rendering.—R.]
[5] John i. 34.
[6] John i. 33, 34. [R. V., more correctly, " I have seen, and have borne witness," etc. The Greek perfects are to be taken in their grammatical sense, as the comment of Chrysostom implies. —R.]

[1] [δύναμιν.]

saith, "I saw and bare record that this is the Son of God;" as though the one were to all time the clear evidence of the other.

7. Then, as having uttered the gentler part of his message, and soothed and relaxed the hearer, he again binds him up, that he may not become remiss. For such was the nature of the Jewish nation; by all encouraging things they were easily puffed up, and corrupted. Wherefore he again adduces his terrors, saying,

"Whose fan is in His hand." [1]

Thus, as before he had spoken of the punishment, so here he points out the Judge likewise, and introduces the eternal vengeance. For "He will burn the chaff," saith he, "with unquenchable fire." Thou seest that He is Lord of all things, and that He is Himself the Husbandman; albeit in another place He calls His Father the same. For "My Father," saith He, "is the Husbandman." [2] Thus, inasmuch as He had spoken of an axe, lest thou shouldest suppose that the thing needed labor, and the separation was hard to make; by another comparison he suggest the easiness of it, implying that all the world is His; since He could not punish those who were not His own. For the present, it is true, all are mingled together (for though the wheat appears gleaming through, yet it lies with the chaff, as on a threshing floor, not as in a garner), but then, great will be the separation.

Where now are they by whom hell-fire [3] is disbelieved? Since surely here are two points laid down, one, that He will baptize with the Holy Ghost, the other, that He will burn up the disobedient. If then that is credible, so is this too, assuredly. Yea, this is why the two predictions are put by him in immediate connection, that by that which hath taken place already, he might accredit the other, as yet unaccomplished. For Christ too Himself in many places doth so, often of the same things, and often of opposites, setting down two prophecies; the one of which He performs here, the other He promises in the future; that such as are too contentious may, from the one which has already come to pass, believe the other also, which is not yet accomplished. For instance, to them that strip themselves of all that they have for His sake [4] He promised to give an hundred fold in the present world, and life eternal in that which is to come; by the things already given making the future also credible. Which, as we see, John likewise hath done in this place; laying down two things, that He shall both

baptize with the Holy Ghost, and burn up with unquenchable fire. Now then, if He had not baptized with the Spirit the apostles, and all every day who are willing, thou mightest have doubts concerning those other things too; but if that which seems to be greater and more difficult, and which transcends all reason, hath been done, and is done every day; how deniest thou that to be true, which is easy, and comes to pass according to reason? Thus having said, "He shall baptize with the Holy Ghost and with fire," and having thence promised great blessings; lest thou, released wholly from the former things, grow supine, he hath added the fan, and the judgment thereby declared. Thus, "think not at all," saith he, "that your baptism suffices, if ye become ordinary persons [5] hereafter:" for we need both virtue, and plenty of that known self-restraint. [6] Therefore as by the axe he urges them unto grace, and unto the font, so after grace he terrifies them by the fan, and the unquenchable fire. And of the one sort, those yet unbaptized, he makes no distinction, but saith in general, "Every tree that bringeth not forth good fruit is hewn down," [7] punishing all the unbelievers. Whereas after baptism He works out a kind of division, because many of them that believed would exhibit a life unworthy of their faith.

Let no man then become chaff, let no one be tossed to and fro, nor lie exposed to wicked desires, blown about by them easily every way. For if thou continue wheat, though temptation be brought on thee, thou wilt suffer nothing dreadful; nay, for in the threshing floor, the wheels of the car, that are like saws, [8] do not cut in pieces the wheat; but if thou fall away into the weakness of chaff, thou wilt both here suffer incurable ills, being smitten of all men, and there thou wilt undergo the eternal punishment. For all such persons both before that furnace become food for the irrational passions here, as chaff is for the brute animals: and there again they are material and food for the flame.

Now to have said directly, that He will judge men's doings, would not so effectually procure acceptance for His doctrine: but to blend with it the parable, and so to establish it all, was apter to persuade the hearer, and attract him by a more ample encouragement. Wherefore also Christ Himself [9] for the most part so discourses with them; threshing floor,

---

[1] Matt. iii. 12.   [2] John xv. 1.
[3] [γεέννη.]   [4] Mark x. 30; Luke xviii. 30.

[5] [φαῦλοι, "worthless."—R.]   [6] φιλοσοφία.
[7] Matt. iii. 10.   [8] πριστηροειδής, see Is. xl. 15.
[9] [The better supported text seems to be αὐτός, without ὁ χριστός; the latter is an explanatory gloss.—R.]

and harvest, and vineyard, and wine-press, and field, and net, and fishing, and all things familiar, and among which they were busied, He makes ingredients in His discourses. This kind of thing then the Baptist likewise did here, and offered an exceeding great demonstration of his words, the giving of the Spirit. For "He who hath so great power, as both to forgive sins, and to give the Spirit, much more will these things also be within His power:" so he speaks.

Seest thou how now in due order the mystery[1] came to be laid as a foundation, before the resurrection and judgment?[2]

"And wherefore," it may be said, "did he not mention the signs and wonders which were straightway to be done by Him?" Because this was greater than all, and for its sake all those were done. Thus, in his mention of the chief thing, he comprehended all; death dissolved, sins abolished, the curse blotted out, those long wars done away; our entrance into paradise,[3] our ascent into heaven, our citizenship with the angels, our partaking of the good things to come: for in truth this is the earnest of them all. So that in mentioning this, he hath mentioned also the resurrection of our bodies, and the manifestation of His miracles here, and our partaking of His kingdom, and the good things, which "eye hath not seen, nor ear heard, neither have entered into the heart of man."[4] For all these things He bestowed on us by that gift. It was therefore superfluous to speak of the signs that were immediately to ensue, and which sight can judge of; but those were meet to be discoursed on, whereof they doubted; as for instance, that He is the Son of God; that He exceeds John beyond comparison; that He "beareth[5] the sin of the world;" that He will require an account of all that we do; that our interests are not limited to the present, but elsewhere every one will undergo the due penalty. For these things were not as yet proveable by sight.

8. Therefore, knowing these things, let us use great diligence, while we are in the threshing floor; for it is possible while we are here, to change even out of chaff into wheat, even as on the other hand many from wheat have become chaff. Let us not then be supine, nor be carried about with every wind; neither let us separate ourselves from our brethren, though they seem to be small and mean; forasmuch as the wheat also compared

with the chaff is less in measure, but better in nature. Look not therefore to the forms of outward pomp, for they are prepared for the fire, but to this godly humility, so firm and indissoluble, and which cannot be cut, neither is burnt by the fire. It being for their sake that He bears long with the very chaff, that by their intercourse with them they may become better. Therefore judgment is not yet, that we may be all crowned together, that from wickedness many may be converted unto virtue.

Let us tremble then at hearing this parable. For indeed that fire is unquenchable. "And how," it may be said, "is it unquenchable?" Seest thou not this sun ever burning, and never quenched? didst thou not behold the bush burning, and not consumed? If then thou also desirest to escape the flame, lay up alms beforehand, and so thou wilt not even taste of that fire. For if, while here, thou wilt believe what is told thee, thou shalt not so much as see this furnace, after thy departure into that region; but if thou disbelieve it now, thou shalt know it there full well by experience, when no sort of escape is possible. Since in truth no entreaty shall avert the punishment from them who have not shown forth an upright life. For believing surely is not enough, since even the devils tremble at God, but for all that they will be punished.

9. Wherefore our care of our conduct hath need to be great. Why, this is the very reason of our continually assembling you here; not simply that ye should enter in, but that ye should also reap some fruit from your continuance here. But if ye come indeed constantly, but go away again reaping no fruit from thence, ye will have no advantage from your entering in and attendance in this place.

For if we, when sending children to teachers, should we see them reaping no benefit thereby, begin to be severe in blaming the teachers, and remove them often to others; what excuse shall we have for not bestowing upon virtue even so much diligence as upon these earthly things, but forever bringing our tablets home empty? And yet our teachers here are more in number and greater. For no less than prophets and apostles and patriarchs, and all righteous men, are by us set over you as teachers in every Church. And not even so is there any profit, but if you have joined in chanting two or three Psalms, and making the accustomed prayers at random and anyhow, are so dismissed, ye think this enough for your salvation. Have ye not heard the prophet, saying (or rather God by the prophet), "This people honoreth me

[1] "The Mystery:" i. e., Christ's Baptism by Fire, His dwelling in our hearts by His Spirit. Comp. Col. i. 26, 27; Eph. i. 9, 10; iii. 9.   [2] Heb. vi. 1, 2.
[3] ["The loosing of death, the abolition of sins," etc., "the entrance into Paradise," etc. The construction is the same throughout the list.—R.]
[4] 1 Cor. ii. 9.   [5] [See note 3 on sec. 6, p. 71.—R.]

with their lips, but their heart is far from me?"[1]

Therefore, lest this be our case too, wipe thou out the letters, or rather the impressions, which the devil hath engraven in thy soul; and bring me a heart set free from worldly tumults, that without fear I may write on it what I will. Since now at least there is nothing else to discern, except his letters;—rapines, covetings, envy, jealousy. Wherefore of course, when I receive your tablets, I am not able so much as to read them. For I find not the letters, which we every Lord's day inscribe on you, and so let you go; but others, instead of these, unintelligible and misshapen. Then, when we have blotted them out, and have written those which are of the Spirit, ye departing, and giving up your hearts to the works of the devil, give Him again power to substitute his own characters in you. What then will be the end of all this, even without any words of mine, each man's own conscience knoweth. For I indeed will not cease to do my part, and to write in you the right letters. But if ye mar our diligence, for our part our reward is unaltered, but your danger is not small.

Now, though I would fain say nothing to disgust you, yet I beseech again and entreat you,[2] imitate at least the little children's diligence in these matters. For so they first learn the form of the letters, after that they practise themselves in distinguishing them put out of shape, and then at last in their reading they proceed orderly by means of them. Just so let us also do; let us divide virtue, and learn first not to swear, nor to forswear ourselves, nor to speak evil; then proceeding to another row,[3] not to envy, not to lust, not to be gluttonous, not to be drunken, not fierce, not slothful, so that from these we may pass on again to the things of the Spirit, and practise continence, and neglect of the belly, temperance, righteousness, to be above glory, and gentle and contrite in mind; and let us join these one with another, and write them upon our soul.

10. And all these let us practise at home. with our own friends, with our wife, with our children. And, for the present, let us begin with the things that come first, and are easier; as for instance, with not swearing; and let us practise this one letter continually at home. For, in truth, there are many at home to hinder this our practice; sometimes a man's servant provoking him, sometimes

his wife annoying and angering him, sometimes an indocile and disorderly child urges him on to threatening and swearing. If now at home, when thus continually galled, thou shouldest attain not to be tempted into swearing, thou wilt in the market-place also have power with ease to abide unconquered.

Yea, and in like sort, thou will attain to keep thyself from insulting any, by not insulting thy wife, nor thy servants, nor any one else among those in thy house. For a man's wife too not seldom, praising this or that person, or bemoaning herself, stirs him up to speak evil of that other. But do not thou let thyself be constrained to speak evil of him that is praised, but bear it all nobly. And if thou shouldest perceive thy servants praising other masters, be not perturbed, but stand nobly. Let thy home be a sort of lists, a place of exercise for virtue, that having trained thyself well there, thou mayest with entire skill encounter all abroad.

Do this with respect to vainglory also. For if thou train thyself not to be vainglorious in company of thy wife and thy servants, thou wilt not ever afterwards be easily caught by this passion with regard to any one else. For though this malady be in every case grievous and tyrannical, yet is it so especially when a woman is present. If we therefore in that instance put down its power, we shall easily master it in the other cases also.

And with respect to the other passions too, let us do this self-same thing, exercising ourselves against them at home, and anointing ourselves every day.

And that our exercise may be easier, let us further enact a penalty for ourselves, upon our transgressing any of our purposes. And let the very penalty again be such as brings with it not loss, but reward,—such as procures some very great gain. And this is so, if we sentence ourselves to intenser fastings, and to sleeping often on the bare ground, and to other like austerity. For in this way will much profit come unto us from every quarter; we shall both live the sweet life of virtue here, and we shall attain unto the good things to come. and be perpetually friends of God.

But in order that the same may not happen again,—that ye may not, having here admired what is said, go your way, and cast aside at random, wherever it may chance, the tablet of your mind, and so allow the devil to blot out these things;—let each one, on returning home, call his own wife, and tell her these things, and take her to help him; and from this day let him enter into that noble school of exercise, using for oil the supply of the

---

[1] Is. xxix. 13; comp. Mark vii. 6.
[2] [The first clause stands independently in the Greek text, forming the conclusion of the preceding paragraph. The new exhortation begins "But I beseech again," etc.—R.]
[3] στίχον.

Spirit. And though thou fall once, twice, many times in thy training, despair not, but stand again, and wrestle; and do not give up until thou hast bound on thee the glorious crown of triumph over the devil, and hast for the time to come stored up the riches of virtue in an inviolable treasure-house.

For if thou shouldest establish thyself in the habits of this noble self-restraint, then, not even when remiss, wilt thou be able to transgress any of the commandments, habit imitating the solidity of nature. Yea, as to sleep is easy, and to eat, and to drink, and to breathe, so also will the deeds of virtue be easy to us, and we shall reap to ourselves that pure pleasure, resting in a harbor without a wave, and enjoying continual calm, and with a great freight bringing our vessel into haven, in that City, on that day; and we shall attain unto the undecaying crowns, unto which may we all attain, by the grace and love towards man of our Lord Jesus Christ, to whom be all glory and might, now and always, and world without end. Amen.

HOMILY XII.

MATT. III. 13.

" Then cometh Jesus from Galilee to Jordan," etc.

WITH the servants the Lord, with the criminals the Judge, cometh to be baptized. But be not thou troubled; for in these humiliations His exaltation doth most shine forth. For He who vouchsafed to be borne so long in a Virgin's womb, and to come forth thence with our nature, and to be smitten with rods, and crucified, and to suffer all the rest which He suffered;—why marvellest thou if He vouchsafed also to be baptized, and to come with the rest to His servant. For the amazement lay in that one thing, that being God, He would be made Man; but the rest after this all follows in course of reason.

For this cause, let me add, John also by way of anticipation said all that he had said before, that he "was not worthy to unloose the latchet of His shoe;" and all the rest, as for instance, that He is Judge, and rewards every man according to his desert, and that He will bestow His Spirit abundantly on all; in order that when thou shouldest see Him coming to the baptism, thou mightest not suspect anything mean. Therefore he forbids Him, even when He was come, saying,

" I have need to be baptized of Thee, and comest Thou to me." [1] For, because the baptism was "of repentance," and led men to accuse themselves for their offenses, lest any one should suppose that He too "cometh to Jordan" in this sort of mind, John sets it right beforehand, by calling Him both Lamb, and Redeemer from all the sin that is in the world. Since He that was able to take away the sins of the whole race of men, much more was He Himself without sin. For this cause then he said not, "Behold, He that is without sin," but what was much more, He "that beareth the sin of the world," in order that together with this truth thou mightest receive that other with all assurance, and having received it mightest perceive, that in the conduct of some further economy He cometh to the baptism. Wherefore also he said to Him when He came, " I have need to be baptized of Thee, and comest Thou to me ? "

And he said not, "And art Thou baptized of me ? " nay, for this he feared to say: but what ? "And comest Thou to me ? " What then doth Christ ? What He did afterwards with respect to Peter, this did He then also. For so he too would have forbidden Him to wash his feet, but when he had heard, " What I do thou knowest not now, but thou shalt know hereafter, "and " thou hast no part with me," [2] he speedily withdrew from his determination, and went over to the contrary. And this man again in like manner, when he had heard, " Suffer it to be so now, for thus it becometh us to fulfill all righteousness," [3] straightway obeyed. For they were not unduly contentious, but they manifested

---

[1] Matt. iii. 14.

[2] John xiii. 7, 8.
[3] Matt. iii. 15. [R. V., " Suffer it (or me) now, for thus it becometh," etc.—R.]

both love and obedience, and made it their study to be ruled by their Lord in all things.

And mark how He urges him on that very ground which chiefly caused him to look doubtfully on what was taking place; in that He did not say, "thus it is just," but "thus it becometh." For, inasmuch as the point unworthy of Him was in his mind chiefly this, His being baptized by His servant, He stated this rather than anything else, which is directly opposed to that impression: as though He had said, " Is it not as unbecoming that thou avoidest and forbiddest this? nay, for this self-same cause I bid thee suffer it, that it is becoming, and that in the highest degree."

And He did not merely say, " suffer," but He added, " now." " For it will not be so forever," saith He, " but thou shalt see me such as thou desirest; for the present, however, endure this." Next He shows also how this "becometh" Him. How then doth it so? " In that we fulfill the whole law;" and to express this He said, " all righteousness." For righteousness is the fulfilling of the commandments. " Since then we have performed all the rest of the commandments," saith He, " and this alone remains, it also must be added: because I am come to do away the curse that is appointed for the transgression of the law. I must therefore first fulfill it all, and having delivered you from its condemnation, in this way bring it to an end. It becometh me therefore to fulfill the whole law, by the same rule that it becometh me to do away the curse that is written against you in the law: this being the very purpose of my assuming flesh, and coming hither."

2. " Then he suffereth Him. And Jesus, when He was baptized, went up straightway out of the water; and, lo, the heavens were opened unto Him, and he saw the Spirit of God descending like a dove, and lighting upon Him." [1]

For inasmuch as many supposed that John was greater than He, because John had been brought up all his time in the wilderness, and was son of a chief priest, and was clothed with such raiment, and was calling all men unto his baptism, and had been born of a barren mother; while Jesus, first of all, was of a damsel of ordinary rank (for the virgin birth was not yet manifest to all); and besides, He had been brought up in an house, and held converse with all men, and wore this common raiment; they suspected Him to be less than John, knowing as yet nothing of

those secret things;—and it fell out moreover that He was baptized of John, which thing added support to this surmise, even if none of those mentioned before had existed; for it would come into their mind that this man was one of the many (for were He not one of the many, He would not have come with the many to the baptism), but that John was greater than He and far more admirable:—in order therefore that this opinion might not prevail with the multitude, the very heavens are opened, when He is baptized, and the Spirit comes down, and a voice with the Spirit, proclaiming the dignity of the Only Begotten. For since the voice that said, " This is my beloved Son," would seem to the multitude rather to belong to John, for It added not, " This that is baptized," but simply *This*, and every hearer would conceive it to be said concerning the baptizer, rather than the baptized, partly on account of the Baptist's own dignity, partly for all that hath been mentioned; the Spirit came in form of a dove, drawing the voice towards Jesus, and making it evident to all, that *This* was not spoken of John that baptized, but of Jesus who was baptized.

And how was it, one may say, that they did not believe, when these things came to pass? Because in the days of Moses also many wonderful works were done, albeit not such as these; and after all those, the voices, and the trumpets, and the lightnings, they both forged a calf, and " were joined unto Baal-peor." And those very persons too, who were present at the time, and saw Lazarus arise, so far from believing in Him, who had wrought these things, repeatedly attempted even to slay Him. Now if seeing before their eyes one rise from the dead, they were so wicked, why marvel at their not receiving a voice wafted from above? Since when a soul is uncandid and perverse, and possessed by the disease of envy, it yields to none of these things; even as when it is candid it receives all with faith, and hath no great need of these.

Speak not therefore thus, " They believed not," but rather inquire, " Did not all things take place which ought to have made them believe?" For by the prophet also God frames this kind of defense of His own ways in general. That is, the Jews being on the point of ruin, and of being given over to extreme punishment; lest any from their wickedness should calumniate His providence, He saith, " What ought I to have done to this vineyard, that I have not done?" [2] Just so

---

[1] Matt. iii. 15, 16. [R. V., " from the water," and " coming " for " lighting."—R.]

[2] Is. v. 4. [Chrysostom varies from the LXX., introducing με έδει, to strengthen his argument.—R.]

here likewise do thou reflect; "what ought to have been done, and was not done?" And indeed whensoever arguments arise on God's Providence, do thou make use of this kind of defense, against those who from the wickedness of the many try to raise a prejudice against it. See, for instance, what astonishing things are done, preludes of those which were to come; for it is no more paradise, but Heaven that is opened.

But let our argument with the Jews stand over unto some other time; for the present, God working with us, we would direct our discourse to what is immediately before us.

3. "And Jesus, when He was baptized, went up straightway out of the water; and lo! the heavens were opened unto Him."[1]

Wherefore were the heavens opened? To inform thee that at thy baptism also this is done, God calling thee to thy country on high, and persuading thee to have nothing to do with earth. And if thou see not, yet never doubt it. For so evermore at the beginnings of all wonderful and spiritual transactions, sensible visions appear, and such-like signs, for the sake of them that are somewhat dull in disposition, and who have need of outward sight, and who cannot at all conceive an incorporeal nature, but are excited only by the things that are seen: that so, though afterward no such thing occur, what hath been declared by them once for all at the first may be received by thy faith.

For in the case of the apostles too, there was a "sound of a mighty wind,"[2] and visions of fiery tongues appeared, but not for the apostles' sake, but because of the Jews who were then present. Nevertheless, even though no sensible signs take place, we receive the things that have been once manifested by them. Since the dove itself at that time therefore appeared, that as in place of a finger (so to say) it might point out to them that were present, and to John, the Son of God. Not however merely on this account, but to teach thee also, that upon thee no less at thy baptism the Spirit comes. But since then we have no need of sensible vision, faith sufficing instead of all. For signs are "not for them that believe, but for them that believe not."[3]

But why in the fashion of a dove? Gentle is that creature, and pure. Forasmuch then as the Spirit too is "a Spirit of meekness,"[4] He therefore appears in this sort. And besides, He is reminding us of an ancient history. For so, when once a common shipwreck had overtaken the whole world, and our race was in danger of perishing, this creature appeared, and indicated the deliverance from the tempest, and bearing an olive branch,[5] published the good tidings of the common calm of the whole world; all which was a type of the things to come. For in fact the condition of men was then much worse, and they deserved a much sorer punishment. To prevent thy despairing, therefore, He reminds thee of that history. Because then also, when things were desperate, there was a sort of deliverance and reformation; but then by punishment, now, on the contrary, by grace and an unspeakable gift.[6] Therefore the dove also appears, not bearing an olive branch, but pointing out to us our Deliverer from all evils, and suggesting the gracious hopes. For not from out of an ark doth she lead one man only, but the whole world she leads up into heaven at her appearing, and instead of a branch of peace from an olive, she conveys the adoption to all the world's offspring in common.

Reflect now on the greatness of the gift, and do not account His dignity the less for His appearing in such a likeness. For I actually hear some saying,[7] that "such as is the difference between a man and a dove, so great is that between Christ and the Spirit: since the one appeared in our nature, the other in the likeness of a dove." What must we say then to these things? That the Son of God did indeed take upon Him the nature of man, but the Spirit took not on Him the nature of a dove. Therefore the evangelist also said not, "in the nature of a dove," but "in the form of a dove." Accordingly, never after did He so much as appear in this fashion, but at that moment only. And if on this account thou affirmest His dignity to be less, the cherubim too will be made out by this reasoning much His superior, even as much so as an eagle is to a dove: because they too were figured into that visible shape. And the angels too superior again, for they no less have many times appeared in the fashion of men. But these things are not so, indeed they are not. For the truth of an economy is one thing, and the condescension of a temporary vision another.

Do not now, I pray thee, become unthankful towards thy Benefactor, nor with the very contraries[8] requite Him that hath bestowed

---

[1] Matt. iii. 16.   [2] Acts ii. 2.   [3] 1 Cor. xiv. 22.
[4] Gal. vi. 1. [The immediate reference in Gal. vi. 1 is not to the Holy Spirit, yet there is a suggestion of the influence of the Holy Spirit.—R.]
[5] Gen. viii.   [6] 2 Cor. ix. 15.
[7] i. e., the Macedonians, who were censured at Constantinople, A. D. 381.
[8] "The contraries:" for whereas the Spirit came to exalt, and make us partakers of the Divine Nature, the heretics would degrade Him to something like our own.

on thee the fountain of blessedness. For where adoption is vouchsafed, there is also the removing of evils, and the giving of all good things.

4. On this very account the Jewish baptism ceases, and ours takes its beginning. And what was done with regard to the Passover, the same ensues in the baptism also. For as in that case too, He acting with a view to both, brought the one to an end, but to the other He gave a beginning: so here, having fulfilled the Jewish baptism, He at the same time opens also the doors of that of the Church; as on one table then, so in one river now, He had both sketched out the shadow, and now adds the truth. For this baptism alone hath the grace of the Spirit, but that of John was destitute of this gift. For this very cause in the case of the others that were baptized no such thing came to pass, but only in the instance of Him who was to hand on [1] this; in order that, besides what we have said, thou mightest learn this also, that not the purity of the baptizer, but the power of the baptized, had this effect. Not until then, assuredly, were either the heavens opened, nor did the Spirit make His approach.[2] Because henceforth He leads us away from the old to the new polity, both opening to us the gates on high, and sending down His Spirit from thence to call us to our country there; and not merely to call us, but also with the greatest mark of dignity. For He hath not made us angels and archangels, but He hath caused us to become "sons of God," and "beloved," and so He draws us on towards that portion of ours.

Having then all this in thy mind, do thou show forth a life worthy of the love of Him who calls thee, and of thy citizenship in that world, and of the honor that is given thee. Crucified as thou art to the world, and having crucified it to thyself, show thyself with all strictness a citizen of the city of the heavens. And do not, because thy body is not translated unto heaven, suppose that thou hast anything to do with the earth; for thou hast thy Head abiding above. Yea with this very purpose the Lord, having first come here and having brought His angels, did then, taking thee with Him, depart thither; that even before thy going up to that place, thou mightest understand that it is possible for thee to inhabit earth as it were heaven.

Let us then keep watch over that noble birth, which we received from the beginning;

and let us every day seek more and more the palaces there, and account all that is here to be a shadow and a dream. For so, had any king among those on earth, finding thee poor and a beggar, made thee suddenly his son, never wouldest thou have thought upon thy cottage, and thy cottage's mean appointments. Yet surely in that case the difference is not much. Do not then either in this case take account of any of the former things, for thou art called unto much greater. For both He who calls is the Lord of the angels, and the good things that are given surpass all both word and thought. Since not from earth to earth doth He remove thee, as the king doth, but from earth to heaven, and from a mortal nature to an immortal, and to glory unspeakable, then only possible to be properly manifested, when we shall actually enjoy it.

Now then, having to partake of such blessings, do I see thee minding money, and clinging to the pomp which is here? And dost thou not esteem all that is seen to be more vile than beggar's rags? And how wilt thou appear worthy of this honor? And what excuse wilt thou have to plead? or rather, what punishment wilt thou not have to suffer, who after so great a gift art running to thy former vomit? For no longer art thou punished merely as a man, but as a son of God that hath sinned; and the greatness of thy honor becomes a mean of bringing a sorer punishment on thee. Since we too punish not equally slaves that do wrong, and sons committing the same offense; and most of all when they have received some great kindness from us.

For if he who had paradise for his portion, for one disobedience underwent such dreadful things after his honor; we, who have received Heaven, and are become joint heirs with the Only Begotten, what excuse shall we have, for running to the serpent after the dove? For it will be no longer, "Dust thou art, and unto dust shalt thou return," [3] and thou "tillest the ground," [4] and those former words, that will be said to us; [5] but what is far more grievous than these, the "outer darkness," [6] the bonds that may not be burst, the venomous worm, the "gnashing of teeth;" and this with great reason. For he that is not made better even by so great a benefit, would justly suffer the most extreme, and a yet more grievous punishment.

Elias once opened and shut Heaven, but

[1] [παραδιδόναι; "hand down" would express the sense more clearly.—R.]

[2] [The sentence in the Greek is not negative but affirmative: "Then assuredly" both these events occurred.—R.]

[3] Gen. iii. 19.

[4] Gen. iv. 12. [The LXX. has γῆ in both passages. The verbal suggestion of the original may be retained by rendering: "Earth thou art, and unto earth thou shalt return," and thou "tillest the earth."—R.]

[5] [Literally, "that we shall hear."—R.]   [6] Matt. xxv. 30.

that was to bring down rain, and restrain it; whereas to thee the heaven is not so opened, but in order for thee to ascend thither; and what is yet more, not to ascend only, but to lead up others also, if thou wilt; such great confidence and power hath He bestowed on thee in all that is His.

5. Forasmuch then as our house is there, there let us store up all, and leave nothing here, lest we lose it. For here, though thou put a lock on it, and doors, and bars, and set thousands of servants to watch it; though thou get the better of all the crafty ones, though thou escape the eyes of the envious, the worms, the wasting that comes of time;— which is impossible;—death at any rate thou wilt never escape, but wilt be deprived of all those things in one moment of time; and not deprived of them only, but wilt have to transfer them into the hands often of thy very enemies. Whereas if thou wouldest transfer them into that house, thou wilt be far above all. For there is no need to apply either key, or doors, or bars; such is the virtue[1] of that city, so inviolable is this place, and by nature inaccessible to corruption and all wickedness.

How then is it not of the utmost folly, where destruction and waste is the lot of all that is stored, there to heap up all, but where things abide untouched and increase, there not to lay up even the least portion; and this, when we are to live there forever? For this cause the very heathens[2] disbelieve the things that we say, since our doings, not our sayings, are the demonstration which they are willing to receive from us; and when they see us building ourselves fine houses, and laying out gardens and baths, and buying fields, they are not willing to believe that we are preparing for another sort of residence away from our city.

" For if this were so," say they, " they would turn to money all they have here, and lay them up beforehand there; " and this they divine from the things that are done in this world. For so we see those who are very rich getting themselves houses and fields and all the rest, chiefly in those cities in which

they are to stay. But we do the contrary; and with all earnest zeal we get possession of the earth, which we are soon after to leave; giving up not money only, but even our very blood for a few acres and tenements: while for the purchase of Heaven we do not endure to give even what is beyond our wants, and this though we are to purchase it at a small price, and to possess it forever, provided we had once purchased it.

Therefore I say we shall suffer the utmost punishment, departing thither naked and poor; or rather it will not be for our own poverty that we shall undergo these irremediable calamities, but also for our making others to be such as ourselves. For when heathens see them that have partaken of so great mysteries earnest about these matters, much more will they cling themselves to the things present. Wherefore even from this we are heaping much fire upon our head. For when we, who ought to teach them to despise all things that appear, do ourselves most of all urge them to the lust of these things; when shall it be possible for us to be saved, having to give account for the perdition of others? Hearest thou not Christ say, that He left us to be for salt and for lights in this world, in order that we may both brace up[3] those that are melting in luxury, and enlighten them that are darkened by the care of wealth? When therefore we even cast them into more thorough darkness, and make them more dissolute, what hope shall we have of salvation? There is none at all; but wailing and gnashing our teeth, and bound hand and foot, we shall depart into the fire of hell, after being full well worn down by the cares of riches.

Considering then all these things, let us loose the bands of such deceit, that we may not at all fall into those things which deliver us over to the unquenchable fire. For he that is a slave to money, the chains both here and there will have him continually liable to them; but he that is rid of this desire will attain to freedom from both. Unto which that we also may attain, let us break in pieces the grievous yoke of avarice, and make ourselves wings toward Heaven; by the grace and love towards man of our Lord Jesus Christ, to whom be glory and might forever and ever. Amen.

---

[1] [δύναμις.]

[2] ["Ελληνες, " Greeks." But the ecclesiastical use is correctly given in the translation. In the New Testament, the term was equivalent to " Gentiles," as opposed to Jews ; but was afterwards applied to heathen as opposed to Christians. See SOPHOCLES, *Greek Lexicon* of the Roman and Byzantine periods, *sub voce.* —R.]

[3] [ἐπισφίγγωμεν, The verb means " to bind tight," and is variously applied.—R.]

HOMILY XIII.

MATT. IV. 1.

" Then was Jesus led up of the Spirit into the wilderness, to be tempted of the devil."

THEN. When? After the descent of the Spirit, after the voice that was borne from above, and said, " This is My Beloved Son, in whom I am well pleased." And what was marvellous, it was of the Holy Spirit; for this, he here saith, led Him up. For since with a view to our instruction He both did and underwent all things; He endures also to be led up thither, and to wrestle against the devil: in order that each of those who are baptized, if after his baptism he have to endure greater temptations, may not be troubled as if the result were unexpected, but may continue to endure all nobly, as though it were happening in the natural course of things.

Yea, for therefore thou didst take up arms, not to be idle, but to fight. For this cause neither doth God hinder the temptations as they come on, first to teach thee that thou art become much stronger; next, that thou mayest continue modest, neither be exalted even by the greatness of thy gifts, the temptations having power to repress thee; moreover, in order that that wicked demon, who is for a while doubtful about thy desertion of him, by the touchstone of temptations may be well assured that thou hast utterly forsaken and fallen from him; fourthly, that thou mayest in this way be made stronger, and better tempered than any steel; fifthly, that thou mayest obtain a clear demonstration of the treasures entrusted to thee.

For the devil would not have assailed thee, unless he had seen thee brought to greater honor. Hence, for example, from the beginning, he attacked Adam, because he saw him in the enjoyment of great dignity. For this reason he arrayed himself against Job, because he saw him crowned and proclaimed by the God of all.

How then saith He, " Pray that ye enter not into temptation." [1] For this cause he doth not show thee Jesus simply going up, but " led up " according to the principle of the Economy; [2] signifying obscurely by this, that we ought not of ourselves to leap upon it, but being dragged thereto, to stand manfully.

And see whither the Spirit led Him up, when He had taken Him; not into a city and forum, but into a wilderness. That is, He being minded to attract the devil, gives him a handle not only by His hunger, but also by the place. For then most especially doth the devil assail, when he sees men left alone, and by themselves. Thus did he also set upon the woman in the beginning, having caught her alone, and found her apart from her husband. Just as when he sees us with others and banded together, he is not equally confident, and makes no attack. Wherefore we have the greatest need on this very account to be flocking together continually, that we may not be open to the devil's attacks.

2. Having then found Him in the wilderness, and in a pathless wilderness (for that the wilderness was such, Mark hath declared, saying, that He " was with the wild beasts" [3]), behold with how much craft he draws near, and wickedness; and for what sort of opportunity he watches. For not in his fast, but in his hunger he approaches Him; to instruct thee how great a good fasting is, and how it is a most powerful shield against the devil, and that after the font, [4] men should give themselves up, not to luxury and drunkenness, and a full table, but to fasting. For, for this cause even He fasted, not as needing it Himself, but to instruct us. Thus, since our sins before the font [4] were brought in by serving the belly: much as if any one who had made a sick man whole were to forbid his doing those things, from which the distemper arose; so we see here likewise that He Himself after the font brought in fasting. For indeed both Adam by the incontinence of the belly was cast out of paradise; and the flood in Noah's time, this produced; and this brought down the thunders on Sodom. For although there was also a charge of whoredom, nevertheless from this grew the root of each of those punishments; which Ezekiel also signified when he said, " But this was the iniquity of Sodom, that she waxed wanton in pride and in fullness of bread, and in abundance of luxury." [5] Thus the Jews also per-

---

[1] Matt. xxvi. 41. [2] κατὰ τὸν λόγον τῆς οἰκονομίας.

[3] Mark i. 13.
[4] [λουόντρ, " laver ;" here by metonymy for the rite of baptism. — R.]
[5] Ezek. xvi. 49.

petrated the greatest wickedness, being driven upon transgression by their drunkenness and delicacy.[1]

On this account then even He too fasts forty days, pointing out to us the medicines of our salvation; yet proceeds no further, lest on the other hand, through the exceeding greatness of the miracle the truth of His Economy[2] should be discredited. For as it is, this cannot be, seeing that both Moses and Elias, anticipating Him, could advance to so great a length of time, strengthened by the power of God. And if He had proceeded farther, from this among other things His assumption of our flesh would have seemed incredible to many.

Having then fasted forty days and as many nights,

" He was afterwards an hungered;[3] " affording him a point to lay hold of and approach, that by actual conflict He might show how to prevail and be victorious. Just so do wrestlers also: when teaching their pupils how to prevail and overcome, they voluntarily in the lists engage with others, to afford these in the persons of their antagonists the means of seeing and learning the mode of conquest. Which same thing then also took place. For it being His will to draw him on so far, He both made His hunger known to him, and awaited his approach, and as He waited for him, so He dashed him to earth, once, twice, and three times, with such ease as became Him.

3. But that we may not, by hurrying over these victories, mar your profit, let us begin from the first assault, and examine each with exact care.

Thus, after He was an hungered, it is said, " The tempter came, and said unto Him, If Thou be Son of God, command that these stones be made bread."[4]

For, because he had heard a voice borne from above, and saying, " This is My beloved Son;" and had heard also John bearing so large witness concerning Him, and after that saw Him an hungered; he was thenceforth in perplexity, and neither could believe that He was a mere man, because of the things spoken concerning Him; nor on the other hand receive it that He was Son of God, seeing Him as he did in hunger. Whence being in perplexity he utters ambiguous sounds. And much as when coming to Adam at the beginning, he feigns things that are not, that he may learn the things that are; even so here also, not knowing clearly the unutterable mystery of the Economy, and who He may be that is come, he attempts to weave other nets, whereby he thought to know that which was hidden and obscure. And what saith he? " If Thou be Son of God, command that these stones be made bread." He said not, because thou art an hungered, but, " if Thou be Son of God;" thinking to cheat Him with his compliments. Wherefore also he was silent touching the hunger, that he might not seem to be alleging it, and upbraiding Him. For not knowing the greatness of the Economy which was going on, he supposed this to be a reproach to Him. Wherefore flattering Him craftily, he makes mention of His dignity only.

What then saith Christ? To put down his pride, and to signify that there was nothing shameful in what had happened, nor unbecoming His wisdom; that which the other had passed over in silence to flatter Him, He brings forward and sets it forth, saying, " Man shall not live by bread alone."[5]

So that He begins with the necessity of the belly. But mark, I pray thee, the craft of that wicked demon, and whence he begins his wrestlings, and how he doth not forget his proper art. For by what means he cast out also the first man, and encompassed him with thousands of other evils, with the same means here likewise he weaves his deceit; I mean, with incontinence of the belly. So too even now one may hear many foolish ones say their bad words by thousands because of the belly. But Christ, to show that the virtuous man is not compelled even by this tyranny to do anything that is unseemly, first hungers, then submits not to what is enjoined Him; teaching us to obey the devil in nothing. Thus, because the first man did hereby both offend God, and transgress the law, as much and more doth He teach thee:—though it be no transgression which he commands, not even so to obey.

And why say I, "transgression"? "Why, even though something expedient be suggested by the devils,[6] do not thou," saith He, " even so give heed unto them." Thus, for instance, He stopped the mouths of those devils[6] also, proclaiming Him Son of God. And Paul too again[7] rebuked them, crying this self-same thing; and yet what they said was profitable; but he more abundantly dishonoring them, and obstructing their plot against us, drove them away even when doctrines of salvation were preached by them,

---

[1] Isa. v. 11, 12.
[2] οἰκονομία, that is, the assumption of humanity. [Justin Martyr and Ignatius so use the term; see reffs. in Sophocles, *Greek Lexicon*, etc., *sub voce.*—R.]
[3] Matt. iv. 2.   [4] Matt. iv. 3.
6

[5] Matt. iv. 4.
[6] [Here "demons" is the more correct rendering.—R.]
[7] Acts xvi. 18.

closing up their mouths, and bidding them be silent.

And therefore neither in this instance did He consent to what was said. But what saith He? "Man shall not live by bread alone." Now His meaning is like this: "God is able even by a word to nourish the hungry man;" bringing him a testimony out of the ancient Scripture, and teaching us, though we hunger, yea, whatever we suffer, never to fall away from our Lord.

But if a man say, "still He should have displayed Himself;" I would ask him, with what intent, and for what reason? For not at all that he might believe did the other so speak, but that he might, as he thought, over-argue[1] Him into unbelief. Since the first of mankind were in this way beguiled and over-argued by him, not putting earnest faith in God. For the contrary of what God had said he promised them, and puffed them up with vain hopes, and brought them to unbelief, and so cast them out of the blessings they actually possessed. But Christ signifies Himself not to have consented, either to him then or afterwards to the Jews his partisans, in their demand of signs: invariably instructing us, whatever we may have power to do, yet to do nothing vainly and at random; nor even when want urges to obey the devil.

4. What then doth this accursed one? Overcome, and unable to persuade Him to do his bidding, and that when pressed by such violent hunger, he proceeds to another thing, saying,

"If Thou be Son of God, cast Thyself down; for it is written, He shall give His angels charge concerning Thee, and in their hands they shall bear Thee up."[2]

What can the reason be, that at each temptation He adds this, "If Thou be Son of God?" Much the same as he did in that former case, he doth also at this time. That is, as he then slandered God, saying, "In the day ye eat, your eyes shall be opened;"[3] thereby intending to signify, that they were beguiled and overreached, and had received no benefit; even so in this case also he insinuates this same thing, saying, "in vain God hath called Thee Son, and hath beguiled Thee by His gift; for, if this be not so, afford us some clear proof that Thou art of that power." Then, because Christ had reasoned with him from Scripture, he also brings in a testimony of the prophet.

How then doth Christ? He is not indignant, nor provoked, but with that extreme gentleness He reasons with him again from the Scriptures, saying, "Thou shalt not tempt the Lord thy God:"[4] teaching us that we must overcome the devil, not by miracles, but by forbearance and long-suffering, and that we should do nothing at all for display and vainglory.

But mark thou his folly, even by the very testimony which he produced. For while the testimonies cited by the Lord were both of them spoken with exceeding fitness: his, on the other hand, were chance and random sayings, neither did he bring forward on his part that which applied to the matter in hand. For that it is written, "He shall give His angels charge concerning Thee," this surely is not advice to dash and toss one's self down headlong; and moreover, this was not so much as spoken concerning the Lord. However, this for the time He did not expose, although there was both insult in his manner of speech, and great inconsistency. For of God's Son no man requires these things: but to cast one's self down is the part of the devil, and of demons. Whereas God's part is to raise up even them that are down. And if He ought to have displayed His own power, it would not have been by casting and tossing Himself down at random, but by saving others. But to cast ourselves down precipices, and into pits, pertains properly to his troop. Thus, for example, the juggler among them doth everywhere.

But Christ, even when these things are said, doth not yet reveal Himself, but as man for a while discourses with him. For the sayings, "Man shall not live by bread alone;" and, "Thou shalt not tempt the Lord thy God," suited one not greatly revealing Himself, but representing Himself as one of the many.

But marvel thou not, if he in reasoning with Christ oftentimes turn himself about. For as pugilists, when they have received deadly blows, reel about, drenched in much blood, and blinded; even so he too, darkened by the first and the second blow, speaks at random what comes uppermost: and proceeds to his third assault.

5. "And he leadeth Him up into a high mountain, and showeth Him all the kingdoms, and saith, All these things will I give Thee, if Thou wilt fall down and worship me. Then saith He, Get thee behind me, Satan, for it is written, Thou shalt worship the Lord thy God, and Him only shalt thou serve."[5]

For since he was now come to sinning against the Father, saying, that all that is the Father's was his, and was endeavoring to

1 [ἐλέγξῃ, "might convince," "argue over."—R.]
2 Matt. iv. 6.   3 Gen. iii. 5.   4 Matt. iv. 7.   5 Matt. iv. 8–10.

make himself out to be God, as artificer of the universe; He then rebuked him: but not even then with vehemence, but simply, "Get thee hence, Satan;" which itself had in it something of command rather than of rebuke. For as soon as He had said to him, "Get thee hence," He caused him to take to flight; since he brought not against Him any other temptations.

And how saith Luke, that "he ended all temptation."[1] To me it seems that in mentioning the chief of the temptations, he had spoken of all, as though the rest too were included in these. For the things that form the substance of innumerable evils are these: to be a slave to the belly, to do anything for vainglory, to be in subjection to the madness of riches Which accordingly that accursed one considering, set last the most powerful of all, I mean the desire of more: and though originally, and from the beginning, he was travailing to come to this, yet he kept it for the last, as being of more force than the rest. For in fact this is the manner of his wrestling, to apply those things last, which seem more likely to overthrow. And this sort of thing he did with respect to Job likewise. Wherefore in this instance too, having begun with the motives which seem to be viler and weaker, he goes on to the more prevailing.

How then are we to get the better of him? In the way which Christ hath taught us, by fleeing to God for refuge; and neither to be depressed in famine, as believing in God who is able to feed even with a word; nor amidst whatever good things we may receive to tempt Him who gave them, but to be content with the glory which is from above, making no account of that which is of men, and on every occasion to despise what is beyond our need. For nothing doth so make us fall under the power of the devil, as longing for more, and loving covetousness. And this we may see even by what is done now. For now also there are those who say, "All these things will we give thee, if thou wilt fall down and worship;" who are indeed men by nature, but have become his instruments. Since at that time too he approached Him, not by himself only, but also by others. Which Luke also was declaring, when he said, that "he departed from Him for a season;"[2] showing that hereafter he approached Him by his proper instruments.

"And, behold, angels came and ministered unto Him."[3] For when the assault was going on, He suffered them not to appear, that He might not thereby drive away the prey; but after He had convicted him in all points, and caused him to take to flight, then they appear: that thou also mayest learn, that after thy victories which are copied from His, angels will receive thee also, applauding thee, and waiting as guards on thee in all things. Thus, for example, angels take Lazarus[4] away with them, after the furnace of poverty and of famine and of all distress. For as I have already said, Christ on this occasion exhibits many things, which we ourselves are to enjoy.

6. Forasmuch then as all these things have been done for thee, do thou emulate and imitate His victory. And should any one approach thee of those who are that evil spirit's servants, and savor the things that be of him, upbraiding thee and saying, "If thou art marvellous and great, remove the mountain;" be not troubled, nor confounded, but answer with meekness, and say some such thing as thou hast heard thy Lord say: "Thou shalt not tempt the Lord thy God."

Or should he, offering glory and dominion, and an endless amount of wealth, enjoin thee to worship him, do thou stand again manfully. For neither did the devil deal so with the common Lord of us all only, but every day also he brings these his machinations to bear on each of His servants, not in mountains only and in wildernesses, nor by himself: but in cities likewise, in market-places, and in courts of justice, and by means of our own kindred, even men. What then must we do? Disbelieve him altogether, and stop our ears against him, and hate him when he flatters, and when he proffers more, then so much the more shun him. Because in Eve's case also, when he was most lifting her up with hopes, then he cast her down, and did her the greatest evils. Yea, for he is an implacable enemy, and hath taken up against us such war as excludes all treaty. And we are not so earnest for our own salvation, as he is for our ruin. Let us then shun him, not with words only, but also with works; not in mind only, but also in deed; and let us do none of the things which he approves, for so shall we do all those which God approves. Yea, for he makes also many promises, not that he may give, but that he may take. He promises by rapine, that he may deprive us of the kingdom, and of righteousness; and sets treasures in the earth as a kind of gins or

---

[1] [Luke iv. 13. The form of the passage is changed by Chrysostom, but the words are identical. The R. V. renders: "And when the devil had completed every temptation." Chrysostom puts the emphasis on the word "every," as his argument shows. —R.]

[2] Luke iv. 13. [In Luke iv. 13, the reading is ἄχρι καιροῦ, but Chrysostom has ἕως καιροῦ, apparently accepting the sense given in the R. V. margin: "until a season," which has much to recommend it.—R.]

[3] Matt. iv. 11.

[4] Luke xvi. 22.

traps, that he may deprive us both of these and of the treasures in Heaven, and he would have us be rich here, that we may not be rich there.

And if he should not be able by wealth to cast us out of our portion there, he comes another way, the way of poverty; as he did with respect to Job. That is, when he saw that wealth did him no harm, he weaves his toils by poverty, expecting on that side to get the better of him. But what could be more foolish than this? Since he that hath been able to bear wealth with moderation, much more will he bear poverty with manliness; and he who desires not riches when present, neither will he seek them when absent; even as that blessed man did not, but by his poverty, on the other hand, he became still more glorious. For of his possessions that wicked demon had power indeed to deprive him, but his love toward God he not only could not take away, but made it even stronger, and when he had stripped him of all, he caused him to abound with more blessings; wherefore also he was in perplexity. For the more plagues he brought upon him, the more mighty he then saw him become. And therefore, as you know, when he had gone through all, and had thoroughly tried his metal,[1] because he made no way, he ran to his old weapon, the woman, and assumes a mask of concern, and makes a tragical picture of his calamities in most pitiable tone, and feigns that for removal of his evil he is introducing that deadly counsel.[2] But neither so did he prevail; nay, for his bait was perceived by that wondrous man, who with much wisdom stopped the mouth of the woman speaking at his instigation.

Just so we likewise must act: though it be a brother, a tried friend, a wife, whom you will of those nearest to us, whom he hath entered into, and so utters something not convenient,[3] we must not receive the counsel for the person of him who so speaks, but for the deadly counsel turn away from the speaker. Since in fact now also he doth many such things, and puts before him a mask of sympathy, and while he seems to be friendly, he is instilling his pernicious words, more grievous than poisons. Thus, as to flatter for evil is his part, so to chastise for our good, is God's.

7. Let us not then be deceived, neither let us by every mean seek after the life of ease. For "whom the Lord loveth," it is said, "He chasteneth."[4] Wherefore when we enjoy prosperity, living in wickedness, then most of all should we grieve. For we ought ever to be afraid while we sin, but especially when we suffer no ill. For when God exacts our penalties by little and little, he makes our payment for these things easy to us; but when he is long-suffering for each of our negligences, He is storing us up, if we continue in such things, unto a great punishment. Since, if for the well-doers affliction be a necessary thing, much more for them that sin.

See for instance how much long-suffering Pharaoh met with, and afterwards underwent for all most extreme punishment: in how many things Nebuchadnezzar offended, yet at the end expiated all; and the rich man, because he had suffered no great ill here, for this very cause chiefly became miserable, for that having lived in luxury in the present life, he departed to pay the penalty of all these things there, where he could not obtain anything at all to soothe his calamity.

Yet for all this some are so cold and senseless, as to be always seeking only the things that are here, and uttering those absurd sayings, "Let me enjoy all things present for a time, and then I will consider about things out of sight: I will gratify my belly, I will be a slave to pleasures, I will make full use of the present life; give me to-day, and take to-morrow." Oh excess of folly! Why, wherein do they who talk so differ from goats and swine? For if the prophet[5] permits not them to be accounted men, that "neigh after their neighbor's wife," who shall blame us for esteeming these to be goats and swine, and more insensible than asses, by whom those things are held uncertain, which are more evident than what we see? Why, if thou believest nothing else, attend to the devils in their scourging, to them who had our hurt for their object in all their practice, both in word and deed. For thou wilt not, I am sure, contradict this, that they do all to increase our security, and to do away with the fear of hell, and to breed disbelief of the tribunals in that world. Nevertheless, they that are so minded, by cryings and wailings do oftentimes proclaim the torments that are there.[6] Whence is it then that they so speak, and utter things contrary to their own will? From no other cause, but because they are under the pressure of stronger compulsion. For they would have not been minded of their own accord to confess either that they

---

[1] διακωδώνισας. [2] "Curse God and die," Job ii. 9.
[3] [τι τῶν οὐ προςηκόντων.—R.] [4] Heb. xii. 6.
[5] Jerem. v. 8.
[6] St. Cyril (about A. D. 350), Catech. x. 19, says, "The demons who even to this day are being driven out by the faithful bear witness to Christ." St. Augustin (A. D. 426), in many places speaks of the like miracle as no unusual thing in his time, particularly at the tombs of the martyrs. De Civ. Dei. x. 22; xxii. 8; contra Lit. Petil. ii. 55.

are tormented by dead men, or that they at all suffer anything dreadful.

Wherefore now have I said this? Because *evil* demons confess hell, who would fain have hell disbelieved; but thou who enjoyest honor so great, and hast been a partaker in unutterable mysteries, dost not so much as imitate them, but art become more hardened even than they.

8. "But who," one will say, "hath come from those in hell, and hath declared these things?" Why, who hath arrived here from heaven, and told us that there is a God who created all things? And whence is it clear that we have a soul? For plainly, if thou art to believe the things only that are in sight, both God and angels, and mind and soul, will be matter of doubting to thee, and in this way thou wilt find all the doctrines of the truth gone.

Yet surely, if thou art willing to believe what is evident, the things invisible ought to be believed by thee, rather than those which are seen. Even though what I say be a paradox, nevertheless it is true, and among men of understanding is fully acknowledged. For whereas the eyes are often deceived, not in the things unseen only (for of those they do not so much as take cognizance), but even in those which men think they actually see, distance and atmosphere, and absence of mind, and anger, and care, and ten thousand other things impeding their accuracy; the reasoning power of the soul on the other hand, if it receive the light of the divine Scriptures, will prove a more accurate, an unerring standard of realities.

Let us not then vainly deceive ourselves, neither in addition to the carelessness of our life, which is the offspring of such doctrines as these, heap up to ourselves, for the very doctrines themselves, a more grievous fire. For if there be no judgment, and we are not to give account of our deeds, neither shall we receive rewards for our labors. Observe which way your blasphemies tend, when ye say, that God, who is righteous, and loving, and mild, overlooks so great labors and toils. And how can this be reasonable? Why, if by nothing else, at any rate by the circumstances of thine own house, I bid thee weigh these things, and then thou wilt see the absurdity. For though thou wert thyself savage and inhuman beyond measure, and wilder than the very wild beasts, thou wouldest not choose at thy death to leave unhonored the servant that had been affectionate to thee, but requitest him both with freedom, and with a gift of money; and forasmuch as in thine own person hereafter, having de-

parted, thou wilt be able to do him no good, thou givest charge concerning him to the future inheritors of thy substance, beseeching, exhorting, doing everything, so that he may not remain unrewarded.

So then thou, who art evil, art so kind and loving towards thy servant; and will the Infinite Goodness, that is, God, the Unspeakable Love to man, the kindness so vast: will He overlook and leave uncrowned His own servants, Peter and Paul, and James, and John, those who every day for His sake suffered hunger, were bound, were scourged, were drowned in the sea, were given up to wild beasts, were dying, were suffering so great things as we cannot so much as reckon up? And whereas the Olympic judge proclaims and crowns the victor, and the master rewards the servant, and the king the soldier, and each in general him that hath done him service, with what good things he can; shall God alone, after those so great toils and labors, repay them with no good thing great or small? shall those just and pious men, who have walked in every virtue, lie in the same state with adulterers, and parricides, and manslayers, and violators of tombs? And in what way can this be reasonable? Since, if there be nothing after our departure hence, and our interests reach no further than things present, those are in the same case with these, or rather not so much as in the same. For what though hereafter, as thou sayest, they fare alike? yet here, the whole of their time, the wicked have been at ease, the righteous in chastisement. And this what sort of tyrant, what savage and relentless man did ever so devise, touching his own servants and subjects?

Didst thou mark the exceeding greatness of the absurdity, and in what this argument issues? Therefore if thou wilt not any other way, yet by these reasonings be instructed to rid thyself of this wicked thought, and to flee from vice, and cleave to the toils which end in virtue: and then shalt thou know certainly that our concerns are not bounded by the present life. And if any one ask thee, "Who hath come from thence and brought word what is there?" say unto him, "of men not one; for surely he would have been often disbelieved, as vaunting, and exaggerating the thing; but the Lord of the angels hath brought word with exactness of all those things. What need then have we of any man, seeing He, that will demand account of us, crieth aloud every day, that He hath both made ready a hell, and prepared a kingdom; and affords us clear demonstrations of these things? For if He were not hereafter to judge, neither would he have exacted any penalty here.

9. "Well, but as to this very point, how can it be reasonable? that of the wicked some should be punished, others not? I mean, if God be no respecter of persons, as surely He is not, why can it be that of one He exacts a penalty, but another He suffers to go away unpunished? Why, this is again more inexplicable than the former."

Yet if you are willing to hear what we say with candor, we will solve this difficulty also.

What then is the solution? He neither exacts penalty of all here, lest thou shouldest despair of the resurrection, and lose all expectation of the judgment, as though all were to give account here; nor doth He suffer all to go away unpunished, lest on the other hand thou shouldest account all to be without His providence; but He both punishes and abstains from punishing: by those whom He punishes, signifying that in that world also He will exact a penalty of such as are unpunished here; and by those whom He doth not punish, working upon thee to believe that there is some fearful trial after our departure hence.

But if He were altogether indifferent about our former deeds, He neither would have punished any here, nor have conferred benefits. But now thou seest Him for thy sake stretching out the heaven, kindling the sun, founding the earth, pouring forth the sea, expanding the air, and appointing for the moon her courses, setting unchangeable laws for the seasons of the years, and all other things too performing their own courses exactly at a sign from Him. For both our nature, and that of creatures irrational, of them that creep, that walk, that fly, that swim, in marshes, in springs, in rivers, in mountains, in forests, in houses, in the air, in plains; plants also, and seeds, and trees, both wild and cultivated, both fruitful and unfruitful; and all things in general, moved by that unwearied Hand, make provision for our life, affording to us of themselves their ministry, not for our need only, but also for our feeling of high station.[1]

Seeing therefore order so great and fair (and yet we have not mentioned so much as the least portion thereof), darest thou say, that He who for thy sake hath wrought things so many and great, will overlook thee in the most critical points, and suffer thee when dead to lie with the asses and swine: and that having honored thee with so great a gift, that of godliness, whereby He hath even equalled thee with the angels, He will overlook thee after thy countless labors and toils?

And how can this be reasonable? Why, these things, if we be silent, "the stones will immediately cry out;"[2] so plain are they, and manifest, and more lucid than the sunbeam itself.

Having then considered all these things, and having convinced our own soul, that after our departure hence, we shall both stand at the fearful judgment-seat, and give account of all that we have done, and shall bear our penalty, and submit to our sentence, if we continue in our negligences; and shall receive crowns and unutterable blessings, if we are willing to give a little heed to ourselves; let us both stop the mouths of them who gainsay these things, and ourselves choose the way of virtue; that with due confidence departing to that tribunal, we may attain unto the good things that are promised us, by the grace and love towards man of our Lord Jesus Christ, to whom be glory and dominion, now and ever, world without end. Amen.

---

[1] φιλοτιμίαν.   [2] Luke xix. 40.

HOMILY XIV.

MATT. IV. 12.

"Now when Jesus had heard that John was delivered up, He departed into Galilee."

1. WHEREFORE doth He depart? Again instructing us not to go to meet temptations,[1] but to give place and withdraw ourselves. For it is no reproach, the not casting one's self into danger, but the failing to stand manfully when fallen into it. To teach us this accordingly, and to soothe the envy of the Jews, He retires to Capernaum; at once fulfilling the prophecy,[2] and making haste to catch the teachers of the world: for they, as

---

[1] [τοῖς πειρασμοῖς: here including "trials" of every kind.—R.]   [2] Matt. iv. 14, and Is. ix. 1, 2.

you know, were abiding there, following their craft.

But mark, I pray thee, how in every case when He is about to depart unto the Gentiles, He hath the occasion given Him by Jews. For so in this instance, by plotting against His forerunner, and casting him into prison, they thrust out Christ into the Galilee of the Gentiles. For to show that He neither speaks of the Jewish nation by a part of it, nor signifies obscurely all the tribes; mark how the Prophet distinguishes that place, saying " The land of Nephthalim, by the way of the sea,[1] beyond Jordan, Galilee of the Gentiles, the people which sat in darkness, saw great light: "[2] by darkness here not meaning that which is sensible, but men's errors and ungodliness. Wherefore he also added, " They which sat in the region and shadow of death, to them light is sprung up." For that thou mightest learn that neither the light nor the darkness which he speaks of are sensible, in discoursing of the light, he called it not merely light, but " a great light," which elsewhere he expresses by the word, True:[3] and in describing the darkness, he termed it, " a shadow of death."

Then implying that they did not of themselves seek and find, but that God showed Himself to them from above, he saith to them, " Light is sprung up; " that is, the light of itself sprang up and shone forth: it was not that they first ran to the light. For in truth the condition of men was at the worst before Christ's coming. Since they more than " walked in darkness; " they " sat in darkness; " a kind of sign that they did not even hope to be delivered. For as persons not even knowing where to put a step forward, so they sat, overtaken by the darkness, not being able so much as to stand any more.

2. " From that time Jesus began to preach and to say, Repent; for the kingdom of heaven is at hand."

" From that time: " what time? After John was cast into prison. And wherefore did He not preach to them from the beginning? Indeed what occasion for John at all, when the witness of His works was proclaiming Him?

That hence also thou mightest learn His dignity; namely, that as the Fathers, so He too hath prophets; to which purpose Zacharias also spake; " And thou, child, shalt be called a prophet of the Highest."[4] And that he might leave no occasion to the shameless Jews; which motive He Himself alleged, saying, " John came neither eating nor drinking, and they say, he hath a devil. The Son of Man came eating and drinking, and they say, Behold a man gluttonous and a winebibber, a friend of publicans and sinners. But wisdom is justified of her children."[5]

And moreover it was necessary that what concerned Him should be spoken by another first and not by Himself. For if even after both testimonies and demonstrations so many and so great, they sad, " Thou bearest record of Thyself, Thy record is not true: "[6] had He, without John's saying anything, come into the midst, and first borne record Himself; what would they not have said? For this cause, neither did He preach before John, nor did He work miracles, until John was cast into prison; lest in this way the multitude should be divided. Therefore also John did no miracle at all; that by this means also might give over the multitude to Jesus, His miracles drawing them unto Him.

Again, if even after so many divine precautions,[7] John's disciples, both before and after his imprisonment, were jealously disposed towards Him, and the people too suspected not Him but John to be the Christ; what would not the result have been, had none of these things taken place? For this cause both Matthew distinctly notes, that " from that time He began to preach; " and when He began His preaching, He Himself also taught this same doctrine, which the other used to preach; and no word as yet concerning Himself doth the doctrine which he preached say. Because it was for the time a great thing even for this to be received, forasmuch as they had not as yet the proper opinion about Him. Therefore also at the beginning He puts nothing severe or grievous, as the other did, mentioning an axe, and a tree cut down; a fan, and a threshing-floor, and unquenchable fire; but *His* preludes are gracious: the Heavens and the kingdom there are the good tidings which he declares to His hearers.

3. "And walking by the sea of Galilee, He saw two brethren, Simon that was surnamed Peter, and Andrew his brother, casting a net into the sea; for they were fishers. And He saith unto them, Come ye after me, and I will make you fishers of men. And they left their nets, and followed Him."[8]

And yet John saith that they were called

---

[1] [R. V., " Toward the sea, *Greek*, the way of the sea." The text is cited accurately in the Homily.—R.]

[2] Matt. iv. 15, 16 · see Is. ix. 1, 2.　　[3] John i. 9.

[4] Luke i. 76.

[5] Matt. xi. 18, 19. [The citation is from Matthew, not Luke, but the last clause in the R. V. reads : " And wisdom is justified by her works." Comp., however, the margin and Luke vii. 35. —R.]

[6] John viii. 13.　　[7] τοσούτων οἰκονομηθέντων.

[8] Matt. iv. 18, 19.

in another manner. Whence it is evident that this was a second call; and from many things one may perceive this. For there it is said, that they came to Him when "John was not yet cast into prison;" but here, after he was in confinement. And there Andrew calls Peter, but here Jesus calls both. And John saith, Jesus seeing Simon coming, saith, "Thou art Simon, the Son of Jona, thou shalt be called Cephas, which is by interpretation, a stone."[1] But Matthew saith that he was already called by that name; for his words are, "Seeing Simon that was called Peter." And from the place whence they were called, and from many other things, one may perceive this; and from their ready obedience, and abandonment of all. For now they were well instructed beforehand. Thus, in the other case, Andrew is seen coming into His house, and hearing many things; but here, having heard one bare word, they followed immediately. Since neither was it unnatural[2] for them to follow Him at the beginning, and then leave Him again and return anew to their own craft, when they saw both John thrown into prison, and Himself departing. Accordingly you see that He finds them actually fishing. But He neither forbad them at the first when minded to withdraw, nor having withdrawn themselves, did He let them go altogether; but He gave way when they started aside from Him, and comes again to win them back; which kind of thing is the great point in fishing.[3]

But mark both their faith, and their obedience. For though they were in the midst of their work (and ye know how greedy a thing fishing is), when they heard His command, they delayed not, they procrastinated not, they said not, "let us return home, and converse with our kinsfolk," but "they forsook all and followed," even as Elisha did to Elijah."[4] Because such is the obedience which Christ seeks of us, as that we delay not even a moment of time, though something absolutely most needful should vehemently press on us. Wherefore also when some other had come unto Him, and was asking leave to bury his own father,[5] not even this did He permit him to do: to signify that before all we ought to esteem the following of Himself.

But if thou should say, "the promise is very great;" even for this do I most admire them, for that when they had not as yet seen any sign, they believed in so great a reach of promise, and accounted all but second to that

attendance. And this, because they believed that by what words they were caught, by the same they would be able to catch others also.

To these, then, such was His promise: but to James and John He saith no such thing. For the obedience of those that had gone before had by this time paved the way for these. And besides they had also heard many things before concerning Him.

And see how he doth with exact care intimate unto us their poverty also: in that He found them sewing up their nets. So exceeding great was their poverty, that they were mending what was worn out, not being able to buy others. And this too was for the time no small proof of virtue, their bearing poverty with ease, their supporting themselves by honest labor, their being bound one to another by the power of love, their having their father with them, and attending upon them.

4. When therefore He had caught them, then He begins in their presence to work miracles, by His deeds confirming the words of John concerning Him. And He was continually frequenting their synagogues, even by this instructing them that He was not a sort of adversary of God and deceiver, but that He was come in accordance with the Father.

And while frequenting them, He did not preach only, but also showed forth miracles. And this, because on every occasion, whensoever anything is done strange and surprising, and any polity is introduced, God is wont to work miracles, as pledges of his power, which He affords to them that are to receive His laws. Thus, for instance, when He was about to make man, He created a whole world, and then gave him that law which he had in Paradise. And when He was to give laws to Noah, He showed forth anew great miracles, in that He reduced again the whole creation to its elements,[6] and made that fearful sea to prevail for a full year; and in that, amid so great a tempest, He preserved that righteous man. And in the time of Abraham too He vouchsafed many signs; as his victory in the war, the plague upon Pharaoh, his deliverance from dangers. And when about to legislate for the Jews, He showed forth those marvellous and great prodigies, and then gave the law. Just so in this case also, being to introduce a certain high polity, and to tell them what they had never heard, by the display of the miracles He confirms what He saith.

Thus because the kingdom He was preach-

---

[1] John i. 42.
[2] ["it was natural."—R.]
[3] μέγιστος τρόπος ἀλείας.
[4] 1 Kings xix. 20, 21.
[5] Matt. viii. 21, 22.
[6] ἀνεστοιχείου.

ing appeared not, by the things that appear, He makes it, though invisible, manifest.

And mark the evangelist's care to avoid superfluity of words;[1] how he tells us not of every one of them that are healed, but in a few words speeds over showers of miracles.[2]

For "they brought unto Him," saith he, "all that were sick with divers diseases, and torments, and those which were possessed with devils, and those which were lunatic, and those that had the palsy, and He healed them."

But our inquiry is this; why it can have been that He demanded faith of none of them? For He said not, what we find Him saying after this, "Believe ye that I am able to do this?"[3] because He had not as yet given proof of His power. And besides, the very act of approaching Him, and of bringing others to Him, exhibited no common faith. For they brought them even from far; whereas they would never have brought them, unless they had persuaded themselves of great things concerning Him.

Now then, let us too follow Him; for we also have many diseases of our soul, and these especially He would fain heal. Since with this intent He corrects that other sort, that He may banish these out of our soul.

5. Let us therefore come unto Him, and let us ask nothing pertaining to this life, but rather remission of sins. For indeed He gives it even now, if we be in earnest. Since as then "His fame went out into Syria," so now into the whole world. And they indeed ran together on hearing that He healed persons possessed: and thou, after having much more and greater experience of His power, dost thou not rouse thyself and run?

But whereas they left both country, and friends, and kinsfolk; endurest thou not so much as to leave thy house for the sake of drawing near, and obtaining far greater things? Or rather we do not require of thee so much as this, but leave thy evil habits only, and thou canst easily be made whole, remaining at home with thy friends.

But as it is, if we have any bodily ailment, we do and contrive everything to be rid of what pains us; but when our soul is indisposed, we delay, and draw back. For which cause neither from the other sort are we delivered: since the things that are indispensable are becoming to us secondary, and the secondary indispensable; and letting alone the fountain of our ills, we would fain cleanse out the streams.

For that our bodily ills are caused by the wickedness of the soul, is shown both by him that had the palsy thirty and eight years, and by him that was let down through the roof, and by Cain also before these; and from many other things likewise one may perceive this. Let us do away then with the well-spring of our evils, and all the channels of our diseases will be stayed. For the disease is not palsy only, but also our sin; and this more than that, by how much a soul is better than a body.

Let us therefore now also draw nigh unto Him; let us entreat Him that He would brace our paralyzed soul, and leaving all things that pertain to this life, let us take account of the things spiritual only. Or if thou cleave unto these also, yet think of them after the other.

Neither must thou think lightly of it, because thou hast no pain in sinning; rather on this very account most of all do thou lament, that thou feelest not the anguish of thine offenses. For not because sin bites not, doth this come to pass, but because the offending soul is insensible. Regard with this view them that have a feeling of their own sins, how they wail more bitterly than such as are being cut, or burned; how many things they do, how many suffer, how greatly they mourn and lament, in order to be delivered from their evil conscience. They would not do any such thing, unless they were exceedingly pained in soul.

The best thing then is, to avoid sin in the first instance: the next to it, is to feel that we sin, and thoroughly amend ourselves. But if we have not this, how shall we pray to God, and ask forgiveness of our sins, we who take no account of these matters? For when thou thyself who hast offended art unwilling to know so much as this very fact, that thou hast sinned; for what manner of offenses wilt thou entreat God for pardon? For what thou knowest not? And how wilt thou know the greatness of the benefit? Tell therefore thine offenses in particular, that thou mayest learn for what thou receivest forgiveness, that so thou mayest become grateful towards thy Benefactor.

But thou, when it is a man whom thou hast provoked, entreatest friends, neighbors, and door-keepers, and spendest money, and consumest many days in visiting and petitioning, and though he that is provoked utterly reject thee once, twice, ten thousand times over, thou despondest not, but becoming more earnest thou makest the more entreaty; but when the God of all is provoked, we gape, and throw ourselves back, and live in luxury and in drunkenness, and do

---

all things as usual. And when shall we be able to propitiate Him? and how shall we by this very thing fail to provoke Him so much the more? For not so much sinning, as sinning without even pain, causes in Him indignation and wrath. Wherefore it were meet after all this to sink into the very earth, and not so much as to behold this sun, nor to breathe at all, for that having so placable a Master, we provoke Him first, and then have no remorse for provoking Him. And yet He assuredly, even when He is wroth, doeth not so as hating and turning away from us, but in order that in this way at least He may win us over to Himself. For if He continued after insult befriending thee, thou wouldest the more despise Him. Therefore in order that this may not be, He turns away for a little while, to have thee ever with Himself.

6. Let us now, I pray you, take courage at His love to man, and let us show forth an anxious repentance, before the day come on, which permits us not to profit thereby. For as yet all depends on us, but then He that judges hath alone control over the sentence. " Let us therefore come before His face with confession;"[1] let us bewail, let us mourn. For if we should be able to prevail upon the Judge before the appointed day to forgive us our sins, then we need not so much as enter into the court; as on the other hand, if this be not done, He will hear us publicly in the presence of the world, and we shall no longer have any hope of pardon. For no one of those who have not done away with their sins here, when he hath departed thither shall be able to escape his account for them; but as they who are taken out of these earthly prisons are brought in their chains to the place of judgment, even so all souls, when they have gone away hence bound with the manifold chains of their sins, are led to the awful judgment-seat. For in truth our present life is nothing better than a prison. But as when we have entered into that apartment, we see all bound with chains; so now if we withdraw ourselves from outward show, and enter into each man's life, into each man's soul, we shall see it bound with chains more grievous than iron: and this most especially if thou enter into the souls of them that are rich. For the more men have about them, so much the more are they bound. As therefore with regard to the prisoner, when thou seest him with irons on his back, on his hands, and often on his feet too, thou dost therefore most of all account him miserable; so also as to the rich man, when thou seest him encompassed with innumerable affairs, let him not be therefore rich, but rather for these very things wretched, in thine account. For together with these bonds, he hath a cruel jailor too, the wicked love of riches; which · suffers him not to pass out of this prison, but provides for him thousands of fetters, and guards, and doors, and bolts; and when he hath cast him into the inner prison, persuades him even to feel pleasure in these bonds; that he may not find so much as any hope of deliverance from the evils which press on him.

And if in thought thou wert to lay open that man's soul, thou wouldest see it not bound only, but squalid, and filthy, and teeming with vermin. For no better than vermin are the pleasures of luxury, but even more abominable, and destroy the body more, together with the soul also; and upon the one and upon the other they bring ten thousand scourges of sickness.

On account then of all these things let us entreat the Redeemer of our souls, that He would both burst asunder our bands, and remove this our cruel jailor, and having set us free from the burden of those iron chains, He would make our spirits lighter than any wing. And as we entreat Him, so let us contribute our own part, earnestness, and consideration, and an excellent zeal. For thus we shall be able both in a short time to be freed from the evils which now oppress us, and to learn in what condition we were before, and to lay hold on the liberty which belongs to us; unto which God grant we may all attain, by the grace and love towards man of our Lord Jesus Christ, to whom be glory and power forever and ever. Amen.

[1] Ps. xcv. 2, LXX.

HOMILY XV.

Matt. V. 1, 2.

"And Jesus seeing the multitudes went up into the mountain, and when He was set, His disciples came unto Him. And He opened His mouth, and taught them saying, Blessed," etc.

See how unambitious He was, and void of boasting: in that He did not lead people about with Him, but whereas, when healing was required, He had Himself gone about everywhere, visiting both towns and country places; now when the multitude is become very great, He sits in one spot: and that not in the midst of any city or forum, but on a mountain and in a wilderness; instructing us to do nothing for display, and to separate ourselves from the tumults of ordinary life,[1] and this most especially, when we are to study wisdom, and to discourse of things needful to be done.

But when He had gone up into the mount, and " was set down, His disciples came unto Him." Seest thou their growth in virtue? and how in a moment[2] they became better men? Since the multitude were but gazers on the miracles, but these from that hour desired also to hear some great and high thing. And indeed this it was set Him on His teaching, and made Him begin this discourse.

For it was not men's bodies only that He was healing, but He was also amending their souls; and again from the care of these He would pass to attendance on the other. Thus He at once varied the succor that He gave, and likewise mingled with the instruction afforded by His words, the manifestation of His glory from His works; and besides, He stopped the shameless mouths of the heretics, signifying by this His care of both parts of our being, that He Himself is the Maker of the whole creation. Therefore also on each nature He bestowed abundant providence, now amending the one, now the other.

And in this way He was then employed. For it is said, that " He opened His mouth, and taught them." And wherefore is the clause added, " He opened His mouth"? To inform thee that in His very silence He gave instruction, and not when He spoke only: but at one time by " opening His mouth," at another uttering His voice by the works which He did.

But when thou hearest that He taught *them*, do not think of Him as discoursing with His disciples only, but rather with all through them.

For since the multitude was such as a multitude ever is,[3] and consisted moreover of such as creep on the ground,[4] He withdraws the choir of His disciples, and makes His discourse unto them: in His conversation with them providing that the rest also, who were yet very far from the level of His sayings, might find His lesson of self-denial no longer grievous unto them. Of which indeed both Luke gave intimation, when he said, that He directed His words unto them:[5] and Matthew too, clearly declaring the same, wrote, " His disciples came unto Him, and He taught them." For thus the others also were sure to be more eagerly attentive to Him, than they would have been, had He addressed Himself unto all.

2. Whence then doth He begin? and what kind of foundations of His new polity doth He lay for us?

Let us hearken with strict attention unto what is said. For though it was spoken unto them, it was written for the sake also of all men afterwards. And accordingly on this account, though He had His disciples in His mind in His public preaching, yet unto them He limits not His sayings, but applies all His words of blessing without restriction. Thus He said not, " Blessed are ye, if ye become poor," but " Blessed are the poor." And I may add that even if He had spoken of them, the advice would still be common to all. For so, when He saith, "Lo! I am with you always, even unto the end of the world,"[6] He is discoursing not with them only, but also, through them, with all the world. And in pronouncing them blessed, who are persecuted, and chased, and suffer

---

[1] τῶν ἐν μέσῳ θορύβων.   [2] [ἀθρόον, " all at once."--R.]

[3] δημῶδες.   [4] χάμαι συρομένων, al. ἐρχομένων.
[5] Luke vi. 20. " And He lifted up His eyes on His disciples, and said." And ver. 27, " I say unto you which hear.'
[6] Matt. xxviii. 20.

all intolerable things; not for them only, but also for all who arrive at the same excellency, He weaves His crown.

However, that this may be yet plainer, and to inform thee that thou hast great interest in His sayings, and so indeed hath all mankind, if any choose to give heed; hear how He begins these wondrous words.

"Blessed are the poor in spirit; for theirs is the kingdom of Heaven."[1]

What is meant by "the poor in spirit?" The humble and contrite in mind. For by "spirit" He hath here designated the soul, and the faculty of choice. That is, since many are humble not willingly, but compelled by stress of circumstances; letting these pass (for this were no matter of praise), He blesses them first, who by choice humble and contract themselves.

But why said he not, "the humble," but rather "the poor?" Because this is more than that. For He means here them who are awestruck, and tremble at the commandments of God. Whom also by His prophet Isaiah God earnestly accepting said, "To whom will I look, but to him who is meek[2] and quiet, and trembleth at My words?"[3] For indeed there are many kinds of humility: one is humble in his own measure, another with all excess of lowliness. It is this last lowliness of mind which that blessed prophet commends, picturing to us the temper that is not merely subdued, but utterly broken, when he saith, "The sacrifice for God is a contrite spirit, a contrite and an humble heart God will not despise."[4] And the Three Children also offer this unto God as a great sacrifice, saying, "Nevertheless, in a contrite soul, and in a spirit of lowliness, may we be accepted."[5] This Christ also now blesses.

3. For whereas the greatest of evils, and those which make havoc of the whole world, had their entering in from pride:—for both the devil, not being such before, did thus become a devil; as indeed Paul plainly declared, saying, "Lest being lifted up with pride, he fall into the condemnation of the devil:"[6]—and the first man, too, puffed up by the devil with these hopes, was made an example of,[7] and became mortal (for expecting to become a god, he lost even what he had; and God also upbraiding him with this, and mocking his folly, said, "Behold, Adam is become as one of us"[8]); and each one of those that came after did hereby wreck himself in impiety, fancying some equality with God:—since, I say, this was the stronghold of our evils, and the root and fountain of all wickedness, He, preparing a remedy suitable to the disease, laid this law first as a strong and safe foundation. For this being fixed as a base, the builder in security lays on it all the rest. But if this be taken away, though a man reach to the Heavens in his course of life,[9] it is all easily undermined, and issues in a grievous end. Though fasting, prayer, almsgiving, temperance, any other good thing whatever, be gathered together in thee; without humility all fall away and perish.

It was this very thing that took place in the instance of the Pharisee. For even after he had arrived at the very summit, he "went down"[10] with the loss of all, because he had not the mother of virtues: for as pride is the fountain of all wickedness, so is humility the principle of all self-command. Wherefore also He begins with this, pulling up boasting by the very root out of the soul of His hearers.

"And what," one may ask, "is this to His disciples, who were on every account humble? For in truth they had nothing to be proud of, being fishermen, poor, ignoble, and illiterate." Even though these things concerned not His disciples, yet surely they concerned such as were then present, and such as were hereafter to receive the disciples, lest they should on this account despise them. But it were truer to say that they did also concern His disciples. For even if not then, yet by and by they were sure to require this help, after their signs and wonders, and their honor from the world, and their confidence towards God. For neither wealth, nor power, nor royalty itself, had so much power to exalt men, as the things which they possessed in all fullness. And besides, it was natural that even before the signs they might be lifted up, at that very time when they saw the multitude, and all that audience surrounding their Master; they might feel some human weakness. Wherefore He at once represses their pride.

And He doth not introduce what He saith by way of advice or of commandments, but by way of blessing, so making His word less burthensome, and opening to all the course of His discipline. For He said not, "This or that person," but "they who do so, are all of them *blessed.*" So that though thou be a slave, a beggar, in poverty, a stranger, unlearned,[11] there is nothing to hinder thee from being blessed, if thou emulate this virtue.

---

[1] Matt. v. 3.   [2] ταπεινόν, LXX.
[3] Isa. lxvi. 2, LXX.   [4] Ps. li. 17, LXX.
[5] Dan. iii. 39, LXX.; or Song of the Three Holy Children, ver. 16.
[6] 1 Tim. iii. 6.   [7] ἐξετραχηλίσθη.   [8] Gen. iii. 22.

[9] πολιτευόμενος.   [10] Luke xviii. 14.   [11] [ἰδιώτης.]

4. Now having begun, as you see, where most need was, He proceeds to another commandment, one which seems to be opposed to the judgment of the whole world. For whereas all think that they who rejoice are enviable, those in dejection, poverty, and mourning, wretched, He calls these blessed rather than those; saying thus,

" Blessed are they that mourn." [1]

Yet surely all men call them miserable. For therefore He wrought the miracles beforehand, that in such enactments as these He might be entitled to credit.

And here too again he designated not simply all that mourn, but all that do so for sins: since surely that other kind of mourning is forbidden, and that earnestly, which relates to anything of this life. This Paul also clearly declared, when he said, " The sorrow of the world worketh death, but godly sorrow worketh repentance unto salvation, not to be repented of." [2]

These then He too Himself calls blessed, whose sorrow is of that kind; yet not simply them that sorrow did He designate, but them that sorrow intensely. Therefore He did not say, " they that sorrow," but " they that mourn." For this commandment again is fitted to teach us entire self-control. For if those who grieve for children, or wife, or any other relation gone from them, have no fondness for gain or pleasure during that period of their sorrow; if they aim not at glory, are not provoked by insults, nor led captive by envy, nor beset by any other passion, their grief alone wholly possessing them; much more will they who mourn for their own sins, as they ought to mourn, show forth a self-denial greater than this.

Next, what is the reward for these ? " For they shall be comforted,"saith He.

Where shall they be comforted ! tell me. Both here and there. For since the thing enjoined was exceeding burthensome and galling, He promised to give that, which most of all made it light. Wherefore, if thou wilt be comforted, mourn: and think not this a dark saying. For when God doth comfort, though sorrows come upon thee by thousands like snow-flakes, thou wilt be above them all. Since in truth, as the returns which God gives are always far greater than our labors; so He hath wrought in this case, declaring them that mourn to be blessed, not after the value of what they do, but after His own love towards man   For they that mourn, mourn

for misdoings, and to such it is enough to enjoy forgiveness, and obtain wherewith to answer for themselves. But forasmuch as He is full of love towards man, He doth not limit His recompense either to the removal of our punishments, or to the deliverance from our sins, but He makes them even blessed, and imparts to them abundant consolation.

But He bids us mourn, not only for our own, but also for other men's misdoings. And of this temper were the souls of the saints: such was that of Moses, of Paul, of David; yea, all these many times mourned for evils not their own.

5. " Blessed are the meek, for they shall inherit the earth." [3] Tell me, what kind of earth? Some [4] say a figurative earth, but it is not this, for nowhere in Scripture do we find any mention of an earth that is merely figurative. [5] But what can the saying mean ? He holds out a sensible prize; even as Paul also doth, in that when he had said, " Honor thy father and thy mother," [6] he· added, " For so shalt thou live long upon the earth." And He Himself unto the thief again, " To-day shalt thou be with me in Paradise." [7]

Thus He doth not incite us by means of the future blessings only, but of the present also, for the sake of the grosser sort of His hearers, and such as before the future seek those others.

Thus, for example, further on also He said, "Agree with thine adversary." [8] Then He appoints the reward of such self-command, and saith, " Lest at any time the adversary deliver thee to the judge, and the judge to the officer." [9] Seest thou whereby He alarmed us ? By the things of sense, by what happens before our eyes. And again, " Whosoever shall say to his brother, Raca, shall be in danger of the council." [10]

And Paul too sets forth sensible rewards at great length, and uses things present in his exhortations; as when he is discoursing about virginity. For having said nothing about the heavens there, for the time he urges it by things present, saying, " Because of the present distress," and, " But I spare you," and, " I would have you without carefulness." [11]

Thus accordingly Christ also with the things spiritual hath mingled the sensible. For whereas the meek man is thought to lose all his own, He promises the contrary, saying,

---

[1] Matt. v. 4.
[2] 2 Cor. vii. 10. [R. V., " *a repentance* which bringeth no regret," in the margin, " unto a salvation which bringeth no regret." —R.]

[3] Or, " the land.'
[4] So St. Aug. *de Serm. Dom. in Monte,* lib. i. c. 4 ; St. Jerome *in loc.;* Op. Imperf. *in loc.;* St. Hilar. *in loc.;* Orig. *in Levit.,* Hom. XV. 2, *et alibi.*
[5] νοητήν.   [6] Eph. vi. 2,   [7] Luke xxiii. 43.
[8] Matt. v. 25.   [9] Matt. v. 25   [10] Matt. v. 22.
[11] 1 Cor. vii. 26, 28, 32

" Nay, but this is he who possesses his goods in safety, namely, he who is not rash, nor boastful: while that sort of man shall often lose his patrimony, and his very life."

And besides, since in the Old Testament the prophet used to say continually, " The meek shall inherit the earth;"[1] He thus weaves into His discourse the words to which they were accustomed, so as not everywhere to speak a strange language.

And this He saith, not as limiting the rewards to things present, but as joining with these the other sort of gifts also.   For neither in speaking of any spiritual thing doth He exclude such as are in the present life; nor again in promising such as are in our life, doth He limit his promise to that kind.   For He saith, " Seeκ ye the kingdom of God, and all these things shall be added unto you."[2] And again: " Whosoever hath left houses or brethren, shall receive an hundred fold in this world, and in the future shall inherit everlasting life."[3]

6. " Blessed are they which do hunger and thirst after righteousness."[4]

What sort of righteousness?   He means either the whole of virtue, or that particular virtue which is opposed to covetousness.[5] For since He is about to give commandment concerning mercy, to show how we must show mercy, as, for instance, not of rapine or covetousness, He blesses them that lay hold of righteousness.

And see with what exceeding force He puts it.   For He said not, " Blessed are they which keep fast by righteousness," but, " Blessed are they which do hunger and thirst after righteousness: " that not merely anyhow, but with all desire we may pursue it. For since this is the most peculiar property of covetousness, and we are not so enamored of meat and drink, as of gaining, and compassing ourselves with more and more, He bade us to transfer this desire to a new object, freedom from covetousness.

Then He appoints the prize, again from things sensible; saying, " for they shall be filled."   Thus, because it is thought that the rich are commonly made such by covetousness, " Nay," saith He, " it is just contrary: for it is righteousness that doeth this. Wherefore, so long as thou doest righteously, fear not poverty, nor tremble at hunger. For the extortioners, they are the very persons who lose all, even as he certainly who is in love with righteousness, possesses himself the goods of all men in safety."

But if they who covet not other men's goods enjoy so great abundance,[6] much more they who give up their own.

" Blessed are the merciful."[7]

Here He seems to me to speak not of those only who show mercy in giving of money, but those likewise who are merciful in their actions.   For the way of showing mercy is manifold, and this commandment is broad.

What then is the reward thereof?

" For they shall obtain mercy."

And it seems indeed to be a sort of equal recompence, but it is a far greater thing than the act of goodness.   For whereas they themselves show mercy as men, they obtain mercy from the God of all; and it is not the same thing, man's mercy, and God's; but as wide as is the interval between wickedness and goodness, so far is the one of these removed from the other.

" Blessed are the pure in heart, for they shall see God."[8]

Behold again the reward is spiritual.   Now He here calls " pure," either those who have attained unto all virtue, and are not conscious to themselves of any evil; or those who live in temperance.   For there is nothing which we need so much in order to see God, as this last virtue.   Wherefore Paul also said, " Follow peace with all men, and holiness, without which no man shall see the Lord."[9]   He is here speaking of such sight as it is possible for man to have.

For because there are many who show mercy, and who commit no rapine, nor are covetous, who yet are guilty of fornication and uncleanness; to signify that the former alone suffices not, He hath added this, much in the same sense as Paul, writing to the Corinthians, bore witness of the Macedonians, that they were rich not only in almsgiving, but also in all other virtue.   For having spoken of the noble spirit[10] they had shown in regard of their goods, he saith, " They gave also their own selves to the Lord, and to us."[11]

7. " Blessed are the peace-makers."[12]

Here He not only takes away altogether our own strife and hatred amongst ourselves, but he requires besides this something more, namely, that we should set at one again others, who are at strife.

And again, the reward which He annexes is spiritual.   Of what kind then is it.

" For they shall be called the children of God."

---

[1] Ps. xxxvii. 11.   [2] Matt. vi. 33
[3] Matt. xix. 29.   See also Mark x. 29, 30; and Luke xviii. 29, 30.
[4] Matt. v. 6.   [5] See Aristot. *Eth. Nic.* v. 2.

[6] Not that St. Chrysostom limited this or any of the Gospel promises to a temporal sense.   See below, sec. 7.
[7] Matt. v. 7   [8] Matt. v. 8.   [9] Heb. xii. 14.
[10] [φιλοτιμίας.   The term in later Greek means " munificence," and is so rendered below, in sec. 13.—R.]
[11] 2 Cor. viii. 5.   [12] Matt. v. 9.

Yea, for this became the work of the Only Begotten, to unite the divided, and to reconcile the alienated.

Then, lest thou shouldest imagine peace in all cases a blessing, He hath added,

" Blessed are they which are persecuted for righteousness' sake." [1]

That is, for virtue's sake, for succor [2] given to others, and for godliness: it being ever His wont to call by the name of " righteousness " the whole practical wisdom of the soul.

" Blessed are ye, when men shall revile you and persecute you, and say all manner of evil against you falsely, for my sake. Rejoice, and be exceeding glad." [3]

As if He said, " Though they should call you sorcerers, deceivers, pestilent persons, or whatever else, blessed are ye ": so He speaks. What could be newer than these injunctions? wherein the very things which all others avoid, these He declares to be desirable; I mean, being poor, mourning, persecution, evil report. But yet He both affirmed this, and convinced not two, nor ten, nor twenty, nor an hundred, nor a thousand men, but the whole world. And hearing things so grievous and galling, so contrary to the accustomed ways of men, the multitudes " were astonished." So great was the power of Him who spake.

However, lest thou shouldest think that the mere fact of being evil spoken of makes men blessed, He hath set two limitations; when it is for His sake, and when the things that are said are false: for without these, he who is evil spoken of, so far from being blessed, is miserable.

Then see the prize again: " Because your reward is great in heaven." But thou, though thou hear not of a kingdom given in each one of the blessings, be not discouraged. For although He give different names to the rewards, yet He brings all into His kingdom. Thus, both when He saith, " they that mourn shall be comforted; " and, " they that show mercy shall obtain mercy; " and, " the pure in heart shall see God; " and, the peace-makers " shall be called the children of God; " nothing else but the Kingdom doth He shadow out by all these sayings. For such as enjoy these, shall surely attain unto that. Think not therefore that this reward is for the poor in spirit only, but for those also who hunger after righteousness, for the meek, and for all the rest without exception.

Since on this account He hath set His blessing on them all, that thou mightest not look for anything sensible: for that man can-not be blessed, who is crowned with such things as come to an end with this present life, and hurry by quicker than a shadow.

8. But when He had said, " your reward is great," he added also another consolation, saying, " For so persecuted they the prophets which were before you."

Thus, since that first, the promise of the Kingdom, was yet to come, and all in expectation, He affords them comfort from this world; from their fellowship with those who before them had been ill-treated.

For " think not," saith He, " that for something inconsistent in your sayings and enactments ye suffer these things: or, as being teachers of evil doctrines, ye are to be persecuted by them; the plots and dangers proceed not of any wickedness in your sayings, but of the malice of those who hear you. Wherefore neither are they any blame to you who suffer wrong, but to them who do the wrong. And to the truth of these things all preceding time bears witness. For against the prophets they did not even bring any charge of transgressing the law, and of sentiments of impiety, that they stoned some, chased away others, encompassed others with innumerable afflictions. Wherefore let not this trouble you, for of the very same mind they do all that is done now." Seest thou how He raised up their spirits, by placing them near to the company of Moses and Elias?

Thus also Paul writing to the Thessalonians, saith, " For ye became followers of the Churches of God, which are in Judea; for ye also have suffered the same things of your own fellow-countrymen, even as they have of the Jews: who both killed the Lord Jesus, and their own prophets, and have driven us out; and they please not God, and are contrary to all men." [4] Which same point here also Christ hath established.

And whereas in the other beatitudes, He said, " Blessed are the poor," and " the merciful; " here He hath not put it generally, but addresses His speech unto themselves, saying, " Blessed are ye, when they shall revile you, and persecute you, and say every evil word: " signifying that this is an especial privilege of theirs; and that beyond all others, teachers have this for their own.

At the same time He here also covertly signifies His own dignity, and His equality in honor with Him who begat Him. For " as they on the Father's account, " saith He, " so shall ye also for me suffer these things." But when He saith, " the prophets which

---

[1] Matt. v. 10.   [2] προστασίας.   [3] Matt. v. 11, 12.   [4] 1 Thess. ii. 14, 15.

were before you," He implies that they were also by this time become prophets.

Next, declaring that this above all profits them, and makes them glorious, He did not say, "they will calumniate and persecute you, but I will prevent it." For not in their escaping evil report, but in their noble endurance thereof, and in refuting them by their actions, He will have their safety stand: this being a much greater thing than the other; even as to be struck and not hurt, is much greater than escaping the blow.

9. Now in this place He saith, "Your reward is great in heaven." But Luke[1] reports Him to have spoken this, both earnestly, and with more entire consolation; for He not only, as you know, pronounces them blessed, who are evil spoken of for God's sake, but declares them likewise wretched, who are well spoken of by all men. For, "Woe unto you," saith He, "when all men shall speak well of you." And yet the apostles were well spoken of, but not by all men. Wherefore He said not, "Woe unto you, when men shall speak well of you," but, "when all men" shall do so: for it is not even possible that those who live in the practice of virtue should be well spoken of by all men.

And again He saith, "When they shall cast out your name as evil, rejoice ye, and leap for joy."[2] For not only of the dangers they underwent, but of the calumny also, He appoints the recompence to be great. Wherefore He said not, "When they shall persecute, and kill you," but, "When they shall revile you, and say all manner of evil." For most assuredly, men's evil reports have a sharper bite than their very deeds. For whereas, in our dangers, there are many things that lighten the toil, as to be cheered[3] by all, to have many to applaud, to crown, to proclaim our praise; here in our reproach even this consolation is destroyed. Because we seem not to have achieved anything great; and this galls the combatant more than all his dangers: at least many have gone on even to hang themselves, not bearing evil report. And why marvellest thou at the others? since that traitor, that shameless and accursed one, he who had ceased to blush for anything whatever, was wrought upon by this chiefly to hurry to the halter. And Job again, all adamant as he was, and firmer than a rock; when he had been robbed of all his possessions, and had become on a sudden childless, and when he saw his body pouring out worms like a fountain, and his wife attacking him, he

repelled it all with ease; but when he saw his friends reproaching and trampling upon him, and entertaining an evil opinion of him, and saying that he suffered those things for some sins, and was paying the penalty of wickedness: then was there trouble, then commotion, even in that great and noble-hearted man.[4]

And David also, letting pass all that he had suffered, sought of God a retribution for the calumny alone. For, "Let him curse," saith he, "for the Lord hath bidden him: that the Lord may see my humiliation, and requite me for this cursing of his on this day."[5]

And Paul too proclaims the triumph not of those only who incur danger, or are deprived of their goods, but of these also, thus saying, "Call to remembrance the former days, in which after ye were illuminated ye endured a great fight of afflictions; partly whilst ye were made a gazing stock by reproaches, and afflictions."[6] On this account then Christ hath appointed the reward also to be great.

After this, lest any one should say, "Here thou givest no redress, nor stoppest men's mouths; and dost thou assign a reward there?" He hath put before us the prophets, to show that neither in their case did God give redress. And if, where the rewards were at hand, He cheered them with things to come; much more now, when this hope is become clearer, and self-denial is increased.

And observe too, after how many commandments He hath put this: for surely He did it not without reason, but to show that it is not possible for one unprovided, and unarmed with all those other virtues, to go forth unto these conflicts. Therefore, you see, in each instance, by the former precept making way for the following one, He hath woven a sort of golden chain for us. Thus, first, he that is "humble," will surely also "mourn" for his own sins: he that so "mourns," will be both "meek," and "righteous," and "merciful;" he that is "merciful," and "righteous," and "contrite," will of course be also "pure in heart:" and such a one will be "a peacemaker" too: and he that hath attained unto all these, will be moreover arrayed against dangers, and will not be troubled when evil is spoken of him, and he is enduring grievous trials innumerable.

10. Now then, after giving them due exhortation, He refreshes them again with

---

[4] [Literally, "then was disturbed, then was troubled, that noble and great man."—R.]

[5] 2 Sam. xvi. 11, 12.

[6] Heb. x. 32, 33. [R. V., "in which, after ye were enlightened, ye endured a great conflict of sufferings; partly, being made a gazing-stock both by reproaches and afflictions." The text of the Homily omits "both."—R.]

---

[1] See Luke vi. 23, 26.   [2] Luke vi. 22, 23.   [3] ἀλείφεσθαι.

praises. As thus: the injunctions being high, and far surpassing those in the Old Testament; lest they should be disturbed, and confounded, and say, "How shall we be able to achieve these things?" hear what He saith:

"Ye are the salt of the earth."[1]

Implying, that of absolute necessity He enjoins all this. For "not for your own life apart," saith He, "but for the whole world, shall your account be. For not to two cities, nor to ten or twenty, nor to a single nation am I sending you, as I sent the prophets; but to earth, and sea, and the whole world; and that in evil case." For by saying, "Ye are the salt of the earth," He signified all human nature to have "lost its savor,"[2] and to be decayed by our sins. For which cause, you see, He requires of them such virtues, as are most necessary and useful for the superintendence of the common sort. For first, the meek, and yielding, and merciful, and righteous, shuts not up his good deeds unto himself only, but also provides that these good fountains should run over for the benefit of others. And he again who is pure in heart, and a peacemaker, and is persecuted for the truth's sake; he again orders his way of life for the common good. "Think not then," He saith, "that ye are drawn on to ordinary conflicts, or that for some small matters you are to give account." "Ye are the salt of the earth."

What then? did they restore the decayed? By no means; for neither is it possible to do any good to that which is already spoilt, by sprinkling it with salt. This therefore they did not. But rather, what things had been before restored, and committed to their charge, and freed from that ill savor, these they then salted, maintaining and preserving them in that freshness,[3] which they had received of the Lord. For that men should be set free from the rottenness of their sins was the good work of Christ; but their not returning to it again any more was the object of these men's diligence and travail.

Seest thou how by degrees He indicates their superiority to the very prophets? in that He saith they are teachers, not of Palestine, but of the whole world; and not simply teachers, but awful ones too. For this is the marvellous thing, that not by flattering, nor soothing, but by sharply bracing[4] them, as salt, even so they became dear to all men.

"Now marvel not," saith He, "if leaving all others, I discourse to you, and draw you on to so great dangers. For consider over how many cities, tribes, and nations, I am to send you to preside. Wherefore I would have you not only be prudent yourselves, but that you should also make others the same. And such persons have great need to be intelligent, in whom the salvation of the rest is at stake: they ought so much to abound in virtue, as to impart of the profit to others also. For if ye do not become such as this, ye will not suffice even for your own selves.

"Be not then impatient, as though my sayings were too burdensome. For while it is possible for others who have lost their savor to return by your means, you, if you should come to this, will with yourselves destroy others also. So that in proportion as the matters are great, which ye have put into your hands, you need so much the greater diligence." Therefore He saith,

"But if the salt have lost its savor, wherewith shall it be salted? it is thenceforth good for nothing, but to be cast out, and to be trodden under foot of men."[5]

For other men, though they fall never so often, may possibly obtain indulgence: but the teacher, should this happen to him, is deprived of all excuse, and will suffer the most extreme vengeance. Thus, lest at the words, "When they shall revile you, and persecute you, and say all manner of evil against you," they should be too timid to go forth: He tells them, "unless ye are prepared to combat with all this, ye have been chosen in vain." For it is not evil report that ye should fear, but lest ye should prove partners in dissimulation.[6] For then, "Ye will lose your savor, and be trodden under foot:" but if ye continue sharply to brace them up, and then are evil spoken of, rejoice; for this is the very use of salt, to sting the corrupt,[7] and make them smart And so their censure follows of course, in no way harming you, but rather testifying your firmness. But if through fear of it you give up the earnestness that becomes you, ye will have to suffer much more grievously, being both evil spoken of, and despised by all. For this is the meaning of "trodden under foot."

11. After this He leads on to another, a higher image.

"Ye are the light of the world."[8]

"Of the world" again; not of one nation, nor of twenty states,[9] but of the whole inhabited earth. And "a light" to the mind, far better than this sunbeam: like as they were also a spiritual *salt*. And before they are *salt*, and now *light;* to teach thee how great

---

[1] Matt. v. 13.   [2] μωρανθεῖσαν.   [3] νεαρότητι.
[4] [ἐπιστύφοντες, used of astringents.—R.]

[5] Matt. v. 13.   [6] συνυποκρινομένους, cf. Gal. ii. 13.
[7] χαύνους.   [8] Matt. v. 14.   [9] [πόλεων.]

is the gain of these strict[1] precepts, and the profit of that grave discipline: how it binds, and permits not to become dissolute; and causes clear sight, leading men on to virtue.

"A city that is set on a hill cannot be hid, neither do men light a candle, and put it under the bushel."[2]

Again, by these words He trains them to strictness of life, teaching them to be earnest in their endeavors, as set before the eyes of all men, and contending in the midst of the amphitheatre of the world. For, "look not to this," He saith, "that we are now sitting here, that we are in a small portion of one corner. For ye shall be as conspicuous to all as a city set on the ridge of a hill, as a candle in a house on the candlestick, giving light."[3]

Where now are they who persevere in disbelieving the power of Christ? Let them hear these things, and let them adore His might, amazed at the power of the prophecy. For consider how great things he promised to them, who were not known even in their own country: that earth and sea should know them, and that they should by their fame reach to the limits of the inhabited world; or rather, not by their fame, but by the working of the good they wrought. For it was not fame that bearing them everywhere made them conspicuous, but also the actual demonstration by their works. Since, as though they had wings, more vehemently than the sunbeam did they overrun the whole earth, sowing the light of godliness.[4]

But here He seems to me to be also training them to boldness of speech. For to say, "A city set on a hill cannot be hid," is to speak as declaring His own powers.[5] For as that city can by no means be hidden, so it was impossible that what they preached should sink into silence and obscurity. Thus, since He had spoken of persecutions and calumnies, of plots and wars, for fear they might think that these would have power to stop their mouths; to encourage them, He saith, that so far from being hid, it should overshine the whole world; and that on this very account they should be illustrious and renowned.

By this then He declares His own power. In what follows, He requires that boldness of speech which was due on their part; thus saying,

"Neither do men light a candle and put it under the bushel, but on the candlestick, and it giveth light unto all that are in the house. Let your light so shine before men, that they may see your good works, and glorify your Father which is in Heaven."[6]

"For I," saith He, "it is true, have kindled the light, but its continuing to burn, let that come of your diligence: not for your own sakes alone, but also for their sake, who are to profit by these rays, and to be guided unto the truth. Since the calumnies surely shall not be able to obscure your brightness, if you be still living a strict life, and as becomes those who are to convert the whole world. Show forth therefore a life worthy of His grace; that even as it is everywhere preached, so this light may everywhere accompany the same.

Next He sets before them another sort of gain, besides the salvation of mankind, enough to make them strive earnestly, and to lead them unto all diligence. As thus, "Ye shall not only," saith He, "amend the world, if ye live aright, but ye will also give occasion that God shall be glorified; even as if ye do the contrary, ye will both destroy men, and make God's name to be blasphemed."

And how, it may be asked, shall God be glorified through us, if at least men are to speak evil of us? Nay, not all men, and even they themselves who in envy do this, will in their conscience admire and approve you; even as the outward flatterers of such as live in wickedness do in mind accuse them.

What then? Dost thou command us to live for display and vain glory? Far from it; I say not this; for I did not say, "Give ye diligence to bring forward your own good deeds," neither did I say, "Show them;" but "Let your light shine." That is, "Let your virtue be great, and the fire abundant, and the light unspeakable." For when virtue is so great, it cannot lie hid, though its pursuer shade it over ten thousand fold. Present unto them an irreprehensible life, and let them have no true occasion of evil speaking; and then, though there be thousands of evil-speakers, no man shall be able to cast any shade upon you. And well did He say, "your light," for nothing makes a man so illustrious, how manifold soever his will to be concealed, as the manifestation of virtue. For as if he were clad with the very sunbeam, so he shines, yet brighter than it; not spending his rays on earth, but surmounting also Heaven itself.

---

[1] κατεστυμμένων.
[2] Matt. v. 14, 15. [R. V., "lamp."—R.]
[3] ["a lamp in a house, giving light (φαίνων) on the lampstand."—.]
[4] *Lumine conserit arva, Lucr.*
[5] [Or, "is spoken of manifesting His power."—R.]

[6] Matt. v. 15, 16. [R. V., "Neither do men light a lamp, and put it under the bushel, but on the stand; and it shineth unto all that are in the house. Even so let your light shine," etc.—R.]

Hence also He comforts them more abundantly. For, "What though the slander pain you," saith He; "yet shall ye have many to honor God on your account. And in both ways your recompence is gathering, as well because God is glorified through you, as because ye are defamed for God's sake. Thus, lest we should on purpose seek to be reproached, on hearing that there is a reward for it: first, He hath not expressed that sentiment simply, but with two limitations, namely, when what is said is false, and when it is for God's sake:—and next He signifies how not that only, but also good report, hath its great profit, the glory of it passing on to God. And He holds out to them those gracious hopes. "For," saith He, "the calumny of the wicked avails not so much as to put all others in the dark, in respect of seeing your light. For then only when you have "lost your savor" shall they tread you under foot; but not when you are falsely accused, doing right. Yea, rather then shall there be many admiring, not you only, but for your sake your Father also." And He said not "God," but "your Father;" already sowing beforehand the seeds of that noble birth, which was about to be bestowed upon them. Moreover, indicating His parity in honor, as He said above, "Grieve not when ye are evil spoken of, for it is enough for you that for my sake you are thus spoken of;" so here He mentions the Father: every where manifesting His equality.

12. Since then we know the gain that arises from this earnestness, and the danger of indolence (for if our Lord be blasphemed because of us, that were far worse than our perdition), let us "give none offense, neither to the Jews, nor to the Gentiles, nor to the Church of God."[1] And while the life which we present before them is brighter than the sun, yet if any one will speak evil of us, let us not grieve at being defamed, but only if we be defamed with justice.

For, on the one hand, if we live in wickedness, though there be none to speak ill of us, we shall be the most wretched of all men: on the other hand, if we apply ourselves to virtue, though the whole world speak evil of us, at that very time we shall be more enviable than any. And we shall draw on to follow us all who choose to be saved, for not the calumny of the wicked, but our good life, will draw their attention. For indeed no trumpet is so clear as the proof that is given by our actions: neither is the light itself so transparent as a pure life, though our calumniators be beyond number.

I say, if all the above-mentioned qualities be ours; if we be meek and lowly and merciful; if we be pure, and peacemakers; if hearing reproach, we revile not again, but rather rejoice; then shall we attract all that observe us no less than the miracles do. And all will be kindly disposed towards us, though one be a wild beast, a demon, or what you will.

Or if there should even be some who speak evil of thee, be not thou at all troubled thereat, nor because they revile thee in public, regard it; but search into their conscience, and thou shalt see them applauding and admiring thee, and numbering up ten thousand praises.

See, for instance, how Nebuchadnezzar praises the children in the furnace; yet surely he was an adversary and an enemy. But upon seeing them stand nobly, he proclaims their triumph, and crowns them: and that for nought else, but because they disobeyed him, and hearkened unto the law of God. For the devil, when he sees himself effecting nothing, from that time departs, fearing lest he should be the cause of our winning more crowns. And when he is gone, even one who is abominable and depraved will recognize virtue, that mist being withdrawn. Or if men still argue perversely, thou shalt have from God the greater praise and admiration.

Grieve not now, I pray thee, neither despond; since the very apostles were to some a "savor of death;"[2] to others, a "savor of life." And if there be nothing to lay hold of in thyself, thou art rid of all their charges; or rather, thou art become the more blessed. Shine out therefore in thy life, and take no account of them who speak evil of thee. For it cannot, it cannot be, that one careful of virtue, should not have many enemies. However, this is nothing to the virtuous man. For by such means his brightness will increase the more abundantly.

Let us then, bearing these things in mind, look to one object only; how to order our own life with strictness. For thus we shall also guide to the life that is there, such as are now sitting in darkness. For such is the virtue of that light, as not only to shine here, but also to conduct its followers thither. For when men see us despising all things present, and preparing ourselves for that which is to come, our actions will persuade them sooner than any discourse. For who is there so senseless, that at sight of one, who within a day or two was living in luxury and wealth, now stripping himself of all, and putting on wings, and arrayed to meet both hunger and poverty, and all hardship, and dangers, and

---

[1] 1 Cor. x. 32.

[2] 1 Cor. ii. 16.

blood, and slaughter, and everything that is counted dreadful; will not from this sight derive a clear demonstration of the things which are to come?

But if we entangle ourselves in things present, and plunge ourselves in them more and more, how will it be possible for them to be persuaded that we are hastening to another sojourn?[1]

And what excuse after this shall we have, if the fear of God avail not so much with us, as human glory availed with the Greek philosophers? For some of them did really both lay aside wealth, and despised death, that they might make a show before men; wherefore also their hopes became vain. What plea then shall deliver us, when with so great things set before us, and with so high a rule of self-denial laid open to us, we are not able even to do as they did, but ruin both ourselves and others besides? For neither is the harm so great when a heathen commits transgression, as when a Christian doeth the same. Of course not; for their character is already lost, but ours, by reason of the grace of God, is even among the ungodly venerable and glorious. Therefore when they would most revile us, and aggravate their evil speech, they add some such taunt as, "Thou Christian:" a taunt which they would not utter, did they not secretly entertain a great opinion of our doctrine.

Hast thou not heard how many, and how great precepts Christ enjoined? Now when wilt thou be able to fulfill one of those commandments, while thou leavest all, and goest about gathering interest, tacking together usuries, setting on foot transactions of business, buying herds of slaves, procuring silver vessels, purchasing houses, fields, goods without end? And I would this were all. But when to these unseasonable pursuits, thou addest even injustice, removing landmarks,[2] taking away houses by violence, aggravating poverty, increasing hunger, when wilt thou be able to set thy foot on these thresholds?

13. But sometimes thou showest mercy to the poor. I know it as well as thou. But even in this again great is the mischief. For thou doest this either in pride or in vainglory, so as not to profit even by thy good deeds. What can be more wretched than this, to be making thy shipwreck in the very harbor? To prevent this, when thou hast done any good action, seek not thanks from me, that thou mayest have God thy debtor. For,

"Lend," saith He, "unto them from whom ye do not expect to receive."[3]

Thou hast thy Debtor; why leave Him, and require it of me, a poor and wretched mortal? What? is that Debtor displeased, when the debt is required of Him? What? is He poor? Is He unwilling to pay? Seest thou not His unspeakable treasures? Seest thou not His indescribable munificence? Lay hold then on Him, and make thy demand; for He is pleased when one thus demands the debt of Him. Because, if He see another required to pay for what He Himself owes, He will feel as though He were insulted, and repay thee no more; nay, He justly finds fault, saying, "Why, of what ingratitude hast thou convicted me? what poverty dost thou know to be in me, that thou hastenest by me, and resortest unto others? Hast thou lent to One, and dost thou demand the debt of another?"

For although man received it, it was God that commanded thee to bestow; and His will is to be Himself, and in the original sense,[4] debtor, and surety, affording thee ten thousand occasion to demand the debt of Him from every quarter. Do not thou then let go so great facility and abundance, and seek to receive of me who have nothing. Why, to what end dost thou display to me thy mercy shown to the poor. What! was it I that said to thee, Give? was it from me that thou didst hear this; that thou shouldest demand it back of me? He Himself hath said, "He that hath pity upon the poor lendeth to God."[5] Thou hast lent to God:[6] put it to His account.

"But He doth not repay the whole now." Well, this too He doth for thy good. For such a debtor is He: not as many, who are anxious simply to repay that which is lent; whereas He manages and doeth all things, with a view of investing likewise in security that which hath been given unto Him. Therefore some, you see, He repays here: some He assigns[7] in the other place.

14. Knowing therefore as we do these things, let us make our mercifulness abundant, let us give proof of much love to man, both by the use of our money, and by our actions. And if we see any one ill-treated and beaten in the market-place, whether we can pay down money, let us do it: or whether by words we may separate them, let us not be backward. For even a word has its re-

---

[1] ἀποδημίαν.
[2] [γῆν ἀποτεμνόμενος. There is no reference to the Old Testament phrase in the original, which simply means "cutting off land for one's self," i. e., to appropriate it wrongfully.—R.]

[3] [Comp. Luke vi. 34.]
[4] πρωτότυπος, archetypal : the word seems to imply the symbolical use to be made of all visible things and their relations : as here, the relation of debtor and creditor is a sort of token of God's mercy, in binding Himself to do us good.
[5] Prov. xix. 17.   [6] αὐτῷ περίθες.   [7] ταμιεύεται.

ward, and still more have sighs. And this the blessed Job said; "But I wept for every helpless one, and I sighed when I saw a man in distress."[1] But if there be a reward for tears and sighs; when words also, and an anxious endeavor, and many things besides are added, consider how great the recompence becomes. Yea, for we too were enemies to God, and the Only-begotten reconciled us, casting himself between, and for us receiving stripes, and for us enduring death.

Let us then likewise do our diligence to deliver from countless evils such as are incurring them; and not as we now do, when we see any beating and tearing one another: we are apt to stand by, finding pleasure in the disgrace of others, and forming a devilish amphitheatre around: than which what can be more cruel? Thou seest men reviled, tearing each other to pieces, rending their clothes, smiting each other's faces, and dost thou endure to stand by quietly?

What! is it a bear that is fighting? a wild beast? a serpent? It is a man, one who hath in every respect fellowship with thee: a brother, a member.[2] Look not on, but separate them. Take no pleasure, but amend the evil. Stir not up others to the shameful sight, but rather drive off and separate those who are assembled. It is for shameless persons, and born slaves,[3] to take pleasure in such calamities; for those that are mere refuse, for asses without reason.

Thou seest a man behaving himself unseemly, and dost thou not account the unseemliness thine own? Dost thou not interpose, and scatter the devil's troop, and put an end to men's miseries?

"That I may receive blows myself," saith one; "is this also thy bidding?" Thou wilt not have to suffer even this; but if thou shouldest, the thing would be to thee a sort of martyrdom; for thou didst suffer on God's behalf. And if thou art slow to receive blows, consider that thy Lord was not slow to endure the cross for thee.

Since they for their part are drunken and in darkness, wrath being their tyrant and commander; and they need some one who is sound to help them, both the wrong-doer, and he who is injured; the one that he may be delivered from suffering evil, the other that he may cease to do it. Draw nigh, therefore, and stretch forth the hand, thou that art sober to him that is drunken. For there is a drunkenness of wrath too, and that more grievous than the drunkenness of wine.

Seest thou not the seamen, how, when they see any meeting with shipwreck, they spread their sails, and set out with all haste, to rescue those of the same craft out of the waves? Now, if partakers in an art show so much care one for another, how much more ought they who are partakers of the same nature to do all these things! Because in truth here too is a shipwreck, a more grievous one than that; for either a man under provocation blasphemes, and so throws all away: or he forswears himself under the sway of his wrath, and that way falls into hell: or he strikes a blow and commits murder, and thus again suffers the very same shipwreck. Go thou then, and put a stop to the evil; pull out them that are drowning, though thou descend into the very depth of the surge; and having broken up the theatre of the devil, take each one of them apart, and admonish him to quell the flame, and to lull the waves.

But if the burning pile wax greater, and the furnace more grievous, be not thou terrified; for thou hast many to help thee, and stretch forth the hand, if thou furnish but a beginning; and above all thou surely hast with thee the God of peace. And if thou wilt first turn aside the flames, many others also will follow, and of what they do well, thou wilt thyself receive the reward.

Hear what precept Christ gave to the Jews, creeping as they did upon the earth: "If thou see," saith He, "thine enemy's beast of burden falling down, do not hasten by, but raise it."[4] And thou must see that to separate and reconcile men that are fighting is a much lighter thing than to lift up the fallen beast. And if we ought to help in raising our enemies' ass, much more our friends' souls: and most when the fall is more grievous; for not into mire do these fall, but into the fire of hell, not bearing the burden of their wrath. And thou, when thou seest thy brother lying under the load, and the devil standing by, and kindling the pile, thou runnest by, cruelly and unmercifully; a kind of thing not safe to do, even where brutes are concerned.

And whereas the Samaritan, seeing a wounded man, unknown, and not at all appertaining to him, both staid, and set him on a beast, and brought him home to the inn, and hired a physician, and gave some money, and promised more: thou, seeing one fallen not among thieves, but amongst a band of demons, and beset by anger; and this not in a wilderness, but in the midst of the forum;

---

[1] Job xxx. 25   [2] Eph. iv. 25.   [3] οἰκοτρίβων.

[4] Exod. xxiii. 5; Deut. xxii. 4. [The citation is made very freely from the LXX. The former passage was probably in the mind of the preacher.—R.]

not having to lay out money, nor to hire a beast, nor to bring him on a long way, but only to say some words:—art thou slow to do it? and holdest back, and hurriest by cruelly and unmercifully? And how thinkest thou, calling upon God, ever to find Him propitious?

15. But let me speak also to you, who publicly disgrace yourselves: to him who is acting despitefully, and doing wrong. Art tnou inflicting blows? tell me; and kicking, and biting? art thou become a wild boar, and a wild ass? and art thou not ashamed? dost thou not blush at thus being changed into a wild beast, and betraying thine own nobleness? For though thou be poor, thou art free; though thou be a working man, thou art a Christian.

Nay, for this very reason, that thou art poor, thou shouldest be quiet. For fightings belong to the rich, not to the poor; to the rich, who have many causes to force them to war. But thou, not having the pleasure of wealth, goest about gathering to thyself the evils of wealth, enmities, and strifes, and fightings; and takest thy brother by the throat, and goest about to strangle him, and throwest him down publicly in the sight of all men: and dost thou not think that thou art thyself rather disgraced, imitating the violent passions of the brutes; nay rather, becoming even worse than they? For they have all things in common; they herd one with another, and go about together: but we have nothing in common, but all in confusion: fightings, strifes, revilings, and enmities, and insults. And we neither reverence the heaven, unto which we are called all of us in common; nor the earth, which He hath left free to us all in common; nor our very nature; but wrath and the love of money sweeps all away.

Hast thou not seen him who owed the ten thousand talents, and then, after he was forgiven that debt, took his fellow-servant by the throat for an hundred pence, what great evils he underwent, and how he was delivered over to an endless punishment? Hast thou not trembled at the example? Hast thou no fear, lest thou too incur the same? For we likewise owe to our Lord many and great debts: nevertheless, He forbears, and suffers long, and neither urges us, as we do our fellow-servants, nor chokes and takes us by the throat; yet surely had he been minded to exact of us but the least part thereof, we had long ago perished.

16. Let us then, beloved, bearing these things in mind, be humbled, and feel thankful to those who are in debt to us. For they become to us, if we command ourselves, an occasion of obtaining most abundant pardon; and giving a little, we shall receive much. Why then exact with violence, it being meet, though the other were minded to pay, for thee of thine accord to excuse him, that thou mayest receive the whole of God? But now thou doest all things, and art violent, and contentious,[1] to have none of thy debts forgiven thee; and whilst thou art thinking to do despite unto thy neighbor, thou art thrusting the sword into thyself, so increasing thy punishment in hell: whereas if thou wilt show a little self-command here, thou makest thine own accounts easy. For indeed God therefore wills us to take the lead in that kind of bounty, that He may take occasion to repay us with increase.

As many therefore as stand indebted to thee, either for money, or for trespasses, let them all go free, and require of God the recompense of such *thy* magnanimity. For so long as they continue indebted to thee, thou canst not have God thy debtor. But if thou let them go free, thou wilt be able to detain thy God, and to require of Him the recompense of so great self-restraint in bountiful measure. For suppose a man had come up and seeing thee arresting thy debtor, had called upon thee to let him go free, and transfer to himself thy account with the other: he would not choose to be unfair[2] after such remission, seeing he had passed the whole demand to himself: how then shall God fail to repay us manifold, yea, ten thousand fold, when for His commandment's sake, if any be indebted to us, we urge no complaint against them, great or small, but let them go exempt from all liability? Let us not then think of the temporary pleasure that springs up in us by exacting of our debtors, but of the loss, rather, how great! which we shall thereby sustain hereafter, grievously injuring ourselves in the things which are eternal. Rising accordingly above all, let us forgive those who must give account to us, both their debts and their offenses; that we may make our own accounts prove indulgent, and that what we could not reach by all virtue besides, this we may obtain by not bearing malice against our neighbors; and thus enjoy the eternal blessings, by the grace and love towards man of our Lord Jesus Christ, to whom be glory and might now and always, even forever and ever. Amen.

---

[1] [ὥστε.]   [2] ἀγνωμονεῖν.

HOMILY XVI.

MATT. V. 17.

"Think not that I am come to destroy the Law or the Prophets."

WHY, who suspected this? or who accused Him, that He should make a defense against this charge? Since surely from what had gone before [1] no such suspicion was generated. For to command men to be meek, and gentle, and merciful, and pure in heart, and to strive for righteousness, indicated no such design, but rather altogether the contrary.

Wherefore then can He have said this? Not at random, nor vainly: but inasmuch as He was proceeding to ordain commandments greater than those of old, saying, "It was said to them of old time, Thou shalt not kill;[2] but I say unto you, Be not even angry;" and to mark out a way for a kind of divine and heavenly conversation;[3] in order that the strangeness thereof might not disturb the souls of the hearers, nor dispose them quite to mutiny against what He said, He used this means of setting them right beforehand.

For although they fulfilled not the law, yet nevertheless they were possessed with much conscientious regard to it; and whilst they were annulling it every day by their deeds, the letters thereof they would have remain unmoved, and that no one should add anything more to them. Or rather, they bore with their rulers adding thereto, not however for the better, but for the worse. For so they used to set aside the honor due to our parents by additions of their own, and very many others also of the matters enjoined them, they would free themselves of [4] by these unseasonable additions.

Therefore, since Christ in the first place was not of the sacredotal tribe, and next, the things which He was about to introduce were a sort of addition, not however lessening, but enhancing virtue; He knowing beforehand that both these circumstances would trouble them, before He wrote in their mind those wondrous laws, casts out that which was sure to be harboring there. And what was it that was harboring there, and making an obstacle?

2. They thought that He, thus speaking, did so with a view to the abrogation of the ancient institutions. This suspicion therefore He heals; nor here only doth He so, but elsewhere also again. Thus, since they accounted Him no less than an adversary of God, from this sort of reason, namely, His not keeping the sabbath; He, to heal such their suspicion, there also again sets forth His pleas, of which some indeed were proper to Himself; as when He saith, "My Father worketh, and I work;"[5] but some had in them much condescension, as when He brings forward the sheep lost on the sabbath day,[6] and points out that the law is disturbed for its preservation, and makes mention again of circumcision, as having this same effect.[7]

Wherefore we see also that He often speaks words somewhat beneath Him, to remove the semblance of His being an adversary of God.

For this cause He who had raised thousands of the dead with a word only, when He was calling Lazarus, added also a prayer; and then, lest this should make Him appear less than Him that begat Him, He, to correct this suspicion, added, "I said these things, because of the people which standeth by, that they may believe that thou hast sent me."[8] And neither doth He work all things as one who acted by His own power, that He might thoroughly correct their weakness; nor doth He all things with prayer, lest He should leave matter of evil suspicion to them that should follow, as though He were without strength or power: but He mingles the latter with the former, and those again with these. Neither doth He this indiscriminately, but with His own proper wisdom. For while He doeth the greater works authoritatively, in the less He looks up unto Heaven. Thus, when absolving sins, and revealing His secrets, and opening Paradise, and driving away devils, and cleansing lepers, and bridling death, and raising the dead by thousands, He did all by way of command: but when, what was much less than these, He

---

[1] [τῶν εἰρημένων.]
[2] [The text has also "Ye have heard that,' as in Matt. v. 22: the latter half is not a direct quotation.—R']
[3] [πολιτείας.]   ἐξέλνον.

[5] John v. 17.   [6] Matt. xii. 11.   [7] John vii. 23.
[8] John xi. 42. ["These things" does not occur in the New Testament passage, but is inserted here to complete the sense. Comp. R. V., "but because of the multitude which standeth around I said it, that they may believe that thou didst send me." —R.]

was causing many loaves to spring forth out of few, then He looked up to Heaven: signifying that not through weakness He doth this. For He who could do the greater with authority, how in the lesser could He need prayer? But as I was saying, He doeth this to silence their shamelessness. The same reckoning, then, I bid thee make of His words also, when thou hearest Him speak lowly things. For many in truth are the causes both for words and for actions of that cast: as, for instance, that He might not be supposed alien from God; His instructing and waiting on all men; His teaching humility; His being encompassed with flesh; the Jews' inability to hear all at once; His teaching us to utter no high word of ourselves. For this cause many times, having in His own person said much that is lowly of Himself, the great things He leaves to be said by others. Thus He Himself indeed, reasoning with the Jews, said, "Before Abraham was, I AM:"[1] but His disciple not thus, but, "In the beginning was the Word, and the Word was with God, and the Word was God."[2]

Again, that He Himself made Heaven, and earth, and sea, and all things visible and invisible, in His own person He nowhere expressly said: but His disciple, speaking plainly out, and suppressing nothing, affirms this once, twice, yea often: writing that "all things were made by Him;" and, "without Him was not one thing made;" and, He was in the world, and the world was made by Him."[3]

And why marvel, if others have said greater things of Him than He of Himself; since (what is more) in many cases, what He showed forth by His deeds, by His words He uttered not openly? Thus that it was Himself who made mankind He showed clearly even by that blind man; but when He was speaking of our formation at the beginning, He said not, "I made," but "He who made them, made them male and female."[4] Again, that He created the world and all things therein, He demonstrated by the fishes, by the wine, by the loaves, by the calm in the sea, by the sunbeam which He averted on the Cross; and by very many things besides: but in words He hath nowhere said this plainly, though His disciples are continually declaring it, both John, and Paul, and Peter.

For if they who night and day hear Him discourse, and see Him work marvels; to whom He explained many things in private, and gave so great power as even to raise the dead; whom He made so perfect, as to forsake all things for Him: if even they, after so great virtue and self-denial, had not strength to bear it all, before the supply of the Spirit; how could the people of the Jews, being both void of understanding, and far behind such excellency, and only by hazard present when He did or said anything, how could they have been persuaded but that He was alien from the God of all, unless he had practised such great condescension throughout?

For on this account we see that even when He was abrogating the sabbath, He did not as of set purpose bring in such *His* legislation, but He puts together many and various pleas of defense. Now if, when He was about to cause one commandment to cease, He used so much reserve in His language,[5] that He might not startle the hearers; much more, when adding to the law, entire as it was, another entire code of laws, did He require much management and attention, not to alarm those who were then hearing Him.

For this same cause, neither do we find Him teaching everywhere clearly concerning His own Godhead. For if His adding to the law was sure to perplex them so greatly, much more His declaring Himself God.

3. Wherefore many things are uttered by Him, far below His proper dignity, and here when He is about to proceed upon His addition to the law, He hath used abundance for correction beforehand. For neither was it once only that He said, "I do not abrogate the law," but He both repeated it again, and added another and a greater thing; in that, to the words, "Think not that I am come to destroy," He subjoined, "I am not come to destroy, but to fulfill."

Now this not only obstructs the obstinacy of the Jews, but stops also the mouths of those heretics,[6] who say that the old covenant is of the devil. For if Christ came to destroy his tyranny, how is this covenant not only not destroyed, but even fulfilled by Him? For He said not only, "I do not destroy it;" though this had been enough; but "I even fulfill it:" which are the words of one so far from opposing himself, as to be even establishing it.

And how, one may ask, did He not destroy it? in what way did He rather fulfill either the law or the prophets? The prophets He fulfilled, inasmuch as He confirmed by His actions all that had been said concerning Him; wherefore also the evangelist used to say in each case, "That it might be

---

[1] John viii. 58.   [2] John i. 1.
[3] John i. 3, 10.   [4] Matt. xix. 4.
[5] λόγων οἰκονομίᾳ.
[6] The Gnostic and Manichæan sects

fulfilled which was spoken by the prophet." Both when He was born,[1] and when the children sung that wondrous hymn to Him, and when He sat on the ass,[2] and in very many more instances He worked this same fulfillment: all which things must have been unfulfilled, if He had not come.

But the law He fulfilled, not in one way only, but in a second and third also. In one way, by transgressing none of the precepts of the law. For that He did fulfill it all, hear what He saith to John, "For thus it becometh us to fulfill all righteousness."[3] And to the Jews also He said, "Which of you convinceth me of sin."[4] And to His disciples again, "The prince of this world cometh, and findeth nothing in me."[5] And the prophet too from the first had said that "He did no sin."[6]

This then was one sense in which He fulfilled it. Another, that He did the same through us also; for this is the marvel, that He not only Himself fulfilled it, but He granted this to us likewise. Which thing Paul also declaring said, "Christ is the end of the law for righteousness to every one that believeth."[7] And he said also, that "He judged sin in the flesh, that the righteousness of the law might be fulfilled in us who walk not after the flesh."[8] And again, "Do we then make void the law through faith? God forbid! yea, we establish the law."[9] For since the law was laboring at this, to make man righteous, but had not power, He came and brought in the way of righteousness by faith, and so established that which the law desired: and what the law could not by letters, this He accomplished by faith. On this account He saith, "I am not come to destroy the law."

4. But if any one will inquire accurately, he will find also another, a third sense, in which this hath been done. Of what sort is it then? In the sense of that future code of laws, which He was about to deliver to them.

For His sayings were no repeal of the former, but a drawing out, and filling up of them. Thus, "not to kill," is not annulled by the saying, Be not angry, but rather is filled up and put in greater security: and so of all the others.

Wherefore, you see, as He had before unsuspectedly cast the seeds of this teaching; so at the time when from His comparison of the old and new commandments, He would be more distinctly suspected of placing them in opposition, He used His corrective before-hand. For in a covert way He had indeed already scattered those seeds, by what He had said. Thus, "Blessed are the poor," is the same as that we are not to be angry; and, "Blessed are the pure in heart," as not to "look upon a woman for lust;" and the "not laying up treasures on earth," harmonizes with, "Blessed are the merciful;" and "to mourn" also, "to be persecuted" and "reviled,"" coincide with "entering in at the strait gate;" and, "to hunger and thirst after righteousness," is nothing else than that which He saith afterwards, "Whatsoever ye would that men should do to you, do ye also to them." And having declared "the peace-maker blessed," He again almost said the same, when He gave command "to leave the gift," and hasten to reconciliation with him that was grieved, and about "agreeing with our adversary."

But there He set down the rewards of them that do right, here rather the punishments of them who neglect practice.[10] Wherefore as in that place He said, "The meek shall inherit earth;" so here, "He who calleth his brother fool, shall be in danger of hell-fire;" and there, "The pure in heart shall see God;" here, he is a complete adulterer who looks unchastely. And having there called "the peace-makers, sons of God;" here He alarms us from another quarter, saying, "Lest at any time the adversary deliver thee to the judge." Thus also, whereas in the former part He blesses them that mourn, and them that are persecuted; in the following, establishing the very same point, He threatens destruction to them that go not that way; for, "They that walk 'in the broad way,' saith He, 'make their end there.'" And, "Ye cannot serve God and mammon," seems to me the same with, "Blessed are the merciful," and, "those that hunger after righteousness."

But as I said, since He is going to say these things more clearly, and not only more clearly, but also to add again more than had been already said (for He no longer merely seeks a merciful man, but bids us give up even our coat; not simply a meek person, but to turn also the other cheek to him that would smite us): therefore He first takes away the apparent contradiction.

On this account, then, as I have already stated, He said this not once only, but once and again; in that to the words, "Think not that I am come to destroy," He added, "I am not come to destroy, but to fulfill."

"For verily I say unto you, Till Heaven

---

1 Matt. i. 22, 23.　2 Matt. xxi. 5-16.　3 Matt. iii. 15.
4 John viii. 46.　5 John xiv. 30.　6 Isa. liii. 9.
7 Rom. x. 4.　8 Rom. viii. 3, 4.　9 Rom. iii. 31.

10 [τῶν μὴ ποιούντων.]

and earth pass, one jot or one tittle shall in no wise pass from the law, till all come to pass." [1]

Now what He saith is like this: it cannot be that it should remain unaccomplished, but the very least thing therein must needs be fulfilled. Which thing He Himself performed, in that He completed [2] it with all exactness.

And here He signifies to us obscurely that the fashion of the whole world is also being changed. Nor did He set it down without purpose, but in order to arouse the hearer, and indicate, that He was with just cause introducing another discipline; if at least the very works of the creation are all to be transformed, and mankind is to be called to another country, and to a higher way of practising how to live. [3]

5. "Whosoever therefore shall break one of these least commandments, and shall teach men so, he shall be called least in the kingdom of Heaven." [4]

Thus, having rid Himself of the evil suspicion, and having stopped the mouths of them who would fain gainsay, then at length He proceeds to alarm, and sets down a heavy denunciation in support of the enactments He was entering on.

For as to His having said this in behalf not of the ancient laws, but of those which He was proceeding to enact, listen to what follows, "For I say unto you," saith he, "Except your righteousness shall exceed the righteousness of the Scribes and Pharisees, ye shall in no case enter into the kingdom of Heaven." [5]

For if He were threatening with regard to the ancient laws, how said He, "except it shall exceed?" since they who did just the same as those ancients, could not exceed them on the score of righteousness.

But of what kind was the required excess? Not to be angry, not even to look upon a woman unchastely.

For what cause then doth He call these commandments "least," though they were so great and high? Because He Himself was about to introduce the enactment of them; for as He humbled Himself, and speaks of Himself frequently with measure, so likewise of His own enactments, hereby again teaching us to be modest in everything. And besides, since there seemed to be some sus-

picion of novelty, He ordered His discourse for a while with reserve. [6]

But when thou hearest, "least in the kingdom of Heaven," surmise thou nothing but hell and torments. For He was used to mean by "the kingdom," not merely the enjoyment thereof, but also the time of the resurrection, and that awful coming. And how could it be reasonable, that while he who called his brother fool, and transgressed but one commandment, falls into hell; the breaker of them all, and instigator of others to the same, should be within the kingdom. This therefore is not what He means, but that such a one will be at that time *least*, that is, cast out, last. And he that is last will surely then fall into hell. For, being God, He foreknew the laxity of the many, He foreknew that some would think these sayings were merely hyperbolical, and would argue about the laws, and say, What, if any one call another a fool, is he punished? If one merely look on a woman, doth he become an adulterer? For this very cause He, destroying such insolence beforehand, hath set down the strongest denunciation against either sort, as well them who transgress, as them who lead on others so to do.

Knowing then His threat as we do, let us neither ourselves transgress, nor discourage such as are disposed to keep these things.

"But whosoever shall do and teach," saith He, "shall be called great."

For not to ourselves alone, should we be profitable, but to others also; since neither is the reward as great for him who guides himself aright, as for one who with himself adds also another. For as teaching without doing condemns the teacher (for "thou which teachest another," it is said, "teachest thou not thyself" [7]?) so doing but not guiding others, lessens our reward. One ought therefore to be chief in either work, and having first set one's self right, thus to proceed also to the care of the rest. For on this account He Himself hath set the doing before the teaching; to intimate that so most of all may one be able to teach, but in no other way. For one will be told, "Physician, heal thyself." [8] Since he who cannot teach himself, yet attempts to set others right, will have many to ridicule him. Or rather such a one will have no power to teach at all, his actions uttering their voice against him. But if he be complete in both respects, "he shall be called great in the kingdom of Heaven."

6. "For I say unto you, Except your righteousness shall exceed the righteousness

---

[1] Matt. v. 18. [R. V., "Till Heaven and earth pass away, one jot or one tittle shall in no wise pass away from the law, till all things be accomplished."—R.]
[2] ἀπαρτίσας.   [3] βίου παρασκευὴν ὑψηλοτέραν.
[4] Matt. v. 19.
[5] [Matt. v. 20. The citation is accurate ; the phrase "the righteousness" is supplied in English ; see R. V.—R.]

[6] ὑπεσταλμένως.   [7] Rom. ii. 21.   [8] Luke iv. 23.

of the Scribes and Pharisees, ye shall in no case enter into the kingdom of Heaven."[1]

Here by righteousness He means the whole of virtue; even as also discoursing of Job, He said, " He was a blameless man, righteous."[2] According to the same signification of the word, Paul also called that man " righteous " for whom, as he said, no law is even set. " For," saith he, " a law is not made for a righteous man."[3] And in many other places too one might find this name standing for virtue in general.

But observe, I pray thee, the increase of grace; in that He will have His newly-come disciples better than the teachers in the old covenant. For by " Scribes and Pharisees " here, He meant not merely the lawless, but the well-doers. For, were they not doing well, He would not have said they have a righteousness; neither would He have compared the unreal to the real.

And observe also here, how He commends the old law, by making a comparison between it and the other; which kind of thing implies it to be of the same tribe and kindred. For *more* and *less*, is in the same kind. He doth not, you see, find fault with the old law, but will have it made stricter. Whereas, had it been evil,[4] He would not have required more of it; He would not have made it more perfect, but would have cast it out.

And how one may say, if it be such, doth it not bring us into the Kingdom? It doth not now bring in them who live after the coming of Christ, favored as they are with more strength, and bound to strive for greater things: since as to its own foster-children, them it doth bring in one and all. Yea, for " many shall come," saith He, " from east and west, and shall lie down in the bosoms of Abraham, Isaac, and Jacob."[5] And Lazarus also receiving the great prize, is shown dwelling in Abraham's bosom. And all, as many as have shone forth with excellency in the old dispensation, shone by it, every one of them. And Christ Himself, had it been in anything evil or alien from Him, would not have fulfilled it all when He came. For if only to attract the Jews He was doing this, and not in order to prove it akin to the new law, and concurrent therewith; wherefore did He not also fulfill the laws and customs of the Gentiles, that He might attract the Gentiles also ?

So that from all considerations it is clear,

that not from any badness in itself doth it fail to bring us in, but because it is now the season of higher precepts.

And if it be more imperfect than the new, neither doth this imply it to be evil: since upon this principle the new law itself will be in the very same case. Because in truth our knowledge of this, when compared with that which is to come, is a sort of partial and imperfect. thing, and is done away on the coming of that other. " For when," saith He, " that which is perfect is come, then that which is in part shall be done away:"[6] even as it befell the old law through the new. Yet we are not to blame the new law for this, though that also gives place on our attaining unto the Kingdom: for " then," saith He, " that which is in part shall be done away:" but for all this we call it great.

Since then both the rewards thereof are greater, and the power given by the Spirit more abundant, in reason it requires our graces to be greater also. For it is no longer " a land that floweth with milk and honey," nor a comfortable[7] old age, nor many children, nor corn and wine, and flocks and herds: but Heaven, and the good things in the Heavens, and adoption and brotherhood with the Only-Begotten, and to partake of the inheritance and to be glorified and to reign with Him, and those unnumbered rewards. And as to our having received more abundant help, hear thou Paul, when he saith, " There is therefore no condemnation now to them which are in Christ Jesus, who walk not after the flesh, but after the Spirit:[8] for the law of the Spirit of life hath made me free from the law of sin and death."[9]

7. And now after threatening the transgressors, and setting great rewards for them that do right, and signifying that He justly requires of us something beyond the former measures; He from this point begins to legislate, not simply, but by way of comparison with the ancient ordinances, desiring to intimate these two things: first, that not as contending with the former, but rather in great harmony with them, He is making these enactments; next, that it was meet and very seasonable for Him to add thereto these second precepts.

And that this may be made yet clearer, let us hearken to the words of the Legislator.

What then doth He Himself say ?

" Ye have heard that it was said to them of old time, Thou shalt not kill."[10]

---

[1] Matt. v. 20.
[2] Job i. 1, LXX.   " That man was true, blameless, righteous, devout, refraining from every evil deed."
[3] 1 Tim. i. 9.
[4] There is MS. authority for reading " of an evil one."
[5] Matt. viii. 11.

[6] 1 Cor. xiii. 10.   [7] λιπαρόν.
[8] [This addition to Rom. viii. 1 (" who walk," etc.), now rejected by all critical editors, is not found in any patristic authority older than Chrysostom. The argument above shows how it was added from an assumed application to sanctification.—R.]
[9] Rom. viii. 1, 2.   [10] Matt. v. 21.

And yet it was Himself who gave those laws also, but so far He states them impersonally. For if on the one hand He had said, " Ye have heard that I said to them of old," the saying would have been hard to receive, and would have stood in the way of all the hearers. If again, on the other hand, after having said, " Ye have heard that it was said to them of old by my Father," He had added, " But I say," He would have seemed to be taking yet more on Himself.

Wherefore He hath simply stated it, making out thereby one point only; the proof that in fitting season He had come saying these things. For by the words, " It was said to them of old," He pointed out the length of the time, since they received this commandment. And this He did to shame the hearer, shrinking from the advance to the higher class of His commandments; as though a teacher should say to a child that was indolent, " Knowest thou not how long a time thou hast consumed in learning syllables?" This then He also covertly intimates by the expression, "them of old time," and thus for the future summons them on to the higher order of His instructions: as if He had said, " Ye are learning these lessons long enough, and you must henceforth press on to such as are higher than these."

And it is well that He doth not disturb the order of the commandments, but begins first with that which comes earlier, with which the law also began. Yea, for this too suits with one showing the harmony between them.

" But I say unto you, that whosoever is angry with his brother without a cause, shall be in danger of the judgment." [1]

Seest thou authority in perfection? Seest thou a bearing suited to a legislator? Why, which among prophets ever spake on this wise? which among righteous men? which among patriarchs? None; but, " Thus saith the Lord." But the Son not so. Because they were publishing their Master's commands, He His Father's. And when I say, " His Father's," I mean His own. " For mine," saith He, " are thine, and thine are mine." [2] And they had their fellow-servants to legislate for, He His own servants.

Let us now ask those who reject the law, " is, ' Be not angry ' contrary to ' Do no murder '? or is not the one commandment the completion and the development of the other?" Clearly the one is the fulfilling of the other, and that is greater on this very

account. Since he who is not stirred up to anger, will much more refrain from murder; and he who bridles wrath will much more keep his hands to himself. For wrath is the root of murder. And you see that He who cuts up the root will much more remove the branches; or rather, will not permit them so much as to shoot out at all. Not therefore to abolish the law did He make these enactments, but for the more complete observation of it. For with what design did the law enjoin these things? Was it not, that no one might slay his neighbor? It follows, that he who was opposing the law would have to enjoin murder. For to murder, were the contrary to doing no murder. But if He doth not suffer one even to be angry, the mind of the law is established by Him more completely. For he that studies to avoid murder will not refrain from it equally with him that hath put away even anger; this latter being further removed from the crime.

8. But that we may convict them in another way also, let us bring forward all their allegations. What then do they affirm? They assert that the God who made the world, who " makes His sun to rise on the evil and on the good, who sends the rain on the just and on the unjust," is in some sense an evil being. [3] But the more moderate (forsooth) among them, though declining this, yet while they affirm Him to be just, they deprive Him of being good. And some other one, who is not, nor made any of the things that are, they assign for a Father to Christ. And they say that he, who is not good, abides in his own, and preserves what are his own; but that He, that is good, seeks what are another's, and desires of a sudden to become a Saviour to them whose Creator He was not. [4] Seest thou the children of the devil, how they speak out of the fountain of their father, alienating the work of creation from God: while John cries out, " He came

---

[1] Matt. v. 22. [Chrysostom reads εικη̣ in this verse, and interprets accordingly ; see also Homily XVII. 2. The term is wanting in the two oldest MSS. of the Greek Testament, and in the Vulgate. Comp. R. V. *in loco.*—R.]
[2] John xvii. 10.

[3] Epiph. Hær. 41, sec. 1. " Cerdon [circ. A. D. 150] with others preached two first principles, and so in fact two Gods : the one good, and unknown to all : whom he also called the Father of Jesus : the other, the Demiurgus, or artificer, evil, and open to knowledge, who spake in the law, and appeared in the prophets, and hath often become visible." In this he agreed with the Oriental heretics generally. Marcion, his disciple, within a few years improved on him (Hær. 42, sec. 3), " saying, that there are three principles : one, that on high, unnamed, and unseen, which it pleases them to call the good God (this, however, was not the Creator of any of the things that are in the world) : another, a visible God, Creator and Artificer : and, in the third place, the devil. . . . . Now the Creator, and Artificer, and visible One, they say, is the God of the Jews, and is also the Judge." Cf. *ibid.* sec. 6 ; St. Aug. *de Hæres.* 22 ; Tertull. contr. Marc. i. 10 [*Ante-Nicene Fathers,* vol. III. p. 278]; St. Iren. i. 28, 29 [*Ante-Nicene Fathers,* vol. I. pp. 352, 353].
[4] St. Iren. v. 2. " Vain also are those who say that the Lord came to what was another's, as though coveting it, in order to present that man who had been made by another, to that God, who had neither made nor ordered him, yea, rather, who had deserted him from men's first original formation. His coming, therefore, is not just, coming as He did by their account to what was none of His." [*Ibid.* pp. 527, 528.] In Lib. iii. 11, he specifies Marcion as teaching this doctrine.

unto His own," and, "The world was made by Him?"[1]

In the next place, they criticise the law in the old covenant, which bids put out "an eye for an eye,"and "a tooth for a tooth;"[2] and straightway they insult and say, "Why, how can He be good who speaks so?"

What then do we say in answer to this? That it is the highest kind of philanthropy. For He made this law, not that we might strike out one another's eyes, but that fear of suffering by others might restrain us from doing any such thing to them. As therefore He threatened the Ninevites with overthrow, not that He might destroy them, (for had that been His will, He ought to have been silent), but that He might by fear make them better, and so quiet His wrath: so also hath He appointed a punishment for those who wantonly assail the eyes of others, that if good principle dispose them not to refrain from such cruelty, fear may restrain them from injuring their neighbors' sight.

And if this be cruelty, it is cruelty also for the murderer to be restrained, and the adulterer checked. But these are the sayings of senseless men, and of those that are mad to the extreme of madness. For I, so far from saying that this comes of cruelty, should say, that the contrary to this would be unlawful, according to men's reckoning. And whereas, thou sayest, "Because He commanded to pluck out "an eye for an eye," therefore He is cruel;" I say, that if He had not given this commandment, then He would have seemed, in the judgment of most men, to be that which thou sayest He is.

For let us suppose that this law had been altogether done away, and that no one feared the punishment ensuing thereupon, but that license had been given to all the wicked to follow their own disposition in all security, to adulterers, and to murderers,[3] to perjured persons, and to parricides; would not all things have been turned upside down? would not cities, market-places, and houses, sea and land, and the whole world, have been filled with unnumbered pollutions and murders? Every one sees it. For if, when there are

laws, and fear, and threatening, our evil dispositions are hardly checked; were even this security taken away, what is there to prevent men's choosing vice? and what degree of mischief would not then come revelling upon the whole of human life?

The rather, since cruelty lies not only in allowing the bad to do what they will, but in another thing too quite as much; to overlook, and leave uncared for, him who hath done no wrong, but who is without cause or reason suffering ill. For tell me; were any one to gather together wicked men from all quarters, and arm them with swords, and bid them go about the whole city, and massacre all that came in their way, could there be anything more like a wild beast than he? And what if some other should bind, and confine with the utmost strictness those whom that man had armed, and should snatch from those lawless hands them, who were on the point of being butchered; could anything be greater humanity than this?

Now then, I bid thee transfer these examples to the law likewise; for He that commands to pluck out "an eye for an eye," hath laid the fear as a kind of strong chain upon the souls of the bad, and so resembles him, who detains those assassins in prison; whereas he who appoints no punishment for them, doth all but arm them by such security, and acts the part of that other, who was putting the swords in their hands, and letting them loose over the whole city.

Seest thou not, how the commandments, so far from coming of cruelty, come rather of abounding mercy? And if on account of these thou callest the Lawgiver grievous, and hard to bear with; tell me which sort of command is the more toilsome and grievous, "Do no murder," or, "Be not even angry"? Which is more in extreme, he who exacts a penalty for murder, or for mere anger? He who subjects the adulterer to vengeance after the fact, or he who enjoins a penalty even for the very desire, and that penalty everlasting? See ye not how their reasoning comes round to the very contrary? how the God of the old covenant, whom they call cruel, will be found mild and meek: and He of the new, whom they acknowledged to be good, will be hard and grievous, according to their madness? Whereas we say, that there is but one and the same Legislator of either covenant, who dispensed all meetly, and adapted to the difference of the times the difference between the two systems of law. Therefore neither are the first commandments cruel, nor the second hard and grievous, but all of one and the same providential care.

---

[1] John i. 11, 10.

[2] Tertull. adv. Marcion. ii. 18 ; Exod. xxi. 24. "Which of the good rules of the law should I rather defend, than those which heresy hath craved for her own purposes? As the rule of retaliation, requiring eye for eye, tooth for tooth, and bruise for bruise. There is no tinge here of any permission for repaying an injury in kind, but the whole drift of it is to restrain violence. That is, because that most stubborn and faithless people would count it hard or even inconceivable to await God's redress, which the prophet was afterwards to proclaim, in the words, 'Vengeance is mine, I will repay, saith the Lord;' the commission of wrong during the interval was to be in a manner smothered by the fear of immediate retribution." [*Ante-Nicene Fathers*, vol. III. p. 311.] St. Augustin (contr. Adim. c. 8), says the same in reply to the Manichæans.

[3] ["And to thieves" should be inserted here. The omission was probably accidental.—R.]

For that He Himself gave the old covenant also, hear the affirmation of the prophet, or rather (so we must speak), of Him who is both the one and the other: "I will make a covenant with you, not according to the covenant which I made with your fathers." [1]

But if he receive not this, who is diseased with the Manichæan doctrines,[2] let him hear Paul saying the very same in another place, "For Abraham had two sons, one by the bondmaid, and another by the freewoman; and these are two covenants."[3] As therefore in that case the wives are different, the husband the same; so here too the covenants are two, the Lawgiver one.

And to prove to thee that it was of one and the same mildness; in the one He saith, "An eye for an eye," but in this other,

"If one smite thee on thy right cheek, turn to him the other also."[4]

For as in that case He checks him that doth the wrong with the fear of this suffering, even so also in this. "How so," it may be said, "when He bids turn to him the other cheek also?" Nay, what of that? Since not to take away his fear did He enjoin this, but as charging yourself to allow him to take his fill entirely. Neither did He say, that the other continues unpunished, but, "do not thou punish;" at once both enhancing the fear of him that smiteth, if he persist, and comforting him who is smitten.

9. But these things we have said, as one might say them incidentally, concerning all the commandments. Now we must go on to that which is before us, and keep to the thread of what had been affirmed. "He that is angry with his brother without a cause shall be in danger of the judgment:" so He speaks. Thus He hath not altogether taken the thing away: first, because it is not possible, being a man, to be freed from passions: we may indeed get the dominion over them, but to be altogether without them is out of the question.

Next, because this passion is even useful, if we know how to use it at the suitable time.[5] See, for instance, what great good was wrought by that anger of Paul, which he felt against the Corinthians, on that well-known occasion; and how, as it delivered them from a grievous pest, so by the same means again he recovered the people of the Galatians likewise, which had fallen aside; and others too beside these.

What then is the proper time for anger?

When we are not avenging ourselves, but checking others in their lawless freaks, or forcing them to attend in their negligence.

And what is the unsuitable time? When we do so as avenging ourselves: which Paul also forbidding, said "Avenge not yourselves, dearly beloved, but rather give place unto wrath."[6] When we are contending for riches: yea, for this hath he also taken away, where he saith, "Why do ye not rather take wrong? why do ye not rather suffer yourselves to be defrauded?"[7] For as this last sort is superfluous, so is the first necessary and profitable. But most men do the contrary; becoming like wild beasts when they are injured themselves, but remiss and cowardly when they see despite done to another: both which are just opposite to the laws of the Gospel.

Being angry then is not a transgression, but being so unseasonably. For this cause the prophet also said, "Be ye angry, and sin not."[8]

10. And whosoever shall say to his brother, Raca, shall be in danger of the council."

By the council in this place He means the tribunal of the Hebrews: and He hath mentioned this now, on purpose that He might not seem everywhere to play the stranger and innovator.

But this word, "Raca," is not an expression of a great insolence, but rather of some contempt and slight on the part of the speaker. For as we, giving orders either to our servants, or to any very inferior person, say, "Away with thee; you here, tell such an one:"[9] so they who make use of the Syrians' language say, "Raca," putting that word in stead of "thou." But God, the lover of man, roots up even the least faults, commanding us to behave to one another in seemly manner, and with due respect; and this with a view of destroying hereby also the greater.

"But whosoever shall say, Thou fool, shall be in danger of hell fire."[10]

To many this commandment hath appeared grievous and galling, if for a mere word we are really to pay so great a penalty. And some even say that it was spoken rather hyperbolically. But I fear lest, when we have deceived ourselves with words here, we may in deeds there suffer that extreme punishment.

---

1 Jer. xxxi. 31, 32.
2 Because they denied the authority of the Old Testament, but received the New, including St. Paul's Epistles.
3 Gal. iv. 22.   4 Matt. v. 39.
5 See Bp. Butler's Sermon on Resentment.

6 Rom. xii. 19.   7 1 Cor. vi. 7.
8 Ps. iv. 5, LXX., comp. Eph. iv. 26. "Stand in awe, and sin not," in our version. Another part of the same Hebrew verb is, however, rendered "rage" in our translation: 2 Kings xix. 27, 28; Is. xxxvii. 28, 29. [The R. V. has the marginal rendering, "Be ye angry," in Ps. iv. 5. In Eph. iv. 26, the LXX. is accurately cited.—R.]
9 [The original repeats the emphatic and contemptuous σύ.—R.]
10 [εἰς τὴν γέενναν τοῦ πυρός. Comp. R. V. in loco.—R.]

For wherefore, tell me, doth the commandment seem overburdensome? Knowest thou not that most punishments and most sins have their beginning from words? Yea, for by words are blasphemies, and denials are by words, and revilings, and reproaches, and perjuries, and bearing false witness.[1] Regard not then its being a mere word, but whether it have not much danger, this do thou inquire. Art thou ignorant that in the season of enmity, when wrath is inflamed, and the soul kindled, even the least thing appears great, and what is not very reproachful is counted intolerable? And often these little things have given birth even to murder, and overthrown whole cities. For just as where friendship is, even grievous things are light, so where enmity lies beneath, very trifles appear intolerable. And however simply a word be spoken, it is surmised to have been spoken with an evil meaning. And as in fire: if there be but a small spark, though thousands of planks lie by, it doth not easily lay hold of them; but if the flame have waxed strong and high, it readily seizes not planks only, but stones, and all materials that fall in its way; and by what things it is usually quenched, by the same it is kindled the more (for some say that at such a time not only wood and tow, and the other combustibles, but even water darted forth upon it doth but fan its power the more); so is it also with anger; whatever any one may say, becomes food in a moment for this evil conflagration. All which kind of evils Christ checking beforehand, had condemned first him that is angry without a cause to the judgment, (this being the very reason why He said, " He that is angry shall be in danger of the judgment ") ; then him that saith " Raca," to the council. But as yet these are no great things; for the punishments are here. Therefore for him who calleth "fool" He hath added the fire of hell, now for the first time mentioning the name of hell. For having before discoursed much of the kingdom, not until then did He mention this; implying, that the former comes of His own love and indulgence towards man, this latter of our negligence.

11. And see how He proceeds by little and little in His punishments, all but excusing Himself unto thee, and signifying that His desire indeed is to threaten nothing of the kind, but that we drag Him on to such denunciations. For observe: " I bade thee," saith He, " not be angry for nought, because thou art in danger of the judgment. Thou hast despised the former commandment: see what anger hath produced; it hath led thee on straightway to insult, for thou hast called thy brother 'Raca.' Again, I set another punishment, ' the council.' If thou overlook even this, and proceed to that which is more grievous, I visit thee no longer with these finite punishments, but with the undying penalty of hell, lest after this thou shouldest break forth[2] even to murder." For there is nothing, nothing in the world more intolerable than insolence; it is what hath very great power[3] to sting a man's soul. But when the word too which is spoken is in itself more wounding than the insolence, the blaze becomes twice as great. Think it not then a light thing to call another " fool." For when of that which separates us from the brutes, and by which especially we are human beings, namely, the mind and the understanding,—when of this thou hast robbed thy brother, thou hast deprived him of all his nobleness.

Let us not then regard the words merely, but realizing the things themselves, and his feeling, let us consider how great a wound is made by this word, and unto how much evil it proceeds. For this cause Paul likewise cast out of the kingdom not only " the adulterous" and " the effeminate," but " the revilers "[4] also. And with great reason: for the insolent man mars all the beauty of charity, and casts upon his neighbor unnumbered ills, and works up lasting enmities, and tears asunder the members of Christ, and is daily driving away that peace which God so desires: giving much vantage ground unto the devil by his injurious ways, and making him the stronger. Therefore Christ Himself, cutting out the sinews of the devil's power, brought in this law.

For indeed He makes much account of love: this being above all things the mother of every good, and the badge of His disciples, and the bond which holds together our whole condition. With reason therefore doth He remove with great earnestness the roots and the sources of that hatred which utterly spoils it.

Think not therefore that these sayings are in any wise hyperbolical, but consider the good done by them, and admire the mildness of these laws. For there is nothing for which God takes so much pains, as this; that we should be united and knit together one with another. Therefore both in His own person, and by His disciples, as well those in the

---

[1] [One MS. adds here καὶ ἀναιρεῖν ("and murdering"). The words are bracketed in Field's Greek text; while the Latin version has *ipsa homicidia*.--R.]

[2] ἀποπηδήσῃς.
[3] ὁ μάλιστα δύναται δάκνειν.
[4] 1 Cor. vi. 9, 10.

Old, as in the New Testament, He makes so much account of this commandment; and is a severe avenger and punisher of those who despise the duty. For in truth nothing so effectually gives entrance and root to all wickedness, as the taking away of love. Wherefore He also said, "When iniquity abounds, the love of the many shall wax cold."[1] Thus Cain became his brother's murderer; thus Esau; thus Joseph's brethren; thus our unnumbered crimes have come revelling in, this bond being dissevered. You see why He Himself also roots out whatever things injure this, on every side, with great exactness.

12. Neither doth He stop at those precepts only which have been mentioned, but adds also others more than those: whereby He signifies how much account He makes thereof. Namely, having threatened by "the council," by "the judgment," and by "hell," He added other sayings again in harmony with the former, saying thus:

"If thou bring thy gift to the altar, and there rememberest that thy brother hath ought against thee; leave there thy gift before the altar, and go away;[2] first be reconciled to thy brother, and then come and offer thy gift."[3]

O goodness! O exceeding love to man! He makes no account of the honor due unto Himself, for the sake of our love towards our neighbor; implying that not at all from any enmity, nor out of any desire to punish, had He uttered those former threatenings, but out of very tender affection. For what can be milder than these sayings? "Let my service," saith he, "be interrupted, that thy love may continue; since this also is a sacrifice, thy being reconciled to thy brother." Yea, for this cause He said not, "after the offering," or "before the offering;" but, while the very gift lies there, and when the sacrifice is already beginning, He sends thee to be reconciled to thy brother; and neither after removing that which lies before us,[4] nor before presenting the gift, but while it lies in the midst, He bids thee hasten thither.

With what motive then doth He command so to do, and wherefore? These two ends, as it appears to me, He is hereby shadowing out and providing for. First, as I have said, His will is to point out that He highly values charity,[5] and considers it to be the greatest sacrifice: and that without it He doth not receive even that other; next, He is imposing such a necessity of reconciliation, as admits of no excuse. For whoso hath been charged not to offer before he be reconciled, will hasten, if not for love of his neighbor, yet, that this may not lie unconsecrated,[6] to run unto him who hath been grieved, and do away the enmity. For this cause He hath also expressed it all most significantly, to alarm and thoroughly to awaken him. Thus, when He had said, "Leave thy gift," He stayed not at this, but added, "before the altar" (by the very place again causing him to shudder); "and go away." And He said not merely, "Go away," but He added, "first, and then come and offer thy gift." By all these things making it manifest, that this table receives not them that are at enmity with each other.

Let the initiated hear this, as many as draw nigh in enmity: and let the uninitiated hear too: yea, for the saying hath some relation to them also. For they too offer a gift and a sacrifice: prayer, I mean, and almsgiving. For as to this also being a sacrifice, hear what the prophet saith: "A sacrifice of praise will glorify me;"[7] and again, "Sacrifice to God a sacrifice of praise;"[8] and, "The lifting up of mine hands is an evening sacrifice."[9] So that if it be but a prayer, which thou art offering in such a frame of mind, it were better to leave thy prayer, and become reconciled to thy brother, and then to offer thy prayer.

For to this end were all things done: to this end even God became man, and took order for all those works, that He might set us at one.

And whereas in this place He is sending the wrong doer to the sufferer, in His prayer He leads the sufferer to the wrong doer, and reconciles them. For as there He saith, "Forgive men their debts;" so here, "If he hath ought against thee, go thy way unto him."

Or rather, even here too He seems to me to be sending the injured person: and for some such reason He said not, "Reconcile thyself to thy brother," but, "Be thou rec-

---

[1] Matt. xxiv. 12. ["Shall be multiplied" is a more exact rendering of the verb in the first clause. Comp. R. V.—R.]

[2] ἀπελθε, St. Chrys. ὕπαγε, rec. text. [There is no MSS. authority for the former reading in the New Testament passage, but the authorities for the text of the Homilies are divided between ἀπελθε and ἀπελθών.—R.]

[3] Matt. v. 23, 24.

[4] συνελθόντα τὰ προκείμενα. Mr. Field translates this, "quickly doing the work in hand:" alleging that the word συναιρεῖν cannot well stand for "removing." But its strict meaning seems to be "to pack up," or "put into a small compass." So Odyss. xx. 95. χλαῖναν μὲν συνελὼν καὶ κώεα, τοῖσιν ἔνευδεν. And this meaning suits well enough with the word προκείμενα, taken in its liturgical sense. [The technical sense of the verb is "to contract," and the context favors Field's view. The command was neither "after hastening through the service (Latin, nec propere confecto sacrificio) nor before beginning it."—R.]

[5] [τὴν ἀγάπην, properly rendered "love" in the next sentence. —R.]

[6] ἀτελεστον.

[7] Ps. l. 23.

[8] Ps. l. 14.

[9] Ps. cxli. 2.

onciled." And while the saying seems to pertain to the aggressor, the whole of it really pertains to him that is aggrieved. Thus, "If thou art reconciled to him," saith Christ, "through thy love to him thou wilt have me also propitious, and wilt be able to offer thy sacrifice with great confidence. But if thou art still irritated, consider that even I readily command that which is mine to be lightly esteemed, that ye may become friends; and let these thoughts be soothing to thine anger."

And He said not, "When thou hast suffered any of the greater wrongs, then be reconciled; but, "Though it be some trifle that he hath against thee." And He added not, "Whether justly or unjustly; but merely, "If he hath ought against thee." For though it be justly, not even in that case oughtest thou to protract the enmity; since Christ also was justly angered with us, yet nevertheless He gave Himself for us to be slain, "not imputing those trespasses." [1]

For this cause Paul also, when urging us in another way to reconciliation, said, "Let not the sun go down upon your wrath." [2] For much as Christ by this argument of the sacrifice, so there Paul by that of the day, is urging us on to the self-same point. Because in truth he fears the night, lest it overtake him that is smitten alone, and make the wound greater. For whereas in the day there are many to distract, and draw him off; in the night, when he is alone, and is thinking it over by himself, the waves swell, and the storm becomes greater. Therefore Paul, you see, to prevent this, would fain commit him to the night already reconciled, that the devil may after that have no opportunity, from his solitude, to rekindle the furnace of his wrath, and make it fiercer. Thus also Christ permits not, though it be ever so little delay, lest, the sacrifice being accomplished, such an one become more remiss, procrastinating from day to day: for He knows that the case requires very speedy treatment. And as a skillful physician exhibits not only the preventives of our diseases, but their correctives also, even so doth He likewise. Thus, to forbid our calling "fool," is a preventive of enmity; but to command reconciliation is a means of removing the diseases that ensue on the enmity.

And mark how both commands are set forth with earnestness. For as in the former case He threatened hell, so here He receives not the gift before the reconciliation, indicating great displeasure, and by all these

methods destroying both the root and the produce.

And first of all He saith, "Be not angry;" and after that, "revile not." For indeed both these are augmented, the one by the other: from enmity is reviling, from reviling enmity. On this account then He heals now the root, and now the fruit; hindering indeed the evil from ever springing up in the first instance: but if perchance it may have sprouted up and borne its most evil fruit, then by all means He burns it down the more.

13. Therefore, you see, having mentioned, first the judgment, then the council, then hell, and having spoken of His own sacrifice, He adds other topics again, thus speaking: "Agree with thine adversary quickly, whilst thou art in the way with him." [3]

That is, that thou mayest not say, "What then, if I am injured;" "what if I am plundered, and dragged too before the tribunal?" even this occasion and excuse He hath taken away: for He commands us not even so to be at enmity. Then, since this injunction was great, He draws His advice from the things present, which are wont to restrain the grosser sort more than the future. "Why, what sayest thou?" saith He. "That thine adversary is stronger, and doeth thee wrong? Of course then he will wrong thee more, if thou do not make it up, but art forced to go into court. For in the former case, by giving up some money, thou wilt keep thy person free; but when thou art come under the sentence of the judge, thou wilt both be bound, and pay the utmost penalty. But if thou avoid the contest there, thou wilt reap two good results: first, not having to suffer anything painful; and secondly, that the good done will be thereafter thine own doing, and no longer the effect of compulsion on his part. But if thou wilt not be ruled by these sayings, thou wrongest not him, so much as thyself."

And see here also how He hastens him; for having said, "Agree with thine adversary," He added, "quickly;" and He was not satisfied with this, but even of this quickness He hath required a further increase, saying, "Whilst thou art in the way with him;" pressing and hastening him hereby with great earnestness. For nothing doth so much turn our life upside down, as delay and procrastination in the performance of our good works. Nay, this hath often caused us to lose all. Therefore, as Paul for his part saith, "Before the sun set, do away the enmity;" and as He Himself had said above,

---

"Before the offering is completed, be reconciled;" so He saith in this place also, "Quickly, whilst thou art in the way with him," before thou art come to the doors of the court; before thou standest at the bar, and art come to be thenceforth under the sway of him that judgeth. Since, before entering in, thou hast all in thine own control; but if thou set thy foot on that threshold, thou wilt not by ever so earnest efforts be able to arrange thy matters at thy will, having come under the constraint of another.

But what is it "to agree?" He means either, consent rather to suffer wrong?" or, "so plead the cause, as if thou wert in the place of the other;" that thou mayest not corrupt justice by self-love, but rather, deliberating on another's cause as thine own, mayest so proceed to deliver thy vote in this matter. And if this be a great thing, marvel not; since with this view did He set forth all those His blessings, that having beforehand smoothed and prepared the hearer's soul, he might render it apter to receive all His enactments.

Now some say that He obscurely signifies the devil himself, under the name of the adversary; and bids us have nothing of his, (for this, they say, is to "agree" with him): no compromise being possible after our departure hence, nor anything awaiting us, but that punishment, from which no prayers can deliver. But to me He seems to be speaking of the judges in this world, and of the way to the court of justice, and of this prison.

For after he had abashed men by higher things, and things future, he alarms them also by such as are in this life. Which thing Paul also doth, using both the future and the present to sway his hearer: as when, deterring from wickedness, he points out to him that is inclined to evil, the ruler armed: thus saying, "But if thou do that which is evil, be afraid; for he beareth not the sword in vain; for he is a minister of God."[1] And again, enjoining us to be subject unto him, he sets forth not the fear of God only, but the threatening also of the other party, and his watchful care. "For ye must needs be subject, not only for wrath, but also for conscience sake."[2] Because the more irrational, as I have already said, are wont to be sooner corrected by these things, things which appear and are at hand. Wherefore Christ also made mention, not of hell only, but also of a court of justice, and of being dragged thither, and of the prison, and of all the suffering there; by all these means destroying the

roots of murder. For he who neither reviles, nor goes to law, nor prolongs enmity, how will he ever commit murder? So that from hence also it is evident, that in the advantage of our neighbor stands our own advantage. For he that agrees with his adversary, will benefit himself much more; becoming free, by his own act, from courts of law, and prisons, and the wretchedness that is there.

14. Let us then be obedient to His sayings; let us not oppose ourselves, nor be contentious; for first of all, even antecedently to their rewards, these injunctions have their pleasure and profit in themselves. And if to the more part they seem to be burdensome, and the trouble which they cause, great; have it in thy mind that thou art doing it for Christ's sake, and the pain will be pleasant. For if we maintain this way of reckoning at all times, we shall experience nothing burdensome, but great will be the pleasure we reap from every quarter; for our toil will no longer seem toil, but by how much it is enhanced, so much the sweeter and pleasanter doth it grow.

When therefore the custom of evil things, and the desire of wealth, keep on bewitching thee; do thou war against them with that mode of thinking which tells us, "Great is the reward we shall receive, for despising the pleasure which is but for a season;" and say to thy soul; "Art thou quite dejected because I defraud thee of pleasure? Nay, be of good cheer, for I am introducing thee into Heaven. Thou doest it not for man's sake, but for God's. Be patient therefore a little while, and thou shalt see how great is the gain. Endure for the present life, and thou shalt receive an unspeakable confidence." For if we would thus discourse with our own soul, and not only consider that which is burdensome in virtue, but take account also of the crown that comes thereof, we shall quickly withdraw it from all wickedness.

For if the devil, holding out pleasure for a season, but pain for ever, is yet strong, and prevails; seeing our case is just the reverse in these matters, the labor temporary, the pleasure and profit immortal, what plea shall we have, if we follow not virtue after so great encouragement? Why, the object of our labors is enough to set against all, and our clear persuasion that for God's sake we are enduring all this. For if one having the king his debtor, thinks he hath sufficient security for all his life; consider how great will he be, who hath made the Gracious and Everlasting God a debtor to himself, for good deeds both small and great. Do not then allege to me labors and sweats; for not by the hope only

---

[1] Rom. xiii. 4.   [2] Rom. v. 5.

of the things to come, but in another way also, God hath made virtue easy, assisting us everywhere, and putting His hand to our work. And if thou wilt only contribute a little zeal, everything else follows. For to this end He will have thee too to labor a little, even that the victory may be thine also. And just as a king would have his own son present indeed in the array; he would have him shoot with the bow,[1] and show himself, that the trophy may be reckoned his, while he achieves it all Himself: even so doth God in our war against the devil: He requires of thee one thing alone, that thou show forth a sincere hatred against that foe. And if thou contribute this to Him, He by Himself brings all the war to an end. Though thou burn with anger, with desire of riches, with any tyrannical passion whatever; if He see thee only stripping thyself and prepared against it, He comes quickly to thee, and makes all things easy, and sets thee above the flame, as He did those children of old in the Babylonian furnace: for they too carried in with them nought but their good will.

In order then that we also may extinguish all the furnace of disordered pleasure here, and so escape the hell that is there, let these each day be our counsels, our cares, and our practice, drawing towards us the favor of God, both by our full purpose concerning good works, and by our frequent prayers.

For thus even those things which appear insupportable now, will be most easy, and light, and lovely. Because, so long as we are in our passions, we think virtue rugged and morose and arduous, vice desirable and most pleasing; but if we would stand off from these but a little, then both vice will appear abominable and unsightly, and virtue easy, mild, and much to be desired. And this you may learn plainly from those who have done well. Hear, for instance, how of those passions Paul is ashamed, even after his deliverance from them, saying, "For what fruit had ye then in those things, whereof ye are now ashamed?"[2] But virtue, even after his labor, he affirms to be light, calling[3] the laboriousness of our affliction momentary and "light," and rejoicing in his sufferings, and glorying in his tribulations, and taking a pride in the marks wherewith he had been branded for Christ's sake.

In order then that we too may establish ourselves in this habit, let us order ourselves each day by what hath been said, and "forgetting those things which are behind, and reaching forth unto those things which are before, let us press on towards the prize of the high calling:"[4] unto which God grant that we may all attain, by the grace and love towards man of our Lord Jesus Christ, to whom be glory and power for ever and ever. Amen.

---

[1] [This clause is not found in the Greek text of Field, nor noticed in the critical notes. The Latin version has *jacula vibrare*, and was probably inadvertently followed by the translator.—R.]

[2] Rom. vi. 21.
[3] 2 Cor. iv. 17, xii. 10; Rom. v. 3; Gal. vi. 17; Col. i. 24.
[4] Phil. iii. 13, 14.

HOMILY XVII.

MATT. V. 27, 28.

"Ye have heard that it was said to them of old time,[1] Thou shalt not commit adultery; but I say unto you, that every one who looketh upon a woman to lust after her, hath committed adultery with her already in his heart."

HAVING now finished the former commandment, and having extended it unto the height of self-denial, He, advancing in course and order, proceeds accordingly unto the second, herein too obeying the law.

"And yet," it may be said, "this is not the second, but the third; for neither is the first, "Thou shalt not kill." but "The Lord thy God is one Lord."[2]

Wherefore it is worth inquiring too, why He did not begin with that. Why was it then? Because, had He begun from thence, He must have enlarged it also, and have brought in Himself together with His Father.[3]

---

[1] [The phrase "to them of old time" (τοῖς ἀρχαίοις) is not found in the oldest MSS. of the New Testament, in Matt. v. 27. It would be readily inserted from similar passages.—R.]

[2] Deut. vi. 4. [Comp. Mark xii. 29, and the renderings of the R. V. text and margin in both passages.—R.]
[3] [ἑαυτὸν συνεισαγαγεῖν.]

But it was not as yet time to teach any such thing about Himself.

And besides, He was for a while practising His moral doctrine only, being minded from this first, and from His miracles, to convince the hearers that He was the Son of God. Now, if He had said at once, before He had spoken or done anything, "Ye have heard that it was said to them of old time, "I am the Lord thy God, and there is none other but me," but I say unto you, Worship me even as Him; this would have made all regard Him as a madman. For if, even after His teaching, and His so great miracles, while not even yet was He saying this openly, they called Him possessed with a devil;[1] had He before all these attempted to say any such thing, what would they not have said? what would they not have thought?

But by keeping back at the proper season His teaching on these subjects, He was causing that the doctrine should be acceptable to the many. Wherefore now He passed it by quickly, but when He had everywhere established it by His miracles, and by His most excellent teaching, He afterwards unveiled it in words also.

For the present, however, by the manifestation of His miracles, and by the very manner of His teaching, He unfolds it on occasion, gradually and quietly. For His enacting such laws, and such corrections of laws, with authority, would lead on the attentive and understanding hearer, by little and little, unto the word of His doctrine. For it is said, "they were astonished at Him, because He taught not as their Scribes."[2]

2. For beginning from those passions, which most belong to our whole race, anger, I mean, and desire (for it is these chiefly that bear absolute sway within us, and are more natural than the rest); He with great authority, even such as became a legislator, both corrected them, and reduced them to order with all strictness. For He said not that the adulterer merely is punished; but what He had done with respect to the murderer, this He doth here also, punishing even the unchaste look: to teach thee wherein lies what He had more than the scribes. Accordingly, He saith, "He that looketh upon a woman to lust after her hath already committed adultery with her:" that is, he who makes it his business to be curious about bright forms, and to hunt for elegant features, and to feast his soul with the sight, and to fasten his eyes on fair countenances.

For He came to set free from all evil deeds not the body only, but the soul too before the body. Thus, because in the heart we receive the grace of the Spirit, He cleanses it out first.

"And how," one may say, "is it possible to be freed from desire?" I answer, first, if we were willing, even this might be deadened, and remain inactive.

In the next place, He doth not here take away desire absolutely, but that desire which springs up in men from sight. For he that is curious to behold fair countenances, is himself chiefly the enkindler of the furnace of that passion, and makes his own soul a captive, and soon proceeds also to the act.

Thus we see why He said not, "whosoever shall lust to commit adultery," but, "whosoever shall look to lust." And in the case of anger He laid down a certain distinction, saying, "without a cause," and "for nought;" but here not so; rather once for all He took away the desire. Yet surely both are naturally implanted, and both are set in us for our profit; both anger, and desire: the one that we may chastise the evil, and correct those who walk disorderly; the other that we may have children, and that our race may be recruited by such successions.

Why then did He not make a distinction here also? Nay, very great is the distinction which, if thou attend, thou wilt see here also included. For He said not simply, "whosoever shall desire," since it is possible for one to desire even when sitting in the mountains; but, "Whosoever shall look to lust;" that is to say, he who gathers in lust unto himself; he who, when nothing compels him, brings in the wild beast upon his thoughts when they are calm. For this comes no longer of nature, but of self-indulgence. This even the ancient Scripture corrects from the first, saying, "Contemplate not beauty which is another's."[3] And then, lest any one should say, "what then, if I contemplate, and be not taken captive," He punishes the look, lest confiding in this security thou shouldest some time fall into sin. "What then," one may say, "if I should look, and desire indeed, but do no evil?" Even so thou art set among the adulterers. For the Lawgiver hath pronounced it, and thou must not ask any more questions. For thus looking once, twice, or thrice, thou wilt perhaps have power to refrain; but if thou art continually doing this, and kindling the furnace, thou wilt assuredly be taken; for thy station is not beyond that nature which is common to men. As we then, if we see a child holding a knife,

1 John viii. 48.   2 Matt. vii. 28, 29.   3 Ecclus. ix. 8.

though we do not see him hurt, beat him, and forbid his ever holding it; so God likewise takes away the unchaste look even before the act, lest at any time thou shouldest fall in act also. For he who hath once kindled the flame, even when the woman whom he hath beheld is absent, is forming by himself continually images of shameful things, and from them often goes on even to the deed. For this cause Christ takes away even that embrace which is in the heart only.

What now can they say, who have those virgin inmates?[1] Why, by the tenor of this law they must be guilty of ten thousand adulteries, daily beholding them with desire. For this cause the blessed Job[2] also laid down this law from the beginning, blocking out from himself on all sides this kind of gazing.

For in truth greater is the struggle on beholding, and not possessing the object of fondness: nor is the pleasure so great which we reap from the sight, as the mischief we undergo from increasing this desire; thus making our opponent strong, and giving more scope to the devil, and no longer[3] able to repulse him, now that we have brought him into our inmost parts, and have thrown our mind open unto him. Therefore He saith, "commit no adultery with thine eyes, and thou wilt commit none with thy mind."

For one may indeed behold in another way, such as are the looks of the chaste; wherefore he did not altogether prohibit our seeing, but that seeing which is accompanied with desire. And if He had not meant this, He would have said simply, "He who looketh on a woman." But now He said not thus, but, "He who looketh to lust," "he who looketh to please his sight."

For not at all to this end did God make thee eyes, that thou shouldest thereby introduce adultery, but that, beholding His creatures, thou shouldest admire the Artificer.

Just then as one may feel wrath at random, so may one cast looks at random; that is, when thou doest it for lust. Rather, if thou desirest to look and find pleasure, look at thine own wife, and love her continually; no law forbids that. But if thou art to be curious about the beauties that belong to another, thou art injuring both thy wife by letting thine eyes wander elsewhere, and her on whom thou hast looked, by touching her unlawfully. Since, although thou hast not touched her with the hand, yet hast thou caressed her with thine eyes; for which cause this also is accounted adultery, and before that great penalty draws after it no slight one of its own. For then all within him is filled with disquiet and turmoil, and great is the tempest, and most grievous the pain, and no captive nor person in chains can be worse off than a man in this state of mind. And oftentimes she who hath shot the dart is flown away, while the wound even so remains. Or rather, it is not she who hath shot the dart, but thou gavest thyself the fatal wound, by thine unchaste look. And this I say to free modest women from the charge: since assuredly, should one deck herself out, and invite towards herself the eyes of such as fall in her way; even though she smite not him that meets with her, she incurs the utmost penalty: for she mixed the poison, she prepared the hemlock, even though she did not offer the cup. Or rather, she did also offer the cup, though no one were found to drink it.

3. "Why then doth He not discourse with them also?" it may be said. Because the laws which He appoints are in every case common, although He seem to address Himself unto men only. For in discoursing with the head, He makes His admonition common to the whole body also. For woman and man He knows as one living creature, and nowhere distinguishes their kind.

But if thou desirest to hear also His rebuke for them in particular, listen to Isaiah,[4] in many words inveighing against them, and deriding their habit, their aspect, their gait, their trailing garments, their tripping feet, their drooping necks. Hear with him the blessed Paul[5] also, setting many laws for them; and both *about garments, and ornaments of gold*,[6] and plaiting of hair, and luxurious[7] living, and all other such things, vehemently rebuking this sex. And Christ too, by what follows next, obscurely intimated this very same; for when He saith, "pluck out and cut off the eye that offendeth thee,"[8] He speaks as indicating His anger against them.

3. Wherefore also He subjoins,

---

[1] τὰς συνοίκους παρθένους, they were often called συνείσακτοί. The practice of unmarried men, especially of the clergy, having single young women in their houses, is a frequent object of warning and censure both in the Homilies of the Fathers and in Church Canons. The earliest mention of such a thing, and of the sad abuse consequent on it, appears to be in St. Irenæus, i. 6, 3 : who lays it to the charge of the Valentinian heretics. Tertullian (*de Jejun. ad fin.*) imputes it to the Catholics. St. Cyprian's fourth Epistle (ed. Fell.) was written to repress and punish an instance of it in the Church of Carthage. It was one of the charges against Paul of Samosata, and was forbidden by the third canon of Nicæa. See Dr. Routh's *Reliquiæ Sacræ*, 2,506, to which the editor is indebted for this note. The custom seems to have prevailed particularly at Antioch, *ib.* 482. See also an oration of Chrysostom on this subject, vi. 214.

[2] Job xxxi. 1.
[3] [οὐκέτι ἰσχύοντες, "no longer having strength."—R.]

[4] Isa. iii. 16.   [5] 1 Tim. ii. 9 ; Titus ii. 3, 4, 5.
[6] [The words in italics are a translation of the Latin version; nothing corresponding to these terms occurs in the Greek text of the Homily.—R.]
[7] Or, *wantonness.* See 1 Tim. v. 6.
[8] [The text has simply τὸν σκανδαλίζοντα. The precept is thus made more general.—R.]

" If thy right eye offend thee, pluck it out, and cast it from thee." [1]

Thus, lest thou shouldest say, " But what if she be akin to me? what if in any other way she belong to me?" therefore He hath given these injunctions; not discoursing about our limbs;—far from it,—for nowhere doth He say that our flesh is to be blamed for things, but everywhere it is the evil mind that is accused. For it is not the eye that sees, but the mind and the thought. Often, for instance, we being wholly turned elsewhere, our eye sees not those who are present. So that the matter does not entirely depend upon its working. Again, had He been speaking of members of the body, He would not have said it of one eye, nor of the right eye only, but of both. For he who is offended by his right eye, most evidently will incur the same evil by his left also. Why then did He mention the right eye, and add the hand? To show thee that not of limbs is He speaking, but of them who are near unto us. Thus, " If," saith He, "thou so lovest any one, as though he were in stead of a right eye; if thou thinkest him so profitable to thee as to esteem him in the place of a hand, and he hurts thy soul; even these do thou cut off." And see the emphasis; for He saith not, " Withdraw from him," but to show the fullness of the separation, " pluck it out," saith He, " and cast it from thee."

Then, forasmuch as His injunction was sharp, He shows also the gain on either hand, both from the benefits and from the evils, continuing in the metaphor.

" For it is profitable for thee," saith He, " that one of thy members should perish, and not that thy whole body should be cast into hell." [2]

For while he neither saves himself, nor fails to destroy thee too, what kindness is it for both to sink, whereas if they were separated, one at least might have been preserved?

But why did Paul then, it may be said, choose to become accursed? [3] Not on condition of gaining nothing, but with a view to the salvation of others. But in this case the mischief pertains to both. And therefore He said not, " pluck out" only, but also " cast from thee:" to receive him again no more, if he continue as he is. For so shalt thou both deliver him from a heavier charge, and free thyself from ruin.

But that thou mayest see yet more clearly the profit of this law; let us, if you please,

try what hath been said, in the case of the body itself, by way of supposition. I mean, if choice were given, and thou must either, keeping thine eye, be cast into a pit and perish, or plucking it out, preserve the rest of thy body; wouldest thou not of course accept the latter? It is plain to everyone. For this were not to act as one hating the eye, but as one loving the rest of the body. This same reckoning do thou make with regard to men also and women: that if he who harms thee by his friendship should continue incurable, his being thus cut off will both free thee from all mischief, and he also will himself be delivered from the heavier charges, not having to answer for thy destruction along with his own evil deeds.

Seest thou how full the law is of gentleness and tender care, and that which seems to men in general to be severity, how much love towards man it discloses?

Let them hearken to these things, who hasten to the theatres, and make themselves adulterers every day. For if the law commands to cut off him, whose connexion with us tends to our hurt; what plea can they have, who, by their haunting those places, attract towards them daily those even that have not yet become known to them, and procure to themselves occasions of ruin without number?

For henceforth, He not only forbids us to look unchastely, but having signified the mischief thence ensuing, He even straitens the law as He goes on, commanding to cut off, and dissever, and cast somewhere far away. And all this He ordains, who hath uttered [4] words beyond number about love, that in either way thou mightest learn His providence, and how from every source He seeks thy profit.

4. " Now it hath been said, Whosoever shall put away his wife, let him give her a writing of divorcement. [5] But I say unto you, Whosoever shall put away his wife, saving for the cause of fornication, causeth her to commit adultery; and whosoever marrieth her that is put away, committeth adultery." [6]

He goes not on to what lies before Him, until He have well cleared out the former topics. For, lo, He shows us yet another kind of adultery. And what is this? There was an ancient law made, [7] that he who hated his wife, for whatever kind of cause, should not be forbidden to cast her out, and to bring

---

[1] Matt. v. 29. [R. V., "If thy right eye causeth thee to stumble," and so everywhere in rendering σκανδαλίζειν.—R.]
[2] [Matt. v. 29, 30.]   [3] Rom. ix. 3.

[4] κινήσας.
[5] βιβλίον ἀποστασίου, St. Chrys. Comp. Mark x. 4: ἀποστάσιον, rec. Text. [There is no variation in the text of Matthew here, but in verse 32 the best authorities read πᾶς ὁ ἀπολύων, " every one that putteth away" (so R. V.). Chrysostom repeats ὃς ἂν ἀπολύσῃ, as in text. rec.--R.]
[6] Matt. vi. 31, 32.   [7] Deut. xxiv. 1-4.

home another instead of her. The law however did not command him simply to do this,
but after giving the woman a writing of
divorcement, that it might not be in her
power to return to him again; that so at least
the figure of the marriage might remain.

For if He had not enjoined this, but it were
lawful first to cast her out, and take another,
then afterwards to take back the former, the
confusion was sure to be great, all men continually taking each others' wives; and the
matter thenceforth would have been direct
adultery. With a view to this, He devised,
as no small mitigation, the writing of divorcement.

But these things were done by reason of
another, a far greater wickedness; I mean,
had He made it necessary to keep in the
house her even that was hated, the husband,
hating, would have killed her. For such was
the race of the Jews. For they who did not
spare children, who slew prophets, and " shed
blood as water,"[1] much more would they
have showed no mercy to women. For this
cause He allowed the less, to remove the
greater evil. For that this was not a primary[2]
law, hear Him saying, " Moses wrote these
things according to the hardness of your
hearts,"[3] that ye might not slay them in the
house, but rather put them out. But forasmuch as He had taken away all wrath, having
forbidden not murder only, but even the
mere feeling of anger, He with ease introduces this law likewise. With this view also
He is ever bringing to mind the former words,
to signify that His sayings are not contrary
to them, but in agreement: that He is en-
forcing, not overthrowing them; perfecting,
not doing them away.

And observe Him everywhere addressing
His discourse to the man. Thus, " He that
putteth away his wife," saith He, " causeth
her to commit adultery, and he that marrieth
a woman put away, committeth adultery."
That is, the former, though he take not another wife, by that act alone hath made himself liable to blame, having made the first an
adulteress; the latter again is become an
adulterer by taking her who is another's.
For tell me not this, " the other hath cast
her out;" nay, for when cast out she continues to be the wife of him that expelled her.
Then lest He should render the wife more
self-willed, by throwing it all upon him who
cast her out, He hath shut against her also
the doors of him who was afterwards receiving her; in that He saith, " He who marrieth
her that is put away committeth adultery;"

and so makes the woman chaste even though
unwilling, and blocks up altogether her access
to all, and suffers her not to give an occasion for jealousy.[4] For she who hath been
made aware that she positively must either
keep the husband, who was originally allotted
to her, or being cast out of that house, not
have any other refuge;—she even against her
will was compelled to make the best of her
consort.

And if He discourse not at all unto her
concerning these things, marvel not; for the
woman is rather a weak creature.[5] For this
cause letting her go, in his threatening
against the men He fully corrects her remissness. Just as if any one who had a prodigal
child, leaving him, should rebuke those who
make him such, and forbid them to have intercourse, or to approach him. And if that
be galling, call to mind, I pray thee, His
former sayings, on what terms He had
blessed His hearers; and thou wilt see that
it is very possible and easy. For he that is
meek, and a peacemaker, and poor in spirit,
and merciful, how shall he cast out his wife?
He that is used to reconcile others, how shall
he be at variance with her that is his own?

And not thus only, but in another way also
He hath lightened the enactment: forasmuch
as even for him He leaves one manner of
dismissal, when He saith, " Except for the
cause of fornication;" since the matter had
else come round again to the same issue.
For if He had commanded to keep her in the
house, though defiling herself with many,
He would have made the matter end again
in adultery.

Seest thou how these sayings agree with
what had gone before? For he who looks
not with unchaste eyes upon another woman,
will not commit whoredom; and not committing whoredom, he will give no occasion to
the husband to cast out his wife.

Therefore, you see, after this He presses
the point without reserve, and builds up this
fear as a bulwark, urging on the husband the
great danger, if he do cast her out, in that he
makes himself accountable for her adultery.
Thus, lest thou being told, " pluck out the
eye," shouldest suppose this to be said even
of a wife: He added in good time this corrective, in one way only giving leave to cast
her out, but no otherwise.

5. " Again, ye have heard that it was said
to them of old time, Thou shalt not forswear
thyself, but shalt perform unto the Lord

---

[1] Ps. lxxix. 3.　　　　　　[2] προηγούμενος.
[3] Matt. xix. 8. [R. V. " for your hardness of heart." —R.]

[4] μικροψυχίας.
[5] [ἀσθενέστερον γὰρ ἡ γυνή. The translator paraphrases this
as above, giving an unnecessary tone of depreciation to the language.—R.]

thine oaths. But I say unto you, swear not at all." [1]

Why did He go straightway not to theft, but to false witness, passing over that commandment? Because he that steals, doth upon occasion swear also; but he that knows not either swearing or speaking falsehood, much less will he choose to steal. So that by this He hath overthrown the other sin likewise: since falsehood comes of stealing.

But what means, " Thou shalt perform unto the Lord thine oaths?" [2] It is this, "thou shalt be true in swearing." "But I say unto you, swear not at all."

Next, to lead them farther away from swearing by God, He saith, " Neither by Heaven, for it is God's throne, nor by the earth, for it is the footstool of His feet; nor by Jerusalem, for it is the city of the great King:" [3] still speaking out of the prophetical writings, and signifying Himself not to be opposed to the ancients. This was because they had a custom of swearing by these objects, and he intimates this custom near the end of his Gospel.[4]

But mark, I pray thee, on what ground He magnifies the elements; not from their own nature, but from God's relation to them, such as it had been in condescension declared. For because the tyranny of idolatry was great, that the elements might not be thought worthy of honor for their own sake, He hath assigned this cause, which we have mentioned, which again would pass on to the glory of God. For He neither said, "because Heaven is beautiful and great," nor, "because earth is profitable;" but "because the one is God's throne, the other His footstool;" on every side urging them on towards their Lord.

" Neither by thy head," saith He, "because thou canst not make one hair white or black." [5]

Here again, not as wondering at man, hath He withdrawn him from swearing by his head (for so man himself would be worshipped), but as referring the glory to God, and signifying that thou art not master even of thyself, and of course therefore not of the oaths made by thy head. For if no one would give up his own child to another, much more will not God give up His own work to thee. For though it be thy head, yet is it the property of another; and so far from being master thereof, thou shalt not be able to do with it, no not the least thing of all. For He said not, " Thou canst not make one

hair grow;" but, "Not so much as change its quality."

"But what," it may be said, "if any one should require an oath, and apply constraint?" Let the fear of God be more powerful than the constraint: since, if thou art to bring forward such excuses, thou wilt keep none of the things which are enjoined.

Yea, for first with respect to thy wife thou wilt say, "what if she be contentious and extravagant;" and then as to the right eye, "what if I love it, and am quite on fire?" and of the unchaste look, "what then, if I cannot help seeing?" and of our anger against a brother, "what if I be hasty, and not able to govern my tongue?" and in general, all His sayings thou mayest on this wise trample under foot. Yet surely with regard to human laws thou darest not in any case use this allegation, nor say, "what then if this or that be the case," but, willing or unwilling, thou receivest what is written.

And besides, thou wilt never have compulsion to undergo at all. For he that hath hearkened unto those former blessings, and hath framed himself to be such as Christ enjoined, will have no such constraint to endure from any, being held in reverence and veneration by all.

" But let your yea, be yea; and your nay, nay: for that which exceedeth these cometh of the evil one." [6]

What is it then that " exceeds yea " and " nay "? it is the oath, not the perjury. For this latter is quite acknowledged, and no man needs to learn that it is of the evil one; and it is not an excess, but an opposite: whereas an excess means something more, and added over and above: which kind of thing swearing is.

" What then," saith one, " was it of the evil one? and if it was of the evil one, how was it a law?" Well, this same thing thou wilt say concerning the wife also; how is that now accounted adultery, which was before permitted?

What now may one reply to this? That the precepts then uttered had reference to the weakness of them who were receiving the laws; since also to be worshipped with the vapor of sacrifice is very unworthy of God, just as to lisp is unworthy of a philosopher. That kind of thing accordingly was now laid down to be adultery, and swearing to be of the evil one, now that the principles of virtue

---

[1] Matt. v. 33, 34.   [2] See Num. xxx. 2 ; Deut. xxiii. 23.
[3] Isa. lxxvi. 1 ; Ps. xlviii. 2.   [4] Matt. xxiii. 16, et seq.
[5] Matt. v. 36.

[6] Matt. v. 37. St. Chrysostom deviates from the received text here: as if he were thinking also of James v. 12. [The variation is in the first half of the verse, but the resemblance to James v. 12 is not marked. In the latter half the citation is exact, and Chrysostom explains ἐκ τοῦ πονηροῦ as the R. V. does: " of the evil one."—R.]

have advanced. But if these things had been, from the first, laws of the devil, they would not have attained to so great goodness. Yea, for had those not been forerunners in the first place, these which we now have would not have been so easily received. Do not thou then require their excellency now, when their use is past: but then, when the time was calling for them. Or rather, if thou wilt, even now: yea, for now also is their virtue shown: and most of all for the very cause, by reason of which we find fault with them. For their appearing such now, is the greatest commendation of them. For had they not brought us up well, and made us meet for the reception of the greater precepts, they would not have appeared such.

Therefore as the breast, when it hath fulfilled all its part, and is dismissing the child to the more manly diet, after that appears useless; and the parents who before thought it necessary for the babe, now abuse it with ten thousand mockeries (and many even not content with words of abuse, anoint it also with bitter drugs; that when their words have not power to remove the child's unseasonable propensity towards it, the real things may quench their longing) : so also Christ saith, that they are of the evil one, not to indicate that the old law is of the devil, but in order that with most exceeding earnestness He might lead them away from their ancient poverty. And to them He saith these things; but with regard to the Jews, who were insensible and persevered in the same ways, He hath anointed their city all round with the terror of captivity, as with some bitter drug, and made it inaccessible. But since not even this had power to restrain them, but they desired to see it again, running to it, just as a child to the breast, He hid it from them altogether; both pulling it down, and leading away the more part of them far from it: as it is with our cattle; many, by shutting out the calves, in time induce them to forego their old familiar use of the milk.

But if the old law had belonged to the devil, it would not have led people away from idolatry, but rather would have drawn them on and cast them into it; for this did the devil desire. But now we see the opposite effect produced by the old law. And indeed this very thing, the oath, was ordained of old for this cause, that they might not swear by the idols. For " ye shall swear," saith He, " by the true God."[1] They were then no small advantages which the law effected, but rather very great. For that they came unto the " strong meat," was the work of its care.

" What then," it may be said, " is not swearing of the evil one?" Yes, indeed it is altogether of the evil one; that is, now, after so high a rule of self-restraint; but then not so.

" But how," one may say, " should the same thing become at one time good, at another time not good?" Nay, I say the very contrary: how could it help becoming good and not good, while all things are crying aloud, that they are so: the arts, the fruits of the earth, and all things else?

. See it, for example, taking place first in our own kind. Thus, to be carried, in the earliest age of life, is good, but afterwards pernicious; to eat food that hath been softened in the mouth, in the first scene of our life, is good, but afterwards it is full of disgust; to be fed upon milk and to fly to the breast, is at first profitable and healthful, but tends afterwards to decay and harm. Seest thou how the same actions, by reason of the times, appear good, and again not so? Yea, and to wear the robe of a child is well as long as you are a boy, but contrariwise, when you are become a man, it is disgraceful. Wouldest thou learn of the contrary case too, how to the child again the things of the man are unsuited? Give the boy a man's robe, and great will be the laughter; and greater the danger, he being often upset in walking after that fashion. Allow him to handle public affairs, and to traffic, and sow, and reap, and great again will be the laughter.

And why do I mention these things? when killing, which among all is acknowledged to be an invention of the evil one, killing, I say, having found its proper occasion, caused Phinehas, who committed it, to be honored with the priesthood.[2] For that killing is a work of him whom I just now mentioned, hear what Christ saith; " Ye will do the works of your Father; he was a manslayer from the beginning."[3] But Phinehas became a manslayer, and " it was counted unto him " (so He speaks) " for righteousness:"[4] and Abraham again on becoming not a manslayer only, but (which was far worse) the slayer of his child, won more and more approbation. And Peter too wrought a twofold slaughter, nevertheless what he did was of the Spirit.[5]

Let us not then examine simply the acts, but the season too, and the causes, and the mind, and the difference of persons, and whatsoever else may accompany them, these

[1] Jer. iv. 2, LXX. καὶ ὀμόσῃ, Ζῇ Κύριος, μετὰ ἀληθείας ἐν, κρίσει, καὶ ἐν δικαιοσύνῃ.

[2] Num. xxv. 8.   [3] John viii. 44.
[4] Ps. cvi. 31.   [5] Acts v.

let us search out with all exactness: for there is no arriving at the truth otherwise.

And let us be diligent, if we would attain unto the kingdom, to show forth something more than the old commandments; since we cannot otherwise lay hold of the things of Heaven. For if we arrive but at the same measure, that of the ancients, we shall stand without that threshold; for "except your righteousness shall exceed the righteousness of the Scribes and Pharisees, ye cannot enter into the kingdom of Heaven."[1]

6. Yet, although so heavy a threat is set down, there are some who so far from over-passing this righteousness, even come short of it; so far from shunning oaths, they even swear falsely; so far from avoiding an unchaste gaze, they even fall into the very act of wickedness. And all the rest of the things which are forbidden, they dare to do, as though past feeling: waiting for one thing only, the day of punishment, and the time when they are to pay the most extreme penalty for their misdoings. And this is the portion of those only who have ended their lives in wickedness. For these have reason to despair, and thenceforth to expect nothing else but punishment; whereas they who are yet here, may have power both to renew the fight and to conquer and be crowned with ease.

Despond not therefore, O man, neither put away thy noble earnestness; for in truth the things are not grievous, which are enjoined. What trouble is it, I pray thee, to shun an oath? What, does it cost any money? Is it sweat and hardship? It is enough to have willed only, and the whole is done.

But if you allege to me thine habit; for this very reason most of all do I say, that thy doing right is easy. For if thou bring thyself to another habit, thou hadst effected all.

Consider, for example, how among the Greeks, in many instances, persons lisping have entirely cured by much practice their halting tongue; while others, who were used to shrug up their shoulders in an unseemly way, and to be continually moving them, by putting a sword over them, have broken themselves of it.[2]

For since you are not persuaded out of the Scriptures, I am compelled to shame you by them that are without. This God also did unto the Jews, when He said, "Go ye forth unto the Isles of Chittim, and send unto Kedar, and know if nations will change their gods; which yet are no gods."[3] And to the

brutes likewise He sends us oftentimes, saying on this wise, "Go to the ant, thou sluggard, and emulate her ways:" and "go forth to the bee."[4]

This therefore I also now say unto you; consider the philosophers of the Greeks; and then ye will know of how great punishment we are worthy, who disobey the laws of God: in that they for seemliness before men have taken exceeding pains, and you bestow not the same diligence, no, not for the things of Heaven.

But if thou shouldest reply, "Habit has a wonderful power to beguile even those who are very much in earnest:" this I likewise acknowledge; however, there is another thing which I say with it; that as it is powerful to beguile, so also is it easy to be corrected. For if thou wilt set over thyself at home many to watch thee, such as thy servant, thy wife, thy friend, thou wilt easily break off from the bad habits, being hard pressed and closely restrained by all. If thou succeed in doing this for ten days only, thou wilt after that no longer need any further time, but all will be secured to thee, rooted anew in the firmness of the most excellent habit.

When therefore thou art beginning to correct this, though thou shouldest transgress thy law a first, a second, a third, a twentieth time, do not despair, but rise up again, and resume the same diligence, and thou wilt surely prevail.

For perjury surely is no trifling mischief. If to swear is of the evil one, how great the penalty which false swearing will bring! Did ye give praise to what hath been said?[5] Nay, I want not applause, nor tumults, nor noise. One thing only do I wish, that quietly and intelligently listening, you should do what is said. This is the applause, this the panegyric for me. But if thou praisest what I say, but doest not what thou applaudest, greater is the punishment, more aggravated the accusation: and to us it is shame and ridicule. For the things here present are no dramatic spectacle; neither do ye now sit gazing on actors, that ye may merely applaud. This place is a spiritual school. Wherefore also there is but one thing aimed at, duly to perform the things that have been spoken, and to show forth our obedience by our works. For then only shall we have obtained all. Since as things are,

---

[1] Matt. v. 20.
[2] He clearly alludes to the history of Demosthenes.
[3] Jer. ii. 10, 11. [The citation is much abbreviated from the LXX., which does not vary materially from the Hebrew.—R.]

[4] Prov. vi. 6-8, LXX. "Or go to the bee, and learn how industrious she is, and how honorable she maketh her work; whose labors kings and private men make use of for health: and she is desirable to all and glorious, although she be weak in strength; for holding wisdom precious she is preferred." [This is the addition to Prov. vi. 8, found in the LXX., but not in the Vulgate.—R.]
[5] See St. Chrys. on 1 Cor. Hom. IV. and the note there.

to say the truth, we have fairly given up in despair. For I have not ceased giving these admonitions either to those whom I meet in private, or in discourse with you all in common. Yet I see no advantage at all gained, but you are still clinging to the former rude beginnings, which thing is enough to fill the teacher with weariness.

See, for example, Paul himself, hardly bearing it, because his scholars were delaying a long time in their earlier lessons: "For when for the time," saith he, "ye ought to be teachers, ye have need to be taught again which be the first principles of the oracles of God.[1]"

Wherefore we too mourn and lament. And if I see you persisting, I will forbid you for the future to set foot on this sacred threshold, and partake of the immortal mysteries; as we do fornicators and adulterers, and persons charged with murder. Yea, for it is better to offer our accustomed prayers, with two or three, who keep the laws of God, than to sweep together[2] a multitude of trangressors and corrupters of others.

Let me have no rich man, no potentate, puffing at me here, and drawing up his eyebrows; all these are to me a fable, a shade, a dream. For no one of those who are now rich, will stand up for me there, when I am called to account and accused, as not having thoroughly vindicated the laws of God, with all due earnestness. For this, this ruined even that admirable old man,[3] though in his own life giving no handle for blame; yet for all that, because he overlooked the treading under foot of God's laws, he was chastised with his children, and paid that grievous penalty. And if, where the absolute authority of nature was so great, he who failed to treat his own children with due firmness endured so grievous a punishment; what indulgence shall we have, freed as we are from that dominion, and yet ruining all by flattery?

In order therefore that ye may not destroy both us and your own selves with us, be persuaded, I entreat you; set very many to watch over you, and call you to account, and so free yourselves from the habit of oaths; that going on orderly from thence, ye may both with all facility succeed in attaining unto all other virtue, and may enjoy the good things to come; which God grant that we may all win, by the grace and love towards man of our Lord Jesus Christ, to whom be glory and might now and always, even for ever and ever. Amen.

---

[1] Heb. v. 12　[The text of Heb. v. 12 is modified, διδάσκεσθαι being substituted for διδάσκειν. The Vulgate also has the passive. The R. V. takes τινα as the indefinite pronoun: "that some one teach you;" but compare the margin. Notice, too, the acceptance of the Pauline authorship of the Epistle.—R.]

[2] ἐπισύρεσθαι.

[3] 1 Sam. iii. 13.

HOMILY XVIII.

MATT. V. 38, 39, 40..

"Ye have heard that it hath been said, An eye for an eye, and a tooth for a tooth. But I say unto you, that ye resist not the evil:[1] but whosoever shall smite thee on the right cheek, turn to him the other also. And if any man will sue thee at the law, and take away thy coat, let him have thy cloak also."

SEEST thou that it was not of an eye that He was speaking before, when He made the law to pluck out the offending eye, but of him who by his friendship is harming us, and casting us into the gulf of destruction? For He who in this place uses so great strength of expression, and who, not even when another is plucking out your eye, permits you to strike out his; how should He have made it a law to strike out one's own?

But if any one accuses the ancient law, because it commands such retaliation, he seems to me very unskillful in the wisdom that becomes a legislator, and ignorant of the virtue of opportunities, and the gain of condescension. For if he considered who were the hearers of these sayings, and how they

---

[1] [R. V. text, "him that is evil." Chrysostom interprets τῷ πονηρῷ, "the evil one." In verse 40 the R. V. renders "would go to law with thee."—R.]

were disposed, and when they received this code of laws, he will thoroughly admit the wisdom of the Lawgiver, and will see that it is one and the same, who made both those laws and these, and who wrote each of them exceeding profitably, and in its due season. Yes, for if at the beginning He had introduced these high and most weighty commandments, men would not have received either these, or the others; but now ordaining them severally in their due time, He hath by the two corrected the whole world.

And besides, He commanded this, not that we might strike out one another's eyes, but that we might keep our hands to ourselves. For the threat of suffering hath effectually restrained our inclination to be doing.

And thus in fact He is silently dropping seed of much self-restraint, at least in that He commands to retaliate with just the same acts. Yet surely he that began such transgression were worthy of a greater punishment, and this the abstract nature of justice[1] demands. But forasmuch as He was minded to mingle mercy also with justice, He condemns him whose offenses were very great to a punishment less than his desert: teaching us even while we suffer to show forth great consideration.

Having therefore mentioned the ancient law, and recognized it all, He signifies again, that it is not our brother who hath done these deeds, but the evil one. For this cause he hath also subjoined, "But I say unto you, that ye resist not the evil one." He did not say, "resist not your brother," but "the evil one," signifying that on his motion men dare so to act; and in this way relaxing and secretly removing most of our anger against the aggressor, by transferring the blame to another.

"What then?" it is said, "ought we not to resist the evil one?" Indeed we ought, but not in this way, but as He hath commanded, by giving one's self up to suffer wrongfully; for thus shalt thou prevail over him. For one fire is not quenched by another, but fire by water. And to show thee that even under the old law he that suffered rather prevails, that he it is who wins the crown; examine just what is done, and thou wilt see that his advantage is great. For as he that hath begun with unjust acts, will have himself destroyed the eyes of both, his neighbor's and his own (wherefore also he is justly hated of all, and ten thousand accusations are aimed at him): so he that hath been injured, even after his equal retaliation, will

have done nothing horrible. Wherefore also he hath many to sympathize with him, as being clear from that offense even after he hath retaliated. And though the calamity be equal to both parties, yet the sentence passed on it is not equal, either with God, or with men. It should seem then, that neither is the calamity equal in the end.

Now whereas at the beginning He said, "he that is angry with his brother without a cause," and "he that calleth him fool shall be in danger of hell fire," here He requires yet more entire self-restraint, commanding him that suffers ill not merely to be quiet, but even to be more exceedingly earnest in his turn,[2] by offering the other cheek.

And this He saith, not as legislating about such a blow as this only, but as teaching also what forbearance we should practise in all our other trials. For just as when He saith, "whoso calleth his brother fool, is in danger of hell," He speaks not of this word only, but also of all reviling; even so here also He is making a law, not so much for our bearing it manfully, when smitten, as that we should be undisturbed, whatever we suffer. Because of this He both there singled out the extremest insult, and here hath set down that which seems to be of all blows most opprobrious, the blow on the cheek, so full of all insolence. And He commands this as having regard both of him that strikes and of him that is stricken. Since both he that is insulted will not think that he suffers any harm, being thus framed to self-restraint (nay, he will not even have any sense of the insult, as striving rather for a prize than as receiving a blow); and he that is offering the affront will be made ashamed, and not add a second blow, though he be fiercer than any wild beast, yea, rather will condemn himself heartily for the former. For nothing so restrains the wrong doers, as when the injured bear what is done with gentleness. And it not only restrains them from rushing onward, but works upon them also to repent for what has gone before, and in wonder at such forbearance to draw back. And it makes them more our own, and causes them to be slaves, not merely friends, instead of haters and enemies; even as avenging one's self does just the contrary: for it both disgraces each of the two, and makes them worse, and their anger it heightens into a greater flame; yea, often no less than death itself is the end of it, going on from bad to worse. Wherefore He not only forbade thee to be angry when smitten, but even enjoined thee to satiate the

---

[1] ὁ τοῦ δικαίου λόγος.

[2] ἀντιφιλοτιμεῖσθαι.

other's desire, that so neither may the former blow appear to have befallen thee against thy will. For thus, lost as he may be to shame, thou wilt be able to smite him with a mortal blow, rather than if thou hadst smitten him with thine hand; or if his shamelessness be still greater, thou wilt make him gentle in proportion.

2. "And if any man will sue thee at the law, and take away thy coat, let him have thy cloak also."[1]

For not in the matter of blows only, but of our goods also, He would have such forbearance exhibited. Wherefore He again employs the same strong figure.[2] That is, as in the other case He commands to overcome in suffering, so here again, by allowing ourselves to be deprived of more than the wrong doer expected. However, He did not put it so merely, but with something to enhance it: not saying, "give thy cloak to him that asketh," but "to him that would sue thee at the law," that is, "if he drag thee into court, and give thee trouble."

And just as, after He had bidden not to call another fool, nor to be angry without cause, He went on and required more, in that He commanded to offer the right cheek also; even so here, having said, "Agree with thine adversary," He again amplifies the precept. For now He orders us not only to give what the other would have, but even to show forth a greater liberality.

"What then!" one may say, "am I to go about naked?" We should not be naked, if we obeyed these sayings with exactness; rather more abundantly than any should we be clothed. For first, no one would attack men of this disposition; and next, if there chanced to be any one so savage and ungentle, as to proceed even so far, yet many more would be found to clothe him, who acted with such self-denial, not with garments only, but even with their own flesh, if it were possible.

Further: even though one were of necessity to go about naked on account of this sort of self-denial, neither so were it any disgrace. Since Adam too was "naked"[3] in paradise, "and was not ashamed;" and Isaiah was "naked, and barefoot," and more glorious than all the Jews;[4] and Joseph[5] also, when he stripped himself, did then more than ever shine forth. For to be thus naked is no evil, but to be so clad, as we now are, with costly garments, this is both disgraceful and ridiculous. For this cause, you see, those

had praise of God, but these He blames, both by prophets and by apostles.

Let us not therefore suppose His injunctions impossible. Nay, for besides their expediency, they are very easy, if we are sober-minded; and the profit of them is so great as to be an exceeding help, not to ourselves only, but to those also who are using us despitefully. And in this chiefly stands their excellence, that while they induce us to suffer wrong, they by the same means teach them also that do the wrong to control themselves. For while he on his part thinks it a great thing to take what belongs to others, but thou signifiest to him, that to thee it is easy to give even what he doth not ask: while thou bringest in liberality for a counterpoise to his meanness, and a wise moderation to his covetousness: consider what a lesson he will get, being taught not by sayings, but by actual deeds, to scorn vice and to seek after virtue.

For God will have us profitable not to ourselves alone, but to all our neighbors as well. Now if thou givest, and abstainest from suing, thou hast sought thine own advantage only; but if thou give him some other thing, thou hast made him too better, and so sent him away. Of this nature is salt, which is what He would have them to be; seeing it both recruits[6] itself, and keeps all other bodies with which it may associate: of this nature is light; for it shows objects both to a man's self and to all others. Forasmuch then as He hath set thee in the rank of these things, help thou likewise him who is sitting in darkness, and teach him that neither before did he take any thing by force: persuade him that he hath done no despite. Yea, for thus thou thyself also wilt be had in more respect and reverence, if thou signify that thou gavest freely and wert not robbed. Make therefore his sin, through thy moderation, an instance of thine own bounty.

3. And if thou think this a great thing, wait, and thou wilt see clearly, that neither yet hast thou attained to perfection. For not even here doth He stop with thee, who is laying down the laws of patient endurance, but He proceeds even further, thus saying,

"If any one shall compel thee to go one mile, go with him twain."[7]

Seest thou the height of self-denial? in this at least, that after giving thy coat, and thy cloak, not even if thine enemy should wish to use thy naked body for hardships and labors, not even so (saith He), must thou forbid him. For He would have us possess

---

[1] Matt. v. 40.　　　[2] ὑπερβολήν.　　　[3] Gen. ii. 25.
[4] Isa. xx. 2, 3.　　[5] Gen. xxxix. 12.　　　[6] συγκροτεῖ.　　　[7] Matt. v. 41.

all things in common, both our bodies and our goods, as with them that are in need, so with them that insult us: for the latter comes of manliness, the former of mercifulness.

Because of this, He said, " If any one shall compel thee to go one mile, go with him twain: " again leading thee higher up, and commanding thee to show forth the same kind of ambition.

For if the things of which He spake at the beginning, being far less than these, have so great blessings pronounced on them; consider what sort of portion awaits them, who duly perform these, and what they become even before their rewards, in a human and passible [1] body winning entire freedom from passion. Since when neither insult, nor blows, nor the spoiling of their property, galls them; while they give way to no such thing, but rather add in large measure to their endurance; reflect what kind of training their soul is undergoing.

On this account then, as in regard of blows, as in regard of our goods, so in this case also, He hath bidden us act. " For why," saith He, " do I mention insult, and property? Though he should want to make use of thy very own limbs for toil and weary work, and this unjustly, do thou again conquer and overpass His unjust desire."

For " to compel " [2] is this, to drag unjustly and without any reason, and by way of despite. Nevertheless, for this also be thou ready in thy station, so as to suffer more than the other would fain do to thee.

" Give to him that asketh thee, and from him that would borrow of thee, turn not thou away." [3]

These last are less than what went before; but marvel not, for this He is ever wont to do, mingling the small with the great. And if these be little in comparison with those, let them hearken, who take the goods of others, who distribute their own among harlots, and kindle to themselves a double fire, both by the unrighteous income, and by the pernicious outlay.

But by " borrowing," here, He means not the compact with usury, but the use merely. And elsewhere He even amplifies it, saying that we should give to them, from whom we do not expect to receive. [4]

4. " Ye have heard that it hath been said,

Thou shalt love thy neighbor, and hate thine enemy. But I say unto you, love your enemies, and pray for them which despitefully use you: bless them that curse you, do good to them that hate you. That ye may become like [5] your Father which is in Heaven; for He maketh His sun to rise on the evil and on the good, and sendeth rain on the just and on the unjust." [6]

See how He hath set the highest pinnacle on our good deeds. For this is why He teaches not only to endure a blow, but to offer the right cheek also; not only to add the cloak to the coat, but to travel also two miles with him who compels thee to go one; in order that thou mightest receive with all facility that which is much more than these. " But what," one may say, " is more than these?" Not even to count as an enemy him who is doing these things: or rather even somewhat else more than this. For He said not, " do not hate," but " love;" He said not, " do not injure," but " do good."

And if any one should examine accurately, he will see that even to these things somewhat is added, much greater than they are. For neither did He simply command to love, but to pray.

Seest thou how many steps He hath ascended, and how He hath set us on the very summit of virtue? Nay, mark it, numbering from the beginning. A first step is, not to begin with injustice: a second, after he hath begun, to vindicate one's self by equal retaliation; a third, not to do unto him that is vexing us the same that one hath suffered, but to be quiet; a fourth, even to give one's self up to suffer wrongfully; a fifth, to give up yet more than the other, who did the wrong, wishes; a sixth, not to hate him who hath done so; a seventh, even to love him; an eighth, to do him good also; a ninth, to entreat God Himself on his behalf. Seest thou, what height of self-command? Wherefore glorious too, as we see, is the reward which it hath. That is, because the thing enjoined was great, and needed a fervent [7] soul, and much earnestness, He appoints for it also such a reward, as for none of the former. For He makes not mention here of earth, as with respect to the meek; nor of comfort and mercy, as with regard to the mourners and the merciful; nor of the kingdom of Heaven; but of that which was more thrilling than all; our becoming like God, in

---

[1] [παθητῷ. There is a paranomasia in the original, indicated here by the word " passible."—·R.]

[2] ἀγγαρεῦσαι. [R. V. marg., "impress," a legal act of oppression. The Greek work is of Persian origin, and was transferred into Latin also ; see Vulgate, Matt. v. 41.—R.]

[3] Matt. v. 42.

[4] Luke vi. 35. " Do good and lend, hoping for nothing again." [But the R.V. renders "never despairing," with the margin, "Some ancient authorities read despairing of no man."—R.]

[5] ὅμοιοι, Chrys. υἱοὶ, rec. text. [For the former reading in the New Testament there is no MS. authority.—R.]

[6] Matt. v. 43-45. [The briefer form of verse 44 is now accepted by critical editors (so Vulgate). The longer reading is from Luke vi. 27, 28. Comp. R. V.—R.]

[7] νεανικῆς.

such wise as men might become so. For He saith, "That ye may become like unto your Father which is in Heaven."

And observe, I pray thee, how neither in this place, nor in the preceding parts, doth He call Him His own Father, but in that instance, "God," and "a great King," when he was discoursing about oaths, and here, "their Father." And this He doth, as reserving for the proper season what He had to say touching these points.

5. Then, bringing the likeness yet closer, He saith,

"Because He maketh His sun to rise on the evil and on the good, and sendeth rain upon just and unjust." [1]

"For He too, so far from hating," so He speaks, "even pours benefits on those that insult Him." Yet surely in no respect is the case parallel, not only because of the surpassing nature of His benefits, but also by reason of the excellence of His dignity. For thou indeed art despised by thy fellow-slave, but He by His slave, who hath also received ten thousand benefits from Him: and thou indeed givest words, in praying for him, but He, deeds, very great and marvellous, kindling the sun, and giving the annual showers. "Nevertheless, even so I grant thee to be mine equal, in such wise as it is possible for a man so to be."

Hate not then the man that doeth thee wrong, who is procuring thee such good things, and bringing thee to so great honor. Curse not him that uses thee despitefully; for so hast thou undergone the labor, but art deprived of the fruit; thou wilt bear the loss, but lose the reward; which is of the utmost folly, having borne the more grievous, not to bear what is less than it. "But how," saith one, "is it possible for this to take place?" Having seen God become man, and descend so far, and suffer so much for thy sake, dost thou still inquire and doubt, how it is possible to forgive thy fellow-servants their injuriousness? Hearest thou not Him on the cross, saying, "Forgive them, for they know not what they do?" [2] Hearest thou not Paul, when he saith, "He who is gone up on high, and is sitting on the right hand intercedeth for us?" [3] Seest thou not that even after the cross, and after He had been received up, He sent the apostles unto the Jews that had slain Him, to bring them His ten thousand blessings, and this, though they were to suffer ten thousand terrors at their hands?

6. But hast thou been greatly wronged?

Nay, what hast thou endured like thy Lord, bound, beaten with whips, with rods, spit upon by servants, enduring death, and that death, which is of all deaths the most shameful, after ten thousand favors shown? And even if thou hast been greatly wronged, for this very cause most of all do thou do him good, that thou mayest both make thine own crown more glorious, and set thy brother free from the worst infirmity. For so too the physicians, when they are kicked, and shamefully handled by the insane, then most of all pity them, and take measures for their perfect cure, knowing that the insult comes of the extremity of their disease. Now I bid thee too have the same mind touching them that are plotting against thee, and do thou so treat them that are injuring thee. For it is they above all that are diseased, it is they who are undergoing all the violence. Deliver him then from this grievous contumely, and grant him to let go his anger, and set him free from that grievous demon, wrath. Yea, for if we see persons possessed by devils, we weep for them; we do not seek to be ourselves also possessed.

Now let us do this too likewise with respect to them that are angry; for in truth the enraged are like the possessed; yea rather, are more wretched than they, being mad with consciousness of it. Wherefore also their frenzy is without excuse. Trample not then on the fallen, but rather pity him. For so, should we see any one troubled with bile, blinded and giddy, and straining to cast up this evil humor, we stretch forth a hand, and continue to support him through his struggles, and though we stain our garments, we regard it not, but seek one thing only, how we may set him free from this grievous distress. This then let us do with respect to the angry also, and continue to bear them up when vomiting and struggling; nor let him go, until he put from him all the bitterness. And then shall he feel toward thee the greatest thankfulness; when he is at rest, then he will know clearly from how great trouble thou hast released him.

But why do I speak of the thanks from him? for God will straightway crown thee, and will requite thee with ten thousand honors, because thou hast freed thy brother from a grievous disease; and that brother too will honor thee as a master, ever reverencing thy forbearance.

Seest thou not the women that are in travail, how they bite those that stand by, and they are not pained? or rather they are pained, but bear it bravely, and sympathize with them who are in sorrow and are torn by

---

[1] Matt. v. 45.   [2] Luke xxiii. 34.   [3] Rom. viii. 34.

those pangs. These do thou too emulate, and prove not softer than women. For after these women have brought forth (for these men are more feeble minded than women), then they will know thee to be a man in comparison.[1]

And if the things enjoined be grievous, consider that to this end Christ came, that He might implant these things in our mind, that He might render us profitable both to enemies and friends. Wherefore also He commands us to have a care of both these: of our brethren, when He saith, "If thou bring thy gift;" of our enemies, when He makes a law both to love them, and to pray for them.

7. And not only from the example they have in God, doth He urge them on to this, but also from the contrary.

"For if ye love those," saith He, "that love you, what reward have ye? do not even the publicans the same?"[2] This Paul also saith, "Ye have not yet resisted unto blood, striving against sin."[3] If then thou doest these things, thou hast taken thy stand with God; but if thou forsakest them, with the publicans. Seest thou how that the interval between the commandments is not so great as the difference between the persons? Let us not therefore infer this, "the injunction is hard;" but let us consider also the reward, and think whom we are like, if we duly perform it, and to whom equal, if we wander from it.

Thus then to our brother He commands us to be reconciled, and not to desist till we have removed the enmity: but when He is discoursing of persons generally, He subjects us no longer to this necessity, but requires only what is on our part; in this way also making the law easy. For inasmuch as He had said, "They persecuted the prophets which were before you;" lest on occasion of those very words they should be unfavorably disposed towards them, He bids them not only to endure such as do so, but even to love them.

8. Seest thou how He pulls up by the roots wrath, and sensual lusts, as well as that of riches, that of glory, all that belongs to this life? For this he had done indeed from the first, but much more now. For the poor, and the meek, and the mourner, empties himself of his anger; the just and the merciful, of the lust of riches; the pure in heart is delivered from wicked lusts; he that is persecuted and suffers insults, and is evil spoken of, is practising of course entire contempt of

things present, and is clear from pride and vainglory.

Having therefore loosed the hearer from these bonds, and having anointed him for the conflicts, again in another way He roots up these passions, and with increased strictness. For having begun by anger, and having cut out on every side the sinews of this passion; having said, "he that is angry with his brother," and "he that calleth fool," or "Raca," let him be punished: and "he that is offering his gift, let him not approach the table until he have done away the enmity;" and "he that hath an adversary, before he see the tribunal, let him make the enemy a friend:" He makes a transition to lust again, and saith, "he that beholds with unchaste eyes, let him be punished as an adulterer;" whoso is offended by an unchaste woman, or by a man, or by any other of those belonging to him, let him cut off all these; "he that hath a woman by law of marriage, let him never cast her out, and look to another." For hereby He hath pulled up the roots of wicked lust. Then after this He restrains the love of riches, commanding neither to swear, nor to lie, nor to keep hold of the very cloak with which one may chance to be clad, but rather to give up one's coat too, to him who would have it, and one's bodily services; completely and more than completely taking away our longing for riches. Then after all these things, and the varied garland of these commandments, He goes on to say "pray for them which despitefully use you:" leading us up to the very highest summit of self-control.

For as being meek is not so much as to take smiting, nor being merciful, as to give one's coat also together with one's cloak, nor being just, as to bear injury, nor being a peacemaker, as to follow even when smitten and compelled; so also to suffer persecution is not so much as to bless when persecuted. Seest thou how by degrees He leads us up into the very arches[4] of Heaven?

9. What then can we deserve, who are commanded to emulate God, and are perhaps in a way not so much as to equal the publicans? For if "to love them that love us" be the part of publicans, sinners, and heathens: when we do not even this (and we do it not, so long as we envy our brethren who are in honor), what penalty shall we not incur, commanded as we are to surpass the scribes, and taking our place below the heathens? How then shall we behold the kingdom, I pray thee? how shall we set foot on that holy

---

[1] σε τὸν ἄνδρα εἴσονται, "they will know thee to be the man."
[2] Matt. v. 46.   [3] Heb. xii. 4.   [4] ἀψῖδας.

threshold, who are not surpassing even the publicans? For this He covertly signified, when He said, "Do not even the publicans the same?"

And this thing most especially we may admire in His teaching, that while in each instance He sets down with very great fullness the prizes of the conflicts; such as "to see God," and "to inherit the kingdom of Heaven," and "to become sons of God," and "like God," and "to obtain mercy," and "to be comforted," and "the great reward:" if anywhere He must needs mention things grievous, He doth this in a subdued tone. Thus in the first place, the name of hell He hath set down once only in so many sentences; and in some other instances too, it is with reserve that He corrects the hearer, and as though he were managing His discourse rather in the way of shaming than threatening him; where He saith, "do not even the publicans the same?" and, "if the salt have lost its savor;" and, "he shall be called least in the kingdom of Heaven."

And there are places where He puts down the sin itself by way of punishment, leaving to the hearer to infer the grievousness of the punishment: as when He saith, "he hath committed adultery with her in his heart;" and, "he that putteth away causeth her to commit adultery;" and, "That which is more than these is of the evil one." For to them that have understanding, instead of the mention of the punishment, the very greatness of the sin is sufficient for correction.

Wherefore also He here brings forward the heathens and the publicans, by the quality of the person putting the disciple to shame. Which Paul too did, saying, "Sorrow not, even as the rest which have no hope;"[1] and, "Even as the Gentiles which know not God."[2]

And to signify that He requires nothing very overpowering, but a little more than was accustomed, He saith,

"Do not even the Gentiles[3] the same?"[4]

Yet nevertheless He stops not the discourse at this, but makes it end with His rewards, and those good hopes, saying,

"Be ye therefore perfect, as your Heavenly Father."[5]

And He intersperses everywhere abundantly the name of the heavens, by the very place thoroughly elevating their minds. For as yet, I know not how, they were somewhat weak and dull.

10. Let us then, bearing in mind all the things which have been said, show forth great love even towards our enemies; and let us cast away that ridiculous custom, to which many of the more thoughtless give way, waiting for those that meet them to address them first. Towards that which hath a great blessing, they have no zeal; but what is ridiculous, that they follow after.

Wherefore now dost thou not address him first? "Because he is waiting for this," is the reply. Nay, for this very reason most of all thou shouldest have sprung forward to him, that thou mightest win the crown. "No," saith he, "since this was his object." And what can be worse than this folly? That is, "Because this," saith he, "was his object;—to become procurer of a reward for me;—I will not put my hand to what he has thus suggested." Now if he first address thee, thou gainest nothing, even though thou accost him. But if thou be first to spring forward and speak to him, thou hast made thyself profit of his pride, and hast gathered in a manner abundant fruit from his obstinacy.[6] What is it then but the utmost folly, when we are to reap so large fruit from bare words, to give up the gain; and condemning him, to stumble at the very same thing? For if thou blamest him for this, that he first waits to be addressed by another, wherefore dost thou emulate that same thing which thou accusest? That which thou saidst was evil, why art thou to imitate the same as good? Seest thou how that nothing is more senseless than a man who associates with wickedness? Wherefore, I entreat, let us flee this evil and ridiculous practice. Yea, for ten thousand friendships hath this pestilence overthrown, many enmities hath it wrought.

For this cause then let us anticipate them. Since we who are commanded to take blows, and be compelled to journey,[7] and to be stripped by enemies, and to bear it; what kind of indulgence should we deserve, exhibiting so great contentiousness in a mere formal address?

11. "Why," saith one, "we are despised and spit upon, the moment we have given him up this." And in order that man may not despise thee, dost thou offend God? And in order that thy frenzied fellow servant may not despise thee, dost thou despise the Lord, who hath bestowed on thee benefits so great? Nay, if it be amiss that thine equal

---

[1] 1 Thess. iv. 13. [2] 1 Thess. iv. 5.
[3] τελῶναι, rec. text. [But οἱ ἐθνικοί, the reading accepted by Chrysostom, is supported by the best authorities of every class. Comp. R. V.—R.]
[4] Matt. v. 47.
[5] Matt. v. 48. [The text of the Homily has γίνεσθε, which is probably imperative, but in Matt. v. 48, ἔσεσθε is the undisputed reading: comp. R. V., "Ye therefore shall be perfect,' etc.—R.]

[6] ἀπονοίας.   [7] ἀγγαρευέσθαι. [See note on sec. 3.—R.]

should despise thee, how much more that thou shouldest despise the God that made thee?

And together with this, consider that other point also; that when he despises thee, he is at that very moment employed in procuring to thee a greater reward. Since for God's sake thou submittest to it, because thou hast hearkened to His laws. And this, to what kind of honor is it not equal? to how many diadems? Be it my portion both to be insulted and despised for God's sake, rather than to be honored by all kings; for nothing, nothing is equal to this glory.

This then let us pursue, in such wise as Himself commanded, and making no account of the things of men, but showing forth per-fect self restraint in all things, let us so direct our own lives. For so even now, from this very time, we shall enjoy the good things of the heavens, and of the crowns that are there, walking as angels among men, going about in the earth like the angelic powers, and abiding apart from all lust, from all turmoil.

And together with all these things we shall receive also the unutterable blessings: unto which may we all attain, by the grace and love towards man of our Lord Jesus Christ, to whom be glory, and power, and worship, with the unoriginate Father, and the Holy and Good Spirit, now and always, even forever and ever. Amen

---

HOMILY XIX.

MATT. VI. 1.

"Take heed that ye do not your alms[1] before men, to be seen of them."

HE roots out in what remains the most tyrannical passion of all, the rage and madness with respect to vainglory, which springs up in them that do right. For at first He had not at all discoursed about it; it being indeed superfluous, before He had persuaded them to do any of the things which they ought, to teach in which way they should practise and pursue them.

But after He had led them on to self-command, then He proceeds to purge away also the alloy which secretly subsists with it. For this disease is by no means of random birth; but when we have duly performed many of the commandments.

It behooved therefore first to implant virtue, and then to remove the passion which mars its fruit.

And see with what He begins, with fasting, and prayer, and almsgiving: for in these good deeds most especially it is wont to make its haunt. The Pharisee, for instance, was hereby puffed up, who saith, "I fast twice a week, I give tithes of my substance."[2] And he was vainglorious too in his very prayer, making it for display. For since there was no one else present, he pointed himself out to the publican,[3] saying, "I am not as the rest of men, nor even as this publican."[4]

And mark how Christ began, as though He were speaking of some wild beast, hard to catch, and crafty to deceive him who was not very watchful. Thus, "take heed," saith He, "as to your alms." So Paul also speaks to the Philippians; "Beware of dogs."[5] And with reason, for[6] the evil beast comes in upon us secretly, and without noise puffs all away, and unobservedly carries out all that is within.

Forasmuch then as He had made much discourse about almsgiving, and brought forward God, "Who maketh His sun to rise on the evil and the good,"[7] and by motives from all quarters had urged them on to this, and had persuaded them to exult in the abundance of their giving; He finishes by taking away also all things that encumber this fair olive tree. For which same cause He saith, "Take heed that ye do not your alms before men," for that which was before mentioned, is "God's" almsgiving.

---

[1] [All authorities of an early period, including many fathers prior to Chrysostom, read δικαιοσύνην (comp. R. V.). It seems likely that the apparent homiletical advantage of the other reading made it the common one.—R.]

[2] Luke xviii. 12.

[3] Or, "by the publican:" τῷ τελώνῃ ἐνεδείκνυτο. [The dative is correctly rendered in the text, but the verb is used in a figurative sense.—R.]

[4] Luke xviii. 11. [5] Phil. iii. 2. ["The dogs," so R. V.—R.]

[6] [Καὶ γάρ.] [7] Matt. v. 45.

2. And when He had said, "not to do it before men," He added, "to be seen of them." And though it seems as if the same thing were said a second time, yet if any one give particular attention, it is not the same thing, but one is different from the other; and it hath great security, and unspeakable care and tenderness. For it may be, both that one doing alms before men may not do it to be seen of them, and again that one not doing it before men may do it to be seen of them. Wherefore it is not simply the thing, but the intent, which He both punishes and rewards. And unless such exactness were employed, this would make many more backward about the giving of alms, because it is not on every occasion altogether possible to do it secretly. For this cause, setting thee free from this restraint, He defines both the penalty and the reward not by the result of the action, but by the intention of the doer.

That is, that thou mayest not say, "What? am I then the worse, should another see?" —"it is not this," saith He, "that I am seeking, but the mind that is in thee, and the tone of what thou doest." For His will is to bring our soul altogether into frame, and to deliver it from every disease. Now having, as you see, forbidden men's acting for display, and having taught them the penalty thence ensuing, namely, to do it vainly, and for nought, He again rouses their spirits by putting them in mind of the Father, and of Heaven, that not by the loss alone He might sting them, but also shame them by the recollection of Him who gave them being.

"For ye have no reward," saith He, "with your Father which is in Heaven."[1]

Nor even at this did He stop, but proceeds yet further, by other motives also increasing their disgust. For as above He set forth publicans and heathens, by the quality of the person shaming their imitators, so also in this place the hypocrites.

"Therefore when thou doest thine alms," saith He, "do not sound a trumpet before thee, as the hypocrites do."[2]

Not that they had trumpets, but He means to display the greatness of their frenzy, by the use of this figure of speech, deriding and making a show[3] of them hereby.

And well hath He called them "hypocrites" for the mask was of mercy, but the spirit of cruelty and inhumanity. For they do it, not because they pity their neighbors, but that they themselves may enjoy credit; and this came of the utmost cruelty; while another was perishing with hunger, to be seeking vainglory, and not putting an end to his suffering.

It is not then the giving alms which is required, but the giving as one ought, the giving for such and such an end.[4]

Having then amply derided those men, and having handled them so, that the hearer should be even ashamed of them, He again corrects thoroughly the mind which is so distempered: and having said how we ought not to act, He signifies on the other hand how we ought to act. How then ought we to do our alms?[5]

"Let not thy left hand know," saith He, "what thy right hand doeth."[6]

Here again His enigmatical meaning is not of the hands, but He hath put the thing hyperbolically. As thus: "If it can be," saith He, "for thyself not to know it, let this be the object of thine endeavor; that, if it were possible, it may be concealed from the very hands that minister." It is not, as some say, that we should hide it from wrongheaded[7] men, for He hath here commanded that it should be concealed from all.

And then the reward too; consider how great it is. For after He had spoken of the punishment from the one, He points out also the honor derived from the other; from either side urging them, and leading them on to high lessons. Yea, for He is persuading them to know that God is everywhere present, and that not by our present life are our interests limited, but a yet more awful tribunal will receive us when we go hence, and the account of all our doings, and honors, and punishments: and that no one will be hid in doing anything either great or small, though he seem to be hid from men. For all this did He darkly signify, when He said,

"Thy Father which seeth in secret shall reward thee openly."[8]

Setting for him a great and august assemblage of spectators, and what He desires, that very thing bestowing on him in great abundance. "For what," saith He, "dost thou wish? is it not to have some to be spectators of what is going on? Behold then, thou hast some; not angels, nor archangels, but the God of all." And if thou desire to have men also as spectators, neither of this desire doth He deprive thee at the fitting season, but rather in greater abundance affords it

---

4 [διὰ τοῦτο.]
5 [As in the previous clause, "ought we to act."—R.]
6 Matt. vi. 3.
7 σκαιούς, literally, "on the left hand."
8 Matt. vi. 4. [The phrase ἐν τῷ φανερῷ is poorly supported in verses 4, 6, 18. It seems, however, to be accepted by Chrysostom. The R. V. properly renders "recompense thee" to distinguish from the word "reward" (μισθόν), which occurs in verse 2 and similar passages.—R.]

---

1 Matt. vi. 1.   2 Matt. vi. 2.   3 ἐκπομπεύων.

unto thee. For, if thou shouldest now make a display, thou wilt be able to make it to ten only, or twenty, or (we will say) a hundred persons: but if thou take pains to lie hid now, God Himself will then proclaim thee in the presence of the whole universe. Wherefore above all, if thou wilt have men see thy good deeds, hide them now, that then all may look on them with the more honor, God making them manifest, and extolling them, and proclaiming them before all. Again, whereas now they that behold will rather condemn thee as vainglorious; when they see thee crowned, so far from condemning, they will even admire thee, all of them. When therefore by waiting a little, thou mayest both receive a reward, and reap greater admiration; consider what folly it is to cast thyself out of both these; and while thou art seeking thy reward from God, and while God is beholding, to summon men for the display of what is going on. Why, if display must be made of our love, to our Father above all should we make it; and this most especially, when our Father hath the power both to crown and to punish.

And let me add, even were there no penalty, it were not meet for him who desires glory, to let go this our theatre, and take in exchange that of men. For who is there so wretched, as that when the king was hastening to come and see his achievements, he would let him go, and make up his assembly of spectators of poor men and beggars? For this cause then, He not only commands to make no display, but even to take pains to be concealed: it not being at all the same, not to strive for publicity, and to strive for concealment.

3. "And when ye pray," saith He, "ye shall not be as the hypocrites, for they love to pray standing in the synagogues, and in the corners of the streets. Verily I say unto you, they have their reward."[1]

"But thou, when thou prayest, enter into thy closet, and when thou hast shut thy door, pray to thy Father which is in secret."[2]

These too again He calls "hypocrites," and very fitly; for while they are feigning to pray to God, they are looking round after men; wearing the garb not of suppliants, but of ridiculous persons. For he, who is to do a suppliant's office, letting go all other, looks to him alone, who hath power to grant his request. But if thou leave this one, and go about wandering and casting around thine eyes everywhere, thou wilt depart with empty hands. For this was thine own will. Wherefore He said not, "such shall not receive a reward," but, "they have it out:" that is, they shall indeed receive one, but from those of whom they themselves desire to have it. For God wills not this: He rather for His part was willing to bestow on men the recompence that comes from Himself; but they seeking that which is from men, can be no longer justly entitled to receive from Him, for whom they have done nothing.

But mark, I pray thee, the lovingkindness of God, in that He promises to bestow on us a reward, even for those good things which we ask of Him.

Having then discredited them, who order not this duty as they ought, both from the place and from their disposition of mind, and having shown that they are very ridiculous: He introduces the best manner of prayer, and again gives the reward, saying, "Enter into thy closet."

"What then," it may be said, "ought we not to pray in church?" Indeed we ought by all means, but in such a spirit as this. Because everywhere God seeks the intention of all that is done. Since even if thou shouldest enter into thy closet, and having shut the door, shouldest do it for display, the doors will do thee no good.

It is worth observing in this case also, how exact the definition, which He made when He said, "That they may appear unto men." So that even if thou shut the doors, this He desires thee duly to perform, rather than the shutting of the doors, even to shut the doors of the mind. For as in everything it is good to be freed from vainglory, so most especially in prayer. For if even without this, we wander and are distracted, when shall we attend unto the things which we are saying, should we enter in having this disease also? And if we who pray and beseech attend not, how do we expect God to attend?

4. But yet some there are, who after such and so earnest charges, behave themselves so unseemly in prayer, that even when their person is concealed, they make themselves manifest to all by their voice, crying out disorderly,[3] and rendering themselves objects of ridicule both by gesture and voice. Seest thou not that even in a market place, should any one come up doing like this, and begging clamorously, he will drive away him whom he is petitioning; but if quietly, and with the proper gesture, then he rather wins over him that can grant the favor?

[1] Matt. vi. 5. [R. V., "to stand and pray," and, "They have received their reward."—R.]
[2] Matt. vi. 6. [R. V., "Enter into thine inner chamber, and having shut thy door, pray," etc.—R.]
[3] συρφετωδῶς.

Let us not then make our prayer by the gesture of our body, nor by the loudness of our voice, but by the earnestness of our mind: neither with noise and clamor and for display, so as even to disturb those that are near us, but with all modesty,[1] and with contrition in the mind, and with inward tears.

But art thou pained in mind, and canst not help crying aloud? yet surely it is the part of one exceedingly pained to pray and entreat even as I have said. Since Moses too was pained, and prayed in this way and was heard; for this cause also God said unto him, "Wherefore criest thou unto me."[2] And Hannah too again, her voice not being heard, accomplished all she wished, forasmuch as her heart cried out.[3] But Abel prayed not only when silent, but even when dying, and his blood sent forth a cry more clear than a trumpet.[4]

Do thou also then groan, even as that holy one, I forbid it not. "Rend," as the prophet commanded,[5] "thine heart, and not thy garments." Out of deeps call upon God, for it is said, "Out of the depths have I cried to Thee, O Lord."[6] From beneath, out of the heart, draw forth a voice, make thy prayer a mystery. Seest thou not that even in the houses of kings all tumult is put away, and great on all sides is the silence? Do thou also therefore, entering as into a palace,—not that on the earth, but what is far more awful than it, that which is in heaven, —show forth great seemliness. Yea, for thou art joined to the choirs of angels, and art in communion with archangels, and art singing with the seraphim. And all these tribes show forth much goodly order, singing with great awe that mystical strain, and their sacred hymns to God, the King of all. With these then mingle thyself, when thou art praying, and emulate their mystical order.

For not unto men art thou praying, but to God, who is everywhere present, who hears even before the voice, who knows the secrets of the mind. If thou so pray, great is the reward thou shalt receive.

"For thy Father," saith He, "who seeth in secret, shall reward thee openly."[7]

He said not, "shall freely give thee," but, "shall reward thee;" yea, for He hath made Himself a debtor to thee, and even from this hath honored thee with great honor. For because He Himself is invisible, He would have thy prayer be so likewise.

5. Then He speaks even the very words of the prayer.

"When ye pray," saith He, "use no vain repetitions, even as the heathen do."[8]

You see that when He was discoursing of almsgiving, He removed only that mischief which comes of vainglory, and added nothing more; neither did He say whence one should give alms; as from honest labor, and not from rapine nor covetousness: this being abundantly acknowledged among all. And also before that, He had thoroughly cleared up this point, when He blessed them "that hunger after righteousness."

But touching prayer, He adds somewhat over and above; "not to use vain repetitions." And as there He derides the hypocrites, so here the heathen; shaming the hearer everywhere most of all by the vileness of the persons. For since this, in most cases, is especially biting and stinging, I mean our appearing to be likened to outcast persons; by this topic He dissuades them; calling frivolousness, here, by the name of "vain repetition:" as when we ask of God things unsuitable, kingdoms, and glory, and to get the better of enemies, and abundance of wealth, and in general what does not at all concern us.

"For He knoweth," saith He, "what things ye have need of."[9]

And herewith He seems to me to command in this place, that neither should we make our prayers long; long, I mean, not in time, but in the number and length of the things mentioned. For perseverance indeed in the same requests is our duty: His word being, "continuing instant in prayer."[10]

And He Himself too, by that example of the widow, who prevailed with the pitiless and cruel ruler, by the continuance of her intercession;[11] and by that of the friend, who came late at night time, and roused the sleeper from his bed,[12] not for his friendship's, but for his importunity's sake; what did He, but lay down a law, that all should continually make supplication unto Him? He doth not however bid us compose a prayer of ten thousand clauses, and so come to Him and merely repeat it. For this He obscurely signified when He said, "They think that they shall be heard for their much speaking."

"For He knoweth," saith He, "what things ye have need of." And if He know, one may say, what we have need of, wherefore must we pray? Not to instruct Him, but to prevail with Him; to be made intimate with Him, by continuance in supplication; to be humbled; to be reminded of thy sins.

---

[1] ἐπιεικείας.   [2] Exod. xiv. 15.   [3] 1 Sam. i. 13.
[4] Gen. iv. 10.   [5] Joel ii. 13.   [6] Ps. cxxxi. 1.
[7] Matt. vi. 6. [See note on sec. 2, verse 4.—R.]

[8] Matt. vi. 7. [R. V., "And in praying use not vain repetitions, as the Gentiles do."—R.]
[9] Matt. vi. 8.   [10] Rom. xii. 12.
[11] Luke xviii. 1.   [12] Luke xi. 5.

6. "After this manner, therefore, pray ye," saith He: "Our Father, which art in heaven."[1]

See how He straightway stirred up the hearer, and reminded him of all God's bounty in the beginning. For he who calls God Father, by him both remission of sins, and taking away of punishment, and righteousness, and sanctification, and redemption, and adoption, and inheritance, and brotherhood with the Only-Begotten, and the supply of the Spirit, are acknowledged in this single title. For one cannot call God Father, without having attained to all those blessings. Doubly, therefore, doth He awaken their spirit, both by the dignity of Him who is called on, and by the greatness of the benefits which they have enjoyed. But when He saith, "in Heaven," He speaks not this as shutting up God there, but as withdrawing him who is praying from earth, and fixing him in the high places, and in the dwellings above.

He teaches, moreover, to make our prayer common, in behalf of our brethren also. For He saith not, "my Father, which art in Heaven," but, "our Father," offering up his supplications for the body in common, and nowhere looking to his own, but everywhere to his neighbor's good. And by this He at once takes away hatred, and quells pride, and casts out envy, and brings in the mother of all good things, even charity, and exterminates the inequality of human things, and shows how far the equality reaches between the king and the poor man, if at least in those things which are greatest and most indispensable, we are all of us fellows. For what harm comes of our kindred below, when in that which is on high we are all of us knit together, and no one hath aught more than another; neither the rich more than the poor, nor the master than the servant, neither the ruler than the subject, nor the king than the common soldier, nor the philosopher than the barbarian, nor the skillful than the unlearned? For to all hath He given one nobility, having vouchsafed to be called the Father of all alike.

7. When therefore He hath reminded us of this nobility, and of the gift from above, and of our equality with our brethren, and of charity; and when He hath removed us from earth, and fixed us in Heaven; let us see what He commands us to ask after this.

Not but, in the first place, even that saying alone is sufficient to implant instruction in all virtue. For he who hath called God Father, and a common Father, would be justly bound to show forth such a conversation, as not to appear unworthy of this nobility, and to exhibit a diligence proportionate to the gift. Yet is He not satisfied with this, but adds, also another clause, thus saying,

"Hallowed be Thy name."

Worthy of him who calls God Father, is the prayer to ask nothing before the glory of His Father, but to account all things secondary to the work of praising Him. For "hallowed" is *glorified*. For His own glory He hath complete, and ever continuing the same, but He commands him who prays to seek that He may be glorified also by our life. Which very thing He had said before likewise, "Let your light so shine before men, that they may see your good works, and glorify your Father which is in heaven."[2] Yea, and the seraphim too, giving glory, said on this wise, "Holy, holy, holy."[3] So that "hallowed" means this, *viz.* "glorified." That is, "vouchsafe," saith he, "that we may live so purely, that through us all may glorify Thee." Which thing again appertains unto perfect self-control, to present to all a life so irreprehensible, that every one of the beholders may offer to the Lord the praise due to Him for this.

"Thy kingdom come."[4]

And this again is the language of a right-minded child, not to be rivetted to things that are seen, neither to account things present some great matter; but to hasten unto our Father, and to long for the things to come. And this springs out of a good conscience, and a soul set free from things that are on earth. This, for instance, Paul himself was longing after every day: wherefore he also said, that "even we ourselves, who have the first-fruits of the Spirit, groan, waiting for an adoption, the redemption of our body."[5] For he who hath this fondness,[6] can neither be puffed up by the good things of this life, nor abashed by its sorrows; but as though dwelling in the very heavens, is freed from each sort of irregularity.[7]

"Thy will be done in earth, as it is in Heaven."

Behold a most excellent train of thought! in that He bade us indeed long for the things

---

[1] Matt. vi. 9. [In Latin editions of the Homilies a division has been made at this point, so as to separate the comments on the Lord's Prayer into a distinct Homily. But the Greek mss. have no such division. The latter half is numbered Homily XX., and the enumeration of all the subsequent Homilies modified. In Migne's edition, two sets of numbers are given to the Homilies which follow.—R.]

[2] Matt. v. 16.   [3] Is. vi. 3 ; Rev. iv. 8.   [4] Matt. vi. 10.
[5] Rom. viii. 23. [The citation is slightly abridged, but the latter part agrees exactly with the Greek text followed in the R. V., which renders : " waiting for *our* adoption, *to wit*, the redemption of our body."—R.]
[6] ἔρωτα.   [7] ἀνωμαλίας.

to come, and hasten towards that sojourn; and, till that may be, even while we abide here, so long to be earnest in showing forth the same conversation as those above. For ye must long, saith He, for heaven, and the things in heaven; however, even before heaven, He hath bidden us make the earth a heaven and do and say all things, even while we are continuing in it, as having our conversation there; insomuch that these too should be objects of our prayer to the Lord. For there is nothing to hinder our reaching the perfection of the powers above, because we inhabit the earth; but it is possible even while abiding here, to do all, as though already placed on high. What He saith therefore is this: "As there all things are done without hindrance, and the angels are not partly obedient and partly disobedient, but in all things yield and obey (for He saith, 'Mighty in strength, performing His word') ;[1] so vouchsafe that we men may not do Thy will by halves, but perform all things as Thou willest."

Seest thou how He hath taught us also to be modest, by making it clear that virtue is not of our endeavors only, but also of the grace from above? And again, He hath enjoined each one of us, who pray, to take upon himself the care of the whole world. For He did not at all say, " Thy will be done" *in me*, or *in us*, but everywhere on the earth; so that error may be destroyed, and truth implanted, and all wickedness cast out, and virtue return, and no difference in this respect be henceforth between heaven and earth. " For if this come to pass," saith He, " there will be no difference between things below and above, separated as they are in nature; the earth exhibiting to us another set of angels."

8. " Give us this day our daily bread."[2]

What is " *daily bread* " ? That for one day.[3]

For because He had said thus, " Thy will be done in earth as it is in heaven," but was discoursing to men encompassed with flesh, and subject to the necessities of nature, and

incapable of the same impassibility with the angels:—while He enjoins the commands to be practised by us also, even as they perform them; He condescends likewise, in what follows, to the infirmity of our nature. Thus, " perfection of conduct," saith He, " I require as great, not however freedom from passions; no, for the tyranny of nature permits it not: for it requires necessary food." But mark, I pray thee, how even in things that are bodily, that which is spiritual abounds. For it is neither for riches, nor for delicate living, nor for costly raiment, nor for any other such thing, but for bread only, that He hath commanded us to make our prayer. And for " daily bread," so as not to " take thought for the morrow."[4] Because of this He added, " *daily* bread," that is, bread for one day.

And not even with this expression is He satisfied, but adds another too afterwards, saying, " Give us *this day;*" so that we may not, beyond this, wear ourselves out with the care of the following day. For that day, the interval[5] before which thou knowest not whether thou shalt see, wherefore dost thou submit to its cares?

This, as He proceeded, he enjoined also more fully, saying, " Take no thought for the morrow." He would have us be on every hand unencumbered and winged for flight, yielding just so much to nature as the compulsion of necessity requires of us.

9. Then forasmuch as it comes to pass that we sin even after the washing of regeneration, He, showing His love to man to be great even in this case, commands us for the remission of our sins to come unto God who loves man, and thus to say,

" Forgive us our debts, as we also forgive our debtors."[6]

Seest thou surpassing mercy? After taking away so great evils, and after the unspeakable greatness of His gift, if men sin again, He counts them such as may be forgiven. For that this prayer belongs to believers, is taught us both by the laws of the church, and by the beginning of the prayer. For the uninitiated could not call God Father. If then the prayer belongs to believers, and they pray, entreating that sins may be forgiven them, it is clear that not even after the laver is the profit of repentance taken away. Since, had He not meant to signify this, He would not have made a law that we should so pray. Now He who both brings sins to

---

[1] Ps. ciii. 20.   [2] Matt. vi. 11.
[3] [This is one of the most important passages in these Homilies, from a lexical point of view. The Greek text is, Τί ἐστι, Τον ἄρτον τὸν ἐπιούσιον ; Τοὺ ἐφήμερον. The word ἐπιούσιος is found only in Matt. vi. 11, Luke xi. 3, and in the Christian literature based on these passages. As all Biblical scholars are aware, the etymology and meaning are still open to discussion. See Thayer's *Greek Lexicon, New Testament, sub voce*. The Fathers generally gave it a spiritual or mystical sense, and Chrysostom's position is, therefore, the more important. The modern views may be inferred from the R. V., which in the text of both renders the word " daily," with the margin " Greek, our bread for the coming day," but the American Company add as a second marginal rendering, " our needful bread." These two marginal renderings represent two distinct etymologies, while " daily " is an explanatory or inferential rendering, for which the authority of Chrysostom has furnished strong support.—R.]

[4] Matt. vi. 34.   [5] τὸ διάστημα.
[6] Matt. vi. 12. [R. V., " have forgiven our debtors," following a different and better supported reading than that accepted by Chrysostom.—R.]

remembrance, and bids us ask forgiveness, and teaches how we may obtain remission, and so makes the way easy; it is perfectly clear that He introduced this rule of supplication, as knowing, and signifying, that it is possible even after the font[1] to wash ourselves from our offenses; by reminding us of our sins, persuading us to be modest; by the command to forgive others, setting us free from all revengeful passion; while by promising in return for this to pardon us also, He holds out good hopes, and instructs us to have high views[2] concerning the unspeakable mercy of God toward man.

But what we should most observe is this, that whereas in each of the clauses He had made mention of the whole of virtue, and in this way had included also the forgetfulness of injuries (for so, that " His name be hallowed," is the exactness of a perfect conversation; and that " His will be done," declares the same thing again; and to be able to call God " Father," is the profession of a blameless life; in all which things had been comprehended also the duty of remitting our anger against them that have transgressed): still He was not satisfied with these, but meaning to signify how earnest He is in the matter, He sets it down also in particular, and after the prayer, He makes mention of no other commandment than this, saying thus:

" For if ye forgive men their trespasses, your heavenly Father also will forgive you."[3]

So that the beginning is of us, and we ourselves have control over the judgment that is to be passed upon us. For in order that no one, even of the senseless, might have any complaint to make, either great or small, when brought to judgment; on thee, who art to give account, He causes the sentence to depend; and " in what way soever thou hast judged for thyself,[4] in the same," saith He, " do I also judge thee." And if thou forgive thy fellow servant, thou shalt obtain the same favor from me; though indeed the one be not equal to the other. For thou forgivest in thy need, but God, having need of none: thou, thy fellow slave; God, His slave: thou liable to unnumbered charges; God, being without sin. But yet even thus doth He show forth His lovingkindness towards man.

Since He might indeed, even without this, forgive thee all thine offenses; but He wills thee hereby also to receive a benefit; affording thee on all sides innumerable occasions

of gentleness and love to man, casting out what is brutish in thee, and quenching wrath, and in all ways cementing thee to him who is thine own member.

For what canst thou have to say? that thou hast wrongfully endured some ill of thy neighbor? (For these only are trespasses, since if it be done with justice, the act is not a trespass.) But thou too art drawing near to receive forgiveness for such things, and for much greater. And even before the forgiveness, thou hast received no small gift, in being taught to have a human soul, and in being trained to all gentleness. And herewith a great reward shall also be laid up for thee elsewhere, even to be called to account for none of thine offenses.

What sort of punishment then do we not deserve, when after having received the privilege, we betray our salvation? And how shall we claim to be heard in the rest of our matters, if we will not, in those which depend on us, spare our own selves?

10. "And lead us not into temptation; but deliver us from the evil one: for Thine is the kingdom, and the power, and the glory, for ever. Amen."[5]

Here He teaches us plainly our own vileness, and quells our pride, instructing us to deprecate all conflicts, instead of rushing upon them. For so both our victory will be more glorious, and the devil's overthrow more to be derided. I mean, that as when we are dragged forth, we must stand nobly; so when we are not summoned, we should be quiet, and wait for the time of conflict; that we may show both freedom from vainglory, and nobleness of spirit.

And He here calls the devil " the wicked one," commanding us to wage against him a war that knows no truce, and implying that he is not such by nature. For wickedness[6] is not of those things that are from nature, but of them that are added by our own choice. And he is so called pre-eminently, by reason of the excess of his wickedness, and because he, in no respect injured by us, wages against us implacable war. Wherefore neither said He, " deliver us from the wicked ones," but, " from the wicked one;" instructing us in no case to entertain displeasure against our neighbors, for what wrongs soever we may suffer at their hands, but to transfer our enmity from these to him, as being himself the cause of all our wrongs.

---

1 [μετὰ τὸ λουτρόν, rendered above, "after the laver."—R.]
2 φιλοσοφεῖν.   3 Matt. vi. 14.
4 Many MSS. read hast given judgment on him.

5 Matt. vi. 13. [Two points of great interest are to be noticed here : (1) that the interpretation " of the evil one " is unqualifiedly accepted ; (2) that the doxology is given without any suggestion of doubt respecting the genuineness of it. Here, as so often, the exegetical accuracy of Chrysostom appears to exceed his critical estimate of the Greek text of the New Testament.—R.]
6 πονηρία.

Having then made us anxious as before conflict, by putting us in mind of the enemy, and having cut away from us all our remissness; He again encourages and raises our spirits, by bringing to our remembrance the King under whom we are arrayed, and signifying Him to be more powerful than all. "For Thine," saith He, "is the kingdom, and the power, and the glory."

Doth it not then follow, that if His be the kingdom, we should fear no one, since there can be none to withstand, and divide the empire with him. For when He saith, "Thine is the kingdom," He sets before us even him, who is warring against us, brought into subjection, though he seem to oppose, God for a while permitting it. For in truth he too is among God's servants, though of the degraded class, and those guilty of offense; and he would not dare set upon any of his fellow servants, had he not first received license from above. And why say I, "his fellow servants?" Not even against swine did he venture any outrage, until He Himself allowed him;[1] nor against flocks, nor herds, until he had received permission from above.[2]

"And the power," saith He. Therefore, manifold as thy weakness may be, thou mayest of right be confident, having such a one to reign over thee, who is able fully to accomplish all, and that with ease, even by thee.

"And the glory, for ever. Amen." Thus He not only frees thee from the dangers that are approaching thee, but can make thee also glorious and illustrious. For as His power is great, so also is His glory unspeakable, and they are all boundless, and no end of them. Seest thou how He hath by every means anointed His Champion, and hath framed Him to be full of confidence?

11. Then, as I said before, meaning to signify, that of all things He most loathes and hates bearing malice, and most of all accepts the virtue which is opposite to that vice; He hath after the prayer also again put us in mind of this same point of goodness; both by the punishment set, and by the reward appointed, urging the hearer to obey this command.

"For if ye forgive men," saith He, "your heavenly Father will also forgive you. But if ye forgive not, neither will He forgive you."[3]

With this view He hath again mentioned

heaven also, and their Father; to abash the hearer by this topic likewise; that he of all people, being of such a Father, should be made a wild beast of; and summoned as he is to heaven, should cherish an earthly and ordinary[4] sort of mind. Since not by grace only, you see, ought we to become His children, but also by our works. And nothing makes us so like God, as being ready to forgive the wicked and wrong-doers; even as indeed He had taught before, when He spake of His "making the sun to shine on the evil and on the good."[5]

For this same cause again in every one of the clauses He commands us to make our prayers common, saying, "Our Father," and "Thy will be done in earth as it is in heaven," and "Give us the bread, and forgive us our debts," and "lead us not into temptation," and "deliver us;" everywhere commanding us to use this plural word, that we may not retain so much as a vestige of anger against our neighbor.

How great punishment then must they deserve, who after all this, so far from themselves forgiving, do even entreat God for vengeance on their enemies, and diametrically as it were transgress this law; and this while He is doing and contriving all, to hinder our being at variance one with another? For since love is the root of all that is good, He removing from all sides whatever mars it, brings us together, and cements us to each other. For there is not, there is not one, be he father, or mother, or friend, or what you will, who so loved us as the God who created us. And this, above all things, both His daily benefits and His precepts make manifest. But if thou tell me of the pains, and of the sorrows, and of the evils of life; consider in how many things thou offendest Him every day, and thou wilt no longer marvel, though more than these evils should come upon thee, but if thou shouldest enjoy any good, then thou wilt marvel, and be amazed. But as it is, we look upon the calamities that come upon us, but the offenses, whereby we offend daily, we consider not: therefore we are perplexed. Since if we did but reckon up with strictness our sins of one day only, in that case we should know well how great evils we must be liable to.

And to let pass the other misdoings of which we have been guilty, each one for himself, and to speak of what have been committed this day; although of course I know not in what each of us may have sinned, yet such is the abundance of our misdoings, that

---

[1] Luke viii. 32.   [2] Job i. 12.
[3] Matt. vi. 14, 15. [The latter verse is abridged, but there are variations in the MSS. of the New Testament ; comp. Tischendorf, *in loco.*—R.]

[4] βιωτικόν [here in the sense of "secular."—R.]
[5] Matt. v. 45.

not even he who knew all exactly would be able to choose from among these only. Which of us, for instance, hath not been careless in his prayers? Which hath not been insolent, or vainglorious? Who hath not spoken evil of his brother, hath not admitted a wicked desire, hath not looked with unchaste eyes, hath not remembered things with hostile feeling, even till he made his heart swell?

And if while we are in church, and in a short time we have become guilty of so great evils; what shall be when we are gone out from hence? If in the harbor the waves are so high, when we are gone forth into the channel of wickednesses, the forum I mean, and to public business, and our cares at home, shall we indeed be able so much as to know ourselves again?

But yet from our so great and so many sins, God hath given us a short and easy way of deliverance, and one that is free from all toil. For what sort of toil is it to forgive him that hath grieved us? Nay, it is a toil not to forgive, but to keep up our enmity: even as to be delivered from the anger, both works in us a great refreshment, and is very easy to him that is willing. For there is no sea to be crossed, nor long journey to be travelled, nor summits of mountains to be passed over, nor money to be spent, no need to torment thy body; but it suffices to be willing only, and all our sins are done away.

But if so far from forgiving him thyself, thou makest intercession to God against him, what hope of salvation wilt thou then have, if at the very time when thou oughtest rather to appease God, even then thou provokest Him; putting on the garb of a suppliant, but uttering the cries of a wild beast, and darting out against thyself those shafts of the wicked one? Wherefore Paul also, making mention of prayer, required nothing so much as the observance of this commandment; for He saith, "lifting up holy hands without wrath and doubting."[1] And if when thou hast need of mercy, not even then wilt thou let go thine anger, but art rather exceedingly mindful of it, and that, although thou knowest thou art thrusting the sword into thyself; when will it be possible for thee to become merciful, and to spew out the evil venom of this wickedness?

But if thou hast not yet seen this outrageousness in its full extent, suppose it happening among men, and then thou wilt perceive the excess of the insolence. As thus: should one approach thee who are a man, seeking to

obtain mercy, and then, in the midst of his lying on the ground, should see an enemy, and leaving off to supplicate thee, begin to beat him; wouldest thou not make thyself more angry with him? This do thou consider as taking place with regard to God also. For so thou likewise, making supplication unto God, leavest thy supplication in the midst, and smitest thine enemy with thy words, and insultest the laws of God. Him who made a law to dismiss all anger, thou art summoning against those that have vexed thee, and requiring Him to do things contrary to His own commandments. Is it not enough for thee in the way of revenge, that thou thyself transgressest the law of God, but entreatest thou Him likewise to do so? What? hath He forgotten what He commanded? What? is He a man who spake these things? It is God, who knows all things, and whose will is, that His own laws be kept with the utmost exactness, and who, so far from doing these things which thou art requiring of Him, doth even regard thee who sayest these things, merely because thou sayest them, with aversion and hatred, and exacts of thee the most extreme penalty. How then seekest thou to obtain of Him things, from which He very seriously bids thee refrain?

Yet some there are, who have come to such a point of brutishness, as not only to make intercession against their enemies, but even to curse their children, and to taste, if only it might be, of their very flesh; or rather they are even tasting thereof. For tell me not this, that thou hast not fixed thy teeth in the body of him that vexed thee; since thou hast done, at least as far as concerned thee, what is much more grievous; in claiming that wrath from above should fall upon him, and that he should be delivered over to undying punishment, and be overthrown with his whole house.

Why, what sort of bites are as ferocious as this? what kind of weapons as bitter? Not so did Christ instruct thee; not so did He command thee to stain thy mouth with blood. Nay, mouths made bloody with human flesh are not so shocking as tongues like these.

How then wilt thou salute thy brother? how wilt thou touch the sacrifice? how taste the Lord's blood, when thou hast so much venom upon thy mind? Since when thou sayest, "Rend him in pieces, and overthrow his house, and destroy all," when thou art imprecating on him ten thousand deaths, thou art in nothing different from a murderer, or rather from a wild beast that devours men.

Let us cease then from this disease and madness, and that kindliness which He com-

---

[1] 1 Tim. ii. 8. [R. V., "disputing," with margin, "doubting."—R.]

manded let us show forth towards them that have vexed us: that we may become like " our Father which is in heaven." And we shall cease therefrom, if we call to mind our own sins; if we strictly search out all our misdeeds at home, abroad, and in the market, and in church.

12. For if for nothing else, surely for our disrespectfulness here we are worthy to undergo the utmost punishment. For when prophets are chanting, and apostles singing hymns, and God is discoursing, we wander without, and bring in upon us a turmoil of worldly business. And we do not afford to the laws of God so great stillness, even as the spectators in the theatres to the emperor's letters, keeping silence for them. For there, when these letters are being read, deputies at once, and governors, and senate, and people, stand all upright, with quietness hearkening to the words. And if amid that most profound silence any one should suddenly leap up and cry out, he suffers the utmost punishment, as having been insolent to the emperor. But here, when the letters from heaven are being read, great is the confusion on all sides. And yet both He who sent the letters is much greater than this our king,[1] and the assembly more venerable: for not men only, but angels too are in it; and these triumphs, of which the letters bear us the good tidings, are much more awful than those on earth. Wherefore not men only, but angels also and archangels; both the nations of heaven, and all we on the earth, are commanded to give praise. For, " Bless the Lord," it is said, " all His works."[2] Yea, for His are no small achievements, rather they surpass all speech, and thought, and understanding of man.

And these things the prophets proclaim every day, each of them in a different way publishing this glorious triumph. For one saith, " Thou hast gone up on high, Thou hast led captivity captive, and hast received gifts amongst men."[3] And, " The Lord strong and mighty in battle."[4] And another saith, " He shall divide the spoils of the strong."[5] For indeed to this purpose He came, that He might " preach deliverance to captives, and recovery of sight to the blind."[6] And raising aloud the cry of victory over death, he said, " Where, O Death, is thy victory? Where, O Grave, is thy sting?"[7] And another again, declaring glad tidings of

the most profound peace, said, " They shall beat their swords into ploughshares, and their spears into pruning hooks."[8] And while one calls on Jerusalem, saying, " Rejoice greatly, O daughter of Sion, for lo ! thy King cometh to thee meek, riding upon an ass, and a young colt; "[9] another proclaims His second coming also, saying on this wise, " The Lord, whom ye seek, will come, and who will abide the day of His coming ?[10] Leap ye as calves set free from bonds."[11] And another again, amazed at such things, said, " This is our God; there shall none other be accounted of in comparison of Him."[12]

Yet, nevertheless, while both these and many more sayings than these are being uttered, while we ought to tremble, and not so much as account ourselves to be on the earth; still, as though in the midst of a forum, we make an uproar and disturbance, and spend the whole time of our solemn assembly[13] in discoursing of things which are nothing to us.

When therefore both in little things, and in great, both in hearing, and in doing, both abroad, and at home, in the church, we are so negligent; and together with all this, pray also against our enemies: whence are we to have any hope of salvation, adding to so great sins yet another grievous enhancement, and equivalent to them all, even this unlawful prayer ?

Have we then hereafter any right to marvel, if aught befall us of the things which are unexpected and painful ? whereas we ought to marvel when no such thing befalls us. For the former is in the natural order of things, but the latter were beyond all reason and expectation. For surely it is beyond reason, that they who are become enemies of God, and are provoking Him to anger, should enjoy sunshine and showers, and all the rest; who being men surpass the barbarity of wild beasts, setting themselves one against another, and by the biting of their neighbors staining their own tongues with blood: after the spiritual table, and His so great benefits, and His innumerable injunctions.

Therefore, considering these things, let us cast up that venom; let us put an end to our enmities, and let us make the prayers that become such as we are. Instead of the brutality of devils, let us take upon us the mildness of angels; and in whatsoever things we may have been injured, let us, consider-

---

[1] [τοῦ βασιλέως, the Greek title of the emperor. The term is so rendered above.—R.]

[2] Ps. ciii. 22.　　　[3] Ps. lxviii. 18.　　　[4] Ps. xxiv. 8.

[5] Isa. liii. 12.　　　[6] Isa. lxi. 1 ; Luke iv. 19.

[7] Hosea xiii. 14. [The LXX. has been modified in this citation to accord, in the first clause, with 1 Cor. xv. 55.—R.]

[8] Isa. ii. 4 ; Micah iv. 3.　　[9] Zech. ix. 9.　　[10] Mal. iii. 1, 2.

[11] Mal. iv. 2. The present reading of the LXX. is σκιρτήσετε, " ye shall leap." [So the Hebrew ; comp. R. V.—R.]

[12] Baruc. iii. 35.

[13] τῆς συνάξεως : " of the Holy Communion." [But see note 1 in Homily V., p. 31, and comp. Homily LXXXVIII. at the close. —R.]

ing our own case, and the reward appointed us for this commandment, soften our anger; let us assuage the billows, that we may both pass through the present life calmly, and when we have departed thither, may find our Lord such as we have been towards our fellow-servants. And if this be a heavy and fearful thing, let us make it light and desirable; and let us open the glorious gates of confidence towards Him; and what we had not strength to effect by abstaining from sin, that let us accomplish by becoming gentle to them who have sinned against us (for this surely is not grievous, nor burdensome) ; and let us by doing kindnesses to our enemies, lay up beforehand much mercy for ourselves.

For so both during this present life all will love us, and above all others, God will both befriend and crown us, and will count us worthy of all the good things to come; unto which may we all attain, by the grace and love towards man of our Lord Jesus Christ, to whom be glory and might for ever and ever. Amen.

HOMILY XX.[1]

MATT. VI. 16.

"And when ye fast, be not as the hypocrites, of a sad countenance. For they disfigure their faces, that they may appear unto men to fast."

HERE it were well to sigh aloud, and to wail bitterly: for not only do we imitate the hypocrites, but we have even surpassed them. For I know, yea I know many, not merely fasting and making a display of it, but neglecting to fast, and yet wearing the masks of them that fast, and cloaking themselves with an excuse worse than their sin.

For " I do this," say they, " that I may not offend the many." What sayest thou? There is a law of God which commands these things, and dost thou talk of offense? And thinkest thou that in keeping it thou art offending, in transgressing it, delivering men from offense? And what can be worse than this folly?

Wilt thou not leave off becoming worse than the very hypocrites, and making thine hypocrisy double? And when thou considerest the great excess of this evil, wilt thou not be abashed at the force of the expression now before us? In that He did not say, "they act a part," merely, but willing also to touch them more deeply, He saith, " For they disfigure their faces;" that is, they corrupt, they mar them.

But if this be a disfiguring of the face, to appear pale for vainglory, what should we say concerning the women who corrupt their faces with colorings and paintings to the ruin of the unchaste sort of young men? For while those harm themselves only, these women harm both themselves and them who behold them. Wherefore we should fly both from the one pest and from the other, keeping at distance enough and to spare. For so He not only commanded to make no display, but even to seek to be concealed. Which thing He had done before likewise.

And whereas in the matter of almsgiving, He did not put it simply, but having said, " Take heed not to do it before men," He added, " to be seen of them;" yet concerning fasting and prayer, He made no such limitation. Why could this have been? Because for almsgiving to be altogether concealed is impossible, but for prayer and fasting, it is possible.

As therefore, when He said, " Let not thy left hand know what thy right hand doeth," it was not of hands that He was speaking, but of the duty of being strictly concealed from all; and as when He commanded us to enter into our closet, not there alone absolutely, nor there primarily, did He command us to pray, but He covertly intimated the same thing again; so likewise here, in commanding us " to be anointed," He did not enact that we positively must anoint ourselves; for then we should all of us be found transgressors of this law; and above all, surely, they who have taken the most pains to keep it, the societies of the monks, who have taken up their dwelling on the mountains. It was not this then that He enjoined, but, forasmuch as the ancients had a custom to anoint themselves continually, when they were taking their pleasure and rejoicing (and this one may see clearly from David[1] and from Daniel) ;[2] He said that we were to anoint ourselves, not that we should positively do this, but that by all means we might endeavor, with great strictness, to hide this our acquisition. And to convince thee that so it is, He Himself, when by action exhibiting what He enjoined in words, having fasted forty days, and fasted in secret, did neither anoint nor wash Himself: nevertheless, though He did not these things, He most assuredly fulfilled the whole without vainglory. It is this then that He enjoins on us likewise, both bringing before us the hypocrites, and by a twice repeated charge dissuading the hearers.

And somewhat else He signified by this name, this of hypocrites,[3] I mean. That is, not only by the ridiculousness of the thing, nor by its bringing an extreme penalty, but also by showing that such deceit is but for a season, doth He withdraw us from that evil desire. For the actor seems glorious just so long as the audience is sitting; or rather not even then in the sight of all. For the more part of the spectators know who it is, and what part he is acting. However, when the audience is broken up, he is more clearly discovered to all. Now this, you see, the vainglorious must in all necessity undergo. For even here they are manifest to the majority, as not being that which they appear to be, but as wearing a mask only; but much more will they be detected hereafter, when all things appear " naked and open."[4]

And by another motive again He withdraws them from the hypocrites, by showing that His injunction is light. For He doth not make the fast more strict, nor command us to practise more of it, but not to lose the crown thereof. So that what seems hard to bear, is common to us and to the hypocrites, for they also fast; but that which is lightest, namely, not to lose the reward after our labors, " this is what I command," saith He; adding nothing to our toils, but gathering our wages for us with all security, and not suffering us to go away unrewarded, as they do. Nay, they will not so much as imitate them that wrestle in the Olympic games, who although so great a multitude is sitting there, and so many princes, desire to

please but one, even him who adjudges the victory amongst them; and this, though he be much their inferior. But thou, though thou hast a twofold motive for displaying the victory to Him, first, that He is the person to adjudge it, and also, that He is beyond comparison superior to all that are sitting in the theatre,—thou art displaying it to others, who so far from profiting, do privily work thee the greatest harm.

However, I do not forbid even this, saith He. Only, if thou art desirous to make a show to men, also, wait, and I will bestow on thee this too in fuller abundance, and with great profit. For as it is, this quite breaks thee off from the glory which is with me, even as to despise these things unites thee closely; but then shalt thou enjoy all in entire security; having, even before that last, no little fruit to reap in this world also, namely, that thou hast trodden under foot all human glory, and art freed from the grievous bondage of men, and art become a true worker of virtue. Whereas now, as long at least as thou art so disposed, if thou shouldest be in a desert, thou wilt be deserted by all thy virtue, having none to behold thee. This is to act as one insulting virtue itself, if thou art to pursue it not for its own sake, but with an eye to the ropemaker, and the brazier, and the common people of the baser sort, that the bad and they that are far removed from virtue may admire thee. And thou art calling the enemies of virtue to the display and the sight thereof, as if one were to choose to live continently, not for the excellency of continence, but that he might make a show before prostitutes. Thou also, it would seem, wouldest not choose virtue, but for the sake of virtue's enemies; whereas thou oughtest indeed to admire her on this very ground, that she hath even her enemies to praise her, — yet to admire her (as is meet), not for others, but for her own sake. Since we too, when we are loved not for our own, but for others' sake, account the thing an insult. Just so I bid thee reckon in the case of virtue as well, and neither to follow after her for the sake of others, nor for men's sake to obey God; but men for God's sake. Since if thou do the contrary, though thou seem to follow virtue, thou hast provoked equally with him who follows her not. For just as he disobeyed by not doing, so thou by doing unlawfully.

2 " Lay not up for yourselves treasures upon earth."[5]

Thus, after He hath cast out the disease

---

[1] 2 Sam. xii. 20.   [2] Dan. x. 3.   [3] Literally, "actors."
[4] Heb. iv. 13. [R. V., "laid open," τετραχηλισμένα.—R.]

[5] Matt. vi. 19. [" upon the earth," so R. V.—R.]

of vainglory, and not before, He seasonably introduces His discourse of voluntary poverty.[1] For nothing so trains men to be fond of riches, as the fondness for glory. This, for instance, is why men devise those herds of slaves, and that swarm of eunuchs, and their horses with trappings of gold, and their silver tables, and all the rest of it, yet more ridiculous; not to satisfy any wants, nor to enjoy any pleasure, but that they may make a show before the multitude.

Now above He had only said, that we must show mercy; but here He points out also how great mercy we must show, when He saith, " Lay not up treasure." For it not being possible at the beginning to introduce all at once His discourse on contempt of riches, by reason of the tyranny of the passion, He breaks it up into small portions, and having set free the hearer's mind, instills it therein, so as that it shall become acceptable. Wherefore, you see, He said first, " Blessed are the merciful;" and after this, "Agree with thine adversary;" and after that again, " If any one will sue thee at the law, and take thy coat, give him thy cloak also;" but here, that which is much greater than all these. For there His meaning was, " if thou see a law-suit impending, do this; since to want and be freed from strife, is better than to possess and strive;" but here, supposing neither adversary nor any one at law with thee, and without all mention of any other such party, He teaches the contempt of riches itself by itself, implying that not so much for their sake who receive mercy, as for the giver's sake, He makes these laws: so that though there be no one injuring us, or dragging us into a court of justice, even so we may despise our possessions, bestowing them on those that are in need.

And neither here hath He put the whole, but even in this place it is gently spoken; although He had in the wilderness shown forth to a surpassing extent His conflicts in that behalf.[2] However He doth not express this, nor bring it forward; for it was not yet time to reveal it; but for a while He searches out for reasons, maintaining the place of an adviser rather than a lawgiver, in His sayings on this subject.

For after He had said, " Lay not up treasures upon the earth," He added, " where moth and rust doth corrupt, and where thieves break through and steal."

For the present He signifies the hurtfulness of the treasure here, and the profit of what is there, both from the place, and from the things which mar it. And neither at this point doth He stop, but adds also another argument.

And first, what things they most fear, from these He urges them. For " of what art thou afraid?" saith He: " lest thy goods should be spent, if thou give alms? Nay, then give alms, and so they will not be spent; and, what is more, so far from being spent, they will actually receive a greater increase; yea, for the things in heaven are added unto them."

However, for a time He saith it not, but puts it afterwards. But for the present, what had most power to persuade them, that He brings forward, namely, that the treasure would thus remain for them unspent.

And on either hand He attracts them. For He said not only, " If thou give alms, it is preserved:" but He threatened also the opposite thing, that if thou give not, it perishes.

And see His unspeakable prudence. For neither did He say, " Thou dost but leave them to others;" since this too is pleasant to men: He alarms them however on a new ground, by signifying that not even this do they obtain: since though men defraud not, there are those which are sure to defraud, " the moth " and " the rust." For although this mischief seem very easy to restrain, it is nevertheless irresistible and uncontrollable, and devise what thou wilt, thou wilt be unable to check this harm.

" What then, doth moth[3] make away with the gold?" Though not moth,[3] yet thieves do. " What then, have all been despoiled?" Though not all, yet the more part.

3. On this account then He adds another argument, which I have already mentioned, saying,

" Where the man's treasure is, there is his heart also."[4]

For though none of these things should come to pass, saith He, thou wilt undergo no small harm, in being nailed to the things below, and in becoming a slave instead of a freeman, and casting thyself out of the heavenly things, and having no power to think on aught that is high, but all about money, usuries and loans, and gains, and ignoble traffickings. Than this what could be more wretched? For in truth such an one will be worse off than any slave, bringing upon himself a most grievous tyranny, and giving up

---

[1] ἀκτημοσύνης.   [2] Matt. iv. 9, 10.

[3] σής. The Oxford version has inadvertently rendered it " rust."—R.]
[4] Matt. vi. 21. [The correct text of Matt. vi. 21 is rendered, " For where thy treasure is, there will thy heart be also " (R. V.), but Chrysostom varies from this both here and below. The plural form has little authority.—R.]

the chiefest thing of all, even the nobleness and the liberty of man. For how much soever any one may discourse unto thee, thou wilt not be able to hear any of those things which concern thee, whilst thy mind is nailed down to money; but bound like a dog to a tomb, by the tyranny of riches, more grievously than by any chain, barking at all that come near thee, thou hast this one employment continually, to keep for others what thou hast laid up. Than this what can be more wretched?

However, forasmuch as this was too high for the mind of His hearers, and neither was the mischief within easy view of the generality, nor the gain evident, but there was need of a spirit of more self-command to perceive either of these; first, He hath put it after those other topics, which are obvious, saying, "Where the man's treasure is, there is his heart also;" and next He makes it clear again, by withdrawing His discourse from the intellectual to the sensible, and saying,

"The light of the body is the eye."[1]

What He saith is like this: Bury not gold in the earth, nor do any other such thing, for thou dost but gather it for the moth, and the rust, and the thieves. And even if thou shouldest entirely escape these evils, yet the enslaving of thine heart, the nailing it to all that is below, thou wilt not escape: "For wheresoever thy treasure may be, there is thine heart also." As then, laying up stores in heaven, thou wilt reap not this fruit only, the attainment of the rewards for these things, but from this world thou already receivest thy recompence, in getting into harbor there, in setting thine affections on the things that are there, and caring for what is there (for where thou hast laid up thy treasures, it is most clear thou transferrest thy mind also); so if thou do this upon earth, thou wilt experience the contrary.

But if the saying be obscure to thee, hear what comes next in order.

"The light of the body is the eye; if therefore thine eye be single, thy whole body shall be full of light. But if thine eye be evil, thy whole body shall be full of darkness. But if the light that is in thee be darkness, how great is the darkness!"[2]

He leads His discourse to the things which are more within the reach of our senses. I mean, forasmuch as He had spoken of the mind as enslaved and brought into captivity, and there were not many who could easily discern this, He transfers the lesson to things outward, and lying before men's eyes, that by these the others also might reach their understanding. Thus, "If thou knowest not," saith He, "what a thing it is to be injured in mind, learn it from the things of the body; for just what the eye is to the body, the same is the mind to the soul." As therefore thou wouldest not choose to wear gold, and to be clad in silken garments, thine eyes withal being put out, but accountest their sound health more desirable than all such superfluity (for, shouldest thou lose this health or waste it, all thy life besides will do thee no good): for just as when the eyes are blinded, most of the energy of the other members is gone, their light being quenched; so also when the mind is depraved, thy life will be filled with countless evils:[3]—as therefore in the body this is our aim, namely, to keep the eye sound, so also the mind in the soul. But if we mutilate this, which ought to give light to the rest, by what means are we to see clearly any more? For as he that destroys the fountain, dries up also the river, so he who hath quenched the understanding hath confounded all his doings in this life. Wherefore He saith, "If the light that is in thee be darkness, how great is the darkness?"

For when the pilot is drowned, and the candle is put out, and the general is taken prisoner; what sort of hope will there be, after that, for those that are under command?

Thus then, omitting now to speak of the plots to which wealth gives occasion, the strifes, the suits (these indeed He had signified above, when He said, "The adversary shall deliver thee to the judge, and the judge to the officer"); and setting down what is more grievous than all these, as sure to occur, He so withdraws us from the wicked desire. For to inhabit the prison is not nearly so grievous, as for the mind to be enslaved by this disease; and the former is not sure to happen, but the other is connected as an immediate consequent with the desire of riches. And this is why He puts it after the first, as being a more grievous thing, and sure to happen.

For God, He saith, gave us understanding, that we might chase away all ignorance, and have the right judgment of things, and that using this as a kind of weapon and light against all that is grievous or hurtful, we might remain in safety. But we betray the gift for the sake of things superfluous and useless.

---

[1] Matt. vi. 22. [R. V., "The lamp of the body," etc.—R.]
[2] Matt. vi. 22, 23. [In verse 23, "If therefore" is the correct reading, and some MSS. of the Homilies have this reading here. —R.]

[3] [In the Greek text, the parenthesis extends to this place.—R.]

For what is the use of soldiers arrayed in gold, when the general is dragged along a captive? what the profit of a ship beautifully equipped, when the pilot is sunk beneath the waves? what the advantage of a well-proportioned body, when the sight of the eyes is stricken out? As therefore, should any one cast into sickness the physician (who should be in good health, that he may end our diseases), and then bid him lie on a silver couch, and in a chamber of gold, this will nothing avail the sick persons; even so, if thou corrupt the mind (which hath power to put down our passions),[1] although thou set it by a treasure, so far from doing it any good, thou hast inflicted the very greatest loss, and hast harmed thy whole soul.

4. Seest thou how by those very things, through which most especially men everywhere affect wickedness, even by these most of all He deters them from it. and brings them back to virtue? "For with what intent dost thou desire riches?" saith He; "is it not that thou mayest enjoy pleasure and luxury? Why now, this above all things thou wilt fail to obtain thereby, it will rather be just contrary." For if, when our eyes are stricken out, we perceive not any pleasant thing, because of such our calamity; much more will this be our case in the perversion and maiming of the mind.

Again, with what intent dost thou bury it in the earth? That it may be kept in safety? But here too again it is the contrary, saith He.

And thus, as in dealing with him that for vainglory fasts and gives alms and prays, by those very things which he most desires He had allured him not to be vainglorious: — "for with what intent," saith He, "dost thou so pray and give alms? for love of the glory that may be had from men? then do not pray thus," saith He, "and so thou shalt obtain it in the day that is to come:"—so He hath taken captive the covetous man also, by those things for which he was most earnest. Thus: "what wouldest thou?" saith He, "to have thy wealth preserved, and to enjoy pleasure? Both these things I will afford thee in great abundance, if thou lay up thy gold in that place, where I bid thee."

It is true that hereafter He displayed more clearly the evil effect of this on the mind, I mean, when He made mention of the thorns;[2] but for the present, even here He hath strikingly intimated[3] the same, by representing him as darkened who is beside himself in this way.

And as they that are in darkness see nothing distinct, but if they look at a rope, they suppose it to be a serpent, if at mountains and ravines, they are dead with fear; so these also: what is not alarming to them that have sight, that they regard with suspicion. Thus among other things they tremble at poverty: or rather not at poverty only, but even at any trifling loss. Yea, and if they should lose some little matter, those who are in want of necessary food do not so grieve and bewail themselves as they. At least many of the rich have come even to the halter, not enduring such ill fortune: and to be insulted also, and to be despitefully used, seems to them so intolerable, that even because of this again many have actually torn themselves from this present life. For to everything wealth had made them soft, except to the waiting on it. Thus, when it commands them to do service unto itself, they venture on murders, and stripes, and revilings, and all shame. A thing which comes of the utmost wretchedness; to be of all men most effeminate, where one ought to practise self-command, but where more caution was required, in these cases again to become more shameless and obstinate. Since in fact the same kind of thing befalls them, as one would have to endure who had spent all his goods on unfit objects. For such an one, when the time of necessary expenditure comes on, having nothing to supply it, suffers incurable evils, forasmuch as all that he had hath been ill spent beforehand.

And as they that are on the stage, skilled in those wicked arts, do in them go through many things strange and dangerous, but in other necessary and useful things none so ridiculous as they; even so is it with these men likewise. For so such as walk upon a stretched rope, making a display of so much courage, should some great emergency demand daring or courage, they are not able, neither do they endure even to think of such a thing. Just so they likewise that are rich, daring all for money, for self-restraint's sake endure not to submit to anything, be it small or great. And as the former practise both a hazardous and fruitless business; even so do these undergo many dangers and downfalls, but arrive at no profitable end. Yea, they undergo a twofold darkness, both having their eyes put out by the perversion of their mind, and being by the deceitfulness of their cares involved in a great mist. Wherefore neither can they easily so much as see through it. For he that is in darkness, is

---

[1] [These clauses are not parenthetical, but in the Greek define what precedes.—R.]
[2] Matt. xiii. 22.   [3] [εὐχ ὡς ἔτυχε.]

freed from the darkness by the mere appearance of the sun; but he that hath his eyes mutilated not even when the sun shines; which is the very case of these men: not even now that the Sun of Righteousness hath shone out, and is admonishing, do they hear, their wealth having closed their eyes. And so they have a twofold darkness to undergo, part from themselves, part from disregard to their teacher.

5. Let us then give heed unto Him exactly, that though late we may at length recover our sight. And how may one recover sight? If thou learn how thou wast blinded. How then wast thou blinded? By thy wicked desire. For the love of money, like an evil humor[1] which hath collected upon a clear eyeball, hath caused the cloud to become thick.

But even this cloud may be easily scattered and broken, if we will receive the beam of the doctrine of Christ; if we will hear Him admonishing us, and saying, "Lay not up for yourselves treasures upon earth."

"But," saith one, "what avails the hearing to me, as long as I am possessed by the desire?" Now in the first place, there will be power in the continual hearing to destroy even the desire. Next, if it continue to possess thee, consider that this thing is not really so much as a desire. For what sort of desire is this, to be in grievous bondage, and to be subject to a tyranny, and to be bound on all sides, and to dwell in darkness, and to be full of turmoil, and to endure toils without profit, and to keep thy wealth for others, and often for thy very enemies? with what sort of desire do these things agree? or rather of what flight and aversion are they not worthy? What sort of desire, to lay up treasure in the midst of thieves? Nay, if thou dost at all desire wealth, remove it where it may remain safe and unmolested. Since what you are now doing is the part of one desiring, not riches, surely, but bondage, and affront,[2] and loss, and continual vexation. Yet thou, were any one among men on earth to show thee a place beyond molestation, though he lead thee out into the very desert, promising security in the keeping of thy wealth,—thou art not slow nor backward; thou hast confidence in him, and puttest out thy goods there; but when it is God instead of men who makes thee this promise, and when He sets before thee not the desert, but Heaven, thou acceptest the contrary. Yet surely, how manifold soever be their security below, thou canst never become free from the care

of them. I mean, though thou lose them not, thou wilt never be delivered from anxiety lest thou lose. But there thou wilt undergo none of these things: and mark, what is yet more, thou dost not only bury thy gold, but plantest it. For the same is both treasure and seed; or rather it is more than either of these. For the seed remains not for ever, but this abides perpetually. Again, the treasure germinates not, but this bears thee fruits which never die.

6. But if thou tellest me of the time, and the delay of the recompence, I too can point out and tell how much thou receivest back even here: and besides all this, from the very things of this life, I will try to convict thee of making this excuse to no purpose. I mean, that even in the present life thou providest many things which thou art not thyself to enjoy; and should any one find fault, thou pleadest thy children and their children, and so thinkest thou hast found palliation enough for thy superfluous labors. For when in extreme old age thou art building splendid houses, before the completion of which (in many instances) thou wilt have departed; when thou plantest trees, which will bear their fruit after many years;[3] when thou art buying properties and inheritances, the ownership of which thou wilt acquire after a long time, and art eagerly busy in many other such things, the enjoyment whereof thou wilt not reap; is it indeed for thine own sake, or for those to come after, that thou art so employed? How then is it not the utmost folly, here not at all to hesitate[4] at the delay of time; and this though thou art by this delay to lose all the reward of thy labors: but there, because of such waiting to be altogether torpid; and this, although it bring thee the greater gain, and although it convey not thy good things on to others, but procure the gifts for thyself.

But besides this, the delay itself is not long; nay, for those things are at the doors, and we know not but that even in our own generation all things which concern us may have their accomplishment, and that fearful day may arrive, setting before us the awful and incorruptible tribunal. Yea, for the more part of the signs are fulfilled, and the gospel moreover hath been preached in all parts of the world, and the predictions of wars, and of earthquakes, and of famines, have come to pass, and the interval is not great.

---

[1] χυμός.   ἐπηρείας.   [4] ἀλύειν.

[3] [In the Greek text, bracketted by Field, and in the Latin, occurs this clause: "when" [or "for when") "thou plantest trees in the field, the fruit of which will yield after many (μυρία) years." —R.]

But is it that thou dost not see any signs? Why, this self-same thing is a very great sign. For neither did they in Noah's time see any presages of that universal destruction, but in the midst of their playing, eating, marrying, doing all things to which they were used, even so they were overtaken by that fearful judgment. And they too in Sodom in like manner, living in delight, and suspecting none of what befell them, were consumed by those lightnings, which then came down upon them.

Considering then all these things, let us betake ourselves unto the preparation for our departure hence.

For even if the common day of the consummation never overtake us, the end of each one is at the doors, whether he be old or young; and it is not possible for men after they have gone hence, either to buy oil any more, or to obtain pardon by prayers, though he that entreats be Abraham,[1] or Noah, or Job, or Daniel.[2]

While then we have opportunity, let us store up for ourselves beforehand much confidence, let us gather oil in abundance, let us remove all into. Heaven, that in the fitting time, and when we most need them, we may enjoy all: by the grace and love towards man of our Lord Jesus Christ, to whom be the glory, and the might, now and always, and forever and ever. Amen.

---

[1] Luke xvi. 24. [2] Ezek. xiv. 14.

HOMILY XXI.

Matt. VI. 24.

" No man can serve two masters, for either he will hate the one and love the other, or else he will hold to one and despise the other."

Seest thou how by degrees He withdraws us from the things that now are, and at greater length introduces what He hath to say, touching voluntary poverty, and casts down the dominion of covetousness?

For He was not contented with His former sayings, many and great as they were, but He adds others also, more and more alarming.[1]

For what can be more alarming than what He now saith, if indeed we are for our riches to fall from the service of Christ? or what more to be desired, if indeed, by despising wealth, we shall have our affection towards Him and our charity perfect?[2] For what I am continually repeating, the same do I now say likewise, namely, that by both kinds He presses the hearer to obey His sayings; both by the profitable, and by the hurtful; much like an excellent physician, pointing out both the disease which is the consequence of neglect, and the good health which results from obedience.

See, for instance, what kind of gain He signifies this to be, and how He establishes the advantage of it by their deliverance from the contrary things. Thus, " wealth," saith He, " hurts you not in this only, that it arms robbers against you, nor in that it darkens your mind in the most intense degree, but also in that it casts you out of God's service, making you captive of lifeless riches, and in both ways doing you harm, on the one hand, by causing you to be slaves of what you ought to command; on the other, by casting you out of God's service, whom, above all things, it is indispensable for you to serve." For just as in the other place, He signified the mischief to be twofold, in both laying up here, " where moth corrupteth," and in not laying up there, where the watch kept is impregnable; so in this place, too, He shows the loss to be twofold, in that it both draws off from God, and makes us subject to mammon.

But He sets it not down directly, rather He establishes it first upon general considerations, saying thus; " No man can serve two masters:" meaning here two that are enjoining opposite things; since, unless this were the case, they would not even be two. For so, " the multitude of them that believed

---

[1] [" More in number and more terrible."—R.] [2] [ἀκριβῆ.]

were of one heart and of one soul," [1] and yet were they divided into many bodies; their unanimity however made the many one.

Then, as adding to the force of it, He saith, "so far from serving, he will even hate and abhor:" "For either he will hate the one," saith He, "and love the other, or else he will hold to the one and despise the other." And it seems indeed as if the same thing were said twice over; He did not however choose this form without purpose, but in order to show that the change for the better is easy. I mean, lest thou shouldest say, "I am once for all made a slave; I am brought under the tyranny of wealth," He signifies that it is possible to transfer one's self, and that as from the first to the second, so also from the second one may pass over to the first.

2. Having thus, you see, spoken generally, that He might persuade the hearer to be an uncorrupt judge of His words, and to sentence according to the very nature of the things; when he hath made sure of his assent, then, and not till then, He discovers Himself. Thus He presently adds,

"Ye cannot serve God and mammon."

Let us shudder to think what we have brought Christ to say; with the name of God, to put that of gold. But if this be shocking, its taking place in our deeds, our preferring the tyranny of gold to the fear of God, is much more shocking.

"What then? Was not this possible among the ancients?" By no means. "How then," saith one, "did Abraham, how did Job obtain a good report?" Tell me not of them that are rich, but of them that serve riches. Since Job also was rich, but he served not mammon, but possessed it and ruled over it, and was a master, not a slave. Therefore he so possessed all those things, as if he had been the steward of another man's goods; not only not extorting from others, but even giving up his own to them that were in need. And what is more, when he had them they were no joy to him: so he also declared, saying, "If I did so much as rejoice when my wealth waxed great:" [2] wherefore neither did he grieve when it was gone. But they that are rich are not now such as he was, but are rather in a worse condition than any slave, paying as it were tribute to some grievous tyrant. Because their mind is as a kind of citadel occupied by the love of money, which from thence daily sends out unto them its commands full of all iniquity, and there is none to disobey. Be not there-

fore thus over subtle.[3] Nay, for God hath once for all declared and pronounced it a thing impossible for the one service and the other to agree. Say not thou, then, "it is possible." Why, when the one master is commanding thee to spoil by violence, the other to strip thyself of thy possessions; the one to be chaste, the other to commit fornication; the one to be drunken and luxurious, the other to keep the belly in subjection; the one again to despise the things that are, the other to be rivetted to the present; the one to admire marbles, and walls, and roofs, the other to contemn these, but to honor self-restraint: how is it possible that these should agree?

Now He calls mammon here "a master," not because of its own nature, but on account of the wretchedness of them that bow themselves beneath it. So also He calls "the belly a god," [4] not from the dignity of such a mistress, but from the wretchedness of them that are enslaved: it being a thing worse than any punishment, and enough, before the punishment, in the way of vengeance on him who is involved in it. For what condemned criminals can be so wretched, as they who having God for their Lord, do from that mild rule desert to this grievous tyranny, and this when their act brings after it so much harm even here? For indeed their loss is unspeakable by so doing: there are suits, and molestations, and strifes, and toils, and a blinding of the soul; and what is more grievous than all, one falls away from the highest blessings; for such a blessing it is to be God's servant.

3. Having now, as you see, in all ways taught the advantage of contemning riches, as well for the very preservation of the riches, as for the pleasure of the soul, and for acquiring self-command, and for the securing of godliness; He proceeds to establish the practicability of this command. For this especially pertains to the best legislation, not only to enjoin what is expedient, but also to make it possible. Therefore He also goes on to say,

"Take no thought [5] for your life,[6] what ye shall eat."

That is, lest they should say, "What then? if we cast all away, how shall we be able to live?" At this objection, in what follows, He makes a stand, very seasonably. For as

---

[1] Acts iv. 32.   [2] Job xxxi. 25.

[3] [Μὴ τοίνυν περιττὰ φιλοσόφει.]   [4] Phil. iii. 19.
[5] [R. V., more correctly, "Be not anxious," and so throughout the chapter.—R.]
[6] τῇ ψυχῇ, "your soul." [So Chrysostom interprets (see below); but the New Testament passage must refer to physical life. In the latter part of the verse the higher "life" is suggested. But to understand the argument of Chrysostom, ψυχή must be rendered "soul" throughout this passage.—R.]

surely as if at the beginning He had said, "Take no thought," the word would have seemed burdensome; so surely, now that He hath shown the mischief arising out of covetousness, His admonition coming after is made easy to receive. Wherefore neither did He now simply say, "Take no thought," but He added the reason, and so enjoined this. After having said, "Ye cannot serve God and mammon," He added, "therefore I say unto you, take no thought. Therefore;" for what? Because of the unspeakable loss. For the hurt you receive is not in riches only, rather the wound is in the most vital parts, and in that which is the overthrow of your salvation; casting you as it does out from God, who made you, and careth for you, and loveth you.

"Therefore I say unto you, take no thought." Thus, after He hath shown the hurt to be unspeakable, then and not before He makes the commandment stricter; in that He not only bids us cast away what we have, but forbids to take thought even for our necessary food, saying, "Take no thought for your soul, what ye shall eat." Not because the soul needs food, for it is incorporeal; but He spake according to the common custom. For though it needs not food, yet can it not endure to remain in the body, except that be fed. And in saying this, He puts it not simply so, but here also He brings up arguments, some from those things which we have already, and some from other examples.

From what we have already, thus saying: "Is not the soul more than meat, and the body more than the raiment?"[1]

He therefore that hath given the greater, how shall He not give the less? He that hath fashioned the flesh that is fed, how shall He not bestow the food? Wherefore neither did He simply say, "Take no thought what ye shall eat," or "wherewithal ye shall be clothed;" but, "for the body," and, "for the soul:" forasmuch as from them He was to make His demonstrations, carrying on His discourse in the way of comparison. Now the soul He hath given once for all, and it abides such as it is; but the body increases every day. Therefore pointing out both these things, the immortality of the one, and the frailty of the other, He subjoins and says,

"Which of you can add one cubit unto his stature?"[2]

Thus, saying no more of the soul, since it receives not increase, He discoursed of the body only; hereby making manifest this point also, that not the food increases it, but the providence of God. Which Paul showing also in other ways, said, "So then, neither is he that planteth any thing, neither he that watereth; but God that giveth the increase."[3]

From what we have already, then, He urges us in this way: and from examples of other things, by saying, "Behold the fowls of the air."[4] Thus, lest any should say, "we do good by taking thought," He dissuades them both by that which is greater, and by that which is less; by the greater, i. e. the soul and the body; by the less, i. e. the birds. For if of the things that are very inferior He hath so much regard, how shall He not give unto you? saith He. And to them on this wise, for as yet it was an ordinary[5] multitude: but to the devil not thus; but how? "Man shall not live by bread alone, but by every word that proceedeth out of the mouth of God."[6] But here He makes mention of the birds, and this in a way greatly to abash them; which sort of thing is of very great value for the purpose of admonition.

4. However, some of the ungodly have come to so great a pitch of madness, as even to attack His illustration. Because, say they, it was not meet for one strengthening[7] moral principle, to use natural advantages as incitements to that end. For to those animals, they add, this belongs by nature. What then shall we say to this? That even though it is theirs by nature, yet possibly we too may attain it by choice. For neither did He say, "behold how the birds fly," which were a thing impossible to man; but that they are fed without taking thought, a kind of thing easy to be achieved by us also, if we will. And this they have proved, who have accomplished it in their actions.

Wherefore it were meet exceedingly to admire the consideration of our Lawgiver, in that, when He might bring forward His illustration from among men, and when He might have spoken of Moses and Elias and John, and others like them, who took no thought; that He might touch them more to the quick, He made mention of the irrational beings. For had He spoken of those righteous men, these would have been able to say, "We are not yet become like them." But now by passing them over in silence, and bringing forward the fowls of the air, He hath cut off from them every excuse, imitating in this place also the old law. Yea, for the old covenant

---

[1] Matt. vi. 25. [R. V., "Is not the life more than the food," i. e., the food that sustains it.—R.]
[2] Matt. vi. 27.

[3] 1 Cor. iii. 7.   [4] Matt. vi. 26.   [5] δημώδης.
[6] Matt. iv. 4.   [7] ἀλείφοντα.

likewise sends to the bee, and to the ant,[1] and to the turtle, and to the swallow.[2] And neither is this a small sign of honor, when the same sort of things, which those animals possess by nature, those we are able to accomplish by an act of our choice. If then He take so great care of them which exist for our sakes, much more of us; if of the servants, much more of the master. Therefore He said, " Behold the fowls," and He said not, " for they do not traffic, nor make merchandise,"[3] for these were among the things that were earnestly forbidden. But what? "they sow not, neither do they reap." " What then?" saith one, " must we not sow?" He said not, " we must not sow," but " we must not *take thought;*" neither that " one ought not to work, but not to be low-minded, nor to rack one's self with cares. Since He bade us also be nourished, but not in " taking thought."

Of this lesson David also lays the foundation from old time, saying enigmatically on this wise, " Thou openest Thine hand, and fillest every living thing with bounty; "[4] and again, " To Him that giveth to the beasts their food, and to the young ravens that call upon Him."[5]

" Who then," it may be said, " have not taken thought "? Didst thou not hear how many of the righteous I adduced? Seest thou not with them Jacob, departing from his father's house destitute of all things? Dost thou not hear him praying and saying, " If the Lord give me bread to eat and raiment to put on?"[6] which was not the part of one taking thought, but of one seeking all of God. This the apostles also attained, who cast away all, and took no thought: also, the " five thousand," and the " three thousand."[7]

5. But if thou canst not bear, upon hearing so high words, to release thyself from these grievous bonds, consider the unprofitableness of the thing, and so put an end to thy care. For

" Which of you by taking thought " (saith He) " can add one cubit unto his stature."[8]

Seest thou how by that which is evident, He hath manifested that also which is obscure? Thus, "As unto thy body," saith He, " thou wilt not by taking thought be able to add, though it be ever so little; so neither to gather food; think as thou mayest otherwise."

Hence it is clear that not our diligence, but the providence of God, even where we seem to be active, effects all. So that, were He to forsake us, no care, nor anxiety, nor toil, nor any other such thing, will ever appear to come to anything, but all will utterly pass away.

Let us not therefore suppose His injunctions are impossible: for there are many who duly perform them, even as it is. And if thou knowest not of them, it is nothing marvellous, since Elias too supposed he was alone, but was told, " I have left unto myself seven thousand men."[9] Whence it is manifest that even now there are many who show forth the apostolical life; like as the " three thousand " then, and the " five thousand."[10] And if we believe not, it is not because there are none who do well, but because we are far from so doing. So that just as the drunkard would not easily believe, that there exists any man who doth not taste even water (and yet this hath been achieved by many solitaries in our time[11]) ; nor he who connects himself with numberless women, that it is easy to live in virginity; nor he that extorts other men's goods, that one shall readily give up even his own: so neither will those, who daily melt themselves down with innumerable anxieties, easily receive this thing.

Now as to the fact, that there are many who have attained unto this, we might show it even from those, who have practised this self-denial even in our generation.

But for you, just now, it is enough to learn not to covet, and that almsgiving is a good thing; and to know that you must impart of what ye have. For these things if thou wilt duly perform, beloved, thou wilt speedily proceed to those others also.

6. For the present therefore let us lay aside our excessive sumptuousness, and let us endure moderation, and learn to acquire by honest labor all that we are to have: since even the blessed John, when he was discoursing with those that were employed upon the tribute, and with the soldiery, enjoined them " to be content with their wages."[12] Anxious though he were to lead them on to another, and a higher self-command, yet since they were still unfit for this, he speaks of the lesser things. Because, if he had mentioned what are higher than these, they would have failed to apply themselves to them, and would have fallen from the others.

For this very reason we too are practising you[13] in the inferior duties. Yes, because

[1] Prov. vi. 6-8, LXX. See before, Hom. XVII., 6, note.
[2] Jer. viii. 7.
[3] καπηλεύουσιν, ἐμπορεύονται : two words which in the New Testament are always used in a bad sense.
[4] Ps. cxlv. 16.   [5] Ps. cxlvii. 9.   [6] Gen. xxviii. 20.
[7] Acts iv. 4, and ii. 41.   [8] Matt. vi. 27.

[9] 1 Kings xix. 18 ; Rom. xi. 4.   [10] Acts ii. 41, iv. 5.
[11] See Sulpicius Severus, Dial. i. c. 14. " It is told of a certain holy man that he constantly and entirely abstained from all drink: and that by way of food, he lived upon seven figs only."
[12] Luke iii. 14.
[13] [ὑμᾶς γυμνάζομεν, " we are exercising you."—R.]

as yet, we know, the burden of voluntary poverty is too great for you, and the heaven is not more distant from the earth, than such self-denial from you. Let us then lay hold, if it be only of the lowest commandments, for even this is no small encouragement. And yet some amongst the heathens have achieved even this, though not in a proper spirit, and have stripped themselves of all their possessions.[1] However, we are contented in your case, if alms are bestowed abundantly by you; for we shall soon arrive at those other duties too, if we advance in this way. But if we do not so much as this, of what favor shall we be worthy, who are hidden to surpass those under the old law, and yet show ourselves inferior to the philosophers among the heathens? What shall we say, who when we ought to be angels and sons of God, do not even quite maintain our being as men? For to spoil and to covet comes not of the gentleness of men, but of the fierceness of wild beasts; nay, worse than wild beasts are the assailers of their neighbor's goods. For to them this comes by nature, but we who are honored with reason, and yet are falling away unto that unnatural vileness, what indulgence shall we receive?

Let us then, considering the measures of that discipline which is set before us, press on at least to the middle station, that we may both be delivered from the punishment which is to come, and proceeding regularly, may arrive at the very summit of all good things; unto which may we all attain, by the grace and love towards man of our Lord Jesus Christ, to whom be glory and dominion for ever and ever. Amen.

[1] So Aristippus: vid. Hor. Serm. 2, 3, 100.

HOMILY XXII.

MATT. VI. 28, 29.

"Consider the lilies of the field, how they grow; they toil not, neither do they spin. And yet I say unto you, That even Solomon in all his glory was not arrayed like one of these."

HAVING spoken of our necessary food, and having signified that not even for this should we take thought, He passes on in what follows to that which is more easy. For raiment is not so necessary as food.

Why then did He not make use here also of the same example, that of the birds, neither mention to us the peacock, and the swan, and the sheep? for surely there were many such examples to take from thence. Because He would point out how very far the argument may be carried both ways:[1] both from the vileness[2] of the things that partake of such elegance, and from the munificence vouchsafed to the lilies, in respect of their adorning. For this cause, when He hath decked them out, He doth not so much as call them lilies any more, but "grass of the field."[3] And He is not satisfied even with this name, but again adds another circum-stance of vileness, saying, "which to-day is." And He said not, "and to-morrow is not," but what is much baser yet, "is cast into the oven." And He said not, "clothe," but "so clothe."

Seest thou everywhere how He abounds in amplifications and intensities? And this He doth, that He may touch them home: and therefore He hath also added, "shall He not much more clothe you?" For this too hath much emphasis: the force of the word, "you," being no other than to indicate covertly the great value set upon our race, and the concern shown for it; as though He had said, "you, to whom He gave a soul, for whom He fashioned a body, for whose sake He made all the things that are seen, for whose sake He sent prophets, and gave the law, and wrought those innumerable good works; for whose sake He gave up His only begotten Son."

And not till He hath made His proof clear, doth He proceed also to rebuke them, say-

[1] ἐκατέρωθεν δεῖξαι τὴν ὑπερβολήν.
[2] [εὐτελείας, "cheapness" first, then "meanness."—R.]
[3] Matt. vi. 30.

ing, "O ye of little faith." For this is the quality of an adviser: He doth not admonish only, but reproves also, that He may awaken men the more to the persuasive power of His words.

Hereby He teaches us not only to take no thought, but not even to be dazzled at the costliness of men's apparel. Why, such comeliness is of grass, such beauty of the green herb: or rather, the grass is even more precious than such apparelling. Why then pride thyself on things, whereof the prize rests with the mere plant, with a great balance in its favor?

And see how from the beginning He signifies the injunction to be easy; by the contraries again, and by the things of which they were afraid, leading them away from these cares. Thus, when He had said, "Consider the lilies of the field," He added, "they toil not:" so that in desire to set us free from toils, did He give these commands. In fact, the labor lies, not in taking no thought, but in taking thought for these things. And as in saying, "they sow not," it was not the sowing that He did away with, but the anxious thought; so in saying, "they toil not, neither do they spin," He put an end not to the work, but to the care.

But if Solomon was surpassed by their beauty, and that not once nor twice, but throughout all his reign:—for neither can one say, that at one time He was clothed with such apparel, but after that He was so no more; rather not so much as on one day did He array Himself so beautifully: for this Christ declared by saying, "in all his reign:" and if it was not that He was surpassed by this flower, but vied with that, but He gave place to all alike (wherefore He also said, "as one of these:" for such as between the truth and the counterfeit, so great is the interval between those robes and these flowers):—if then he acknowledged his inferiority, who was more glorious than all kings that ever were: when wilt thou be able to surpass, or rather to approach even faintly to such perfection of form?

After this He instructs us, not to aim at all at such ornament. See at least the end thereof; after its triumph "it is cast into the oven:" and if of things mean, and worthless, and of no great use, God hath displayed so great care, how shall He give up thee, of all living creatures the most important?

Wherefore then did He make them so beautiful? That He might display His own wisdom and the excellency of His power; that from everything we might learn His glory. For not "the Heavens only declare the glory of God,"[1] but the earth too; and this David declared when he said, "Praise the Lord, ye fruitful trees, and all cedars."[2] For some by their fruits, some by their greatness, some by their beauty, send up praise to Him who made them: this too being a sign of great excellency of wisdom, when even upon things that are very vile (and what can be viler than that which to-day is, and to-morrow is not?) He pours out such great beauty. If then to the grass He hath given that which it needs not (for what doth the beauty thereof help to the feeding of the fire?) how shall He not give unto thee that whch thou needest? If that which is the vilest of all things, He hath lavishly adorned, and that as doing it not for need, but for munificence, how much more will He honor thee, the most honorable of all things, in matters which are of necessity.

2. Now when, as you see, He had demonstrated the greatness of God's providential care, and they were in what follows to be rebuked also, even in this He was sparing, laying to their charge not want, but poverty, of faith. Thus, "if God," saith He, "so clothe the grass of the field, much more you, O ye of little faith."[3]

And yet surely all these things He Himself works. For "all things were made by Him, and without Him was not so much as one thing made."[4] But yet He nowhere as yet makes mention of Himself: it being sufficient for the time, to indicate His full power, that He said at each of the commandments, "Ye have heard that it hath been said to them of old time, but I say unto you."

Marvel not then, when in subsequent instances also He conceals Himself, or speaks something lowly of Himself: since for the present He had but one object, that His word might prove such as they would readily receive, and might in every way demonstrate that He was not a sort of adversary of God, but of one mind, and in agreement with the Father.

Which accordingly He doth here also; for through so many words as He hath spent He ceases not to set Him before us, admiring His wisdom, His providence, His tender care extending through all things, both great and small. Thus, both when He was speaking of Jerusalem, He called it "the city of the Great King;"[5] and when He mentioned Heaven, He spake of it again as "God's throne;"[6] and when He was discoursing of His economy in the world, to Him again He attributes it all, saying, "He maketh His sun

---

1 Ps. xix. 1.　　2 Ps. cxlviii. 9.　　3 Matt. vi. 30
4 John i. 3.　　5 Matt. v. 35.　　6 Matt. v. 34

to rise on the evil and on the good, and sendeth rain on the just and on the unjust."[1] And in the prayer too He taught us to say, His "is the kingdom and the power and the glory." And here in discoursing of His providence, and signifying how even in little things He is the most excellent of artists, He saith, that "He clothes the grass of the field." And nowhere doth He call Him His own Father, but theirs; in order that by the very honor He might reprove them, and that when He should call Him His Father, they might no more be displeased.

Now if for bare necessaries one is not to take thought, what pardon can we[2] deserve, who take thought for things expensive? Or rather, what pardon can they deserve, who do even without sleep, that they may take the things of others?

3. "Therefore take no thought, saying, what shall we eat? or, what shall we drink? or, wherewithal shall we be clothed? For after all these things do the nations of the world seek."[3]

Seest thou how again He hath both shamed them the more, and hath also shown by the way, that He had commanded nothing grievous nor burdensome? As therefore when He said, "If ye love them which love you," it is nothing great which ye practise, for the very Gentiles do the same; by the mention of the Gentiles He was stirring them up to something greater: so now also He brings them forward to reprove us, and to signify that it is a necessary debt which He is requiring of us. For if we must show forth something more than the Scribes or Pharisees, what can we deserve, who so far from going beyond these, do even abide in the mean estate of the Gentiles, and emulate their littleness of soul?

He doth not however stop at the rebuke, but having by this reproved and roused them, and shamed them with all strength of expression, by another argument He also comforts them, saying, "For your Heavenly Father knoweth that ye have need of all these things." He said not, "God knoweth," but, "your Father knoweth;" to lead them to a greater hope. For if He be a Father, and such a Father, He will not surely be able to overlook His children in extremity of evils; seeing that not even men, being fathers, bear to do so.

And He adds along with this yet another argument. Of what kind then is it? That "ye have need" of them. What He saith is like this. What! are these things superfluous, that He should disregard them? Yet not even in superfluities did He show Himself wanting in regard, in the instance of the grass: but now are these things even necessary. So that what thou considerest a cause for thy being anxious, this I say is sufficient to draw thee from such anxiety. I mean, if thou sayest, "Therefore I must needs take thought, because they are necessary;" on the contrary, I say, "Nay, for this self-same reason take no thought, because they are necessary." Since were they superfluities, not even then ought we to despair, but to feel confident about the supply of them; but now that they are necessary, we must no longer be in doubt. For what kind of father is he, who can endure to fail in supplying to his children even necessaries? So that for this cause again God will most surely bestow them.

For indeed He is the artificer of our nature, and He knows perfectly the wants thereof. So· that neither canst thou say, "He is indeed our Father, and the things we seek are necessary, but He knows not that we stand in need of them." For He that knows our nature itself, and was the framer of it, and formed it such as it is; evidently He knows its need also better than thou, who art placed in want of them: it having been by His decree, that our nature is in such need. He will not therefore oppose Himself to what He hath willed, first subjecting it of necessity to so great want, and on the other hand again depriving it of what it wants, and of absolute necessaries

Let us not therefore be anxious, for we shall gain nothing by it, but tormenting ourselves. For whereas He gives both when we take thought, and when we do not, and more of the two, when we do not; what dost thou gain by thy anxiety, but to exact of thyself a superfluous penalty? Since one on the point of going to a plentiful feast, will not surely permit himself to take thought for food; nor is he that is walking to a fountain anxious about drink. Therefore seeing we have a supply more copious than either any fountain, or innumerable banquets made ready, the providence of God; let us not be beggars, nor little minded.

4. For together with what hath been said, He puts also yet another reason for feeling confidence about such things, saying,

"Seek ye the kingdom of Heaven, and all these things shall be added unto you."[4]

---

[1] Matt. v. 45.

[2] [Or, "they," as in the next sentence.—R.]

[3] Matt. vi. 31, 32. [The text of Chrysostom is in doubt here; one MS. omits "of the world." The longer reading is probably due to a recollection of Luke xii. 30, where this form occurs.—R.]

[4] Matt. vi. 33. [The reading of this verse given by Chrysostom is peculiar. The best authorities support the form accepted in the R. V., "his kingdom and his righteousness." But the read-

Thus when He had set the soul free from anxiety, then He made mention also of Heaven. For indeed He came to do away with the old things, and to call us to a greater country. Therefore He doeth all, to deliver us from things unnecessary, and from our affection for the earth. For this cause He mentioned the heathens also, saying that "the Gentiles seek after these things;" they whose whole labor is for the present life, who have no regard for the things to come, nor any thought of Heaven. But to you not these present are the chief things,[1] but other than these. For we were not born for this end, that we should eat and drink and be clothed, but that we might please God, and attain unto the good things to come. Therefore as things here are secondary in our labor, so also in our prayers let them be secondary. Therefore He also said, "Seek ye the kingdom of Heaven, and all these things shall be added unto you."

And He said not, "shall be given," but "shall be added," that thou mightest learn, that the things present are no great part of His gifts, compared with the greatness of the things to come. Accordingly, He doth not bid us so much as ask for them, but while we ask for other things,to have confidence, as though these also were added to those. Seek then the things to come, and thou wilt receive the things present also; seek not the things that are seen, and thou shalt surely attain unto them. Yea, for it is unworthy of thee to approach thy Lord for such things. And thou, who oughtest to spend all thy zeal and thy care for those unspeakable blessings, dost greatly disgrace thyself by consuming it on the desire of transitory things.

"How then?" saith one, "did He not bid us ask for bread?" Nay, He added, "daily," and to this again, "this day," which same thing in fact He doth here also. For He said not, "Take no thought," but, "Take no thought for the morrow," at the same time both affording us liberty, and fastening our soul on those things that are more necessary to us.

For to this end also He bade us ask even those, not as though God needed reminding by us, but that we might learn that by His help we accomplish whatever we do accomplish, and that we might be made more His own by our continual prayer for these things.

Seest thou how by this again He would persuade them, that they shall surely receive the things present? For He that bestows the greater, much more will He give the less. "For not for this end," saith He, "did I tell you not to take thought nor to ask, that ye should suffer distress, and go about naked, but in order that ye might be in abundance of these things also:" and this, you see, was suited above all things to attract them to Him. So that like as in almsgiving, when deterring them from making a display to men, he won upon them chiefly by promising to furnish them with it more liberally;—"for thy Father," saith He, "who seeth in secret, shall reward thee openly;"[2]—even so here also, in drawing them off from seeking these things, this is His persuasive topic, that He promises to bestow it on them, not seeking it, in greater abundance. Thus, to this end, saith He, do I bid thee not seek, not that thou mayest not receive, but that thou mayest receive plentifully; that thou mayest receive in the fashion[3] that becomes thee, with the profit which thou oughtest to have; that thou mayest not, by taking thought, and distracting thyself in anxiety about these, render thyself unworthy both of these, and of the things spiritual; that thou mayest not undergo unnecessary distress, and again fall away from that which is set before thee.

5. "Take therefore no thought for the morrow: for sufficient unto the day is the evil thereof:" that is to say, the affliction, and the bruising thereof.[4] Is it not enough for thee, to eat thy bread in the sweat of thy face? Why add the further affliction that comes of anxiety, when thou art on the point to be delivered henceforth even from the former toils?

By "evil" here He means, not wickedness, far from it, but affliction, and trouble, and calamities; much as in another place also He saith, "Is there evil in a city, which the Lord hath not done?"[5] not meaning rapines, nor injuries,[6] nor any thing like these, but the scourges which are borne from above. And again, "I," saith He, "make peace, and create evils:"[7] For neither in this place doth He speak of wickedness,[8] but of famines, and pestilences, things accounted evil by most men: the generality being wont to call these things evil. Thus, for example, the priests and prophets of those five lordships, when having yoked the kine to the ark, they let them go without their calves,[9] gave the name of "evil" to those heaven-sent plagues, and

---

ing of the received text is ancient. Some other Fathers agree with Chrysostom. The phrase "kingdom of heaven" is peculiar to Matthew.—R.]
[1] προηγούμενα.

[2] Matt. vi. 4.   [3] σχήματος.   [4] Matt. v. 34.   [5] συντριβή.
[6] Amos iii. 6.   [πλεονεξίας ; but one mss. reads δυναστείας, referring to oppressive oligarchies, Latin, principatus.—R.]
[7] Isa. xlv. 7.
[8] [κακίαν, the word rendered "evil" throughout this passage. —R.]
[9] 1 Sam. vi. 9.

the dismay and anguish which thereby sprang up within them.

This then is His meaning here also, when He saith, "sufficient unto the day is the evil thereof." For nothing so pains the soul, as carefulness and anxiety. Thus did Paul also, when urging to celibacy, give counsel, saying, "I would have you without carefulness."[1]

But when He saith, "the morrow shall take thought for itself," He saith it not, as though the day took thought for these things, but forasmuch as He had to speak to a people somewhat imperfect, willing to make what He saith more expressive, He personifies the time, speaking unto them according to the custom of the generality.

And here indeed He advises, but as He proceeds, He even makes it a law, saying, "provide neither gold nor silver, nor scrip for your journey."[2] Thus, having shown it all forth in His actions, then after that He introduces the verbal enactment of it more determinately, the precept too having then become more easy of acceptance, confirmed as it had been previously by His own actions. Where then did He confirm it by His actions? Hear Him saying, "The Son of Man hath not where to lay His head."[3] Neither is He satisfied with this only, but in His disciples also He exhibits His full proof of these things, by fashioning them too in like manner, yet not suffering them to be in want of anything.

But mark His tender care also, how He surpasses the affection of any father. Thus, "This I command," saith He, "for nothing else, but that I may deliver you from superfluous anxieties. For even if to-day thou hast taken thought for to-morrow, thou wilt also have to take thought again to-morrow. Why then what is over and above? Why force the day to receive more than the distress which is allotted to it, and together with its own troubles add to it also the burden of the following day; and this, when there is no chance of thy lightening the other by the addition so taking place, but thou art merely to exhibit thyself as coveting superfluous troubles?" Thus, that He may reprove them the more, He doth all but give life to the very time, and brings it in as one injured, and exclaiming against them for their causeless despite. Why, thou hast received the day, to care for the things thereof. Wherefore then add unto it the things of the other day also? Hath it not then burden enough in its own anxiety? Why now, I pray, dost

thou make it yet heavier? Now when the Lawgiver saith these things, and He that is to pass judgment on us, consider the hopes that He suggests to us, how good they are; He Himself testifying, that this life is wretched and wearisome, so that the anxiety even of the one day is enough to hurt and afflict us.

6. Nevertheless, after so many and so grave words, we take thought for these things, but for the things in Heaven no longer: rather we have reversed His order, on either side fighting against His sayings. For mark; "Seek ye not the things, present," saith He, "at all;" but we are seeking these things for ever: "seek the things in Heaven," saith He; but those things we seek not so much as for a short hour, but according to the greatness of the anxiety we display about the things of the world, is the carelessness we entertain in things spiritual; or rather even much greater. But this doth not prosper for ever; neither can this be for ever. What if for ten days we think scorn? if for twenty? if for an hundred? must we not of absolute necessity depart, and fall into the hands of the Judge?

"But the delay hath comfort." And what sort of comfort, to be every day looking for punishment and vengeance? Nay, if thou wouldest have some comfort from this delay, take it by gathering for thyself the fruit of amendment after repentance. Since if the mere delay of vengeance seem to thee a sort of refreshment, far more is it gain not to fall into the vengeance. Let us then make full use of this delay, in order to have a full deliverance from the dangers that press upon us. For none of the things enjoined is either burdensome or grievous, but all are so light and easy, that if we only bring a genuine purpose of heart, we may accomplish all, though we be chargeable with countless offenses. For so Manasses had perpetrated innumerable pollutions, having both stretched out his hands against the saints, and brought abominations into the temple, and filled the city with murders, and wrought many other things beyond excuse; yet nevertheless after so long and so great wickedness, he washed away from himself all these things.[4] How and in what manner? By repentance, and consideration.

For there is not, yea, there is not any sin, that doth not yield and give way to the power of repentance, or rather to the grace of Christ. Since if we would but only change, we have Him to assist us. And if thou art desirous to become good, there is none to

---

[1] 1 Cor. vii. 32. [R. V., "to be free from care;" ἀμερίμνους, a compound of the same origin as the word rendered "take no thought" in the A. V.—R.]
[2] Matt. x. 9, 10.   [3] Matt. viii. 20.   [4] 2 Chron. xxxiii. 1–20 ; 2 Kings xxi. 1–18.

hinder us; or rather there is one to hinder us, the devil, yet hath he no power, so long as thou choosest what is best, and so attract est God to thine aid. But if thou art not thyself willing, but startest aside, how shall He protect thee? Since not of necessity or compulsion, but of thine own will, He wills thee to be saved. For if thou thyself, having a servant full of hatred and aversion for thee, and continually going off, and fleeing away from thee, wouldest not choose to keep him, and this though needing his services; much less will God, who doeth all things not for His own profit, but for thy salvation, choose to retain thee by compulsion; as on the other hand, if thou show forth a right intention only, He would not choose ever to give thee up, no, not whatever the devil may do. So that we are ourselves to blame for our own destruction. Because we do not approach, nor beseech, nor entreat Him, as we ought: but even if we do draw nigh, it is not as persons who have need to receive, neither is it with the proper faith, nor as making demand, but we do all in a gaping and listless way.

7. And yet God would have us demand things of Him, and for this accounts Himself greatly bound to thee.[1] For He alone of all debtors, when the demand is made, counts it a favor, and gives what we have not lent Him. And if He should see him pressing earnestly that makes the demand, He pays down even what He hath not received of us; but if sluggishly, He too keeps on making delays; not through unwillingness to give, but because He is pleased to have the demand made upon Him by us. For this cause He told thee also the example of that friend, who came by night, and asked a loaf;[2] and of the judge that feared not God, nor regarded men.[3] And He stayed not at similitudes, but signified it also in His very actions, when He dismissed that Phœnician woman, having filled her with His great gift.[4] For through her He signified, that He gives to them that ask earnestly, even the things that pertain not to them. "For it is not meet," saith He, "to take the children's bread, and to give[5] it unto the dogs." But for all that He gave, because she demanded of him earnestly. But by the Jews He showed, that to them that are careless, He gives not even their own. They accordingly received nothing, but lost what was their own. And while these, because they asked not, did not receive so much as their very own; she, because she assailed Him with earnestness, had power to obtain even what pertained to others, and the dog received what was the children's. So great a good is importunity. For though thou be a dog, yet being importunate, thou shalt be preferred to the child being negligent: for what things affection accomplishes not, these, all of them, importunity did accomplish. Say not therefore, "God is an enemy to me, and will not hearken." He doth straightway answer thee, continually troubling him, if not because thou art His friend, yet because of thine importunity. And neither the enmity, or the unseasonable time, nor anything else becomes an hindrance. Say not, "I am unworthy, and do not pray;" for such was the Syrophœnician woman too. Say not, "I have sinned much, and am not able to entreat Him whom I have angered;" for God looks not at the desert, but at the disposition. For if the ruler that feared not God, neither was ashamed of men, was overcome by the widow, much more will He that is good be won over by continual entreaty.

So that though thou be no friend, though thou be not demanding thy due, though thou hast devoured thy Father's substance, and have been a long time out of sight, though without honor, though last of all, though thou approach Him angry, though much displeased; be willing only to pray, and to return, and thou shalt receive all, and shall quickly extinguish the wrath and the condemnation.

But, "behold, I pray," saith one, "and there is no result." Why, thou prayest not like those; such I mean as the Syrophœnician woman, the friend that came late at night, and the widow that is continually troubling the judge, and the son that consumed his father's goods. For didst thou so pray, thou wouldest quickly obtain. For though despite have been done unto Him, yet is He a Father; and though He have been provoked to anger, yet is He fond of His children; and one thing only doth He seek, not to take vengeance for our affronts, but to see thee repenting and entreating Him. Would that we were warmed in like measure, as those bowels are moved to the love of us. But this fire seeks a beginning only, and if thou afford it a little spark, thou kindlest a full flame of beneficence. For not because He hath been insulted, is He sore vexed, but because it is thou who art insulting Him, and so becoming frenzied. For if we being evil, when our children molest[6] us, grieve on their account; much more is God, who can-

---

1 [καὶ χάριν ἔχει σοι τούτου πολλήν.]   2 Luke xi. 5-8.
3 Luke xviii. 1-8.   4 Matt. xv. 21-28; Mark vii. 24-30.
5 δοῦναι. See Hom. LII.

6 [The Greek word is that rendered "insult" in this and the preceding sentence.—R.]

not so much as suffer insult, sore vexed on account of thee, who hast committed it. If we, who love by nature, much more He, who is kindly affectioned beyond nature. "For though," saith He, "a woman should forget the fruits of her womb, yet will I not forget thee."[1]

8. Let us therefore draw nigh unto Him, and say, "Truth, Lord; for even the dogs eat of the crumbs which fall from their masters' table."[2] Let us draw nigh "in season, out of season:" or rather, one can never draw nigh out of season, for it is unseasonable not to be continually approaching. For of Him who desires to give it is always seasonable to ask: yea, as breathing is never out of season, so neither is praying unseasonable, but rather not praying. Since as we need this breath, so do we also the help that comes from Him; and if we be willing, we shall easily draw Him to us. And the prophet, to manifest this, and to point out the constant readiness of His beneficence, said, "We shall find Him prepared as the morning."[3] For as often as we may draw nigh, we shall see Him awaiting our movements. And if we fail to draw from out of His ever-springing goodness, the blame is all ours. This, for example, was His complaint against certain Jews, when He said, "My mercy is as a morning cloud, and as the early dew it goeth away."[4] And His meaning is like this; "I indeed have supplied all my part, but ye, as

a hot sun coming over scatters both the cloud and the dew, and makes them vanish, so have ye by your great wickedness restrained the unspeakable Beneficence."

Which also itself again is an instance of providential care: that even when He sees us unworthy to receive good, He withholds His benefits, lest He render us careless. But if we change a little, even but so much as to know that we have sinned, He gushes out beyond the fountains, He is poured forth beyond the ocean; and the more thou receivest, so much the more doth He rejoice; and in this way is stirred up again to give us more. For indeed He accounts it as His own wealth, that we should be saved, and that He should give largely to them that ask. And this, it may seem, Paul was declaring when He said, that He is "rich unto all and over all that call upon Him."[5] Because when we pray not, then He is wroth; when we pray not, then doth He turn away from us. For this cause "He became poor, that He might make us rich;"[6] for this cause He underwent all those sufferings, that He might incite us to ask.

Let us not therefore despair, but having so many motives and good hopes, though we sin every day, let us approach Him, entreating, beseeching, asking the forgiveness of our sins. For thus we shall be more backward to sin for the time to come; thus shall we drive away the devil, and shall call forth the lovingkindness of God, and attain unto the good things to come, by the grace and love towards man of our Lord Jesus Christ, to whom be glory and might forever and ever. Amen.

---

[1] Isa. xlix. 15.   [2] Matt. xv. 27.

[3] Hosea vi. 3, LXX. "His going forth is prepared as the morning," agreeing with the present Hebrew copies. The sentiment of both readings (as we so often find, apparently by a special Providence) is the same. [R. V., "His going forth is sure as the morning." This, too, conveys the same general sentiment, but is a more accurate rendering of the Hebrew.—R.]

[4] Hosea vi. 4. A.V., "Your goodness is as the morning cloud;" and so also LXX. τὸ ἔλεος ὑμῶν. And with this the Hebrew copies agree, as did St. Jerome's (in loc. t. vi. 63, Venet. 1768). But St. Cyril (in loc. t. iii. 96, reads τὸ ἔλεος μοῦ. And St. Jerome's Commentary shows that according to his interpretation the two readings came to the same meaning. "Your mercy, that wherewith I have always had mercy upon you, hath passed by . . . for now is the captivity near." [R. V., "For your goodness (or, kindness) is as a morning cloud." In the Homily δέ occurs, but is not translated.—R.]

[5] Rom. x. 12. καὶ ἐπὶ πάντας is omitted in our present copies. Mr. Field refers to Rom. iii. 22; "unto all and upon all them that believe." [There is no authority for καὶ ἐπὶ πάντας in Rom. x. 12, and in iii. 22 the weight of authority is against the phrase (see R. V. in loco); but Chrysostom undoubtedly accepted the longer reading in the latter passage, and seems to have combined the two in the present instance.—R.]

[6] 2 Cor. viii. 9. [The citation is not accurate, probably the variation is intentional.—R.]

HOMILY XXIII.

MATT. VII. 1.

"Judge not, that ye be not judged."

WHAT then? Ought we not to blame them that sin? Because Paul also saith this self-same thing: or rather, there too it is Christ, speaking by Paul, and saying,[1] "Why dost thou judge thy brother? And thou, why dost thou set at nought thy brother?" and, "Who art thou that judgest another man's servant?"[2] And again, "Therefore judge nothing before the time, until the Lord come."[3]

How then doth He say elsewhere, "Reprove, rebuke, exhort,"[4] and, "Them that sin rebuke before all?"[5] And Christ too to Peter, "Go and tell him his fault between thee and him alone," and if he neglect to hear, add to thyself another also; and if not even so doth he yield, declare it to the church likewise?"[6] And how hath He set over us so many to reprove; and not only to reprove, but also to punish? For him that hearkens to none of these, He hath commanded to be "as a heathen man and a publican."[7] And how gave He them the keys also? since if they are not to judge, they will be without authority in any matter, and in vain have they received the power to bind and to loose.

And besides, if this were to obtain, all would be lost alike, whether in churches, or in states,[8] or in houses. For except the master judge the servant, and the mistress the maid, and the father the son, and friends one another, there will be an increase of all wickedness. And why say I, friends? unless we judge our enemies, we shall never be able to put an end to our enmity, but all things will be turned upside down.

What then can the saying be? Let us carefully attend, lest the medicines of salvation, and the laws of peace, be accounted by any man laws of overthrow and confusion. First of all, then, even by what follows, He hath pointed out to them that have understanding the excellency of this law, saying, "Why beholdest thou the mote that is in thy brother's eye, but considerest not the beam that is in thine own eye?"[9]

But if to many of the less attentive, it seem yet rather obscure, I will endeavor to explain it from the beginning. In this place, then, as it seems at least to me, He doth not simply command us not to judge any of men's sins, neither doth He simply forbid the doing of such a thing, but to them that are full of innumerable ills, and are trampling upon other men for trifles. And I think that certain Jews too are here hinted at, for that while they were bitter accusing their neighbors for small faults, and such as came to nothing, they were themselves insensibly committing deadly[10] sins. Herewith towards the end also He was upbraiding them, when He said, "Ye bind heavy burdens, and grievous to be borne, but ye will not move them with your finger,"[11] and, "ye pay tithe of mint and anise, and have omitted the weightier matters of the law, judgment, mercy, and faith."[12]

Well then, I think that these are comprehended in His invective; that He is checking them beforehand as to those things, wherein they were hereafter to accuse His disciples. For although His disciples had been guilty of no such sin, yet in them were supposed to be offenses; as, for instance, not keeping the sabbath, eating with unwashen hands, sitting at meat with publicans; of which He saith also in another place, "Ye which strain at the gnat, and swallow the camel."[13] But yet it is also a general law that He is laying down on these matters.

And the Corinthians[14] too Paul did not absolutely command not to judge, but not to judge their own superiors, and upon grounds that are not acknowledged; not absolutely to refrain from correcting them that sin. Neither indeed was He then rebuking all without distinction, but disciples doing so to their teachers were the object of His reproof; and they who, being guilty of innumerable sins, bring an evil report upon the guiltless.

This then is the sort of thing which Christ also in this place intimated; not intimated merely, but guarded[15] it too with a great ter-

---

[1] Rom. xiv. 10.　　　[2] Rom. xiv. 4.　　　[3] 1 Cor. iv. 5.
[4] 2 Tim. iv. 2.
[5] 1 Tim. v. 20. [R. V., "reprove." The Greek verb is the same in Matt. xviii. 15 also.—R.]
[6] Matt. xviii. 15, 16, 17.　　　[7] Matt. xviii. 17.　　　[8] [πόλεσι.]
[9] Matt. vii. 3.

[10] τὰ μεγαλά. The article implies the distinction.
[11] Matt. xxiii. 4.　　　[12] Matt. xxiii. 23.
[13] Matt. xxiii. 24. [R. V., more correctly, "strain out; the word "at" is probably a typographical blunder of the A. V.—R.]
[14] 1 Cor. iv. 5　　　　　　　　　　　　ἐπέστησε.

ror, and the punishment from which no prayers can deliver.

2. "For with what judgment ye judge," saith He, "ye shall be judged."[1]

That is, "it is not the other," saith Christ, "that thou condemnest, but thyself, and thou art making the judgment-seat dreadful to thyself, and the account strict." As then in the forgiveness of our sins the beginnings are from us, so also in this judgment, it is by ourselves that the measures of our condemnation are laid down. You see, we ought not to upbraid nor trample upon them, but to admonish; not to revile, but to advise; not to assail with pride, but to correct with tenderness. For not him, but thyself, dost thou give over to extreme vengeance, by not sparing him, when it may be needful to give sentence on his offenses.

Seest thou, how these two commandments are both easy, and fraught with great blessings to the obedient, even as of evils on the other hand, to the regardless? For both he that forgives his neighbor, hath freed himself first of the two from the grounds of complaint, and that without any labor; and he that with tenderness and indulgence inquires into other men's offenses, great is the allowance[2] of pardon, which he hath by his judgment laid up beforehand for himself.

"What then!" say you: "if one commit fornication, may I not say that fornication is a bad thing, nor at all correct him that is playing the wanton?" Nay, correct him, but not as a foe, nor as an adversary exacting a penalty, but as a physician providing medicines. For neither did Christ say, "stay not him that is sinning," but "judge not;" that is, be not bitter in pronouncing sentence.

And besides, it is not of great things (as I have already observed), nor of things prohibited, that this is said, but of those which are not even counted offenses. Wherefore He said also,

"Why beholdest thou the mote that is in thy brother's eye?"[3]

Yea, for many now do this; if they see but a monk wearing an unnecessary garment, they produce against him the law of our Lord,[4] while they themselves are extorting without end, and defrauding men every day. If they see him but partaking rather largely of food, they become bitter accusers, while they themselves are daily drinking to excess and surfeiting: not knowing, that besides their own sins, they do hereby gather up for themselves a greater flame, and deprive themselves of every plea. For on this point,

that thine own doings must be strictly inquired into, thou thyself hast first made the law, by thus sentencing those of thy neighbor. Account it not then to be a grievous thing, if thou art also thyself to undergo the same kind of trial.

"Thou hypocrite, first cast out the beam out of thine own eye."[5]

Here His will is to signify the great wrath, which He hath against them that do such things. For so, wheresoever He would indicate that the sin is great, and the punishment and wrath in store for it grievous, He begins with a reproach.[6] As then unto him that was exacting the hundred pence, He said in His deep displeasure, "Thou wicked servant, I forgave thee all that debt;"[7] even so here also, "Thou hypocrite." For not of protecting care comes such a judgment, but of ill will to man; and while a man puts forward a mask of benevolence, he is doing a work of the utmost wickedness, causing reproaches without ground, and accusations, to cleave unto his neighbors, and usurping a teacher's rank, when he is not worthy to be so much as a disciple. On account of this He called him "hypocrite." For thou, who in other men's doings art so bitter, as to see even the little things; how hast thou become so remiss in thine own, as that even the great things are hurried over by thee?

"First cast out the beam out of thine own eye."

Seest thou, that He forbids not judging, but commands to cast out first the beam from thine eye, and then to set right the doings of the rest of the world? For indeed each one knows his own things better than those of others; and sees the greater rather than the less; and loves himself more than his neighbor. Wherefore, if thou doest it out of guardian care, I bid thee care for thyself first, in whose case the sin is both more certain and greater. But if thou neglect thyself, it is quite evident that neither dost thou judge thy brother in care for him, but in hatred, and wishing to expose him. For what if he ought to be judged? it should be by one who commits no such sin, not by thee.

Thus, because He had introduced great and high doctrines of self denial, lest any man should say, it is easy so to practise it in words; He willing to signify His entire confidence, and that He was not chargeable with any of the things that had been mentioned, but had duly fulfilled all, spake this parable. And that, because He too was afterwards to

---

[1] Matt. vii. 2. [2] ἔρανον.
[3] Matt. vii. 3. [4] Matt. x. 10. [5] Matt. vii. 5. [6] ὕβρεως. [7] Matt. xviii. 32.

judge, saying, "Woe unto you, Scribes and Pharisees, hypocrites."[1] Yet was not he chargeable with what hath been mentioned; for neither did He pull out a mote, nor had He a beam on His eyes, but being clean from all these, He so corrected the faults of all. "For it is not at all meet," saith He, "to judge others, when one is chargeable with the same things." And why marvel at His establishing this law, when even the very thief knew it upon the cross, saying to the other thief, "Dost not thou fear God, seeing we are in the same condemnation;"[2] expressing the same sentiments with Christ?

But thou, so far from casting out thine own beam, dost not even see it, but another's mote thou not only seest, but also judgest, and essayest to cast it out; as if any one seized with a grievous dropsy, or indeed with any other incurable disease, were to neglect this, and find fault with another who was neglecting a slight swelling. And if it be an evil not to see one's own sins, it is a twofold and threefold evil to be even sitting in judgment on others, while men themselves, as if past feeling, are bearing about beams in their own eyes: since no beam is so heavy as sin.

His injunction therefore in these words is as follows, that he who is chargeable with countless evil deeds, should not be a bitter censor of other men's offenses, and especially when these are trifling. He is not overthrowing reproof nor correction, but forbidding men to neglect their own faults, and exult over those of other men.

For indeed this was a cause of men's going unto great vice, bringing in a twofold wickedness. For he, whose practice it had been to slight his own faults, great as they were, and to search bitterly into those of others, being slight and of no account, was spoiling himself two ways: first, by thinking lightly of his own faults; next, by incurring enmities and feuds with all men, and training himself every day to extreme fierceness, and want of feeling for others.

3. Having then put away all these things, by this His excellent legislation, He added yet another charge, saying,

"Give not that which is holy unto the dogs, neither cast ye your pearls before swine."[3]

"Yet surely further on," it will be said, "He commanded, "What ye have heard in the ear, that preach ye upon the housetops."[4] But this is in no wise contrary to the former. For neither in that place did He simply command to tell all men, but to whom it should be spoken, to them He bade speak with freedom.[5] And by "dogs" here He figuratively described them that are living in incurable ungodliness, and affording no hope of change for the better; and by "swine," them that abide continually in an unchaste life, all of whom He hath pronounced unworthy of hearing such things. Paul also, it may be observed, declared this when He said, "But a natural man receiveth not the things of the Spirit, for they are foolishness unto him."[5] And in many other places too He saith that corruption of life is the cause of men's not receiving the more perfect doctrines. Wherefore He commands not to open the doors to them; for indeed they become more insolent after learning. For as to the well-disposed and intelligent, things appear venerable when revealed, so to the insensible, when they are unknown rather. "Since then from their nature, they are not able to learn them, "let the thing be hidden," saith He, "that[6] at least for ignorance they may reverence them. For neither doth the swine know at all what a pearl is. Therefore since he knows not, neither let him see it, lest he trample under foot what he knows not."

For nothing results, beyond greater mischief to them that are so disposed when they hear; for both the holy things are profaned[7] by them, not knowing what they are; and they are the more lifted up and armed against us. For this is meant by, "lest they trample them under their feet, and turn again and rend you."[8]

Nay, "surely," saith one, "they ought to be so strong as to remain equally impregnable after men's learning them, and not to yield to other people occasions against us." But it is not the things that yield it, but that these men are swine; even as when the pearl is trampled under foot, it is not so trampled, because it is really contemptible, but because it fell among swine.

And full well did He say, "turn again and rend you:" for they feign gentleness,[9] so as to be taught: then after they have learnt,

---

[1] Matt. xxiii. 1.
[2] Luke xxiii. 40, 41. [R. V., "Dost thou not even fear God, seeing thou art in the same condemnation." In several places Chrysostom gives the plural form, as here, but there is little authority for it in the New Testament text.—R.]
[3] Matt. vii. 6. [R. V., "the swine," the article is in the Greek text of the Homily.]

[4] Matt. x. 27.
[5] 1 Cor. ii. 14. In the verse before that to which reference is here made, our Saviour says, "Fear them not therefore." And again in the verse after, "Fear not them which kill the body:" whence the natural conclusion is, that His chief purpose here was to caution His disciples against the fear of man.
[6] The words in italics are omitted in the manuscripts. [The construction of the Greek is very difficult, if the MSS. text is accepted. One MS., however, has an imperative in the last clause: "let them reverence them," thus relieving the difficulty.—R.]
[7] ἐμπαροινεῖται.　　[8] [R. V., properly omits "again."—R.]
[9] ἐπιείκειαν.

quite changing from one sort to another, they jeer, mock and deride us, as deceived persons. Therefore Paul also said to Timothy,[1] "Of whom be thou ware also; for he hath greatly withstood our words;" and again in another place, "From such turn away,"[2] and, "A man that is an heretic, after the first and second admonition, reject."[3]

It is not, you see, that those truths furnish them with armor, but they become fools in this way of their own accord, being filled with more willfulness. On this account it is no small gain for them to abide in ignorance, for so they are not such entire scorners. But if they learn, the mischief is twofold. For neither will they themselves be at all profited thereby, but rather the more damaged, and to thee they will cause endless difficulties.

Let them hearken, who shamelessly associate with all, and make the awful things contemptible. For the mysteries we too therefore celebrate with closed doors, and keep out the uninitiated, not for any weakness of which we have convicted our rites, but because the many are as yet imperfectly prepared for them. For this very reason He Himself also discoursed much unto the Jews in parables, "because they seeing saw not." For this, Paul likewise commanded "to know how we ought to answer every man."[4]

4. "Ask, and it shall be given you; seek, and ye shall find; knock, and it shall be opened unto you."[5]

For inasmuch as He had enjoined things great and marvellous, and had commanded men to be superior to all their passions, and had led them up to Heaven itself, and had enjoined them to strive after the resemblance, not of angels and archangels, but (as far as was possible) of the very Lord of all; and had bidden His disciples not only themselves duly to perform all this, but also to correct others, and to distinguish between the evil and them that are not such, the dogs and them that are not dogs (although there be much that is hidden in men):—that they might not say, "these things are grievous and intolerable," (for indeed in the sequel Peter did utter some such things, saying, "Who can be saved?"[6] and again, "If the case of the man be so, it is not good to marry): in order therefore that they might not now likewise say so; as in the first place even by what had gone before He had proved it all to be easy, setting down many reasons one upon another, of power to persuade men:

so after all He adds also the pinnacle of all facility, devising as no ordinary relief to our toils, the assistance derived from persevering prayers. Thus, we are not ourselves, saith He, to strive alone, but also to invoke the help from above: and it will surely come and be present with us, and will aid us in our struggles, and make all easy. Therefore He both commanded us to ask, and pledged Himself to the giving.

However, not simply to ask did He command us, but with much assiduity and earnestness. For this is the meaning of "seek." For so he that seeks, putting all things out of his mind, is taken up with that alone which is sought, and forms no idea of any of the persons present. And this which I am saying they know, as many as have lost either gold, or servants, and are seeking diligently after them.

By "seeking," then, He declared this; by "knocking," that we approach with earnestness and a glowing mind.

Despond not therefore, O man, nor show less of zeal about virtue, than they do of desire for wealth. For things of that kind thou hast often sought and not found, but nevertheless, though thou know this, that thou art not sure to find them, thou puttest in motion every mode of search; but here, although having a promise that thou wilt surely receive, thou dost not show even the smallest part of that earnestness. And if thou dost not receive straightway, do not even thus despair. For to this end He said, "knock," to signify that even if He should not straightway open the door, we are to continue there.

5. And if thou doubt my affirmation, at any rate believe His example.

"For what man is there of you," saith He, "whom if his son ask bread, will he give him a stone?"[7]

Because, as among men, if thou keep on doing so, thou art even accounted troublesome, and disgusting: so with God, when thou doest not so, then thou dost more entirely provoke Him. And if thou continue asking, though thou receive not at once, thou surely wilt receive. For to this end was the door shut, that He may induce thee to knock; to this end He doth not straightway assent, that thou mayest ask. Continue then to do these things, and thou wilt surely receive. For that thou mightest not say, "What then if I should ask and not receive?" He hath

---

[1] 2 Tim. iv. 15.
[2] 2 Tim. iii. 5. [The citation is modified.—R.]
[3] Titus iii. 10. [R. V., "A man that is heretical (or factious) after a first and second admonition, refuse (or avoid)."—R.]
[4] Col. iv. 6.   [5] Matt. vii. 6.   [6] Matt. xix. 25, and 10.

[7] Matt. vii. 9. [The citation is not exact. Here, as below, Chrysostom gives the form : " For which is there of you," omitting " man." The Oxford translator follows the A. V. here but not below. " Of whom " (in R. V.) is better English (see below); the Greek is the same in both passages.—R.]

blocked up[1] thy approach with that similitude, again framing arguments, and by those human things urging us to be confident on these matters; implying by them that we must not only ask, but ask what we ought.[2]

"For which of you is there, a father, of whom if his son shall ask bread, will he give him a stone?" So that if thou receive not, thy asking a stone is the cause of thy not receiving. For though thou be a son, this suffices not for thy receiving: rather this very thing even hinders thy receiving, that being a son, thou askest what is not profitable.

Do thou also therefore ask nothing worldly, but all things spiritual, and thou wilt surely receive. For so Solomon,[3] because he asked what he ought, behold how quickly he received. Two things now, you see, should be in him that prays, asking earnestly, and asking what he ought: "since ye too," saith He, "though ye be fathers, wait for your sons to ask: and if they should ask of you anything inexpedient, ye refuse the gifts; just as, if it be expedient, ye consent and bestow it." Do thou too, considering these things, not withdraw until thou receive; until thou have found, retire not; relax not thy diligence, until the door be opened. For if thou approach with this mind, and say, "Except I receive, I depart not;" thou wilt surely receive, provided thou ask such things, as are both suitable for Him of whom thou askest to give, and expedient for thee the petitioner. But what are these? To seek the things spiritual, all of them; to forgive them that have trespassed, and so to draw nigh asking forgiveness; "to lift up holy hands without wrath and doubting."[4] If we thus ask, we shall receive. As it is, surely our asking is a mockery, and the act of drunken rather than of sober men.

"What then," saith one, "if I ask even spiritual things, and do not receive?" Thou didst not surely knock with earnestness; or thou madest thyself unworthy to receive; or didst quickly leave off.

"And wherefore," it may be inquired, "did He not say, what things we ought to ask"? Nay verily, He hath mentioned them all in what precedes, and hath signified for what things we ought to draw nigh. Say not then, "I drew nigh, and did not receive." For in no case is it owing to God that we receive not, God who loves us so much as to surpass even fathers, to surpass them as far as goodness doth this evil nature.

"For if ye, being evil, know how to give good gifts unto your children, how much more your heavenly Father."[5]

Now this He said, not to bring an evil name on man's nature, nor to condemn our race as bad; but in contrast to His own goodness He calls paternal tenderness evil,[6] so great is the excess of His love to man.

Seest thou an argument unspeakable, of power to arouse to good hopes even him that hath become utterly desperate?

Now here indeed He signifies His goodness by means of our fathers, but in what precedes by the chief among His gifts, by the "soul,"[7] by the body. And nowhere doth He set down the chief of all good things, nor bring forward His own coming:—for He who thus made speed to give up His Son to the slaughter, "how shall He not freely give us all things?"—because it had not yet come to pass. But Paul indeed sets it forth, thus saying, "He that spared not His own Son, how shall He not also with Him freely give us all things."[8] But His discourse with them is still from the things of men.

6. After this, to indicate that we ought neither to feel confidence in prayer, while neglecting our own doings; nor, when taking pains, trust only to our own endeavors; but both to seek after the help from above, and contribute withal our own part; He sets forth the one in connection with the other. For so after much exhortation, He taught also how to pray, and when He had taught how to pray, He proceeded again to His exhortation concerning what we are to do; then from that again to the necessity of praying continually, saying, "Ask," and "seek," and "knock." And thence again, to the necessity of being also diligent ourselves.

"For all things," saith He, "whatsoever ye would that men should do to you, do ye also to them."[9]

Summing up all in brief, and signifying, that virtue is compendious, and easy, and readily known of all men.

And He did not merely say, "All things whatsoever ye would," but, "Therefore all things whatsoever ye would." For this word, "therefore," He did not add without purpose, but with a concealed meaning: "if ye desire," saith He, "to be heard, together with what I have said, do these things also." What then are these? "Whatsoever ye

---

[1] ἐπετείχισε.
[2] [οὐκ αἰτεῖν χρὴ μόνον, ἀλλὰ καὶ ἃ χρὴ αἰτεῖν, "not only is it fitting to ask, but to ask what "is fitting."—R.]
[3] 1 Kings iii. 10-14 ; 2 Chron. i. 11, 12.
[4] 1 Tim. ii. 8, perhaps "disputing" rather than "doubting." [R. V. text "disputing," in the margin "doubting." Comp. Homily XIX. 11, p. 138.—R.]

[5] Matt. vii. 11. ["Heavenly" is substituted for "which is in Heaven."—R.]
[6] πονηρίαν.   7 Or "life:" see Matt. vi. 25.
[8] Rom. viii. 32.
[9] Matt. vii. 12. [οὕτως is omitted ; so the Vulgate.—R.]

would that men should do to you." Seest thou how He hath hereby also signified that together with prayer we need exact conversation?[1] And He did not say, "whatsoever things thou wouldest to be done unto thee of God, those do unto thy neighbor;" lest thou should say, "But how is it possible? He is God and I am man:" but, "whatsoever thou wouldest to be done unto thee of thy fellow servant, these things do thou also thyself show forth towards thy neighbor." What is less burdensome than this? what fairer?

Then the praise also, before the rewards, is exceeding great.

"For this is the law and the prophets."

Whence it is evident, that virtue is according to our nature; that we all, of ourselves, know our duties; and that it is not possible for us ever to find refuge in ignorance.

7. "Enter ye in at the strait gate, for wide is the gate and broad is the way that leadeth to destruction, and many there be which go in thereat: and strait is the gate and narrow[2] is the way which leadeth unto life, and few there be that find it."[3]

And yet after this He said, "My yoke is easy, and my burden is light."[4] And in what He hath lately said also, He intimated the same: how then doth He here say it is strait and confined? In the first place, if thou attend, even here He points to it as very light, and easy, and accessible. "And how," it may be said, "is the narrow and confined way easy?" Because it is a way and a gate; even as also the other, though it be wide, though spacious, is also a way and a gate. And of these there is nothing permanent, but all things are passing away, both the pains and the good things of life.

And not only herein is the part of virtue easy, but also by the end again it becomes yet easier. For not the passing away of our labors and toils, but also their issuing in a good end (for they end in life) is enough to console those in conflict. So that both the temporary nature of our labors, and the perpetuity of our crowns, and the fact that the labors come first, and the crowns after, must prove a very great relief in our toils. Wherefore Paul also called their affliction "light"; not from the nature of the events, but because of the mind of the combatants, and the hope of the future. "For our light affliction," saith he, "worketh an eternal weight of glory, while we look not at the things which are seen, but at the things which are not seen."[5] For if to sailors the waves and the seas, to soldiers their slaughters and wounds, to husbandmen the winters and the frosts, to boxers the sharp blows, be light and tolerable things, all of them, for the hope of those rewards which are temporary and perishing; much more when heaven is set forth, and the unspeakable blessings, and the eternal rewards, will no one feel any of the present hardships. Or if any account it, even thus, to be toilsome, the suspicion comes of nothing but their own remissness.

See, at any rate, how He on another side also makes it easy, commanding not to hold intercourse with the dogs, nor to give one's self over to the swine, and to "beware of the false prophets;" thus on all accounts causing men to feel as if in real conflict. And the very fact too of calling it narrow contributed very greatly towards making it easy; for it wrought on them to be vigilant. As Paul then, when he saith, "We wrestle not against flesh and blood,"[6] doth so not to cast down, but to rouse up the spirits of the soldiers: even so He also, to shake the travellers out of their sleep, called the way rough. And not in this way only did He work upon men to be vigilant, but also by adding, that it contains likewise many to supplant them; and, what is yet more grievous, they do not even attack openly, but hiding themselves; for such is the race of the false prophets. "But look not to this," saith He, "that it is rough and narrow, but where it ends; nor that the opposite is wide and spacious, but where it issues."

And all these things He saith, thoroughly to awaken our alacrity; even as elsewhere also He said, "Violent men take it by force."[7] For whoever is in conflict, when he actually sees the judge of the lists marvelling at the painfulness of his efforts, is the more inspirited.

Let it not then bewilder us, when many things spring up hence, that turn to our vexation. For the way is strait, and the gate narrow, but not the city.[8] Therefore must one neither look for rest here, nor there expect any more aught that is painful.

Now in saying, "Few there be that find it," here again He both declared the careless-

[1] [πολιτείας.]   [2] Confined, τεθλιμμένη.
[3] Matt. vi. 13, 14. [R. V., "by the narrow gate;" "enter in thereby;" "For narrow is the gate, and straitened the way," &c. Chrysostom introduces verse 14 with καί; and in some MSS. of the Homilies τί is added. Comp. R.V. margin: "How narrow," etc. —R.]
[4] Matt. xi. 30.

[5] 2 Cor. iv. 17, 18.
[6] Eph. vi. 12. [R. V., "our wrestling is not," etc.—R.]
[7] Matt. xi. 12. [R. V., "men of violence," etc.—R.]
[8]
          'They pass in stooping low,
For strait and narrow was the way, which he did shew.

          Each goodly thing is hardest to begin:
          But entered in, a spacious court they see,
          Both plaine, and pleasant to be walked in.
                    Spenser's Faery Queen, b. i. c. x. 5, 6.

ness of the generality, and instructed His hearers not to regard the felicities of the many, but the labors of the few. For the more part, saith He, so far from walking this way, do not so much as make it their choice: a thing of most extreme criminality. But we should not regard the many, nor be troubled thereat, but emulate the few; and, by all means equipping[1] ourselves, should so walk therein.

For besides that it is strait, there are also many to overthrow us in the way that leads thither. Wherefore He also added,

8. "Beware of false prophets, for they will come to you in sheep's clothing, but inwardly they are ravening wolves."[2] Behold together with the dogs and swine another kind of ambush and conspiracy, far more grievous than that. For those are acknowledged and open, but these shaded over. For which cause also, while from those He commanded to hold off, these He charged men to watch with exact care, as though it were not possible to see them at the first approach. Wherefore He also said, "beware"; making us more exact to discern them.

Then, lest when they had heard that it was narrow and strait, and that they must walk on a way opposite to the many, and must keep themselves from swine and dogs, and together with these from another more wicked kind, even this of wolves; lest, I say, they should sink down at this multitude of vexations, having both to go a way contrary to most men, and therewith again to have such anxiety about these things: He reminded them of what took place in the days of their fathers, by using the term, "false prophets," for then also no less did such things happen. Be not now, I pray you, troubled (so He speaks), for nothing new nor strange is to befall you. Since for all truth the devil is always secretly substituting its appropriate deceit.

And by the figure of "false prophets," here, I think He shadows out not the heretics, but them that are of a corrupt life, yet wear a mask of virtue; whom the generality are wont to call by the name of impostors.[3] Wherefore He also said further,

"By their fruits ye shall know them."[4]

For amongst heretics one may often find actual goodness,[5] but amongst those whom I was mentioning, by no means.

"What then," it may be said, "if in these things too they counterfeit?" "Nay, they will be easily detected; for such is the nature of this way, in which I commanded men to walk, painful and irksome; but the hypocrite would not choose to take pains, but to make a show only; wherefore also he is easily convicted." Thus, inasmuch as He had said, "there be few that find it," He clears them out again from among those, who find it not, yet feign so to do, by commanding us not to look to them that wear the masks only, but to them who in reality pursue it.

"But wherefore," one may say, "did He not make them manifest, but set us on the search for them?" That we might watch, and be ever prepared for conflict, guarding against our disguised as well as against our open enemies: which kind indeed Paul also was intimating, when he said, that "by their good words they deceive the hearts of the simple."[6] Let us not be troubled therefore, when we see many such even now. Nay, for this too Christ foretold from the beginning.

And see His gentleness: how He said not, "Punish them," but, "Be not hurt by them," "Do not fall amongst them unguarded." Then that thou mightest not say, "it is impossible to distinguish that sort of men," again He states an argument from a human example, thus saying,

"Do men gather grapes of thorns, or figs of thistles? even so every good tree bringeth forth good fruit, but the corrupt tree bringeth forth evil fruit. A good tree cannot bring forth evil fruit, neither can a corrupt tree bring forth good fruit."[7]

Now what He saith is like this: they have nothing gentle nor sweet; it is the sheep only so far as the skin; wherefore also it is easy to discern them. And lest thou shouldest have any the least doubt, He compares it to certain natural necessities, in matters which admit of no result but one. In which sense Paul also said, "The carnal mind is death; for it is not subject to the law of God, neither indeed can be."[8]

And if He states the same thing twice, it is not tautology. But, lest any one should say, "Though the evil tree bear evil fruit, it bears also good, and makes the distinction difficult, the crop being twofold:" "This is not so," saith He, "for it bears evil fruit only, and

---

[1] συγκροτοῦντας.

[2] Matt. vii. 15. [" For they will come " is substituted by Chrysostom for " which come," but without any MSS. authority known to us.—R.]

[3] ἐπιθετῶν.   [4] Matt. vii. 16.

[5] βιόν. Comp. Hom. XLVI. p. 486, Ben. [In the passage referred to, the word is rendered "practice." For the ethical sense of βιός in classical usage, see Trench, *Synonymes New Testament, sub voce.*—R.]

[6] Rom. xvi. 18. [R. V., " by their smooth and fair speech they beguile the hearts of the innocent." But Chrysostom omits καὶ εὐλογίας, agreeing with the reading of the four principal Græco-Latin MSS. of the Pauline Epistles.—R.]

[7] Matt. vii. 16–18.

[8] Rom. viii. 6, 7. [R. V., " For the mind of the flesh," etc. The translator has not rendered γάρ, which occurs in the Greek of the Homily, as in Rom. viii. 6.—R.]

never can bear good: as indeed in the contrary case also."

"What then? Is there no such thing as a good man becoming wicked? And the contrary again takes place, and life abounds with many such examples."

But Christ saith not this, that for the wicked there is no way to change, or that the good cannot fall away, but that so long as he is living in wickedness, he will not be able to bear good fruit. For he may indeed change to virtue, being evil; but while continuing in wickedness, he will not bear good fruit.

What then? did not David, being good, bear evil fruit? Not continuing good, but being changed; since, undoubtedly, had he remained always what he was, he would not have brought forth such fruit. For not surely while abiding in the habit of virtue, did he commit what he committed.

Now by these words He was also stopping the mouths of those who speak evil at random, and putting a bridle on the lips of all calumniators. I mean, whereas many suspect the good by reason of the bad, He by this saying hath deprived them of all excuse. "For thou canst not say, 'I am deceived and beguiled;' since I have given thee exactly this way of distinguishing them by their works, having added the injunction to go to their actions, and not to confound all at random."

9. Then forasmuch as He had not commanded to punish, but only to beware of them, He, at once both to comfort those whom they vex, and to alarm and change them, set up as a bulwark against[1] them the punishment they should receive at His hands, saying,

"Every tree that bringeth not forth good fruit is hewn down, and cast into the fire."[2]

Then, to make the saying less grievous, He added,

"Wherefore by their fruits ye shall know them."[3]

That He might not seem to introduce the threatening as His leading topic, but to be stirring up their mind in the way of admonition and counsel.

Here He seems to me to be hinting at the Jews also, who were exhibiting such fruits. Wherefore also He reminded them of the sayings of John, in the very same terms delineating their punishment. For he too said the very same, making mention to them of an "axe," and of a "tree cut down," and of "unquenchable fire."

And though it appear indeed to be some single judgment, the being burnt up, yet if one examine carefully, these are two punishments. For he that is burnt is also cast of course out of God's kingdom; and this latter punishment is more grievous than the other. Now I know indeed that many tremble only at hell, but I affirm the loss of that glory to be a far greater punishment than hell. And if it be not possible to exhibit it such in words, this is nothing marvellous. For neither do we know the blessedness of those good things, that we should on the other hand clearly perceive the wretchedness ensuing on being deprived of them; since Paul, as knowing these things clearly, is aware, that to fall from Christ's glory is more grievous than all. And this we shall know at that time, when we shall fall into the actual trial of it.

But may this never be our case, O thou only-begotten Son of God, neither may we ever have any experience of this irremediable punishment. For how great an evil it is to fall from those good things, cannot indeed be accurately told: nevertheless, as I may be able, I will labor and strive by an example to make it clear to you, though it be but in some small degree.

Let us then imagine a wondrous child, having besides His virtue the dominion of the whole world, and in all respects so virtuous, as to be capable of bringing all men to the yearning of a father's affection. What then do you think the father of this child would not gladly suffer, not to be cast out of His society? And what evil, small or great, would he not welcome, on condition of seeing and enjoying Him? Now let us reason just so with respect to that glory also. For no child, be he never so virtuous, is so desirable and lovely to a father, as the having our portion in those good things, and "to depart and be with Christ."[4]

No doubt hell, and that punishment, is a thing not to be borne. Yet though one suppose ten thousand hells, he will utter nothing like what it will be to fail of that blessed glory, to be hated of Christ, to hear "I know you not,"[5] to be accused for not feeding Him when we saw Him an hungered.[6] Yea, better surely to endure a thousand thunderbolts, than to see that face of mildness turning away from us, and that eye of peace not enduring to look upon us. For if He, while I was an enemy, and hating Him, and turning from Him, did in such wise follow after me, as not to spare even Himself, but to give

---

ἐπετείχισεν αὐτοῖς.   [2] Matt. vii. 19.
Matt. vii. 20. [There is here a slight variation from the New Testament text.—R.]

[4] Phil. i. 23.   [5] Matt. xxv. 12.   [6] Matt. xxv. 42.

Himself up unto death: when after all this I do not vouchsafe to Him so much as a loaf in His hunger, with what kind of eyes shall I ever again behold Him?

But mark even here His gentleness; in that He doth not at all speak of His benefits, nor say, "Thou hast despised Him that hath done thee so much good:" neither doth He say, "Me, who brought thee from that which is not into being, who breathed into thee a soul, and set thee over all things on earth, who for thy sake made earth, and heaven, and sea, and air, and all things that are, who had been dishonored by thee, yea accounted of less honor than the devil, and did not even so withdraw Himself, but had innumerable thoughts for thee after it all; who chose to become a slave, who was beaten with rods and spit upon, who was slain, who died the most shameful death, who also on high makes intercession for thee, who freely gives thee His Spirit, who vouchsafes to thee a kingdom, who makes thee such promises, whose will it is to be unto thee Head, and Bridegroom, and Garment, and House, and Root, and Meat, and Drink, and Shepherd, and King, and who hath taken thee to be brother, and heir, and joint-heir with Himself; who hath brought thee out of darkness into the dominion of light." These things, I say, and more than these He might speak of, but He mentions none of these; but what? only the sin itself.

Even here He shows His love, and indicates the yearning which He hath toward thee: not saying, "Depart into the fire prepared for you," but "prepared for the devil." And before He tells them what wrongs they had done, and neither so doth He endure to mention all, but a few. And before these He calls the other sort, those who have done well, to signify from this too that He is blaming them justly.

What amount of punishment, then, is so grievous as these words? For if any one seeing but a man who was his benefactor an hungered, would not neglect him; or if he should neglect him, being upbraided with it, would choose rather to sink into the earth than to hear of it in the presence of two or three friends; what will be our feelings, on hearing these words in the presence of the whole world; such as He would not say even then, were He not earnestly accounting for His own doings? For that not to upbraid did He bring these things forward, but in self-defense, and for the sake of showing, that not without ground nor at random was He saying, "depart from me;" this is evident from His unspeakable benefits. For if He

had been minded to upbraid, He would have brought forwards all these, but now He mentions only what treatment He had received.

10. Let us therefore, beloved, fear the hearing these words. Life is not a plaything: or rather our present life is a plaything, but the things to come are not such; or perchance our life is not a plaything only, but even worse than this. For it ends not in laughter, but rather brings exceeding damage on them who are not minded to order their own ways strictly. For what, I pray thee, is the difference between children who are playing at building houses, and us when we are building our fine houses? what again between them making out their dinners, and us in our delicate fare? None, but just that we do it at the risk of being punished. And if we do not yet quite perceive the poverty of what is going on, no wonder, for we are not yet become men; but when we are become so, we shall know that all these things are childish.

For so those other things too, as we grow to manhood, we laugh to scorn; but when we are children we account them to be worth anxiety; and while we are gathering together potsherds and mire we think no less of ourselves than they who are erecting their great circuits of walls Nevertheless they straightway perish and fall down, and not even when standing can they be of any use to us, as indeed neither can those fine houses. For the citizen of Heaven they cannot receive, neither can he bear to abide in them, who hath his country above; but as we throw down these with our feet, so he too those by his high spirit. And as we laugh at the children, weeping at that overthrow, even so these also, when we are bewailing it all, do not laugh only, but weep also: because both their bowels are compassionate, and great is the mischief thence arising.

Let us therefore become men. How long are we to crawl on the earth, priding ourselves on stones and stocks? How long are we to play? And would we played only! But now we even betray our own salvation; and as children when they neglect their learning, and practise themselves in these things at their leisure, suffer very severe blows; even so we too, spending all our diligence herein, and having then our spiritual lessons required of us in our works, and not being able to produce them, shall have to pay the utmost penalty. And there is none to deliver us; though he be father, brother, what you will. But while these things shall all pass away, the torment ensuing upon them remains immortal and unceasing; which sort of thing indeed takes place with respect to the children as well, their father destroying their childish toys altogether for their idleness, and causing them to weep incessantly.

11. And to convince thee that these things are such, let us bring before us wealth, that which more than anything seems to be worthy of our pains, and let us set against it a virtue of the soul (which soever thou wilt), and then shalt thou see most clearly the vileness thereof. Let us, I say, suppose there are two men (and I do not now speak of injuriousness,¹ but as yet of honest wealth); and of these two, let the one get together money, and sail on the sea, and till the land, and find many other ways of merchandise (although I know not quite, whether, so doing, he can make honest gains); nevertheless let it be so, and let it be granted that his gains are gotten with honesty; that he buys fields, and slaves, and all such things, and suppose no injustice connected therewith. But let the other one, possessing as much, sell fields, sell houses, and vessels of gold and silver, and give to the poor; let him supply the necessitous, heal the sick, free such as are in straits, some let him deliver from bonds, others let him release that are in mines, these let him bring back from the noose, those, who are captives, let him rescue from their punishment. Of whose side then would you be? And we have not as yet spoken of the future, but as yet of what is here. Of whose part then would ye be? his that is gathering gold, or his that is doing away with calamities? with him that is purchasing fields, or him who is making himself a harbor of refuge for the human race? him that is clothed with much gold, or him that is crowned with innumerable blessings? Is not the one like some angel come down from Heaven for the amendment of the rest of mankind; but the other not so much as like a man, but like some little child that is gathering all together vainly and at random?

But if to get money honestly be thus absurd, and of extreme madness; when not even the honesty is there, how can such a man choose but be more wretched than any? I say, if the absurdity be so great; when hell is added thereto, and the loss of the kingdom, how great wailings are due to him, both living and dead?

12. Or wilt thou that we take in hand some other part also of virtue? Let us then introduce again another man, who is in power, commanding all, invested with great dignity, having a gorgeous herald, and girdle, and lictors, and a large company of attendants. Doth not this seem great, and meet to be called happy? Well then, against this man

again let us set another, him that is patient of injuries, and meek, and lowly, and long suffering; and let this last be despitefully used, be beaten, and let him bear it quietly, and bless them that are doing such things.

Now which is the one to be admired, I pray thee? he that is puffed up, and inflamed, or he that is self-subdued? Is not the one again like the powers above, that are so free from passion, but the other like a blown bladder, or a man who hath the dropsy, and great inflammation? The one like a spiritual physician, the other, a ridiculous child that is puffing out his cheeks?

For why dost thou pride thyself, O man? Because thou art borne on high in a chariot? Because a yoke of mules is drawing thee? And what is this? Why, this one may see befalling mere logs of wood and stones. Is it that thou art clothed with beautiful garments? But look at him that is clad with virtue for garments, and thou wilt see thyself to be like withering hay, but him like a tree that bears marvellous fruit, and affords much delight to the beholders. For thou art bearing about food for worms and moths, who, if they should set upon thee, will quickly strip thee bare of this adorning (for truly garments and gold and silver, are the one, the spinning of worms; the other earth and dust, and again become earth and nothing more): but he that is clothed with virtue hath such raiment, as not only worms cannot hurt, but not even death itself. And very naturally; for these virtues of the soul have not their origin from the earth, but are a fruit of the Spirit; wherefore neither are they subject to the mouths of worms. Nay, for these garments are woven in Heaven, where is neither moth, nor worm, nor any other such thing.

Which then is better, tell me? To be rich, or to be poor? To be in power, or in dishonor? In luxury, or in hunger? It is quite clear; to be in honor, and enjoyment, and wealth. Therefore, if thou wouldest have the things and not the names, leave the earth and what is here, and find thee a place to anchor in Heaven: for what is here is a shadow, but all things there are immovable, stedfast, and beyond any assault.

Let us therefore choose them with all diligent care, that we may be delivered from the turmoil of the things here, and having sailed into that calm harbor, may be found with our lading abundant, and with that unspeakable wealth of almsgiving; unto which God grant we may all attain, by the grace and love towards man of our Lord Jesus Christ, to whom be the glory and the might, world without end. Amen.

---

¹ [πλεονεξίας.]

HOMILY XXIV.

MATT. VII. 21.

"Not every one that saith unto me, Lord, Lord, shall enter into the kingdom of Heaven, but he that doeth the will of my Father which is in Heaven."

WHEREFORE said He not, "but he that doeth my will?" Because for the time it was a great gain[1] for them to receive even this first; yea it was very great, considering their weakness. And moreover He intimated the one also by the other. And withal this may be mentioned, that in fact there is no other will of the Son besides that of the Father.

And here He seems to me to be censuring the Jews chiefly, laying as they did the whole stress upon the doctrines, and taking no care of practice. For which Paul also blames them, saying, "Behold thou art called a Jew, and restest in the law, and makest thy boast of God, and knowest His will:"[2] but thou art nothing advantaged thereby, so long as the manifestation by life and by works is not there.

But He Himself staid not at this, but said also what was much more: that is,

"Many will say to me in that day, Lord, Lord, have we not prophesied in thy name?"[3] For "not only," saith He, "is he that hath faith, if his life be neglected, cast out of Heaven, but though, besides his faith, he have wrought many signs, yet if he have done nothing good, even this man is equally shut out from that sacred porch." "For many will say unto me in that day, Lord, Lord, have we not prophesied in thy name?" Seest thou how He secretly brings in Himself also here and afterwards, having now finished His whole exhortation? how He implies Himself to be judge? For that punishment awaits such as sin, He hath signified in what precedes; and now who it is that punishes, He here proceeds to unfold.

And He said not openly, I am He, but, "Many will say unto me;" making out again the same thing. Since were He not the judge, how could He have told them,

"And then will I profess unto them, depart from me, I never knew you?"[4]

"Not only in the time of the judgment, but not even then, when ye were working miracles," saith He. Therefore He said also to His disciples, Rejoice not, that the devils are subject unto you, but because your names are written in Heaven."[5] And everywhere He bids us practise great care of our way of life. For it is not possible for one living rightly, and freed from all the passions, ever to be overlooked; but though he chance to be in error, God will quickly draw him over to the truth.

But there are some who say, "they made this assertion falsely;" and this is their account why such men are not saved. Nay then it follows that His conclusion is the contrary of what He intends. For surely His intention is to make out that faith is of no avail without works. Then, enhancing it, He added miracles also, declaring that not only faith, but the exhibiting even of miracles, avails nothing for him who works such wonders without virtue. Now if they had not wrought them, how could this point have been made out here? And besides, they would not have dared, when the judgment was come, to say these things to His face: and the very reply too, and their speaking in the way of question, implies their having wrought them: I mean, that they, having seen the end contrary to their expectation, and after they had been here admired among all for their miracles, beholding themselves there with nothing but punishment awaiting them;—as amazed and marvelling they say, "Lord, have we not prophesied in thy name?" how then dost thou turn from us now? What means this strange and unlooked-for end?

2. But though they marvel because they are punished after working such miracles, yet do not thou marvel. For all the grace was of the free gift of Him that gave it, but they contributed nothing on their part; wherefore

---

[1] [ἀγαπητόν: probably the sense is rather: "it must suffice them," etc.—R.]

[2] Rom. ii. 17, 18. [R. V., "But if thou bearest the name of a Jew," etc., following the reading εἰ δέ, which is abundantly attested. Chrysostom has ἴδε, as in the received text.—R.]

[3] Matt. vii. 22. [R. V., "did we not prophesy," etc. The Greek verb is an aorist.—R.]

[4] Matt. vii. 23.   [5] Luke x. 20.

also they are justly punished, as having been ungrateful and without feeling towards Him that had so honored them as to bestow His grace upon them though unworthy.

" What then," saith one, "did they perform such things while working iniquity?" Some indeed say that it was not at the time when they did these miracles that they also committed iniquity, but that they changed afterwards, and wrought their iniquity. But if this be so, a second time the point at which He is laboring fails to be established. For what He took pains to point out is this, that neither faith nor miracles avail where practise is not: to which effect Paul also said, "Though I have faith, so that I could remove mountains, and understand all mysteries, and all knowledge, and have not charity, I am nothing." [1] "Who then are these men?" you ask. Many of them that believed received gifts such as He that was casting out devils, [2] and was not with Him; such as Judas; for even he too, wicked as he was, had a gift. And in the Old Testament also this may be found, in that grace hath oftentimes wrought upon unworthy persons, that it might do good to others. That is, since all men were not meet for all things, but some were of a pure life, not having so great faith, and others just the contrary; by these sayings, while He urges the one to show forth much faith, the others too He was summoning by this His unspeakable gift to become better men. Wherefore also with great abundance did He bestow that grace. For "we wrought," it is said, "many mighty works." But "then will I profess unto them, I knew you not." For "now indeed they suppose they are my friends; but then shall they know, that not as to friends did I give to them."

And why marvel if He hath bestowed gifts on men that have believed on Him, though without life suitable to their faith, when even on those who have fallen from both these, He is unquestionably found working? For so Balaam was an alien both from faith and from a truly good life; nevertheless grace wrought on him for the service [3] of other men. And Pharaoh too was of the same sort: yet for all that even to him He signified the things to come. And Nebuchadnezzar was very full of iniquity; yet to him again He revealed what was to follow after many generaions. [4] And again to the son of this last, though surpassing his father in iniquity, He

signified the things to come, ordering a marvellous and great dispensation. [5] Accordingly because then also the beginnings of the gospel were taking place, and it was requisite that the manifestation of its power should be abundant, many even of the unworthy used to receive gifts. Howbeit, from those miracles no gain accrued to them; rather they are the more punished. Wherefore unto them did He utter even that fearful saying, "I never knew you:" there being many for whom His hatred begins already even here; whom He turns away from, even before the judgment.

Let us fear therefore, beloved; and let us take great heed to our life, neither let us account ourselves worse off, in that we do not work miracles now. For that will never be any advantage to us, as neither any disadvantage in our not working them, if we take heed to all virtue. Because for the miracles we ourselves are debtors; but for our life and our doings we have God our debtor.

3. Having now, you see, finished all, having discoursed accurately of all virtue, and pointed out the pretenders to it, of divers kinds, both such as for display fast and make prayers, and such as come in the sheep's hide; and them too that spoil it, whom He also called swine and dogs: He proceeds to signify how great is the profit of virtue even here, and how great the mischief of wickedness, by saying,

"Whosoever therefore heareth these sayings of mine, and doeth them, shall be likened unto a wise man." [6]

As thus: What they shall suffer who do not (although they work miracles), ye have heard; but ye should know also what such as obey all these sayings shall enjoy; not in the world to come, but even here. " For whosoever," saith He, " heareth these sayings of mine, and doeth them, shall be likened to a wise man."

Seest thou how He varies His discourse; at one time saying, "Not every one that saith unto me, Lord, Lord," and revealing Himself; at another time, " He that doeth the will of my Father;" and again, bringing in Himself as judge, " For many will say to me in that day, Lord, Lord, have we not prophesied in thy name, and I will say, I know you not." And here again He indicates Himself to have the power over all, this being why He said, " Whosoever heareth these sayings of mine."

---

[1] 1 Cor. xiii. 2. [R. V., " love," as the uniform rendering of ἀγάπη.—R.]

[2] Mark ix. 38 ; Luke ix. 49. [" Demons," so in the New Testament passages.—R.]

[3] οἰκονομίαν.   [4] Dan. iii.

[5] Dan. v.

[6] Matt. vii. 24. [R. V., " Every one, therefore, which heareth these words of mine, and doeth them, shall be likened." The Greek text in the Homily is identical with that accepted in the R. V.—R.]

Thus whereas all His discourse had been touching the future; of a kingdom, and an unspeakable reward and consolation, and the like; His will is, out of things here also to give them their fruits, and to signify how great is the strength of virtue even in the present life. What then is this her strength? To live in safety, to be easily subdued by no terror, to stand superior to all that despitefully use us. To this what can be equal? For this, not even he that wears the diadem can provide for himself, but that man who follows after virtue. For he alone is possessed of it in full abundance: in the ebb and flow [1] of the things present he enjoys a great calm. The truly marvellous thing being this, that not in fair weather, but when the storm is vehement, and the turmoil great, and the temptations continual, he cannot be shaken ever so little.

"For the rain descended," saith He, "the floods came, the winds blew, and beat upon that house; and it fell not: for it was founded upon the rock." [2]

By "rain" here, and "floods," and "winds," He is expressing metaphorically the calamities and afflictions that befall men; such as false accusations, plots, bereavements, deaths, loss of friends, vexations from strangers, all the ills in our life that any one could mention. "But to none of these," saith He, "doth such a soul give way; and the cause is, it is founded on the rock." He calls the stedfastness of His doctrine a rock; because in truth His commands are stronger than any rock, setting one above all the waves of human affairs. For he who keeps these things strictly, will not have the advantage of men only when they are vexing him, but even of the very devils plotting against him. And that it is not vain boasting so to speak, Job is our witness, who received all the assaults of the devil, and stood unmoveable; and the apostles too are our witnesses, for that when the waves of the whole world were beating against them, when both nations and princes, both their own people and strangers, both the evil spirits, and the devil, and every engine was set in motion, they stood firmer than a rock, and dispersed it all.

And now, what can be happier than this kind of life? For this, not wealth, not strength of body, not glory, not power, nor ought else will be able to secure, but only the possession of virtue. For there is not, nay there is not another life we may find free from all evils, but this alone. And ye are

witnesses, who know the plots in king's courts, the turmoils and the troubles in the houses of the rich. But there was not among the apostles any such thing.

What then? Did no such thing befall them? Did they suffer no evil at any man's hand? Nay, the marvel is this above all things, that they were indeed the object of many plots, and many storms burst upon them, but their soul was not overset by them, nor thrown into despair, but with naked bodies they wrestled, prevailed, and triumphed.

Thou then likewise, if thou be willing to perform these things exactly, shalt laugh all ills to scorn. Yea, for if thou be but strengthened with such philosophy as is in these admonitions, nothing shall be able to hurt thee. Since in what is he to harm thee, who is minded to lay plots? Will he take away thy money? Well, but before their threatening thou wast commanded to despise it, and to abstain from it so exceedingly, as not so much as even to ask any such thing of thy Lord. But doth he cast thee into prison? Why, before thy prison, thou wast enjoined so to live, as to be crucified even to all the world. But doth he speak evil? Nay, from this pain also Christ hath delivered thee, by promising thee without toil a great reward for the endurance of evil, and making thee so clear from the anger and vexation hence arising, as even to command thee to pray for them. But doth he banish thee and involve thee in innumerable ills? Well, he is making th crown more glorious for thee. But doth he destroy and murder thee? Even hereby he profits thee very greatly, procuring for thee the rewards of the martyrs, and conducting thee more quickly into the untroubled haven, and affording thee matter for a more abundant recompence, and contriving for thee to make a gain of the universal penalty. [3] Which thing indeed is most marvellous of all, that the plotters, so far from injuring at all, do rather make the objects of their despite more approved. To this what can be comparable? I mean, to the choice of such a mode of life as this, and no other, is.

Thus whereas He had called the way strait and narrow; to soothe our labors on this side also, He signifies the security thereof to be great, and great the pleasure; even as of the opposite course great is the unsoundness, and

---

[1] [εὐρίπῳ, a strait, where the ebb and flow is great and frequent. See Liddell and Scott, Greek Lexicon.—R.]

[2] Matt. vii. 25.

[3] τὴν κοινὴν δίκην πραγματεύεσθαί σε παρασκευάζων. "The universal penalty," i. e., Death. See Hom. XXXIV., as quoted by Mr. Field, for this sense of πραγματεύεσθαι. [The verb means "to engage in business," and it is an easy transition to the successful result of trading. The Latin rendering of Montfaucon is: ac tibi providens, ut a communi illa reddenda ratione te expedias.—R.]

the detriment. For as virtue even from things here was signified by Him to have her rewards, so vice also her penalties. For what I am ever saying, that I will say now also: that in both ways He is everywhere bringing about the salvation of His hearers, on the one hand by zeal for virtue, on the other by hatred of vice. Thus, because there would be some to admire what He said, while they yield no proof of it by their works, He by anticipation awakens their fears, saying, Though the things spoken be good, hearing is not sufficient for security, but there is need also of obedience in actions, and the whole lies chiefly in this. And here He ends His discourse, leaving the fear at its height in them.

For as with regard to virtue, not only from the things to come did He urge them (speaking of a kingdom, and of Heaven, and an unspeakable reward, and comfort, and the unnumbered good things): but also from the things present, indicating the firm and immoveable quality of the Rock; so also with respect to wickedness, not from the expected things only doth He excite their fears (as from the tree that is cut down, and the unquenchable fire, and the not entering into the kingdom, and from His saying, "I know you not ") : but also from the things present, the downfall, I mean, in what is said of the house.

4. Wherefore also He made His argument more expressive, by trying its force[1] in a parable; for it was not the same thing to say, " The virtuous man shall be impregnable, but the wicked easily subdued," as to suppose a rock, and a house, and rivers, and rain, and wind, and the like.

"And every one," saith He, " that heareth these sayings of mine, and doeth them not, shall be likened to a foolish man, which built his house upon the sand."[2]

And well did He call this man " foolish ": for what can be more senseless than one building a house on the sand, and while he submits to the labor, depriving himself of the fruit and refreshment, and instead thereof undergoing punishment? For that they too, who follow after wickedness, do labor, is surely manifest to every one: since both the extortioner, and the adulterer, and the false accuser, toil and weary themselves much to bring their wickedness to effect; but so far from reaping any profit from these their labors, they rather undergo great loss. For Paul too intimated this when he said, " He that soweth to his flesh, shall of his flesh reap

corruption."[3] To this man are they like also, who build on the sand; as those that are given up to fornication, to wantonness, to drunkenness, to anger, to all the other things.

Such an one was Ahab, but not such Elijah (since when we have put virtue and vice along side of one another, we shall know more accurately the difference): for the one had built upon the rock, the other on the sand; wherefore though he were a king, he feared and trembled at the prophet, at him that had only his sheepskin. Such were the Jews but not the apostles; and so though they were few and in bonds, they exhibited the steadfastness of the rock; but those, many as they were, and in armor, the weakness of the sand. For so they said, "What shall we do to these men? "[4] Seest thou those in perplexity, not who are in the hands of others, and bound, but who are active in holding down and binding? And what can be more strange than this? Hast thou hold of the other, and art yet in utter perplexity? Yes, and very naturally. For inasmuch as they had built all on the sand, therefore also were they weaker than all. For this cause also they said again, " What do ye, seeking to bring this man's blood upon us? "[5] What saith he? Dost thou scouge, and art thou in fear? entreatest thou despitefully, and art in dismay? Dost thou judge, and yet tremble? So feeble is wickedness.

But the Apostles not so, but how? " We cannot but speak the things which we have seen and heard."[6] Seest thou a noble spirit? seest thou a rock laughing waves to scorn? seest thou a house unshaken? And what is yet more marvellous; so far from turning cowards themselves at the plots formed against them, they even took more courage, and cast the others into greater anxiety. For so he that smites adamant, is himself the one smitten; and he that kicks against the pricks, is himself the one pricked, the one on whom the severe wounds fall: and he who is forming plots against the virtuous, is himself the one in jeopardy. For wickedness becomes so much the weaker, the more it sets itself in array against virtue. And as he who wraps up fire in a garment, extinguishes not the flame, but consumes the garment; so he that is doing despite to virtuous men, and oppressing them, and binding them, makes them more glorious, but destroys himself.[7] For the more ills thou sufferest, living righteously, the stronger art thou become; since the more we honor self-restraint, the less we need anything; and the

---

[1] γυμνάζων.   [2] Matt. vii. 26. [R. V., " these words."—R.]

[3] Gal. vi. 8.   [4] Acts iv. 16.
[5] Acts v. 28.   [6] Acts iv. 20.
[7] [ἑαυτὸν δὲ ἠφάνισε, " but obliterates himself."—R.]

less we need anything, the stronger we grow, and the more above all. Such a one was John; wherefore him no man pained, but he caused pain to Herod; so he that had nothing prevailed against him that ruled; and he that wore a diadem, and purple, and endless pomp, trembles, and is in fear of him that is stripped of all, and not even when beheaded could he without fear see his head. For that even after his death he had the terror of him in full strength, hear what He saith, " This is John, whom I slew."[1] Now the expression, " I slew," is that of one not exulting, but soothing his own terror, and persuading his troubled soul to call to mind, that he himself slew him. So great is the force of virtue, that even after death it is more powerful than the living. For this same cause again, when he was living, they that possessed much wealth came unto him, and said, " What shall we do ?"[2] Is so much yours, and are ye minded to learn the way of your prosperity from him that hath nothing ? the rich from the poor ? the soldiers from him that hath not even a house ?

Such an one was Elias too: wherefore also with the same freedom did he discourse to the people. For as the former said, " Ye generation of vipers;"[3] so this latter, " How long will ye halt upon both your hips ?"[4] And the one said, " Hast thou killed, and inherited ?"[5] the other, " It is not lawful for thee to have thy brother Philip's wife."[6]

Seest thou the rock ? Seest thou the sand; how easily it sinks down, how it yields to calamities ? how it is overthrown, though it

have the support of royalty, of number, of nobility ? For them that pursue it, it makes more senseless than all.

And it doth not merely fall, but with great calamity: for " great indeed," He saith, " was the fall of it." The risk not being of trifles, but of the soul, of the loss of Heaven, and those immortal blessings. Or rather even before that loss, no life so wretched as he must live that follows after this; dwelling with continual despondencies, alarms, cares, anxieties; which a certain wise man also was intimating when he said, " The wicked fleeth, when no man is pursuing."[7] For such men tremble at their shadows, suspect their friends, their enemies, their servants, such as know them, such as know them not; and before their punishment, suffer extreme punishment here. And to declare all this, Christ said, "And great was the fall of it;" shutting up these good commandments with that suitable ending, and persuading even by the things present the most unbelieving to flee from vice.

For although the argument from what is to come be vaster, yet is this of more power to restrain the grosser sort, and to withdraw them from wickedness. Wherefore also he ended with it, that the profit thereof might make its abode in them.

Conscious therefore of all these things, both the present, and the future, let us flee from vice, let us emulate virtue, that we may not labor fruitlessly and at random, but may both enjoy the security here, and partake of the glory there: unto which God grant we may all attain, by the grace and love towards man of our Lord Jesus Christ, to whom be the glory and the might forever and ever. Amen.

---

[1] Matt. xiv. 2 ; Luke ix. 9. [The verb ἀνεῖλον, which occurs here, is not found in the New Testament accounts of Herod's language.—R.]
[2] Luke iii. 10, 14.   [3] Matt. iii. 7.
[4] 1 Kings xviii. 21, LXX.   [5] 1 Kings xxi. 19, LXX.
[6] Mark vi. 18.

[7] Prov. xxviii. 1.

HOMILY XXV.

Matt. VII. 28.

"And it came to pass, when Jesus had ended these sayings, the people were astonished at His doctrine."[1]

Yet was it rather natural for them to grieve at the unpleasantness of His sayings, and to shudder at the loftiness of His injunctions; but now so great was the power of the Teacher, that many of them were even caught thereby, and thrown into very great admiration, and persuaded by reason of the sweetness of His sayings, not even when He ceased to speak, to depart from Him at all afterwards. For neither did the hearers depart, He having

---

[1] [R. V., " When Jesus ended these words, the multitudes were astonished at his teaching."—R.]

come down from the mountain, but even then the whole auditory followed Him; so great a love for His sayings had He instilled into them.

But they were astonished most of all at His authority. For not with reference to another, like the prophet and Moses, did He say what He said; but everywhere indicating Himself to be the person that had the power of deciding. For so, when setting forth His laws, He still kept adding, "But I say unto you." And in reminding them of that day, He declared Himself to be the judge, both by the punishments, and by the honors.

And yet it was likely that this too would disturb them. For if, when they saw Him by His works showing forth His authority, the scribes were for stoning and persecuting Him; while there were words only to prove this, how was it other than likely for them to be offended? and especially when at first setting out these things were said, and before He had given proof of His own power? But however, they felt nothing of this; for when the heart and mind is candid, it is easily persuaded by the words of the truth. And this is just why one sort, even when the miracles were proclaiming His power, were offended; while the other on hearing mere words were persuaded and followed Him. This, I would add, the evangelist too is intimating, when he saith, "great multitudes followed Him,"[1] not any of the rulers, nor of the scribes, but as many as were free from vice, and had their judgment uncorrupted. And throughout the whole gospel thou seest that such clave unto Him. For both while He spake, they used to listen in silence, not making any intrusion, nor breaking in upon the connexion of His sayings, nor tempting Him, and desiring to find a handle like the Pharisees; and after His exhortation they followed Him again, marvelling.

But do thou mark, I pray thee, the Lord's consideration, how He varies the mode of profiting His hearers, after miracles entering on words, and again from the instruction by His words passing to miracles. Thus, both before they went up into the mountain, He healed many, preparing the way for His sayings; and after finishing that long discourse to the people, He comes again to miracles, confirming what had been said by what was done. And so, because He was teaching as "one having authority," lest His so teaching should be thought boasting and arrogant, He doth the very same in His works also, as having authority to heal; that they might no

more be perplexed at seeing Him teach in this way, when He was working His miracles also in the same.

2. "For when He was come down from the mountain, there came a leper, saying, Lord, if Thou wilt, Thou canst make me clean."[2] Great was the understanding and the faith of him who so drew near. For he did not interrupt the teaching, nor break through the auditory, but awaited the proper time, and approaches Him "when He is come down." And not at random, but with much earnestness, and at His knees, he beseeches Him,[3] as another evangelist saith, and with the genuine faith and right opinion about him. For neither did he say, "If Thou request it of God," nor, "If Thou pray," but, "If Thou wilt, Thou canst make me clean." Nor did he say, "Lord, cleanse me," but leaves all to Him, and makes His recovery depend on Him, and testifies that all the authority is His

"What then," saith one, "if the leper's opinion was mistaken?" It were meet to do away with it, and to reprove, and set it right. Did He then so do? By no means; but quite on the contrary, He establishes and confirms what had been said. For this cause, you see, neither did He say, "Be thou cleansed," but, "I will, be thou clean;" that the doctrine might no longer be a thing of the other's surmising, but of His own approval.

But the apostles not so: rather in what way? The whole people being in amazement, they said, "Why give heed to us, as though by our own power or authority we had made him to walk?"[4] But the Lord, though He spake oftentimes many things modestly, and beneath His own glory, what saith He here, to establish the doctrine of them that were amazed at Him for His authority? "I will, be thou clean." Although in the many and great signs which He wrought, He nowhere appears to have uttered this word. Here however, to confirm the surmise both of all the people and of the leper touching His authority, He purposely added, "I will."

And it was not that He said this, but did it not; but the work also followed immediately. Whereas, if he had not spoken well, but the saying had been a blasphemy, the work ought to have been interrupted. But now nature herself gave way at His command, and that speedily, as was meet, even more speedily

---

[1] Matt. viii. 1.

[2] Matt. vii. 2. [The first clause is from verse 1; and the passages are joined to point the lesson from the assumed delay. But there can be little doubt that the healing of the leper took place earlier. Comp. Mark i. 40-42; Luke v. 12-16.—R.]
[3] Mark i. 40. Comp. Luke v. 12.
[4] Acts iii. 12. [The New Testament passage has been modified in the citation.—R.]

than the evangelist hath said. For the word, "immediately," falls far short of the quickness that there was in the work.

But He did not merely say, "I will, be thou clean," but He also "put forth His hand, and touched him;" a thing especially worthy of inquiry. For wherefore, when cleansing him by will and word, did He add also the touch of His hand? It seems to me, for no other end, but that He might signify by this also, that He is not subject to the law, but is set over it; and that to the clean, henceforth, nothing is unclean.[1] For this cause, we see, Elisha did not so much as see Naaman, but though he perceived that he was offended at his not coming out and touching him, observing the strictness of the law, he abides at home, and sends him to Jordan to wash. Whereas the Lord, to signify that He heals not as a servant, but as absolute master, doth also touch. For His hand became not unclean from the leprosy, but the leprous body was rendered clean by His holy hand.

Because, as we know, He came not to heal bodies only, but also to lead the soul unto self-command. As therefore He from that time forward no more forbad to eat with unwashen hands, introducing that excellent law, which relates to the indifference of meats; just so in this case also, to instruct us for the future, that the soul must be our care;—that leaving the outward purifications, we must wipe that clean, and dread the leprosy thereof alone, which is sin (for to be a leper is no hindrance to virtue):—He Himself first touches the leper, and no man finds fault. For the tribunal was not corrupt, neither were the spectators under the power of envy. Therefore, so far from blaming, they were on the contrary astonished at the miracle, and yielded thereto: and both for what He said, and for what He did, they adored his uncontrollable power.

3. Having therefore healed his body, He bids him,

"Tell no man, but show himself to the priest, and offer the gift that Moses commanded, for a testimony unto them." [2]

Now some say, that for this intent He bade him tell no man, that they might practise no craft about the discerning of his cure; a very foolish suspicion on their part. For He did not so cleanse as to leave the cleansing questionable, but He bids him "tell no man," teaching us to avoid boasting and vainglory. And yet He well knew that the other would not obey, but would proclaim his benefactor: nevertheless He doth His own part.

"How then elsewhere doth He bid them tell of it?" one may ask. Not as jostling with or opposing Himself, but as teaching men to be grateful. For neither in that place did He give command to proclaim Himself, but to "give glory to God;" [3] by this leper training us to be clear of pride and vainglory, by the other to be thankful and grateful; and instructing on every occasion to offer to the Lord the praise of all things that befall us. That is, because men for the most part remember God in sickness, but grow slacker after recovery; He bids them continually both in sickness and in health to give heed to the Lord, in these words, "give glory to God."

But wherefore did He command him also to show himself to the priest, and to offer a gift? To fulfill the law here again.[4] For neither did He in every instance set it aside, nor in every instance keep it, but sometimes He did the one, sometimes the other; by the one making way for the high rule [5] of life that was to come, by the other checking for a while the insolent speech of the Jews, and condescending to their infirmity. And why marvel, if just at the beginning He Himself did this, when even the very apostles, after they were commanded to depart unto the Gentiles, after the doors were opened for their teaching throughout the world, and the law shut up, and the commandments made new, and all the ancient things had ceased, are found sometimes observing the law, sometimes neglecting it?

But what, it may be said, doth this saying, "Show thyself to the priest," contribute to the keeping of the law? No little. Because it was an ancient law, that the leper when cleansed should not entrust to himself the judgment of his cleansing, but should show himself to the priest, and present the demonstration thereof to his eyes, and by that sentence be numbered amongst the clean. For if the priest said not "The leper is cleansed," he remained still with the unclean without the camp. Wherefore he saith, "Show thyself to the priest, and offer the gift that Moses commanded." He said not, "which I command," but for a time remits him to the law, by every means stopping their mouths. Thus, lest they should say, He had seized upon the priests' honor; though He performed the work Himself, yet the approving it He entrusted to them, and made them sit as judges of His own miracles "Why, I

---

[1] Titus i. 15.　　　[2] Matt. viii. 4.

[3] Luke xvii. 18. [This is the passage probably referred to. The Oxford edition refers to Luke vii. 18, and the Latin version to John ix. 24, where the exact phrase occurs, but in the mouths of Christ's opposers.—R.]

[4] Lev. xiv. 1–32.　　　[5] φιλοσοφία.

am so far," He saith, "from striving either with Moses or with the priests, that I guide the objects of my favor to submit themselves unto them."

But what is, "for a testimony unto them"? For reproof, for demonstration, for accusation, if they be unthankful. For since they said, as a deceiver and impostor we persecute Him, as an adversary of God, and a transgressor of the law; "Thou shalt bear me witness," saith He, "at that time, that I am not a transgressor of the law. Nay, for having healed thee, I remit thee to the law, and to the approval of the priests;" which was the act of one honoring the law, and admiring Moses, and not setting himself in opposition to the ancient doctrines.

And if they were not in fact to be the better, hereby most of all one may perceive His respect for the law, that although He foreknew they would reap no benefit, He fulfilled all His part. For this very thing He did indeed foreknow, and foretold it: not saying, "for their correction," neither, "for their instruction," but, "for a testimony unto them," that is, for accusation, and for reproof, and for a witness that all hath been done on my part; and though I foreknew they would continue incorrigible, not even so did I omit what ought to be done; only they continued keeping up to the end their own wickedness.[1]

This, we may observe, He saith elsewhere also; "This gospel shall be preached in all the world for a testimony to all the nations, and then shall the end come;"[2] to the nations, to them that obey not, to them that believe not. Thus, lest any one should say, "And wherefore preach to all, if all are not to believe?"—it is that I may be found to have done all my own part, and that no man may hereafter be able to find fault, as though he had not heard. For the very preaching shall bear witness against them, and they will not be able hereafter to say, "We heard not;" for the word of godliness "hath gone out unto the ends of the world."[3]

4. Therefore bearing these things in mind, let us also fulfill all our duties to our neighbor, and to God let us give thanks continually. For it is too monstrous, enjoying as we do His bounty in deed every day, not so much as in word to acknowledge the favor; and this, though the acknowledgment again yield all its profit to us. Since He needs not, be sure, anything of ours: but we stand in need of all things from Him. Thus thanksgiving

itself adds nothing to Him, but causes us to be nearer to Him. For if men's bounties, when we call them to memory, do the more warm us with their proper love-charm;[4] much more when we are continually bringing to mind the noble acts of our Lord towards us, shall we be more diligent in regard of His commandments.

For this cause Paul also said, "Be ye thankful."[5] For the best preservative of any benefit is the remembrance of the benefit, and a continual thanksgiving.

For this cause even the awful mysteries, so full of that great salvation, which are celebrated at every communion, are called a sacrifice of thanksgiving,[6] because they are the commemoration of many benefits, and they signify the very sum of God's care for us, and by all means they work upon us to be thankful. For if His being born of a virgin was a great miracle, and the evangelist said in amaze, "now all this was done;" His being also slain, what place shall we find for that? tell me. I mean, if to be born is called "all this;" to be crucified, and to pour forth His blood, and to give Himself to us for a spiritual feast and banquet,—what can that be called? Let us therefore give Him thanks continually, and let this precede both our words and our works.

But let us be thankful not for our own blessings alone, but also for those of others; for in this way we shall be able both to destroy our envy, and to rivet our charity, and make it more genuine. Since it will not even be possible for thee to go on envying them, in behalf of whom thou givest thanks to the Lord.

Wherefore, as you know, the priest also enjoins to give thanks for the world, for the former things, for the things that are now, for what hath been done to us before, for what shall befall us hereafter, when that sacrifice[7] is set forth.

For this is the thing both to free us from earth, and to remove us into heaven, and to make us angels instead of men. Because they too form a choir, and give thanks to God for His good things bestowed on us, saying, "Glory to God in the highest, and on earth peace, good will towards men."[8] "And what is this to us, that are not upon earth, nor are men?" "Nay, it is very much to us, for we have been taught so to love our fellow serv-

---

[1] [This interpretation is scarcely admissible, nor does Chrysostom notice the disobedience of the healed man (Mark i. 45). The "testimony" is that commanded by Moses.—R.]
[2] Matt. xxiv. 14
[3] Ps. xix 4; Rom. x. 18.

[4] τῷ φίλτρῳ.   [5] Col. iii. 15.
[6] εὐχαριστία. [The translator has paraphrased the passage. Literally, "which are at every assembly (σύναξιν), are called Eucharist." There is no suggestion of "sacrifice" in the Greek at this point.—R.]
[7] [Here the word meaning "sacrifice" is used.—R.]
[8] Luke ii. 14. [The form is that of the received text; but "among men" is the correct rendering even of this reading.—R.]

ants, as even to account their blessings ours."

Wherefore Paul also, everywhere in his epistles, gives thanks for God's gracious acts to the world.

Let us too therefore continually give thanks, for our own blessings, and for those of others, alike for the small and for the great. For though the gift be small, it is made great by being God's gift, or rather, there is nothing small that cometh from Him, not only because it is bestowed by Him, but also in its very nature.

And to pass over all the rest, which exceed the sand in multitude; what is equal to the dispensation[1] that hath taken place for our sake? In that what was more precious to Him than all, even His only-begotten Son, Him He gave for us His enemies; and not only gave, but after giving, did even set Him before us as food;[2] Himself doing all things that were for our good, both in giving Him, and in making us thankful for all this. For because man is for the most part unthankful, He doth Himself everywhere take in hand and bring about what is for our good. And what He did with respect to the Jews, by places, and times, and feasts, reminding them of His benefits, that He did in this case also, by the manner of the sacrifice bringing us to a perpetual remembrance of His bounty in these things.

No one hath so labored that we should be approved, and great, and in all things right-minded, as the God who made us. Wherefore both against our will He befriends us often, and without our knowledge oftener than not. And if thou marvel at what I have said, I point to this as having occurred not to any ordinary person, but to the blessed Paul. For even that blessed man, when in much danger and affliction, often besought God that the temptations might depart from him: nevertheless God regarded not his request, but his profit, and to signify this He said, "My grace is sufficient for thee, for my strength is made perfect in weakness."[3] So that before He hath told him the reason, He benefits him against his will, and without his knowing it.

5. Now what great thing doth He ask, in requiring us to be thankful in return for such tender care? Let us then obey, and everywhere keep up this. Since neither were the Jews by anything ruined so much, as by being unthankful; those many stripes, one after another, were brought upon them by nothing else than this; or rather even before those stripes this had ruined and corrupted their soul. "For the hope of the unthankful," saith one, "is like the winter's hoar frost;"[4] it benumbs and deadens the soul, as that doth our bodies.

And this springs from pride, and from thinking one's self worthy of something. But the contrite will acknowledge grounds of thanksgiving to God, not for good things only, but also for what seem to be adverse; and how much soever he may suffer, will count none of his sufferings undeserved. Let us then also, the more we advance in virtue, so much the more make ourselves contrite; for indeed this, more than anything else is virtue. Because, as the sharper our sight is, the more thoroughly do we learn how distant we are from the sky; so the more we advance in virtue, so much the more are we instructed in the difference between God and us. And this is no small part of true wisdom,[5] to be able to perceive our own desert. For he best knows himself, who accounts himself to be nothing. Thus we see that both David and Abraham, when they were come up to the highest pitch of virtue, then best fulfilled this; and would call themselves, the one, "earth and ashes,"[6] the other, "a worm;"[7] and all the saints too, like these, acknowledge their own wretchedness. So that he surely who is lifted up in boasting, is the very person to be most ignorant of himself. Wherefore also in our common practice we are wont to say of the proud, "he knows not himself," "he is ignorant of himself." And he that knows not himself, whom will he know? For as he that knows himself will know all things, so he who knows not this, neither will he know the rest.

Such an one was he that saith, "I will exalt my throne above the Heavens."[8] Being ignorant of himself, he was ignorant of all else. But not so Paul; he rather used to call himself "one born out of due time,"[9] and last of the saints,[10] and did not account himself to be worthy so much as of the title of the apostles, after so many and so great deeds of goodness.

Him therefore let us emulate and follow. And we shall follow him, if we rid ourselves of earth, and of things on earth. For nothing makes a man to be so ignorant of himself, as the being rivetted to worldly concerns: nor does anything again so much cause men to be rivetted to worldly concerns, as ignorance of one's self: for these things depend upon each other. I mean, that as he that is fond of outward glory, and highly esteems

---

[1] οἰκονομίας. [2] τράπεζαν, a table. [3] 2 Cor. xii. 9.

[4] Wisdom xvi. 29. [5] φιλοσοφίας. [6] Gen. xviii. 27
[7] Ps. ii. 7. [8] Isa. xiv. 13, τῶν ἀστέρων τοῦ οὐρανοῦ, LXX.
[9] 1 Cor. xv. 8, 9. [10] Eph. iii. 8, ἐλαχιστοτέρον, here ἐσχάτον.

the things present, if he strive for ever, is not permitted to understand himself; so he that overlooks these things will easily know himself; and having come to the knowledge of himself, he will proceed in order to all the other parts of virtue.

In order therefore that we may learn this good knowledge, let us, disengaged from all the perishable things that kindle in us so great flame, and made aware of their vileness, show forth all lowliness of mind, and self-restraint: that we may attain unto blessings, both present and future: by the grace and love towards man of our Lord Jesus Christ, with whom be glory, might, and honor, to the Father, together with the Holy and Good Spirit, now and ever, and world without end. Amen.

HOMILY XXVI.

MATT. VIII. 5.

"And when He was entered into Capernaum, there came unto Him a centurion, beseeching Him, and saying, Lord, my servant lieth at home[1] sick of the palsy, grievously tormented."

THE leper came unto Him "when He was come down from the mountain," but this centurion, "when He was entered into Capernaum." Wherefore then did neither the one nor the other go up into the mountain? Not out of remissness, for indeed the faith of them both was fervent, but in order not to interrupt His teaching.

But having come unto Him, he saith, "My servant lieth at home sick of the palsy, grievously tormented." Now some say, that by way of excuse he mentioned also the cause, why he had not brought him. "For neither was it possible," saith he, "paralyzed as he was, and tormented, and at his last gasp, to lift and convey him." For that he was at the point of expiring, Luke saith; "He was even ready to die."[2] But I say, this is a sign of his having great faith, even much greater than theirs, who let one down through the roof.[3] For because he knew for certain, that even a mere command was enough for the raising up of the patient, he thought it superfluous to bring him.

What then doth Jesus? What He had in no case done before, here He doeth. For whereas on every occasion He was used to follow the wish of His supplicants, here He rather springs toward it, and offers not only to heal him, but also to come to the house. And this He doth, that we might learn the virtue of the centurion. For if He had not made this offer, but had said, "Go thy way, let thy servant be healed;" we should have known none of these things.

This at least He did, in an opposite way, in the case also of the Phœnician woman. For here, when not summoned to the house, of His own accord He saith, He will come, that thou mightest learn the centurion's faith and great humility; but in the case of the Phœnician woman, He both refuses the grant, and drives her, persevering therein, to great perplexity.

For being a wise physician and full of resources, He knows how to bring about contraries the one by the other.[4] And as here by His freely-offered coming, so there by His peremptory putting off and denial, He unfolds the woman's faith. So likewise He doth in Abraham's case, saying, "I will by no means hide from Abraham my servant;"[5] to make thee know that man's kindly affection, and his care for Sodom. And in the instance of Lot,[6] they that were sent refuse to enter into his house, to make thee know the greatness of that righteous man's hospitality.

What then saith the centurion? "I am not worthy that thou shouldest come under my roof."[7] Let us hearken, as many as are

---

[1] [R. V., "in the house."]
[2] Luke vii. 2. [R. V., "and at the point of death; καί in the citation means "and," not "even."—R.]
[3] Luke v. 19.

[4] διὰ τῶν ἐναντίων τὰ ἐναντία. The argument seems to require τὰ αὐτά, "the same things by opposite means:" but no MS. authority appears for such a change.
[5] Gen. xviii. 17 [LXX.].   [6] Gen. xix. 2.   [7] Matt. viii. 8.

to receive Christ: for it is possible to receive Him even now. Let us hearken, and emulate, and receive Him with as great zeal; for indeed, when thou receivest a poor man who is hungry and naked, thou hast received and cherished Him.

2. "But say in a word only,[1] and my servant shall be healed."

See this man also, how, like the leper, he hath the right opinion touching Him. For neither did this one say, "entreat," nor did he say, "pray, and beseech," but "command only." And then from fear lest out of modesty He refuse, He saith,

"For I also am a man under authority, having under me soldiers; and I say to this man, go, and he goeth; and to another, come, and he cometh; and to my servant, do this, and he doeth it."[2]

"And what of that," saith one, "if the centurion did suspect it to be so? For the question is, whether Christ affirmed and ratified as much." Thou speakest well, and very sensibly. Let us then look to this very thing; and we shall find what happened in the case of the leper, the same happening here likewise. For even as the leper said, "If thou wilt" (and not from the leper only are we positive about His authority, but also from the voice of Christ; in that, so far from putting an end to the suspicion, He did even confirm it more, by adding what were else superfluous to say, in the phrase, "I will, be thou cleansed," in order to establish that man's doctrine): so here too, it is right to see whether any such thing occurred. In fact, we shall find this same thing again taking place. For when the centurion had spoken such words, and had testified His so great prerogative; so far from blaming, He did even approve it, and did somewhat more than approve it. For neither hath the evangelist said, that He praised the saying only, but declaring a certain earnestness in His praise, that He even "marvelled;" and neither did He simply marvel, but in the presence also of the whole people, and set Him as an example to the rest, that they should emulate Him.

Seest thou how each of them that bore witness of His authority is "marvelled at? And the multitudes were astonished at His doctrine, because He taught as one having authority;"[3] and so far from blaming them, He both took them with Him when He came down, and by His words of cleansing to the leper, confirmed their judgment. Again,

that leper said, "If thou wilt, thou canst make me clean;"[4] and so far from rebuking, He on the contrary cleansed him by such treatment as He had said. Again, this centurion saith, "Speak the word only, and my servant shall be healed:"[5] and "marvelling" at him, He said, "I have not found so great faith, no, not in Israel."[6]

Now, to convince thee of this by the opposite also; Martha having said nothing of this sort, but on the contrary, "Whatsoever thou wilt ask of God, He will give Thee;"[7] so far from being praised, although an acquaintance, and dear to Him, and one of them that had shown great zeal toward Him, she was rather rebuked and corrected by Him, as not having spoken well; in that He said to her, "Said I not unto thee, that if thou wouldest believe, thou shouldest see the glory of God?"[8] blaming her, as though she did not even yet believe. And again, because she had said, "Whatsoever Thou wilt ask of God, He will give Thee;" to lead her away from such a surmise, and to teach her that He needs not to receive from another, but is Himself the fountain of all good things, He saith, "I am the resurrection and the life;"[9] that is to say, "I wait not to receive active power,[10] but work all of myself."

Wherefore at the centurion He both marvels, and prefers him to all the people, and honors him with the gift of the kingdom, and provokes the rest to the same zeal. And to show thee that for this end He so spake, viz. for the instructing of the rest to believe in like manner, listen to the exactness of the evangelist, how he hath intimated it. For,

"Jesus," saith He, "turned Him about, and said to them that followed Him, I have not found so great faith, no, not in Israel."[11]

It follows, that to have high imaginations concerning Him, this especially is of faith, and tends to procure the kingdom and His other blessings. For neither did His praise reach to words only, but He both restored the sick man whole, in recompence of his faith, and weaves for him a glorious crown, and promises great gifts, saying on this wise,

"Many shall come from the east and west, and shall sit down in the bosoms of Abraham, and Isaac, and Jacob; but the children of the kingdom shall be cast out."[12]

---

[1] [R. V., "only say the word," "Gr. with a word." Chrysostom varies from the order, placing "only" last.—R.]
[2] Matt. viii. 4.   [3] Matt. vii. 29.
[4] Matt. viii. 2.   [5] Matt. viii. 8.
[6] Matt. viii. 10. [The reading of the received text is found here. Comp. R. V. margin for the reading of the Vatican MS., accepted by Augustin.—R.]
[7] John xi. 22.   [8] John xi. 40.
[9] John xi. 25.   [10] ἐνεργείαν.
[11] Matt. viii. 10. Comp. Luke vii. 9. ["Turned him about," στραφείς, is taken from the latter passage.—R.]
[12] Matt. viii. 11, 12. [For "with" Chrysostom substitutes "in

Thus, since He had shown many miracles, He proceeds to talk with them more unreservedly.

Then, that no one might suppose His words to come of flattery, but that all might be aware that such was the mind of the centurion, He saith,

"Go thy way; as thou hast believed, so be it done unto thee."[1]

And straightway the work followed, bearing witness to his character.[2]

"And his servant was healed from that hour."

Which was the result in the case of the Syrophœnician woman also; for to her too He saith, "O woman, great is thy faith; be it unto thee even as thou wilt. And her daughter was made whole."[3]

3. But since Luke, also relating this miracle, inserts by the way a good many other things, which seem to indicate some disagreement; these too must be explained by us.

What then saith Luke? He sent elders of the Jews unto Him entreating Him to come.[4] But Matthew saith, that he approached himself, and said, "I am not worthy." And some indeed say, the one is not the same as the other, though they have many points of resemblance. Thus, of the one it is said, that "He both hath builded our synagogue, and loveth our nation;"[5] but concerning this other Jesus Himself saith, "I have not found so great faith, no not in Israel." And touching the former, He did not say, "many shall come from the east;" whence it is likely that he was a Jew.

What then are we to say? That this solution is indeed easy, but the question is, whether it be true. To me this one seems to be the same as the other. How then, it may be asked, doth Matthew relate, that he himself said, "I am not worthy that thou shouldest come under my roof," but Luke, that he sent for Christ to come? To me Luke seems to be intimating to us the flattery of the Jews; and that persons in affliction, being unsettled, form to themselves many different counsels. For it is likely that the centurion, when he wished to have gone, was stopped by the Jews, flattering him, and saying, "We will go and bring Him."

See at least that even their entreaty is full of flattering. "For He loveth our nation" (so it runs), "and our synagogue He builded:"[6] neither know they for what to praise the man. For whereas they ought to

have said, He was minded himself to come and entreat Thee, "but we forbad him, seeing his affliction, and the calamity lying upon his house;" and so they should have set forth the greatness of his faith; this they say not, for neither were they willing, for envy, to declare the man's faith: but they chose rather to cast a shade over his virtue, for whom they had come to make their supplication, lest He who was entreated, should seem to be some great one; than by proclaiming the other's faith, to accomplish that for which they had come. For envy is enough to blind the understanding. But He who knows the secret things, even against their will proclaimed that centurion.

And that this is true, hear Luke himself again, interpreting it. For he himself saith on this wise : "When He was now not far off, he sent, saying, O Lord, trouble not Thyself: for I am not worthy that Thou shouldest enter under my roof."[7] That is, when he was freed from their importunity, then he sends, saying, "Think not it was for sloth that I came not, but I accounted myself unworthy to receive Thee in my house." And if Matthew saith that not by his friends, but by himself did he say this; that proves[8] nothing; for the question is, whether each of them has set before us the zealousness of the man, and his having had the right opinion concerning Christ. But it is likely, that after sending his friends, he himself also came and said these things. And if Luke did not speak of the one, no more did Matthew of the other; and this is not the part of men disagreeing amongst themselves, but rather of those that are filling up the things omitted by one another. But see by another thing also how Luke hath proclaimed his faith, saying that his servant "was ready to die."[9] Nevertheless, not even this cast him into despondency, neither did it cause him to give up: but even so he trusted that he should prevail. And if Matthew affirm Christ to have said, "I have not found so great faith, no, not in Israel," and hereby to show clearly that he was not an Israelite; while Luke saith, "He built our synagogue;" neither is this a contradiction. For it was possible for one, even though not a Jew, both to build the synagogue, and to love the nation.

4. But do not thou, I pray thee, merely inquire what was said by him, but add thereto his rank also, and then thou wilt see the man's excellency. Because in truth great is the pride of them that are in places of command, and not even in afflictions do they take

---

the bosom of " (εἰς τοὺς κόλπους), commenting upon the term below (sec. 5). There is no authority for this reading, so far as now known.—R.]

[1] Matt. viii. 13.　　[2] τῇ προαιρέσει.　　[3] Matt. xv. 28.
[4] Luke vii. 2.　　[5] Luke vii. 5.　　[6] Luke vii. 5.

[7] Luke vii. 6.　　　　[8] ποιεῖ.　　　　[9] Luke vii. 2.

lower ground. He, for example, who is set down in John, is for dragging Him unto his house, and saith, "Come down, for my child is ready to die."[1] But not so this man; rather he is far superior both to him, and to those who let down the bed through the roof. For he seeks not for His bodily presence, neither did He bring the sick man near the physician; a thing which implied no mean imaginations concerning Him, but rather a suspicion of His divine dignity. And he saith, "speak the word only." And at the beginning he saith not even, "speak the word," but only describe his affliction: for neither did he, of great humility, expect that Christ would straightway consent, and inquire for his house. Therefore, when he heard Him say, "I will come and heal him," then, not before, he saith, "speak the word." Nor yet did the suffering confound him, but still under calamity he reasons coolly,[2] not looking so much to the health of the servant, as to the avoiding all appearance of doing anything irreverent.

And yet it was not he that pressed it, but Christ that offered it: nevertheless even so he feared, lest perchance he should be thought to be going beyond his own deservings, and to be drawing upon himself a thing above his strength.[3] Seest thou his wisdom? Mark the folly of the Jews, in saying, "He was worthy for whom He should do the favor."[4] For when they should have taken refuge in the love of Jesus towards man, they rather allege this man's worthiness; and know not so much as on what ground to allege it. But not so he, but he affirmed himself even in the utmost degree unworthy, not only of the benefit, but even of receiving the Lord in his house. Wherefore even when he said, "My servant lieth sick," he did not add, "speak," for fear lest he should be unworthy to obtain the gift; but he merely made known his affliction. And when he saw Christ zealous in His turn, not even so did he spring forward, but still continues to keep to the end his own proper measure.

And if any one should say, "wherefore did not Christ honor him in return?" we would say this, that He did make return to him in honor, and that exceedingly: first by bringing out his mind, which thing chiefly appeared by His not coming to his house; and in the second place, by introducing him into His kingdom, and preferring him to the whole Jewish nation. For because he made himself out unworthy even to receive Christ into his house, he became worthy both of a kingdom, and of attaining unto those good things which Abraham enjoyed.

"But wherefore," one may say, "was not the leper commended, who showed forth things greater than these?" For he did not so much as say, "speak the word," but what was far more, "be willing only," which is what the prophet saith concerning the Father, "He hath done whatsoever He pleased."[5] But he also was commended. For when He said, "Offer the gift that Moses commanded, for a testimony unto them,"[6] He means nothing else but, "thou shalt be an accuser of them, in that thou didst believe." And besides, it was not the same for one that was a Jew to believe, and for one from without that nation. For that the centurion was not a Jew is evident, both from his being a centurion and from its being said, "I have not found so great faith, no, not in Israel." And it was a very great thing for a man who was out of the list of the Jewish people to admit so great a thought. For he did no less than imagine to himself, as it seems to me, the armies in Heaven; or that the diseases and death, and everything else, were so subject to Him, as his soldiers to himself.

Wherefore he said likewise, "For I also am a man set under authority;" that is, Thou art God, and I man; I under authority, but Thou not under authority. If I therefore, being a man, and under authority, can do so much; far more He, both as God, and as not under authority. Thus with the strongest expression He desires to convince Him, that he saith this, as one giving not a similar example, but one far exceeding. For if I (said he), being equal in honor to them whom I command, and under authority, yet by reason of the trifling superiority of my rank am able to do such great things; and no man contradicts me, but what I command, that is done, though the injunctions be various ("for I say to this man, go, and he goeth; and to another, come, and he cometh":[7]) much more wilt Thou Thyself be able.

And some actually read the place in this way, "For if I, being a man," and having inserted a stop, they add, "having soldiers under authority under me."

But mark thou, I pray thee, how he signified that Christ is able both to overcome even death as a slave, and to command it as its master. For in saying, "come, and he cometh," and "go, and he goeth;" he expresses this: "If Thou shouldest command his end not to come upon him, it will not come."

[1] John iv. 49.   [2] φιλοσοφεῖ.
[3] βαρὺ πρᾶγμα.   [4] Luke vii. 4   [5] Ps. cxv 3.   [6] Matt. viii. 4.   [7] Matt. viii. 9.

Seest thou how believing he was? For that which was afterwards to be manifest to all, here is one who already hath made it evident; that He hath power both of death and of life, and "leadeth down to the gates of hell, and bringeth up again."[1] Nor was he speaking of soldiers only, but also of slaves; which related to a more entire obedience.

5. But nevertheless, though having such great faith, he still accounted himself to be unworthy. Christ however, signifying that he was worthy to have Him enter into his house, did much greater things, marvelling at him, and proclaiming him, and giving more than he had asked. For he came indeed seeking for his servant health of body, but went away, having received a kingdom. Seest thou how the saying had been already fulfilled, "Seek ye the kingdom of heaven, and all these things shall be added unto you."[2] For, because he evinced great faith, and lowliness of mind, He both gave him heaven, and added unto him health.

And not by this alone did He honor him, but also by signifying upon whose casting out he is brought in. For now from this time forth He proceeds to make known to all, that salvation is by faith, not by works of the law. And this is why not to Jews only, but to Gentiles also the gift so given shall be proffered, and to the latter rather than to the former. For "think not," saith He, "by any means, that so it hath come to pass in regard of this man alone; nay, so it shall be in regard of the whole world. And this He said, prophesying of the Gentiles, and suggesting to them good hopes. For in fact there were some following Him from Galilee of the Gentiles. And this He said, on the one hand, not letting the Gentiles despair, on the other, putting down the proud spirits of the Jews.

But that His saying might not affront[3] the hearers, nor afford them any handle; He neither brings forward prominently what He hath to say of the Gentiles, but upon occasion taken from the centurion; nor doth He use nakedly the term, Gentiles: not saying, "many of the Gentiles," but, "many from east and west:"[4] which was the language of one pointing out the Gentiles, but did not so much affront the hearers, because His meaning was under a shadow.

Neither in this way only doth He soften the apparent novelty of His doctrine, but also

by speaking of "Abraham's bosom" instead of "the kingdom." For neither was that term familiar to them:[5] moreover, the introduction of Abraham would be a sharper sting to them. Wherefore John also spake nothing at first concerning hell, but, what was most apt to grieve them, He saith, "Think not to say, we are children of Abraham."[6]

He is providing for another point also; not to seem in any sense opposed to the ancient polity. For he that admires the patriarchs, and speaks of their bosom as an inheritance of blessings, doth much more than sufficiently remove also this suspicion.

Let no man therefore suppose that the threat is one only, for both the punishment of the one and the joy of the other is double: of the one, not only that they fell away, but that they fell away from their own; of the other, not only that they attained, but that they attained what they had no expectation of: and there is a third together with these, that the one received what pertained to the other. And he calls them "children of the kingdom," for whom the kingdom had been prepared: which also more than all was apt to gall them; in that having pointed to them as being in their bosom by His offer and promise, after all He puts them out.

6. Then, because what He had said was mere affirmation, He confirms it by the miracle; as indeed He shows the miracles in their turn, by the subsequent accomplishment of the prediction. He accordingly, who disbelieves the health which the servant then received, let him from the prophecy, which hath this day come to pass, believe that other also. For so that prophecy again, even before the event, was made manifest to all by the sign which then took place. To this end, you see, having first uttered that prediction, then and not before He raised up the sick of the palsy; that He might make the future credible by the present, and the less by the greater. Since for virtuous men to enjoy His good things, and for the contrary sort to undergo His penalties, were nothing improbable, but a reasonable event, and according to the tenor of laws: but to brace up the feeble, and to raise the dead, was something beyond nature.

But nevertheless, unto this great and marvellous work the centurion too contributed no little; which thing, we see, Christ also declared, saying, "Go thy way, and as thou hast believed, so be it done unto thee." Seest thou how the health of the servant proclaimed

---

[1] 1 Sam. xxvi.
[2] Matt. vi. 33. [Comp. Hom. XXII. 4, p. 148, on the reading "kingdom of heaven."—R.]
[3] προσστῆναι, "disagree with, be nauseous to."
[4] Matt. viii. 11.

[5] [Both terms were current in Jewish theological language; but it is implied in the argument that "Abraham's bosom" was not so well known, or so definitely apprehended.—R.]
[6] Matt. iii. 9.

aloud both Christ's power, and the faith of the centurion, and also became a pledge of the future? Or rather it was all a proclamation of Christ's power. For not only did He quite heal the servant's body, but the soul also of the centurion He did Himself bring over unto the faith by His miracles.

And do thou look not to this only, that the one believed, and the other was healed, but marvel how quickly also. For this too the evangelist declared, saying, "And his servant was healed in the self-same hour:" even as of the leper also he said, " he was straightway cleansed." For not by healing, but by doing so both in a wonderful manner and in a moment of time, did He display His power. Neither in this way only doth He profit us, but also by his constant practice, in the manifestation of His miracles, of opening incidentally His discourses about His kingdom, and of drawing all men towards it. For those even whom He was threatening to cast out, He threatened not in order to cast them out, but in order that through such fear, He might draw them into it by His words. And if not even hereby were they profited, theirs is the whole blame, as also of all who are in the like distemper.

For not at all among Jews only may one see this taking place, but also among them that have believed. For Judas too was a child of the kingdom, and it was said to him with the disciples, "Ye shall sit on twelve thrones;"[1] yet he became a child of hell; whereas the Ethiopian, barbarian as he was, and of them " from the east and west," shall enjoy the crowns with Abraham, and Isaac, and Jacob. This takes place among us also now. " For many," saith He, "that are first shall be last, and the last first."[2] And this He saith, that neither the one may grow languid, as unable to return; nor the others be confident, as standing fast. This John also declared before from the beginning, when he said, " God is able of these stones to raise up children unto Abraham."[3] Thus, since it was so to come to pass, it is proclaimed long before; that no one may be confounded at the strangeness of the event. But he indeed speaks of it as a possible thing (for he was first); Christ on the other hand as what will surely be, affording the proof of it from His works.

7. Let us not then be confident, who stand, but let us say to ourselves, " Let him that thinketh he standeth take heed lest he fall;"[4] neither let us who are fallen despair, but let us say to ourselves, " He that falleth, doth

he not arise?"[5] For many even who have mounted to the very summit of Heaven, and have shown forth all austerity, and had made their abode in the deserts, nor saw any woman so much as in a dream; having become a little remiss, have been tripped up, and have come unto the very gulf of wickedness. While others again from thence have gone up to Heaven, and from the stage and orchestra have passed over unto the discipline of angels, and have displayed so great virtue, as to drive away devils, and to work many other such miracles. And of these examples both the Scriptures are full, and our life is also full. Even whoremongers and effeminate persons stop the mouths of the Manichæans, who say that wickedness is immoveable, enrolling themselves on the devil's side, and weakening the hands of them that would wish to be in earnest, and overturning all our life.

For they who inculcate these things, not only injure men as to the future, but here also turn all things upside down, for their own part at least. Because when will any regard virtue, from among those that are living in wickedness, so long as he accounts his return that way, and His change for the better, a thing impossible? For if now, when both laws exist, and penalties are threatened, and there is common opinion to recall the ordinary sort, and hell is looked for, and a kingdom promised, and wrong things reproached, and the good praised; hardly do any choose the labors that are to be undergone for virtue's sake: shouldest thou take away all these things, what is there to hinder ruin and corruption universal?

Knowing therefore the devil's craft, and that as well the lawgivers of the Gentiles as the oracles of God, and the reasonings of nature, and the common opinion of all men, yea barbarians, and Scythians, and Thracians, and generally all, are directly opposed both to these, and to such as strive to enact the doctrines of fate: let us be sober, beloved, and bidding farewell to all those, let us travel along the narrow way, being both confident and in fear: in fear because of the precipices on either side, confident because of Jesus our guide. Let us travel on, sober and wakeful. For though but for a little while one slumber, he is swept away quickly.

8. For we are not more perfect than David, who by a little carelessness was hurled into the very gulf of sin. Yet he arose again quickly. Look not then to his having sinned only, but also to his having washed away his

---

[1] Matt. xix. 28.   [2] Matt. xix. 30.
[3] Matt. iii. 9.   [4] 1 Cor. x. 12.   [5] Jer. viii. 4.

sin. For to this end He wrote that history, not that thou shouldest behold him fallen, but admire him risen; to teach thee, when thou art fallen, how thou shouldest arise. Thus, as physicians choose out the most grievous diseases, and write them in their books, and teach their method of cure in similar cases; if so be men having practised on the greater, may easily master the less; even so God likewise hath brought forward the greatest of sins, that they also who offend in small things may find the cure of these easy, by means of the other: since if those admitted of healing, much more the less.

Let us look then to the manner both of the sickness, and of the speedy recovery of that blessed man. What then was the manner of his sickness? He committed adultery and murder. For I shrink not from proclaiming these things with a loud voice. Since if the Holy Ghost thought it no shame to record [1] all this history, much less ought we to draw any shade over it. Wherefore I not only proclaim it, but I add another circumstance also. For in fact, whosoever hide these things, they most of all men throw his virtue into the shade. And as they that say nothing of the battle with Goliath deprive him of no small crowns, so also they that hurry by this history. Doth not my saying seem a paradox? Nay, wait a little, and then ye shall know that with reason have we said this. For to this end do I magnify the sin, and make my statement stranger, that I may the more abundantly provide the medicines.

What is it then which I add? The man's virtue; which makes the fault also greater. For all things are not judged alike in all men. "For mighty" men (it is said) "shall be mightily tormented:"[2] and "He that knew his Lord's will, and doeth it not, shall be beaten with many stripes."[3] So that more knowledge is a ground of more punishment. For this same reason the priest, if he commit the same sin as those under government, shall not have the same to endure, but things far more grievous.

Perhaps, seeing the charge against him amplified, ye tremble and fear, and marvel at me, as though I were going down a precipice. But I am so confident on that righteous man's behalf, that I will proceed even farther; for the more I aggravate the charge, so much the more shall I be able to show forth the praise of David.

"And what more than this," you will say, "can be uttered?" Abundantly more. For as in the case of Cain, what was done was not a murder only, but worse than even many murders; for it was not a stranger, but a brother, whom he slew; and a brother who had not done but suffered wrong; not after many murderers, but having first originated the horrid crime: so here too that which was perpetrated was not murder only. For it was no ordinary man that did it, but a prophet: and he slays not him that had done wrong, but him that had suffered wrong; for indeed he had been mortally wronged, by the forcing away his wife: nevertheless after that he added this also.

9. Perceive ye, how I have not spared that righteous one? how without any the least reserve I have mentioned his offenses? But yet, so confident am I concerning his defense, that after so great load as this of his sin, I would there were present both the Manichæans who most deride all this, and they that are diseased in Marcion's way,[4] that I might fully stop their mouths. For they indeed say "he committed murder and adultery;" but I say not this only, but have also proved the murder to be twofold, first from him who suffered the wrong, then from the quality of the person who offended. For it is not the same thing, for one to whom the Spirit was vouchsafed, and on whom so great benefits had been conferred, and who had been admitted to such freedom of speech, and at such a time of life, to venture on crimes of that sort; as without all these, to commit this self-same thing. Nevertheless even in this respect is that illustrious man most of all worthy of admiration, that when he had fallen into the very pit of wickedness, he did not sink nor despair, nor cast himself down in supineness, on receiving of the devil so fatal a wound; but quickly, or rather straightway, and with great force, he gave a more fatal blow than he had received.

And the same thing occurred, as if in war and in battle some barbarian had struck his spear into the heart of a chieftain, or shot an arrow into his liver, and had added to the former wound a second more fatal than it, and he that had received these grievous blows, when fallen, and wallowing in much blood all about him, were first to rise up quickly, then to hurl a spear at him that wounded him, and exhibit him dead on the ground in a moment. Even so in this case also, the greater thou declarest the wound, so much the more admirable dost thou imply the soul of him that was wounded to be, that he

---

[1] ἀναθεῖναι.   [2] ἐτασθήσονται. Wisdom vi. 6.
[3] Luke xii. 47.

[4] Both these sects ascribed the Old Testament to an evil principle, and argued against it from such cases as this of David. Of Marcion, see St. Iren. i. 29, iv. 45. Of Manes, St. Aug. *contra Faustum*, xxii. 5, 66. [*Nicene and Post-Nicene Fathers*, first series, vol. iv. p. 297.]

had power after this grievous wound both to rise up again, and to stand in the very forefront of the battle array, and bear down him that had wounded him.

And how great a thing this is, they best know, whosoever are fallen into grievous sins. For it is not so much a proof of a generous and vigorous soul to walk upright, and to run all the way (for such a soul hath the good hope going along with it, to cheer and to rouse it, to nerve and render it more zealous); as after those innumerable crowns, and so many trophies, and victories, having undergone the utmost loss, to be able to resume the same course. And that what I say may be made plain, I will endeavor to bring before you another example, not at all inferior to the former.

For imagine, I pray thee, some pilot, when he had compassed seas without number, and sailed over the whole ocean; after those many storms, and rocks and waves, to sink, having with him a great freight, in the very mouth of the harbor, and hardly with his naked body to escape this grievous shipwreck; how would he naturally feel towards the sea, and navigation, and such labors? Will such a one then ever choose, unless he be of a very noble soul, to see a beach, or a vessel, or a harbor? I trow not; but he will lie hiding his face, seeing night all through the day, and shrinking from all things; and he will choose rather to live by begging, than to put his hand to the same labors.

But not such was this blessed man; but though he had undergone such a shipwreck, after those innumerable troubles and toils, he stayed not with his face covered, but launched his vessel, and having spread his sails, and taken the rudder in hand, he applies himself to the same labors, and hath made his wealth more abundant again. Now if to stand be so admirable, and not to lie down for ever after one has fallen; to rise up again, and to do such deeds, what crowns would not this deserve?

And yet surely there were many things to drive him to despair; as first, the greatness of his sins; secondly, that not at the beginning of life, when our hopes also are more abundant, but near the end, these things befell him. For neither doth the merchant, who hath just gone out of the harbor and been wrecked, grieve equally with him, who after very many traffickings strikes on a rock. Thirdly, that when he had already obtained great wealth, he incurred this. Yea, for by that time he had stored up no small merchandise: for instance, the deeds of his early youth, when he was a shepherd;

those about Goliath, when he set up the glorious trophy; those pertaining to his self-command respecting Saul. Since he showed forth even the evangelical long-suffering, in that he got his enemy ten thousand times into his hands, and continually spared him; and chose rather to be an outcast from his country and from liberty, and from life itself, than to slay him that was unjustly plotting against him. Likewise after his coming to the kingdom, there were noble deeds of his to no small amount.

And besides what I have said, his credit also among the many, and his fall from glory so bright, would cause no ordinary perplexity. For the purple did by no means so much adorn him, as the stain of his sin disgraced him. And ye know of course what a great thing it is for evil deeds to be exposed, and how great a soul is required in such an one, not to despond after the censure of the multitude, and when he hath so many witnesses of his own offenses.

Nevertheless all these darts that noble person drew out of his soul, and so shone forth after this, so wiped out the stain, became so pure, that his offspring even after his death had their sins mitigated by him: and that which was said of Abraham, we find God saying the same of this man also; or rather, much more of the latter. For with respect to the patriarch it is said, "I remembered my covenant with Abraham;"[1] but here He saith not "the covenant," but how? "I will defend this city for my servant David's sake."[2] And besides, on account of His favor towards him, He suffered not Solomon to fall from the kingdom, great as the sin was which he had committed. And so great was the glory of the man, that Peter, so many years after, in exhorting the Jews, spake on this wise: "Let me freely speak unto you of the patriarch David, that he is both dead and buried."[3] And Christ too, discoursing with the Jews, signifies him after his sin to have had the Spirit vouchsafed to such a degree, that he was counted worthy to prophesy again even concerning His Godhead; and thereby stopping their mouths, He said, "How then doth David in spirit call Him Lord, saying, The Lord said unto my Lord, Sit thou on my right hand?"[4] And much as with Moses, so it fell out also with David. For as Miriam, even against Moses' will, was punished by God for insolence to her brother,[5] because He greatly loved the holy man; even so this man, injuriously treated by his son,

---

[1] Exod. ii. 24.   [2] Isa. xxxvii. 35.   [3] Acts ii. 29.
[4] Matt. xxii. 43; Ps. cx. 1.   [5] Numb. xii. 13, 14.

God did swiftly avenge, and that against his will.

These things then are sufficient, yea rather before all others these are sufficient to indicate the man's excellency. For when God pronounces His judgment, we ought to inquire no further. But if ye would become particularly acquainted with His self command, ye may by perusing his history after his sin, perceive his confidence towards God, his benevolence, his growth in virtue, his strictness unto his last breath.

10. Having then these examples, let us be sober, and let us strive not to despond, and if at any time we fall, not to lie prostrate. For not to cast you into slothfulness, did I speak of the sins of David, but to work in you more fear. For if that righteous man through a little remissness received such wounds, what shall we have to suffer, who are every day negligent? Do not therefore look at his fall, and be remiss, but consider what great things he did even after this, what great mournings, how much repentance he showed forth, adding his nights to his days, pouring forth fountains of tears, washing his couch with his tears, withal clothing himself in sackcloth.

Now if he needed so great a conversion, when will it be possible for us to be saved, feeling insensible after so many sins? For he that hath many good deeds, would easily even by this throw a shade over his sins; but he that is unarmed, wherever he may receive a dart, receives a mortal wound.

In order therefore that this may not be so, let us arm ourselves with good works; and if any offense have befallen us, let us wash it away: that we may be counted worthy, after having lived the present life to the glory of God, to enjoy the life to come; unto which may we all attain, by the grace and love towards man of our Lord Jesus Christ, to whom be glory and might forever and ever. Amen.

HOMILY XXVII.

Matt. VIII. 14, 15.

"And when Jesus was come into Peter's house, He saw his wife's mother laid and sick of a fever:[1] and He touched her hand, and the fever left her, and she arose and ministered unto Him."[2]

But Mark adds also, "immediately,"[3] meaning to declare the time as well; but this evangelist hath set down only the miracle, without signifying besides the time. And whereas the others say, that she that lay ill did also entreat Him, this too he hath passed over in silence. But this comes not of any dissonance, but the one of brevity, the other of exact narrative. But for what intent did He go into Peter's house? As it seems to me, to take food. This at least is declared when it is said,

"She arose and ministered unto Him."[4]

For He used to visit His disciples (as Matthew likewise, when He had called him), so honoring them and making them more zealous.

But do thou mark, I pray thee, herein also Peter's reverence towards Him. For though he had his wife's mother at home lying ill, and very sick of a fever, he drew Him not into his house, but waited first for the teaching to be finished, then for all the others to be healed; and then when He had come in, besought Him. Thus from the beginning was he instructed to prefer the things of all others to his own.

Therefore neither doth he himself bring Him in, but He entered of His own accord (after the centurion had said, "I am not worthy that Thou shouldest come under my roof"[5]): to show how much favor He bestowed on His disciple. And yet consider of

----

[1] [R. V., "lying sick of a fever."]
[2] A. V., "unto them." [The Oxford edition has "rec. vers." here. But the word "received" is now applied, in matters of text, only to the editions of Stephens and Elzevir and the readings they contain. The reference is, of course, to the authorized version, and that version in Matt. viii. 15 follows the received text. —R.]
[3] Mark i. 31. See Luke iv. 39. [Mark's favorite term, εὐθύς, is rendered "straightway" in the R. V., passim. –R.]
[4] Matt. viii. 15.

[5] Matt. viii. 8.

what sort were the houses of these fisher-men; but for all that, He disdained not to enter into their mean huts, teaching thee by all means to trample under foot human pride.

And sometimes He heals by words only, sometimes He even stretches forth His hand, sometimes He doeth both these things, to bring into sight His way of healing. For it was not His will always to work miracles in the more surpassing manner: it being needful for Him to be concealed awhile, and espec-ially as concerned His disciples; since they out of their great delight would have pro-claimed everything. And this was evident from the fact, that even after coming to the mount, it was needful to charge them that they should tell no man.

Having therefore touched her body, He not only quenched the fever, but also gave her back perfect health. Thus, the disease being an ordinary one, He displayed His power by the manner of healing; a thing which no physician's art could have wrought. For ye know that even after the departing of fevers, the patients yet need much time to return to their former health. But then all took place at once.

And not in this case only, but also in that of the sea. For neither there did He quiet the winds only and the storm, but He also stayed at once the swelling of the waves; and this also was a strange thing. For even if the tempest should cease, the waves continue to swell for a long time.

But with Christ it was not so, but all at once was ended: and so it befell this woman also. Wherefore also the evangelist, to de-clare this, said, "She arose and ministered unto Him;"[1] which was a sign both of Christ's power, and of the disposition of the woman, which she showed towards Christ.

And another thing together with these we may hence observe, that Christ grants the healing of some to the faith even of others. Since in this case too, others besought Him, as also in the instance of the centurion's servant. And this grant He makes, when there is no unbelief in him that is to be healed, but either through disease he cannot come unto Him, or through ignorance imag-ines nothing great of Him, or because of His immature age.

2. "When the even was come, they brought unto Him many that were possessed with devils: and He cast out the spirits from them with a word, and healed all that were sick: that it might be fulfilled which was spoken by the Prophet Esaias, that He took our infirmities, and bare our sicknesses."[2]

Seest thou the multitude, by this time growing in faith? For not even when the time pressed could they endure to depart, nor did they account it unseasonable to bring their sick to Him at eventide.

But mark, I pray thee, how great a multi-tude of persons healed the evangelists pass quickly over, not mentioning one by one, and giving us an account of them, but in one word traversing an unspeakable sea of miracles. Then lest the greatness of the wonder should drive us again to unbelief, that even so great a people and their various diseases should be delivered and healed by Him in one moment of time, He brings in the prophet also to bear witness to what is going on: indicating the abundance of the proof we have, in every case, out of the Scriptures; such, that from the miracles themselves we have no more; and He saith, that Esaias also spake of these things; "He took our infirmities, and bare our sicknesses."[3] He said not, "He did them away," but "He took and bare them;" which seems to me to be spoken rather of sins, by the prophet, in harmony with John, where he saith, "Behold the Lamb of God, that beareth the sin of the world."[4]

How then doth the evangelist here apply it to diseases? Either as rehearsing the pas-sage in the historical sense,[5] or to show that most of our diseases arise from sins of the soul. For if the sum of all, death itself, hath its root and foundation from sin, much more the majority of our diseases also: since our very capability of suffering did itself originate there.

3. "Now when Jesus saw great multitudes about Him, He gave commandment to depart unto the other side."[6]

Seest thou again His freedom from osten-tation? in that as the others say, "He charged the devils not to say it was He,"[7] so this writer saith, He repels the multitudes from Him. Now in so doing, He was at once both training us to be moderate,[8] and at the same time allaying the envy of the Jews, and teach-ing us to do nothing for display. For He was not, we know, a healer to bodies only,

---

[1] Matt. viii. 15.

[2] Matt. viii. 16, 17. [R. V., " our diseases."]
[3] Isa. liii. 4. The Evangelist seems to quote the Hebrew, not the LXX. [The explanation given in the Homily agrees with the LXX., " he bare our sins and suffered pain (ὀδυνᾶται) in our behalf." Hebrew has " sorrows " instead of " sicknesses " or " diseases." —R.]
[4] John i. 29.
[5] κατὰ ἱστορίαν τὴν μαρτυρίαν ἀναγινώσκων, " reading the text in that sense, to which the actual knowledge of the facts concern-ing Christ, apart from what faith teaches, might guide a man." See Suicer in v. ἱστορία.
[6] Matt. viii. 18.   [7] Mark i. 34 ; Luke iv. 41.
[8] i. e., " moderate, as receivers, in what we expect from Him ; and averse to all display, when we give in His Name."

but a curer also of the soul, and a teacher of self-restraint; by both disclosing Himself, both by putting away their diseases, and by doing nought for display. Because they indeed were cleaving unto Him, loving Him, and marvelling at Him, and desiring to look upon Him. For who would depart from one who was doing such miracles? Who would not long, were it only to see the face, and the mouth that was uttering such words?

For not by any means in working wonders only was He wonderful, but even when merely showing Himself, He was full of great grace; and to declare this the prophet said, " Fair [1] in beauty beyond the children of men." [2] And if Esaias saith, " He hath no form nor comeliness," [3] he affirms it either in comparison of the glory of His Godhead, which surpasses all utterance and description; or as declaring what took place at His passion, and the dishonor which He underwent at the season of the cross, and the mean estate which throughout His life He exemplified in all respects.

Further: He did not first give " commandment to depart unto the other side," nor until He had healed them. For surely they could not have borne it. As therefore on the mountain they not only continued with Him while exhorting them, but also when it was silence followed Him; so here too, not in His miracles only did they wait on Him, but also when He had ceased again, from His very countenance receiving no small benefit. For if Moses had his face made glorious, and Stephen like that of an angel; consider thou our common Lord, what manner of person it was likely He would appear at such a time.

Many now perchance have fallen into a passionate desire of seeing that form; but if we are willing we shall behold one far better than that. For if we can pass through our present life with Christian boldness,[4] we shall receive Him in the clouds, meeting Him in an immortal and incorruptible body.

But observe how He doth not simply drive them away, lest He should hurt them. For He did not say, " withdraw," but " gave commandment to depart to the other side," giving them to expect that He would surely come thither.

4. And the multitudes for their part evinced this great love, and were following with much affection; but some one person, a slave of wealth, and possessed with much arrogance, approaches Him, and saith,

" Master, I will follow Thee whithersoever Thou goest." [5]

Seest thou how great his arrogance? For as not deigning to be numbered with the multitude, and indicating that he is above the common sort, so he comes near. Because such is the Jewish character; full of unseasonable confidence. So too another afterwards, when all men were keeping silence, of his own accord springs up, and saith, " Which is the first commandment?" [6]

Yet nevertheless the Lord rebuked not his unseasonable confidence, teaching us to bear even with such as these. Therefore He doth not openly convict them who are devising mischief, but replies to their secret thought, leaving it to themselves only to know that they are convicted, and doubly doing them good, first by showing that He knows what is in their conscience, next by granting unto them concealment after this manifestation, and allowing them to recover themselves again, if they will: which thing He doth in the case of this man also.

For he, seeing the many signs, and many drawn after Him, thought to make a gain out of such miracles; wherefore also he was forward to follow Him. And whence is this manifest? From the answer which Christ makes, meeting not the question, as it stands verbally, but the temper shown in its meaning. For, " What?" saith He, " dost thou look to gather wealth by following me? Seest thou not then that I have not even a lodging, not even so much as the birds have?"

For " the foxes," saith He, " have holes, and the birds of the air have nests, but the Son of Man hath not where to lay His head." [7]

Now these were not the words of one turning Himself away, but of one who while putting to the proof his evil disposition, yet permitted him (if he were willing with such a prospect) to follow Him. And to convince thee of his wickedness, when he had heard these things, and had been proved, he did not say, " I am ready to follow Thee."

5. And in many other places also Christ is clearly doing this; He doth not openly convict, but by His answer He manifests the purpose of them that are coming unto Him. Thus to him again that said, " Good Master," and had thought by such flattery to gain His favor, according to his purpose He made answer, saying, " Why callest thou me good? There is none good but one, that is, God." [8]

---

[1] ὡραῖος.   [2] Ps. xlv. 2, LXX.
[3] Isa. liii. 2, LXX. [So the Hebrew.]   [4] μετὰ παρρησίας.
[5] Matt. viii. 19.

[6] Matt. xxii. 36 ; Luke x. 25. [The passage in Luke tells of an entirely different incident. The citation from Matthew is not exact, though " first " occurs in the answer of our Lord.—R.]
[7] Matt. viii. 20.
[8] Matt. xix. 16, 17 ; Luke xviii. 18, 19. [The citation agrees more exactly with Mark x. 18. In Matthew, according to the best MSS. authorities, and also the Latin versions and fathers, another form of the answer occurs. Even in Homily LXIII., where the

And when they said unto Him, "Behold, Thy mother and Thy brethren seek Thee;"[1] forasmuch as these were under the influence of some human infirmity, not desiring to hear something profitable, but to make a display of their relationship to Him, and therein to be vainglorious; hear what He saith: "Who is my mother, and who are my brethren?"

And again to His brethren themselves, saying unto Him, "Show thyself to the world,"[2] and wishing thence to feed their vainglory, He said, "Your time" (so He speaks) "is always ready, but my time is not yet come."

And in the opposite cases too He doth so; as in that of Nathanael, saying, "Behold an Israelite indeed, in whom is no guile."[3] And again, "Go and show John again those things which ye do hear and see."[4] For neither in this did He reply to the words, but to the intention of him that sent them. And with the people again in like manner, He addresses His discourse unto their conscience, saying, "What went ye out into the wilderness to see?"[5] That is, because they were probably feeling about John, as though he had been a sort of easy and wavering person; to correct this their suspicion, He saith, "What went ye out into the wilderness to see? A reed shaken with the wind?" or, "a man clothed with soft raiment?" by both these figures declaring, that he was neither of himself a waverer, nor would be softened by any luxury. Thus then in the present case also He makes His answer to their meaning.

And see how in this also He shows forth great moderation: in that He said not, "I have it indeed, but despise it," but "I have it not." Seest thou what exact care goes along with His condescension? Even as when He eats and drinks, when He seems to be acting in an opposite way to John, this too He doeth for the sake of the Jews' salvation, or rather for that of the whole world, at once both stopping the mouths of the heretics,[6] and desiring to win also more abundantly those of that day to Himself.

6. But a certain other one, we read, said unto Him,

"Lord, suffer me first to go and bury my father."[7]

Didst thou mark the difference? how one impudently saith, "I will follow Thee whithersoever Thou goest;" but this other, although asking a thing of sacred duty,[8] saith, "Suffer me." Yet He suffered him not, but saith, "Let the dead bury their dead, but do thou follow me." For in every case He had regard to the intention. And wherefore did He not suffer him? one may ask. Because, on the one hand, there were those that would fulfill that duty, and the dead was not going to remain unburied; on the other, it was not fit for this man to be taken away from the weightier matters. But by saying, "their own dead," He implies that this is not one of His dead. And that because he that was dead, was, at least as I suppose, of the unbelievers.

Now if thou admire the young man, that for a matter so necessary he besought Jesus, and did not go away of his own accord; much rather do thou admire him for staying also when forbidden.

Was it not then, one may say, extreme ingratitude, not to be present at the burial of his father? If indeed he did so out of negligence, it was ingratitude, but if in order not to interrupt a more needful work, his departing would most surely have been of extreme inconsideration. For Jesus forbad him, not as commanding to think lightly of the honor due to our parents, but signifying that nothing ought to be to us more urgent than the things of Heaven, and that we ought with all diligence to cleave to these, and not to put them off for ever so little, though our engagements be exceeding indispensable and pressing. For what can be more needful than to bury a father? what more easy? since it would not even consume any long time.

But if one ought not to spend even as much time as is required for a father's burial, nor is it safe to be parted even so long from our spiritual concerns; consider what we deserve, who all our time stand off from the things that pertain to Christ, and prefer things very ordinary to such as are needful, and are remiss, when there is nothing to press on us?

And herein too we should admire the instructiveness[9] of His teaching, that He nailed him fast to His word, and with this freed him from those endless evils, such as lamentations, and mournings, and the things that follow thereafter. For after the burial he must of necessity proceed to inquire about the will, then about the distribution of the inheritance, and all the other things that follow thereupon; and thus waves after waves coming in succession upon him, would bear him away very far from the harbor of truth. For this cause He draws him, and fastens him to Himself.

---

incident is commented upon, Chrysostom does not directly attribute this language, as given above, to Matthew's Gospel.—R.]
[1] Matt. xii. 47, 48.　　[2] John vii. 4, 6.　　[3] John i. 47.
[4] Matt. xi. 4.　　[5] Matt. xi. 7.
[6] *i. e.*, of those heretics who "commanded to abstain from meats," as though possessed with some evil principle: the Manichæan and Marcionite schools. Comp. St. Chrys. on 1 Tim. i. 5.
[7] Matt. viii. 21.　　[8] ὅσιον.
[9] φιλοσοφίαν.

But if thou still marvellest, and art perplexed, that he was not permitted to be present at his father's burial; consider that many suffer not the sick, if it be a father that is dead, or a mother, or a child, or any other of their kinsmen, to know it, nor to follow him to the tomb; and we do not for this charge them with cruelty nor inhumanity: and very reasonably. For, on the contrary, it were cruelty to bring out to the funeral solemnity men in such a state.

But if to mourn and be afflicted in mind for them that are of our kindred is evil, much more our being withdrawn from spiritual discourses. For this same cause He said elsewhere also, "No man having put his hand to the plough, and looking back, is fit for the kingdom of Heaven."[1] And surely it is far better to proclaim the kingdom, and draw back others from death, than to bury the dead body, that is nothing advantaged thereby; and especially, when there are some to fulfill all these duties.

7 Nothing else then do we learn hereby, but that we must not wantonly lose any, no not the smallest time, though there be ten thousand things to press on us; but to set what is spiritual before all, even the most indispensable matters, and to know both what is life, and what is death. Since many even of them that seem to live are nothing better than dead men, living as they do in wickedness; or rather these are worse than the dead; "For he that is dead," it is said, "is freed from sin,"[2] but this man is a slave to sin. For tell me not of this, that he is not eaten of worms, nor lies in a coffin, nor hath closed his eyes, nor is bound in graveclothes. Nay, for these things he undergoes more grievously than the dead, no worms devouring him, but the passions of his soul tearing him to pieces more fiercely than wild beasts.

And if his eyes be open, this too again is far worse than having closed them. For those of the dead see no evil thing, but this man is gathering unto himself diseases without number, while his eyes are open. And whereas the other lies in a coffin, unmoved by anything, this one is buried in the tomb of his innumerable distempers.

But thou seest not his body in a state of decay. And what of that? Since before his body, his soul is corrupted and destroyed, and undergoes greater rottenness. For the other stinketh a few[3] days, but this for the whole of his life exhales evil odors, having a mouth more foul than sewers.

And so the one differs from the other, by just so much as this, that the dead indeed undergoes that decay only which comes of nature, but this man together with that, brings in also that rottenness which is from intemperance, devising each day unnumbered causes of corruption.

But is he borne on horseback? And what of that? Why, so is the other on a couch. And what is very hard, while the other is seen by no one in his dissolution and decay, but hath his coffin for a veil, this man is going about everywhere with his evil savor, bearing about a dead soul in his body as in a tomb.

And if one could but once see a man's soul who is living in luxury and vice, thou wouldest perceive that it is far better to lie bound in a grave than to be rivetted by the chains of our sins; and to have a stone laid over thee, than that heavy cover[4] of insensibility. Wherefore above all things it behooves the friends of these dead men, seeing that they are past feeling, to come near to Jesus in their behalf, as Mary then did in the case of Lazarus. Though he "stinketh," though he be "dead four days," do not despair, but approach, and remove the stone first. Yea, for then thou shalt see him lying as in a tomb, and bound in his grave clothes.

And if ye will, let it be some one of them that are great and distinguished, whom we bring before you. Nay, fear not, for I will state the example without a name: or rather, though I should mention the name, not even so need there be any fear: for who ever fears a dead man? seeing that whatever one may do, he continues dead, and the dead cannot injure the living either little or much.

Let us then behold their head bound up. For indeed, when they are for ever drunken, even as the dead by their many wrappers and grave-clothes, so are all their organs of sense closed and bound up. And if thou wilt look at their hands too, thou shalt see these again bound to their belly, like those of the dead, and fastened about not with grave-clothes, but what is far more grievous, with the bands of covetousness: obtaining as they do no leave from her to be stretched out for alms-giving, or for any other of such like good deeds; rather she renders them more useless than those of the dead. Wouldest thou also see their feet bound together? See them again fastened about with cares, and for this cause never able to run unto the house of God.

---

[1] Luke ix, 62, ἐν τῇ βασιλείᾳ. [The citation is peculiar: (1) ἐν is not found in any of our MSS. of the New Testament, the received text is εἰς τὴν βασιλείαν, while the dative alone is better supported. (2) τῶν οὐρανῶν is substituted for τοῦ θεοῦ; the former occurring in Matthew only in connection with βασιλεία.—R.]

[2] Rom. vi. 7.   [3] [More exactly, "ten days."—R.]

[4] πῶμα, the lid of a coffer of any kind: here of a sarcophagus.

Hast thou seen the dead? behold also the embalmer. Who then is the embalmer of these? The devil, who carefully fastens them about, and suffers not the man any longer to appear a man, but a dry stock. For where there is no eye, nor hands, nor feet, nor any other such thing, how can such an one appear a man? Even so may we see their soul also swaddled up, and rather an image[1] than a soul.

Forasmuch then as they are in a sort of senseless state, being turned to dead men, let us in their behalf draw nigh unto Jesus, let us entreat Him to raise them up, let us take away the stone, let us loosen the grave clothes. For if thou take away the stone, that is, their insensibility to their own miseries, thou wilt quickly be able to bring them also out of the tomb; and having brought them out, thou wilt more easily rid them of their bonds. Then shall Christ know thee, when thou art risen, when unbound; then will He call thee even unto His own supper.[2] As many therefore of you as are friends of Christ, as many as are disciples, as many as love him that is gone, draw near unto Jesus, and pray. For even though his ill savor abound and be ever so intense, nevertheless not even so should we, his friends, forsake him, but so much the rather draw near; even as the sisters of Lazarus then did; neither should we leave interceding, beseeching, entreating, until we have received Him alive.

For if we thus order our own affairs, and those of our neighbors, we shall also attain speedily unto the life to come; unto which may we all attain, by the grace and love to man of our Lord Jesus Christ, to whom be glory forever and ever. Amen.

---

[1] εἴδωλον. The classical use of this word is well known: see e. g. Odyss. xi. 602. "A shadow or phantom: not a true substantial soul."

[2] Alluding to John xii. 2.

HOMILY XXVIII.

MATT. VIII. 23, 24.

"And when He was entered into a ship, His disciples followed Him. And, behold, there arose a great tempest in the sea, insomuch that the ship was covered with the waves, but He was asleep."

Now Luke,[1] to free himself from having the order of time required of Him, saith thus, "And it came to pass on a certain day that He went into a ship with His disciples;" and Mark in like manner.[2] But this evangelist not so, but he maintains the order in this place also. For they did not all of them write all things in this way. And these things I have mentioned before, lest any one from the omission should suppose there was a discordance.

The multitudes then He sent on, but the disciples He took with Himself: for the others mention this too. And He took them with Him, not for nought, nor at hazard, but in order to make them spectators of the miracle that was to take place. For like a most excellent trainer, He was anointing them with a view to both objects; as well to be undismayed in dangers, as to be modest in honors. Thus, that they might not be high minded, because having sent away the rest, He retained them, He suffers them to be tossed with the tempest; at once correcting this, and disciplining them to bear trials nobly.

For great indeed were the former miracles too, but this contained also in it a kind of discipline, and that no inconsiderable one, and was a sign akin to that of old.[3] For this cause He takes the disciples only with Himself. For as, when there was a display of miracles, He suffers the people also to be present; so when trials and terrors were rising up against Him, then He takes with Him none but the champions of the whole world, whom He was to discipline.

---

[1] Luke viii. 22.

[2] See Mark iv. 35. [But Mark is very specific as to time. This event is placed very much out of chronological position in Matthew's account. But Chrysostom does not discuss such questions with any fullness. Indeed, the order of Matthew seems to have been accepted up to his time. The earliest harmonies were based upon Matthew. Comp. even Augustin, *Harmony, Nicene and Post-Nicene Fathers*, vol. vi., first series, pp. 67–69, and elsewhere.—R.]

[3] *i. e.*, the miracle at the Red Sea, afterwards mentioned.

And while Matthew merely mentioned that "He was asleep,"[1] Luke saith that it was "on a pillow;" signifying both His freedom from pride, and to teach us hereby a high degree of austerity.[2]

The tempest therefore being thoroughly excited, and the sea raging, "They awake Him, saying, Lord, save us: we perish"[3] But He rebuked them before He rebuked the sea. Because as I said, for discipline these things were permitted, and they were a type of the temptations that were to overtake them. Yea, for after these things again, He often suffered them to fall into more grievous tempests of fortune,[4] and bare long with them. Wherefore Paul also said, "I would not, brethren, have you ignorant, that we were pressed out of measure beyond strength, insomuch that we despaired even of life;"[5] and after this again, "Who delivered us from so great deaths." Signifying therefore hereby, that they ought to be confident, though the waves rise high, and that He orders all things for good, He first of all reproves them. For indeed their very alarm was a profitable occurrence, that the miracle might appear greater, and their remembrance of the event be rendered lasting. Since when anything strange is about to happen, there are prepared beforehand many things to cause remembrance, lest after the miracle hath passed by, men should sink into forgetfulness.

Thus Moses also first is in fear of the serpent, and not merely in fear, but even with much distress: and then he sees that strange thing come to pass.[6] So these too, having first looked to perish, were then saved, that having confessed the danger, they might learn the greatness of the miracle.

Therefore also He sleeps: for had He been awake when it happened, either they would not have feared, or they would not have besought Him, or they would not so much as have thought of His being able to do any such thing. Therefore He sleeps, to give occasion for their timidity, and to make their perception of what was happening more distinct. For a man looks not with the same eyes on what happens in the persons of others, as in his own. Therefore since they had seen all benefitted, while themselves had enjoyed no benefit, and were supine (for neither were they lame, nor had they any other such infirmity); and it was meet they should enjoy His benefits by their own perception: He permits the storm, that by their deliverance they might attain to a clearer perception of the benefit.

Therefore neither doth He this in the presence of the multitudes, that they might not be condemned for little faith, but He has them apart, and corrects them, and before the tempest of the waters He puts an end to the tempests of their soul, rebuking them, and saying,

"Why are ye fearful, O ye of little faith:" instructing them also, that men's fear is wrought not by the approach of the temptations, but by the weakness of their mind.

But should any one say, that it was not fearfulness, or little faith, to come near and awaken Him; I would say this, that that very thing was an especial sign of their wanting the right opinion concerning Him. That is, His power to rebuke when awakened they knew, but that He could do so even sleeping, they knew not as yet.

And why at all marvel that it was so now, when even after many other miracles their impressions were still rather imperfect? wherefore also they are often rebuked; as when He saith, "Are ye also yet without understanding?"[7] Marvel not then, if when the disciples were in such imperfect dispositions, the multitudes had no exalted imagination of Him. For

"They marvelled, saying, What manner of man is this, that even the sea and the winds obey Him?"[8]

But Christ chode not with them for calling Him a man, but waited to teach them by His signs, that their supposition was mistaken. But from what did they think Him a man? First from His appearance, then from His sleeping, and His making use of a ship. So on this account they were cast into perplexity, saying, "What manner of man is this?" since while the sleep and the outward appearance showed man, the sea and the calm declared Him God.

For because Moses had once done some such thing, in this regard also doth He signify His own superiority, and that the one works miracles as a slave, the other as Lord. Thus, He put forth no rod, as Moses did, neither did He stretch forth His hands to Heaven, nor did He need any prayer, but, as was meet for a master commanding His handmaid, or a creator His creature, so did He quiet and curb it by word and command only; and all the surge was straightway at an

---

[1] See Mark iv. 38.   [2] φιλοσοφίαν.   [3] Matt. viii. 25.
[4] πραγμάτων, "of things."   [5] 2 Cor. i. 8, 10.
[6] Exod. iv. 3, 4.

[7] Matt. xv. 16. ["For" is part of the citation, in the Greek text of the Homily, but does not occur in the Gospel narratives. The order, "the sea and the winds," is also peculiar to the text of the Homily. The Oxford translator gives the order of the A. V., which is well attested, but not followed here.—R.]
[8] Matt. viii. 27.

end, and not one trace of the disturbance remained. For this the evangelist declared, saying, "And there was a great calm." [1] And that which had been spoken of the Father as a great thing, this He showed forth again by His works. And what had been said concerning Him? "He spake," it saith, "and the stormy wind ceased." [2] So here likewise, He spake, and "there was a great calm." And for this most of all did the multitudes marvel at him; who would not have marvelled, had He done it in such manner as did Moses.

2. Now when He is departed from the sea, there follows another miracle yet more awful. For men possessed with devils, [3] like wicked runaways at sight of their master, said,

"What have we to do with Thee, Jesus, Thou Son of God? Art Thou come hither to torment us before the time?" [4]

For, because the multitudes called Him man, the devils came proclaiming His Godhead, and they that heard not the sea swelling and subsiding, heard from the devils the same cry, as it by its calm was loudly uttering.

Then, lest the thing might seem to come of flattery, according to their actual experience they cry out and say, "Art Thou come hither to torment us before the time?" With this view, then, their enmity is avowed beforehand, that their entreaty may not incur suspicion. For indeed they were invisibly receiving stripes, and the sea was not in such a storm as they; galled, and inflamed, and suffering things intolerable from His mere presence. Accordingly, no man daring to bring them to Him, Christ of Himself goes unto them.

And Matthew indeed relates that they said, "Art Thou come hither before the time to torment us?" but the other evangelists have added, that they also entreated and adjured Him not to cast them into the deep. [5] For they supposed that their punishment was now close upon them, and feared, as even now about to fall into vengeance.

And though Luke and those who follow him [6] say that it was one person, but this evangelist two, this doth not exhibit any discrepancy at all. I grant if they had said, there was only one, and no other, they would appear to disagree with Matthew; but if that spake of the one, this of the two, the statement comes not of disagreement, but of a different manner of narration. That is, I for my part think, Luke singled out the fiercest one of them for his narrative, wherefore also in more tragical wise doth he report their miserable case; as, for instance, that bursting his bonds and chains he used to wander about the wilderness. And Mark saith, that he also cut himself with the stones.

And their words too are such as well betray their implacable and shameless nature. For, saith he, "Art thou come hither to torment us before the time?" You see, that they had sinned, they could not deny, but they demand not to suffer their punishment before the time. For, since He had caught them in the act of perpetrating those horrors so incurable and lawless, and deforming and punishing [7] His creature in every way; and they supposed that He, for the excess of their crimes, would not await the time of their punishment: therefore they besought and entreated Him: and they that endured not even bands of iron come bound, and they that run about the mountains, are gone forth into the plain; and those who hinder all others from passing, at sight of Him blocking up the way, stand still.

3. But what can be the reason that they love also to dwell in the tombs? They would fain suggest to the multitude a pernicious opinion, as though the souls of the dead become demons, [8] which God forbid we should ever admit into our conception. "But what then wilt thou say," one may ask, "when many of the sorcerers take children and slay them, in order to have the soul afterwards to assist them?" Why, whence is this evident? for of their slaying them, indeed, many tell us, but as to the souls of the slain being with them, whence knowest thou it, I pray thee? "The possessed themselves," it is replied, "cry out, I am the soul of such a one." But this too is a kind of stage-play, and devilish deceit. For it is not the spirit of the dead that cries out, but the evil spirit that feigns these things in order to deceive the hearers. For if it were possible for a soul to enter into the substance of an evil spirit, much more into its own body.

And besides, it stands not to reason that

---

[1] Matt. viii. 26. [2] Ps. cvii. 25, LXX.
[3] [R. V., "demons," and so the translator in many places in this Homily.—R.]
[4] Matt. viii. 29. [5] Mark v. 10; Luke viii. 31.
[6] οἱ περὶ τὸν Λουκᾶν.

[7] τιμωρουμένους.
[8] So St. Augustin de Civitate Dei, ix. 11. "Plotinus says that the souls of men are demons, and of men become Lares, if they are of good desert; if of bad, Lemures or Larvæ." Mr. Field refers to St. Chrys. 2 Hom. on Lazarus, vi. 235, 6 (Savile). "Many of the simpler sort imagine that the souls of such as die violent deaths are turned into demons, whereas the souls which really become such are theirs who are yet living in their sins, not by change of substance, but by imitating their evil mind. . . . Why did the devil introduce this wicked doctrine? He tried to undermine the glory of the martyrs. I mean, because they die violent deaths, he wishing to diffuse an evil impression of them, did this. This, however, he could not do, but another very grievous result he did accomplish. He induced, by these doctrines, the sorcerers that minister to him to butcher the bodies of many tender youths, in the hope that they would become demons, and in return minister to them." He proceeds to argue against the superstition much as in the text here.

the injured soul should co-operate with the wrong-doer, or that a man should be able to change an incorporeal power into another substance. For if in bodies this were impossible, and one could not make a man's body become that of an ass; much more were this impossible in the invisible soul; neither could one transform it into the substance of an evil spirit. So that these are the sayings of besotted old wives, and spectres to frighten children.

Nor indeed is it possible for a soul, torn away from the body, to wander here any more. For "the souls of the righteous are in the hand of God;"[1] and if of the righteous, then those children's souls also; for neither are they wicked: and the souls too of sinners are straightway led away hence. And it is evident from Lazarus and the rich man; and elsewhere too Christ saith, "This day they require thy soul of thee."[2] And it may not be that a soul, when it is gone forth from the body, should wander here; nor is the reason hard to see. For if we, going about on the earth which is familiar and well known to us, being encompassed with a body, when we are journeying in a strange road, know not which way to go unless we have some one to lead us; how should the soul, being rent away from the body, and having gone out from all her accustomed region, know where to walk without one to show her the way?

And from many other things too one might perceive, that it is not possible for a disembodied soul to remain here. For both Stephen saith, "Receive my spirit;"[3] and Paul, "To depart and to be with Christ is far better;"[4] and of the patriarch too the Scripture saith, that "he was gathered unto his fathers, being cherished in a good old age."[5] And as to the proof, that neither can the souls of sinners continue here; hear the rich man making much entreaty for this, and not obtaining it; since had it been at all possible, he would have come, and have told what had come to pass there.[6] Whence it is evident that after their departure hence our souls are led away into some place, having no more power of themselves to come back again, but awaiting that dreadful day.

4. Now, should any one say, "And wherefore did Christ fulfill the devils' request, suffering them to depart into the herd of swine?" this would be our reply, that He did so, not as yielding to them, but as providing for many objects thereby. One, to teach them that are delivered from those wicked

tyrants, how great the malice of their insidious enemies: another, that all might learn, how not even against swine are they bold, except He allow them; a third, that they would have treated those men more grievously than the swine, unless even in their calamity they had enjoyed much of God's providential care. For that they hate us more than the brutes is surely evident to every man. So then they that spared not the swine, but in one moment of time cast them all down the precipice, much more would they have done so to the men whom they possessed, leading them towards the desert, and carrying them away, unless even in their very tyranny the guardian care of God had abounded, to curb and check the excess of their violence. Whence it is manifest that there is no one, who doth not enjoy the benefit of God's providence. And if not all alike, nor after one manner, this is itself a very great instance of providence; in that according to each man's profit, the work also of providence is displayed.

And besides what hath been mentioned, there is another thing also, which we learn from this; that His providence is not only over all in common, but also over each in particular; which He also declared with respect to His disciples, saying, "But the very hairs of your head are numbered."[7] And from these demoniacs too, one may clearly perceive this; who would have "been choked" long before, if they had not enjoyed the benefit of much tender care from above.

For these reasons then He suffered them to depart into the herd of swine, and that they also dwelt in those places should learn His power. For where His name was great, He did not greatly display Himself: but where no one knew Him, but they were still in an insensible condition, He made His miracles to shine out, so as to bring them over to the knowedge of His Godhead. For it is evident from the event that the inhabitants of that city were a sort of senseless people; for when they ought to have adored and marvelled at His power, they sent Him away, and "besought Him that He would depart out of their coasts."[8]

But for what intent did the devils destroy the swine? Everywhere they have labored to drive men to dismay, and everywhere they rejoice in destruction. This, for instance, the devil did with respect to Job, although in that case too God suffered it, but neither in that case as complying with the devil, but willing to show His own servant the more

---

[1] Wisd. iii. 1.   [2] Luke xii. 20.   [3] Acts vii. 59.   [7] Matt. x. 30.
[4] Phil. i. 23.   [5] Gen. xv. 15, in LXX.   [6] Luke xvi. 27, 28.   [8] Matt. viii. 34. [R. V., "from their borders."]

glorious, cutting off from the evil spirit all pretext for his shamelessness, and turning on his own head what was done against the righteous man. Because now also the contrary of what they wished came to pass. For the power of Christ was gloriously proclaimed, and the wickedness of the demons, from which He delivered those possessed by them, was more plainly indicated; and how they want power to touch even swine, without permission from the God of all.

And if any would take these things in a hidden sense,[1] there is nothing to hinder. For the history indeed is this, but we are to know assuredly, that the swinish sort of men are especially liable to the operations of the demons. And as long as they are men that suffer such things, they are often able yet to prevail; but if they are become altogether swine, they are not only possessed, but are also cast down the precipice. And besides, lest any should suppose what was done to be mere acting, instead of distinctly believing that the devils[2] were gone out; by the death of the swine this is rendered manifest.

And mark also His meekness together with His power. For when the inhabitants of that country, after having received such benefits, were driving Him away, He resisted not, but retired, and left those who had shown themselves unworthy of His teaching, having given them for teachers them that had been freed from the demons, and the swine-herds, that they might of them learn all that had happened; whilst Himself retiring leaves the fear vigorous in them. For the greatness withal of the loss was spreading the fame of what had been done, and the event penetrated their mind. And from many quarters were wafted sounds, proclaiming the strangeness of the miracle; from the cured, and from the drowned, from the owners of the swine, from the men that were feeding them.

5. These things any one may see happening now also, even many in the tombs possessed of evil spirits, whom nothing restrains from their madness; not iron, nor chain, nor multitude of men, nor advice, nor admonition, nor terror, nor threat, nor any other such thing.

For so when any man is dissolute, eager after all embraces,[3] he differs not at all from the demoniac, but goes about naked like him, clad indeed in garments, but deprived of the true covering, and stripped of his proper glory; cutting himself not with stones, but with sins more hurtful than many stones. Who then shall be able to bind such a one? Who, to stay his unseemliness and frenzy, his way of never coming to himself, but forever haunting the tombs? For such are the resorts of the harlots, full of much evil savor, of much rottenness.

And what of the covetous man? Is he not like this? For who will be able ever to bind him? Are there not fears and daily threats, and admonitions, and counsels? Nay, all these bonds he bursts asunder; and if any one come to set him free, he adjures him that he may not be freed, accounting it the greatest torture not to be in torture: than which what can be more wretched? For as to that evil spirit, even though he despised men, yet he yielded to the command of Christ, and quickly sprang out of the man's body; but this man yields not even to His commandment. See at least how he daily hears Him saying, "Ye cannot serve God and mammon,"[4] and threatening hell, and the incurable torments, and obeys not: not that He is stronger than Christ, but because against our will Christ corrects us not.[5] Therefore such men live as in desert places, though they be in the midst of cities. For who, that hath reason, would choose to be with such men? I for my part would sooner consent to dwell with ten thousand demoniacs, than with one diseased in this way.

And that I am not mistaken in saying this, is manifest from their respective feelings. For these last account him an enemy that hath done them no wrong, and desire even to take him for a slave when he is free, and encompass him with ten thousand evils; but the demoniacs do no such thing, but toss their disease to and fro within themselves. And while these overturn many houses, and cause the name of God to be blasphemed, and are a pest to the city and to the whole earth; they that are troubled by evil spirits, deserve rather our pity and our tears. And the one for the more part act in insensibility, but the others are frantic while they reason, keeping their orgies in the midst of cities, and maddened with some new kind of madness. For what do all the demoniacs so bad, as what Judas dared to do, when he showed forth that extremity of wickedness? And all too that imitate him, like fierce wild beasts escaped from their cage, trouble their cities, no man restraining them. For these also have bonds upon them on every side; such as the fears of the judges, the threatening of the laws, the condemnation of the multitude,

---

[1] κατὰ ἀναγωγήν. [Comp. the "analogical" sense of Scripture in the later Hermeneutics. But Origen and others had already made the term ἀναγωγή familiar and technical in the usage of ecclesiastical Greek.—R.]

[2] ["demons."]   [3] σώματά.   [4] Matt. vi. 24.   [5] [οὐ σωφρονίζει.]

and other things more than these; yet bursting asunder even these, they turn all things upside down. And should any one remove these altogether from them, then would he know assuredly the demon that is in them to be far fiercer, and more frantic than he who is just now gone forth.

But since this may not be, let us for the time suppose it for argument's sake: and let us take off from him all his chains, and then shall we clearly know his manifest madness. But be not afraid of the monster, when we uncover it; for it is the representation in word, not the thing in truth. Let there be then some man, darting fire from his eyes, black, having from either shoulder serpents hanging down instead of hands; and let him have also a mouth, with sharp swords set in it instead of teeth, and for a tongue a gushing fountain of poison and some baneful drug; and a belly more consuming than any furnace, devouring all that is cast unto it, and a sort of winged feet more vehement than any flame; and let his face be made up of a dog and of a wolf; and let him utter nothing human, but something discordant, and unpleasing, and terrible; and let him have also in his hands a firebrand. Perhaps what we have said seems to you to be terrible, but we have not even yet fashioned him worthily; for together with these things we must add others besides. I mean, that he is also to slay them that meet with him, to devour them, to fasten upon their flesh.

Yet is the covetous man much more fierce even than this, assailing all like hell, swallowing all up, going about a common enemy to the race of men. Why, he would have no man exist, that he may possess all things. And he stops not even at this, but when in his longing he shall have destroyed all men, he longs also to mar the substance of the earth, and to see it all become gold; nay, not the earth only, but hills also, and woods, and fountains, and in a word all things that appear.

And to convince you that not even yet have we set forth his madness, let there be no man to accuse and frighten him, but take away the terror of the laws in supposition awhile, and thou wilt see him snatching up a sword, laying violent hands on all, and sparing none; neither friend, nor kinsman, nor brother, nor even his very parent. Nay rather, in this case there is not even need of supposing, but let us ask him, if he is not for ever framing to himself such imaginations, and if he does not in thought range among all men to destroy them; both friends and kinsmen, and even his very parents. Nay rather there is

no need even to ask, because in truth all men know that they who are under the power of this disease are wearied even of their father's old age; and that which is sweet, and universally desirable, the having children, they esteem grievous and unwelcome: many at least with this view have even paid money to be childless, and have maimed their nature, not only by slaying their children after birth, but by not suffering them even to be born at all.

6. Marvel not, therefore, if we have thus sketched the covetous man (for in truth he is far worse than what we have said); but let us consider how we shall deliver him from the demon. How then shall we deliver him? If he may be clearly made aware, that his love of money stands very much in his way in respect of this very object, the gaining of money; for they that wish to gain in little things undergo great losses; whence accordingly a proverb hath been put forth to this same effect.[1] Many, for instance, on many occasions, wishing to lend at large usury, and through the expectation of gain not having inquired about them who receive their money, have together with the interest lost also all their capital. Others again falling into dangers, and not willing to give up a little, have together with the substance lost their life too.

Again, when it has been in men's power to purchase either gainful offices, or some other such thing, by some trifling meanness they have lost all. For because they know not how to sow, but have ever practised reaping, they of course continually fail of their harvest. For no man can be always reaping, as neither can he be always gaining. Therefore since they are not willing to spend, neither do they know how to gain. And should they have to take a wife, the same thing again befalls them; for either they are deceived into taking a poor wife for a rich one, or when they have brought home one that is rich, but full of faults without number, here too they have incurred more loss than gain. For it is not superfluity, but virtue, that causes wealth. For what profit is there of her wealth, when she is expensive and dissolute, and scatters all abroad more vehemently than any wind? What if she be unchaste, and bring in numberless lovers? what if she be drunken? Will she not quickly make her husband the poorest of men? But they do not only marry, but also buy at great risk, from their great covetousness, laboring to find not good slaves, but cheap ones.

---

[1] Perhaps the χρύσεα χαλκείων, of which Erasmus says, "*Conveniet uti, quoties officium aut munus longe impari munere pensatur. . . . Admissus est in amicitiam principis, sed excidit ex amicitia Christi.*" Adag. Chil. 1, Cent. ii. Prov. 1.

Consider then all these things (for the words concerning hell and the kingdom ye are not yet able to hear), and bearing in mind the losses which ye have often undergone from your love of money, in loans, and in purchases, and in marriages, and in offices of power, and in all the rest; withdraw yourselves from doating on money.

For so shall ye be able to live the present life in security, and after a little advance to hear also the words that treat on self-government, and see through and look upon the very Sun of Righteousness, and to attain unto the good things promised by Him; unto which God grant we may all attain, by the grace and love towards man of our Lord Jesus Christ, to whom be glory and might forever and ever.   Amen.

HOMILY XXIX.

MATT. IX. 1, 2.

"And He entered into a ship, and passed over, and came into His own city.   And, behold, they brought to Him a man sick of the palsy, lying on a bed: and Jesus seeing their faith said unto the sick of the palsy; Son, be of good cheer; thy sins be forgiven thee." [1]

By His own city here he means Capernaum. For that which gave Him birth was Bethlehem; that which brought Him up, Nazareth; that which had Him continually inhabiting it, Capernaum.

This paralytic, however, was different from that one who is set forth in John.[2]   For he lay at the pool, but this at Capernaum; and that man had his infirmity thirty and eight years, but concerning this, no such thing is mentioned; and the other was in a state destitute of protectors, but this had some to take care of him, who also took him up, and carried him.   And to this He saith, "Son, thy sins be forgiven thee,"[1] but to that He saith, "Wilt thou be made whole?"[3]   And the other He healed on a sabbath day, but this not on a sabbath, for else the Jews would have laid this also to His charge; and in the case of this man they were silent, but in that of the other they were instant in persecuting him.

And this I have said, not without purpose, lest any one should think there is a discrepancy from suspecting it to be one and the same paralytic.

But do thou, I pray thee, mark the humility and meekness of our Lord.   For He had also before this put away the multitudes from Him, and moreover when sent away by them at Gadara, He withstood not, but retired, not however to any great distance.

And again He entered into the ship and passed over, when He might have gone over afoot.   For it was His will not to be always doing miracles, that He might not injure the doctrine of His humanity.[4]

Now Matthew indeed saith, that "they brought him," but the others, that they also broke up the roof, and let him down.[5]   And they put the sick man before Christ, saying nothing, but committing the whole to Him. For though in the beginning He Himself went about, and did not require so much faith of them that came unto Him; yet in this case they both approached Him, and had faith required on their part.   For, "Seeing," it is said, "their faith;" that is, the faith of them that had let the man down.   For He doth not on all occasions require faith on the part of the sick only: as for instance, when they are insane, or in any other way, through their disease, are out of their own control.   Or rather, in this case the sick man too had part in the faith; for he would not have suffered himself to be let down, unless he had believed.

Forasmuch then as they had evinced so great faith, He also evinces His own power, with all authority absolving his sins, and signifying in all ways that He is equal in honor with Him that begat Him.   And mark; He implied it from the beginning, by His teaching, when He taught them as one having

---

[1] [R. V., accepting the same Greek text with Chrysostom, 'thy sins are forgiven.'—R.]

[2] John v. 1.   [3] John v. 6.

[4] τῷ τῆς οἰκονομίας λόγῳ.   ["Incarnation" expresses better the technical sense of the Greek term, as here used.   Comp. Homily XIII. 2, p. 81, note.—R.]

[5] Mark ii. 4; Luke v. 19.

authority; by the leper, when He said, "I will, be thou clean,"[1] by the centurion, when upon his saying, "Speak the word only, and my servant shall be healed, He marvelled at him,"[2] and celebrated him above all men; by the sea, when He curbed it with a mere word; by the devils, when they acknowledged Him as their judge, and He cast them out with great authority.

Here again in another and a greater way He constrains His very enemies to confess His equality in honor, and by their own mouth He makes it manifest. For He, to signify His indifference to honor (for there stood a great company of spectators shutting up the entrance, wherefore also they let him down from above), did not straightway hasten to heal the visible body, but He takes His occasion from them; and He healed first that which is invisible, the soul, by forgiving his sins; which indeed saved the other, but brought no great glory to Himself. They themselves rather, troubled by their malice, and wishing to assail Him, caused even against their will what was done to be conspicuous. He, in fact, in His abundance of counsel, made use of their envy for the manifestation of the miracle.

Upon their murmuring,[3] then, and saying, "This man blasphemeth; who can forgive sins but God only?"[4] let us see what He saith. Did He indeed take away the suspicion? And yet if He were not equal, He should have said, "Why fix upon me a notion which is not convenient? I am far from this power." But now hath He said none of these things, but quite the contrary He hath both affirmed and ratified, as well by His own voice, as by the performance of the miracle. Thus, it appearing that His saying certain things of himself gave disgust to his hearers, He affirms what He had to say concerning Himself by the others; and what is truly marvellous, not by His friends only, but also by His enemies; for this is the excellency of His wisdom. By His friends on the one hand, when He said, "I will, be thou clean,"[5] and when He said, "I have not found so great faith, no, not in Israel;"[6] but by His enemies, now. For because they had said, "No man can forgive sins but God only," He subjoined,

"But that ye may know that the Son of Man hath power to forgive sins upon the earth (then saith He to the sick of the palsy),

Arise, and take up thy bed, and go unto thine house."[7]

And not here only, but also in another case again, when they were saying, "For a good work we stone thee not, but for blasphemy, and because that thou, being a man, makest thyself God."[8] neither in that instance did He put down this opinion, but again confirmed it, saying, "If I do not the works of my Father, believe me not; but if I do, though ye believe not me, believe the works."[9]

2. In this case indeed He discloses also another sign, and that no small one, of His own Godhead, and of His equality in honor with the Father. For whereas they said, "To unbind sins pertains to God only," He not only unbinds sins, but also before this He makes another kind of display in a thing which pertained to God only; the publishing the secrets in the heart. For neither had they uttered what they were thinking.

For "behold, certain of the scribes," it saith," said within themselves, This man blasphemeth. And Jesus knowing their thoughts, said, Wherefore think ye evil in your hearts?"[10]

But that it belongs to God only to know men's secrets, hear what saith the prophet, "Thou most entirely alone[11] knowest the hearts;"[12] and again, "God trieth the hearts and reins;[13]" and Jeremiah too saith, "The heart is deep above all things, and it is man, and who shall know him?"[14] and, "Man shall look on the face, but God on the heart."[15] And by many things one may see, that to know what is in the mind belongs to God alone.

Implying therefore that He is God, equal to Him that begat Him; what things they were reasoning in themselves (for through fear of the multitude, they durst not utter their mind), this their opinion He unveils and makes manifest, evincing herein also His great gentleness.[16]

"For wherefore," saith He, "think ye evil in your hearts?"[17]

And yet if there were cause for displeasure, it was the sick man who should have been displeased, as being altogether deceived, and should have said, "One thing I came to have healed, and amendest Thou another? Why, whence is it manifest that my sins are forgiven?"

But now he for his part utters no such word, but gives himself up to the power of

1 Matt. viii. 3.   2 Matt. viii. 8.
3 [ἐθορυβοῦντο ; a stronger word than the Gospel narratives suggest. The translator tones it down, as above.—R.]
4 Matt. viii. 3. Comp. Mark ii. 7 [from which the latter part of the citation is taken.--R.]
5 Matt. viii. 3.   6 Matt. viii. 10.
7 Matt. viii. 6. [" Upon the earth "' is placed in this peculiar' position by Chrysostom here. In the next reference to the passage the correct order is followed.—R.]
8 John x. 33.   9 John x. 37, 38.   10 Matt. ix. 3, 4.
11 μονώτατος.   12 2 Chron. vi. 30.   13 Ps. vii. 9.
14 Jer. xvii. 9, LXX.   15 1 Sam. xvi. 7.   16 τὸ ἀνεπαχθές.
17 Matt. ix. 4.

the healer; but these being curious and envious, plot against the good deeds of others. Wherefore He rebukes them indeed, but with all gentleness. "Why, if ye disbelieve," saith He, "what went before, and account my saying a boast; behold I add to it also another, the uncovering of your secrets; and after that again another." What then is this? The giving tone to the body of the paralyzed.

And whereas, when He spake unto the sick of the palsy, He spake without clearly manifesting His own authority: for He said not, "I forgive thee thy sins," but, "thy sins be forgiven thee:" upon their constraining, He discloses His authority more clearly, saying, "But that ye may know that the Son of Man hath power [1] on earth to forgive sins."

Seest thou, how far He was from unwillingness to be thought equal to the Father? For He said not at all, "The Son of Man hath need of another;" or, "He hath given Him authority," but, "He hath authority." Neither doth He say it for love of honor, but "to convince you," so He speaks, "that I do not blaspheme in making myself equal with God."

Thus everywhere His will is to offer proofs clear and indisputable; as when He saith, "Go thy way, show thyself to the priest;" [2] and when He points to Peter's wife's mother ministering, and permits the swine to cast themselves down headlong. And in the same manner here also; first, for a certain token of the forgiveness of his sins, He provides the giving tone to his body: and of that again, his carrying his bed; to hinder the fact from being thought a mere fancy. And He doeth not this, before He had asked them a question. "For whether is easier," saith He, "to say, Thy sins be forgiven thee? or to say, Take up thy bed, and go unto thine house?" [3] Now what He saith is like this, "Which seems to you easier, to bind up a disorganized [4] body, or to undo [5] the sins of a soul? It is quite manifest; to bind up a body. For by how much a soul is better than a body, by so much is the doing away sins a greater work than this; but because the one is unseen, the other in sight, I throw in that, which although an inferior thing, is yet more open to sense; that the greater also and the unseen may thereby receive its proof;" thus by His works anticipating even

now the revelation of what had been said by John, that "He taketh away the sins of the world."

Well then, having raised him up, He sends him to His house; here again signifying His unboastfulness, [6] and that the event was not a mere imagination; for He makes the same persons witnesses of his infirmity, and also of his health. For I indeed had desired, saith He, through thy calamity to heal those also, that seem to be in health, but are diseased in mind; but since they will not, depart thou home, to heal them that are there.

Seest thou how He indicates Him [7] to be Creator both of souls and bodies? He heals therefore the palsy in each of the two substances, and makes the invisible evident by that which is in sight. But nevertheless they still creep upon the earth.

"For when the multitudes saw it, they marvelled, and glorified God, which" (it is said) "had given such power unto men:" [8] for the flesh was an offense unto them. [9] But He did not rebuke them, but proceeds by His works to arouse them, and exalt their thoughts. Since for the time it was no small thing for Him to be thought greater than all men, as having come from God. For had they well established these things in their own minds, going on orderly they would have known, that He was even the Son of God. But they did not retain these things clearly, wherefore neither were they able to approach Him. For they said again, "This man is not of God;" [10] "how is this man of God?" And they were continually harping on these things, putting them forward as cloaks for their own passions.

3. Which thing many now also do; and thinking to avenge God, fulfill their own passions, when they ought to go about all with moderation. For even the God of all, having power to launch His thunderbolt against them that blaspheme Him, makes the sun to rise, and sends forth the showers, and affords them all other things in abundance; whom we ought to imitate, and so to entreat, advise, admonish, with meekness, not angry, not making ourselves wild beasts.

For no harm at all ensues unto God by their blasphemy, that thou shouldest be angered, but he who blasphemed hath himself also received the wound. Wherefore groan, bewail, for the calamity indeed deserves tears. And the wounded man, again,—noth-

---

[1] [R. V., margin, "authority;" compare the next paragraph. On the order, see note 7, p. 196.—R]
[2] Matt. viii. 4.   [3] Matt. ix. 5, 6.
[4] διῳκισμένον, literally, "distributed into different habitations;" as when the population of Mantinea was broken up by the Lacedæmonians, διῳκίσθη ἡ Μαντινεία: see Xen. Hellenic, v. 2, 7; comp. Dem. de Pace, i. 59, ed. Reiske; de Fals. Leg. i. 366.
[5] λῦσαι.

[6] [τὸ ἄτυφον.]
[7] [The reference here seems to be to God, but a reflexive sense is not improbable; "indicates that He Himself is," etc.—R.]
[8] Matt. ix. 8. [R. V., "they were afraid," for "they marvelled" (A. V.) But Chrysostom's text agrees with that of the received, followed by the A. V.]
[9] προσίστατο αὐτοῖς.   [10] John ix. 16.

ing can so heal him as gentleness: gentleness, I say, which is mightier than any force.

See, for example, how He Himself, the insulted one, discourses with us, both in the Old Testament, and in the New; in the one saying, "O my people, what have I done unto thee?"[1] in the other, "Saul, Saul, why persecutest thou me."[2] And Paul too bids, "In meekness instruct those that oppose themselves."[3] And Christ again, when His disciples had come to Him, requiring fire to come down from heaven, strongly rebuked them, saying, "Ye know not what manner of spirit ye are of."[4]

And here again He said not, "O accursed, and sorcerers as ye are; O ye envious, and enemies of men's salvation;" but, "Wherefore think ye evil in your hearts?"

We must, you see, use gentleness to eradicate the disease. Since he who is become better through the fear of man, will quickly return to wickedness again. For this cause He commanded also the tares to be left, giving an appointed day of repentance. Yea, and many of them in fact repented, and became good, who before were bad; as for instance, Paul, the Publican, the Thief; for these being really tares turned into kindly wheat. Because, although in the seeds this cannot be, yet in the human will it is both manageable and easy; for our will is bound by no limits of nature, but hath freedom of choice for its privilege.

Accordingly, when thou seest an enemy of the truth, wait on him, take care of him, lead him back into virtue, by showing forth an excellent life, by applying "speech that cannot be condemned,"[5] by bestowing attention and tender care, by trying every means of amendment, in imitation of the best physicians. For neither do they cure in one manner only, but when they see the wound not yield to the first remedy, they add another, and after that again another; and now they use the knife, and now bind up. And do thou accordingly, having become a physician of souls, put in practice every mode of cure according to Christ's laws; that thou mayest receive the reward both of saving thyself and of profiting others, doing all to the glory of God, and so being glorified also thyself. "For them that glorify me," saith He, "I will glorify; and they that despise me, shall be lightly esteemed."[6]

Let us, I say, do all things unto His glory; that we may attain unto that blessed portion, unto which God grant we may all attain, by the grace and love towards man of our Lord Jesus Christ, to whom be glory and might forever and ever. Amen.

---

[1] Micah vi. 3.   [2] Acts ix. 4.   [3] 2 Tim. ii. 25.
[4] Luke ix. 55. [This clause is not found in the oldest Greek MSS. of the New Testament. Comp. R. V. text and margin.—R.]

[5] Tit. ii. 8.
[6] 1 Sam. ii. 30. ["Shall be despised," according to the form given in the text. But in the LXX. the last verb is not the same as the preceding one.—R.]

HOMILY XXX.

MATT. IX. 9.

"And as Jesus passed forth from thence, He saw a man sitting at the receipt of custom,[1] named Matthew; and He saith unto him, Follow me."

FOR when He had performed the miracle, He did not remain, lest, being in sight, He should kindle their jealousy the more; but He indulges them by retiring, and soothing their passion. This then let us also do, not encountering them that are plotting against us; let us rather soothe their wound, giving way and relaxing their vehemence.

But wherefore did He not call him together with Peter and John and the rest? As in their case He had come at that time, when He knew the men would obey Him; so Matthew also He then called when He was assured he would yield himself. And therefore Paul again He took, as a fisher his prey, after the resurrection. Because He who is acquainted with the hearts, and knows the secrets of each man's mind, knew also when each of these would obey. Therefore not at the beginning did He call him, when he was yet in

---

[1] [R. V., "at the place of toll."]

rather a hardened state, but after His count-less miracles, and the great fame concerning Him, when He knew him to have actually become more prepared for obedience.

And we have cause also to admire the self-denial[1] of the evangelist, how he disguises not his own former life, but adds even his name, when the others had concealed him under another appellation.[2]

But why did he say he was "sitting at the receipt of custom?" To indicate the power of Him that called him, that it was not when he had left off or forsaken this wicked trade, but from the midst of the evils He drew him up; much as He converted the blessed Paul also when frantic and raging, and darting fire; which thing he himself makes a proof of the power of Him that called him, saying to the Galatians, "Ye have heard of my conver-sation in time past in the Jews' religion, how that beyond measure I persecuted the church of God." [3]   And the fishermen too He called when they were in the midst of their business. But that was a craft not indeed in bad report, but of men rather rudely bred, not mingling with others, and endowed with great simplic-ity; whereas the pursuit now in question was one full of all insolence and boldness, and a mode of gain whereof no fair account could be given, a shameless traffic, a robbery under cloak of law: yet nevertheless He who uttered the call was ashamed of none of these things.

And why talk I of His not being ashamed of a publican? since even with regard to a harlot woman, so far from being ashamed to call her, He actually permitted her to kiss His feet, and to moisten them with her tears.[4] Yea, for to this end He came, not to cure bodies only, but to heal likewise the wicked-ness of the soul.   Which He did also in the case of the paralytic; and having shown clearly that He is able to forgive sins, then, not before, He comes to him whom we are now speaking of; that they might no more be troubled at seeing a publican chosen into the choir of the disciples.   For He that hath power to undo all our offenses, why marvel if He even make this man an apostle?

But as thou hast seen the power of Him that called, so consider also the obedience of him that was called: how he neither resisted, nor disputing said, "What is this?   Is it not indeed a deceitful calling, wherewith He calls me, being such as I am?" nay; for this humility again had been out of season: but he obeyed straightway, and did not even re-quest to go home, and to communicate with his relations concerning this matter; as

neither indeed did the fishermen; but as they left their net and their ship and their father, so did he his receipt of custom and his gain, and followed, exhibiting a mind prepared for all things; and breaking himself at once away from all worldly things, by his complete obe-dience he bare witness that He who called him had chosen a good time.

And wherefore can it be, one may say, that he hath not told us of the others also, how and in what manner they were called; but only of Peter and James, and John and Philip, and nowhere of the others?[5]

Because these more than others were in so strange and mean ways of life.   For there is nothing either worse than the publican's bus-iness, or more ordinary than fishing.   And that Philip also was among the very ignoble, is manifest from his country.   Therefore these especially they proclaim to us, with their ways of life, to show that we ought to believe them in the glorious parts of their his-tories also.   For they who choose not to pass by any of the things whch are accounted re-proachful, but are exact in publishing these more than the rest, whether they relate to the Teacher or to the disciples; how can they be suspected in the parts which claim reverence? more especially since many signs and miracles are passed over by them, while the events of the cross, accounted to be reproaches, they utter with exact care and loudly; and the disciples' pursuits too, and their faults, and those of their Master's ancestry who were notorious for sins,[6] they discover with a clear voice.   Whence it is manifest that they made much account of truth, and wrote nothing for favor, nor for display.

2. Having therefore called him, He also honored him with a very great honor by par-taking straightway of his table; for in this way He would both give him good hope for the future, and lead him on to a greater con-fidence.[7]   For not in a long time, but at once, He healed his vice.   And not with him only doth He sit down to meat, but with many others also; although this very thing was accounted a charge against Him, that He chased not away the sinners.   But neither do they conceal this point, what sort of blame is endeavored to be fixed on His proceedings.

Now the publicans come together as to one of the same trade; for he, exulting[8] in the entrance of Christ, had called them all to-gether.   The fact is, Christ used to try every kind of treatment; and not when discoursing only, nor when healing, nor when reproving

---

[1] φιλοσοφίαν.   [2] Mark ii. 14 ; Luke v. 27.
[3] Gal. i. 13.   [4] Luke vii. 38.

[5] It appears by this that St. Chrysostom did not consider Na-thanael to be the same with St. Bartholomew.
[6] Matt. iii. 6.   [7] παρῥησίαν.   [8] ἐγκαλλωπιζόμενος.

His enemies, but even at His morning meal, He would often correct such as were in a bad way; hereby teaching us, that every season and every work may by possibility afford us profit. And yet surely what was then set before them came of injustice and covetousness; but Christ refused not to partake of it, because the ensuing gain was to be great: yea rather He becomes partaker of the same roof and table with them that have committed such offenses. For such is the quality of a physician; unless he endure the corruption of the sick, he frees them not from their infirmity.

And yet undoubtedly He incurred hence an evil report; first by eating with him, then in Matthew's house, and thirdly, in company with many publicans. See at least how they reproach Him with this. "Behold a man gluttonous, and a winebibber, a friend of publicans and sinners."[1]

Let them hear, as many as are striving to deck themselves with great honor for fasting, and let them consider that our Lord was called "a man gluttonous and a winebibber," and He was not ashamed, but overlooked all these things, that he might accomplish what He had set before him; which indeed was accordingly done. For the publican was actually converted, and thus became a better man.

And to teach thee that this great thing was wrought by his partaking of the table with Him, hear what Zacchæus saith, another publican. I mean, when he heard Christ saying, "To-day, I must abide in thy house," the delight gave him wings, and he saith, "The half of my goods I give to the poor, and if I have taken anything from any man by false accusation, I restore him fourfold."[2] And to him Jesus saith, "This day is salvation come to this house." So possible is it by all ways to give instruction.

But how is it, one may say, that Paul commands, "If any man that is called a brother be a fornicator or covetous, with such an one no, not to eat?"[3] In the first place, it is not as yet manifest, whether to teachers also he gives this charge, and not rather to brethren only. Next, these were not yet of the number of the perfect,[4] nor of those who had become brethren. And besides, Paul commands, even with respect to them that had become brethren, then to shrink from them, when they continue as they were, but these had now ceased, and were converted.

3. But none of these things shamed the Pharisees, but they accuse Him to His disciples, saying,

"Why eateth your Master with publicans and sinners?"[5]

And when the disciples seem to be doing wrong, they intercede with Him, saying, "Behold thy disciples do that which is not lawful to do on the sabbath-day;"[6] but here to them they discredit Him. All which was the part of men dealing craftily, and wishing to separate from the Master the choir of the disciples.

What then saith Infinite Wisdom?

"They that be whole need not a physician," saith He, "but they that are sick."[7]

See how He turned their reasoning to the opposite conclusion. That is, while they made it a charge against Him that He was in company with these men: He on the contrary saith, that His not being with them would be unworthy of Him, and of His love of man; and that to amend such persons is not only blameless, but excellent, and necessary, and deserving of all sorts of praise.

After this, that He might not seem to put them that were bidden to shame, by saying, "they that are sick;" see how He makes up for it again, by reproving the others, and saying,

"Go ye and learn what that meaneth, I will have mercy, and not sacrifice."[8]

Now this He said, to upbraid them with their ignorance of the Scriptures. Wherefore also He orders His discourse more sharply, not Himself in anger, far from it; but so as that the publicans might not be in utter perplexity.

And yet of course He might say, "Did ye not mark, how I remitted the sins of the sick of the palsy, how I braced up his body?" But He saith no such thing, but argues with them first from men's common reasonings, and then from the Scriptures. For having said, "They that be whole need not a physician, but they that are sick;" and having covertly indicated that He Himself was the Physician; after that He said, "Go ye and learn what that meaneth, I will have mercy, and not sacrifice." Thus doth Paul also: when he had first established his reasoning by illustrations from common things, and had said, "Who feedeth a flock, and eateth not of the milk thereof?"[9] then he brings in the Scriptures also, saying, "It is written in the law of Moses, Thou shalt not muzzle the ox that treadeth out the corn;"[10] and again, "Even so hath the Lord ordained, that they

---

[1] Matt. xi. 19.
[2] Luke xix. 5, 8, 9.
[3] 1 Cor. v. 11.
[4] ἀπηρτισμένων.
[5] Matt. ix. 11.
[6] Matt. xii. 2.
[7] Matt. ix. 12. [R. V., "They that are whole have no need of a physician."]
[8] Matt. ix. 13.
[9] 1 Cor. ix. 7.
[10] 1 Cor. ix. 9. [R. V., "when he treadeth."] See Deut. xxv. 4.

which preach the gospel should live of the gospel." [1]

But to His disciples not so, but He puts them in mind of His signs, saying on this wise, "Do ye not yet remember the five loaves of the five thousand, and how many baskets ye took up?" [2] Not so however with these, but He reminds them of our common infirmity, and signifies them at any rate to be of the number of the infirm; who did not so much as know the Scriptures, but making light of the rest of virtue, laid all the stress on their sacrifices; which thing He is also earnestly intimating unto them, when He sets down in brief what had been affirmed by all the prophets,[3] saying, "Learn ye what that meaneth, I will have mercy, and not sacrifice."

The fact is, He is signifying hereby that not He was transgressing the law, but they; as if He had said, "Wherefore accuse me? Because I bring sinners to amendment? Why then ye must accuse the Father also for this." Much as He said also elsewhere, establishing this point: "My Father worketh hitherto, and I work:" [4] so here again, "Go ye and learn what that meaneth, I will have mercy, and not sacrifice." "For as this is His will, saith Christ, so also mine." Seest thou how the one is superfluous, the other necessary? For neither did He say, "I will have mercy, and sacrifice," but, "I will have mercy, and not sacrifice." That is, the one thing He allowed, the other He cast out; and proved that what they blamed, so far from being forbidden, was even ordained by the law, and more so than sacrifice; and He brings in the Old Testament, speaking words and ordaining laws in harmony with Himself.

Having then reproved them, both by common illustrations and by the Scriptures, He adds again,

"I am not come to call righteous men, but sinners to repentance." [5]

And this He saith unto them in irony; as when He said, "Behold, Adam is become as one of us;" [6] and again, "If I were hungry, I would not tell thee." [7] For that no man on earth was righteous, Paul declared, saying, "For all have sinned, and come short of the glory of God." [8] And by this too the others were comforted, I mean, the guests. "Why, I am so far," saith He, "from loathing sinners, that even for their sakes only am I

come." Then, lest He should make them more careless, He staid not at the word "sinners," but added, "unto repentance." "For I am not come that they should continue sinners, but that they should alter, and amend."

4. He then having stopped their mouths every way, as well from the Scriptures as from the natural consequence of things; and they having nothing to say, proved as they were obnoxious to the charges which they had brought against Him, and adversaries of the law and the Old Testament; they leave Him, and again transfer their accusation to the disciples.

And Luke indeed affirms that the Pharisees said it, but this evangelist, that it was the disciples of John; [9] but it is likely that both said it. That is, they being, as might be expected, in utter perplexity, take the other sort with them; as they did afterwards with the Herodians likewise. Since in truth John's disciples were always disposed to be jealous of Him, and reasoned against Him: being then only humbled, when first John abode in the prison. They came at least then, "and told Jesus;" [10] but afterwards they returned to their former envy.

Now what say they? "Why do we and the Pharisees fast oft, but thy disciples fast not?" [11]

This is the disease, which Christ long before was eradicating, in the words, "When thou fastest, anoint thy head, and wash thy face;" [12] foreknowing the evils that spring therefrom. But yet He doth not rebuke even these, nor say, "O ye vainglorious and over-busy;" but He discourses to them with all gentleness, saying, "The children of the bridechamber cannot fast, as long as the bridegroom is with them." [13] Thus, when others were to be spoken for, the publicans I mean, to soothe their wounded soul, He was more severe in His reproof of their revilers; but when they were deriding Himself and His disciples, He makes His reply with all gentleness.

Now their meaning is like this; "Granted," say they, "Thou doest this as a physician; why do Thy disciples also leave fasting, and cleave to such tables?" Then, to make the accusation heavier, they put themselves first, and then the Pharisees; wishing by the comparison to aggravate the charge. For indeed "both we," it is said, "and the Pharisees, fast oft." And in truth they did fast, the one having learnt it from John, the other

---

[1] 1 Cor. ix. 14 ; comp. Matt. x. 10.   [2] Matt. xvi. 9.
[3] See Hosea vi. 6; Ps. l. 8-15 ; Prov. xxi. 3 ; Isa. i. 11-15 ; Micah vi. 6, 7, 8.
[4] John v. 17.
[5] Matt. ix. 13. [The best Greek MSS., with the Vulgate (so Augustin) do not sustain the reading: "unto repentance." Comp. Luke v. 32.—R.]
[6] Gen. iii. 22, LXX.   [7] Ps. l. 12.   [8] Rom. iii. 23.

[9] Comp. Matt. ix. 14 ; Luke v. 33, &c., and Mark ii. 18, &c.
[10] See Matt. xiv. 12.   [11] Matt. ix. 14.   [12] Matt. vi. 17.
[13] Matt. ix. 15. Comp. Mark ii. 19 ; Luke v. 33.

from the law; even as also the Pharisee said, "I fast twice in the week."[1]

What then saith Jesus? "Can the children of the bridechamber fast, while the bridegroom is with them." Before, He called Himself a physician, but here a bridegroom; by these names revealing His unspeakable mysteries. Yet of course He might have told them, more sharply, "These things depend not on you, that you should make such laws. For of what use is fasting, when the mind is full of wickedness; when ye blame others, when ye condemn them, bearing about beams in your eyes, and do all for display? Nay, before all this ye ought to have cast out vainglory, to be proficients in all the other duties, in charity, meekness, brotherly love." However, nothing of this kind doth He say, but with all gentleness, "The children of the bridechamber cannot fast, so long as the bridegroom is with them;" recalling to their mind John's words, when he said, "He that hath the bride, is the bridegroom, but the friend of the bridegroom, which standeth and heareth Him, rejoiceth greatly because of the bridegroom's voice."[2]

Now His meaning is like this: The present time is of joy and gladness, therefore do not bring in the things which are melancholy. For fasting is a melancholy thing, not in its own nature, but to them that are yet in rather a feeble state; for to those at least that are willing to practise self-command, the observance is exceedingly pleasant and desirable. For as when the body is in health, the spirits are high,[3] so when the soul is well conditioned, the pleasure is greater. But according to their previous impression He saith this. So also Isaiah,[4] discoursing of it, calls it "an affliction of the soul;" and Moses too in like manner.

Not however by this only doth He stop their mouths, but by another topic also, saying,

"Days will come, when the bridegroom shall be taken from them, and then shall they fast."[5]

For hereby He signifies, that what they did was not of gluttony, but pertained to some marvellous dispensation. And at the same time He lays beforehand the foundation of what He was to say touching His passion, in His controversies with others instructing His disciples, and training them now to be versed in the things which are deemed sorrowful. Because for themselves already to have this said to them, would have been grievous and galling, since we know that afterwards, being

uttered, it troubled them;[6] but spoken to others, it would become rather less intolerable to them.

It being also natural for them to pride themselves on John's calamity, He from this topic represses likewise such their elation: the doctrine however of His resurrection He adds not yet, it not being yet time. For so much indeed was natural, that one supposed to be a man should die, but that other was beyond nature.

5. Then what He had done before, this He doth here again. I mean, that as He, when they were attempting to prove Him blameable for eating with sinners, proved to them on the contrary, that His proceeding was not only no blame, but an absolute praise to Him: so here too, when they wanted to show of Him, that He knows not how to manage His disciples, He signifies that such language was the part of men not knowing how to manage their inferences,[7] but finding fault at random.

"For no man," saith He, putteth a piece of new cloth unto an old garment."[8]

He is again establishing His argument by illustrations from common life. And what He saith is like this, "The disciples have not yet become strong, but still need much condescension. They have not yet been renewed by the Spirit, and on persons in that state one ought not to lay any burden of injunctions."

And these things He said, setting laws and rules for His own disciples, that when they should have to receive as disciples those of all sorts that should come from the whole world, they might deal with them very gently.

"Neither do men put new wine into old bottles."[9]

Seest thou His illustrations, how like the Old Testament? the garment? the wine skins? For Jeremiah too calls the people "a girdle," and makes mention again of "bottles" and of "wine."[10] Thus, the discourse being about gluttony and a table, He takes His illustrations from the same.

But Luke[11] adds something more, that the new also is rent, if thou put it upon the old. Seest thou that so far from any advantage taking place, rather the mischief is increased?

---

[6] Matt. xvi. 22, xvii. 23.
[7] κεχρῆσθαι τοῖς ἑπομένοις, "to treat their followers." The last editor thinks there is a designed play upon the words, by way of rhetorical turn, here.
[8] Matt. ix. 15. [The three accounts of the sayings in verses 15-17 vary greatly in form, and the authorities for the Greek text present a great number of various readings. It will be sufficient to refer to the R. V., and to note a few verbal changes.—R.]
[9] Matt. ix. 17. [R. V., "wine-skins." Comp. the next paragraph.]
[10] Jer. xiii. 10-12.   [11] See Luke v. 36, 37.   τὸ καινὸν σχίζει.

[1] Luke xviii. 12.   [2] John iii. 29.   [3] [πολλὴ ἡ εὐφροσύνη.]
[4] Lit., "humiliation."   Isa. lviii. 3 ; Numb. xxix. 7.
[5] Matt. ix. 15.

And while He speaks of the present, He foretells also the future; as that they shall hereafter be new, but until that come to pass, nothing austere and grievous ought to be imposed on them. For he, saith Christ, that seeks to instill the high doctrines before the proper time, thenceforth not even when the time calls will he find them to his purpose, having once for all made them unprofitable. And this comes to pass not by any fault of the wine, nor of the deceivers, but from the unseasonable act of them that put it in.

Hereby He hath taught us also the cause of those lowly expressions, which He was continually using in discourse with them. That is, by reason of their infirmity He said many things very short of His proper dignity: which John also pointing out, relates Him to have said, "I have many things to say unto you, but ye cannot bear them now."[1] Here, that they might not suppose those things only to be which He had spoken, but might imagine to themselves others also, and far greater; He set before them their own infirmity, with a promise that when they should have become strong, He would tell them also the rest; which thing He saith here too, "Days will come, when the bridegroom shall be taken from them, and then shall they fast."

6. Therefore neither let us require all things of all men in the beginning, but so much as is possible; and soon shall we have made our way to the rest. But if thou art urgent and in haste, for this very cause I bid thee urge not, because thou art in haste. And if the saying seem to thee a riddle, learn it from the very nature of the things, and then wilt thou see the whole force thereof.

And let none move thee of those who find fault unseasonably; since here too the censurers were Pharisees, and the reproached, disciples; nevertheless, none of these things persuaded Christ to reverse His judgment, neither did He say, "it is a shame for these to fast, and for those not to fast." But as the perfect pilot heeds not the troubled waves, but his own art; so at that time did Christ. For in truth it was a shame, not that they should forbear fasting, but that on account of the fast they should be wounded in vital points, and be cut off, and broken away.

These things then let us also bear in mind, and treat accordingly all those that belong to us. Yea, if thou have a wife fond of dress, gaping and eager after modes of painting the face, and dissolved in great luxury, and talkative, and foolish (although it is not

of course possible that all these should concur in one woman; however let us frame in our discourse a woman of that sort).

"Why then is it," some one may say, "that thou fashionest a woman, and not a man?" There are men too worse than this woman. But forasmuch as the authority is intrusted to men, we accordingly are framing a woman, for the present, not as though vice more abounded in them. For there are many things to be found in men also, which are not amongst women; as for instance man-slaying, breaking open of tombs, fighting with wild beasts, and many such like things. Think not therefore that we do this as undervaluing the sex; it is not, it is not this, but thus it was convenient at present to sketch out the picture.

Let us then suppose such a woman, and let her husband endeavor in every way to reform her. How then shall he reform her? Not by enjoining all at once, but the easier things first, and in matters by which she is not vehemently possessed. For if thou hasten to reform her entirely at the beginning, thou hast ruined all. Do not accordingly take off her golden ornaments at once, but let her have them, and wear them for a time, for this seems a less evil than her paintings and shadings. Let these therefore be first taken away, and not even these by fear and threatening, but by persuasion and mildness, and by blaming of others, and by your own opinion and judgment. And tell her continually, that to thee a countenance so decked up is not lovely, but rather in a high degree unpleasing, and persuade her above all things that this vexes thee. And after thine own suffrage, bring in also the judgment expressed by others, and say that even beautiful women are wont to be disfigured by this; that thou mayest root out the passion. And say nothing yet of hell, or of the kingdom, for thou wilt talk of these things in vain: but persuade her that she pleases thee more by displaying the work of God undisguised; but she who tortures, and strains, and daubs her countenance, doth not even to people in general appear fair and beautiful. And first by common reasonings and the suffrages of all men expel the pest, and when thou hast softened her down by these words, add also the other considerations. And though thou shouldest speak once and not persuade her, do not grow weary of pouring in[2] the same words, a second and a third time and often; not however in a wearisome kind of way, but sport-

---

[1] John xvi. 12.

[2] ἐπαντλῶν, "using fomentation." See Mr. Field's note on the place.

ively; and do thou now turn from her, now flatter and court her.

Seest thou not the painters, how much they rub out, how much they insert, when they are making a beautiful portrait? Well then, do not thou prove inferior to these. For if these, in drawing the likeness of a body, used such great diligence, how much more were it meet for us, in fashioning a soul, to use every contrivance. For if thou shouldest fashion well the form of this soul, thou wilt not see the countenance of the body looking unseemly, nor lips stained, nor a mouth like a bear's mouth dyed with blood, nor eyebrows blackened as with the smut of some kitchen vessel, nor cheeks whitened with dust like the walls of the tombs. For all these things are smut, and cinders, and dust, and signals of extreme deformity.

But stay: I have been led on unobserving, I know not how, into these expressions; and while admonishing another to teach with gentleness, I have been myself hurried away[1] into wrath. Let us return therefore again unto the more gentle way of admonition, and let us bear with all the faults of our wives, that we may succeed in doing what we would. Seest thou not how we bear with the cries of children, when we would wean them from the breast, how we endure all for this object only, that we may persuade them to despise their former food? Thus let us do in this case also, let us bear with all the rest, that we may accomplish this. For when this hath been amended, thou wilt see the other too proceeding in due order, and thou wilt come again unto the ornaments of gold, and in the same way wilt reason concerning them likewise, and thus by little and little bringing thy wife unto the right rule, thou wilt be a beautiful painter, a faithful servant, an excellent husbandman.

Together with these things remind her also of the women of old, of Sarah, of Rebecca, both of the fair and of them that were not so, and point out how all equally practised modesty. For even Leah, the wife of the patriarch, not being fair, was not constrained to devise any such thing, but although she were uncomely, and not very much beloved by her husband, she neither devised any such thing, nor marred her countenance, but continued to preserve the lineaments thereof undisfigured, and this though brought up by Gentiles.[2]

But thou that art a believing woman, thou that hast Christ for thine head, art thou bringing in upon us a satanic art? And dost thou not call to mind the water that dashed over thy countenance, the sacrifice that adorns thy lips, the blood that hath reddened thy tongue? For if thou wouldest consider all these things, though thou wert fond of dress to the ten thousandth degree, thou wilt not venture nor endure to put upon thee that dust and those cinders. Learn that thou hast been joined unto Christ, and refrain from this unseemliness. For neither is He delighted with these colorings, but He seeks after another beauty, of which He is in an exceeding degree a lover, I mean, that in the soul. This the prophet likewise hath charged thee to cherish, and hath said, "So shall the King have pleasure in thy beauty."[3]

Let us not therefore be curious in making ourselves unseemly. For neither is any one of God's works imperfect, nor doth it need to be set right by thee. For not even if to an image of the emperor, after it was set up, any one were to seek to add his own work, would the attempt be safe, but he will incur extreme danger. Well then, man works and thou addest not; but doth God work, and dost thou amend it? And dost thou not consider the fire of hell? Dost thou not consider the destitution of thy soul? For on this account it is neglected, because all thy care is wasted on the flesh.

But why do I speak of the soul? For to the very flesh everything falls out contrary to what ye have sought. Consider it. Dost thou wish to appear beautiful? This shows thee uncomely. Dost thou wish to please thy husband? This rather grieves him; and causes not him only, but strangers also, to become thine accusers. Wouldest thou appear young? This will quickly bring thee to old age. Wouldest thou wish to array thyself honorably? This makes thee to be ashamed. For such an one is ashamed not only before those of her own rank, but even those of her maids who are in her secret, and those of her servants who know; and, above all, before herself.

But why need I say these things? For that which is more grievous than all I have now omitted, namely, that thou dost offend God; thou underminest modesty, kindlest the flame of jealousy, emulatest the harlot women at their brothel.

All these things then consider, ye women, and laugh to scorn the pomp of Satan and the craft of the devil; and letting go this adorning, or rather disfiguring, cultivate that beauty in your own souls which is lovely even to angels, and desired of God, and delightful

---

[1] ἐξεκυλίσθην.
[2] ['Ελλήνων ; see note on Homily XII. 5, p. 79.--R.]

[3] Ps. xlv. 11.

to your husbands; that ye may attain both unto present glory, and unto that which is to come. To which God grant that we may all attain, by the grace and love towards man of our Lord Jesus Christ, to whom be glory and might forever and ever. Amen.

HOMILY XXXI.

MATT. IX. 18.

" While He spake these things unto them, behold, there came in [1] a ruler, and worshipped Him, saying, My daughter is even now dead; but come and lay Thy hand upon her, and she shall live."

THE deed overtook the words; so that the mouths of the Pharisees were the more stopped. For both he that came was a ruler of the synagogue, and his affliction terrible. For the young damsel was both his only child, and twelve years old, the very flower of her age; on which account especially He raised her up again, and that immediately.

And if Luke say that men came, saying, " Trouble not the Master, for she is dead; " [2] we will say this, that the expression, " she is even now dead," was that of one conjecturing from the time of his journeying, or exaggerating his affliction. For it is an usual thing with persons in need to heighten their own evils by their report, and to say something more than is really true, the more to attract those whom they are beseeching.

But see his dullness: how he requires of Christ two things, both His actual presence, and the laying on of His hand: and this by the way is a sign that he had left her still breathing. This Naaman also, that Syrian, required of the prophet. " For I thought," saith he, " he will surely come out, and will lay on his hand." [3] For in truth they who are more or less dull of temper, require sight and sensible things.

And whereas Mark [4] saith, He took the three disciples, and so doth Luke; [5] our evangelist merely saith, " the disciples." Wherefore then did He not take with Him Matthew, though he had but just come unto Him? To bring him to a more earnest longing, and because he was yet rather in an imperfect state. For to this intent doth He honor those, that these may grow such as those are. But for him it sufficed for the present, to see what befell the woman with the issue of blood, and to be honored by His table, and by His partaking of his salt.

And when He had risen up many followed Him, as for a great miracle, both on account of the person who had come, and because the more part being of a grosser disposition were seeking not so much the care of the soul, as the healing of the body; and they flowed together, some urged by their own afflictions, some hastening to behold how other men's were cured: however, there were as yet but few in the habit of coming principally for the sake of His words and doctrine. Nevertheless, He did not suffer them to enter into the house, but His disciples only; and not even all of these, everywhere instructing us to repel the applause of the multitude.

2. "And, behold," it is said, " a woman that had an issue of blood twelve years, came behind Him, and touched the hem of His garment. For she said within herself, If I may but touch His garment, I shall be whole." [6]

Wherefore did she not approach Him boldly? She was ashamed on account of her affliction, accounting herself to be unclean. For if the menstruous woman was judged not to be clean, much more would she have the same thought, who was afflicted with such a disease; since in fact that complaint was under the law accounted a great uncleanness. [7] Therefore she lies hidden, and conceals herself. For neither had she as yet the proper and correct opinion concerning Him: else she

---

[1] [εἰϛελθών, " came in," so Tischendorf, but the R. V. accepts the reading εἰϛ ἐλθών, " there came one ruler."—R.]
[2] Luke viii. 49.   [3] 2 Kings v. 11, LXX.
[4] Mark v. 37.   [5] Luke viii. 51.

[6] Matt. ix. 21, 22. [R. V., " border " for " hem ;" " do " for " may ;" " made whole " for " whole."]
[7] Levit. xv. 25.

would not have thought to be concealed. And this is the first woman that came unto Him in public, having heard of course that He heals women also, and that He is on His way to the little daughter that was dead.

And she durst not invite him to her house, although she was wealthy;[1] nay, neither did she approach publicly, but secretly with faith she touched His garments. For she did not doubt, nor say in herself, " Shall I indeed be delivered from the disease? shall I indeed fail of deliverance?" But confident of her health, she so approached Him. " For she said," we read, " in herself, If I may only touch His garment, I shall be whole." Yea, for she saw out of what manner of house He was come, that of the publicans, and who they were that followed Him, sinners and publicans; and all these things made her to be of good hope.

What then doth Christ? He suffers her not to be hid, but brings her into the midst, and makes her manifest for many purposes.

It is true indeed that some of the senseless ones say, " He does this for love of glory. For why," say they, " did He not suffer her to be hid?" What sayest thou, unholy, yea, all unholy one? He that enjoins silence, He that passes by miracles innumerable, is He in love with glory?

For what intent then doth He bring her forward? In the first place He puts an end to the woman's fear, lest being pricked by her conscience, as having stolen the gift, she should abide in agony. In the second place, He sets her right, in respect of her thinking to be hid. Thirdly, He exhibits her faith to all, so as to provoke the rest also to emulation; and His staying of the fountains of her blood was no greater sign than He affords in signifying His knowledge of all things. Moreover the ruler of the synagogue, who was on the point of thorough unbelief, and so of utter ruin, He corrects by the woman. Since both they that came said, " Trouble not the Master, for the damsel is dead;" and those in the house laughed Him to scorn, when He said, " She sleepeth;" and it was likely that the father too should have experienced some such feeling. Therefore to correct this weakness beforehand, He brings forward the simple woman. For as to that ruler being quite of the grosser sort, hear what He

saith unto him: " Fear not, do thou believe only, and she shall be made whole."[2]

Thus He waited also on purpose for death to come on, and that then He should arrive; in order that the proof of the resurrection might be distinct. With this view He both walks more leisurely, and discourses more with the woman; that He might give time for the damsel to die, and for those to come, who told of it, and said, " Trouble not the Master."[3] This again surely the evangelist obscurely signifies, when he saith, " While He yet spake, there came from the house certain which said, Thy daughter is dead, trouble not the Master." For His will was that her death should be believed, that her resurrection might not be suspected. And this He doth in every instance. So also in the case of Lazarus, He waited a first and a second and a third day.[4]

On account then of all these things He brings her forward, and saith, " Daughter, be of good cheer,"[5] even as He had said also to the paralyzed person, " Son, be of good cheer." Because in truth the woman was exceedingly alarmed; therefore He saith, " be of good cheer," and He calls her " daughter;" for her faith had made her a daughter. After that comes also her praise: " Thy faith hath made thee whole."

But Luke tells us also other things more than these concerning the woman. Thus, when she had approached Him, saith he, and had received her health, Christ did not immediately call her, but first He saith, " Which is he that touched me?" Then when Peter and they that were with Him said, Master, the multitude throng Thee, and press Thee, and sayest Thou, who touched me?"[6] (which was a very sure sign both that He was encompassed with real flesh, and that He trampled on all vainglory, for they did not follow Him at all afar off, but thronged Him on every side); He for His part continued to say, " Somebody hath touched me, for I perceive that virtue is gone out of me;"[7] answering after a grosser manner according to the impression of His hearers. But these things He said, that He might also induce her of herself to make confession. For on this account neither did He immediately convict her, in order that having signified that He knows all things clearly, He might induce her of her own accord to publish all, and work upon her to proclaim herself what had been done, and that He might not incur suspicion by saying it.

---

[1] Eusebius, E. H., viii. 18, mentions a tradition that she belonged to Cæsarea Philippi, otherwise called Paneas, and that certain brazen statues, of a man holding out his hand and a woman kneeling, which were there in his time, were set up at her expense, that being her native place. He adds, that a certain plant which grew by the Saviour's statue, when it came to touch the hem of His garment, stopped growing; and that it was endowed with virtue to cure all manner of diseases.

[2] Luke viii. 50.　　[3] Mark v. 35 ; Luke viii. 49.
[4] John xi. 6, 39.　　[5] Matt. ix. 22 ; see verse 2.
[6] Luke viii. 45.　　[7] Luke viii. 46. [R. V., " power."]

Seest thou the woman superior to the ruler of the synagogue? She detained Him not, she took no hold of Him, but touched Him only with the end of her fingers, and though she came later, she first went away healed. And he indeed was bringing the Physician altogether to his house, but for her a mere touch suffered. For though she was bound by her affliction, yet her faith had given her wings. And mark how He comforts her, saying, "Thy faith hath saved thee." Now surely, had He drawn her forward for display, He would not have added this; but He saith this, partly teaching the ruler of the synagogue to believe, partly proclaiming the woman's praise, and affording her by these words delight and advantage equal to her bodily health.

For that He did this as minded to glorify her, and to amend others, and not to show Himself glorious, is manifest from hence; that He indeed would have been equally an object of admiration even without this (for the miracles were pouring around Him faster than the snow-flakes, and He both had done and was to do far greater things than these): but the woman, had this not happened, would have gone away hid, deprived of those great praises. For this cause He brought her forward, and proclaimed her praise, and cast out her fear, (for "she came," it is said, "trembling"[1]); and He caused her to be of good courage, and together with health of body, He gave her also other provisions for her journey, in that He said, "Go in peace."[2]

3. "And when He came into the ruler's house, and saw the minstrels and the people making a noise, He saith unto them, Give place, for the maid is not dead, but sleepeth. And they laughed Him to scorn."[3]

Noble tokens, surely, these, of the rulers of synagogues; in the moment of her death pipes and cymbals raising a dirge! What then doth Christ? All the rest He cast out, but the parents He brought in; to leave no room for saying that He healed her in any other way. And before her resurrection too, He raises her in His word; saying, "The maid is not dead, but sleepeth." And in many instances besides He doeth this. As then on the sea He expels tumult from the mind of the by-standers, at the same time both signifying that it is easy for Him to raise the dead (which same thing He did with respect to Lazarus also, saying, "Our friend Lazarus sleepeth[4]);" and also teaching us

not to fear death; for that it is not death, but is henceforth become a sleep. Thus, since He Himself was to die, He doth in the persons of others prepare His disciples beforehand to be of good courage, and to bear the end meekly. Since in truth, when He had come, death was from that time forward a sleep.

But yet they laughed Him to scorn: He however was not indignant at being disbelieved by those for whom He was a little afterwards to work miracles; neither did He rebuke their laughter, in order that both it and the pipes, and the cymbals, and all the other things, might be a sure proof of her death. For since for the most part, after the miracles are done, men disbelieve, He takes them beforehand by their own answers; which was done in the case both of Lazarus and of Moses. For to Moses first He saith, "What is that in thine hand?"[5] in order that when he saw it become a serpent, He should not forget that it was a rod before, but being reminded of his own saying, might be amazed at what was done. And with regard to Lazarus He saith, "Where have ye laid him?"[6] that they who had said, "Come and see," and "he stinketh, for he hath been dead four days," might no longer be able to disbelieve His having raised a dead man.

Seeing then the cymbals and the multitude, He put them all out, and in the presence of the parents works the miracle; not introducing another soul, but recalling the same that had gone out, and awakening her as it were out of a sleep.

And He holds her by the hand, assuring the beholders; so as by that sight to make a way for the belief of her resurrection. For whereas the father said, "Lay thy hand upon her;"[7] He on His part doth somewhat more, for He lays no hand on her, but rather takes hold of her, and raises her, implying that to Him all things are ready. And He not only raises her up, but also commands to give her meat, that the event might not seem to be an illusion. And He doth not give it Himself, but commands them; as also with regard to Lazarus He said, "Loose him, and let him go,"[8] and afterwards makes him partaker of His table.[9] For so is He wont always to establish both points, making out with all completeness the demonstration alike of the death and of the resurrection.

But do thou mark, I pray thee, not her resurrection only, but also His commanding "to tell no man;" and by all learn thou this especially, His freedom from haughtiness

---

[1] Luke viii. 47. [The English rendering has been modified to indicate more exactly the words cited.--R.]
[2] Luke viii. 48.
[3] Matt. ix. 23, 24. [R. V., "the flute-players, and the crowds making a tumult."]   [4] John xi. 11.

[5] Ex. iv. 2.   [6] John xi. 34, 39.   [7] Matt. ix. 18.
[8] John xi. 44.   [9] John xii. 2.

and vainglory. And withal learn this other thing also, that He cast them that were beating themselves out of the house, and declared them unworthy of such a sight; and do not thou go out with the minstrels, but remain with Peter, and John, and James.

For if He cast them out then, much more now. For then it was not yet manifest that death was become a sleep, but now this is clearer than the very sun itself. But is it that He hath not raised thy daughter now? But surely He will raise her, and with more abundant glory. For that damsel, when she had risen, died again; but thy child, if she rise again, abides thenceforth in immortal being.

4. Let no man therefore beat himself any more, nor wail, neither disparage Christ's achievement. For indeed He overcame death. Why then dost thou wail for nought? The thing is become a sleep. Why lament and weep? Why, even if Greeks[1] did this, they should be laughed to scorn; but when the believer behaves himself unseemly in these things, what plea hath he? What excuse will there be for them that are guilty of such folly, and this, after so long a time, and so clear proof of the resurrection?

But thou, as though laboring to add to the charge against thee, dost also bring us in heathen women singing dirges, to kindle thy feelings, and to stir up the furnace thoroughly: and thou hearkenest not to Paul, saying, "What concord hath Christ with Belial? or what part hath he that believeth with an infidel?"[2]

And while the children of heathens, who know nothing of resurrection, do yet find words of consolation, saying, "Bear it manfully, for it is not possible to undo what hath taken place, nor to amend it by lamentations;" art not thou, who hearest sayings wiser and better than these, ashamed to behave thyself more unseemly than they? For we say not at all, "Bear it manfully, because it is not possible to undo what hath taken place," but, "bear it manfully, because he will surely rise again;" the child sleeps and is not dead; he is at rest and hath not perished. For resurrection will be his final lot, and eternal life, and immortality, and an angel's portion. Hearest thou not the Psalm that saith, "Return unto thy rest, O my soul, for the Lord hath dealt bountifully with thee?"[3] God calleth it "bountiful dealing," and dost thou make lamentation?

And what more couldest thou have done,

if thou wert a foe and an enemy of the dead? Why, if there must be mourning, it is the devil that ought to mourn. He may beat himself, he may wail, at our journeying to greater blessings. This lamentation becomes his wickedness, not thee, who art going to be crowned and to rest. Yea, for death is a fair haven. Consider, at any rate, with how many evils our present life is filled; reflect how often thou thyself hast cursed our present life. For indeed things go on to worse, and from the very beginning thou wert involved in no small condemnation. For, saith He, "In sorrow thou shalt bring forth children;" and, "In the sweat of thy face shalt thou eat thy bread;"[4] and, "In the world ye shall have tribulation."[5]

But of our state there, no such word at all is spoken, but all the contrary; that "grief and sorrow and sighing have fled away."[6] And that "men shall come from the east and from the west, and shall recline in the bosoms of Abraham and Isaac and Jacob."[7] And that the region there is a spiritual bride-chamber, and bright lamps, and a translation to Heaven.

5. Why then disgrace the departed? Why dispose the rest to fear and tremble at death? Why cause many to accuse God, as though He had done very dreadful things? Or rather, why after this invite poor persons, and entreat priests to pray?[8] "In order," saith he, "that the dead may depart into rest; that he may find the Judge propitious." For these things then art thou mourning and wailing? Thou art therefore fighting and warring with thyself: exciting a storm against thyself on account of his having entered into harbor.

"But what can I do?" saith he: "such a thing is nature." The blame is not nature's, neither doth it belong to the necessary consequence of the thing; but it is we that are turning all things upside down, are overcome with softness, are giving up our proper nobility, and are making the unbelievers worse. For how shall we reason with another concerning immortality? how shall we persuade the heathen, when we fear death, and shudder at it more than he? Many, for instance, among the Greeks[9] although they knew nothing of course about immortality, have crowned themselves at the decease of their children, and appeared in white garments,

---

[1] [Probably "Gentiles" or "heathen" would be a better reading. The contrast is with "believer."—R.]
[2] 2 Cor. vi. 15. [R. V., "unbeliever."]　　　[3] Ps. cxvi. 7.

[4] Gen. iii. 16, 19.　　　　　　　　[5] John xvi. 33.
[6] Is. xxxv. 10.　　　　　　　　　[7] Matt. viii. 11.
[8] Because the feasts and prayers for the dead being supposed to benefit those only who have fallen asleep in the Lord, and whose final happiness was therefore sure, it was an inconsistency in those who celebrated them to sorrow as if they had no hope. See Bingham, b. xxiii. c. iii. secs. 13, 15.
[9] [Or, "Gentiles."]

that they might reap the present glory; but thou not even for the future glory's sake ceasest thy woman's behavior and wailing.

But hast thou no heirs, nor any to succeed to thy goods? And which wouldest thou rather, that he should be heir of thy possessions, or of Heaven? And which didst thou desire, that he should succeed to the things that perish, which he must have let go soon after, or to things that remain, and are immoveable? Thou hadst him not for heir, but God had him instead of thee; he became not joint-heir with his own brethren, but he became " joint-heir with Christ."

" But to whom," saith he, " are we to leave our garments, to whom our houses, to whom our slaves and our lands?" To him again, and more securely than if he lived; for there is nothing to hinder. For if barbarians burn the goods of the departed together with them, much more were it a righteous thing for thee to send away with the dead what things he hath: not to be turned to ashes, like those, but to invest him with more glory; and that if he departed a sinner, it may do away his sins;[1] but if righteous, that it may become an increase of reward and recompense.

But dost thou long to see him? Then live the same life with him, and thou wilt soon obtain that sacred vision.

And herewith consider this also, that though thou shouldest not hearken to us, thou wilt certainly yield to time. But no reward then for thee; for the consolation comes of the number of the days. Whereas if thou art willing now to command thyself, thou wilt gain two very great points: first, thou wilt deliver thyself from the intervening ills, next, thou wilt be crowned with the brighter crown from God. For indeed neither almsgiving nor anything else is nearly so great as bearing affliction meekly.

Bear in mind, that even the Son of God died: and He indeed for thee, but thou for thyself. And when He said, " If it be possible, let the cup pass from me,"[2] and suffered pain, and was in agony, nevertheless He shunned not the end, but underwent it, and that with its whole course of exceeding woe.[3] That is, He did by no means simply endure death, but the most shameful death; and before His death, stripes; and before His stripes, upbraidings, and jeers, and revilings; instructing thee to bear all manfully.

And though He died, and put off His body, He resumed it again in greater glory, herein also holding out to thee good hopes. If these things be not a fable, lament not. If thou account these things to be sure, weep not; but if thou dost weep, how wilt thou be able to persuade the Greek that thou believest?

6. But even so doth the event still appear intolerable to thee? Well then, for this very cause it is not meet to lament for him, for he is delivered from many such calamities. Grudge not therefore against him, neither envy him: for to ask death for yourself because of his premature end, and to lament for him that he did not live to endure many such things, is rather the part of one grudging and envying.

And think not of this, that he will no more return home: but that thyself also art a little while after to go to him. Regard not this, that he returns here no more, but that neither do these things that are seen remain such as they are, but these too are being transformed. Yea, for heaven, and earth, and sea, and all, are being put together afresh,[4] and then shalt thou recover thy child in greater glory.

And if indeed he departed a sinner, his wickedness is stayed; for certainly, had God known that he was being converted, He would not have snatched him away before his repentance: but if he ended his life righteous, he now possesses all good in safety. Whence it is manifest that thy tears are not of kindly affection, but of unreasoning passion. For if thou lovedst the departed, thou shouldest rejoice and be glad that he is delivered from the present waves.

For what is there more, I pray thee? What is there fresh and new? Do we not see the same things daily revolving? Day and night, night and day, winter and summer, summer and winter, and nothing more. And these indeed are ever the same; but our evils are fresh, and newer. Wouldest thou then have him every day drawing up more of these things, and abiding here, and sickening, and mourning, and in fear and trembling, and enduring some of the ills of life, dreading others lest he some time endure them? Since assuredly thou canst not say this, that one sailing over this great sea might possibly be free from despondency and cares, and from all other such things.

And withal take this also into account, that thou didst not bring him forth immortal; and that if he had not died now, he must have endured it soon after. But is it that thou hadst not thy fill of him? But thou wilt of a

---

[1] Not that St. Chrysostom imagined that anything could be done to change the relative condition of those who have died in the favor or displeasure of God: see *e. g.*, Hom. XXXVI. p. 506, ed. Field. Indeed, the same is implied in the words which immediately follow, " Dost thou long to see him? Then live the same life with him," &c.

[2] Matt. xxvi. 39.　　　[3] μετὰ πολλῆς τῆς τραγῳδίας.

[4] μεθαρμόζεται.

certainty enjoy him there. But longest thou to see him here also? And what is there to hinder thee? For thou art permitted even here, if thou be watchful; for the hope of the things to come is clearer than sight.

But thou, if he were in some king's court wouldest not ever seek to see him, so long as thou heardest of his good report: and seeing him departed to the things that are far better, art thou faint-hearted about a little time; and that, when thou hast in his place one to dwell with thee?

But hast thou no husband? yet hast thou a consolation, even the Father of the orphans, and Judge of the widows. Hear even Paul pronouncing this widowhood blessed, and saying, "Now she that is a widow indeed and desolate, trusteth in the Lord."[1] Because such an one will appear more approved, evincing as she doth greater patience. Mourn not therefore for that which is thy crown, that for which thou demandest a reward.

Since thou hast also restored His deposit, if thou hast exhibited the very thing entrusted to thee. Be not in care any more, having laid up the possession in an inviolable treasure-house.

But if thou wouldest really learn, both what is our present being, and what our life to come; and that the one is a spider's web and a shadow, but the things there, all of them, immoveable and immortal; thou wouldest not after that want other arguments. For whereas now thy child is delivered from all change; if he were here, perhaps he might continue good, perhaps not so. Seest thou not how many openly cast off[2] their own children? how many are constrained to keep them at home, although worse than the open outcasts?

Let us make account of all these things and practise self-command; for so shall we at once show regard to the deceased, and enjoy much praise from men, and receive from God the great rewards of patience, and attain unto the good things eternal; unto which may we all attain, by the grace and love towards man of our Lord Jesus Christ, to whom be glory and might forever and ever. Amen.

[1] 1 Tim. v. 5. [R. V., "hath her hope set on God." Chrysostom reads κύριον, and Augustin followed the same reading.—R.]

[2] ἀποκηρύττουσι.

HOMILY XXXII.

Matt. IX. 27—30.

"And when Jesus departed thence, two blind men followed Him, crying, and saying, Thou Son of David, have mercy on us.[1] And when He was come into the house, the blind men came to Him: and Jesus saith unto them, Believe ye that I am able to do this? They say unto Him, Yea, Lord. Then touched He their eyes, saying, According to your faith be it[2] unto you. And their eyes were opened."

Wherefore can it be that He puts them off,[3] and they crying out? Here again teaching us utterly to repel the glory that cometh from the multitude. For because the house was near, He leads them thither to heal them in private. And this is evident from the fact, that He charged them moreover to tell no man.

But this is no light charge against the Jews; when these men, though their eyes were struck out, receive the faith by hearing alone, but they beholding the miracles, and having their sight to witness what was happening, do all just contrary. And see their earnestness also, both by their cry, and by their prayer itself. For they did not merely approach Him, but with loud cries, and alleging nought else but "mercy."

And they called Him "Son of David," because the name was thought to be honorable. In many passages, for instance, did the prophets[4] likewise so call the kings, whom

[1] [R. V. (and Chrysostom), "Have mercy on us, thou Son of David."]

[2] [R. V., "be it done."]

[3] παρέλκει.

[4] Perhaps Isa. xxxvii. 35.

they wished to honor, and to declare great.

And having brought them into the house, He puts to them a further question. For in many cases He made a point of healing on entreaty, lest any should suppose Him to be rushing[1] upon these miracles through vainglory: and not on this account alone, but to indicate also that they deserve healing, and that no one should say, " If it was of mere mercy that He saved, all men ought to be saved." For even His love to man hath a kind of proportion; depending on the faith of them that are healed. But not for these causes only doth He require faith of them, but forasmuch as they called Him " Son of David," He to lead them up to what is higher, and to teach them to entertain the imaginations they ought of Himself, saith, " Believe ye that I am able to do this ? " He did not say, " Believe ye that I am able to entreat my Father, that I am able to pray " but, " that I am able to do this ? "

What then is their word ? " Yea, Lord." They call Him no more Son of David, but soar higher, and acknowledge His dominion.

And then at last He for His part lays His hand upon them, saying, "According to your faith be it unto you." And this He doth to confirm their faith, and to show that they are participators in the good work, and to witness that their words were not words of flattery. For neither did He say, " Let your eyes be opened," but, "According to your faith be it unto you; " which He saith to many of them that came unto Him; before the healing of their bodies, hastening to proclaim the faith in their soul; so as both to make them more approved, and to render others more serious.

Thus with respect to the sick of the palsy also; for there too before giving nerve to the body, He raises up the fallen soul, saying, " Son, be of good cheer, thy sins be forgiven thee." [2] And the young damsel too, when He had raised her up, He detained, and by the food taught her her Benefactor; and in the case of the centurion also He did in like manner, leaving the whole to his faith; and as to His disciples again, when delivering them from the storm on the sea, He delivered them first from their want of faith. Just so likewise in this case: He knew indeed, even before their cry, the secrets of their mind; but that He might lead on others also to the same earnestness, He makes them known to the rest as well, by the result of their cure proclaiming their hidden faith.

Then after their cure He commands them to tell no man; neither doth He merely command them, but with much strictness.

" For Jesus," it is said, " straitly charged them, saying, See that no man know it. But they, when they were departed, spread abroad His fame in all that country."[3]

They however did not endure this, but became preachers, and evangelists; and when bidden to hide what had been done, they endured it not.

And if in another place we find Him saying, " Go thy way, and declare the glory of God," [4] that is not contrary to this, but even highly in agreement herewith. For He instructs us to say nothing ourselves, concerning ourselves, but even to forbid them that would eulogise us: but if the glory be referred to God, then not only not to forbid, but to command men to do this.

2. "And as they went out," it is said, " behold, they brought unto Him a dumb man possessed with a devil."[5]

For the affliction was not natural, but the device of the evil Spirit; wherefore also he needs others to bring him. For he could neither make entreaty himself, being speechless, nor supplicate others, when the evil spirit had bound his tongue, and together with his tongue had fettered his soul.

For this cause neither doth He require faith of him, but straightway heals the disease.

" For when the devil was cast out," it saith, " the dumb spake: and the multitudes marvelled, saying, It was never so seen in Israel." [6]

Now this especially vexed the Pharisees, that they preferred Him to all, not only that then were, but that had ever been. And they preferred Him, not for His healing, but for His doing it easily and quickly, and to diseases innumerable and incurable.

And thus the multitude; but the Pharisees quite contrariwise; not only disparaging the works, but saying things contradictory to themselves, and not ashamed. Such a thing is wickedness. For what say they ?

" He casteth out devils through the prince of the devils." [7]

What can be more foolish than this ? For in the first place, as He also saith further on, it is impossible that a devil should cast out a devil for that being is wont to repair what belongs to himself, not to pull it down. But

---

[1] ἐπιπηδᾶν.
[2] Matt. ix. 2. [" Thy sins are forgiven." Comp. Homily XXIX. 1.—R.]

[3] Matt. ix. 30, 31.   [4] Mark v. 19 ; Luke viii. 39.
[5] Matt. ix. 32. [" Demon " is more correct, here and throughout the passage.—R.]
[6] Matt. ix. 33.
[7] Matt. ix. 34. [R. V., " By (or, in) the prince of the devils (Greek, demons) he casteth out devils."]

He did not cast out devils only, but also cleansed lepers, and raised the dead, and curbed the sea, and remitted sins, and preached the kingdom, and brought men unto the Father; things which a demon would never either choose, or at any time be able to effect. For the devils bring men to idols, and withdraw them from God, and persuade them to disbelieve the life to come. The devil doth not bestow kindness when he is insulted; forasmuch as even when not insulted, he harms those that court and honor him.

But He doeth the contrary. For after these their insults and revilings,

3. "He went about," it is said, "all the cities and villages, teaching in their synagogues, and preaching the gospel of the kingdom, and healing every sickness and every disease." [1]

And so far from punishing them for their insensibility, He did not even simply rebuke them; at once both evincing His meekness, and so refuting the calumny; and at the same time minded also by the signs which followed to exhibit His proof more completely: and then to adduce also the refutation by words. He went about therefore both in cities, and in countries, and in their synagogues; instructing us to requite our calumniators, not with fresh calumnies, but with greater benefits. Since, if not for man's sake, but God's, thou doest good to thy fellow-servants; whatsoever they may do, leave not thou off doing them good, that thy reward may be greater; since he surely, who upon their calumny leaves off his doing good, signifies that for their praise' sake, not for God's sake, he applies himself to that kind of virtue.

For this cause Christ, to teach us that of mere goodness He had entered on this, so far from waiting for the sick to come to Him, of Himself hastened unto them, bearing them two of the greatest blessings; one, the gospel of the kingdom; another, the perfect cure of all their diseases. And not a city did He overlook, not a village did He hasten by, but visited every place.

4. And not even at this doth He stop, but He exhibits also another instance of His forethought. That is,

"When He saw," it is said, "the multitudes, He was moved with compassion on them, because they were troubled,[2] and scattered abroad, as sheep having no shepherd. Then saith He unto His disciples, The har-

vest truly is plenteous, but the laborers are few, pray ye therefore the Lord of the harvest, that He will send forth laborers into His harvest."[3]

See again His freedom from vainglory. That He may not draw all men unto Himself, He sends out His disciples.

And not with this view only, but that He might also teach them, after practising in Palestine, as in a sort of training-school, to strip themselves for their conflicts with the world. For this purpose then He makes the exercises even more serious than the actual conflicts, so far as pertained to their own virtue; that they might more easily engage in the struggles that were to ensue; as it were a sort of tender nestlings whom He was at length leading out to fly. And for the present He makes them physicians of bodies, dispensing to them afterwards the cure of the soul, which is the principal thing.

And mark how He points out the facility and necessity of the thing. For what saith He? "The harvest truly is plenteous, but the laborers are few." That is, "not to the sowing," saith He, "but to the reaping do I send you." Which in John He expressed by, "Other men labored, and ye are entered into their labors."[4]

And these things he said, at once repressing their pride, and preparing them to be of good courage, and signifying that the greater part of the labor came first.

And contemplate Him here too beginning from love to man, not with any requital. "For He had compassion, because they were troubled and scattered abroad as sheep having no shepherd." This is His charge against the rulers of the Jews, that being shepherds they acted the part of wolves. For so far from amending the multitude, they even marred their progress. For instance, when they were marvelling and saying, "It was never so seen in Israel:" these were affirming the contrary, "He casteth out devils through the prince of the devils."[5]

But of what laborers doth He speak here? Of the twelve disciples. What then? whereas He had said, "But the laborers are few," did He add to their number? By no means, but He sent them out alone. Wherefore then did He say, "Pray ye the Lord of the harvest, that He would[6] send forth laborers into His harvest; and made no addition to their number? Because though they were but twelve, He made them many from that time

---

[1] Matt. ix. 35. [R. V., "all manner of disease and all manner of sickness." In the Homily, as in the best New Testament mss. ἐν τῷ λαῷ is not found.—R.]

[2] ἐσκυλμένοι, vexati, the reading of the Vulgate, and of most mss. and Fathers: adopted by Griesbach into the text. [The R. V. renders this "distressed."]

[3] Matt. ix. 36–38. ["will" is unnecessary.—R.]
[4] John iv. 38.
[5] Matt. xii. 23, 24. [See on verse 34, in sec. 2.]
[6] [Omit "would."]

forward, not by adding to their number, but by giving them power.

Then to signify how great the gift is, He saith, "Pray ye the Lord of the harvest;" and indirectly declares it to be His own prerogative. For after having said, "Pray ye the Lord of the harvest;" when they had not made any entreaty nor prayer, He Himself at once ordains them, reminding them also of the sayings of John,[1] of the threshing floor, and of the Person winnowing, and of the chaff, and of the wheat. Whence it is evident that Himself is the husbandman, Himself the Lord of the harvest, Himself the master and owner of the prophets. For if He sent them to reap, clearly it was not to reap what belongs to another, but what Himself had sown by the prophets.

But not in this way only was He indirectly encouraging them, in calling their ministry a harvest; but also by making them able for the ministry.

"And when He had called unto Him," it saith, "His twelve disciples, He gave them power against[2] unclean spirits, to cast them out, and to heal all manner of sickness, and all manner of disease."[3]

Still the Spirit was not yet given. For "there was not yet," it saith, "a Spirit, because that Jesus was not yet glorified."[4] How then did they cast out the spirits? By His command, by His authority.

And mark, I pray thee, also, how well timed was the mission. For not at the beginning did He send them; but when they had enjoyed sufficiently the advantage of following Him, and had seen a dead person raised, and the sea rebuked, and devils expelled, and a paralytic new-strung, and sins remitted, and a leper cleansed, and had received a sufficient proof of His power, both by deeds and words, then He sends them forth: and not to dangerous acts, for as yet there was no danger in Palestine, but they had only to stand against evil speakings. However, even of this He forewarns them, I mean of their perils; preparing them even before the time, and making them feel as in conflict by His continual predictions of that sort.

5. Then, since He had mentioned to us two pairs of apostles, that of Peter, and that of John, and after those had pointed out the calling of Matthew, but had said nothing to us either of the calling or of the name of the other apostles; here of necessity He sets down the list of them, and their number, and makes known their names, saying thus:

"Now the names of the twelve apostles are these; first, Simon, who is called Peter."[5]

Because there was also another Simon, the Canaanite; and there was Judas Iscariot, and Judas the brother of James; and James the son of Alphæus, and James the son of Zebedee.

Now Mark doth also put them according to their dignity; for after the two leaders, He then numbers Andrew; but our evangelist not so, but without distinction; or rather He sets before himself even Thomas who came far short of him.

But let us look at the list of them from the beginning.

"First, Simon, who is called Peter, and Andrew his brother."

Even this is no small praise. For the one he named from his virtue, the other from his high kindred, which was in conformity to his disposition.

Then, "James the son of Zebedee, and John his brother."

Seest thou how He arranges them not according to their dignity. For to me John seems to be greater, not only than the others, but even than his brother.

After this, when he had said, "Philip, and Bartholomew," he added, "Thomas, and Matthew the Publican."[6]

But Luke not so, but in the opposite order, and he puts him before Thomas

Next, "James the son of Alphæus." For there was, as I have already said, the son of Zebedee also. Then after having mentioned "Lebbæus, whose surname was Thaddæus,"[7] and "Simon" Zelotes, whom he calls also "the Canaanite," he comes to the traitor. And not as a sort of enemy or foe, but as one writing a history, so hath he described him. He saith not, "the unholy, the all unholy one," but hath named him from his city, "Judas Iscariot." Because there was also another Judas, "Lebbæus, whose surname was Thaddæus," who, Luke saith, was the brother of James, saying, "Judas the brother of James."[8] Therefore to distinguish him from this man, it saith, "Judas Iscariot, who also betrayed Him."[9] And he is not ashamed to say, "who also betrayed Him." So far were they from ever disguising aught even of

---

[1] Matt. iii. 12.   [2] [R. V., "authority over."]
[3] Matt. x. 1. ["Sickness" and "disease" should be transposed. Comp. on chap. ix. 35, and R. V.—R.]
[4] John vii. 39. [Chrysostom accepts the reading sustained by our best authorities; but the literal rendering given above does not represent his view. In Homily LI., in John, he distinctly says: "For the Holy Ghost was not yet, that is, 'was not yet given.'"—R.]

[5] Matt. x. 2.   [6] Matt. x. 3.
[7] [R. V., "Thaddæus." The longer reading arose quite early. Tischendorf accepts "Lebbæus," though it is not strongly supported, mainly because Mark has "Thaddæus."—R.]
[8] Luke vi. 16.   [9] Matt. x. 4.

those things that seem to be matters of reproach.

And first of all, and leader of the choir,[1] is the "unlearned, the ignorant man."[2]

But let us see whither, and to whom, He sends them.

"These twelve," it is said, "Jesus sent forth."[3]

What manner of men were these? The fishermen, the publicans: for indeed four were fishermen and two publicans, Matthew and James, and one was even a traitor. And what saith He to them? He presently charges them, saying,

"Go not into the way [4] of the Gentiles, and into any city of the Samaritans enter ye not; but go rather to the lost sheep of the house of Israel."[5]

"For think not at all," saith He, "because they insult me, and call me demoniac, that I hate them and turn away from them. Nay, as I sought earnestly to amend them in the first place, so keeping you away from all the rest, to them do I send you as teachers and physicians. And I not only forbid you to preach to others before these, but I do not suffer you so much as to touch upon the road that leads thither, nor to enter into such a city." Because the Samaritans too are in a state of enmity with the Jews. And yet it was an easier thing to deal with them, for they were much more favorably disposed to the faith; but the case of these was more difficult. But for all this, He sends them on the harder task, indicating his guardian care of them, and stopping the mouths of the Jews, and preparing the way for the teaching of the apostles, that people might not hereafter blame them for "entering in to men uncircumcised,"[6] and think they had a just cause for shunning and abhorring them. And he calls them "lost," not "stray," "sheep," in every way contriving how to excuse them, and winning their mind to himself.

6. "And as ye go," saith He, "preach, saying, The kingdom of Heaven is at hand."[7]

Seest thou the greatness of their ministry? Seest thou the dignity of apostles? Of nothing that is the object of sense are they commanded to speak, nor such as Moses spake of, and the prophets before them, but of some new and strange things. For while the former preached no such things, but earth, and the good things in the earth, these preached the kingdom of Heaven, and whatever is there.

And not from this circumstance only were these the greater, but also from their obedience: in that they shrink not, nor are they backward, like those of old;[8] but, warned as they are of perils, and wars, and of those insupportable evils, they receive with great obedience His injunctions, as being heralds of a kingdom.

"And what marvel," saith one, "if having nothing to preach that is dismal or grievous, they readily obeyed?" What sayest thou? nothing grievous enjoined them? Dost thou not hear of the prisons, the executions, the civil wars, the hatred of all men? all which, He said a little while after, they must undergo.

True, as to other men, He sent them to be procurers and heralds of innumerable blessings: but for themselves, He said and proclaimed beforehand, that they were to suffer terrible and incurable ills.

After this, to make them trustworthy,[9] He saith,

"Heal the sick, cleanse the lepers,[10] cast out devils: freely ye have received, freely give."

See how He provides for their conduct, and that no less than for their miracles, implying that the miracles without this are nothing. Thus He both quells their pride by saying, "Freely ye have received, freely give;" and takes order for their being clear of covetousness. Moreover, lest it should be thought their own work,[11] and they be lifted up by the signs that were wrought, He saith, "freely ye have received." "Ye bestow no favor on them that receive you, for not for a price did ye receive these things, nor after toil: for the grace is mine. In like manner therefore give ye to them also, for there is no finding a price worthy of them."

7. After this plucking up immediately the root of the evils,[12] He saith,

"Provide neither gold, nor silver, nor brass in your purses, nor scrip for your journey, neither two coats, neither shoes, nor yet a staff."[13]

He said not, "take them not with you," but, "even if you can obtain them from another, flee the evil disease." And you see that hereby He was answering many good pur-

---

[1] κορυφαῖος.   [2] Acts iv. 13.   [3] Matt. x. 5.
[4] [R. V., "any way."]   [5] Matt. x. 5, 6.
[6] Acts xi. 3.   [7] Matt. x. 7.

[8] See Exod. iv. 10–14 ; Jerem. i. 6.
[9] [ἀξιοπίστους, worthy of the confidence of those to whom they preached.—R.]
[10] Matt. x. 8. "Raise the dead," is added in our copies. [There is some authority for omitting this clause in the New Testament, but recent critical editors retain it.—R.]
[11] κατόρθωμα ; nearly answering, perhaps, both here and in other places, to meritum.
[12] 1 Tim. vi. 10.
[13] Matt. x. 9, 10. [R. V., "Get you no gold, nor silver, nor brass in your purses (Greek, girdles); no wallet for your journey, neither two coats, nor shoes, nor staff."]

poses; first setting His disciples above suspicion; secondly, freeing them from all care, so that they might give all their leisure to the word; thirdly, teaching them His own power. Of this accordingly He quite speaks out to them afterwards, "Lacked ye anything, when I sent you naked and unshod?" [1]

He did not at once say, "Provide not," but when He had said, "Cleanse the lepers, cast out devils," then He said, "Provide nothing; freely ye have received, freely give;" by His way of ordering things consulting at once for their interest, their credit, and their ability.

But perhaps some one may say, that the rest may not be unaccountable, but "not to have a scrip for the journey, neither two coats, nor a staff, nor shoes," why did He enjoin this? Being minded to train them up unto all perfection; since even further back, He had suffered them not to take thought so much as for the next day. For even to the whole world He was to send them out as teachers. Therefore of men He makes them even angels (so to speak); releasing them from all worldly care, so that they should be possessed with one care alone, that of their teaching; or rather even from that He releases them, saying, "Take no thought how or what ye shall speak." [2]

And thus, what seems to be very grievous and galling, this He shows to be especially light and easy for them. For nothing makes men so cheerful as being freed from anxiety and care; and especially when it is granted them, being so freed, to lack nothing, God being present, and becoming to them instead of all things.

Next, lest they should say, "whence then are we to obtain our necessary food?" He saith not unto them, "Ye have heard that I have told you before, 'Behold the fowls of the air;'" [3] (for they were not yet able to realise [4] this commandment in their actions); but He added what came far short of this, saying, "For the workman is worthy of his meat;" [5] declaring that they must be nourished by their disciples, that neither they might be high minded towards those whom they were teaching, as though giving all and receiving nothing at their hands; nor these again break away, as being despised by their teachers.

After this, that they may not say, "Dost thou then command us to live by begging?" and be ashamed of this, He signifies the thing

to be a debt, both by calling them "workmen," and by terming what was given, "hire." [6] For "think not," saith He, "because the labor is in words, that the benefit conferred by you is small; nay, for the thing hath much toil; and whatsoever they that are taught may give, it is not a free gift which they bestow, but a recompence which they render: "for the workman is worthy of his meat." But this He said, not as declaring so much to be the worth of the apostles' labors, far from it; God forbid: but as both making it a law for them to seek nothing more, and as convincing the givers, that what they do is not an act of liberality, but a debt.

8. "And into whatsoever city or town ye shall enter, inquire who in it is worthy: and there abide till ye go thence." [7]

That is, "it follows not," saith He, "from my saying, 'The workman is worthy of his meat,' that I have opened to you all men's doors: but herein also do I require you to use much circumspection. For this will profit you both in respect of your credit, and for your very maintenance. For if he is worthy, he will surely give you food; more especially when ye ask nothing beyond mere necessaries."

And He not only requires them to seek out worthy persons, but also not to change house for house, whereby they would neither vex him that is receiving them, nor themselves get the character of gluttony and self-indulgence. [8] For this He declared by saying, "There abide till ye go thence." And this one may perceive from the other evangelists also. [9]

Seest thou how He made them honorable by this also, and those that received them careful; by signifying that they rather are the gainers, both in honor, and in respect of advantage?

Then pursuing again the same subject, He saith,

"And when ye come into an house, salute it. And if the house be worthy, let your peace come upon it; but if it be not worthy, let your peace return to you." [10]

Seest thou how far He declines not to carry His injunctions? And very fitly. For as champions of godliness, and preachers to the whole world, was He training them. And in that regard disposing them to practise moderation, and making them objects of love, He saith,

"And whosoever shall not receive you, nor hear your words, when ye depart out of that

---

[1] Luke xxii. 35. [The passage is paraphrased by Chrysostom. —R.]
[2] Matt. x. 19. [R. V., "Be not anxious," etc.]
[3] Matt. vi. 26.   [4] ἐπιδείξασθαι.
[5] Matt. x. 10. [R. V., "For the laborer is worthy of his food."]

[6] See Luke x. 7.
[7] Matt. x. 11. [R. V., "Search out who, etc.]
[8] εὐκολίας.   [9] Luke x. 7.   [10] Matt. x. 12, 13.

house or city, shake off the dust of your feet. Verily I say unto you, it shall be more tolerable for the land of Sodom and Gomorrah in the day of judgment, than for that city."[1]

That is, "do not," saith He, "because ye are teachers, therefore wait to be saluted by others, but be first in showing that respect." Then, implying that this is not a mere salutation, but a blessing, He saith, "If the house be worthy, it shall come upon it," but if it deal insolently, its first punishment will be, not to have the benefit of your peace; and the second, that it shall suffer the doom of Sodom." "And what," it will be said, "is their punishment to us?" Ye will have the houses of such as are worthy.

But what means, "Shake off the dust of your feet?" It is either to signify their having received nothing of them, or to be a witness to them of the long journey, which they had travelled for their sake.

But mark, I pray thee, how He doth not even yet give the whole to them. For neither doth He as yet bestow upon them foreknowledge, so as to learn who is worthy, and who is not so; but He bids them inquire, and await the trial. How then did He Himself abide with a publican? Because he was become worthy by his conversion.

And mark, I pray thee, how when He had stripped them of all, He gave them all, by suffering them to abide in the houses of those who became disciples, and to enter therein, having nothing. For thus both themselves were freed from anxiety, and they would convince the others, that for their salvation only are they come; first by bringing in nothing with them, then by requiring no more of them than necessaries, lastly, by not entering all their houses without distinction.

Since not by the signs only did He desire them to appear illustrious, but even before the signs, by their own virtue. For nothing so much characterizes strictness of life,[2] as to be free from superfluities, and so far as may be, from wants. This even the false apostles knew. Wherefore Paul also said, "That wherein they glory, they may be found even as we."[3]

But if when we are in a strange country, and are going unto persons unknown to us, we must seek nothing more than our food for the day, much more when abiding at home.

9. These things let us not hear only, but also imitate. For not of the apostles alone are they said, but also of the saints afterwards. Let us therefore become worthy to entertain them. For according to the dispo-

sition of the entertainers this peace both comes and flies away again. For not only on the courageous speaking of them that teach, but also on the worthiness of them that receive, doth this effect follow.

Neither let us account it a small loss, not to enjoy such peace. For this peace the prophet also from of old proclaims, saying, "How beautiful are the feet of them that bring good tidings of peace."[4] Then to explain the value thereof he added, "That bring good tidings of good things."

This peace Christ also declared to be great, when He said, "Peace I leave with you, my peace I give unto you."[5] And we should do all things, so as to enjoy it, both at home and in church. For in the very church too the presiding minister gives peace.[6] And this which we speak of is a type of that. And you should receive it with all alacrity, in heart[7] before the actual communion.[8] For if not to impart it after the communion[9] be disgusting, how much more disgusting to repel from you him that pronounces it!

For thee the presbyter sits, for thee the teacher stands, laboring and toiling. What plea then wilt thou have, for not affording him so much welcome as to listen to Him? For indeed the church is the common home of all, and when ye have first occupied it, we enter in, strictly observing the type which they exhibited. For this cause we also pronounce "peace" in common to all, directly as we enter, according to that law.

Let no one therefore be careless, no one inattentive,[10] when the priests have entered in and are teaching; for there is really no small punishment appointed for this. Yea, and I for one would rather enter into any of your houses ten thousand times, and find myself

---

[1] Matt. x. 14, 15. [2] φιλοσοφίαν. [3] 2 Cor. xi. 12.

[4] Isa. lii. 7; Rom. x. 15. [5] John xiv. 27.
[6] See Bingham 13, 10, 8, quoting St. Chrys. Hom. *in eos qui primum Pascha jejunant*, P. vi. 383. Sav. "There is nothing like peace and harmony. Therefore our Father (the Bishop) mounts not up to this throne, until he have invoked peace upon you all: nor when he stands up, doth he begin his instruction to you, until he have given peace to all; and the priests, when about to consecrate, first make this prayer for you, and so begin the blessing: and the deacon also, when he bids you pray, joins this with the rest as matter of your prayer, that you should ask for the angel of peace, and that all the things set before you should be for your peace: also in dismissing you from this assembly, this is what he implores for you, saying, 'Depart in peace.' And in a word, we may not say or do any thing without this peace." See also Bingham, 14, 4, 6; 4, 14; 15, 3, 1, 2; and the authors quoted by him, especially St. Chrysostom in various places: from which it is evident that "the table" here means the holy table, and that his argument is, "We should receive our brethren's salutations as home and elsewhere with a brotherly mind, that we may be fit to impart to him the kiss of peace in the holy mysteries: the one is a type of, and a preparation for, the other: as was the salutation here enjoined to the apostles. Especially ought we to be ready and attentive at the many salutations which the ministers offer to us in the earlier part of the service, that we may lose none of the benefit of that mysterious salutation which we know will come in the end and most awful part of it."
[7] [τῇ γνώμῃ.] [8] τῆς Τραπέζης.
[9] *i. e.*, to refuse the kiss of peace, which was always a part of the altar service.
[10] μετέωρος.

baffled, than not be heard when I speak here. This latter is to me harder to bear than the other, by how much this house is of greater dignity; our great possessions being verily laid up here, here all the hopes we have. For what is here, that is not great and awful? Thus both this table is far more precious and delightful than the other,[1] and this candlestick than the candlestick there. And this they know, as many as have put away diseases by anointing themselves with oil[2] in faith and in due season. And this coffer too is far better and more indispensable than that other chest; for it hath not clothes but alms shut up in it; even though they be few that own them. Here too is a couch better than that other; for the repose of the divine Scriptures is more delightful than any couch.

And had we attained to excellence in respect of concord, then had we no other home beside this. And that there is nothing overburdensome in this saying, the "three thousand,"[3] bear witness, and the "five thousand,"[4] who had but one home, one table, one soul; for "the multitude of them that believed," we read, "were of one heart and of one soul."[5] But since we fall far short of their virtue, and dwell scattered in our several homes, let us at least, when we meet here, be earnest in so doing. Because though in all other things we be destitute and poor, yet in these we are rich. Wherefore here at least receive us with love when we come in unto you. And when I say, "Peace be unto you,"[6] and ye say, "And with thy spirit," say it not with the voice only, but also with the mind; not in mouth, but in understanding also. But if, while here thou sayest, "Peace also to thy spirit," out of doors thou art mine enemy, spitting at and calumniating me, and secretly aspersing me with innumerable reproaches; what manner of peace is this?

For I indeed, though thou speak evil of me ten thousand times, give thee that peace with a pure heart, with sincerity of purpose, and I can say nothing evil at any time of thee; for

I have a father's bowels. And if I rebuke thee at any time, I do it out of concern for thee. But as for thee, by thy secret carping at me, and not receiving me in the Lord's house, I fear lest thou shouldest in return add to my despondency; not for thine insulting me, not for thy casting me out, but for thy rejecting our peace, and drawing down upon thyself that grievous punishment.

For though I shake not off the dust, though I turn not away, what is threatened remains unchanged. For I indeed oftentimes pronounce peace to you, and will not cease from continually speaking it; and if, besides your insults, ye receive me not, even then I shake not off the dust; not that I am disobedient to our Lord, but that I vehemently burn for you. And besides, I have suffered nothing at all for you; I have neither come a long journey, nor with that garb and that voluntary poverty am I come (therefore we first blame ourselves), nor without shoes and a second coat; and perhaps this is why ye also fail of your part. However, this is not a sufficient plea for you; but while our condemnation is greater, to you it imparts no excuse.

10. Then the houses were churches, but now the church is become a house. Then one might say nothing worldly in a house, now one may say nothing spiritual in a church, but even here ye bring in the business from the market place, and while God is discoursing, ye leave off listening in silence to His sayings, and bring in the contrary things, and make discord. And I would it were your own affairs, but now the things which are nothing to you, those ye both speak and hear.

For this I lament, and will not cease lamenting. For I have no power to quit this house, but here we must needs remain until we depart from this present life. "Receive us"[7] therefore, as Paul commanded. For his language in that place related not to a meal, but to the temper and mind. This we also seek of you, even love, that fervent and genuine affection. But if ye endure not even this, at least love yourselves, and lay aside your present remissness. This is sufficient for our consolation, if we see you approving yourselves, and becoming better men. So will I also myself show forth increased love, even "though the more abundantly I love you, the less I be loved."[8]

For indeed there are many things to bind us together. One table is set before all, one

---

[1] i. e., than the common tables in your own houses.
[2] See James v. 14, 15; Tertull. ad Scapul. c. 4. "Severus sought out one Proculus, a Christian, who had cured him at a certain time with oil, and kept him in his court until he died." St. Jerome, vit. St. Hilarion, c. 32. "Very many, wounded by serpents, having had recourse to Hilarion, indeed all the husbandmen and shepherds, upon touching their wounds with consecrated oil, recovered lasting health." Other cases occur in church history, and illustrate the importance which the early writers attribute to the sacred oil in the church ritual, and the account of the miracle of St. Narcissus in Euseb. E. H. vi. 9. This statement of St. Chrysostom should be borne in mind, as qualifying what he so often seems to affirm or imply, that miraculous gifts had been withdrawn.
[3] Acts ii. 41.　　[4] Acts iv. 4.　　[5] Acts iv. 32.
[6] See St. Chrys. on Coloss. Hom. III. (as quoted by Mr. Field). "When the bishop enters the church, immediately he says, 'Peace be to all;' when he exhorts, 'Peace to all,' when he consecrates, 'Peace to all;' when he enjoins the salutation, 'Peace to all;' when the sacrifice is ended, 'Peace to all:' and at intervals again, 'Grace to you and Peace.'"

[7] 2 Cor. vii. 2.
[8] 2 Cor. xii. 15. [R. V., "Am I loved the less?" The reading accepted by Chrysostom agrees better with this interpretation. —R.]

Father begat us, we are all the issue of the same throes, the same drink hath been given to all; or rather not only the same drink, but also to drink out of one cup. For our Father desiring to lead us to a kindly affection, hath devised this also, that we should drink out of one cup; a thing which belongs to intense love.

But "there is no comparison between the apostles and us." I confess it too, and would never deny it. For I say not, to themselves, but not even to their shadows are we comparable.

But nevertheless, let your part be done. This will have no tendency to disgrace you, but rather to profit you the more. For when even to unworthy persons ye show so much love and obedience, then shall ye receive the greater reward.

For neither are they our own words which we speak, since ye have no teacher at all on earth; but what we have received, that we also give, and in giving we seek for nothing else from you, but to be loved only. And if we be unworthy even of this, yet by our loving you we shall quickly be worthy. Although we are commanded to love not them only that love us, but even our enemies. Who then is so hardhearted, who so savage, that after having received such a law, he should abhor and hate even them that love him, full as he may be of innumerable evils?

We have partaken of a spiritual table, let us be partakers also of spiritual love. For if robbers, on partaking of salt, forget their character; what excuse shall we have, who are continually partaking of the Lord's body, and do not imitate even their gentleness? And yet to many, not one table only, but even to be of one city, hath sufficed for friendship; but we, when we have the same city, and the same house, and table, and way, and door, and root, and life, and head, and the same shepherd, and king, and teacher, and judge, and maker, and father, and to whom all things are common; what indulgence can we deserve, if we be divided one from another?

11. But the miracles, perhaps, are what ye seek after, such as they wrought when they entered in; the lepers cleansed, the devils driven out, and the dead raised? Nay, but this is the great indication of your high birth, and of your love, that ye should believe God without pledges. And in fact this, and one other thing, were the reasons why God made miracles to cease. I mean, that if when miracles are not performed, they that plume themselves on other advantages,—for instance, either on the word of wisdom, or on show of piety,—grow vainglorious, are puffed up, are separated one from another; did miracles also take place, how could there but be violent rendings? And that what I say is not mere conjecture, the Corinthians bear witness, who from this cause were divided into many parties.

Do not thou therefore seek signs, but the soul's health. Seek not to see one dead man raised; nay, for thou hast learnt that the whole world is arising. Seek not to see a blind man healed, but behold all now restored unto that better and more profitable sight; and do thou too learn to look chastely, and amend thine eye.

For in truth, if we all lived as we ought, workers of miracles would not be admired so much as we by the children of the heathen. For as to the signs, they often carry with them either a notion of mere fancy, or another evil suspicion, although ours be not such. But a pure life cannot admit of any such reproach; yea, all men's mouths are stopped by the acquisition of virtue.

Let virtue then be our study: for abundant are her riches, and great the wonder wrought in her. She bestows the true freedom, and causes the same to be discerned even in slavery, not releasing from slavery, but while men continue slaves, exhibiting them more honorable than freemen; which is much more than giving them freedom: not making the poor man rich, but while he continues poor, exhibiting him wealthier than the rich.

But if thou wouldest work miracles also, be rid of transgressions, and thou hast quite accomplished it. Yea, for sin is a great demon, beloved; and if thou exterminate this, thou hast wrought a greater thing than they who drive out ten thousand demons. Do thou listen to Paul, how he speaks, and prefers virtue to miracles. "But covet earnestly," saith he, "the best gifts: and yet show I unto you a more excellent way."[1] And when he was to declare this "way," he spoke not of raising the dead, not of cleansing of lepers, not of any other such thing; but in place of all these he set charity. Hearken also unto Christ, saying, "Rejoice not that the demons obey you, but that your names are written in Heaven."[2] And again before this, "Many will say to me in that day, Have we not prophesied in Thy name, and cast out devils, and done many mighty works, and then I will profess unto them, I know you not."[3] And when He was about to be crucified, He called His disciples, and said unto them, "By this shall all men know that ye

---

[1] 1 Cor. xii. 31. [2] Luke x. 20. [3] Matt. vii. 22, 23.

are my disciples," not " if ye cast out devils," but " if ye have love one to another." [1]   And again, " Hereby shall all men know that Thou hast sent me;" not " if these men raise the dead," but, " if they be one." [2]

For, as to miracles, they oftentimes, while they profited another, have injured him who had the power, by lifting him up to pride and vainglory, or haply in some other way: but in our works there is no place for any such suspicion, but they profit both such as follow them, and many others.

These then let us perform with much diligence.   For if thou change from inhumanity to almsgiving, thou hast stretched forth the hand that was withered.   If thou withdraw from theatres and go to the church, thou hast cured the lame foot.   If thou draw back thine eyes from an harlot, and from beauty not thine own, thou hast opened them when they were blind.   If instead of satanical songs, thou hast learnt spiritual psalms, being dumb, thou hast spoken.

These are the greatest miracles, these the wonderful signs.   If we go on working these signs, we shall both ourselves be a great and admirable sort of persons through these, and shall win over all the wicked unto virtue, and shall enjoy the life to come; unto which may we all attain, by the grace and love towards man of our Lord Jesus Christ, to whom be glory and might forever and ever.   Amen.

---

[1] John xiii. 35.   [2] John xvii. 23, 22.

HOMILY XXXIII.

MATT. X. 16.

" Behold, I send you forth as sheep in the midst of wolves; be ye therefore wise as serpents, and harmless as doves."

HAVING made them feel confident about their necessary food, and opened unto them all men's houses, and having invested their entrance with an appearance to attract veneration, charging them not to come in as wanderers, and beggars, but as much more venerable than those who received them (for this He signifies by His saying, " the workman is worthy of his hire;" and by His commanding them to inquire, who was worthy, and there to remain, and enjoining them to salute such as receive them; and by His threatening such as receive them not with those incurable evils): having I say, in this way cast out their anxiety, and armed them with the display of miracles, and made them as it were all iron and adamant, by delivering them from all worldly things, and enfranchising them from all temporal care: He speaks in what follows of the evils also that were to befall them; not only those that were to happen soon after, but those too that were to be in long course of time; from the first, even long beforehand, preparing them for the war against the devil. Yea, and many advantages were hence secured; and first, that they learnt the power of His foreknowledge; secondly, that no one should suspect, that through weakness of their Master came these evils upon them; thirdly, that such as undergo these things should not be dismayed by their falling out unexpectedly, and against hope; fourthly, that they might not at the very time of the cross be troubled on hearing these things. For indeed, they were just so affected at that time; when also He upbraided them, saying, " Because I have said these things unto you, sorrow hath filled your hearts; and none of you asketh me, whither goest Thou ?" [1]   And yet He had said nothing as yet touching Himself, as that He should be bound, and scourged, and put to death, that He might not hereby also confound their minds; but for the present He announces before what should happen to themselves.

Then, that they might learn that this system of war is new, and the manner of the array unwonted; as He sends them bare, and with one coat, and unshod, and without staff, and without girdle or scrip, and bids them be maintained by such as receive them; so neither here did He stay His speech, but to

---

[1] John xvi. 6, 5.

signify His unspeakable power, He saith, "Even thus setting out, exhibit the gentleness of "sheep," and this, though ye are to go unto "wolves;" and not simply unto wolves, but "into the midst of wolves."

And He bids them have not only gentleness as sheep, but also the harmlessness of the dove. "For thus shall I best show forth my might, when sheep get the better of wolves, and being in the midst of wolves, and receiving a thousand bites, so far from being consumed, do even work a change on them: a thing far greater and more marvellous than killing them, to alter their spirit, and to reform their mind; and this, being only twelve, while the whole world is filled with the wolves."

Let us then be ashamed, who do the contrary, who set like wolves upon our enemies. For so long as we are sheep, we conquer: though ten thousand wolves prowl around, we overcome and prevail. But if we become wolves, we are worsted, for the help of our Shepherd departs from us: for He feeds not wolves, but sheep: and He forsakes thee, and retires, for neither dost thou allow His might to be shown. Because, as He accounts the whole triumph His own, if thou being ill used, show forth gentleness; so if thou follow it up and give blows, thou obscurest His victory.

2. But do thou consider, I pray thee, who they are that hear these injunctions, so hard and laborious: the timid and ignorant; the unlettered and uninstructed; such as are in every respect obscure, who have never been trained up in the Gentile laws, who do not readily present themselves in the public places; the fishermen, the publicans, men full of innumerable deficiencies. For if these things were enough to confound even the lofty and great, how were they not enough to cast down and dismay them that were in all respects untried, and had never entertained any noble imagination? But they did not cast them down.

"And very naturally," some one may perhaps say; "because He gave them power to cleanse lepers, to drive out devils." I would answer as follows: Nay, this very thing was enough especially to perplex them, that for all their raising the dead, they were to undergo these intolerable evils, both judgments, and executions, and the wars which all would wage on them, and the common hatred of the world; and that such terrors await them, while themselves are working miracles.

3. What then is their consolation for all these things? The power of Him that sends them. Wherefore also He puts this before

all, saying, "Behold, I send you." This suffices for your encouragement, this for confidence, and fearing none of your assailants.

Seest thou authority? seest thou prerogative? seest thou invincible might? Now His meaning is like this: "Be not troubled" (so He speaks), "that sending you among wolves, I command you to be like sheep and like doves. For I might indeed have done the contrary, and have suffered you to undergo nothing terrible, nor as sheep to be exposed to wolves; I might have rendered you more formidable than lions; but it is expedient that so it should be. This makes you also more glorious; this proclaims also my power."

This He said also unto Paul: "My grace is sufficient for thee, for my strength is made perfect in weakness."[1] "It is I, now mark it, who have caused you so to be." For in saying, "I send you forth as sheep," He intimates this. "Do not therefore despond, for I know, I know certainly, that in this way more than any other ye will be invincible to all."

After this, that they may contribute something on their own part also, and that all might not seem to be of His grace, nor they supposed to be crowned at random, and vainly, He saith, "Be ye therefore wise as serpents, and harmless as doves." "But what," it might be said, "will our wisdom avail in so great dangers? nay, how shall we be able to have wisdom at all, when so many waves are drenching us all over? For let a sheep be ever so wise, when it is in the midst of wolves, and so many wolves, what will it be able to do? Let the dove be ever so harmless, what will it profit, when so many hawks are assailing it?" In the brutes indeed, not at all: but in you as much as possible.

But let us see what manner of wisdom He here requires. That of the serpent, He saith. For even as that animal gives up everything, and if its very body must be cut off, doth not very earnestly defend it, so that it may save its head; in like manner do thou also, saith He, give up every thing but the faith; though goods, body, life itself, must be yielded. For that is the head and the root; and if that be preserved, though thou lose all, thou wilt recover all with so much the more splendor.[2]

On this account then He neither commanded to be merely a simple and single-hearted sort of person, nor merely wise; but hath mixed up both these, so that they may become virtue; taking in the wisdom of the

---

[1] 2 Cor. xii. 9.   [2] περιφανείας.

serpent that we may not be wounded in our vitals; and the harmlessness of the dove, that we may not retaliate on our wrongdoers, nor avenge ourselves on them that lay snares; since wisdom again is useless, except this be added. Now what, I ask, could be more strict than these injunctions? Why, was it not enough to suffer wrong? Nay, saith He, but I do not permit thee so much as to be indignant. For this is "the dove." As though one should cast a reed into fire, and command it not to be burnt by the fire, but to quench it.

However, let us not be troubled; nay, for these things have come to pass, and have had an accomplishment, and have been shown in very deed, and men became wise as serpents, and harmless as doves; not being of another nature, but of the same with us.

Let not then any one account His injunctions impracticable. For He beyond all others knows the nature of things; He knows that fierceness is not quenched by fierceness, but by gentleness. And if in men's actual deeds too thou wouldest see this result, read the book of the Acts of the Apostles, and thou wilt see how often, when the people of the Jews had risen up against them and were sharpening their teeth, these men, imitating the dove, and answering with suitable meekness, did away with their wrath, quenched their madness, broke their impetuosity. As when they said, "Did not we straitly command you, that ye should not speak in this name?"[1] although able to work any number of miracles, they neither said nor did anything harsh, but answered for themselves with all meekness, saying, "Whether it be right to hearken unto you more than unto God, judge ye."[2]

Hast thou seen the harmlessness of the dove? Behold the wisdom of the serpent. "For we cannot but speak the things, which we know and have heard."[3] Seest thou how we must be perfect on all points, so as neither to be abased by dangers, nor provoked by anger?

4. Therefore He said also,[4]

"Beware of men, for they shall deliver you up to councils, and they shall scourge you in their synagogues: and ye shall be brought before governors and kings for my sake, for a testimony to them and the Gentiles."

Thus again is He preparing them to be vigilant, in every case assigning to them the sufferance of wrong, and permitting the infliction of it to others; to teach thee that the victory is in suffering evil, and that His glori-

ous trophies are thereby set up. For He said not at all, "Fight ye also, and resist them that would vex you," but only, "Ye shall suffer the utmost ills."

O how great is the power of Him that speaks! How great the self-command of them that hear! For indeed we have great cause to marvel, how they did not straightway dart away from Him on hearing these things, apt as they were to be startled at every sound, and such as had never gone further than that lake, around which they used to fish; and how they did not reflect, and say to themselves, "And whither after all this are we to flee? The courts of justice against us, the kings against us, the governors, the synagogues of the Jews, the nations of the Gentiles, the rulers, and the ruled." (For hereby He not only forewarned them of Palestine, and the ills therein, but discovered also the wars throughout the world, saying, "Ye shall be brought before kings and governors;" signifying that to the Gentiles also He was afterwards to send them as heralds.) "Thou hast made the world our enemy, Thou hast armed against us all them that dwell on the earth, peoples, tyrants, kings."

And what follows again is much more fearful, since men are to become on our account murderers of brothers, of children, of fathers.

"For the brother," saith He, "shall deliver up the brother to death, and the father the child; and children shall rise up against their parents, and cause them to be put to death."[5]

"How, then," one might say, "will the rest of men believe, when they see on our account, children slain by their fathers, and brethren by brethren, and all things filled with abominations?" What? will not men, as though we were destructive demons, will they not, as though we were devoted, and pests of the world, drive us out from every quarter, seeing the earth filled with blood of kinsmen, and with so many murderers? Surely fair is the peace (is it not?) which we are to bring into men's houses and give them, while we are filling those houses with so many slaughters. Why, had we been some great number of us, instead of twelve; had we been, instead of "unlearned and ignorant," wise, and skilled in rhetoric, and mighty in speech; nay more, had we been even kings, and in possession of armies and abundance of wealth; how could we have persuaded any, while kindling up civil wars, yea, and other wars far worse than they? Why, though we were to despise our own safety, which of all other men will give heed to us?"

---

[1] Acts v. 28. [2] Acts iv. 19.
[3] Acts iv. 20. [4] Matt. x. 17, 18. [5] Matt. x. 21.

But none of these things did they either think or say, neither did they require any account of His injunctions, but simply yielded and obeyed. And this came not from their own virtue only, but also of the wisdom of their Teacher. For see how to each of the fearful things He annexed an encouragement; as in the case of such as received them not, He said, " It shall be more tolerable for the land of Sodom and Gomorrha in the day of judgment, than for that city;" so here again, when He had said, " Ye shall be brought before governors and kings," He added, " for my sake, for a testimony to them, and the Gentiles." And this is no small consolation, that they are suffering these things both for Christ, and for the Gentiles' conviction. Thus God, though no one regard, is found to be everywhere doing His own works. Now these things were a comfort to them, not that they desired the punishment of other men, but that they might have ground of confidence, as sure to have Him everywhere present with them, who had both foretold and foreknown these things; and because not as wicked men, and as pests, were they to suffer all this.

And together with these, He adds another, and that no small consolation for them, saying,

" But when they deliver you up, take no thought[1] how or what ye shall speak, for it shall be given you in that hour what ye shall speak. For it is not ye that speak, but the Spirit of your Father that speaketh in you."[2]

For lest they should say, " How shall we be able to persuade men, when such things are taking place?" He bids them be confident as to their defense also. And elsewhere indeed He saith, "I will give you a mouth and wisdom;"[3] but here, " It is the Spirit of your Father that speaketh in you," advancing them unto the dignity of the prophets. Therefore, when He had spoken of the power that was given, then He added also the terrors, the murders, and the slaughters.

"For the brother shall deliver up the brother," saith He, " to death, and the father the child, and the children shall rise up against their parents, and cause them to be put to death."[4]

And not even at this did He stop, but added also what was greatly more fearful, and enough to shiver a rock to pieces: "And ye shall be hated of all men." And here again the consolation is at the doors, for, " For my name's sake," saith He, " ye shall suffer these things." And with this again another,

" But he that endureth to the end, the same shall be saved."[5]

And these things in another point of view likewise were sufficient to rouse up their spirits; since at any rate the power of their gospel was to blaze up so high, as that nature should be despised, and kindred rejected, and the Word preferred to all, chasing all mightily away. For if no tyranny of nature is strong enough to withstand your sayings, but it is dissolved and trodden under foot, what else shall be able to get the better of you? Not, however, that your life will be in security, because these things shall be; but rather ye will have for your common enemies and foes them that dwell in the whole world.

5. Where now is Plato? Where Pythagoras? Where the long chain[6] of the Stoics? For the first, after having enjoyed great honor, was so practically refuted, as even to be sold out of the country,[7] and to succeed in none of his objects, no, not so much as in respect of one tyrant: yea, he betrayed his disciples, and ended his life miserably. And the Cynics, mere pollutions as they were, have all passed by like a dream and a shadow. And yet assuredly no such thing ever befell them, but rather they were accounted glorious for their heathen philosophy, and the Athenians made a public monument of the epistles of Plato, sent them by Dion; and they passed all their time at ease, and abounded in wealth not a little. Thus, for instance, Aristippus was used to purchase costly harlots; and another made a will, leaving no common inheritance; and another, when his disciples had laid themselves down like a bridge, walked on them; and he of Sinope, they say, even behaved himself unseemly in the market place.

Yea, these are their honorable things. But there is no such thing here, but a strict temperance, and a perfect decency, and a war against the whole world in behalf of truth and godliness, and to be slain every day, and not until hereafter their glorious trophies.

But there are some also, one may say, skilled in war amongst them; as Themistocles, Pericles. But these things too are children's toys, compared with the acts of the fishermen. For what canst thou say? That he persuaded the Athenians to embark in their ships, when Xerxes was marching upon Greece? Why in this case, when it is not Xerxes marching, but the devil with the whole world, and his evil spirits innumerable

---

[1] [R. V., "be not anxious."]   [2] Matt. x. 19, 20.
[3] Luke xxi. 15.   [4] Matt. x. 21.

[5] Matt. x. 22.   [6] ὁρμαθὸς.
[7] For the story of Plato's slavery, see Diogen. Laertius, lib. 3 ; St. Chrys. in 1 Cor. Hom. IV. sec. 9 ; and Plutarch (as there quoted) in his Life of Dion. as to its authenticity, see Mitford's Greece, iv. c. 31, sec. 8.

assailing these twelve men, not at one crisis only, but throughout their whole life, they prevailed and vanquished; and what was truly marvellous, not by slaying their adversaries, but by converting and reforming them.

For this especially you should observe throughout, that they slew not, nor destroyed such as were plotting against them, but having found them as bad as devils, they made them rivals of angels, enfranchising human nature from this evil tyranny, while as to those execrable demons that were confounding all things, they drave them out of the midst of markets, and houses, or rather even from the very wilderness. And to this the choirs of the monks bear witness, whom they have planted everywhere, clearing out not the habitable only, but even the uninhabitable land. And what is yet more marvellous, they did not this in fair conflict, but in the enduring of evil they accomplished it all. Since men actually had them in the midst, twelve unlearned persons, binding, scourging, dragging them about, and were not able to stop their mouths; but as it is impossible to bind the sunbeam, so also their tongue. And the reason was, " it was not they " themselves " that spake," but the power of the Spirit. Thus for instance did Paul overcome Agrippa, and Nero, who surpassed all men in wickedness. " For the Lord," saith he, " stood with me, and strengthened me, and delivered me out of the mouth of the lion." [1]

But do thou also admire them, how when it was said to them, " Take no thought," they yet believed, and accepted it, and none of the terrors amazed them. And if thou say, He gave them encouragement enough, by saying, " It shall be the Spirit of your Father that shall speak;" even for this am I most amazed at them, that they doubted not, nor sought deliverance from their perils; and this, when not for two or three years were they to suffer these things, but all their life long. For the saying, " He that endureth to the end, the same shall be saved," is an intimation of this.

For His will is, that not His part only should be contributed, but that the good deeds should be also done of them. Mark, for instance, how from the first, part is His, part His disciples'. Thus, to do miracles is His, but to provide nothing is theirs. Again, to open all men's houses, was of the grace from above; but to require no more than was needful, of their own self-denial. " For the workman is worthy of his hire." Their bestowing peace was of the gift of God, their

inquiring for the worthy, and not entering in without distinction unto all, of their own self command. Again, to punish such as received them not was His, but to retire with gentleness from them, without reviling or insulting them, was of the apostles' meekness. To give the Spirit, and cause them not to take thought, was of Him that sent them, but to become like sheep and doves, and to bear all things nobly, was of their calmness and prudence. To be hated and not to despond, and to endure, was their own; to save them that endured, was of Him who sent them.

Wherefore also He said, " He that endureth to the end, the same shall be saved." That is, because the more part are wont at the beginning indeed to be vehement, but afterwards to faint, therefore saith He, " I require the end." For what is the use of seeds, flourishing indeed at first, but a little after fading away? Therefore it is continued patience that He requires of them. I mean, lest any say, He wrought the whole Himself, and it was no wonder that they should prove such, suffering as they did nothing intolerable; therefore He saith unto them, " There is need also of patience on your part. For though I should rescue you from the first dangers, I am reserving you for others more grievous, and after these again others will succeed; and ye shall not cease to have snares laid for you, so long as ye have breath. For this He intimated in saying, " But he that endureth to the end, the same shall be saved."

For this cause then, though He said, " Take no thought what ye shall speak;" yet elsewhere He saith, " Be ready to give an answer to every man that asketh you a reason of the hope that is in you." [2] That is, as long as the contest is among friends, He commands us also to take thought; but when there is a terrible tribunal, and frantic assemblies, and terrors on all sides, He bestows the influence from Himself, that they may take courage and speak out, and not be discouraged, nor betray the righteous cause.

For in truth it was a very great thing, for a man occupied about lakes, and skins, and receipt of custom, when tyrants were on their thrones, and satraps, and guards standing by them, and the swords drawn, and all standing on their side; to enter in alone, bound, hanging down his head, and yet be able to open his mouth. For indeed they allowed them neither speech nor defense with respect to their doctrines, but set about torturing them to death, as common pests of the world.

---

[1] 2 Tim. iv. 17.

[2] 1 Peter iii. 15.

For "They," it is said, "that have turned the world upside down, are come hither also;" and again, "They preach things contrary to the decrees of Cæsar, saying that Jesus Christ is king."[1] And everywhere the courts of justice were preoccupied by such suspicions, and much influence from above was needed, for their showing both the truth of the doctrine they preached, and that they are not violating the common laws; so that they should neither, while earnest to speak of the doctrine, fall under suspicion of overturning the laws; nor again, while earnest to show that they were not overturning the common government, corrupt the perfection of their doctrines: all which thou wilt see accomplished with all due consideration, both in Peter and in Paul, and in all the rest. Yea, and as rebels and innovators, and revolutionists, they were accused all over the world; yet nevertheless they both repelled this impression, and invested themselves with the contrary, all men celebrating them as saviors, and guardians, and benefactors. And all this they achieved by their much patience. Wherefore also Paul said, "I die daily;"[2] and he continued to "stand in jeopardy" unto the end.

6. What then must we deserve, having such high patterns, and in peace giving way to effeminacy, and remissness? With none to make war (it is too evident) we are slain; we faint when no man pursues, in peace we are required to be saved, and even for this we are not sufficient. And they indeed, when the world was on fire, and the pile was being kindled over the whole earth, entering, snatched from within, out of the midst of the flame, such as were burning; but thou art not able so much as to preserve thyself.

What confidence then will there be for us? What favor? There are no stripes, no prisons, no rulers, no synagogues, nor aught else of that kind to set upon us; yea, quite on the contrary we rule and prevail. For both kings are godly, and there are many honors for Christians, and precedences, and distinctions, and immunities, and not even so do we prevail. And whereas they being daily led to execution, both teachers and disciples, and bearing innumerable stripes, and continual brandings, were in greater luxury than such as abide in Paradise; we who have endured no such thing, not even in a dream, are softer than any wax. "But they," it will be said, "wrought miracles." Did this then keep them from the scourge? did it free them from persecution? Nay, for this is the strange thing, that they suffered such things often even at the hands of them whom they benefited, and not even so were they confounded, receiving only evil for good. But thou if thou bestow on any one any little benefit, and then be requited with anything unpleasant, art confounded, art troubled, and repentest of that which thou hast done.

If now it should happen, as I pray it may not happen nor at any time fall out, that there be a war against churches, and a persecution, imagine how great will be the ridicule, how sore the reproaches. And very naturally; for when no one exercises himself in the wrestling school, how shall he be distinguished in the contests? What champion, not being used to the trainer, will be able, when summoned by the Olympic contests, to show forth anything great and noble against his antagonist? Ought we not every day to wrestle and fight and run? See ye not them that are called Pentathli, when they have no antagonists, how they fill a sack with much sand, and hanging it up try their full strength thereupon? And they that are still younger, practise the fight against their enemies upon the persons of their companions.

These do thou also emulate, and practise the wrestlings of self denial. For indeed there are many that provoke to anger, and incite to lust, and kindle a great flame. Stand therefore against thy passions, bear nobly the mental pangs, that thou mayest endure also those of the body.

7. For so the blessed Job, if he had not exercised himself well before his conflicts, would not have shone so brightly in the same. Unless he had practised freedom from all despondency, he would have uttered some rash word, when his children died. But as it was, he stood against all the assaults, against ruin of fortune, and destruction of so great affluence: against loss of children, against his wife's commiseration, against plagues in body, against reproaches of friends, against revilings of servants.

And if thou wouldest see his ways of exercise also, hear him saying, how he used to despise wealth: "If I did but rejoice," saith he, "because my wealth was great: if I set gold up for a heap, if I put my trust in a precious stone."[3] Therefore neither was he confounded at their being taken away, since he desired them not when present.

Hear how he also managed what related to his children, not giving way to undue softness, as we do, but requiring of them all circumspection. For he who offered sacrifice

---

[1] Acts xvii. 6, 7.   [2] 1 Cor. xv. 31, 30.   [3] Job xxxi. 25, 24, LXX.

even for their secret sins, imagine how strict a judge he was of such as were manifest.[1]

And if thou wouldest also hear of his strivings after continence, hearken to him when he saith, " I made a covenant with mine eyes, that I should not think upon a maid."[2] For this cause his wife did not break his spirit, for he loved her even before this, not however immoderately, but as is due to a wife.

Wherefore I am led even to marvel, whence it came into the devil's thought to stir up the contest, knowing as he did of his previous training. Whence then did it occur to him? The monster is wicked, and never despairs: and this turns out to us a very great condemnation, that he indeed never gives up the hope of our destruction, but we despair of our own salvation.

But for bodily mutilation and indignity, mark how he practised himself. Why, inasmuch as he himself had never undergone any such thing, but had continued to live in wealth and luxury, and in all other splendor, he used to divine other men's calamities, one by one. And this he declared, when he said, " For the thing which I greatly feared is come upon me; and that which I was afraid of is come unto me."[3] And again, " But I wept for every helpless man, and groaned when I saw a man in distress."[4]

So because of this, nothing of what happened confounded him, none of those great and intolerable ills. For I bid thee not look at the ruin of his substance, nor at the loss of his children, nor at that incurable plague, nor at his wife's device against him; but at those things which are far more grievous than these.

"And what," saith one, " did Job suffer more grievous than these? for from his history there is nothing more than these for us to learn." Because we are asleep, we do not learn, since he surely that is anxious, and searches well for the pearl, will know of many more particulars than these. For the more grievous, and apt to infuse greater perplexity, were different.

And first, his knowing nothing certain about the kingdom of heaven, and the resurrection; which indeed he also spoke of, lamenting. " For I shall not live alway, that I should suffer long."[5] Next, his being conscious to himself of many good works. Thirdly, his being conscious of no evil thing. Fourthly, his supposing that at God's hands he was undergoing it; or if at the devil's, this again was enough to offend him. Fifthly, his hearing his friends accusing him of wickedness, " For thou hast not been scourged," say they, " according to what thy sins deserve."[6] Sixthly, his seeing such as lived in wickedness prospering, and exulting over him. Seventhly, not having any other to whom he might look as even having ever suffered such things.

8. And if thou wouldest learn how great these things are, consider our present state. For if now, when we are looking for a kingdom, and hoping for a resurrection, and for the unutterable blessings, and are conscious to ourselves of countless evil deeds, and when we have so many examples, and are partakers of so high a philosophy; should any persons lose a little gold, and this often, after having taken it by violence, they deem life not to be lived in, having no wife to lay sore on them, nor bereaved of children, nor reproached by friends, nor insulted by servants, but rather having many to comfort them, some by words, some by deeds; of how noble crowns must not he be worthy, who seeing what he had gotten together by honest labor, snatched away from him for nought and at random, and after all that, undergoing temptations without number, like sleet, yet throughout all abides unmoved, and offers to the Lord his due thanksgiving for it all?

Why, though no one had spoken any of the other taunts, yet his wife's words alone were sufficient utterly to shake a very rock. Look, for example, at her craft. No mention of money, none of camels, and flocks, and herds, (for she was conscious of her husband's self command with regard to these), but of what was harder to bear than all these, I mean, their children; and she deepens the tragedy, and adds to it her own influence.

Now if when men were in wealth, and suffering no distress, in many things and oft have women prevailed on them: imagine how courageous was that soul, which repulsed her, assaulting him with such powerful weapons, and which trod under foot the two most tyrannical passions, desire and pity. And yet many having conquered desire, have yielded to pity. That noble Joseph, for instance, held in subjection the most tyrannical of pleasures, and repulsed that strange woman, plying him as she did with innumerable devices; but his tears he contained not, but when he saw his brethren that had wronged him, he was all on fire with that passion, and quickly cast off the mask, and discovered the part he had been playing.[7] But when first of all she is his wife, and when her words are piteous, and the moment favorable for her,

---

[1] Job i. 5.   [2] Job xxxi. 1.   [3] Job iii. 25.
[4] Job xxx. 25.   [5] Job vii. 16, LXX.

15

[6] Job xi. 6.   [7] δρᾶμα.

as well as his wounds and his stripes, and those countless waves of calamities; how can one otherwise than rightly pronounce the soul impassive to so great a storm to be firmer than any adamant?

Allow me freely to say, that the very apostles, if not inferior to this blessed man, are at least not greater than he was. For they indeed were comforted by the suffering for Christ; and this medicine was so sufficient daily to relieve them, that the Lord puts it everywhere, saying, "for me, for my sake," and, "If they call me, the master of the house, Beelzebub." [1] But he was destitute of this encouragement, and of that from miracles, and of that from grace; for neither had he so great power of the Spirit.

And what is yet greater, nourished in much delicacy, not from amongst fishermen, and publicans, and such as lived frugally, but after enjoyment of so much honor, he suffered all that he did suffer. And what seemed hardest to bear in the case of the apostles, this same he also underwent, being hated of friends, of servants, of enemies, of them who had received kindness of him: and the sacred anchor, the harbor without waves, namely, that which was said to the apostles, "for my sake," of this he had no sight.

I admire again the three children, for that they dared the furnace, that they stood up against a tyrant. But hear what they say,

"We serve not thy Gods, nor worship the image which thou hast set up." [2] A thing which was the greatest encouragement to them, to know of a certainty that for God they are suffering all whatsoever they suffer. But this man knew not that it was all conflicts, and a wrestling; for had he known it, he would not have felt what was happening. At any rate, when he heard, "Thinkest thou that I have uttered to thee mine oracles for nought, or that thou mightest be proved righteous?" [3] consider how straightway, at a bare word, he breathed again, how he made himself of no account, how he accounted himself not so much as to have suffered what he had suffered, thus saying, "Why do I plead any more, being admonished and reproved of the Lord, hearing such things, I being nothing?" [4] And again, "I have heard of Thee before, as far as hearing of the ear; but now mine eye hath seen Thee; wherefore I have made myself vile, and have melted away; and I accounted myself earth and ashes." [5]

This fortitude then, this moderation, of him that was before law and grace, let us also emulate, who are after law and grace; that we may also be able to share with him the eternal tabernacles; unto which may we all attain, by the grace and love towards man of our Lord Jesus Christ, to whom be the glory and the victory forever and ever. Amen.

---

[1] Matt. x. 25.

[2] Dan. iii. 18.
[4] Job xl. 4, LXX.

[3] Job xl. 3, LXX.
[5] Job xlii. 5, 6, LXX.

HOMILY XXXIV.

MATT. X. 23.

"But when they persecute you in this city, flee ye into the other; for verily I say unto you, ye shall not have gone over the cities of Israel, till the Son of Man be come."

HAVING spoken of those fearful and horrible things, enough to melt very adamant, which after His cross, and resurrection, and assumption, were to befall them, He directs again His discourse to what was of more tranquil character, allowing those whom He is training to recover breath, and affording them full security. For He did not at all command them, when persecuted, to close with the enemy, but to fly. That is, it being so far but a beginning, and a prelude, He gave His discourse a very condescending

turn. For not now of the ensuing persecutions is He speaking, but of those before the cross and the passion. And this He showed by saying, "Ye shall not have gone over the cities of Israel, till the Son of Man be come." That is, lest they should say, "What then, if when persecuted we flee, and there again they overtake us, and drive us out?"—to destroy this fear, He saith, "Ye shall not have gone round Palestine first, but I will straightway come upon you."

And see how here again He doeth not

away with the terrors, but stands by them in their perils. For He said not, "I will snatch you out, and will put an end to the persecutions;' but what? "Ye shall not have gone over the cities of Israel, till the Son of Man be come." Yea, for it sufficed for their consolation, simply to see Him.

But do thou observe, I pray thee, how He doth not on every occasion leave all to grace, but requires something also to be contributed on their part. "For if ye fear," saith He, "flee," for this He signified by saying, "flee ye," and "fear not."[1] And He did not command them to flee at first, but when persecuted to withdraw; neither is it a great distance that He allows them, but so much as to go about the cities of Israel.

Then again, He trains them for another branch of self-command; first, casting out all care for their food: secondly, all fear of their perils; and now, that of calumny. Since from that first anxiety He freed them, by saying, "The workman is worthy of his hire,"[2] and by signifying that many would receive them; and from their distress about their dangers, by saying, "Take no thought how or what ye shall speak," and, "He that endureth unto the end, the same shall be saved."[3]

But since withal it was likely that they should also bring upon themselves an evil report, which to many seems harder to bear than all; see whence He comforts them even in this case, deriving the encouragement from Himself, and from all that had been said touching Himself; to which nothing else was equal. For as He said in that other place, "Ye shall be hated of all men," and added, "for my name's sake," so also here.

And in another way He mitigates it, joining a fresh topic to that former. What kind of one then is it?

"The disciple," saith He, "is not above his Master, nor the servant above his Lord It is enough for the disciple that he be as his Master, and the servant as his Lord. If they have called the Master of the house Beelzebub, how much more shall they call them of His household? Fear them not therefore."[4]

See how He discovers Himself to be the Lord and God and Creator of all things. What then? Is there not any disciple above his Master, or servant above his Lord?[5] So long as he is a disciple, and a servant, he is not, by the nature of that honor. For tell me not here of the rare instances, but take the principle from the majority. And He saith

not, "How much more His servants," but "them of His household," to show how very near He felt them to be to Him.[6] And elsewhere too He said, "Henceforth I call you not servants; ye are my friends."[7] And He said not, If they have insulted the Master of the house, and calumniated Him; but states also the very form of the insult, that they "called Him Beelzebub."

Then He gives also another consolation, not inferior to this: for this indeed is the greatest; but because for them who were not yet living strictly, there was need also of another, such as might have special power to refresh them, He states it likewise. And the saying seems indeed in form to be an universal proposition, nevertheless not of all matters, but of those in hand only, is it spoken. For what saith He?

"There is nothing covered, that shall not be revealed; nor hid, that shall not be known."[8] Now what He saith is like this. It is indeed sufficient for your encouragement, that I also shared with you in the same reproach; I who am your Master and Lord. But if it still grieve you to hear these words, consider this other thing too, that even from this suspicion ye will soon be released. For why do ye grieve? At their calling you sorcerers and deceivers? But wait a little, and all men will address you as saviors, and benefactors of the world. Yea, for time discovers all things that are concealed, it will both refute their false accusation, and make manifest your virtue. For when the event shows you saviors, and benefactors, and examples of all virtue, men will not give heed to their words, but to the real state of the case; and they will appear false accusers, and liars, and slanderers, but ye brighter than the sun, length of time revealing and proclaiming you, and uttering a voice clearer than a trumpet, and making all men witnesses of your virtue. Let not therefore what is now said humble you, but let the hope of the good things to come raise you up. For it cannot be, that what relates to you should be hid.

2. Then, having rid them of all distress, and fears, and anxiety, and set them above men's reproaches, then, and not till then, He seasonably discourses to them also of boldness in their preaching.

For, "What I tell you," saith He, "in darkness, that speak ye in light; and what ye have heard in the ear, that preach ye[9] upon the housetops."[10]

Yet it was not at all darkness, when He was saying these things; neither was He dis-

---

[1] Matt. x. 26.
[2] Matt. x. 10.
[3] Matt. x. 19, 22.
[4] Matt. x. 24-26.
[5] [In the Greek this seems to be a repetition of verse 24, and not a question.—R.]

[6] γνησιότητα ἐπιδεικνύμενος.
[7] John xv. 15, 14.
[8] Matt. x. 16.
[9] [R. V., "proclaim."]
[10] Matt. x. 27.

coursing unto them in the ear; but He used a strong figure, thus speaking. That is, because He was conversing with them alone, and in a small corner of Palestine, therefore He said, "in darkness," and "in the ear;" contrasting the boldness of speech, which He was hereafter to confer on them, with the tone of the conversation which was then going on. "For not to one, or two, or three cities, but to the whole world ye shall preach," saith He, "traversing land and sea, the inhabited country, and the desert; to princes alike and tribes, to philosophers and orators, saying all with open face,[1] and with all boldness of speech." Therefore, He said, "On the house tops," and, "In the light," without any shrinking, and with all freedom.

And wherefore said He not only, "Preach on the housetops," and "Speak in the light," but added also, "What I tell you in darkness," and "What ye hear in the ear"? It was to raise up their spirits. As therefore when He said, "He that believeth on me, the works that I do shall he do also, and greater works than these shall he do;"[2] even so here too, to signify that He will do it all by them, and more than by Himself, He inserted this. For "the beginning indeed," saith He, "I have given, and the prelude; but the greater part it is my will to effect through you." Now this is the language of one not commanding only, but also declaring beforehand what was to be, and encouraging them with His sayings, and implying that they should prevail over all, and quietly also removing[3] again their distress at the evil report. For as this doctrine, after lying hid for a while, shall overspread all things, so also the evil suspicion of the Jews shall quickly perish.

Then, because He had lifted them up on high, He again gives warning of the perils also, adding wings to their mind, and exalting them high above all. For what saith He? "Fear not them which kill the body, but are not able to kill the soul."[4] Seest thou how He set them far above all things, persuading them to despise not anxiety only and calumny, dangers and plots, but even that which is esteemed of all things most terrible, death? And not death alone, but by violence too? And He said not, "ye shall be slain," but with the dignity that became Him, He set this before them, saying, "Fear not them which kill the body, but are not able to kill the soul; but rather fear Him[5] which is able to destroy both soul and body

in hell;" bringing round the argument, as He ever doth, to its opposite. For what? is your fear, saith He, of death? and are ye therefore slow to preach? Nay for this very cause I bid you preach, that ye fear death: for this shall deliver you from that which is really death. What though they shall slay you? yet over the better part they shall not prevail, though they strive ten thousand ways. Therefore He said not, "Who do not kill the soul," but, who "are not able to kill." For wish it as they may, they shall not prevail. Wherefore, if thou fear punishment, fear that, the more grievous by far.

Seest thou how again He doth not promise them deliverance from .death, but permits them to die, granting them more than if He had not allowed them to suffer it? Because deliverance from death is not near so great as persuading men to despise death. You see now, He doth not push them into dangers, but sets them above dangers, and in a short sentence fixes in their mind the doctrines that relate to the immortality of the soul, and having in two or three words implanted a saving doctrine, He comforts them also by other considerations.

Thus, lest they should think, when killed and butchered, that as men forsaken they suffered this, He introduces again the argument of God's providence, saying on this wise: "Are not two sparrows sold for a farthing? And one of them shall not fall into a snare[6] without your Father. But the very hairs of your head are all numbered."[7] "For what is viler than they?" saith He; "nevertheless, not even these shall be taken without God's knowledge." For He means not this, "by His operation they fall," for this were unworthy of God; but, "nothing that is done is hid from Him." If then He is not ignorant of anything that befalls us, and loves us more truly than a father, and so loves us, as to have numbered our very hairs; we ought not to be afraid. And this He said, not that God numbers our hairs, but that He might indicate His perfect knowledge,.and His great providence over them. If therefore He both knows all the things that are done, and is able to save you, and willing; whatever ye may have to suffer, think not that as persons forsaken ye suffer. For neither is it His will to deliver you from the terrors, but to persuade you to despise them, since this is, more than anything, deliverance from the terrors.

---

[1] γυμνῇ τῇ κεφαλῇ.   [2] John xiv. 12.
[3] ὑπορύττοντος.   [4] Matt. x. 28.
[5] [Chrysostom plainly refers this to God, not Satan. Hence the capital letter of the Oxford translator.—R].

[6] See received text above, Hom. IX. 4. [The reading here followed is accepted by several others of the Fathers, but has no MSS. authority. See Tischendorf, in loco. In Homily IX. 4, there is no variation from the Greek text, as now attested.—R.]
[7] Matt. x. 29, 30.

3. " Fear ye not therefore; ye are of more value than many sparrows."[1] Seest thou that the fear had already prevailed over them? Yea, for He knew the secrets of the heart; therefore He added, " Fear them not therefore;" for even should they prevail, it will be over the inferior part, I mean, the body; which though they should not kill, nature will surely take with her and depart. So that not even this depends on them, but men have it from nature. And if thou fear this, much more shouldest thou fear what is greater, and dread " Him who is able to destroy both soul and body in hell." And He saith not openly now, that it is Himself, " Who is able to destroy both soul and body," but where He before declared Himself to be judge, He made it manifest.

But now the contrary takes place: Him, namely, who is able to destroy the soul, that is, to punish it, we fear not, but those who slay the body, we shudder at. Yet surely while He together with the soul punishes the body also, they cannot even chasten the body, much less the soul; and though they chasten it ever so severely, yet in that way they rather make it more glorious. Seest thou how He signifies the conflicts to be easy? Because in truth, death did exceedingly agitate their souls, inspiring terror for a time, for that it had not as yet been made easy to overcome, neither had they that were to despise it partaken of the grace of the Spirit.

Having, you see, cast out the fear and distress that was agitating their soul; by what follows He also encourages them again, casting out fear by fear; and not by fear only, but also by the hope of great prizes; and He threatens with much authority, in both ways urging them to speak boldly for the truth; and saith further,

" Whosoever therefore shall confess me before men, him[2] will I also confess before my Father which is in Heaven. But whosoever shall deny me before men, him will I also deny before my Father which is in Heaven."[3]

Thus not from the good things only, but also from the opposites, doth He urge them; and He concludes with the dismal part.

And mark His exact care; He said not " me," but " in me," implying that not by a power of his own, but by the help of grace from above, the confessor makes his confession. But of him that denies, He said not,

" in me," but " me;" for he having become destitute of the gift, his denial ensues.

" Why then is he blamed," one may say, " if being forsaken, he denies?" Because the being forsaken is the fault of the forsaken person himself.

But why is He not satisfied with the faith in the mind, but requires also the confession with the mouth? To train us up to boldness in speech, and a more abundant love and determination, and to raise us on high. Wherefore also He addresses Himself to all. Nor doth He at all apply this to the disciples only in person, for not them, but their disciples too, He is now rendering noble hearted. Because he that hath learnt this lesson will not only teach with boldness, but will likewise suffer all things easily, and with ready mind. This at any rate brought over many to the apostles, even their belief in this word. Because both in the punishment the infliction is heavier, and in the good things the recompense greater. I mean, whereas he that doeth right hath the advantage in time,[4] and the delay of the penalty is counted for gain by the sinner: He hath introduced an equivalent, or rather a much greater advantage, the increase of the recompenses. " Hast thou the advantage," saith He, " by having first confessed me here? I also will have the advantage of thee, by giving thee greater things, and unspeakably greater; for I will confess thee there." Seest thou that both the good things and the evil things are there to be dispensed? Why then hasten and hurry thyself? and why seek thy rewards here, thou who art " saved by hope?"[5] Wherefore, whether thou hast done anything good, and not received its recompense here, be not troubled (for with increase, in the time to come, the reward thereof awaits thee): or whether thou hast done any evil, and not paid the penalty, be not easy; for there will vengeance receive thee, if thou turn not and amend.

But if thou believe it not, from the things here form thy conjecture about things to come also. Why, if in the season of the conflicts they that confess are so glorious, imagine what they will be in the season of the crowns. If the enemies here applaud, how shall that tenderest of all fathers fail to admire and proclaim thee? Yea, then shall we have both our gifts for the good, and our punishments for the evil. So that such as deny shall suffer harm, both here and there;

---

[1] Matt. x. 31.
[2] [R. V., "Every one, therefore, who shall confess me (Greek, in me) before men, him (Greek, in him)," etc. See the use made in the Homily of the Greek preposition " in."—R.]
[3] Matt. x. 32, 33.

[4] τῷ χρόνῳ πλεονεκτεῖ, " he is beforehand with his rewarder:" his sufferings, and the sinner's enjoyment, come respectively first.
[5] Rom. viii. 24. [" Saved in hope " or " for hope " expresses the meaning better, and agrees with the argument in the Homily. —R.]

here living with an evil conscience, though they were never to die, they shall be surely dead; and there, undergoing the last penalty: but the other sort will profit both here and there, both here making a gain of their death, and in this way becoming more glorious than the living, and there enjoying those unspeakable blessings.

God then is in no wise prompt to punish only, but also to confer benefits; and for this last more than for the first. But why hath He put the reward once only, the punishment twice? He knows that this would be more apt to correct us. For this cause when He had said, "Fear Him which is able to destroy both soul and body in hell," He saith again, "Him will I also deny." So doth Paul also, continually making mention of hell.

Thus we see that He, having by all ways trained on His scholar (both by opening Heaven to him, and by setting before him that fearful judgment-seat, and by pointing to the amphitheatre of angels, and how in the midst of them the crowns shall be proclaimed, which thing would thenceforth prepare the way for the word of godliness to be very easily received); in what follows, lest they grow timid and the word be hindered, He bids them be prepared even for slaughter itself; to make them aware that such as continue in their error, will have to suffer (among other things) for plotting against them.

4. Let us therefore despise death, although the time be not come that requires it of us; for indeed it will translate us to a far better life. "But the body decays." Why, on this account most especially we ought to rejoice, because death decays, and mortality perishes, not the substance of the body. For neither, shouldest thou see a statue being cast, wouldest thou call the process destruction, but an improved formation. Just so do thou reason also concerning the body, and do not bewail. Then it were right to bewail, had it remained in its chastisement.

"But," saith one, "this ought to take place without the decay of our bodies; they should continue entire." And what would this have advantaged either the living or the departed? How long are ye lovers of the body? How long are ye rivetted to the earth and gaping after shadows? Why, what good would this have done? or rather, what harm would it not have done? For did our bodies not decay, in the first place the greatest of all evils, pride, would have continued with many. For if even while this is going on, and worms gushing out, many have earnestly sought to be gods; what would not have been the result did the body continue?

In the second place, it would not be believed to be of earth; for if, its end witnessing this, some yet doubt; what would they not have suspected if they did not see this? Thirdly, the bodies would have been excessively loved; and most men would have become more carnal and gross; and if even now some cleave to men's tombs and coffins, after that themselves have perished, what would they not have done, if they had even their image preserved? Fourthly, they would not have earnestly desired the things to come. Fifthly, they that say the world is eternal, would have been more confirmed, and would have denied God as Creator. Sixthly, they would not have known the excellence of the soul, and how great a thing is the presence of a soul in a body. Seventhly, many of them that lose their relations would have left their cities, and have dwelt in the tombs, and have become frantic, conversing continually with their own dead. For if even now men form to themselves images, since they cannot keep the body (for neither is it possible, but whether they will or no it glides and hurries from them), and are rivetted to the planks of wood; what monstrous thing would they not then have devised? To my thinking, the generality would have even built temples for such bodies, and they that are skilled in such sorceries would have persuaded evil spirits to speak through them; since at least even now, they that venture on the arts of necromancy attempt many things more out of the way than these. And how many idolatries would not have arisen from hence? when men even after the dust and ashes, are yet eager in those practices.

God therefore, to take away all our extravagances, and to teach us to stand off from all earthly things, destroys the bodies before our eyes. For even he that is enamored of bodies, and is greatly affected at the sight of a beautiful damsel, if he will not learn by discourse the deformity of that substance, shall know it by the very sight. Yea, many of the like age with her whom he loves, and oftentimes also fairer, being dead, after the first or second day, have emitted an ill savor, and foul matter, and decay with worms. Imagine then what sort of beauty thou lovest, and what sort of elegance has power so to disturb thee. But if bodies did not decay, this would not be well known: but as evil spirits run unto men's graves, so also many of our lovers, continually sitting by the tombs, would have received evil spirits in their soul, and would quickly have perished in this grievous madness.

But as it is, together with all other things

this also comforts the soul, that the form is not seen: it brings men to forgetfulness of their affliction. Indeed, if this were not so, there would be no tombs at all, but thou wouldest see our cities having corpses instead of statues, each man desiring to look upon his own dead. And much confusion would arise hence, and none of the ordinary sort would attend to his soul, nor would give room to the doctrine of immortality to enter in: and many other things too, more shocking than these, would have resulted, which even to speak of were unseemly. Wherefore it decays presently, that thou mightest see unveiled the beauty of the soul. For if she be the procurer of all that beauty and life, much more excellent must she herself be. And if she preserve that which is so deformed and unsightly, much more herself.

5. For it is not the body wherein the beauty lies, but the expression,[1] and the bloom which is shed over its substance by the soul. Now then, I bid thee love that which makes the body also to appear such as it is. And why speak I of death? Nay even in life itself, I would have thee mark how all is hers that is beautiful. For whether she be pleased, she showers roses over the cheeks; or whether she be pained, she takes that beauty, and involves it all in a dark robe. And if she be continually in mirth, the body improves in condition; if in grief, she renders the same thinner and weaker than a spider's web; if in wrath, she hath made it again abominable and foul; if she show the eye calm, great is the beauty that she bestows; if she express envy, very pale and livid is the hue she sheds over us; if love, abundant the gracefulness she at once confers. Thus in fact many women, not being beautiful in feature, have derived much grace from the soul; others again of brilliant bloom, by having an ungracious soul, have marred their beauty. Consider how a face that is pale grows red, and by the variation of color produces great delight, when there is need of shame and blushing. As, on the other hand, if it be shameless, it makes the countenance more unpleasing than any monster.

For nothing is fairer, nothing sweeter than a beauteous soul. For while as to bodies, the longing is with pain, in the case of souls the pleasure is pure and calm. Why then let go the king, and be wild about the herald? Why leave the philosopher, and gape after his interpreter? Hast thou seen a beautiful eye? acquaint thyself with that which is within; and if that be not beautiful, despise this likewise. For surely, didst thou see an illfavored woman wearing a beautiful mask, she would make no impression on thee: just as on the other hand, neither wouldest thou suffer one fair and beautiful to be disguised by the mask, but wouldest take it away, as choosing to see her beauty unveiled.

This then I bid thee do in regard of the soul also, and acquaint thyself with it first; for this is clad with the body instead of a mask; wherefore also that abides such as it is; but the other, though it be mishapen, may quickly become beautiful. Though it have an eye that is unsightly, and harsh, and fierce, it may become beautiful, mild, calm, sweettempered, gentle.

This beauty therefore let us seek, this countenance let us adorn; that God also may " have pleasure in our beauty,"[2] and impart to us of His everlasting blessings, by the grace and love towards man of our Lord Jesus Christ, to whom be glory and might forever and ever. Amen.

----

[1] διάπλασις, " the moulding of it by the informing soul."

[2] Ps. xlv. 12, LXX.

HOMILY XXXV.

Matt. X. 34.

" Think not that I am come[1] to send peace on earth; I am not come[2] to send peace, but a sword."

Again, He sets forth the things that are more painful, and that with great aggravation: and the objection they were sure to meet Him with, He prevents them by stating. I mean, lest hearing this, they should say, " For this then art Thou come, to destroy both us, and them that obey us, and to fill the earth with war?" He first saith Himself, " I am not come to send peace on earth."

[1] [R. V., " came."]   [2] [R. V., " came not."]

How then did He enjoin them to pronounce peace on entering into each house? And again, how did the angels say, "Glory to God in the highest, and on earth peace"?[1] And how came all the prophets too to publish it for good tidings? Because this more than anything is peace, when the diseased is cut off, when the mutinous is removed. For thus it is possible for Heaven to be united to earth. Since the physician too in this way preserves the rest of the body, when he amputates the incurable part; and the general, when he has brought to a separation them that were agreed in mischief. Thus it came to pass also in the case of that famous tower; for their evil peace[2] was ended by their good discord, and peace made thereby. Thus Paul also divided them that were conspiring against him.[3] And in Naboth's case that agreement was at the same time more grievous than any war.[4] For concord is not in every case a good thing, since even robbers agree together.

The war is not then the effect of His purpose, but of their temper. For His will indeed was that all should agree in the word of godliness; but because they fell to dissension, war arises. Yet He spake not so; but what saith He? "I am not come to send peace;" comforting them. As if He said, For think not that ye are to blame for these things; it is I who order them so, because men are so disposed. Be not ye therefore confounded, as though the events happened against expectation. To this end am I come, to send war among men; for this is my will. Be not ye therefore troubled, when the earth is at war, as though it were subject to some hostile device. For when the worse part is rent away, then after that Heaven is knit unto the better.

And these things He saith, as strengthening them against the evil suspicion of the multitude.

And He said not "war," but what was more grievous than it, "a sword." And if there be somewhat painful in these expressions, and of an alarming emphasis, marvel not. For, it being His will to train their ears by the severity of His words, lest in their difficult circumstances they should start aside, He fashioned His discourse accordingly; lest any one should say it was by flattery He persuaded them, and by concealing the hardships; therefore even to those things which merited to be otherwise expressed, He gave by His words the more galling and painful

turn. For it is better to see persons' gentleness in things, than in words.

2. Wherefore neither with this was He satisfied, but unfolds also the very nature of the war, signifying it to be far more grievous even than a civil war; and He saith,

"I am come to set a man at variance against his father, and the daughter against her mother, and the daughter-in-law against her mother-in-law."[5]

For not friends only, saith He, nor fellow citizens, but even kinsmen shall stand against one another, and nature shall be divided against herself. "For I am come," saith He, "to set a man at variance against his father, and the daughter against her mother, and a daughter-in-law against her mother-in-law." That is, not merely among those of the same household is the war, but among those that are dearest, and extremely near to each other. And this more than anything signifies His power, that hearing these things, they both accepted Him, and set about persuading all others.

Yet was it not He that did this: of course not: but the wickedness of the other sort: nevertheless He saith it is His own doing. For such is the custom of the Scripture. Yea, and elsewhere also He saith, "God hath given them eyes that they should not see:"[6] and here He speaks in this way, in order that having, as I said before, exercised themselves in these words, they might not be confounded on suffering reproaches and insults.

But if any think these things intolerable, let them be reminded of an ancient history. For in times of old also this came to pass, which thing especially shows the old covenant to be akin to the new, and Him who is here speaking, the same with the giver of those commands. I mean that in the case of the Jews also, when each had slain his neighbor, then He laid aside His anger against them; both when they made the calf, and when they were joined to Baal Peor.[7] Where then are they that say, "That God is evil, and this good?" For behold He hath filled the world with blood, shed by kinsmen. Nevertheless even this we affirm to be a work of great love towards man.

Therefore, you see, implying that it was He who approved those other acts also, He makes mention also of a prophecy, which if not spoken for this end, yet involves the same meaning. And what is this?

"A man's foes shall be they of his own household."[8]

---

1 Luke ii. 14.
3 Acts xxiii. 6, 7

2 Gen. xi. 7, 8.
4 1 Kings xxi.

5 Matt. x. 35. [R. V., "I came," etc.]
7 Exod. xxxii. 29; Numb. xxv. 7-11.

6 Rom. xi. 8.
8 Matt. x. 36.

For indeed among the Jews also something of the kind took place. That is, there were prophets, and false prophets, and the people was divided, and families were in dissension; and some believed the one, and some the other. Wherefore the prophet admonishes, saying, "Trust ye not in friends, have not hope in guides; yea, even of her that lieth in thy bosom beware, in respect of communicating aught to her:" and, "A man's enemies are the men that are in his own house."[1]

And this He said, preparing him that should receive the word to be above all. For to die is not evil, but to die an evil death. On this account He said moreover, "I am come to cast fire upon the earth."[2] And this He said, to declare the vehemence and warmth of the love which He required. For, because He loved us very much, so He will likewise be loved of us. And these sayings would strengthen[3] the persons present also, and lift them higher. "For if those others," saith He, "are to despise kinsmen, and children, and parents, imagine what manner of men ye their teachers ought to be. Since neither will the hardships stop with you, but will also pass on to the rest. For since I am come bringing great blessings, I demand also great obedience, and purpose of heart."

3. "He that loveth father or mother more than me, is not worthy of me; and he that loveth son or daughter more than me, is not worthy of me; and he that taketh not his cross and followeth after me, is not worthy of me."[4]

Seest thou a teacher's dignity? Seest thou, how He signifies himself a true Son of Him that begat Him, commanding us to let go all things beneath, and to take in preference the love of Him?

"And why speak I," saith He, "of friends and kinsmen? Even if it be thine own life which thou preferrest to my love, thy place is far from my disciples." What then? Are not these things contrary to the Old Testament? Far from it, rather they are very much in harmony therewith. For there too He commands not only to hate the worshippers of idols, but even to stone them; and in Deuteronomy again, admiring these, He saith, "Who said unto his father, and to his mother, I have not seen thee; neither did he acknowledge his brethren, and his own sons he disowned: he kept Thy oracles."[5] And if Paul gives many directions touching parents, commanding us to obey them in all things, marvel not; for in those things only doth he

mean us to obey, as many as do not hinder godliness.[6] For indeed it is a sacred duty to render them all other honors: but when they demand more than is due, one ought not to obey. For this reason Luke saith, "If any man come to me, and hate not his father, and mother, and wife, and children, and brethren, and sisters, yea, and his own life also, he cannot be my disciple;"[7] not commanding simply to hate them, since this were even quite contrary to the law; but "when one desires to be loved more than I am, hate him in this respect. For this ruins both the beloved himself, and the lover." And these things He said, both to render children more determined, and to make fathers more gentle, that would hinder them. For when they saw He had such strength and power as to sever their children from them, they, as attempting things impossible, would even desist. Wherefore also He leaves the fathers, and addresses His discourse to the children, instructing the former not to make the attempt, as attempting things impracticable.

Then lest they should be indignant, or count it hard, see which way He makes His argument tend: in that having said, "Who hateth not father and mother," He adds, "and his own life." For why dost thou speak to me of parents, saith He, and brothers, and sisters, and wife? Nothing is nearer than the life to any man: yet if thou hate not this also, thou must bear in all things the opposite of his lot who loveth me.

And not even simply to hate it was His command, but so as to expose it to war, and to battles, and to slaughters, and blood. "For he that beareth not his cross, and cometh after me, cannot be my disciple."[8] Thus He said not merely that we must stand against death, but also against a violent death; and not violent only, but ignominious too.

And He discourses nothing as yet of His own passion, that when they had been for a time instructed in these things, they might more easily receive His word concerning it. Is there not, therefore, cause for amazement, how on their hearing these things, their soul did not wing its way from the body, the hardships being everywhere at hand, and the good things in expectation? How then did it not flee away? Great was both the power of the speaker, and the love of the hearers. Wherefore though hearing things far more intolera-

---

[1] Micah vii. 5, 6.   [2] Luke xii. 49.
[3] ἤλειφε, " would anoint them for action."
[4] Matt. x. 37, 38.   [5] Deut. xxxiii. 9.

[6] Eph. vi. 1. See there St. Chrysostom's explanation of the expression, "in the Lord."
[7] Luke xiv. 26.
[8] Matt. x. 38. Comp. Luke xiv. 27. [The word "beareth" (from Luke) is here substituted for "taketh."—R.]

ble and galling than those great men, Moses and Jeremiah, they continued to obey, and to say nothing against it.

"He that findeth his life," saith He, "shall lose it: and he that loseth his life for my sake, shall find it."[1] Seest thou how great the damage to such as love it unduly? how great the gain to them that hate it? I mean, because the injunctions were disagreeable, when He was bidding them set themselves against parents, and children, and nature, and kindred, and the world, and their very soul, He sets forth the profit also, being very great. Thus, "These things," saith He, "so far from harming, will very greatly profit; and their opposites will injure;" urging them, as He ever doth, by the very things which they desire. For why art thou willing to despise thy life?[2] Because thou lovest it? Then for that very reason despise it, and so thou wilt advantage it in the highest degree, and do the part of one that loves it.

And mark an instance of unspeakable consideration. For not in respect of our parents only doth He practise this reasoning, nor of our children, but with regard to our life, which is nearer than all; that the other point may thenceforth become unquestionable, and they may learn that they will in this way profit those of their kindred likewise, as much as may be; since so it is in the case even of our life, which is more essential to us than all.

4. Now these things were enough to recommend men to receive them, their appointed healers. Yea, who would choose but receive with all readiness them that were so noble, such true heroes, and as lions running about the earth, and despising all that pertained to themselves, so that others might be saved? Yet nevertheless He proffers also another reward, indicating that He is caring here for the entertainers more than for the guests.

And the first honor He confers is by saying,

"He that receiveth you, receiveth me, and he that receiveth me, receiveth Him that sent me."[3]

With this, what may compare? that one should receive the Father and the Son!

But He holds out herewith another reward also.

"He," saith He, "that receiveth a prophet in the name of a prophet, shall receive a prophet's reward; and he that receiveth a righteous man in the name of a righteous man, shall receive a righteous man's reward."[4]

And as before He threatens punishment to such as do not receive them, here He defines also a certain refreshment[5] for the good. And to teach thee His greater care for them, He said not simply, "He that receiveth a prophet," or "He that receiveth a righteous man," but subjoined, "in the name of a prophet," and, "in the name of a righteous man;" that is, if not for any worldly preferment, nor for any other temporal thing, he receive him, but because he is either a prophet or a righteous man, he shall receive a prophet's reward, and a righteous man's reward; such as it were meet for him to have, that hath received a prophet, or a righteous man; or, such as that other is himself to receive. Which kind of thing Paul also said: "That your abundance may be a supply for their want, that their abundance also may be a supply for your want."[6]

Then, lest any one should allege poverty, He saith,

"Or whosoever shall give to drink unto one of these little ones a cup of cold water only in the name of a disciple, verily I say unto you, he shall in no wise lose his reward."[7]

"Though a cup of cold water be thy gift, on which there is nothing laid out, even of this shall a reward be stored up for thee. For I do all things for the sake of you the receivers."

Seest thou what mighty persuasions He used, and how He opened to them the houses of the whole world? Yea, He signified that men are their debtors: first, by saying, "The workman is worthy of his hire;" secondly, by sending them forth having nothing; thirdly, by giving them up to wars and fightings in behalf of them that receive them; fourthly, by committing to them miracles also; fifthly, in that He did by their lips introduce peace, the cause of all blessings, into the houses of such as receive them; sixthly, by threatening things more grievous than Sodom to such as receive them not: seventhly, by signifying that as many as welcome them are receiving both Himself and the Father; eighthly, by promising both a prophet's and a righteous man's reward: ninthly, by undertaking that the recompenses shall be great, even for a cup of cold water. Now each one of these things, even by itself, were enough to attract them. For who, tell me, when a

---

[1] Matt. x. 39.
[2] Or "soul;" the same word standing in the Greek for both "soul" and "life;" which makes it impossible to give the full force of the passage in English.
[3] Matt. x. 40.

[4] Matt. x. 41.
[5] ἄνεσιν, opposed to κόλασιν, "punishment," in the same way, Hom. XIII. 8, in the Benedictine edition, p. 176, c.; and elsewhere.
[6] 2 Cor. viii. 14.   [7] Matt. x. 43.

leader of armies wounded in innumerable places, and dyed in blood, came in sight, returning after many trophies from war and conflict, would not receive him, throwing open every door in his house?

5. But who now is like this? one may say. Therefore He added, "In the name of a disciple, and of a prophet, and of a righteous man;" to instruct thee that not for the worthiness of the visitor, but for the purpose of him that gives welcome, is His reward appointed. For though here He speak of prophets, and righteous men, and disciples, yet elsewhere He bids men receive the veriest outcasts, and punishes such as fail to do so. For, "Inasmuch as ye did it not to one of the least of these, ye did it not to me;"[1] and the converse again He affirms with respect to the same persons.

Since though he may be doing no such great work, he is a man, inhabiting the same world with thee, beholding the same sun, having the same soul, the same Lord, a partaker with thee of the same mysteries, called to the same heaven with thee; having a strong claim, his poverty, and his want of necessary food. But now they that waken thee with flutes and pipes in the winter season, and disturb thee without purpose or fruit, depart from thee receiving many gifts.[2] And they that carry about swallows,[3] and smut themselves over,[4] and abuse every one, receive a reward for this their conjuration. But if there come to thee a poor man wanting bread, there is no end of revilings, and reproaches, and charges of idleness, and upbraidings, and insults, and jeers; and thou considerest not with thyself, that thou too art idle, and yet God giveth thee His gifts. For tell me not this, that thou too art doing somewhat, but point me out this rather, if it be anything really needful that thou doest, and art busy about. But if thou tellest one of money-getting, and of traffic, and of the care and increase of thy goods, I also would

say unto thee, Not these, but alms, and prayers, and the protection of the injured, and all such things, are truly works, with respect to which we live in thorough idleness. Yet God never told us, "Because thou art idle, I light not up the sun for thee; because thou doest nothing of real consequence, I quench the moon, I paralyze the womb of the earth, I restrain the lakes, the fountains, the rivers, I blot out the atmosphere, I withhold the annual rains:" but He gives us all abundantly. And to some that are not merely idle, but even doing evil, He freely gives the benefit of these things.

When therefore thou seest a poor man, and sayest, "It stops my breath that this fellow, young as he is and healthy, having nothing, would fain be fed in idleness; he is surely some slave and runaway, and hath deserted his proper master:" I bid thee speak these same words to thyself; or rather, permit him freely to speak them unto thee, and he will say with more justice, "It stops my breath that thou, being healthy, art idle, and practisest none of the things which God hath commanded, but having run away from the commandments of thy Lord, goest about dwelling in wickedness, as in a strange land, in drunkenness, in surfeiting, in theft, in extortion, in subverting other men's houses." And thou indeed imputest idleness, but I evil works; in thy plotting, in thy swearing, in thy lying, in thy spoiling, in thy doing innumerable such things.

And this I say, not as making a law in favor of idleness, far from it; but rather very earnestly wishing all to be employed; for sloth is the teacher of all wickedness: but I beseech you not to be unmerciful, nor cruel. Since Paul also, having made infinite complaints, and said, "If any will not work, neither let him eat," stopped not at this, but added, "But ye, be not weary in well doing."[5] "Nay, but these things are contradictory. For if thou hast commanded for them not to eat, how exhortest thou us to give?" I do so, saith He, for I have also commanded to avoid them, and "to have no company with them;" and again I said, "Count them not as enemies, but admonish them;"[6] not making contradictory laws, but such as are quite in unison with each other. Because, if thou art prompt to mercy, both he, the poor man, will soon be rid of his idleness, and thou of thy cruelty.

"But he hath many lies and inventions," you reply. Well, hence again is he pitiable, for that he hath fallen into such distress, as

1 Matt. xxv. 45.
2 This was part of the festivities of the Saturnalia; "it began on the 13th of January, when the flute players used to run about the city with much license and wantonness in female apparel; as at this time, about the Epiphany season, pipers and singers are wont to come into the houses of the rich, to sing for largesses, with some in masks at their head. *Vid.* Liv. lib. ix. c. 30." Francisc. Modius *de Ludis et Spect. Veterum*, ii. 28, ap. Gronov. Thes. xi. 1055.
3 Here Mr. Field quotes from Bois as follows: "It is a description of certain jugglers, who used to carry about swallows trained to come and go when let loose, and settle on their heads, and take meat out of their mouths. So I conjecture." Mr. Field adds, "I have nothing to add to this. For those whom Athanæus" (from Theognis) "mentions, as *gathering a dole for the swallow* (p. 360, B.) seem not to answer to what is here meant. They, by way of begging, used to chant a sort of song about the coming of the swallow. It was the custom of the Rhodians particularly."
4 Scaliger, Poet i. 10, says, "Some actors in low comedy were not masked, but smeared with soot; . . . and used to dance to music in honor of Bacchus, and bounding forward, to jeer at every one." ap. Hoffman, *voc. Mimus.*

5 2 Thess. iii. 10, 13.	6 2 Thess. iii. 14, 15.

to be hardened even in such doings. But we, so far from pitying, add even those cruel words, "Hast thou not received once and again?" so we talk. What then? because he was once fed, hath he no need to be fed again? Why dost thou not make these laws for thine own belly also, and say to it likewise, Thou wert filled yesterday, and the day before, seek it not now? But while thou fillest that beyond measure, even to bursting,[1] from him thou turnest away, when he asks but what is moderate; whereas thou oughtest therefore to pity him, because he is constrained to come to thee every day. Yea, if nought else incline thee to him, thou shouldest pity him because of this; for by the constraint of his poverty he is forced on these things, and doeth them. And thou dost not pity him, because, being so spoken to, he feels no shame: the reason being, that his want is too strong for him.

Nay, thou instead of pitying, dost even make a show of him; and whereas God hath commanded to give secretly, thou standest exposing publicly him that hath accosted thee, and upbraiding him, for what ought to move thy pity. Why, if thou art not minded to give, to what end add reproach, and bruise that weary and wretched soul? He came as into a harbor, seeking help at thine hands; why stir up waves, and make the storm more grievous? Why dost thou condemn him of meanness? What? had he thought to hear such things, would he have come to thee? Or if he actually came foreseeing this, good cause therefore both to pity him, and to shudder at thine own cruelty, that not even so, when thou seest an inexorable necessity laid upon him, dost thou become more gentle, nor judgest him to have a sufficient excuse for his importunity in the dread of hunger, but accusest him of impudence: and yet hast thou often thyself practised greater impudence, yea in respect of grievous matters. For while here the very impudence brings with it ground of pardon, we, often doing things punishable, brazen it out: and when we ought to bear all that in mind, and be humble, we even trample on those miserable men, and when they ask medicines, we add to their wounds. I say, if thou wilt not give, yet why dost thou strike? If thou wilt not be bounteous, yet why be insolent?

"But he submits not to be put off in any other way." Well then, as that wise man commanded,[2] so do. "Answer him peaceable words with meekness." For not of his own accord, surely, is he so very importu-

nate. For there is not, there cannot be, any man desiring to be put to shame for its own sake. How much soever any may contend, I cannot yield ever to be convinced that a man who was living in plenty would choose to beg.

6. Let no man then beguile us with arguments. But although Paul saith, "If any will not work, neither let him eat,"[3] to them he saith it; but to us he saith not this, but, on the contrary, "Be not weary in well doing."[4] Even thus do we at home; when any two are striving with each other, we take each apart, and give them the opposite advice. This did God also, and Moses. For while to God he said, "If thou wilt forgive them their sin, forgive it; else blot me out also;"[5] them on the contrary he commanded to slay one another, and all that pertained to them. Yet these things are contrary; nevertheless, both looked to one end.

Again, God said to Moses in the hearing of the Jews, "Let me alone, that I may consume the people,"[6] (for though they were not present when God was saying this, yet they were to hear it afterwards): but privately He gives him directions of the opposite tenor. And this, Moses upon constraint revealed afterwards, thus saying, "What? did I conceive them, that thou sayest to me, Carry them, as a nurse would carry the sucking child in her bosom?"[7]

These things are done also in houses, and often a father while he blames the tutor in private for having used his child reproachfully, saying, "Be not rough, nor hard," to the youth speaks in the contrary way, "Though thou be reproached unjustly, bear it;" out of those opposites making up some one wholesome result. Thus also Paul said to such as are in health and beg, "If any man will not work, neither let him eat," that he may urge them into employment: but to such as can show mercy, "Ye, for your part, be not weary in well doing:" that he may lead them to give alms.

So also, when he was admonishing those of the Gentiles, in his Epistle to the Romans, not to be highminded against the Jews, he brought forward also the wild olive, and he seems to be saying one thing to these, another to those.[8]

Let us not therefore fall away into cruelty, but let us listen to Paul, saying, "Be not weary in well doing;" let us listen to the Lord, who saith, "Give to every man that asketh of thee,"[9] and, "Be ye merciful as

---

[1] [ὑπὲρ τὸ μέτρον διαρρηγνύεις.]   [2] Ecclus. iv. 8.

[3] 2 Thess. iii. 10.   [4] 2 Thess. iii. 13.
[5] Exod. xxxii. 32 [LXX.].   [6] Exod. xxxii. 10.
[7] Numb. xi. 12 [LXX.].   [8] Rom. xi. 17.
[9] Luke vi. 30.

your Father."[1]   And though He hath spoken of many things, He hath nowhere used this expression, but with regard to our deeds of mercy only.   For nothing so equals us with God, as doing good.

"But nothing is more shameless," saith one, "than a poor man."   Why, I pray thee? Because he runs up, and cries out after thee? Wilt thou then let me point out, how we are more importunate than they, and very shameless?   Remember, I say, now at the season of the fast, how often, when thy table was spread at eventide, and thou hadst called thy ministering servant; on his moving rather leisurely,[2] thou hast overset everything, kicking, insulting, reviling, merely about a little delay; although fully assured, that if not immediately, yet a little after thou shalt enjoy thy victuals.   Upon which thou dost not call thyself impudent, changed as thou art into a wild beast for nothing; but the poor man, alarmed and trembling about his greater interests (for not about delay, but about famine, is all his fear), him dost thou call audacious, and shameless, and impudent, and all the most opprobrious names?   Nay, how is this anything but extreme impudence.

But these things we do not consider: therefore we account such men troublesome: since if we at all searched into our own doings, and compared them with theirs, we should not have thought them intolerable.

Be not then a severe judge.   Why, if thou wert clear of all sins, not even then would the law of God permit thee to be strict in searching out other men's sins.   And if the Pharisee perished on this account, what defense are we to find?   If He suffer not such as have done well to be bitter in searching out other men's doings, much less them that have offended.

7. Let us not then be savage, nor cruel, not without natural feeling, not implacable, not worse than wild beasts.   For I know many to have gone even so far in brutishness, as for a little trouble to slight famishing persons, and to say these words: "I have no servant now with me; we are far from home; there is no money-changer that I know." Oh cruelty !   Didst thou promise the greater, and dost thou not fulfill the less?   To save thy walking a little way, doth he perish with hunger?   Oh insolence ! Oh pride ! Why, if it were ten furlongs to be walked, oughtest thou to be backward?   Doth it not even come into thy mind that so thy reward is made greater?   For whereas, when thou givest,

thou receivest reward for the gift only: when thou thyself also goest, for this again is appointed thee a recompense.

Yea, the patriarch himself we admire for this, that in his own person be ran to the herd, and snatched up the calf,[3] and that, when he had three hundred and eighteen servants born in his house.[4]   But now some are filled with so much pride, as to do these things by servants, and not to be ashamed. "But dost thou require me to do these things myself?" one may say.   "How then shall I not seem to be vainglorious ?"   Nay, but as it is, thou art led by another kind of vainglory to do this, being ashamed to be seen talking with a poor man.

But I am in no respect strict about this; only give, whether by thyself or by another thou art minded to do so; and do not accuse, do not smite, do not revile.   For medicines, not wounds, doth he need who comes unto thee; mercy, not a sword.   For tell me, if any one who had been smitten with a stone, and had received a wound in his head, were to let go all others, and run unto thy knees, drenched in his blood; wouldest thou indeed smite him with another stone, and add unto him another wound?   I, for my part, think not; but even as it was, thou wouldest endeavor to cure it.   Why then doest thou the contrary with respect to the poor?   Knowest thou not how much power a word hath, both to raise up, and to cast down?   "For a word," it is said, "is better than a gift."[5]

Dost thou not consider that thou art thrusting the sword into thyself, and art receiving a more grievous wound, when he, being reviled, silently withdraws, with groans and many tears?   Since indeed of God he is sent unto thee.   Consider then, in insulting him, upon whom thou art causing the insult to pass; when God indeed sends him unto thee, and commands thee to give, but thou, so far from giving, dost even insult him on his coming.

And if thou art not aware how exceedingly amiss this is, look at it as among men, and then thou wilt fully know the greatness of the sin.   As thus: if a servant of thine had been commanded by thee to go to another servant, who had money of thine, to receive it, and were to come back not only with empty hands, but also with despiteful usage; what wouldest thou not do to him that had wrought the insult?   What penalty wouldest thou not exact, as though, after this, it were thyself that had been ill used?

This reckoning do thou make in regard of

---

[1] Luke vi. 36.
[2] [The construction is difficult : ἵνα σχολαιότερον βαδίσῃ.   We must accept here a causal sense of ἵνα.—R.]

[3] Gen. xviii. 7.   [4] Gen. xiv. 14.   Comp. ep. of Barn. c. 9.
[5] Ecclus. xviii. 16.

God also; for truly it is He that sends the poor to us, and of His we give, if indeed we do give. But if, besides not giving, we also send them away insulted, consider how many bolts, how many thunders, that which we are doing deserves.

Duly considering then all these things, let us both bridle our tongue, and put away inhumanity, and let us stretch forth the hand to give alms, and not with money only, but with words also, let us relieve such as are in need; that we may both escape the punishment for reviling, and may inherit the kingdom which is for blessing and almsgiving, by the grace and love towards man of our Lord Jesus Christ, to whom be glory and might forever and ever. Amen.

HOMILY XXXVI.

MATT. XI. 1.

"And it came to pass, when Jesus had made an end of commanding His twelve disciples, He departed thence to teach and to preach in their cities."

THAT is, after He had sent them, He proceeded to withdraw Himself, to give them room and opportunity to do what He had enjoined. For while He was present and healing, no one would be willing to approach them.

"Now when John had heard in the prison the works of Jesus,[1] he sent two of[2] his disciples, and asked Him, saying, Art thou He that should come,[3] or do we look for another?"[4]

But Luke saith, they also told John of the miracles, and then he sent them.[5] However, this contains no matter of difficulty, but of consideration only; for this, among other things, indicates their jealousy towards Him.

But what follows is completely among the controverted points. Of what nature then is this? Their saying, "Art Thou He that should come, or do we look for another?" That is, he that knew Him before His miracles, he that had learned it of the Spirit, he that heard it of the Father, he who had proclaimed Him before all men; doth he now send to learn of Him, whether it be Himself or no? And if yet thou didst not know that it is surely He, how thinkest thou thyself credible, affirming as thou dost concerning things, whereof thou art ignorant? For he that is to bear witness to others, must be first worthy of credit himself. Didst thou not say, "I am not meet to loose the latchet of His shoe?"[6] Didst thou not say, "I knew Him not, but He that sent me to baptize with water, the same said unto me, Upon whom thou shalt see the Spirit descending and resting upon Him, the same is He which baptizeth with the Holy Ghost?"[7] Didst thou not see the Spirit in form of a dove? didst thou not hear the voice? Didst thou not utterly forbid Him, saying, "I have need to be baptized of Thee?"[8] Didst thou not say even to thy disciples, "He must increase, I must decrease?"[9] Didst thou not teach all the people, that "He should baptize them with the Holy Ghost and with fire?"[10] and that He "is the Lamb of God that taketh away the sin of the world?"[11] Didst thou not before His signs and miracles proclaim all these things? How then now, when He hath been made manifest to all, and the fame of Him hath gone out everywhere, and dead men have been raised, and devils driven away, and a display made of so great miracles, dost thou after this send to learn of Him?

What then is the fact? Were all these sayings a kind of fraud: a stage play and fables? Nay, who that hath any understanding would say so? I say not, John, who leaped in the womb, who before his own birth proclaimed Him, the citizen of the wilderness, the exhibitor of the conversation of

---

[1] [R. V., "Of the Christ," as in nearly all authorities, but Chrysostom reads τοῦ Ἰησοῦ.—R.]
[2] [R. V., "by his disciples," but some ancient authorities (Vulgate also) support "two." Taken from Luke vii. 19.—R.]
[3] [R. V., "He that cometh."]   [4] Matt. xi. 2, 3.
[5] Luke vii. 18.

[6] John i. 27.   [7] John i. 33.   [8] Matt. iii. 14.
[9] John iii. 30.   [10] Matt. iii. 11.
[11] John i. 29. [R. V., "Or, beareth the sin," etc.]

angels; but even though he were one of the common sort, and of them that are utterly outcast, he would not have hesitated, after so many testimonies, both on his own part and on the part of others.

Whence it is evident, that neither did he send as being himself in doubt, nor did he ask in ignorance. Since no one surely could say this, that though he knew it fully, yet on account of his prison he was become rather timid: for neither was he looking to be delivered therefrom, nor if he did look for it, would he have betrayed his duty to God, armed as he was against various kinds of death. For unless he had been prepared for this, he would not have evinced so great courage towards a whole people, practised in shedding blood of prophets; nor would he have rebuked that savage tyrant with so much boldness in the midst of the city and the forum, severely chiding him, as though he were a little child, in hearing of all men. And even if he were grown more timid, how was he not ashamed before his own disciples, in whose presence he had so often borne witness unto Him, but asked his question by them, which he should have done by others? And yet surely he knew full well, that they too were jealous of Christ, and desired to find some handle against Him. And how could he but be abashed before the Jewish people, in whose presence he had proclaimed such high things? Or what advantage accrued to him thereby, towards deliverance from his bonds? For not for Christ's sake had he been cast into prison, nor for having proclaimed His power, but for his own rebuke touching the unlawful marriage. And what child so silly, what person so frantic, but that so he would have put on himself their character?[1]

2. What then is it which he is bringing about? For that it belongs not to John to have doubt hereupon, no nor to any ordinary person, nor even to one extremely foolish and frenzied; so much is evident from what we have said. And now we have only to add the solution.

For what intent then did he send to ask? John's disciples were starting aside from Jesus, and this surely any one may see, and they had always a jealous feeling towards Him. And it is plain, from what they said to their master: "He that was with thee," it is said, "beyond Jordan, to whom thou barest witness, behold, the same baptizeth, and all men come unto Him."[2] And again, "There arose a question between John's dis-

ciples and the Jews about purifying."[3] And again they came unto Him, and said, "Why do we and the Pharisees fast oft, but Thy disciples fast not?"[4] For as yet they knew not who Christ was, but imagining Jesus to be a mere man, but John greater than after the manner of man, were vexed at seeing the former held in estimation, but the latter, as he had said, now ceasing. And this hindered them from coming unto Him, their jealousy quite blocking up the access. Now so long as John was with them, he was exhorting them continually and instructing them, and not even so did he persuade them; but when he was now on the point of dying, he uses the more diligence: fearing as he did lest he might leave a foundation for bad doctrine, and they continue broken off from Christ. For as he was diligent even at first to bring to Christ all that pertained to himself; so on his failing to persuade them, now towards his end he does but exert the more zeal.

Now if he had said, "Go ye away unto Him, He is better than I," he would not have persuaded them, minded as they were not easily to be separated from him, but rather he would have been thought to say it out of modesty, and they would have been the more rivetted to him; or if he had held his peace, then again nothing was gained. What then doth he? He waits to hear from them that Christ is working miracles, and not even so doth he admonish them, nor doth he send all, but some two (whom he perhaps knew to be more teachable than the rest); that the inquiry might be made without suspicion, in order that from His acts they might learn the difference between Jesus and himself. And he saith, Go ye, and say, "Art thou He that should come, or do we look for another?"[5]

But Christ knowing the purpose of John, did not say, I am He; for this would again have offended the hearers, although this was what it naturally followed for Him to say, but He leaves them to learn it from His acts. For it saith, "when these were come to Him, then "He cured many."[6] And yet what congruity was there, that being asked, "Art thou He," He should say nothing to that, but should presently cure them that were sick; unless it had been His mind to establish this which I have mentioned? Because they of course would account the testimony of His deeds surer, and more above suspicion than that of His words.

Knowing therefore, as being God, the mind

---

[1] [οὐκ ἂν ἑαυτῷ δόξαν περιέθηκε.]   [2] John iii. 26.

[3] John iii. 25. [R. V., "with a Jew." So one ms. here. In Homily XXIX. on John, Chrysostom distinctly accepts the singular, as do nearly all Greek mss.—R.]
[4] Matt ix. 14.   [5] Matt. xi. 3.   [6] Luke vii. 21.

with which John had sent them, He straight-way cured blind, lame, and many others; not to teach him (for how should He him that was convinced), but these that were doubting: and having healed them, He saith,

"Go and show John again those things which ye do hear and see; the blind receive their sight, and the lame walk, and the lepers are cleansed, and the deaf hear, and the dead are raised up, and the poor have the gospel preached unto them."[1] And he added, "And blessed is he, whosoever shall not be offended in me;"[2] implying that He knows even their unuttered thoughts. For if He had said, "I am He," both this would have offended them, as I have already said; and they would have thought, even if they had not spoken, much as the Jews said to Him, "Thou bearest record of Thyself."[3] Where-fore He saith not this Himself, but leaves them to learn all from the miracles, freeing what He taught from suspicion, and making it plainer. Wherefore also He covertly added His reproof of them. That is, because they were "offended in Him," He by setting forth their case and leaving it to their own con-science alone, and by calling no witness of this His accusation, but only themselves that knew it all, did thus also draw them the more unto Himself, in saying, "Blessed is he, whosoever shall not be offended in me." For indeed His secret meaning was of them when He said this.

3. But in order to our making the truth more evident to you by the comparison of the several statements, producing not only our own sayings, but also what is stated by others; we must needs add some account of them.

What then do some affirm? That this which we have stated was not the cause, but that John was in ignorance, yet not in ignor-ance of all; but that He was the Christ, he knew, but whether He was also to die for mankind, he knew not, therefore he said, "Art Thou He that should come?" that is, He that is to descend into hell.[4] But this is not tenable; for neither of this was John ignorant. This at least he proclaimed even before all the others, and bare record of this first, "Behold," saith he, "the Lamb of God, which taketh away the sin of the world."[5] Now he called Him a lamb, as pro-claiming the cross, and again in saying,

"That taketh away the sin of the world," he declared this same thing. For not otherwise than by the cross did He effect this; as Paul likewise said: "And the handwriting which was contrary to us, even it He took out of the way, nailing it to His cross."[6] And his say-ing too, "He shall baptize you with the Spirit,"[7] is that of one who was foretelling the events after the resurrection.

Well: that He was to rise again, he knew, say they, and that He was to give the Holy Ghost; but that He should likewise be cruci-fied, he knew not. How then was He to rise again, who had not suffered, nor been cruci-fied? And how was this man greater than a prophet, who knew not even what the pro-phets knew? For that he was greater than a prophet, even Christ Himself bare record,[8] but that the prophets knew of the passion is surely plain to every one. For so Isaiah saith, "He is brought as a lamb to the slaughter, and as a sheep before her shearer is dumb."[9] And before this testimony also he saith, "There shall be a root of Jesse, and He that shall rise again to rule the Gentiles, in Him shall the Gentiles trust."[10] Then speaking of His passion, and of the ensuing glory, he added, "And His rest shall be honor." And this prophet foretold not only that He should be crucified, but also with whom. "For," saith he, "He was numbered with the trans-gressors."[11] And not this only, but that He should not even plead for Himself; "For this man," he saith, "openeth not His mouth:" and that He should be unjustly condemned; "For in His humiliation," saith he, "His judgment was taken away."[12] And before this again, David both saith this, and describes the judgment hall. "Why," saith he, "do the heathen rage, and the people imagine a vain thing? The kings of the earth stand up, and the rulers are gathered together against the Lord, and against His anointed."[13] And elsewhere he mentions also the image of the cross, saying on this wise, "They pierced my hand and my feet,"[14] and those things which the soldiers were embold-ened to do, he adds with all exactness, "For they parted my garments," saith he, "among them, and for my vesture they did cast lots."[15] And elsewhere again he saith, that they also offered Him vinegar; "For they gave me," saith He, "gall for my meat, and for my thirst they made me drink vinegar."[16] So then the prophets, so many years be-fore, speak of the hall of judgment, and of the condemnation, and of them that were

---

[1] Matt. iv. 5.
[2] Matt. xi. 6. [R. V., "shall find none occasion of stumbling in me."]
[3] John viii. 13. [R. V., "witness."]
[4] See Origen, 2 Hom. in *Reg.* t. ii. p. 495, 6 ; St. Ambr. in *Luc.* vii. 19 ; St. Jerome in *loc.* [The Greek term used is "Hades," not "Gehenna."—R.]
[5] John i. 29.

[6] Col. ii. 14. [Comp. R. V., in *loco.*]
[7] Matt. iii. 11.
[8] Matt. xi. 9.
[9] Isa. liii. 7.
[10] Isa. xi. 10.
[11] Isa. liii. 12.
[12] Isa. liii. 8, from LXX.
[13] Ps. ii. 1, 2.
[14] Ps. xxii. 16.
[15] Ps. xxii. 18.
[16] Ps. lxix. 21.

crucified with Him, and of the division of the garments, and of the lot cast upon them, and of many more things besides (for indeed it is unnecessary to allege all now, lest we make our discourse long): and was this man, greater than them all, ignorant of all these things? Nay, how should this be reasonable?

And why did he not say, "Art thou He that should come to hell,"[1] but simply, "He that should come?" Although this were far more absurd than the others, I mean their saying, "he therefore said these things, that he might preach there also after his departure." To whom it were seasonable to say, "Brethren, be not children in understanding, howbeit in malice be ye children."[2] For the present life indeed is the season for right conversation, but after death is judgment and punishment. "For in hell," it is said, "who will confess unto thee?"[3]

How then were "the gates of brass burst, and the bars of iron broken in sunder"?[4] By His body; for then first was a body shown, immortal, and destroying the tyranny of death. And besides, this indicates the destruction of the might of death, not the loosing of the sins of those who had died before His coming. And if this were not so, but He have delivered all that were before Him from hell,[5] how saith He, "It shall be more tolerable for the land of Sodom and Gomorrah?"[6] For this saying supposes that those are also to be punished; more mildly indeed, yet still that they are to be punished. And yet they did also suffer here the most extreme punishment, nevertheless not even this will deliver them. And if it is so with them, much more with such as have suffered nothing.

"What then?" one may say, "were they wronged, who lived before His coming?" By no means, for men might then be saved, even though they had not confessed Christ. For this was not required of them, but not to worship idols, and to know the true God. "For the Lord thy God," it is said, "is one Lord."[7] Therefore the Maccabees were admired, because for the observance of the law they suffered what they did suffer; and the three children, and many others too amongst the Jews, having shown forth a very virtuous life, and having maintained the standard of this their knowledge, had nothing more required of them. For then it was sufficient for salvation, as I have said already, to know God only; but now it is so no more, but there is need also of the knowledge of Christ.

Therefore He said, "If I had not come and spoken unto them, they had not had sin, but now they have no cloak for their sin."[8]

So likewise with regard to the rule of practice. Then murder was the destruction of him that committed it, but now even to be angry. And then to commit adultery, and to lie with another man's wife, brought punishment, but now even to look with unchaste eyes. For as the knowledge, so also the rule of life is now made stricter. So that there was no need of a forerunner there.

And besides, if unbelievers are after death to be saved on their believing, no man shall ever perish. For all will then repent and adore. And in proof that this is true, hear Paul saying, "Every tongue shall confess, and every knee shall bow, of things in heaven, and things in earth, and things under the earth."[9] And, "The last enemy that shall be destroyed is death."[10] But there is no advantage in that submission, for it comes not of a rightly disposed choice, but of the necessity of things, as one may say, thenceforth taking place.

Let us not then any more bring in such old wives' doctrines, and Jewish fables. Hear at least what Paul saith touching these things. "For as many as have sinned without law, shall also perish without law;"[11] where his discourse is of those who lived in the time before the law; and, "As many as have sinned in the law, shall be judged by the law,"[12] speaking of all after Moses. And, "That the wrath of God is revealed from heaven against all ungodliness, and unrighteousness of men,"[13] and, "indignation and wrath, tribulation and anguish upon every soul of man that worketh evil, of the Jew first, and also of the Gentile."[14] And yet countless were the evils which the Gentiles have suffered in this world, and this is declared alike by the histories of the heathens, and by the Scriptures that are in our hands. For who could recount the tragic calamities of the Babylonians, or those of the Egyptians? But in proof that they who, not having known Christ before His coming in the flesh, yet refrained from idolatry and worshipped God only, and showed forth an excellent life, shall enjoy all the blessings; hear what is said: "But glory, and honor, and peace to every one that worketh good, to the Jew first, and also to the Gentile." Seest thou that for their good deeds there are many rewards, and chastisements again, and penalties for such as have done the contrary?

---

[1] [εἰς τὸν ᾅδην.] [2] 1 Cor. xiv. 20. [3] Ps. vi. 5 [ᾅδη].
[4] Ps. cvii. 16. [5] [γεέννης.] [6] Matt. x. 15.
[7] Deut. vi. 4.
16

[8] John xv. 22. [R. V., "excuse."] [9] Phil. ii. 10, 11.
[10] 1 Cor. xv. 26. [11] Rom. ii. 12. [12] Rom. ii. 12.
[13] Rom. i. 18. [14] Rom. ii. 8, 9.

4. Where now, tell me, are the utter unbelievers in hell? Why, if those before Christ's coming, who had not so much as heard the name of hell,[1] nor of a resurrection, and were punished here, shall suffer punishment there also; how much more we that have been nurtured in so many lessons of strict virtue?[2]

And how is it reasonable, asks one, that they that have never heard of hell,[3] should fall into hell? For they will say, "If thou hadst threatened hell, we should have feared more, and have been sobered." To be sure; (is it not so?) at our rate of living now, who hear daily the sayings about hell, and give no heed at all.

And besides, there is this also to be said; that he who is not restrained by the judgments in sight, much less will he be restrained by those others. For the less reasonable sort, and those of a grosser disposition, are wont to be sobered rather by things which are at hand, and straightway to happen, than by such as will come to pass a long time after. "But over us," one may say, "a greater fear is suspended, and herein were they wronged." By no means. For first, there are not the same measures[4] set to us as to them, but much greater for us. Now they that have undertaken greater labors, ought to enjoy greater help. And it is no little help, that our fear has been increased. And if we have an advantage over them in knowing things to come, they have an advantage over us in that the severe punishments are presently laid upon them.

But there is something else, which the multitude say with respect to this also. For "where," say they, "is God's justice, when any one for sinning here, is punished both here and there?" Would ye then I should put you in mind of your own sayings, that ye may no longer give us trouble, but furnish the solution from within yourselves. I have heard many of our people, if haply they were told of a murderer cut off in a court of justice, how they had indignation, and talked in this way: "This unholy and accursed wretch, having perpetrated thirty murders, or even many more, hath himself undergone one death only; and where is the justice of it?" So that ye yourselves confess, that one death is not sufficient for punishment; how give ye

then an opposite sentence now. Because not others but yourselves are the objects of your judgment: so great a hindrance is self-love to our perceiving what is just. Because of this, when we are judging others, we search out all things with strictness, but when we are sitting in judgment on ourselves, we are blinded. Since if we were to search into these things in our own case too, as we do with regard to other men, we should give an uncorrupt sentence. For we also have sins, deserving not two or three, but ten thousand deaths. And to pass over all the rest, let us recollect ourselves, as many of us as partake unworthily of the mysteries; such men being guilty of the body and blood of Christ. Wherefore, when thou art talking of the murderer, take account of thyself also. For he indeed hath murdered a man, but thou art under the guilt of slaying the Lord; and he, not having partaken of mysteries, but we, while enjoying the benefit of the sacred table.

And what are they that bite and devour their brethren, and pour out such abundance of venom? What is he that robs the poor of their food? For if he who imparts not of his own, is such as I have said, *much more he that takes the things of others*.[5] How many robbers do the covetous surpass in wickedness! how many murderers and robbers of tombs, the rapacious! and how many after spoiling men are desirous even of their blood!

"Nay," saith he, "God forbid." Now thou sayest, God forbid. When thou hast an enemy, then say, God forbid, and call to mind what hath been said, and show forth a life full of great strictness; lest the portion of Sodom await us also, lest we suffer the lot of Gomorrha, lest we undergo the ills of the Tyrians and Sidonians; or rather, lest we offend Christ, which were a thing more grievous *and more to be feared* than all.

For though to many hell[6] seem to be a fearful thing, yet I for my part will not cease continually to say, that this is more grievous and fearful than any hell; and you I entreat to be of the same mind. For so shall we both be delivered from hell, and enjoy the glory that is bestowed of Christ; unto which may we all attain, by the grace and love towards man of our Lord Jesus Christ, to whom be glory and might forever and ever. Amen.

---

[1] [γεέννης.]
[2] φιλοσοφίας.
[3] [γεέννης, and so throughout the paragraph.—R.]
[4] σκάμματα.

[5] The words in italics, both here and below, are omitted in several MSS.
[6] [γέεννα, and similarly throughout the paragraph.—R.]

HOMILY XXXVII.

Matt. X. 7, 8, 9.

"And as they departed, Jesus began to say unto the multitudes concerning John, What went ye out into the wilderness to see? A reed shaken with the wind? But what went ye out for to see? A man clothed in soft raiment; behold, they that wear soft clothing are in kings' houses. But what went ye out for to see? A prophet?[1] yea, I say unto you, and more than a prophet."

For the matter indeed of John's disciples had been ordered well, and they were gone away assured by the miracles which had just been performed; but there was need after that of remedy as regarded the people. For although they could not suspect anything of the kind of their own master, the common people might from the inquiry of John's disciples form many strange suspicions, not knowing the mind with which he sent his disciples. And it was natural for them to reason with themselves, and say, " He that bore such abundant witness, hath he now changed his persuasion, and doth he doubt whether this or another be He that should come? Can it be, that in dissension with Jesus he saith this? that the prison hath made him more timid? that his former words were spoken vainly, and at random?" It being then natural for them to suspect many such things, see how He corrects their weakness, and removes these their suspicions. For " as they departed, He began to say to the multitudes." Why, " as they departed?" That He might not seem to be flattering the man.

And in correcting the people, He doth not publish their suspicion, but adds only the solution of the thoughts that were mentally disturbing them: signifying that He knew the secrets of all men. For He saith not, as unto the Jews, " Wherefore think ye evil?"[2] Because if they had it in their minds, not of wickedness did they so reason, but of ignorance on the points that had been spoken of. Wherefore neither doth He discourse unto them in the way of rebuke, but merely sets right their understanding, and defends John, and signifies that he is not fallen away from his former opinion, neither is he changed, not being at all a man easily swayed and fickle, but steadfast and sure, and far from being such as to betray the things committed unto him.

And in establishing this, He employs not at first his own sentence, but their former testimony, pointing out how they bare record of his firmness, not by their words only, but also by their deeds.

Wherefore He saith, " What went ye out into the wilderness to see?" as though He had said, Wherefore did ye leave your cities, and your houses, and come together all of you into the wilderness? To see a pitiful and flexible kind of person? Nay, this were out of all reason, this is not what is indicated by that earnestness, and the concourse of all men unto the wilderness. So much people and so many cities would not have poured themselves out with so great zeal towards the wilderness and the river Jordan at that time, had ye not expected to see some great and marvellous one, one firmer than any rock. Yea, it was not " a reed " surely, that " ye went out to see shaken by the wind:" for the flexible and such as are lightly brought round, and now say one thing, now another, and stand firm in nothing, are most like that.

And see how He omits all wickedness, and mentions this, which then especially haunted[3] them; and removes the suspicion of lightness.

" But what went ye out for to see? a man clothed in soft raiment? Behold, they that wear soft clothing are in kings' houses."[4]

Now His meaning is like this: He was not of himself a waverer; and this ye yourselves showed by your earnestness. Much less could any one say this, that he was indeed firm, but having made himself a slave to luxury, he afterwards became languid. For among men, some are such as they are of themselves, others become so; for instance, one man is passionate by nature, and another from having fallen into a long illness gets this infirmity. Again, some men are flexible

[1] [R. V. text, " But wherefore went ye out? to see a prophet?" In the margin the received reading is given. Chrysostom gives the latter here, but has the other in his comments. See sec. 2. —R.]

[2] Matt. ix. 4.

[3] ὑφορμοῦσαν.

[4] Matt. xi. 8.

and fickle by nature, while others become so by being slaves to luxury, and by living effeminately. "But John," saith He, "neither was such a character by nature, for neither was it a reed that ye went out to see; nor by giving himself to luxury did he lose the advantage he possessed." For that he did not make himself a slave to luxury, his garb shows, and the wilderness, and the prison. Since, had he been minded to wear soft raiment, he would not have lived in the wilderness, nor in the prison, but in the king's courts: it being in his power, merely by keeping silence, to have enjoyed honor without limit. For since Herod so reverenced him, even when he had rebuked him, and was in chains, much more would he have courted him, had he held his peace. You see, he had indeed given proof of his firmness and fortitude; and how could he justly incur suspicions of that kind?

2. When therefore as well by the place, as by his garments, and by their concourse unto Him, He had delineated his character, He proceeds to bring in the prophet. For having said, "Why went ye out? To see a prophet? Yea I say unto you, and more than a prophet;"[1] He goes on, "For this is he of whom it is written,[2] Behold, I send my messenger before Thy face, which shall prepare Thy way before Thee."[3] Having before set down the testimony of the Jews, He then applies that of the prophets; or rather, He puts in the first place the sentence of the Jews, which must have been a very strong demonstration, the witness being borne by his enemies; secondly, the man's life; thirdly, His own judgment; fourthly, the prophet; by all means stopping their mouths.

Then lest they should say, "But what if at that time indeed he were such an one, but now is changed?" He added also what follows; his garments, his prison, and together with these the prophecy.

Then having said, that he is greater than a prophet, He signifies also in what he is greater. And in what is he greater? In being near Him that was come. For, "I send," saith He, "my messenger before Thy face;" that is, nigh Thee. For as with kings, they who ride near the chariot, these are more illustrious than the rest, just so John also appears in his course near the advent itself. See how He signified John's excellency by this also; and not even here doth He stop, but adds afterwards His own suffrage as well, saying,

"Verily I say unto you, among them that are born of women, there hath not arisen a greater than John the Baptist."[4]

Now what He said is like this: "woman hath not borne a greater than this man." And His very sentence is indeed sufficient; but if thou art minded to learn from facts also, consider his table, his manner of life, the height of his soul.[5] For he so lived as though he were in heaven: and having got above the necessities of nature, he travelled as it were a new way, spending all his time in hymns and prayers, and holding intercourse with none among men, but with God alone continually. For he did not so much as see any of his fellow-servants, neither was he seen by any one of them; he fed not on milk, he enjoyed not the comfort of bed, or roof, or market, or any other of the things of men; and yet he was at once mild and earnest. Hear, for example, how considerately he reasons with his own disciples, how courageously with the people of the Jews, how openly with the king. For this cause He said also, "There hath not risen among them that are born of women a greater than John the Baptist."

3. But lest the exceeding greatness of His praises should produce a sort of extravagant feeling, the Jews honoring John above Christ; mark how He corrects this also. For as the things which edified His own disciples did harm to the multitudes, they supposing Him an easy kind of person; so again the remedies employed for the multitudes might have proved more mischievous, they deriving from Christ's words a more reverential opinion of John than of Himself.

Wherefore this also, in an unsuspected way, He corrects by saying, "He that is less,[6] in the kingdom of Heaven is greater than he." Less in age, and according to the opinion of the multitude, since they even called Him "a gluttonous man and a winebibber;"[7] and, "Is not this the carpenter's son?"[8] and on every occasion they used to make light of Him.

"What then?" it may be said, is it by comparison that He is greater than John?" Far from it. For neither when John saith, He is mightier than I,"[9] doth he say it as comparing them; nor Paul, when remembering Moses he writes, For this man was counted worthy of more glory than Moses,"[10] doth he so write by way of comparison; and He Himself too, in saying, Behold, a greater than

1 Matt. xi. 9. [See note 1, p. 243.]   2 See Mal. iii. 1.
3 Matt. xi. 10.

4 Matt. xi. 11.
5 [τῆς γνώμης; "zeal" would be a better rendering, though there is no precise English equivalent.—R.]
6 [R. V., "but little;" Gr. "lesser."]   7 Matt. xi. 19.
8 Matt. xiii. 55.   9 Matt. iii. 11.
10 Heb. iii. 3.

Solomon is here,"[1] speaks not as making a comparison.

Or if we should even grant that this was said by Him in the way of comparison, this was done in condescension,[2] because of the weakness of the hearers. For the men really had their gaze very much fixed upon John; and then he was rendered the more illustrious both by his imprisonment, and by his plainness of speech to the king; and it was a great point for the present, that even so much should be received among the multitude. And so too, the Old Testament uses in the same way to correct the souls of the erring, by putting together in a way of comparison things that cannot be compared; as when it saith, "Among the gods there is none like unto Thee, O Lord:"[3] and again, "There is no god like our God."[4]

Now some affirm, that Christ said this of the apostles, others again, of angels.[5] Thus, when any have turned aside from the truth, they are wont to wander many ways. For what sort of connexion hath it, to speak either of angels or of apostles? And besides, if He were speaking of the apostles, what hindered his bringing them forward by name? whereas, when He is speaking of Himself, He naturally conceals His person, because of the still prevailing suspicion, and that He may not seem to say anything great of Himself; yea, and we often find Him doing so.

But what is, "In the kingdom of heaven?" Among spiritual beings, and all them that are in heaven.

And moreover His saying, "There hath not risen among them that are born of women a greater than John," suited one contrasting John with Himself, and thus tacitly excepting Himself. For though He too were born of a woman, yet not as John, for He was not a mere man, neither was He born in like manner as a man, but by a strange and wondrous kind of birth.

4. "And from the days of John the Bap-

tist," saith He, "until now, the kingdom of heaven suffereth violence, and the violent take it by force."[6]

And what sort of connexion may this have with what was said before? Much, assuredly, and in full accordance therewith. Yea, by this topic also He proceeds to urge and press them into the faith of Himself; and at the same time likewise, He is speaking in agreement with what had been before said by John. "For if all things are fulfilled even down to John, I am "He that should come."

"For all the prophets," saith He, "and the law prophesied until John."[7]

For the prophets would not have ceased, unless I were come. Expect therefore nothing further, neither wait for any one else. For that I am He is manifest both from the prophets ceasing, and from those that every day "take by force" the faith that is in me. For so manifest is it and certain, that many even take it by force. Why, who hath so taken it? tell me. All who approach it with earnestness of mind.

Then He states also another infallible sign, saying, "If ye will receive it, he is Elias, which was for to come." For "I will send you," it is said, "Elias the Tishbite, who shall turn the heart of the father to the children."[8] This man then is Elias, if ye attend exactly, saith He. For "I will send," saith He, "my messenger before Thy face."[9]

And well hath He said, "If ye will receive it," to show the absence of force. For I do not constrain, saith He. And this He said, as requiring a candid mind, and showing that John is Elias, and Elias John. For both of them received one ministry, and both of them became forerunners. Wherefore neither did He simply say, "This is Elias," but, "If ye are willing to receive it, this is he," that is, if with a candid mind ye give heed to what is going on. And He did not stop even at this, but to the words, "This is Elias, which was for to come," He added, to show that understanding is needed, "He that hath ears to hear, let him hear."[10]

Now He used so many dark sayings, to stir them up to inquiry. And if not even so were they awakened, much more, had all been plain and clear. For this surely no man could say, that they dared not ask Him, and that He was difficult of approach. For they that were asking him questions, and

---

[1] Matt. xii. 42.   [2] Or, "by way of economy;" οἰκονομικῶς.
[3] Ps. lxxxvi. 8.   [4] Ps. lxxvii. 13.
[5] "Many will understand this of the Saviour; that he who is less in time is greater in dignity. But let us simply understand, that every saint who is already with God is greater than he whose post is yet in the battle. For it is one thing to possess the crown of victory, another still to fight in the battle. Some will take it that the lowest angel serving God in Heaven is greater than any even the first of men who as yet dwells on earth." St. Jerome, in loco.
"Finally, it is so utterly impossible that there should be any comparison between John and the Son of God, that the former is of less esteem even than the angels. Thus, on the one hand, inasmuch as He had called him an angel" (Mal. iii. 1), "He is of course set above men; on the other, because he had declared him chief among those born of women, He therefore added, For he who is lesser in the kingdom of heaven is greater than he : that you might know he could not compare with the angels." St. Ambr. on St. Luke, vii. 27 ; St. Aug. Contr. Advers. Legis et Proph. ii. xx, states both interpretations, without any preference for either. But in his 13 Tract. on St. John, c. ii. he gives the same as St. Chrysostom.

[6] Matt. xi. 12.   [R. V., "men of violence."]
[7] Matt. xi. 13.
[8] Mal. iv. 5, 6 [LXX., but with "children" substituted for "son."—R.]
[9] Mal. iii. 1. ["My face," in Mal. iii. 1, but "thy face" in the New Testament citations. Comp. verse 10, Mark i. 2, Luke vii. 27.—R.]
[10] Matt. xi. 15.

tempting Him about common matters, and whose mouths were stopped a thousand times, yet they did not withdraw from Him; how should they but have inquired of Him, and besought Him touching the indispensable things, had they indeed been desirous to learn? For if concerning the matters of the law they asked, "Which is the first commandment," and all such questions, although there was of course no need of His telling them that; how should they but ask the meaning of what He Himself said, for which also He was bound to give account in His answers? And especially when it was He Himself that was encouraging and drawing them on to do this. For by saying, "The violent take it by force," He stirs them up to earnestness of mind; and by saying, "He that hath ears to hear, let him hear," He doth just the same thing.

5. "But whereunto shall I liken this generation?" saith He, "It is like unto children sitting in the market place, and saying, We have piped unto you, and ye have not danced; we have mourned unto you, and ye have not lamented."[1] This again seems to be unconnected with what came before, but it is the most natural consequence thereof. Yea, He still keeps to the same point, the showing that John is acting in harmony with Himself, although the results were opposite; as indeed with respect to his inquiry also. And He implies that there was nothing that ought to have been done for their salvation, and was omitted; which thing the prophet[2] saith of the vineyard; "What ought I to have done to this vineyard, and have not done it? For whereunto," saith He, "shall I liken this generation? It is like unto children sitting in the market, and saying, We have piped unto you, and ye have not danced, we have mourned unto you, and ye have not lamented. For John came neither eating nor drinking, and they say, He hath a devil.[3] The Son of Man came eating and drinking, and they say, Behold a man gluttonous, and a winebibber, a friend of publicans and sinners."[4]

Now what He saith is like this: We have come each of us an opposite way, I and John; and we have done just as if it were some hunters with a wild beast that was hard to catch, and which might by two ways fall into the toils; as if each of the two were to cut it off his several way, and drive it, taking his stand opposite to the other; so that it must needs fall into one of the two snares. Mark,

for instance, the whole race of man, how it is astonished at the wonder of men's fasting, and at this hard and self-denying life. For this reason it had been so ordered, that John should be thus brought up from his earliest youth, so that hereby (among other things) his sayings might obtain credit.

But wherefore, it may be asked, did not He Himself choose that way? In the first place He did also Himself proceed by it, when He fasted the forty days, and went about teaching, and not having where to lay His head. Nevertheless He did also in another mode accomplish this same object, and provide for the advantage thence accruing. For to be testified of by him that came this way was the same thing, or even a much greater thing than to have come this way Himself.

And besides, John indeed exhibited no more than his life and conversation; for "John," it is said, "did no sign,"[5] but He Himself had the testimony also from signs and from miracles. Leaving therefore John to be illustrious by his fasting, He Himself came the opposite way, both coming unto publicans' tables, and eating and drinking.

Let us ask the Jews then, "Is fasting a good thing, and to be admired? you should then have obeyed John, and received him, and believed his sayings. For so would those sayings have led you towards Jesus. Is fasting, on the other hand, a thing grievous, and burdensome? then should you have obeyed Jesus, and have believed in Him that came the opposite way. Thus, either way, ye would have found yourselves in the kingdom." But, like an intractable wild beast, they were speaking evil of both. The fault is not then theirs who were not believed, but they are to be blamed who did not believe. For no man would ever choose to speak evil of opposite things, any more than he would on the other hand commend them. I mean thus: he that approves the cheerful and free character, will not approve him that is sad and grave; he that commends the man of a sad countenance will not commend the cheerful man. For it is a thing impossible to give your vote both ways at once. Therefore also He saith, "We have piped unto you, and ye have not danced;" that is, "I have exhibited the freer kind of life, and ye obeyed not:" and, "We have mourned, and ye have not lamented;" that is, "John followed the rugged and grave life, and ye took no heed." And He saith not, "he this, I that," but the purpose of both being one, although their

---

[1] Matt. xi. 16, 17. [The former verse is abridged. R. V. (ver. 17), "We piped unto you, and ye did not dance; we wailed, and ye did not mourn (Greek, beat the breast)."—R.]
[2] Isa. v. 4 [LXX.]   [3] ["demon."]
[4] Matt. xi. 16-19 [see note 1].

[5] John x. 41.

modes of life were opposite, for this cause He speaks of their doings as common. Yea, for even their coming by opposite ways arose out of a most exact accordance, such as continued looking to one and the same end. What sort of excuse then can ye have after all this?

Wherefore He subjoined, "And wisdom is justified of her children;"[1] that is, though ye be not persuaded, yet with me after this ye cannot find fault. As the prophet saith touching the Father, "That Thou mightest be justified in Thy sayings."[2] For God, though He should effect nothing more by His care over us, fulfills all His part, so as to leave to them that will be shameless not so much as a shadow of excuse for uncandid doubt.

And if the similitudes be mean, and of an ill sound, marvel not, for He was discoursing with a view to the weakness of His hearers. Since Ezekiel too mentions many similitudes like them, and unworthy of God's majesty.[3] But this too especially becomes His tender care.

And mark them, how in another respect also they are carried about into contradictory opinions. For whereas they had said of John, "he hath a devil,"[4] they stopped not at this, but said the very same again concerning Him,[5] taking as He did the opposite course; thus were they forever carried about into conflicting opinions.

But Luke herewith sets down also another and a heavier charge against them, saying, "For the publicans justified God, having received the baptism of John."[6]

6. Then He proceeds to upbraid the cities; now that wisdom hath been justified; now that He hath shown all to be fully performed. That is, having failed to persuade them, He now doth but lament over them; which is more than terrifying. For He had exhibited both His teaching by His words, and His wonder-working power by His signs. But forasmuch as they abode in their own unbelief, He now does but upbraid.

For "then," it is said, "began Jesus to upbraid the cities, wherein most of His mighty works were done, because they repented not; saying, Woe unto thee, Chorazin! woe unto thee, Bethsaida!"[7]

Then, to show thee that they are not such by nature, He states also the name of the city out of which proceeded five apostles.

For both Philip, and those two pairs of the chief apostles, were from thence.[8]

"For if," saith He, "the mighty works which were done in you had been done in Tyre and Sidon, they would have repented in sackcloth and ashes. But I say unto you, It shall be more tolerable for Tyre and Sidon, at the day of judgment, than for you. And thou, Capernaum, which art exalted unto heaven, shalt be brought down to hell,[9] for if the mighty works which have been done in thee had been done in Sodom, it would have remained until this day. But I say unto you, It shall be more tolerable for the land of Sodom in the day of judgment, than for thee."[10]

And He adds not Sodom with the others for nought, but to aggravate the charge against them. Yea, for it is a very great proof of wickedness, when not only of them that now are, but even of all those that ever were wicked, none are found so bad as they.

Thus elsewhere also He makes a comparison, condemning them by the Ninevites, and by the Queen of the south; there, however, it was by them that did right, here, even by them that sinned; a thing far more grievous. With this law of condemnation, Ezekiel too was acquainted: wherefore also he said to Jerusalem, "Thou hast justified thy sisters in all thy sins."[11] Thus everywhere is He wont to linger in the Old Testament, as in a favored place. And not even at this doth He stay His speech, but makes their fears yet more intense, by saying, that they should suffer things more grievous than Sodomites and Tyrians, so as by every means to gather them in, both by bewailing, and by alarming them.

7. To these same things let us also listen: since not for the unbelievers only, but for us also, hath He appointed a punishment more grievous than that of the Sodomites, if we will not receive the strangers that come in unto us; I mean, when He commanded to shake off the very dust: and very fitly. For as to the Sodomites, although they committed a great transgression, yet it was before the law and grace; but we, after so much care shown towards us, of what indulgence should we be worthy, showing so much inhospitality, and shutting our doors against them that are in need, and before our doors, our ears? or rather not against the poor only, but against the apostles themselves? For therefore we

---

[1] Matt. xi. 19. [The text of the Homily agrees with the received text. Comp. Luke vii. 35, where this reading is undoubtedly the correct one.—R.]
[2] Ps. li. 4.   [3] See Ezek. iv. 5, 12, 13, 24, &c.
[4] Matt. xi. 18.   [5] John vii. 20; viii. 48, 52; x. 20.
[6] Luke vii. 29, 30. [δεξάμενοι for βαπτισθέντες in Luke.]
[7] Matt. xi. 20, 21.

[8] John i. 44.   [9] [R. V., "Hades."]
[10] Matt. xi. 21-24. [The Greek here agrees with the received text. In verse 23 the R. V. follows a different and better established reading.—R.]
[11] Ezek. xvi. 51. [The LXX. is not cited with verbal accuracy. —R.]

do it to the poor, because we do it to the very apostles. For whereas Paul is read, and thou attendest not; whereas John preaches, and thou hearest not: when wilt thou receive a poor man, who wilt not receive an apostle?

In order then that both our houses may be continually open to the one, and our ears to the others, let us purge away the filth from the ears of our soul. For as filth and mud close up the ears of our flesh, so do the harlot's songs, and worldly news, and debts, and the business of usury and loans, close up the ear of the mind, worse than any filth; nay rather, they do not close it up only, but also make it unclean. And they are putting dung in your ears, who tell you of these things. And that which the barbarian threatened, saying, "Ye shall eat your own dung," and what follows;[1] this do these men also make you undergo, not in word, but in deeds; or rather, somewhat even much worse. For truly those songs are more loathsome even than all this; and what is yet worse, so far from feeling annoyance when ye hear them, ye rather laugh, when ye ought to abominate them and fly.

But if they be not abominable, go down unto the stage, imitate that which thou praisest; or rather, do thou merely take a walk with him that is exciting that laugh. Nay, thou couldest not bear it. Why then bestow on him so great honor? Yea, while the laws that are enacted by the Gentiles would have them to be dishonored, thou receivest them with thy whole city, like ambassadors and generals, and dost convoke all men, to receive dung in their ears. And thy servant, if he say anything filthy in thy hearing, will receive stripes in abundance; and be it a son, a wife, whoever it may, that doth as I have said, thou callest the act an affront; but if worthless fellows, that deserve the scourge, should invite thee to hear the filthy words, not only art thou not indignant, thou dost even rejoice and applaud. And what could be equal to this folly?

But dost thou thyself never utter these base words? Why what is the profit? or rather, this very fact, whence is it manifest? For if thou didst not utter these things, neither wouldest thou at all laugh at hearing them, nor wouldest thou run with such zeal to the voice that makes thee ashamed.

For tell me, art thou pleased at hearing men blaspheme? Dost thou not rather shudder, and stop thine ears? Surely I think thou dost. Why so? Because thou blasphemest not thyself. Just so do thou act

with respect to filthy talking also; and if thou wouldest show us clearly, that thou hast no pleasure in filthy speaking, endure not so much as to hear them. For when wilt thou be able to become good, bred up as thou art with such sounds in thine ears? When wilt thou venture to undergo such labors as chastity requires, now that thou art falling gradually away through this laughter, these songs, and filthy words? Yea, it is a great thing for a soul that keeps itself pure from all this, to be able to become grave and chaste; how much more for one that is nourished up in such hearings? Know ye not, that we are of the two more inclined to evil? While then we make it even an art, and a business, when shall we escape that furnace?

8. Heardest thou not what Paul saith, "Rejoice in the Lord?"[2] He said not, "in the devil." When then wilt thou be able to hear Paul? when, to gain a sense of thy wrong actions? drunken as thou art, ever and incessantly, with the spectacle I was speaking of. For thy having come here is nothing wonderful nor great; or rather it is wonderful. For here thou comest any how, and so as just to satisfy a scruple,[3] but there with diligence and speed, and great readiness. And it is evident from what thou bringest home, on returning thence.

For even all the mire that is there poured out for you, by the speeches, by the songs, by the laughter, ye collect and take every man to his home, or rather not to his home only, but every man even into his own mind.

And from things not worthy of abhorrence thou turnest away; while others which are to be abhorred, so far from hating, thou dost even court. Many, for instance, on coming back from tombs, are used to wash themselves, but on returning from theatres they have never groaned, nor poured forth any fountains of tears; yet surely the dead man is no unclean thing, whereas sin induces such a blot, that not even with ten thousand fountains could one purge it away, but with tears only, and with confessions. But no one hath any sense of this blot. Thus because we fear not what we ought, therefore we shrink from what we ought not.

And what again is the applause? what the

---

[2] Philip. iv. 4.
[3] ἀφοσιούμενος, "just saying, 'God forgive me;' just doing enough to come without scruple." Vid. Suicer in verb. who quotes St. Chrys. on Ps. 41. "Let us not come in hither any how, nor make our responses ἀφοσιούμενοι, just well enough to keep off a curse" (i. 617, Sav.) Also Hom. XXIX. on Acts, t. iv. p. 777. "How may one form a judgment of a church? If we go away daily with some profit, great or small, not simply satisfying a rule and ἀφοσιούμενοι, quitting ourselves of a scruple." Again, ibid. "What we do, is turned into a mere regulation and ἀφοσίωσις, a formal deprecation of a curse." Cf. Isæus de Appollodori Hered. p. 185. Ed. Reiske, "not ἀφοσιούμενος, but preparing himself as well as possible."

tumult, and the satanical cries, and the devilish gestures? For first one, being a young man, wears his hair long behind, and changing his nature into that of a woman, is striving both in aspect, and in gesture, and in garments, and generally in all ways, to pass into the likeness of a tender damsel.[1] Then another who is grown old, in the opposite way to this, having his hair shaven, and with his loins girt about, his shame cut off before his hair, stands ready to be smitten with the rod, prepared both to say and do anything. The women again, their heads uncovered, stand without a blush, discoursing with a whole people, so complete is their practice in shamelessness; and thus pour forth all effrontery and impurity into the souls of their hearers. And their one study is, to pluck up all chastity from the foundations, to disgrace our nature, to satiate the desire of the wicked demon. Yea, and there are both foul sayings, and gestures yet fouler; and the dressing of the hair tends that way, and the gait, and apparel, and voice, and flexure of the limbs; and there are turnings of the eyes, and flutes, and pipes, and dramas, and plots; and all things, in short, full of the most extreme impurity. When then wilt thou be sober again, I pray thee, now that the devil is pouring out for thee so much of the strong wine of whoredom, mingling so many cups of unchastity? For indeed both adulteries and stolen marriages are there, and there are women playing the harlot, men prostituting, youths corrupting themselves: all there is iniquity to the full, all sorcery, all shame. Wherefore they that sit by should not laugh at these things, but weep and groan bitterly.

"What then? Are we to shut up the stage?" it will be said, "and are all things to be turned upside down at thy word?" Nay, but as it is, all things are turned upside down. For whence are they, tell me, that plot against our marriages? Is it not from this theatre? Whence are they that dig through into chambers? Is it not from that stage? Comes it not of this, when husbands are insupportable to their wives? of this, when the wives are contemptible to their husbands? of this, that the more part are adulterers? So that the subverter of all things is he that goes to the theatre; it is he that brings in a grievous tyranny. "Nay," thou wilt say, "this is appointed by the good order of the laws." Why, to tear away men's wives, and to insult young boys, and to overthrow houses, is proper to those who have

seized on citadels.[2] "And what adulterer," wilt thou say, "hath been made such by these spectacles?" Nay, who hath not been made an adulterer? And if one might but mention them now by name, I could point out how many husbands those harlots have severed from their wives, how many they have taken captive, drawing some even from the marriage bed itself, not suffering others so much as to live at all in marriage.

"What then? I pray thee, are we to overthrow all the laws?" Nay, but it is overthrowing lawlessness, if we do away with these spectacles. For hence are they that make havoc in our cities; hence, for example, are seditions and tumults. For they that are maintained by the dancers, and who sell their own voice to the belly, whose work it is to shout, and to practise everything that is monstrous, these especially are the men that stir up the populace, that make the tumults in our cities. For youth, when it hath joined hands with idleness, and is brought up in so great evils, becomes fiercer than any wild beast. The necromancers too, I pray thee, whence are they? Is it not from hence, that in order to excite the people who are idling without object, and make the dancing men have the benefit of much and loud applause, and fortify the harlot women against the chaste, they proceed so far in sorcery, as not even to shrink from disturbing the bones of the dead? Comes it not hence, when men are forced to spend without limit on that wicked choir of the devil? And lasciviousness, whence is that, and its innumerable mischiefs? Thou seest, it is thou who art subverting our life, by drawing men to these things, while I am recruiting it by putting them down.

"Let us then pull down the stage," say they. Would that it were possible to pull it down; or rather, if ye be willing, as far as regards us, it is pulled down, and digged up. Nevertheless, I enjoin no such thing. Standing as these places are, I bid you make them of no effect; which thing were a greater praise than pulling them down.

9. Imitate at least the barbarians, if no one else; for they verily are altogether clean from seeking such sights. What excuse then can we have after all this, we, the citizens of Heaven, and partners in the choirs of the cherubim, and in fellowship with the angels, making ourselves in this respect worse even than the barbarians, and this, when innumerable other pleasures, better than these, are within our reach?

---

[1] The women in plays were personated by men: those mentioned below were singers; the slave's part is described in the next sentence.

[2] i. e., to tyrants, such as Pisistratus and others.

Why, if thou desirest that thy soul may find delight, go to pleasure grounds, to a river flowing by, and to lakes, take notice of gardens, listen to grasshoppers as they sing, be continually by the coffins of martyrs, where is health of body and benefit of soul, and no hurt, no remorse after the pleasure, as there is here.

Thou hast a wife, thou hast children; what is equal to this pleasure? Thou hast a house, thou hast friends, these are the true delights: besides their purity, great is the advantage they bestow. For what, I pray thee, is sweeter than children? what sweeter than a wife, to him that will be chaste in mind?

To this purpose, we are told, that the barbarians uttered on some occasion a saying full of wise severity. I mean, that having heard of these wicked spectacles, and the unseasonable delight of them; "why the Romans," say they, "have devised these pleasures, as though they had not wives and children;" implying that nothing is sweeter than children and wife, if thou art willing to live honestly.

"What then," one may say, "if I point to some, who are nothing hurt by their pastime in that place?" In the first place, even this is a hurt, to spend one's time without object or fruit, and to become an offense to others. For even if thou shouldest not be hurt, thou makest some other more eager herein. And how canst thou but be thyself hurt, giving occasion to what goes on? Yea, both the fortune-teller, and the prostitute boy, and the harlot woman, and all those choirs of the devil, cast upon thy head the blame of their proceedings. For as surely as, if there were no spectators, there would be none to follow these employments; so, since there are, they too have their share of the fire due to such deeds. So that even if in chastity thou wert quite unhurt (a thing impossible), yet for others' ruin thou wilt render a grievous account; both the spectators', and that of those who assemble them.

And in chastity too thou wouldest profit more, didst thou refrain from going thither. For if even now thou art chaste, thou wouldest have become chaster by avoiding such sights. Let us not then delight in useless argument, nor devise unprofitable apologies: there being but one apology, to flee from the Babylonian furnace, to keep far from the Egyptian harlot, though one must escape her hands naked.[1]

For so shall we both enjoy much delight, our conscience not accusing us, and we shall live this present life with chastity, and attain unto the good things to come, by the grace and love towards man of our Lord Jesus Christ; to whom be glory and might, now and ever, and world without end. Amen.

---

[1] Gen. xxxix. 12.

HOMILY XXXVIII.

Matt. XI. 25, 26.

"At that time Jesus answered and said, I make acknowledgment unto Thee,[1] O Father, Lord of Heaven and earth; because Thou hast hid these things from the wise and prudent, and hast revealed them unto babes. Even so, Father, for so it seemed good in Thy sight." [2]

Seest thou, how many ways He leads them on to the faith? First,[3] by His praises of John. For by pointing to him as a great and marvellous one, He proved likewise all his sayings credible, whereby he used to draw them on to the knowledge of Him. Secondly,[4] by saying, "The kingdom of Heaven suffereth violence, and the violent take it by force;" for this is the language of one who is pressing and urging them. Thirdly,[5] by signifying that the number of the prophets was finished; for this too manifested Himself to be the person that was announced beforehand by them. Fourthly,[6] by pointing out that whatsoever things should be done by him, were all accomplished; at which time

---

[1] [A. V., "I thank thee," so R. V., with margin, "Or, praise." The Oxford translator gives the exact sense of the Greek verb, but below reverts to the rendering "thank," in accordance with the explanation of Chrysostom.—R.]
[2] [R. V., "Yea, Father, for (or, that) so it was well-pleasing in thy sight." Comp. the explanation in the Homily.—R.]
[3] Matt. xi. 7-11.   [4] Matt. xi. 12.

[5] Matt. vi. 13.   [6] Matt. vi. 14-19.

also He made mention of the parable of the children. Fifthly, by His upbraiding them that had not believed, and by His alarming and threatening them greatly.[1] Sixthly, by His giving thanks for them that believed. For the expression, " I make acknowledgment to Thee," here is, " I thank Thee." " I thank Thee," He saith, " because Thou hast hid these things from the wise and prudent."

What then ? doth He rejoice in destruction, and in the others not having received this knowledge ? By no means; but this is a most excellent way of His to save men, His not forcing them that utterly reject, and are not willing to receive His sayings; that, since they were not bettered by His call, but fell back, and despised it, His casting them out might cause them to fall into a longing for these things. And so likewise the attentive would grow more earnest.

And while His being revealed to these was fit matter of joy, His concealment from those was no more of joy but of tears. Thus at any rate He acts, where He weeps for the city. Not therefore because of this doth He rejoice, but because what wise men knew not, was known to these. As when Paul saith, " I thank God, that ye were servants of sin, but ye obeyed from the heart the form of doctrine which was delivered unto you."[2] You see, neither doth Paul therefore rejoice, because they were " servants of sin," but because being such, they had been so highly favored.

Now by the " wise," here, He means the Scribes, and the Pharisees. And these things He saith, to make the disciples more earnest, and to show what had been vouchsafed to the fishermen, when all those others had missed of it. And in calling them " wise," He means not the true and commendable wisdom, but this which they seemed to have through natural shrewdness. Wherefore neither did He say, " thou hast revealed it to fools," but " to babes;" to unsophisticated, that is, to simple-minded men; and He implies that so far from their missing these privileges contrary to their desert, it was just what might be expected. And He instructs us throughout, to be free from pride, and to follow after simplicity. For this cause Paul also expressed it with more exceeding earnestness, writing on this wise: " If any man among you seemeth to be wise in this world,

let him become a fool, that he may be wise."[3] For thus is God's grace manifested.

But wherefore doth He give thanks to the Father, although of course it was Himself who wrought this ? As He prays and intercedes with God, showing His great love towards us, in the same way doth He this too: for this also is of much love. And He signifies, that not from Him only had they fallen away, but also from the Father. Thus, what He said, speaking to His disciples, " Cast not the holy things unto dogs,"[4] this He Himself anticipated them in performing.

Moreover He signifies hereby both His own principal[5] will, and that of the Father; His own, I say, by His giving thanks and rejoicing at what had taken place; His Father's, by intimating that neither had He done this upon entreaty, but of Himself upon His own will; " For so," saith He, " it seemed good in Thy sight:" that is, " so it pleased Thee."

And wherefore was it hidden from them ? Hear Paul, saying, that " Seeking to establish their own righteousness, they have not submitted themselves to the righteousness of God."[6]

Consider now how it was likely the disciples should[7] be affected, hearing this; that what wise men knew not, these knew, and knew it continuing babes, and knew it by God's revelation. But Luke saith, that " at the very hour," when the seventy came telling Him about the devils, then He " rejoiced" and spake these things,[8] which, besides increasing their diligence, would also dispose them to be modest. That is, since it was natural for them to pride themselves on their driving away devils, on this among other grounds He refrains them; that it was a revelation, whatever had been done, no diligence on their part. Wherefore also the scribes, and the wise men, thinking to be intelligent for themselves, fell away through their own vanity. Well then, if for this cause it was hidden from them, " do you also," saith He, " fear, and continue babes." For this caused you to have the benefit of the revelation, as indeed on the other hand the contrary made them be deprived of it. For by

---

[1] Matt. xi. 20-24.
[2] Rom. vi. 17. [R. V., " that form of teaching whereunto ye were delivered." The A. V. renders the passage incorrectly: there being no doubt as to the Greek text. The R. V. also brings out the thought which the Homily indicates.—R.]

[3] 1 Cor. iii. 18.   [4] Matt. vii. 6.
[5] προηγούμενον. In the same sense in which Hooker says, " He willeth positively that which Himself worketh ; He willeth by permission that which His creatures do." E. P. v. App. No. 1, p. 714, cf. in Walton's Life, p. 29. " That in God there were two wills, an antecedent and a consequent will ; His first will, that all mankind should be saved ; His second, that those only should be saved, who lived answerable to that degree of grace which He had offered."
[6] Rom. x. 3.
[7] [" would ;" but the whole clause has been freely paraphrased. —R.]
[8] Luke x. 21.

no means, when He saith, "Thou hast hid," doth He mean that it is all God's doing: but as when Paul saith, "He gave them over to a reprobate mind,"[1] and, "He hath blinded their minds,"[2] it is not meant to bring Him in as the doer of it, but those who gave the occasion: so here also He uses the expression, "Thou hast hid."

For since He had said, "I thank[3] Thee, because Thou hast hid them, and hast revealed them unto babes;" to hinder thy supposing that as being Himself deprived of this power, and unable to effect it, so He offers thanks, He saith,

"All things are delivered unto me of my Father."[4] And to them that are rejoicing, because the devils obey them, "Nay, why marvel," saith He,[5] "that devils yield to you? All things are mine; "All things are delivered unto me."

But when thou hearest, "they are delivered," do not surmise anything human. For He uses this expression, to prevent thine imagining two unoriginate Gods. Since, that He was at the same time both begotten, and Lord of all, He declares in many ways, and in other places also.

2. Then He saith what is even greater than this, lifting up thy mind; "And no man knoweth the Son, but the Father; neither knoweth any man the Father, but the Son." Which seems indeed to the ignorant unconnected with what went before, but hath full accordance therewith. As thus: having said, "All things are delivered unto me of my Father," He adds, "And what marvel," so He speaks, "if I be Lord of all? I who have also another greater privilege, the knowing the Father, and being of the same substance." Yea, for this too He covertly signifies by His being the only one who so knew Him. For this is His meaning, when He saith, "No man knoweth the Father but the Son."

And see at what time He saith this. When they by His works had received the certain proof of His might, not only seeing Him work miracles, but endowed also in His name with so great powers. Then, since He had said, "Thou hast revealed them to babes," He signifies this also to pertain to Himself; for "neither knoweth any man the Father," saith He, "save the Son, and he to whomsoever the Son is willing[6] to reveal Him;[7] not "to whomsoever He may be enjoined," "to whomsoever He may be commanded." But

if He reveals Him, then Himself too. This however He let pass as acknowledged, but the other He hath set down. And everywhere He affirms this; as when He saith, "No man cometh unto the Father, but by me."[8]

And thereby he establishes another point also, His being in harmony and of one mind with Him. "Why," saith He, "I am so far from fighting and warring with Him, that no one can even come to Him but by me." For because this most offended them, His seeming to be a rival God, He by all means doth away with this; and interested Himself about this not less earnestly, but even more so, than about His miracles.

But when He saith, "Neither knoweth any man the Father, save the Son," He means not this, that all men were ignorant of Him, but that with the knowledge wherewith He knows[9] Him, no man is acquainted with Him; which may be said of the Son too.[10] For it was not of some God unknown, and revealed to no man, that He was so speaking, as Marcion saith;[11] but it is the perfection of knowledge that He is here intimating, since neither do we know the Son as He should be known; and this very thing, to add no more, Paul was declaring, when he said, "We know in part, and we prophesy in part."[12]

3. Next, having brought them by His words to an earnest desire, and having signified His unspeakable power, He after that invites them, saying, "Come unto me, all ye that labor and are heavy laden, and I will give you rest."[13] Not this or that person, but all that are in anxiety, in sorrows, in sins. Come, not that I may call you to account, but that I may do away your sins; come, not that I want your honor, but that I want your salvation. "For I," saith He, "will give you rest." He said not, "I will save you," only; but what was much more, "I will place you in all security."

"Take my yoke upon you, and learn of me, for I am meek and lowly in heart; and ye shall find rest unto your souls. For my yoke is easy, and my burden is light."[14] Thus, "be not afraid," saith He, "hearing of a yoke, for it is easy: fear not, because I said, "a burden," for it is light.

And how said He before, "The gate is

---

[1] Rom. i. 28.
[2] 2 Cor. iv. 4. [This passage is irrelevant, since it speaks of "the god of this world."—R.]
[3] [See above, and note 1, p. 250.—R.]
[4] Matt. xi. 27.   [5] Luke x. 22.
[6] βούληται. [R. V., "willeth."]   [7] Matt. xi. 27.

[8] John xiv. 6.   [9] ἐπίσταται.
[10] That is, that none but the Father has full knowledge of Him.
[11] Tertull. adv. Marc. i. 8. "The Marcionites bring forward a new God, as if we were ashamed of the ancient One. . . . I hear them talk of a new God, in the old world and in the old age, and under that ancient God, unknown and unheard of." [Ante-Nicene Fathers, vol. iii. p. 276.] It seems to have been common to all the Oriental sects, to speak of the Supreme God as utterly unknown until the Christian dispensation began.
[12] 1 Cor. xiii. 9.   [13] Matt. xi. 28.   [14] Matt. xi. 29, 30.

narrow and the way strait?"[1] Whilst thou art careless, whilst thou art supine; whereas, if thou duly perform His words, the burden will be light; wherefore also He hath now called it so.

But how are they duly performed? If thou art become lowly, and meek, and gentle. For this virtue is the mother of all strictness of life. Wherefore also, when beginning those divine laws, with this He began.[2] And here again He doeth the very same, and exceeding great is the reward He appoints. "For not to another only dost thou become serviceable; but thyself also above all thou refreshest," saith He. "For ye shall find rest unto your souls."

Even before the things to come, He gives thee here thy recompense, and bestows the prize already, making the saying acceptable, both hereby, and by setting Himself forward as an example. For, "Of what art thou afraid?" saith He, "lest thou shouldest be a loser by thy low estate? Look to me, and to all that is mine; learn of me, and then shalt thou know distinctly how great thy blessing." Seest thou how in all ways He is leading them to humility? By His own doings: "Learn of me, for I am meek." By what themselves are to gain; for, "Ye shall find," saith He, "rest unto your souls." By what He bestows on them; for, "I too will refresh you," saith He. By rendering it light; "For my yoke is easy, and my burden is light." So likewise doth Paul, saying, "For the present light affliction, which is but for a moment, worketh a far more exceeding and eternal weight of glory."[3]

And how, some one may say, is the burden light, when He saith, "Except one hate father and mother;" and, "Whosoever taketh not up his cross, and followeth after me, is not worthy of me:" and, "Whosoever forsaketh not all that he hath, cannot be my disciple:"[4] when He commands even to give up our very life?[5] Let Paul teach thee, saying, "Who shall separate us from the love of Christ? Shall tribulation, or distress, or persecution, or famine, or nakedness, or peril, or sword?"[6] And that, "The sufferings of this present time are not worthy to be compared with the glory that shall be revealed in us."[7] Let those teach thee, who return from the council of the Jews after plenty of stripes, and "rejoice that they were counted worthy to suffer shame for the name of Christ."[8] And if thou art still afraid and tremblest at hearing of the yoke and the burden, the fear

comes not of the nature of the thing, but of thy remissness; since if thou art prepared, and in earnest, all will be easy to thee and light. Since for this cause Christ also, to signify that we too must needs labor ourselves, did not mention the gracious things only, and then hold His peace, nor the painful things only, but set down both. Thus He both spake of "a yoke," and called it "easy;" both named a burden, and added that it was "light;" that thou shouldest neither flee from them as toilsome, nor despise them as over easy.

But if even after all this, virtue seem to thee an irksome thing, consider that vice is more irksome. And this very thing He was intimating, in that He said not first, "Take my yoke upon you," but before that, "Come, ye that labor and are heavy laden;" implying that sin too hath labor, and a burden that is heavy and hard to bear. For He said not only, "Ye that labor," but also, "that are heavy laden." This the prophet too was speaking of, when in that description of her nature, "As an heavy burden they weighed heavy upon me."[9] And Zacharias too, describing her, saith she is "A talent of lead."[10]

And this moreover experience itself proves. For nothing so weighs upon the soul, and presses it down, as consciousness of sin; nothing so much gives it wings, and raises it on high, as the attainment of righteousness and virtue.

And mark it: what is more grievous, I pray thee, than to have no possessions? to turn the cheek, and when smitten not to smite again? to die by a violent death? Yet nevertheless, if we practise self-command, all these things are light and easy, and pleasurable.

But be not disturbed; rather let us take up each of these, and inquire about it accurately; and if ye will, that first which many count most painful. Which then of the two, tell me, is grievous and burdensome, to be in care for one belly, or to be anxious about ten thousand? To be clothed with one outer garment, and seek for nothing more; or having many in one's house, to bemoan one's self every day and night in fear, in trembling, about the preservation of them, grieved, and ready to choke about the loss of them; lest one should be moth-eaten, lest a servant purloin and go off with them?

4. But whatever I may say, my speech will present no such proof as the actual trial. Wherefore I would there were present here with us some one of those who have attained unto that summit of self-restraint, and then

[1] Matt. vii. 13.   [2] Matt. v. 3.   [3] 2 Cor. iv. 17.
[4] Luke xiv. 26, 27, 33; Matt. x. 37, 38.   [5] Matt. xvi. 25.
[6] Rom. viii. 35.   [7] Rom. viii. 18.   [8] Acts v. 41.

[9] Ps. xxxviii. 4.   [10] Zech. v. 7, 8.

you would know assuredly the delight thereof; and that none of those that are enamored of voluntary poverty would accept wealth, though ten thousand were to offer it.

But would these, say you, ever consent to become poor, and to cast away the anxieties which they have? And what of that? This is but a proof of their madness and grievous disease, not of anything very pleasurable in the thing. And this even themselves would testify to us, who are daily lamenting over these their anxieties, and accounting their life to be not worth living. But not so those others; rather they laugh, leap for joy, and the wearers of the diadem do not so glory, as they do in their poverty.

Again, to turn the cheek is, to him that gives heed, a less grievous thing than to smite another; for from this the contest hath beginning, in that termination: and whereas by the former thou hast kindled the other's pile too, by the latter thou hast quenched even thine own flames. But that not to be burnt is a pleasanter thing than to be burnt, is surely plain to every man. And if this hold in regard of bodies, much more in a soul.

And whether is lighter, to contend, or to be crowned? to fight, or to have the prize? and to endure waves, or to run into harbor? Therefore also, to die is better than to live. For the one withdraws us from waves and dangers, while the other adds unto them, and makes a man subject to numberless plots and distresses, which have made life not worth living in thine account.

And if thou disbelievest our sayings, hearken to them that have seen the countenances of the martyrs in the time of their conflicts, how when scourged and flayed, they were exceeding joyful and glad, and when exposed upon hot irons, rejoiced, and were glad of heart, more than such as lie upon a bed of roses. Wherefore Paul also said, when he was at the point of departing hence, and closing his life by a violent death, "I joy, and rejoice with you all; for the same cause also do ye joy, and rejoice with me."[1] Seest thou with what exceeding strength of language he invites the whole world to partake in his gladness? So great a good did he know his departure hence to be, so desirable, and lovely, and worthy of prayer, that formidable thing, death.

5. But that virtue's yoke is sweet and

light, is manifest many other ways also; but to conclude, if you please, let us look also at the burdens of sin. Let us then bring forward the covetous, the retailers and second-hand dealers in shameless bargains. What now could be a heavier burden than such transactions? how many sorrows, how many anxieties, how many disappointments, how many dangers, how many plots and wars, daily spring up from these gains? how many troubles and disturbances? For as one can never see the sea without waves, so neither such a soul without anxiety, and despondency, and fear, and disturbance; yea, the second overtakes the first, and again others come up, and when these are not yet ceased, others come to a head.

Or wouldest thou see the souls of the revilers, and of the passionate? Why, what is worse than this torture? what, than the wounds they have within? what, than the furnace that is continually burning, and the flame that is never quenched?

Or of the sensual, and of such as cleave unto this present life? Why, what more grievous than this bondage? They live the life of Cain, dwelling in continual trembling and fear at every death that happens; the kinsmen of the dead mourn not so much, as these do for their own end.

What again fuller of turmoil, and more frantic, than such as are puffed up with pride? "For learn," saith He, "of me, for I am meek and lowly in heart, and ye shall find rest unto your souls." Because long-suffering is the mother of all good things.

Fear thou not therefore, neither start away from the yoke that lightens thee of all these things, but put thyself under it with all forwardness, and then thou shalt know well the pleasure thereof. For it doth not at all bruise thy neck, but is put on thee for good order's sake only, and to persuade thee to walk seemly, and to lead thee unto the royal road, and to deliver thee from the precipices on either side, and to make thee walk with ease in the narrow way.

Since then so great are its benefits, so great its security, so great its gladness, let us with all our soul, with all our diligence, draw this yoke; that we may both here "find rest unto our souls," and attain unto the good things to come, by the grace and love towards man of our Lord Jesus Christ, to whom be glory and might, now and ever, and world without end. Amen.

---

[1] Phil. ii. 17, 18. [R. V., "and in the same manner also," etc.]

HOMILY XXXIX.

MATT. XII. 1.

"At that time Jesus went on the Sabbath day through the corn; and His disciples were an hungered, and began to pluck the [1] ears of corn, and to eat."

But Luke saith, " On a double Sabbath." [2] Now what is a double Sabbath? When the cessation from toil is twofold, both that of the regular Sabbath, and that of another feast coming upon it. For they call every cessation from toil, a sabbath.

But why could He have led them away from it, who foreknew all, unless it had been His will that the Sabbath should be broken? It was His will indeed, but not simply so; wherefore He never breaks it without a cause, but giving reasonable excuses: that He might at once bring the law to an end, and not startle them. But there are occasions on which He even repeals it directly, and not with circumstance: as when He anoints with the clay the eyes of the blind man; [3] as when He saith, " My Father worketh hitherto, and I work." [4] And He doth so, by this to glorify His own Father, by the other to soothe the infirmity of the Jews. At which last He is laboring here, putting forward as a plea the necessity of nature; although in the case of acknowledged sins, that could not of course ever be an excuse. For neither may the murderer make his anger a plea, nor the adulterer allege his lust, no, nor any other excuse; but here, by mentioning their hunger, He freed them from all blame.

But do thou, I pray thee, admire the disciples, how entirely they control themselves, and make no account of the things of the body, but esteem the table of the flesh a secondary thing, and though they have to struggle with continual hunger, do not even so withdraw themselves. For except hunger had sorely constrained them, they would not have done so much as this.

What then do the Pharisees? " When they saw it," it is said, " they said unto Him, Behold, Thy disciples do that which is not lawful to do upon the Sabbath day." [5]

Now here indeed with no great vehemence (yet surely that would have been consistent in them),—nevertheless they are not vehemently provoked, but simply find fault. But when He stretched out the withered hand and healed it, [6] then they were so infuriated, as even to consult together about slaying and destroying Him. For where nothing great and noble is done, they are calm; but where they see any made whole, they are savage, and fret themselves, and none so intolerable as they are: such enemies are they of the salvation of men.

How then doth Jesus defend His disciples? " Have ye not read," saith He, " what David did in the temple, [7] when he was an hungered, himself and all they that were with him? how he entered into the house of God, and did eat the show-bread, which was not lawful for him to eat, neither for them which were with him, but only for the priests?" [8]

Thus, whereas in pleading for His disciples, He brings forward David; for Himself, it is the Father. [9]

And observe His reproving manner: " Have ye not read what David did?" For great indeed was that prophet's glory, so that Peter also afterwards pleading with the Jews, spake on this wise, " Let me freely speak unto you of the patriarch David, that he is both dead and buried." [10]

But wherefore doth He not call him by the name of his rank, either on this occasion or afterwards? Perhaps because He derived His race from him.

Now had they been a candid sort of persons, He would have turned His discourse to the disciples' suffering from hunger; but abominable as they were and inhuman, He rather rehearses unto them a history.

But Mark saith, " In the days of Abiathar the High Priest: " [11] not stating what was con-

---

[1] [With our best mss. authorities, the article is omitted in the Homily. Comp. R. V., *in loco.*—R.]
[2] δευτεροπρώτω, Luke vi. 1. [On the textual difficulty, see Tischendorf (viii.) and Westcott and Hort. The former retains it, giving the patristic comments upon it. The latter put it in the margin, regarding it as spurious.—R.]
[3] John ix. 6, 14.
[4] John v. 17. [R. V., " even until now," etc.]
[5] Matt. xii. 2.

[6] Matt. xii. 10, 14.
[7] [ἐν τῷ ἱερῷ is inserted here (not in Homily XL.) by Chrysostom, but does not occur in any of our mss. of the New Testament. --R.]
[8] Matt. xii. 3, 4.　　[9] John v. 17.　　[10] Acts ii. 29.
[11] Mark ii. 26. [The Homily reads τοῦ ἀρχιερέως, which is to be thus rendered. The R. V. follows the best mss. in rejecting τοῦ, rendering " when Abiathar was high priest;" but gives the other reading in the margin.—R.]

trary to the history, but implying that he had two names; and adds that "he gave unto him,"[1] indicating that herein also David had much to say for himself, since even the very priest suffered him; and not only suffered, but even ministered unto him. For tell me not that David was a prophet, for not even so was it lawful, but the privilege was the priests': wherefore also He added, "but for the priests only." For though he were ten thousand times a prophet, yet was he not a priest; and though he were himself a prophet, yet not so they that were with him; since to them too we know that he gave.

"What then," it might be said, "were they all one with David?" Why talk to me of dignity, where there seems to be a transgression of the law, even though it be the constraint of nature? Yea, and in this way too He hath the more entirely acquitted them of the charges, in that he who is greater is found to have done the same.

"And what is this to the question," one may say; "for it was not surely the Sabbath, that he transgressed?" Thou tellest me of that which is greater, and which especially shows the wisdom of Christ, that letting go the Sabbath, He brings another example greater than the Sabbath. For it is by no means the same, to break in upon a day, and to touch that holy table, which it was not lawful for any man to touch. Since the Sabbath indeed hath been violated, and that often; nay rather it is continually being violated, both by circumcision, and by many other works; and at Jericho[2] too one may see the same to have happened; but this happened then only. So that He more than obtains the victory. How then did no man blame David, although there was yet another ground of charge heavier than this, that of the priests' murder, which had its origin from this? But He states it not, as applying himself to the present subject only.

2. Afterwards again He refutes it in another way also. For as at first He brought in David, by the dignity of the person quelling their pride; so when He had stopped their mouths, and had put down their boasting, then He adds also the more appropriate refutation. And of what sort is this? "Know ye not, that in the temple the priests profane the Sabbath, and are blameless?"[3] For in that other instance indeed, saith He, the emergency made the relaxation, but here is the relaxation even without emergency. He did not however at once thus refute them, but first by way of permission, afterwards as insisting upon his argument. Because it was meet to draw the stronger inference last, although the former argument also had of course its proper weight.

For tell me not, that it is not freeing one's self from blame, to bring forward another who is committing the same sin. For when the doer incurs no blame, the act on which he hath ventured becomes a rule for others to plead.

Nevertheless He was not satisfied with this, but subjoins also what is more decisive, saying that the deed is no sin at all; and this more than anything was the sign of a glorious victory, to point to the law repealing itself, and in two ways doing so, first by the place, then by the Sabbath; or rather even in three ways, in that both the work is twofold[4] that is done, and with it goes also another thing, its being done by the priests; and what is yet more, that it is not even brought as a charge. "For they," saith He, "are blameless."

Seest thou how many points He hath stated? the place; for He saith, "In the temple;" the persons, for they are "the priests;" the time, for He saith, "the Sabbath;" the act itself, for "they profane;" (He not having said, "they break," but what is more grievous, "they profane;") that they not only escape punishment, but are even free from blame, "for they," saith He, "are blameless."

Do not ye therefore account this, He saith, like the former instance. For that indeed was done both but once, and not by a priest, and was of necessity; wherefore also they were deserving of excuse; but this last is both done every Sabbath, and by priests, and in the temple, and according to the law. And therefore again not by favor, but in a legal way, they are acquitted of the charges. For not at all as blaming them did I so speak, saith He, nor yet as freeing them from blame in the way of indulgence, but according to the principle of justice.

And He seems indeed to be defending them, but it is His disciples whom He is clearing of the alleged faults. For when He saith, "those are blameless," He means, "much more are these."

"But they are not priests." Nay, they are greater than priests. For the Lord of the temple Himself is here: the truth, not the type. Wherefore He said also, "But I say unto you, That in this place is one greater than the temple."[5]

---

[1] Abimelech, 1 Sam. xxi. 6.   [2] Josh. vi. 15.   [3] Matt. xii. 5.
[4] As being done, 1, in the holy place; 2, on the holy day.
[5] Matt. xii. 6. [R. V., "that one greater (Greek, a greater thing) than the temple is here."]

Nevertheless, great as the sayings were which they heard, they made no reply, for the salvation of men was not their object.

Then, because to the hearers it would seem harsh, He quickly draws a veil over it, giving His discourse, as before, a lenient turn, yet even so expressing Himself with a rebuke. "But if ye had known what this meaneth, I will have[1] mercy and not sacrifice, ye would not have condemned the guiltless."[2]

Seest thou how again He inclines His speech to lenity, yet again shows them to be out of the reach of lenity? "For ye would not have condemned," saith He, "the guiltless." Before indeed He inferred the same from what is said of the priests, in the words, "they are guiltless;" but here He states it on His own authority; or rather, this too is out of the law, for He was quoting a prophetic saying.[3]

3. After this He mentions another reason likewise; "For the Son of man," saith He, "is Lord of the Sabbath day;"[4] speaking it of Himself. But Mark relates Him to have said this of our common nature also; for He said, "The Sabbath was made for man, not man for the Sabbath."[5]

Wherefore then was he punished that was gathering the sticks?[6] Because if the laws were to be despised even at the beginning, of course they would scarcely be observed afterwards.

For indeed the Sabbath did at the first confer many and great benefits; for instance, it made them gentle towards those of their household, and humane; it taught them God's providence and the creation, as Ezekiel saith;[7] it trained them by degrees to abstain from wickedness, and disposed them to regard the things of the Spirit.

For because they could not have borne it,[8] if when He was giving the law for the Sabbath, He had said, "Do your good works on the Sabbath, but do not the works which are evil," therefore He restrained them from all alike· for, "Ye must do nothing at all," saith He: and not even so were they kept in order. But He Himself, in the very act of giving the law of the Sabbath, did even therein darkly signify that He will have them refrain from the evil works only, by the saying, "Ye must do no work, except what shall be done for your life."[9] And in the temple too all went on, and with more diligence and double toil.[10] Thus even by the very shadow

He was secretly opening unto them the truth.

Did Christ then, it will be said, repeal a thing so highly profitable? Far from it; nay, He greatly enhanced it. For it was time for them to be trained in all things by the higher rules, and it was unnecessary that his hands should be bound, who was freed from wickedness, winged for all good works; or that men should hereby learn that God made all things; or that they should so be made gentle, who are called to imitate God's own love to mankind (for He saith, "Be ye merciful, as your Heavenly Father");[11] or that they should make one day a festival, who are commanded to keep a feast all their life long; ("For let us keep the feast," it is said, "not with old leaven, neither with leaven of malice and wickedness; but with unleavened bread of sincerity and truth");[12] as neither need they stand by an ark and a golden altar, who have the very Lord of all for their inmate, and in all things hold communion with Him; by prayer, and by oblation, and by scriptures, and by almsgiving, and by having Him within them. Lo now, why is any Sabbath required, by him who is always keeping the feast, whose conversation is in Heaven?

4. Let us keep the feast then continually, and do no evil thing; for this is a feast: and let our spiritual things be made intense, while our earthly things give place: and let us rest a spiritual rest, refraining our hands from covetousness; withdrawing our body from our superfluous and unprofitable toils, from such as the people of the Hebrews did of old endure in Egypt. For there is no difference betwixt us who are gathering gold, and those that were bound in the mire, working at those bricks, and gathering stubble, and being beaten. Yea, for now too the devil bids us make bricks, as Pharaoh did then. For what else is gold, than mire? and what else is silver, than stubble? Like stubble, at least, it kindles the flame of desire; like mire, so doth gold defile him that possesses it.

Wherefore He sent us, not Moses from the wilderness, but His Son from Heaven. If then, after He is come, thou abide in Egypt, thou wilt suffer with the Egyptians: but if leaving that land thou go up with the spiritual Israel, thou shalt see all the miracles.

Yet not even this suffices for salvation. For we must not only be delivered out of Egypt, but we must also enter into the promise. Since the Jews too, as Paul saith, both went through the Red Sea,[13] and ate manna,

---

[1] [R. V., "desire."]   [2] Matt. xii. 7.   [3] Hosea vi. 6.
[4] Matt. xii. 8.   [5] Mark ii. 27.
[6] Numb. xv. 32-36.   [7] Ezek. xx. 12.
[8] The meaning seems to be, it would have been too hard a trial of their religious discretion.
[9] Exod. xii. 16, LXX.   [10] Numb. xxviii. 9, 10.

[11] Luke vi. 36.   [12] 1 Cor. v. 8.   [13] 1 Cor. x. 1, &c.

17

and drank spiritual drink, but nevertheless they all perished.

Lest then the same befall us also, let us not be slow, neither draw back; but when thou hearest wicked spies even now bringing up an evil report against the strait and narrow way, and uttering the same kind of talk as those spies of old, let not the multitude, but Joshua, be our pattern, and Caleb the son of Jephunneh; and do not thou give up, until thou have attained the promise, and entered into the Heavens.

Neither account the journey to be difficult. "For if when we were enemies, we were reconciled to God, much more, being reconciled, shall we be saved."[1] "But this way," it will be said, "is strait and narrow." Well, but the former, through which thou hast come, is not strait and narrow only, but even impassable, and full of savage wild beasts. And as there was no passing through the Red Sea, unless that miracle had been wrought, so neither could we, abiding in our former life, have gone up into Heaven, but only by baptism intervening. Now if the impossible hath become possible, much more will the difficult be easy.

"But that," it will be said, "was of grace only." Why, for this reason especially thou hast just cause to take courage. For if, where it was grace alone, He wrought with you; will He not much more be your aid, where ye also show forth laborious works? If He saved thee, doing nothing, will He not much more help thee, working?

Above[2] indeed I was saying, that from the impossibilities thou oughtest to take courage about the difficulties also; but now I add this, that if we are vigilant, these will not be so much as difficult. For mark it: death is trodden under foot, the devil hath fallen, the law of sin is extinguished, the grace of the Spirit is given, life is contracted into a small space, the heavy burdens are abridged.

And to convince thee hereof by the actual results, see how many have overshot the injunctions of Christ; and art thou afraid of that which is just their measure? What plea then wilt thou have, when others are leaping beyond the bounds, and thou thyself too slothful for what is enacted?

Thus, thee we admonish to give alms of such things as thou hast, but another hath even stripped himself of all his possessions: thee we require to live chastely with thy wife, but another hath not so much as entered into marriage: and thee we entreat not to be envious, but another we find giving up even his own life for charity: thee again we entreat to be lenient in judgments, and not severe to them that sin, but another, even when smitten, hath turned the other cheek also.

What then shall we say, I pray thee? What excuse shall we make, not doing even these things, when others go so far beyond us? And they would not have gone beyond us, had not the thing been very easy. For which pines away, he who envies other men's blessings, or he who takes pleasure with them, and rejoices? Which eyes all things with suspicion and continual trembling, the chaste man, or the adulterer? Which is cheered by good hopes, he that spoils by violence, or he that shows mercy, and imparts of his own to the needy?

Let us then bear in mind these things, and not be torpid in our career for virtue's sake; but having stripped ourselves with all readiness for these glorious wrestlings, let us labor for a little while, that we may win the perpetual and imperishable crowns; unto which may we all attain, by the grace and love towards man of our Lord Jesus Christ, to whom be glory and might forever and ever. Amen.

---

[1] Rom. v. 10.
[2] ['Ἀνωτέρω; but "before" agrees better with English usage in public address.—R.]

HOMILY XL.

MATT. XII. 9, 10.

"And when He was departed thence, He went into their synagogue: and, behold, a man which had his hand withered."

AGAIN He heals on a Sabbath day, vindicating what had been done by His disciples. And the other evangelists indeed say, that He "set" the man "in the midst," and asked them, "If it was lawful to do good on the Sabbath days."[1]

See the tender bowels of the Lord. "He set him in the midst," that by the sight He might subdue them; that overcome by the spectacle they might cast away their wickedness, and out of a kind of shame towards the man, cease from their savage ways. But they, ungentle and inhuman, choose rather to hurt the fame of Christ, than to see this person made whole: in both ways betraying their wickedness; by their warring against Christ, and by their doing so with such contentiousness, as even to treat with despite His mercies to other men.

And while the other evangelists say, He asked the question, this one saith, it was asked of Him. "And they asked Him," so it stands, "saying, Is it lawful to heal on the Sabbath days? that they might accuse Him."[2] And it is likely that both took place. For being unholy wretches, and well assured that He would doubtless proceed to the healing, they hastened to take Him beforehand with their question, thinking in this way to hinder Him. And this is why they asked, "Is it lawful to heal on the Sabbath days?" not for information, but that "they might accuse Him." Yet surely the work was enough, if it were really their wish to accuse Him; but they desired to find a handle in His words too, preparing for themselves beforehand an abundance of arguments.

But He in His love towards man doth this also: He answers them, teaching His own meekness, and turning it all back upon them; and points out their inhumanity. And He "setteth" the man "in the midst;" not in fear of them, but endeavoring to profit them, and move them to pity.

But when not even so did He prevail with them, then was He grieved, it is said, and

wroth with them for the hardness of their heart, and He saith,

"What man is there among you that shall have one sheep, and if this fall into a pit on the Sabbath days, will he not lay hold of it, and lift it out? How much then is a man better than a sheep?[3] Wherefore it is lawful to do well[4] on the Sabbath days."[5]

Thus, lest they have ground of obstinacy, and of accusing him again of transgression, He convicts them by this example. And do thou mark, I pray thee, how variously and suitably in each case, He introduces His pleas for the breaking of the sabbath. Thus, first, in the case of the blind man,[6] He doth not so much as defend Himself to them, when He made the clay: and yet then also were they blaming Him; but the manner of the creation was enough to indicate the Lord and Owner[7] of the law. Next, in the case of the paralytic, when he carried his bed, and they were finding fault,[8] He defends Himself, now as God, and now as man; as man, when He saith, "If a man on the Sabbath day receive circumcision, that the law should not be broken;" (and He said not "that a man should be profited"); "are ye angry at me, because I have made a man every whit whole on the Sabbath day?"[9] As God again, when He saith, "My Father worketh hitherto, and I work."[10]

But when blamed for His disciples, He said, "Have ye not read what David did, when he was an hungered, himself and they that were with him, how he entered into the house of God, and did eat the show-bread?"[11] He brings forward the priests also.

And here again; "Is it lawful to do good on the Sabbath days, or to do evil?[12] Which of you shall have one sheep?" For He knew their love of wealth, that they were all

---

[3] [R. V., "How much, then, is a man of more value than a sheep!"]
[4] [R. V., "to do good."]   [5] Matt. xii. 3.   [6] John ix. 6.
[7] [τὸν Δεσπότην, not two titles, as the English rendering would suggest.—R.]
[8] John v. 9, 10.   [9] John vii. 23.
[10] John v. 17.   [11] Matt. xii. 3, 4.
[12] [So Mark and Luke, but not Matthew.—R.]

[1] See Mark iii. 3, 4, and Luke vi. 8, 9.   [2] Matt. xii. 10.

taken up with it, rather than with love of mankind. And indeed the other evangelist saith,[1] that He also looked about upon them when asking these questions, that by His very eye He might win them over; but not even so did they become better.

And yet here He speaks only; whereas elsewhere in many cases He heals by laying on of hands also. But nevertheless none of these things made them meek; rather, while the man was healed, they by his health became worse.

For His desire indeed was to cure them before him, and He tried innumerable ways of healing, both by what He did in their presence, and by what He said: but since their malady after all was incurable, He proceeded to the work. "Then saith He to the man, Stretch forth thine hand. And he stretched it forth, and it was restored whole, like as the other."[2]

2. What then did they? They go forth, it is said, and take counsel together to slay Him. For "the Pharisees," saith the Scripture, "went out and held a council against Him, how they might destroy Him."[3] They had received no injury, yet they went about to slay Him. So great an evil is envy. For not against strangers only, but even against our own, is it ever warring. And Mark saith, they took this counsel with the Herodians.[4]

What then doth the gentle and meek One? He withdrew, on being aware of it. "But when Jesus knew their devices,[5] He withdrew Himself," it is said, "from them"[6] Where now are they who say, miracles ought to be done? Nay, by these things He signified, that the uncandid soul is not even thereby persuaded; and He made it plain that His disciples too were blamed by them without cause. This however we should observe, that they grow fierce especially at the benefits done to their neighbors; and when they see any one delivered either from disease or from wickedness, then is the time for them to find fault, and become wild beasts. Thus did they calumniate Him, both when He was about to save the harlot, and when He was eating with publicans, and now again, when they saw the hand restored.

But do thou observe, I pray thee, how He neither desists from His tender care over the infirm, and yet allays their envy. "And great multitudes[7] followed Him, and He

healed them all; and He charged them that were healed, that they should make Him known to no man."[8] Because, while the multitudes everywhere both admire and follow Him, they desist not from their wickedness.

Then, lest thou shouldest be confounded at what is going on, and at their strange frenzy, He introduces the prophet also, foretelling all this. For so great was the accuracy of the prophets, that they omit not even these things, but foretell His very journeyings, and changes of place, and the intent with which He acted therein; that thou mightest learn, how they spake all by the Spirit. For if the secrets of men cannot by any art be known, much more were it impossible to learn Christ's purpose, except the Spirit revealed it.[9]

What then saith the prophet? Nay, it is subjoined: "That it might be fulfilled which was spoken by Esaias the Prophet, saying, Behold my servant, whom I have chosen; my beloved, in whom my soul is well pleased. I will put my Spirit upon Him, and He shall show judgment to the Gentiles. He shall not strive nor cry,[10] neither shall any man hear His voice in the streets. A bruised reed shall He not break, and smoking flax shall He not quench, till He send forth judgment unto victory. And in His name shall the Gentiles trust."[11]

The prophet celebrates His meekness, and His unspeakable power, and opens to the Gentiles "a great door and effectual;" he foretells also the ills that are to overtake the Jews, and signifies His unanimity with the Father. For "behold," saith He, "my servant, whom I have chosen, my beloved, in whom my soul is well pleased." Now if He chose Him, not as an adversary doth Christ set aside the law, nor as being an enemy of the lawgiver, but as having the same mind with Him, and the same objects.

Then proclaiming His meekness, he saith, "He shall not strive nor cry." For His desire indeed was to heal in their presence; but since they thrust Him away, not even against this did He contend.

And intimating both His might, and their weakness, he saith, "A bruised reed shall He not break." For indeed it was easy to break them all to pieces like a reed, and not a reed merely, but one already bruised.

"And smoking flax shall He not quench." Here he sets forth both their anger that is kindled, and His might that is able to put

---

1 Mark iii. 5; Luke vi. 10.   2 Matt xii. 13.
3 Matt. xii. 14. [R. V., "took counsel," etc.]
4 Mark iii. 6.
4 ["Their devices" is borrowed from verse 25, where the Greek phrase occurs ("their thoughts," A. V.)—R.]
6 Matt. xii. 15.
7 [So Chrysostom, with the received text. Comp. R. V.—R.]

8 Matt. xii. 15, 16. ["To no man," peculiar to Chrysostom.—R.]
9 Cf. 1 Cor. ii. 11.   10 [R. V., "cry aloud."]
11 Matt. xii. 17-21; see Isa. xlii. 1-4. [R. V., "hope" for "trust."]

down their anger, and to quench it with all ease; whereby His great mildness is signified.

What then? Shall these things always be? And will He endure them perpetually, forming such frantic plots against Him? Far from it; but when He hath performed His part, then shall He execute the other purposes also. For this He declared by saying "Till He send forth judgment unto victory: and in His name shall the Gentiles trust." As Paul likewise saith, "Having in a readiness to revenge all disobedience, when your obedience is fulfilled." [1]

But what is, "when He sends forth judgment unto victory?" When He hath fulfilled all His own part, then, we are told, He will bring down upon them His vengeance also, and that a perfect vengeance. Then shall they suffer His terrors, when His trophy is gloriously set up, and the ordinances that proceed from Him have prevailed, and He hath left them no plea of contradiction, however shameless. For He is wont to call righteousness, "judgment."

But not to this will His dispensation be confined, to the punishment of unbelievers only, but He will also win to Himself the whole world. Wherefore He added, "And in His name shall the Gentiles trust."

Then, to inform thee that this too is according to the purpose of the Father, in the beginning the prophet had assured us of this likewise, together with what had gone before; saying, " My well-beloved, in whom my soul is well pleased." For of the well-beloved it is quite evident that He did these things also according to the mind of the beloved.[2]

3. "Then they brought unto Him one possessed with a devil, blind and dumb, and He healed him, insomuch that the blind and dumb both spake and saw."[3]

O wickedness of the evil spirit! he had barred up both entrances, whereby that person should have believed, as well sight as hearing; nevertheless, both did Christ open.

"And all the people were amazed, saying, Is not this the Son of David?[4] But the Pharisees said, This fellow doth[5] not cast out devils, but by Beelzebub, the prince of the devils."[6]

And yet what great thing had been said? Nevertheless, not even this did they endure:

to such a degree, as I have already remarked, are they ever stung by the good works done to their neighbors, and nothing grieves them so much as the salvation of men. And yet He had actually retired, and had given room for their passion to subside; but the evil was again rekindled, because a benefit was again conferred: and the evil spirit was not so indignant as they. For he indeed departed from the body, and gave place and fled away, uttering now no sound; but these were endeavoring now to slay, now to defame Him. That is, their first aim not succeeding, they would fain hurt His good name.

Such a thing is envy, than which no worse evil can exist. For the adulterer indeed enjoys some pleasure, such as it is, and in a short time accomplishes his proper sin; but the envious man punishes himself, and takes vengeance upon himself more than on the person whom he envies, and never ceases from his sin, but is continually engaged in the commission thereof. For as a sow in mire, and evil spirits in our hurt, so also doth he delight in his neighbor's ills; and if anything painful take place, then is he refreshed, and takes breath; accounting the calamities of others his own joys, and the blessings of others his own ills; and he considers not what pleasure may accrue to himself, but what pain to his neighbor. These men therefore were it not meet to stone and beat to death, like mad dogs, like destroying demons, like the very furies?

For as beetles feed on dung, so do these men on the calamities of others, being a sort of common foes and enemies of our nature. And whereas the rest of mankind pity even a brute when it is killed, dost thou, on seeing a man receive benefits, become like a wild beast, tremble, and turn pale? Why, what can be worse than this madness? Therefore, you see, whoremongers and publicans were able to enter into the kingdom, but the envious, being within it, went out: For " the children of the kingdom," it is said, " shall be cast out." [7] And the former, once freed from their present wickedness, attained to things which they never looked for, while these latter lost even the good things which they had; and very reasonably. For this turns a man into a devil, this renders one a savage demon. Thus did the first murder arise; thus was nature forgotten; thus the earth defiled; thus afterwards did it open its mouth, to receive yet living, and utterly destroy, Dathan, and Korah, and Abiram, and all that multitude.[8]

---

[1] 2 Cor. x. 6. [R. V., " being in readiness to avenge all disobedience, when your obedience shall be fulfilled."]

[2] ὁ ἀγαπητὸς—τοῦ φιλουμένου. See Isa. v. 1. [" well-beloved " answers to the former term, rendered " beloved " above.—R.]

[3] Matt. xii. 22. [" Then was brought " (A. V. and R. V.), but the other form occurs in the Homily. R. V. omits " both."—R.]

[4] [R. V., " Is this the Son of David?"]

[5] [R. V., " this man."]　　　[6] Matt. xii. 23, 24.

[7] Matt. viii. 12.　　　[8] Numb. xvi.

4. But to declaim against envy, one may say, is easy; but we ought to consider also how men are to be freed from the disease. How then are we to be rid of this wickedness? If we bear in mind, that as he who hath committed fornication cannot lawfully enter the church, so neither he that envies; nay, and much less the latter than the former. For as things are, it is accounted even an indifferent thing; wherefore also it is little thought of; but if its real badness be made evident, we should easily refrain from it.

Weep then, and groan; lament, and entreat God. Learn to feel and to repent for it, as for a grievous sin. And if thou be of this mind, thou wilt quickly be rid of the disease.

And who knows not, one may say, that envy is an evil thing? No one indeed is ignorant of it: yet they have not the same estimation of this passion as of adultery and fornication. When, at least, did any one condemn himself bitterly for having envied? when did he entreat God concerning this pest, that He would be merciful to him? No man at any time: but if he shall fast and give a little money to a poor man, though he be envious to the thousandth degree, he counts himself to have done nothing horrid, held as he is in subjection by the most accursed passion of all. Whence, for example, did Cain become such as he was? Whence Esau? Whence the children of Laban? Whence the sons of Jacob? Whence Korah, Dathan, and Abiram, with their company? Whence Miriam? Whence Aaron? Whence the devil himself?

Herewith consider this also; that thou injurest not him whom thou enviest, but into thyself art thrusting the sword. For wherein did Cain injure Abel? Did he not even against his own will send him the more quickly into the kingdom? but himself he pierced through with innumerable evils. Wherein did Esau harm Jacob? Did not Jacob grow wealthy, and enjoy unnumbered blessings; while he himself both became an outcast from his father's house, and wandered in a strange land, after that plot of his?[1] And wherein did Jacob's sons again make Joseph the worse, and this, though they proceeded even unto blood? had not they to endure famine, and encounter peril to the utmost, whereas he became king of all Egypt? For the more thou enviest, the more dost thou become a procurer of greater blessing to the object of thine envy. For there is a God who beholds these things; and when He sees him injured, that doeth no injury,

him He exalts the more, and so makes him glorious, but thee He punishes.

For if them that exult over their enemies, He suffer not to go unpunished ("For rejoice not," it is said, "when thine enemies fall, lest at any time the Lord see it, and it displease Him"[2]); much more such as envy those who have done no wrong.

Let us then extirpate the many-headed wild beast. For in truth many are the kinds of envy. Thus, if he that loves one that is a friend to him hath no more than the publican,[3] where shall he stand who hates him that doeth him no wrong? and how shall he escape hell,[4] becoming worse than the heathens? Wherefore also I do exceedingly grieve, that we who are commanded to copy the angels, or rather the Lord of the angels, emulate the devil. For indeed there is much envy, even in the church; and more among us, than among those under authority. Wherefore we must even discourse unto ourselves.

5. Tell me then, why dost thou envy thy neighbor? Because thou seest him reaping honor, and words of good report? Then dost thou not bear in mind how much evil honors bring on the unguarded? lifting them up to pride, to vainglory, to arrogance, to contemptuousness; making them more careless? and besides these evils, they wither also lightly away. For the most grievous thing is this, that the evils arising therefrom abide immortal, but the pleasure at the moment of its appearing, is flown away. For these things then dost thou envy? tell me.

"But he hath great influence with the Ruler, and leads and drives all things which way he will, and inflicts pain on them that offend him, and benefits his flatterers, and hath much power." These are the sayings of secular persons, and of men that are riveted to the earth. For the spiritual man nothing shall be able to hurt.

For what serious harm shall he do to him? vote him out of his office? And what of that? For if it be justly done, he is even profited; for nothing so provokes God, as for one to hold the priest's office unworthily. But if unjustly, the blame again falls on the other, not on him; for he who hath suffered anything unjustly, and borne it nobly, obtains in this way the greater confidence towards God.

Let us not then aim at this, how we may be in places of power, and honor, and authority, but that we may live in virtue and self denial. For indeed places of authority persuade men to do many things which are

---

[1] Gen. xxvii. 41. [2] Prov. xxiv. 17, 18. [3] Matt. v. 46. [4] [γέενναν.]

not approved of God; and great vigor of soul is needed, in order to use authority aright. For as he that is deprived thereof, practises self restraint, whether with or against his will, so he that enjoys it is in some such condition, as if any one living with a graceful and beautiful damsel were to receive rules never to look upon her unchastely. For authority is that kind of thing. Wherefore many, even against their will, hath it induced to show insolence; it awakens wrath, and removes the bridle from the tongue, and tears off the door of the lips; fanning the soul as with a wind, and sinking the bark in the lowest depth of evils. Him then who is in so great danger dost thou admire, and sayest thou he is to be envied? Nay, how great madness is here! Consider, at any rate (besides what we have mentioned), how many enemies and accusers, and how many flatterers this person hath besieging him. Are these then, I pray thee, reasons for calling a man happy? Nay, who can say so?

"But the people," you say, "hold high account of him." And what is this? For the people surely is not God, to whom he is to render account: so that in naming the people, thou art speaking of nothing else than of other breakers, and rocks, and shoals, and sunken ridges. For to be in favor with the people, the more it makes a man illustrious, the greater the dangers, the cares, the despondencies it brings with it. For such an one has no power at all to take breath or stand still, having so severe a master. And why say I, "stand still and take breath"? Though such an one have never so many good works, hardly doth he enter into the kingdom. For nothing is so wont to overthrow[1] men, as the honor which comes of the multitude, making them cowardly, ignoble, flatterers, hypocrites.

Why, for instance, did the Pharisees say that Christ was possessed? Was it not because they were greedy of the honor of the multitude?

And whence did the multitude pass the right judgment on Him? Was it not because this disease had no hold on them? For nothing, nothing so much tends to make men lawless and foolish, as gaping after the honor of the multitude. Nothing makes them glorious and immoveable, like despising the same.

Wherefore also great vigor of soul is needed for him who is to hold out against such an impulse, and so violent a blast. For as when things are prosperous, he prefers himself to all, so when he undergoes the contrary, he would fain bury himself alive: and this is to

him both hell, and the kingdom, when he hath come to be overwhelmed by this passion.

Is all this then, I pray thee, matter of envyings, and not rather of lamentations and tears? Every one surely can see. But thou doest the same, in envying one in that kind of credit, as if a person, seeing another bound and scourged and torn by innumerable wild beasts, were to envy him his wounds and stripes. For in fact, as many men as the multitude comprises, so many bonds also, so many tyrants hath he: and, what is yet more grievous, each of these hath a different mind: and they all judge whatever comes into their heads concerning him that is a slave to them, without examining into anything; but whatever is the decision of this or that person, this they also confirm.

What manner of waves then, what tempest so grievous as this? Yea, such a one is both puffed up in a moment by the pleasure, and is under water again easily, being ever in fluctuation, in tranquillity never. Thus, before the time of the assembly, and of the contests in speaking, he is possessed with anxiety and fear; but after the assembly he is either dead with despondency, or rejoices on the contrary without measure; a worse thing than sorrow. For that pleasure is not a less evil than sorrow is plain from the effect it has on the soul; how light it makes it, and unsteady, and fluttering.

And this one may see even from those of former times. When, for instance, was David to be admired; when he rejoiced, or when he was in anguish? When, the people of the Jews? groaning and calling upon God, or exulting in the wilderness, and worshipping the calf? Wherefore Solomon too, who best of all men knew what pleasure is, saith, "It is better to go to the house of mourning, than to the house of laughter."[2] Wherefore Christ also blesses the one, saying, "Blessed are they that mourn,"[3] but the other sort He bewails, saying, "Woe unto you that laugh, for ye shall weep."[4] And very fitly. For in delight the soul is more relaxed and effeminate, but in mourning it is braced up, and grows sober, and is delivered from the whole swarm of passions, and becomes higher and stronger.

Knowing then all these things, let us shun the glory that comes from the multitude, and the pleasure that springs therefrom, that we may win the real and everlasting glory; unto which may we all attain, by the grace and love towards man of our Lord Jesus Christ, to whom be glory and might, forever and ever. Amen.

---

[1] ἐκτραχηλιάζειν.   [2] Eccles. vii. 2.   [3] Matt. v. 4.   [4] Luke vi. 25.

HOMILY XLI.

MATT. XII. 25, 26.

"And Jesus knew their thoughts, and said unto them, Every kingdom divided against itself shall be brought to desolation; and every city or house divided against itself, shall not stand: and if Satan cast out Satan, he is divided against himself; how shall then his kingdom stand?"

EVEN before now they had accused Him of this, that "by Beelzebub He casteth out the devils." [1] But whereas then He did not rebuke them, allowing them both to know His power by His more numerous miracles, and by His teaching to learn His majesty: now, since they continued saying the same, He proceeds also to rebuke them, showing His Godhead by this first, that He made their secrets public; and secondly, by the very act of casting out the devils with ease.

And indeed the accusation too was very shameless. Because, as I have said, envy seeks not what to say, but only that it may say somewhat. Yet for all that, not even so did Christ despise them, but defends Himself with the forbearance proper to Him, teaching us to be meek to our enemies; and though they say such things, as we are neither conscious of, nor have they any the least probability, not to be disturbed, nor troubled, but with all long suffering to render them an account. This then He did most especially on that very occasion, affording the strongest proof, that the things were false that were said by them. For neither was it a demoniac's part to exhibit so much meekness; it was not a demoniac's part to know men's secrets.

For, in truth, both because of the exceeding impudence of such a suspicion, and because of the fear of the multitude, they durst not publicly make these charges, but were turning them in their mind. But He, to show them that He knew all that likewise, doth not set down the accusation, nor doth He expose their wickedness; but the refutation He adds, leaving it to the conscience of them that had said it to convict them. For on one thing only was He bent, to do good to them that were sinning, not to expose them.

Yet surely, if He had been minded to extend his speech in length, and to make them ridiculous, and withal to have exacted of them also the most extreme penalty, there was nothing to hinder Him. Nevertheless He put aside all these things, and looked to one object only, not to render them more contentious, but more candid, and so to dispose them better toward amendment.

How then doth He plead with them? Not by allegation out of the Scriptures (for they would not so much as attend, but were sure rather to distort their meaning), but by the events of ordinary life. For "every kingdom," saith He, "divided against itself shall not stand: and a city and a house, if it be divided, is soon dissolved." [2]

For the wars from without are not so ruinous as the civil ones. Yea, and this is the case in bodies too; it is the case even in all things; but for this time He takes His illustration from those that are more publicly known.

And yet, what is there more powerful on earth than a kingdom? Nothing, but nevertheless it perishes if in dissension. And if in that case one throw the blame on the great burden of the affairs thereof, as breaking down by its own weight; what wouldest thou say of a city? and what of a house? Thus, whether it be a small thing, or a great, if at dissension with itself, it perishes. If then I, having a devil, do by him cast out the devils, there is dissension and fighting among devils, and they take their stand one against another. But if they stand one against another, their strength is wasted and destroyed. "For if Satan cast out Satan" (and He said not "the devils," implying their great unanimity one with another), "he is then divided against himself;" so He speaks. But if he be divided, he is become weaker, and is ruined; and if he be ruined, how can he cast out another?

Seest thou how great the absurdity of the accusation, how great the folly, the inconsistency? Since it is not for the same persons to say first, that He stands, and casts out devils, and then to say, that He stands by

---

that, which it was likely would be the cause of His undoing.

2. This then being the first refutation, the next after it is that which relates to the disciples. For not always in one way only, but also in a second and third, He solves their objections, being minded most abundantly to silence their shamelessness. Which sort of thing He did also with respect to the Sabbath, bringing forward David, the priests, the testimony that saith, "I will have mercy, and not sacrifice," the cause of the Sabbath, for which it was ordained; "for the Sabbath," saith He," was for man."[1] This then He doth in the present case also: where after the first He proceeds to a second refutation, plainer than the former.

"For if I," saith He, "by Belezebub cast out devils, by whom do your sons cast them out?"[2]

See here too His gentleness. For He said not, "my disciples," nor, "the apostles," but "your sons;" to the end that if indeed they were minded to return to the same nobleness [3] with them, they might derive hence a powerful spring that way; but if they were uncandid, and continued in the same course, they might not thenceforth be able to allege any plea, though ever so shameless.

But what He saith is like this, "By whom do the apostles cast them out?" For in fact they were doing so already, because they had received authority from Him, and these men brought no charge against them; their quarrel not being with the acts, but with the person only. As then it was His will to show that their sayings arose only from their envy against Him, He brings forward the apostles; thus: If I so cast them out, much more those, who have received their authority from me. Nevertheless, no such thing have ye said to them. How then bring ye these charges against me, the author of their doings, while acquitting them of the accusations? This, however, will not free you from your punishment, rather it will condemn you the more. Therefore also He added, "They shall be your judges." For when persons from among you, and having been practised in these things, both believe me and obey, it is most clear that they will also condemn those who are against me both in deed and word.

"But if I cast out devils by the Spirit of God, then the Kingdom of God is come unto you."[4]

What means "the Kingdom"? "My coming." See how again He conciliates and

soothes them, and draws them to the knowledge of Himself, and signifies that they are warring with their own good, and contentious against their own salvation. "For whereas ye ought to rejoice," saith He, "and leap for joy, that One is come bestowing those great and unutterable blessings, hymned of old by the prophets, and that the time of your prosperity is at hand; ye do the contrary; so far from receiving the blessings, you do even speak ill of them, and frame accusations that have no real being."

Now Matthew indeed saith, "If I by Spirit of God cast out"; but Luke, "If I by the finger of God cast out the devils:"[5] implying that to cast out devils is a work of the greatest power, and not of any ordinary grace. And He means indeed that from these things they should infer and say, If this be so, then the Son of God is come. This, however, He saith not, but in a reserved way, and so as not to be galling to them, He darkly intimates it by saying, "Then the kingdom of God is come unto you."

Seest thou exceeding wisdom? By the very things which they were blaming, He showed His presence shining forth.

Then, to conciliate them, He said not simply, "The Kingdom is come," but, "unto you,"[6] as though He had said, To you the good things are come; wherefore then feel displeased at your proper blessings? why war against your own salvation? This is that time, which the prophets long ago foretold: this, the sign of that advent which was celebrated by them, even these things being wrought by divine power. For the fact indeed, that they are wrought, yourselves know; but that they are wrought by divine power, the deeds themselves cry out. Yea, and it is impossible that Satan should be stronger now; rather he must of absolute necessity be weak. But it cannot be, that he who is weak should, as though he were strong, cast out the strong devil.

Now thus speaking He signified the power of charity, and the weakness of separation and contentiousness. Wherefore He was Himself also continually charging His disciples, on every occasion, concerning charity, and teaching them that the devil, to subvert it, leaves nothing undone.

3. Having then uttered His second refutation, He adds also a third, thus saying:

"How can one enter into the strong man's house, and spoil his goods, except he first bind the strong man, and then spoil his goods?"[7]

---

[1] See Matt. xii. 3, 5, 7, and Mark ii. 27.　　[2] Matt. xii. 27.
[3] εὐγένειαν, "hereditary good feeling." [Comp. Acts xvii. 11.]
[4] Matt. xii. 28. [R. V., " upon you."]

[5] Luke xi. 20.　　[6] [" upon you," see note 1.]
[7] Matt. xii. 29. [The R. V and A. V. follow a different reading in the last clause.—R.]

For that Satan cannot possibly cast out Satan is evident from what hath been said; but that neither in any other way is it possible to cast him out, except one first get the better of him, this too is acknowledged by all.

What then is established hereby? The former statement, with more abundant evidence. "Why, I am so far," saith He, "from using the devil as an ally, that I make war upon him, and bind him; and an infallible proof thereof is the plundering of his goods." See how the contrary is proved, of what they were attempting to establish. For whereas they wished to show, that not by His own power doth He cast out devils, He shows that not only the devils, but even their very chief leader is held by Him bound with all authority; and that over him, before them, did He prevail by His own power. And this is evident from the things that are done. For if he be the prince, and they subjects, how, except he were worsted, and made to bow down, could they have been spoiled?

And here His saying seems to me to be a prophecy likewise. For not only, I suppose, are the evil spirits the goods of the devil, but also the men that are doing his works. Therefore to declare that He doth not only cast out devils, but also will drive away all error from the world, and will put down his sorceries, and make all his arts useless, He said these things.

And He said not, He will take away, but "He will spoil," to express what is done with authority. But He calls him "strong," not because he is so by nature, God forbid, but declaring his former tyranny, which arose from our remissness.

4. "He that is not with me is against me, and he that gathereth not with me scattereth abroad."[1]

Behold also a fourth refutation. For what is my desire? saith He. To bring men to God, to teach virtue, to proclaim the kingdom. What, that of the devil, and the evil spirits? The contrary to these. How then should he that gathers not with me, nor is at all with me, be likely to co-operate with me? And why do I say co-operate? Nay, on the contrary, his desire is rather to scatter abroad my goods. He then who is so far from co-operating that he even scatters abroad, how should he have exhited such unanimity with me, as with me to cast out the devils?

Now it is a natural surmise that He said this not of the devil only, but Himself also of Himself, as being for His part against the

devil, and scattering abroad his goods. And how, one may say, is he that is not with me against me? By this very fact, of his not gathering. But if this be true, much more he that is against him. For if he that doth not co-operate is an enemy, much more he that wages war.

But all these things He saith, to indicate His enmity against the devil, how great and unspeakable it is. For tell me, if thou must go to war with any one, he that is not willing to fight on thy side, by this very fact is he not against thee? And if elsewhere He saith, "He that is not against you is for you,"[2] it is not contrary to this. For here He signified one actually against them, but there He points to one who in part is on their side: "For they cast out devils," it is said "in Thy name."[3]

But to me He seems here to be hinting also at the Jews, setting them on the devil's side. For they too were against Him, and were scattering what He gathered. As to the fact that He was hinting at them also, He declared it by speaking thus,

"Therefore I say unto you, that all manner of sin and blasphemy shall be forgiven unto men."[4]

5. Thus having defended Himself, and refuted their objection, and proved the vanity of their shameless dealings, He proceeds to alarm them. For this too is no small part of advice and correction, not only to plead and persuade, but to threaten also; which He doth in many passages, when making laws and giving counsel.

And though the saying seem to have much obscurity, yet if we attend, its solution will prove easy.

First then it were well to listen to the very words: "All manner of sin and blasphemy shall be forgiven unto men; but the blasphemy of the Holy Ghost shall not be forgiven unto them. And whosoever speaketh a word against the Son of Man, it shall be forgiven him; but whosoever speaketh against the Holy Ghost, it shall not be forgiven him, neither in this world, neither in the world to come."[5]

What now is it that He affirms? Many things have ye spoken against me; that I am a deceiver, an adversary of God. These things I forgive you on your repentance, and exact no penalty of you; but blasphemy against the Spirit shall not be forgiven, no,

---

[1] Matt. xii. 30.

[2] Mark ix. 40; Luke ix. 50. [In Mark "us" is better supported.—R.]
[3] Mark ix. 38; Luke ix. 49.
[4] Matt. xii. 31. [R. V., "every sin," etc.]
[5] Matt. xii. 31, 32. [The Greek text is almost identical with that followed in the R. V.—R.]

not to those who repent. And how can this be right? For even this was forgiven upon repentance. Many at least of those who said these words believed afterward, and all was forgiven them. What is it then that He saith? That this sin is above all things unpardonable. Why so? Because Himself indeed they knew not, who He might be, but of the Spirit they received ample experience. For the prophets also by the Spirit said whatever they said; and indeed all in the Old Testament had a very high notion of Him.

What He saith, then, is this: Be it so: ye are offended at me, because of the flesh with which I am encompassed: can ye say of the Spirit also, We know it not? And therefore is your blasphemy unpardonable, and both here and hereafter shall ye suffer punishment. For many indeed have been punished here only (as he who had committed fornication,[1] as they who partook unworthily of the mysteries,[1] amongst the Corinthians); but ye, both here and hereafter.

Now as to your blasphemies against me, before the cross, I forgive them: and the daring crime too of the cross itself; neither shall ye be condemned for your unbelief alone. (For neither had they, that believed before the cross, perfect faith. And on many occasions He even charges them to make Him known to no man before the Passion; and on the cross He said that this sin was forgiven them.) But as to your words touching the Spirit, they will have no excuse. For in proof that He is speaking of what was said of Him before the crucifixion, He added, "Whosoever shall speak a word against the Son of Man, it shall be forgiven him; but whosoever shall speak against the Holy Ghost," there is no more forgiveness. Wherefore? Because this is known to you; and the truths are notorious which you harden yourselves against. For though ye say that ye know not me; yet of this surely ye are not ignorant, that to cast out devils, and to do cures, is a work of the Holy Ghost. It is not then I only whom ye are insulting, but the Holy Ghost also. Wherefore your punishment can be averted by no prayers, neither here nor there.

For so of men, some are punished both here, and there, some here only, some there only, others neither here nor there. Here and there, as these very men (for both here did they pay a penalty, when they suffered those incurable ills at the taking of their city, and there shall they undergo a very grievous one), as the inhabitants of Sodom;

as many others. There only, as the rich man who endured the flames,[2] and had not at his command so much as a drop of water. Here, as he that had committed fornication amongst the Corinthians. Neither here nor there, as the apostles, as the prophets, as the blessed Job; for their sufferings were not surely in the way of punishment, but as contests and wrestlings.

Let us labor, therefore, to be of the same part with these: or if not with these, at least with them that wash away their sins here. For fearful indeed is that other judgment, and inexorable the vengeance, and incurable the punishment.

6. But if thou desire not to be punished even here, pass judgment on thyself, exact thine own penalty. Listen to Paul, when he saith, "If we would judge ourselves, we should not be judged."[3] If thou do this, proceeding in order thou shalt even arrive at a crown.

But how are we to exact our own penalty? one may ask. Lament, groan bitterly, humble, afflict thyself, call to remembrance thy sins in their particulars. This thing is no small torture to a man's soul. If any man hath been in a state of contrition, he knows that the soul is punished by this more than anything. If any hath been living in remembrance of sins, he knows the anguish thence arising. Therefore doth God appoint righteousness as a reward for such repentance, saying, "Be thou first to tell thy sins, that thou mayest be justified."[4] For it is not, it is not indeed, a small step towards amendment, to lay together all our sins, and to be continually revolving and reckoning them up with their particulars. For he that is doing this will be so heart-broken, as not to think himself worthy so much as to live; and he that thinks thus, will be tenderer than any wax. For tell me not of acts of fornication only, nor of adulteries, nor of these things that are manifest, and acknowledged amongst all men: but lay together also thy secret crafts, and thy false accusations, and thine evil speakings, and thy vain gloryings, and thine envy, and all such things. For neither will these bring a trifling punishment. For the reviler too shall fall into hell; and the drunkard hath no part in the kingdom; and he that lovest not his neighbor so offends God, as to find no help even in his own martyrdom; and he that neglects his own hath denied the faith, and he who overlooks the poor is sent into the fire.

---

[1] See 1 Cor. v. and vi.

[2] ἀποτηγανιζόμενος, "was broiling."
[3] 1 Cor. xi. 31. [The Greek text of 1 Cor. xi. 31 is slightly modified here.—R.]
[4] Isa. xliii. 26 [LXX.].

Account not then these things to be little, but put all together, and write them as in a book. For if thou write them down, God blots them out; even as on the other hand, if thou omit writing them, God both inscribes them, and exacts their penalty. It were then far better for them to be written by us, and blotted out above, than on the contrary, when we have forgotten them, for God to bring them before our eyes in that day.

Therefore that this may not be so, let us reckon up all with strictness, and we shall find ourselves answerable for much. For who is clear from covetousness? Nay, tell me not of the quantity, but since even in a small amount we shall pay the same penalty, consider this and repent. Who is rid of all insolence? Yet this casts into hell. Who hath not secretly spoken evil of his neighbor? Yet this deprives one of the Kingdom.[1] Who hath not been self-willed? Yet this man is more unclean than all. Who hath not looked with unchaste eyes? Yet this is a complete adulterer. Who hath not been "angry with his brother without a cause"? Yet such an one is "in danger of the council." Who hath not sworn? Yet this thing is of the evil one. Who hath not forsworn himself? but this man is something

more than of the evil one. Who hath not served mammon? but this man is fallen away from the genuine service of Christ.

I have also other things greater than these to mention: but even these are enough, and able, if a man be not made of stone, nor utterly past feeling, to bring him to compunction. For if each one of them casts into hell, what will they not bring to pass when all are met together?

How then can one be saved? it may be asked. By application of the countervailing remedies: alms, prayers, compunction, repentance, humility, a contrite heart, contempt of possessions. For God hath marked out for us innumerable ways of salvation, if we be willing to attend. Let us then attend, and let us every way cleanse out our wounds, showing mercy, remitting our anger against them that have displeased us, giving thanks for all things to God, fasting acccording to our power, praying sincerely, "making unto ourselves friends of the mammon of unrighteousness."[2] For so shall we be able to obtain pardon for our offenses, and to win the promised good things; whereof may we all be counted worthy, by the grace and love toward man of our Lord Jesus Christ, to whom be glory and might forever and ever. Amen.

---

[1] [This clause is wanting in three MSS.—R.]

[2] Luke xvi. 9. [R. V., "by means of," with margin, "Greek, out of."]

HOMILY XLII.

MATT. XII. 33

"Either make the tree good, and his fruit good, or else make the tree corrupt, and his fruit corrupt; for the tree is known by his fruit."

AGAIN in another way He shames them, and is not content with His former refutations. But this He doth, not freeing Himself from accusations, (for what went before was quite enough), but as wishing to amend them.

Now His meaning is like this: none of you hath either found fault about the persons healed, as not being healed; nor hath said, that it is an evil thing to deliver one from a devil. For though they had been ever so shameless, they could not have said this.

Since therefore they brought no charge against the works, but were defaming the

Doer of them, He signifies that this accusation is against both the common modes of reasoning, and the congruity of the circumstances. A thing of aggravated shamelessness, not only to interpret maliciously, but also to make up such charges as are contrary to men's common notions.

And see how free He is from contentiousness. For He said not, "Make the tree good, forasmuch as the fruit also is good;" but, most entirely stopping their mouths, and exhibiting His own considerateness, and their insolence, He saith, Even if ye are minded to find fault with my works, I forbid it not at all, only bring not inconsistent and contradictory charges. For thus were they sure to be most clearly detected, persisting against what was too palpable. Wherefore to no purpose is your maliciousness, saith He, and your self-contradictory statements. Because in truth the distinction of the tree is shown by the fruit, not the fruit by the tree; but ye do the contrary. For what if the tree be the origin of the fruit; yet it is the fruit that makes the tree to be known. And it were consistent, either in blaming us to find fault with our works too, or praising these, to set us who do them free from these charges. But now ye do the contrary; for having no fault to find with the works, which is the fruit, ye pass the opposite judgment upon the tree, calling me a demoniac; which is utter insanity.

Yea, and what He had said before,[1] this He establishes now also; that a good tree cannot bring forth evil fruit, nor again can the converse be. So that their charges were against all consistency and nature.

Then since He is arguing not for Himself, but for the Spirit, He hath dealt out His reproof even as a torrent, saying, "O generation of vipers, how can ye, being evil, speak good things?"[2]

Now this is at once to accuse, and to give demonstration of His own sayings from their case. For behold, saith He, ye being evil trees, cannot bring forth good fruit. I do not then marvel at your talking thus: for ye were both ill nurtured, being of wicked ancestors, and ye have acquired a bad mind.

And see how carefully, and without any hold for exception, He hath expressed His accusations: in that He said not, "How can ye speak good things, being a generation of vipers? (for this latter is nothing to the former): but, "How can ye, being evil, speak good things?"

But He called them "broods of vipers," because they prided themselves on their forefathers. To signify therefore that they had no advantage thereby, He both casts them out from their relationship to Abraham, and assigns them forefathers of kindred disposition, having stripped them of that ground of illustriousness.

"For out of the abundance of the heart the mouth speaketh." Here again He indicates His Godhead, which knew their secrets: and that not for words only, but also for wicked thoughts, they shall suffer punishment; and that He knows it all, as God. And He saith,

that it is possible even for men to know these things; for this is a natural consequence, that when wickedness is overflowing within, its words should be poured forth through the lips. So that when thou hearest a man speak wicked words, do not suppose only so much wickedness to be in him as the words display, but conjecture the fountain to be much more abundant; for that which is spoken outwardly, is the superabundance of that which is within.

See how vehemently He reprehends them. For if what they had said is so evil, and is of the very mind of the devil, consider the root and well-spring of their words, how far that must reach. And this is naturally the case; for while the tongue through shame often pours not forth all its wickedness at once, the heart having no human witness, fearlessly gives birth to whatever evils it will; for of God it hath not much regard.[3] Since then men's sayings come to examination, and are set before all, but the heart is concealed; therefore the evils of the former grow less, while those of the latter increase. But when that within is multiplied, all that hath been awhile hidden comes forth with a violent gushing. And as persons vomiting strive at first to keep down the humors that force their way out, but, when they are overcome, cast forth much abomination; so do they that devise evil things, and speak ill of their neighbors.

"A good man out of his good treasure," saith He, "bringeth forth good things, and an evil man out of his evil treasure bringeth forth evil things."[4]

For think not by any means, saith He, that it is so in respect of wickedness only, for in goodness also the same occurs: for there too the virtue within is more than the words without. By which He signified, that both they were to be accounted more wicked than their words indicated, and Himself more perfectly good than His sayings declared. And He calls it "a treasure," indicating its abundance.

Then again He fences them in with great terror. For think not at all, saith He, that the thing stops at this, that is, at the condemnation of the multitude; nay, for all that do wickedly in such things shall suffer the utmost punishment. And He said not, "ye," partly in order to instruct our whole race, partly to make His saying the less burdensome.

"But I say unto you," this is His word,

---

[1] Matt. vii. 16-18.   [2] Matt. xii. 34.

[3] [οὐ πολὺς λόγος αὐτῇ, "it takes not much account."—R.]
[4] Matt. xii. 35. [R. V., "The good man . . . the evil man," etc.]

"that every idle word that men shall speak, they shall give account thereof in the day of judgment."[1]

And that is idle, which is not according to the fact, which is false, which hath in it unjust accusation; and some say, that which is vain also, for instance, provoking inordinate laughter, or what is filthy, and immodest, and coarse.

"For by thy words thou shalt be justified, and by thy words thou shalt be condemned."[2]

Seest thou how far the tribunal is from invidiousness? how favorable the account required? For not upon what another hath said of thee, but from what thou hast thyself spoken, will the Judge give His sentence; which is of all things the very fairest: since surely with thee it rests, either to speak, or not to speak.

2. Wherefore not those that are slandered, but the slanderers, have need to be anxious and to tremble. For the former are not constrained to answer for themselves touching the evil things which are said of them, but the latter will, for the evil they have spoken; and over these impends the whole danger. So that the persons censured should be without anxiety, not being to give account of the evil that others have said; but the censurers have cause to be in anxiety, and to tremble, as being themselves to be dragged before the judgment-seat in that behalf. For this is indeed a diabolical snare, and a sin having in it no pleasure, but harm only. Yea, and such an one is laying up an evil treasure in his soul. And if he that hath an evil humor in him doth himself first reap the fruits of the malady, much more he that is treasuring up in himself what is more bitter than any bile, I mean, wickedness, will suffer the utmost evils, gathering unto himself a grievous disease. And it is evident from the things that He vomits out. For if they pain others so much, far more the soul that gives them birth.

Thus the plotter destroys himself first; just as he that treads[3] on fire burns up himself, and he that smites adamant spites himself, and he that kicks against the pricks draws blood from himself. For somewhat of this kind is he that knows how to suffer wrong, and to bear it manfully; he is adamant, and the pricks, and fire; but he that hath used himself to do wrong is feebler than any clay.

Not therefore to suffer wrong is evil, but to do it, and not to know how to bear being wronged. For instance, how great wrongs did David endure! How great wrongs[4] did Saul commit! Which then was the stronger and happier? which the more wretched and miserable? was it not he that did wrong? And mark it. Saul had promised, if David should slay the Philistine, to take him for his son-in law, and to give him his daughter with great favor. He slew the Philistine; the other broke his engagements, and so far from bestowing her, did even go about to slay him. Which then became the more glorious? Was not the one choking with despair and the evil demon, while the other shone brighter than the sun with his trophies, and his loyalty to God? Again, before the choir of the women, was not the one suffocated with envy, while the other enduring all in silence, won all men, and bound them unto himself? And when he had even gotten him into his hands, and spared him, which again was happy? and which wretched? which was the weaker? which the more powerful? Was it not this man, who did not avenge himself even justly? And very naturally. For the one had armed soldiers, but the other, righteousness, that is more mighty than ten thousand armies, for his ally and helper. And for this reason, though unjustly conspired against, he endured not to slay him even justly. For he knew by what had taken place before, that not to do evil, but to suffer evil, this is what makes men more powerful. So it is with bodies also, so also with trees.

And what did Jacob? Was he not injured by Laban, and suffered evil? Which then was the stronger? he that had gotten the other into his hands, and durst not touch him, but was afraid and trembling;[5] or he whom we see without arms and soldiers proving more terrible to him than innumerable kings?

But that I may give you another demonstration of what I have said, greater than this, let us again in the instance of David himself try the reasoning on the opposite side. For this man who being injured was so strong, afterwards upon committing an injury became on the contrary the weaker party. At least, when he had wronged Uriah, his position was changed again, and the weakness passed to the wrong doer, and the might to the injured; for he being dead laid waste the other's house. And the one being a king, and alive, could do nothing, but the other, being but a soldier, and slain, turned upside down all that pertained to his adversary.

---

[1] Matt. xii. 36.   [2] Matt. xii. 37.
[3] πατῶν. Bened. from MSS. ἀνάπτων, "he that kindles:" which seems to agree with the tenor of the sentence better. [There are other various readings: ἅπτων, ἄπτων. All can be more readily accounted for, if πατῶν is accepted as the original form.—R.]

[4] [Oxford version: "things;" probably a misprint, the Greek being the same as before.—R.]
[5] Gen. xxxi. 29.

Would ye that in another way also I should make what I say plainer? Let us look into their case, who avenge themselves even justly. For as to the wrong doers, that they are the most worthless of all men, warring against their own soul; this is surely plain to every one.

But who avenged himself justly, yet kindled innumerable ills, and pierced himself through with many calamities and sorrows? The captain of David's host. For he both stirred up a grievous war, and suffered unnumbered evils; not one whereof would have happened, had he but known how to command himself.[1]

Let us flee therefore from this sin, and neither in words nor deeds do our neighbors wrong. For He said not, If thou slander, and summon a court of justice, but simply, If thou speak evil, though within thyself, even so shalt thou suffer the utmost punishment. Though it be true which thou hast said, though thou have spoken upon conviction, even so shall vengeance come upon thee. For not according to what the other hath done, but according to what thou hast spoken, will God pass sentence; "for by thy words thou shalt be condemned," saith He. Art thou not told that the Pharisee also spake the truth, and affirmed what was manifest to all men, without discovering what was hidden? Nevertheless, he paid the utmost penalty.

But if we ought not to accuse men of things which are acknowledged, much less of those which are disputed; nay, for the offender hath a judge. Do not now, I warn thee, seize upon the privilege of the Only Begotten. For Him is the throne of judgment reserved.

3. Wouldest thou however be a judge? Thou hast a court of judgment which hath great profit, and bears no blame. Make consideration, as judge, to sit down upon thy conscience, and bring before it all thy transgressions, search out the sins of thy soul, and exact with strictness the account thereof, and say, "wherefore didst thou dare to do this and that?" And if she shun these, and be searching into other men's matters, say to her, "Not about these am I judging thee, not for these art thou come here to plead. For what, if such a one be a wicked man? Thou, why didst thou commit this and that offense? Answer for thyself, not to accuse; look to thine own matters, do not those of others." And be thou continually urging her to this anxious trial. Then, if she have nothing to say, but shrink back, wear her out with the scourge, like some restless and unchaste handmaid. And this tribunal do thou cause to sit every day, and picture the river of fire, the venomous worm, the rest of the torments.

And permit her not to be with the devil any more, nor bear with her shameless sayings, " he comes to me, he plots against me, he tempts me;" but tell her, "If thou wert not willing, all that would be to no purpose." And if she say again, "I am entangled with a body, I am clothed with flesh, I dwell in the world, I abide on earth;" tell her, "All these are excuses and pretexts. For such an one too was encompassed with flesh, and such another dwelling in the world, and abiding on earth, is approved; and thou thyself too, when thou doest well, doest it encompassed with flesh." And if she be pained at hearing this, take not off thine hand; for she will not die, if thou smite her, but thou wilt save her from death. And if she say again, " Such an one provoked me," tell her, " But it is in thy power not to be provoked; often at least thou hast restrained thine anger." And if she say, " The beauty of such a woman moved me;" tell her, " Yet wast thou able to have mastered thyself." Bring forward those that have got the better, bring forward the first woman, who said, " The serpent beguiled me,"[2] and yet was not acquitted of the blame.

And when thou art searching out these things, let no man be present, let no man disturb thee; but as the judges sit under curtains to judge, so do thou too, instead of curtains, seek a time and place of quiet. And when after thy supper thou art risen up, and art about to lie down, then hold this thy judgment; this is the time convenient for thee, and the place, thy bed, and thy chamber. This the prophet likewise commanded, saying, " For the things which ye say in your hearts, be ye moved to compunction upon your beds."[3] And for small offenses require great satisfaction, that unto the great thou mayest never even approach. If thou do this every day, thou wilt with confidence stand at that fearful judgment-seat.

In this way Paul became clean; therefore also he said, "For if we judged ourselves, we should not be judged."[4] Thus did Job cleanse his sons.[5] For he that offered sacrifices for secret sins, much more did he require an account of such as were manifest.

4. But we do not so, but altogether the contrary. For as soon as we are laid down to rest, we rather think over all our worldly maters; and some introduce unclean thoughts, some usuries, and contracts, and temporal cares.

---

[1] See 2 Samuel iii. 23-30, and xx. 9, 10; 1 Kings ii. 5, 6.

[2] Gen. iii. 13.
[4] 1 Cor. xi. 31.
[3] Ps. iv. 4, LXX.
[5] Job. i. 5.

And if we have a daughter, a virgin, we watch her strictly; but that which is more precious to us than a daughter, our soul, her we suffer to play the harlot and defile herself, introducing to her innumerable wicked thoughts. And whether it be the love of covetousness, or that of luxury, or that of fair persons, or that of wrath, or be it what you will else that is minded to come in, we throw open the doors, and attract and invite it, and help it to defile our soul at its leisure. And what can be more barbarous than this, to overlook our soul that is more precious than all, abused by so many adulterers, and so long companying with them, even until they are sated? which will never be. So it is, therefore, that when sleep overtakes us, then only do they depart from her; or rather not even then, for our dreams and imaginations furnish her with the same images. Whence also, when day is come, the soul stored with such images often falls away to the actual performance of those fancies.

And thou, while into the apple of thine eye thou sufferest not so much as a grain of dust to enter, dost thou pass unnoticed thy soul, gathering to itself a heap of so great evils? When shall we then be able to clear out this filth, which we are daily laying up within us? when to cut up the thorns? when to sow the seed? Knowest thou not that henceforth the time of harvest is at hand? But we have not yet so much as ploughed our fields. If then the husbandman should come and find fault, what shall we say? and what answer shall we make? That no man gave us the seed? Nay, this is sown daily. That no man, then, hath cut up the thorns? Nay, every day we are sharpening the sickle. But

do the necessary engagements of life distract thee? And why hast thou not crucified thyself to the world? For if he that repays that only, which is given him, is wicked, because he did not double it; he that hath wasted even this, what will be said to him? If that person was bound, and cast out where is gnashing of teeth, what shall we have to suffer, who, when numberless motives are drawing us toward virtue, shrink back and are unwilling?

For what is there, that hath not enough in it to persuade thee? Seest thou not the vileness of the world, the uncertainty of life, the toil, the sweat, for things present? What? is it the case that virtue must be toiled for, but may vice be had without toil? If then both in the one and in the other there is toil, why didst thou not choose this, which hath so great profit?

Or rather, there are some parts of virtue, which are free even from toil. For what kind of toil is it, not to calumniate, not to lie, not to swear, to lay aside our anger against our neighbor? Nay, on the contrary, to do these things is toilsome, and brings much anxiety.

What plea then shall we have, what excuse, not doing right even in these matters? For hereby it is plain, that out of remissness and sloth the more toilsome duties also altogether escape us.

All these things let us consider; let us flee vice, let us choose virtue, that we may attain both unto the good things that are present, and unto those that are to come, by the grace and love towards man of our Lord Jesus Christ, to whom be glory and might forever and ever. Amen.

HOMILY XLIII.

MATT. XII. 38, 39.

" Then certain of the Scribes and Pharisees answered Him, saying, Master, we would see a sign from Thee. But He answered and said,[1] An evil and adulterous generation seeketh after a sign, and there shall no sign be given to it, but the sign of the Prophet Jonas."

COULD then anything be more foolish than these men (not more impious only), who after so many miracles, as though none had

been wrought, say, "We would see a sign from Thee?" With what intent then did they so speak? That they might lay hold of Him again. For since by His words He had stopped their mouths, once and twice

---

[1] [" Unto them " is omitted in the Greek text here, against all our New Testament codices.—R.]

and often, and had checked their shameless tongue, they come to His works again. At which also the evangelist marvelling again, said,

"Then certain of the scribes answered Him, asking a sign."

"Then," when? When they ought to be stooping before Him, to admire, to be amazed and give way, "then" they desist not from their wickedness.

And see their words too, teeming with flattery and dissimulation. For they thought to draw Him towards them in that way. And now they insult, now they flatter Him; now calling Him a demoniac, now again "Master," both out of an evil mind, how contrary soever the words they speak.

Wherefore also He rebukes them severely. And when they were questioning Him roughly and insulting Him, He reasoned with them gently; when they were flattering, reproachfully, and with great severity; implying that He is superior to either passion, and is neither at the one time moved to anger, nor at the other softened by flattery. And see His reproach, that it is not merely hard words, but contains a demonstration of their wickedness. For what saith He?

"An evil and adulterous generation seeketh after a sign." Now what He saith is to this effect: What marvel if ye behave so to me, who have been hitherto unknown to you, when even to the Father, of whom ye have had so much experience, ye have done the very same? forsaking Him, ye have run unto the devils, drawing to yourselves wicked lovers. With this Ezekiel too was continually upbraiding them.[1]

Now by these sayings He signified Himself to be of one accord with His Father, and them to be doing nothing new; He was also unfolding their secrets, how with hypocrisy and as enemies they were making their demand. Therefore He called them "an evil generation," because they have been always ungrateful towards their benefactors; because upon favors they become worse, which belongs to extreme wickedness.

And He called it "adulterous," declaring both their former and their present unbelief; whereby He implies Himself again to be equal to the Father, if at least the not believing Him makes it "adulterous."

2. Then, after His reproach, what saith He? "There shall no sign be given to it, but the sign of Jonas the prophet." Now is He striking the first note of the doctrine of His resurrection, and confirming it by the type.

What then? one may say; was no sign given it? None was given to it on asking. For not to bring in them did He work His signs (for He knew them to be hardened), but in order to amend others. Either then this may be said, or that they were not to receive such a sign as that was. For a sign did befall them, when by their own punishment they learnt His power. Here then He speaks as threatening, and with this very meaning obscurely conveyed: as if He said, innumerable benefits have I showed forth, none of these hath drawn you to me, neither were ye willing to adore my power. Ye shall know therefore my might by the contrary tokens, when ye shall see your city cast down to the ground, the walls also dismantled, the temple become a ruin; when ye shall be cast out both from your former citizenship and freedom, and shall again go about everywhere, houseless and in exile. (For all these things came to pass after the cross.) These things therefore shall be to you for great signs. And indeed it is an exceeding great sign, that their ills remain unchanged; that although ten thousand have attempted it, no one hath been able to reverse[2] the judgment once gone forth against them.

All this however He saith not, but leaves it to after time to make it clear to them, but for the present He is making trial of[3] the doctrine of His resurrection, which they were to come to know by the things which they should afterwards suffer.

"For as Jonas," saith He, "was three days and three nights in the whale's belly, so shall the Son of Man be three days and three nights in the heart of the earth."[4] Thus, He said not indeed openly that He should rise again, since they would have even laughed Him to scorn, but He intimated it in such manner, that they might believe Him to have foreknown it. For as to their being aware of it, they say to Pilate, "That deceiver said," these are their words, "while He was yet alive, After three days I will rise again;"[5] and yet we know His disciples were ignorant of this; even as they had been beforehand more void of understanding than these: wherefore also these became self-condemned.

But see how exactly He expresses it, even though in a dark saying. For He said not, "In the earth," but, "In the heart of the earth;" that He might designate His very sepulchre, and that no one might suspect a mere semblance.[6] And for this intent too

---

[1] See Ezek. xvi. 23, etc.
18

[2] διορθῶσαι.   [3] γυμνάζει.   [4] Matt. xxii. 40.
[5] Matt. xxvii. 63. [The citation is not exact: at the close a different verb, in a different tense, is given.—R.]
[6] δόκησιν: so Δοκηταί was the name of those heretics who denied the reality of our Lord's incarnation and death.

did He allow three days, that the fact of His death might be believed. For not by the cross only doth He make it certain, and by the sight of all men, but also by the time of those days. For to the resurrection indeed all succeeding time was to bear witness; but the cross, unless it had at the time many signs bearing witness to it, would have been disbelieved; and with this disbelief would have gone utter disbelief of the resurrection also. Therefore He calls it also a sign. But had He not been crucified, the sign would not have been given. For this cause too He brings forward the type, that the truth may be believed. For tell me, was Jonah in the whale's belly a mere appearance? Nay, thou canst not say so. Therefore neither was Christ in the heart of the earth such. For surely the type is not in truth, and the truth in mere appearance. For this cause we every where show forth His death, both in the mysteries, and in baptism, and in all the rest. Therefore Paul also cries with a clear voice, "God forbid that I should glory, save in the cross of our Lord Jesus Christ."[1]

Whence it is clear, that they who are diseased in Marcion's way are children of the devil, blotting out these truths, to avoid the annulling whereof Christ did so many things, while to have them annulled the devil took such manifold pains: I mean, His cross and His passion.

3. Therefore He said elsewhere also, "Destroy this temple, and in three days I will raise it up:"[2] and, "The days will come when the Bridegroom shall be taken away from them:"[3] and here, "There shall no sign be given it, but the sign of Jonas the prophet:" declaring both that He should die[4] for them, and that they would profit nothing; for this He afterwards declared. Nevertheless, even with this knowledge He died: so great was His tender care.

For to hinder thy supposing that the result would be such with the Jews as with the Ninevites; that they would be converted, and that as in their case He established the tottering city, and converted the barbarians, so these too should turn unto Him after His resurrection; hear how He declares altogether the contrary. For that they should reap no good from hence in respect of their own benefit, but rather suffer incurable ills, this too He went on to declare by the parable of the evil spirit.

But for the present He is justifying their future sufferings, signifying that they would suffer justly. For their calamities and their desolation He represents by that similitude; but up to this time He is indicating the justice of their having to suffer all these things: which also in the Old Testament was His wont. Thus when about to destroy Sodom, He first defended Himself to Abraham, by showing the desolation and rareness of virtue, when indeed not even ten men were found in so many cities, who had made it their rule to live chastely. And to Lot also in like manner, He first signifies their inhospitality and their unnatural lusts, and then He brings the fire on them. And with regard to the deluge again He did the self-same thing, by His acts excusing Himself to Noah. And also to Ezekiel[5] in like manner, when He caused him dwelling in Babylon to see men's evil deeds in Jerusalem. And yet again to Jeremiah, when He said, "Pray not," excusing Himself He added, "Seest thou not what they do?"[6] And everywhere He doeth the selfsame thing, as here also.

For what saith He? "The men of Nineveh shall rise up,[7] and shall condemn this generation, because they repented at the preaching of Jonas, and, behold, a greater than Jonas is here."[8]

For he was a servant, but I am the Master; and he came forth from the whale, but I rose from death; and he proclaimed destruction, but I am come preaching the good tidings of the kingdom. And they indeed believed without a sign, but I have exhibited many signs. And they indeed heard nothing more than those words, but I have given a spring to every kind of self-denial. And he came being ministered unto, but I the very Master and Lord of all am come not threatening, not demanding an account, but bringing pardon. And they were barbarians, but these have conversed with unnumbered prophets. And of him no man had foretold, but of me all, and the facts agreed with their words. And he indeed, when he was to go forth, ran away that he might not be ridiculed; but I, knowing that I am both to be crucified and mocked, am come. And while he did not endure so much as to be reproached for them that were saved, I underwent even death, and that the most shameful death, and after this I sent others again. And he was a strange sort of person, and an alien, and unknown; but I a kinsman after the flesh, and of the same forefathers. And many more topics too might any one collect, were he to seek diligently for more.

---

[1] Gal. vi. 14. [R. V. "Far be it from me to glory." etc.]
[2] John ii. 19.   [3] Matt. ix. 15
[4] [πείσεται, "suffer," as it is rendered below.—R.]

[5] Ezek. viii. 5, etc.   [6] Jer. vii. 16, 17.
[7] [R. V., "stand up."]
[8] Matt. xii. 41. [The citation is not verbally exact: some phrases are omitted, and the order is varied.—R.]

But He stops not even at this, but adds also another example, saying,

"And the queen of the south shall rise up in judgment [1] with this generation, and shall condemn them, because she came from the uttermost parts of the earth to hear the wisdom of Solomon, and behold a greater than Solomon is here." [2]

This was more than the former. For Jonah went unto them, but the queen of the south waited not for Solomon to come to her, but went herself unto him, although she was both a woman, and a barbarian, and at so great a distance, no threat laid upon her, nor being in fear of death, but simply through the love of wise words. "But behold even a greater than Solomon is here." For in that case the woman came, but here I have come. And she indeed rose up from the uttermost parts of the earth, but I go about cities and villages. And his discourse was of trees and various kinds of wood, which could do no great good to his visitor: but mine, of secret things, and most awful mysteries.

4. When therefore He had condemned them, having proved most amply that they were sinning inexcusably, and that their disobedience arose from their own perverseness, not from their Teacher's inability, and when He had demonstrated this as well by many other arguments, as also by the Ninevites, and by the queen: then He speaks also of the punishment that should overtake them, darkly indeed, yet He doth speak of it, interweaving an intense fear in His narration.

"For when," saith He, "the unclean spirit is gone out of the man, he walketh through dry places, seeking rest; and finding none, he saith, I will return to my house from whence I came out; and when he is come, he findeth it empty, and swept and garnished. Then goeth he, and taketh with himself seven other spirits more wicked than himself, and they enter in and dwell there, and the last state of that man is worse than the first. Even so shall it be also unto this generation." [3]

By this He signifies, that not only in the world to come, but here too they should suffer most grievously. For since He had said, "The men of Nineveh shall rise up in judgment, and shall condemn this generation;" lest, on account of the postponement of the time, they should despise and grow more careless, by this He brings His terror close upon them. Wherewith the prophet Hosea likewise threatening them said, that they

should be "even as the prophet that is beside himself, the man that is carried away by a spirit;" [4] that is to say, as the madmen, and distracted by evil spirits, even the false prophets. For here, by "a prophet that is beside himself," he means the false prophet, such as are the augurs. Much to the same effect Christ also tells them, that they shall suffer the utmost evils.

Seest thou how from everything He urges them to attend to His sayings; from things present, from things to come; by those who had approved themselves (the Ninevites, I mean, and that queen), and by the offending Tyrians and Sodomites? This did the prophets likewise, bringing forward the sons of the Rechabites, [5] and the bride that forgetteth not her proper ornament and her girdle, [6] and "the ox that knoweth his owner, and the ass that remembereth his crib." [7] Even so here too, when He had by a comparison set forth their perverseness, He speaks afterwards of their punishment also.

What then can the saying mean? As the possessed, saith He, when delivered from that infirmity, should they be at all remiss, draw upon themselves their delusion more grievous than ever: even so is it with you. For before also ye were possessed by a devil, when ye were worshipping idols, and were slaying your sons to the devils, exhibiting great madness; nevertheless I forsook you not, but cast out that devil by the prophets; and again in my own person I am come, willing to cleanse you more entirely. Since then you will not attend, but have wrecked yourselves in greater wickedness (for to kill prophets was a crime not nearly so great and grievous as to slay Him); therefore your sufferings will be more grievous than the former, those at Babylon, I mean, and in Egypt, and under the first Antiochus. Because what things befell them in the time of Vespasian and Titus, were very far more grievous than those. Wherefore also He said, "There shall be great tribulation, such as never was, neither shall be." [8] But not this only doth the illustration declare, but that they should be also utterly destitute of all virtue, and more assailable by the power of the devils, than at that time. For then even although they sinned, yet were there also among them such as acted uprightly, and God's providence was present with them, and the grace of the Spirit, tending, correcting, fulfilling all its part; but now of this guardianship too they shall be utterly deprived; so He tells them; so that there is now both a greater scarcity

---

[1] [R. V., "in the judgment."]　　　　[2] Matt. xii. 42.
[3] Matt. xii. 43-45. ["Evil" is omitted in the text ; in other respects the citation is in accordance with our present Greek text of verses 43-45. Even "and," which is inserted above before "swept," is omitted in some mss of the Homily.—R.]

[4] Hosea ix. 7, LXX.　　　　[5] Jer. xxxv. 2.
[6] Jer. ii. 32, στηθοδεσμίδος.　　[7] Is. i. 3.　　[8] Matt. xxiv. 21.

of virtue, and a more intense affliction, and a more tyrannical operation of the devils.

Ye know accordingly even in our generation, when he who surpassed all in impiety, I mean Julian, was transported with his fury, how they ranged themselves with the heathens, how they courted their party. So that, even if they seem to be in some small degree chastened now, the fear of the emperors makes them quiet; since, if it were not for that, far worse than the former had been their daring. For in all their other evil works they surpass their predecessors; sorceries, magic arts, impurities, they exhibit in great excess. And amongst the rest, moreover, strong as is the curb which holds them down, they have often made seditions, and risen up against kings, which has resulted in their being pierced through with the worst of evils.

Where now are they that seek after signs? Let them hear that a considerate mind is needed, and if this be wanting, signs are of no profit. See, for instance, how the Ninevites without signs believed, while these, after so many miracles, grew worse, and made themselves an habitation of innumerable devils, and brought on themselves ten thousand calamities; and very naturally. For when a man, being once delivered from his ills, fails to be corrected, he will suffer far worse than before. Yea, therefore He said, "he finds no rest," to indicate, that positively and of necessity such an one will be overtaken by the ambush of the devils. Since surely by these two things he ought to have been sobered, by his former sufferings, and by his deliverance; or rather a third thing also is added, the threat of having still worse to endure. But yet by none of these were they made better.

5. All this might be seasonably said, not of them only, but of us also, when after having been enlightened,[1] and delivered from our former ills, we again cleave unto the same wickedness, for more grievous also thenceforth will be the punishment of our subsequent sins. Therefore to the sick of the palsy also Christ said, "Behold, thou art made whole; sin no more, lest a worse thing come unto thee;"[2] and this to a man who was thirty-eight years in his infirmity. And what, one might ask, was he to suffer worse than this? Something far worse, and more intolerable. For far be it from us, that we should endure as much as we are capable of enduring. For God is at no loss for inflictions. For according to the greatness of His mercy, so also is His wrath.

With this He charges Jerusalem also by Ezekiel. "I saw thee," saith He, "polluted in blood; and I washed thee, and anointed thee; and thou hadst renown for thy beauty; and thou pouredst out thy fornications," saith He, "on those who dwell near thee,"[3] wherefore also the more grievous are His threatenings to thee when thou sinnest.

But from hence infer not thy punishment only, but also the boundless longsuffering of God. How often at least have we put our hands to the same evil deeds, and yet He suffers long! But let us not be sanguine, but fear; since Pharaoh too, had he been taught by the first plague, would not have experienced the later ones; he would not afterwards have been drowned, his host and all together.

And this I say, because I know many, who like Pharaoh are even now saying, "I know not God,"[4] and making those that are in their power cleave to the clay and to the bricks. How many, though God bids them assuage their "threatening,"[5] cannot bear so much as to relax the toil!

"But we have no Red Sea now, to pass through afterwards." But we have a sea of fire, a sea not like that, either in kind or in size, but far greater and fiercer, having its waves of fire, of some strange and horrible fire. A great abyss is there, of most intolerable flame. Since everywhere fire may be seen roving quickly round, like some savage wild beast. And if here this sensible and material fire leaped like a wild beast out of the furnace, and sprang upon those who were sitting without,[6] what will not that other fire do to such as have fallen into it?

Concerning that day, hear the prophets, saying, "The day of the Lord is incurable, full of anger and wrath."[7] For there will be none to stand by, none to rescue, nowhere the face of Christ, so mild and calm. But as those who work in the mines are delivered over to certain cruel men, and see none of their friends, but those only that are set over them; so will it be then also: or rather not so, but even far more grievous. For here it is possible to go unto the king, and entreat, and free the condemned person: but there, no longer; for He permits it not, but they continue in the scorching torment,[8] and in so great anguish, as it is not possible for words to tell. For if, when any are in flames here, no speech can describe their sharp pangs, much less theirs, who suffer it in that place: since here indeed all is over in a brief point

---

[1] Heb. vi. 4.   [2] John v. 14.

[3] Ezek. xvi. 6, 9, 14, 26.   [4] Exod. v. 2.
[5] Ephes. vi. 9.   [6] Dan. iii. 22.   [7] Is. xiii. 9.
[8] ἀποτηγανιζόμενοι.

of time, but in that place there is burning indeed, but what is burnt is not consumed.

What then shall we do there? For to my self also do I say these things.

6. "But if thou," saith one, "who art our teacher, speakest so of thyself, I care no more; for what wonder, should I be punished?" Nay, I entreat, let no man seek this consolation; for this is no refreshment at all. For tell me; was not the devil an incorporeal power? Was he not superior to men? Yet he fell away. Is there any one who will derive consolation from being punished along with him? By no means. What of all who were in Egypt? did they not see those also punished who were in high places, and every house in mourning? Were they then hereby refreshed, and comforted? No surely; and it is manifest by what they did afterwards, as men tortured by some kind of fire, rising up together against the king, and compelling him to cast out the people of the Hebrews.

Yea, and very unmeaning is this saying, to suppose that it gives comfort to be punished with all men, to say, "As all, so I too." For why should I speak of hell? Think, I pray you, of those that are seized with gout, how, when they are racked by sharp pain, though you show them ten thousand suffering worse, they do not so much as take it into their mind. For the intensity of their anguish allows not their reason any leisure for thinking of others, and so finding consolation. Let us not then feed ourselves with these cold hopes. For to receive consolation from the ills of our neighbors, takes place in ordinary sufferings; but when the torment is excessive, and all our inward parts full of tempest, and the soul is now come to be unable so much as to know itself, whence shall it derive consolation? So that all these sayings are an absurdity, and fables of foolish children. For this, of which thou speakest, takes place in dejection, and in moderate dejection, when we are told, "the same thing hath befallen such an one;" but sometimes not even in dejection: now if in that case it hath no strength, much less in the anguish and burden unspeakable, which "the gnashing of teeth" indicates.

And I know that I am galling you, and giving you pain by these words; but what can I do? For I would fain not speak thus, but be conscious of virtue both in myself, and in all of you; but since we are in sins, the more part of us, who will grant me ability to pain you indeed, and to penetrate the understanding of them that hear me? Then might I so be at rest. But now I fear lest any despise my sayings, and their punishments become the

greater for their indifferent way of hearing. Since, when a master utters a threat, should one of the fellow-servants hear and make light of his menace, not without punishment would he hasten by him, provoked as he is, but rather it would be a ground for increasing his chastisement. Wherefore I entreat you, let us pierce our own hearts, when we hear His sayings regarding hell. For nothing is more delightful than this discourse, by how much nothing is more bitter than the reality. But how delightful to be told of hell? one may ask. Because it were so far from delight to fall into hell, which result, our words that appear so galling, keep off. And before this they furnish another pleasure: in that they brace up our souls, and make us more reverent, and elevate the mind, and give wings to the thoughts, and cast out the desires that so mischievously beset us; and the thing becomes a cure.

7. Wherefore, to proceed, together with the punishment let me speak also of the shame. For as the Jews shall then be condemned by the Ninevites, so we too by many that seem beneath us now.

Let us imagine then how great the mockery, how great the condemnation; let us imagine, and cast some foundation at length, some door of repentance.

To myself I say these things, to myself first I give this advice, and let no one be angry, as though he were condemned. Let us enter upon the narrow way. How long shall it be luxury? how long sloth? Have we not had enough of indolence, mirth, procrastination? Will it not be the same over again, feasting, and surfeiting, and expense, and wealth, and acquisitions, and buildings? And what is the end? Death. What is the end? Ashes, and dust, and coffins, and worms.

Let us show forth then a new kind of life. Let us make earth, heaven; let us hereby show the Greeks, of how great blessings they are deprived. For when they behold in us good conversation, they will look upon the very face of the kingdom of Heaven. Yea, when they see us gentle, pure from wrath, from evil desire, from envy, from covetousness, rightly fulfilling all our other duties, they will say, "If the Christians are become angels here, what will they be after their departure hence? if where they are strangers they shine so bright, how great will they become when they shall have won their native land!" Thus they too will be reformed, and the word of godliness "will have free course,"[1] not less than in the apostles' times.

---

[1] 2 Thess. iii. 1.

For if they, being twelve, converted entire cities and countries; were we all to become teachers by our careful conduct, imagine how high our cause will be exalted. For not even a dead man raised so powerfully attracts the Greek, as a person practising self-denial. At that indeed he will be amazed, but by this he will be profited. That is done, and is past away; but this abides, and is constant culture to his soul.

Let us take heed therefore to ourselves, that we may gain them also. I say nothing burdensome. I say not, do not marry. I say not, forsake cities, and withdraw thyself from public affairs; but being engaged in them, show virtue. Yea, and such as are busy in the midst of cities, I would fain have more approved than such as have occupied the mountains. Wherefore? Because great is the profit thence arising. "For no man lighteth a candle, and setteth it under the bushel." [1] Therefore I would that all the candles were set upon the candlestick, that the light might wax great.

Let us kindle then His fire; let us cause them that are sitting in darkness to be delivered from their error. And tell me not, "I have a wife, and children belonging to me, and am master of a household, and cannot duly practise all this." For though

thou hadst none of these, yet if thou be careless, all is lost; though thou art encompassed with all these, yet if thou be earnest, thou shalt attain unto virtue. For there is but one thing that is wanted, the preparation of a generous mind; and neither age, nor poverty, nor wealth, nor reverse of fortune, nor anything else, will be able to impede thee. Since in fact both old and young, and men having wives, and bringing up children, and working at crafts, and serving as soldiers, have duly performed all that is enjoined. For so Daniel was young, and Joseph a slave, and Aquila wrought at a craft, and the woman who sold purple was over a workshop, and another was the keeper of a prison, and another a centurion, as Cornelius; and another in ill health, as Timothy; and another a runaway, as Onesimus; but nothing proved an hindrance to any of these, but all were approved, both men and women, both young and old, both slaves and free, both soldiers and people.

Let us not then make vain pretexts, but let us provide a thoroughly good mind, and whatsoever we may be, we shall surely attain to virtue, and arrive at the good things to come; by the grace and love towards man of our Lord Jesus Christ, with whom be unto the Father, together with the Holy Ghost, glory, might, honor, now and ever, and world without end. Amen.

---

[1] Matt. v. 15; Luke xi. 33.

HOMILY XLIV.

Matt. XII. 46—49.

"While He yet talked to the people, behold, His mother and His brethren stood without, desiring to speak with Him. Then one said unto Him, Behold, Thy mother and Thy brethren stand without, desiring to speak with Thee. But He answered and said unto him that told Him, Who is my mother, and [1] my brethren? And He stretched forth His hand towards His disciples, and said, Behold my mother and my brethren."

That which I was lately saying, that when virtue is wanting all things are vain, this is now also pointed out very abundantly. For I indeed was saying, that age and nature, and to dwell in the wilderness, and all such things, are alike unprofitable, where there is not a good mind; but to-day we learn in addition

another thing, that even to have borne Christ in the womb, and to have brought forth that marvellous birth, hath no profit, if there be not virtue.

And this is hence especially manifest. "For while He yet talked to the people," it is said, "one told Him, Thy mother and Thy brethren seek Thee. But He saith, who is my mother, and who are my brethren?"

And this He said, not as being ashamed of

---

[1] [In the text here τίνες εἰσίν is omitted, but is inserted in the comment. There is no MSS. authority for the omission in Matthew. The other variations are slight.—R.]

His mother, nor denying her that bare Him; for if He had been ashamed of her, He would not have passed through that womb; but as declaring that she hath no advantage from this, unless she do all that is required to be done. For in fact that which she had essayed to do, was of superfluous vanity; in that she wanted to show the people that she hath power and authority over her Son, imagining not as yet anything great concerning Him; whence also her unseasonable approach. See at all events both her self-confidence[1] and theirs.[2] Since when they ought to have gone in, and listened with the multitude; or if they were not so minded, to have waited for His bringing His discourse to an end, and then to have come near; they call Him out, and do this before all, evincing a superfluous vanity, and wishing to make it appear, that with much authority they enjoin Him. And this too the evangelist shows that he is blaming, for with this very allusion did he thus express himself, "While He yet talked to the people;" as if he should say, What? was there no other opportunity? Why, was it not possible to speak with Him in private?

And what was it they wished to say? For if it were touching the doctrines of the truth, they ought to have propounded these things publicly, and stated them before all, that the rest also might have the benefit: but if about other matters that concerned themselves, they ought not to have been so urgent. For if He suffered not the burial of a father, lest the attendance on Him should be interrupted, much less ought they to have stopped His discourse to the people, for things that were of no importance. Whence it is clear, that nothing but vainglory led them to do this; which John too declares, by saying, "Neither did His brethren believe on Him;"[3] and

[1] ἀπόνοιαν.

[2] "It seems to me that the person bringing the message was not simply doing so on occasion given, but was laying a snare for our Saviour, to see whether he would prefer flesh and blood to His spiritual task. Our Lord therefore did not think scorn to come out, as disavowing mother and brethren, but He speaks as answering one who was laying a snare for Him. . . . Not, as Marcion and Manichæus say, did He deny His mother, that we should esteem Him born of a phantom, but He preferred the apostles to His kindred." St. Jer. in loc. "Some pestilent heretics maintain from this passage, that our Lord had no mother, and do not perceive that it follows, on comparison of another text" (St. Matt. xxiii. 9), "that neither have His disciples fathers. Because, as He said Himself, "Who is my mother?" so He taught them, saying, "Call no man your father on earth." St. Aug. in Ps. ix. sec. 31. [He speaks] "not as defrauding His mother of her due honor, but indicates for what kind of maternity the Virgin is pronounced to be blessed. For if he who hears the Word of God and keeps it is His brother, and sister, and mother, and Christ's mother had both these, evidently this was the maternity in respect of which His mother was to be blessed. For to hear the Word of God and keep it belongs to a pure soul, looking altogether towards God And since it was no ordinary woman whom God selected to become the mother of Christ, but her who in virtues held a place higher than all women, therefore Christ also willed His mother to be called blessed from this virtue, whereby she was deemed worthy to become a virgin mother." Quæst. et Resp. ad Orthod. ap. St. Just. Mart. p. 485. Ed. Morell. 1736.

[3] John vii. 5.

some sayings too of theirs he reports, full of great folly; telling us that they were for dragging Him to Jerusalem, for no other purpose, but that they themselves might reap glory from His miracles. "For if thou do these things," it is said, "show Thyself to the world. For there is no man that doeth anything in secret, and seeketh himself to be manifest;"[4] when also He Himself rebuked them, attributing it to their carnal mind. That is, because the Jews were reproaching Him, and saying, "Is not this the carpenter's son, whose father and mother we know? and His brethren, are not they with us?"[5] they, willing to throw off the disparagement caused by His birth, were calling Him to the display of His miracles.

For this cause He quite repels them, being minded to heal their infirmity; since surely, had it been His will to deny His mother, He would have denied her then, when the Jews were reproaching Him. But as it is, we see that He takes so great care of her, as even at the very cross to commit her to the disciple whom He loved most of all, and to give him a great charge concerning her.

But now He doth not so, out of care for her, and for His brethren. I mean, because their regard for Him was as towards a mere man, and they were vainglorious, He casts out the disease, not insulting, but correcting them.

But do thou, I pray, examine not the words only, which contain a moderate reproof, but also the unbecoming conduct of His brethren, and the boldness wherewith they had been bold and who was the person reproving it, no mere man, but the only-begotten Son of God; and with what purpose He reproved; that it was not with intent to drive them to perplexity, but to deliver them from the most tyrannical passion and to lead them on by little and little to the right idea concerning Himself, and to convince her that He was not her Son only, but also her Lord: so wilt thou perceive that the reproof is in the highest degree both becoming Him and profitable to her, and withal having in it much gentleness. For He said not, "Go thy way, tell my mother, thou art not my mother," but He addresses Himself to the person that told Him; saying, "Who is my mother?" together with the things that have been mentioned providing for another object also. What then is that? That neither they nor others confiding in their kindred, should neglect virtue. For if she is nothing profited

[4] John vii. 4. φανερὸς εἶναι. rec. text, ἐν παρρησίᾳ εἶναι. [The latter reading is that of all our authorities.—R.]

[5] Matt. xiii. 55, 56. [Comp. Mark vi. 3. But the citation is freely made.—R.]

by being His mother, were it not for that quality in her, hardly will any one else be saved by his kindred. For there is one only nobleness, to do the will of God. This kind of noble birth is better than the other, and more real.

2. Knowing therefore these things, let us neither pride ourselves on children that are of good report, unless we have their virtue; nor upon noble fathers, unless we be like them in disposition. For it is possible, both that he who begat a man should not be his father, and that he who did not beget him should be. Therefore in another place also, when some woman had said, "Blessed is the womb that bare Thee, and the paps which Thou hast sucked;" He said not, "The womb bare me not, neither did I suck the paps," but this, "Yea rather, blessed are they that do the will of my Father."[1] Seest thou how on every occasion He denies not the affinity by nature, but adds that by virtue? And His forerunner too, in saying, "O generation of vipers, think not to say, We have Abraham to our father,"[2] means not this, that they were not naturally of Abraham, but that it profits them nothing to be of Abraham, unless they had the affinity by character; which Christ also declared, when He said, "If ye were Abraham's children, ye would do the works of Abraham;"[3] not depriving them of their kindred according to the flesh, but teaching them to seek after that affinity which is greater than it, and more real.

This then He establishes here also, but in a manner less invidious, and more measured, as became Him speaking to His mother. For He said not at all, "She is not my mother, nor are those my brethren, because they do not my will;" neither did He declare and pronounce judgment against them; but He yet left in it their own power to choose, speaking with the gentleness that becomes Him.

"For he that doeth," saith He, "the will of my Father, this is my brother, and sister, and mother."[4]

Wherefore if they desire to be such, let them come this way. And when the woman again cried out, saying, "Blessed is the womb that bare Thee," He said not, "She is not my mother," but, "If she wishes to be blessed, let her do the will of my Father. For such a one is both brother, and sister, and mother."

Oh honor! oh virtue! Unto what a height doth she lead up him that follows after her! How many women have blessed that holy Virgin, and her womb, and prayed that they might become such mothers, and give up all! What then is there to hinder? For behold, He hath marked out a spacious road for us; and it is granted not to women only, but to men also, to be of this rank, or rather of one yet far higher. For this makes one His mother much more, than those pangs did. So that if that were a subject for blessing, much more this, inasmuch as it is also more real. Do not therefore merely desire, but also in the way that leads thee to thy desire walk thou with much diligence.

3. Having then said these words, "He came out of the house." Seest thou, how He both rebuked them, and did what they desired? Which He did also at the marriage.[5] For there too He at once reproved her asking unseasonably, and nevertheless did not gainsay her; by the former correcting her weakness, by the latter showing His kindly feeling toward His mother. So likewise on this occasion too, He both healed the disease of vainglory, and rendered the due honor to His mother, even though her request was unseasonable. For, "in the same day," it is said, "went Jesus out of the house, and sat by the sea."[6]

Why, if ye desire, saith He, to see and hear, behold I come forth and discourse. Thus having wrought many miracles, He affords again the benefit of His doctrine. And He "sits by the sea," fishing and getting into His net them that are on the land.

But He "sat by the sea," not without a purpose; and this very thing the evangelist has darkly expressed. For to indicate that the cause of His doing this was a desire to order His auditory with exactness, and to leave no one behind His back, but to have all face to face,

"And great multitudes," saith He, "were gathered together unto Him, so that He went into a ship and sat, and the whole multitude stood on the shore."[7]

And having sat down there, He speaks by parables.

"And He spake," it says, "many things unto them in parables."[8]

And yet on the mount, we know, He did no such thing, neither did He weave His discourse with so many parables, for then there were multitudes only, and a simple people; but here are also Scribes and Pharisees.

---

[1] Luke xi. 27, 28. [According to many Harmonists this occurred about the same time, probably as His mother was seen approaching.—R.]

[2] Matt. iii. 7, 9.   [3] John viii. 39.

[4] Matt. xiii. 50. [Slightly altered.]

[5] John ii. 1-11.

[6] Chap. xiii. 1. [R. V., "On that day," etc.]

[7] Matt. xiii. 2. [R. V., "all the multitude stood on the beach."]   [8] Matt. xiii. 3.

But do thou mark, I pray thee, what kind of parable He speaks first, and how Matthew puts them in their order. Which then doth He speak first? That which it was most necessary to speak first, that which makes the hearer more attentive. For because He was to discourse unto them in dark sayings, He thoroughly rouses His hearers' mind first by His parable. Therefore also another evangelist saith that He reproved them, because they do not understand; saying, "How knew ye not the parable?"[1] But not for this cause only doth He speak in parables, but that He may also make His discourse more vivid, and fix the memory of it in them more perfectly, and bring the things before their sight. In like manner do the prophets also.

4. What then is the parable? "Behold," saith He, "a sower[2] went forth to sow." Whence went He forth, who is present everywhere, who fills all things? or how went He forth? Not in place, but in condition and dispensation to usward, coming nearer to us by His clothing Himself with flesh. For because we could not enter, our sins fencing us out from the entrance, He comes forth unto us. And wherefore came He forth? to destroy the ground teeming with thorns? to take vengeance upon the husbandmen? By no means; but to till and tend it, and to sow the word of godliness. For by seed here He means His doctrine, and by land, the souls of men, and by the sower, Himself.

What then comes of this seed? Three parts perish, and one is saved.

"And when He sowed, some seeds fell," He saith, "by the way side; and the fowls came and devoured them up."[3]

He said not, that He cast them, but that "they fell."

"And some upon the rock, where they had not much earth; and forthwith they sprang up, because they had no deepness of earth; and when the sun was up, they were scorched; and because they had no root, they withered away. And some fell among the thorns, and the thorns sprang up, and choked them. But others fell on the good ground, and brought forth fruit, some an hundredfold, some sixtyfold, some thirtyfold. Who hath ears to hear let him hear."[4]

A fourth part is saved; and not this all alike, but even here great is the difference.

Now these things He said, manifesting that He discoursed to all without grudging. For as the sower makes no distinction in the land submitted to him, but simply and indifferently casts his seed; so He Himself too makes no distinction of rich and poor, of wise and unwise, of slothful or diligent, of brave or cowardly; but He discourses unto all, fulfilling His part, although foreknowing the results; that it may be in His power to say, "What ought I to have done, that I have not done?"[5] And the prophets speak of the people as of a vine; "For my beloved," it is said, "had a vineyard;"[6] and, "He brought a vine out of Egypt;"[7] but He, as of seed. What could this be to show? That obedience now will be quick and easier, and will presently yield its fruit.

But when thou hearest, "The sower went forth to sow," think it not a needless repetition. For the sower frequently goes forth for some other act also, either to plough, or to cut out the evil herbs, or to pluck up thorns, or to attend to some such matter; but He went forth to sow.

Whence then, tell me, was the greater part of the seed lost? Not through the sower, but through the ground that received it; that is, the soul that did not hearken.

And wherefore doth He not say, Some the careless received, and lost it; some the rich, and choked it, and some the superficial, and betrayed it? It is not His will to rebuke them severely, lest He should cast them into despair, but He leaves the reproof to the conscience of His hearers.

And this was not the case with the seed only, but also with the net; for that too produced many that were unprofitable.

5. But this parable He speaks, as anointing His disciples, and to teach them, that even though the lost be more than such as receive the word yet they are not to despond. For this was the case even with their Lord, and He who fully foreknew that these things should be, did not desist from sowing.

And how can it be reasonable, saith one, to sow among the thorns, on the rock, on the wayside? With regard to the seeds and the earth it cannot be reasonable; but in the case of men's souls and their instructions, it hath its praise, and that abundantly. For the husbandman indeed would reasonably be blamed for doing this; it being impossible for the rock to become earth, or the wayside not to be a wayside, or the thorns, thorns; but in the things that have reason it is not so. There is such a thing as the rock changing, and becoming rich land; and the wayside being no longer trampled on, nor lying

[1] Mark iv. 13. [Freely cited.]
[2] [R. V., "the sower."]
[3] Matt. xiii. 4. [R. V., "And as he sowed," etc.]
[4] Matt. xiii. 5–9. [The Greek text here differs slightly from that of the New Testament passage, as well as from the accounts of Mark and Luke.—R.]

[5] Is. v. 4.   [6] Is. v. 1.   [7] Ps. lxxx. 8.

open to all that pass by, but that it may be a fertile field; and the thorns may be destroyed, and the seed enjoy full security. For had it been impossible, this Sower would not have sown. And if the change did not take place in all, this is no fault of the Sower, but of them who are unwilling to be changed: He having done His part: and if they betrayed what they received of Him, He is blameless, the exhibitor of such love to man.

But do thou mark this, I pray thee; that the way of destruction is not one only, but there are differing ones, and wide apart from one another. For they that are like the way-side are the coarse-minded,[1] and indifferent, and careless; but those on the rock such as fail from weakness only.

For "that which is sown upon the stony places," saith He, "the same is he that heareth the word, and anon with joy receiveth it. Yet hath he not root in himself, but dureth for a while; but when tribulation or persecution ariseth because of the word, by and by he is offended! When any one," so He saith, "heareth the word of truth and understandeth it not, then cometh the wicked one, and catcheth that which was sown out of his heart. This is he that is sown by the way-side."[2]

Now it is not the same thing for the doctrine to wither away, when no man is evil entreating, or disturbing its foundations, as when temptations press upon one. But they that are likened to the thorns, are much more inexcusable than these.

6. In order then that none of these things may befall us, let us by zeal and continual remembrance cover up the things that are told us. For though the devil do catch them away, yet it rests with us, whether they be caught away; though the plants wither, yet it is not from the heat this takes place (for He did not say, because of the heat it withered, but, "because it had no root"); although His sayings are choked, it is not because of the thorns, but of them who suffer them to spring up. For there is a way, if thou wilt, to check this evil growth, and to make the right use of our wealth. Therefore He said not, "the world," but "the care of the world;" nor "riches," but "the deceitfulness of riches."

Let us not then blame the things, but the corrupt mind. For it is possible to be rich and not to be deceived; and to be in this world, and not to be choked with its cares. For indeed riches have two contrary disad-

vantages; one, care, wearing us out, and bringing a darkness over us; the other, luxury, making us effeminate.

And well hath He said, "The deceitfulness of riches." For all that pertains to riches is deceit; they are names only, not attached to things. For so pleasure and glory, and splendid array, and all these things, are a sort of vain show, not a reality.

Having therefore spoken of the ways of destruction, afterwards He mentions the good ground, not suffering them to despair, but giving a hope of repentance, and indicating that it is possible to change from the things before mentioned into this.

And yet if both the land be good, and the Sower one, and the seed the same, wherefore did one bear a hundred, one sixty, one thirty? Here again the difference is from the nature of the ground, for even where the ground is good, great even therein is the difference. Seest thou, that not the husbandman is to be blamed, nor the seed, but the land that receives it? not for its nature, but for its disposition. And herein too, great is His mercy to man, that He doth not require one measure of virtue, but while He receives the first, and casts not out the second, He gives also a place to the third.

And these things He saith, lest they that followed Him should suppose that hearing is sufficient for salvation. And wherefore, one may say, did He not put the other vices also, such as lust, vainglory? In speaking of "the care of this world, and the deceitfulness of riches," He set down all. Yea, both vainglory and all the rest belong to this world, and to the deceitfulness of riches; such as pleasure, and gluttony, and envy, and vainglory, and all the like.

But He added also the "way" and the "rock," signifying that it is not enough to be freed from riches only, but we must cultivate also the other parts of virtue. For what if thou art free indeed from riches, yet are soft and unmanly? and what if thou art not indeed unmanly, but art remiss and careless about the hearing of the word? Nay, no one part is sufficient for our salvation, but there is required first a careful hearing, and a continual recollection; then fortitude, then contempt of riches, and deliverance from all worldly things.

In fact, His reason for putting this before the other, is because the one is first required (for "How shall they believe except they hear?"[3] just as we too, except we mind what is said, shall not be able so much as to

---

[1] βάναυσοι.
[2] Matt. xiii. 20, 21, 19. [There are some variations in the Greek text, not found in any New Testament mss. In verse 19 ἀληθείας is substituted for βασιλείας.—R.]

[3] Rom. x. 14.

learn what we ought to do): after that, fortitude, and the contempt of things present.

7. Hearing therefore these things, let us fortify ourselves on all sides, regarding His instructions, and striking our roots deep, and cleansing ourselves from all worldly things. But if we do the one, neglecting the other, we shall be nothing bettered; for though we perish not in one way, yet shall we in some other. For what signifies our not being ruined by riches, if we are by indolence: or not by indolence, if we are by softness. For so the husbandman, whether this way or that way he lose his crop, equally bewails himself. Let us not then soothe ourselves upon our not perishing in all these ways, but let it be our grief, in whichever way we are perishing.

And let us burn up the thorns, for they choke the word. And this is known to those rich men, who not for these matters alone, but for others also prove unprofitable. For having become slaves and captives of their pleasures, they are useless even for civil affairs, and if for them, much more for those of Heaven. Yea, and in two ways hereby our thoughts are corrupted; both by the luxury, and by the anxiety too. For either of these by itself were enough to overwhelm the bark; but when even both concur, imagine how high the billow swells.

And marvel not at His calling our luxury, "thorns." For thou indeed art not aware of it, being intoxicated with thy passion, but they that are in sound health know that it pricks sharper than any thorn, and that luxury wastes the soul worse than care, and causes more grievous pains both to body and soul. For one is not so sorely smitten by anxiety, as by surfeiting. Since when watchings, and throbbings of the temples, and heaviness in the head, and pangs of the bowels, lay hold of such a man, you may imagine how many thorns these surpass in grievousness. And as the thorns, on whichever side they are laid hold of, draw blood from the hands that seize them, just so doth luxury plague both feet, and hands, and head, and eyes, and in general all our members; and it is withered also, and unfruitful, like the thorn, and hurts much more than it, and in our vital parts. Yea, it brings on premature old age, and dulls the senses, and darkens our reasoning, and blinds the keen-sighted mind, and makes the body tumid,[1] rendering excessive the deposition of that which is cast away, and gathering together a great accumulation of evils; and it makes the burden too great, and the load overwhelming; whence

our falls are many and continual, and our shipwrecks frequent.

For tell me, why pamper thy body? What? are we to slay thee in sacrifice, to set thee on the table? The birds it is well for thee to pamper: or rather, not so well even for them; for when they are fattened, they are unprofitable for wholesome food. So great an evil is luxury, that its mischief is shown even in irrational beings. For even them by luxury we make unprofitable, both to themselves and to us. For their superfluous flesh is indigestible, and the moister kind of corruption is engendered by that kind of fatness. Whereas the creatures that are not so fed, but live, as one may say, in abstinence, and moderate diet, and in labor and hardship, these are most serviceable both to themselves and to others, as well for food, as for everything else. Those, at any rate, who live on them, are in better health; but such as are fed on the others are like them, growing dull and sickly, and rendering their chain more grievous. For nothing is so hostile and hurtful to the body, as luxury; nothing so tears it in pieces, and overloads and corrupts it, as intemperance.

Wherefore above all may this circumstance make one amazed at them for their folly, that not even so much care as others show towards their wine skins, are these willing to evince towards themselves. For those the wine merchants do not allow to receive more than is fit, lest they should burst; but to their own wretched belly these men do not vouchsafe even so much forethought, but when they have stuffed it and distended it, they fill all, up to the ears, up to the nostrils, to the very throat itself, thereby pressing into half its room the spirit, and the power that directs the living being. What? was thy throat given thee for this end, that thou shouldest fill it up to the very mouth, with wine turned sour, and all other corruption? Not for this, O man, but that thou shouldest above all things sing to God, and offer up the holy prayers, and read out the divine laws, and give to thy neighbors profitable counsel. But thou, as if thou hadst received it for this end, dost not suffer it to have leisure for that ministry, so much as for a short season, but for all thy life subjectest it to this evil slavery. And as if any man having had a lyre given him with golden strings, and beautifully constructed, instead of awakening with it the most harmonious music, were to cover it over with much dung and clay; even so do these men. Now the word, dung, I use not of living, but of luxurious living, and of that great wantonness. Because what is more than necessary is not

---

[1] πλαδαρόν.

nourishment, but merely injurious. For in truth the belly alone was made merely for the reception of food; but the mouth, and the throat, and tongue, for other things also, far more necessary than these: or rather, not even the belly for the reception of food simply, but for the reception of moderate food. And this it makes manifest by crying out loudly against us, when we tease it by this greediness; nor doth it clamor against us only, but also avenging that wrong exacts of us the severest penalty. And first it punishes the feet, that bear and conduct us to those wicked revels, then the hands that minister to it, binding them together for having brought unto it such quantities and kinds of provisions; and many have distorted even their very mouth, and eyes, and head. And as a servant receiving an order beyond his

power, not seldom out of desperation becomes insolent to the giver of the order: so the belly too, together with these members, often ruins and destroys, from being overstrained, the very brain itself. And this God hath well ordered, that from excess so much mischief should arise; that when of thine own will thou dost not practise self-restraint, at least against thy will, for fear of so great ruin, thou mayest learn to be moderate.

Knowing then these things, let us flee luxury, let us study moderation, that we may both enjoy health of body, and having delivered our soul from all infirmity, may attain unto the good things to come, by the grace and love towards man of our Lord Jesus Christ, to whom be glory and might forever and ever. Amen.

HOMILY XLV.

MATT. XIII. 10, 11.

"And the disciples came and said unto Him, Why speakest Thou unto them in parables? He answered and said unto them, Because it is given unto you[1] to know the mysteries of the Kingdom of Heaven, but to them it is not given."

WE have good cause to admire the disciples, how, longing as they do to learn, they know when they ought to ask. For they do it not before all: and this Matthew shows by saying, "And they came." And, as to this assertion not being conjecture, Mark hath expressed it more distinctly, by saying, that "they came to Him privately."[2] This then His brethren and His mother should also have done, and not have called Him out, and made a display.

But mark their kindly affection also, how they have much regard for the others, and seek their good first, and then their own. "For why," it is said, "speakest Thou unto them in parables?" They did not say, why speakest thou unto us in parables? Yea, and on other occasions also their kindliness towards men appears in many ways; as when they say, "Send the multitude away;"[3] and, "Knowest thou that they were offended?"[4]

What then saith Christ? "Because it is

given unto you," so He speaks, "to know the mysteries of the Kingdom of Heaven, but to them it is not given."[5] But this He said, not bringing in necessity, or any allotment[6] made causelessly and at random, but implying them to be the authors of all their own evils, and wishing to represent that the thing is a gift, and a grace bestowed from above.

It by no means follows, however, because it is a gift, that therefore free will is taken away; and this is evident from what comes after. To this purpose, in order that neither the one sort may despair, nor the other grow careless, upon being told that "it is given," He signifies the beginning to be with ourselves.

"For whosoever hath, to him shall be given, and he shall have more abundance; but whosoever hath not, from him shall be taken away, even that which he seemeth to have."[7]

1 [R. V., "Unto you it is given," omitting "Because."]
2 Mark iv. 10.   3 Luke ix. 12.   4 Matt. xv. 12.

5 Matt. xiii. 11. [R. V., "Unto you it is given," etc.]
6 ἀποκλήρωσις.
7 Matt. xiii. 12. See Luke viii. 18. [δοκεῖ is inserted from the latter passage, and repeated in the comments.– R.]

And although the saying be full of much obscurity, yet it indicates unspeakable justice. For what He saith is like this: When any one hath forwardness and zeal, there shall be given unto him all things on God's part also: but if he be void of these, and contribute not his own share, neither are God's gifts bestowed. For even "what he seemeth to have," so He saith, "shall be taken away from him;" God not so much taking it away, as counting him unworthy of His gifts. This we also do; when we see any one listening carelessly, and when with much entreaty we cannot persuade him to attend, it remains for us to be silent. For if we are still to go on, his carelessness is aggravated. But him that is striving to learn, we lead on, and pour in much.

And well said He, "Even that which he seemeth to have." For he hath not really even this.

Then He also made what He had said more distinct, pointing out the meaning of, "To him that hath, shall be given, but from him that hath not, even that which he seemeth to have, shall be taken away."

"Therefore," saith He, "speak I to them in parables; because they seeing see not." [1]

"It were meet then," one may say, "to have opened their eyes, if they see not." Nay, if the blindness were natural, it were meet to open them; but because it was a voluntary and self-chosen blindness, therefore He said not simply, "They see not," but, "seeing, they see not;" so that the blindness is of their own wickedness. For they saw even devils cast out, and said, "By Beelzebub, prince of the devils, He casteth out the devils." [2] They heard Him guiding them unto God, and evincing His great unanimity with Him, and they say, "This man is not of God." [3] Since then the judgment they pronounced was contrary both to their sight and hearing, therefore, saith He, the very hearing do I take away from them. For they derive thence no advantage, but rather greater condemnation. For they not only disbelieved, but found fault also, and accused, and laid snares. However, He saith not this, for it is not His will to give disgust in accusing them. Therefore neither at the beginning did He so discourse to them, but with much plainness; but because they perverted themselves, thenceforth He speaks in parables.

2. After this, lest any one should suppose His words to be a mere accusation, and lest men should say, Being our enemy He is bringing these charges and calumnies against us; He introduces the prophet also, pronouncing the same judgment as Himself.

"For in them is fulfilled," saith He, "the prophecy of Esaias, which saith, By hearing ye shall hear, and shall not understand, and seeing ye shall see, and shall not perceive." [4]

Seest thou the prophet likewise, accusing them with this same accuracy? for neither did He say, Ye see not, but "Ye shall see and not perceive;" nor again, Ye shall not hear, but "Ye shall hear and not understand." So that they first inflicted the loss on themselves, by stopping their ears, by closing their eyes, by making their heart fat. For they not only failed to hear, but also "heard heavily," and they did this, He saith,

"Lest at any time they should be converted, and I should heal them;" [5] describing their aggravated wickedness, and their determined defection from Him. And this He saith to draw them unto Him, and to provoke them, and to signify that if they would convert [6] He would heal them: much as if one should say, "He would not look at me, and I thank him; for if he had vouchsafed me this, I should straightway have given in:" and this he saith, to signify how he would have been reconciled. Even so then here too it is said, "Lest at any time they should convert, [7] and I should heal them;" implying that both their conversion was possible, and that upon their repentance they might be saved, and that not for His own glory, but for their salvation, He was doing all things.

For if it had not been His will that they should hear and be saved, He ought to have been silent, not to have spoken in parables; but now by this very thing He stirs them up, even by speaking under a veil. "For God willeth not the death of the sinner, but that he should turn unto Him and live." [8]

For in proof that our sin belongs not to nature, nor to necessity and compulsion, hear what He saith to the apostles, "But blessed are your eyes, for they see, and your ears, for they hear;" [9] not meaning this kind of sight nor hearing, but that of the mind. For indeed these too were Jews, and brought up in the same circumstances; but nevertheless they took no hurt from the prophecy, because they had the root of His blessings well settled in them, their principle of choice, I mean, and their judgment.

Seest thou that, "unto you it is given," was not of necessity? For neither would

---

[1] Matt. xiii. 13.   [2] Matt. xii. 24.   [3] John ix. 16.

[4] Matt. xiii. 14. See Is. vi. 9, 10.
[5] Matt xiii. 15. [The passage is abridged. R. V., "should turn again" (so in Isaiah). Chrysostom takes it in this sense, as the context shows.—R.]
[6] ["turn again."]   [7] [τὸ ἐπιστραφῆναι.]
[8] Ezek. xviii. 23. [Freely cited in the first part.—R.]
[9] Matt. xiii. 16.

they have been blessed, unless the well-doing had been their own. For tell me not this, that it was spoken obscurely; for they might have come and asked Him, as the disciples did: but they would not, being careless and supine. Why say I, they would not? nay, they were doing the very opposite, not only disbelieving, not only not hearkening, but even waging war, and disposed to be very bitter against all He said: which He brings in the prophet laying to their charge, in the words, "They heard heavily."

But not such were these; wherefore He also blessed them. And in another way too He assures them again, saying,

"For verily I say unto you, many prophets and righteous men have desired to see those things which ye see, and have not seen them, and to hear those things which ye hear, and have not heard them;"[1] my coming, He means; my very miracles, my voice, my teaching. For here He prefers them not to these depraved only, but even to such as have done virtuously; yea, and He affirms them to be more blessed even than they. Why can this be? Because not only do these see what the Jews saw not, but even what those of old desired to see. For they indeed beheld by faith only: but these by sight too, and much more distinctly.

Seest thou how again He connects the old dispensation with the new, signifying that those of old not only knew the things to come, but also greatly desired them? But had they pertained to some strange and opposing God, they would never have desired them.

"Hear ye therefore the parable of the sower,"[2] saith He; and He speaks what we before mentioned, of carelessness and attention, of cowardice and fortitude, of wealth and voluntary poverty; pointing out the hurt from the one, and the benefit from the other.

Then of virtue also He brings forward different forms. For being full of love to man, He marked out not one only way, nor did He say, "unless one bring forth an hundred, he is an outcast;" but he that brings forth sixty is saved also, and not he only, but also the producer of thirty. And this He said, making out salvation to be easy.

3. And thou then, art thou unable to practise virginity? Be chaste in marriage. Art thou unable to strip thyself of thy possessions? Give of thy substance. Canst thou not bear that burden? Share thy goods with Christ. Art thou unwilling to yield Him up all? Give Him but the half, but the third part. He is thy brother, and joint-heir, make Him joint-heir with thee here too. Whatsoever thou givest Him, thou wilt give to thyself. Hearest thou not what saith the prophet? "Them that pertain to thy seed thou shalt not overlook."[3] But if we must not overlook our kinsmen, much less our Lord, having towards thee, together with His authority as Lord, the claim also of kindred, and many more besides. Yea, for He too hath made thee a sharer in His goods, having received nothing of thee, but having begun with this unspeakable benefit. What then can it be but extreme senselessness, not even by this gift to be made kind towards men, not even to give a return for a free gift, and less things for greater? Thus whereas He hath made thee heir of Heaven, impartest thou not to Him even of the things on earth? He, when thou hadst done no good work, but wert even an enemy, reconciled thee: and dost thou not requite Him, being even a friend and benefactor?

Yet surely, even antecedently to the kingdom, and to all the rest, even for the very fact of His giving, we ought to feel bound to Him. For so servants too, when bidding their masters to a meal, account themselves not to be giving but receiving; but here the contrary hath taken place: not the servant the Lord, but the Lord hath first bidden the servant unto His own table; and dost thou not bid Him, no not even after this? He first hath introduced thee under His own roof; dost thou not take Him in, so much as in the second place? He clad thee, being naked; and dost thou not even after this receive Him being a stranger? He first gave thee to drink out of His own cup, and dost thou not impart to Him so much as cold water? He hath made thee drink of the Holy Spirit, and dost thou not even soothe His bodily thirst? He hath made thee drink of the Spirit, when thou wast deserving of punishment; and dost thou neglect Him even when thirsty, and this when it is out of His own, that thou art to do all these things? Dost thou not then esteem it a great thing, to hold the cup out of which Christ is to drink, and to put it to His lips? Seest thou not that for the priest alone is it lawful[4] to give the cup of His blood? But I am by no means strict about this, saith He; but though thyself should give, I receive; though thou be a layman, I refuse it not. And I do not require such as I have given: for not blood do I seek, but cold water. Consider to whom thou art giving drink, and tremble. Consider, thou art become a priest of Christ, giv-

---

[1] Matt. xiii. 17.   [2] Matt. xiii. 18.   [3] Isa. lviii. 7, LXX.   [4] θέμις.

ing with thine own hand, not flesh but bread, not blood, but a cup of cold water. He clothed thee with a garment of salvation, and clothed thee by Himself; do thou at least by thy servant clothe Him. He made thee glorious in Heaven, do thou deliver Him from shivering, and nakedness, and shame. He made thee a fellow-citizen of angels, do thou impart to Him at least of the covering of thy roof, give house-room to Him at least as to thine own servant. "I refuse not this lodging and that, having opened to thee the whole Heaven. I have delivered thee from a most grievous prison; this I do not require again, nor do I say, deliver me; but if thou wouldest look upon me only, when I am bound, this suffices me for refreshment. When thou wert dead, I raised thee; I require not this again of thee, but I say, visit me only when sick."

Now when His gifts are so great, and His demands exceeding easy, and we do not supply even these; what deep of hell must we not deserve? Justly shall we depart into the fire that is prepared for the devil and his angels, being more insensible than any rock. For how great insensibility is it, tell me, for us, who have received, and are to receive so much, to be slaves of money, from which we shall a little while hence be separated even against our will? And others indeed have given up even their life, and shed their blood; and dost thou not even give up thy superflui-

ties for Heaven's sake, for the sake of so great crowns?

And of what favor canst thou be worthy? of what justification? who in thy sowing of the earth, gladly pourest forth all, and in lending to men at usury sparest nothing; but in feeding thy Lord through His poor art cruel and inhuman?

Having then considered all these things, and calculated what we have received, what we are to receive, what is required of us, let us show forth all our diligence on the things spiritual. Let us become at length mild and humane, that we may not draw down on ourselves the intolerable punishment. For what is there that hath not power to condemn us? Our having enjoyed so many and such great benefits; our having no great thing required of us; our having such things required, as we shall leave here even against our will; our exhibiting so much liberality in our worldly matters. Why each one of these, even by itself, were enough to condemn us; but when they all meet together, what hope will there be of salvation?

In order then that we may escape all this condemnation, let us show forth some bounty towards those who are in need. For thus shall we enjoy all the good things, both here, and there; unto which may we all attain, by the grace and love towards man of our Lord Jesus Christ, to whom be glory and might forever and ever. Amen.

HOMILY XLVI.

MATT. XIII. 24—30.

"Another parable put He forth unto them, saying, The Kingdom of Heaven is likened unto a man which sowed good seed in his field. But while men slept, his enemy came and sowed tares among the wheat, and went his way. But when the blade was sprung up, and brought forth fruit, then appeared the tares. So the servants of the householder came and said unto him, Sir, didst thou not sow good seed in thy field? whence then hath it tares? He said unto them, An enemy hath done this. The servants said unto him, Wilt thou then that we go and gather them up? But he said, Nay, lest while ye gather up the tares, ye root up also the wheat with them. Let both therefore grow together until the harvest." [1]

WHAT is the difference between this, and the parable before it? There He speaks of

them that have not at all holden with Him, but have started aside, and have thrown away the seed; but here He means the societies of the heretics. For in order that not even this might disturb His disciples, He foretells it

---

[1] [The citation agrees exactly with the Received text; οὖν is however inserted in verse 30, against nearly all our New Testament authorities. In several minor variations the text differs from that of Tischendorf and other recent editors.—R.]

also, after having taught them why He speaks in parables. The former parable then means their not receiving Him; this, their receiving corrupters. For indeed this also is a part of the devil's craft, by the side of the truth always to bring in error, painting thereon many resemblances, so as easily to cheat the deceivable. Therefore He calls it not any other seed, but tares; which in appearance are somewhat like wheat.

Then He mentions also the manner of his device. For "while men slept," saith He. It is no small danger, which He hereby suspends over our rulers, to whom especially is entrusted the keeping of the field; and not the rulers only, but the subjects too.

And He signifies also that the error comes after the truth, which the actual event testifies. For so after the prophets, were the false prophets; and after the apostles, the false apostles; and after Christ, Antichrist. For unless the devil see what to imitate, or against whom to plot, he neither attempts, nor knows how. Now then also, having seen that "one brought forth a hundred, another sixty, another thirty," he proceeds after that another way. That is, not having been able to carry away what had taken root, nor to choke, nor to scorch it up, he conspires against it by another craft, privily casting in his own inventions.

And what difference is there, one may say, between them that sleep, and them that resemble the wayside? That in the latter case he immediately caught it away; yea, he suffered it not even to take root; but here more of his craft was needed.

And these things Christ saith, instructing us to be always wakeful. For, saith He, though thou quite escape those harms, there is yet another harm. For as in those instances "the wayside," and "the rock," and "the thorns," so here again sleep occasions our ruin; so that there is need of continual watchfulness. Wherefore He also said, "He that endureth to the end, the same shall be saved." [1]

Something like this took place even at the beginning. Many of the prelates, I mean, bringing into the churches wicked men, disguised heresiarchs, gave great facility to the laying that kind of snare. For the devil needs not even to take any trouble, when he hath once planted them among us.

And how is it possible not to sleep? one may say. Indeed, as to natural sleep, it is not possible; but as to that of our moral faculty, it is possible. Wherefore Paul also said, "Watch ye, stand fast in the faith." [2]

After this He points out the thing to be superfluous too, not hurtful only; in that, after the land hath been tilled, and there is no need of anything, then this enemy sows again; as the heretics also do, who for no other cause than vainglory inject their proper venom.

And not by this only, but by what follows likewise, He depicts exactly all their acting. For, "When the blade was sprung up, saith He, "and brought forth fruit, then appeared the tares also;" which kind of thing these men also do. For at the beginning they disguise themselves; but when they have gained much confidence, and some one imparts to them the teaching of the word, then they pour out their poison.

But wherefore doth He bring in the servants, telling what hath been done? That He may pronounce it wrong to slay them.

And He calls him "an enemy," because of his harm done to men. For although the despite is against us, in its origin it sprang from his enmity, not to us, but to God. Whence it is manifest, that God loves us more than we love ourselves.

And see from another thing also, the malicious craft of the devil. For he did not sow before this, because he had nothing to destroy, but when all had been fulfilled, that he might defeat the diligence of the Husbandman; in such enmity against Him did he constantly act.

And mark also the affection of the servants. I mean, what haste they are in at once to root up the tares, even though they do it indiscreetly; which shows their anxiety for the crop, and that they are looking to one thing only, not to the punishment of that enemy, but to the preservation of the seed sown. For of course this other is not the urgent consideration.

Wherefore how they may for the present extirpate the mischief, this is their object. And not even this do they seek absolutely, for they trust not themselves with it, but await the Master's decision, saying, "Wilt Thou?"

What then doth the Master? He forbids them, saying, "Lest haply ye root up the wheat with them." And this He said, to hinder wars from arising, and blood and slaughter. For it is not right to put a heretic to death, since an implacable war would be brought into the world. By these two reasons then He restrains them; one, that the wheat be not hurt; another, that punishment will surely overtake them, if incurably diseased. Wherefore, if thou wouldest have them punished, yet without harm to the wheat, I bid thee wait for the proper season.

---

[1] Matt. x. 22.   [2] 1 Cor. xvi. 13.

But what means, "Lest ye root up the wheat with them?" Either He means this, If ye are to take up arms, and to kill the heretics, many of the saints also must needs be overthrown with them; or that of the very tares it is likely that many may change and become wheat. If therefore ye root them up beforehand, ye injure that which is to become wheat, slaying some, in whom there is yet room for change and improvement. He doth not therefore forbid our checking heretics, and stopping their mouths, and taking away their freedom of speech, and breaking up their assemblies and confederacies, but our killing and slaying them.

But mark thou His gentleness, how He not only gives sentence and forbids, but sets down reasons.

What then, if the tares should remain until the end? "Then I will say to the reapers, Gather ye together first the tares, and bind them in bundles to burn them."[1] He again reminds them of John's words,[2] introducing Him as judge; and He saith, So long as they stand by the wheat, we must spare them, for it is possible for them even to become wheat; but when they have departed, having profited nothing, then of necessity the inexorable punishment will overtake them. "For I will say to the reapers," saith He, "Gather ye together first the tares." Why, "first?" That these may not be alarmed, as though the wheat were carried off with them. "And bind them in bundles to burn them, but gather the wheat into my barn."[3]

2. "Another parable put He forth unto them, saying, The Kingdom of Heaven is like to a grain of mustard seed."[4]

That is, since He had said, that of the crop three parts are lost, and but one saved, and in the very part again which is saved so great damage ensues; lest they should say, "And who, and how many will be the faithful?" this fear again He removes, by the parable of the mustard seed leading them on to belief, and signifying that in any case the gospel[5] shall be spread abroad.

Therefore He brought forward the similitude of this herb, which has a very strong resemblance to the subject in hand; "Which indeed is the least," He saith, "of all seeds, but when it is grown, it is the greatest among herbs, and becometh a tree, so that the birds of the air come and lodge in the branches thereof."[6]

Thus He meant to set forth the most decisive sign of its greatness. "Even so then shall it be with respect to the gospel too," saith He. Yea, for His disciples were weakest of all, and least of all; but nevertheless, because of the great power that was in them, It hath been unfolded[7] in every part of the world.

After this He adds the leaven to this similitude, saying,

"The Kingdom of Heaven is like unto leaven, which a woman took, and hid in three measures of meal, until the whole was leavened."[8]

For as this converts the large quantity of meal into its own quality,[9] even so shall ye convert the whole world.

And see His wisdom, in that He brings in things natural, implying that as the one cannot fail to take place, so neither the other. For say not this to me: "What shall we be able to do, twelve men, throwing ourselves upon so vast a multitude?" Nay, for this very thing most of all makes your might conspicuous, that ye mix with the multitude and are not put to flight. As therefore the leaven then leavens the lump when it comes close to the meal, and not simply close, but so as to be actually mixed with it (for He said not, "put," simply, but "hid"); so also ye, when ye cleave to your enemies, and are made one with them, then shall ye get the better of them. And as the leaven, though it be buried, yet is not destroyed, but by little and little transmutes all into its own condition; of like sort will the event be here also, with respect to the gospel. Fear ye not then, because I said there would be much injurious dealing: for even so shall ye shine forth, and get the better of all.

But by "three measures," here, He meant many, for He is wont to take this number for a multitude.

And marvel not, if discoursing about the kingdom, He made mention of a little seed and of leaven; for He was discoursing with men inexperienced and ignorant, and such as needed to be led on by those means. For so simple were they, that even after all this, they required a good deal of explanation.

Where now are the children of the Greeks? Let them learn Christ's power, seeing the verity of His deeds, and on either ground let them adore Him, that He both foretold so great a thing, and fulfilled it. Yea, for it is He that put the power into the leaven. With

---

[1] Matt. xiii. 30.　　　　[2] Matt. iii. 12.
[3] [μου is omitted from the text of the Homily.—R.]
[4] [Matt. xiii. 31. [R. V., "set he before them," etc.]
[5] κήρυγμα.
[6] Matt. xiii. 31, 32. [R. V., "is less than all," "is greater than."]

[7] ἐξηπλώθη.
[8] Matt. xiii. 33. [ἔκρυψεν (see Luke xiii. 21) is the reading here, and in the comment. Our best New Testament mss. read ἐνέκρυψεν.—R.]
[9] ἰσχύν.

19

this intent He mingled also with the multitude those who believe on Him, that we might impart unto the rest of our wisdom. Let no one therefore reprove us for being few. For great is the power of the gospel, and that which hath been once leavened, becomes leaven again for what remains. And as a spark, when it hath caught in timber, makes what hath been burnt up already increase the flame, and so proceeds to the rest; even so the gospel likewise. But He said not fire, but "leaven." Why might this be? Because in that case the whole effect is not of the fire, but partly of the timber too that is kindled, but in this the leaven doth the whole work by itself.

3. Now if twelve men leavened the whole world, imagine how great our baseness, in that when we being so many are not able to amend them that remain; we, who ought to be enough for ten thousand worlds, and to become leaven to them. "But they," one may say, "were apostles." And what then? Were they not partakers with thee? Were they not brought up in cities? Did they not enjoy the same benefits? Did they not practise trades? What, were they angels? What, came they down from Heaven?

"But they had signs," it will be said. It was not the signs that made them admirable. How long shall we use those miracles as cloaks for our own remissness? *Behold the choir of the Saints, that they shone not by those miracles.*[1] Why, many who had actually cast out devils, because they wrought iniquity, instead of being admired, did even incur punishment.

And what can it be then, he will say, that showed them great? Their contempt of wealth, their despising glory, their freedom from worldly things. Since surely, had they wanted these qualities, and been slaves of their passions, though they had raised ten thousand dead, so far from doing any good, they would even have been accounted deceivers. Thus it is their life, so bright on all sides, which also draws down the grace of the Spirit.

What manner of miracle did John work, that he fixed on himself the attention[2] of so many cities? For as to the fact that he did no wondrous works, hear the evangelist, saying, "John did no miracle."[3] And whence did Elias become admirable? Was it not

from his boldness towards the king? from his zeal towards God? from his voluntary poverty? from his garment of sheep's skin, and his cave, and his mountains? For his miracles He did after all these. And as to Job, what manner of miracle did he work in sight of the devil, that he was amazed at him? No miracle indeed, but a life that shone and displayed an endurance firmer than any adamant. What manner of miracle did David, yet being young, that God should say, "I have found David the son of Jesse, a man after mine own heart?"[4] And Abraham, and Isaac, and Jacob, what dead body did they raise? what leper did they cleanse? Knowest thou not that the miracles, except we be sober, do even harm in many cases? Thus many of the Corinthians were severed one from another; thus many of the Romans were carried away with pride; thus was Simon cast out. Thus he, who at a certain time had a desire to follow Christ, was rejected, when he had been told, "The foxes have holes, and the birds of the air nests."[5] For each of these, one aiming at the wealth, another at the glory, which the miracles bring, fell away and perished. But care of practice, and love of virtue, so far from generating such a desire, doth even take it away when it exists.

And Himself too, when He was making laws for His own disciples, what said He? "Do miracles, that men may see you"? By no means. But what? "Let your light shine before men, that they may see your good works, and glorify your Father which is in Heaven."[6] And to Peter again He said not, "If thou lovest me," "do miracles," but "feed my sheep."[7] And whereas He everywhere distinguishes him with James and John above all the rest, for what, I pray thee, did He distinguish them? For their miracles? Nay, all alike cleansed the lepers, and raised the dead; and to all alike He gave that authority.

Whence then had these the advantage? From the virtue in their soul. Seest thou how everywhere practice is required, and the proof by works? "For by their fruits," saith He, "ye shall know them."[8] And what commends our own life? Is it indeed a display of miracles, or the perfection of an excellent conversation? Very evidently it is the second; but as to the miracles, they both have their origin from hence, and terminate herein. For both He that shows forth an excellent life, draws to Himself this gift, and he that receives the gift, receives it for this end, that he may amend other men's lives.

---

[1] This sentence is printed in italics, as not appearing in many of the mss. It is evidently a marginal note by some copyist. [It is not found in any of the mss. collated by Field, and was bracketed as doubtful by earlier editors.—R.]

[2] ἀνηρτήσατο.

[3] John x. 41. [R. V., "sign," and so elsewhere in this edition of the Homilies. The same term (σημεῖον) occurs frequently in the present context, and is uniformly rendered "miracle."—R.]

[4] Acts xiii. 22.   [5] Matt. viii. 20.   [6] Matt. v. 16.
[7] John xxi. 16.   [8] Matt. vii. 16.

Since even Christ for this end wrought those miracles, that having made Himself thereby credible, and drawn men unto Him, He might bring virtue into our life. Wherefore also He lays more stress of the two on this. For He is not at all satisfied with the signs only, but He also threatens hell, and promises a kingdom, and lays down those startling laws, and all things He orders to this end, that He may make us equal to the angels.

And why say I, that Christ doth all for this object? Why, even thou, should one give thee thy choice, to raise dead men by His name, or to die for His name; which I pray thee, of the two wouldest thou rather accept? Is it not quite plain, the latter? and yet the one is a miracle, the other but a work. And what, if one offered thee to make grass gold, or to be able to despise all wealth as grass, wouldest thou not rather accept this latter? and very reasonably. For mankind would be attracted by this more than any way. For if they saw the grass changed into gold, they would covet themselves also to acquire that power, as Simon did, and the love of money would be increased in them; but if they saw us all contemning and neglecting gold, as though it were grass, they would long ago have been delivered from this disease.

4. Seest thou that our practice has more power to do good? By practice I mean, not thy fasting, nor yet thy strewing sackcloth and ashes under thee, but if thou despise wealth, as it ought to be despised; if thou be kindly affectioned, if thou give thy bread to the hungry, if thou control anger, if thou cast out vainglory, if thou put away envy. So He Himself used to teach: for, "Learn of me," saith He, "for I am meek and lowly in heart."[1] He did not say, "for I fasted," although surely He might have spoken of the forty days, yet He saith not this; but, "I am meek and lowly in heart." And again, when sending them out, He said not, "Fast," but, "Eat of all that is set before you."[2] With regard to wealth, however, He required of them great strictness, saying, "Provide not gold, or silver, or brass, in your purses."[3]

And all this I say, not to depreciate fasting, God forbid, but rather highly to commend it. But I grieve when other duties being neglected, ye think it enough for salvation, having but the last place in the choir of virtue. For the greatest thing is charity, and moderation, and almsgiving; which hits a higher mark even than virginity.

Wherefore, if thou desire to become equal to the apostles, there is nothing to hinder thee. For to have arrived at this virtue only suffices for thy not at all falling short of them. Let no one therefore wait for miracles.[4] For though the evil spirit is grieved, when he is driven out of a body, yet much more so, when he sees a soul delivered from sin. For indeed this is his great power.[5] This power caused Christ to die, that He might put an end to it. Yea, for this brought in death; by reason of this all things have been turned upside down. If then thou remove this, thou hast cut out the nerves of the devil, thou hast "bruised his head," thou hast put an end to all his might, thou hast scattered his host, thou hast exhibited a sign greater than all signs.

The saying is not mine, but the blessed Paul's. For when he had said, "Covet earnestly the best gifts, and yet show I unto you a more excellent way;"[6] he did not speak next of a sign, but of charity, the root of all our good things. If then we practise this, and all the self-denial that flows from it, we shall have no need of signs; even as on the other hand, if we do not practise it, we shall gain nothing by the signs.

Bearing in mind then all this, let us imitate those things whereby the apostles became great. And whereby did they become great? Hear Peter, saying, "Behold we have forsaken all, and followed Thee; what shall we have therefore?"[7] Hear also Christ saying to them, Ye shall sit upon twelve thrones," and, "every one that hath forsaken houses, or brethren, or father, or mother, shall receive an hundredfold in this world, and shall inherit everlasting life."[8] From all worldly things, therefore, let us withdraw ourselves, and dedicate ourselves to Christ, that we may both be made equal to the apostles according to His declaration, and may enjoy eternal life; unto which may we all attain, by the grace and love towards man of our Lord Jesus Christ to whom be glory and might forever and ever. Amen.

---

[1] Matt. xi. 29.
[2] Luke x. 7, 8 ; compare 1 Cor. x. 27. [The two passages are combined.—R.]
[3] Matt. x. 9.
[4] ἀναβαλλέσθω εἰς σημεῖα.
[5] Acts. viii. 10.
[6] 1 Cor. xii. 31.
[7] Matt. xix. 27.
[8] Matt. v. 29 ; compare Mark x. 30, Luke viii. 30.

HOMILY XLVII.

Matt. XIII. 34, 35.

" All these things spake Jesus unto the multitudes in parables, and without a parable spake He not[1] unto them; that it might be fulfilled which was spoken by the prophet, saying, I will open my mouth in parables; I will utter things that have been kept secret[2] from the foundation of the world." [3]

But Mark saith, " As they were able to hear it, He spake the word unto them in parables." [4]

Then pointing out that He is not making a new thing, He brings in the Prophet also, proclaiming beforehand this His manner of teaching. And to teach us the purpose of Christ, how He discoursed in this manner, not that they might be ignorant, but that He might lead them to inquiry, he added, " And without a parable spake He nothing unto them." Yet surely He did say many things without a parable; but then nothing. And for all this no man asked Him questions, whereas the Prophets, we know, they were often questioning: as Ezekiel,[5] for instance; as many others: but these did no such thing. Yet surely His sayings were enough to cast them into perplexity, and to stir them up to the inquiry; for indeed a very sore punishment was threatened by those parables: however, not even so were they moved.

Wherefore also He left them and went away. For,

" Then," saith he, " Jesus sent the multitudes away,[6] and went into His house." [7]

And not one of the Scribes follows Him; whence it is clear that for no other purpose did they follow, than to take hold of Him.[8] But when they marked not His sayings, thenceforth He let them be.

" And His disciples come unto Him, asking Him concerning the parable of the tares; " [9] although at times wishing to learn, and afraid[10] to ask. Whence then arose their confidence in this instance? They had been told, " To you it is given to know the mysteries of the kingdom of Heaven; " and they were emboldened. Wherefore also they ask in private; not as grudging the multitude, but observing their Master's law. For, " To these," saith He, " it is not given."

And why may it be that they let pass the parable of the leaven, and of the mustard seed, and inquire concerning this? They let those pass, as being plainer; but about this, as having an affinity to that before spoken, and as setting forth something more than it, they are desirous to learn (since He would not have spoken the same to them a second time) ; for indeed they saw how severe was the threatening therein uttered.[11] Wherefore neither doth He blame them, but rather completes His previous statements.

And, as I am always saying, the parables must not be explained throughout word for word, since many absurdities will follow; this even He Himself is teaching us here in thus interpreting this parable. Thus He saith not at all who the servants are that came to Him, but, implying that He brought them in, for the sake of some order, and to make up the picture, He omits that part, and interprets those that are most urgent and essential, and for the sake of which the parable was spoken; signifying Himself to be Judge and Lord of all.

" And He answered," so it is said, " and said unto them, He that soweth the good seed is the Son of Man; the field is the world, the good seed, these are the children of the kingdom, but the tares are the children of the wicked one; the enemy that soweth them is the devil; and the harvest is the end of the world, and the reapers are angels. As there fore the tares are gathered and burned in the fire; so shall it be in the end of this world. The Son of Man shall send His angels, and they shall gather out of His kingdom all things that offend, and them which do iniquity; " [12]

---

[1] [R. V., " nothing," following a reading accepted by Chrysostom, both here and in the comments. The received text has "not." —R.]

[2] [R. V., " things hidden."]

[3] Comp. Ps. lxxviii. 2.   [4] Matt. iv. 33.

[5] Ezek. xii. 9, xxiv. 19, xxxvii. 18.

[6] [R. V., " he left the multitudes." Compare the previous sentence. But Chrysostom, with the rec. text, inserts " Jesus."—R.]

[7] Matt. xiii. 36, the house (rec. text).   [8] ἐπιλαβέσθαι.

[9] [Matt. xiii. 36, freely cited.]   [10] Mark ix. 32.

[11] This passage is translated according to a conjectural emendation of Mr. Field. [The Greek text seems to be corrupt here. The mss. readings yield no intelligible sense that can be considered correct.—R.]

[12] Or, " produce lawlessness," τοὺς ποιοῦντας τὴν ἀνομίαν, in which sense it seems more directly applicable to heretics, who

and shall cast them into the furnace of fire, there shall be weeping and gnashing of teeth. Then shall the righteous shine forth as the sun in the kingdom of their Father." [1]

For whereas He Himself is the sower, and that of His own field, and out of His own kingdom He gathers, it is quite clear that the present world also is His.

But mark His unspeakable love to man, and His leaning to bounty, and His disinclination to punishment; in that, when He sows, He sows in His own person, but when He punishes, it is by others, that is, by the angels.

"Then shall the righteous shine forth as the sun in the kingdom of their Father." Not because it will be just so much only, but because this star is surpassed in brightness by none that we know. He uses the comparisons that are known to us.

And yet surely elsewhere He saith, the harvest is already come; as when He saith of the Samaritans, "Lift up your eyes, and look on the fields; for they are white already to harvest" [2] And again, "The harvest truly is plenteous, but the laborers are few." [3] How then saith He there, that the harvest is already come, while here He said, it is yet to be? According to another signification.

And how having elsewhere said, "One soweth, and another reapeth," [4] doth He here say, it is Himself that soweth? Because there again, He was speaking, to distinguish the apostles, not from Himself, but from the prophets, and that in the case of the Jews and Samaritans. Since certainly it was He who sowed through the prophets also.

And at times He calls this self-same thing both harvest and sowing, naming it with relation, now to one thing, now to another. Thus when He is speaking of the conviction and obedience of His converts, [5] He calls the thing "a harvest," as though He had accomplished all; but when He is seeking after the fruit of their hearing, He calls it seed, and the end, harvest.

And how saith He elsewhere, that "the righteous are caught up first?" [6] Because they are indeed caught up first, but Christ being come, those others are given over to punishment, and then the former depart into the kingdom of heaven. For because they must be in heaven, but He Himself is to come and judge all men here; having passed sentence upon these, like some king He rises

with His friends, leading them to that blessed portion. Seest thou that the punishment is twofold, first to be burnt up, and then to fall from that glory?

2. But wherefore doth He still go on, when the others have withdrawn, to speak to these also in parables? They had become wiser by His sayings, so as even to understand. At any rate, to them He saith afterwards, "Have ye understood all these things? They say unto Him, Yea, Lord." [7] So completely, together with its other objects, did the parable effect this too, that it made them more clear sighted.

What then saith He again?

"The Kingdom of Heaven is like unto treasure hid in a field, the which when a man hath found, he hideth, and for joy thereof selleth all that he hath, and buyeth that field. Again, the Kingdom of Heaven is like unto a merchant man seeking goodly pearls, who, when he had found one pearl of great price, went and sold all that he had, and bought it." [8]

Much as in the other place, the mustard seed and the leaven have but some little difference from each other, so here also these two parables, that of the treasure and that of the pearl. This being of course signified by both, that we ought to value the gospel above all things. And the former indeed, of the leaven and of the mustard seed, was spoken with a view to the power of the gospel, and to its surely prevailing over the world; but these declare its value, and great price. For as it extends itself like mustard seed, and prevails like leaven, so it is precious like a pearl, and affords full abundance like a treasure. We are then to learn not this only, that we ought to strip ourselves of everything else, and cling to the gospel, but also that we are to do so with joy; and when a man is dispossessing himself of his goods, he is to know that the transaction is gain, and not loss.

Seest thou how both the gospel is hid in the world, and the good things in the gospel?

Except thou sell all, thou buyest not; except thou have such a soul, anxious and inquiring, thou findest not. Two things therefore are requisite, abstinence from worldly matters, and watchfulness. For He saith "One seeking goodly pearls, who when he had found one of great price, sold all and bought it." For the truth is one, and not in many divisions.

And much as he that hath the pearl knows

---

may not be vicious in their own lives, but produce a contempt of God's law by their false doctrines. *Transl.*
[1] Matt. xiii. 37-43. [The long citation presents few textual variations of any kind, none that affect the sense.—R.]
[2] John iv. 35.   [3] Matt. ix. 37 ; Luke x. 2.
[4] John iv. 37.   [5] ὑπακουσάντων.   [6] Thess. iv. 17.

[7] Matt. xiii. 51. [R. V., omits "Lord," so the oldest MSS. and the Vulgate.—R.]
[8] Matt. xiii. 44-46. [Here also the Greek text presents few peculiarities ; τῷ is omitted before ἀγρῷ in verse 44, as in a few MSS. of the New Testament.—R.]

indeed himself that he is rich, but others know not, many times, that he is holding it in his hand (for there is no corporeal bulk); just so also with the gospel, they that have hold of it know that they are rich, but the unbelievers, not knowing of this treasure, are in ignorance also of our wealth.

3. After this, that we may not be confident in the gospel merely preached, nor think that faith only suffices us for salvation, He utters also another, an awful parable. Which then is this? That of the net.

"For the kingdom of Heaven is like unto a net, that was cast into the sea, and gathered of every kind; which, when it was full, they drew to shore, and sat down, and gathered the good into vessels, but cast the bad away."[1]

And wherein doth this differ from the parable of the tares? For there too the one are saved, the other perish; but there, for choosing of wicked doctrines; and those before this again, for not giving heed to His sayings, but these for wickedness of life; who are the most wretched of all, having attained to His knowledge, and being caught, but not even so capable of being saved.

Yet surely He saith elsewhere, that the shepherd Himself separates them, but here He saith the angels do this;[2] and so with respect to the tares. How then is it? At one time He discourses to them in a way more suited to their dullness,[3] at another time in a higher strain.

And this parable He interprets without so much as being asked, but of His own motion He explained it by one part of it, and increased their awe. For lest, on being told, "They cast the bad away," thou shouldest suppose that ruin to be without danger; by His interpretation He signified the punishment, saying, "They will cast them into the furnace."[4] And He declared the gnashing of teeth, and the anguish, that it is unspeakable.

Seest thou how many are the ways of destruction? By the rock, by the thorns, by the wayside, by the tares, by the net. Not without reason therefore did He say, "Broad is the way that leadeth to destruction, and many there be which go away[5] by it."[6]

4. Having then uttered all this, and concluded His discourse in a tone to cause fear, and signified that these are the majority of cases (for He dwelt more on them). He saith,

"Have ye understood all these things? They say unto Him, Yea, Lord."[7]

Then because they understood, He again praises them, saying,

"Therefore every Scribe, which is instructed in the Kingdom of Heaven,[8] is like unto a man that is an householder, which bringeth forth out of his treasure things new and old."[9]

Wherefore elsewhere also He saith, "I will send you wise men and scribes."[10] Seest thou how so far from excluding the Old Testament, He even commends it, and speaks publicly in favor of it, calling it "a treasure"?

So that as many as are ignorant of the divine Scriptures cannot be "householders;" such as neither have of themselves, nor receive of others, but neglect their own case, perishing with famine. And not these only, but the heretics too,[11] are excluded from this blessing. For they bring not forth things new and old. For they have not the old things, wherefore neither have they the new; even as they who have not the new, neither have they the old, but are deprived of both. For these are bound up and interwoven one with another.

Let us then hear, as many of us as neglect the reading of the Scriptures, to what harm we are subjecting ourselves, to what poverty. For when are we to apply ourselves to the real practice of virtue, who do not so much as know the very laws according to which our practice should be guided? But while the rich, those who are mad about wealth, are constantly shaking out their garments, that they may not become moth-eaten; dost thou, seeing forgetfulness worse than any moth wasting thy soul, neglect conversing with books? dost thou not thrust away from thee the pest, adorn thy soul, look continually upon the image of virtue, and acquaint thyself with her members and her head? For she too hath a head and members more seemly than any graceful and beautiful body.

What then, saith one, is the head of virtue? Humility. Wherefore Christ also begins with it, saying, "Blessed are the poor."[12] This head hath not locks and ringlets, but beauty, such as to gain God's favor. For, "Unto whom shall I look," saith He, "but unto him that is meek and humble, and trembleth at my words?"[13] And, "Mine eyes are upon the meek of the earth."[14] And, "The Lord is nigh unto them that are of a contrite heart."[15] This head, instead of

---

[1] Matt. xiii. 47, 48. [R. V., "which, when it was filled, they drew up on the beach," etc.]
[2] Matt. xxv. 32.   [3] παχύτερον.   [4] Matt. xiii. 50.
[5] ἀπερχόμενοι, rec. text, εἰσερχόμενοι.   [6] Matt. vii. 13.
[7] Matt. xiii. 51. [See note 7, p. 293.—R.]

[8] [R. V., "hath been made a disciple to the Kingdom of Heaven." Chrysostom reads ἐν, the received text has εἰς with the accusative.—R.]
[9] Matt. xiii. 52.   [10] Matt. xxiii. 34.
[11] i.e. in particular the Manichæans, and other sects which deny the divinity of the Old Testament.
[12] Matt. v. 3; Luke vi. 20.   [13] Is. lxvi. 2.
[14] Ps. ci. 6, comp. Ps. lxxvi. 9.   [15] Ps. xxxiv. 18.

locks, and flowing hair, bears sacrifices acceptable to God. It is a golden altar, and a spiritual place of sacrifice;[1] "For a contrite spirit is a sacrifice to God."[2] This is the mother of wisdom. If a man have this, he will have the rest also.

Hast thou seen a head such as thou hadst never seen? Wilt thou see the face too, or rather mark it? Mark then for the present its color, how ruddy, and blooming, and very engaging; and observe what are its ingredients. "Well, and what are they?" Shamefacedness and blushing. Wherefore also some one saith, "Before a shamefaced man shall go favor."[3] This sheds much beauty over the other members also. Though thou mix ten thousand colors, thou wilt not produce such a bloom.

And if thou wilt see the eyes also, behold them exactly delineated with decency and temperance. Wherefore they become also so beautiful and sharpsighted, as to behold even the Lord Himself. For, "Blessed," saith He, "are the pure in heart, for they shall see God."[4]

And her mouth is wisdom and understanding, and the knowledge of spiritual hymns. And her heart, acquaintance with Scripture, and maintenance of sound doctrines, and benevolence, and kindness. And as without this last there is no living, so without that other is never any salvation. Yea, for from that all her excellencies have birth. She hath also for feet and hands the manifestations of her good works. She hath a soul too, godliness. She hath likewise a bosom of gold, and firmer than adamant, even fortitude; and all may be taken captive more easily than that bosom may be riven asunder. And the spirit that is in the brain and heart, is charity[5]

5. Wilt thou that in her actual deeds also I show thee her image? Consider, I pray thee, this very evangelist: although we have not his whole life in writing, nevertheless even from a few facts one may see his image shine forth.

First, as to his having been lowly and contrite, hear him, after his gospel, calling himself a publican; for his being also merciful, see him stripping himself of all and following Jesus; and as to his piety, it is evident from his doctrines. And his wisdom again it is easy to see from the gospel which he composed, and his charity[6] (for he cared for the whole world); and the manifestation of his good works, from the throne on which he is to sit;[7] and his courage too, "by his departing with joy from the presence of the council."[8]

Let us imitate then this virtue, and most of all his humility and almsgiving, without which one cannot be saved. And this is shown by the five virgins, and together with them by the Pharisee. For without virginity indeed it is possible to see the kingdom, but without almsgiving it cannot be. For this is among the things that are essential, and hold all together. Not unnaturally then have we called it the heart of virtue. But this heart, unless it supply breath to all, is soon extinguished. In the same way then as the fountain also, if it confine its streams to itself, grows putrid; so it is with the rich also, when they keep their possessions to themselves. Wherefore even in our common conversation we say, "great is the consumption[9] of wealth with such a man;" instead of saying, "great is the abundance, great the treasure." For in truth there is a consumption, not of the possessors only, but of the riches themselves. Since both garments laid by spoil, and gold is cankered, and corn is eaten up, and the soul too of their owner is more than they all cankered and corrupted by the cares of them.

And if thou be willing to produce in the midst a miser's soul; like a garment eaten by inumerable worms, and not having any sound part, even so wilt thou find it, perforated on all sides by cares; rotted, cankered by sins.

But not such the poor man's soul, the soul of him, I mean, that is voluntarily poor; but it is resplendent as gold, it shines like a pearl, and it blooms like a rose. For no moth is there, no thief is there, no worldly care, but as angels converse, so do they.

Wouldest thou see the beauty of this soul? Wouldest thou acquaint thyself with the riches of poverty? He commands not men, but he commands evil spirits. He stands not at a king's side, but he hath taken his stand near to God. He is the comrade, not of men, but of angels. He hath not chests, two, or three, or twenty, but such an abundance as to account the whole world as nothing. He hath not a treasure, but heaven. He needs not slaves, or rather hath his passions for slaves, hath for slaves the motives[10] that rule over kings. For that which commands him who wears the purple, that motive shrinks before him.[11] And royalty, and gold, and all

---

[1] βῶμος, θυσιαστήριον. These two words are commonly used, the former in a bad, the other in a good sense, of Heathen, and Christian, or Jewish, altars respectively. This seems to be an invariable rule, as to the word βῶμος, in the Greek Bible, except that it is used of the Jewish altar in the following places of the Apocrypha : Ecclus. l. 12, 14 ; 2 Macc. ii. 19 xiii. 8, which may suffice to show that it was occasionally employed, as by St. Chrysostom here, with no unholy association.
[2] Ps. li. 17.   [3] Ecclus. xxxii. 10.
[4] Matt. v. 3.   [5] [ἀγάπῃ]

[6] [ἀγάπην.]   [7] Luke xxii. 30.   [8] Acts. v. 41.
[9] σῆψις, q. d. "the wear and tear."   [10] λογισμούς.
[11] [The translator has omitted a clause : "and dares not face him," καὶ ἀντιβλέψαι οὐ τολμᾷ.—R.]

such things, he laughs at, as at children's toys; and like hoops, and dice, and heads, and balls, so doth he count all these to be contemptible. For he hath an adorning, which they who play with these things cannot even see.

What then can be superior to this poor man? He hath at least heaven for his pavement; but if the pavement be like this, imagine the roof! But hath he not horses and chariots? Why, what need hath he of these, who is to be borne upon the clouds, and to be with Christ?

Having these things then impressed on our minds, let us, both men and women, seek after that wealth, and the plenty that cannot be rifled; that we may attain also unto the kingdom of heaven, by the grace and love towards man of our Lord Jesus Christ, to whom be glory and might forever and ever. Amen.

HOMILY XLVIII.

MATT. XIII. 53.

"And it came to pass, that, when Jesus had finished these parables, He departed thence."

WHEREFORE said He, "these"? Because He was to speak others besides. And wherefore, again, doth He depart? Desiring to sow the word everywhere.

"And when He was come into His own country, He taught them in their synagogue." [1]

And what doth he now call His country? As it seems to me, Nazareth. "For He did not many mighty works there," [2] it is said, but in Capernaum He did miracles: wherefore He said also, "And thou, Capernaum, which art exalted unto Heaven, shalt be brought down to hell; for if the mighty works, which have been done in thee, had been done in Sodom, it would have remained until this day." [3]

But having come there, while He slackens somewhat in His miracles; so as not to inflame them unto more envy, nor to condemn them more grievously, by the aggravation of their unbelief: He yet puts forth a doctrine, having no less of wonder in it than the miracles. For these utterly senseless men, when they ought to have marvelled, and to have been amazed at the power of His words, they on the contrary hold Him cheap, because of him who seemed to be His father; yet we know they had many examples of these things in the former times, and from fathers of no note had seen illustrious children. For so David was the son of a certain mean husbandman, Jesse; and Amos, the child of a goatherd, and himself a goatherd; [4] and Moses too, the lawgiver, had a father very inferior to himself. When they therefore, for this especially, ought to adore and be amazed, that being of such parents He spake such things, it being quite manifest, that so it was not of man's care, but of God's grace: yet they, what things they should admire Him for, for those they despise Him.

He is moreover continually frequenting the synagogues, lest if He were always abiding in the wilderness, they should the more accuse Him as making a schism, and fighting against their polity.

Being amazed therefore, and in perplexity, they said, "Whence hath this man this wisdom, and these powers?" [5] either calling the miracles powers, or even the wisdom itself. "Is not this the carpenter's son?" [6] The greater then the marvel, and the more abundant the ground of amaze. "Is not His mother called Mary, and His brethren James, and Joses, [7] and Simon, and Judas? and His sisters, are they not all with us? Whence hath this man these things? And they were offended in Him." [8]

Seest thou that Nazareth was where He was discoursing? "Are not his brethren," it is said, "such a one, and such a one?" And

---

[1] Matt. xiii. 54.   [2] Matt. xiii. 58.   [3] Matt. xi. 23.

[4] Amos. vii. 14, 15.
[5] Matt. xiii. 54.   [R. V., margin, "Greek, powers."]
[6] Matt. xiii. 55.
[7] [R. V., "Joseph," following a reading better supported than that of the recorded text, which agrees with that in the Homily. —R.]
[8] Matt. xiii. 55, 56.

what of this? Why, by this especially you ought to have been led on to faith. But envy you see is a poor base thing, and often falls foul of itself. For what things were strange and marvellous, and enough to have gained them over, these offended them.

What then saith Christ unto them? "A prophet," saith He, "is not without honor, save in his own country, and in his own house: and He did not," it is said, "many mighty works, because of their unbelief."[1] But Luke saith, "And He did not there many miracles."[2] And yet it was to be expected He should have done them. For if the feeling of wonder towards Him was gaining ground (for indeed even there He was marvelled at), wherefore did He not do them? Because He looked not to the display of Himself, but to their profit. Therefore when this succeeded not, He overlooked what concerned Himself, in order not to aggravate their punishment.

And yet see after how long a time He came to them, and after how great a display of miracles: but not even so did they endure it, but were inflamed again with envy.

Wherefore then did He yet do a few miracles? That they might not say, "Physician, heal thyself."[3] That they might not say, "He is a foe and an enemy to us, and overlooks His own;" that they might not say, "If miracles had been wrought, we also should have believed." Therefore He both wrought them, and stayed: the one, that He might fulfill His own part; the other, that He might not condemn them the more.

And consider thou the power of His words, herein at least, that possessed as they were by envy, they did yet admire. And as with regard to His works, they do not find fault with what is done, but feign causes which have no existence, saying, "In Beelzebub He casteth out the devils;" even so here too, they find no fault with the teaching, but take refuge in the meanness of His race.

But mark thou, I pray thee, the Master's gentleness, how He reviles them not, but with great mildness saith, "A prophet is not without honor, save in his own country." And neither here did He stop, but added, "And in his own house." To me it appears, that with covert reference to His very own brethren, He made this addition.

But in Luke He puts examples also of this, saying, that neither did Elias come unto His own, but to the stranger widow; neither by Eliseus was any other leper healed, but the stranger Naaman;[4] and Israelites neither received benefit, nor conferred benefit, but the foreigners. And these things He saith, signifying in every instance their evil disposition, and that in His case nothing new is taking place.

2. "At that time Herod the tetrarch heard of the fame of Jesus."[5] For Herod the king, this man's father, he that slew the children, was dead.

But not without a purpose doth the evangelist signify the time, but to make thee observe also the haughtiness of the tyrant, and his thoughtlessness, in that not at the beginning did he inform himself about Christ, but after a very long time.[6] For such are they that are in places of power, and are encompassed with much pomp, they learn these things late, because they do not make much account of them.

But mark thou, I pray thee, how great a thing virtue is, that he was afraid of him even when dead, and out of his fear he speaks wisely even concerning a resurrection.

"For he said," it is mentioned, "unto his servants, This is John, whom I slew, he is risen from the dead, and therefore the mighty powers do work in him."[7] Seest thou the intensity of his fear? for neither then did he dare to publish it abroad, but he still speaks but to his own servants.

But yet even this opinion savored of the soldier, and was absurd. For many besides had risen from the dead, and no one had wrought anything of the kind. And his words seem to me to be the language both of vanity, and of fear. For such is the nature of unreasonable souls, they admit often a mixture of opposite passions.

But Luke affirms that the multitudes said, "This is Elias, or Jeremias, or one of the old prophets,"[8] but he, as uttering forsooth something wiser than the rest, made this assertion.

But it is probable that before this, in answer to them that said He was John (for many had said this too), he had denied it, and said, "I slew him," priding himself and glorying in it. For this both Mark and Luke report that he said, "John I beheaded."[9] But when the rumor prevailed, then he too saith the same as the people.

Then the evangelist relates to us also the history. And what might his reason be for

---

[1] Matt. xiii. 57, 58. [Chrysostom omits "there."]
[2] Mark vi. 5. [σημεῖα, "signs;" but even in Mark this expression does not occur in this connection.—R.]
[3] Luke iv. 23.
[4] Luke iv. 25-27.
[5] Matt. xiv. 1. [R. V., "the report concerning Jesus."]
[6] "Perspicuum est prædicationem Christi reges mundi audire novissimos." St. Jerome, in Jonam. c. iii.
[7] Matt. xiii. 2.   [8] Luke ix. 8. Comp. Matt. xvi. 14.
[9] Mark vi. 16 ; Luke ix. 9

not introducing it as a subject by itself?[1] Because all their labor entirely was to tell what related to Christ, and they made themselves no secondary work besides this, except it were again to contribute to the same end. Therefore neither now would they have mentioned the history were it not on Christ's account, and because Herod said, "John is risen again."

But Mark saith, that Herod exceedingly honored the man, and this, when reproved.[2] So great a thing is virtue.

Then his narrative proceeds thus: "For Herod had laid hold on John, and bound him, and put him in prison, for Herodias' sake, his brother Philip's wife. For John said unto him, It is not lawful for thee to have her. And when he would have put him to death, he feared the people, because they counted him as a prophet."[3]

And wherefore doth he not address his discourse at all to her, but to the man? Because it depended more on him.

But see how inoffensive he makes his accusation, as relating a history rather than bringing a charge.

4. "But when Herod's birth-day was kept,"[4] saith he, "the daughter of Herodias danced before them,[5] and pleased Herod."[6] O diabolical revel! O satanic spectacle! O lawless dancing! and more lawless reward for the dancing. For a murder more impious than all murders was perpetrated, and he that was worthy to be crowned and publicly honored, was slain in the midst, and the trophy of the devils was set on the table.

And the means too of the victory were worthy of the deeds done. For,

"The daughter of Herodias," it is said, "danced in the midst, and pleased Herod. Whereupon he swore[7] with an oath to give her whatsoever she would ask. And she being before instructed of[8] her mother, said, Give me here John Baptist's head in a charger."[9]

Her reproach is twofold; first, that she danced, then that she pleased him, and so pleased him, as to obtain even murder for her reward.

Seest thou how savage he was? how senseless? how foolish? in putting himself under the obligation of an oath, while to her he gives full power over her request.

But when he saw the evil actually ensuing,

"he was sorry,"[10] it is said; and yet in the first instance he had put him in bonds. Wherefore then is he sorry? Such is the nature of virtue, even amongst the wicked admiration and praises are its due. But alas for her madness! When she too ought to admire, yea, to bow down to him, for trying to redress her wrong, she on the contrary even helps to arrange the plot, and lays a snare, and asks a diabolical favor.

But he was afraid "for the oath's sake," it is said, "and them that sat at meat with him." And how didst thou not fear that which is more grievous? Surely if thou wast afraid to have witnesses of thy perjury, much more oughtest thou to fear having so many witnesses of a murder so lawless.

But as I think many are ignorant of the grievance itself, whence the murder had its origin, I must declare this too, that ye may learn the wisdom of the lawgiver. What then was the ancient law, which Herod indeed trampled on, but John vindicated? The wife of him that died childless was to be given to his brother.[11] For since death was an incurable ill, and all was contrived for life's sake; He makes a law that the living brother should marry her, and should call the child that is born by the name of the dead, so that his house should not utterly perish. For if the dead were not so much as to leave children, which is the greatest mitigation of death, the sorrow would be without remedy. Therefore you see, the lawgiver devised this refreshment for those who were by nature deprived of children, and commanded the issue to be reckoned as belonging to the other.

But when there was a child, this marriage was no longer permitted. "And wherefore?" one may say, "for if it was lawful for another, much more for the brother." By no means. For He will have men's consanguinity extended, and the sources multiplied of our interest in each other.

Why then, in the case also of death without offspring, did not another marry her? Because it would not so be accounted the child of the departed; but now his brother begetting it, the fiction became probable. And besides, any other man had no constraining call to build up the house of the dead, but this had incurred the claim by relationship.

Forasmuch then as Herod had married his brother's wife, when she had a child, therefore John blames him, and blames him with moderation, showing together with his boldness, his consideration also.

---

[1] προηγουμένως.   [2] Mark vi. 20.   [3] Matt. xiii. 3-5.
[4] [R. V., "come;" rec. text as in Homily.]
[5] [R. V., "in the midst;" so Homily, see below.—R.]
[6] Matt. xiii. 6.
[7] ["Swore" is substituted for "promised;" peculiar to Chrysostom, but probably borrowed from Mark vi. 23.—R.]
[8] [R. V., "being put forward by."]
[9] Matt. xiii. 6-8.

[10] Matt. xiii. 9. [R. V., "was grieved."]   [11] Deut. xxv. 5.

But mark thou, I pray thee, how the whole theatre was devilish. For first, it was made up of drunkenness and luxury, whence nothing healthful could come. Secondly, the spectators in it were depraved, and he that gave the banquet the worst transgressor of all. Thirdly, there was the irrational pleasure. Fourthly, the damsel, because of whom the marriage was illegal, who ought even to have hid herself, as though her mother were dishonored by her, comes making a show, and throwing into the shade all harlots, virgin as she was.

And the time again contributes no little to the reproof of this enormity. For when he ought to be thanking God, that on that day He had brought him to light, then he ventures upon those lawless acts. When one in chains ought to have been freed by him, then he adds slaughter to bonds.

Hearken, ye virgins, or rather ye wives also, as many as consent to such unseemliness at other person's weddings, leaping, and bounding, and disgracing our common nature. Hearken, ye men too, as many as follow after those banquets, full of expense and drunkenness, and fear ye the gulf of the evil one. For indeed so mightily did he seize upon that wretched person just then, that he sware even to give the half of his kingdom: this being Mark's statement, "He sware unto her, Whatsoever thou shalt ask of me, I will give it thee, unto the half of my kingdom."[1]

Such was the value he set upon his royal power; so was he once for all made captive by his passion, as to give up *his kingdom* for a dance.[2]

And why marvel at these things so happening then, since even now, after the coming in of so high a wisdom, for a dance' sake many of these effeminate young men give up their very souls, and that without constraint of any oath? For being made captive by the pleasure, they are led like sheep, wheresoever the wolf may drag them; which was then the case with that frenzied man, who was guilty of two extreme acts of madness; first, in making it depend on her that was so maddened, and intoxicated with her passion, and shrinking from nothing; next, in making the deed fast with the constraint of an oath.

5. But albeit he was so wicked, that base woman was more wicked than all of them, both the damsel and the tyrant. For she was the very first contriver of all the mischiefs, and the framer of the whole plot (she who

most of all ought to have been thankful to the prophet); since it was in obedience to her that her daughter both disgraced herself, and danced, and sought the murder; and Herod was entrapped by her.

Seest thou how justly Christ said, "He that loveth father or mother more than me, is not worthy of me."[3] For had she kept this law, she would not have transgressed so many laws, she would not have perpetrated this foul murder.

For what could be worse than this brutal fierceness? to ask a murder by way of a favor, a lawless murder, a murder in the midst of a banquet, a murder publicly, and without shame? Since she went not unto him privately to speak of these things, but publicly, and with her mask thrown off, barefaced, and having got the devil to plead with her, in this guise she saith whatever she saith. Yea, and he it was that caused her at all to get credit by her dancing, and to catch Herod at that moment. For where dancing is, there is the evil one. For neither did God give us feet for this end, but that we may walk orderly: not that we may behave ourselves unseemly, not that we may jump like camels (for even they too are disagreeable when dancing, much more women), but that we may join the choirs of angels.

For if the body is base, thus making itself unseemly, much more the soul. Like this is the dancing of the demons, like this, the jesting of such as are servants of the demons.

And mark too the very mode of asking. "Give me here John Baptist's head in a charger." Dost thou see her lost to all shame, become altogether the devil's? She mentions his very office, and not even so does she hide her face, but as if it were some viand she is speaking of, just so doth she ask for that sacred and blessed head to be brought in in a charger.

And she doth not so much as assign a cause, for neither had she one to mention, but she claims simply to be complimented by the calamities of others. And she said not, "Bring him in here, and slay him," for she could not have endured his bold language even when he was about to die. Yea, and she dreaded to hear his awful voice, even when enduring slaughter; for not on the very point of being beheaded would he have kept silence. Therefore she saith, "Give me here in a charger," for "I long to see that tongue silent:" her object being, not simply to be rid of his reproofs, but also to trample upon him, and deride him when fallen.

---

[1] Mark vi. 23.
[2] [δι᾽ ὄρχησιν αὐτῆς παραχωρῆσαι, " to concede for the sake of her dance."—R.]

[3] Matt. x. 37.

Yet God endured it, and neither discharged His thunderbolt from above to scorch her shameless countenance, nor commanded the earth to open, and receive that wicked revel; at once both crowning the righteous man more signally, and leaving much consolation to them that hereafter suffer anything unjustly.

6. Let us hearken therefore, as many as suffer ill, living in virtue, at the hands of wicked men. For then too God endured that even he in the wilderness, he in the leathern girdle, in the garment of hair, the prophet, the man greater than all prophets, who had no superior among those born of women, should actually be murdered, and that by an immodest damsel, and a corrupt harlot, and all in vindicating the laws of God. These things then let us consider, and bear all nobly, whatever we may suffer.

For then too this bloodthirsty and lawless woman, as far as she desired to take vengeance on him that had grieved her, so far did she prevail, and satiated all her anger, and God permitted it. And yet to her he had said nothing, nor had he accused her, but he found fault with the man only. But her conscience was a bitter accuser. Wherefore also she was led on in frenzy to greater evils, being grieved, and stung, and she disgraced all at once, herself, her daughter, her departed husband, her living paramour, and tried to surpass her former acts. For "if thou art vexed," saith she, "at his committing adultery, I make him a murderer also, and cause him to be the slayer of his reprover."

Hearken, as many as are unduly excited about women.

Hearken, as many as proffer oaths about things uncertain, and give others power for your own destruction, and dig a pit for yourselves.

Yea, for so came this man's ruin. I mean, he surely expected her to ask some request suitable to the feast, and that being a damsel, and asking a favor at a banquet, and revel, and solemn assembly, she would ask something cheerful, and gracious, and surely not a head; and he was deceived.

But nevertheless none of these things will be a plea for him. And what if she had attained the spirit of the men that fight with wild beasts? nevertheless he ought not to have been deceived, nor to have ministered to such tyrannical injunctions.

For, in the first place, who would not have shuddered to see that sacred head, dropping blood, set forth at the feast? But not so the lawless Herod, nor the woman more accured than he. For such is the nature of the unchaste among women; none so audacious and so savage as they.

For if we shudder at hearing these things, what must we suppose of the effect of that sight at the time? what of the feeling of those who sat with him at meat, on seeing blood dropping from a newly-severed head in the midst of the revel? But as for that bloodthirsty woman, and fiercer than furies, she had no feeling at that spectacle, but even took delight in it, yet if nothing else, surely the mere sight, it was to be expected, would effectually turn her cold. But no such feeling had she, the murderess, and full of thirst after prophets' blood.

For such is the nature of whoredom. It makes men not wanton only, but murderous also. Those women at all events, who desire to commit adultery, are prepared even for the slaying of their injured husbands, and not one only, nor two, but ten thousand murders are they ready to venture upon. And of this sort of tragic plots there are many witnesses.

Which thing she also did at that time, looking to be concealed after this, and to hide her crime. The very contrary whereunto was the result; for John's cry was heard more loudly after these things. But wickedness looks to the present only, like fevered persons unseasonably asking for cold water. For in fact, if she had not slain her accuser, her crime would not have been so completely discovered. His disciples at least, when she had thrown him into prison, said nothing of the kind; but when she had slain him, then they were compelled to mention the cause also. For willing as they were to have concealed the adulteress, and not inclined to expose their neighbor's calamities; yet when they found themselves compelled to give an account of it, then they tell the whole crime. For lest any one should suspect that the cause of his slaughter was a discreditable one, as in the case of Theudas and Judas,[1] they are constrained to tell the occasion also of the murder. So that the more thou wouldest dissemble a sin in this way, so much the more dost thou expose it. For sin is not hidden by the addition of sin, but by repentance and confession.

7. But see the evangelist, how he relates all without invidiousness, and as far as he can, absolutely makes out an excuse. Thus first in behalf of Herod he saith, "For the oath's sake, and them which sat with him at meat," and that "he was sorry;" then of the damsel, "Being before instructed of her

---

[1] Acts v. 36. 37.

mother," and that "she brought the head to her mother;" as though he had said, it was her command that she was fulfilling. Since not for the sufferers but for the wrongdoers do all righteous men grieve, since in fact these are they who properly speaking suffer ill. For neither was John injured, but these the contrivers of such proceedings.

Them let us also imitate, and not trample upon our neighbors' sins, but so far as is right, shadow them over. Let us take to ourselves a soul severe in goodness. For so the very evangelist, speaking of a harlot and a blood-stained woman, avoided harshness, as far as might be. For neither did he say, "by the blood-stained and accursed woman," but "being before instructed of her mother,"[1] using such names as have rather an innocent sound.

But thou dost even insult and revile thy neighbor, and couldest never endure to make mention of a brother that had grieved thee in such terms, as he hath done of the harlot, but with much brutal fierceness, and reproaches, calling him the wicked one, the malefactor, the crafty, the fool, and many other names more grievous than these. For so we make ourselves more and more like wild beasts, and talk of him as of a man of monstrous origin,[2] vilifying, reviling, insulting. But not so the saints; they on the contrary mourn for such as sin, rather than curse them.

8. This then let us also do, and let us weep for Herodias, and for them that imitate her. For many such revels now also take place, and though John be not slain, yet the members of Christ are, and in a far more grievous way. For it is not a head in a charger that the dancers of our time ask, but the souls of them that sit at the feast. For in making them slaves, and leading them to unlawful loves, and besetting them with harlots, they do not take off the head, but slay the soul, making them adulterers, and effeminate, and whoremongers.

For thou wilt not surely tell me, that when full of wine, and drunken, and looking at a woman who is dancing and uttering base words, thou dost not feel anything towards her, neither art hurried on to profligacy, overcome by thy lust. Nay, that awful thing befalls thee, that thou "makest the members of Christ members of an harlot."[3]

For though the daughter of Herodias be not present, yet the devil, who then danced in her person, in theirs also holds his choirs now, and departs with the souls of those guests taken captive.

But if ye are able to keep clear of drunkenness, yet are ye partakers of another most grievous sin; such revels being also full of much rapine. For look not, I pray thee, on the meats that are set before them, nor on the cakes; but consider whence they are gathered, and thou wilt see that it is of vexation, and covetousness, and violence, and rapine.

"Nay, ours are not from such sources," one may say. God forbid they should be: for neither do I desire it. Nevertheless, although they be clear of these, not even so are our costly feasts freed from blame. Hear, at all events, how even apart from these things the prophet finds fault with them, thus speaking, "Woe to them that drink wine racked off, and anoint themselves with the chief ointments."[4] Seest thou how He censures luxury too? For it is not covetousness which He here lays to their charge, but prodigality only.

And thou eatest to excess, Christ not even for need; thou various cakes, He not so much as dry bread; thou drinkest Thasian wine, but on Him thou hast not bestowed so much as a cup of cold water in His thirst. Thou art on a soft and embroidered bed, but He is perishing with the cold.

Wherefore, though the banquets be clear from covetousness, yet even so are they accursed, because, while for thy part thou doest all in excess, to Him thou givest not even His need; and that, living in luxury upon things that belong to Him. Why, if thou wert guardian to a child, and having taken possession of his goods, were to neglect him in extremities, thou wouldest have ten thousand accusers, and wouldest suffer the punishment appointed by the laws; and now having taken possession of the goods of Christ, and thus consuming them for no purpose, dost thou not think thou wilt have to give account?

9. And these things I say not of those who introduce harlots to their tables (for to them I have nothing to say, even as neither have I to the dogs), nor of those who cheat some, and pamper others (for neither with them have I anything to do, even as I have not with the swine and with the wolves); but of those who enjoy indeed their own property, but do not impart thereof to others; of those who spend their patrimony at random. For neither are these clear from reprehension.

For how, tell me, wilt thou escape reprov-

---

[1] [R V., "being put forward by her mother."

[2] ἀλλογενοῦς, which seems to be opposed to αὐθιγενοῦς, "of genuine origin."

[3] 1 Cor. vi. 15.

[4] Amos vi. 6, LXX. [τὸν διυλισμένον οἶνον.]

ing and blame, while thy parasite is pampered, and the dog that stands by thee, but Christ's worth appears to thee even not equal to theirs? when the one receives so much for laughter's sake, but the other for the Kingdom of Heaven not so much as the smallest fraction thereof. And while the parasite, on saying something witty, goes away filled; this Man, who hath taught us, what if we had not learnt we should have been no better than the dogs,—is He counted unworthy of even the same treatment with such an one?

Dost thou shudder at being told it? Shudder then at the realities. Cast out the parasites, and make Christ to sit down to meat with thee. If He partake of thy salt, and of thy table, He will be mild in judging thee: He knows how to respect a man's table.[1] Yea, if robbers know this, much more the Lord. Think, for instance, of that harlot, how at a table He justified her, and upbraids Simon, saying, "Thou gavest me no kiss."[2] I say, if He feed thee, not doing these things, much more will He reward thee, doing them. Look not at the poor man, that he comes to thee filthy and squalid, but consider that Christ by him is setting foot in thine house, and cease from thy fierceness, and thy relentless words, with which thou art even aspersing such as come to thee, calling them impostors, idle, and other names more grievous than these.

And think, when thou art talking so, of the parasites; what kind of works do they accomplish? in what respect do they profit thine house? Do they really make thy dinner pleasant to thee? pleasant, by their being beaten and saying foul words? Nay, what can be more unpleasing than this, when thou smitest him that is made after God's likeness, and from thine insolence to him gatherest enjoyment for thyself, making thine house a theatre, and filling thy banquet with stage-players, thou who art well born and free imitating the actors with their heads shaven?[3] For among them too is laughter, and rude blows.

These things then dost thou call pleasure, I pray thee, which are deserving of many tears, of much mourning and lamentation? And when it were fit to urge them to a good life, to give timely advice, dost thou lead them on to perjuries, and disorderly language,

and call the thing a delight? and that which procures hell, dost thou account a subject of pleasure? Yea, and when they are at a loss for witty sayings, they pay the whole reckoning with oaths and false swearing. Are these things then worthy of laughter, and not of lamentations and tears? Nay, who would say so, that hath understanding?

And this I say, not forbidding them to be fed, but not for such a purpose. Nay, let their maintenance have the motive of kindness, not of cruelty; let it be compassion, not insolence. Because he is a poor man, feed him; because Christ is fed, feed him; not for introducing satanical sayings, and disgracing his own life. Look not at him outwardly laughing, but examine his conscience, and then thou wilt see him uttering ten thousand imprecations against himself, and groaning, and wailing. And if he do not show it, this also is due to thee.

10. Let the companions of thy meals then be men that are poor and free, not perjured persons, nor stage-players. And if thou must needs ask of them a requital for their food, enjoin them, should they see anything done that is amiss, to rebuke, to admonish, to help thee in thy care over thine household, in the government of thy servants. Hast thou children? Let these be joint fathers to them, let them divide thy charge with thee, let them yield thee such profits as God loveth. Engage them in a spiritual traffic. And if thou see one needing protection, bid them succor, command them to minister. By these do thou track the strangers out, by these clothe the naked, by these send to the prison, put an end to the distresses of others.

Let them give thee, for their food, this requital, which profits both thee and them, and carries with it no condemnation.

Hereby friendship also is more closely riveted. For now, though they seem to be loved, yet for all that they are ashamed, as living without object in thy house; but if they accomplish these purposes, both they will be more pleasantly situated, and thou wilt have more satisfaction in maintaining them, as not spending thy money without fruit; and they again will dwell with thee in boldness and due freedom, and thy house, instead of a theatre, will become to thee a church, and the devil will be put to flight, and Christ will enter, and the choir of the angels. For where Christ is, there are the angels too, and where Christ and the angels are, there is Heaven, there is a light more cheerful than this of the sun.

And if thou wouldest reap yet another consolation through their means, command them,

---

[1] That is, to respect the obligation incurred by having been a person's guest.
[2] Luke vii. 54.
[3] Comp. Homily XXXVII. 8. Of such parasites Juvenal says, (Sat. v. 170.)

Omnia ferre
Si potes, et debes. Pulsandum *vertice raso*
Præbebis quandoque caput, nec dura timebis
Flagra pati, his epulis et tali dignus amico.
See Mr. Field's note.

when thou art at leisure, to take their books and read the divine law. They will have more pleasure in so ministering to you, than in the other way. For these things add respect both to thee and to them, but those bring disgrace upon all together; upon thee as an insolent person and a drunkard, upon them as wretched and gluttonous. For if thou feed in order to insult them, it is worse than if thou hadst put them to death; but if for their good and profit, it is more useful again than if thou hadst brought them back from their way to execution. And now indeed thou dost disgrace them more than thy servants, and thy servants enjoy more liberty of speech, and freedom of conscience, than they do; but then thou wilt make them equal to the angels.

Set free therefore both them and thine own self, and take away the name of parasite, and call them companions of thy meals;[1] cast away the appellation of flatterers, and bestow on them that of friends. With this intent indeed did God make our friendships, not for evil to the beloved and loving, but for their good and profit.

But these friendships are more grievous than any enmity. For by our enemies, if we will, we are even profited; but by these we must needs be harmed, no question of it.

Keep not then friends to teach thee harm; keep not friends who are enamored rather of thy table than of thy friendship. For all such persons, if thou retrench thy good living, retrench their friendship too; but they that associate with thee for virtue's sake, remain continually, enduring every change.

And besides, the race of the parasites doth often take revenge upon thee, and bring upon thee an ill fame. Hence at least I know many respectable persons to have got bad characters, and some have been evil reported of for sorceries, some for adulteries and corrupting of youths. For whereas they have no work to do, but spend their own life unprofitably; their ministry is suspected by the multitude as being the same with that of corrupt youths.

Therefore, delivering ourselves both from evil report, and above all from the hell that is to come, and doing the things that are well-pleasing to God, let us put an end to this devilish custom, that "both eating and drinking we may do all things to the glory of God,"[2] and enjoy the glory that cometh from Him; unto which may we all attain, by the grace and love towards man of our Lord Jesus Christ, to whom be glory and might, now and ever, and world without end. Amen.

---

[1] συσσίτους.

[2] 1 Cor. x. 31.

HOMILY XLIX.

Matt. XIV. 13.

"But when Jesus heard of it, He departed thence by ship into a desert place apart; and when the multitudes had heard thereof, they followed Him on foot out of all the cities."

See Him on every occasion "departing,"[2] both when John was delivered up,[3] and when he was slain, and when the Jews heard that He was making more disciples.[4] For it is His will ordinarily to conduct things after the manner of a man, the time not yet calling Him to reveal His Godhead plainly. Wherefore also He bade His disciples "tell no man that He is the Christ;"[5] for His will was that this should be better known after His resurrection. Wherefore upon those of the Jews that were for a time obstinate in their unbelief He was not very severe, but even disposed to be indulgent to them.

And on retiring, He departs not into a city, but into a wilderness, and in a vessel, so that no man should follow.

But do thou mark, I pray thee, how the disciples of John had now come to be more

---

[1] R. V., "from the cities;" the word "all" is not found in the text of Matthew, but in Mark vi. 33.—R.]
[2] ["withdrawing;" so the R. V. properly renders ἀναχωρεῖν.—R.]
[3] Matt. iv. 12.   [4] John iv. 1-3.   [5] Matt. xvi. 20.

attached to Jesus. For it was they that told Him of the event; for indeed they have left all, and take refuge henceforth in Him. Thus, besides their calamity, His provision before made in that answer[1] did no small good.

But wherefore did He not retire before they brought Him the tidings, when yet He knew the fact before they reported it? To signify all means the reality of His economy.[2] For not by His appearance only, but by His actions He would have this confirmed, because He knew the devil's craft, and that he would leave nothing undone to destroy this doctrine.

He then for this end retires; but the multitudes not even so withdraw themselves from Him, but they follow, riveted to Him, and not even John's tragical end alarmed them. So great a thing is earnest desire, so great a thing is love; in such wise doth it overcome and dispel all dangers.

Therefore they straightway also received their reward. For "Jesus," it is said, "went forth, and saw a great multitude, and was moved with compassion toward them, and He healed their sick."[3]

For great as their assiduity was, yet nevertheless His doings exceeded what any diligence could earn. Wherefore He sets forth also His motive for so healing them, His mercy, intense mercy: and He healeth all.

And He requires not faith here. For both by coming to Him, and by leaving their cities, and by diligently seeking Him, and by abiding with Him even when hunger was pressing, they display their own faith.

But He is about to feed them also. And He doth not this of Himself, but waits to be entreated; on every occasion, as I have said, maintaining this rule, not to spring onward to His miracles, preventing them, but upon some call.[4]

And why did none of the multitude come near and speak for them? They reverenced Him exceedingly, and felt not even their hunger, through their longing to stay with Him. Neither indeed do His disciples, when they were come to Him, say, "Feed them;" for as yet they were rather in an imperfect state; but what?

"And when it was evening,' it is said, "His disciples came to Him, saying, This is a desert place, and the time is now passed; send the multitude away, that they may go and buy themselves victuals."[5]

For if even after the miracle they forgot what had been done, and after the baskets, supposed Him to be speaking of loaves, when He gave the name of "leaven" to the doctrine of the Pharisees;[6] much less, when they had never yet had experience of such a miracle, would they have expected any such thing. And yet He had made a beginning by actually healing many sick; but nevertheless, not even from this did they expect the miracle of the loaves; so imperfct were they as yet.

But mark thou, I pray, the Teacher's skill, how distinctly He summons them on towards believing. For He said not at once, "I feed them;" which indeed would not have been easily received; but what?

"But Jesus," so it is written, "said unto them, "They need not depart; give ye them to eat."[7]

He said not, "I give them," but, "Give ye them;" for as yet their regard to Him was as to a man. But they not even so are awakened, but still reason as with a man, saying,

"We have but five loaves, and two fishes."[8]

Wherefore Mark also saith, "They understood not the saying, for their heart was hardened."[9]

They continuing therefore to crawl on the ground, then at length He brings in His own part, and saith, "Bring them hither to me." For although the place be desert, yet He that feeds the world is here; and although the time be now past, yet He that is not subject to time is discoursing with you.

But John saith also, that they were "barley loaves,"[10] not mentioning it without object, but teaching us to trample under foot the pride of costly living. Such was the diet of the prophets also.[11]

2. "He took therefore the five loaves, and the two fishes, and commanded the multitude," it is said, "to sit down upon the grass, and looking up to Heaven, He blessed, and brake, and gave to His disciples, and the disciples to the multitude.[12] And they did all eat and were filled, and they took up of the fragments that remained twelve baskets full. And they that had eaten were about five thousand men, beside women and children."[13]

Wherefore did He look up to Heaven, and bless? It was to be believed of Him, both that He is of the Father, and that He is equal to Him. But the proofs of these things

---

[1] Matt. xi. 2.
[2] οἰκονομίας, that is, of His incarnation and manhood.
[3] Matt. xiv. 14.
[4] [τὸ μὴ πρότερος ἐπιπηδᾷν τοῖς θαύμασιν, ἀλλὰ καλούμενος.]
[5] Matt. xiv. 15.

[6] Matt. xvi. 6.   [7] Matt. xiv. 16.   [8] Matt. xiv. 17.
[9] Matt. vi. 52. [Slightly altered.]   [10] John vi. 9.
[11] See 2 Kings iv. 42 ; v. 19-21.
[12] [In verse 19 τοίνυν is inserted ; the order of the clauses changed, and τοὺς ἄρτους omitted.--R.]
[13] Verses 20, 21 are verbally exact. The R. V. renders more accurately the last clause of ver. 20, "that which remained over of the broken pieces, twelve baskets full."—R.]

seemed to oppose one another. For while His equality was indicated by His doing all with authority, of His origin from the Father they could no otherwise be persuaded, than by His doing all with great lowliness, and with reference to Him, and invoking Him on His works. Wherefore we see that He neither did these actions only, nor those, that both might be confirmed; and now He works miracles with authority, now with prayer.

Then again, that what He did might not seem an inconsistency, in the lesser things He looks up to Heaven, but in the greater doth all with authority; to teach thee in the lesser also, that not as receiving power from elsewhere, but as honoring Him that begat Him, so He acts. For example: when He forgave sins, and opened paradise, and brought in the thief, and most utterly set aside the old law, and raised innumerable dead, and bridled the sea, and reproved the un-uttered thoughts of men, and created an eye;—which are achievements of God only and of none else;—we see Him in no instance pray-ing: but when He provided for the loaves to multiply themselves, a far less thing than all these, then He looks up to Heaven; at once establishing these truths which I have spoken of, and instructing us not to touch a meal, until we have given thanks to Him who giveth us this food.

And why doth He not make it of things that are not? Stopping the mouth of Marcion, and of Manichæus, who alienate His creation from Him, and teaching by His very works, that even all the things that are seen are His works and creatures, and signifying that it is Himself who gives the fruits, who said at the beginning, "Let the earth put forth the herb of grass," and "Let the waters bring forth things moving with living souls."[1]

For this is not at all a less work than the other. For though those were made of things that are not, yet nevertheless were they of water; and it was no greater thing to produce fruits out of the earth, and moving things with life out of the water, than out of five loaves to make so many; and of fishes again, which was a sign that He was ruler both of the earth and of the sea.

Thus, since the sick were constantly the subject of His miracles, He works also a general benefit, that the many might not be spectators only of what befell others, but themselves also partakers of the gift.

And that which in the wilderness seemed to the Jews marvellous, (they said at least, "Can He give bread also? or prepare a table in the wilderness?)"[2] this He shows forth in His works. With this view also He leads them into the wilderness, that the miracle might be very far beyond suspicion, and that no one might think that any village lying near contributed ought to the meal. For this reason He mentions the hour also, not the place only.

And another thing too we learn, the self-restraint of the disciples which they practised in necessary things, and how little they ac-counted of food. For being twelve, they had five loaves only and two fishes; so secondary to them were the things of the body: so did they cling to the things spiritual only.

And not even that little did they hold fast, but gave up even it when asked. Whereby we should be taught, that though we have but little, this too we ought to give up to them that are in need. Thus, when commanded to bring the five loaves, they say not, "and whence are we to have food? whence to ap-pease our own hunger?" but they obey at once.

And besides what I have mentioned, to this end, as I at least think, He makes it out of the materials which they had, namely, that He might lead them to faith; for as yet they were rather in a weak state.[3]

Wherefore also "He looks up to Heaven." For of the other miracles they had many ex-amples, but of this none.[3]

3. "He took the loaves," therefore, "and brake them, and gave them by His disciples," hereby to honor them; and not in honor to them only, but also that, when the miracle had been done they might not disbelieve it, nor forget it when it had past, their own hands bearing them witness.[3]

Wherefore also He suffers the multitudes first to have a sense of hunger, and waits for these to come to Him first and ask Him, and by them makes the people sit down, and by them distributes; being minded by their own confessions and actions to prepossess them every one.[3]

Therefore also, from them He receives the loaves, that the testimonies of what was doing might be many, and that they might have memorials of the miracle. For if even after these occurrences they forgot,[4] what would not have been their case, had He omitted those provisions?

And He commands them to sit down on the trampled grass, instructing the multitudes in self-denial. For His will was not to feed

---

[1] Gen. i. 11, 20. [LXX., ἑρπετὰ ψυχῶν ζωσῶν.]
20

[2] Ps. lxxviii. 20.
[3] In these and other places of this Homily there may be per-haps a tacit reference to the Holy Eucharist, and to the aptitude of the miracle of the loaves as a preparation of the apostles for it.
[4] Matt. xvi. 9.

their bodies only, but also to instruct their souls. As well by the place therefore, as by His giving them nothing more than loaves and fishes, and by setting the same before all, and making it common, and by affording no one more than another, He was teaching them humility, and temperance, and charity, and to be of like mind one towards another, and to account all things common.

"And He brake and gave to the disciples, and the disciples to the multitude." The five loaves He brake and gave, and the five multiplied themselves in the hands of the disciples. And not even here doth He stay the miracle, but He made them even to exceed; to exceed, not as whole loaves, but as fragments; to signify that of those loaves these were remains, and in order that the absent might learn what had been done.

For this purpose indeed He suffered the multitudes to hunger, that no one might suppose what took place to be illusion.

For this also He caused just twelve baskets to remain over, that Judas also might bear one. For He was able indeed to have appeased their hunger, but the disciples would not have known His power, since in Elijah's case also this took place.[1]

At all events, so greatly were the Jews amazed at Him for this, that they wished even to make Him a king,[2] although with regard to the other miracles they did not so in any instance.

What reasoning now may set forth, how the loaves multiplied[3] themselves; how they flowed together in the wilderness; how they were enough for so many (for there were "five thousand men beside women and children;" which was a very great commendation of the people, that both women and men attended Him); how the remnants had their being (for this again is not less than the former), and became so abundant, that the baskets were equal in number to the disciples, and neither more nor less?

Having then taken the fragments, He gave them not to the multitudes, but to the disciples, and that, because the multitudes were in a more imperfect state than the disciples.

And, having wrought the miracle, "straightway He constrained His disciples to get into a ship, and to go before Him unto the other side, while He sent the multitudes away."[4]

For even if He had seemed, when in sight, to be presenting an illusion, and not to have wrought a truth; yet surely not in His absence also. For this cause then, submitting His proceedings to an exact test, He commanded those that had got the memorials, and the proof of the miracles, to depart from Him.

And besides this, when He is doing great works, He disposes elsewhere of the multitudes and the disciples, instructing us in nothing to follow after the glory that comes from the people, nor to collect a crowd about us.

Now by saying, "He constrained them," He indicates the very close attendance of the disciples.

And His pretext indeed for dismissing them was the multitude, but He was Himself minded to go up into the mountain; and He did this, instructing us neither to be always in intercourse with multitudes, nor always to fly from the crowd, but each of the two as may be expedient, and giving each duly his turn.

4. Let us learn therefore ourselves also to wait upon Jesus; but not for His bounty in things sensible, lest we be upbraided like the Jews. For "ye seek me," saith He, "not because ye saw the miracles,[5] but because ye did eat of the loaves, and were filled."[6] Therefore neither doth He work this miracle continually, but a second time only; that they might be taught not to be slaves to their belly, but to cling incessantly to the things of the Spirit.

To these then let us also cling, and let us seek the heavenly bread, and having received it, let us cast away all worldly care. For if those men left houses, and cities, and kinsmen, and all, and abode in the wilderness, and when hunger was pressing, withdrew not; much more ought we, when approaching such a table, to show forth a more abundant self-command, and to set our love on the things of the Spirit, and to seek the things of sense as secondary to these.

Since even they were blamed, not because they sought Him for the bread, but because it was for this only they sought Him, and for this primarily. For should any one despise the great gifts, but cling to the small, and to those which the giver would have him despise, He loses these latter too: as on the other hand, if we love those, He adds these also. For these are but an appendage to the others; so vile are they and trifling, compared with those, although they be great. Let us not therefore spend our diligence on them, but account both the acquisition and loss of them alike indifferent, even as Job also neither clung to them when present, nor sought them

---

[1] Kings xvii 16.   [2] John vi. 15.   [3] ἐπήγαζον.
[4] Matt. xiv. 22. [R. V., "till he should send," etc.]   [5] [R. V., "ye saw signs."]   [6] John vi. 26.

absent. For on this account, they are called χρήματα,[1] not that we should bury them in the earth, but that we should use them aright.

And as of artisans every one hath his peculiar skill, even so the rich man, as he knows not how to work in brass, nor to frame ships, nor to weave, nor to build houses, nor any such thing;—let him learn then to use his wealth aright, and to pity the poor; so shall he know a better art than all those.

For indeed this is above all those arts. Its workshop is builded in Heaven. It hath its tools not of iron and brass, but of goodness and of a right will. Of this art Christ is the Teacher, and His Father. "For be ye merciful," saith He, "as your Father which is in Heaven."[2]

And what is indeed marvellous, being so much superior to the rest, it needs no labor, no time for its perfection; it is enough to have willed, and the whole is accomplished.

But let us see also the end thereof, what it is. What then is the end of it? Heaven, the good things in the heavens, that unspeakable glory, the spiritual bride-chambers, the bright lamps, the abiding with the Bridegroom; the other things, which no speech, nor even understanding, is able to set forth.

So that herein likewise great is its difference from all others. For most of the arts profit us for the present life, but this for the life to come also.

5. But if it so far excels the arts that are necessary to us for the present, as medicine, for instance, and house-building, and all others like them: much more the rest, which if any one were nicely to examine, he would not even allow them to be arts. Wherefore I at least would not call those others, as they are unnecessary, so much as arts at all. For wherein is delicate cookery and making sauces profitable to us? Nowhere: yea, they are greatly unprofitable and hurtful, doing harm both to body and soul, by bringing upon us the parent of all diseases and sufferings, luxury, together with great extravagance.[3]

But not these only, but not even painting, or embroidery, would I for one allow to be an art, for they do but throw men into useless expense. But the arts ought to be concerned with things necessary and important to our life, to supply and work them up. For to this end God gave us skill at all, that we might invent methods, whereby to furnish out our life. But that there should be figures[4] either on walls, or on garments, wherein is it useful, I pray thee? For this same cause the sandal-makers too, and the weavers, should have great retrenchments made in their art. For most things in it they have carried into vulgar ostentation,[5] having corrupted its necessary use, and mixed with an honest art an evil craft; which has been the case with the art of building also. But even as to this, so long as it builds houses and not theatres, and labors upon things necessary, and not superfluous, I give the name of an art; so the business of weaving too, as long as it makes clothes, and coverlids, but does not imitate the spiders, and overwhelm men with much absurdity, and unspeakable effeminacy, so long I call it an art.

And the sandal-makers' trade, so long as it makes sandals, I will not rob of the appellation of art; but when it perverts men to the gestures of women, and causes them by their sandals to grow wanton and delicate, we will set it amidst the things hurtful and superfluous, and not so much as name it an art.

And I know well, that to many I seem over-minute in busying myself about these things; I shall not however refrain for this. For the cause of all our evils is this, such faults being at all counted trifling, and therefore disregarded.

And what sin, say you, can be of less account than this, of having an ornamented and glittering sandal, which fits the foot; if indeed it seem right at all to denominate it a sin?

Will ye then that I let loose my tongue upon it, and show its unseemliness, how great it is? and will ye not be angry? Or rather, though ye be angry, I care not much. Nay, for yourselves are to blame for this folly, who do not so much as think it is a sin, and hereby constrain us to enter upon the reproof of this extravagance. Come then, let us examine it, and let us see what sort of an evil it is. For when the silken threads, which it is not seemly should be even inwoven in your garments, these are sewn by you into your shoes, what reproach, what derision do these things deserve?

And if thou despise our judgments, hear the voice of Paul, with great earnestness forbidding these things, and then thou wilt perceive the absurdity of them. What then saith he? "Not with braided hair, or gold, or pearls, or costly array."[6] Of what favor then canst thou be worthy; when, in spite of Paul's prohibiting the married woman to have costly clothing, thou extendest this effeminacy even to thy shoes, and hast no end of contri-

---

[1] That is, "things for use."
[2] Luke vi. 36.   [3] φιλοτιμίας.
[4] ζωδίων. See Herod. i. 70, and Schweighæuser's note, as quoted here by Mr. Field.
[5] τὸ βάναυσον.   [6] 1 Tim. ii. 9.

vances for the sake of this ridicule and reproach? Yes: for first a ship is built, then rowers are mustered, and a man for the prow, and a helmsman, and a sail is spread, and an ocean traversed, and, leaving wife and children and country, the merchant commits his very life to the waves, and comes to the land of the barbarians, and undergoes innumerable dangers for these threads, that after it all thou mayest take them, and sew them into thy shoes, and ornament the leather. And what can be done worse than this folly?

But the old ways are not like these, but such as become men. Wherefore I for my part expect that in process of time the young men amongst us will wear even women's shoes, and not be ashamed. And what is more grievous, men's fathers seeing these things are not much displeased, but do even account it an indifferent matter.

Would ye that I should add what is still more grievous; that these things are done even when there are many poor? Would ye that I bring before you Christ, an hungered, naked, wandering everywhere, in chains? And how many thunderbolts must ye not deserve, overlooking Him in want of necessary food, and adorning these pieces of leather with so much diligence? And He indeed, when He was giving law to His disciples, would not so much as suffer them to have shoes at all, but we cannot bear to walk, I say not barefooted, but even with feet shod as they ought to be.

7. What then can be worse than this unseemliness, this absurdity? For the thing marks a soul, in the first place effeminate, then unfeeling and cruel, then curious and idly busy. For when will he be able to attend to any necessary matter, who is taken up with these superfluous things? when will such a youth endure to take heed to his soul, or to consider so much as that he hath a soul? Yes, he surely will be a trifler who cannot help admiring such things; he cruel, who for their sake neglects the poor; he void of virtue, who spends all his diligence on them.

For he that is curious about the beauty of threads, and the bloom of colors, and the tendrils made of such woven work, when will he be able to look upon the heaven? when will he admire the beauty there, who is excited about a kind of beauty that belongs to pieces of leather, and who is bending to the earth? And whereas God hath stretched out the Heaven, and lighted up the sun, drawing thy looks upwards; thou constrainest thyself to look downwards, and to the earth, like the swine, and obeyest the devil. For indeed this wicked demon hath devised this unseem-

liness, to draw thee off from that beauty. For this intent hath he drawn thee this way; and God, showing Heaven, is outvied by a devil showing certain skins, or rather not even skins (for indeed these too are God's works), but effeminacy and a bad kind of skill.

And the young man goes about bending down towards the earth, he that is required to seek wisdom concerning the things in Heaven; priding himself more on these trifles than if he had accomplished some great and good work, and walking on tiptoe in the forum, and hereby begetting to himself superfluous sorrows and distresses, lest he should stain them with the mud when it is winter; lest he should cover them with the dust, when summer is come.

What sayest thou, O man? Hast thou cast thy whole soul into the mire through this extravagance, and dost thou overlook it trailing on the ground, and art thou so anxious about a pair of shoes? Mark their use, and respect the verdict thou passest on them. For to tread on mud and mire, and all the spots on the pavement, for this were thy shoes made. Or if thou canst not bear this, take and hang them from thy neck, or put them on thy head.

And ye indeed laugh at hearing this. But I am inclined to weep for these men's madness, and their earnest care about these matters. For in truth they would rather stain their body with mud, than those pieces of leather.

Triflers then they become in this way, and fond of money again in another way. For he that has been used to be frantic and eager upon such matters, requires also for his clothes and for all other things much expense, and a large income.

And if he have a munificent father, his thraldom becomes worse, his absurd fancy more intense; but if a parsimonious one, he is driven to other unseemliness, by way of getting together a little money for such expenses.

Hence many young men have even sold their manhood, and have become parasites to the rich, and have undertaken other servile offices, purchasing thereby the fulfillment of such desires.

So then, that this man is sure to be at once fond of money, and a trifler, and about important things the most indolent of all men, and that he will be forced to commit many sins, is hereby evident. And that he is cruel and vainglorious, neither this will any one gainsay: cruel, in that when he sees a poor man, through the love of finery he makes as though he did not even see him, but while he is decking out these things with gold, overlooks him perishing of hunger; vainglorious, since even in such little matters he trains himself to hunt after the admiration of the beholders. For I suppose no general prides himself so much on his legions and trophies, as our profligate youths on the decking out of their shoes, on their trailing garments, on the dressing of their hair; yet surely all these are works of other persons, in their trades. But if men do not cease from vain boasting in the works of others, when will they cease from it in their own?

8. Shall I mention yet other things more grievous than these? or are even these enough for you? Well then; I must end my speech here; since even this have I said, because of the disputatious, who maintain the thing not to be so very wrong.

And although I know that many of the young will not so much as attend to what I have said, being once for all intoxicated with this fancy, I yet ought not therefore to keep silence. For such fathers as have understanding, and are as yet sound, will be able to force them, even against their will, to a becoming decency.

Say not then, "this is of no consequence, that is of no consequence;" for this, this hath ruined all. For even hereby ought you to train them, and by the things which seem trifling to make them grave, great of soul, superior to outward habiliments; so shall we find them approved in the great things also. For what is more ordinary than the learning of letters? nevertheless thereby do men become rhetoricians,[1] and sophists, and philosophers, and if they know not their letters, neither will they ever have that knowledge.

And this we have spoken not to young men only, but to women also, and to young damsels. For these too are liable to the like charges, and much more, inasmuch as seemliness is a thing appropriate to a virgin.

---

[1] [ῥήτορες.]

What has been said therefore to the others; do ye account to have been said to you also, that we may not repeat again the same things.

For it is full time now to close our discourse with prayer. All of you then pray with us, that the young men of the church above all things may be enabled to live orderly, and to attain an old age becoming them. Since for those surely who do not so live, it were well not to come to old age at all. But for them that have grown old even in youth, I pray that they may attain also to the very deep of gray hairs, and become fathers of approved children, and may be a joy to them that gave them birth, and above all surely to the God that made them, and may exterminate every distempered fancy, not that about their shoes, nor about their clothes only, but every other kind also.

For as untilled land, such is also youth neglected, bringing forth many thorns from many quarters. Let us then send forth on them the fire of the Spirit, and burn up these wicked desires, and let us break up our fields, and make them ready for the reception of the seed, and the young men amongst us let us exhibit with soberer minds than the old elsewhere. For this in fact is the marvellous thing, when temperance shines forth in youth; since he surely that is temperate in old age cannot have a great reward, having in perfection the security from his age. But what is wonderful, is to enjoy a calm amidst waves, and in a furnace not to be burnt, and in youth not to run wanton.

With these things then in our minds, let us emulate that blessed Joseph, who shone through all these trials, that we may attain unto the same crowns with him; unto which may we all attain, by the grace and love towards man of our Lord Jesus Christ, with whom be glory unto the Father, together with the Holy Ghost, now and always, and world without end. Amen.

HOMILY L.

MATT. XIV. 23, 24.

"And when He had sent the multitudes away, He went up into the mountain apart to pray: and when the evening was come, He was there alone. But the ship was now in the midst of the sea, tossed with waves:[1] for the wind was contrary."

For what purpose doth He go up into the mountain? To teach us, that loneliness and retirement is good, when we are to pray to God. With this view, you see, He is continually withdrawing into the wilderness, and there often spends the whole night in prayer, teaching us earnestly to seek such quietness in our prayers, as the time and place may confer. For the wilderness is the mother of quiet; it is a calm and a harbor, delivering us from all turmoils.

He Himself then went up thither with this object, but the disciples are tossed with the waves again, and undergo a storm, equal even to the former. But whereas before they had Him in the ship when this befell them, now they were alone by themselves. Thus gently and by degrees He excites and urges them on for the better, even to the bearing all nobly. Accordingly we see, that when they were first near that danger, He was present, though asleep, so as readily to give them relief; but now leading them to a greater degree of endurance, He doth not even this, but departs, and in mid sea permits the storm to arise, so that they might not so much as look for a hope of preservation from any quarter; and He lets them be tempest-tost all the night, thoroughly to awaken, as I suppose, their hardened heart.

For such is the nature of the fear, which the time concurs with the rough weather in producing. And together with the compunction, He cast them also into a greater longing for Himself, and a continual remembrance of Him.

Accordingly, neither did He present Himself to them at once. For, "in the fourth watch," so it is said, "of the night, He went unto them, walking upon the sea;"[2] instructing them not hastily to seek for deliverance from their pressing dangers, but to bear all occurrences manfully. At all events, when they looked to be delivered, then was their fear again heightened. For,

"When the disciples," it is said, "saw Him walking on the sea, they were troubled, saying, It is a spirit: and they cried out for fear."[3]

Yea, and He constantly doth so; when He is on the point of removing our terrors, He brings upon us other worse things, and more alarming: which we see took place then also. For together with the storm, the sight too troubled them, no less than the storm. Therefore neither did He remove the darkness, nor straightway make Himself manifest, training them, as I said, by the continuance of these fears, and instructing them to be ready to endure.

This He did in the case of Job also; for when He was on the point of removing the terror and the temptation, then He suffered the end to grow more grievous; I mean not for his children's death, or the words of his wife, but because of the reproaches, both of his servants and of his friends. And when He was about to rescue Jacob from his affliction in the strange land, He allowed his trouble to be awakened and aggravated; in that his father-in-law first overtook him and threatened death, and then his brother coming immediately after, suspended over him the extremest danger.

For since one cannot be tempted both for a long time and severely; when the righteous are on the point of coming to an end of their conflicts, He, willing them to gain the more, enhances their struggles. Which He did in the case of Abraham too, appointing for his last conflict that about his child. For thus even things intolerable will be tolerable, when they are so brought upon us, as to have their removal near, at the very doors.

So did Christ at that time also, and did not discover Himself before they cried out. For the more intense their alarm, the more did they welcome His coming. Afterward when they had exclaimed, it is said,

---

[1] [R. V., " distressed by the waves."]   [2] Matt. xiv. 25.

[3] Matt. xiv. 26. [R. V., " It is an apparition," but Chrysostom has the indirect form, " saying that it is an apparition." The Greek term is φάντασμα, not πνεῦμα.—R.]

"Straightway Jesus spake unto them, saying, Be of good cheer, it is I; be not afraid."[1]

This word removed their fear, and caused them to take confidence. For as they knew Him not by sight, because of His marvellous kind of motion, and because of the time, He makes Himself manifest by His voice.

2. What then saith Peter, everywhere ardent, and ever starting forward before the rest?

"Lord, if it be Thou," saith he, "bid me come unto Thee on the water."[2]

He said not, "Pray and entreat," but, "bid." Seest thou how great his ardor, how great his faith? Yet surely he is hereby often in danger, by seeking things beyond his measure. For so here too he required an exceedingly great thing, for love only, not for display. For neither did he say, "Bid me walk on the water," but what? "Bid me come unto Thee." For none so loved Jesus.

This he did also after the resurrection; he endured not to come with the others, but leapt forward.[3] And not love only, but faith also doth he display. For he not only believed that He was able Himself to walk on the sea, but that He could lead upon it others also; and he longs to be quickly near Him.

"And he said, Come. And when Peter was come down out of the ship, he walked on the water, and came[4] to Jesus. But when he saw the wind boisterous,[5] he was afraid; and beginning to sink, he cried, saying, Lord, save me. And immediately Jesus stretched forth His hand and caught him, and saith unto him, O thou of little faith, wherefore didst thou doubt?"[6]

This is more wonderful than the former. Therefore this is done after that. For when He had shown that He rules the sea, then He carries on the sign to what is yet more marvellous. Then He rebuked the winds only; but now He both walks Himself, and permits another to do so; which thing if He had required to be done at the beginning, Peter would not have so well received it, because he had not yet acquired so great faith.

Wherefore then did Christ permit him? Why, if He had said, "thou canst not," Peter being ardent would have contradicted Him again. Wherefore by the facts He convinces him, that for the future he may be sobered.

But not even so doth he endure. Therefore having come down, he becomes dizzy;

for he was afraid. And this the surf caused, but his fear was wrought by the wind.

But John saith, that "they willingly received Him into the ship; and immediately the ship was at the land whither they went,"[7] relating this same circumstance. So that when they were on the point of arriving at the land, He entered the ship.

Peter then having come down from the ship went unto Him, not rejoicing so much in walking on the water, as in coming unto Him. And when he had prevailed over the greater, he was on the point of suffering evil from the less, from the violence of the wind, I mean, not of the sea. For such a thing is human nature; not seldom effecting great things, it exposes itself in the less; as Elias felt toward Jezebel, as Moses toward the Egyptian, as David toward Bathsheba. Even so then this man also; while their fear was yet at the height, he took courage to walk upon the water, but against the assault of the wind he was no longer able to stand; and this, being near Christ. So absolutely nothing doth it avail to be near Christ, not being near Him by faith.

And this also showed the difference between the Master and the disciple, and allayed the feelings of the others. For if in the case of the two brethren they had indignation, much more here; for they had not yet the Spirit vouchsafed unto them.

But afterwards they were not like this. On every occasion, for example, they give up the first honors to Peter, and put him forward in their addresses to the people, although of a rougher vein than any of them.[8]

And wherefore did He not command the winds to cease, but Himself stretched forth His hand and took hold of him? Because in him faith was required. For when our part is wanting, then God's part also is at a stand.

Signifying therefore that not the assault of the wind, but his want of faith had wrought his overthrow, He saith, "Wherefore didst thou doubt, O thou of little faith?" So that if his faith had not been weak, he would have stood easily against the wind also. And for this reason, you see, even when He had caught hold of Him, He suffers the wind to blow, showing that no hurt comes thereby, when faith is steadfast.

And as when a nestling has come out of the nest before the time, and is on the point of falling, its mother bears it on her wings, and brings it back to the nest; even so did Christ.

[1] Mat. xiv. 27.   [2] Matt. xiv. 28.   [3] John xxi. 7.
[4] [So R. V. margin. The rec. text has ἐλθεῖν.—R.]
[5] [R. V. text, with a few of the oldest authorities, omits "boisterous," ἰσχυρόν, which Chrysostom accepts.—R.]
[6] Matt. xiv. 29-31.
[7] John vi. 21. [R.V., "They were willing to receive him into the boat: and straightway the boat was at the land whither they were going."]
[8] Compare Acts iv. 13.

"And when they were come into the ship, then the wind ceased."[1]

Whereas before this they had said, "What manner of man is this, that even the winds and the sea obey Him!"[2] now it is not so. For "they that were in the ship," it is said, "came and worshipped Him, saying, Of a truth Thou art Son of God."[3] Seest thou, how by degrees he was leading them all higher and higher? For both by His walking on the sea, and by His commanding another to do so, and preserving him in jeopardy; their faith was henceforth great. For then indeed He rebuked the sea, but now He rebukes it not, in another way signifying His power more abundantly. Wherefore also they said, "Of a truth Thou art Son of God."

What then? Did He rebuke them on their so speaking? Nay, quite the contrary, He rather confirmed what they said, with greater authority healing such as approached Him, and not as before.

"And when they were gone over," so it is said, "they came into the land of Gennesaret. And when the men of that place had knowledge of Him, they sent out into all that country round about, and brought unto Him all that were diseased; and besought Him that they might touch the hem of His garment; and as many as touched were made perfectly whole."[4]

For neither did they approach Him as before, dragging Him into their houses, and seeking a touch of His hand, and directions from Him in words; but in a far higher strain, and with more of self-denial, and with a more abundant faith did they try to win themselves a cure; for she that had the issue of blood taught them all to be severe in seeking wisdom.

And the evangelist, implying also that at long intervals He visited the several neighborhoods, saith, "The men of that place took knowledge of Him, and sent out into the country round about, and brought unto Him them that were diseased." But yet the interval, so far from abolishing their faith, made it even greater, and preserved it in vigor.

3. Let us also then touch the hem of His garment, or rather, if we be willing, we have Him entire. For indeed His body is set before us now, not His garment only, but even His body; not for us to touch it only, but also to eat, and be filled. Let us now then draw near with faith, every one that hath an infirmity. For if they that touched the hem

of His garment drew from Him so much virtue, how much more they that possess Him entire? Now to draw near with faith is not only to receive the offering, but also with a pure heart to touch it; to be so minded, as approaching Christ Himself. For what, if thou hear no voice? Yet thou seest Him laid out; or rather thou dost also hear His voice, while He is speaking by the evangelists.

Believe, therefore, that even now it is that supper, at which He Himself sat down. For this is in no respect different from that. For neither doth man make this and Himself the other; but both this and that is His own work. When therefore thou seest the priest delivering it unto thee, account not that it is the priest that doeth so, but that it is Christ's hand that is stretched out.

Even as when he baptizes, not he doth baptize thee, but it is God that possesses thy head with invisible power, and neither angel nor archangel nor any other dare draw nigh and touch thee; even so now also. For when God begets, the gift is His only. Seest thou not those who adopt to themselves sons here, how they commit not the act to slaves, but are themselves present at the judgment-seat? Even so neither hath God committed His gift to angels, but Himself is present, commanding and saying, "Call no man Father on earth;"[5] not that thou shouldest dishonor them that gave thee birth, but that thou shouldest prefer to all those Him that made thee, and enrolled thee amongst His own children. For He that hath given the greater, that is, hath set Himself before thee, much more will He not think scorn to distribute unto thee of His body. Let us hear therefore, both priests and subjects, what we have had vouchsafed to us; let us hear and tremble. Of His own holy flesh He hath granted us our fill; He hath set before us Himself sacrificed.

What excuse shall we have then, when feeding on such food, we commit such sins? when eating a lamb, we become wolves? when feeding on a sheep, we spoil by violence like the lions?

For this mystery He directs to be always clear, not from violence only, but even from bare enmity. Yea, for this mystery is a mystery of peace; it allows us not to cling to wealth. For if He spared not Himself for us, what must we deserve, sparing our wealth, and being lavish of a soul, in behalf of which He spared not Himself?

Now upon the Jews God every year bound

---

[1] Matt. xiv. 32.   [2] Matt. viii. 27.   [3] Matt. xiv. 33.
[4] Matt. xiv. 34-36. [In verse 34, R. V., following a different reading, as: "to the land, unto Gennesaret." In verse 36, Chrysostom omits "only," and reads ἐσώθησαν for διεσώθησαν.—R.]

[5] Matt. xxiii. 9.

in their feasts a memorial of His peculiar favors to them: but for thee, every day, as I may say, through these mysteries.

Be not therefore ashamed of the cross: for these are our venerable things, these our mysteries; with this gift do we adorn ourselves, with this we are beautified.

And if I say, He stretched out the heaven, He spread out the earth and the sea, He sent prophets and angels, I say nothing in comparison. For the sum of His benefits is this, that "He spared not His own Son,"[1] in order to save His alienated servants.

4. Let no Judas then approach this table, no Simon; nay, for both these perished through covetousness. Let us flee then from this gulf; neither let us account it enough for our salvation, if after we have stripped widows and orphans, we offer for this table a gold and jewelled cup. Nay, if thou desire to honor the sacrifice, offer thy soul, for which also it was slain; cause that to become golden; but if that remain worse than lead or potter's clay, while the vessel is of gold, what is the profit?

Let not this therefore be our aim, to offer golden vessels only, but to do so from honest earnings likewise. For these are of the sort that is more precious even than gold, these that are without injuriousness. For the church is not a gold foundry nor a workshop for silver, but an assembly of angels. Wherefore it is souls which we require, since in fact God accepts these for the souls' sake.

That table at that time was not of silver, nor that cup of gold, out of which Christ gave His disciples His own blood; but precious was everything there, and awful, for that they were full of the Spirit.[2]

Wouldest thou do honor to Christ's body? Neglect Him not when naked; do not, while here thou honorest Him with silken garments, neglect Him perishing without of cold and nakedness. For He that said, "This is my body," and by His word confirmed the fact, "This same said, "Ye saw me an hungered, and fed me not;" and, "Inasmuch as ye did it not to one of the least of these, ye did it not to me."[3] For This indeed needs not coverings, but a pure soul; but that requires much attention.

Let us learn therefore to be strict in life, and to honor Christ as He Himself desires. For to Him who is honored that honor is most pleasing, which it is His own will to have, not that which we account best. Since Peter too thought to honor Him by forbidding Him to wash his feet, but his doing so was not an honor, but the contrary.

Even so do thou honor Him with this honor, which He ordained, spending thy wealth on poor people. Since God hath no need at all of golden vessels, but of golden souls.

And these things I say, not forbidding such offerings to be provided; but requiring you, together with them, and before them, to give alms. For He accepts indeed the former, but much more the latter. For in the one the offerer alone is profited, but in the other the receiver also. Here the act seems to be a ground even of ostentation; but there all is mercifulness, and love to man.

For what is the profit, when His table indeed is full of golden cups, but He perishes with hunger? First fill Him, being an hungered, and then abundantly deck out His table also. Dost thou make Him a cup of gold, while thou givest Him not a cup of cold water? And what is the profit? Dost thou furnish His table with cloths bespangled with gold, while to Himself thou affordest not even the necessary covering? And what good comes of it? For tell me, should you see one at a loss for necessary food, and omit appeasing his hunger, while you first overlaid his table with silver; would he indeed thank thee, and not rather be indignant? What, again, if seeing one wrapped in rags, and stiff with cold, thou shouldest neglect giving him a garment, and build golden columns, saying, "thou wert doing it to his honor," would he not say that thou wert mocking, and account it an insult, and that the most extreme?

Let this then be thy thought with regard to Christ also, when He is going about a wanderer, and a stranger, needing a roof to cover Him; and thou, neglecting to receive Him, deckest out a pavement, and walls, and capitals of columns, and hangest up silver chains by means of lamps,[4] but Himself bound in prison thou wilt not even look upon.

5. And these things I say, not forbidding munificence in these matters, but admonishing you to do those other works together with these, or rather even before these. Because for not having done these no one was ever blamed, but for those, hell is threatened, and unquenchable fire, and the punishment with evil spirits. Do not therefore while adorning His house overlook thy brother in distress, for he is more properly a temple than the other.

---

[1] Rom. viii. 32.   [2] Comp. Eph. v. 18.   [3] Matt. xxv. 42, 45.

[4] St. Jerome (ad Eustoch. Ep. 108 sec. 30) says, "Let others boast of their money, and coin cast into the treasury of God, *Funalibusque aureis dona pendentia*, 'and of their gifts hanging upon golden sconces,' or perhaps brackets for lamps, on which the Anathemata, or votive offerings, were suspended." See Bingh. 8, 8, 1.

And whereas these thy stores will be subject to alienation, both by unbelieving kings, and tyrants, and robbers; whatever thou mayest do for thy brother, being hungry, and a stranger, and naked, not even the devil will be able to despoil, but it will be laid up in an inviolable treasure.

Why then doth He Himself say, "The poor always ye have with you, but me ye have not always?"[1] Why, for this reason most of all should we give alms, that we have Him not always an hungered, but in the present life only. But if thou art desirous to learn also the whole meaning of the saying, understand that this was said not with a view to His disciples, although it seem so, but to the woman's weakness. That is, her disposition being still rather imperfect, and they doubting about her; to revive her He said these things. For in proof that for her comfort He said it, He added, "Why trouble ye the woman?"[2] And with regard to our having Him really always with us, He saith, "Lo, I am with you alway, even unto the end of the world."[3] From all which it is

evident, that for no other object was this said, but that the rebuke of the disciples might not wither the faith of the woman, just then budding.

Let us not then bring forward these things now, which were uttered because of some economy, but let us read all the laws, those in the New and those in the Old Testament, that are set down about almsgiving, and let us be very earnest about this matter. For this cleanses from sin. For "give alms, and all things will be clean unto you."[4] This is a greater thing than sacrifice. "For I will have mercy, and not sacrifice."[5] This opens the heavens. For "thy prayers and thine alms are come up for a memorial before God."[6] This is more indispensable than virginity: for thus were those virgins cast out of the bridechamber; thus were the others brought in.

All which things let us consider, and sow liberally, that we may reap in more ample abundance, and attain unto the good things to come, by the grace and love towards man of our Lord Jesus Christ, to whom be glory forever. Amen.

---

[1] Matt. xxvi. 11; John xii. 8.
[3] Matt. xxviii. 2.
[2] Matt. xxvi. 10.
[4] Luke xi. 41.
[6] Acts x. 4.
[5] Hosea vi. 6; Matt. ix. 18.

HOMILY LI.

Matt. XV. 1.

"Then came to Jesus Scribes and Pharisees, which were of Jerusalem, saying, Why do Thy disciples," etc.[1]

Then; when? when He had wrought His countless miracles; when He had healed the infirm by the touch of the hem of His garment. For even with this intent doth the evangelist mark the time, that He might signify their unspeakable wickedness, by nothing repressed.

But what means, "The Scribes and Pharisees, which were of Jerusalem?"[2] In every one of the tribes were they scattered abroad,

and divided into twelve parts; but they who occupied the chief city were worse than the others, as both enjoying more honor, and having contracted much haughtiness.

But mark, I pray thee, how even by the question itself they are convicted; in not saying, "Why do they transgress the law of Moses," but, "the tradition of the elders." Whence it is evident that the priests were inventing many novelties, although Moses, with much terror and with much threatening, had enjoined neither to add nor take away. "For ye shall not add," saith he, "unto the word which I command you this day, and ye shall not take away from it."[3]

---

[1] In the Oxford edition verses 1-6 are printed here in full from the A. V. But in the Greek text of the Homily only the first part of ver. 1 appears. As the larger part of the other verses is given below, and as several questions of text and interpretation arise, the passage has been printed here to correspond with the Greek.—R.]
[2] [R. V., "from Jerusalem Pharisees and Scribes." But Chrysostom's text is as above, agreeing with the received. The omission of the article affects the sense, as indicated in the R. V.—R.]
[3] Deut. iv. 2.

But not the less were they innovating; as in this instance, that one ought not to eat with unwashen hands, that we must wash cups and brazen vessels, that we must wash also ourselves. Thus, when men were henceforth, as time advanced, to be freed from their observances, at that very time they bound them with the same in more and more instances, fearing lest any one should take away their power, and wishing to strike more dread, as though they were themselves also lawgivers. The thing in fact proceeded so far in enormity, that while their own commandments were kept, those of God were transgressed; and they so far prevailed, that the matter had actually become a ground of accusation. Which was a twofold charge against them, in that they both invented novelties, and were so strict exactors on their own account, while of God they made no reckoning.

And omitting to speak of the other things, the pots and the brazen vessels (for it was too ridiculous), what seemed more reasonable than the rest, that they bring forward, wishing, as seems at least to me, in that way to provoke Him to anger. Wherefore also they made mention of the elders, in order that He, as setting them at nought, might give occasion against Himself.

But it were meet first to inquire, why the disciples ate with unwashen hands. Wherefore then did they so eat? Not as making a point of it, but as overlooking henceforth the things that are superfluous, and attending to such as are necessary; having no law to wash or not to wash, but doing either as it happened. For they that despised even their own necessary food, how were they to hold these things worth much consideration? This then having often happened unintentionally,—for instance, when they ate in the wilderness, when they plucked the ears of corn,—is now put forward as a charge by these persons, who are always transgressing in the great things, and making much account of the superfluous.

2. What then saith Christ? He did not set Himself against it, neither made He any defense, but straightway blames them again, plucking down their confidence, and signifying that he who commits great sins ought not to be strict with others concerning small matters. "What? when you ought to be blamed," saith He, "do ye even blame?"

But do thou observe, how when it is His will to set aside any of the things enjoined by the law, He does it in the form of an apology; and so He did in that case. For by no means doth He proceed at once to transgress it, nor doth He say, "It is nothing;" for surely He would have made them more audacious; but first He clean cuts away their boldness, bringing forward the far heavier charge, and directing it upon their head. And He neither saith, "they do well in transgressing it," lest He should give them a hold on Him; nor doth He speak ill of their proceeding, lest He should confirm the law: nor again, on the other hand, doth He blame the elders, as lawless and unholy men; for doubtless they would have shunned Him as a reviler and injurious: but all these things He gives up, and proceeds another way. And He seems indeed to be rebuking the persons themselves who had come to Him, but He is reprehending them that enacted these laws; nowhere indeed making mention of the elders, but by His charge against the Scribes casting down them also, and signifying that their sin is twofold, first in disobeying God, next in doing so on men's account; as though He had said, "Why, this hath ruined you, your obeying the elders in all things."

Yet He saith not so, but this is just what He intimates, by answering them as follows:

"Why do ye also transgress the commandment of God by[1] your tradition? For God commanded, saying, Honor thy father and thy mother: and, He that curseth father or mother, let him die the death. But ye say, Whosoever shall say to his father or his mother, It is a gift, by whatsoever thou mightest be profited by me, and[2] honor not his father or his mother[3]—. And ye have made void the commandment[4] of God by your tradition. [5]

And He said not, "the elders' tradition," but "your own." And, "ye say;" again He said not, "the elders say:" in order to make His speech less galling. That is, because they wanted to prove the disciples transgressors of the law, He signifies that they themselves are doing so, but that these are free from blame. For of course that is not a law, which is enjoined by men (wherefore also He calls it "a tradition"), and especially by men that are transgressors of the law.

And since this had no shade of contrariety to the law, to command men to wash their hands, He brings forward another tradition, which is opposed to the law. And what He

---

[1] [R. V., "because of."]
[2] [Chrysostom reads καί, with the rec. text, thus making the sentence break off. The A. V. supplies "he shall be free." R. V., omitting "and," with the best authorities, makes this clause the conclusion: "he shall not honor," etc.—R.]
[3] [R. V. text omits "and his mother."]
[4] [So rec. text, but R. V. reads "word" in the text, with "law" in the margin.—R.]
[5] Matt. xv. 3-6. [R. V., "because of your tradition."]

saith is like this. "They taught the young, under the garb of piety, to despise their fathers." How, and in what way? "If one of their parents said to his child, Give me this sheep that thou hast, or this calf, or any such thing, they used to say, 'This is a gift to God, whereby thou wouldest be profited by me, and thou canst not have it.' And two evils hence arose: on the one hand they did not bring them to God, on the other they defrauded their parents under the name of the offering, alike insulting their parents for God's sake, and God for their parents' sake." But He doth not say this at once, but first rehearses the law, by which He signifies His earnest desire that parents should be honored. For, "honor," saith He, "thy father and thy mother, that thou mayest live long upon the earth."[1] And again, "He that curseth father or mother, let him die the death."[2]

But He, omitting the first, the reward appointed for them that honor their parents, states that which is more awful, the punishment, I mean, threatened to such as dishonor them; desiring both to dismay them, and to conciliate such as have understanding; and He implies them to be for this worthy of death. For if he who dishonors them in word is punished, much more ye, who do so in deed, and who not only dishonor, but also teach it to others. "Ye then who ought not so much as to live, how find ye fault with the disciples?"

"And what wonder is it, if ye offer such insults to me, who am as yet unknown, when even to the Father ye are found doing the like?" For everywhere He both asserts and implies, that from Him they began with this their arrogance.

But some do also otherwise interpret, "It is a gift, by whatsoever thou mightest be profited by me;" that is, I owe thee no honor, but it is a free gift from me to thee, if indeed I do honor thee. But Christ would not have mentioned an insult of that sort. And Mark again makes this plainer, by saying, "It is Corban, by whatsoever thou mightest be profited by me;"[3] which means, not a gift and present, but properly an offering.

Having then signified that they who were trampling on the law could not be justly entitled to blame men for transgressing a command of certain elders, He points out this same thing again from the prophet likewise. Thus, having once laid hold of them severely, He proceeds further: as on every occasion He doth, bringing forward the Scriptures, and

so evincing Himself to be in accordance with God.

And what saith the prophet? "This people honoreth me with their lips, but their heart is far from me. But in vain do they worship me, teaching for doctrines the commandments of men."[4]

Seest thou a prophecy in exact accordance with His sayings, and from the very first proclaiming beforehand their wickedness? For what Christ laid to their charge now, of this Isaiah also spake from the very first; that the words of God they despise, "for in vain do they worship me," saith He; but of their own they make much account, "teaching," saith He, "for doctrines the commandments of men." Therefore with reason the disciples keep them not.

3. Having, you see, given them their mortal blow; and from the facts first, then from their own suffrage, then from the prophet having aggravated the charge, with them indeed He discourses not at all, incorrigibly disposed as they are now come to be, but directs His speech to the multitudes, so as to introduce His doctrine, great and high, and full of much strictness; and taking occasion from the former topic, He proceeds to insert that which is greater, casting out also the observance of meats.

But see when. When He had cleansed the leper, when He had repealed the Sabbath, when He had shown Himself King of earth and sea, when He had made laws, when He had remitted sins, when He had raised dead men, when He had afforded them many proofs of His Godhead, then He discourses of meats.

For indeed all the religion of the Jews is comprised in this; if thou take this away, thou hast even taken away all. For hereby He signifies, that circumcision too must be abrogated. But of Himself He doth not prominently introduce this (forasmuch as that was older than the other commandments, and had higher estimation), but He enacts it by His disciples. For so great a thing was it, that even the disciples after so long a time being minded to do it away, first practise it, and so put it down.[5]

But see how He introduces His law: how "He called the multitude, and said unto them, Hear and understand."[6]

Thus He doth by no means simply reveal it to them, but by respect and courtesy, first, He makes His saying acceptable (for this the evangelist declares by saying, "He called

---

[1] Exod. xx. 12. See also Ephes. vi. 1, 2.
[2] Exod. xxi. 17. [3] Mark vii. 11.

[4] Matt. xv. 8, 9. See Is. xxix. 13. [R. V., "teaching *as their* doctrines the precepts of men."]
[5] Acts xvi. 3. [6] Matt. xv. 11.

them unto Him"): and secondly, by the time also; in that after their refutation, and His victory over them, and the accusation by the prophet, then He begins His legislation, when they too would more easily receive His sayings.

And He doth not merely call them unto Him, but also makes them more attentive. For "understand," saith He, that is, "consider, rouse yourselves; for of that sort is the law now about to be enacted. For if they set aside the law, even unseasonably, for their own tradition, and ye hearkened; much more ought ye to hearken unto me, who at the proper season am leading you unto a higher rule of self restraint."

And He did not say, "The observance of meats is nothing, neither that Moses had given wrong injunctions, nor that of condescension He did so;" but in the way of admonition and counsel, and taking His testimony from the nature of the things, He saith: "Not the things that go into the mouth, defile the man, but the things that go out of the mouth;"¹ resorting to nature herself both in His enactment and in His demonstration. Yet they hearing all this, made no reply, neither did they say, "What sayest Thou? When God hath given charges without number concerning the observance of meats, dost thou make such laws?" But since He had utterly stopped their mouths, not by refuting them only, but also by publishing their craft, and exposing what was done by them in secret, and revealing the secrets of their mind; their mouths were stopped, and so they went away.

But mark, I pray thee, how He doth not yet venture distinctly to set Himself with boldness against the meats. Therefore neither did He say "the meats," but, "the things that enter in defile not the man;" which it was natural for them to suspect concerning the unwashen hands also. For He indeed was speaking of meats, but it would be understood of these matters too.

Why, so strong was the feeling of scruple about the meats, that even after the resurrection Peter said, "Not so, Lord, for I have never eaten anything common or unclean."² For although it was for the sake of others that He said this, and in order to leave Himself a justification against his censurers, by pointing out that he actually remonstrated, and not even so was excused, nevertheless it implies the depth of their impression on that point.

Wherefore you see He Himself also at the beginning spake not openly concerning meats, but, "The things that go into the mouth;" and again, when He had seemed afterwards to speak more plainly, He veiled it by His conclusion, saying, "But to eat with unwashen hands defileth not the man:"³ that He might seem to have had His occasion from thence, and to be still discoursing of the same. Therefore He said not, "To eat meats defileth not a man," but is as though He were speaking on that other topic; that they may have nothing to say against it.

4. When therefore they had heard these things, "the Pharisees," it is said, "were offended,"⁴ not the multitudes. For "His disciples," so it is said, "came and said unto Him, Knowest thou that the Pharisees were offended, when they heard the saying?" Yet surely nothing had been said unto them.

What then saith Christ? He did not remove the offense in respect of them, but reproved them, saying, "Every plant which my heavenly Father hath not planted, shall be rooted up."⁵ For He is wont both to despise offenses, and not to despise them. Elsewhere, for example, He saith, "But lest we should offend them, cast an hook into the sea:"⁶ but here He saith, "Let them alone, they be blind leaders of the blind: and if the blind lead the blind, both shall fall into the ditch."⁷

But these things His disciples said, not as grieving for those men only, but as being themselves also slightly perplexed. But because they durst not say so in their own person, they would fain learn it by their telling Him of others. And as to its being so, hear how after this the ardent and ever-forward Peter came to Him, and saith, "Declare unto us this parable,"⁸ discovering the trouble in his soul, and not indeed venturing to say openly, "I am offended," but requiring that by His interpretation he should be freed from his perplexity; wherefore also he was reproved.

What then saith Christ? "Every plant which my heavenly Father hath not planted, shall be rooted up."

This, they that are diseased with the Manichæan pest affirm to be spoken of the law; but their mouths are stopped by what had been said before. For if He was speaking of the law, how doth He further back defend it, and fight for it, saying, "Why do ye transgress the commandments of God for your tradition?" And how doth He bring for-

---

¹ Matt. xv. 11.　　² Acts x. 14.

³ Matt. xv. 20.　　⁴ Matt. xv. 12.
⁵ Matt. xv. 13.　　⁶ Matt. xvii. 27.
⁷ Matt. xv. 14. [So rec. text. The R. V. follows a briefer reading, but properly substitutes "a pit" for "the ditch."—R.]
⁸ Matt. xv. 15.

ward the prophet? But of themselves and of their traditions He so speaks. For if God said, "Honor thy father and thy mother," how is not that of God's planting, which was spoken by God?

And what follows also indicates, that of themselves it was said, and of their traditions. Thus He added, "They are blind leaders of the blind." Whereas, had He spoken it of the law, He would have said, "It is a blind leader of the blind." But not so did He speak, but, "They are blind leaders of the blind:" freeing it from the blame, and bringing it all round upon them.

Then to sever the people also from them, as being on the point of falling into a pit by their means, He saith, "If the blind lead the blind, both shall fall into the ditch."

It is a great evil merely to be blind, but to be in such a case and have none to lead him, nay, to occupy the place of a guide, is a double and triple ground of censure. For if it be a dangerous thing for the blind man not to have a guide, much more so that he should even desire to be guide to another.

What then saith Peter? He saith not, "What can this be which Thou hast said?" but as though it were full of obscurity, he puts his question. And he saith not, "Why hast thou spoken contrary to the law?" for he was afraid, lest he should be thought to have taken offense, but asserts it to be obscure. However, that it was not obscure, but that he was offended, is manifest, for it had nothing of obscurity.

Wherefore also He rebukes him, saying, "Are ye also yet without understanding?"[1] For as to the multitude, they did not perhaps so much as understand the saying; but themselves were the persons offended. Wherefore, whereas at first, as though asking in behalf of the Pharisees, they were desirous to be told; when they heard Him denouncing a great threat, and saying, "Every plant, which my heavenly Father hath not planted, shall be rooted up," and, "They are blind leaders of the blind," they were silenced. But he, always ardent, not even so endures to hold his peace, but saith, "Declare unto us this parable."[2]

What then saith Christ? With a sharp rebuke He answers, "Are ye also yet without understanding? Do ye not yet understand?"

But these things He said, and reproved them, in order to cast out their prejudice; He stopped not however at this, but adds other things also, saying,

"That whatsoever entereth in at the mouth goeth into the belly, and is cast out into the draught; but those things which proceed out of the mouth come forth from the heart, and they defile the man. For out of the heart proceed evil thoughts, murders, adulteries, fornications, thefts, blasphemies, false-witnessings: and these are the things that defile the man: but to eat with unwashen hands defileth not the man."[3]

Seest thou how sharply He deals with them, and in the way of rebuke?

Then He establishes His saying by our common nature, and with a view to their cure. For when He saith, "It goeth into the belly, and is cast out into the draught," he is still answering according to the low views of the Jews. For He saith, "it abides not, but goes out:" and what if it abode? it would not make one unclean. But not yet were they able to hear this.

And one may remark, that because of this the lawgiver allows just so much time, as it may be remaining within one, but when it is gone forth, no longer. For instance, at evening He bids you wash yourself, and so be clean; measuring the time of the digestion, and of the excretion.[4] But the things of the heart, He saith, abide within, and when they are gone forth they defile, and not when abiding only. And first He puts our evil thoughts, a kind of thing which belonged to the Jews; and not as yet doth He make His refutation from the nature of the things, but from the manner of production from the belly and the heart respectively, and from the fact that the one sort remains, the other not; the one entering in from without, and departing again outwards, while the others are bred[5] within, and having gone forth they defile, and then more so, when they are gone forth. Because they were not yet able, as I said, to be taught these things with all due strictness.

But Mark saith, that "cleansing the meats,"[6] He spake this. He did not however express it, nor at all say, "but to eat such and such meats defileth not the man," for neither could they endure to be told it by Him thus distinctly. And accordingly

---

3 Matt. xv. 17–20.   4 Lev. xi. 24, 25.
5 [τίκτεται; the Oxford edition has "bad," which is probably a misprint for "bred."—R.]
6 Mark vii. 19. Origen in his commentary on this passage of St. Matthew, refers also to St. Mark, where he reads as St. Chrysostom here, καθαρίζων instead of καθαρίζον. The word "cleansing" or "purging" is therefore referred to our Lord, and our Saviour's words will stand as a parenthesis. See Field *in loc.* [The translator doubtless means that this view makes our Lord's own words a parenthetical explanation of the evangelist. So the R. V. gives the clause. That καθαρίζων is the correct reading is quite certain, but German commentators refer it to ἀφεδρῶνα, accepting a change of construction. The evangelist Mark rarely inserts explanations. The citation from Origen will be found in Tischendorf, VIII., note on Mark vii. 19. Despite the authority of Origen and Chrysostom, the rendering of the R. V. is of doubtful propriety.—R.]

---

1 Matt. xv. 16.   2 Matt. xv. 15.

His conclusion was, "But to eat with un-washen hands defileth not the man."[1]

5. Let us learn then what are the things that defile the man; let us learn, and let us flee them. For even in the church we see such a custom prevailing amongst the generality, and men giving diligence to come in clean garments, and to have their hands washed; but how to present a clean soul to God, they make no account.

And this I say, not forbidding them to wash hands or mouth; but willing men so to wash as is meet, not with water only, but in-stead of water, with all virtues. For the filth of the mouth is evil speaking, blasphemy, reviling, angry words, filthy talking, laughter, jesting: if then thou art conscious to thyself of uttering none of them, neither of being defiled with this filth, draw near with confi-dence; but if thou hast times out of number received these stains, why dost thou labor in vain, washing thy tongue indeed with water, but bearing about on it such deadly and hurt-ful filth? For tell me, hadst thou dung on thy hands, and mire, wouldest thou indeed venture to pray? By no means. And yet this were no hurt; but that is ruin. How then art thou reverential in the different things, but in the forbidden remiss?

What then? should not we pray? saith one. We should indeed, but not while de-filed, and having upon us mire of that sort.

"What then, if I have been overtaken?" saith one. Cleanse thyself. "How, and in what way?" Weep, groan, give alms, apol-ogize to him that is affronted, reconcile him to thyself hereby, wipe clean thy tongue, lest thou provoke God more grievously. For so if one had filled his hands with dung, and then should lay hold of thy feet, entreating thee, far from hearing him, thou wouldest rather spurn him with thy foot; how then durst thou in such sort draw nigh to God? Since in truth the tongue is the hand of them that pray, and by it we lay hold on the knees of God. Defile it not therefore, lest to thee also He say, "Though ye make many prayers, I will not hearken."[2] Yea, and "in the power of the tongue are death and life;"[3] and, "By thy words thou shalt be justified, and by thy words thou shalt be condemned."[4]

I bid thee then watch thy tongue more than the apple of thine eye. The tongue is a royal steed. If then thou put a bridle on it, and teach it to pace orderly, the King will rest and take His seat thereon; but if thou suffer it to rush about unbridled and leap wantonly, it becomes a beast for the devil and bad spirits to ride on. And while thou, fresh from the company of thine own wife, darest not pray, although this is no blame at all; dost thou lift up thine hands, fresh from re-viling and insult, which brings after it no less than hell, before thou hast well cleansed thy-self? And how dost thou not shudder? tell me. Hast thou not heard Paul, saying, "Marriage is honorable, and the bed unde-filed?"[5] But if on rising from the undefiled bed, thou darest not draw nigh in prayer, how dost thou coming from the bed of the devil call on that awful and terrible name? For it is truly the devil's bed, to wallow in insults and reviling. And like some wicked adulterer, wrath dallies with us in great delight, casting into us deadly seed, and making us give birth to diabolical enmity, and doing all things in a way opposite to marriage. For whereas marriage causes the two to be-come one flesh, wrath severs into many parts them that were united, and cleaves and cuts in pieces the very soul.

That thou mayest therefore with confidence draw nigh to God, receive not wrath, when it comes in upon thee, and desires to be with thee, but drive it away like a mad dog.

For so Paul too commanded: his phrase being, "lifting up holy hands without wrath and disputing."[6] Dishonor not then thy tongue, for how will it entreat for thee, when it hath lost its proper confidence? but adorn it with gentleness, with humility, make it worthy of the God who is entreated, fill it with blessing, with much almsdoing. For it is possible even with words to do alms. "For a word is a better thing than a gift,"[7] and "answer the poor man peaceably with meek-ness."[8] And all the rest of thy time too adorn it with the rehearsing of the laws of God; "Yea, let all thy communication be in the law of the Most High."[9]

Having thus adorned ourselves, let us come to our King, and fall at His knees,[10] not with the body only, but also with the mind. Let us consider whom we are approaching, and on whose behalf, and what we would accom-plish. We are drawing nigh unto God, whom the seraphim behold and turn away their faces, not bearing His brightness; at sight of whom the earth trembles. We draw nigh unto God, "who dwelleth in the light, which no man can approach unto."[11] And we draw nigh unto Him for deliverance from hell, for remission of sins, for escape from those in-

---

[1] Matt. xv. 20.   [2] Is. i. 15.
[3] Prov. xviii. 21.   [4] Matt. xii. 37.

[5] Heb. xiii. 4.   [6] 1 Tim. ii. 8.   [7] Ecclus. xviii. 16.
[8] Ecclus. iv. 8.   [9] Ecclus. ix. 15.
[10] [πίπτωμεν ἐπὶ γόνατα, "fall on our knees" seems to be the more probable sense, as the context indicates. Compare the last sentence in the paragraph.—R.]
[11] 1 Tim. vi. 16.

tolerable punishments, for attaining to the Heavens, and to the good things that are there. Let us, I say, fall down before Him both in body and in mind, that He may raise us up when we are down; let us converse with all gentleness and meekness.

And who is so wretched and miserable, one may say, as not to become gentle in prayer? He that prays with an imprecation, and fills himself with wrath, and cries out against his enemies.

6. Nay, if thou wilt accuse, accuse thyself. If thou wilt whet and sharpen thy tongue, let it be against thine own sins. And tell not what evil another hath done to thee, but what thou hast done to thyself; for this is most truly an evil; since no other will really be able to injure thee, unless thou injure thyself. Wherefore, if thou desire to be against them that wrong thee, approach as against thyself first; there is no one to hinder; since by coming into court against another, thou hast but the greater injury to go away with.

And what injury at all hast thou really to mention? That such an one insulted and spoiled thee by violence, and encompassed thee with dangers? Nay, this is receiving not injury, but if we be sober, the very greatest benefit; the injured being he that did such things, not he that suffered them. And this is more than any one thing the cause of all our evils, that we do not so much as know at all who is the injured, and who the injurious person. Since if we knew this well, we should not ever injure ourselves, we should not pray against another, having learnt that it is impossible to suffer ill of another. For not to be spoiled, but to spoil, is an evil. Wherefore, if thou hast spoiled, accuse thyself; but if thou hast been spoiled, rather pray for him that spoiled thee, because he hath done thee the greatest good. For although the intent of the doer was not such, yet thou hast received the greatest benefit, if thou hast endured it nobly. For him, both men, and the laws of God declare to be wretched, but thee, the injured party, they crown, and proclaim thy praise.

For so if any one sick of a fever had violently taken from any other a vessel containing water, and had had his fill of his pernicious desire, we should not say that the despoiled had been injured, but the spoiler; for he has aggravated his fever, and made his disease more grievous. Now in this way I bid thee reason concerning him also that loves wealth and money. For he too, having a far worse fever than the other, has by this rapine fanned the flame in himself.

Again, were some madman to snatch a sword from any one, and destroy himself, which again is the injured? He that hath been robbed, or the robber? It is quite clear, he that did the robbery.

Well then, in the case of seizing property also, let us give the same suffrage. For what a sword is to a madman, much the same is wealth to a covetous man; nay, it is even a worse thing. For the madman, when he has taken the sword, and thrust it through himself, is both delivered from his madness, and hath no second blow to receive; but the lover of money receives daily ten thousand wounds more grievous than his, without delivering himself from his madness, but aggravating it more exceedingly: and the more wounds he receives, the more doth he give occasion for other more grievous blows.

Reflecting then on these things, let us flee this sword; let us flee the madness; though late, let us become temperate. For this virtue too ought to be called temperance, not less than that which is used to be so called among all men. For whereas there the dominion of one lust is to be struggled against, here we have to master many lusts, and those of all kinds.

Yea, nothing, nothing is more foolish [1] than the slave of wealth. He thinks he overcomes when he is overcome. He thinks he is master, when he is a slave, and putting bonds on himself, he rejoices; making the wild beast fiercer, he is pleased; and becoming a captive, he prides himself, and leaps for joy; and seeing a dog rabid and flying at his soul, when he ought to bind him and weaken him by hunger, he actually supplies him with abundance of food, that he may leap upon him more fiercely, and be more formidable.

Reflecting then on all these things, let us loose the bonds, let us slay the monster, let us drive away the disease, let us cast out this madness; that we may enjoy a calm and pure health, and having with much pleasure sailed into the serene haven, may attain unto the eternal blessings; unto which may we all attain, by the grace and love towards man of our Lord Jesus Christ, to whom be glory and might, now and always, and world without end. Amen.

---

[1] ἀφρονέστερον opposed to σωφροσύνη.

HOMILY LII.

MATT. XV. 21, 22.

"And Jesus went thence, and departed into the coasts of Tyre and Sidon. And, behold, a woman of Canaan came out of the same coasts, and cried unto Him,[1] saying, Have mercy on me, O Lord, Thou Son of David; my daughter is grievously vexed with a devil."

BUT Mark saith, that "He could not be hid,"[2] though He had entered into the house.

And why did He go at all into these parts? When He had set them free from the observance of meats, then to the Gentiles also He goes on to open a door, proceeding in due course; even as Peter, having been first directed to annul this law, is sent to Cornelius.[3]

But if any one should say, "How then, while saying to His disciples, "Go not into the way of the Gentiles,"[4] doth He Himself admit her?" first, this would be our reply, that what He enjoined upon His disciples, He was not Himself also tied to; secondly, that not in order to preach did He depart; which indeed Mark likewise intimating said, He even hid Himself, yet was not concealed.

For as His not hastening to them first was a part of the regular course of His proceedings, so to drive them away when coming to Him was unworthy of His love to man. For if the flying ought to be pursued, much more ought the pursuing not to be avoided.

See at any rate how worthy this woman is of every benefit. For she durst not even come to Jerusalem, fearing, and accounting herself unworthy. For were it not for this, she would have come there, as is evident both from her present earnestness, and from her coming out of her own coasts.

And some also taking it as an allegory say, that when Christ came out of Judea, then the church ventured to approach Him, coming out herself also from her own coasts. For it is said, "Forget thine own people and thy father's house."[5] For both Christ went out of His borders, and the woman out of her borders, and so it became possible for them to fall in with each other: thus He saith,

"Behold a woman of Canaan coming out of her own coasts."

The evangelist speaks against the woman, that he may show forth her marvellous act, and celebrate her praise the more. For when thou hearest of a Canaanitish woman, thou shouldest call to mind those wicked nations, who overset from their foundations the very laws of nature. And being reminded of these, consider also the power of Christ's advent. For they who were cast out, that they might not pervert any Jews, these appeared so much better disposed than the Jews, as even to come out of their coasts, and approach Christ; while those were driving Him away, even on His coming unto them.

2. Having then come unto Him, she saith nothing else, but "Have mercy on me," and by her cry brings about them many spectators. For indeed it was a pitiful spectacle to see a woman crying aloud in so great affliction, and that woman a mother, and entreating for a daughter, and for a daughter in such evil case: she not even venturing to bring into the Master's sight her that was possessed, but leaving her to lie at home, and herself making the entreaty.

And she tells her affliction only, and adds nothing more; neither doth she drag the physician to her house, like that nobleman, saying, "Come and lay thy hand upon her," and, "Come down ere my child die."[6] But having described both her calamity, and the intensity of the disease, she pleads the Lord's mercy, and cries aloud; and she saith not, "Have mercy on my daughter," but, "Have mercy on me." For she indeed is insensible of her disease, but it is I that suffer her innumerable woes; my disease is with consciousness, my madness with perception of itself.

2. "But He answered her not a word."[7]

What is this new and strange thing? the Jews in their perverseness He leads on, and

[1] [R. V., "And Jesus went out thence and withdrew into the parts of Tyre and Sidon. And behold, a Canaanitish woman came out from those borders, and cried." But Chrysostom agrees with the rec. text, in adding "unto Him." There is some doubt as to the correct form of the Greek verb rendered "cried," both in the New Testament and in Chrysostom's text.—R.]

[2] Mark vii. 24.　　　　　[3] Acts x. 15, 20.
[4] Matt. x. 5.　[R. T. "any way."]　[5] Ps. xlv. 10.

[6] See John iv. 49, and comp. Matt. ix. 18.
[7] Matt. xv. 23.

blaspheming He entreats them, and tempting Him He dismisses them not; but to her, running unto Him, and entreating, and beseeching Him, to her who had been educated neither in the law, nor in the prophets, and was exhibiting so great reverence; to her He doth not vouchsafe so much as an answer.

Whom would not this have offended, seeing the facts so opposite to the report? For whereas they had heard, that He went about the villages healing, her, when she had come to Him, He utterly repels. And who would not have been moved by her affliction, and by the supplication she made for her daughter in such evil case? For not as one worthy, nor as demanding a due, not so did she approach Him, but she entreated that she might find mercy, and merely gave a lamentable account of her own affliction; yet is she not counted worthy of so much as an answer.

Perhaps many of the hearers were offended, but she was not offended. And why say I, of the hearers? For I suppose that even the very disciples must have been in some degree affected at the woman's affliction, and have been greatly troubled, and out of heart.

Nevertheless not even in this trouble did they venture to say, "Grant her this favor," but, "His disciples came and besought Him, saying, Send her away, for she crieth after us." For we too, when we wish to persuade any one, oftentimes say the contrary.

But Christ saith, "I am not sent, but unto the lost sheep of the house of Israel."[1]

What then did the woman, after she heard this? Was she silent, and did she desist? or did she relax her earnestness? By no means, but she was the more instant. But it is not so with us; rather, when we fail to obtain, we desist; whereas it ought to make us the more urgent.

And yet, who would not have been driven to perplexity by the word which was then spoken? Why His silence were enough to drive her to despair, but His answer did so very much more. For together with herself, to see them also in utter perplexity that were pleading with her, and to hear that the thing is even impossible to be done, was enough to cast her into unspeakable perplexity.

Yet nevertheless the woman was not perplexed, but on seeing her advocates prevail nothing, she made herself shameless with a goodly shamelessness.

For whereas before this she had not ventured so much as to come in sight (for "she crieth," it is said, "after us"), when one might expect that she should rather depart further off in utter despair, at that very time she comes nearer, and worships, saying, "Lord, help me."[2]

What is this, O woman? Hast thou then greater confidence than the apostles? more abundant strength? "Confidence and strength," saith she, "by no means; nay, I am even full of shame. Yet nevertheless my very shamelessness do I put forward for entreaty; He will respect my confidence." And what is this? Heardest thou not Him saying, "I am not sent but unto the lost sheep of the house of Israel?" "I heard," saith she, "but He Himself is Lord." Wherefore neither did she say, "Entreat and beseech," but, "Help me."

3. What then saith Christ? Not even with all this was He satisfied, but He makes her perplexity yet more intense again, saying,

"It is not meet to take the children's bread and to cast it to the dogs."[3]

And when He vouchsafed her a word, then He smote her more sharply than by His silence. And no longer doth He refer the cause to another, nor say, "I am not sent," but the more urgent she makes her entreaty, so much the more doth He also urge His denial. And He calls them no longer "sheep," but "children," and her "a dog."

What then saith the woman? Out of His own very words she frames her plea. "Why, though I be a dog," said she, "I am not an alien."

Justly did Christ say, "For judgment am I come."[4] The woman practises high self-command, and shows forth all endurance and faith, and this, receiving insult; but they, courted and honored, requite it with the contrary.

For, "that food is necessary for the children," saith she, "I also know; yet neither am I forbidden, being a dog. For were it unlawful to receive, neither would it be lawful to partake of the crumbs; but if, though in scanty measure, they ought to be partakers, neither am I forbidden, though I be a dog; nay, rather on this ground am I most surely a partaker, if I am a dog."

With this intent did Christ put her off, for He knew she would say this; for this did He deny the grant, that He might exhibit her high self-command.

For if He had not meant to give, neither would He have given afterwards, nor would He have stopped her mouth again. But as He doth in the case of the centurion, saying, "I will come and heal him,"[5] that we might learn the godly fear of that man, and might hear him say, "I am not worthy that Thou shouldest come under my roof;"[1] and as He doth in the case of her that had the issue of blood, saying, "I perceive that virtue hath gone out of me,"[2] that He might make her faith manifest; and as in the case of the Samaritan woman, that He might show how not even upon reproof she desists:[3] so also here, He would not that so great virtue in the woman should be hid. Not in insult then were His words spoken, but calling her forth, and revealing the treasure laid up in her.

But do thou, I pray thee, together with her faith see also her humility. For He had called the Jews "children," but she was not satisfied with this, but even called them "masters;" so far was she from grieving at the praises of others.

"Why, the dogs also,"[4] saith she, "eat of the crumbs that fall from their master's table."[5]

Seest thou the woman's wisdom, how she did not venture so much as to say a word against it, nor was stung by other men's praises, nor was indignant at the reproach? Seest thou her constancy? He said, "It is not meet," and she said, "Truth, Lord;" He called them "children," but she "masters;" He used the name of a dog, but she added also the dog's act. Seest thou this woman's humility?

Hear the proud language of the Jews. "We be Abraham's seed, and were never in bondage to any man;"[6] and, "We be born of God."[7] But not so this woman, rather she calls herself a dog, and them masters; so for this she became a child.

What then saith Christ?

"O woman, great is thy faith."[8]

Yea, therefore did He put her off, that He might proclaim aloud this saying, that He might crown the woman.

"Be it unto thee even as thou wilt." Now what He saith is like this: "Thy faith indeed is able to effect even greater things than these; nevertheless, Be it unto thee even as thou wilt."

This was akin to that voice that said, "Let the Heaven be, and it was."[9]

"And her daughter was made whole from that very hour."

Seest thou how this woman too contributed not a little to the healing of her daughter? For to this purpose neither did Christ say, "Let thy little daughter be made whole," but, "Great is thy faith, be it unto thee even

as thou wilt;" to teach thee that the words were not used at random, nor were they flattering words, but great was the power of her faith.

The certain test, however, and demonstration thereof, He left to the issue of events. Her daughter accordingly was straightway healed.

But mark thou, I pray thee, how when the apostles had failed, and had not succeeded, this woman had success. So great a thing is assiduity in prayer. Yea, He had even rather be solicited by us, guilty as we are, for those who belong to us, than by others in our behalf. And yet they had more liberty to speak; but she exhibited much endurance.

And by the issue He also excused Himself to His disciples for the delay, and showed that with reason He had not assented to their request.

4. "And Jesus departed from thence, and came nigh unto the sea of Galilee; and went up into the mountain, and sat down there. And great multitudes came unto Him, having with them those that were lame, blind, maimed, dumb; and cast them [10] at His feet; and He healed them, insomuch that the multitudes wondered, when they saw the dumb speak, the maimed to be whole, the lame to walk, and the blind to see, and they glorified the God of Israel."[11]

Now He goes about Himself, now sits awaiting the diseased, and hath the lame brought up unto the mountain. And no longer do they touch so much as His garment, but advance a higher step, being cast at His feet: and they showed their faith doubly, first, by going up into the mountain though lame, then by wanting nothing else but to be cast at His feet only.

And great was the marvel and strange, to see them that were carried walking, the blind needing not any to lead them by the hand. Yea, both the multitude of the healed, and the facility of their cure amazed them.

Seest thou, how the woman indeed He healed with so much delay, but these immediately? not because these are better than she is, but because she is more faithful than they. Therefore, while in her case He defers and delays, to manifest her constancy; on these He bestows the gift immediately, stopping the mouths of the unbelieving Jews, and cutting away from them every plea. For the greater favors one hath received, so much the more is he liable to punishment, if he be insensible, and the very honor make him no

---

[1] Matt. viii. 8.   [2] Luke viii. 46.   [3] John iv. 18.
[4] [R. V., "for even the dogs," etc.]   [5] Matt. xv. 27.
[6] John viii. 33.   [7] John viii. 41.
[8] Matt. xv. 28.   [9] Gen. i. 3.

[10] ["cast them down."]
[11] Matt. xv. 29-31. [Comp. the more exact rendering of the R. V., "the dumb speaking," etc.]

better. Therefore you see the rich also proving wicked, are more punished than the poor, for not being softened even by their prosperity. For tell me not that they gave alms. Since if they gave not in proportion to their substance, not even so shall they escape; our alms being judged not by the measure of our gifts, but by the largeness [1] of our mind. But if these suffer punishment, much more they that are eager about unnecessary things; who build houses of two and three stories, but despise the hungry; who give heed to covetousness, but neglect almsgiving.

5. But since the discourse hath fallen on almsgiving, come then, let us resume again to-day that argument, which I was making three days ago concerning benevolence, and left unfinished. Ye remember, when lately I was speaking of vanity about your shoes, and of that empty trouble, and the luxury of the young, that it was from almsgiving that our discourse passed on to those charges *against you*. What were the matters then at that time brought forward? That almsgiving is a kind of art, having its workshop in Heaven, and for its teacher, not man, but God. Then inquiring what is an art, and what not an art, we came upon fruitless labors, and evil devices, amongst which we made mention also of this art concerning men's shoes.

Have ye then recalled it to mind? Come now, let us to-day also resume what we then said, and let us show how almsgiving is an art, and better than all arts. For if the peculiarity of art is to issue in something useful, and nothing is more useful than almsgiving, very evidently this is both an art, and better than all arts. For it makes for us not shoes, nor doth it weave garments, nor build houses that are of clay; but it procures life everlasting, and snatches us from the hands of death, and in either life shows us glorious, and builds the mansions that are in Heaven, and those eternal tabernacles.

This suffers not our lamps to go out, nor that we should appear at the marriage having filthy garments, but washes them, and renders them purer than snow. "For though your sins be as scarlet, I will make them white as snow." [2] It suffers us not to fall, where that rich man fell, nor to hear those fearful words, but it leads us into the bosom of Abraham.

And indeed of the arts of this life, each severally takes and keeps one good work; as agriculture the feeding us; weaving the cloth-ing us; or rather not so much as this; for it is in no wise sufficient alone to contribute to us its own part. And, if thou wilt, let us try agriculture first. Why, if it hath not the smith's art, that it may borrow from it spade, and ploughshare, and sickle, and axe, and other things besides; and that of the carpenter, so as both to frame a plough, and to prepare a yoke and a cart to bruise the ears; and the currier's, to make also the leathern harness; and the builder's, to build a stable for the bullocks that plough, and houses for the husbandmen that sow; and the woodman's, to cut wood; and the baker's after all these, it is found nowhere.

So also the art of weaving, when it produces anything, calls many arts, together with itself, to assist it in the works set before it; and if they be not present and stretch forth the hand, this too stands, like the former, at a loss. And indeed every one of the arts stands in need of the other.

But when alms is to be given, we want nothing else, but the disposition only is required. And if thou say that money is needed, and houses and clothes and shoes; read those words of Christ, which He spake concerning the widow,[3] and cease from this anxiety. For though thou be exceedingly poor, and of them that beg, if thou cast in two mites, thou hast effected all; though thou give but a barley cake, having only this, thou art arrived at the end of the art.

This science then let us receive, and bring to perfection. For truly it is a better thing to know this, than to be a king, and to wear a diadem. For this is not its only advantage, that it needs not other things, but it is also able to accomplish a variety of objects, both many and of all kinds. Thus, it both builds houses that continue forever in Heaven; and teaches them that have brought it to perfection, how they may escape the never-dying death; and bestows on thee treasures that are never spent, but escape all injury, both from robbers, and from worms, and from moths, and from time.

And yet, were it but for the preservation of wheat that any one had taught thee this, what wouldest thou not have given, to be able to preserve thy grain unconsumed for many years? But behold, this teaches thee the same not concerning wheat only, but concerning all things, and shows how both thy goods and thy soul and thy body may remain unconsumed.

And why should we rehearse particularly all the good effects of this art? For this

---

[1] δαψιλεία.　　　　[2] Isaiah i. 18.　　　　[3] Mark xii. 43; Luke xxi. 3, 4.

teaches thee how thou mayest become like God, which is the sum of all good things whatsoever.

Seest thou how the work thereof is not one, but many? Without needing any other art, it builds houses, it weaves garments, it stores up treasures which cannot be taken from us, it makes us get the better of death, and prevail over the devil; it renders us like God.

What now can be more profitable than this art? For while the other arts, as well as what I have mentioned, both end with our present life, and when the artists are diseased, are found nowhere; and their works have no power to endure, and they need much labor and time, and innumerable other things; this one, when the world hath passed away, then it becomes more than ever conspicuous; when we are dead, then it shines out brighter than ever, and exhibits the works which it hath accomplished. And neither time nor labor, nor any such travail, doth it need; but is active even in thy sickness, and in thine old age, and migrates with thee into the life to come, and never forsakes thee. This makes thee to surpass in ability both sophists and rhetoricians. For such as are approved in those arts have many to envy them, but they who shine in this have thousands to pray for them. And those indeed stand at men's judgment seat, pleading for them that are wronged, and often too for them that do wrong; but this virtue stands by the judgment seat of Christ, not only pleading, but persuading the judge Himself to plead for him that is judged, and to give sentence in his favor: though his sins have been very many, almsgiving doth both crown and proclaim him. For "give alms, and all things shall be clean."[1]

And why do I speak of the things to come? Since in our present life, should we ask men which they would rather, that there should be many sophists and rhetoricians, or many that give alms, and love their fellow men, thou wilt hear them choose the latter; and very reasonably. For if oratory were taken away, our life will be nothing the worse; for indeed even before this, it had continued a long time; but if thou take away the showing of mercy, all is lost and undone. And as men could not sail on the sea, if harbors and roadsteads were blocked up; so neither could this life hold together, if thou take away mercy, and compassion, and love to man.

6. Therefore God hath not at all left them to reasoning only, but many parts thereof He hath implanted by the absolute power of nature herself. Thus do fathers pity children, thus mothers, thus children parents; and not in the case of men only, but of all the brutes also; thus brothers pity brothers, and kinsmen, and connexions; thus man pities man. For we have somewhat even from nature prone to mercy.

Therefore also we feel indignation in behalf of them that are wronged, and seeing men killed we are overcome, and beholding them as they mourn, we weep. For because it is God's will that it should be very perfectly performed, He commanded nature to contribute much hereunto, signifying that this is exceedingly the object of His care.

Considering then these things, let us bring both ourselves and our children and them that pertain to us unto the school of mercy, and this above all things let man learn, since even this is man. "For a man is a great thing, and a merciful man a precious thing;"[2] so that unless one hath this, one hath fallen away even from being a man. This renders them wise. And why marvel at this being man? This is God. For, "be ye," saith He, "merciful as your Father."[3]

Let us learn therefore to be merciful on all accounts, but chiefly, because we too need much mercy. And let us reckon ourselves as not even living, at such time as we are not showing mercy. But by mercy, I mean that which is free from covetousness. For if he that is contented with his own, and imparts to no man, is not merciful, how is he that takes the goods of other men merciful, though he give without limit? For if merely to enjoy one's own be inhumanity, much more to defraud others. If they that have done no wrong are punished, because they imparted not, much more they, who even take what is others.

Say not therefore this, "One is injured, another receives mercy." For this is the grievous thing. Since it were meet that the injured should be the same with the receiver of the mercy: but now, while wounding some, thou art healing them whom thou hast not wounded, when thou oughtest to heal the same; or rather not so much as to wound them. For he is not humane who smites and heals, but he that heals such as have been smitten by others. Heal therefore thine own evil acts, not another's; or rather do not smite at all, nor cast down (for this is the conduct of a mocker), but raise up them that are cast down.

For neither is it possible by the same

---

[1] Luke xi. 41. [The verse reads: "Howbeit give for alms those things which are within (or, ye can), and behold, all things are clean unto you." The connection scarcely warrants the unqualified use made of the passage in the Homily.—R.]

[2] Prov. xx. 6, LXX.   [3] Luke vi. 36.

measure of almsgiving to cure the evil result of covetousness. For if thou hast unjustly gotten a farthing, it is not a farthing that thou needest again for almsgiving, to remove the sin that comes of thine unjust gain, but a talent. Therefore the thief being taken pays fourfold, but he that spoils by violence is worse than he that steals. And if this last ought to give fourfold[1] what he stole, the extortioner should give tenfold and much more; and it is much if even so he can make atonement for his injustice; for of almsgiving not even then will he receive the reward. Therefore saith Zacchæus, "I will restore what I have taken by false accusation fourfold, and the half of my goods I will give to the poor."[2] And if under the law one ought to give fourfold, much more under grace; if he that steals, much more he that spoils by violence. For besides the damage, in this case the insult too is great. So that even if thou give an hundredfold, thou hast not yet given the whole.

Seest thou how not without cause I said, If thou take but a farthing by violence, and pay back a talent, scarcely even so dost thou remedy it? But if scarcely by doing this; when thou reversest the order, and hast taken

by violence whole fortunes, yet bestowest but little, and not to them either that have been wronged, but to others in their stead; what kind of plea wilt thou have? what favor? what hope of salvation?

Wouldest thou learn how bad a deed thou doest in so giving alms? Hear the Scripture that saith, "As one that killeth the son before his father's eyes, so is he that bringeth a sacrifice of the goods of the poor."[3]

This denunciation then let us write in our minds before we depart, this let us write on our walls, this on our hands, this in our conscience, this everywhere; that at least the fear of it being vigorous in our minds, may restrain our hands from daily murders. For extortion is a more grievous thing than murder, consuming the poor man by little and little.

In order then that we may be pure from this pollution, let us exercise ourselves in these thoughts, both by ourselves and to one another. For so shall we both be more forward to show mercy, and receive undiminished the reward for it, and enjoy the eternal good things, by the grace and love towards man of our Lord Jesus Christ; to whom be glory and might with the Father, and the Holy Ghost, now and always, and world without end. Amen.

[1] Exod. xxii. 1.
[2] Luke xix. 8. [The future tense is given by Chrysostom, and other variations made in the New Testament passage.—R.]

[3] Ecclus. xxxiv. 20.

HOMILY LIII.

Matt. XV. 32.

"But Jesus called His disciples unto Him, and said, I have compassion on the multitude, because they continue with me now three days, and have nothing to eat: and I will[1] not send them away fasting, lest they faint in the way."

Both above, when going to do this miracle, He first healed them that were maimed in body, and here He doth the self-same thing; from the healing of the blind and the lame, He goes on to this again.

But why might it be, that then His disciples said, "Send away the multitude," but now they said not so; and this, though three days had past? Either being themselves improved by this time, or seeing that the people

had no great sense of hunger; for they were glorifying God for the things that were done.

But see how in this instance too He doth not proceed at once to the miracle, but calls them forth thereunto. For the multitudes indeed who had come out for healing durst not ask for the loaves; but He, the benevolent and provident one, gives even to them that ask not, and saith unto His disciples, "I have compassion, and will not send them away fasting."

For lest they should say that they came

[1] [R. V., "would," θέλω.]

having provisions for the way, He saith, "They continue with me now three days;" so that even if they came having any, it is all spent. For therefore He Himself did not this on the first and second day, but when all had been consumed by them, in order that having first been in want, they might more eagerly accept His work.

Therefore He saith, "Lest they faint in the way;" implying both their distance to be great, and that they had nothing left.

"Then, if thou art not willing to send them away fasting, wherefore dost thou not work the miracle?" That by this question and by their answer He might make the disciples more heedful, and that they might show forth their faith, coming unto Him, and saying, "Make loaves."

But not even so did they understand the motive of His question; wherefore afterwards He saith to them, as Mark relates, "Are your hearts so hardened? Having eyes, see ye not? and having ears, hear ye not?"[1]

Since, if this were not so, wherefore doth He speak to the disciples, and signify the multitude's worthiness to receive a benefit, and add also the pity He Himself feels?

But Matthew saith, that after this He also rebuked them, saying, "O ye of little faith, do ye not yet understand, nor remember the five loaves of the five thousand, and how many baskets ye took up? nor the seven loaves of the four thousand, and how many baskets ye took up?"[2] So completely do the evangelists harmonize one with another.

What then say the disciples? Still they creep on the ground, although He had done so very many things in order that that miracle might be kept in memory; as by His question, and by the answer, and by making them minister herein, and by distributing the baskets; but their state of mind was yet rather imperfect.

Wherefore also they say to Him, "Whence should we have so many loaves in the wilderness?"[3]

Both before this, and now, they make mention of the wilderness; themselves in a weak way of argument so speaking, yet even hereby putting the miracle above suspicion. That is, lest any should affirm (as I have indeed already said), that they obtained it from some neighboring village, the place is acknowledged, that the miracle may be believed. With this view, both the former miracle and this He works in a wilderness, at a great distance from the villages.

The disciples, considering none of all this,

said, "Whence should we have so many loaves in a wilderness?" For they thought verily He had said it as purposing next to enjoin them to feed the people; most foolishly; since with this intent He had said, and that lately, "Give ye them to eat,"[4] that He might bring them to an urgent need of entreating Him.

But now He saith not this, "Give ye them to eat," but what? "I have compassion on them, and will not send them away fasting;" bringing the disciples nearer, and provoking them more, and granting them clearer sight, to ask these things of Him. For in truth they were the words of one signifying that He hath power not to send them away fasting; of one manifesting His authority. For the expression, "I will not," implies such a purpose in Him.

2. Since however they still spake of the multitude merely, and the place, and the wilderness (for "whence," it is said, "should we have in a wilderness so many loaves, as to fill so great a multitude"?); and not even so understood what He said, He proceeds to contribute His own part, and saith unto them,

"How many loaves have ye? And they say, Seven, and a few little fishes."[5]

And they no more say, "But what are these among so many?"[6] as they had said before. So that although they reached not His whole meaning, yet nevertheless they became higher by degrees. For so He too, arousing their mind hereby, puts the question much as He had done before, that by the very form of the inquiry He might remind them of the works already done.

But as thou hast seen their imperfection hereby, so do thou observe the severity of their spirit, and admire their love of truth, how, writing themselves, they conceal not their own defects, great as they were. For it was no small blame to have presently forgotten this miracle, which had so recently taken place; wherefore they are also rebuked.

And herewith consider also their strictness in another matter, how they were conquerors of their appetite; how disciplined to make little account of their diet. For being in the wilderness and abiding there three days, they had seven loaves.

Now all the rest He doth as on the former occasion; thus He both makes them sit down on the ground, and He makes the loaves multiply themselves in the hands of the disciples.

For, "He commanded," it is said, "the

---

[1] Mark viii. 17, 18.   [2] Matt. xvi. 8-10.
[3] Matt. xv. 33. [R. V., "in a desert place."]

[4] Matt. xiv. 16.   [5] Matt. xv. 34.   [6] John vi. 9.

multitude to sit down on the ground. And He took the seven loaves, and the fishes, and gave thanks, and brake, and gave to His disciples, and the disciples to the multitude."[1]

But when we come to the end, there is a difference.

For, "they did all eat," so it is said, "and were filled, and they took up of the broken meat that was left,[2] seven baskets full. And they that did eat were four thousand men, besides women and children."[3]

But why at the former time, when there were five thousand, did twelve baskets full remain over and above, whereas here, when there were four thousand, it was seven baskets full? For what purpose, I say, and by what cause, were the remnants less, the guests not being so many?

Either then one may say this, that the baskets on this last occasion[4] were greater than those used before,[5] or if this were not so, lest the equality of the miracle should again cast them into forgetfulness, He rouses their recollection by the difference, that by the variation they might be reminded of both one and the other. Accordingly, in that case, He makes the baskets full of fragments equal in number to His disciples, in this, the other baskets equal to the loaves; indicating even hereby His unspeakable power, and the ease wherewith He exercised His authority, in that it was possible for Him to work such miracles, both in this way and in the other. For neither was it of small power, to maintain the exact number, both then and now; then when there were five thousand, now when there were four thousand; and not suffer the remnants to be more than the baskets used on the one occasion or on the other, although the number of the guests was different.

And the end again was like the former. For as then He left the multitude and withdrew in a ship, so also now; and John also saith this.[6] For since no sign did so work upon them to follow Him, as the miracle of the loaves; and they were minded not only to follow Him, but also to make Him a king;[7] avoiding all suspicion of usurping royalty, He hastens away after this work of wonder: and He doth not even go away afoot, lest they should follow Him, but by entering into a ship.

"And He sent away the multitudes," so it saith, "and went on board the ship, and came into the coasts of Magdala."[8]

3. "And the Pharisees and Sadducees came and[9] desired Him to show them a sign from Heaven. But He saith, When it is evening, ye say, Fair weather, for the sky is red; and in the morning, Foul weather to-day, for the sky is red and lowering. Ye can discern the face of the sky, but can ye not the signs of the times?[10] A wicked and adulterous generation seeketh after a sign, and there shall no sign be given unto it, but the sign of the prophet Jonas. And He left them, and departed."[11]

But Mark saith, that when they were come unto Him, and were questioning with Him, "He sighed deeply in His spirit, and saith, Why doth this generation seek after a sign?"[12]

And yet surely their inquiry was deserving of anger and great displeasure; yet nevertheless the benevolent and provident One is not angry, but pities and bewails them as incurably diseased, and after so full a demonstration of His power, tempting Him.

For not in order to believe did they seek, but to lay hold of Him. Since had they come unto Him as ready to believe, He would have given it. For He who said to the woman, "It is not meet,"[13] and afterwards gave, much more would He have shown His bounty to these.

But since they did not seek to believe, therefore He also calls them hypocrites, because in another place they said one thing, and meant another. Yea, had they believed, they would not even have asked. And from another thing too it is evident that they believed not; that when reproved and exposed, they abode not with Him, nor said, "We are ignorant and seek to learn."

But for what sign from Heaven were they asking? Either that He should say the sun, or curb the moon, or bring down thunderbolts, or work a change in the air, or some other such thing.

What then saith He to all this? "Ye can discern the face of the sky, but can ye not discern the signs of the times?"[14]

See His meekness and moderation. For

---

[1] Matt. xv. 35, 36. [The imperfect ἐδίδου, "kept giving," is found here, against the rec. text.—R.]
[2] [R. V., "that which remained over of the broken pieces."]
[3] Matt. xv. 37, 38.
[4] σπυρίδες. That the σπυρίς was of large size would appear from Acts ix. 25, where this word is again used. Κόφινος is the word commonly used by the LXX. for basket; that it was in common use among the Jews seems proved by the well-known line in Juvenal, Sat. iii. 14. "Judæis, quorum cophinus fænumque suppellex." See also Sat. vi. 541, 542. Tr.
[5] κόφινοι.   [6] John vi. 17.   [7] John vi. 15.

[8] Matt. xv. 39. [R. V., "Magadan," following a better supported reading; so Jerome, Augustin, and others.—R.]
[9] ["tempting him" is omitted.]
[10] ["hypocrites" is omitted; so R. V., "ye know how to discern the face of the heavens; but ye cannot *discern* the signs of the times." The last clause is not a question.—R.]
[11] Chap. xvi. 1–4.   [12] Mark viii. 12.   [13] Matt. xv. 26.
[14] [See above, note 10. Were the sentence a question, it would imply an affirmative answer, but it is plainly implied that they could not discern the signs of the times.—R.]

not even as before did He refuse merely, and say, "There shall none be given them," but He states also the cause why He gives it not, even though they were not asking for information.

What then was the cause? "Much as in the sky," saith He, "one thing is a sign of a storm, another of fair weather, and no one when he saw the sign of foul weather would seek for a calm, neither in calm and fair weather for a storm; so should you reckon with regard to me also. For this present time of my coming, is different from that which is to come. Now there is need of these signs which are on the earth, but those in Heaven are stored up against that time. Now as a physician am I come, then I shall be here as a judge; now to seek that which is gone astray, then to demand an account. Therefore in a hidden manner am I come, but then with much publicity, folding up the heaven, hiding the sun, not suffering the moon to give her light. Then 'the very powers of the heavens shall be shaken,'[1] and the manifestation of my coming shall imitate lightning that appears at once to all.[2] But not now is the time for these signs; for I am come to die, and to suffer all extremities."

Heard ye not the prophet, saying, "He shall not strive nor cry, neither shall His voice be heard without?"[3] and another again, "He shall come down as rain upon a fleece of wool?"[4]

And if men speak of the signs in Pharaoh's time, there was an enemy then from whom deliverance was needed, and it all took place in due course. But to Him that came among friends there was no need of those signs.

"And besides, how shall I give the great signs, when the little are not believed?" Little, I mean, as regards display, since in power these latter were much greater than the former. For what could be equal to remitting sins, and raising the dead, and driving away devils, and creating a body, and ordering all other things aright?

But do thou see their hardened heart, how on being told, that "no sign should be given them but the sign of the prophet Jonas," they do not ask. And yet, knowing both the prophet, and all that befell him, and having been told this a second time, they ought to have inquired and learnt what the saying could mean; but, as I said, there is no desire of information in these their doings. For this cause "He also left them, and departed."

4. "And when His disciples," so it is said, "were come to the other side, they forgot to take bread. Then Jesus said unto them, Take heed and beware of the leaven of the Pharisees and of the Sadducees."[5]

And why said He not plainly, Beware of their teaching? His will is to remind them of what had been done, for He knew they had forgotten. But for accusing them at once there seemed to be no reasonable ground, but to take the occasion from themselves, and so to reprove them, would make the charge admissible. "And why did He not then reprove them, when they said, 'Whence should we have so many loaves in the wilderness?' for it seemed a good time then to say what He says here." That He might not seem to rush hastily on the miracle. And besides, He would not blame them before the multitude, nor seek honor in their presence. And now too the accusation had greater reason, for that after repetition of the miracle they were so minded.

Wherefore also He works another miracle, and then and not till then He reproves; I mean, He brings forward what they were reasoning in their hearts. But what were their reasonings? "Because," so it is said, "we have taken no bread."[6] For as yet they were full of trepidation about the purifications of the Jews, and the observances of meats.

Wherefore on all accounts He attacks them even with severity, saying, "Why reason ye in yourselves, O ye of little faith, because ye have brought no bread?[7] Perceive ye not yet, neither understand? Have ye your heart hardened? Having eyes, see ye not? Having ears, hear ye not?[8] Do ye not remember the five loaves of the five thousand, and how many baskets ye took up? neither the seven loaves of the four thousand, and how many baskets ye took up?"[9]

Seest thou intense displeasure? For nowhere else doth He appear to have so rebuked them. Wherefore then doth He so? In order again to cast out their prejudice about the meats. I mean that with this view, whereas then He had only said, "Perceive ye not, neither understand?" in this place, and with a strong rebuke, He saith, "O ye of little faith."[10]

For not everywhere is lenity a good thing. And as He used to allow them freedom of

---

[1] Matt. xxiv. 29.　　　[2] Matt. xxiv. 27.
[3] Is. xlii. 2.　　　[4] Ps. lxxii. 6. [LXX.]

[5] Matt. xvi. 5, 6.
[6] Matt. xvi. 7. [R. V., "We took no bread;" ὅτι being *recitantis*.]
[7] Matt. xiv. 8. [R. V., "because ye have no bread?" Chrysostom agrees with the rec. text.—R.]
[8] Mark viii. 17, 18.　　　[9] Matt. xvi. 9, 10.
[10] [Both the citations are from Matthew, but probably the former occasion referred to is that narrated in Matt. xv. 16, 17. —R.]

speech, so doth He also reprove, by this variety providing for their salvation. And mark thou at once His reproof, how strong, and His mildness. For all but excusing Himself to them for His severe reproofs to them, He saith, "Do ye not yet consider the five loaves, and how many baskets ye took up; and the seven loaves, and how many baskets ye took up?" And to this end He sets down also the numbers, as well of the persons fed as of the fragments, at once both bringing them to recollection of the past, and making them more attentive to the future.

And to teach thee how great the power of His reproof, and how it roused up their slumbering mind, hear what saith the evangelist. For Jesus having said no more, but having reproved them, and added this only, "How is it that ye do not understand, that I spake it not to you concerning bread that ye should beware, but of the leaven of the Pharisees and Sadducees;"[1] He subjoined, saying, "Then understood they that He bade them not beware of the leaven of bread, but of the doctrine of the Pharisees and Sadducees,"[2] although He had not uttered that interpretation.

See how much good His reproof wrought. For it both led them away from the Jewish observances, and when they were remiss, made them more heedful, and delivered them from want of faith;[3] so that they were not afraid nor in alarm, if at any time they seemed to have few loaves; nor were they careful about famine, but despised all these things.

5. Neither let us then for our part be in all ways flattering those under our charge, nor seek to be flattered of them that have the rule over us. Since, in truth, the soul of men stands in need of medicines in both these kinds. Therefore even in the whole world we may see that God doth so order things, now doing this, now the other, and permits neither our good things to be permanent, nor our adversities to be by themselves. Yea, as now it is night, now day, and now winter, now summer; so also within us, now pain, now pleasure, now sickness, and now health. Let us not then marvel when we are sick, since rather when we are in health we should marvel. Neither let us be troubled when we are in sorrow, since when we are glad rather it is reasonable to be troubled; all coming to pass according to nature and in order.

And why marvel, if in thy case so it be,

when even in regard of those saints one may see this happening?

And that thou mayest learn it, the life which thou accountest to be most full of pleasure and free from troubles, that let us bring forward. Wilt thou that we examine Abraham's life from the beginning? What then at the very first was said to him? "Get thee out of thy country, and from thy kindred."[4] Didst thou see what a painful thing is enjoined him? But look also on the good coming after it: "And come hither unto a land that I will show thee, and I will make thee a great nation."

What then? after he had come to the land, and reached the harbor, did his troubles cease? By no means; but others again, more grievous than the former, succeed, a famine, and a removal, and a violent seizure of his wife; and after these other prosperities befell him, the plague upon Pharaoh, and her liberation, and the honor, and those many gifts, and the return to his house. And the subsequent events too all form the same kind of chain, prosperities and troubles entwined together.

And the like befell the apostles too. Wherefore also Paul said, "Who comforteth us in all our tribulation, that we may be able to comfort them which are in any trouble."[5]

"What then is this to me," some one will say, "who am always in sorrow?" Be not uncandid, nor unthankful; nay, it is out of the question for one to be in troubles always, nature being unequal to it; but because we want to be always in joy, therefore we account ourselves always in sorrow. Not however on this account alone, but because we presently forget our advantages and blessings, but are always remembering our troubles, therefore we say we are in sorrow. Whereas it is impossible, being a man, to be always in sorrow.

6. And if ye will, let us examine both the life of luxury, so delicate and dissipated, and the other, so grievous and galling, and painful. For we will show you that both the former hath sorrows, and the latter refreshments Nay, be not disturbed. Let there be set before us a man who is in bonds, and another who is a king, youthful, an orphan, having succeeded to a great substance; and let there also be set before us one toiling for hire through the whole day, and another living in luxury continually.

Wilt thou then that we tell first the vexations of that one, who lives in luxury? Consider how his mind must naturally be rocked

[1] Matt. xvi. 11. [See R. V., for a different reading.]
[2] Matt. xiv. 12.
[3] [Some MSS. insert φιλοτιμίας καί, "from ambition and want of faith." It is lectio difficilior, but not accepted by Field. —R.]

[4] Gen. xii. 1.   [5] 2 Cor. i. 4.

as with a tempest, when he longs for a glory beyond him, when he is despised by his servants, when he is insulted by his inferiors, when he hath ten thousand to accuse him, and to blame his costly living. And all the rest too, which is likely to occur in such wealth, one cannot even tell; the vexations, the affronts, the accusations, the losses, the devices of the envious, who, because they cannot transfer his wealth to themselves, drag and tear in pieces the young man on every side, and excite against him storms without end.

Wilt thou have me tell also of the pleasure of this other, the hired laborer? From all this he is free; though one insult him, he grieves not, for he counts not himself greater than any; he is not in fear about wealth, he eats with pleasure, he sleeps with great comfort. Not so luxurious are the drinkers of Thasian wine, as he in going to fountains, and enjoying those springs. But the state of the other is not such.

Now if what I have said suffice thee not, to make my victory more complete, come let us compare the king and the prisoner, and thou wilt often see the latter in pleasure and sporting and leaping, while the former with his diadem and purple robe is in despair, and hath innumerable cares, and is dead with fear.

For we may not, we may not find any one's life without sorrow, nor again without its share of pleasure; for our nature would not have been equal to it, as I have already said. But if one joys more, and another grieves more, this is due to the person himself that grieves, being mean of soul, not to the nature of the case. For if we would rejoice continually, we have many means thereto.

Since, had we once laid hold on virtue, there would be nothing to grieve us any more. For she suggests good hopes to them that possess her, and makes them well pleasing to God, and approved among men, and infuses unspeakable delight. Yea, though in doing right virtue hath toil, yet doth it fill the conscience with much gladness, and lays up within so great pleasure, as no speech shall be able to express.

For which of the things in our present life seems to thee pleasant? A sumptuous table, and health of body, and glory, and wealth? Nay, these delights, if thou set them by that pleasure, will prove the bitterest of all things, compared thereunto. For nothing is more pleasurable than a sound conscience, and a good hope.

7. And if ye would learn this, let us inquire of him who is on the point of departing hence, or of him that is grown old; and when

we have reminded him of sumptuous banqueting which he hath enjoyed, and of glory and honor, and of good works which he hath some time practised and wrought, let us ask in which he exults the more; and we shall see him for the other ashamed, and covering his face, but for these soaring and leaping with joy.

So Hezekiah, too, when he was sick, called not to mind sumptuous feasting, nor glory, nor royalty, but righteousness. For " remember," saith he, " how I walked before Thee in an upright way."[1] See Paul again for these things leaping with joy, and saying, " I have fought the good fight, I have finished my course, I have kept the faith."[2] " Why, what had he to speak of besides?" one may say. Many things, and more than these; even the honors wherewith he was honored, what attendance and great respect he had enjoyed. Hearest thou not him saying, " Ye received me as an angel of God, as Christ Jesus"? and, " If it were possible, ye would have plucked out your eyes, and given them to me"?[3] and that " Men had laid down their neck for his life"?[4] But none of those things doth he bring forward, but his labors, and perils, and his crowns in requital for them; and with much reason. For while the one sort are left here, the other migrate with us; and for those we shall give account, but for these we shall ask reward.

Know ye not in the day of death how sins make the soul shrink? how they stir up the heart from beneath? At that time therefore, when such things are happening, the remembrance of good works stands by us, like a calm in a storm, and comforts the perturbed soul.

For if we be wakeful, even during our life this fear will be ever present with us; but, insensible as we are, it will surely come upon us when we are cast out from hence. Because the prisoner too is then most grieved, when they are leading him out to the court; then most trembles, when he is near the judgment-seat, when he must give his account. For the same kind of reason most persons may be then heard relating horrors, and fearful visions, the sight whereof they that are departing may not endure, but often shake their very bed with much vehemence, and gaze fearfully on the bystanders, the soul urging itself inwards, unwilling to be torn away from the body, and not enduring the sight of the coming angels. Since if human beings that are awful strike terror into us beholding them; when we see angels threat-

---

[1] 2 Kings xx. 3.
[3] Gal. iv. 14, 15.
[2] 2 Tim. iv. 7.
[4] Rom. xvi. 4.

ening, and stern powers, among our visitors; what shall we not suffer, the soul being forced from the body, and dragged away, and bewailing much, all in vain? Since that rich man too, after his departure, mourned much, but derived no profit therefrom.

All these things then let us picture to ourselves, and consider, lest we too suffer the same, and thus let us keep the fear thence arising in vigor; that we may escape the actual punishment, and attain unto the eternal blessings; unto which God grant we may all attain, by the grace and love towards man of our Lord Jesus Christ, with whom be glory unto the Father, together with the Holy and Life-giving Spirit, now and ever, and world without end. Amen.

HOMILY LIV.

MATT. XIV. 13.

"Now when Jesus had gone forth into the coasts[1] of Cæsarea Philippi, He asked His disciples, saying, Whom do men say that I the Son of Man am?"[2]

WHEREFORE hath he mentioned the founder of the city? Because there was another besides, Cæsarea Stratonis. But not in that, but in this doth He ask them, leading them far away from the Jews, so that being freed from all alarm, they might speak with boldness all that was in their mind.

And wherefore did He not ask them at once their own opinion, but that of the people? In order that when they had told the people's opinion, and then were asked, "But whom[3] say ye that I am?" by the manner of His inquiry they might be led up to a sublimer notion, and not fall into the same low view as the multitude. Accordingly He asks them not at all in the beginning of His preaching, but when He had done many miracles, and had discoursed with them of many and high doctrines, and had afforded so many clear proofs of His Godhead, and of His unanimity with the Father, then He puts this question to them.

And He said not, "Whom say the Scribes and Pharisees that I am?" often as these had come unto Him, and discoursed with Him; but, "Whom do men say that I am?" inquiring after the judgment of the people, as unbiassed. For though it was far meaner than it should be, yet was it free from malice, but the other was teeming with much wickedness.

And signifying how earnestly He desires His Economy[4] to be confessed, He saith, "The Son of Man;" thereby denoting His Godhead, which He doth also in many other places. For He saith, "No man hath ascended up to Heaven, but the Son of Man, which is in Heaven."[5] And again, "But when ye shall see the Son of Man ascend up, where He was before."[6]

Then, since they said, "Some John the Baptist, some Elias, some Jeremias, or one of the prophets,"[7] and set forth their mistaken opinion, He next added, "But whom say ye that I am?"[8] calling them on by His second inquiry to entertain some higher imagination concerning Him, and indicating that their former judgment falls exceedingly short of His dignity. Wherefore He seeks for another judgment from themselves, and puts a second question, that they might not fall in with the multitude, who, because they saw His miracles greater than human, accounted Him a man indeed, but one that had appeared after a resurrection, as Herod also said.[9] But He, to lead them away from this notion, saith, "But whom say ye that I am?" that is, "ye that are with me always, and see me working miracles, and have yourselves done many mighty works by me."

2. What then saith the mouth of the apos-

---

[1] [R. V., "came into the parts," etc.]
[2] [R. V. text, "who do men say that the Son of Man is?" But Chrysostom, with the rec. text, reads με. So R. V. margin, "that I the Son of Man am," as in the parallel passages.—R.]
[3] [The A. V. is ungrammatical; "whom" is simply a transfer of the Greek accusative (with the infinitive in the passage) into the English finite clause.—R.]

[4] i. e. His Incarnation.   [5] John iii. 13.   [6] John vi. 62.
[7] Matt. xvi. 14.   [8] Matt. xvi. 15.   [9] Matt. xiv. 2.

tles, Peter, the ever fervent, the leader of the apostolic choir?[1] When all are asked, he answers. And whereas when He asked the opinion of the people, all replied to the question; when He asked their own, Peter springs forward, and anticipates them, and saith, "Thou art the Christ, the Son of the living God."[2]

What then saith Christ? "Blessed art thou, Simon Barjona, for flesh and blood hath not revealed it unto thee."[3]

Yet surely unless he had rightly confessed Him, as begotten of the very Father Himself, this were no work of revelation; had he accounted our Lord to be one of the many, his saying was not worthy of a blessing. Since before this also they said, "Truly He is Son of God,"[4] those, I mean, who were in the vessel after the tempest, which they saw, and were not blessed, although of course they spake truly. For they confessed not such a Sonship as Peter, but accounted Him to be truly Son as one of the many, and though peculiarly so beyond the many, yet not of the same substance.

And Nathanael too said, "Rabbi, Thou art the Son of God, Thou art the King of Israel;"[5] and so far from being blessed, he is even reproved by Him, as having said what was far short of the truth. He replied at least, "Because I said unto thee, I saw thee under the fig-tree, believest thou? thou shalt see greater things than these."[6]

Why then is this man blessed? Because he acknowledged Him very Son. Wherefore you see, that while in those former instances He had said no such thing, in this case He also signifies who had revealed it. That is, lest his words might seem to the many (because he was an earnest lover of Christ) to be words of friendship and flattery, and of a disposition to show favor to Him, he brings forward the person who had made them ring[7] in his soul; to inform thee that Peter indeed spake, but the Father suggested, and that thou mightest believe the saying to be no longer a human opinion, but a divine doctrine.

And wherefore doth He not Himself declare it, nor say, "I am the Christ," but by His question establish this, bringing them in to confess it? Because so to do was both more suitable to Him, yea necessary at that time, and it drew them on the more to the belief of the things that were said.

Seest thou how the Father reveals the Son, how the Son the Father? For "neither knoweth any man the Father," saith He, "save the Son, and he to whomsoever the Son will reveal Him."[8] It cannot therefore be that one should learn the Son of any other than of the Father; neither that one should learn the Father of any other than of the Son. So that even hereby, their sameness of honor and of substance is manifest.

3. What then saith Christ? "Thou art Simon, the son of Jonas; thou shalt be called Cephas."[9] "Thus since thou hast proclaimed my Father, I too name him that begat thee;" all but saying, "As thou art son of Jonas, even so am I of my Father." Else it were superfluous to say, "Thou art Son of Jonas;" but since he had said, "Son of God," to point out that He is so Son of God, as the other son of Jonas, of the same substance with Him that begat Him, therefore He added this, "And I say unto thee, Thou art Peter, and upon this rock will I build my Church;"[10] that is, on the faith of his confession. Hereby He signifies that many were now on the point of believing, and raises his spirit, and makes him a shepherd. "And the gates of hell[11] shall not prevail against it." "And if not against it, much more not against me. So be not troubled because thou art shortly to hear that I shall be betrayed and crucified."

Then He mentions also another honor. "And I also[12] will give thee the keys of the heavens."[13] But what is this, "And I also will give thee?" "As the Father hath given thee to know me, so will I also give thee."

And He said not, "I will entreat the Father" (although the manifestation of His authority was great, and the largeness of the gift unspeakable), but, "I will give thee." What dost Thou give? tell me. "The keys of the heavens, that whatsoever thou shalt bind on earth, shall be bound in Heaven,[14] and whatsoever thou shalt loose on earth, shall be loosed in Heaven." How then is it not "His to give to sit on His right hand, and on His left,"[15] when He saith, "I will give thee"?

Seest thou how He, His own self, leads Peter on to high thoughts of Him, and reveals Himself, and implies that He is Son of God by these two promises? For those things which are peculiar to God alone, (both to absolve sins, and to make the church in-

---

[1] ὁ κορυφαῖος.
[2] Matt. xvi. 16
[3] Matt. xvi. 17.
[4] Matt. xiv. 33.
[5] John i. 49.
[6] John i. 50.
[7] ἐνηχήσαντα.
[8] Matt. xi. 27 ; Luke x. 22.
[9] Matt. xvi. 17, 18 ; see John i. 42.
[10] Matt. xvi. 18.
[11] [R. V., "Hades."]
[12] [Chrysostom reads καὶ ἐγὼ δέ, probably from verse 18, as none of our authorities have this fuller form.—R.]
[13] Matt. xvi. 19. [The text is peculiar in omitting τῆς βασιλείας. The translator has here rendered τὴν οὐρανῶν, "the heavens ;" but not in all similar instances. The English versions generally disregard the plural form.—R.]
[14] [τοῖς οὐρανοῖς.]
[15] Matt. xx. 23.

capable of overthrow in such assailing waves, and to exhibit a man that is a fisher more solid than any rock, while all the world is at war with him), these He promises Himself to give; as the Father, speaking to Jeremiah, said, He would make him as "a brazen pillar, and as a wall;"[1] but him to one nation only, this man in every part of the world.

I would fain inquire then of those who desire to lessen the dignity of the Son, which manner of gifts were greater, those which the Father gave to Peter, or those which the Son gave him? For the Father gave to Peter the revelation of the Son; but the Son gave him to sow that of the Father and that of Himself in every part of the world; and to a mortal man He entrusted the authority over all things in Heaven, giving him the keys; who extended the church to every part of the world, and declared it to be stronger than heaven. "For heaven and earth shall pass away, but my word shall not pass away."[2] How then is He less, who hath given such gifts, hath effected such things?

And these things I say, not dividing the works of Father and Son ("for all things are made by Him, and without Him was nothing made which was made"):[3] but bridling the shameless tongue of them that dare so to speak.

But see, throughout all, His authority: "I say unto thee, Thou art Peter; I will build the Church; I will give thee the keys of Heaven."[4]

4. And then, when He had so said, "He charged them that they should tell no man that He was the Christ."[5]

And why did He charge them? That when the things which offend are taken out of the way, and the cross is accomplished, and the rest of His sufferings fulfilled, and when there is nothing any more to interrupt and disturb the faith of the people in Him, the right opinion concerning Him may be engraven pure and immovable in the mind of the hearers. For, in truth, His power had not yet clearly shone forth. Accordingly it was His will then to be preached by them, when both the plain truth of the facts, and the power of His deeds were pleading in support of the assertions of the apostles. For it was by no means the same thing to see Him in Palestine, now working miracles, and now insulted and persecuted (and especially when the very cross was presently to follow the miracles that were

happening); and to behold him everywhere in the world, adored and believed, and no more suffering anything, such as He had suffered.

Therefore He bids them "tell no man." For that which hath been once rooted and then plucked up, would hardly, if planted, again be retained among the many; but that which, once fixed, hath remained immovable, and hath suffered injury from no quarter, easily mounts up, and advances to a greater growth.

And if they who had enjoyed the benefit of many miracles, and had had part in so many unutterable mysteries, were offended by the mere hearing of it; or rather not these only, but even the leader[6] of them all, Peter; consider what it was likely the common sort should feel, being first told that He is the Son of God, then seeing Him even crucified and spit upon, and that without knowledge of the secret of those mysteries, or participation in the gift of the Holy Ghost. For if to His disciples He said, "I have many things to say unto you, but ye cannot bear them now;"[7] much more would the rest of the people have utterly failed, had the chiefest of these mysteries been revealed to them before the proper time. Accordingly He forbids them to tell.

And to instruct thee how great a thing it was, their afterwards learning His doctrine complete, when the things that offend had passed by; learn it from this same leader of theirs. For this very Peter, he who after so many miracles proved so weak as even to deny Him, and to be in fear of a mean damsel; after the cross had come forth, and he had received the certain proofs of the resurrection, and there was nothing more to offend and trouble him, retained the teaching of the Spirit so immovable, that more vehemently than a lion he sprang upon the people of the Jews, for all the dangers and innumerable deaths which were threatened.

With reason then did He bid them not tell the many before the crucifixion, since not even to them that were to teach did He venture to commit all before the crucifixion. "For I have many things to say unto you," saith He, "but ye cannot bear them now."

And of the things too that He did say, they do not understand many, which He did not make plain before the crucifixion. At least when He was risen from the dead, then and not before they knew some of His sayings.

5. "From that time forth began He to show unto them that He must suffer.[8] From

[1] Jer. i. 18.   [2] Matt. xxiv. 35.
[3] John i. 3. [The Greek text omits ὁ γέγονεν "which was made."]
[4] [The singular is retained here by the translator, though the Greek form is the same, τῶν οὐρανῶν.—R.]
[5] Matt. xvi. 20.

[6] ὁ κορυφαῖος   [7] John xvi. 12.   [8] Matt. xvi. 21.

that time." What time? When He had fixed the doctrine in them; when He had brought in the beginning of the Gentiles.[1]

But not even so did they understand what He said. "For the saying," it is said, "was hid from them;"[2] and they were as in a kind of perplexity, not knowing that He must rise again. Therefore He rather dwells on the difficulties, and enlarges His discourse, that He may open their mind, and they may understand what it can be that He speaks of.

"But they understood not, but the saying was hid from them, and they feared to ask this;"[3] not whether He should die, but how, and in what manner, and what this mystery could be. For they did not even know what was this same rising again, and supposed it much better not to die. Therefore, the rest being troubled and in perplexity, Peter again, in his ardor, alone ventures to discourse of these things; and not even he openly, but when he had taken Him apart; that is, having separated himself from the rest of the disciples; and he saith, "Be it far from Thee, Lord, this shall not be unto Thee."[4] What ever is this? He that obtained a revelation, he that was blessed, hath he so soon fallen away, and suffered overthrow, so as to fear His passion? And what marvel, that one who had not on these points received any revelation, should have that feeling? Yea, to inform thee that not of himself did he speak those other things either, see in these matters that were not revealed to him how he is confounded and overthrown, and being told ten thousand times, knows not what the saying can mean.

For that He is Son of God he had learnt, but what the mystery of the cross and of the resurrection might be, was not yet manifest to him: for "the saying," it is said, "was hid from them."

Seest thou that with just cause He bade them not declare it to the rest? For if it so confounded them, who must needs be made aware of it, what would not all others have felt?

6. He however, to signify that He is far from coming to the passion against His will, both rebuked Peter, and called him Satan.

Let them hear, as many as are ashamed of the suffering of the cross of Christ. For if the chief apostle, even before he had learnt all distinctly, was called Satan for feeling this, what excuse can they have, who after so abundant proof deny His economy? I say, when he who had been so blessed, who made

such a confession, has such words addressed to him; consider what they will suffer, who after all this deny the mystery of the cross.

And He said not, "Satan spake by thee," but, "Get thee behind me, Satan."[5] For indeed it was a desire of the adversary that Christ should not suffer. Therefore with such great severity did He rebuke him, as knowing that both he and the rest are especially afraid of this, and will not easily receive it.

Therefore He also reveals the thoughts of his mind, saying, "Thou savorest[6] not the things that be of God, but those that be of men."

But what means, "Thou savorest[6] not the things that be of God, but those that be of men"? Peter examining the matter by human and earthly reasoning, accounted it disgraceful to Him and an unmeet thing. Touching him therefore sharply,[7] He saith, "My passion is not an unmeet thing, but thou givest this sentence with a carnal mind; whereas if thou hadst hearkened to my sayings in a godly manner, disengaging thyself from thy carnal understanding, thou wouldest know that this of all things most becometh me. For thou indeed supposest that to suffer is unworthy of me; but I say unto thee, that for me not to suffer is of the devil's mind;" by the contrary statements repressing his alarm.

Thus as John, accounting it unworthy of Christ to be baptized by him, was persuaded of Christ to baptize Him, He saying, "Thus it becometh us,"[8] and this same Peter too, forbidding Him to wash his feet, by the words, "Thou hast no part with me, unless I wash thy feet;"[9] even so here too He restrained him by the mention of the opposite, and by the severity of the reproof repressed his fear of suffering.

7. Let no man therefore be ashamed of the honored symbols of our salvation, and of the chiefest of all good things, whereby we even live, and whereby we are; but as a crown, so let us bear about the cross of Christ. Yea, for by it all things are wrought, that are wrought among us. Whether one is to be new-born, the cross is there; or to be nourished with that mystical food, or to be ordained, or to do anything else, everywhere our symbol of victory is present. Therefore both on house, and walls, and windows, and upon our forehead, and upon our mind, we inscribe it with much care.

For of the salvation wrought for us, and of our common freedom, and of the goodness of our Lord, this is the sign. "For as a

---

[1] i. e., the woman of Canaan.
[2] Luke xviii. 34.   [3] Luke ix. 45.
[4] Matt. xvi. 22. [R. V., "this shall never be unto thee."]

[5] Matt. xvi. 23.   [6] [R. V., "mindest."]   [7] καθικνούμενος.
[8] Matt. iii. 15.   [9] John xiii. 8.

sheep was He led to the slaughter." [1] When therefore thou signest thyself, think of the purpose of the cross, and quench anger, and all the other passions. When thou signest thyself, fill thy forehead with all courage, make thy soul free. And ye know assuredly what are the things that give freedom. Wherefore also Paul leading us there, I mean unto the freedom that beseems us, did on this wise lead us unto it, having reminded us of the cross and blood of our Lord. " For ye are bought," saith he, " with a price; be not ye the servants of men." [2] Consider, saith he, the price that hath been paid for thee, and thou wilt be a slave to no man; by the price meaning the cross.

Since not merely by the fingers ought one to engrave it, but before this by the purpose of the heart with much faith. And if in this way thou hast marked it on thy face, none of the unclean spirits will be able to stand near thee, seeing the blade whereby he received his wound, seeing the sword which gave him his mortal stroke. For if we, on seeing the places in which the criminals are beheaded, shudder; think what the devil must endure, seeing the weapon, whereby Christ put an end to all his power, and cut off the head of the dragon.

Be not ashamed then of so great a blessing, lest Christ be ashamed of thee, when He comes with His glory, and the sign appears before Him, shining beyond the very sunbeam. [3] For indeed the cross cometh then, uttering a voice by its appearance, and pleading with the whole world for our Lord, and signifying that no part hath failed of what pertained to Him.

This sign, both in the days of our forefathers and now, hath opened doors that were shut up; [4] this hath quenched poisonous drugs; [5] this hath taken away the power of hemlock; this hath healed bites of venomous beasts. For if it opened the gates of hell, and threw wide the archways of Heaven, and made a new entrance into Paradise, and cut away the nerves of the devil; what marvel, if it prevailed over poisonous drugs, and venomous beasts, and all other such things.

This therefore do thou engrave upon thy mind, and embrace the salvation of our souls. For this cross saved and converted the world, drove away error, brought back truth, made earth Heaven, fashioned men into angels. Because of this, the devils are no longer terrible, but contemptible; neither is death,

death, but a sleep; because of this, all that warreth against us is cast to the ground, and trodden under foot.

If any one therefore say to thee, Dost thou worship the crucified? say, with your voice all joy, and your countenance gladdened, " I do both worship Him, and will never cease to worship." And if he laugh, weep for him, because he is mad. Thank the Lord, that He hath bestowed on us such benefits, as one cannot so much as learn without His revelation from above. Why, this is the very reason of his laughing, that "the natural man receiveth not the things of the Spirit." [6] Since our children too feel this, when they see any of the great and marvellous things; and if thou bring a child into the mysteries, he will laugh. Now the heathen are like these children; or rather they are more imperfect even than these; wherefore also they are more wretched, in that not in an immature age, but when full grown, they have the feelings of babes; wherefore neither are they worthy of indulgence.

But let us with a clear voice, shouting both loud and high, cry out and say (and should all the heathen be present, so much the more confidently), that the cross is our glory, and the sum of all our blessings, and our confidence, and all our crown. I would that also with Paul I were able to say, " By which the world is crucified unto me, and I unto the world; " [7] but I cannot, restrained as I am by various passions.

8. Wherefore I admonish both you, and surely before you myself, to be crucified to the world, and to have nothing in common with the earth, but to set your love on your country above, and the glory and the good things that come from it. For indeed we are soldiers of a heavenly King, and are clad with spiritual arms. Why then take we upon ourselves the life of traders, and mountebanks, nay rather of worms? For where the King is, there should also the soldier be. Yea, we are become soldiers, not of them that are far off, but of them that are near. For the earthly king indeed would not endure that all should be in the royal courts, and at his own side, but the King of the Heavens willeth all to be near His royal throne.

And how, one may say, is it possible for us, being here, to stand by that throne? Because Paul too being on earth was where the seraphim, where the cherubim are; and nearer to Christ, than these the body guards to the king. For these turn about their faces in many directions, but him nothing beguiled

---

[1] Isaiah liii. 7.
[2] Cor. vii. 23. [R. V., "become not bondservants of men."]
[3] See S. Cyril, *Catech.* xiii. 41. Oxf. Trans. and the note there: see also aspecially hereafter on S. Matth. xxiv. 30, Hom. LXXVI.
[4] S. Greg. Nyss. Life of S. Greg. Thaum. Works, t. iii. p. 573. Paris, 1638.
[5] Sim. Metaphr. Life of St. John, p. 47, etc. Oxon. 1597.
[6] 1 Cor. ii. 14.   [7] Gal. vi. 14.

nor distracted, but he kept his whole mind intent upon the king. So that if we would, this is possible to us also.

For were He distant from us in place, thou mightest well doubt, but if He is present everywhere, to him that strives and is in earnest He is near. Wherefore also the prophet said, "I will fear no evil, for Thou art with me;[1]" and God Himself again, "I am a God nigh at hand, and not a God afar off."[2] Then as our sins separate us from Him, so do our righteousnesses draw us nigh unto Him. "For while thou art yet speaking," it is said, "I will say, Here I am."[3] What father would ever be thus obedient to his offspring? What mother is there, so ready, and continually standing, if haply her children call her? There is not one, no father, no mother: but God stands continually waiting, if any of his servants should perchance call Him; and never, when we have called as we ought, hath He refused to hear. Therefore He saith, "While thou art yet speaking," I do not wait for thee to finish, and I straightway hearken.

9. Let us call Him therefore, as it is His will to be called. But what is this His will? "Loose," saith He, "every band of iniquity, unloose the twisted knots of oppressive covenants, tear in pieces every unjust contract. Break thy bread to the hungry, and bring in the poor that are cast out to thy house. If thou seest one naked, cover him, and them that belong to thy seed thou shalt not overlook. Then shall thy light break forth in the morning, and thine healings shall spring forth speedily, and thy righteousness shall go before thee, and the glory of the Lord shall cover thee. Then thou shalt call upon me, and I will give ear unto thee; whilst thou art yet speaking, I will say, Lo! here I am."[4]

And who is able to do all this? it may be asked. Nay, who is unable, I pray thee? For which is difficult of the things I have mentioned? Which is laborious? Which not easy?

Why, so entirely are they not possible only, but even easy, that many have actually overshot the measure of those sayings, not only tearing in pieces unjust contracts, but even stripping themselves of all their goods; making the poor welcome not to roof and table, but even to the sweat of their body, and laboring in order to maintain them; doing good not to kinsmen only, but even to enemies.

But what is there at all even hard in these sayings? For neither did He say, "Pass over the mountain, go across the sea, dig through so many acres of land, abide without food, wrap thyself in sackcloth;" but, "Impart to the poor,[5] impart of thy bread, cancel the contracts unjustly made."

What is more easy than this? tell me. But even if thou account it difficult, look, I pray thee, at the rewards also, and it shall be easy to thee.

For much as our emperors at the horse races heap together before the combatants crowns, and prizes, and garments, even so Christ also sets His rewards in the midst of His course, holding them out by the prophet's words, as it were by many hands. And the emperors, although they be ten thousand times emperors, yet as being men, and the wealth which they have in a course of spending, and their munificence of exhaustion, are ambitious of making the little appear much; wherefore also they commit each thing severally into the hand of the several attendants, and so bring it forward. But our King contrariwise, having heaped all together (because He is very rich, and doeth nothing for display), He so brings it forward, and what He so reaches out is indefinitely great, and will need many hands to hold it. And to make thee aware of this, examine each particular of it carefully.

"Then," saith He, "shall thy light break forth in the morning."[6] Doth not this gift appear to thee as some one thing? But it is not one; nay, for it hath many things in it, both prizes, and crowns, and other rewards. And, if ye are minded, let us take it to pieces and show all its wealth, as it shall be possible for us to show it; only do not ye grow weary.

And first, let us learn the meaning of "It shall break forth." For He said not at all, "shall appear," but "shall break forth;" declaring to us its quickness and plentifulness, and how exceedingly He desires our salvation, and how the good things themselves travail to come forth, and press on; and that which would check their unspeakable force shall be nought; by all which He indicates their plentifulness, and the infinity of His abundance. But what is "the morning." It means, "not after being in life's temptations, neither after our evils have come upon us;" nay, it is quite beforehand with them. For as in our fruits, we call that early, which has shown itself before its season; so also here again, declaring its rapidity, he has spoken

---

[1] Ps. xxiii. 4.   [2] Jerem. xxiii. 23.
[3] Is. lviii. 9, lxv. 24. [The citation is from the former passage; but "I will say" from the latter is substituted for "he will say." So in the last part of the longer citation below.—R.]
[4] Is. lviii. 6-9. [LXX., see note above.]
22

[5] [τοῖς οἰκείοις, "thy kinsmen," taken from Isa. lviii. 7., LXX., last clause (see above).—R.]
[6] [πρωΐμον, explained below. Our versions render "as the morning."—R.]

in this way, much as above He said, "Whilst thou art yet speaking, I will say, Lo! here I am."

But of what manner of light is He speaking, and what can this light be? Not this, that is sensible; but another far better, which shows us Heaven, the angels, the archangels, the cherubim, the seraphim, the thrones, the dominions, the principalities, the powers, the whole host, the royal palaces, the tabernacles. For shouldest thou be counted worthy of this light, thou shalt both see these, and be delivered from hell, and from the venomous worm, and from the gnashing of teeth, and from the bonds that cannot be broken, and from the anguish and the affliction, from the darkness that hath no light, and from being cut asunder, and from the river of fire, and from the curse, and from the abodes of sorrow; and thou shalt depart, "where sorrow and woe are fled away,"[1] where great is the joy, and the peace, and the love, and the pleasure, and the mirth; where is life eternal, and unspeakable glory, and inexpressible beauty; where are eternal tabernacles, and the untold glory of the King, and those good things, "which

eye hath not seen, nor ear heard, neither have entered into the heart of man;"[2] where is the spiritual bridechamber, and the apartments of the heavens, and the virgins that bear the bright lamps, and they who have the marriage garment; where many are the possessions of our Lord, and the storehouses of the King.

Seest thou how great the rewards, and how many He hath set forth by one expression, and how He brought all together?

So also by unfolding each of the expressions that follow, we shall find our abundance great, and the ocean immense. Shall we then still delay, I beg you; and be backward to show mercy on them that are in need? Nay, I entreat, but though we must throw away all, be cast into the fire, venture against the sword, leap upon daggers, suffer what you will; let us bear all easily, that we may obtain the garment of the kingdom of Heaven, and that untold glory; which may we all attain, by the grace and love towards man of our Lord Jesus Christ, to whom be glory and might, world without end. Amen.

[1] Isaiah xxxv. 10.

[2] 1 Cor. ii. 9.

HOMILY LV.

MATT. XVI. 24.

"Then said Jesus unto His disciples, If any man will come after me, let him renounce himself,[1] and take up his cross and follow me."

THEN; when? When Peter said, 'Be it far from Thee, this shall not be unto Thee; and was told, "Get thee behind me, Satan."[2] For He was by no means satisfied with the mere rebuke, but, willing also more abundantly to show both the extravagance of what Peter had said, and the benefit of His passion, He saith, "Thy word to me is, "Be it far from Thee, this shall not be unto Thee:" but my word to thee is, "Not only is it hurtful to thee, and destructive, to hinder me and to be displeased at my Passion, but it will be impossible for thee even to be saved, unless

thou thyself too be continually prepared for death."

Thus, lest they should think His suffering unworthy of Him, not by the former things only, but also by the events that were coming on, He teaches them the gain thereof. Thus in John first, He saith, "Except the corn of wheat fall into the ground and die, it abideth alone; but if it die, it bringeth forth much fruit;"[3] but here more abundantly working it out, not concerning Himself only doth He bring forward the statement that it is meet to die, but concerning them also. "For so great is the profit thereof, that in your case also unwillingness to die is grievous, but to be ready for it, good."

[1] [R. V., "If any man would come after me, let him deny himself," etc. The Oxford translator substitutes "renounce" to bring out the distinction between ἀπαρνεῖσθαι and ἀρνεῖσθαι, which is pointed out in the Homily, sec. 2.—R.]
[2] Matt. xvi. 22, 23.

[3] John xii. 24.

This however He makes clear by what follows, but for the present He works it out on one side only. And see how He also makes His discourse unexceptionable: not saying at all, "whether you will, or no, you must suffer this," but how? "If any man will come after me." "I force not, I compel not, but each one I make lord of his own choice; wherefore also I say, 'If any man will.' For to good things do I call you, not to things evil, or burdensome; not to punishment and vengeance, that I should have to compel. Nay, the nature of the thing is alone sufficient to attract you."

Now, thus saying, He drew them unto Him the more. For he indeed that uses compulsion oftens turns men away, but he that leaves the hearer to choose attracts him more. For soothing is a mightier thing than force. Wherefore even He Himself said, "If any man will." "For great," saith He, "are the good things which I give you, and such as for men even to run to them of their own accord. For neither if one were giving gold, and offering a treasure, would he invite with force. And if that invitation be without compulsion, much more this, to the good things in the Heavens. Since if the nature of the thing persuade thee not to run, thou art not worthy to receive it at all, nor if thou shouldest receive it, wilt thou well know what thou hast received."

Wherefore Christ compels not, but urges, sparing us. For since they seemed to be murmuring much, being secretly disturbed at the saying, He saith, "No need of disturbance or of trouble. If ye do not account what I have mentioned to be a cause of innumerable blessings, even when befalling yourselves, I use no force, nor do I compel, but if any be willing to follow, him I call.

"For do not by any means imagine that this is your following of me; I mean, what ye now do attending upon me. Ye have need of many toils, many dangers, if ye are to come after me. For thou oughtest not, O Peter, because thou hast confessed me Son of God, therefore only to expect crowns, and to suppose this enough for thy salvation, and for the future to enjoy security, as having done all. For although it be in my power, as Son of God, to hinder thee from having any trial at all of those hardships; yet such is not my will, for thy sake, that thou mayest thyself too contribute something, and be more approved."

For so, if one were a judge at the games, and had a friend in the lists, he would not wish to crown him by favor only, but also for his own toils; and for this reason especially, because he loves him. Even so Christ also; whom He most loves, those He most of all will have to approve themselves by their own means also, and not from His help alone.

But see how at the same time He makes His saying not a grievous one. For He doth by no means compass them only with His terror, but He also puts forth the doctrine generally to the world, saying, "If any one will," be it woman or man, ruler or subject, let him come this way.

2. And though he seem to have spoken but one single thing, yet His sayings are three, "Let him renounce himself," and "Let him bear his cross," and "Let him follow me;" and two of them are joined together, but the one is put by itself.

But let us see first what it can be to deny one's self. Let us learn first what it is to deny another, and then we shall know what it may be to deny one's self. What then is it to deny another? He that is denying another,—for example, either brother, or servant, or whom you will,—should he see him either beaten, or bound, or led to execution, or whatever he may suffer, stands not by him, doth not help him, is not moved, feels nothing for him, as being once for all alienated from him. Thus then He will have us disregard our own body, so that whether men scourge, or banish, or burn, or whatever they do, we may not spare it. For this is to spare it. Since fathers too then spare their offspring, when committing them to teachers, they command not to spare them.

So also Christ; He said not, "Let him not spare himself," but very strictly, "Let him renounce himself;" that is, let him have nothing to do with himself, but give himself up to all dangers and conflicts; and let him so feel, as though another were suffering it all.

And He said not, "Let him deny,"[1] but "Let him renounce;"[2] even by this small addition intimating again, how very far it goes. For this latter is more than the former.

"And let him take up his cross." This arises out of the other. For to hinder thy supposing that words, and insults, and reproaches are to be the limits of our self-renunciation, He saith also how far one ought to renounce one's self; that is, unto death, and that a reproachful death. Therefore He said not, "Let him renounce himself unto death," but, "Let him take up his cross;" setting forth the reproachful death; and that not once, nor twice, but throughout all life one ought so to do. "Yea," saith He, "bear about this death continually, and day by day

---

[1] ἀρνησάσθω.   [2] ἀπαρνησάσθω. [Comp. note, p. 338.]

be ready for slaughter. For since many have indeed contemned riches, and pleasure, and glory, but death they despised not, but feared dangers; I," saith He, " will that my champion should wrestle even unto blood, and that the limits of his course should reach unto slaughter; so that although one must undergo death, death with reproach, the accursed death, and that upon evil surmise, we are to bear all things nobly, and rather to rejoice in being suspected."

"And let him follow me." That is, it being possible for one to suffer, yet not to follow Him, when one doth not suffer for Him (for so robbers often suffer grievously, and violaters of tombs, and sorcerers); to hinder thy supposing that the mere nature of thy calamities is sufficient, He adds the occasion of these calamities.

And what is it? In order that, so doing and suffering, thou mayest follow Him; that for Him thou mayest undergo all things; that thou mayest possess the other virtues also. For this too is expressed by " Let him follow me;" so as to show forth not fortitude only, such as is exercised in our calamities, but temperance also, and moderation, and all self-restraint. This being properly " to follow," the giving heed also to the other virtues, and for His sake suffering all.

For there are who follow the devil even to the endurance of all this, and for his sake give up their own lives; but we for Christ, or rather for our own sakes: they indeed to harm themselves both here and there; but we, that we may gain both lives.

How then is it not extreme dullness, not to show forth even the same fortitude with them that perish; and this, when we are to reap from it so many crowns? Yet with us surely Christ Himself is present to be our help, but with them no one.

Now He had indeed already spoken this very injunction, when He sent them, saying, " Go not into the way of the Gentiles" (for, saith He, " I send you as sheep in the midst of wolves," and, " ye shall be brought before kings and governors "),[1] but now with more intensity and severity. For then He spake of death only, but here He hath mentioned a cross also, and a continual cross. For " let him take up," saith He, " his cross;" that is, " let him carry it continually and bear it." And this He is wont to do in everything; not in the first instance, nor from the beginning, but quietly and gradually, bringing in the greater commandments, that the hearers may not count it strange.

3. Then, because the saying seemed to be vehement, see how He softens it by what follows, and sets down rewards surpassing our toils; and not rewards only, but also the penalties of vice: nay, on these last He dwells more than on those, since not so much His bestowing blessings, as His threat of severities, is wont to bring ordinary men to their senses. See at least how He both begins here from this, and ends in this.

" For whosoever will save his life shall lose it," saith He, " but whosoever shall lose his life for my sake, shall find it. For what is a man profited,[2] if he should gain the whole world, and lose his own soul? Or what shall a man give in exchange for his soul?"[3]

Now what He saith is like this: " not as unsparing towards you, but rather as exceedingly sparing you, I enjoin these things. For he who spares his child, ruins it; but he who spares it not, preserves." To which effect also a certain wise man said, " If thou beat thy son with a rod, he shall not die, but thou shalt deliver his soul from death."[4] And again, " He that refresheth his son, shall bind up his wounds."[5]

This takes place in the camp also. For if the general, sparing the soldiers, commands them to remain within the place always, he will destroy with them the inhabitants too.

" In order then that this may not happen in your case also," saith He, " ye must be arrayed against continual death. For now too a grievous war is about to be kindled. Sit not therefore within, but go forth and fight; and shouldest thou fall in thy post, then hast thou obtained life." For if in the visible wars he that in his post meets slaughter, is both more distinguished than the rest, and more invincible, and more formidable to the enemy; although we know that after death the king, in behalf of whom he takes his station, is not able to raise him up again: much more in these wars, when there are such hopes of resurrection besides, will he who exposes his own life unto death, find it; in one sense, because he will not be quickly taken; in a second, because even though he fall, God[6] will lead his life on to a higher life.

4. Then, because he had said, " He who will save shall lose it, but whosoever shall lose shall save it," and on that side had set salvation and destruction, and on this salva-

---

[1] Matt. x. 5, 16, 18.

[2] [R. V., " shall a man be profited;" so the Homily here, against rec. text.—R.]
[3] Matt. xvi. 25, 26. [Chrysostom inserts ὑπέρ, and takes ψυχή in ver. 26 as " soul," but in his comment in ver. 25 recognizes the obvious contrast between lower and higher life.—R.]
[4] Prov. xxiii. 13, 14.   [5] Ecclus. xxx. 7.
[6] [The word " God " is supplied by the translator, but this is not necessarily the sense; the subject may be the man himself.—R.]

tion and destruction; to prevent any one's imagining the one destruction and salvation to be all the same with the other, and to teach thee plainly that the difference between this salvation and that is as great as between destruction and salvation; from the contraries also He makes an inference once for all to establish these points. "For what is a man profited,"[1] saith He, "if he gain the whole world, and lose his own soul?"

Seest thou how the wrongful preservation of it is destruction, and worse than all destruction, as being even past remedy, from the want of anything more to redeem it? For "tell me not this," saith He, "that he that hath escaped such dangers hath saved his life; but together with his life put also the whole world, yet what profit hath he thereby, if the soul perish?"

For tell me, shouldest thou see thy servants in luxury, and thyself in extreme calamity, wilt thou indeed profit aught by being master? By no means. Make this reckoning then with regard to thy soul also, when the flesh is in luxury and wealth, and she awaiting the destruction to come.

"What shall a man give in exchange for his soul?"[2]

Again, He dwells upon the same point. What? hast thou another soul to give for this soul? saith He. Why, shouldest thou lose money, thou wilt be able to give money; or be it house, or slaves, or any other kind of possession, but for thy soul, if thou lose it, thou wilt have no other soul to give: yea, though thou hadst the world, though thou wast king of the whole earth, thou wouldest not be able, by paying down all earthly goods, with the earth itself, to redeem but one soul.

And what marvel, if it be so with the soul? Since even in the body one may see that so it turns out. Though thou wear ten thousand diadems, but have a body sickly by nature, and incurable, thou wilt not be able, not by giving all thy kingdom, to recover this body, not though thou add innumerable persons, and cities, and goods.

Now thus I bid thee reason with regard to thy soul also; or rather even much more with regard to the soul; and do thou, forsaking all besides, spend all thy care upon it. Do not then while taking thought about the things of others, neglect thyself and thine own things; which now all men do, resembling them that work in the mines. For neither do these receive any profit from this labor, nor from the wealth; but rather great

harm, both because they incur fruitless peril, and incur it for other men, reaping no benefit from such their toils and deaths. These even now are objects of imitation to many, who are digging up wealth for others; or rather we are more wretched even than this, inasmuch as hell itself awaits us after these our labors. For they indeed are staid from those toils by death, but to us death proves a beginning of innumerable evils.

But if thou say, thou hast in thy wealth the fruit of thy toils: show me thy soul gladdened, and then I am persuaded. For of all things in us the soul is chief. And if the body be fattened, while she is pining away, this prosperity is nothing to thee (even as when the handmaiden is glad, the happiness of the maidservant is nothing to her mistress perishing, nor is the fair robe anything compared with the weak flesh); but Christ will say unto thee again, "What shall a man give in exchange for his soul?" on every hand commanding thee to be busied about that, and to take account of it only.

5. Having alarmed them therefore hereby, He comforts them also by His good things.

"For the Son of Man shall come," saith He, "in the glory of His Father with His holy angels, and then He shall reward every man according to his works."[3]

Seest thou how the glory of the Father and of the Son is all one? But if the glory be one, it is quite evident that the substance also is one. For if in one substance there be a difference of glory ("for there is one glory of the sun, and another glory of the moon, and another glory of the stars; for one star differeth from another star in glory;"[4] although the substance be one), how may the substance of those differ, whereof the glory is one? For He said not at all, "In glory such as the Father's," whereby thou mightest suppose again some variation; but implying entire perfection, "In that same glory," saith He, "will He come;" for it to be deemed one and the same.

"Now, why fear, O Peter" (so He speaks), "on being told of death? Why, then shalt thou see me in the glory of the Father. And if I am in glory, so are ye; your interests are no wise limited to the present life, but another sort of portion will take you up, a better one." Nevertheless, when He had spoken of the good things, He stayed not at this, but mingled the fearful things also, bringing forward that judgment-seat, and the inexorable account, and the inflexible sentence, and the judgment that cannot be deceived.

---

[1] Here the citation agrees with the rec. text.—R.]
[2] [Here ὑπέρ does not occur, the text agreeing with the received.—R.]

[3] Matt. xvi. 37. [Some MSS. of the Homily omit ἁγίων, and read τὴν πρᾶξιν for τὰ ἔργα (see note 1, p. 342.). So R. V.—R.]
[4] 1 Cor. xv. 41.

He suffered not however His discourse to appear only dismal, but tempered it also with good hopes. For neither did He say, "then shall He punish them that sinned," but, "He shall reward every man according to his doings." [1] And this He said, reminding not only the sinners of punishment, but also them that have done well of prizes and crowns.

6. And He indeed spake it, in part to refresh the good, but I ever shudder at hearing it, for I am not of them that are crowned, and I suppose that others also share with us in our fear and anxiety. For whom is this saying not enough to startle, when he hath entered into his own conscience; and to make him shudder, and convince him that we have need of sackcloth, and of prolonged fasting, more than the people of the Ninevites? For not for an overthrow of·a city, and the common end, are we concerned, but for eternal punishment, and the fire that is never quenched.

Wherefore also I praise and admire the monks that have occupied the desert places, as for the rest, so for this saying. For they after having made their dinners, or rather after supper (for dinner they know not at any time, because they know that the present time is one of mourning and fasting); after supper then, in saying certain hymns of thanksgiving unto God, they make mention of this expression also. And if ye would hear the very hymns themselves, that ye too may say them continually, I will rehearse to you the whole of that sacred song. The words of it then stand as follows: "Blessed God, who feedest me from my youth up, who givest food to all flesh; fill our hearts with joy and gladness, that always having all sufficiency we may abound unto every good work in Christ Jesus our Lord; with whom be unto Thee glory, honor and might, with the Holy Spirit, forever. Amen. Glory to Thee, O Lord, glory to Thee, O Holy One, glory to Thee, O King, that Thou hast given us meat to make us glad. Fill us with the Holy Ghost, that we may be found well-pleasing before Thee, not being ashamed, when Thou renderest to every man according to his works."

Now this hymn is in all parts worthy of admiration, but especially the above ending of it. That is, because meals and food are wont to dissipate and weigh down, they put this saying as a kind of bridle upon the soul, at the time of indulgence reminding it of the time of judgment. For they have learnt what befell Israel through a costly table. "For

my beloved," saith He, "ate, and waxed fat, and kicked." [2] Wherefore also Moses said, "When thou shalt have eaten and drunk and art full, remember the Lord thy God." [3]

For after that feast, then they ventured on those acts of lawless daring.

Do thou therefore also look to it, lest something like it befall thee. For though thou sacrifice not to stone nor to gold, either sheep or bullocks, see lest to wrath thou sacrifice thine own soul, lest to whoredom or other like passions, thou sacrifice thine own salvation. Yea—on this account, you see, they being afraid of these downfalls, when they have enjoyed their meal, or rather fasting (for their meal is in fact fasting), remind themselves of the terrible judgment-seat, and of that day. And if they who correct themselves both with fasting, and with nights spent on the ground, with watchings, and with sackcloth, and with ten thousand means, do yet require also this reminding, when will it be possible for us to live virtuously; who set forth tables loaded with innumerable wrecks, and do not so much as pray at all, neither in the beginning nor the end?

7. Wherefore to put an end to these shipwrecks, let us bring before us that hymn and unfold it all, that seeing the profit thereof, we too may chant it constantly over our table, and quell the rude motions of the belly, introducing both the manners and laws of those angels into our houses. For you ought indeed to go there and reap these fruits; but since ye are not willing, at least through our words, hear this spiritual melody, and let every one after his meal say these words, beginning thus.

"Blessed God." For the apostolic law they straightway fulfill, that commands, "Whatsoever we do in word or in deed, that we do it in the name of our Lord Jesus Christ, giving thanks to God and the Father by Him." [4]

Next, the thanksgiving takes place not for that one day only, but for all their life. For, "Who feedest me," it is said, "from my youth up." And a lesson of self-command is drawn thence, that when God feeds, we must not take thought. For if upon a king's promising thee to furnish thy daily food out of his own stores, thou wouldest be of good hope for the future; much more, when God gives, and all things pour upon thee as out of fountains, shouldest thou be freed from all anxiety. Yea, and to this very intent they so speak, that they may persuade

---

[1] [τὴν πρᾶξιν, the reading accepted in R. V.—R.]

[2] Deut. xxxii. 15 [LXX.]   [3] Deut. vi. 11, 12.
[4] Colos. iii. 17.

both themselves, and those that are made disciples by them, to put off all worldly care.

Then, not to have thee suppose that for themselves only they offer up this thanksgiving, they further say, " Who givest food to all flesh," giving thanks in behalf of all the world; and as fathers of the whole earth, so do they offer up their praises for all, and train themselves to a sincere brotherly love. For it is not even possible they should hate them, in behalf of whom they thank God, that they are fed.

Seest thou both charity introduced by their thanksgiving, and worldly care cast out, both by the preceding words, and by these? For if He feed all flesh, much more them that are devoted to him; if them that are entangled in worldly cares, much more them that are freed from the same.

To establish this, Christ Himself said, " How many sparrows do ye exceed in value?"[1]   And He said it, teaching them not to put their confidence in wealth and land and seeds; for it is not these that feed us, but the word of God.[2]

Hereby they stop the mouths, both of the Manichæans, and of them of Valentinus, and of all that are diseased in their way. For sure this Being is not evil, who sets his own stores before all, even before them that blaspheme Him.

Then comes the petition: " Fill our hearts with joy and gladness." With what manner of joy then, doth it mean? the joy of this world? God forbid: for had they meant this, they would not have occupied summits of mountains, and deserts, nor wrapt themselves in sackcloth; but that joy they mean, which hath nothing in common with this present life, the joy of angels, the joy above.

And they do not simply ask for it, but in great excess; for they say not, " give," but, " fill," and they say not " us," but " our hearts." For this is especially a heart's joy; " For the fruit of the Spirit is love, joy, peace."[3]

Thus, because sin brought in sorrow, they request that through joy righteousness may be implanted in them, for no otherwise might joy be engendered.

" That, always having all sufficiency, we may abound unto every good work."[4] See how they fulfill that word of the gospel which saith, " Give us this day our daily bread," and how they seek even this for spiritual ends. For their phrase is, " That we may abound unto every good work." They said not, " That we may do our duty only," but

" even more than what is enjoined," for, " that we may abound," means this. And while of God they seek sufficiency in things needful, themselves are willing to obey not in sufficiency only, but with much abundance, and in all things. This is the part of well-disposed servants, this of men strict in goodness, to abound always, and in all things.

Then again reminding themselves of their own weakness, and that without the influence from above nothing noble can be done; having said, " that we may abound unto every good work," they add, " in Christ Jesus our Lord, with whom unto Thee be glory, honor, and might forever. Amen;" framing this end like their commencement by a thread of thanksgiving.

8. After this again, they seem to begin afresh, but they are keeping to the same argument. As Paul also in the beginning of an epistle, having closed with a doxology, where he says, " According to the will of our God and Father, to whom be glory forever. Amen;"[5] begins the subject again on which he was writing. And again in another place when he had said, " They worshipped and served the creature more than the Creator, who is blessed forever: Amen;"[6] he completed not his discourse, but begins again.

Therefore neither let us blame these our angels, as acting disorderly, for that having closed with a doxology they begin again the sacred hymns. For they follow apostolical laws, beginning from a doxology, and ending therein, and after that end making a commencement again.

Wherefore they say, " Glory be to Thee, O Lord; glory be to Thee, O Holy One; glory be to Thee, O King; that Thou hast given us food to make us glad."

Since not for the greater things only, but also for the lesser, we ought to give thanks. And they do give thanks for these also, putting to shame the heresy of the Manichæans, and of as many as affirm our present life to be evil. For lest for their high self-command, and contempt of the belly, thou shouldest suspect them as abhorring the meat, like the heretics aforesaid, who choke themselves[7] to death; they by their prayer teach thee, that not from abhorrence of God's creatures they abstain from most of them, but as exercising self-restraint.

And see how after thanksgiving for His past gifts, they are importunate also for the greater things, and dwell not upon the mat-

---

[1] Luke xii. 7. [Very freely cited.]
[2] Deut. viii. 3 ; Matt. iv. 4.   [3] Gal. v. 22.   [4] 2 Cor. ix. 8.

[5] Gal. i. 4, 5.   [6] Rom. i. 25
[7] ἀπαγχονιζόντων, a strong figurative expression, as it seems, for the unhallowed self-tormenting of the Manichæans. In Hom. XLII., the word is applied to Saul, " choking with envy " towards David.

ters of this life, but mount above the heavens, and say, " Fill us with the Holy Ghost." For it is not even possible to approve one's self as one ought, not being filled with that grace; as there is no doing anything noble or great, without the benefit of Christ's influences.

As therefore when they had said, " That we may abound unto every good work," they added, " In Christ Jesus;" so here also they say, " Fill us with the Holy Ghost, that we may be found to have been well-pleasing before Thee."[1]

Seest thou how for the things of this life they pray not, but give thanks only; but for the things of the Spirit, they both give thanks and pray. For, "seek ye," saith He, " the kingdom of heaven, and all these things shall be added unto you."[2]

And mark too another kind of severe goodness in them; their saying, namely, " That we may be found to have been well-pleasing in Thy sight, not being ashamed." For " we care not," say they, " for the shame that proceeds from the many, but whatever men may say of us, laughing, upbraiding, we do not so much as regard it; but our whole endeavor is not to be put to shame then." But in these expressions, they bring in also the river of fire, and the prizes, and the rewards.

They said not, "that we be not punished," but, "that we be not ashamed."[3] For this is to us far more fearful than hell, to seem to have offended our Lord."

But since the more part and the grosser sort are not in fear of this, they add, "When Thou renderest to every man according to his works." Seest thou how greatly these strangers and pilgrims have benefitted us, these citizens of the wilderness, or rather citizens of the Heavens? For whereas we are strangers to the Heavens, but citizens of the earth, these are just the contrary.

And after this hymn, being filled with much compunction, and with many and fervent tears, so they proceed to sleep, snatching just so much of it as a little to refresh themselves. And again, the nights they make days, spending them in thanksgivings and in the singing of psalms.

But not men only, but women also practise this self-denial, overcoming the weakness of their nature by the abundance of their zeal.

Let us be abashed then at their earnestness, we who are men, let us cease to be fastened to the things present, to shadow, to dreams, to smoke. For the more part of our life is passed in insensibility.

For both the first period of our life is full of much folly, and that again which travels on to old age, makes all the feeling that is in us wither away, and small is the space between, that is able feelingly to enjoy pleasure; or rather, not even that hath a pure participation thereof, by reason of innumerable cares and toils, that harrass it.

Wherefore, I pray, let us seek the unmovable and eternal goods, and the life that never has old age.

For even one dwelling in a city may imitate the self-denial of the monks; yea, one who has a wife, and is busied in a household, may pray, and fast, and learn compunction. Since they also, who at the first were instructed by the apostles, though they dwelt in cities, yet showed forth the piety of the occupiers of the deserts: and others again who had to rule over workshops, as Priscilla and Aquila.

And the prophets too, all had both wives and households, as Isaiah, as Ezekiel, as the great Moses, and received no hurt therefrom in regard of virtue.

These then let us also imitate, and continually offer thanksgiving to God, continually sing hymns to Him; let us give heed to temperance, and to all other virtues, and the self-denial that is practised in the deserts, let us bring into our cities; that we may appear both well-pleasing before God, and approved before men, and attain unto the good things to come, by the grace and love towards man of our Lord Jesus Christ, through whom and with whom be unto the Father, glory, honor, and might, together with the holy and life-giving Spirit, now and always and world without end. Amen.[4]

---

[1] [In some MSS. the two paragraphs which follow are omitted, " and not be ashamed" being joined with this clause.—R.]

[2] Matt. vi. 33. [Here, also, the peculiar reading " Kingdom of Heaven" occurs. Comp. Homily XXII. 4.—R.]

[3] [See above, note 1.—R.]

[4] The grace here commented on is in its commencement the same with one still used *before meat* in collegiate bodies: *e. g.* in Oriel College, Oxford. " *Benedicte Deus qui pascis nos in juventute nostra, et præbes cibum omni carni: reple gaudio et lætitia corda nostra, ut nos affatim quod satis est habentes, abundemus ad omne opus bonum: Per Jesum Christum Dominum nostrum:* Amen." The conclusion of St. Chrysostom's grace seems to be referred to by St. Just. Mart. Apol. 1. p. 83 C. and p. 50 E. as quoted by Mr. Field here.

HOMILY LVI.

Matt. XVI. 28.

" Verily, verily, I say unto you, There are some of them that stand here, which shall not taste of death, until they see the Son of Man coming in His kingdom."

Thus, inasmuch as He had discoursed much of dangers and death, and of His own passion, and of the slaughter of the disciples, and had laid on them those severe injunctions; and these were in the present life and at hand, but the good things in hope and expectation: —for example, " They save their life who lose it;" " He is coming in the glory of His Father;" " He renders His rewards: "—He willing to assure their very sight, and to show what kind of glory that is wherewith He is to come, so far as it was possible for them to learn it; even in their present life He shows and reveals this; that they should not grieve any more, either over their own death, or over that of their Lord, and especially Peter in His sorrow.

And see what He doth. Having discoursed of hell,[1] and of the kingdom (for as well by saying, " He that findeth his life shall lose it, and whosoever will lose it for my sake, shall find it;"[2] as by saying, " He shall reward every man according to his works,"[3] He had manifested both of these): having, I say, spoken of both, the kingdom indeed He shows in the vision, but hell not yet.

Why so? Because had they been another kind of people, of a grosser sort, this too would have been necessary; but since they are approved and considerate, He leads them on the gentler way. But not therefore only doth He make this disclosure, but because to Himself also it was far more suitable.

Not however that He passes over this subject either, but in some places He almost brings even before our eyes the very realities of hell; as when He introduces the picture of Lazarus, and mentions him that exacted the hundred pence, and him that was clad in the filthy garments, and others not a few.

2. " And after six days He taketh with Him Peter and James and John.[4]

Now another says, " after eight,"[5] not contradicting this writer, but most fully agreeing with him. For the one expressed both the very day on which He spake, and that on which He led them up; but the other, the days between them only.

But mark thou, I pray thee, the severe goodness of Matthew, not concealing those who were preferred to himself. This John also often doth, recording the peculiar praises of Peter with great sincerity. For the choir of these holy men was everywhere pure from envy and vainglory.

Having taken therefore the leaders, " He bringeth them up into a high mountain apart, and was transfigured before them: and His face did shine as the sun, and His raiment was[6] white as the light. And there appeared unto them Moses and Elias talking with Him.[7]

Wherefore doth He take with Him these only? Because these were superior to the rest. And Peter indeed showed his superiority by exceedingly loving Him; but John by being exceedingly loved of Him; and James again by his answer which he answered with his brother, saying, " We are able to drink the cup;[8] nor yet by his answer only, but also by his works; both by the rest of them, and by fulfilling, what he said. For so earnest was he, and grievous to the Jews, that Herod himself supposed that he had bestowed herein a very great favor on the Jews, I mean in slaying him.

But wherefore doth He not lead them up straightway? To spare the other disciples any feeling of human weakness: for which cause He omits also the names of them that are to go up. And this, because the rest would have desired exceedingly to have followed, being to see a pattern of that glory; and would have been pained, as overlooked. For though it was somewhat in a corporeal way that He made the disclosure, yet nevertheless the thing had much in it to be desired.

Wherefore then doth He at all foretell it? That they might be readier to seize the high meaning, by His foretelling it; and being filled with the more vehement desire in that round of days, might so be present with their mind quite awake and full of care.

---

[1] [γεέννης.]
[3] Matt. xvi. 27. [τὴν πρᾶξιν αὐτοῦ.]
[4] Matt. xvii. 1.
[2] Matt. xvi. 25.
[5] Luke ix. 28.
[6] [R. V., " his garments became," etc.]
[7] Matt. xvii. 2, 3.
[8] Matt. xx. 20, 22.

3. But wherefore doth He also bring forward Moses and Elias? One might mention many reasons. And first of all this: because the multitudes said He was, some Elias, some Jeremias, some one of the old prophets, He brings the leaders of His choir, that they might see the difference even hereby between the servants and the Lord; and that Peter was rightly commended for confessing Him Son of God.

But besides that, one may mention another reason also: that because men were continually accusing Him of transgressing the law, and accounting Him to be a blasphemer, as appropriating to Himself a glory which belonged not to Him, even the Father's, and were saying, "This Man is not of God, because He keepeth not the Sabbath day;"[1] and again, "For a good work we stone Thee not, but for blasphemy, and because that Thou, being a man, makest Thyself God:"[2] that both the charges might be shown to spring from envy, and He be proved not liable to either; and that neither is His conduct a transgression of the law, nor His calling Himself equal to the Father an appropriation of glory not His own; He brings forward them who had shone out in each of these respects: Moses, because he gave the law, and the Jews might infer that he would not have overlooked its being trampled on, as they supposed, nor have shown respect to the transgressor of it, and the enemy of its founder: Elias too for his part was jealous for the glory of God, and were any man an adversary of God, and calling himself God, making himself equal to the Father, while he was not what he said, and had no right to do so; he was not the person to stand by, and hearken unto him.

And one may mention another reason also, with those which have been spoken of. Of what kind then is it? To inform them that He hath power both of death and life, is ruler both above and beneath. For this cause He brings forward both him that had died, and him that never yet suffered this.

But the fifth motive, (for it is a fifth, besides those that have been mentioned), even the evangelist himself hath revealed. Now what was this? To show the glory of the cross, and to console Peter and the others in their dread of the passion, and to raise up their minds. Since having come, they by no means held their peace, but "spake," it is said, "of the glory[3] which He was to accomplish at Jerusalem;[4]" that is, of the passion, and the cross; for so they call it always.

And not thus only did He cheer them, but also by the excellency itself of the men, being such as He was especially requiring from themselves. I mean, that having said, "If any man will come after me, let him take up his cross, and follow me;" them that had died ten thousand times for God's decrees, and the people entrusted to them, these persons He sets before them. Because each of these, having lost his life, found it. For each of them both spake boldly unto tyrants, the one to the Egyptian, the other to Ahab; and in behalf of heartless and disobedient men; and by the very persons who were saved by them, they were brought into extreme danger; and each of them wishing to withdraw men from idolatry; and each being unlearned; for the one was of a "slow tongue,"[5] and dull of speech, and the other for his part also somewhat of the rudest in his bearing: and of voluntary poverty both were very strict observers; for neither had Moses made any gain, nor had Elias aught more than his sheepskin; and this under the old law, and when they had not received so great a gift of miracles. For what if Moses clave a sea? yet Peter walked on the water, and was able to remove mountains, and used to work cures of all manner of bodily diseases, and to drive away savage demons, and by the shadow of his body to work those wonderful and great prodigies; and changed the whole world. And if Elias too raised a dead man, yet these raised ten thousand; and this before the spirit was as yet vouchsafed to them. He brings them forward accordingly for this cause also. For He would have them emulate their winning ways toward the people, and their presence of mind and inflexibility; and that they should be meek like Moses, and jealous for God like Elias, and full of tender care, as they were. For the one endured a famine of three years for the Jewish people; and the other said, "If thou wilt forgive them their sin, forgive; else blot me too out of the book, which thou hast written."[6] Now of all this He was reminding them by the vision.

For He brought those in glory too, not that these should stay where they were, but that they might even surpass their limitary lines. For example, when they said, "Should we command fire to come down from heaven," and made mention of Elias as having done so, He saith, "Ye know not what manner of spirit ye are of;"[7] training them to forbearance by the superiority in their gift.

---

1 John ix. 16.   2 John x. 33.
3 δόξαν: in our copies of St. Luke ἔξοδον, but St. Chrysostom's reading is that of a good many MSS. [None of the recent critical editions of the New Testament refer to any Greek MSS., uncial or cursive, with this reading. Chrysostom alludes to it again in Homily LVIII. 1.—R.]

4 Luke ix. 31.   5 Exod. iv. 10.   6 Exod. xxxii. 32.
7 Luke ix. 54, 55. [The latter clause is omitted in the R. V. text.—R.]

And let none suppose us to condemn Elias as imperfect; we say not this; for indeed he was exceedingly perfect, but in his own times, when the mind of men was in some degree childish, and they needed this kind of schooling. Since Moses too was in this respect perfect; nevertheless these have more required of them than he. For " except your righteousness shall exceed the righteousness of the Scribes and Pharisees, ye shall in no case enter into the kingdom of Heaven." [1] For not into Egypt did they enter, but into the whole world, worse disposed than the Egyptians; neither were they to speak with Pharaoh, but to fight hand to hand with the devil, the very prince of wickedness. Yea, and their appointed struggle was, both to bind him, and to spoil all his goods; and this they did cleaving not the sea, but an abyss of ungodliness, through the rod of Jesse,—an abyss having waves far more grievous. See at any rate how many things there were to put the men in fear; death, poverty, dishonor, their innumerable sufferings; and at these things they trembled more than the Jews of old at that sea. But nevertheless against all these things He persuaded them boldly to venture, and to pass as along dry ground with all security.

To train them therefore for all this, He brought forward those who shone forth under the old law.

4. What then saith the ardent Peter? " It is good for us to be here." [2] For because he had heard that Christ was to go to Jerusalem and to suffer, being in fear still and trembling for Him, even after His reproof, he durst not indeed approach and say the same thing again, " Be it far from thee; [3] but from that fear obscurely intimates the same again in other words. That is, when he saw a mountain, and so great retirement and solitude, his thought was, " He hath great security here, even from the place; and not only from the place, but also from His going away no more unto Jerusalem." For he would have Him be there continually: wherefore also he speaks of " tabernacles." For " if this may be," saith he, " we shall not go up to Jerusalem; and if we go not up, He will not die, for there He said the scribes would set upon Him."

But thus indeed he durst not speak; but desiring however to order things so, he said undoubtingly, " It is good for us to be here," where Moses also is present, and Elias; Elias who brought down fire on the mountain, and Moses who entered into the thick darkness,

and talked with God; and no one will even know where we are."

Seest thou the ardent lover of Christ? For look not now at this, that the manner of his exhortation was not well weighed, but see how ardent he was, how burning his affection to Christ. For in proof that not so much out of fear for himself he said these things, hear what he saith, when Christ was declaring beforehand His future death, and the assault upon Him: " I will lay down my life for Thy sake. [4] Though I should die with Thee, yet will I not deny Thee. [5]

And see how even in the very midst of the actual dangers he counselled amiss [6] for himself. We know that when so great a multitude encompassed them, so far from flying, he even drew the sword, and cut off the ear of the high priest's servant. To such a degree did he disregard his own interest, and fear for his Master. Then because he had spoken as affirming a fact, he checks himself, and thinking, what if he should be again reproved, he saith, " If Thou wilt, let us make [7] here three tabernacles, one for Thee and one for Moses, and one for Elias."

What sayest thou, O Peter? didst thou not a little while since distinguish Him from the servants? Art thou again numbering Him with the servants? Seest thou how exceedingly imperfect they were before the crucifixion? For although the Father had revealed it to him, yet he did not always retain the revelation, but was troubled by his alarm; not this only, which I have mentioned, but another also, arising from that sight. In fact, the other evangelists, to declare this, and to indicate that the confusion of his mind, with which he spake these things, arose from that alarm, said as follows; mark, " He wist not what to say, for they were sore afraid;" [8] but Luke after his saying, " Let us make three tabernacles," added, " not knowing what he said." [9] Then to show that he was holden with great fear, both he and the rest, he saith, " They were heavy with sleep, and when they were awake they saw His glory;" [10] meaning by deep sleep here, the deep stupor engendered in them by that vision. For as eyes are darkened by an excessive splendor, so at that time also did they feel. For it was not, I suppose, night, but day; and the exceeding greatness of the light weighed down the infirmity of their eyes.

5. What then? He Himself speaks

---

[1] Matt. v. 20.　　[2] Matt. xvi. 4.　　[3] Matt. xvi. 22.

[4] John xiii. 37.　　　　　　[5] Matt. xxvi. 35.
[6] παρεβούλευετο. Comp. Philip. ii. 30.
[7] [R. V., " I will make" (ποιήσω), with the earliest MSS. Mark and Luke: " Let us make."—R.]
[8] Mark ix. 6.　　　　　　[9] Luke ix. 33.
[10] Luke ix. 32. [R. V., margin, " having remained awake."]

nothing, nor Moses, nor Elias, but He that is greater than all, and more worthy of belief, the Father, uttereth a voice out of the cloud.

Wherefore out of the cloud? Thus doth God ever appear. "For a cloud and darkness are round about Him;"[1] and, "He sitteth on a light cloud;"[2] and again, "Who maketh clouds His chariot;"[3] and, "A cloud received Him out of their sight;"[4] and, "As the Son of Man coming in the clouds."[5]

In order then that they might believe that the voice proceeds from God, it comes from thence.

And the cloud was bright. For "while he yet spake, behold, a bright cloud overshadowed them; and, behold, a voice out of the cloud, which said, This is My beloved Son, in whom I am well pleased; hear ye Him."[6]

For as, when He threatens, He shows a dark cloud;—as on Mount Sinai; for "Moses," it is said, "entered into the cloud, and into the thick darkness; and as a vapor, so went up the smoke;"[7] and the prophet said, when speaking of His threatening, "Dark water in clouds of the air;"[8]—so here, because it was His desire not to alarm, but to teach, it is a bright cloud.

And whereas Peter had said "Let us make three tabernacles," He showed a tabernacle not made with hands. Wherefore in that case it was smoke, and vapor of a furnace; but in this, light unspeakable and a voice.

Then, to signify that not merely concerning some one of the three was it spoken, but concerning Christ only; when the voice was uttered, they were taken away. For by no means, had it been spoken merely concerning any one of them, would this man have remained alone, the two being severed from Him.

Why then did not the cloud likewise receive Christ alone, but all of them together? If it had received Christ alone, He would have been thought to have Himself uttered the voice. Wherefore also the evangelist, making sure this same point, saith, that the voice was from the cloud, that is, from God.

And what saith the voice? "This is my beloved Son." Now if He is beloved, fear not thou, O Peter. For thou oughtest indeed to know His power already, and to be fully assured touching His resurrection; but since thou knowest not, at least from the voice of the Father take courage. For if God be mighty, as surely He is mighty, very evidently the Son is so likewise. Be not afraid then of those fearful things.

But if as yet thou receive it not, consider at least that other fact, that He is both a Son, and is beloved. For "This," it is said, "is My beloved Son." Now if He is beloved, fear not. For no one gives up one whom he loves. Be not thou therefore confounded; though thou lovest Him beyond measure, thou lovest Him not as much as He that begat Him.

"In whom I am well pleased." For not because He begat Him only, doth He love Him, but because He is also equal to Him in all respects, and of one mind with Him. So that the charm of love is twofold, or rather even threefold, because He is the Son, because He is beloved, because in Him He is well pleased.

But what means, "In whom I am well pleased?" As though He had said, "In whom I am refreshed, in whom I take delight;" because He is in all respects perfectly equal with Himself, and there is but one will in Him and in the Father, and though He continue a Son, He is in all respects one with the Father.

"Hear ye Him." So that although He choose to be crucified, you are not to oppose Him.

6. "And when they heard it, they fell on their face, and were sore afraid. And Jesus came and touched them, and said, Arise, and be not afraid. And when they lifted up their eyes, they saw no man, save Jesus only."[9]

How was it that, when they heard these words, they were dismayed? And yet before this also a like voice was uttered at Jordan, and a multitude was present, and no one felt anything of the kind; and afterwards again, when also they said, "It thundered,"[10] yet neither at that time did they experience anything like this. How then did they fall down in the mount? Because there was solitude, and height, and great quietness, and a transfiguration full of awe, and a pure light, and a cloud stretched out; all which things put them in great alarm. And the amazement came thick on every side, and they fell down both in fear at once and in adoration.

But that the fear abiding so long might not drive out their recollection, presently He puts an end to their alarm, and is seen Himself alone, and commands them to tell no man this, until He is risen from the dead.

For "as they came down from the mount, He charged them to tell the vision to no man, until He were risen from the dead."[11]

For the greater the things spoken of Him,

---

[1] Ps. xcvii. 2.   [2] Is. xix. 1.   [3] Ps. civ. 3.
[4] Acts i. 9.   [5] Dan. vii. 13.   [6] Matt. xvii. 5.
[7] Exod. xx. 21, xix. 18.   [8] Ps. xviii. 11.

[9] Matt. xvii. 6–8.   [10] John xii. 28, 29.
[11] Matt. xvii. 9. [In the last clause "the Son of Man" is omitted, and ἀναστῇ is substituted for ἐγερθῇ. The former is the usual term in Mark, not in Matthew.—R.]

the harder to be received by the generality at that time; and the offense also from the cross was the more increased thereby.

Therefore He bids them hold their peace; and not merely so, but He again reminds them of the passion, and all but tells them also the cause, for which indeed He requires them to keep silence. For He did not, you see, command them never to tell any man, but "until He were risen from the dead." And saying nothing of the painful part, He expresses the good only.

What then? Would they not afterwards be offended? By no means. For the point required was the time before the crucifixion. Since afterwards they both had the spirit vouchsafed them, and the voice that proceeded from the miracles pleading with them, and whatsoever they said was thenceforth easy to be received, the course of events proclaiming His might more clearly than a trumpet, and no offense of that sort interrupting [1] what they were about.

7. Nothing then is more blessed than the apostles, and especially the three, who even in the cloud were counted worthy to be under the same roof with the Lord.

But if we will, we also shall behold Christ, not as they then on the mount, but in far greater brightness. For not thus shall He come hereafter. For whereas then, to spare His disciples, He discovered so much only of His brightness as they were able to bear; hereafter He shall come in the very glory of the Father, not with Moses and Elias only, but with the infinite host of the angels, with the archangels, with the cherubim, with those infinite tribes, not having a cloud over His head, but even heaven itself being folded up.

For as it is with the judges; when they judge publicly, the attendants drawing back the curtains show them to all; even so then likewise all men shall see Him sitting, and all the human race shall stand by, and He will make answers to them by Himself; and to some He will say, "Come, ye blessed of my Father; for I was an hungered, and ye gave me meat;" [2] to others, "Well done, thou good and faithful servant, thou hast been faithful over a few things, I will set thee over many things. [3]

And again passing an opposite sentence, to some He will answer, "Depart into the everlasting fire, that is prepared for the devil and his angels," [4] and to others, "O thou wicked and slothful servants." [5] And some He will "cut asunder," and "deliver to the tormentors;" but others He will command to

"be bound hand and foot, and cast into outer darkness. [6] And after the axe the furnace will follow; and all out of the net, that is cast away, will fall therein.

"Then shall the righteous shine forth as the sun;" [7] or rather more than the sun. But so much is said, not because their light is to be so much and no more, but since we know no other star brighter than this, He chose by the known example to set forth the future brightness of the saints.

Since on the mount too, when He says, "He did shine as the sun," for the same cause did He so speak. For that the comparison did not come up to His light, the apostles showed by falling down. For had the brightness not been unalloyed, but comparable to the sun; they would not have fallen, but would easily have borne it.

The righteous therefore will shine as the sun, and more than the sun in that time; but the sinners shall suffer all extremities. Then will there be no need of records, proofs, witnesses. For He who judges is Himself all, both witness, and proof, and judge. For He knows all things exactly; "For all things are naked and opened unto His eyes." [8]

No man will there appear rich or poor, mighty or weak, wise or unwise, bond or free; but these masks will be dashed in pieces, and the inquiry will be into their works only. For if in our courts, when any one is tried for usurpation, or murder, whatever he may be, whether governor, or consul, or what you will, all these dignities fleet away, and he that is convicted suffers the utmost penalty; much more will it be so there.

8. Therefore that this may not be so, let us lay aside our filthy garments, let us put on the armor of light, and the glory of God will wrap us around. For what is even grievous in the injunctions? or what is there not easy? Hear, for instance, the prophet speaking, and then thou shalt know the easiness thereof. "Neither though thou bow as a collar thy neck, and strew beneath thee sackcloth and ashes, not even so shalt thou call a fast acceptable; but loose every bond of iniquity, unloose the twisted knots of oppressive bargains." [9]

See a prophet's wisdom, how stating first whatever was irksome, and removing it, he exhorts them to obtain salvation by the duties that are easy; signifying, that God needs not toils, but obedience.

Then implying that virtue is easy, but vice grievous and galling, he makes it out by the

---

[1] μεσολαβοῦντος. [2] Matt. xxv. 34, 35. [3] Matt. xxv. 23.
[4] Matt. xxv. 41. [5] Matt. xxv. 26.
[6] Matt. xxii. 13.
[7] Matt. xiii. 43.
[8] Heb. iv. 13.
[9] Is. lviii. 6.

bare names; "For," saith he, "vice is a bond," and "a twisted knot," but virtue is a disengagement and release from all these.

"Tear in sunder every unjust compact;" thus calling men's bills about the interest due to them, and the sums they have lent.

"Set at liberty them that are bruised;" them that are afflicted. For such a being is the debtor; when he sees his creditor, his mind is broken, and he fears him more than a wild beast.

"Bring in the poor that are cast out to thy house; if thou seest one naked, clothe him, and them that belong to thy seed thou shalt not overlook."[1]

Now in our late discourse which we made unto you when declaring the rewards, we showed the wealth arising from these acts; but now let us see if any of the injunctions be grievous, and transcending our nature. Nay, nothing of the kind shall we discover, but quite the contrary; that while these courses are very easy, those of vice are full of labor. For what is more vexatious than to be lending, and taking thought about usuries and bargains, and demanding sureties, and fearing and trembling about securities, about the principal, about the writings, about the interest, about the bondsmen?

For such is the nature of worldly things; yea, nothing is so unsound and suspicious as that which is accounted security, and contrived for that purpose; but to show mercy is easy, and delivers from all anxiety.

Let us not then traffic in other men's calamities, nor make a trade of our benevolence. And I know indeed that many hear these words with displeasure; but what is the profit of silence? For though I should hold my peace, and give no trouble by my words, I could not by this silence deliver you from your punishment; rather it has altogether the opposite result; the penalty is enhanced, and not to you only, but to me also, doth such a silence procure punishment. What then signify our gracious words, when in our works they help us not, but rather do harm? What is the good of delighting men in word, while we vex them in deed, bringing pleasure to the ears, and punishment to the soul? Wherefore I must needs make you sorry here, that we may not suffer punishment there.

9. For indeed a dreadful disease, beloved, dreadful and needing much attendance, hath fallen on the church. Those, namely, who are enjoined not even by honest labors to lay up treasures, but to open their houses to the needy, make a profit of other men's poverty, devising a specious robbery, a plausible covetousness.

For tell me not of the laws that are without; since even the publican fulfills the law that is without, but nevertheless is punished: which will be the case with us also, unless we refrain from oppressing the poor, and from using their need and necessity as an occasion for shameless trafficking.

For to this intent thou hast wealth, to relieve poverty, not to make a gain of poverty; but thou with show of relief makest the calamity greater, and sellest benevolence for money.

Sell it, I forbid thee not, but for a heavenly kingdom. Receive not a small price for so good a deed, thy monthly one in the hundred,[2] but that immortal life. Why art thou beggarly, and poor, and mean, selling thy great things for a little, even for goods that perish, when it should be for an everlasting kingdom? Why dost thou leave God, and get human gains? Why dost thou pass by the wealthy one, and trouble him that hath not? and leaving the sure paymaster make thy bargain with the unthankful? The other longs to repay, but this even grudges in the act of repaying. This hardly repays a hundredth part, but the other "an hundredfold and eternal life." This with insults and revilings, but the other with praises and auspicious words. This stirs up envy against thee, but the other even weaves for thee crowns. This hardly here, but the other both there and here.

Surely then is it not the utmost senselessness, not so much as to know how to gain? How many have lost their very principal for the interest's sake? How many have fallen into perils for usurious gains. How many have involved both themselves and others in extreme poverty through their unspeakable covetousness!

For tell me not this, that he is pleased to receive, and is thankful for the loan. Why, this is a result of thy cruelty. Since Abraham too,[3] contriving how his plan might take with the barbarians, did himself give up his wife to them; not however willingly, but through fear of Pharaoh. So also the poor man, because thou countest him not even worth so much money, is actually compelled to be thankful for cruelty.

And it seems to me as though, shouldest thou deliver him from dangers, thou wouldest exact of him a payment for this deliverance. "Away," saith he; "let it not be." What sayest thou? Delivering him from the greater evil, thou art unwilling to exact money, and

---

[2] Τόκος ἑκατοστιαῖος, *centesima usura*, 1 per cent. per month.
[3] Gen. xii. 11, etc.

for the lesser dost thou display so much inhumanity?

Seest thou not how great a punishment is appointed for the deed? hearest thou not that even in the old law this is forbidden?[1] But what is the plea of the many? "When I have received the interest, I give to the poor;" one tells me. Speak reverently, O man; God desires not such sacrifices. Deal not subtilly with the law. Better not give to a poor man, than give from that source; for the money that hath been collected by honest labors, thou often makest to become unlawful because of that wicked increase; as if one should compel a fair womb to give birth to scorpions.

And why do I speak of God's law? Do not even ye call it "filth"? But if ye, the gainers, give your voice so, consider what suffrage God will pass upon you.

And if thou wilt ask the Gentile lawgivers too, thou wilt be told that even by them this thing is deemed a proof of the most utter shamelessness. Those, for example, who are in offices of honor, and belong to the great council, which they call the senate, may not legally disgrace themselves with such gains; there being a law among them which prohibits the same.[2]

How then is it not a horrible thing, if thou ascribe not even so much honor to the polity of Heaven, as the legislators to the council of the Romans; but Heaven is to obtain less than earth, and thou art not ashamed even of the very folly of the thing? For what could be more foolish than this, unless one without land, rain, or plough, were to insist upon sowing?[3] Tares therefore, to be committed to the fire, do they reap, who have devised this evil husbandry.

Why, are there not many honest trades? in the fields, the flocks, the herds, the breeding of cattle, in handicrafts, in care of property? Why rave and be frantic, cultivating thorns for no good? What if the fruits of the earth are subject to mischance; hail, and blight, and excessive rain? yet not to such an extent as are money dealings. For in whatsoever cases of that sort occur, the damage of course concerns the produce, but the principal remains, I mean, the land. But herein many often have suffered shipwreck in their principal; and before the loss too they are in continual dejection. For never doth the moneylender enjoy his possessions, nor find pleasure in them; but when the interest is brought, he rejoices not that he hath received gain, but is grieved that the interest hath not yet come up to the principal. And before this evil offspring is brought forth complete, he compels it also to bring forth,[4] making the interest principal, and forcing it to bring forth its untimely and abortive brood of vipers. For of this nature are the gains of usury; more than those wild creatures do they devour and tear the souls of the wretched.[5] This "is the bond of iniquity:" this "the twisted knot of oppressive bargains."

Yea, "I give," he seems to say, "not for thee to receive, but that thou mayest repay more." And whereas God commands not even to receive what is given (for "give," saith He, "to them from whom ye look not to receive "),[6] thou requirest even more than is given, and what thou gavest not, this as a debt, thou constrainest the receiver to pay.

And thou indeed supposest thy substance to be increased hereby, but instead of substance thou art kindling the unquenchable fire.

That this therefore may not be, let us cut out the evil womb of usurious gains, let us deaden these lawless travailings, let us dry up this place of pernicious teeming, and let us pursue the true and great gains only. "But what are these?" Hear Paul saying "Godliness with contentment is great gain."[7]

Therefore in this wealth alone let us be rich, that we may both here enjoy security, and attain unto the good things to come, by the grace and love towards man of our Lord Jesus Christ, to whom be glory and might with the Father and the Holy Spirit, now and always, and world without end. Amen.

---

[1] Exod. xxii. 25 ; Lev. xxv. 35, 36 : Deut. xxiii. 19.
[2] See Bingham, *Antiq.* vi. ii. 6, who refers to a Law of Honorius, A.D. 397. *Cod. Theod.* lib. 2, tit. 33, *de usuris*, leg. 3; and Gibbon, c. 44; who quotes several of the Fathers to prove that all lending with interest was forbidden; but most or all of them seem to be speaking of exorbitant interest, or of lending to the poor.
[3] So St. Basil, as quoted below. "The husbandman having reaped the ear, seeks not again the seed under the root. But thou having the fruits, still givest not up that of which they grew. Thou plantest without land, thou reapest without seed."

[4] St. Basil, *Hom. in Ps.* 14 (15), c. 3. "Interest upon interest, a bad offspring of bad parents. These may be well called *a generation of vipers*, I mean what our usuries bring forth. Vipers, they say, are yeaned, eating through their mother's womb: and these usurious gains devour the debtors' houses, and so have their birth."
[5] There is here and afterwards a play upon the word τόκος, gain, as a derivative of τίκτειν, *to bring forth*, which can hardly be expressed in English.
[6] Luke vi. 35. [Cited very freely.]	[7] 1 Tim vi. 6.

HOMILY LVII.

MATT. XVII. 10.

" And His disciples asked Him, saying, Why then say the Scribes that Elias must first come ? "

NOT then from the Scriptures did they know this, but the Scribes used to explain themselves, and this saying was reported abroad amongst the ignorant people; as about Christ also.

Wherefore the Samaritan woman also said, " Messiah cometh; when He is come, He will tell us all things: " [1] and they themselves asked John, " Art thou Elias, or the Prophet ? " [2] For the saying, as I said, prevailed, both that concerning the Christ and that concerning Elias, not however rightly interpreted by them.

For the Scriptures speak of two advents of Christ, both this that is past, and that which is to come; and declaring these Paul said, " The grace of God, that bringeth salvation, hath appeared, teaching us, that, denying ungodliness and worldly lusts, we should live soberly, and righteously, and godly." [3] Behold the one, hear how he declares the other also; for having said these things, he added, " Looking for the blessed hope and appearing of our great God and Saviour Jesus Christ." [4] And the prophets too mention both; of the one, however, that is, of the second, they say Elias will be the forerunner. For of the first, John was forerunner; whom Christ called also Elias, not because he was Elias, but because he was fulfilling the ministry of that prophet. For as the one shall be forerunner of the second advent, so was the other too of the first. But the Scribes, confusing these things and perverting the people, made mention of that other only to the people, the second advent, and said, " If this man is the Christ, Elias ought to have come beforehand." Therefore the disciples too speak as follows, " How then say the Scribes, Elias must first come ? "

Therefore also the Pharisees sent unto John, and asked him, " Art thou Elias ? " [5] making no mention anywhere of the former advent.

What then is the solution, which Christ al- leged ? " Elias indeed cometh then, before my second advent; and now too is Elias come; " so calling John.

In this sense Elias is come: but if thou wouldest seek the Tishbite, he is coming. Wherefore also He said, " Elias truly cometh, and shall restore all things." [6] All what things ? Such as the Prophet Malachi spake of; for " I will send you," saith He, " Elias the Tishbite, who shall restore the heart of father to son, lest I come and utterly smite the earth." [7]

Seest thou the accuracy of prophetical language ? how, because Christ called John, Elias, by reasoning of their community of office, lest thou shouldest suppose this to be the meaning of the prophet too in this place, He added His country also, saying, " the Tishbite; " [8] whereas John was not a Tishbite. And herewith He sets down another sign also, saying, " Lest I come and utterly smite the earth," signifying His second and dreadful advent. For in the first He came not to smite the earth. For, " I came not," saith He, " to judge the world, but to save the world." [9]

To show therefore that the Tishbite comes before that other advent, which hath the judgment, He said this. And the reason too of his coming He teaches withal. And what is this reason ? That when He is come, he may persuade the Jews to believe in Christ, and that they may not all utterly perish at His coming. Wherefore He too, guiding them on to that remembrance, saith, "And he shall restore all things; " that is, shall correct the unbelief of the Jews that are then in being.

Hence the extreme accuracy of his expression; in that he said not, " He will restore the heart of the son to the father," but " of the father to the son." [10] For the Jews being fathers of the apostles, his meaning is, that he will restore to the doctrines of their sons, that is, of the apostles, the hearts of the fathers, that is, the Jewish people's mind. [11]

---

[1] John iv. 25.　　　　　　　　[2] John i. 21.
[3] Titus ii. 11, 12. [The Homily omits " to all men."]
[4] Tit. ii. 13.　　　　　　　　[5] John i. 21.

[6] Matt. xvii. 11. [R. V., " Elijah indeed cometh," etc.]
[7] Mal. iv. 5, 6, LXX.
[8] [The Hebrew does not have this; the argument rests on the inaccurate rendering of the LXX.]
[9] John xii. 47.　　　　　　　　[10] See LXX.
[11] As to Elijah's future coming, see St. Just. Mart. *Dial. adv.*

"But I say unto you, that Elias is come already, and they knew him not, but have done unto him whatsoever they listed. Likewise shall also the Son of Man suffer of them. Then they understood that He spake to them of John."[1]

And yet neither the Scribes said this, nor the Scriptures; but because now they were sharper and more attentive to His sayings, they quickly caught His meaning.

And whence did the disciples know this? He had already told them, "He is Elias, which was for to come;"[2] but here, that he hath come; and again, that "Elias cometh and will restore all things." But be not thou troubled, nor imagine that His statement wavers, though at one time He said, "he will come," at another, "he hath come." For all these things are true. Since when He saith, "Elias indeed cometh, and will restore all things," He means Elias himself, and the conversion of the Jews which is then to take place; but when He saith, "Which was for to come," He calls John, Elias, with regard to the manner of his administration. Yea, and so the prophets used to call every one of their approved kings, David;[3] and the Jews, "rulers of Sodom,"[4] and "sons of Ethiopians;"[5] because of their ways. For as the other shall be forerunner of the second advent, so was this of the first.

2. And not for this only doth He call him Elias everywhere, but to signify His perfect agreement with the Old Testament, and that this advent too is according to prophecy.

Wherefore also He adds again, "He came, and they knew him not, but have done unto him all things whatsoever they listed."[6] What means, "all things whatsoever they listed?" They cast him into prison, they used him despitefully, they slew him, they brought his head in a charger.

"Likewise shall also the Son of Man suffer of them." Seest thou how again He in due season reminds them of His passion, laying up for them great store of comfort from the passion of John. And not in this way only, but also by presently working great miracles. Yea, and whensoever He speaks of His passion, presently He works miracles, both after those sayings and before them; and in many places one may find Him to have kept this rule.

"Then," for instance, it saith, "He began to signify how that He must go unto Jerusalem, and be killed, and suffer many things."[7] "Then:" when? when He was confessed to be Christ, and the Son of God.

Again on the mountain, when He had shown them the marvellous vision, and the prophets had been discoursing of His glory, He reminded them of His passion. For having spoken of the history concerning John, He added, "Likewise shall also the Son of Man suffer of them."

And after a little while again, when He had cast out the devil, which His disciples were not able to cast out; for then too, "As they abode in Galilee," so it saith, "Jesus said unto them, The Son of Man shall be betrayed into the hands of sinful[8] men, and they shall kill Him, and the third day He shall rise again."[9]

Now in doing this, He by the greatness of the miracles was abating the excess of their sorrow, and in every way consoling them; even as here also, by the mention of John's death, He afforded them much consolation.

But should any one say, "Wherefore did He not even now raise up Elias and send him, witnessing as He doth so great good of his coming?" we should reply, that even as it was, while thinking Christ to be Elias, they did not believe Him. For "some say," such are the words, "that Thou art Elias, and others, Jeremias."[10] And indeed between John and Elias, there was no difference but the time only. "Then how will they believe at that time?" it may be said. Why, "he will restore all things," not simply by being recognized, but also because the glory of Christ will have been growing more intense up to that day, and will be among all clearer than the sun. When therefore, preceded by such an opinion and expectation, he comes making the same proclamation as John, and himself also announcing Jesus, they will more easily receive his sayings. But in saying, "They knew him not," He is excusing also what was done in His own case.[11]

And not in this way only doth He console them, but also by pointing out that John's sufferings at their hands, whatever they are, are undeserved; and by His throwing into the shade what would annoy them, by means of two signs, the one on the mountain, the other just about to take place.

But when they heard these things, they do not ask Him when Elias cometh; being

Tryph. p. 268, ed. Paris, 1636: Tert. *de Anim.* 35; *de Resur. Carnis,* 22; Origen (more doubtfully) *in St. Matt.* tom. 13, iii. 572; *in St. Joan.* tom. 3, iv. 92. St. Jer. *in St. Matt.* xi, 15, (t. 7, 70. Vallars. 1771), but doubtingly; *in loco,* p. 132, more positively; St. Aug. *in St. Joan.* Tr. iv. 5, 6. *de Civ. Dei,* 20, 29 : who speaks positively of his coming to convert the Jews, as being "a most common topic in the mouths and hearts of the faithful."

[1] Matt. xvii. 12, 13.   [2] Matt. xi. 14.
[3] This refers apparently to such texts as Jer. xxx. 9; Ezek. xxxiv. 23, 24, xxxvii. 24; Hos. iii. 5.
[4] Isa. i. 10.   [5] Amos ix. 7.   [6] Matt. xvii. 12.

[7] Matt. xvi. 21.
[8] ["Sinful" (ἁμαρτωλῶν) is omitted in some MSS. of the Homily. It does not occur in Matt. xvii. 22, but is taken from Luke xxiv. 7. Comp. Homily LVIII. at the beginning.—R.]
[9] Matt. xvii. 23.   [10] Matt. xvi. 14.   [11] Comp. Luke xxiii. 24.

23

straitened either by grief at His passion, or by fear. For on many occasions, upon seeing Him unwilling to speak a thing clearly, they are silent, and so an end. For instance, when during their abode in Galilee He said, "The Son of Man shall be betrayed, and they shall kill Him;"[1] it is added by Mark, "That they understood not the saying, and were afraid to ask Him;"[2] by Luke, "That it was hid from them, that they might not perceive it, and they feared to ask Him of that saying."[3]

3. "And when they were come to the multitude, there came to Him a man, kneeling down to Him, and saying, Lord, have mercy on my son, for he is lunatic, and sore vexed;[4] for ofttimes he falleth into the fire, and oft into the water. And I brought him unto Thy disciples, and they could not cure him."[5]

This man the Scripture signifies to be exceedingly weak in faith; and this is many ways evident; from Christ's saying, "All things are possible to him that believeth;"[6] from the saying of the man himself that approached, "Help Thou mine unbelief:"[7] from Christ's commanding the devil to "enter no more into him;"[8] and from the man's saying again to Christ, "If Thou canst."[9] "Yet if his unbelief was the cause," it may be said, "that the devil went not out, why doth He blame the disciples?" Signifying, that even without persons to bring the sick in faith, they might in many instances work a cure. For as the faith of the person presenting oftentimes availed for receiving the cure, even from inferior ministers; so the power of the doers oftentimes sufficed, even without belief in those who came to work the miracle.

And both these things are signified in the Scripture. For both they of the company of Cornelius by their faith drew unto themselves the grace of the Spirit; and in the case of Eliseus[10] again, when none had believed, a dead man rose again. For as to those that cast him down, not for faith but for cowardice did they cast him, unintentionally and by chance, for fear of the band of robbers, and so they fled: while the person himself that was cast in was dead, yet by the mere virtue of the holy body the dead man arose.

Whence it is clear in this case, that even the disciples were weak; but not all; for the pillars[11] were not present there. And see this man's want of consideration, from another circumstance again, how before the multitude he pleads to Jesus against His disciples, saying, "I brought him to Thy disciples, and they could not cure him."

But He, acquitting them of the charges before the people, imputes the greater part to him. For, "O faithless and perverse generation," these are His words, "how long shall I be with you?"[12] not aiming at his person only, lest He should confound the man, but also at all the Jews. For indeed many of those present might probably be offended, and have undue thoughts of them.

But when He said, "How long shall I be with you," He indicates again death to be welcome to Him, and the thing an object of desire, and His departure longed for, and that not crucifixion, but being with them, is grievous.

He stopped not however at the accusations; but what saith He? "Bring him hither to me."[13] And Himself moreover asks him, "how long time he is thus;" both making a plea for His disciples, and leading the other to a good hope, and that he might believe in his attaining deliverance from the evil.

And He suffers him to be torn, not for display (accordingly, when a crowd began to gather, He proceeded to rebuke him), but for the father's own sake, that when he should see the evil spirit disturbed at Christ's mere call, so at least, if in no other way, he might be led to believe the coming miracle.

And because he had said, "Of a child," and, "If thou canst help me," Christ saith, "To him that believeth, all things are possible,"[14] again giving the complaint a turn against him. And whereas when the leper said, "If Thou wilt, Thou canst make me clean,"[15] bearing witness to His authority Christ commending him, and confirming His words, said, "I will, be thou clean;" in this man's case, upon his uttering a speech in no way worthy of His power,—"If Thou canst, help me,"—see how He corrects it, as not rightly spoken. For what saith He? "If thou canst believe, all things are possible to him that believeth."[16] What He saith is like this: "Such abundance of power is with me, that I can even make others work these miracles. So that if thou believe as one ought, even thou thyself art able," saith He, "to heal both this one, and many others." And having thus said, He set free the possessed of the devil.

But do thou not only from this observe His providence and His beneficence, but also from that other time, during which He allowed the

---

1 Matt. xvii. 22, 23.   2 Mark ix. 32.   3 Luke ix. 45.
4 [R. V., "for he is epileptic, and suffereth grievously."]
5 Matt. xvii. 14–16.   6 Mark ix. 23.   7 Mark ix. 24.
8 Mark ix. 25.   9 Mark ix. 22.   10 2 Kings xiii. 21.
11 Gal. ii. 9.

12 Matt. xvii. 17.   13 Mark ix. 21.
14 Mark ix. 23.   15 Matt. viii. 2.
16 Mark ix. 23.   [The word πιστεῦσαι is read here ; the R. V. has a briefer reading. The entire passage in Mark shows many variations of text.—R.]

devil to be in him. Since surely, unless the man had been favored with much providential care even then, he would have perished long ago; for "it cast him both into the fire," so it is said, "and into the water." And he that dared this would assuredly have destroyed the man too, unless even in so great madness God had put on him His strong curb: as indeed was the case with those naked men that were running in the deserts and cutting themselves with stones.

And if he call him "'a lunatic," trouble not thyself at all, for it is the father of the possessed who speaks the word. How then saith the evangelist also, "He healed many that were lunatic?"[1] Denominating them according to the impression of the multitude. For the evil spirit, to bring a reproach upon nature,[2] both attacks them that are seized, and lets them go, according to the courses of the moon; not as though that were the worker of it;—away with the thought;—but himself craftily doing this to bring a reproach on nature. And an erroneous opinion hath gotten ground among the simple, and by this name do they call such evil spirits, being deceived; for this is by no means true.

4. "Then came His disciples unto Him apart, and asked Him, why they could not themselves cast out the devil."[3] To me they seem to be in anxiety and fear, lest haply they had lost the grace, with which they had been entrusted. For they received power against unclean spirits.[4] Wherefore also they ask, coming to Him apart; not out of shame (for if the fact had gone abroad, and they were convicted, it were superfluous after that to be ashamed of confessing it in words); but it was a secret and great matter they were about to ask Him of. What then saith Christ? "Because of your unbelief," saith He; "for if ye have faith as a grain of mustard seed, ye shall say unto this mountain, Remove, and it shall remove; and nothing shall be impossible unto you."[5] Now if you say, "Where did they remove a mountain?" I would make this answer, that they did far greater things, having raised up innumerable dead. For it is not at all the same thing, to remove a mountain, and to remove death from a body. And certain saints after them, far inferior to them, are said actually to have removed mountains, when necessity called for it."[6] Whereby we see that these also would have done the same, need calling on them.

But if there was then no need for it, do not thou find fault. And besides, He Himself said not, "ye shall surely remove it," but "ye shall be able to do even this." And if they did it not, it was not because they were unable (how could this be, when they had power to do the greater things?), but because they would not, there being no need.

And it is likely that this too may have been done, and not have been written; for we know that not all the miracles they wrought were written. Then however they were in a state by comparison very imperfect. What then? Had they not at that time so much as this faith? They had not, for neither were they always the same men, since even Peter is now pronounced blessed, now reproved; and the rest also are mocked by Him for folly, when they understood not His saying concerning the leaven.[7] And so it was, that then also the disciples were weak, for they were but imperfectly minded before the cross.

But by faith here He means that which related to the miracles, and mentions a mustard seed, to declare its unspeakable power. For though in bulk the mustard seed seem to be small, yet in power it is the strongest of all things. To indicate therefore that even the least degree of genuine faith can do great things, He mentioned the mustard seed; neither by any means did He stop at this only, but added even mountains, and went on beyond that. "For nothing," saith He, "shall be impossible to you."

But do thou herein also marvel at their self-denial, and the might of the Spirit; their self-denial in not hiding their fault, and the might of the Spirit in so leading on by degrees them who had not so much as a grain of mustard seed, that rivers and fountains of faith sprang up within them.

"Howbeit, this kind goeth not out, but by prayer and fasting;"[8] meaning the whole kind of evil spirits, not that of lunatics only.

Seest thou how He now proceeds to lay beforehand in them the foundation of His doctrine about fasting? Nay, argue not with me from rare cases, that some even without fasting have cast them out. For although one might say this, in one or two instances, of them that rebuke the evil spirits, yet for the patient it is a thing impossible, living luxuriously, to be delivered from such madness: this thing being especially necessary for him that is diseased in that way.

"And yet, if faith be requisite," one may

---

[1] Matt. iv. 24. [σεληνιαζομένους; the same term occurs here, and is the basis of the comment.—R.]
[2] τοῦ στοιχείου, the Element.   [3] Matt. xvii. 19.
[4] See Matt. x. 1.   [5] Matt. xvii. 20.
[6] St. Gregory Thaumaturgus : see his life by Nyssen.

[7] Matt. xvi. 6-12.
[8] Matt. xvii. 21 [This verse, which is wanting in several of the oldest and best N. T. MSS. (in Matthew), was undoubtedly accepted by Chrysostom, and by Origen before him. But the testimony from the canons of Eusebius is against its genuineness.—R.]

say, "what need of fasting?" Because, together with our faith, that also brings no small power. For it both implants much strictness, and of a man makes one an angel, and fights against the incorporeal powers: yet not by itself, but prayer too is needed, and prayer must come first.

5. See, at any rate, how many blessings spring from them both. For he that is praying as he ought, and fasting, hath not many wants, and he that hath not many wants, cannot be covetous; he that is not covetous, will be also more disposed for almsgiving. He that fasts is light, and winged, and prays with wakefulness, and quenches his wicked lusts, and propitiates God, and humbles his soul when lifted up. Therefore even the apostles were almost always fasting. He that prays with fasting hath his wings double, and lighter than the very winds. For neither doth he gape, nor stretch himself, nor grow torpid in prayer, as is the case with most men, but is more vehement than fire, and rises above the earth. Wherefore also such a one is most especially a hater and an enemy to the evil spirits. For nothing is mightier than a man who prays sincerely. For if a woman[1] had power to prevail with a savage ruler, one neither fearing God, nor regarding man; much more will he prevail with God, who is continually waiting upon Him, and controlling the belly, and casting out luxury. But if thy body be too weak to fast continually, still it is not too weak for prayer, nor without vigor for contempt of the belly. For although thou canst not fast, yet canst thou avoid luxurious living; and even this is no little thing, nor far removed from fasting, but even this is enough to pluck down the devil's madness. For indeed nothing is so welcome to that evil spirit, as luxury and drunkenness; since it is both fountain and parent of all our evils. Hereby, for example, of old he drove the Israelites to idolatry;[2] hereby he made the Sodomites to burn in unlawful lust. For, "this," it is said, "was the iniquity of Sodom; in pride, and in fullness of bread, and in banquetings they waxed wanton."[3] Hereby he hath destroyed ten thousand others, and delivered them to hell.

For what evil doth not luxury work? It makes swine of men, and worse than swine. For whereas the sow wallows in the mire and feeds on filth, this man lives on food more abominable than that, devising forbidden intercourse, and unlawful lusts.

Such an one is in no respect different from a demoniac, for like him he is lost to shame, and raves. And the demoniac at any rate we pity, but this man is the object of our aversion and hatred. Why so? Because he brings upon himself a self-chosen madness, and makes his mouth, and his eyes, and nostrils, and all, in short, mere sewers.

But if thou wert to see what is within him also, thou wilt behold his very soul as in a kind of wintry frost, stiff and torpid, and in nothing able to help its vessel through the excess of the storm.

I am ashamed to say how many ills men and women suffer from luxury, but I leave it to their own conscience, which knows it all more perfectly. For what is viler than a woman drunken, or at all led away[4] by wine? For the weaker the vessel, the more entire the shipwreck, whether she be free or a slave. For the free woman behaves herself unseemly in the midst of her slaves as spectators, and the slave again in like manner in the midst of the slaves, and they cause the gifts of God to be blasphemously spoken of by foolish men.

For instance, I hear many say, when these excesses happen, "Would there were no wine." O folly! O madness! When other men sin, dost thou find fault with God's gifts? And what great madness is this? What? did the wine, O man, produce this evil? Not the wine, but the intemperance of such as take an evil delight in it. Say then, "Would there were no drunkenness, no luxury;" but if thou say, "Would there were no wine," thou wilt say, going on by degrees, "Would there were no steel, because of the murderers; no night, because of the thieves; no light, because of the informers; no women, because of adulteries;" and, in a word, thou wilt destroy all.

But do not so; for this is of a satanical mind; do not find fault with the wine, but with the drunkenness; and when thou hast found this self-same man sober, sketch out all his unseemliness, and say unto him, Wine was given, that we might be cheerful, not that we might behave ourselves unseemly; that we might laugh, not that we might be a laughing-stock; that we might be healthful, not that we might be diseased; that we might correct the weakness of our body, not cast down the might of our soul.

God honored thee with the gift, why disgrace thyself with the excess thereof? Hear what Paul saith, "Use a little wine for thy stomach's sake, and thine often infirmities"[5] But if that saint, even when oppressed with disease, and enduring successive sicknesses, partook not of wine, until his Teacher suffered

---

[1] Luke xviii. 1-5.   [2] Exod. xxxii. 6.
[3] Ezek. xvi. 49. [LXX., but freely cited.]
[4] παραφερομένης.   [5] 1 Tim. v. 23.

him; what excuse shall we have, who are drunken in health? To him indeed He said, "Use a little wine for thy stomach's sake;" but to each of you who are drunken, He will say, "Use little wine, for thy fornications, thy frequent filthy talking, for the other wicked desires to which drunkenness is wont to give birth." But if ye are not willing, for these reasons, to abstain; at least on account of the despondencies which come of it, and the vexations, do ye abstain. For wine was given for gladness, "Yea, wine," so it is said, "maketh glad the heart of man:"[1] but ye mar even this excellence in it. For what kind of gladness is it to be beside one's self, and to have innumerable vexations, and to see all things whirling round, and to be oppressed with giddiness, and like those that have a fever, to require some who may drench their heads with oil?[2]

6. These things are not said by me to all: or rather they are said to all, not because all are drunken, God forbid; but because they who do not drink take no thought of the drunken. Therefore even against you do I rather inveigh, that are in health; since the physician too leaves the sick, and addresses his discourse to them that are sitting by them. To you therefore do I direct my speech, entreating you neither to be at any time overtaken by this passion, and to draw up[3] as by cords those who have been so overtaken, that they be not found worse than the brutes. For they indeed seek nothing more than what is needful, but these have become even more brutish than they, overpassing the boundaries of moderation. For how much better is the ass than these men? how much better the dog! For indeed each of these animals, and of all others, whether it need to eat, or to drink, acknowledges sufficiency for a limit, and goes not on beyond what it needs; and though there are innumerable persons to constrain, it will not endure to go on to excess.

In this respect then we are worse even than the brutes, by the judgment not of them that are in health only, but even by our own. For that ye have judged yourselves to be baser than both dogs and asses,[4] is evident from thence: that these brutes thou dost not compel to partake of food, beyond their measure; and should any one say, "Wherefore?" "Lest I should hurt them," thou wilt reply. But upon thyself thou bestowest not so much as this forethought. Thus thou accountest thyself

viler even than they are, and permittest thyself to be continually tossed as with a tempest.

For neither in the day of thy drunkenness only dost thou undergo the harm of drunkenness, but also after that day. And as when a fever is passed by, the mischievous consequences of the fever remain; so also when drunkenness is past, the disturbance of intoxication is whirling round both the soul and body; and while the wretched body lies paralyzed, like the hull of a vessel after a shipwreck, the soul yet more miserable than it, even when this is ended, stirs up the storm, and kindles the desire; and when one seems to be sober, then most of all is he mad, imagining to himself wine and casks, cups and goblets. And like as in a storm when the raging of the waters hath ceased, the loss by reason of the storm remains; so likewise here too. For as there of our freight, so here too is there a casting away of nearly all our good things. Whether it be temperance, or modesty, or understanding, or meekness, or humility, which the drunkenness finds there, it casts all away into the sea of iniquity.

But in what follows there is no more any likeness. Since there indeed upon the casting out the vessel is lightened, but here it is weighed down the more. For in its former place of wealt hit takes on board sand, and salt water, and all the accumulated filth of drunkenness; enough to sink the vessel at once, with the mariners and the pilot.

That we may not then suffer these things, let us deliver ourselves from that tempest. It is not possible with drunkenness to see the kingdom of Heaven. "Be not deceived," it is said, "no drunkards, no revilers, shall inherit the kingdom of God."[5] And why do I speak of a kingdom? Why, with drunkenness one cannot see so much as the things present. For in truth drunkenness makes the days nights to us, and the light darkness. And though their eyes be opened, the drunken see not even what is close at hand.

And this is not the only frightful thing, but with these things they suffer also another most grievous punishment, continually undergoing unreasonable despondencies, madness, infirmity, ridicule, reproach.

What manner of excuse is there for them that pierce themselves through with so many evils? There is none.

Let us fly then from that pest, that we may attain both unto the good things here, and unto those to come, by the grace and love towards man of our Lord Jesus Christ, to whom be glory and might with the Father and the Holy Spirit, world without end. Amen.

---

[1] Ps. civ. 15.

[2] Lightfoot, *Harmony*, A. D., 43. t. i. p. 333, seems to show from Talmudic writers, that anointing was regularly used among the Jews, either as a remedy or as a charm, in complaints of the head especially; and he uses the fact to explain St. James v. 15.

[3] ἀνιμᾶσθαι.

[4] [The Oxford edition reads "apes," obviously a typographical error. The Greek word is ὄνων.—R.]

[5] 1 Cor. vi. 9, 10.

HOMILY LVIII.

MATT. XVII. 22, 23.

"And while they abode in Galilee, Jesus said unto them, The Son of Man shall be betrayed into the hands of men, and they shall kill Him, and the third day He shall be raised again. And they were exceeding sorry."

THAT is, to hinder their saying, "wherefore do we abide here continually," He speaks to them again of the passion; on hearing which they had no wish so much as to see Jerusalem. And it is remarkable how, when both Peter had been rebuked, and Moses and Elias had discoursed concerning it, and had called the thing glory, and the Father had uttered a voice from above, and so many miracles had been done, and the resurrection was at the doors (for He said, He should by no means abide any long time in death, but should be raised the third day); not even so did they endure it, but were sorry; and not merely sorry, but exceeding sorry.

Now this arose from their being ignorant as yet of the force of His sayings. This Mark and Luke indirectly expressing said, the one, "They understood not the saying, and were afraid to ask Him:"[1] the other, "It was hid from them, that they perceived it not, and they feared to ask Him of that saying."[2]

And yet if they were ignorant, how were they sorry? Because they were not altogether ignorant; that He was to die they knew, continually hearing it, but what this death might be, and that there would be a speedy release from it, and that it would work innumerable blessings, as yet they knew not clearly; nor what this resurrection might be: but they understood it not, wherefore they grieved; for indeed they clung very earnestly to their Master.

"And when they were come to Capernaum, they that received the didrachma came to Peter, and said, Doth not your Master pay the didrachma?"[3]

And what is this "didrachma?" When God had slain the firstborn of the Egyptians, then He took the tribe of Levi in their stead.[4] Afterwards, because the number of the tribe was less than of the firstborn among the Jews,

for them that are wanting to make up the number, He commanded[5] a shekel to be contributed: and moreover a custom came thereby in force, that the firstborn should pay this tribute.

Because then Christ was a firstborn child, and Peter seemed to be first of the disciples, to him they come: their way being, as I suppose, to exact it in every city; wherefore also in His native place they approached Him; for Capernaum was accounted His native place.

And Him indeed they durst not approach, but Peter; nor him either with much violence, but rather gently. For not as blaming, but as inquiring, they said, "Doth not your Master pay the didrachma?" For the right opinion of Him they had not as yet, but as concerning a man, so did they feel; yet they rendered Him some reverence and honor, because of the signs that went before.

2. What then saith Peter? "He saith, Yea:" and to these indeed he said, that He payeth, but to Him he said it not, blushing perhaps to speak to Him of these things. Wherefore that gentle one, well knowing as He did all things, prevented him,[6] "saying, What thinkest thou, Simon? Of whom do the kings of the earth take custom or tribute? of their own sons, or of strangers;" and when he said "of strangers," He replied, "Then are the sons free."[7]

For lest Peter should suppose Him to say so, being told it by the others, He prevents him, partly indicating what hath been said, partly giving him leave to speak freely, backward as he was to speak first of these things.

And what He saith is like this, "I am indeed free from paying tribute. For if the kings of the earth take it not of their sons, but of their subjects; much more ought I to be freed from this demand, I who am Son, not of an earthly king, but of the King of Heaven, and myself a King."

Seest thou how He hath distinguished the

---

[1] Mark ix. 32.
[2] Luke ix. 45. [R. V. "It was concealed from them, that they should not perceive it: and they were afraid to ask him about this saying." Chrysostom reads, "the saying," and omits "it" after "perceive."—R.]
[3] Matt. xvii. 24.   [4] Num. iii. 11–13, 41–45.

[5] Num. iii. 46–51; xviii. 16.
[6] [R. V., "spake first to him." This is the sense here, but the citation begins at "saying," another Greek term than that of Matthew being used here.—R.]
[7] Matt. xvii. 25, 26.

sons from them that are not sons? And if He were not a Son, to no purpose hath He brought in the example also of the kings. "Yea," one may say, "He is a Son, but not truly begotten." Then is He not a Son; and if not a Son, nor truly begotten, neither doth He belong to God, but to some other. But if He belong to another, then neither hath the comparison its proper force. For He is discoursing not of the sons generally, but of the genuine sons, men's very own; of them that share the kingdom with their parents.

Wherefore also in contradistinction He hath mentioned the "strangers;" meaning by "strangers," such as are not born of them, but by "their own," those whom they have begotten of themselves.

And I would have thee mark this also; how the high doctrine,[1] revealed to Peter, He doth hereby again confirm. And neither at this did He stop, but by His very condescension declares this self-same truth; an instance of exceeding wisdom.

For after thus speaking, He saith, "But lest we should offend them, go thou and cast an hook into the sea, and take up the fish that first cometh up, and thou shalt find therein a piece of money;[2] that take, and give unto them for me and thee."[3]

See how He neither declines the tribute, nor simply commands to pay it, but having first proved Himself not liable to it, then He gives it: the one to save the people, the other, those around Him, from offense. For He gives it not at all as a debt, but as doing the best[4] for their weakness. Elsewhere, however, He despises the offense, when He was discoursing of meats,[5] teaching us to know at what seasons we ought to consider them that are offended, and at what to disregard them.

And indeed by the very mode of giving He discloses Himself again. For wherefore doth He not command him to give of what they have laid up? That, as I have said, herein also He might signify Himself to be God of all, and the sea also to be under His rule. For He had indeed signified this even already, by His rebuke, and by His commanding this same Peter to walk on the waves; but He now again signifies the self-same thing, though in another way, yet so as to cause herein great amazement. For neither was it a small thing, to foretell that the first, who out of those depths should come in his way, would be the fish that would pay the tribute; and having cast forth His commandment like a net into

that abyss, to bring up the one that bore the piece of money; but it was of a divine and unutterable power, thus to make even the sea bear gifts, and that its subjection to Him should be shown on all hands, as well when in its madness it was silent,[6] and when, though fierce, it received its fellow servant;[7] as now again, when it makes payment in His behalf to them that are demanding it.

"And give unto them," He saith, "for me and thee." Seest thou the exceeding greatness of the honor? See also the self-command of Peter's mind. For this point Mark, the follower of this apostle, doth not appear to have set down, because it indicated the great honor paid to him; but while of the denial he wrote as well as the rest, the things that make him illustrious he hath passed over in silence, his master perhaps entreating him not to mention the great things about himself. And He used the phrase, "for me and thee," because Peter too was a firstborn child.

Now as thou art amazed at Christ's power, so I bid thee admire also the disciple's faith, that to a thing beyond possibility he so gave ear. For indeed it was very far beyond possibility by nature. Wherefore also in requital for his faith, He joined him to Himself in the payment of the tribute.

3. "In that hour came the disciples unto Jesus, saying, Who then is the greatest in the kingdom of heaven?"[8]

The disciples experienced some feeling of human weakness; wherefore the evangelist also adds this note, saying, "In that hour;" when He had preferred him to all. For of James too, and John, one was a firstborn son, but no such thing as this had He done for them.

Then, being ashamed to avow their feeling, they say not indeed openly, "Wherefore hast thou preferred Peter to us?" or, "Is he greater than we are?" for they were ashamed; but indefinitely they ask, "Who then is greater?" For when they saw the three preferred, they felt nothing of the kind; but now that the honor had come round to one, they were vexed. And not for this only, but there were many other things which they put together to kindle that feeling. For to him He had said, "I will give thee the keys;"[9] to him, "Blessed art thou, Simon Barjona;" to him here, "Give unto them for me and thee;" and seeing too in general how freely he was allowed to speak, it somewhat fretted them.

And if Mark saith,[10] that they did not ask,

---

[1] τὴν γνῶσιν.
[2] Literally, a stater, = 4 drachmas. [R. V., "shekel, Greek, stater."]
[3] Matt. xvii. 27. [Slightly abridged.]
[4] διορθούμενος. [5] Matt. xv. 11.

[6] Matt. viii. 26. [7] Matt. xiv. 29.
[8] Matt. xviii. 1. [R. V., "Who then is greatest (Greek, greater)." Compare the comment.—R.]
[9] Matt. xvi. 19. [10] Mark ix. 34.

but reasoned in themselves, that is nothing contrary to this. For it is likely that they did both the one and the other, and whereas before, on another occasion, they had had this feeling, both once and twice, that now they did both declare it, and reason among themselves.

But to thee I say, "Look not to the charge against them only, but consider this too; first, that they seek none of the things of this world; next, that even this passion they afterwards laid aside, and give up the first place one to another." But we are not able to attain so much as unto their faults, neither do we seek, "who is greatest[1] in the kingdom of heaven;" but, who is greatest[2] in the earthly kingdom, who is wealthiest, who most powerful.

What then saith Christ? He unveils their conscience, and replies to their feeling, not merely to their words. "For He called a little child unto Him," saith the Scripture, "and said, Except ye be converted, and become as this little child, ye shall not enter into the kingdom of heaven."[3] "Why, you," He saith, "inquire who is greatest, and are contentious for first honors; but I pronounce him, that is not become lowest of all, unworthy so much as to enter in thither."

And full well doth He both allege that pattern, and not allege it only, but also set the child in the midst, by the very sight abashing them, and persuading them to be in like manner lowly and artless. Since both from envy the little child is pure, and from vainglory, and from longing for the first place; and he is possessed of the greatest of virtues, simplicity, and whatever is artless and lowly.

Not courage then only is wanted, nor wisdom, but this virtue also, humility I mean, and simplicity. Yea, and the things that belong to our salvation halt even in the chiefest point, if these be not with us.

The little child, whether it be insulted and beaten, or honored and glorified, neither by the one is it moved to impatience or envy, nor by the other lifted up.

Seest thou how again He calls us on to all natural excellencies, indicating that of free choice it is possible to attain them, and so silences the wicked frenzy of the Manichæans? For if nature be an evil thing, wherefore doth He draw from hence His patterns of severe goodness?

And the child which He set in the midst I suppose to have been a very young child indeed, free from all these passions. For such a little child is free from pride and the mad desire of glory, and envy, and contentiousness, and all such passions, and having many virtues, simplicity, humility, unworldliness,[4] prides itself upon none of them; which is a twofold severity of goodness; to have these things, and not to be puffed up about them.

Wherefore He brought it in, and set it in the midst; and not at this merely did He conclude His discourse, but carries further this admonition, saying, "And whoso shall receive such a little child in my name, receiveth me."[5]

"For know," saith He, "that not only, if ye yourselves become like this, shall ye receive a great reward; but also if for my sake ye honor others who are such, even for your honor to them do I appoint unto you a kingdom as your recompence." Or rather, He sets down what is far greater, saying, "he receiveth me." So exceedingly dear to me is all that is lowly and artless." For by "a little child," here, He means the men that are thus simple and lowly, and abject and contemptible in the judgment of the common sort.

4. After this, to obtain yet more acceptance for His saying, He establishes it not by the honor only, but also by the punishment, going on to say, "And whoso shall offend one of these little ones, it were better for him that a millstone were hanged about his neck, and that he were drowned in the depth of the sea."[6]

"For as they," saith He, "who honor these for my sake, have heaven, or rather an honor greater than the very kingdom; even so they likewise who dishonor them (for this is to offend them), shall suffer the extremity of punishment. And marvel thou not at His calling the affront "an offense;"[7] for many feeble-minded persons have suffered no ordinary offense from being treated with slight and insult. To heighten therefore and aggravate the blame, He states the mischief arising therefrom.

And He doth not go on to express the punishment in the same way, but from the things familiar to us, He indicates how intolerable it is. For when He would touch the grosser sort most sharply, He brings sensible images. Wherefore here also, meaning to

---

[1] [μείζων "greater."]
[2] [R. V., "Except ye turn, and become as little children," but Chrysostom substitutes "this little child."—R.]
[3] Matt. xviii. 2, 3.

[4] ἀπραγμοσύνην.
[5] Matt. xviii. 5. ["one such little child," rec. text.; so R. V.]
[6] Matt. xviii. 6. [R. V., but whoso shall cause one of these little ones which believe in me to stumble, it is profitable for him that a great millstone (Greek, a millstone turned by an ass) should be hanged about his neck, and that he should be sunk in the depth of the sea." The Greek text of Chrysostom agrees very closely with the received, but omits "which believe in me."—R.]
[7] [σκάνδαλον, "stumbling block."]

indicate the greatness of the punishment they shall undergo, and to strike into the arrogance of those that despise them, He brought forward a kind of sensible punishment, that of the millstone, and of the drowning. Yet surely it were suitable to what had gone before to have said, " He that receiveth not one of these little ones, receivoth not me;" a thing bitterer than any punishment; but since the very unfeeling, and exceeding gross, were not so much penetrated by this, terrible as it is, He puts "a millstone," and "a drowning." And He said not, "A millstone shall be hanged about his neck," but, "It were better for him"[1] to undergo this; implying that another evil, more grievous than this, awaits him; and if this be unbearable, much more that.

Seest thou how in both respects He made His threat terrible, first by the comparison with the known image rendering it more distinct, then by the excess on its side presenting it to the fancy as far greater than that visible one. Seest thou how He plucks up by the root the spirit of arrogance; how He heals the ulcer of vainglory; how He instructs us in nothing to set our heart on the first honors; how He persuades such as covet them in everything to follow after the lowest place?

5. For nothing is worse than arrogance.[2] This even takes men out of their natural senses, and brings upon them the character of fools; or rather, it really makes them to be utterly like idiots.

For like as, if any one, being three cubits in stature, were to strive to be higher than the mountains, or actually to think it, and draw himself up, as overpassing their summits, we should seek no other proof of his being out of his senses; so also when thou seest a man arrogant, and thinking himself superior to all, and accounting it a degradation to live with other people, seek not thou after that to see any other proof of that man's madness. Why, he is much more ridiculous than any natural fool, inasmuch as he absolutely creates this his disease on purpose. And not in this only is he wretched, but because he doth without feeling it fall into the very gulf of wickedness.

For when will such an one come to due knowledge of any sin? when will he perceive that he is offending? Nay, rather he is as a vile and captive slave, whom the devil having caught goes off with, and makes him altogether a prey, buffetting him on every side, and encompassing him with ten thousand insults.

For unto such great folly doth he lead them in the end, as to get them to be haughty towards their children, and wives, and towards their own forefathers. And others, on the contrary, He causes to be puffed up by the distinction of their ancestors. Now, what can be more foolish than this? when from opposite causes people are alike puffed up, the one sort because they had mean persons for fathers, grandfathers, and ancestors; and the other because theirs were glorious and distinguished? How then may one abate in each case the swelling sore? By saying to these last, " Go farther back than your grandfather, and immediate ancestors, and you will find perchance many cooks, and drivers of asses, and shopkeepers:" but to the former, that are puffed up by the meanness of their forefathers, the contrary again; "And thou again, if thou proceed farther up among thy forefathers, wilt find many far more illustrious than thou art."

For that nature hath this course, come let me prove it to thee even from the Scriptures. Solomon was son of a king, and of an illustrious king, but that king's father was one of the vile and ignoble. And his grandfather on his mother's side in like manner; for else he would not have given his daughter to a mere soldier. And if thou wert to go up again higher from these mean persons, thou wilt see the race more illustrious and royal. So in Saul's case too, so in many others also, one shall come to this result. Let us not then pride ourselves herein. For what is birth? tell me. Nothing, but a name only without a substance; and this ye will know in that day. But because that day is not yet come, let us now even from the things present persuade you, that hence arises no superiority. For should war overtake us, should famine, should anything else, all these inflated conceits of noble birth are put to the proof: should disease, should pestilence come upon us, it knows not how to distinguish between the rich and the poor, the glorious and inglorious, the high born and him that is not such; neither doth death, nor the other reverses of fortune, but they all rise up alike against all; and if I may say something that is even marvellous, against the rich more of the two. For by how much they are less exercised in these things, so much the more do they perish, when overtaken by them. And the fear too is greater with the rich. For none so tremble at princes as they; and at multitudes, not less than at princes. yea rather much more; many such houses in fact have been subverted alike by the wrath of multitudes and the threatening of princes. But

---

[1] [συμφερεῖ αὐτῷ, " it is profitable for him."]   [2] ἀπονοίας.

the poor man is exempt from both these kinds of troubled waters.

6. Wherefore let alone this nobility, and if thou wouldest show me that thou art noble, show the freedom of thy soul, such as that blessed man had (and he a poor man), who said to Herod, "It is not lawful for thee to have thy brother Philip's wife;"[1] such as he was possessed of, who before him was like him, and after him shall be so again; who said to Ahab, "I do not trouble Israel, but thou, and thy father's house;"[2] such as the prophets had, such as all the apostles.

But not like this are the souls of them that are slaves to wealth, but as they that are under ten thousand tutors, and taskmasters, so these dare not so much as lift up their eye, and speak boldly in behalf of virtue. For the love of riches, and that of glory, and that of other things, looking terribly on them, make them slavish flatterers; there being nothing which so takes away liberty, as entanglement in worldly affairs, and the wearing what are accounted marks of distinction. For such an one hath not one master, nor two, nor three, but ten thousand.

And if ye would fain even number them, let us bring in some one of those that are in honor in kings' courts, and let him have both very much wealth, and great power, and a birthplace excelling others, and distinction of ancestry, and let him be looked up to by all men. Now then let us see, if this be not the very person to be more in slavery than all; and let us set in comparison with him, not a slave merely, but a slave's slave, for many though servants have slaves. This slave's slave then for his part hath but one master. And what though that one be not a freeman? yet he is but one, and the other looks only to his pleasure. For albeit his master's master seem to have power over him, yet for the present he obeys one only; and if matters between them two are well, he will abide in security all his life. But our man hath not one or two only, but many, and more griev-ous masters. And first he is in care about the sovereign himself. And it is not the same to have a mean person for a master, as to have a king, whose ears are buzzed into by many, and who becomes a property now to this set and now to that.

Our man, though conscious of nothing, suspects all; both his comrades and his sub-ordinates; both his friends and his enemies.

But the other man too, you may say, fears his master. But how is it the same thing, to have one or many, to make one timorous?

Or rather, if a man inquire carefully, he will not find so much as one. How, and in what sense? Whereas that slave hath no one that desires to put him out of that service of his, and to introduce himself (whence neither hath he any one to plot against him therein); these have not even any other pursuit, but to unsettle him that is more approved and more beloved by their ruler. Wherefore also he must needs flatter all, his superiors, his equals, his friends. For where envy is, and love of glory, there even sincere friendship has no strength. For as those of the same craft cannot love one another with a perfect and genuine love, so is it with rivals in honor also, and with them that long for the same among worldly objects. Whence also great is the war within.

Seest thou what a swarm of masters, and of hard masters? Wilt thou that I show thee yet another, more grievous than this? They that are behind him, all of them strive to get before him: all that are before him, to hinder him from coming nearer them, and passing them by.

7. But O marvel! I undertook indeed to show you masters, but our discourse, we find, coming on and waxing eager, hath performed more than my undertaking, pointing out foes instead of masters; or rather the same per-sons both as foes and as masters. For while they are courted like masters, they are terri-ble as foes, and they plot against us as enemies. When then any one hath the same persons both as masters, and as enemies, what can be worse than this calamity? The slave indeed, though he be subject to com-mand, yet nevertheless hath the advantage of care and good-will on the part of them who give him orders; but these, while they receive commands, are made enemies, and are set one against another; and that so much more grievously than those in battles, in that they both wound secretly, and in the mask of friends they treat men as their enemies would do, and oftentimes make themselves credit of the calamity of others.

But not such are our circumstances; rather should another fare ill, there are many to grieve with him: should he obtain distinction, many to find pleasure with him. Not so again the apostle: "For whether," saith he, "one member suffer, all the members suffer with it; or one member be honored, all the members rejoice with it."[3] And the words of him who gives these admonitions, are at one time, "What is my hope or joy? are not even ye?"[4] at another, "Now we live, if ye

---

[1] Mark vi. 18.   [2] 1 Kings xviii. 18.   [3] 1 Cor. xii. 26.   [4] 1 Thes. ii. 19.

stand fast in the Lord;''[1] at another, "Out of much affliction and anguish of heart I wrote unto you;''[2] and, "Who is weak, and I am not weak? Who is offended, and I burn not?''[3]

Wherefore then do we still endure the tempest and the billows of the world without, and not run to this calm haven, and leaving the names of good things, go on to the very things themselves? For glory, and dignity, and wealth, and credit, and all such things, are names with them, but with us realities; just as the grievous things, death and dishonor and poverty, and whatever else is like them, are names indeed with us, but realities with them.

And, if thou wilt, let us first bring forward glory, so lovely and desirable with all of them. And I speak not of its being short-lived, and soon put out, but when it is in its bloom, then show it me. Take not away the daubings and colored lines of the harlot, but bring her forward decked out, and exhibit her to us, for me thereupon to expose her deformity. Well then, of course thou wilt tell of her array, and her many lictors, and the heralds' voice, and the listening of all classes, and the silence kept by the populace, and the blows given to all that come in one's way, and the universal gazing. Are not these her splendors? Come then, let us examine whether these things be not vain, and a mere unprofitable imagination. For wherein is the person we speak of the better for these things, either in body, or in soul? for this constitutes the man. Will he then be taller hereby, or stronger, or healthier, or swifter, or will he have his senses keener, and more piercing? Nay, no one could say this. Let us go then to the soul, if haply we may find there any advantage occurring herefrom. What then? Will such a one be more temperate, more gentle, more prudent, through that kind of attendance? By no means, but rather quite the contrary. For not as in the body, so also is the result here. For there the body indeed gains nothing in respect of its proper excellence; but here the mischief is not only the soul's reaping no good fruit, but also its actually receiving much evil therefrom: hurried as it is by such means into haughtiness, and vainglory, and folly, and wrath, and ten thousand faults like them.

"But he rejoices," thou wilt say, "and exults in these things, and they brighten him up." The crowning point[4] of his evils lies in that word of thine, and the incurable part of the disease. For he that rejoices in these things, would be unwilling however easily to

be released from that which is the ground of his evils; yea, he hath blocked up against himself the way of healing by this delight. So that here most of all is the mischief, that he is not even pained, but rather rejoices, when the diseases are growing upon him.

For neither is rejoicing always a good thing; since even thieves rejoice in stealing, and an adulterer in defiling his neighbor's marriage bed, and the covetous in spoiling by violence, and the manslayer in murdering. Let us not then look whether he rejoice, but whether it be for something profitable, lest[5] perchance we find his joy to be such as that of the adulterer and the thief.

For wherefore, tell me, doth he rejoice? For his credit with the multitude, because he can puff himself up, and be gazed upon? Nay, what can be worse than this desire, and this ill-placed fondness? or if it be no bad thing, ye must leave off deriding the vain-glorious and aspersing them with continual mockeries: ye must leave off uttering imprecations on the haughty and contemptuous. But ye would not endure it. Well then, they too deserve plenty of censure, though they have plenty of lictors. And all this I have said of the more tolerable sort of rulers; since the greater part of them we shall find transgressing more grievously than either robbers, or murderers, or adulterers, or spoilers of tombs, from not making a good use of their power. For indeed both their thefts are more shameless, and their butcheries more hardened, and their impurities far more enormous than the others; and they dig through, not one wall, but estates and houses without end, their prerogative making it very easy to them.

And they serve a most grievous servitude, both stooping basely under their passions,[6] and trembling at all their accomplices. For he only is free, and he only a ruler, and more kingly than all kings, who is delivered from his passions.

Knowing then these things, let us follow after the true freedom, and deliver ourselves from the evil slavery, and let us account neither pomp of power nor dominion of wealth, nor any other such thing, to be blessed; but virtue only. For thus shall we both enjoy security here, and attain unto the good things to come, by the grace and love towards man of our Lord Jesus Christ, to whom be glory and might, with the Father and the Holy Spirit, world without end. Amen.

---

[1] 1 Thes. iii. 8.   [2] 2 Cor. ii. 4.
[3] 2 Cor. xi. 29.   [4] κολοφῶνα.
[5] [The Greek text has διασκεψώμεθα, which the translator has ignored: "Let us consider well, lest," etc.—R.]
[6] [Some MSS. insert here: καὶ τοὺς συνδούλους τύπτοντες ἀφειδῶς, "and beating the fellow servants unsparingly." But it is put in brackets by Field.—R.]

HOMILY LIX.

MATT. XVIII. 7.

"Woe unto the world because of offenses:[1] for it must needs be that offenses come: but woe to that man by[2] whom the offense cometh."

"And if 'it must needs be that offenses come,'" (some one of our adversaries may perchance say), "why doth He lament over the world, when He ought rather to afford succor, and to stretch forth His hand in its behalf? For this were the part of a physician, and a protector, whereas the other might be looked for even from any ordinary person."

What then could we possibly say, in answer to so shameless a tongue? nay what dost thou seek for equal to this healing care of His? For indeed being God He became man for thee, and took the form of a slave, and underwent all extremities, and left undone none of those things which it concerned Him to do. But inasmuch as unthankful men were nothing the better for this, He laments over them, for that after so much fostering care they continued in their unsoundness.

It was like as if over the sick man, that had had the advantage of much attendance, and who had not been willing to obey the rules of the physician, any one were to lament and say, "Woe to such a man from his infirmity, which he has increased by his own remissness." But in that case indeed there is no advantage from the bewailing, but here this too is a kind of healing treatment to foretell what would be, and to lament it. For many oftentimes, though, when advised, they were nothing profited, yet, when mourned for, they amended.

For which reason most of all He used the word "Woe," thoroughly to rouse them, and to make them in earnest, and to work upon them to be wakeful. And at the same time He shows forth the good will He had towards those very men and His own mildness, that He mourns for them even when gainsaying, not taking mere disgust at it, but correcting them, both with the mourning, and with the prediction, so as to win them over.

But how is this possible? he may say. For if "it must needs be that offenses come," how is it possible to escape these?

Because that the offenses come indeed must needs be, but that men should perish is not altogether of necessity. Like as though a physician should say (for nothing hinders our using the same illustration again), it must needs be that this disease should come on, but it is not a necessary consequence that he who gives heed should be of course destroyed by the disease. And this He said, as I mentioned, to awaken together with the others His disciples. For that they may not slumber, as sent unto peace and unto untroubled life, He shows many wars close upon them, from without, from within. Declaring this, Paul said, "Without were fightings, within were fears;"[3] and, "In perils among false brethren;"[4] and in his discourse to the Milesians too He said, "Also of you shall some arise speaking perverse things;"[5] and He Himself too said, "The man's foes shall be they of his own household."[6] But when He said, "It must needs be," it is not as taking away the power of choosing for themselves, nor the freedom of the moral principle, nor as placing man's life under any absolute constraint of circumstances, that He saith these things, but He foretells what would surely be; and this Luke hath set forth in another form of expression, "It is impossible but that offenses should come."[7]

But what are the offenses?[8] The hindrances on the right way. Thus also do those on the stage call them that are skilled in those matters, them that distort their bodies.

It is not then His prediction that brings the offenses; far from it; neither because He foretold it, therefore doth it take place; but because it surely was to be, therefore He foretold it; since if those who bring in the offenses had not been minded to do wickedly, neither would the offenses have come; and if they had not been to come, neither would they have been foretold. But because those men did evil, and were incurably diseased, the offenses came, and He foretells that which is to be.

---

3 2 Cor. vii. 5. 4 2 Cor. xi. 26. 5 Acts xx. 30.
6 Matt. x. 36. 7 Luke xvii. 1. 8 σκάνδαλα.

But if these men had been kept right, it may be said, and there had been no one to bring in an offense, would not this saying have been convicted of falsehood? By no means, for neither would it have been spoken. For if all were to have been kept right, He would not have said, "it must needs be that they come," but because He foreknew they would be of themselves incorrigible, therefore He said, the offenses will surely come.

And wherefore did He not take them out of the way? it may be said. Why, wherefore should they have been taken out of the way? For the sake of them that are hurt? But not thence is the ruin of them that are hurt, but from their own remissness. And the virtuous prove it, who, so far from being injured thereby, are even in the greatest degree profited, such as was Job, such as was Joseph, such as were all the righteous, and the apostles. But if many perish, it is from their own slumbering. But if it were not so, but the ruin was the effect of the offenses, all must have perished. And if there are those who escape, let him who doth not escape impute it to himself. For the offenses, as I have said, awaken, and render more quick-sighted, and sharper, not only him that is preserved; but even him that hath fallen into them, if he rise up again quickly, for they render him more safe, and make him more difficult to overcome; so that if we be watch-ful, no small profit do we reap from hence, even to be continually awake. For if when we have enemies, and when so many dangers are pressing upon us, we sleep, what should we be if living in security. Nay, if thou wilt, look at the first man. For if having lived in paradise a short time, perchance not so much as a whole day, and having enjoyed delights, he drove on to such a pitch of wickedness, as even to imagine an equality with God, and to account the deceiver a benefactor, and not to keep to one commandment; if he had lived the rest of his life also without affliction, what would he not have done?

2. But when we say these things, they make other objections again, asking, And why did God make him such? God did not make him such, far from it, since then neither would He have punished him. For if we in those matters in which we are the cause, do not find fault with our servant, much more will not the God of all. "But whence did this come to pass?" one may say. Of himself and his own remissness. "What means, of himself?" Ask thyself. For if it be not of themselves the bad are bad, do not punish thy servant nor reprove thy wife for what errors she may commit, neither beat thy son,

nor blame thy friend, nor hate thine enemy that doth despite to thee: for all these deserve to be pitied, not to be punished, unless they offend of themselves. "But I am not able to practise self-restraint," one may say. And yet, when thou perceivest the cause not to be with them, but of another necessity, thou canst practise self-restraint. When at least a servant being taken with sickness doth not the things enjoined him, so far from blaming thou dost rather excuse him. Thus thou art a witness, that the one thing is of one's self, the other not of one's self. So that here too, if thou knewest that he was wicked from being born such, so far from blaming, thou wouldest rather have shown him indulgence. For surely, when thou makest him allowance for his illness, it could not be that thou wouldest have refused to make allowance for God's act of creation, if indeed he had been made such from the very first.

And in another way too it is easy to stop the mouths of such men, for great is the abounding power of the truth. For where-fore dost thou never find fault with thy serv-ant, because he is not of a beautiful counte-nance, that he is not of fine stature in his body, that he is not able to fly? Because these things are natural. So then from blame against his nature he is acquitted, and no man gainsays it. When therefore thou blamest, thou showest that the fault is not of nature but of his choice. For if in those things, which we do not blame, we bear wit-ness that the whole is of nature, it is evident that where we reprove, we declare that the offense is of the choice.

Do not then bring forward, I beseech thee, perverse reasonings, neither sophistries and webs slighter than the spider's, but answer me this again: Did God make all men? It is surely plain to every man. How then are not all equal in respect of virtue and vice? whence are the good, and gentle, and meek? whence are the worthless and evil? For if these things do not require any purpose, but are of nature, how are the one this, the others that? For if by nature all were bad, it were not possible for any one to be good, but if good by nature, then no one bad. For if there were one nature of all men, they must needs in this respect be all one, whether they were to be this, or whether they were to be that.

But if we should say that by nature the one are good, the other bad, which would not be reasonable (as we have shown), these things must be unchangeable, for the things of nature are unchangeable. Nay, mark. All mortals are also liable to suffering; and no one is free from suffering, though he strive without end. But now we see of good many becoming worthless, and of worthless good, the one through remissness, the other by earnestness; which thing most of all indicates that these things do not come of nature.

For the things of nature are neither changed, nor do they need diligence for their acquisition. For like as for seeing and hearing we do not need labor, so neither should we need toils in virtue, if it had been apportioned by nature.

"But wherefore did He at all make worthless men, when He might have made all men good? Whence then are the evil things?" saith he. Ask thyself; for it is my part to show they are not of nature, nor from God.

"Come they then of themselves?" he saith. By no means. "But are they unoriginated?" Speak reverently, O man, and start back from this madness, honoring with one honor God and the evil things, and that honor the highest. For if they be unoriginate they are mighty, and cannot so much as be plucked up, nor pass into annihilation. For that what is unoriginate is imperishable, is surely manifest to all.

3. And whence also are there so many good, when evil hath such great power? how are they that have an origin stronger than that which is unoriginate?

"But God destroys these things," he saith. When? And how will He destroy what are of equal honor, and of equal strength, and of the same age, as one might say, with Himself?

Oh malice of the devil! how great an evil hath he invented! With what blasphemy hath he persuaded men to surround God! with what cloak of godliness hath he devised another profane account? For desiring to show, that not of Him was the evil, they brought in another evil doctrine, saying, that these things are unoriginate.

"Whence then are evils?" one may say. From willing and not willing. "But the very thing of our willing and not willing, whence is it?" From ourselves. But thou dost the same in asking, as if when thou hadst asked, whence is seeing and not seeing? then when I said, from closing the eyes or not closing the eyes, thou wert to ask again; the very closing the eyes or not, whence is it? then having heard that it was of ourselves, and our will, thou wert to seek again another cause.

For evil is nothing else than disobedience to God. "Whence then," one may say, "did man find this?" "Why, was it a task to find this? I pray thee." "Nay, neither do I say this, that this thing is difficult; but whence became he desirous to disobey." "From remissness. For having power for either, he inclined rather to this."

But if thou art perplexed yet and dizzy at hearing this, I will ask thee nothing difficult nor involved, but a simple and plain question. Hast thou become some time bad? and hast thou become some time also good? What I mean, is like this. Didst thou prevail some time over passion, and wast thou taken again by passion? Has thou been overtaken by drunkenness, and hast thou prevailed over drunkenness? Wast thou once moved to wrath, and again not moved to wrath? Didst thou overlook a poor man, and not overlook him? Didst thou commit whoredom once? and didst thou become chaste again? Whence then are all these things? tell me, whence? Nay if thou thyself do not tell, I will say. Because at one time thou didst restrain thyself and strive, but after that thou becamest remiss and careless. For to those that are desperate, and are continually in wickedness, and are in a state of senselessness, and are mad, and who are not willing so much as to hear what will amend them, I will not even discourse of self restraint; but to them that have been sometimes in the one, and sometimes in the other, I will gladly speak. Didst thou once take by violence the things that belonged not to thee; and after this, subdued by pity, didst impart even of thine unto him that was in need? Whence then this change? Is it not quite plain it is from the mind, and the choice of will?

It is quite plain, and there is no one who would not say this. Wherefore I entreat you to be in earnest, and to cleave to virtue, and ye will have no need of these questions. For our evils are mere names, if we be willing. Inquire not then whence are evils, neither perplex thyself; but having found that they are from remissness only, flee the evil deeds.

And if any one should say, that these things come not from us; whenever thou seest him angry with his servants, and provoked with his wife, and blaming a child, and condemning them who injure him, say to him, how then saidst thou, that evils come not from us? For if they be not from us, wherefore dost thou find fault? Say again; is it of thyself thou revilest, and insultest? For if it be not of thyself, let no man be angry with thee; but if it be of thyself, of thyself and of thy remissness are thy evil deeds.

But what? thinkest thou there are some good men? For if indeed no man is good, whence hast thou this word? whence are praises? But if there are good men, it is quite plain that they will also reprove the bad. Yet if no one is voluntarily wicked, nor of himself, the good will be found to be unjustly reproving the bad, and they themselves too will be in this way bad again. For what can be worse than to subject the guiltless to accusations? But if they continue in our estimation good men, though reproving, and this especially is a proof of their goodness, even to the very fools it is hereby plain, that no one is ever by necessity bad.

But if after all this thou wouldest still inquire, whence are evils? I would say, from remissness, from idleness, from keeping company with the bad, from contempt of virtue; hence are both the evils themselves, and the fact that some inquire, whence are the evils. Since of them surely who do right no one inquires about these things, of them that are purposed to live equitably and temperately; but they, who dare to commit wicked acts, and wish to devise some foolish comfort[1] to themselves by these discussions, do weave spiders' webs.

But let us tear these in pieces not by our words only, but by our deeds too. For neither are these things of necessity. For if they were of necessity, He would not have said, "Woe to the man, by whom the offense cometh."[2] For those only doth he bewail, who are wicked by their choice.

And if He saith "by whom,"[3] marvel not. For not as though another were bringing in it by him, doth He say this, but viewing him as himself causing the whole. For the Scripture is wont to say, "by whom," for "of whom;"[4] as when it saith, "I have gotten a man by God,"[5] putting not the second cause, but the first; and again, "Is not the interpretation of them by God,"[6] and, "God is faithful, by whom ye are called unto the fellowship of His Son."[7]

4. And that thou mayest learn that it is not of necessity, hear also what follows. For after bewailing them, He saith, "If thy hand, or thy foot offend thee, cut them off, and cast them from thee: for it is better for thee to enter into life halt or maimed, rather than having two hands or feet to be cast into the fire. And if thy right eye offend thee, pluck it out; it is better for thee to enter into life with one eye, than having two eyes to be cast into the furnace of fire;"[8] not saying these

things of limbs; far from it; but of friends, of relations, whom we regard in the rank of necessary members. This He had both said further back, and now He saith it. For nothing is so hurtful as bad company. For what things compulsion cannot, friendship can often effect, both for hurt, and for profit. Wherefore with much earnestness He commands us to cut off them that hurt us, intimating these that bring the offenses.

Seest thou how He hath put away the mischief that would result from the offenses? By foretelling that there surely will be offenses, so that they might find no one in a state of carelessness, but that looking for them men might be watchful. By showing the evils to be great (for He would not have said without purpose, "Woe to the world because of the offenses," but to show that great is the mischief therefrom), by lamenting again in stronger terms over him that brings them in. For the saying, "But woe to that man," was that of one showing that great was the punishment, but not this only, but also by the comparison which He added He increased the fear.

Then He is not satisfied with these things, but He showeth also the way, by which one may avoid the offenses.

But what is this? The wicked, saith He, though they be exceeding dear friends to thee, cut off from thy friendship.

And He giveth a reason that cannot be gainsaid. For if they continue friends, thou wilt not gain them, but thou wilt lose thyself besides; but if thou shouldest cut them off, thine own salvation at least thou wilt gain. So that if any one's friendship harms thee, cut it off from thee. For if of our own members we often cut off many, when they are both in an incurable state, and are ruining the rest, much more ought one to do this in the case of friends.

But if evils were by nature, superfluous were all this admonition and advice, superfluous the precaution by the means that have been mentioned. But if it be not superfluous, as surely it is not superfluous, it is quite clear that wickedness is of the will.[9]

"Take heed that ye despise not one of these little ones; for I say unto you, that their angels do always behold the face of my Father which is in Heaven."[10]

He calleth little ones not them that are really little, but them that are so esteemed by the multitude, the poor, the objects of contempt, the unknown (for how should he be little who is equal in value to the whole

---

[1] παραμυθίαν, Field.　　[2] Matt. xviii. 7.　　[3] δι᾽ οὗ.
[4] [δι᾽ οὗ and ὑφ᾽ οὗ, i. e., "through whom" for "by whom," the latter phrase referring to the personal agent.—R.]
[5] Gen. iv. 1, LXX. [διὰ τοῦ θεοῦ.]　　[6] Gen. xl. 8.
[7] 1 Cor. i. 9.
[8] Matt. xviii. 8, 9. [The variations from the received text appear in the English rendering as given above.—R.]

[9] γνώμης.　　[10] Matt. xviii. 10. [R. V., "See," etc.]

world; how should he be little, who is dear to God?); but them who in the imagination of the multitude are so esteemed.

And He speaks not of many only, but even of one, even by this again warding off the hurt of the many offenses. For even as to flee the wicked, so also to honor the good, hath very great gain, and would be a twofold security to him who gives heed, the one by rooting out the friendships with them that offend, the other from regarding these saints with respect and honor.

Then in another way also He makes them objects of reverence, saying, "That their angels do always behold the face of my Father which is in Heaven."

Hence it is evident, that the saints have angels, or even all men. For the apostle too saith of the woman, "That she ought to have power on her head because of the angels."[1] And Moses, "He set the bounds of the nations according to the number of the angels[2] of God."[3]

But here He is discoursing not of angels only, but rather of angels that are greater than others. But when He saith, "The face of my Father," He means nothing else than their fuller confidence, and their great honor.

"For the Son of Man is come to save that which was lost."[4]

Again, He is putting another reason stronger than the former, and connects with it a parable, by which He brings in the Father also as desiring these things. "For how think ye?" saith He; "If a man have an hundred sheep, and one of them be gone astray, doth he not leave the ninety and nine, and goeth into the mountains, and seeketh that which is gone astray? And if so be that he find it,[5] he rejoiceth over it more than over the ninety and nine, which went not astray. Even so it is not will before your Father,[6] that one of these little ones should perish."[7]

Seest thou by how many things He is urging to the care of our mean brethren. Say not then, "Such a one is a blacksmith, a shoemaker, he is a ploughman, he is a fool," and so despise him. For in order that thou shouldest not feel this, see by how many motives He persuades thee to practise mode-ration, and presses thee into a care for these. He set a little child, and saith, "Be ye as

little children." And, "Whosoever receiveth such a little child receiveth me;" and, "Whosoever shall offend," shall suffer the utmost penalties. And He was not even sat-isfied with the comparison of the "mill-stone," but added also His "woe," and com-manded us to cut off such, though they be in the place of hands and eyes to us. And by the angels again that are entrusted with these same mean brethren, He makes them objects of veneration, and from His own will and passion (for when He said, "The Son of Man is come to save that which was lost," He signifies even the cross, like as Paul saith, speaking of a brother, "For whom Christ died"); and from the Father, for that neither to Him doth it seem good that one should perish; and from common custom, because the shepherd leaves them that are safe, and seeks what is lost; and when he hath found what was gone astray, he is greatly delighted at the finding and the saving of this.

5. If then God thus rejoices over the little one that is found, how dost thou despise them that are the objects of God's earnest care, when one ought to give up even one's very life for one of these little ones? But is he weak and mean? Therefore for this very cause most of all, one ought to do everything in order to preserve him. For even He Himself left the ninety and nine sheep, and went after this, and the safety of so many availed not to throw into the shade the loss of one. But Luke saith, that He even brought it on his shoulders, and that "There was greater joy over one sinner that repent-eth, than over ninety and nine just persons"[8] And from His forsaking those that were saved for it, and from His taking more pleasure in this one, He showed His earnestness about it to be great.

Let us not then be careless about such souls as these. For all these things are said for this object. For by threatening, that he who has not become a little child should not so much as at all set foot in the Heavens, and speaking of "the millstone," He hath brought down the haughtiness of the boastful; for nothing is so hostile to love as pride; and by saying, "It must needs be that offenses come," He made them to be wakeful; and by adding, "Woe unto him by whom the offense cometh," He hath caused each to endeavor that it be not by him. And while by com-manding to cut off them that offend He made salvation easy; by enjoining not to despise them, and not merely enjoining, but with

---

[1] 1 Cor. xi. 10.
[2] A. V. "Children of Israel," al. "Sons of God," and hence "Angels."
[3] Deut. xxxii. 8.
[4] Matt. xviii. 11. [This verse, which is passed over without comment, is omitted in Matthew by some of the best MSS. and fathers. Probably taken from Luke xix. 10.—R.]
[5] ["Verily I say unto you," omitted.]
[6] [R.V., margin, Greek: "a thing willed before your Father."]
[7] Matt. xviii. 12–14.

[8] Luke xv. 7.

earnestness (for "take heed," saith He, "that ye despise not one of these little ones"), and by saying, "Their angels behold the face of my Father," and, "For this end am I come," and "my Father willeth this," He hath made those who should take care of them more diligent.

Seest thou what a wall He hath set around them, and what earnest care He taketh of them that are contemptible and perishing, at once threatening incurable ills to them that make them fall, and promising great blessings to them that wait upon them, and take care of them, and bringing an example from Himself again and from the Father?

Him let us also imitate, refusing none of the tasks that seem lowly and troublesome for our brethren's sake; but though we have to do service, though he be small, though he be mean for whom this is done, though the work be laborious, though we must pass over mountains and precipices, let all things be held endurable for the salvation of our brother. For a soul is an object of such earnest care to God, that "He spared not His own Son."[1]

Wherefore I entreat, when morning hath appeared, straightway as we come out of our house, let us have this one object in view, this earnest care above all, to rescue him that is in danger; I do not mean this danger only that is known by sense, for this is not danger at all, but the danger of the soul, that which is brought upon men by the devil.

For the merchant too, to increase his wealth, crosses the sea; and the artisan, to add to his substance, doeth all things. Let us also then not be satisfied with our own salvation only, since else we destroy even this. For in a war too, and in an engagement, the soldier who is looking to this only how he may save himself by flight, destroys the rest also with himself; much as on the other hand the noble-minded one, and he who stands in arms in defense of the others, with the others preserves himself also. Since then our state too is a war, and of all wars the bitterest, and an engagement and a battle, even as our King commanded us, so let us set ourselves in array in the engagement, prepared for slaughter, and blood, and murders, looking to salvation in behalf of all, and cheering them that stand, and raising up them that are down. For indeed many of our brethren lie fallen in this conflict, having wounds, wallowing in blood, and there is none to heal, not any one of the people, not a priest, no one else, no one to stand by, no friend, no

brother, but we look every man to his own things.

By reason of this we maim our own interests also. For the greatest confidence and means of approval is the not looking to our own things.

Therefore I say, are we weak and easy to be overcome both by men, and by the devil, because we seek the opposite to this, and lock not our shields one with another, neither are fortified with godly love, but seek for ourselves other motives of friendship, some from relationship, some from long acquaintance, some from community of interest, some from neighborhood; and from every cause rather are we friends, than from godliness, when one's friendships ought to be formed upon this only. But now the contrary is done; with Jews and with Greeks[2] we sometimes become friends, rather than with the children of the church.

6. Yes, saith he, because the one is worthless, but the other kind and gentle. What sayest thou? Dost thou call thy brother worthless, who art commanded not to call him so much as Raca? And art thou not ashamed, neither dost thou blush, at exposing thy brother, thy fellow member, him that hath shared in the same birth with thee, that hath partaken of the same table?

But if thou hast any brother after the flesh, if he should perpetrate ten thousand evil deeds, thou laborest to conceal him, and accountest thyself also to partake of the shame, when he is disgraced; but as to thy spiritual brother, when thou oughtest to free him from calumny, thou dost rather encompass him with ten thousand charges against him?

"Why he is worthless and insufferable," thou mayest say. Nay then for this reason become his friend, that thou mayest put an end to his being such a one, that thou mayest convert him, that thou mayest lead him back to virtue. —"But he obeys not," thou wilt say, "neither doth he bear advice."—Whence knowest thou it? What, hast thou admonished him, and attempted to amend him?— "I have admonished him often," thou wilt say. How many times?—Oftentimes, both once, and a second time.—Oh! Is this often? Why, if thou hadst done this throughout all the time, oughtest thou to grow weary, and to give it up? Seest thou not how God is always admonishing us, by the prophets, by the apostles, by the evangelists? What then? have we performed all? and have we been obedient in all things? By no means. Did He then cease admonishing?

---

[1] Rom. viii. 32.

[2] *i. e.* Heathens.

24

Did He hold His peace? Doth He not say each day, "Ye cannot serve God, and mammon"[1] and with many, the superfluity and the tyranny of wealth yet increases? Doth He not cry aloud each day, "Forgive, and ye shall have forgiveness,"[2] and we become wild beasts more and more? Doth He not continually admonish to restrain desire, and to keep the mastery over wicked lust, and many wallow worse than swine in this sin? But nevertheless, He ceases not speaking.

Wherefore then do we not consider these things with ourselves, and say that even with us God reasons, and abstains not from doing this, although we disobey Him in many things?

Therefore He said that, "Few are the saved."[3] For if virtue in ourselves suffices not for our salvation, but we must take with us others too when we depart; when we have saved neither ourselves, nor others, what shall we suffer? Whence shall we have any more a hope of salvation?

But why do I blame for these things, when not even of them that dwell with us do we take any account, of wife, and children, and servants, but we have care of one thing instead of another, like drunken men, that our servants may be more in number, and may serve us with much diligence, and that our children may receive from us a large inheritance, and that our wife may have ornaments of gold, and costly garments, and wealth; and we care not at all for themselves, but for the things that belong to them. For neither do we care for our own wife, nor provide for her, but for the things that belong to the wife; neither for the child, but for the things of the child.

And we do the same as if any one seeing a house in a bad state, and the walls giving way, were to neglect to raise up these, and to make up great fences round it without; or when a body was diseased, were not to take care of this, but were to weave for it gilded garments; or when the mistress was ill, were to give heed to the maidservants, and the looms, and the vessels in the house, and mind other things, leaving her to lie and moan.

For this is done even now, and when our soul is in evil and wretched case, and angry, and reviling, and lusting wrongly, and full of vainglory, and at strife, and dragged down to the earth, and torn by so many wild beasts, we neglect to drive away the passions from her, and are careful about house and servants. And while if a bear has escaped by stealth, we shut up our houses, and run

along by the narrow passages, so as not to fall in with the wild beast; now while not one wild beast, but many such thoughts are tearing in pieces the soul, we have not so much as a feeling of it. And in the city we take so much care, as to shut up the wild beasts in solitary places and in cages, and neither at the senate house of the city, nor at the courts of justice, nor at the king's palace, but far off somewhere at a distance do we keep them chained; but in the case of the soul, where the senate house is, where the King's palace, where the court of justice is, the wild beasts are let loose, crying and making a tumult about the mind itself and the royal throne. Therefore all things are turned upside down, and all is full of disturbance, the things within, the things without, and we are in nothing different from a city thrown into confusion from being overrun by barbarians; and what takes place in us is as though a serpent were setting on a brood of sparrows, and the sparrows, with their feeble cries, were flying about every way affrighted, and full of trouble, without having any place whither to go and end their consternation.

7. Wherefore I entreat, let us kill the serpent, let us shut up the wild beasts, let us stifle them, let us slay them, and these wicked thoughts let us give over to the sword of the Spirit, lest the prophet threaten us also with such things as he threatened Judea, that "The wild asses shall dance there, and porcupines, and serpents."[4]

For there are, there are even men worse than wild asses, living as it were in the wilderness, and kicking; yea the more part of the youth amongst us is like this. For indeed having wild lusts they thus leap, they kick, going about unbridled, and spend their diligence on no becoming object.

And the fathers are to blame, who while they constrain the horsebreakers to discipline their horses with much attention, and suffer not the youth of the colt to go on long untamed, but put upon it both a rein, and all the rest, from the beginning; but their own young ones they overlook, going about for a long season unbridled, and without temperance; disgracing themselves, by fornications, and gamings, and continuings in the wicked theatres, when they ought before fornication to give him to a wife, to a wife chaste, and highly endued with wisdom; for she will both bring off her husband from his most disorderly course of life, and will be instead of a rein to the colt.

---

[1] Matt. vi. 24.   [2] Luke vi. 37.   [3] See Luke xiii. 23.

[4] Isaiah xiii. 21, 22. [The word δράκοντες, here rendered "serpents," is not found in the LXX; nor does the prophecy refer to Judæa, but to Babylon.—R.]

For indeed fornications and adulteries come not from any other cause, than from young men's being unrestrained. For if he have a prudent wife, he will take care of house and honor and character. "But he is young," you say. I know it too. For if Isaac was forty years old when he took his bride, passing all that time of his life in virginity, much more ought young men under grace to practise this self-restraint. But oh what grief! Ye do not endure to take care of their chastity, but ye overlook their disgracing, defiling themselves, becoming accursed; as though ye knew not that the profit of marriage is to preserve the body pure, and if this be not so, there is no advantage of marriage. But ye do the contrary; when they are filled with countless stains, then ye bring them to marriage without purpose and without fruit.

"Why I must wait," thou wilt say, "that he may become approved. that he may distinguish himself in the affairs of the state;" but of the soul ye have no consideration, but ye overlook it as a cast-away. For this reason all things are full of confusion, and disorder, and trouble, because this is made a secondary matter, because necessary things are neglected, but the unimportant obtain much forethought.

Knowest thou not, that thou canst do no such kindness to the youth, as to keep him pure from whorish uncleannness? For nothing is equal to the soul. Because, "What is a man profited," saith He, "if he shall gain the whole world, but lose his own soul."[1] But because the love of money hath overturned and cast down all, and hath thrust aside the strict fear of God, having seized upon the souls of men, like some rebel chief upon a citadel; therefore we are careless both of our children's salvation, and of our own, looking to one object only, that having become wealthier, we may leave riches to others, and these again to others after them, and they that follow these to their posterity, becoming rather a kind of passers on of our possessions and of our money, but not masters.

Hence great is our folly; hence the free are less esteemed than the slaves. For slaves we reprove, if not for their sake, yet for our own; but the free enjoy not the benefit even of this care, but are more vile in our estimation than these slaves. And why do I say, than our slaves? For our children are less esteemed than cattle; and we take care of horses and asses rather than of children. And should one have a mule, great is his anxiety to find the best groom, and not one either harsh, or dishonest, or drunken, or ignorant of his art; but if we have set a tutor[2] over a child's soul, we take at once, and at random, whoever comes in our way. And yet than this art there is not another greater. For what is equal to training the soul, and forming the mind of one that is young? For he that hath this art, ought to be more exactly observant than any painter and any sculptor.[3]

But we take no account of this, but look to one thing only, that he may be trained as to his tongue. And to this again we have directed our endeavors for money's sake. For not that he may be able to speak, but that he may get money, does he learn speaking; since if it were possible to grow rich even without this, we should have no care even for this.

Seest thou how great is the tyranny of riches? how it has seized upon all things, and having bound them like some slaves or cattle, drags them where it will?

But what are we advantaged by such accusations against it? For we indeed shoot at it in words, but it prevails over us in deeds. Nevertheless, not even so shall we cease to shoot at it with words from our tongue. For if any advance is made, both we are gainers and you; but if you continue in the same things, all our part at least hath been performed.

But may God both deliver you from this disease, and cause us to glory in you, for to Him be glory, and dominion, world without end. Amen.

---

[1] Matt. xvi. 26.

[2] παιδαγωγόν, a man-servant who took care of boys.
[3] [ἀνδριαντοποιοῦ, "maker of statuary."]

HOMILY LX.

MATT. XVIII. 15.

"If thy brother shall trespass·against thee, go and tell him his fault² between thee and
him alone. If he shall hear thee, thou hast gained thy brother."

FOR, since He had used vehement language against them that cause offense, and on every hand had moved them to fear; in order that the offended might not in this way on the other hand become supine, neither supposing all to be cast upon others, should be led on to another vice, soften in themselves, and desiring to be humored in everything, and run upon the shoal of pride; seest thou how He again checks them also, and commands the telling of the faults to be between the two alone, lest by the testimony of the many he should render his accusation heavier, and the other, become excited to opposition, should continue incorrigible.

Wherefore He saith, "Between thee and him alone," and, "If he shall hear thee, thou hast gained thy brother." What is, "If he shall hear thee?" If he shall condemn himself, if he shall be persuaded that he has done wrong.

"Thou hast gained thy brother." He did not say, Thou hast a sufficient revenge, but, "Thou hast gained thy brother," to show that there is a common loss from the enmity. For He said not, "He hath gained himself only," but, "thou too hast gained him," whereby He showed that both the one and the other were losers before this, the one of his brother, the other of his own salvation.

This, when He sat on the mount also, He advised; at one time bringing him who has given the pain to him that had been pained, and saying, "Be reconciled to thy brother,"³ and at another commanding him that had been wronged to forgive his neighbor. For He taught men to say, "Forgive us our debts, like as we forgive our debtors."⁴

But here He is devising another mode. For not him that gave the pain, *doth He now call upon*,⁵ but him that was pained He brings to this one. For because this who hath done the wrong would not easily come to make excuse, out of shame, and confusion of face, He draws that other to him, and not merely so, but in such way as also to correct what hath been done. And He saith not, "Accuse," nor "Charge him," nor "Demand satisfaction, and an account," but "Tell him of his fault,"⁶ saith He. For he is held in a kind of stupor through anger and shame with which he is intoxicated; and thou, who art in health, must go thy way to him that is ill, and make the tribunal private, and the remedy such as may be readily received. For to say, "Tell him of his fault," is nothing else than "Remind him of his error," tell him what thou hast suffered at his hand, which very thing, if it be done as it ought, is the part of one making excuse for him, and drawing him over earnestly to a reconciliation.

What then, if he should disobey, and be disposed to abide in hardness? "Take with thyself yet one or two, that in the mouth of two witnesses every word may be established."⁷ For the more he is shameless, and bold, the more ought we to be active for his cure, not in anger and indignation. For the physician in like manner, when he sees the malady obstinate, doth not give up nor grow impatient, but then makes the more preparation; which He commands us to do in this case too.

For since thou appearedst to be too weak alone, make thyself more powerful by this addition. For surely the two are sufficient to convict him that hath sinned. Seest thou how He seeketh not the good of him that hath been pained only, but of him also that hath given the pain. For the person injured is this one who is taken captive by his passion, he it is that is diseased, and weak, and infirm. Wherefore He often sends the other to this one, now alone, and now with others; but if he continue in it, even with the church. For, "Tell it," saith He, "to the Church."⁸

---

¹ [The form of the Greek verb here is peculiar to the text of the Homily. R. V., "sin," for "trespass."—R.]

² Lit. "reprove" or "convict him."

³ Matt. v. 24. [But the citation is fuller : "If thou art standing by the altar and rememberest that thy brother hath aught against thee, go away, be reconciled," etc.—R.]

⁴ Matt. vi. 12.   ⁵ [Supplied by translator.]

⁶ Or, "Convict him."

⁷ Matt. xviii. 16. [The words "or three" are omitted in the Homily here, but not below. In both cases the form of the verb is changed.—R.]

⁸ Matt. xviii. 17.

For if He were seeking this one's advantage only, He would not have commanded to pardon, seventy times seven, one repenting. He would not so often have set so many over him to correct his passion; but if he had remained incorrigible after the first conference, would have let him be; but now once, and twice, and thrice, He commands to attempt his cure, and now alone and now with two, now with more.

Wherefore, with respect to them that are without He saith no such thing, but, "If any one smite thee," He saith, "on thy right cheek, turn to him the other also,"[1] but here not in such wise. For what Paul meaneth, saying, "What have I to do to judge them also that are without?"[2] but the brethren he commands both to tell of their faults, and to avoid them, and to cut them off, not being obedient, that they may be ashamed; this Himself also doeth here, making these laws about the brethren; and He sets three[3] over him for teachers and judges, to teach him the things that are done at the time of his drunkenness. For though it be himself that hath said and done all those unreasonable things, yet he will need others to teach him this, like as the drunken man. For anger and sin is a more frantic thing[4] than any drunkenness, and puts the soul in greater distraction.

Who, for instance, was wiser than David? Yet for all that, when he had sinned he perceived it not, his lust keeping in subjection all his reasoning powers, and like some smoke filling his soul. Therefore he stood in need of a lantern from the prophet, and of words calling to his mind what he had done. Wherefore here also He brings these to him that hath sinned, to reason with him about the things he had done.

2. But for what reason doth He command this one to tell him of his fault, and not another? Because this man he would endure more quietly, this, who hath been wronged, who hath been pained, who hath been despitefully used. For one doth not bear in the same way being told by another of one's fault concerning him that hath been insulted, as by the insulted person himself, especially when this person is alone convicting him. For when he who should demand justice against him, even this one appears to be caring for his salvation, this will have more power than anything in the world to shame him.

Seest thou how this is done not for the sake of just punishment, but of amendment? Therefore He doth not at once command to take with him the two, but when himself hath failed; and not even then doth He send forth a multitude against him; but makes the addition no further than two, or even one; but when he has contemned these too, then and not till then He brings him out to the church.

So much earnestness doth He show, that our neighbor's sins be not exposed by us. And indeed He might have commanded this from the first, but that this might not be, He did not command it, but after a first and second admonition He appoints this.

But what is, "In the mouth of two or three witnesses every word shall be established?" Thou hast a sufficient testimony. His meaning is, that thou hast done all thy part, that thou hast left undone none of the things which it pertained to thee to do.

"But if he shall neglect to hear them also, tell it to the church," that is, to the rulers of it; "but if he neglect to hear the church, let him be to thee as an heathen man and a publican." For after this such a one is incurably diseased.

But mark thou, I pray thee, how everywhere He putteth the publican for an example of the greatest wickedness. For above too He saith, "Do not even the publicans the same?"[5] And further on again, "Even the publicans and the harlots shall go before you into the Kingdom of Heaven,"[6] that is, they who are utterly reprobated and condemned. Let them hearken, who are rushing upon unjust gains, who are counting up usuries upon usuries.

But why did He set him with these? To soothe the person wronged, and to alarm him. Is this only then the punishment? Nay, but hear also what follows. "Whatsoever ye shall bind on earth shall be bound in Heaven."[7] And He did not say to the ruler of the church, "Bind such a man," but, "If thou bind," committing the whole matter to the person himself, who is aggrieved, and the bonds abide indissoluble. Therefore he will suffer the utmost ills; but not he who hath brought him to account is to blame, but he who hath not been willing to be persuaded.

Seest thou how He hath bound him down with twofold constraint, both by the vengeance here, and by the punishment hereafter? But these things hath He threatened, that these circumstances may not arise, but that fearing, at once the being cast out of the

---

[1] Matt. v. 39.   [2] 1 Cor. v. 12.
[3] [Oxford edition, "these," misprint, since the Greek word is τρεῖς.—R.]
[4] ἐκστατικώτερον.

[5] Matt. v. 46.   [6] Matt. xxi. 31.
[7] Matt. xviii. 18. [R. V., "What things soever," etc. But the singular pronoun is substituted in the text of the Homily.—R.]

church, and the danger from the bond, and the being bound in Heaven, he may become more gentle. And knowing these things, if not at the beginning, at any rate in the multitude of the tribunals he will put off his anger. Wherefore, I tell you, He hath set over him a first, and a second, and a third court,[1] so that though he should neglect to hear the first, he may yield to the second; and even if he should reject that, he may fear the third; and though he should make no account of this, he may be dismayed at the vengeance to come, and at the sentence and judgment to proceed from God.

"And again I say unto you, that if two of you shall agree on earth as touching anything that they shall ask, it shall be done for them of my Father which is in Heaven. For where two or three are gathered together in my name, there am I in the midst of them." [2]

Seest thou how by another motive also He puts down our enmities, and takes away our petty dissensions,[3] and draws us one to another, and this not from the punishment only which hath been mentioned, but also from the good things which spring from charity? For having denounced those threats against contentiousness, He putteth here the great rewards of concord, if at least they who are of one accord do even prevail with the Father, as touching the things they ask, and have Christ in the midst of them.

"Are there then indeed nowhere two of one accord?" Nay, in many places, perchance even everywhere. "How then do they not obtain all things?" Because many are the causes of their failing. For either they often ask things inexpedient. And why marvellest thou, if this is the case with some others, whereas it was so even with Paul, when he heard, "My grace is sufficient for thee; for my strength is perfected in weakness."[4] Or they are unworthy to be reckoned with them that heard these words, and contribute not their own part, but He seeks for such as are like them; therefore He saith "of you," of the virtuous, of them that show forth an angelic rule of life.[5] Or they pray against them that have aggrieved them, seeking for redress and vengeance; and this kind of thing is forbidden, for, "Pray," saith He, "for your enemies."[6] Or having sins unrepented they ask mercy, which thing it is impossible to receive, not only if themselves ask it, but although others having much confi-

dence towards God entreat for them, like as even Jeremiah praying for the Jews did hear, "Pray not thou for this people, because I will not hear thee."[7]

But if all things are there, and thou ask things expedient, and contribute all thine own part, and exhibit an apostolical life, and have concord and love towards thy neighbor, thou wilt obtain on thy entreaty; for the Lord is loving towards man.

3. Then because He had said, "Of my Father," in order that He might show that it is Himself that giveth, and not He who begat Him only, He added, "For wheresoever two or three are gathered together in my name, there am I in the midst of them."

What then? are there not two or three gathered together in His name? There are indeed, but rarely. For not merely of the assembling doth He speak, neither this doth He require only; but most surely, as I said before also, the rest of virtue too together with this, and besides, even this itself He requires with great strictness. For what He saith is like this, "If any holds me the principal ground of his love to his neighbors, I will be with Him, if he be a virtuous man in other respects."

But now we see the more part having other motives of friendship. For one loves, because he is loved, another because he hath been honored, a third because such a one has been useful to him in some other worldly matter, a fourth for some other like cause; but for Christ's sake it is a difficult thing to find any one loving his neighbor sincerely, and as he ought to love him. For the more part are bound one to another by their worldly affairs. But Paul did not love thus, but for Christ's sake; wherefore even when not loved in such wise as he loved, he did not cease his love, because he had planted a strong root of his affection; but not so our present state, but on inquiry we shall find with most men anything likely to produce friendship rather than this. And if any one bestowed on me power in so great a multitude to make this inquiry, I would show the more part bound one to another by worldly motives.

And this is evident from the causes that work enmity. For because they are bound one to another by these temporal[8] motives, therefore they are neither fervent towards one another, nor constant, but insult, and loss of money, and envy, and love of vainglory, and every such thing coming upon them, severs the love-tie. For it finds not the root spiritual. Since if indeed it were

---

[1] [A clause is omitted here, "and doth not straightway cut him off."—R.]
[2] Matt. xviii. 19, 20.   [3] μικροψυχίας.
[4] 2 Cor. xii. 9. [R. V., "for my power is made perfect in weakness."]
[5] πολιτείαν.   [6] Matt. v. 44.   [7] Jer. xi. 14.   [8] ἐπικήρων.

such, no worldly thing would dissolve things spiritual. For love for Christ's sake is firm, and not to be broken, and impregnable, and nothing can tear it asunder; not calumnies, not dangers, not death, no other thing of this kind. For though he suffer ten thousand things, who thus loves; looking to the ground of his love, he will not desist. For he who loves because of being loved, should he meet with anything painful, puts an end to his love; but he who is bound by this, will never desist.

Wherefore Paul also said, " Charity never faileth."[1] For what hast thou to say? That when honored he insults? that receiving benefits he was minded to slay thee? But even this works upon thee to love more, if thou lovest for Christ's sake. For what things are in the rest subversive of love, these here become apt to produce it. How? First, because such a one is to thee a cause of rewards; secondly, because he that is so disposed stands in need of more succor, and much attention. Therefore I say, he who thus loves inquires not about race, nor country, nor wealth, nor his love to himself, nor any other such matter, but though he be hated,

though he be insulted, though he be slain, continues to love, having as a sufficient ground for love, Christ; wherefore also he stands steadfast, firm, not to be overthrown, looking unto Him.

For Christ too so loved his enemies, having loved the obstinate, the injurious, the blasphemers, them that hated Him, them that would not so much as see Him; them that were preferring wood and stones to Him, and with the highest love beyond which one cannot find another. " For greater love hath no man than this," He saith, " that one lay down his life for his friends." [2]

And those even that crucified Him, and acted in so many instances with contumely against Him, see how He continues to treat with kindness. For even to His Father He speaks for them, saying, " Forgive them, for they know not what they do." [3] And He sent His disciples moreover, after these things, unto them.

This love then let us also imitate, unto this let us look, that being followers of Christ, we may attain both unto the good things here, and unto those to come, by the grace and love towards man of our Lord Jesus Christ, to whom be glory and might world without end. Amen.

[1] 1 Cor. xiii. 8. [R. V., " Love never faileth." The Greek word is rendered " love " throughout this part of the Homily.—R.]

[2] John xv. 13.

[3] Luke xxiii. 34.

HOMILY LXI.

MATT. XVIII. 21.

" Then came Peter to Him, and said, Lord, how oft shall my brother sin against me, and I forgive him? till seven times? Jesus saith unto him, I say not unto thee, Until seven times, but, Until seventy times seven."[1]

PETER supposed he was saying something great, wherefore also as aiming at greatness he added, " Until seven times?" For this thing, saith he, which Thou hast commanded to do, how often shall I do? For if he forever sins, but forever when reproved repents, how often dost thou command us to bear with this man? For with regard to that other who repents not, neither acknowledges

his own faults, Thou hast set a limit, by saying, " Let him be to thee as the heathen and the publican;" but to this no longer so, but Thou hast commanded to accept him.

How often then ought I to bear with him, being told his faults, and repenting? Is it enough for seven times?

What then saith Christ, the good God, who is loving towards man? " I say not unto thee, until seven times, but, until seventy times seven," not setting a number here, but what is infinite and perpetual and forever. For even as ten thousand times signifies

[1] [R. V. margin, " seventy times and seven." There is no difference of reading, but one of interpretation. Comp. Augustin, vol. vi., p. 107, *Nicene and Post Nicene Fathers.* Chrysostom does not indicate which view he accepts.—R.]

often, so here too. For by saying, "The barren hath borne seven,"[1] the Scripture means many. So that He hath not limited the forgiveness by a number, but hath declared that it is to be perpetual and forever.

This at least He indicated by the parable that is put after. For that He might not seem to any to enjoin great things and hard to bear, by saying, "Seventy times seven," He added this parable, at once both leading them on to what He had said, and putting down him who was priding himself upon this, and showing the act was not grievous, but rather very easy. Therefore let me add, He brought forward His own love to man, that by the comparison, as He saith, thou mightest learn, that though thou forgive seventy times seven, though thou continually pardon thy neighbor for absolutely all his sins, as a drop of water to an endless sea, so much, or rather much more, doth thy love to man come short in comparison of the boundless goodness of God, of which thou standest in need, for that thou art to be judged, and to give an account.

Wherefore also He went on to say, "The Kingdom of Heaven is likened unto a certain king, which would take account of his servants.[2] And when he had begun to reckon, one was brought unto him, which owed him ten thousand talents. But forasmuch as he had not to pay,[3] he commanded him to be sold, and his wife, and his children, and all that he had."[4]

Then after this man had enjoyed the benefit of mercy, he went out, and "took by the throat his fellow-servant, which owed him an hundred pence;"[5] and having by these doings moved his lord, he caused him to cast him again into prison, until he should pay off the whole.

Seest thou how great the difference between sins against man and against God? As great as between ten thousand talents, and a hundred pence, or rather even much more. And this arises both from the difference of the persons, and the constant succession of our sins. For when a man looks at us, we stand off and shrink from sinning: but when God sees us every day, we do not forbear, but do and speak all things without fear.

But not hereby alone, but also from the benefit and from the honor of which we have partaken, our sins become more grievous.

And if ye are desirous to learn how our sins against Him are ten thousand talents, or rather even much more, I will try to show it

briefly. But I fear lest to them that are inclined to wickedness, and love continually to sin, I should furnish still greater security, or should drive the meeker sort to despair, and they should repeat that saying of the disciples, "who can be saved?"[6]

Nevertheless for all that I will speak, that I may make those that attend more safe, and more meek. For they that are incurably diseased, and past feeling, even without these words of mine, do not depart from their own carelessness, and wickedness; and if even from hence they derive greater occasion for contempt, the fault is not in what is said, but in their insensibility; since what is said surely is enough both to restrain those that attend to it, and to prick their hearts; and the meeker sort, when they see on the one hand the greatness of their sins, and learn also on the other hand the power of repentance, will cleave to it the more, wherefore it is needful to speak.

I will speak then, and will set forth our sins, both wherein we offend against God, and wherein against men, and I will set forth not each person's own, but what are common; but his own let each one join to them after that from his conscience.

And I will do this, having first set forth the good deeds of God to us. What then are His good deeds? He created us when we were not, and made all things for our sakes that are seen, Heaven, sea, air, all that in them is, living creatures, plants, seeds; for we must needs speak briefly for the boundless ocean of the works. Into us alone of all that are on earth He breathed a living soul such as we have, He planted a garden, He gave a helpmeet, He set us over all the brutes, He crowned us with glory and honor.

After that, when man had been unthankful towards his benefactor, He vouchsafed unto him a greater gift.

2. For look not to this only, that He cast him out of paradise, but mark also the gain that arose from thence. For after having cast him out of paradise, and having wrought those countless good works, and having accomplished His various dispensations, He sent even His own Son for the sake of them that had been benefited by Him and were hating Him, and opened Heaven to us, and unfolded paradise itself, and made us sons, the enemies, the unthankful.

Wherefore it were even seasonable now to say, "O the depth of the riches both of the wisdom and knowledge of God!"[7]

And He gave us also a baptism of the re-

---

[1] 1 Sam. ii. 5.   [2] [R. V., "make a reckoning."]
[3] [R. V., "wherewith to pay."]
[4] Matt. xviii. 23–25. [The textual variations are slight.—R.]
[5] Matt. xviii. 28.

[6] Matt. xix. 25. [Comp. Mark x. 26.]   [7] Rom. xi. 33.

mission of sins, and a deliverance from vengeance, and an inheritance of a kingdom, and He promised numberless good things on our doing what is right, and stretched forth His hand, and shed abroad His Spirit into our hearts.

What then? After so many and such great blessings, what ought to be our disposition; should we indeed, even if each day we died for Him who so loves us, make due recompense, or rather should we repay the smallest portion of the debt? By no means, for moreover even this again is turned to our advantage.

How then are we disposed, whose disposition ought to be like this? Each day we insult His law. But be ye not angry, if I let loose my tongue against them that sin, for not you only will I accuse, but myself also.

Where then would ye that I should begin? With the slaves, or with the free? with them that serve in the army, or with private persons? with the rulers, or with the subjects? with the women, or with the men? with the aged men, or with the young? with what age? with what race? with what rank? with what pursuit?

Would ye then that I should make the beginning with them that serve as soldiers? What sin then do not these commit every day, insulting, reviling, frantic, making a gain of other men's calamities, being like wolves, never clear from offenses, unless one might say the sea too was without waves. What passion doth not trouble them? what disease doth not lay siege to their soul?

For to their equals they show a jealous disposition, and they envy, and seek after vainglory; and to those that are subject to them, their disposition is covetous; but to them that have suits, and run unto them as to a harbor, their conduct is that of enemies and perjured persons. How many robberies are there with them! How many frauds! How many false accusations, and meannesses! how many servile flatteries!

Come then, let us apply in each case the law of Christ. " He that saith to his brother, Thou fool, shall be in danger of hell fire.[1] He that hath looked on a woman to lust after her, hath already committed adultery with her.[2] Unless one humble himself as the little child, he shall not enter into the Kingdom of Heaven."[3]

But these even study haughtiness, becoming towards them that are subject to them, and are delivered into their hands, and who tremble at them, and are afraid of them,

more fierce than a wild beast; for Christ's sake doing nothing, but all things for the belly, for money, for vainglory.

Can one indeed reckon up in words the trespass of their actions? What should one say of their derisions, their laughter, their unseasonable discourses, their filthy language? But about covetousness one cannot so much as speak. For like as the monks on the mountains know not even what covetousness is, so neither do these; but in an opposite way to them. For they indeed, because of being far removed from the disease, know not the passion, but these, by reason of being exceedingly intoxicated with it, have not so much as a perception how great the evil is. For this vice hath so thrust aside virtue and tyrannises, that it is not accounted so much as a heavy charge with those madmen.

But will ye, that we leave these, and go to others of a gentler kind? Come then, let us examine the race of workmen and artisans. For these above all seem to live by honest labors, and the sweat of their own brow. But these too, when they do not take heed to themselves, gather to themselves many evils from hence. For the dishonesty that arises from buying and selling they bring into the work of honest labor, and add oaths, and perjuries, and falsehoods to their covetousness often, and are taken up with worldly things only, and continue riveted to the earth; and while they do all things that they may get money, they do not take much heed that they may impart to the needy, being always desirous to increase their goods. What should one say of the revilings that are uttered touching such matters, the insults, the loans, the usurious gains, the bargains full of much mean trafficking, the shameless buyings and sellings.

3. But will ye that we leave these too, and go to others who seem to be more just? Who then are they? They that are possessed of lands, and reap the wealth that springs from the earth. And what can be more unjust than these? For if any one were to examine how they treat their wretched and toilworn laborers, he will see them to be more cruel than savages. For upon them that are pining with hunger, and toiling throughout all their life, they both impose constant and intolerable payments, and lay on them laborious burdens, and like asses or mules, or rather like stones, do they treat their bodies, allowing them not so much as to draw breath a little, and when the earth yields, and when it doth not yield, they alike wear them out, and grant them no indulgence. And what can be more pitiable than this, when after

---

[1] Matt. v. 22.　　[2] Matt. v. 28.
[3] Matt. xviii. 3. [Slightly altered.]

having labored throughout the whole winter, and being consumed with frost and rain, and watchings, they go away with their hands empty, yea moreover in debt, and fearing and dreading more than this famine and shipwreck, the torments of the overlookers,[1] and their dragging them about, and their demands, and their imprisonments, and the services from which no entreaty can deliver them!

Why should one speak of the merchandise which they make of them, the sordid gains which they gain by them, by their labors and their sweat filling winepresses, and wine vats, but not suffering them to take home so much as a small measure, but draining off the entire fruits into the casks of their wickedness, and flinging to them for this a little money?

And new kinds of usuries also do they devise, and not lawful even according to the laws of the heathens, and they frame contracts for loans full of many a curse. For not the hundredth part of the sum, but the half of the sum they press for and exact; and this when he of whom it is exacted has a wife, is bringing up children, is a human being, and is filling their threshing floor, and their winepress by his own toils.

But none of these things do they consider. Wherefore now it were seasonable to bring forward the prophet and say, "Be astonished, O Heaven, and be horribly afraid, O earth,"[2] to what great brutality hath the race of man been madly carried away![3]

But these things I say, not blaming crafts, nor husbandry, nor military service,[4] but ourselves. Since Cornelius also was a centurion, and Paul a worker in leather, and after his preaching practised his craft, and David was a king, and Job enjoyed the possession of land and of large revenues, and there was no hindrance hereby to any of these in the way of virtue.

Bearing in mind all these things, and considering the ten thousand talents, let us at least hence hasten to remit to our neighbors their few and trifling debts. For we too have an account to give of the commandments wherewith we have been trusted, and we are not able to pay all, no not whatever we may do. Therefore God hath given us a way to repayment both ready and easy, and which is able to cancel all these things, I mean, not to be revengeful.

In order then that we may learn this well,

let us hear the whole parable, going on regularly through it. "For there was brought unto Him," it saith, "one which owed ten thousand talents, and when he had not to pay, He commanded him to be sold, and his wife, and his children." Wherefore, I pray thee? Not of cruelty, nor of inhumanity (for the loss came back again upon himself, for she too was a slave), but of unspeakable tenderness.

For it is His purpose to alarm him by this threat, that He might bring him to supplication, not that he should be sold. For if He had done it for this intent, He would not have consented to his request, neither would He have granted the favor.

Wherefore then did He not do this, nor forgive the debt before the account? Desiring to teach him, from how many obligations He is delivering him, that in this way at least he might become more mild towards his fellow-servant. For even if when he had learnt the weight of his debt, and the greatness of the forgiveness, he continued taking his fellow-servant by the throat; if He had not disciplined him beforehand with such medicines, to what length of cruelty might he not have gone?

What then saith the other? "Have patience with me, and I will pay thee all. And his Lord[5] was moved with compassion, and loosed him, and forgave him the debt."[6]

Seest thou again surpassing benevolence? The servant asked only for delay and putting off the time, but He gave more than he asked, remission and forgiveness of the entire debt. For it had been his will to give it even from the first, but he did not desire the gift to be his only, but also to come of this man's entreaty, that he might not go away uncrowned. For that the whole was of him, although this other fell unto him and prayed, the motive of the forgiveness showed, for "moved with compassion" he forgave him. But still even so he willed that other also to seem to contribute something, that he might not be exceedingly covered with shame, and that he being schooled in his own calamities, might be indulgent to his fellow-servant.

4. Up to this point then this man was good and acceptable; for he confessed, and promised to pay the debt, and fell down before him, and entreated, and condemned his own sins, and knew the greatness of the debt. But the sequel is unworthy of his former deeds. For going out straightway, not after a long time but straightway, having the bene-

---

[1] [ἐπιτρόπων, "stewards," answering here to "overseers," in the worst sense.—R.]

[2] Jer. ii. 12.   [3] ἐξεβακχεύθη.

[4] [οὐδὲ ἀγρούς occurs here in the Greek, but is ignored by the translator; probably because the thought was implied in "husbandry" (γεωργίαν).—R.]

[5] ["The lord of that servant," according to our authorities; the Homily varies.—R.]

[6] Matt. xviii. 26, 27.

fit fresh[1] upon him, he abused to wickedness the gift, even the freedom bestowed on him by his master.

For, " he found one of his fellow-servants, which owed him an hundred pence, and took him by the throat, saying, Pay me what thou owest."[2]

Seest thou the master's benevolence? Seest thou the servant's cruelty? Hear, ye who do these things for money. For if for sins we must not do so, much more not for money.

What then saith the other? "Have patience with me, and I will pay thee all."[3] But he did not regard even the words by which he had been saved (for he himself on saying this was delivered from the ten thousand talents), and did not recognize so much as the harbor by which he escaped shipwreck; the gesture of supplication did not remind him of his master's kindness, but he put away from him all these things, from covetousness and cruelty and revenge, and was more fierce than any wild beast, seizing his fellow-servant by the throat.

What doest thou, O man? perceivest thou not, thou art making the demand upon thyself, thou art thrusting the sword into thyself, and revoking the sentence and the gift? But none of these things did he consider, neither did he remember his own state, neither did he yield; although the entreaty was not for equal objects.

For the one besought for ten thousand talents, the other for a hundred pence; the one his fellow-servant, the other his lord; the one received entire forgiveness, the other asked for delay, and not so much as this did he give him, for " he cast him into prison."

" But when his fellow-servants saw it, they accused him to their lord." Not even to men is this well-pleasing, much less to God. They therefore who did not owe, partook of the grief.

What then saith their lord? " O thou wicked servant, I forgave thee all that debt, because thou desiredst[4] me; shouldest not thou also have had compassion, even as I had pity on thee?"[5]

See again the lord's gentleness. He pleads with him, and excuses himself, being on the point of revoking his gift; or rather, it was not he that revoked it, but the one who had received it. Wherefore He saith, " I forgave

thee all that debt, because thou desiredst me; shouldest not thou also have had compassion on thy fellow-servant?" For even if the thing doth seem to thee hard; yet shouldest thou have looked to the gain, which hath been, which is to be. Even if the injunction be galling, thou oughtest to consider the reward; neither that he hath grieved thee, but that thou hast provoked God, whom by mere prayer thou hast reconciled. But if even so it be a galling thing to thee to become friends with him who hath grieved thee, to fall into hell is far more grievous; and if thou hadst set this against that, then thou wouldest have known that to forgive is a much lighter thing.

And whereas, when he owed ten thousand talents, he called him not wicked, neither reproached him, but showed mercy on him; when he had become harsh to his fellow-servant, then he saith, " O thou wicked servant."

Let us hearken, the covetous, for even to us is the word spoken. Let us hearken also, the merciless, and the cruel, for not to others are we cruel, but to ourselves. When then thou art minded to be revengeful, consider that against thyself art thou revengeful, not against another; that thou art binding up thine own sins, not thy neighbors. For as to thee, whatsoever thou mayest do to this man, thou doest as a man and in the present life, but God not so, but more mightily will He take vengeance on thee, and with the vengeance hereafter.

" For He delivered him over till he should pay that which was due," that is, for ever; for he will never repay. For since thou art not become better by the kindness shown thee, it remains that by vengeance thou be corrected.

And yet, " The graces and the gifts are without repentance,"[6] but wickedness has had such power as to set aside even this law. What then can be a more grievous thing than to be revengeful, when it appears to overthrow such and so great a gift of God.

And he did not merely " deliver " him, but " was wroth." For when he commanded him to be sold, his were not the words of wrath (therefore neither did he do it), but a very great occasion for benevolence; but now the sentence is of much indignation, and vengeance, and punishment.

What then means the parable? " So likewise shall my Father do also unto you," He saith, " if ye from your hearts forgive not every one his brother their trespasses."[7]

---

1 ἔναυλον.   2 Matt. xviii. 28.
3 Matt. xviii. 29. [R. V. omits "all" in this verse, with the best authorities. Probably taken from verse 26.—R.]
4 [R. V., " besoughtest."]
5 Matt. xviii. 32. [R. V., " have had mercy on thy fellow servant, even as I had mercy on thee." The verb is the same in both clauses. " On thy fellow servant," omitted here, is inserted in the comment.—R.

6 Rom. xi. 29. [Freely cited.]
7 Matt. xviii. 35. [The best New Testament authorities omit " their trespasses," which was readily introduced from similar passages.—R.]

He saith not "your Father," but "my Father." For it is not meet for God to be called the Father of such a one, who is so wicked and malicious.

5. Two things therefore doth He here require, both to condemn ourselves for our sins, and to forgive others; and the former for the sake of the latter, that this may become more easy (for he who considers his own sins is more indulgent to his fellow-servant); and not merely to forgive with the lips, but from the heart.

Let us not then thrust the sword into ourselves by being revengeful. For what grief hath he who hath grieved thee inflicted upon thee, like thou wilt work unto thyself by keeping thine anger in mind, and drawing upon thyself the sentence from God to condemn thee? For if indeed thou art watchful, and keepest thyself under control, the evil will come round upon his head, and it will be he that will suffer harm; but if thou shouldest continue indignant, and displeased, then thyself wilt undergo the harm not from him, but from thyself.

Say not then that he insulted thee, and slandered thee, and did unto thee ills beyond number; for the more thou tellest, so much the more dost thou declare him a benefactor. For he hath given thee an opportunity to wash away thy sins; so that the greater the injuries he hath done thee, so much more is he become to thee a cause of a greater remission of sins.

For if we be willing, no one shall be able to injure us, but even our enemies shall advantage us in the greatest degree. And why do I speak of men? For what can be more wicked than the devil; yet nevertheless, even hence have we a great opportunity of approving ourselves; and Job showeth it. But if the devil hath become a cause of crowns, why art thou afraid of a man as an enemy?

See then how much thou gainest, bearing meekly the spiteful acts of thine enemies. First and greatest, deliverance from sins; secondly, fortitude and patience; thirdly, mildness and benevolence; for he that knoweth not how to be angry with them that grieve him, much more will he be ready to serve them that love him. Fourthly, to be free from anger continually, to which nothing can be equal. For of him that is free from anger, it is quite clear that he is delivered also from the despondency hence arising, and will not spend his life on vain labors and sorrows. For he that knows not how to hate, neither doth he know how to grieve, but will enjoy pleasure, and ten thousand blessings.

So that we punish ourselves by hating others, even as on the other hand we benefit ourselves by loving them.

Besides all these things, thou wilt be an object of veneration even to thy very enemies, though they be devils; or rather, thou wilt not so much as have an enemy whilst thou art of such a disposition.

But what is greater than all, and first, thou gainest the favor of God. Shouldest thou have sinned, thou wilt obtain pardon; shouldest thou have done what is right, thou wilt obtain a greater confidence. Let us accomplish therefore the hating no one, that God also may love us, that, though we be in debt for ten thousand talents, He may have compassion and pity us.

But hast thou been injured by him? Pity him then, do not hate him; weep and mourn, do not turn away from him. For thou art not the one that hath offended against God, but he; but thou hast even approved thyself, if thou endure it. Consider that Christ, when about to be crucified, rejoiced for Himself, but wept for them that were crucifying Him. This ought to be our disposition also; and the more we are injured, so much more should we lament for them that are injuring us. For to us many are the benefits hence arising, but to them the opposites.

But did he insult thee, and strike thee before all? Then hath he disgraced and dishonored himself before all, and hath opened the mouths of a thousand accusers, and for thee hath he woven more crowns, and gathered for thee many to publish thy forbearance.

But did he slander thee to others? And what is this? God is the one that is to demand the account, not they that have heard this. For to himself hath he added occasion of punishment, so that not only for his own sins he should give account, but also of what he said of thee. And upon thee hath he brought evil report with men, but he himself hath incurred evil report with God.

And if these things are not sufficient for thee, consider that even thy Lord [1] was evil reported of both by Satan and by men, and that to those most loved by Him; and His Only-Begotten the same again. Wherefore He said, "If they have called the Master of the house Beelzebub, much more shall they call them of His household." [2]

And that wicked demon did not only slander Him, but was also believed, and slandered Him not in ordinary matters, but with the greatest reproaches and accusations. For he affirmed Him to be possessed, and to be a deceiver, and an adversary of God.

---

[1] Δεσπότης.   [2] Matt. x. 25.

But hast thou also done good, and received evil? Nay, in respect of this most of all lament and grieve for him that hath done the wrong, but for thyself rather rejoice, because thou art become like God, "Who maketh the sun to rise upon evil and good."[1]

But if to follow God is beyond thee, although to him that watcheth not even this is hard; yet nevertheless if this seem to thee to be too great for thee, come let us bring thee to thy fellow-servants, to Joseph, who suffered countless things, and did good unto his brethren; to Moses, who after their countless plots against him, prayed for them; to the blessed Paul, who cannot so much as number what he suffered from them, and is willing to be accursed for them; to Stephen, who is stoned, and entreating this sin may be forgiven them. And having considered all these things, cast away all anger, that God may forgive us also all our trespasses by the grace and love towards man of our Lord Jesus Christ, with whom to the Father and the Holy Ghost be glory, might, honor, now and always, and world without end. Amen.

---

[1] Matt. v. 45.

HOMILY LXII.

MATT. XIX. 1.

"And it came to pass, that when Jesus had finished these sayings, He departed from Galilee, and came into the coasts of Judæa beyond Jordan."

HAVING constantly left Judæa on account of the envy of those men, now He frequents it from this time forth, because the passion was to be nigh at hand; He goeth not up, however, unto Jerusalem for a while, but "into the coasts of Judæa."

"And," when He was come, "great multitudes followed Him, and He healed them."[1]

For neither in the teaching by words doth He continue always, nor in the wonderful working of signs, but He doeth now one now the other, variously working the salvation of them that were waiting upon Him and following Him, so as by the miracles to appear, in what He said, a Teacher worthy of belief, and by the teaching of His word to increase the profit from the miracles; and this was to lead them by the hand to the knowledge of God.

But do thou mark, I pray thee, this too, how the disciples pass over whole multitudes with one word, not declaring by name each of them that are healed. For they said not, that such a one, and such another, but that many, teaching us to be unostentatious. But Christ healed, benefitting both them, and by them many others. For the healing of these men's infirmity was to others a foundation for the knowledge of God.

But not so to the Pharisees, but even for this self-same thing they become more fierce, and come unto Him tempting Him. For because they could not lay hold of the works that were doing, they propose to Him questions. For they "came unto Him, and tempting Him said, Is it lawful for a man to put away his wife for every cause?"[2]

O folly! They thought to silence Him by their questions, although they had already received certain proof of this power in Him. When at least they argued much about the Sabbath, when they said, "He blasphemeth," when they said, "He hath a devil," when they found fault with His disciples as they were walking in the corn fields, when they argued about unwashen hands, on every occasion having sewed fast their mouths, and shut up their shameless tongue, He thus sent them away. Nevertheless, not even so do they keep off from Him. For such is wickedness, such is envy, shameless and bold; though it be put to silence ten thousand times, ten thousand times doth it assault again.

But mark thou, I pray thee, their craft also from the form of their question. For neither did they say unto Him, Thou didst command not to put away a wife, for indeed He had already discoursed about this law; but never-

---

[1] Matt. xix. 2.

[2] Matt. xix. 3.

theless they made no mention of those words; but took occasion from hence, and thinking to make their snare the greater, and being minded to drive Him to a necessity of contradicting the law, they say not, why didst Thou enact this or that? but as though nothing had been said, they ask, "Is it lawful?" expecting that He had forgotten having said it; and being ready if on the one hand He said, "It is lawful to put away," to bring against Him the things He Himself had spoken, and to say, How then didst Thou affirm the contrary? but if the same things now again as before, to bring against Him the words of Moses.

What then said He? He said not, "Why tempt ye me, ye hypocrites?" although afterwards He saith this, but here He speaks not thus. Why can this be? In order that together with His power He might show forth His gentleness also. For He doth neither always keep silence, lest they should suppose they are hidden; nor doth He always reprove, in order that He may instruct us to bear all things with gentleness.

How then doth He answer them? "Have ye not read, that He which made them at[1] the beginning, made them male and female, and said, For this cause shall a man leave his father and his mother, and shall cleave to his wife; and they twain shall be[2] one flesh? So that they are no more twain but one flesh. What therefore God hath joined together, let not man put asunder."[3]

See a teacher's wisdom. I mean, that being asked, Is it lawful? He did not at once say, It is not lawful, lest they should be disturbed and put in disorder, but before the decision by His argument He rendered this manifest, showing that it is itself too the commandment of His·Father, and that not in opposition to Moses did He enjoin these things, but in full agreement with him.

But mark Him arguing strongly not from the creation only, but also from His command. For He said not, that He made one man and one woman only, but that He also gave this command that the one man should be joined to the one woman. But if it had been His will that he should put this one away, and bring in another, when He had made one man, He would have formed many women.

But now both by the manner of the creation, and by the manner of lawgiving, He showed that one man must dwell with one woman continually, and never break off from her.

And see how He saith, "He which made them at the beginning, made them male and female," that is, from one root they sprung. and into one body came they together, "for the twain shall be one flesh."

After this, to make it a fearful thing to find fault with this lawgiving, and to confirm the law, He said not, "Sever not therefore, nor put asunder," but, "What God hath joined together, let not man put asunder."

But if thou put forward Moses, I tell thee of Moses' Lord, and together with this, I rely upon the time also. For God at the beginning made them male and female; and this law is older (though it seem to have been now introduced by me), and with much earnestness established. For not merely did He bring the woman to the man, but also commanded to leave father and mother. And neither did He make it a law for him merely to come to the woman, but also "to cleave to her," by the form of the language intimating that they might not be severed. And not even with this was He satisfied, but sought also for another greater union, "for the twain," He saith, "shall be one flesh."

Then after He had recited the ancient law, which was brought in both by deeds and by words, and shown it to be worthy of respect because of the giver, with authority after that He Himself too interprets and gives the law, saying, "So that they are no more twain, but one flesh." Like then as to sever flesh is a horrible thing,[4] so also to divorce a wife is unlawful. And He stayed not at this, but brought in God also by saying, "What therefore God hath joined together, let not man put asunder," showing that the act was both against nature, and against law; against nature, because one flesh is dissevered; against law, because that when God hath joined and commanded it not to be divided, ye conspire to do this.

2. What then ought they to have done after this? Ought they not to have held their peace, and to have commended the saying? ought they not to have marvelled at His wisdom? ought they not to have stood amazed at His accordance with the Father? But none of these things do they, but as though they were contending for *the law*, they say, "How then did Moses command to give a writing of divorcement, and to put her away?"[5] And yet they ought not now to have brought this forward, but rather He to them; but nevertheless He doth not take advantage of them, nor doth He say to them, "I am not now bound by this," but He solves this too.

---

[1] [R. V., "from."]　　[2] [R. V., "become."]
[3] Matt. xix. 4-6.

[4] ἐναγές.
[5] Matt. xix. 7. ["How" is substituted for "why."]

And indeed if He had been an alien from the old covenant, He would not have striven for Moses, neither would He have argued positively from the things done once for all at the beginning; He would not have studied to show that His own precepts agreed with those of old.

And indeed Moses had given many other commandments besides, both those about meats, and those about the Sabbath; wherefore then do they nowhere bring him forward, as here? From a wish to enlist the multitude of the husbands against him. For this was considered a thing indifferent with the Jews, and all used to do so much as this. Accordingly it was for this reason that when so many things had been said on the mount, they remembered this commandment only now.

Nevertheless, unspeakable wisdom maketh a defense even for these things, and saith, " Moses for the hardness of your hearts" thus made the law. And not even him doth He suffer to remain under accusation, forasmuch as He had Himself given him the law; but delivers him from the charge, and turns the whole upon their head, as everywhere He doth.

For again when they were blaming His disciples for plucking the ears of corn, He shows themselves to be guilty; and when they were laying a trangression to their charge as to their not washing their hands, He shows themselves to be the transgressors, and touching the Sabbath also: both everywhere, and here in like manner.

Then because the saying was hard to bear, and brought on them much blame, He quickly directs back His discourse to that ancient law, saying as He had said before also, " But in the beginning it was not so," that is, God by His acts at the beginning ordained the contrary. For in order that they may not say, Whence is it manifest, that " for our hardness Moses said this?" hereby again He stoppeth their mouths. For if this were the primary law, and for our good, that other would not have been given at the beginning; God in creating would not have so created, He would not have said such things.

" But I say unto you, Whosoever shall put away his wife except it be for fornication, and marry another, committeth adultery." [1] For since he had stopped their mouths, He then gives the law with His own authority, like as touching the meats, like as touching the Sabbath.

For with regard to the meats likewise, when He had overcome them, then, and not till

then, He declared unto the multitude, that, " Not that which goeth in defileth the man;" [2] and with regard to the Sabbath, when He had stopped their mouths, He saith, " Wherefore it is lawful to do well on the Sabbath day;" [3] and here this self-same thing.

But what took place there, this happened here also. For as there, when the Jews had been put to silence the disciples were troubled, and came unto Him with Peter and said, " Declare unto us this parable;" [4] even so now also they were troubled and said, " If the case of the man be so, it is good not to marry." [5]

For now they understood the saying more than before. Therefore then indeed they held their peace, but now when there hath been gainsaying, and answering, and question, and learning by reply, and the law appeared more clear, they ask Him. And openly to contradict they do not dare, but they bring forward what seemed to be a grievous and galling result of it, saying, " If the case of the man be so with his wife, it is not good to marry." For indeed it seemed to be a very hard thing to have a wife full of every bad quality, and to endure a wild beast perpetually shut up with one in the house. And that thou mayest learn that this greatly troubled them, Mark said,[6] to show it, that they spake to Him privately.

3. But what is, " If such be the case of a man with his wife?" That is, if to this end he is joined with her, that they should be one, or, on the other hand, if the man shall get to himself blame for these things, and always transgresses by putting away, it were easier to fight against natural desire and against one's self, than against a wicked woman.

What then saith Christ? He said not, " yea, it is easier, and so do," lest they should suppose that the thing is a law; but He subjoined, " Not all men receive it, but they to whom it is given," [7] raising the thing, and showing that it is great, and in this way drawing them on, and urging them.

But see herein a contradiction. For He indeed saith this is a great thing; but they, that it is easier. For it was meet that both these things should be done, and that it should be at once acknowledged a great thing by Him, that it might render them more forward, and by the things said by themselves it should be shown to be easier, that on this ground too they might the rather choose virginity and continence. For since to speak of

---

[1] [The citation agrees with the briefer reading, accepted by Tischendorf; comp. R. V. margin.—R.]

[2] Matt. xv. 11.   [3] Matt. xii. 12.   [4] Matt. xv. 15.
[5] Matt. xix. 10. [Compare the more exact citation which follows.—R.]
[6] Mark x. 10.   [7] Matt. xix. 11.

virginity seemed to be grievous, by the constraint of this law He drove them to this desire. Then to show the possibility of it, He saith, "There are some eunuchs, who were so born from their mother's womb, there are some eunuchs which were made eunuchs of men, and there be eunuchs which have made themselves eunuchs for the kingdom of Heaven's sake,"[1] by these words secretly leading them to choose the thing, and establishing the possibility of this virtue, and all but saying, Consider if thou wert in such case by nature, or hadst endured this selfsame thing at the hands of those who inflict such wanton injuries, what wouldest thou have done, being deprived indeed of the enjoyment, yet not having a reward? Thank God therefore now, for that with rewards and crowns thou undergoest this, which those men endure without crowns; or rather not even this, but what is much lighter, being supported both by hope, and by the consciousness of the good work, and not having the desire so raging like waves within thee.

For the excision of a member is not able to quell such waves, and to make a calm, like the curb of reason; or rather, reason only can do this.

For this intent therefore He brought in those others, even that He might encourage these, since if this was not what He was establishing, what means His saying concerning the other eunuchs? But when He saith, that they made themselves eunuchs, He means not the excision of the members, far from it, but the putting away of wicked thoughts. Since the man who hath mutilated himself, in fact, is subject even to a curse, as Paul saith, "I would they were even cut off[2] which trouble you."[3] And very reasonably. For such a one is venturing on the deeds of murderers, and giving occasion to them that slander God's creation, and opens the mouths of the Manichæans, and is guilty of the same unlawful acts as they that mutilate themselves amongst the Greeks. For to cut off our members hath been from the beginning a work of demoniacal agency, and satanic device, that they may bring up a bad report upon the work of God, that they may mar this living creature, that imputing all not to the choice, but to the nature of our members, the more part of them may sin in security, as being irresponsible; and doubly harm this living creature, both by mutilating the mem-

bers, and by impeding the forwardness of the free choice in behalf of good deeds.

These are the ordinances of the devil, bringing in, besides the things which we have mentioned, another wicked doctrine also, and making way beforehand for the arguments concerning destiny and necessity even from hence, and everywhere marring the freedom given to us of God, and persuading us that evil deeds are of nature, and hence secretly implanting many other wicked doctrines, although not openly. For such are the devil's poisons.

Therefore I beseech you to flee from such lawlessness. For together with the things I have mentioned, neither doth the force of lust become milder hereby, but even more fierce. For from another origin hath the seed that is in us its sources, and from another cause do its waves swell. And some say from the brain, some from the loins, this violent impulse hath its birth; but I should say from nothing else than from an ungoverned will and a neglected mind: if this be temperate, there is no evil result from the motions of nature.

Having spoken then of the eunuchs that are eunuchs for nought and fruitlessly, unless with the mind they too practise temperance, and of those that are virgins for Heaven's sake, He proceeds again to say, "He that is able to receive it, let him receive it," at once making them more earnest by showing that the good work is exceeding in greatness, and not suffering the thing to be shut up in the compulsion of a law, because of His unspeakable gentleness. And this He said, when He showed it to be most possible, in order that the emulation of the free choice might be greater.

And if it is of free choice, one may say, how doth He say, at the beginning, "All men do not receive it, but they to whom it is given?" That thou mightest learn that the conflict is great, not that thou shouldest suspect any compulsory allotments. For it is given to those, even to the willing.

But He spake thus to show that much influence from above is needed by him who entereth these lists, whereof He that is willing shall surely partake. For it is customary for Him to use this form of speech when the good work done is great, as when He saith, "To you it is given to know the mysteries."

And that this is true, is manifest even from the present instance. For if it be of the gift from above only, and they that live as virgins contribute nothing themselves, for nought did He promise them the kingdom of Heaven, and distinguish them from the other eunuchs.

---

[1] Matt. xix. 12.

[2] ἀποκόψονται, which may mean this. [R. V. margin, " mutilate themselves."]

[3] Gal. v. 12. [Whatever be the meaning of the verb in Galatians, there can be no question that the use here made of the passage is forced.—R.]

But mark thou, I pray, how from some men's wicked doings, other men gain. I mean, that the Jews went away having learnt nothing, for neither did they ask with the intent of learning, but the disciples gained even from hence.

4. "Then were there brought unto Him little children, that He should put His hands on them, and pray: and the disciples rebuked them. But He said unto them, Suffer the little children to come unto me, for of such is the kingdom of Heaven. And He laid His hands on them, and departed thence."[1]

And wherefore did the disciples repel the little children? For dignity. What then doth He? Teaching them to be lowly, and to trample under foot worldly pride, He doth receive them, and takes them in His arms, and to such as them promises the kingdom; which kind of thing He said before also.[2]

Let us also then, if we would be inheritors of the Heavens, possess ourselves of this virtue with much diligence. For this is the limit of true wisdom; to be simple with understanding; this is angelic life; yes, for the soul of a little child is pure from all the passions. Towards them who have vexed him he bears no resentment, but goes to them as to friends, as if nothing had been done; and how much soever he be beaten by his mother, after her he seeks, and her doth he prefer to all. Though thou show him the queen with a diadem, he prefers her not to his mother clad in rags, but would choose rather to see her in these, than the queen in splendor. For he useth to distinguish what pertains to him and what is strange to him, not by its poverty and wealth, but by friendship. And nothing more than necessary things doth he seek, but just to be satisfied from the breast, and then he leaves sucking. The young child is not grieved at what we are grieved, as at loss of money and such things as that, and he doth not rejoice again at what we rejoice, namely, at these temporal things, he is not eager about the beauty of persons.

Therefore He said, "of such is the kingdom of Heaven," that by choice we should practise these things, which young children have by nature. For since the Pharisees from nothing else so much as out of craft and pride did what they did, therefore on every hand He charges the disciples to be single hearted, both darkly hinting at those men, and instructing these. For nothing so much lifts up unto haughtiness, as power and precedence. Forasmuch then as the disciples were to enjoy great honors throughout the whole world, He preoccupies their mind, not suffering them to feel anything after the manner of men, neither to demand honors from the multitude, nor to have men clear the way[3] before them.

For though these seem to be little things, yet are they a cause of great evils. The Pharisees at least being thus trained were carried on into the very summit of evil, seeking after the salutations, the first seats, the middle places,[4] for from these they were cast upon the shoal of their mad desire of glory, then from thence upon impiety. So therefore those men went away having drawn upon themselves a curse by their tempting, but the little children a blessing, as being freed from all these.

Let us then also be like the little children, and "in malice be we babes."[5] For it cannot be, it cannot be for one otherwise to see Heaven, but the crafty and wicked must needs surely be cast into hell.

5. And before hell too, we shall here suffer the utmost ills. "For if thou be evil," it is said, "thou alone shalt endure the evil; but if good, it is for thyself and for thy neighbor."[6] Mark, at any rate, how this took place in the former instances also. For neither was anything more wicked than Saul, nor more simple and single-hearted than David. Which therefore was the stronger? Did not David get him twice into his hands, and having the power to slay him, forebore? Had he not him shut up as in a net and prison, and spared him? And this when both others were urging him, and when he himself was able to accuse him of countless charges; but nevertheless he suffered him to go away safe. And yet the other was pursuing him with all his army, but he was, with a few desperate fugitives, wandering and changing from place to place; nevertheless the fugitive had the advantage of the king, forasmuch as the one came to the conflict with simplicity, the other with wickedness.

For what could be more wicked than that man, who when he was leading his armies, and bringing all his wars to a successful issue, and undergoing the labors of the victory and the trophies, but bringing the crowns to him, assayed to slay him?

6. Such is the nature of envy, it is ever plotting against its own honors, and wasting him that hath it, and encompassing him with countless calamities. And that miserable man, for instance, until David departed, burst not forth into that piteous cry, bewail-

---

[1] Matt. xix. 13-15. [2] Matt. xviii. 3, 4. [3] σοβεῖν. [4] μεσασμούς. [5] 1 Cor. xiv. 20. [6] Prov. ix. 12, LXX.

25

ing himself and saying, "I am sore distressed, and the Philistines make war against me, and the Lord is departed from me."[1] Until he was separated from David, he fell not in war, but was both in safety and in glory; for indeed unto the king passed the glory of the captain. For neither was the man disposed to usurpation, nor did he assay to depose the other from his throne, but for him did he achieve all things, and was earnestly attached to him, and this is evident even from what followed afterwards. For when indeed he was set under him, any one of them who do not search carefully might perhaps suppose these things to be by the usual custom of a subject; but after he had withdrawn himself out of Saul's kingdom, what then was there to restrain him, and to persuade to abstain from war against Saul; or rather what was wanting that could provoke him even to slay? Had not the other been evil towards him once, twice, and often? Was it not after having received benefits from him? Was it not having nothing whereof to accuse him? Was not Saul's kingdom and safety danger and insecurity to himself? must he not needs wander and be a fugitive, and be in trembling for fear of the utmost ills, while the other is alive, and reigning? Nevertheless none of these things constrained him to stain his sword with blood, but when he saw him asleep, and bound, and alone, and in the midst of his own men, and had touched his head, and when there were many rousing him to it, and saying the opportunity thus favorable was a judgment of God, he at once rebuked those who were urging him on, and refrained from the murder, and sent him away both safe and well; and as though he had been rather a body guard of his, and a shield-bearer, not an enemy, so did he chide the host for their treachery towards the king.[2]

What could be equal to this soul? What to that mildness? For this it is possible to see even by the things that have been mentioned; but much more by what are done now. For when we have considered our vileness, then we shall know more perfectly the virtue of those saints. Wherefore I entreat you to hasten towards the emulation of them.

For indeed if thou lovest glory, and for this cause art plotting against thy neighbor, then shalt thou enjoy it more largely, when having spurned it, thou wilt abstain from the plotting. For like as to become rich[3] is contrary to covetousness, so is the loving of glory to

the obtaining of glory. And if ye be minded, let us inquire into each. For since we have no fear of hell, nor much regard for the kingdom, come and even from the things present let us lead you on.

For who are they that are ridiculous? Tell me. Is it not they that are doing anything for the sake of glory from the multitude? And who are the objects of praise? Is it not they who spurn the praise of the multitude? Therefore if the love of vainglory be matter of reproach, and it cannot be concealed that the vainglorious man loves it, he will assuredly be an object of reproach, and the love of glory is become to him a cause of dishonor. And not in this respect only doth he disgrace himself, but also in that he is compelled to do many things shameful, and teeming with the utmost disgrace. And like as with respect to their gains men are wont to suffer harm more than anything from the disease of covetousness (they become at least the subjects of many tricks, and of small gains make great losses, wherefore this saying hath prevailed even to be a proverb); and as to the voluptuous man likewise, his passion becomes a hindrance to the enjoyment of his pleasure. These at least that are exceedingly given up thereto, and are the slaves of women, these above all do women carry about as servants, and will never vouchsafe to treat them as men, buffeting, spurning them, leading, and taking them about everywhere, and giving themselves airs, and in everything merely giving them orders.

Even so also than him that is arrogant and mad about glory, and accounts himself to be high, nothing is more base and dishonored. For the race of man is fond of contention, and against nothing else doth it set itself so much, as against a boaster, and a contemptuous man, and a slave of glory.

And he himself too, in order to maintain the fashion of his pride, exhibits the conduct of a slave to the common sort, flattering, courting them, serving a servitude more grievous than that of one bought for money.

Knowing then all these things, let us lay down these passions, that we may not both pay a penalty here, and there be punished without end. Let us become lovers of virtue. For so both before reaching the kingdom we shall reap the greatest benefits here, and when we are departed thither we shall partake of the eternal blessings; unto which God grant we may all attain by the grace and love towards man of our Lord Jesus Christ, to whom be glory and might world without end. Amen.

---

[1] 1 Sam. xxviii. 15.   [2] 1 Sam. xxvi. 16.
[3] Mss, "not to make money," and presently, "not to love glory;" but Savile's reading is rightly adopted by Mr. Field, with the Latin Translator.

HOMILY LXIII.

MATT. XIX. 16.

"And, behold, one came and said unto Him, Good Master, by doing what, shall I inherit eternal life?"

SOME indeed accuse this young man, as one dissembling and ill-minded, and coming with a temptation to Jesus, but I, though I would not say he was not fond of money, and under subjection to his wealth, since Christ in fact convicted him of being such a character, yet a dissembler I would by no means call him, both because it is not safe to venture on things uncertain, and especially in blame, and because Mark hath taken away this suspicion; for he saith, that "having come running unto Him, and kneeling to Him, he besought Him," and that "Jesus beheld him, and loved him." [1]

But great is the tyranny of wealth, and it is manifest hence; I mean, that though we be virtuous as to the rest, this ruins all besides. With reason hath Paul also affirmed it to be the root of all evils in general. "For the love of money is the root of all evils," [2] he saith.

Wherefore then doth Christ thus reply to him, saying, "There is none good?" [3] Because He came unto Him as a mere man, and one of the common sort, and a Jewish teacher; for this cause then as a man He discourses with him. And indeed in many instances He replies to the secret thoughts of them that come unto Him; as when He saith, "We worship we know what;" [4] and, "If I bear witness of myself, my witness is not true." [5] When therefore He saith, "There is none good;" not as putting Himself out from being good doth He say this, far from it; for he said not, "Why dost thou call me good? I am not good;" but, "there is none good," that is, none amongst men.

And when He saith this self-same thing, He saith it not as depriving even men of goodness, but in contradistinction to the goodness of God. Wherefore also He added, "But one, that is, God;" and He said not,

"but my Father," that thou mightest learn that He had not revealed Himself to the young man. So also further back He called men evil, saying, "If ye, being evil, know how to give good gifts to your children." [6] For indeed there too He called them evil, not as condemning the whole race as evil (for by "ye," He means not "ye men"), but comparing the goodness that is in men with the goodness of God, He thus named it; therefore also He added, "How much more shall your Father give good things to them that ask Him?" And what was there to urge Him,[7] or what the profit that He should answer in this way? He leads him on by little and little, and teaches him to be far from all flattery, drawing him off from the things upon earth, and fastening him upon God, and persuading him to seek after the things to come, and to know that which is really good, and the root and fountain of all things, and to refer the honors to Him.

Since also when He saith, "Call no one master upon earth," it is in contradistinction to Himself He saith this, and that they might learn what is the chief sovereignty over all things that are. For neither was it a small forwardness the young man had shown up to this time in having fallen into such a desire; and when of the rest some were tempting, some were coming to Him for the cure of diseases, either their own or others, he for eternal life was both coming to Him, and discoursing with Him. For fertile was the land and rich, but the multitude of the thorns choked the seed. Mark at any rate how he is prepared thus far for obedience to the commandments. For "By doing what," he saith, "shall I inherit eternal life?" So ready was he for the performance of the things that should be told him. But if he had come unto Him, tempting Him, the evangelist would have declared this also to us, as He doth also with regard to the others, as in the case of the lawyer. And though himself had been silent, Christ could not have suffered

---

[1] Mark x. 17–21.
[2] 1 Tim. vi. 10. [R. V., "a root of all kinds of evil."]
[3] Matt. xix. 17. [This clause is found in the rec. text, but not in the better supported form of the verse, which reads, "Why askest thou me concerning that which is good? One there is who is good." It is probable, but not certain, that Chrysostom accepted the other form of the text. Comp. note on Homily XXVII. 5., p. 186.—R.]
[4] John iv. 22.   [5] John v. 31.
[6] Matt. vii. 11.
[7] [φησίν, "one may say," occurs in the Greek here.—R.]

him to lie concealed, but would have convicted him plainly, or at least would have intimated it, so that he should not seem to have deceived Him, and to be hidden, and thereby have suffered hurt.

If he had come unto Him tempting, he would not have departed sorrowing for what he heard. This was not at any rate ever the feeling of any of the Pharisees, but they grew fierce when their mouths were stopped. But not so this man; but he goeth away cast down, which is no little sign that not with an evil will he had come unto Him, but with one too feeble, and that he did indeed desire life, but was held in subjection by another and most grievous feeling.

Therefore when Christ said, "If thou wilt enter into life, keep the commandments," he saith, "Which?" Not tempting, far from it, but supposing there were some others besides those of the law that should procure him life, which was like one who was very desirous. Then since Jesus mentioned those out of the law, he saith, "All these things have I kept from my youth up."[1] And neither at this did he stop, but again asks, "What lack I yet?" which itself again was a sign of his very earnest desire.[2]

What then saith Christ? Since He was going to enjoin something great, He setteth forth the recompenses, and saith, "If thou wilt be perfect, go and sell that thou hast, and give to the poor, and thou shalt have treasure in Heaven: and come, and follow me."[3]

2. Seest thou how many prizes, how many crowns, He appoints for this race? If he had been tempting, He would not have told him these things. But now He both saith it, and in order to draw him on, He also shows him the reward to be great, and leaves it all to his own will, by all means throwing into the shade that which seemed to be grievous in His advice. Wherefore even before mentioning the conflicts and the toil, He shows him the prize, saying "If thou wilt be perfect," and then saith, "Sell that thou hast, and give to the poor," and straightway again the rewards, "Thou shalt have treasure in Heaven; and come, and follow me." For indeed to follow Him is a great recompense. "And thou shalt have treasure in Heaven."

For since his discourse was of money, even of all did He advise him to strip himself, showing that he loses not what he hath, but adds to his possessions, He gave him more than He required him to give up; and not only more, but also as much greater as Heaven is greater than earth, and yet more so.

But He called it a treasure, showing the plenteousness of the recompense, its permanency, its security, so far as it was possible by human similitudes to intimate it to the hearer. It is not then enough to despise wealth, but we must also maintain poor men, and above all things follow Christ; that is, do all the things that are ordered by Him, be ready for slaughter and daily death. "For if any man will come after me, let him deny himself, and take up his cross, and follow me."[4] So that to cast away one's money is a much less thing than this last commandment, to shed even one's very blood; yet not a little doth our being freed from wealth· contribute towards this.

"But when the young man heard it, he went away sorrowful."[5] After this the evangelist, as it were to show that he hath not felt anything it was unlikely he should feel, saith, "For he had[6] great possessions." For they that have little are not equally held in subjection, as they that are overflowed with great affluence, for then the love of it becomes more tyrannical. Which thing I cease not always saying, that the increase of acquisitions kindles the flame more, and renders the getters poorer, inasmuch as it puts them in greater desire, and makes them have more feeling of their want.

See, for example, even here what strength did this passion exhibit. Him that had come to Him with joy and forwardness, when Christ commanded him to cast away his riches, it so overwhelmed and weighed down, as not to suffer him so much as to answer touching these things, but silenced and become dejected and sullen to go away.

What then saith Christ? "How hardly shall the rich enter into the kingdom of Heaven!"[7] blaming not riches, but them that are held in subjection by them. But if the rich man "hardly," much more the covetous man. For if not to give one's own be an hindrance to entering the kingdom, even to take of other men's goods, think how much fire it heapeth up.

Why can it have been, however, that He said to His disciples, that "hardly shall a rich man enter in," they being poor men, and having no possessions? Instructing them not to be ashamed of their poverty, and, as

---

[1] Matt. xix. 20. [R. V. omits "from my youth up."]
[2] [An important sentence is omitted here : "But that also was not a little thing which he supposed he lacked, nor did he think that what he had said sufficed for attaining what he desired."--R.]
[3] Matt xix. 21. [R. V., "If thou wouldest," etc.]
[4] Matt. xvi. 24.　　　[5] Matt. xix. 22.
[6] [R. V., "he was one that had," etc.]
[7] Matt. xix. 23. [The citation is a combination of this verse and Mark x. 23. The influence of Mark's more striking account is seen throughout the Homily.—R.]

it were, excusing Himself to them for suffering them to have nothing.

But having said it was hard; as He proceeds, He shows that it is even impossible, and not merely impossible, but even in the highest degree impossible; and this He showed by the comparison concerning the camel and the [1] needle.

"It is easier," saith He, "for a camel to enter in by the eye of a needle,[2] than for a rich man to enter into the kingdom of Heaven."[3] Whence it is shown, that there is no ordinary reward for them that are rich, and are able to practise self command. Wherefore also He affirmed it to be a work of God, that He might show that great grace is needed for him who is to achieve this. At least, when the disciples were troubled, He said, "With men this is impossible; but with God all things are possible."[4]

And wherefore are the disciples troubled, being poor, yea, exceedingly poor? Wherefore then are they confounded? Being in pain about the salvation of the rest, and having a great affection for all, and having already taken upon themselves the tender bowels of teachers. They were at least in such trembling and fear for the whole world from this declaration, as to need much comfort.

Therefore, having first "beheld them, He said unto them, The things which are impossible with men, are possible with God." For with a mild and meek look, having soothed their shuddering mind, and having put an end to their distress (for this the evangelist signified by saying, "He beheld them"), then by His words also He relieves them, bringing before them God's power, and so making them feel confidence.

But if thou wilt learn the manner of it likewise, and how what is impossible may become possible, hear. Born either for this end did He say, "The things which are impossible with men, are possible with God," that thou shouldest give it up, and abstain, as from things impossible; but that having considered the greatness of the good work, thou shouldest hasten to it readily, and having besought God to assist thee in these noble contests, shouldest attain unto life.

3. How then should this become possible? If thou cast away what thou hast, if thou empty thyself of thy wealth, if thou refrain from the wicked desire. For in proof that He does not refer it to God alone, but that to this end He said it, that thou shouldest know

the vastness of the good work, hear what follows. For when Peter had said, "Behold, we have forsaken all, and followed Thee," and had asked, "What shall we have therefore?" having appointed the reward for them; He added, "And every one who hath forsaken houses, or lands, or brothers, or sisters, or father, or mother, shall receive an hundred fold, and shall inherit eternal life."[5] Thus that which is impossible becometh possible. But how may this very thing be done, one may say, to forsake these? how is it possible for him that is once sunk in such lust of wealth, to recover himself? If he begin to empty himself of his possessions, and cut off what are superfluous. For so shall he both advance further, and shall run on his course more easily afterwards.

Do not then seek all at once, but gently, and by little and little, ascend this ladder, that leads thee up to Heaven.[6] For like as those in fevers having acrid bile abounding within them, when they cast in thereon meats and drinks, so far from quenching their thirst, do even kindle the flame; so also the covetous, when they cast in their wealth upon this wicked lust more acrid than that bile, do rather inflame it. For nothing so stays it as to refrain for a time from the lust of gain, like as acrid bile is stayed by abstinence and evacuations.

But this itself, by what means will it be done? one may say. If thou consider, that whilst rich, thou wilt never cease thirsting, and pining with the lust of more; but being freed from thy possessions, thou wilt be able also to stay this disease. Do not then encompass thyself with more, lest thou follow after things unattainable, and be incurable, and be more miserable than all, being thus frantic.

For answer me, whom shall we affirm to be tormented and pained? him that longs after costly meats and drinks, and is not able to enjoy them as he will, or him that hath not such a desire? It is quite clear one must say, him that desires, but cannot obtain what he desires. For this is so painful, to desire and not to enjoy, to thirst and not to drink, that Christ desiring to describe hell to us, described it in this way, and introduced the rich man thus tormented. For longing for a drop of water, and not enjoying it, this was his punishment. So then he that despises wealth quiets the desire, but he that desires to be rich[7] hath inflamed it more, and not yet

---

[1] βελόνην.

[2] [R. V., with the same Greek text, renders, "to go through a needle's eye." The variation in the English above seems unnecessary.—R.]

[3] Matt. xix. 24.   [4] Matt. xix. 26.

[5] Matt. xix. 27-29. [The position of the word "lands" is peculiar; "or wife" is not found here, but occurs in Homily LXIV. I.—R.]

[6] [The following clause is omitted in the translation: "though (or, if) as a whole it seems difficult to them."—R.]

[7] [The Greek adds here, καὶ περιβάλλεσθαι πλείω, "and to possess himself of more.—R.]

doth he stay; but though he have got ten thousand talents, he desireth as much more; though he obtain these, again he aims at twice as much more, and going on he desires even the mountains, and the earth, and the sea, and all to become gold for him, being mad with a kind of new and fearful madness, and one that can never thus be extinguished.

And that thou mightest learn, that not by addition but by taking away this evil is stayed; if thou hadst ever had an absurd desire to fly and to be borne through the air, how wouldest thou extinguish this unreasonable desire? By fashioning wings, and preparing other instruments, or by convincing the mind that it is desiring things impossible, and that one should attempt none of these things? It is quite plain, that by convincing the mind. But that, thou mayest say, is impossible. But this again is more impossible, to find a limit for this desire. For indeed it is more easy for men to fly, than to make this lust cease by an addition of more. For when the objects of desire are possible, one may be soothed by the enjoyment of them, but when they are impossible, one must labor for one thing, to draw ourselves off from the desire, as otherwise at least it is not possible to recover the soul.

Therefore that we may not have superfluous sorrows, let us forsake the love of money that is ever paining, and never endures to hold its peace, and let us remove ourselves to another love, which both makes us happy, and hath great facility, and let us long after the treasures above. For neither is the labor here so great, and the gain is unspeakable, and it is not possible for him to fail of them who is but in any wise watchful and sober, and despises the things present; even as on the other hand, as to him that is a slave to these last, and is utterly given up to them, it as altogether of necessity that he fail of those better riches.

4. Considering then all these things, put away the wicked desire of wealth. For neither couldest thou say this, that it gives the things present, though it deprive us of the things to come, albeit even if this were so, this were extreme punishment, and vengeance. But now not even this may be. For besides hell, and before that hell, even here it casts thee into a more grievous punishment. For many houses hath this lust overthrown, and fierce wars hath it stirred up, and compelled men to end their lives by a violent death; and before these dangers it ruins the nobleness of the soul, and is wont often to make him that hath it cowardly, and unmanly, and rash, and false, and calumnious, and ravenous, and over-reaching, and all the worst things.

But seeing perhaps the brightness of the silver, and the multitude of the servants, and the beauty of the buildings, the court paid in the market-place, art thou bewitched thereby? What remedy then may there be for this evil wound? If thou consider how these things affect thy soul, how dark, and desolate, and foul they render it, and how ugly; if thou reckon with how many evils these things were acquired, with how many labors they are kept, with how many dangers: or rather they are not kept unto the end, but when thou hast escaped the attempts of all, death coming on thee is often wont to remove these things into the hand of thine enemies, and goeth and taketh thee with him destitute, drawing after thee none of these things, save the wounds and the sores only, which the soul received from these, before its departing. When then thou seest any one resplendent outwardly with raiment and large attendance, lay open his conscience, and thou shalt see many a cobweb within, and much dust. Consider Paul, Peter. Consider John, Elias, or rather the Son of God Himself, who hath not where to lay His head. Be an imitator of Him, and of His servants, and imagine to thyself the unspeakable riches of these.

But if having obtained a little sight by these, thou shouldest be darkened again, as in any shipwreck when a storm hath come on, hear the declaration of Christ, which affirms, that it is impossible " for a rich man to enter into the kingdom of Heaven." And against this declaration set the mountains, and the earth, and the sea; and all things, if thou wilt, suppose[1] to be gold; for thou shalt see nothing equal to the loss arising to thee from thence. And thou indeed makest mention of acres of land, so many and so many, and of houses ten or twenty or even more, and of baths as many, and of slaves a thousand, or twice as many, and of chariots fastened with silver and overlaid with gold; but I say this, that if each one of you that are rich were to leave this poverty (for these things are poverty compared with what I am about to say), and were possessed of a whole world, and each of them had as many men as are now everywhere on land and sea, and each a world both sea and land, and everywhere buildings, and cities, and nations, and from every side instead of water, instead of fountains, gold flowed up for him, I would not say those who are thus rich are worth three farthings, when they are cast out of the kingdom

For if now aiming at riches that perish,

---

[1] τῷ λόγῳ ποίησον.

when they miss them, they are tormented, if they should obtain a perception of those unspeakable blessings, what then will suffice for consolation for them? There is nothing. Tell me not then of the abundance of their possessions, but consider how great loss the lovers of this abundance undergo in consequence thereof, for these things losing Heaven, and being in the same state, as if any one after being cast out of the highest honor in kings' courts, having a dung heap, were to pride himself on that. For the storing up of money differs nothing from that, or rather that is even the better. For that is serviceable both for husbandry, and for heating a bath, and for other such uses, but the buried gold for none of these things. And would it were merely useless; but as it is, it kindles moreover many furnaces for him that hath it, unless he use it rightly; countless evils at least spring therefrom.

Therefore they that are without used to call the love of money the citadel[1] of evils; but the blessed Paul spake much better, and more vividly, pronouncing it "the root of all evils."[2]

Considering then all these things, let us emulate the things worthy of emulation, not gorgeous buildings, not costly estates, but the men that have much confidence towards God, those that have riches in Heaven, the owners of those treasures, them that are really rich, them that are poor for Christ's sake, that we may attain unto the good things of eternity by the grace and love towards man of our Lord Jesus Christ, with whom be unto the Father, together with the Holy Ghost, glory, might, honor, now and always and world without end. Amen.

---

[1] Mr. Field cites Stobæus, p. 130, 52, of Bion, and Diog. Laert. vi. 50, of Diogenes the cynic, noting that both say μητρόπολις, not ἀκρόπολις. See Adnot. p. 133.
[2] 1 Tim. vi. 10. [R. V., "a root of all kinds of evil."]

HOMILY LXIV.

MATT. XIX. 27.

"Then answered Peter, and said unto Him, Behold, we have forsaken all, and followed Thee; what shall we have therefore?"

ALL which? O blessed Peter; the rod? the net? the boat? the craft? These things dost thou tell me of, as all? Yea, saith he, but not for display do I say these things, but in order that by this question I may bring in the multitude of the poor. For since the Lord had said, "If thou wilt be perfect, sell that thou hast, and give to the poor, and thou shalt have treasure in Heaven;"[1] lest any one of the poor should say, What then? if I have no possessions, can I not be perfect? Peter asks, that thou, the poor man, mayest learn, that thou art made in no respect inferior by this: Peter asks, that thou mayest not learn from Peter, and doubt (for indeed he was imperfect as yet, and void of the Spirit), but that, having received the declaration from Peter's Master, thou mayest be confident.

For like as we do (we make things our own often when speaking of the concerns of others), so did the apostle, when he put to Him this question in behalf of all the world. Since that at least he knew with certainty his own portion, is manifest from what had been said before; for he that had already received the keys of the Heavens, much more might feel confidence about the things hereafter.

But mark also how exactly his reply is according to Christ's demand. For He had required of the rich man these two things, to give that he had to the poor, and to follow Him. Wherefore he also expresses these two things, to forsake, and to follow. "For behold we have forsaken all," saith he, "and have followed Thee." For the forsaking was done for the sake of following, and the following was rendered easier by the forsaking, and made them feel confidence and joy touching the forsaking.

What then saith He? "Verily, I say unto you, that ye which have followed me, in the regeneration when the Son of Man shall sit on the throne of His glory, ye also shall sit

---

[1] Matt. xix. 21.

upon twelve thrones, judging the twelve tribes of Israel." [1] What then, one may say, shall Judas sit there? By no means. How, then, doth He say, "Ye shall sit on twelve thrones?" how shall the terms of the promise be fulfilled?

Hear how, and on what principle. There is a law ordained of God, recited by Jeremiah, the prophet to the Jews, and in these words: "At what instant I shall speak a sentence concerning a nation and kingdom, to pluck up and destroy; if that nation turn from their evil deeds, I also will repent of the evils, which I thought to do unto them. And at what instant I shall speak concerning a nation and kingdom to build and to plant it; and if they do evil in my sight, that they obey not my voice, I also will repent of the good, which I said I would do unto them." [2]

For the same custom do I observe with respect to the good things as well, saith He. For though I spake of building up, should they show themselves unworthy of the promise, I will no longer do it. Which sort of thing was done with respect to man upon his creation, "For the dread of you," it is said, "and the fear of you shall be on the wild beasts," [3] and it came not to pass, for he proved himself unworthy of the sovereignty, even as did Judas also.

For in order that neither at the denunciations of punishment any men should despair, and become more hardened, nor by the promises of good things be rendered causelessly more remiss, He remedies both these evils, by that which I have before mentioned, saying in this way: Though I should threaten, do not despair; for thou art able to repent, and to reverse the denunciation, like the Ninevites. Though I should promise any good thing, grow not remiss because of the promise. For shouldest thou appear unworthy, the fact of my having promised will not advantage thee, but will rather bring punishment. For I promise thee being worthy.

Therefore even then in His discourse with His disciples He did not promise to them simply, for neither did He say, "you," only, but added, "which have followed me," that He might both cast out Judas, and draw towards Him those that should come afterwards. For neither to them only was it said, nor to Judas any more, when he had become unworthy.

Now to the disciples He promised things to come, saying, "Ye shall sit on twelve thrones," for they were now of a higher

stamp, and sought after none of the things of the present world, but to the rest He promises also what are here.

For "every one," He saith, "that hath forsaken brethren, or sisters, or father, or mother, or wife, or children, or lands, or house, for my name's sake, shall receive an hundredfold in this world, and shall inherit eternal life." [4]

For lest any after having heard the word "ye," should suppose this a thing peculiar to the disciples (I mean now the enjoying the greatest and first honors in the things to come), He extended the word, and spread the promise over the whole earth, and from the things present establishes the things to come also. And to the disciples also at the beginning, when they were in a more imperfect state, He reasoned from the things present. For when He drew them from the sea, and took them from their trade, and commanded them to forsake the ships, He made mention not of Heaven, not of thrones, but of the things here, saying, "I will make you fishers of men;" but when He had wrought them to be of higher views, then after that He discourses of the things to come also.

2. But what is, "Judging the twelve tribes of Israel?" This is, "condemning them." For they are not surely to sit as judges, but like as He said the Queen of the South should condemn that generation, and the Ninevites shall condemn them; so now these also. Therefore He said not, the nations, and the world, but the tribes of Israel. For since both the Jews alike and the apostles had been brought up under the same laws, and customs, and polity; when the Jews said, that for this cause they could not believe in Christ, because the law forbade to receive His commandments, by bringing forward these men, who had received the same law, and yet had believed, He condemns all those; like as even already He had said, "therefore they shall be your judges." [5]

And what great thing doth He promise them, it may be said, if what the Ninevites have and the Queen of the South, this these are to have also? In the first place He had promised them many other things before this, and after this doth promise them, and this alone is not their reward.

And besides even in this He intimated by the way something more than these things. For of those He simply said, The men of Nineveh shall rise up and condemn this gen-

---

[1] Matt. xix. 28.   [2] Jer. xviii. 7-10.   [3] Gen. ix. 2.

[4] Matt. xix. 29. [The citation differs from that in the last Homily. The order here is that of Tischendorf (not of R. V. or rec. text); "or wife" occurs here; "house" is substituted for "houses."—R.]

[5] Matt. xii. 27.

eration," [1] and, "The Queen of the South shall condemn it;" but concerning these, not merely thus, but how? "When the Son of Man shall sit upon the throne of His glory, then shall ye also sit upon twelve thrones," saith He, declaring, that they also shall reign with Him, and partake of that glory. "For if we suffer," it is said, "we shall also reign with Him." [2] For neither do the thrones signify a sitting (in judgment), for He alone is the one that shall sit and judge, but honor and glory unspeakable did He intimate by the thrones.

To these then He spake of these things, but to all the rest of eternal life and an hundredfold here. But if to the rest, much more to these too, both these things, and the things in this life.

And this surely came to pass; for when they had left a fishing rod and a net, they possessed with authority the substances of all, the prices of the houses and the lands, and the very bodies of the believers. For often did they choose even to be slain for their sake, as Paul also bears witness to many, when he saith, "If it had been possible ye would have plucked out your eyes, and given them to me." [3] But when He saith, "Every one who hath forsaken wife," He saith not this, for marriages to be broken asunder for nought, but as He saith concerning one's life, "He that loseth his life for my sake shall find it," [4] not that we should destroy ourselves, neither that while yet here we should part it from the body, but that we should prefer godliness to all things; this too He saith also with respect to wife and brethren.

But He seems to me here to intimate also the persecutions. For since there were many instances both of fathers urging their sons to ungodliness, and wives their husbands; when they command these things, saith He, let them be neither wives nor parents, even as Paul likewise said, "But if the unbelieving depart, let him depart." [5]

When He had then raised the spirit of all, and had persuaded them to feel confidence both with respect to themselves and to all the world, He added, that "Many that were first shall be last, and last first." [6] But this although it be spoken also without distinction concerning many others likewise, it is spoken also concerning these men and concerning the Pharisees, who did not believe, even as before also He had said, "Many shall come from east and west and shall sit down with Abraham, and Isaac, and Jacob; but the children of the kingdom shall be cast out." [7]

Then He adds also a parable, as training those who had fallen short to a great forwardness.

"For the kingdom of Heaven," He said, "is like to a man that is an householder, which went out early in the morning to hire laborers into his vineyard. And when he had agreed with them for a penny a day, he sent them into his vineyard."

"And at the third hour he saw others standing idle, and to them too he said, Go ye also into the vineyard, and whatsoever is right I will give you. And about the sixth and ninth hours he did likewise. And about the eleventh hour, he saw others standing idle, and saith unto them, Why stand ye here all the day idle? But they say unto him, No man hath hired us. He saith unto them, Go ye also into my vineyard, and whatsoever is right, ye shall receive."

"So when even was come, the lord of the vineyard saith unto his steward, Call the laborers, and give them their hire, beginning from the last unto the first. And when they came that were hired about the eleventh hour, they received every man a penny. And the first supposed that they should receive more, and they received likewise every man a penny. And when they had received it, they murmured against the good man of the house, saying, These last have wrought but one hour, and thou hast made them equal unto us that have borne the burden and heat of the day. But he answered one of them, and said, Friend, I do thee no wrong; didst thou not agree with me for a penny? Take that thine is, and go thy way; I will give unto this last also, even as unto thee. Is it not lawful for me to do what I will with mine own? Is thine eye evil, because I am good? Thus the last shall be first, and the first last: for many are called, but few chosen." [8]

3. What is to us the intent of this parable? For the beginning doth not harmonize with what is said at the end, but intimates altogether the contrary. For in the first part He shows all enjoying the same, and not some cast out, and some brought in; yet He Himself both before the parable and after the parable said the opposite thing. "That the first shall be last, and the last first," that is, before the very first, those not continuing first, but having become last. For in proof that this is His meaning, He added, "Many are called, but few chosen," so as doubly

---

[1] Matt. xii. 41.   [2] 2 Tim. ii. 12.
[3] Gal. iv. 51.   [4] Matt. x. 39.   [5] 1 Cor. vii. 15.
[6] Matt. xix. 30. ["were" is an emendation of the translator. The Greek is that of the rec. text.—R.

[7] Matt. viii. 11, 12.
[8] Matt. xx. 1. [This long passage agrees closely with the rec. text. In verses 5, 6, the New Testament narrative is abridged, but there are scarcely any other peculiarities.—R.]

both to sting the one, and to soothe and urge on the other.

But the parable saith not this, but that they shall be equal to them that are approved, and have labored much. "For thou hast made them equal unto us," it is said, "that have borne the burden and heat of the day."

What then is the meaning of the parable? For it is necessary to make this first clear, and then we shall clear up that other point. By a vineyard He meaneth the injunctions of God and His commandments: by the time of laboring, the present life: by laborers, them that in different ways are called to the fulfillment of the injunctions: by early in the morning, and about the third and ninth and eleventh hours, them who at different ages have drawn near to God, and approved themselves.

But the question is this, whether the first having gloriously approved themselves, and having pleased God, and having throughout the whole day shone by their labors, are possessed by the basest feeling of vice, jealousy and envy. For when they had seen them enjoying the same rewards, they say, "These last have wrought but one hour, and thou hast made them equal unto us, that have borne the burden and heat of the day." And in these words, when they are to receive no hurt, neither to suffer diminution as to their own hire, they were indignant, and much displeased at the good of others, which was proof of envy and jealousy. And what is yet more, the good man of the house in justifying himself with respect to them, and in making his defense to him that had said these things, convicts him of wickedness and the basest jealousy, saying, "Didst thou not agree with me for a penny? Take that thine is, and go thy way; I will give unto the last even as unto thee. Is thine eye evil, because I am good?"

What then is it which is to be established by these things? For in other parables also this self-same thing may be seen. For the son who was approved is brought in, as having felt this self-same thing, when he saw his prodigal brother enjoying much honor, even more than himself. For like as these enjoyed more by receiving first, so he in a greater degree was honored by the abundance of the things given him; and to these things he that was approved bears witness.

What then may we say? There is no one who is thus justifying himself, or blaming others in the kingdom of Heaven; away with the thought! for that place is pure from envy and jealousy. For if when they are here the saints give their very lives for sinners, much more when they see them there in the enjoyment of these things, do they rejoice and account these to be blessings of their own.

Wherefore then did He so frame His discourse? The saying is a parable, wherefore neither is it right to inquire curiously into all things in parables word by word,[1] but when we have learnt the object for which it was composed, to reap this, and not to busy one's self about anything further.

Wherefore then was this parable thus composed? what is its object to effect? To render more earnest them that are converted and become better men in extreme old age, and not to allow them to suppose they have a less portion. So it is for this cause He introduces also others displeased at their blessings, not to represent those men as pining or vexed, away with the thought! but to teach us that these have enjoyed such honor, as could even have begotten envy in others. Which we also often do, saying, "Such a one blamed me, because I counted thee worthy of much honor," neither having been blamed, nor wishing to slander that other, but hereby to show the greatness of the gift which this one enjoyed.

But wherefore can it have been that He did not hire all at once? As far as concerned Him, He did hire all; but if all did not hearken at once, the difference was made by the disposition of them that were called. For this cause, some are called early in the morning, some at the third hour, some at the sixth, some at the ninth, some at the eleventh, when they would obey.

This Paul also declared when he said, "When it pleased Him, who separated me from my mother's womb."[2] When did it please Him? When he was ready to obey. For He willed it even from the beginning, but because he would not have yielded, then it pleased Him, when Paul also was ready to obey. Thus also did He call the thief, although He was able to have called him even before, but he would not have obeyed. For if Paul at the beginning would not have obeyed, much more the thief.

And if they say, "No man hath hired us," in the first place as I said we must not be curious about all the points in the parables; but here neither is the good man of the house represented to say this, but they; but he doth not convict them, that he might drive them to perplexity, but might win them over. For that He called all, as far as lay in Him, from the first even the parable shows, saying, that "He went out early in the morning to hire."

---

[1] κατὰ λέξιν.

[2] Gal. i. 15.

4. From everything then it is manifest to us, that the parable is spoken with reference to them who from earliest youth, and those who in old age and more tardily, lay hold on virtue; to the former, that they may not be proud, neither reproach those called at the eleventh hour; to the latter, that they may learn that it is possible even in a short time to recover all.

For since He had been speaking about earnestness, and the casting away of riches, and contempt of all one's possessions, but this needed much vigor of mind and youthful ardor; in order to kindle in them a fire of love, and to give vigor to their will, He shows that it is possible even for men coming later to receive the hire of the whole day.

But He doth not say it thus, lest again He should make them proud, but he shows that the whole is of His love to man, and because of this they shall not fail, but shall themselves enjoy the unspeakable blessings.

And this chiefly is what it is His will to establish by this parable. And if He adds, that, "So the last shall be first and the first last; for many are called, but few chosen," marvel not. For not as inferring it from the parable doth He say this, but His meaning is this, that like as this came to pass, so shall that come to pass. For here indeed the first did not become last, but all received the same contrary to hope and expectation. But as this result took place contrary to hope and contrary to expectation, and they that came before were equalled by them that followed, so shall that also come to pass which is more than this, and more strange, I mean, that the last should come to be even before the first, and that the first should be after these. So that that is one thing, and this another.

But He seems to me to say these things, darkly hinting at the Jews, and amongst the believers at those who at first shone forth, but afterwards neglected virtue, and fell back; and those others again that have risen from vice, and have shot beyond many. For we see such changes taking place both with respect to faith and practice.

Wherefore I entreat you let us use much diligence both to stand in the right faith, and to show forth an excellent life. For unless we add also a life suitable to our faith, we shall suffer the extremest punishment.

And this the blessed Paul showed even from times of old, when he said, that "They did all eat the same spiritual meat, and did all drink the same spiritual drink:" and added, that they were not saved; "for they were overthrown in the wilderness."[1] And Christ declared it even in the evangelists, when He brought in some that had cast out devils and prophesied, and are led away to punishment. And all His parables also, as that of the virgins, that of the net, that of the thorns, that of the tree not bringing forth fruit, demand virtue in our works. For concerning doctrines He discourses seldom, for neither doth the subject need labor, but of life often or rather everywhere, for the war about this is continual, wherefore also so is the labor.

And why do I speak of the whole code. For even a part of it overlooked brings upon one great evils; as, for instance, almsgiving overlooked casts into hell them that have come short in it; and yet this is not the whole of virtue, but a part thereof. But nevertheless both the virgins were punished for not having this, and the rich man was for this cause tormented, and they that have not fed the hungry, are for this condemned with the devil. Again, not to revile is a very small part of it, nevertheless this too casts out them that have not attained to it. "For he that saith to his brother, Thou fool, shall be in danger of hell fire."[2] Again, even continence itself is a part, but nevertheless, without this no one shall see the Lord. For, "Follow peace," it is said, "and holiness,[3] without which no man shall see the Lord."[4] And humility too in like manner is a part of virtue; but nevertheless though any one should fulfill other good works, but have not attained to this, he is unclean with God. And this is manifest from the Pharisee, who though abounding with numberless good works, by this lost all.

But I have also something more than these things to say again. I mean, that not only one of them overlooked shuts Heaven against us, but though it be done, yet not in due perfection and abundance, it produces the self-same effect again. "For except your righteousness shall exceed the righteousness of the Scribes and Pharisees, ye shall not enter into the kingdom of Heaven."[5] So that though thou give alms, but not more than they, thou shalt not enter in.

And how much did they bestow in alms? one may ask. For this very thing, I am minded to say now, that they who do not give may be roused to give, and they that give may not pride themselves, but may make increase of their gifts. What then did they give? A tenth of all their possessions, and again another tenth, and after this a third, so that they almost gave away the

[1] 1 Cor. x. 3, 4, 5.

[2] Matt. v. 22.
[3] ἁγιασμόν, comp. 1 Thess. iv. 3. [R. V., "sanctification."]
[4] Heb. xii. 14.　　　　　　　　　　[5] Matt. viii. 20.

third part, for three-tenths put together make up this. And together with these, first fruits, and first born, and other things besides, as, for instance, the offerings for sins, those for purification, those at feasts, those in the jubilee,[1] those by the cancelling of debts, and the dismissals of servants, and the lendings that were clear of usury. But if he who gave the third part of his goods, or rather the half (for those being put together with these are the half), if then he who is giving the half, achieves no great thing, he who doth not bestow so much as the tenth, of what shall he be worthy? With reason He said, "There are few that be saved."

5. Let us not, then, despise the care of our life. For if one portion of it despised brings so great a destruction, when on every hand we are subject to the sentence of condemnation, how shall we escape the punishment? and what manner of penalty shall we not suffer? and what manner of hope of salvation have we, one may ask, if each of the things we have numbered threatens us with hell? I too say this; nevertheless, if we give heed we may be saved, preparing the medicines of almsgiving, and attending to our wounds.

For oil does not so strengthen a body, as benevolence at once strengthens a soul, and makes it invincible to all and impregnable to the devil. For wheresoever he may seize us, his hold then slips, this oil not suffering his grasp to fix on our back.

With this oil therefore let us anoint ourselves continually. For it is the cause of health, and a supply of light, and a source of cheerfulness. "But such a one," thou wilt say, "hath talents of gold so many and so many, and gives away nothing." And what is that to thee? For thus shalt thou appear more worthy of admiration, when in poverty thou art more munificent than he. It was on this ground Paul marvelled at the Macedonians, not because they gave, but because even though they were in poverty they gave.[2]

Look not then at these, but at the common Teacher of all, who "had not where to lay His head."[3] And why, you say, doth not this and that person do so? Do not judge another, but deliver thyself from the charge against thee. Since the punishment is greater when thou at the same time blamest others, and thyself doest not, when judging other men, thou art again thyself also subject to the same judgment. For if even them who do right He permits not to judge others, much more will He not permit offenders.

Let us not therefore judge others, neither let us look to others who are taking their ease, but unto Jesus, and from thence let us draw our examples.

Why! have I been thy benefactor? Why! did I redeem thee, that thou lookest to me? It is another who hath bestowed these things on thee. Why dost thou let go thy Master, and look unto thy fellow-servant? Heardest thou not Him saying, "Learn of me, for I am meek and lowly in heart?"[4] And again, "He that would be first amongst you, let him be servant of all:" and again, "Even as the Son of Man came not to be ministered unto, but to minister."[5] And after these things again, lest taking offense at them who are remiss amongst thy fellow-servants, thou continue in contemptuousness; to draw thee off from that, He saith, "I have made myself an example to you, that as I have done, ye should do also."[6] But hast thou no teacher of virtue amongst those persons that are with thee, neither such a one as to lead thee on to these things? More abundant then will be the praise, the commendation greater, when not even being supplied with teachers thou hast become one to be marvelled at.

For this is possible, nay very easy, if we be willing; and this they show, who first duly performed these things, as for instance, Noah, Abraham, Melchizedeck, Job, and all the men like them. To them it is needful to look every day, and not unto these, whom ye never cease emulating, and passing about their names in your assemblies. For nothing else do I hear you saying everywhere, but such words as these; "Such a one has bought so many acres of land; such a one is rich, he is building." Why dost thou stare, O man, at what is without? Why dost thou look to others? If thou art minded to look to others, look to them that do their duty, to them that approve themselves, to them that carefully fulfill the law, not to those that have become offenders, and are in dishonor. For if thou look to these, thou wilt gather hence many evil things, falling into remissness, into pride, into condemnation of others; but if thou reckon over them that do right, thou wilt lead thyself on unto humility, unto diligence, unto compunction, unto the blessings that are beyond number.

Hear what the Pharisee suffered, because he let pass them that do right, and looked to him that had offended; hear and fear.

See how David became one to be marvelled at, because he looked to his ancestors that were noted for virtue. "For I am a

---

1 Ἰωβηλαίῳ.   2 2 Cor. viii. 1, 2, 3.   3 Matt. viii. 20.   4 Matt. xi. 29.   5 Matt. xx. 27, 28.   6 John xiii. 15.

stranger," saith he, " and a sojourner, as all my fathers were."[1]　For this man, and all that are like him, let pass them that had sinned, and thought of those who had approved themselves.

This do thou also.　For thou art not set to judge of the negligences of which others have been guilty, nor to inquire into the sins which others are committing; thou art required to do judgment on thyself, not on others. " For if we judged ourselves," it is said, " we should not be judged, but when we are judged, we are chastened of the Lord."[2]　But thou hast reversed the order, of thyself requiring no account of offenses great or small, but being strict and curious about the offenses of others.

Let us no more do this, but leaving off this disorderly way, let us set up a tribunal in ourselves for the sins committed by ourselves, becoming ourselves accusers, and judges, and executioners for our offenses.

But if it be thy will to be busy about the things of other men also, busy thyself about their good works, not their sins, that both by the memory of our negligences and by our emulation for the good works they have done, *and by setting before ourselves the judgment-seat from which no prayers can deliver, wounded each day by our conscience as by a kind of goad,*[3] we may lead ourselves on to humility, and a greater diligence, and attain unto the good things to come, by the grace and love towards man of our Lord Jesus Christ; with whom be to the Father, together with the Holy Ghost, glory, might, honor, now and always, and world without end.　Amen.

---

[1] Ps. xxxix. 12.　　　　[2] 1 Cor. xi. 31, 32.　　　[3] The part in italics is omitted in two manuscripts.

HOMILY LXV.

Matt. XX. 17—19.

"And Jesus going up to Jerusalem took the twelve disciples apart in the way, and said unto them, Behold, we go up to Jerusalem; and the Son of Man shall be betrayed unto the chief priests and unto the Scribes, and they shall condemn Him to death, and shall deliver Him to the Gentiles to mock, and to scourge, and to crucify Him; and the third day He shall be raised."

He goeth not up at once to Jerusalem when He is come out of Galilee, but having first wrought miracles, and having stopped the mouths of Pharisees, and having discoursed with His disciples of renouncing possessions: for, " if thou wilt be perfect," saith He, " sell that thou hast:"[1] and of virginity, " He that is able to receive, let him receive it:"[2] and of humility, " For except ye be converted, and become as little children, ye shall not enter into the kingdom of Heaven:"[3] and of a recompense of the things here, " For whoso hath forsaken houses, or brethren, or sisters, shall receive an hundredfold in this world:"[4] and of rewards there, " For he shall also inherit," it is said, " eternal life:" then He assails the city next, and being on the point of going up, discourses again of His passion.　For since it was likely that they, because they were not willing this should come to pass, would forget it, He is continually putting them in remembrance, exercising their mind by the frequency with which He reminded them, and diminishing their pain.

But He speaks with them " apart," necessarily; for it was not meet that His discourse about these things should be published to the many; neither that it should be spoken plainly, for no advantage arose from this. For if the disciples were confounded at hearing these things, much more the multitude of the people.

What then? was it not told to the people? you may say.　It was indeed told to the people also, but not so plainly.　For, " Destroy," saith He, " this Temple, and in three days I will raise it up;"[5] and, " This generation seeketh after a sign, and there shall no sign be given it, but the sign of Jonas;"[6] and

---

[1] Matt. xix. 21.　　　　[2] Matt. xix. 12.
[3] Matt. xviii. 3.　　　　[4] Matt. xix. 29.
[5] John ii. 19.　　　　[6] Matt. xii. 39.

again, "Yet a little while am I with you, and ye shall seek me, and shall not find me."[1]

But to the disciples not so, but as the other things He spake unto them more plainly, so also spake He this too. And for what purpose, if the multitude understood not the force of His sayings, were they spoken at all? That they might learn after these things, that foreknowing it, He came to His passion, and willing it; not in ignorance, nor by constraint. But to the disciples not for this cause only did He foretell it; but, as I have said, in order that having been exercised by the expectation, they might more easily endure the passion, and that it might not confound them by coming upon them without preparation. So for this cause, while at the beginning He spake of His death only, when they were practised and trained to hear of it, He adds the other circumstances also; as, for instance, that they should deliver Him to the Gentiles, that they should mock and scourge Him; as well on this account, as in order that when they saw the mournful events come to pass, they might expect from this the resurrection also. For He who had not cloaked from them what would give pain, and what seemed to be matter of reproach, would reasonably be believed about good things too.

But mark, I pray thee, how with regard to the time also He orders the thing wisely. For neither at the beginning did He tell them, lest He should disquiet them, neither at the time itself, lest by this again He should confound them; but when they had received sufficient proof of His power, when He had given them promises that were very great concerning life everlasting, then He introduces also what He had to say concerning these things, once and twice and often interweaving it with His miracles and His instructions.

But another evangelist saith, that He brought in the prophets also as witnesses;[2] and another again saith, that even they themselves understood not His words, but the saying was hid from them, and that they were amazed as they followed Him.[3]

Surely then, one may say, the benefit of the prediction is taken away. For if they knew not what they were hearing, neither could they look for the event, and not looking for it, neither could they be exercised by their expectations.

But I say another thing also more perplexing than this: If they did not know, how were they sorry. For another saith, they were sorry. If therefore they knew it not, how were they sorry? How did Peter say, "Be

it far from Thee. this shall not be unto Thee?"[4]

What then may we say? That He should die indeed they knew, albeit they knew not clearly the mystery of the Incarnation.[5] Neither did they know clearly about the resurrection, neither what He was to achieve; and this was hid from them.

For this cause also they felt pain. For some they had known to have been raised again by other persons, but for any one to have raised up himself again, and in such wise to have raised himself as not to die any more, they had never known.

This then they understood not, though often said; nay nor of this self-same death did they clearly know what it was, and how it should come on Him. Wherefore also they were amazed as they followed Him, but not for this cause only; but to me at least He seems even to amaze them by discoursing of His passion.

2. Yet none of these things made them take courage, and this when they were continually hearing about His resurrection. For together with His death this also especially troubled them, to hear that men should "mock and scourge Him," and the like. For when they considered His miracles, the possessed persons whom He had delivered, the dead whom He had raised, all the other marvellous works which He was doing, and then heard these things, they were amazed, if He who doeth these works is thus to suffer. Therefore they fell even into perplexity, and now believed, now disbelieved, and could not understand His sayings. So far at least were they from understanding clearly what He said, that the sons of Zebedee at the same time came to Him, and spake to Him of precedence. "We desire," it is said, "that one should sit on Thy right hand, and one on Thy left"[6] How then doth this evangelist ·say, that their mother came to Him? It is probable both things were done. I mean, that they took their mother with them, with the purpose of making their entreaty stronger, and in this way to prevail with Christ.

For in proof that this is true, as I say, and the request was rather theirs, and that being ashamed they put forward their mother, mark how Christ directs His words to them.

But rather let us learn, first, what do they ask, and with what disposition, and whence they were moved to this? Whence then were they moved to this? They saw themselves honored above the rest, and expected from that they should obtain this request also.

---

[1] John vii. 33, 34.   [2] Luke xviii. 31.
[3] Mark x. 32 ; comp. Mark ix. 32, and Luke xviii. 34.

[4] Matt. xvi. 22.   [5] Lit., "economy."
[6] Matt. xx. 21. Comp. Mark x. 37.

But what can it be they ask? Hear another evangelist plainly declaring this. For, "Because He was nigh," it is said, "to Jerusalem, and because they thought the kingdom of God should immediately appear,"[1] they asked these things. For they supposed that this was at the doors, and visible, and that having obtained what they asked, they would undergo none of the painful things. For neither for its own sake only did they seek it, but as though they would also escape the hardships.

Wherefore also Christ in the first place leads them off from these thoughts, commanding them to await slaughter and dangers, and the utmost terrors. For, "Are ye able," saith He, "to drink of the cup that I drink of?"[2]

But let no man be troubled at the apostles being in such an imperfect state. For not yet was the cross accomplished, not yet the grace of the Spirit given. But if thou wouldest learn their virtue, notice them after these things, and thou wilt see them superior to every passion. For with this object He reveals their deficiencies, that after these things thou mightest know what manner of men they became by grace.

That then they were asking, in fact, for nothing spiritual, neither had a thought of the kingdom above, is manifest from hence. But let us see also, how they come unto Him, and what they say. "We would," it is said, "that whatsoever we shall desire of Thee, Thou shouldest do it for us."[3]

And Christ saith to them, "What would ye?"[4] not being ignorant, but that He may compel them to answer, and lay open the wound, and so apply the medicine. But they out of shame and confusion of face, because under the influence of a human passion they were come to do this, took Him privately apart from the disciples, and asked Him. For they went before, it is said, so that it might not be observable to them, and so said what they wished. For it was their desire, as I suppose, because they heard, "Ye shall sit on twelve thrones, to have the first place of these seats. And that they had an advantage over the others, they knew, but they were afraid of Peter, and say, "Command, that one sit on Thy right hand, one on Thy left;" and they urge Him, saying, "Command."

What then saith He? Showing, that they asked nothing spiritual, neither, if they had known again what they were asking, would they have ventured to ask for so much, He saith, "Ye know not what ye ask," how great,

how marvellous, how surpassing even the powers above. After that He adds, "Are ye able to drink of the cup that I shall drink of, and to be baptized with the baptism that I am baptized with?"[5] Seest thou, how He straightway drew them off from their suspicion, by framing His discourse from the contrary topics? For ye, He saith, talk to me of honor and crowns, but I to you of conflicts and labors. For this is not the season for rewards, neither shall that glory of mine appear now, but the present time is one of slaughter, and wars, and dangers.

And see how by the form of His question, He both urges and attracts them. For He said not, "Are ye able to be slain?" "Are ye able to pour forth your blood?" but how? "Are ye able to drink of the cup?" Then to attract them to it, He saith, "Which I shall drink of," that by their fellowship with Him in it they might be made more ready.

And a baptism again calls He it; showing that great was the cleansing the world was to have from the things that were being done.

"They say unto Him, We are able."[6] Out of their forwardness they straightway undertook it, not knowing even this which they were saying, but looking to hear what they had asked.

What then saith He? "Ye shall drink indeed of my cup, and be baptized with the baptism that I am baptized with."[7] Great blessings did He foretell to them. His meaning is, ye shall be counted worthy of martyrdom, and shall suffer these things which I suffer; ye shall close your life by a violent death, and in these things ye shall be partakers with me; "But to sit on my right hand and on my left is not mine to give, but it shall be given to them for whom it is prepared of my Father."

3. Having first elevated their souls, and made them of a higher character, and having rendered them such as sorrow could not subdue, then He reproves their request.

But what can be this present saying? For indeed there are two points that are subjects of inquiry to many: one, if it be prepared for any to sit on His right hand; and then, if the Lord of all hath not power to bestow it on them for whom it is prepared.

What then is the saying? If we solve the former point, then the second also will be clear to the inquirers. What then is this? No one shall sit on His right hand nor on His left. For that throne is inaccessible to all, I

---

[1] Luke xix. 11.　　[2] Matt. xx. 22.
[3] Mark x. 35.　　[4] Mark x. 36.

[5] [The longer reading is here accepted. The R. V. follows a briefer reading here and in verse 23.—R.]
[6] Matt. xx. 22.
[7] Matt. xx. 23. [The latter clause is omitted in the R. V.]

do not say to men only, and saints, and apostles, but even to angels, and archangels, and to all the powers that are on high.

At least Paul puts it· as a peculiar privilege of the Only-Begotten, saying, "To which of the angels said He at any time, Sit thou on my right hand?[1] And of the angels He saith, who maketh His angels spirits;" but unto the Son, 'Thy throne, O God.'"[2]

How then saith He, "To sit on my right hand and on my left is not mine to give," as though there are some that should sit there? Not as though there are; far from it; but He makes answer to the thoughts of them who ask the favor, condescending to their understanding. For neither did they know that lofty throne, and His sitting at the right hand of the Father; how should they, when even the things that were much lower than these, and were daily instilled into them, they understood not? but they sought one thing only, to enjoy the first honors, and to stand before the rest, and that no one should stand before them with Him; even as I have already said before, that, since they heard of twelve thrones, in ignorance wnat the saying could mean, they asked for the first place.

What therefore Christ saith is this: "Ye shall die indeed for me, and shall be slain for the sake of the gospel, and shall be partakers with me, as far as regards the passion: but this is not sufficient to secure you the enjoyment of the first seat, and to cause that ye should occupy the first place. For if any one else should come, together with the martyrdom, possessed of all the other parts of virtue far more fully than you, not because I love you now, and prefer you to the rest, therefore shall I set aside him that is distinguished by his good works, and give the first honors to you."

But thus indeed He did not say it, so as not to pain them, but darkly He intimates the self-same thing, saying, "Ye shall drink indeed of my cup, and ye shall be baptized with the baptism that I am baptized with; but to sit on my right hand and on my left, this is not mine to give, but it shall be given to those for whom it is prepared."

But for whom is it prepared? For them who could become distinguished by their works. Therefore He said not, It is not mine to give, but my Father's, lest any should say that He was too weak, or wanting in vigor for their recompense; but how? It is not mine, but of those for whom it is prepared.

And in order that wnat I say may be more

plain, let us work it on an illustration, and let us suppose there was some master of the games, then that many excellent combatants went down to the contest, and that some two of the combatants that were most nearly connected with the master of the games were to come to him and say, "Cause us to be crowned and proclaimed," confiding in their good-will and friendship with him; and that he were to say to them, "This is not mine to give, but it shall be given to them for whom it is prepared, by their labors, and their toils;" should we indeed condemn him as powerless? By no means, but we should approve him for his justice, and for having no respect of persons. Like then as we should not say that he did not give the crown from want of vigor, but as not wishing to corrupt the law of the games, nor to disturb the order of justice; in like manner now should I say Christ said this, from every motive to compel them, after the grace of God, to set their hopes of salvation and approval on the proof of their own good works.

Therefore He saith, "For whom it is prepared." For what, saith He, if others should appear better than you? What, if they should do greater things? For shall ye, because ye have become my disciples, therefore enjoy the first honors, if ye yourselves should not appear worthy of the choice?

For that He Himself hath power over the whole, is manifest from His having the entire judgment. For to Peter too He speaks thus, "I will give thee the keys of the Heavens."[3] And Paul also makes this clear where he saith, "Henceforth is laid up for me the crown of righteousness, which the Lord, the righteous judge, will give me in that day; and not to me only, but unto all them also which have loved His appearing."[4] But the appearing was of Christ. But that no one will stand before Paul, is surely clear to every one.

And if He hath expressed these things somewhat obscurely, marvel not. For to lead them on by hidden instruction,[5] not to be rudely pressing Him without object or cause for the first honors (for from a human passion they felt this), and not wishing to give them pain, by the obscurity He effects both these objects.

"Then were the ten moved with indignation with respect to the two." Then. When? When He had reproved them. So long as the judgment was Christ's, they were not moved with indignation; but seeing them preferred,

[1] Heb. i. 13.   [2] Heb. i. 7, 8.   [3] Matt. xvi. 19. [This peculiar reading and rendering is commented on in the note on Homily LIV. 3.—R.]
[4] 2 Tim. iv. 8.   [5] οἰκονομικῶς.

they were contented, and held their peace, out of reverence and honor to their Master.

And if they were vexed in mind, yet they dared not utter this. And when they had some feeling of human weakness towards Peter, at the time that He gave the didrachmas, they did not give way to anger, but asked only, "Who then is greatest?" But since here the request was the disciples', they are moved with indignation. And not even here are they straightway moved with indignation, when they asked, but when Christ had reproved them, and had said they should not enjoy the first honors, unless they showed themselves worthy of these.

4. Seest thou how they were all in an imperfect state, when both these were lifting themselves up above the ten, and those envying the two? But, as I said, show me them after these things, and thou wilt see them delivered from all these passions. Hear at least how this same John, he who now came to Him for these things, everywhere gives up the first place to Peter, both in addressing the people, and in working miracles, in the Acts of the Apostles.

And he conceals not Peter's good deeds, but relates both the confession, which he openly made when all were silent,[1] and his entering into the tomb,[2] and puts the apostle before himself. For, because both continued with Him at His crucifixion, taking away the ground of his own commendation, he saith, "That disciple was known unto the high priest."[3]

But James survived not a long time, but from the beginning he was so greatly filled with warmth, and so forsook all the things of men, and mounted up to an height unutterable, as straightway to be slain. Thus, in all respects, they after these things became excellent.[4]

But then, "they were moved with indignation." What then saith Christ? "He called them unto Him, and said, The princes of the Gentiles exercise dominion over them."[5] For, as they were disturbed and troubled, He soothes them by His call before His word, and by drawing them near Him. For the two having separated themselves from the company of the ten, had stood nearer Him, pleading their own interests. Therefore He brings near Him these also, by this very act, and by exposing and revealing it before the rest, soothing the passion both of the one and of the other.

And not as before, so now also doth He

check them. For whereas before He brings little children into the midst, and commands to imitate their simplicity and lowliness; here He reproves them in a sharper way from the contrary side, saying, "The princes of the Gentiles exercise dominion[6] over them, and their great ones exercise authority upon them, but it shall not be so among you;[7] but he that will be great among you, let this man be minister to all; and he that will be first, let him be last of all;"[8] showing that such a feeling as this is that of heathens, I mean, to love the first place. For the passion is tyrannical, and is continually hindering even great men; therefore also it needs a severer stripe. Whence He too strikes deeper into them, by comparison with the Gentiles shaming their inflamed soul, and removes the envy of the one and the arrogance of the other, all but saying, "Be not moved with indignation, as insulted. For they harm and disgrace themselves most, who on this wise seek the first places, for they are amongst the last. For matters with us are not like matters without. 'For the princes of the Gentiles exercise dominion over them,' but with me the last, even he is first."

"And in proof that I say not these things without cause, by the things which I do and suffer, receive the proof of my sayings. For I have myself done something even more. For being King of the powers above, I was willing to become man, and I submitted to be despised, and despitefully entreated. And not even with these things was I satisfied, but even unto death did I come. Therefore," He saith,

"Even as the Son of Man came not to be ministered unto, but to minister, and to give His life a ransom for many."[9] "For not even at this did I stop," saith He, "but even my life did I give a ransom; and for whom? For enemies. But thou if thou art abased, it is for thyself, but I for thee."

Be not then afraid, as though thine honor were plucked down. For how much soever thou humblest thyself, thou canst not descend so much as thy Lord. And yet His descent hath become the ascent of all, and hath made His own glory shine forth. For before He was made man, He was known amongst angels only; but after He was made man and was crucified, so far from lessening that glory, He acquired other besides, even that from the knowledge of the world.

---

[1] John vi. 68, 69.
[2] John xx. 6.
[3] John xviii. 15.
[4] ἄκροι.
[5] Matt. xx. 25. ["Ye know that" omitted.]

[6] [R. V., "lord it."]
[7] [The form of this clause in Greek differs from that of all our New Testament mss.—R.]
[8] Matt. xx. 25-27. [The variations in text, especially in verse 27, are peculiar; compare with the A. V. and R. V.—R.]
[9] Matt. xx. 28.

26

Fear not then, as though thine honor were put down, if thou shouldest abase thyself, for in this way is thy glory more exalted, in this way it becomes greater. This is the door of the kingdom. Let us not then go the opposite way, neither let us war against ourselves. For if we desire to appear great, we shall not be great, but even the most dishonored of all.

Seest thou how everywhere He urges them by the opposite things, giving them what they desire? For in the preceding parts also we have shown this in many instances, and in the cases of the covetous, and of the vainglorious, He did thus. For wherefore, He saith, dost thou give alms before men? That thou mayest enjoy glory? Thou must then not do so, and thou shall surely enjoy it. Wherefore dost thou lay up treasures? That thou mayest be rich? Thou must then not lay up treasures, and thou shalt be rich. Even so here too, wherefore dost thou set thy heart on the first places? That thou mayest be before others? Choose then the last place, and then thou wilt enjoy the first. So that if it be thy will to become great, seek not to become great, and then thou wilt be great. For the other is to be little.

5. Seest thou how He drew them off from the disease, by showing them both from thence failing of their object, and from hence gaining, that they might flee the one, and follow after the other.

And of the Gentiles, too, He for this cause reminded them, that in this way again He might show the thing to be disgraceful and to be abhorred.

For the arrogant is of necessity base, and, on the contrary, the lowly-minded is high. For this is the height that is true and genuine, and exists not in name only, nor in manner of address. And that which is from without is of necessity and fear, but this is like to God's. Such a one, though he be admired by no one, continues high; even as again the other, though he be courted by all, is of all men the basest. And the one is an honor rendered of necessity, whence also it easily passes away; but the other is of principle, whence also it continues steadfast. Since for this we admire the saints also, that being greater than all, they humbled themselves more than all. Wherefore even to this day they continue to be high, and not even death hath brought down that height.

And if ye be minded, let us by reasonings also inquire into this very thing. Any one is said to be high, either when he is so by greatness of stature, or when he hath chanced to be set on a high place, and low in like manner, from the opposite things.

Let us see then who is like this, the boaster, or he that keeps within measure, that thou mayest perceive that nothing is higher than lowliness of mind, and nothing lower than boastfulness.

The boaster then desires to be greater than all, and affirms no one to be equal in worth with him; and how much soever honor he may obtain, he sets his heart on more and claims it, and accounts himself to have obtained none, and treats men with utter contempt, and yet seeks after the honor that comes from them; than which what can be more unreasonable? For this surely is like an enigma. By those, whom he holds in no esteem, he desires to be glorified.

Seest thou how he who desires to be exalted falls down and is set on the ground? For that he accounts all men to be nothing compared with himself, he himself declares, for this is boasting. Why then dost cast thyself upon him who is nothing? why dost thou seek honor of him? Why dost thou lead about with thee such great multitudes?

Seest thou one low, and set on a low place. Come then, let us inquire about the high man. This one knows what man is, and that man is a great thing, and that he himself is last of all, and therefore whatever honor he may enjoy, he reckons this great, so that this one is consistent with himself and is high, and shifts not his judgment; for whom he accounts great, the honors that come from them he esteems great also, though they should chance to be small, because he accounts those who bestow them to be great. But the boastful man accounts them that give the honors to be nothing, yet the honors bestowed by them he reckons to be great.

Again, the lowly man is seized by no passion, no anger can much trouble this man, no love of glory, no envy, no jealousy: and what can be higher than the soul that is delivered from these things? But the boastful man is held in subjection by all these things, like any worm crawling in the mire, for jealousy and envy and anger are forever troubling his soul.

Which then is high? He that is superior to his passions, or he that is their slave? He that trembles at them and is afraid of them, or he that is unsubdued, and never taken by them? Which kind of bird should we say flies higher? that which is higher than the hands and the arrows of the hunter, or that which does not even suffer the hunters to need an arrow, from his flying along the ground, and from not being able ever to elevate himself? Is not then the arrogant man like this? for indeed every net readily catches him as crawling on the ground.

6. But if thou wilt, even from that wicked demon prove thou this. For what can be baser than the devil, because he had exalted himself; what higher than the man who is willing to abase himself? For the former crawls on the ground under our heel (For, " ye tread," He saith,[1] " upon serpents and scorpions "), but the latter is set with the angels on high.

But if thou desirest to learn this from the example of haughty men also, consider that barbarian king, that led so great an army, who knew not so much as the things that are manifest to all; as, for instance, that stone was stone, and the images, images; wherefore he was inferior even to these. But the godly and faithful are raised even above the sun; than whom what can be higher, who rise above even the vaults of heaven, and passing beyond angels, stand by the very throne of the king.

And that thou mayest learn in another way their vileness; who will be abased? He who has God for his ally, or he with whom God is at war? It is quite plain that it is he with whom He is at war. Hear then touching either of these what saith the Scripture. " God res steth the proud, but giveth grace unto the humble." [2]

Again, I will ask you another thing also. Which is higher? He who acts as a priest to God and offers sacrifice? or he who is somewhere far removed from confidence towards Him? And what manner of sacrifice doth the lowly man offer? one may say. Hear David saying, " The sacrifice of God is a contrite spirit; a contrite and humbled heart God will not despise." [3]

Seest thou the purity of this man? Behold also the uncleanness of the other; for " every one that is proud in heart is unclean before God." [4] Besides, the one hath God resting upon him, (" For unto whom will I look," saith He, " but to him that is meek and quiet, and trembleth at my words "),[5] but the other crawls with the devil, for he that is lifted up with pride shall suffer the devil's punishment. Wherefore Paul also said, " Lest, being lifted up with pride, he should fall into the condemnation of the devil." [6]

And the thing opposite to what he wishes, befalls him. For his wish is to be arrogant, that he may be honored; but the most contemned of all is this character. For these most of all are laughing stocks, foes and enemies to all men, the most easy to be subdued by their enemies, the men that easily fall into anger, the unclean before God.

What then can be worse than this, for this is the extremity of evils? And what is sweeter than the lowly, what more blessed, since they are longed after, and beloved of God? And the glory too that cometh of men, these do most of all enjoy, and all honor them as fathers, embrace them as brothers, receive them as their own members.

Let us then become lowly, that we may be high. For most utterly doth arrogance abase. This abased Pharaoh. For, " I know not," he saith, " the Lord," [7] and he became inferior to flies and frogs, and the locusts, and after that with his very arms and horses was he drowned in the sea. In direct opposition to him, Abraham saith, " I am dust and ashes," [8] and prevailed over countless barbarians, and having fallen into the midst of Egyptians, returned, bearing a trophy more glorious than the former, and, cleaving to this virtue, grew ever more high. Therefore he is celebrated everywhere, therefore he is crowned and proclaimed; but Pharaoh is both earth and ashes, and if there is anything else more vile than these. For nothing doth God so abhor as arrogance. For this object hath He done all things from the beginning, in order that He might root out this passion. Because of this are we become mortal, and are in sorrows, and wailings. Because of this are we in toil, and sweat, and in labor continual, and mingled with affliction. For indeed out of arrogance did the first man sin, looking for an equality with God. Therefore, not even what things he had, did he continue to possess, but lost even these.

For arrogance is like this, so far from adding to us any improvement of our life, it subtracts even what we have; as, on the contrary, humility, so far from subtracting from what we have, adds to us also what we have not.

This virtue then let us emulate, this let us pursue, that we may both enjoy present honor, and attain unto the glory to come, by the grace and love towards man of our Lord Jesus Christ, with whom be unto the Father glory and might, together with the Holy Ghost, now and always, and world without end. Amen.

---

[1] Luke x. 19. [Freely cited.]   [2] James iv. 6.
[3] Ps. li. 17. [LXX.]   [4] Prov. xvi. 5. [LXX.]
[5] Is. lxvi. 2.   [6] 1 Tim. iii. 6.

[7] Exod. v. 2.   [8] Gen. xviii. 27.

HOMILY LXVI.

MATT. XX. 29, 30.

"And as they departed from Jericho, great multitudes followed Him. And, behold, two blind men sitting by the wayside, when they heard that Jesus passed by, cried out, saying, Have mercy on us, O Lord, Thou Son of David."

SEE whence He passed unto Jerusalem, and where He abode before this, with regard to which it seems to me especially worthy of inquiry, wherefore He went not away even long before this from thence unto Galilee, but through Samaria. But this we will leave to them that are fond of learning. For if any one were disposed to search the matter out carefully, he will find that John intimates it well, and hath expressed the cause.[1]

But let us keep to the things set before us, and let us listen to these blind men, who were better than many that see. For neither having a guide, nor being able to see Him when come near to them, nevertheless they strove to come unto Him, and began to cry with a loud voice, and when rebuked for speaking, they cried the more. For such is the nature of an enduring soul, by the very things that hinder, it is borne up.

But Christ suffered them to be rebuked, that their earnestness might the more appear, and that thou mightest learn that worthily they enjoy the benefits of their cure. Therefore He doth not so much as ask, " Do ye believe?" as He doth with many; for their cry, and their coming unto Him, sufficed to make their faith manifest.

Hence learn, O beloved, that though we be very vile and outcast, but yet approach God with earnestness, even by ourselves we shall be able to effect whatsoever we ask. See, for instance, these men, how, having none of the apostles to plead with them, but rather many to stop their mouths, they were able to pass over the hindrances, and to come unto Jesus Himself. And yet the evangelist bears witness to no confidence of life[2] in them, but earnestness sufficed them instead of all.

These then let us also emulate. Though God defer the gift, though there be many withdrawing us, let us not desist from asking. For in this way most of all shall we win God to us. See at least even here, how not poverty, not blindness, not their being unheard,

not their being rebuked by the multitude, not anything else, impeded their exceeding earnestness. Such is the nature of a fervent and toiling soul.

What then saith Christ? " He called them, and said, What will ye that I should do unto you? They say unto Him, Lord, that our eyes may be opened."[3] Wherefore doth He ask them? Lest any one should think that when they wish to receive one thing, He giveth them another thing. For indeed it is usual with Him on every occasion, first to make manifest and discover to all the virtue of those He is healing, and then to apply the cure, for one reason, that He might lead on the others likewise to emulation; and for another, that He might show that they were enjoying the gift worthily. This, for instance, He did with respect to the Canaanitish woman also, this too in the case of the centurion, this again as to her that had the issue of blood, or rather that marvellous woman even anticipated the Lord's inquiry; but not so did He pass her by, but even after the cure makes her manifest. Such earnest care had He on every occasion to proclaim the good deeds of them that come to Him, and to show them to be much greater than they are,[4] which He doth here also.

Then, when they said what they wished, He had compassion on them, and touched them. For this alone is the cause of their cure, for which also He came into the world. But nevertheless, although it be mercy and grace, it seeks for the worthy.

But that they were worthy is manifest, both from what they cried out, and from the fact that, when they had received, they did not hasten away, as many do, being ungrateful after the benefits. Nay, they were not like this, but were both persevering before the

---

[1] John iv. 1, and x. 40–42.
[2] παῤῥησίαν βίου. Claim of access on account of good life.

[3] Matt. xx. 32, 33.
[4] The words, "and to show them to be much greater than they are," are rejected by Montfaucon on the authority of two MSS., but defended by Mr. Field. [They are found in all the MSS. collated by the latter editor, with one exception.—R.] It seems to be true that our Lord sometimes encouraged faith, and brought out good example, by putting on an action a higher meaning and intention than was at all fully formed in the mind of the doer.

gift, and after the gift grateful, for "they followed Him."

"And when He drew nigh unto Jerusalem, and was come to Bethphage, unto the Mount of Olives, He sent two of His disciples, saying, Go into the village over against you, and ye shall find an ass tied, and a colt with her: loose them, and bring them unto me. And if any man say aught unto you, ye shall say, The Lord hath need of them; and straightway he sendeth them. And this was done, that it might be fulfilled which was spoken by Zechariah the prophet, Tell ye the daughter of Sion, Behold, thy King cometh to thee, meek, and sitting upon an ass, and a colt the foal of an ass."[1]

And yet He had often entered Jerusalem before, but never with so much circumstance. What then is the cause? It was the beginning then of the dispensation; and neither was He very well known, nor the time of His passion near; wherefore He mixed with them with less distinction, and more disguising Himself. For He would not have been held in admiration, had He so appeared, and He would have excited them to greater anger. But when He had both given them sufficient proof of His power, and the cross was at the doors, He makes Himself then more conspicuous, and doeth with greater circumstance all the things that were likely to inflame them. For it was indeed possible for this to have been done at the beginning also; but it was not profitable nor expedient it should be so.

But do thou observe, I pray thee, how many miracles are done, and how many prophecies are fulfilled. He said, "Ye shall find an ass;" He foretold that no man should hinder them, but that all, when they heard, should hold their peace.

But this is no small condemnation of the Jews, if them that were never known to Him, neither had appeared before Him, He persuades to give up their own property, and to say nothing against it, and that by His disciples, while these, being present with Him at the working of His miracles, were not persuaded.

2. And do not account what was done to be a small thing. For who persuaded them, when their own property was taken from them, and that, when they were perhaps poor men and husbandmen, not to forbid it? Why say I not to forbid it? not to ask, or even if they asked, to hold their peace, and give it

up. For indeed both things were alike marvellous, as well, if they said nothing, when their beasts were dragged away, or if having spoken, and heard, "The Lord hath need of them," they yielded and withstood not, and this when they see not Him, but His disciples.

By these things He teaches them, that it was in His power to have entirely hindered the Jews also, even against their will, when they were proceeding to attack Him, and to have made them speechless, but He would not.

And another thing again together with these doth He teach the disciples, to give whatever He should ask; and, though he should require them to yield up their very life, to give even this, and not to gainsay. For if even strangers gave up to Him, much more ought they to strip themselves of all things.

And besides what we have said, He was fulfilling also another prophecy, one which was twofold, one part in words, and another in deeds. And that in deeds was, by the sitting on the ass; and that by words, the prediction of Zacharias; because he had said, that the King should sit on an ass. And He, having sat and having fulfilled it, gave to the prophecy another beginning again, by what He was doing typifying beforehand the things to come.

How and in what manner? He proclaimed beforehand the calling of the unclean Gentiles, and that He should rest upon them, and that they should yield to Him and follow Him, and prophecy succeeded to prophecy.

But to me He seemeth not for this object only to sit on the ass, but also as affording us a standard of self-denial. For not only did He fulfill prophecies, nor did He only plant the doctrines of the truth, but by these very things He was correcting our practice for us, everywhere setting us rules of necessary use, and by all means amending our life.

For this cause, I say, even when He was to be born He sought not a splendid house, nor a mother rich and distinguished, but a poor woman, and one that had a carpenter as her betrothed husband; and is born in a shed, and laid in a manger: and choosing His disciples, He chose not orators and wise men, not rich men and nobly born, but poor men, and of poor families, and in every way undistinguished; and providing His table, at one time He sets before Himself barley loaves, and at another at the very moment commands the disciples to buy at the market. And making His couch, He makes it of grass, and putting on raiment, He clothes Himself in

---

[1] Matt. xxi. 1–5. [The textual variations are reproduced in the above rendering. The most interesting variation is ἀποστελλει (" he sendeth "), the reading attested in Mark xi. 3. It implies in the latter passage the promise to send back the colt to the owners. —R.]

what is cheap, and in no respect different from the common sort; and a house He did not so much as possess. And if He had to go from place to place, He did this travelling on foot, and so travelling, as even to grow weary. And sitting, He requires no throne nor pillow, but sits on the ground, sometimes in the mountain, and sometimes by the well, and not merely by the well, but also alone, and talks with a Samaritan woman.

Again, setting measures of sorrow, when He had need to mourn, He weeps moderately, everywhere setting us rules, as I have said, and limits how far one ought to proceed, and not any further. So for this intent now also, since it happens that some are weak and have need of beasts to carry them, in this too He fixes a measure, showing that one ought not to yoke horses or mules to be borne by them, but to use an ass, and not to proceed further, and everywhere to be limited by the want.

But let us look also at the prophecy, that by words, that by acts. What then is the prophecy? "Behold, thy King cometh to thee, meek, and riding on an ass, and a young colt;"[1] not driving chariots, like the rest of the kings, not demanding tributes, not thrusting men off, and leading about guards, but displaying His great meekness even hereby.

Ask then the Jew, what King came to Jerusalem borne on an ass? Nay, he could not mention, but this alone.

But He did these things, as I said, signifying beforehand the things to come. For here the church is signified by the colt, and the new people, which was once unclean, but which, after Jesus sat on them, became clean. And see the image preserved throughout. I mean that the disciples loose the asses. For by the apostles, both they and we were called; by the apostles were we brought near. But because our acceptance provoked them also to emulation, therefore the ass appears following the colt. For after Christ hath sat on the Gentiles, then shall they also come moving us to emulation.[2] And Paul declaring this, said, "That blindness[3] in part is happened to Israel, until the fullness of the Gentiles be come in; and so all Israel shall be saved."[4] For that it was a prophecy is evident from what is said. For neither would the prophet have cared to express with such great exactness the age of the ass, unless this had been so.

But not these things only are signified by what is said, but also that the apostles should bring them with ease. For as here, no man gainsaid them so as to keep the asses, so neither with regard to the Gentiles was any one able to prevent them, of those who were before masters of them.

But He doth not sit on the bare colt, but on the apostles' garments. For after they had taken the colt, they then gave up all, even as Paul also said, "I will very gladly spend and be spent for your souls."[5]

But mark how tractable the colt, how being unbroken, and having never known the rein, he was not restive, but went on orderly; which thing itself was a prophecy of the future, signifying the submissiveness of the Gentiles, and their sudden conversion to good order. For all things did that word work, which said, "Loose him, and bring him to me:" so that the unmanageable became orderly, and the unclean thenceforth clean.

3. But see the baseness of the Jews. He had wrought so many miracles, and never were they thus amazed at Him; but when they saw a multitude running together, then they marvel. "For all the city was moved, saying, Who is this? But the multitudes said, This is Jesus the prophet of Nazareth of Galilee."[6] And when they thought they were saying something great, even then were their thoughts earthly, and low, and dragging on the ground.[7]

But these things He did, not as displaying any pomp, but at once, as I have said, both fulfilling a prophecy, and teaching self-denial, and at the same time also comforting His disciples, who were grieving for His death, and showing them that He suffers all these things willingly.

And mark thou, I pray thee, the accuracy of the prophet, how he foretold all things. And some things David, some things Zechariah, had proclaimed beforehand. Let us also do likewise, and let us sing hymns, and give up our garments to them that bear Him. For what should we deserve, when some clothe the ass on which He was set, and others strew the garments even under her feet; but we, seeing him naked, and not being even commanded to strip ourselves, but to spend of what is laid by, not even so are liberal? And when they indeed attend upon Him before and behind, but we, when He cometh unto us, send Him away, and thrust Him off and insult Him.

How sore a punishment do these things

---

1 Zech. ix. 9.　　　2 Or, "emulating us," παραζηλοῦντες.
3 R. V., "a hardening."]　　　4 Rom. xi. 25, 26.

5 2 Cor. xii. 15.
6 Matt. xxi. 10, 11. [The Greek text agrees with that of the received.—R.]
7 σεσυρμένη.

deserve, how great vengeance! Thy Lord cometh unto thee in need, and thou art not willing so much as to listen to His entreaty, but thou blamest and rebukest Him, and this, when thou hast heard such words as these. But if in giving one loaf, and a little money, thou art so mean, and haughty, and backward; if thou hadst to empty out all, what wouldest thou become?

Seest thou not those that show their magnificence in the theatre, how much they give away to the harlots? but thou givest not so much as the half, nay often not the smallest part. But the devil is exhorting to give to whom it may chance, procuring us hell, and thou givest; but Christ to the needy, promising a kingdom, and thou, far from giving, dost rather insult them, and thou choosest rather to obey the devil, that thou mightest be punished, than to submit to Christ, and be saved.

And what could be worse than this frenzy? One procures hell, the other a kingdom, and ye leave the latter, and run unto the former. And this ye send away, when He cometh unto you, that when he is far off, ye call unto you. And what you do is the same as if a king bearing a royal robe, and offering a diadem, did not win your choice, but a robber brandishing a sword at you, and threatening death, were to win it.

Considering these things then, beloved, let us discern the truth at length though late, and let us grow sober. For I am now ashamed of speaking of almsgiving, because that having often spoken on this subject, I have effected nothing worth the exhortation. For some increase indeed hath there been, but not so much as I wished. For I see you sowing, but not with a liberal hand. Wherefore I fear too lest ye also "reap sparingly."[1]

For in proof that we do sow sparingly, let us inquire, if it seem good, which[2] are more numerous in the city, poor or rich; and which they, who are neither[2] poor nor rich, but have a middle place. As, for instance, a tenth part is of rich, and a tenth of the poor that have nothing at all, and the rest of the middle sort.

Let us distribute then amongst the poor the whole multitude of the city, and ye will see the disgrace how great it is. For the very rich indeed are but few, but those that come next to them are many; again, the poor are much fewer than these. Nevertheless, although there are so many that are able to feed the hungry, many go to sleep in their hunger, not because those that have are not able with ease to succor them, but because of their great barbarity and inhumanity. For if both the wealthy, and those next to them, were to distribute amongst themselves those who are in need of bread and raiment, scarcely would one poor person fall to the share of fifty men or even a hundred. Yet nevertheless, though in such great abundance of persons to assist them, they are wailing every day. And that thou mayest learn the inhumanity of the others, when the church is possessed of a revenue of one of the lowest among the wealthy, and not of the very rich, consider how many widows it succors every day, how many virgins; for indeed the list of them hath already reached unto the number of three thousand. Together with these, she succors them that dwell in the prison, the sick in the caravansera, the healthy, those that are absent from their home, those that are maimed in their bodies, those that wait upon the altar; and with respect to food and raiment, them that casually come every day; and her substance is in no respect diminished. So that if ten men only were thus willing to spend, there would be no poor.

4. And what, it will be said, are our children to inherit? The principal remains, and the income again is become more abundant, the goods being stored up for them in Heaven.

But are ye not willing to do this? At least do it by the half, at least by the third part, at least by the fourth part. at least by the tenth. For owing to God's favor, it were possible for our city to nourish the poor of ten cities.

And if ye will, let us make some calculation[3] in proof of this; or rather there is no need so much as of reckoning; for of itself the easiness of the thing is discernible. See at least, upon public occasions, how much one house hath often not been backward to spend, and hath not had so much as a little feeling of the expense, which service if each of the rich were willing to perform for the poor, in a brief moment of time he would have seized on Heaven.

What plea then will there be? what shadow of defense, when not even of the things from which we must assuredly be separated, when taken away from hence, not even of these do we impart to the needy with as much liberality as others to those on the stage, and this when we are to reap so many benefits therefrom? For we ought indeed, even though we were always to be here, not even so to be sparing of this good expenditure; but when after a little time, we are to be removed from

---

[1] 2 Cor. ix. 6.
[2] ["who are more numerous." . . . "and who are they that are neither," etc.—R.]

[3] συλλογισμόν.

hence, and dragged away naked from all, what kind of defense shall we have for not even out of our income giving to the hungry and distressed?[1]

For neither do I constrain thee to lessen thy possessions, not because I do not wish it, but because I see thee very backward. It is not then this I say, but spend of your fruits, and treasure up nothing from these. It is enough for thee to have the money of thine income pouring in on thee as from a fountain; make the poor sharers with thee, and become a good steward of the things given thee of God.

But I pay tribute, one may say. For this cause then dost thou despise, because in this case no one demands it of thee? And the other, who, should the earth bear, or should it not bear, takes by force, and extorts, thou darest not gainsay; but Him that is so mild, and then only demands, when the earth bears, thou answerest not even to a word? And who will deliver thee from those intolerable punishments? There is no one. For if, because in the other case a very sore punishment will ensue to thee for not giving, therefore thou becomest diligent about the payment, consider here too is one more sore; not to be bound, neither to be cast into prison, but to depart into the eternal fire.

For all reasons then let us pay these tributes first: for great is the facility, and greater the reward; and more abundant the gain, and worse the punishments to us if we are obstinate. For a punishment cometh upon us, which hath no end.

But if thou tell me of the soldier's fighting for thee with the barbarians, there is here too a camp, that of the poor, and a war, which the poor are waging for thee. For when they receive, by praying they make God propitious; and making Him propitious, they repulse, instead of barbarians, the assaults of the devils; they suffer not the evil one to be violent, neither to attack us continually, but they relax his might.

5. Seeing therefore these soldiers every day fighting in thy behalf with the devil by their supplications and prayers, demand of thyself this good contribution, their nourishment. For this King being mild hath not assigned thee any to demand it of thee, but desires thou shouldest give it willingly; though thou pay by little and little, He receives it; though being in difficulty, thou shouldest pay after a long time, He doth not press him that hath not.

Let us not then despise His long-suffering; let us treasure up for ourselves, not wrath, but salvation; not death, but life; not punishment and vengeance, but honors and crowns. There is no need in this case to pay a hire for the conveyance of the things contributed; there is no need in this case to labor in turning them into money. If thou givest them up, the Lord Himself removes them into Heaven; He Himself makes the traffic the more gainful for thee.

There is no need here to find one to carry in what thou hast contributed; contribute only, and straightway it goeth up, not that others may be maintained as soldiers, but that it may remain for thee with great profit. For here[2] whatsoever thou mayest have given, it is not possible to recover; but there thou wilt receive them again with much honor, and shalt gain greater, and more spiritual gains. Here the gifts are a demand; there a loan, and money at interest, and a debt.

Yea farther, God hath given thee bonds. For "he that showeth mercy to a poor man," it is said, "lendeth to the Lord."[3] He gave thee also an earnest, and bail, and this being God! What sort of earnest? The things in the present life, the visible, the spiritual things, the foretaste of the things to come.

Why then dost thou delay, and why art thou backward, having received so many things already, looking for so many things?

For what thou hast received are these: He Himself made thee a body, He Himself put in thee a soul, He honored with speech thee alone of the things on the earth, He gave thee the use of all the things that are seen, He bestowed on thee the knowledge of Himself, He gave up His Son for thee, He gave thee a baptism full of so many good things, He gave thee a holy table, He promised a kingdom, and the good things that cannot be told.

Having then received so many good things, having to receive so many, again I say the same thing, art thou making petty reckoning about perishing riches, and what excuse wilt thou have?

But art thou looking altogether at thy children? and dost draw back for the sake of these? Nay, rather teach them also to gain such gains. For if thou hadst money lent out and bearing interest, and thou hadst a grateful debtor, thou wouldest ten thousand times rather choose instead of the gold to leave the bond to thy child, so that he should have the large income from it, and not be constrained to go about, and seek for others to borrow it.

---

[1] ἀγχομένοις.

[2] [The translation has been altered here to conform to the use of "here" and "there" in the original.—R.]

[3] Prov. xix. 17.

And now give this bond to thy children, and leave God a debtor to them. Thou dost not sell thy lands, and give to thy children, but leavest them, that the income may remain, and that they may have a greater increase of riches from thence; but this bond, which is more productive than any land or revenue, and bears so many fruits, this art thou afraid to leave to them? What great folly must this be, and frenzy. And this when thou knowest, that though thou shouldest leave it to them, thou thyself also shalt again take it away with thee.

Of this nature are the things spiritual; they have great munificence. Let us not then be beggarly; neither be inhuman and savage towards ourselves, but let us traffic in that good merchandise; that we may both ourselves take it away with us when we depart, and leave it to our own children, and attain to the good things to come, by the grace and love towards man of our Lord Jesus Christ, with whom be unto the Father, together with the Holy Ghost, glory, might, honor, now and ever, and world without end. Amen.

HOMILY LXVII.

Matt. XXI. 12, 13.

" And Jesus went into the temple,[1] and cast out all them that sold and bought in the temple, and overthrow the tables of the money-changers and the seats of them that sold doves, and saith unto them, It is written, my house shall be called a house of prayer; but ye have made it a den of thieves." [2]

This John likewise saith, but he in the beginning of his Gospel, this at the end. Whence it is probable this was done twice, and at different seasons.

And it is evident both from the times, and from their reply. For there He came at the very passover, but here much before. And there the Jews say, " What sign showe'st thou us?" [3] but here they hold their peace, although reproved, because He was now marvelled at amongst all men.

And this is a heavier charge against the Jews, that when He had done this not once only, but a second time, they continued in their trafficking, and said that He was an adversary of God, when they ought even from hence to have learnt His honor for His Father and His own might. For indeed He also wrought miracles, and they saw His words agreeing with His works.

But not even so were they persuaded, but " were sore displeased," and this while they heard the prophet crying aloud, and the children in a manner beyond their age proclaiming Him. Wherefore also He Himself sets up Isaiah against them as an accuser,

saying, " My house shall be called a house of prayer.[4]

But not in this way only doth He show His authority, but also by His healing divers infirmities. " For the blind and the lame came unto Him, and He healed them," [5] and His power and authority He indicates.

But they not even so would be persuaded, but together with the rest of the miracles hearing even the children proclaiming, were ready to choke, and say, " Hearest thou not what these say? [6] And yet it was Christ's part to have said this to them, " Hear ye not what these say?" for the children were singing to Him as to God.

What then saith He? Since they were speaking against things manifest, He applies His correction more in the way of reproof, saying, " Have ye never read, Out of the mouths of babes and sucklings Thou hast perfected praise?" And well did He say, " Out of the mouth." For what was said was not of their understanding, but of His power giving articulation to their tongue yet immature.

And this was also a type of the Gentiles lisping, and sounding forth at once great things with understanding and faith.

---

[1] [The words " of God " are omitted in the text here. So three of our best Greek mss. and R. V. margin.—R.]

[2] [R. V., " robbers."]

[3] John ii. 18.

[4] Is. lvi. 7.

[5] Matt. xxi. 14.

[6] Matt. xxi. 16. [R. V., " are saying."]

And for the apostles also there was from hence no small consolation. For that they might not be perplexed, how being unlearned they should be able to publish the gospel, the children anticipate them, and remove all their anxiety, teaching them, that He would grant them utterance, who made even these to sing praises.

And not so only, but the miracle showed that He is Creator even of nature. The children then, although of age immature, uttered things that had a clear meaning, and were in accordance with those above, but the men things teeming with frenzy and madness. For such is the nature of wickedness.

Forasmuch then as there were many things to provoke them, from the multitude, from the casting out of the sellers, from the miracles, from the children, He again leaves them, giving room to the swelling passion, and not willing to begin His teaching, lest boiling with envy they should be the more displeased at His sayings.

" Now in the morning as He returned into the city, He was an hungered."[1] How is He an hungered in the morning? When He permits the flesh, then it shows its feeling. " And when He saw a fig tree in the way, He came to it, and found nothing thereon, but leaves only."[2] Another evangelist saith, " The time *of figs* was not yet;"[3] but if it was not time, how doth the other evangelist say, " He came, if haply He might find fruit thereon." Whence it is manifest that this belongs to the suspicion of His disciples, who were yet in a somewhat imperfect state. For indeed the evangelists in many places record the suspicions of the disciples.

Like as this then was their suspicion, so also was it too to suppose it was cursed for this cause, because of having no fruit. Wherefore then was it cursed? For the disciples' sakes, that they might have confidence. For because everywhere He conferred benefits, but punished no man; and it was needful that He should afford them a demonstrative proof of His power to take vengeance also, that both the disciples might learn, and the Jews, that being able to blast them that crucify Him, of His own will He submits, and does not blast them; and it was not His will to show forth this upon men; upon the plant did He furnish the proof of His might in taking vengeance. But when unto places, or unto plants, or unto brutes, any such thing as this is done, be not curious, neither say, how was the fig-tree justly dried up, if it was not the time *of figs*; for this it is the utmost trifling to say; but behold the miracle, and admire and glorify the worker thereof.

Since in the case also of the swine that were drowned, many have said this, working out the argument of justice; but neither there should one give heed, for these again are brutes, even as that was a plant without life.

Wherefore then was the act invested with such an appearance, and with this plea for a curse? As I said, this was the disciple's suspicion.

But if it was not yet time, vainly do some say the law is here meant. For the fruit of this was faith, and then was the time of this fruit, and it had indeed borne it; " For already[4] are the fields white to harvest," saith He; and, " I sent you to reap that whereon ye bestowed no labor."[5]

2. Not any therefore of these things doth He here intimate, but it is what I said, He displays His power to punish, and this is shown by saying, " The time was not yet," making it clear that of this special purpose He went, and not for hunger, but for His disciples' sake, who indeed marvelled exceedingly, although many miracles had been done greater; but, as I said, this was strange, for now first He showed forth His power to take vengeance. Wherefore not in any other, but in the moistest of all planted things did He work the miracle, so that hence also the miracle appeared greater.

And that thou mightest learn, that for their sakes this was done, that He might train them to feel confidence, hear what He saith afterwards. But what saith He? " Ye also shall do greater things, if ye are willing to believe and to be confident in prayer." Seest thou that all is done for their sake, so that they might not be afraid and tremble at plots against them? Wherefore He saith this a second time also, to make them cleave to prayer and faith. For not this only shall ye do, but also shall remove mountains; and many more things shall ye do, being confident in faith and prayer."[6]

But the boastful and arrogant Jews, wishing to interrupt His teaching, came unto Him, and asked, " By what authority doest thou these things?"[7] For since they could not object against the miracles, they bring forward against Him the correction of the traffickers in the temple. And this in John also they appear to ask, although not in these words, but with the same intent. For there too they say, " What sign showest thou unto us? seeing that thou doest these things."

---

[1] Matt. xxi. 18.   [2] Matt. xxi. 19.
[3] Mark xi. 13. [The passage is freely cited ; " of figs " is supplied here and below by the translator.—R.]
[4] John iv. 35.   [5] John iv. 38.
[6] Matt. xxi. 21, 22. [Paraphrased.]   [7] Matt. xxi. 23.

But there He answers them, saying, "Destroy this temple, and I in three days will raise it up,"[1] whereas here He drives them into a difficulty. Whence it is manifest, that then indeed was the beginning and prelude of the miracles, but here the end.

But what they say is this: Hast thou received the teacher's chair? Hast thou been ordained a priest, that thou didst display such authority? it is said. And yet He had done nothing implying arrogance, but had been careful for the good order of the temple, yet nevertheless having nothing to say, they object against this. And indeed when He cast them out, they did not dare to say anything, because of the miracles, but when He showed Himself, then they find fault with Him.

What then saith He? He doth not answer them directly, to show that, if they had been willing to see His authority, they could; but He asks them again, saying, "The baptism of John, whence is it? From heaven, or of men?"[2]

And what sort of inference is this? The greatest surely. For if they had said, from heaven, He would have said unto them, why then did ye not believe him? For if they had believed, they would not have asked these things. For of Him John had said, "I am not worthy to loose the latchet of His shoe; and, "Behold the Lamb of God, which taketh away the sins of the world;" and, "This is the Son of God;"[3] and, "He that cometh from above is above all;"[4] and, "His fan is in His hand, and He will thoroughly purge His floor."[5] So that if they had believed him, there was nothing to hinder them from knowing by what authority Christ doeth these things.

After this, because they, dealing craftily, said, "We know not," He said not, neither know I, but what? "Neither tell I you."[6] For if indeed they had been ignorant it would have been requisite for them to be instructed; but since they were dealing craftily with good reason He answers them nothing.

And how was it they did not say that the baptism was of men? "They feared the people"[7] it is said. Seest thou a perverse heart? In every case they despise God and do all things for the sake of men. For this man too they feared for their sakes not reverencing the saint[8] but on account of men,[9] and they were not willing to believe in Christ, because of men, and all their evils were engendered to them from hence.

After this, He saith, "What think ye? A man had two sons; and he saith to the first, go, work to-day in the vineyard. But he answered and said, I will not: but afterward he repented, and went. And he came to the second, and said likewise. And he answered and said, I go sir: and went not. Whether then of them twain did the will of his father? They say, the first."[10]

Again He convicts them by a parable, intimating both their unreasonable obstinacy, and the submissiveness of those who were utterly condemned by them. For these two children declare what came to pass with respect to both the Gentiles and the Jews. For the former not having undertaken to obey, neither having become hearers of the law, showed forth their obedience in their works; and the latter having said, "All that the Lord shall speak, we will do, and will hearken,"[11] in their works were disobedient. And for this reason, let me add, that they might not think the law would benefit them, He shows that this self-same thing condemns them, like as Paul also saith, "Not the hearers of the law are just before God, but the doers of the law shall be justified."[12] For this intent, that He might make them even self-condemned, He causes the judgment to be delivered by themselves, like as He does also in the ensuing parable of the vineyard.

3. And that this might be done, He makes trial of the accusation in the person of another. For since they were not willing to confess directly, He by a parable drives them on to what He desired.

But when, not understanding His sayings, they had delivered the judgment, He unfolds His concealed meaning after this, and saith, "Publicans and harlots go into the kingdom of Heaven before you. For John came unto you in the way of righteousness, and ye believed him not; but the publicans[13] believed him; and ye, when ye had seen it, repented not afterwards, that ye might believe him.[14]

For if He had said simply, harlots go before you, the word would have seemed to them to be offensive; but now, being uttered after their own judgment it appears to be not too hard.

Therefore He adds also the accusation. What then is this? "John came," He saith, "unto you," not unto them, and not this only, but; also "in the way of righteousness." "For neither with this can ye find fault, that he was

---

[1] John ii. 18, 19. [The emphatic ἐγώ is inserted here.—R.]
[2] Matt. xxi. 25. ["Is" substituted for "was."—R.]
[3] John i. 27, 29, 34.　[4] John iv. 31.　[5] Matt. iii. 12.
[6] Matt. xxi. 27.　[7] Matt. xxi. 26.
[8] τὸν ἄνδρα, the (great) man.　[9] ἀνθρώπους.

[10] Matt. xxi. 28-31. [There are a few slight variations from the received text.]
[11] Exod. xix. 8.
[12] Rom. ii. 13. [The article is given before νόμου in both instances; against the best MSS. authorities in Rom. ii. 13.—R.]
[13] ["and harlots" omitted here.]　[14] Matt. xxi. 31, 32.

some careless one, and of no profit; but both his life was irreprehensible, and his care for you great, and ye gave no heed to him."

And with this there is another charge also, that publicans gave heed; and with this, again another, that "not even after them did ye. For ye should have done so even before them, but not to do it even after them was to be deprived of all excuse;" and unspeakable was both the praise of the one, and the charge against the other. "To you he came, and ye accepted him not; he came not to them, and they receive him, and not even them did ye take for instructors."

See by how many things is shown the commendation of those, and the charge against these. To you he came, not to them. Ye believed not, this offended not them. They believed, this profited not you.

But the word, "go before you," is not as though these were following, but as having a hope, if they were willing. For nothing, so much as jealousy, rouses the grosser sort. Therefore He is ever saying, "The first shall be last, and the last first." Therefore He brought in both harlots and publicans, that they might provoke them to jealousy.

For these two indeed are chief sins, engendered of violent lust, the one of sexual desire, the other of the desire of money. And He indicates that this especially was hearing the law of God, to believe John. For it was not of grace only, that harlots entered in, but also of righteousness. For not, as continuing harlots, did they enter in, but having obeyed and believed, and having been purified and converted, so did they enter in.

Seest thou how He rendered His discourse less offensive, and more penetrating, by the parable, by His bringing in the harlots? For neither did He say at once, wherefore believed ye not John? but what was much more pricking, when, He had put forward the publicans and the harlots, then He added this, by the order of their actions convicting their unpardonable conduct, and showing that for fear of men they do all things, and for vainglory. For they did not confess Christ for fear, lest they should be put out of the synagogue; and again, of John they dared not speak evil, and not even this from reverence, but for fear. All which things He convicted by His sayings, and with more severity afterwards did He go on to inflict the blow, saying, "But ye, when ye knew it, repented not afterwards, that ye might believe him."

For an evil thing it is not at the first to choose the good, but it is a heavier charge not even to be brought round. For this above all maketh many wicked, which I see

to be the case with some now from extreme insensibility.

But let no one be like this; but though he be sunk down to the extremity of wickedness, let him not despair of the change for the better. For it is an easy thing to rise up out of the very abysses of wickedness.

Heard ye not how that harlot, that went beyond all in lasciviousness, outshone all in godly reverence. Not the harlot in the gospels do I mean, but the one in our generation, who came from Phœnice, that most lawless city. For she was once a harlot among us, having the first honors on the stage, and great was her name everywhere, not in our city only, but even as far as the Cilicians and Cappadocians. And many estates did she ruin, and many orphans did she overthrow; and many accused her of sorcery also, as weaving such toils not by her beauty of person only, but also by her drugs. This harlot once won even the brother of the empress, for mighty indeed was her tyranny.

But all at once, I know not how, or rather I do know well, for it was being so minded, and converting, and bringing down upon herself God's grace, she despised all those things, and having cast away the arts of the devils, mounted up to heaven.

And indeed nothing was more vile than she was, when she was on the stage; nevertheless, afterwards she outwent many in exceeding continence, and having clad herself with sackcloth, all her time she thus disciplined herself. On the account of this woman both the governor was stirred up, and soldiers armed, yet they had not strength to carry her off to the stage, nor to lead her away from the virgins that had received her.

This woman having been counted worthy of the unutterable mysteries, and having exhibited a diligence proportionate to the grace (given her) so ended her life, having washed off all through grace, and after her baptism having shown forth much self-restraint. For not even a mere sight of herself did she allow to those who were once her lovers, when they had come for this, having shut herself up, and having passed many years, as it were, in a prison. Thus "shall the last be first, and the first last;" thus do we in every case need a fervent soul, and there is nothing to hinder one from becoming great and admirable:

4. Let no man then of them that live in vice despair; let no man who lives in virtue slumber. Let neither this last be confident, for often the harlot will pass him by; nor let the other despair, for it is possible for him to pass by even the first.

Hear what God saith unto Jerusalem, "I

said, after she had committed all these whore-doms, Turn thou unto me, and she returned not."[1] When we have come back unto the earnest love of God, He remembers not the former things. God is not as man, for He reproaches us not with the past, neither doth He say, Why wast thou absent so long a time? when we repent; only let us approach Him as we ought. Let us cleave to Him earnestly, and rivet our hearts to His fear.

Such things have been done not under the new covenant only, but even under the old. For what was worse than Manasseh? but he was able to appease God. What more blessed than Solomon? but when he slumbered, he fell. Or rather I can show even both things to have taken place in one, in the father of this man, for he the same person became at different times both good and bad. What more blessed than Judas? but he became a traitor. What more wretched than Matthew? but he became an evangelist. What worse than Paul? but he became an apostle. What more to be envied than Simon? but he became even himself the most wretched of all.

How many other such changes wouldest thou see, both to have taken place of old, and now taking place every day? For this reason then I say, Neither let him on the stage despair, nor let him in the church be confident. For to this last it is said, "Let him that thinketh he standeth, take heed lest he fall;"[2] and to the other, "Shall not he that falleth arise?"[3] and, "Lift up the hands which hang down, and the feeble knees."[4] Again, to these He saith, "Watch;" but to those, "Awake, thou that sleepest, and arise from the dead."[5] For these need to preserve what they have, and those to become what they are not; these to preserve their health, those to be delivered from their infirmity, for they are sick; but many even of the sick become healthy, and of the healthy many by remissness grow infirm.

To the one then He saith, "Behold, thou art made whole, sin no more, lest a worse thing come unto thee;"[6] but to these, "Wilt thou be made whole? Arise, take up thy bed, and go unto thine house."[7] For a dreadful, dreadful palsy is sin, or rather it is not palsy only, but also somewhat else more grievous. For such a one is not only in in-activity as to good works, but also in the active doing of evil works. But nevertheless, though thou be so disposed, and be willing to rouse thyself a little, all the terrors are at an end.

Though thou hast been so "thirty and eight years," and art earnest to become whole, there is no one to hinder thee. Christ is present now also, and saith, "Take up thy bed," only be willing to rouse thyself, despair not. Hast thou no man? but thou hast God. Hast thou no one to put thee into the pool? but thou hast Him who suffers thee not to need the pool. Hast thou had no one to cast thee in there? but thou hast Him that com-mands thee to take up thy bed.

Thou mayest not say, "While I am coming, another steppeth down before me."[8] For if it be thy will to go down into the fountain, there is none to hinder thee. Grace is not consumed, is not spent, it is a kind of foun-tain springing up constantly; by His fullness are we all healed both soul and body. Let us come unto it then even now. For Rahab also was a harlot, yet was she saved; and the thief was a murderer, yet he became a citizen of paradise; and while Judas being with his Master perished, the thief being on a cross became a disciple. Such are the wonderful works of God. Thus the magi approved themselves, thus the publican became an evangelist, thus the blasphemer an apostle.

5. Look at these things, and never despair, but be ever confident, and rouse thyself. Lay hold only on the way that leads thither, and thou wilt advance quickly. Shut not up the doors, close not up the entrance. Short is the present life, small the labor. But though it were great, not even so ought one to de-cline it. For if thou toil not at this most glorious toil that is spent upon repentance and virtue, in the world thou wilt assuredly toil and weary thyself in other ways. But if both in the one and the other there be labor, why do we not choose that which hath its fruit abundant, and its recompense greater.

Yet neither is this labor and that the same. For in worldly pursuits are continual perils, and losses one upon another, and the hope uncertain; great is the servility, and the ex-penditure alike of wealth, and of bodies, and of souls; and then the return of the fruits is far below our expectation, if perchance it should grow up.

For neither doth toil upon worldly matters everywhere bear fruit; nay but even, when it hath not failed, but has brought forth its produce even abundantly, short is the time wherein it continues.

For when thou art grown old, and hast no longer after that the feeling of enjoyment in perfection, then and not till then doth the labor bear thee its recompense. And whereas the labor was with the body in its vigor, the

---

[1] Jer. iii. 7.   [2] 1 Cor. x. 12.   [3] Jer. viii. 4.
[4] Heb. xii. 12.   [5] Eph. v. 14.   [6] John v. 14.
[7] John v. 6-8; comp. Matt. ix. 6.

[8] John v. 7.

fruit and the enjoyment is with one grown old and languid, when time has dulled even the feeling, although if it had not dulled it, the expectation of the end suffers us not to find pleasure.

But in the other case not so, but the labor is in corruption and a dying body, but the crown in one incorruptible, and immortal, and having no end. And the labor is both first and short-lived; but the reward both subsequent and endless, that with security thou mayest take thy rest after that, looking for nothing unpleasant.

For neither mayest thou fear change any more or loss as here. What sort of good things, then, are these, which are both insecure, and short-lived, and earthly, and vanishing before they have appeared, and acquired with many toils? And what good things are equal to those, that are immovable, that grow not old, that have no toil, that even at the time of the conflicts bring thee crowns?

For he that despises money even here already receives his reward, being freed from anxiety, from rivalry, from false accusation, from plotting, from envy. He that is temperate, and lives orderly, even before his departure, is crowned and lives in pleasure, being delivered from unseemliness, ridicule, dangers of accusation,[1] and the other things that are to be feared. All the remaining parts of virtue likewise make us a return here already.

In order therefore that we may attain unto both the present and the future blessings, let us flee from vice and choose virtue. For thus shall we both enjoy delight, and obtain the crowns to come, unto which God grant we may all attain, by the grace and love towards man of our Lord Jesus Christ, to whom be glory and might forever and ever. Amen.

---

[1] [The rendering above has been corrected to conform to the punctuation of the Greek text.—R.]

HOMILY LXVIII.

MATT. XXI. 33—44.

" Hear another parable. There was a certain householder, which planted a vineyard, and hedged it round about, and digged a winepress, and built a tower, and let it out to husbandmen, and went into a far country.[1] And when the time of the fruit drew near, he sent his servants to receive the fruits. And the husbandmen took the servants, and beat some, and killed some, and stoned some. Again he sent other servants more than the first: and they did unto them likewise. But last he sent unto them his son, saying, It may be they will reverence my son. But when the husbandmen saw the son, they said among themselves, This is the heir, come, let us kill him, and let us seize on his inheritance. And they cast him out of the vineyard, and slew him. When the Lord therefore of the vineyard cometh, what will he do to those husbandmen? They say unto Him, He will miserably destroy those wicked men, and will let out his vineyard to other husbandmen, which shall render him the fruits in their seasons. Jesus saith unto them, Did ye never read in the Scriptures, The Stone which the builders rejected, the same is become the head of the corner? " [2]

MANY things doth He intimate by this parable, God's providence, which had been exercised towards them from the first; their murderous disposition from the beginning; that nothing had been omitted of whatever pertained to a heedful care of them; that even when prophets had been slain, He had not turned away from them, but had sent His very Son; that the God both of the New and

---

[1] [R. V., "another country."]
[2] [The Greek text agrees, as a rule, with the received: but a few peculiarities appear: αὐτοῦ is omitted at the close of verse 34; the close of verse 35 is altered; ἴσως is inserted from Luke in verse 37, and the beginning of verse 39 is abridged. The Oxford edition adds verses 43. 44, which are not given in the Greek text of the Homily in Migne, but added in Field's edition.—R.]

of the Old Testament was one and the same; that His death should effect great blessings; that they were to endure extreme punishment for the crucifixion, and their crime; the calling of the Gentiles, the casting out of the Jews.

Therefore He putteth it after the former parable, that He may show even hereby the charge to be greater, and highly unpardonable. How, and in what way? That although they met with so much care, they were worse than harlots and publicans, and by so much.

And observe also both His great care, and the excessive idleness of these men. For what pertained to the husbandmen, He Himself did, the hedging it round about, the planting the vineyard, and all the rest, and He left little for them to do; to take care of what was there, and to preserve what was given to them. For nothing was left undone, but all accomplished; and not even so did they gain, and this, when they had enjoyed such great blessings from Him. For when they had come forth out of Egypt, He gave a law, and set up a city, and built a temple, and prepared an altar.

"And went into a far country;" that is, He bore long with them, not always bringing the punishments close upon their sins; for by His going into a far country,[1] He means His great long-suffering.

And "He sent His servants," that is, the prophets, "to receive the fruit;" that is, their obedience, the proof of it by their works. But they even here showed their wickedness, not only by failing to give the fruit, after having enjoyed so much care, which was the sign of idleness, but also by showing anger towards them that came. For they that had not to give when they owed, should not have been indignant, nor angry, but should have entreated. But they not only were indignant, but even filled their hands with blood, and while deserving punishment, themselves inflicted punishment.

Therefore He sent both a second, and a third company, both that the wickedness of these might be shown, and the love towards man of Him who sent them.

And wherefore sent He not His Son immediately? In order that they might condemn themselves for the things done to the others, and leave off their wrath, and reverence Him when He came. There are also other reasons, but for the present let us go on to what is next.

But what means, "It may be they will

reverence?" It is not the language of one ignorant, away with the thought! but of one desiring to show the sin to be great; and without any excuse. Since Himself knowing that they would slay Him, He sent Him. But He saith, "They will reverence," declaring what ought to have been done, that it was their duty to have reverenced Him. Since elsewhere also He saith, "if perchance they will hear;"[2] not in this case either being ignorant, but lest any of the obstinate should say, that His prediction was the thing that necessitated their disobedience, therefore He frames His expressions in this way, saying, "Whether they will," and, "It may be." For though they had been obstinate towards His servants, yet ought they to have reverenced the dignity of the Son.

What then do these? When they ought to have run unto Him, when they ought to have asked pardon for their offenses, they even persist more strongly in their former sins, they proceed to add unto their pollutions, forever throwing into the shade their former offenses by their later; as also He Himself declared when He said, "Fill ye up the measure of your fathers."[3] For from the first the prophets used to charge them with these things, saying, "Your hands are full of blood;"[4] and, "They mingle blood with blood;"[5] and, "They build up Sion with blood."[6]

But they did not learn self-restraint, albeit they received this commandment first, "Thou shalt not kill;" and had been commanded to abstain from countless other things because of this, and by many and various means urged to the keeping of this commandment.

Yet, for all that, they put not away that evil custom; but what say they, when they saw Him? Come, let us kill Him. With what motive, and for what reason? what of any kind had they to lay to His charge, either small or great? Is it that He honored you, and being God became man for your sakes, and wrought His countless miracles? or that He pardoned your sins? or that He called you unto a kingdom?

But see together with their impiety great was their folly, and the reason of His murder was full of much madness. "For let us kill Him," it is said, "and the inheritance shall be ours."

And where do they take counsel to kill Him? "Out of the vineyard."

2. Seest thou how He prophesies even the place where He was to be slain. "And they cast Him out, and slew Him."

---

[1] [The verb ἀπεδήμησε means "went into another country." But Chrysostom here speaks of the ἀποδημίαν as τὴν πολλήν, thus agreeing with the interpretation of the A. V.—R.]

[2] Ezek. ii. 5. [3] Matt. xxiii. 32. [4] Is. i. 15.
[5] Hosea iv. 2. [6] Micah iii. 10.

And Luke indeed saith, that He declared what these men should suffer; and they said, "God forbid;" and He added the testimony [of Scripture]. For "He beheld them, and said, What is it then that is written? The stone which the builders rejected, the same is become the head of the corner; and every one that falleth upon it shall be broken."[1] But Matthew, that they themselves delivered the sentence. But this is not a contradiction. For indeed both things were done, both themselves passed the sentence against themselves; and again, when they perceived what they had said, they added, "God forbid;" and He set up the prophet against them, persuading them that certainly this would be.

Nevertheless, not even so did He plainly reveal the Gentiles, that He might afford them no handle, but signified it darkly by saying, "He will give the vineyard to others." For this purpose then did He speak by a parable, that themselves might pass the sentence, which was done in the case of David also, when He passed judgment on the parable of Nathan. But do thou mark, I pray thee, even hereby how just is the sentence, when the very persons that are to be punished condemn themselves.

Then that they might learn that not only the nature of justice requires these things, but even from the beginning the grace of the Spirit had foretold them, and God had so decreed, He both added a prophecy, and reproves them in a way to put them to shame, saying, "Did ye never read, The stone which the builders rejected, the same is become the head of the corner? this is the Lord's doing, and it is marvellous in our eyes;" by all things showing, that they should be cast out for unbelief, and the Gentiles brought in. This He darkly intimated by the Canaanitish woman also; this again by the ass, and by the centurion, and by many other parables; this also now.

Wherefore He added too, "This is the Lord's doing, and it is marvellous in our eyes," declaring beforehand that the believing Gentiles, and as many of the Jews as should also themselves believe, shall be one, although the difference between them had been so great before.

Then, that they might learn that nothing was opposed to God's will of the things doing, but that the event was even highly acceptable, and beyond expectation, and amazing every one of the beholders (for indeed the miracle was far beyond words), He added and said,

"It is the Lord's doing." And by the stone He means Himself, and by builders the teachers of the Jews; as Ezekiel also saith, "They that build the wall, and daub it with untempered mortar."[2] But how did they reject Him? By saying, "This man is not of God;[3] This man deceiveth the people;"[4] and again, "Thou art a Samaritan, and hast a devil."[5]

Then, that they might know that the penalty is not limited to their being cast out, He added the punishments also, saying, "Every one that falleth on this stone, shall be broken; but upon whomsoever it shall fall, it shall grind him to powder."[6] He speaks here of two ways of destruction, one from stumbling and being offended; for this is, "Whosoever falleth on this stone:" but another from their capture, and calamity, and utter destruction, which also He clearly foretold, saying, "It will grind him to powder." By these words He darkly intimated His own resurrection also.

Now the Prophet Isaiah saith, that He blames the vineyard, but here He accuses in particular the rulers of the people. And there indeed He saith, "What ought I to have done to my vineyard, that I did not;"[7] and elsewhere again, "What transgression have your fathers found in me?"[8] And again, "O my people, what have I done unto thee? and wherein have I grieved thee?"[9] showing their thankless disposition, and that when in the enjoyment of all things, they requited it by the contraries; but here He expresses it with yet greater force. For He doth not plead, Himself, saying, "What ought I to have done that I have not done?" but brings in themselves to judge, that nothing hath been wanting, and to condemn themselves. For when they say, "He will miserably destroy those wicked men, and will let out the vineyard to other husbandmen," they say nothing else than this, publishing their sentence with much greater force.

With this Stephen also upbraids them, which thing most of all stung them, that having enjoyed always much providential care, they requited their benefactor with the contraries, which very thing itself was a very great sign, that not the punisher, but the punished, were the cause of the vengeance brought upon them.

This here likewise is shown, by the parable, by the prophecy. For neither was He

---

[1] Luke xx. 17, 18.

[2] Ezek. xiii. 10.　　　　　　　　[3] John ix. 16.
[4] John vii. 12.　　　　　　　　　[5] John viii. 48.
[6] [R. V., "scatter him as dust." Chrysostom seems to accept verse 44 as part of Matthew's account ; but as he has just cited the parallel passage in Luke (where this occurs), it is not certain that he refers to Matthew's here.—R.]
[7] Is. v. 4.　　　　[8] Jer. ii. 5.　　　　[9] Micah vi. 3.

satisfied with a parable only, but added also a twofold prophecy, one David's, the others from Himself.

What then ought they to have done on hearing these things? ought they not to have adored, to have marvelled at the tender care, that shown before, that afterwards? But if by none of these things they were made better, by the fear of punishment at any rate ought they not to have been rendered more temperate?

But they did not become so, but what do they after these things? "When they had heard it," it is said, "they perceived that He spake of them. And when they sought to lay hands on Him, they were afraid because of the multitudes, for they took Him for a prophet."[1] For they felt afterwards that they themselves were intimated. Sometimes indeed, when being seized, He withdraws through the midst of them, and is not seen; and sometimes while appearing to them He lays a check upon their laboring eagerness; at which indeed men marveled, and said, "Is not this Jesus? Lo, He speaketh boldly, and they say nothing unto Him."[2] But in this instance, forasmuch as they were held in restraint by the fear of the multitude, He is satisfied with this, and doth not work miracles, as before, withdrawing through the midst, and not appearing. For it was not His desire to do all things in a superhuman way, in order that the Dispensation[3] might be believed.

But they, neither by the multitude, nor by what had been said, were brought to a sound mind; they regarded not the prophet's testimony, nor their own sentence, nor the disposition of the people; so entirely had the love of power and the lust of vainglory blinded them, together with the pursuit of things temporal.

3. For nothing so urges men headlong and drives them down precipices, nothing so makes them fail of the things to come, as their being riveted to these decaying things. Nothing so surely makes them enjoy both the one and the other, as their esteeming the things to come above all. For, "Seek ye," saith Christ, "the kingdom of God, and all these things shall be added unto you."[4] And indeed, even if this were not joined, not even in that case ought we to aim at them. But now in obtaining the others, we may obtain these two; and not even so are some per-

suaded, but are like senseless stones, and pursue shadows of pleasure. For what is pleasant of the things in this present life? what is delightful? For with greater freedom do I desire to discourse with you to-day; but suffer it, that ye may learn that this life which seems to you to be a galling and wearisome life, I mean that of the monks and of them that are crucified, is far sweeter, and more to be desired than that which seems to be easy, and more delicate.

And of this ye are witnesses, who often have asked for death, in the reverses and despondencies that have overtaken you, and have accounted happy them that are in mountains, them that are in caves, them that have not married, them that live the unworldly life; ye that are engaged in crafts, ye that are in military services, ye that live without object or rules, and pass your days at the theatres and orchestras. For of these, although numberless fountains of pleasures and mirth seem to spring up, yet are countless darts still more bitter brought forth.

For if any one be seized with a passion for one of the damsels that dance there, beyond ten thousand marches, beyond ten thousand journeys from home, will he undergo a torture more grievous, being in a more miserable state than any besieged city.

However, not to inquire into those things for the present, having left them to the conscience of those that have been taken captive, come let us discourse of the life of the common sort of men, and we shall find the difference between either of these kinds of life as great as between a harbor, and a sea continually beaten about with winds.

And observe from their retreats at once the first signs of their tranquillity. For they have fled from market places, and cities, and the tumults amidst men, and have chosen the life in mountains, that which hath nothing in common with the things present, that which undergoes none of the ills of man, no worldly sorrows, no grief, no care so great, no dangers, no plots, no envy, no jealousy, no lawless lusts, nor any other thing of this kind.

Here already they meditate upon the things of the kingdom, holding converse with groves, and mountains, and springs, and with great quietness, and solitude, and before all these, with God. . And from all turmoil is their cell pure, and from every passion and disease is their soul free, refined and light, and far purer than the finest air.

And their work is what was Adam's also at the beginning and before his sin, when he was clothed with the glory, and conversed freely with God, and dwelt in that place that was

---

[1] Matt. xxi. 45, 46. ["because of" (διά) is peculiar to this citation.—R.]
[2] [John vii. 25. 26.]
[3] Gr. οἰκονομία, i. e., the verity of the Incarnation.
[4] Matt. vi. 33. ["first" is omitted; inserted by the Oxford translator, against the Greek text.—R.]

27

full of great blessedness. For in what respect are they in a worse state than he, when before his disobedience he was set to till the garden? Had he no worldly care? But neither have these. Did he talk to God with a pure conscience? this also do these; or rather they have a greater confidence than he, inasmuch as they enjoy even greater grace by the supply of the Spirit.

Now ye ought indeed by the sight to take in these things; but forasmuch as ye are not willing, but pass your time in turmoils and in markets, by word at least let us teach you, taking one part of their way of living (for it is not possible to go over their whole life). These that are the lights of the world, as soon as the sun is up, or rather even long before its rise, rise up from their bed, healthy, and wakeful, and sober (for neither doth any sorrow and care, nor headache, and toil, and multitude of business, nor any other such thing trouble them, but as angels live ·they in Heaven); having risen then straightway from their bed cheerful and glad, and having made one choir, with their conscience bright, with one voice all, like as out of one mouth, they sing hymns unto the God of all, honoring Him and thanking Him for all His benefits, both particular, and common.[1]

So that if it seem good, let us leave Adam, and inquire what is the difference between the angels and this company of them who on earth sing and say, "Glory to God in the highest, and on earth peace, good will towards men."[2]

And their dress is suitable to their manliness. For not indeed, like those with trailing garments, the enervated and mincing, are they dressed, but like those blessed angels, Elijah, Elisha, John, like the apostles; their garments being made for them, for some of goat's hair, for some of camel's hair, and there are some for whom skins suffice alone, and these long worn.

Then, after they have said those songs, they bow their knees, and entreat the God who was the object of their hymns for things, to the very thought of which some do not easily arrive. For they ask nothing of things present, for they have no regard for these, but that they may stand with boldness before the fearful judgment-seat, when the Only-Begotten Son of God is come to judge quick and dead, and that no one may hear the tearful voice that saith, "I know you not," and that with a pure conscience and many good

deeds they may pass through this toilsome life, and sail over the angry sea with a favorable wind. And he leads them in their prayers, who is their Father, and their ruler.

After this, when they have risen up and finished those holy and continual prayers, the sun being risen, they depart each one to their work, gathering thence a large supply for the needy.

4. Where now are they who give themselves to devilish choirs, and harlot's songs, and sit in theatres? For I am indeed ashamed to make mention of them; nevertheless, because of your infirmity it is needful to do even this. For Paul too saith, "Like as ye have yielded your members servants to uncleanness, even so now yield your members servants to righteousness unto holiness."[3]

Come let us also therefore compare the company that is made up of harlot women, and prostituted youths on the stage, and this same that consists of these blessed ones in regard of pleasure, for which most of all, many of the careless youths are taken in their snares. For we shall find the difference as great as if any one heard angels singing above that all-harmonious melody of theirs, and dogs and swine howling and grunting on the dunghill. For by the mouths of these Christ speaketh, by their tongues[4] the devil.

But is the sound of pipes joined to them with unmeaning noise, and unpleasing show, when cheeks are puffed out, and their strings stretched to breaking? But here the grace of the Spirit pours forth a sound, using, instead of flute or lyre or pipes, the lips of the saints.

Or rather, whatever we may say, it is not possible to set forth the pleasure thereof, because of them that are riveted to their clay, and their brick-making? Therefore I would even wish to take one of those who are mad about these matters, and to lead him off there, and to show him the choir of those saints, and I should have no more need for these words. Nevertheless, though we speak unto miry ones, we will try, though by word, still by little and little, to draw them out of the slime and the fens. For there the hearer receives straightway the fire of illicit love; for as though the sight of the harlot were not enough to set the mind on fire, they add the mischief also from the voice; but here even should the soul have any such thing, it lays it aside straightway. But not their voice only, nor their countenance, but even their clothes do more than these confound the beholders. And should it be some poor man

---

[1] "For all Thy goodness and loving kindness *to us, and to all men*." Thanksgiving Prayer. See the Morning Thanksgiving; Const. Apost. viii. 38, and the Eucharistic Prayer, ib. c. 12.
[2] [Luke ii. 14, as in the received text. But "among men" is the only possible rendering, whichever reading he accepted.—R.]

[3] Rom. vi. 19. [R. V., "sanctification."]
[4] ["by the tongues of those;" there being a contrast in the Greek, which is obscured in the English rendering.—R.]

of the grosser and heedless sort, from the sight he will cry out ten thousand times in bitter despair, and will say to himself, "The harlot, and the prostituted boy, children of cooks and cobblers, and often even of slaves, live in such delicacy, and I a freeman, and born of freemen, choosing honest labor, am not able so much as to imagine these things in a dream;" and thus he will go his way inflamed with discontent.

But in the case of the monks there is no such result, but rather the contrary altogether. For when he shall see children of rich men and descendants of illustrious ancestors clothed in such garments as not even the lowest of the poor, and rejoicing in this, consider how great a consolation against poverty he will receive as he goes away. And should he be rich, he returns sobered, become a better man. Again in the theatre, when they see the harlot clothed with golden ornaments, while the poor man will lament, and bemoan, seeing his own wife having nothing of the kind, the rich will in consequence of this spectacle contemn and despise the partners of their home. For when the harlot present to the beholders garb and look, and voice and step, all luxurious, they depart set on fire, and enter into their own houses, thenceforth captives.

Hence the insults, and the affronts, hence the enmities, the wars, the daily deaths; hence to them that are taken captive, life is insupportable, and the partner of their home thenceforth unpleasing, and their children not as much objects of affection, and all things in their houses turned upside down, and after that they seem to be thrown into disorder by the very sunbeam.

But not from these choirs does any such dissatisfaction arise, but the wife will receive her husband quiet and meek, freed from all unlawful lust, and will find him more gentle to her than before this. Such evil things doth that choir bring forth, but this good things, the one making wolves of sheep, this lambs of wolves. But as yet we have perhaps said nothing hitherto touching the pleasure.

And what could be more pleasant than not to be troubled or grieved in mind, neither to despond and groan? Nevertheless, let us carry on our discourse still further, and examine the enjoyment of either kind of song and spectacle; and we shall see the one indeed continuing until evening, so long as the spectator sits in the theatre, but after this paining him more grievously than any sting; but in the other case forever vigorous in the souls of them that have beheld it. For as well the fashion of the men, and the delight-

fulness of the place, and the sweetness of their manner of life, and the purity, of their rule, and the grace of that most beautiful and spiritual song they have for ever infixed in them. They at least who are in continual enjoyment of those havens, thenceforth flee as from a tempest, from the tumults of the multitude.

But not when singing only, and praying, but also when riveted to their books, they are a pleasing spectacle to the beholders. For after they have ended the choir, one takes Isaiah and discourses with him, another converses with the apostles, and another goes over the labors of other men, and seeks wisdom concerning God, concerning this universe, concerning the things that are seen, concerning the things that are not seen, concerning the objects of sense, and the objects of intellect, concerning the vileness of this present life, and the greatness of that to come.

5. And they are fed on a food most excellent, not setting before themselves cooked flesh of beasts; but oracles of God, beyond honey and the honey comb, a honey marvellous, and far superior to that whereon John fed of old in the wilderness. For this honey no wild bees collect, settling on the flowers, neither do lay it up in hives digesting the dew, but the grace of the Spirit forming it, layeth it up in the souls of the saints, in the place of honeycombs, and hives, and pipes, so that he that will may eat thereof continually in security. These bees then they also imitate, and hover around the honeycombs of those holy books, reaping therefrom great pleasure.

And if thou desirest to learn about their table, be near it, and thou shalt see them bursting forth[1] with such things, all gentle and sweet, and full of a spiritual fragrance. No foul word can those spiritual mouths bring forth, nothing of foolish jesting, nothing harsh, but all worthy of Heaven. One would not be wrong in comparing the mouths of them that crawl about in the market places, and are mad after worldly things, to ditches of some mire; but the lips of these to fountains flowing with honey, and pouring forth pure streams.

But if any felt displeased that I have called the mouths of the multitude ditches of some mire, let him know that I have said it, sparing them very much. For Scripture hath not used this measure, but a comparison far stronger. "For adder's poison," it is said, "is under their lips,[2] and their throat is an open sepulchre." But theirs are not so, but full of much fragrance.

---

[1] ἐρευγομένους.   [2] Ps. cxl. 3 and v. 9.

And their state here is like this, but that hereafter what speech can set before us? what thought shall conceive? the portion of angels, the blessedness unspeakable, the good things untold?

Perchance some are warmed now, and have been moved to a longing after this good rule of life. But what is the profit, when whilst ye are here only, ye have this fire; but when ye have gone forth, ye extinguish the flame, and this desire fades. How then, in order that this may not be? While this desire is warm in you, go your way unto those angels, kindle it more. For the account that we give will not be able to set thee on fire, like as the sight of the things. Say not, I will speak with my wife, and I will settle my affairs first. This delay is the beginning of remissness. Hear, how one desired to bid farewell to them at his house,[1] and the prophet suffered him not. And why do I say, to bid farewell? The disciple desired to bury his father,[2] and Christ allowed not so much as this. And yet what thing seems to thee to be so necessary as the funeral of a father? but not even this did He permit.

Why could this have been? Because the devil is at hand fierce, desiring to find some secret approach; and though it be but a little hindrance or delay he takes hold of, he works a great remissness.

Therefore one adviseth, " Put not off from day to day."[3] For thus shalt thou be able to succeed in most things, thus also shall the things in thine house be well ordered for thee. " For seek ye," it is said, " the kingdom of God, and all these things shall be added unto you."[4] For if we establish in great security them that overlook their own interests, and prefer the care of ours, much more doth God, who even without these things hath a care for us, and provides for us.

Be not thoughtful then about thine interests, but leave them to God. For if thou art thoughtful about them, thou art thoughtful as a man; but if God provide, He provides as God. Be not so thoughtful about them as to let go the greater things, since then He will not much provide for them. In order therefore that He may fully provide for them, leave them to Him alone. For if thou also thyself takest them in hand, having let go the things spiritual, He will not make much provision for them.

In order then that both these things may be well disposed for thee, and that thou mayest be freed from all anxiety, cleave to the things spiritual, overlook the things of the world; for in this way thou shalt have earth also with heaven, and shalt attain unto the good things to come, by the grace and love towards man of our Lord Jesus Christ, to whom be glory and might world without end. Amen.

---

[1] 1 Kings xix. 20. [2] Matt. viii. 21, 22. 3 Ecclus. v. 7. 4 Matt. vi. 33.

HOMILY LXIX.

Matt. XXII. 1—14.

"And Jesus answered and spake again[1] in parables. The kingdom of Heaven is like unto a certain king, which made a marriage[2] for his son; and sent forth his servants to call them which were bidden to the wedding; and they would not come. Again, he sent forth other servants, saying, Tell them which are bidden, I have prepared my dinner; my oxen and my fatlings are killed, and all things are ready; come unto the marriage. But they made light of it, and went their ways, one to his farm, another to his merchandise: and the remnant took his servants, and entreated them spitefully, and slew them."[3]

SEEST thou both in the former parable and in this the difference between the Son and the servants? Seest thou at once the great affinity between both parables, and the great difference also? For this also indicates God's

[1] [The order here is slightly varied, and "unto them" omitted. With these exceptions the entire passage is in verbal agreement with the received text.—R.]
[2] [R. V., " marriage feast."]
[3] [Verses 7-14 do not appear in the Greek text of Migne's edition, but are added in the Oxford translation, and in Field's Greek text.—R.]

long-suffering, and His great providential care, and the Jews' ingratitude.

But this parable hath something also more than the other. For it proclaims beforehand both the casting out of the Jews, and the calling of the Gentiles; and it indicates together with this also the strictness of the life required, and how great the punishment appointed for the careless.

And well is this placed after the other. For since He had said, " It shall be given to a nation bringing forth the fruits thereof," He declares next to what kind of nation; and not this only, but He also again sets forth His providential care towards the Jews as past utterance. For there He appears before His crucifixion bidding them; but here even after He is slain, He still urges them, striving to win them over. And when they deserved to have suffered the most grievous punishment, then He both presses them to the marriage, and honors them with the highest honor. And see how both there He calls not the Gentiles first, but the Jews, and here again. But as there, when they would not receive Him, but even slew Him when He was come, then He gave away the vineyard; thus here too, when they were not willing to be present at the marriage, then He called others.

What then could be more ungrateful than they, when being bidden to a marriage they rush away? For who would not choose to come to a marriage, and that a King's marriage, and of a King making a marriage for a Son?

And wherefore is it called a marriage? one may say. That thou mightest learn God's tender care, His yearning towards us, the cheerfulness of the state of things, that there is nothing sorrowful there, nor sad, but all things are full of spiritual joy. Therefore also John calls Him a bridegroom, therefore Paul again saith, " For I have espoused you to one husband;"[1] and, " This is a great mystery, but I speak concerning Christ and the Church."[2]

Why then is not the bride said to be espoused to Him, but to the Son? Because she that is espoused to the Son, is espoused to the Father. For it is indifferent in Scripture that the one or the other should be said, because of the identity[3] of the substance.

Hereby He proclaimed the resurrection also. For since in what went before He had spoken of the death, He shows that even after the death, then is the marriage, then the bridegroom.

But not even so do these become better

men, nor more gentle, than which what can be worse? For this again is a third accusation. The first that they killed the prophets; then the son; afterwards that even when they had slain Him, and were bidden unto the marriage of Him that was slain, by the very one that was slain, they come not, but feign excuses, yokes of oxen, and pieces of ground, and wives. And yet the excuses seem to be reasonable; but hence we learn, though the things which hinder us be necessary, to set the things spiritual at a higher price than all.

And He not suddenly, but a long time before. For, " Tell, " He saith, " them that are bidden;" and again, " Call them that were bidden;" which circumstance makes the charge against them heavier. And when were they bidden? By all the prophets; by John again; for unto Christ he would pass all on, saying, " He must increase, I must decrease;"[4] by the Son Himself again, " Come unto me, all ye that labor and are heavy laden, and I will refresh you;"[5] and again, " If any man thirst, let him come unto me, and drink."[6]

But not by words only, but also by actions did He bid them, after His ascension by Peter, and those with him. " For He that wrought effectually in Peter, " it is said, "to the apostleship of the circumcision, was mighty also in me towards the Gentiles."[7]

For since on seeing the Son, they were wroth and slew Him, He bids them again by His servants. And unto what doth He bid them? Unto labors, and toils, and sweat? Nay but unto pleasure. For, " My oxen," He saith, " and my fatlings are killed." See how complete His banquet,[8] how great His munificence.

And not even this shamed them, but the more long-suffering He showed, so much the more were they hardened. For not for press of business, but from " making light of it," they did not come.

" How then do some bring forward marriages, others yokes of oxen? these things surely are of want of leisure."

By no means, for when spiritual things call us, there is no press of business that has the power of necessity.

And to me they seem moreover to make use of these excuses, putting forward these things as cloke for their negligence. And not this only is the grievous thing, that they came not, but also that which is a far more violent

[4] John iii. 30.
[5] Matt. xi. 28. [" Refresh " is the rendering of the Greek term answering to " give rest " in the English versions.—R.]
[6] John vii. 37.
[7] Gal. ii. 8. [R. V., " wrought for " twice; the Greek verb is the same in both clauses.—R.]
[8] πόση ἡ πανδαισία.

[1] 2 Cor. xi. 2.　　[2] Eph. v. 32.　　[3] ἀπαράλλακτον.

and furious act, to have even beaten them that came, and to have used them despitefully, and to have slain them; this is worse than the former. For those others came, demanding produce and fruits, and were slain; but these, bidding them to the marriage of Him that had been slain by them, and these again are murdered.

What is equal to this madness? This Paul also was laying to their charge, when he said, "Who both killed the Lord, and their own prophets, and have persecuted us." [1]

Moreover, that they may not say, "He is an adversary of God, and therefore we do not come," hear what they say who are bidding them; that it is the father who is making the marriage, and that it is He who is bidding them.

What then did He after these things? Since they were not willing to come, yea and also slew those that came unto them; He burns up their cities, and sent His armies and slew them.

And these things He saith, declaring beforehand the things that took place under Vespasian and Titus, and that they provoked the father also, by not believing in Him; it is the father at any rate who was avenging.

And for this reason let me add, not straightway after Christ was slain did the capture take place, but after forty years, that He might show His long suffering, when they had slain Stephen, when they had put James to death, when they had spitefully entreated the apostles.

Seest thou the truth of the event, and its quickness? For while John was yet living, and many other of them that were with Christ, these things came to pass, and they that had heard these words were witnesses of the events.

See then care utterable. He had planted a vineyard; He had done all things, and finished; when His servants had been put to death, He sent other servants; when those had been slain, He sent the son; and when He was put to death, He bids them to the marriage. They would not come. After this He sends other servants, and they slew these also.

Then upon this He slays them, as being incurably diseased. For that they were incurably diseased, was proved not by their acts only, but by the fact, that even when harlots and publicans had believed, they did these things. So that, not by their own crimes alone, but also from what others were able to do aright, these men are condemned.

But if any one should say, that not then were they out of the Gentiles called, I mean, when the apostles had been beaten and had suffered ten thousand things, but straightway after the resurrection (for then He said to them, "Go ye and make disciples of all nations." [2]) We would say, that both before the crucifixion, and after the crucifixion, they addressed themselves to them first. For both before the crucifixion, He saith to them, "Go to the lost sheep of the house of Israel;" [3] and after the crucifixion, so far from forbidding, He even commanded them to address themselves to the Jews. For though He said, "Make disciples of all nations," yet when on the point of ascending into Heaven, He declared that unto those first they were to address themselves; For, "ye shall receive power," saith He, "after that the Holy Ghost is come upon you, and ye shall be witnesses unto me both in Jerusalem, and in all Judæa, and unto the uttermost part of the earth;" [4] and Paul again, "He that wrought effectually in Peter to the apostleship of the circumcision, was mighty in me also toward the Gentiles." [5] Therefore the apostles also went first unto the Jews, and when they had tarried a long time in Jerusalem, and then had been driven away by them, in this way they were scattered abroad unto the Gentiles.

2. And see thou even herein His bounty; "As many as ye shall find," saith He, "bid to the marriage. For before this, as I said, they addressed themselves both to Jews and Greeks, tarrying for the most part in Judæa; but since they continued to lay plots against them, hear Paul interpreting this parable, and saying thus, "It was necessary that the word of God should first have been spoken to you, but since ye judge yourselves unworthy, lo, we turn to the Gentiles.[6]

Therefore Christ also saith, "The wedding is ready, but they which were bidden were not worthy."

He knew this indeed even before, but that He might leave them no pretext of a shameless sort of contradiction, although He knew it, to them first He both came and sent, both stopping their mouths, and teaching us to fulfill all our parts, though no one should derive any profit.

Since then they were not worthy, go ye, saith He, into the highways, and as many as ye shall find, bid; both the common sort, and the outcasts. For because He had said in every way,[7] "The harlots and publicans shall inherit heaven;" and, "The first shall

---

[2] Matt. xxviii. 19.   [3] Matt. x. 6.   [4] Acts i. 8.
[5] Gal. ii. 8. [Comp. note 7, p. 421.]
[6] Acts xiii. 46. [Slightly abridged.]
[7] Or, "repeatedly."

be last, and the last first;" He shows that justly do these things come to pass; which more than anything stung the Jews, and goaded them far more grievously than their overthrow, to see those from the Gentiles brought into their privileges, and into far greater than theirs.

Then in order that not even these should put confidence in their faith alone, He discourses unto them also concerning the judgment to be passed upon wicked actions; to them that have not yet believed, of coming unto Him by faith, and to them that have believed, of care with respect to their life. For the garment is life and practice.

And yet the calling was of grace; wherefore then doth He take a strict account? Because although to be called and to be cleansed was of grace, yet, when called and clothed in clean garments, to continue keeping them so, this is of the diligence of them that are called.

The being called was not of merit, but of grace. It was fit therefore to make a return for the grace, and not to show forth such great wickedness after the honor. "But I have not enjoyed," one may say, "so much advantage as the Jews." Nay, but thou hast enjoyed far greater benefits. For what things were being prepared for them throughout all their time, these thou hast received at once, not being worthy. Wherefore Paul also saith, "And that the Gentiles might glorify God for His mercy." [1] For what things were due to them, these thou hast received.

Wherefore also great is the punishment appointed for them that have been remiss. For as they did despite by not coming, so also thou by thus sitting down with a corrupt life. For to come in with filthy garments is this, namely, to depart hence having one's life impure; wherefore also he was speechless.

Seest thou how, although the fact was so manifest, He doth not punish at once, until he himself, who has sinned, has passed the sentence? For by having nothing to reply he condemned himself, and so is taken away to the unutterable torments.

For do not now, on hearing of darkness, suppose he is punished by this, by sending into a place where there is no light only, but where "there is" also "weeping and gnashing of teeth." [2] And this He saith, indicating the intolerable pains.

Hear ye, as many as having partaken of the mysteries, and having been present at the marriage, clothe your souls with filthy deeds Hear whence ye were called.

From the highway. Being what? Lame and halt in soul, which is a much more grievous thing than the mutilation of the body. Reverence the love of Him, who called you, and let no one continue to have filthy garments, but let each of you busy himself about the clothing of your soul.

Hear, ye women; hear, ye men; we need not these garments that are bespangled with gold, *that adorn our outward parts,*[3] but those others, that adorn the inward. Whilst we have these former, it is difficult to put on those latter. It is not possible at the same time to deck both soul and body. It is not possible at the same time both to serve mammon, and to obey Christ as we ought.

Let us put off us therefore this grievous tyranny. For neither if any one were to adorn thy house by hanging it with golden curtains, and were to make thee sit there in rags, naked, wouldest thou endure it with meekness. But lo, now thou doest this to thyself, decking the house of thy soul, I mean the body, with curtains beyond number, but leaving the soul itself to sit in rags. Knowest thou not that the king ought to be adorned more than the city? so therefore while for the city hangings are prepared of linen, for the king there is a purple robe and a diadem. Even so do thou wrap the body with a much meaner dress, but the mind do thou clothe in purple, and put a crown on it, and set it on a high and conspicuous chariot. For now thou art doing the opposite, decking the city in various ways, but suffering the king, the mind, to be dragged bound after the brute passions.

Rememberest thou not, that thou art bidden to a marriage, and to God's marriage? Considerest thou not how the soul that is bidden ought to enter into those chambers, clad, and decked with fringes of gold.

3. Wilt thou that I show thee them that are clad thus, them that have on a marriage garment?

Call to mind those holy persons, of whom I discoursed to you of late, them that wear garments of hair, them that dwell in the deserts. These above all are the wearers of the garments of that wedding; this is evident from hence, that how many soever purple robes thou wert to give them, they would not choose to receive them; but much as a king, if any one were to take the beggar's rags, and exhort him to put them on, would abhor the clothing, so would those persons also his purple robe. And from no other cause have they this feeling, but because of knowing the beauty of their own raiment. Therefore even

---

[1] Rom. xv. 9.   [2] Matt. xxii. 13.

[3] [The clause in italics is not found in the MSS. collated by Field, but occurs in the Benedictine edition.—R.]

that purple robe they spurn like the spider's web. For these things hath their sackcloth taught them; for indeed they are far more exalted and more glorious than the very king who reigns.

And if thou wert able to open the doors of the mind, and to look upon their soul, and all their ornaments within, surely thou wouldest fall down upon the earth, not bearing the glory of their beauty, and the splendor of those garments, and the lightning brightness of their conscience.

For we could tell also of men of old, great and to be admired; but since visible examples lead on more those of grosser souls, therefore do I send you even to the tabernacles of those holy persons. For they have nothing sorrowful, but as if in heaven they had pitched their tents, even so are they encamped far off the wearisome things of this present life, in campaign against the devils; and as in choirs, so do they war against him. Therefore I say, they have fixed their tents, and have fled from cities, and markets, and houses. For he that warreth cannot sit in a house, but he must make his habitation of a temporary kind, as on the point of removing straightway, and so dwell. Such are all those persons, contrary to us. For we indeed live not as in a camp, but as in a city at peace.

For who in a camp ever lays foundation, and builds himself a house, which he is soon after to leave? There is not one; but should any one attempt it, he is put to death as a traitor. Who in a camp buys acres of land, and makes for himself trades? There is not one, and very reasonably. "For thou art come here," they would say, "to fight, not to traffic; why then dost thou trouble thyself about the place, which in a little time thou wilt leave? When we are gone away to our country, do these things."

The same do I now say to thee also. When we have removed to the city that is·above, do these things: or rather thou wilt have no need of labors there; after that the king will do all things for thee. But here it is enough to dig a ditch round only, and to fix a palisade, but of building houses there is no need.

Hear what was the life of the Scythians, that lived in their wagons, such, as they say, are the habits of the shepherd tribes. So ought Christians to live; to go about the world, warring against the devil, rescuing the captives held in subjection by him, and to be in freedom from all worldly things.

Why preparest thou a house, O man, that thou mayest bind thyself more? Why dost thou bury a treasure, and invite the enemy against thyself? Why dost thou compass thyself with walls, and prepare a prison for thyself?

But if these things seem to thee to be hard, let us go away unto the tents of those men, that by their deeds we may learn the easiness thereof. For they having set up huts, if they must depart from these, depart like as soldiers, having left their camp in peace. For so likewise are they encamped, or rather even much more beautifully.

For indeed it is more pleasant to behold a desert containing huts of monks in close succession, than soldiers stretching the canvas in a camp, and fixing spears, and suspending from the point of the spears saffron garments,[1] and a multitude of men having heads of brass, and the bosses of the shields glistening much, and men armed all throughout with steel, and royal courts hastily made, and ground levelled far, and men dining and piping. For neither is this spectacle so delightful as that of which I now speak.

For if we were to go away into the wilderness, and look at the tents of Christ's soldiers, we shall see not canvas stretched, neither points of spears, nor golden garments making a royal pavilion; but like as if any one upon an earth much larger than this earth, yea infinite, had stretched out many heavens, strange and awful would be the sight he showed; even so may one see here.

For in nothing are their lodging-places in a condition inferior to the heavens; for the angels lodge with them, and the Lord of the angels. For if they came to Abraham, a man having a wife, and bringing up children, because they saw him hospitable; when they find much more abundant virtue, and a man delivered from the body, and in the flesh disregarding the flesh, much more do they tarry there, and celebrate the choral feast that becomes them. For there is moreover a table amongst them pure from all covetousness, and full of self-denial.

No streams of blood are amongst them, nor cutting up of flesh, nor heaviness of head, nor dainty cooking, neither are there unpleasing smells of meat amongst them, nor disagreeable smoke, neither runnings and tumults, and disturbances, and wearisome clamors; but bread and water, the latter from a pure fountain, the former from honest labor. But if any time they should be minded to feast more sumptuously, their sumptuousness consists of fruits, and greater is the pleasure there than at royal tables. There is no fear there, or trembling; no ruler accuses, no wife provokes, no child casts into sadness, no dis-

---

[1] φάρη κροκωτά.

orderly mirth dissipates, no multitude of flatterers puffs up; but the table is an angel's table free from all such turmoil.

And for a couch they have grass only beneath them, like as Christ did when making a dinner in the wilderness. And many of them do this, not being even under shelter, but for a roof they have heaven, and the moon instead of the light of a candle, not wanting oil, nor one to attend to it; on them alone does it shine worthily from on high.

4. This table even angels from heaven beholding are delighted and pleased. For if over one sinner that repenteth they rejoice, over so many just men imitating them, what will they not do? There are not master and slave; all are slaves, all free men. And do not think the saying to be a dark proverb, for they are indeed slaves one of another, and masters one of another.

They have no occasion to be in sadness when evening has overtaken them, as many men feel, revolving the anxious thoughts that spring from the evils of the day. They have no occasion after their supper to be careful about robbers, and to shut the doors, and to put bars against them, neither to dread the other ills, of which many are afraid, extinguishing their candles with strict care, lest a spark anywhere should set the house on fire.

And their conversation again is full of the same calm. For they talk not of these things, whereof we discourse, that are nothing to us; such a one is made governor, such a one has ceased to be governor; such a one is dead, and another has succeeded to the inheritance, and all such like, but always about the things to come do they speak, and seek wisdom; and as though dwelling in another world, as though they had migrated unto heaven itself, as living there, even so all their conversation is about the things there, about Abraham's bosom, about the crowns of the saints, about the choiring with Christ; and of things present they have neither any memory nor thought, but like as we should not deign to speak at all of what the ants do in their holes and clefts; so neither do they of what we do; but about the King that is above, about the war in which they are engaged, about the devil's crafts, about the good deeds which the saints have achieved.

Wherein therefore are we different from ants, when compared with them? For like as they care for the things of the body, so also do we; and would it were for these alone; but now it is even for things far worse. For not for necessary things only do we care like them, but also for things superfluous. For those insects pursue a business free from all

blame, but we follow after all covetousness, and not even the ways of ants do we imitate, but the ways of wolves, but the ways of leopards, or rather we are even worse than these. For to them nature has assigned that they should be thus fed, but us God hath honored with speech, and a sense of equity,[1] and we are become worse than the wild beasts.

And whereas we are worse than the brutes, those men are equal to the angels, being strangers and pilgrims as to the things here; and all things in them are made different from us, clothing, and food, and house, and shoes, and speech. And if any one were to hear them conversing and us, then he would know full well, how they indeed are citizens of heaven, but we are not worthy so much as of the earth.

So that therefore, when any one invested with rank is come unto them, then is all inflated pride found utterly vain. For the laborer there, and he that hath no experience of worldly affairs, sits near him that is a commander of troops, and prides himself on his authority, upon the grass, upon a mean cushion. For there are none to extol him, none to puff him up; but the same result takes place, as if any one were to go to a goldsmith, and a garden of roses, for he receives some brightness from the gold and from the roses; so they too, gaining a little from the splendor of these, are delivered from their former arrogance. And like as if any were to go upon a high place, though he be exceedingly short, he appears high; so these too, coming unto their exalted minds, appear like them, so long as they abide there, but when they are gone down are abased again, on descending from that height.

A king is nothing amongst them, a governor is nothing; but like as we, when children are playing at these things, laugh; so do they also utterly spurn the inflamed pride of them who strut without. And this is evident from hence, that if any one would give them a kingdom to possess in security, they would never take it; yet they would take it, unless their thoughts were upon what is greater than it, unless they accounted the thing to be but for a season.

What then? Shall we not go over unto blessedness so great? Shall we not come unto these angels; shall we not receive clean garments, and join in the ceremonies of this wedding feast; but shall we continue begging, in no respect in a better condition than the poor in the streets, or rather in a state far worse and more wretched? For much worse

---

[1] ἰσονομία.

than these are they that are rich in evil ways, and it is better to beg than to spoil, for the one hath excuse, but the other brings punishment; and the beggar in no degree offends God, but this other both men and God; and undergoes the labors of rapine, but all the enjoyment thereof other men often reap.

Knowing then these things, let us lay aside all covetousness, and covet the things above, with great earnestness "taking the kingdom by force."[1] For it cannot be, it cannot be that any one who is remiss should enter therein.

But God grant that we all having become earnest, and watchful, may attain thereto, by the grace and love towards man of our Lord Jesus Christ, to whom be glory and might, world without end. Amen.

[1] Matt. xi. 12.

HOMILY LXX.

MATT. XXII. 15.

" Then went the Pharisees, and took counsel how they might entangle Him in His talk."

THEN. When? When most of all they ought to have been moved to compunction, when they should have been amazed at His love to man, when they should have feared the things to come, when from the past they ought to have believed touching the future also. For indeed the things that had been said cried aloud in actual fulfillment. I mean, that publicans and harlots believed, and prophets and righteous men were slain, and from these things they ought not to have gainsaid touching their own destruction, but even to believe and to be sobered.

But nevertheless not even so do their wicked acts cease, but travail and proceed further. And forasmuch as they could not lay hands on Him (for they feared the multitude), they took another way with the intention of bringing Him into danger, and making Him guilty of crimes against the state.

For "they sent out unto Him their disciples with the Herodians saying, Master, we know that thou art true, and teachest the way of God in truth, neither carest thou for any man; for thou regardest not the person of men. Tell us therefore, What thinkest thou? Is it lawful to give tribute unto Cæsar or not?"[1]

For they were now tributaries, their state having passed under the rule of the Romans. Forasmuch then as they saw that Theudas and Judas[2] with their companies for this cause were put to death, as having prepared for a revolt, they were minded to bring Him too by these words into such a suspicion. Therefore they sent both their own disciples, and Herod's soldiers, digging, as they thought, a precipice on either side, and in every direction setting the snare, so that, whatever He should say, they might lay hold of it; and if He should answer in favor of the Herodians, themselves might find fault with Him, but if in their favor, the others should accuse Him. And yet He had given the didrachmas,[3] but they knew not that.

And in either way indeed they expected to lay hold of Him; but they desired rather that He should say something against the Herodians. Wherefore they send their disciples also to urge Him thereto by their presence, that they might deliver Him to the governor as an usurper. For this Luke also intimates and shows, by saying, that they asked also in the presence of the multitude, so that the testimony should be the stronger.

But the result was altogether opposite; for in a larger body of spectators they afforded the demonstration of their folly.

And see their flattery, and their hidden craft. "We know," their words are, "that Thou art true." How said ye then, "He is a deceiver," and "deceiveth the people," and "hath a devil," and "is not of God?"[4] how a little while before did ye devise to slay Him?

But they are at everything, whatsoever their craft against Him may suggest. For since,

---

[1] Matt. xxii. 16, 17. [2] Acts v. 36, 37. [3] Matt. xvii. 24, 25-27. [4] John vii. 12; viii. 48; ix. 16.

when a little before they had said in self will, "By what authority doest Thou these things?"[1] they did not meet with an answer to the question, they look to puff Him up by their flattery, and to persuade Him to say something against the established laws, and opposed to the prevailing government.

Wherefore also they testify the truth unto Him, confessing what was really so, nevertheless, not with an upright mind, nor willingly; and add thereto, saying, "Thou carest not for any man." See how plainly they are desiring to urge Him to these sayings, that would make Him both offend Herod, and incur the suspicion of being an usurper, as standing up against the laws, so that they might punish Him, as a mover of sedition, and an usurper. For in saying, "Thou carest not for any man," and, "Thou regardest not the person of man," they were hinting at Herod and Cæsar.

"Tell us therefore, what thinkest Thou?" Now ye honor Him, and esteem Him a Teacher, having despised and insulted Him oftentimes, when He was discoursing of the things that concern your salvation. Whence also they are become confederates.

And see their craftiness. They say not, Tell us what is good, what is expedient, what is lawful? but, "What thinkest Thou?" So much did they look to this one object, to betray Him, and to set Him at enmity with the rulers. And Mark declaring this, and more plainly discovering their self-will, and their murderous disposition, affirms them to have said, "Shall we give Cæsar tribute, or shall we not give?"[2] So that they were breathing anger, and travailing with a plot against Him, yet they feigned respect.

What then saith He? "Why tempt ye me, ye hypocrites?" Seest thou how He talks with them with more than usual severity? For since their wickedness was now complete and manifest, He cuts the deeper, first confounding and silencing them, by publishing their secret thoughts, and making it manifest to all with what kind of intent they are coming unto Him.

And these things He did, repulsing their wickedness, so that they might not suffer hurt in attempting the same things again. And yet their words were full of much respect, for they both called Him Master, and bore witness to His truth, and that He was no respecter of persons; but being God, He was deceived by none of these things. Wherefore they also ought to have conjectured, that the rebuke was not the result of conjecture, but a sign of His knowing their secret thoughts.

2. He stopped not, however, at the rebuke, although it was enough merely to have convicted them of their purpose, and to have put them to shame for their wickedness; but He stoppeth not at this, but in another way closes their mouths; for, "Shew me," saith He, "the tribute money." And when they had shown it, as He ever doth, by their tongue He brings out the decision, and causes them to decide, that it is lawful; which was a clear and plain victory. So that when He asks, not from ignorance doth He ask, but because it is His will to cause them to be bound by their own answers. For when, on being asked, "Whose is the image?" they said, "Cæsar's;" He saith, "Render unto Cæsar the things that are Cæsar's."[3] For this is not to give but to render, and this He shows both by the image, and by the superscription.

Then that they might not say, Thou art subjecting us to men, He added, "And unto God the things that are God's." For it is possible both to fulfill to men their claims, and to give unto God the things that are due to God from us. Wherefore Paul also saith, "Render unto all their dues; tribute to whom tribute is due, custom to whom custom, fear to whom fear."[4]

But thou, when thou hearest, "Render unto Cæsar the things which are Cæsar's," know that He is speaking only of those things, which are no detriment to godliness; since if it be any such thing as this, such a thing is no longer Cæsar's tribute, but the devil's.

When they heard these things, their mouths were stopped, and they "marvelled" at His wisdom. Ought they not then to have believed, ought they not to have been amazed. For indeed, He gave them proof of His Godhead, by revealing the secrets of their hearts, and with gentleness did He silence them.

What then? did they believe? By no means, but they "left Him, and went their way;" and after them, "came to Him the Sadducees."

O folly! When the others had been put to silence, these made the attack, when they ought to have been the more backward. But such is the nature of rashness, shameless, and importunate, and attempting things impossible. Therefore the evangelist also, amazed at their folly, signified this very thing, by saying, "On that day came to Him."[5] On that day. On what day? In which He had convicted their craftiness, and put them to shame.

But who are these? A sect of the Jews dif-

---

[1] Matt. xxi. 23. [2] Mark xii. 15.

[3] Matt. xxii. 20, 21. [Abridged.] [4] Rom. xiii. 7.
[5] Matt. xxii. 22, 23. [The article may not form part of the citation. It does not occur in the New Testament passage.—R.]

ferent from the Pharisees, and much worse than they, who said, " that there is no resurrection, nor angel, nor spirit."[1] For these were some of a grosser sort, and eager after the things of the body. For there were many sects even amongst the Jews. Wherefore Paul also saith, " I am a Pharisee, of the strictest sect amongst us."[2]

And they say nothing indeed directly about a resurrection; but they feign a story, and make up a case, which, as I suppose, never so much as had an existence; thinking to drive Him to perplexity, and desiring to overthrow both things, both the existence of a resurrection, and of such a resurrection.

And again, these too attack Him with a show of moderation, saying, " Master, Moses said, If a man die, not having children, his brother shall marry his wife, and raise up seed unto his brother. Now there were with us seven brethren: and the first, when he had married a wife, deceased; and, having no issue,[3] left his wife unto his brother. Likewise the second also, and the third, unto the seventh. And last of all the woman died also. Therefore, in the resurrection, whose wife shall she be of the seven?"[4]

See Him answering these like a teacher. For though out of craft they came unto Him, yet was their question rather one of ignorance. Therefore neither doth He say unto them, " Ye hypocrites."

Moreover, in order that He might not blame, saying, " Wherefore had seven one wife?" they add the authority of Moses; although, as I have said before, it was a fiction, in my judgment at least. For the third would not have taken her, when he saw the two bridegrooms dead; or if the third, yet not the fourth or the fifth; and if even these, much more the sixth or the seventh would not have come unto the woman, but have shrunk from her. For such is the nature of the Jews. For if now many have this feeling, much more then had they; when at least, even without this, they often avoided marrying in this way, and that when the law was constraining them. Thus, at any rate, Ruth, that Moabitish woman, was thrust off to him that was further off from her kindred; and Tamar too was thus compelled to obtain, by stealth, seed from her husband's kinsman.

And wherefore did they not feign two or three, but seven? In order the more abundantly to bring derision, as they thought, upon the resurrection. Wherefore they further

say, " they all had her," as driving Him into some difficulty.

What then saith Christ? He replies unto both, as taking His stand not against the words, but the purpose, and on every occasion revealing the secrets of their hearts; and at one time exposing them, at another time leaving the refutation of them that question Him to their conscience. See, at any rate here, how He proves both points, as well that there will be a resurrection, as that it will not be such a resurrection as they suspect.

For what saith He? " Ye do err, not knowing the Scriptures, nor the power of God."[5] For since, as if they knew them, they put forward Moses and the law, He shows that this question is that of men very ignorant of the Scriptures. For hence also arose their tempting Him, from their being ignorant of the Scriptures, and from their not knowing the power of God as they ought.

" For what marvel then is it," He saith, " if ye tempt me, who am as yet unknown to you, when at least ye know not so much as the power of God, of which ye have had so much experience, and neither from common sense nor from the Scriptures have become acquainted with it;" if indeed even common sense causes us to know this, that to God all things are possible. And in the first place He answers to the question asked. For since this was the cause for their not believing a resurrection, that they think the order of things is like this, He cures the cause, then the symptom also (for thence arose the disease too), and shows the manner of the resurrection. " For in the resurrection," saith He, " they neither marry, nor are given in marriage, but are as angels of God in Heaven."[6] But Luke saith, " As Sons of God."[7]

If then they marry not, the question is vain. But not because they do not marry, therefore are they angels, but because they are as angels, therefore they do not marry. By this He removed many other difficulties also, all which things Paul intimated by one word, saying, " For the fashion of this world passeth away."[8]

And by these words He declared how great a thing the resurrection is; and that moreover there is a resurrection, He proves. And indeed this too was demonstrated at the same time by what He had said, nevertheless over and above He adds again to His word by what He saith now. For neither at their question only did He stop, but at their

[1] Acts xxiii. 8.   [2] Acts xxiii. 6, and xxvi. 5.
[3] [R. V., " seed."]
[4] Matt. xxii. 24-28. [With the trifling variations the Greek of these verses agrees with the received text.—R.]

[5] Matt. xxii. 29.
[6] Matt. xxii. 30. [The second verb is peculiar, but conveys the same sense as the received text.—R.]
[7] Luke xx. 36.   [8] 1 Cor. vii. 31.

thought. Thus when they are not dealing with great craft, but are asking in ignorance, He teaches even over and above, but when it is of wickedness only, not even to their question doth He answer.

And again by Moses doth He stop their mouths, since they too had brought forward Moses; and He saith, " But as touching the resurrection of the dead, have ye not read, I am the God of Abraham, and the God of Isaac, and the God of Jacob? He is not the God of the dead, but of the living." [1] Not of them that are not, His meaning is, and that are utterly blotted out, and are to rise no more. For He said not, I was, but, I am; of them that are, and them that live. For like as Adam, although he lived on the day that he ate of the tree, died in the sentence; even so also these, although they had died, lived in the promise of the resurrection.

How then doth He say elsewhere, "That He might be Lord both of the dead and of the living?" [2] But this is not contrary to that. For here He speaks of the dead, who are also themselves to live. And moreover too, " I am the God of Abraham," is another thing from, " That He might be Lord both of the dead and of the living." He knew of another death too, concerning which He saith, " Let the dead bury their dead." [3]

"And when the multitudes heard this, they were astonished at His doctrine." [4] Yet not even here the Sadducees; but these go away defeated, while the impartial multitude reap the benefit.

Since then the resurrection is like this, come let us do all things, that we may obtain the first honors there. But, if ye will, let us show you some even before the resurrection here pursuing and reaping these blessings, again having made our resort to the deserts. For again will I enter upon the same discourse, since I see you listening with more pleasure.

Let us behold then to-day also the spiritual camps, let us behold their pleasure unalloyed with fear. For not with spears are they encamped like the soldiers, for at this point I lately ended my discourse, neither with shields and breastplates; but bare of all these wilt thou see them, yet achieving such things, as not even with arms do they.

And if thou art able to observe, come and stretch forth thy hand to me, and let us go unto this war, both of us, and let us see their battle array. For these too fight every day, and slay their adversaries, and conquer all the lusts that are plotting against us; and thou wilt see these cast out on the ground, and not able so much as to struggle, but proving by very deed that saying of the apostle, " They that are Christ's have crucified the flesh with the affections and lusts." [5]

Seest thou a multitude of dead lying *there*, slain by the sword of the Spirit? Therefore in that place is no drunkenness nor gluttony. And their table proves it, and the trophy that is set thereon. For drunkenness and gluttony lie dead, put to the rout by the drinking of water, though this be multiform, and a many-headed monster. For like as in the fabled Scylla and Hydra, so in drunkenness may one see many heads, on one side fornication growing up, on another wrath; on one hand sloth, on another lawless lusts; but all these things are taken away. And yet all those other armies, though they get the better in ten thousand wars, are taken captive by these; and neither arms, nor spears, nor whatever else there may be, is able to stand against these phalanxes; but the very giants, the heroes, those that do countless brave deeds, thou wilt find without bonds bound by sleep and drunkenness, without slaughter or wounds lying like the wounded, or rather in more grievous case. For those at least struggle; but these do not even this, but straightway give up.

Seest thou that this host is greater and more to be admired? For the enemies that got the better of the others it destroys by its mere will. For they do so weaken the mother of all their evils, that she cannot even trouble them any more; and the leader being overthrown, and the head removed, the rest of the body also lies still.

And this victory one may see each of them, that abide there, achieving. For it is not as in these wars of ours, where, if any enemy hath received a blow from one, he is no more grievous to another, having been once overthrown; but it is necessary for all to smite this monster; and he that hath not smitten and overthrown her, is surely troubled by her.

Seest thou a glorious victory? For such a trophy as the hosts in all parts of the world having met together have not power to erect, this each one of those men erects; and all things that from the army of drunkenness lie mingled together wounded, delirious words of frenzy, insane thoughts, unpleasing haughtiness. And they imitate their own Lord, at whom the Scripture marvelling saith, " He shall drink of the brook in the way, therefore shall He lift up the head." [6]

---

[1] Matt. xxii. 31, 32. [In the last clause the text differs from the received, ὁ θεός being omitted (so Tischendorf). The R. V. follows a slightly different reading: " God is not the God," etc.—R.]

[2] Rom. xiv. 9.　　[3] Matt. viii. 22.　　[4] Matt. xxii. 33.

[5] Gal. v. 24.　　[6] Ps. cx. 7.

Would ye see also another multitude of dead? Let us see the lusts that arise from luxurious living, those that are cherished by the makers of sauces, by the cooks, the furnishers of feasts, the confectioners. For I am ashamed indeed to speak of all; however, I will tell of the birds from Phasis, the soups that are mixed from various things: the moist, the dry dishes, the laws made about these things. For like as if ordering some city and marshalling hosts, even so these too make laws, and ordain such a thing first, and such a thing second, and some bring in first birds roasted on the embers, filled within with fish; and others make of other material the beginnings of these unlawful feasts; and there is much rivalry about these things, about quality, and about order, and about quantity; and they take a pride in the things, for which they ought to bury themselves for shame; some saying that they have spent the half of the day, some all of it, some that they have added the night too. Behold, O wretched man, the measure of thy belly, and be ashamed of thy unmeasured earnestness!

But there is nothing like this amongst those angels; but all these desires also are dead. For their meals are not unto fullness, and unto luxurious living, but unto necessity. No bird hunters are there, no fishermen, but bread and water. But this confusion, and the disturbance, and the turmoils, are all removed from thence, alike from the house and from the body, and great is the haven, but amongst these great the tempest.

Burst open now in thought the belly of them who feed on such things, and thou wilt see the vast refuse, and the unclean channel, and the whited sepulchre.

But what come after these I am even ashamed to tell, the disagreeable eructations, the vomitings, the discharges downwards and upwards.

But go and see even these desires dead there, and those more violent lusts that spring from these; I mean, those of impurity. For these too thou wilt see all overthrown, with their horses, with their beasts of burden. For the beast of burden, and the weapon, and the horse of a filthy deed, is a filthy word. But thou wilt see such like horse and rider together, and their weapons thrown down; but here quite the contrary, and souls cast down dead. But not at their meal only is the victory of these holy men glorious, but in the other things also, in money, in glory, in envy, in all diseases of the soul.

Surely does not this host seem to thee mightier than that, and the meal better? Nay, who will gainsay it? None, not even of those

persons themselves, though he be very mad. For this guides us on to Heaven, that drags to hell; this the devil lays out, that Christ; for this luxury gives laws, and intemperance, for that self-denial and sobriety, here Christ is present, there the devil. For where there is drunkenness, the devil is there; where there are filthy words, where there is surfeiting, there the devils hold their choirs. Such a table had that rich man, therefore not even of a drop of water was he master.

But these have not such a table, but they already practise the ways of the angels. They marry not, they are not given in marriage, neither do they sleep excessively, nor live luxuriously, but except a few things they are even bodiless.

Now who is there that so easily overcomes his enemies as he that sets up a trophy while at his dinner? Therefore also the prophet saith, "Thou hast prepared a table before me, in the presence of them that trouble me." [1] One could not be wrong in repeating this oracle about this table. For nothing so troubles a soul as disorderly concupiscence, and luxury, and drunkenness, and the evils that spring from these; and this they know full well who have had experience thereof.

And if thou wast to learn also, whence this table is procured, and whence that; then thou wouldest see well the difference between each. Whence then is this procured. From countless tears, from widows defrauded, from orphans despoiled; but the other from honest labor. And this table is like to a fair and well-favored woman, needing nothing external, but having her beauty from nature; but that to some ugly and ill-favored harlot, wearing much paint, but not able to disguise her deformity, but the nearer she is, the more convicted. For this too, when it is nearer to him that is at it, then shows its ugliness more. For look not I tell thee, at the banqueters, as they come only, but also as they go away, and then thou wilt see its ugliness. For that, as being free, suffers them that come unto it to say nothing shameful; but this nothing seemly, as being a harlot, and dishonored. This seeks the profit of him that is at it, that the hurt. And one permits not to offend God, the other permits not but that we must offend Him.

Let us go away therefore unto those men. Thence we shall learn with how many bonds we are encompassed. Thence shall we learn to set before ourselves a table full of countless blessings, most sweet, without cost, delivered from care, free from envy and jealousy and every disease, and full of good hope, and having its many trophies. No turmoil of soul there, no sorrow, no wrath; all is calm, all is peace.

For tell me not of the silence of them that serve in the houses of the rich, but of the clamor of them that dine; I mean, not that which they make one to another (for this too is worthy of derision), but that within, that in the soul, that brings on them a great captivity, the tumults of the thoughts, the sleet, the darkness, the tempest, by which all things are mingled and confused, and are like to some night battle. But not in the monks' tents are such things as these; but great is the calm, great the quietness. And that table is succeeded by a sleep that is like death, but this by sobriety and wakefulness; that by punishment, this by the kingdom of heaven, and the immortal rewards.

This then let us follow, that we may enjoy also the fruits thereof; unto which God grant we may all attain, by the grace and love towards man of our Lord Jesus Christ, to whom be glory and might world without end. Amen.

HOMILY LXXI.

MATT. XXII. 34—36.

"But when the Pharisees had heard that He had put the Sadducees to silence, they were gathered together; and one of them, which was a lawyer, asked Him a question, tempting Him, and saying, Master, which is the great commandment in the law?"

AGAIN doth the evangelist express the cause, for which they ought to have held their peace, and marks their boldness by this also. How and in what way? Because when those others were put to silence, these again assail Him. For when they ought even for this to hold their peace, they strive to urge further their former endeavors,[1] and put forward the lawyer, not desiring to learn, but making a trial of Him, and ask, "What is the first commandment?"

For since the first commandment was this, "Thou shalt love the Lord thy God," thinking that He would afford them some handle, as though He would amend it, for the sake of showing that Himself too was God, they propose the question. What then saith Christ? Indicating from what they were led to this; from having no charity, from pining with envy, from being seized by jealousy, He saith, "Thou shalt love the Lord thy God. This is the first and great commandment.[2] And the second is like unto this,[3] Thou shalt love thy neighbor as thyself."[4]

But wherefore "like unto this?" Because this makes the way for that, and by it is again established; "For every one that doeth evil hateth the light, neither cometh to the light;"[5] and again, "The fool hath said in his heart, There is no God." And what in consequence of this? "They are corrupt, and become abominable in their ways."[6] And again, "The love of money is the root of all evils; which while some coveted after, they have erred from the faith;"[7] and, "He that loveth me, will keep my commandments."[8]

But His commandments, and the sum of them, are, "Thou shalt love the Lord thy God, and thy neighbor as thyself." If therefore to love God is to love one's neighbor, "For if thou lovest me," He saith, "O Peter, feed my sheep,"[9] but to love one's neighbor worketh a keeping of the commandments, with reason doth He say, "On these hang all the law and the prophets."[10]

So therefore what He did before, this He doth here also. I mean, that both there, when asked about the manner of the resurrection, He also taught a resurrection, instruct-

---

[1] ἐπαγωνίζονται τοῖς προτέροις.
[2] [R. V., following a different reading, "great and first."]
[3] [The text varies from the received slightly, as well as from the reading accepted in the R. V.—R.]
[4] Matt. xxii. 37-39.

[5] John iii. 20.　　[6] Ps. liii. 1.　　[7] 1 Tim. vi. 10.
[8] John xiv. 15. [The paraphrase given above confirms the rendering of the R. V., "If ye love me, ye will keep my commandments."—R.]
[9] John xxi. 16, 17.　　[10] Matt. xxii. 40.

ing them beyond what they inquired; and here, being asked the first commandment, He rehearses the second also, which is not much inferior to that (for though second, it is like that), intimating to them, whence the question had arisen, that it was from hatred. "For charity envieth not."[1] By this He shows Himself to be submissive both to the law and to the prophets.

But wherefore doth Matthew say that he asked, tempting Him, but Mark the contrary? "For when Jesus," he saith, "saw that he answered discreetly, He said unto him, Thou art not far from the kingdom of God."[2]

They are not contradicting each other, but indeed fully agreeing. For he asked indeed, tempting, at the beginning, but being benefitted by the answer, was commended. For not at the beginning did He commend him, but when he had said, "That to love his neighbor is more than whole burnt sacrifices," then He saith, "Thou art not far from the kingdom;" because he overlooked low things, and embraced the first principle of virtue. For indeed all those are for the sake of this, as well the Sabbath as the rest.

And not even so did He make His commendation perfect, but yet deficient. For His saying, "Thou art not far off," indicates that he is yet falling short, that he might seek after what was deficient.

But if, when He said, "There is one God, and there is none other but He," He commended him, wonder not, but by this too observe, how He answers according to the opinion of them that come unto Him. For although men say ten thousand things about Christ unworthy of His glory, yet this at any rate they will not dare to say, that He is not God at all. Wherefore then doth He praise him that said, that beside the Father, there is no other God?

Not excepting Himself from being God; away with the thought; but since it was not yet time to disclose His Godhead, He suffers him to remain in the former doctrine, and praises him for knowing well the ancient principles, so as to make him fit for the doctrine of the New Testament, which He is bringing in its season.

And besides, the saying, "There is one God, and there is none other but He," both in the Old Testament, and everywhere, is spoken not to the rejection of the Son, but to make the distinction from idols. So that when praising this man also, who had thus spoken, He praises him in this mind.

Then since He had answered, He asks also in turn, "What think ye of Christ, whose Son is He? They say unto Him, The Son of David."[3]

See after how many miracles, after how many signs, after how many questions, after how great a display of His unanimity with the Father, as well in words, as in deeds; after having praised this man that said, that there is one God, He asks the question, that they may not be able to say, that He did miracles indeed, yet was an adversary to the law, and a foe to God.

Therefore, after so many things, He asks these questions, secretly leading them on to confess Him also to be God. And the disciples He asked first what the others say, and then themselves; but these not so; for surely they would have said a deceiver, and a wicked one, as speaking all things without fear. So for this cause He inquires for the opinion of these men themselves.

For since He was now about to go on to His passion, He sees forth the prophecy that plainly proclaims Him to be Lord; and not as having come to do this without occasion, nor as having made this His aim, but from a reasonable cause.

For having asked them first, since they answered not the truth concerning Him (for they said He was a mere man), to overthrow their mistaken opinion, He thus introduces David proclaiming His Godhead. For they indeed supposed that He was a mere man, wherefore also they said, "the Son of David;"[4] but He to correct this brings in the prophet witnessing to His being Lord, and the genuineness of His Sonship, and His equality in honor with His Father.

And not even at this doth He stop, but in order to move them to fear, He adds what followeth also, saying, "Till I make Thine enemies Thy footstool;"[5] that at least in this way He might gain them over.

And that they may not say, that it was in flattery he so called Him, and that this was a human judgment, see what He saith, "How then doth David in spirit call Him Lord?" See how submissively He introduces the sentence and judgment concerning Himself. First, He had said, "What think ye? Whose Son is He?" so by a question to bring them to an answer. Then since they said, "the Son of David," He said not, "And yet David saith these things," but again in this order of a question, "How then

---

3 Matt. xxii. 42. [R. V., "the Christ."]
4 It may be in this view that it is said of St. Paul, immediately on his conversion, that "he preached Christ in the synagogues, that He is the Son of God." Acts ix. 20.
5 Matt. xxii. 43. [The form is that of the received text. R. V., following strongly preponderant authority, "underneath thy feet."—R.]

doth David in spirit call Him Lord?" in order that the sayings might not give offense to them. Wherefore neither did He say, What think ye of me, but of Christ. For this reason the apostles also reasoned submissively, saying, "Let us speak freely of the Patriarch David, that he is both dead and buried."[1]

And He Himself too in like manner for this cause introduces the doctrine in the way of question and inference, saying, "How then doth David in spirit call Him Lord, saying, The Lord said unto my Lord, Sit Thou on my right hand, until I make Thy foes Thy footstool;"[2] and again, "If David then call Him Lord, how is He then his Son,"[3] not taking away the fact that He is his Son, away with the thought; for He would not then have reproved Peter for this,[4] but to correct their secret thoughts. So that when He saith, "How is He his Son?" He meaneth this, not so as ye say. For they said, that He is Son only, and not also Lord. And this after the testimony, and then submissively, "If David then call Him Lord, how is He his Son?"

But, nevertheless, even when they had heard these things, they answered nothing, for neither did they wish to learn any of the things that were needful. Wherefore He Himself addeth and saith, that "He is his Lord." Or rather not even this very thing doth He say without support, but having taken the prophet with Him, because of His being exceedingly distrusted by them, and evil reported of amongst them. To which fact we ought to have especial regard, and if anything be said by Him that is lowly and submissive, not to be offended, for the cause is this, with many other things also, that He talks with them in condescension.

Wherefore now also He delivers His doctrine in the manner of question and answer; but He darkly intimates even in this way His dignity. For it was not as much to be called Lord of the Jews, as of David.

But mark thou also, I pray thee, how seasonable it is. For when He had said, "There is one Lord," then He spake of Himself that He is Lord, and showed it by prophecy, no more by His works only. And He showeth the Father Himself taking vengeance upon them in His behalf, for He saith, "Until I make Thine enemies Thy footstool," and great unanimity even hereby on the part of Him that begat Him towards Himself, and honor. And upon His reasonings with them He doth set this end high and

great, and sufficient to close fast their mouths.

For they were silent from thenceforth, not willingly, but from their having nothing to say; and they received so deadly a blow, as no longer to dare to attempt the same things any more. For, "no one," it is said, "durst from that day forth ask Him any more questions."[5]

And this was no little advantage to the multitude.[6] Therefore also unto them doth He henceforth direct His word, having removed the wolves, and having repulsed their plots.

For those men gained nothing, taken captive by vainglory, and having fallen upon this terrible passion. For terrible is this passion and many-headed, for some set their heart upon power for the sake of this, some on wealth, some on strength. But proceeding in order it goes on unto almsgiving also, and fasting, and prayers, and teaching, and many are the heads of this monster.

But to be vainglorious indeed about those other things is nothing wonderful; but to be so about fasting and prayer, this is strange and lamentable.

But that we may not again blame only, come and let us tell the means, by which we shall avoid this. Against whom shall we prepare to contend first, against those that are vainglorious of money, or those of dress, or those of places of power, or those of sciences, or those of art, or those of their person, or those of beauty, or those of ornaments, or those of cruelty, or those of humanity and almsgiving, or those of wickedness, or those of death, or those after death? For indeed, as I have said, this passion hath many links,[7] and goes on beyond our life. For such a one, it is said, is dead, and that he may be held in admiration, hath charged that such and such things be done; and therefore such a one is poor, such a one rich.

For the grievous thing is this, that even of opposite things is it made up.

Against whom then shall we stand, and let ourselves in array first? For one and the same discourse suffices not against all. Will ye then that it be against them that are vainglorious about almsgiving?

To me at least it seems well; for exceedingly do I love this thing, and am pained at seeing it marred, and vainglory plotting against it, like a pandering nurse against some royal damsel. For she feeds her in-

---

[1] Acts ii. 29.　　[2] Matt. xxii. 44.　　[3] Matt. xxii. 45.
[4] For being unwilling to admit what belonged to His Humanity; Matt. xvi. 22, 23.

[5] Matt. xxii. 46.
[6] See the parallel place, Mark xii. 37, where it is added, " The common people heard Him gladly." [R. V., margin, "or, the great multitude," etc.]
[7] πλεκτάνας.

28

deed, but for disgrace and mischief, prosti-tuting her and commanding her to despise her father; but to deck herself to please un-holy and often despicable men; and invests her with such a dress, as strangers wish, dis-graceful, and dishonorable, not such as the father.

Come now, then, let us take our aim against these; and let there be an almsgiving made in abundance for display to the multitude. Surely then, first vainglory leads her out of her Father's chamber. And whereas her Father requires not to appear so much as to the left hand,[1] she displays her to the slaves, and to the vulgar, that have not even known her.

Seest thou a harlot, and pander, casting her into the love of foolish men, that accord-ing as they require, so she may order herself? Dost thou desire to see how it renders such a soul not a harlot only, but insane also?

Mark then her mind. For when she lets go heaven and runs after fugitives and menial slaves, pursuing through streets and lanes them that hate her, the ugly and deformed, them that are not willing so much as to look at her, them that, when she burns with love towards them, hate her, what can be more insane than this? For no one do the multi-tude hate so much, as those that want the glory they have to bestow. Countless accu-sations at least do they frame against them, and the result is the same, as if any one were to bring down a virgin daughter of the king from the royal throne, and to require her to prostitute herself to gladiators, who abhorred her. These then, as much as thou pursuest them, so much do they turn away from thee; but God, if thou seek the glory that cometh from Him, so much the more both draws thee unto Himself, and commends thee, and great is the reward He renders unto thee.

But if thou art minded in another way also to discern the mischief thereof, when thou givest for display and ostentation, consider how great the sorrow that then comes upon thee, and how continual the desponding, while Christ's voice is heard in thine ears, saying,[2] "Thou hast lost all thy reward." For in every matter indeed vainglory is a bad thing, yet most of all in beneficence, for it is the utmost cruelty, making a show of the calami-ties of others, and all but upbraiding those in poverty. For if to mention one's own good actions is to upbraid, what dost thou think it is to publish them even to many others.

How then shall we escape the danger? If we learn how to give alms, if we see after whose good report we are to seek. For tell me, who has the skill of almsgiving? Plainly, it is God, who hath made known the thing, who best of all knows it, and practises it without limit. What then? If thou art learning to be a wrestler, to whom dost thou look? or to whom dost thou display thy doings in the wrestling school, to the seller of herbs, and of fish, or to the trainer? And ye they are many, and he is one. What then, if while the admires thee, others deride thee, wilt thou not with him deride them?

What, if thou art learning to box, wilt thou not look in like manner to him who knows how to teach this?

And if thou art practising oratory, wilt thou not accept the praise of the teacher of rhet-oric, and despise the rest.

How then is it other than absurd, in other arts to look to the teacher only, but here to do the contrary? although the loss be not equal. For there, if you wrestle according to the opinion of the multitude, and not that of the teacher, the loss is in the wrestling; but here it is in eternal life. Thou art become like to God in giving alms; be thou then like Him in not making a display. For even He said, when healing, that they should tell no man.

But dost thou desire to be called merciful amongst men? And what is the gain? The gain is nothing; but the loss infinite. For these very persons, whom thou callest to be witnesses, become robbers of thy treasures that are in the heavens; or rather not these, but ourselves, who spoil our own possessions, and scatter what we have laid up above.

O new calamity! this strange passion. Where moth corrupteth not, nor thief break-eth through, vainglory scattereth. This is the moth of those treasures there; this the thief of our wealth in heaven; this steals away the riches that cannot be spoiled; this mars and corrupts all. For because the devil saw that that place is impregnable to thieves and to the worm, and the other plots against them, he by vainglory steals away the wealth.

But dost thou desire glory? Doth not then that suffice thee which is given by the receiver himself, that from our gracious God, but dost thou set thine heart on that from men also? Take heed, lest thou undergo the contrary, lest some condemn thee as not showing mercy, but making a display, and seeking honor, as making a show of the calamities of others.

For indeed the showing of mercy is a mys-tery. Shut therefore the doors, that none may see what it is not pious to display. For our mysteries too are above all things, a

---

[1] Matt. vi. 3.   [2] Matt. vi. 1.

showing of God's mercy and loving-kindness. According to His great mercy, He had mercy on us being disobedient.

And the first prayer too is full of mercy, when we entreat for the energumens; and the second again, for others under penance seeking for much mercy; and the third also for ourselves, and this puts forward the innocent children of the people entreating God for mercy. For since we condemn ourselves for sins, for them that have sinned much and deserve to be blamed we ourselves cry; but for ourselves the children; for the imitators of whose simplicity the kingdom of heaven is reserved. For this image shows this, that they who are like those children, lowly and simple, these above all men are able to deliver the guilty by their prayers.

But the mystery itself, of how much mercy, of how much love to man it is full, the initiated know.

Do thou then, when according to thy power thou art showing mercy to a man, shut the doors, let the object of thy mercy see it only; but if it be possible, not even he. But if thou set them open, thou art profanely exposing thy mystery.

Consider that the very person, whose praise thou seekest, even himself will condemn thee;

and if he be a friend, will accuse thee to himself; but if an enemy, he will deride thee unto others also. And thou wilt undergo the opposite of what thou desirest. For thou indeed desirest that he should call thee the merciful man; but he will not call thee this, but the vainglorious, the man-pleaser, and other names far more grievous than these.

But if thou shouldest hide it, he will call thee all that is opposite to this; the merciful, the kind. For God suffers it not to be hidden; but if thou conceal it, the other will make it known, and greater will be the admiration, and more abundant the gain. So that even for this very object of being glorified, to make a display is against us; for with respect to the thing unto which we most hasten and press, as to this most especially is this thing against us. For so far from obtaining the credit of being merciful, we obtain even the contrary, and besides this, great is the loss we undergo.

For every motive then let us abstain from this, and set our love on God's praise alone. For thus shall we both attain to honor here, and enjoy the eternal blessings, by the grace and love towards man of our Lord Jesus Christ, to whom be glory and might world without end. Amen.

HOMILY LXXII.

MATT. XXIII. 1—3.

" Then spake Jesus to the multitudes and to His disciples, saying, The Scribes and the Pharisees sit in Moses' seat: all therefore whatsoever they bid you do, that do;[1] but do not after their works."

THEN. When? When He had said these things, when He had stopped their mouths; when He had brought them that they should no more dare to tempt Him; when He had shown their state incurable.

And since He had made mention of " the Lord " and " my Lord,"[2] He recurs again to the law. And yet the law said nothing of this kind, but, " The Lord thy God is one

Lord."[3] But Scripture calls the whole Old Testament the law.

But these things He saith, showing by all things His full agreement with Him that begat Him. For if He were opposed, He would have said the opposite about the law; but now He commands so great reverence to be shown towards it, that, even when they that teach it are depraved, He charges them to hold to it.

But here He is discoursing about their life

---

[1] [The Greek text in this clause differs somewhat both from the received and from that followed in the R. V.—R.]

[2] [κυρίου καὶ κυρίου, referring to the two uses of the word in the Old Testament passage cited in Matt. xxii. 44, but not in precise terms.—R.]

[3] Deut. vi. 4.

and morals, since this was chiefly the cause of their unbelief, their depraved life, and the love of glory. To amend therefore His hearers; that which in the first place most contributes to salvation, not to despise our teachers, neither to rise up against our priests, this doth He command with superabundant earnestness. But He does not only command it, but also Himself doth it. For though they were depraved, He doth not depose them from their dignity; to them rendering their condemnation heavier, and to His disciples leaving no cloke for disobedience.

I mean, that lest any one should say, that because my teacher is bad, therefore am I become more remiss, He takes away even this pretext. So much at any rate did He establish their authority, although they were wicked men, as even after so heavy an accusation to say, "All whatsoever they command you to do, do." For they speak not their own words, but God's, what He appointed for laws by Moses. And mark how much honor He showed towards Moses, again showing His agreement with the Old Testament, since indeed even by this doth He make them objects of reverence. "For they sit," He saith, "on Moses' seat." For because He was not able to make them out worthy of credit by their life, He doth it from the grounds that were open to Him, from their seat, and their succession from him. But when thou hearest all, do not understand all the law, as, for instance, the ordinances about meats, those about sacrifices, and the like; for how was He to say so of these things, which He had taken away beforehand? but He meant all things that correct the moral principle, and amend the disposition, and agree with the laws of the New Testament, and suffer them not any more to be under the yoke of the law.

Wherefore then doth He give these things divine authority, not from the law of grace, but from Moses? Because it was not yet time, before the crucifixion, for these things to be plainly declared.

But to me He seems, in addition to what has been said, to be providing for another object, in saying these things. For since He was on the point of accusing them, that He might not seem in the sight of the foolish to set His heart on this authority of theirs, or for enmity to be doing these things, first He removed this thought, and having set himself clear from suspicion, then begins His accusation. And for what intent doth He convict them, and run out into a long discourse against them? To set the multitude on their guard, so that they might not fall into the

same sins. For neither is dissuading like pointing out those that have offended; much as recommending what is right, is not like bringing forward those that have done well. For this cause also He is beforehand in saying, "Do not after their works." For, lest they should suppose, because of their listening to them, they ought also to imitate them, He uses this means of correction, and makes what seems to be their dignity a charge against them. For what can be more wretched than a teacher, when the preservation of his disciples is, not to give heed to his life? So that what seemeth to be their dignity is a most heavy charge against them, when they are shown to live such a life, as they that imitate are ruined.

For this cause He also falls upon His accusations against them, but not for this only, but that He might show, that both their former unbelief wherewith they had not believed, and the crucifixion after this, which they dared to perpetrate, were not a charge against Him who was crucified and disbelieved, but against their perverseness.

But see whence He begins, and whence He aggravates His blame of them. "For they say," He saith, "and do not." For every one is worthy of blame in transgressing the law, but especially he that bears the authority of teaching, for doubly and triply doth he deserve to be condemned. For one cause, because he transgresses; for another, that as he ought to amend others, and then halteth, he is worthy of a double punishment, because of his dignity; and in the third place, that he even corrupts the more, as committing such transgression in a teacher's place.

And together with these He mentions also another charge against them, that they are harsh to those accountable to them.

"For they bind heavy burdens, and grievous to be borne, and lay them on men's shoulders, but they will not move them with their finger."[1] He mentions here a twofold wickedness, their requiring great and extreme strictness of life, without any indulgence, from those over whom they rule, and their allowing to themselves great security; the opposite to which the truly good ruler ought to hold; in what concerns himself, to be an unpardoning and severe judge, but in the matters of those whom he rules, to be gentle and ready to make allowances; the contrary to which was the conduct of these men.

2. For such are all they who practise self restraint in mere words, unpardoning and grievous to bear as having no experience of

---

[1] Matt. xxiii. 4. [" For," as in rec. text.]

the difficulty in actions. And this itself too is no small fault, and in no ordinary way increases the former charge.

But do thou mark, I pray thee, how He aggravates this accusation also. For He did not say, "they cannot," but, "they will not." And He did not say, "to bear," but, "to move with a finger," that is, not even to come near them, nor to touch them.

But wherein are they earnest, and vigorous? In the things forbidden. For, "all their works they do," He saith, "to be seen of men."[1] These things He saith, accusing them in respect of vainglory, which kind of thing was their ruin. For the things before were signs of harshness and remissness, but these of the mad desire of glory. This drew them off from God, this caused them to strive before other spectators, and ruined them. For whatever kind of spectators any one may have, since it hath become his study to please these, such also are the contests he exhibits. And he that wrestles among the noble, such also are the conflicts he takes in hand, but he among the cold and supine, himself also becomes more remiss. For instance, hath any one a beholder that delights in ridicule? he himself too becomes a mover of ridicule, that he may delight the spectator: hath another one who is earnest minded, and practises self-government? he endeavors himself to be such as he is, since such is the disposition of him who praises him.

But see again that here too the charge is with aggravation. For neither is it that they do some things in this way, some in another way, but all things absolutely this way.

Then, having blamed them for vainglory, He shows that it is not even about great and necessary things they are vainglorious (for neither had they these, but were destitute of good works), but for things without warmth or worth, and such as were certain proofs of their baseness, the phylacteries, the borders of their garments. "For they make broad their phylacteries," He saith, "and enlarge the borders of their garments."[1]

And what are these phylacteries, and these borders? Since they were continually forgetting God's benefits, He commanded His marvellous works to be inscribed on little tablets, and that these should be suspended from their hands (wherefore also He said, "They shall be immoveable in thine eyes "),[2] which they called phylacteries; as many of our women now wear Gospels hung from their necks.

And in order that by another thing again

they may be reminded, like as many often do, binding round their finger with a piece of linen or a thread, as being likely to forget, this God enjoined them as children to do, "to sew a ribbon of blue on their garments, upon the fringe that hung round their feet, that they might look at it, and remember the commandments; "[3] and they were called "borders."

In these things then they were diligent, making wide the strips of the tablets, and enlarging the borders of their garments; which was a sign of the most extreme vanity. For wherefore art thou vainglorious, and dost make these wide? what, is this thy good work? what doth it profit thee at all, if thou gain not the good results from them. For God seeks not the enlarging of these and making them wide, but our remembering His benefits. But if for almsgiving and prayer, although they be attended with labor, and be good deeds on our parts, we must not seek vainglory, how dost thou, O Jew, pride thyself in these things, which most of all convict thy remissness.

But they not in these only, but in other little things, suffered from this disease.

For, "they love," He saith, "the uppermost rooms [4] at feasts, and the chief seats in the synagogues, and greetings in the markets, and to be called of men, Rabbi."[5] For these things, although one may think them small, yet are they a cause of great evils. These things have overthrown both cities and churches.

And it comes upon me now even to weep, when I hear of the first seats, and the greetings, and consider how many ills were hence engendered to the churches of God, which it is not necessary to publish to you now; nay rather as many as are aged men do not even need to learn these things from us.[6]

But mark thou, I pray thee, how vainglory prevailed; when they were commanded not to be vainglorious, even in the synagogues, where they had entered to discipline others.

For to have this feeling at feasts, to howsoever great a degree, doth not seem to be so dreadful a thing; although even there the teachers ought to be held in reverence, and not in the church only, but everywhere. And like as a man, wherever he may appear, is manifestly distinguished from the brutes; so also ought the teacher, both speaking and

---

[1] Matt. xxiii. 5.
[2] Deut. vi. 8; so LXX. A. V. "as frontlets between."

[3] Numb. xv. 38, 39. [The passage is freely given from the LXX.]
[4] [R. V., "the chief place."]
[5] With the oldest New Testament MSS. the word "Rabbi" is not repeated.—R.]
[6] This passage has afforded grounds for a conjecture as to the date of the Homily, but the language is too general to prove anything; see Montfaucon's Preface.

holding his peace, and dining, and doing whatever it may be, to be distinguished as well by his gait, as by his look, and by his garb, and by all things generally. But they were on every account objects of ridicule, and in every respect disgraced themselves, making it their study to follow what they ought to flee. For they love them, it is said; but if the loving them be a matter of blame, what a thing must the doing them be; and to hunt and strive after them, how great an evil.

3. The other things then He carried no further than to accuse them, as being small and trifling, and as though His disciples needed not at all to be corrected about these matters; but what was a cause of all the evils, even ambition, and the violent seizing of the teacher's chair, this He brings forward, and corrects with diligence, touching this vehemently and earnestly charging them.

For what saith He? " But be not ye called Rabbi." Then follows the cause also; " For one is your master, and all ye are brethren;"[1] and one hath nothing more than another, in respect of his knowing nothing from himself. Wherefore Paul also saith, " For who is Paul, and who is Apollos, but ministers?"[2] He said not masters. And again, " Call not, father,"[3] not that they should not call, but they may know whom they ought to call Father, in the highest sense. For like as the master is not a master principally; so neither is the father. For He is cause of all, both of the masters, and of the fathers.

And again He adds, " Neither be ye called guides, for one is your guide, even Christ;"[4] and He said not, I. For like as above He said, " What think ye of Christ?"[5] and He said not, " of me," so here too.

But I should be glad to ask here, what they would say, who are repeatedly applying the term one, one, to the Father alone, to the rejection of the Only-begotten. Is the Father guide? All would declare it, and none would gainsay it. And yet " one," He saith, " is your guide, even Christ." For like as Christ, being called the one guide, casts not out the Father from being guide; even so the Father, being called Master, doth not cast out the Son from being Master. For the expression, one, one, is spoken in contradistinction to men, and the rest of the creation.

Having warned them therefore against this grievous pest, and amended them, He instructs also how they may escape it; by

humility. Wherefore He adds also, " He that is greatest among you shall be your servant. For whosoever shall exalt himself shall be abased, and whosoever shall abase himself shall be exalted."[6]

For nothing is equal to the practice of modesty, wherefore He is continually reminding them of this virtue, both when He brought the children into the midst, and now. And, when on the mount, beginning the beatitudes, He began from hence. And in this place, He plucks it up by the roots hereby, saying, " He that abaseth himself shall be exalted."

Seest thou how He draws off the hearer right over to the contrary thing. For not only doth He forbid him to set his heart upon the first place, but requires him to follow after the last. For so shalt thou obtain thy desire, He saith. Wherefore he that pursues his desire for the first, must folllow after the last place. " For he that abaseth himself shall be exalted."

And where shall we find this humility? Will ye that we go again to the city of virtue, the tents of the holy men, the mountains. I mean, and the groves? For there too shall we see this height of humility.

For men, some illustrious from their rank in the world, some from their wealth, in every way put themselves down, by their vesture, by their dwelling, by those to whom they minister; and, as in written characters, they throughout all things inscribe humility.

And the things that are incentives of arrogance, as to dress well, and to build houses splendidly, and to have many servants, things which often drive men even against their will to arrogance; these are all taken away. For they themselves light their fire, they themselves cleave the logs, themselves cook, themselves minister to those that come there.

No one can be heard insulting there, nor seen insulted, nor commanded, nor giving commands; but all are devoted to those that are waited on, and every one washes the strangers' feet, and there is much contention about this. And he doeth it, not inquiring who it is, neither if he be a slave, nor if he be free; but in the case of every one fulfills this service. No man there is great nor mean. What then? Is there confusion? Far from it, but the highest order. For if any one be mean, he that is great seeth not this, but hath accounted himself again to be inferior even to him, and so becomes great.

There is one table for all, both for them that are served, and for them that serve; the

---

[1] Matt. xxiii. 8.   [2] 1 Cor. iii. 5.   [3] Matt. xxiii. 9.
[4] Matt. xxiii. 10. [The word καθηγητής is rendered " Master" in our English versions, but " guide" is more literal; " the Christ " (R. V.), is preferable, especially in view of the context here.— R.]
[5] Matt. xxii. 42. [R. V., " the Christ."]

[6] Matt. xxiii. 11, 12. [R. V. " humbled," and " humble." The A. V. here uses both "abase " and "humble."—R.]

same food, the same clothes, the same dwellings, the same manner of life. He is great there, who eagerly seizes the mean task. There is not mine and thine, but this expression is exterminated, that is a cause of countless wars.

4. And why dost thou marvel, if there be one manner of life and table and dress for all, since indeed there is even one soul to all, not in substance only (for this is with all men also), but in love? how then should it ever be lifted up itself against itself? There is no wealth and poverty there, honor and dishonor; how then should haughtiness and arrogance find an entrance? For they are indeed little and great in respect of their virtue; but, as I have said, no one seeth this. He that is little, feels not pain, as despised; for neither is there any one to despise him; and should any one spurn him, this above all are they taught, to be despised, to be spurned, to be set at nought, in word and in deed. And with the poor and maimed do they associate, and their tables are full of these guests; so that for this are they worthy of the heavens. And one tends the wounds of the mutilated, another leads the blind by the hand, a third bears him that is lamed of his leg.

There is no multitude of flatterers or parasites there; or rather they know not even what flattery is; whence then could they be lifted up at any time? For there is great equality amongst them, wherefore also there is much facility for virtue.

For by these are they of an inferior sort better instructed, than if they were compelled to give up the first place to them.

For like as the impetuous man derives instruction from him that is smitten, and submits to it; so the ambitious from him that claims not glory, but despises it. This they do there abundantly, and as the strife is great with us to obtain the first place, so great is it with them not to obtain it, but utterly to refuse it; and great is their earnest desire who shall have the advantage in honoring, not in being honored.

And besides, even their very employments persuade them to practise moderation, and not to be high-swollen. For who, I pray thee, digging in the earth, and watering, and planting, or making baskets, or weaving sackcloth, or practising any other handy works, will ever be proud? Who dwelling in poverty and wrestling with hunger, will ever be sick of this disease? There is not one. Therefore humility is easy to them. And like as here, it is a hard thing to be lowly minded, for the multitude of them who applaud and admire us, so there it is exceedingly easy.

And that man gives heed only to the wilderness, and sees birds flying, and trees waving, and a breeze blowing, and streams rushing through glens. Whence then should he be lifted up who dwells in solitude so great?

Not however that therefore we have from this an excuse, in that we are proud when living in the midst of men. For surely Abraham, when amidst Canaanites, said, "I am but dust and ashes;"[1] and David, when in the midst of camps,[2] "I am a worm, and no man;"[3] and the apostle, in the midst of the world, "I am not meet to be called an apostle."[4] What comfort shall we have then; what plea, when even, having such great examples, we do not practise moderation? For even as they are worthy of countless crowns, having been the first that went the way of virtue, even so are we deserving of countless punishments, who not even after those that are departed, and are set before us in books, no nor even after these that are living, and held in admiration through their deeds, are drawn on to the like emulation.

For what couldest thou say, for not being amended? Art thou ignorant of letters, and hast not looked into the Scriptures that thou mightest learn the virtues of them of old? To say the truth, this is itself blameworthy, when the church is constantly standing open, not to enter in, and partake of those sacred streams.

However, although thou know not the departed by the Scriptures, these living men thou oughtest to see. But is there no one to lead thee? Come to me, and I will show thee the places of refuge of these holy men; come and learn thou of them something useful. Shining lamps are these in every part of the earth; as walls are they set about the cities. For this cause have they occupied the deserts, that they may instruct thee to despise the tumults in the midst of the world.

For they, as being strong, are able even in the midst of the raging of the waters to enjoy a calm; but thou, who art leaky on every side, hast need of tranquility, and to take breath a little, after the successive waves. Go then there continually, that, having purged away the abiding stain by their prayers and admonitions, thou mayest both pass in the best manner the present life, and attain unto the good things to come, by the grace and love towards man of our Lord Jesus Christ, by whom and with whom, be unto the Father, together with the Holy Ghost, glory, might, honor, now and ever, and world without end. Amen.

---

[1] Gen. xviii. 27.
[2] Or, "courts." [στρατοπέδοις; in earlier Greek "camps," but in Byzantine Greek applied to the suite of the Emperor.—R.]
[3] Ps. xxii. 6.   [4] 1 Cor. xv. 9.

HOMILY LXXIII.

MATT. XXIII. 14.

"Woe unto you, Scribes and Pharisees, hypocrites! for ye devour widows' houses, and for a pretense make long prayers: therefore ye shall receive greater damnation."

AFTER this, next He derides them for gluttony: and the grievous thing was, that not from rich men's goods, but from the poor they indulged their own belly, and aggravated their poverty, which they should have relieved. For neither did they merely eat, but devoured.

Moreover also the manner of their overreaching was yet more grievous, "for a pretense making long prayers."

For every one is worthy of vengeance who doeth any evil thing; but he that is deriving even the reason for so doing from godliness, and is using this cloke for his wickedness, is justly liable to a far more grievous punishment. And wherefore did He not depose them? Because the time suffered it not as yet. So therefore He lets them alone for a time, but by His sayings, He secures that the people be not deceived, lest, through the dignity of those men, they be drawn on to the same emulation.

For as He had said, "Whatsoever they bid you do, that do;" He shows how many things they do amiss, lest from thence He should be supposed amongst the unwise to commit all to them.

"Woe unto you, for ye shut up the kingdom against men; for ye neither go in yourselves, neither suffer ye them that are entering to go in."[2] But if to profit no one be a charge against a man, even to hurt and hinder, what plea hath that? But what means, "them that are entering in?" Them that are fit for it. For when they were to lay injunctions on others, they used to make the burdens intolerable, but when they themselves were to do any of the things required, on the contrary, so far from doing anything, they went much beyond this in wickedness, they even used to corrupt others. These are they that are called pests,[3] who make their employment the ruin of others, standing right contrary to teachers. For if it be the part of a teacher to save that which is perishing, to destroy that which is on the point of being saved is that of a destroyer.

After this, again another charge: "Ye compass sea and land to make one proselyte, and when he is made, ye make him twofold more the child of hell than yourselves;"[4] that is, not even the fact that hardly ye have taken him, and with endless toils, induces you to be sparing towards him, although of the things we have hardly acquired, we are more sparing, but you not even this renders more gentle.

Here He lays to their charge two things; one, that they are unprofitable for the salvation of the many, and need much toil in order to win over even one; another, that they were remiss in the preservation of him whom they had gained, or rather that they were not only careless, but even traitors, by their wickedness in their life corrupting him, and making him worse. For when the disciple sees his teachers to be such as these, he becomes worse than they. For he stops not at his teacher's wickedness; but as when his teacher is virtuous, he imitates him, so when he is bad, he even goes beyond him, by reason of our proneness to what is evil.

And He calls him "a child of hell," that is, a very hell. And He said "twofold more than you," that He might both alarm those, and make these feel the more severely, because they are teachers of wickedness. And not this only, but because they labor to instill into their disciples a greater wickedness, hardening them to a much greater depravity than they have, and this is above all a mark of a depraved soul.

Then He derides them for folly also, because they bade them disregard the greater commandments. And yet before He had said the opposite, that "they bind heavy burdens, and grievous to be borne." But these things too they did again and were doing everything for the corruption of those

---

[1] [This verse is omitted in the best authorities, and its position varies in the later MSS. and versions which give it. In this Homily it is placed before our verse 13. It is well attested in Mark xii. 40, and Luke xx. 47.—R.]

[2] Matt. xxiii. 13. [See note 1. "Of heaven" is omitted here, but in none of our New Testament authorities.—R.]

[3] λοιμοί.

[4] Matt. xxiii. 15. [R. V., "a son of hell," with the margin, "Greek, Gehenna."]

who were subject to them, in little things requiring strictness, and despising the great.

"For ye pay tithe," He saith, "of mint and anise, and have omitted[1] the weightier matters of the law, judgment, and mercy, and faith. These ought ye to have done, and not to leave the others undone."[2]

Here then He naturally saith it, where it is tithe and almsgiving, for what doth it hurt to give alms? But not to keep the law; for neither doth it say thus. Therefore here indeed He saith, "These ought ye to have done;" but where He is speaking about clean and unclean, He no longer adds this, but makes a distinction, and shows that the inward purity is necessarily followed by the outward, but the converse is no longer so.

For where there is a plea of love to man, He passes it over lightly, for this very reason, and because it was not yet time expressly and plainly to revoke the things of the law. But where it is an observance of bodily purification, He overthrows it more plainly.

So, therefore, while with respect to alms He saith, "These ought ye to have done, and not to leave the others undone," touching purifications He speaks not on this wise, but what? "Ye make clean," He saith, "the outside of the cup and the platter, but within they are full of extortion, and injustice. Cleanse that which is within the cup, that the outside may be clean also."[3] And He took it from a thing confessed and manifest, from a cup and platter.

2. Then, to show that there is no harm arising from despising bodily cleansings, but very great vengeance from not regarding the purifications of the soul, which is virtue, He called these "a gnat," for they are small and nothing, but those other a camel, for they were beyond what men could bear. Wherefore also He saith, "Straining at the gnat, and swallowing the camel."[4] For indeed the one were enacted for the sake of the other, I mean of mercy and judgment; so that not even then did they profit being done alone. For whereas the little things were mentioned for the sake of the great, and after that these last were neglected, and labor was spent on those alone, nothing was gained even then by this. For the greater followed not the lesser, but the lesser were sure to follow these greater.

But these things He saith to show, that even before grace was come, these were not among the principal things, or amongst those upon which men should spend their labor, but the matters required were different. But if before the grace they were so, much more when high commandments had come, were these things unprofitable, and it was not meet to practise them at all.

In every case then is vice a grievous thing, but especially when it does not so much as think it needs amendment; and it is yet more grievous, when it thinks itself sufficient even to amend others; to express which Christ calls them "blind guides." For if for a blind man not to think he needs a guide be extreme misery and wretchedness; when he wishes himself to guide others, see to what a gulf it leads.

But these things He said, by all intimating their mad desire of glory, and their exceeding frenzy concerning this pest. For this became a cause to them of all their evils, namely, that they did all things for display. This both led them away from the faith, and caused them to neglect what really is virtue, and induced them to busy themselves about bodily purifyings only, neglecting the purifications of the soul. So therefore to lead them into what really is virtue, and to the purifyings of the soul, He makes mention of mercy, and judgment, and faith. For these are the things that comprise our life, these are what purify the soul, justice, love to man, truth; the one inclining us to pardon[5] and not suffering us to be excessively severe and unforgiving to them that sin (for then shall we gain doubly, both becoming kind to man, and hence meeting also ourselves with much kindness from the God of all), and causing us both to sympathize with them that are despitefully entreated, and to assist them; the other not suffering them to be deceitful, and crafty.

But neither when He saith, "These ought ye to have done, and not to leave the others undone," doth He say it as introducing a legal observance; away with the thought;[6] neither with regard to the platter and the cup, when He said, "Cleanse that which is within the cup and platter, that the outside of them may be clean also," doth He bring us unto the old regard for little things, but on the contrary indeed, He doth all things to show it to be superfluous. For He said not, Cleanse the outside of them also, but that which is within, and the outside is sure to follow.

---

[1] [R. V., "have left undone."]

[2] Matt. xxiii. 23. [R. V., "to have left the others undone." "And cummin" is omitted.—R.]

[3] Matt. xxiii. 25, 26. [The minor textual variations appear in the above English rendering.]

[4] [Matt. xxiii. 24. R. V., correctly, "strain out the gnat," etc.]

[5] [The Oxford edition has "candor," probably a misprint, since the Greek term is συγγνώμην.—R.]

[6] [The clause, "for this we showed before," is omitted by the translator.—R.]

And besides, neither is it concerning a cup and platter he is speaking, but of soul and body, by the outside meaning the body, by the inside the soul. But if with regard to the platter there be need of that which is within much more with regard to thee.

But ye do the contrary, saith He, observing things trifling and external, ye neglect what are great and inward; whence very great mischief arises, for that thinking ye have duly performed all, ye despise the other things; and despising them, ye do not so much as strive or attempt to perform them.

After this, He again derides them for vainglory, calling them "whited sepulchres,"[1] and unto all adding, "ye hypocrites;" which thing is the cause of all their evils, and the origin of their ruin. And He did not merely call them whited sepulchres, but said, that they were full of uncleanness and hypocrisy. And these things He spake, indicating the cause wherefore they did not believe, because they were full of hypocrisy and iniquity.

But these things not Christ only, but the prophets also constantly lay to their charge, that they spoil, that their rulers judge not according to the rule of justice, and every where you may find the sacrifices indeed refused, but these things required. So that there is nothing strange, nothing new, neither in the lawgiving, nor in the accusation, nay not even in the comparison of the sepulchre. For the prophet makes mention thereof, neither did he call them merely a sepulchre, "but their throat an open sepulchre."[2]

Such are many men now also, decking themselves indeed outwardly, but full of iniquity within. For now too there is many a mode, and many a care for outward purifications, but of those in the soul not so much as one. But if indeed any one should tear open each man's conscience, many worms and much corruption would he find, and an ill savor beyond utterance; unreasonable and wicked lusts I mean, which are more unclean than worms.

3. But that "they" should be such persons is not "so" dreadful a thing (although it be dreadful), but that "you," that have been counted worthy to become temples of God, should of a sudden have become sepulchres, having as much ill savor, this is extreme wretchedness. He in whom Christ dwells, and the Holy Spirit hath worked, and such great mysteries, that this man should be a sepulchre, what wretchedness is this? What mournings and lamentations doth this call

for, when the members of Christ have become a tomb of uncleanness? Consider how thou wast born, of what things thou hast been counted worthy, what manner of garment thou hast received, how thou wast built a temple without a breach! how fair! not adorned with gold, neither with pearls, but with the spirit that is more precious than these.

Consider that no sepulchre is made in a city, so then neither shalt thou be able to appear in the city above. For if here this is forbidden, much more there. Or rather even here thou art an object of scorn to all, bearing about a dead soul, and not to be scorned only, but also to be shunned. For tell me, if any one were to go round, bearing about a dead body, would not all have rushed away? would not all have fled? Think this now likewise. For thou goest about, bearing a spectacle far more grievous than this, a soul deadened by sins, a soul paralyzed.

Who now will pity such a one? For when thou dost not pity thine own soul, how shall another pity him that is so cruel, such an enemy to himself?[3] If any one, where thou didst sleep and eat, had buried a dead body, what wouldest thou not have done? but thou art burying a dead soul, not where thou dinest, nor where thou sleepest, but in the members of Christ: and art thou not afraid lest a thousand lightnings and thunderbolts be hurled from above upon thine head?

And how dost thou even dare to set foot in the churches of God, and in holy temples, having within thee the savor of so much abomination? For if one bearing a dead body into the king's courts and burying it would have suffered the utmost punishment, thou setting thy foot in the sacred courts, and filling the house with so much ill savor, consider what a punishment thou wilt undergo.

Imitate that harlot who anointed with ointment the feet of Christ, and filled the whole house with the odor, the opposite to which thou doest to His house! For what though thou be not sensible of the ill savor? For this most of all is the grievous part of the disease; wherefore also thou art incurably diseased, and more grievously than they that are maimed in their bodies, and become fetid. For that disease indeed is both felt by the sick and is without any blame, nay even is deserving of pity; but this of hatred and punishment.

Since then both in this respect it is more grievous, and from the sick not being sensi-

---

[1] Matt. xxiii. 27.   [2] Ps. v. 9.   [3] [πολέμιον ὄντα ἑαυτῷ καὶ ἐχθρόν.]

ble of it as he ought to be; come, give thyself to my words, that I may teach thee plainly the mischief of it.

But first listen to what thou sayest in the Psalm, "Let my prayer be set forth in Thy sight as incense."[1] When then not incense, but a stinking smoke arises from thee, and from thy deeds, what punishment dost thou not deserve to undergo?

What then is the stinking smoke? Many come in gazing about at the beauty of women; others curious about the blooming youth of boys. After this, dost thou not marvel, how bolts are not launched, and all things are not plucked up from their foundations? For worthy both of thunderbolts and hell are the things that are done; but God, who is long-suffering, and of great mercy, forbears awhile His wrath, calling thee to repentance and amendment.

What doest thou, O man? Art thou curiously looking after women's beauty, and dost thou not shudder at thus doing despite unto the temple of God? Doth the church seem to thee a brothel, and less honorable than the market-place. For in a market-place indeed thou art afraid and ashamed to appear to be looking after any woman, but in God's temple, when God Himself is discoursing unto thee, and threatening about these things, thou art committing whoredom and adultery at the very time in which thou art being told not to do this. And dost thou not shudder, nor stand amazed?

These things do the spectacles of wantonness teach you, the pest that is so hard to put down, the deleterious sorceries, the grievous snares of the thoughtless, the pleasurable destruction of the unchaste

Therefore the prophet also blaming thee, said, "Thine eyes are not good, neither is thine heart."[2]

It were better for such men to be blind; it were better to be diseased, than to abuse thine eyes for these purposes.

It were meet indeed that ye had within you the wall to part you from the women; but since ye are not so minded, our fathers thought it necessary by these boards[3] to wall you off; since I hear from the elder ones, that of old there were not so much as these partitions; "For in Christ Jesus there is neither male nor female."[4] And in the apostle's time also both men and women were together. Because the men were men, and the women women, but now altogether the contrary; the women have urged themselves into the manners of courtezans, but the men are in no better state than frantic horses.

Heard ye not, that the men and women were gathered together in the upper room, and that congregation was worthy of the heavens? And very reasonably. For even women then practised much self-denial, and the men gravity and chastity. Hear, for instance, the seller of purple saying, "If ye have judged me to be faithful to the Lord, come in, and abide with me."[5] Hear the women, who went about with the apostles, having taken unto themselves manly courage, Priscilla, Persis, and the rest; from whom our present women are as far removed as our men from their men.

4. For then indeed even travelling into far countries women brought not on themselves evil report; but now even though brought up in a chamber, they hardly escape this suspicion. But these things arise from their decking of themselves, and their luxury. Then the business of those women was to spread the word; but now to appear beauteous, and fair, and comely in countenance. This is glory to them, this salvation; but of lofty and great works they do not even dream.

What woman exerts herself to make her husband better? what man hath taken to himself this care to amend his wife? There is not one: but the woman's whole study is upon the care of ornaments of gold, and raiment, and the other adornments of the person, and how to increase their substance; but the man's both this, and others more than this, all however worldly.

Who, when about to marry, inquires about the disposition and nurture of the damsel? No one; but straightway about money, and possessions, and measures of property of various and different kinds; like as if he were about to buy something, or to settle some common contract.

Therefore they do even so call marriage. For I have heard many say, such a man has contracted with such a woman, that is, has married. And they offer insult to the gifts of God, and as though buying and selling, so do they marry, and are given in marriage.

And writings there are, requiring greater security than those about buying and selling. Learn how those of old married, and imitate them. How then did they marry? They inquired about ways of life, and morals, and virtue of the soul. Therefore they had no need of writings, nor of security by parch-

---

[1] Ps. cxli. 2.   [2] Jer. xxii. 17, LXX.   [3] σάνισι.
[4] Gal. iii. 28. [The passage is inexactly cited, the form being altered to correspond with the previous part of the verse. Comp. R. V.—R.]

[5] Acts xvi. 15. [Two MSS. have a reading more exactly agreeing with the New Testament text.—R.]

ment and ink; for the bride's disposition sufficed them in the place of all.

I therefore entreat you likewise not to seek
after wealth and affluence, but a good disposition, and gentleness. Seek for a pious and
self-denying damsel, and these will be to thee
better than countless treasures. If thou seek
the things of God, these others will come
also; but if thou pass by those, and hasten
unto these, neither will these follow.

But such a man, one will say, became rich
by his wife! Art thou not ashamed of bringing forward such examples? I had ten
thousand times sooner become a poor man,
as I have heard many say, than gain wealth
from a wife. For what can be more unpleasing than that wealth? What more painful
than the abundance? What more shameful
than to be notorious from thence, and for it
to be said by all, such a man became rich by
a wife? For the domestic discomforts I pass
by, all that must needs result from hence,
the wife's pride, the servility, the strifes, the
reproaches of the servants. "The beggar,"
"the ragged one." "the base one, and
sprung of base." "Why, what had he when
he came in?" "Do not all things belong to
our mistress?" But thou dost not care at all
about these sayings, for neither art thou a
freeman. Since the parasites likewise hear
worse things than these, and are not pained
wherefore neither are these, but rather pride
themselves in their disgrace; and when we tell
them of these things, "Let me have," saith one
of them, "something pleasant and sweet, and
let it choke me." Alas! the devil, what proverbs
hath he brought into the world, of power to
overturn the whole life of such persons. See
at least this self-same devilish and pernicious
saying; of how much ruin it is full. For it
means nothing else than these words, Have
thou no regard to what is honorable; have
thou no regard to what is just; let all those
things be cast aside, seek one thing alone,

pleasure. Though the thing stifle thee, let it
be thy choice; though all that meet thee
spurn thee, though they smear thy face with
mire, though they drive thee away as a dog,
bear all. And what else would swine say, if
they had a voice? What else would filthy
dogs? But perhaps not even they would have
said such things, as the devil hath persuaded
men to rave.

Wherefore I entreat you, being conscious
of the senselessness of such words as these,
to flee such proverbs, and to choose out those
in the Scriptures that are contrary to them.

But what are these? "Go not," it is said,
"after thy lusts, and refrain thyself from
thine appetites."[1] And, touching an harlot
again, it is said in opposition to this proverb,
"Give not heed to a bad woman: for honey
droppeth from the lips of a woman that is an
harlot, which, for a season, is luscious unto
thy throat; but afterwards thou shalt find it
more bitter than gall, and sharper than a two-
edged sword."[2] Unto these last then let us
listen, not unto those. For hence indeed
spring our mean, hence our slavish thoughts,
hence men become brutes, because in everything they will follow after pleasure according
to this proverb, which, even without arguments of ours, is of itself ridiculous. For
after one is choked, what is the gain of
sweetness?

Cease, therefore, to set up such great absurdity, and to kindle hell and unquenchable
fire; and let us look steadfastly (at length
though late) as we ought, unto the things to
come, having put away the film on our eyes,
that we may both pass the present life
honestly, and with much reverence and godly
fear, and attain unto the good things to
come, by the grace and love towards man of
our Lord Jesus Christ, to whom be glory
world without end. Amen.

---

[1] Ecclus. xviii. 30.   [2] Prov. v. 2-4, LXX.

HOMILY LXXIV.

MATT. XXIII. 29, 30.

"Woe unto you, because ye build the tombs of the prophets, and garnish their sepulchres,[1] and say, If we had been in the days of our fathers, we would not have been partakers with them in the blood of the prophets."

NOT because they build, nor because they blame the others, doth He say, woe, but because, while both thus, and by what they say, they are pretending to condemn their fathers, they do worse. For in proof that the condemnation was a pretense, Luke saith, ye do allow because ye build; for, "Woe unto you," saith He, "for ye build the sepulchres of the prophets, and your fathers killed them. Truly ye bear witness, and ye allow the deeds of your fathers, for they indeed killed them, and ye build their sepulchres."[2] For here He reproves their purpose, wherewith they built, that it was not for the honoring of them that were slain, but as making a show of the murders, and afraid, lest, when the tombs had perished by time, the proof and memory of such daring should fade away, setting up these glorious buildings, as a kind of trophy, and priding themselves in the daring deeds of those men, and displaying them.

For the things that ye now dare to do, show that ye do these things also in this spirit. For, though ye speak the contrary, saith He, as condemning them, as, for instance, "We should not, if we had been in their days, have been partakers with them;" yet the disposition is evident wherewith ye say these things. Wherefore also unfolding it, though darkly, still He hath expressed it. For when He had said, ye say, "If we had been in the days of our fathers, we should not have been partakers with them in the blood of the prophets;" He added, "Wherefore ye be witnesses unto yourselves, that ye are the children of them that slew the prophets." And what blame is it to be a murderer's son, if one partake not in the mind of one's father? None. Whence it is evident, that for this same thing He brings it forward against them, hinting at their affinity in wickedness.

And this is manifest too by what comes after; He adds at least, "Ye serpents, ye generation of vipers."[3] For as those beasts are like their parents, in the destructiveness of their venom, so also are ye like your fathers in murderousness.

Then, because He was searching their temper of mind, which is to the more part obscure, He doth, from those things also which they were about to perpetrate, which would be manifest to all, establish His words. For, because He had said, "Wherefore ye be witnesses unto yourselves that ye are the children of them which killed the prophets," making it evident, that of their affinity in wickedness He is speaking, and that it was a pretense to say, "We should not have been partakers with them," He added, "Fill ye up therefore the measure of your fathers,"[4] not commanding, but declaring beforehand, what was to be, that is, His own murder.

Therefore, having brought in their refutation, and having shown that they were pretenses which they said in their own defense, as, for instance, "We would not have been partakers with them," (for they who refrain not from the Lord, how should they have refrained from the servants), He makes after this His language more condemnatory,[5] calling them "serpents, and generation of vipers," and saying, "How shall ye escape the damnation of hell,"[6] at once perpetrating such things, and denying them, and dissembling your purpose?

Then rebuking them more exceedingly from another cause also, He saith, "I will send unto you prophets, and wise men, and scribes, and some of them shall ye kill and crucify, and some of them shall ye scourge in your synagogues."[7] For that they should not say, "Though we crucified the Lord, yet from the servants we should have refrained, if we had been then;" "Behold," He saith, "I send servants also to you, prophets likewise themselves, and neither will ye spare them." But these things He saith, showing that it was nothing strange, that He should

---

[1] [There are two variations in the text of verse 29: the omission of "Scribes and Pharisees, hypocrites!" and the substitution of "their" for "of the righteous."—R.]

[2] Luke xi. 47, 48.   [3] Matt. xxiii. 33.

[4] Matt. xxiii. 32.   [5] καταφορικωτέρῳ.
[6] Matt. xxiii. 33. [R. V., "judgment of hell. Greek, Gehenna."]
[7] Matt. xxiii. 34. [The reading "will send" is peculiar; in the next citation of the passage "send" occurs, as in our New Testament authorities.—R.]

be murdered by those sons, being both murderous and deceitful, and having much guile, and surpassing their fathers in their outrages.

And besides what hath been said, He shows them to be also exceedingly vainglorious. For when they say, "If we had been in the days of our fathers, we should not have been partakers with them," they spake out of vainglory, and were practising virtue in words only, but in their works doing the contrary.

Ye serpents, ye generation of vipers, that is, wicked sons of wicked men, and more wicked than those who begat them. For He showeth that they are committing greater crimes, both by their committing them after those others, and by their doing much more grievous things than they, and this, while positively affirming that they never would have fallen into the same. For they add that which is both the end and the crown of their evil deeds. For the others slew them that came to the vineyard, but these, both the son, and them that were bidding them to the wedding.

But these things He saith, to separate them off from the affinity to Abraham, and to show that they had no advantage from thence, unless they followed his works; wherefore also He adds, "How can ye flee[1] from the damnation of hell," when following them that have committed such acts?

And here He recalls to their remembrance John's accusation, for he too called them by this name, and reminded them of the judgment to come. Then, because they are nothing alarmed by judgment and hell, by reason of their not believing them, and because the thing is future, He awes them by the things present, and saith, "Wherefore, behold, I send unto you prophets and scribes: and some of them shall ye kill and crucify, and scourge;[2] that upon you may come all the righteous blood shed upon the earth, from the blood of righteous Abel, unto the blood of Zacharias the son of Barachias, whom ye slew between the temple[3] and the altar. Verily I say unto you, that all these things shall come upon this generation."[4]

2. See by how many things He has warned them. He said, Ye condemn your fathers, in that ye say, "We would not have been partakers with them;" and this is no little thing to shame them. He said, While ye condemn them, ye do worse things, even ye yourselves; and this is sufficient to cover them with disgrace. He said, These things shall not be without punishment; and hence

he implants in them fear beyond words. He hath reminded them at least of hell. Then because that was to come, He brought home to them the terrors as even present. "For all these things shall come," He saith, "upon this generation."

He added also unspeakable severity to the vengeance, saying, that they shall suffer more grievous things than all; yet by none of these things did they become better. But if any one say, And why do they suffer more grievously than all? we would say, Because they have first committed more grievous things than all, and by none of the things that have been done to them have they been brought to a sound mind.

Heardest thou not Lamech saying, "Of Lamech vengeance shall be taken seventy times sevenfold;"[5] that is, "I am deserving of more punishment than Cain." Why could this be? Yet he did not slay his brother; but because not even by his example was he brought to a better mind. And this is what God saith elsewhere, "Requiting the sins of fathers upon children for the third and fourth generation of them that hate me."[6] Not as though one were to suffer punishment for the crimes committed by others, but inasmuch as they who, after many sin and have been punished, yet have not grown better, but have committed the same offenses, are justly worthy to suffer their punishments also.

But see how seasonably he also mentioned Abel, indicating that this murder likewise is of envy. What then have ye to say? Know ye not what Cain suffered? Did God hold His peace at his deeds? Did He not exact the severest penalty? Heard ye not what things your fathers suffered, when they slew the prophets; were they not delivered over to punishments, and inflictions of vengeance without number? How then did ye not become better? And why do I speak of the punishments of your fathers, and what they suffered? Thou who thyself condemnest thy fathers, how is it thou doest worse? For moreover even ye yourselves have declared that "He will miserably destroy those wicked men."[7] What favor then will ye have after this, committing such things after such a sentence?

But who is this Zacharias? Some say, the father of John; some, the prophet; some, a priest with two different names, whom the Scripture also calls, the son of Jehoiada.[8]

---

[1] ["escape," as before, the verb being the same, though the tense is changed; see note 6, p. 445.—R.]
[2] [The close of verse 34 is abridged.—R.]
[3] [R. V., "sanctuary."]   [4] Matt. xxiii. 34-36.

[5] Gen. iv. 24.
[6] Exod. xx. 5. [The LXX. reads ἕως, which is here altered to ἐπί. The rendering above is not literal: "upon children, upon a third and fourth generation to them that hate me."—R.]
[7] Matt. xxi. 41.
[8] Or, "calls Jehoiada." 2 Chron. xxiv. 21. The name being indeclinable, may be read in the nominative or genitive.

But do thou mark this, that the outrage was twofold. For not only did they slay holy men, but also in a holy place. And saying these things, He did not only alarm them, but also comfort His disciples, showing that the righteous men also who were before them suffered these things. But these He alarmed, foretelling that like as they paid their penalty, even so should these too suffer the utmost extremities. Therefore He calls them [1] "prophets, and wise men, and scribes," even hereby again taking away every plea of theirs. "For ye cannot say," He saith, "Thou didst send from among the Gentiles, and therefore we were offended;" but they were led on unto this by being murderous, and thirsting for blood. Wherefore He also said beforehand, "For this cause do I send prophets and scribes." This did the prophets also lay to their charge, saying, "They mingle blood with blood," [2] and that they are men of blood. Therefore also did He command the blood to be offered to Him, showing that if in a brute it be thus precious, much more in a man. Which He saith to Noah likewise, "I will require all blood that is shed." [3] And ten thousand other such things might one find Him enjoining with regard to their not committing murder; wherefore He commanded them not even to eat that which was strangled.

Oh the love of God towards man! that though He foreknew they would profit nothing, He still doeth His part. For I will send, He saith, and this knowing they would be slain. So that even hereby they were convicted of saying vainly, "We should not have been partakers with our fathers." For these too slew prophets even in their synagogues, and reverenced neither the place, nor the dignity of the persons. For not merely ordinary persons did they slay, but prophets and wise men, such that they had nothing to lay to their charge. And by these He meaneth the apostles, and those after them, for, indeed, many prophesied. Then, willing to aggravate their fears, He saith, "Verily, verily I say unto you, All these things shall come upon this generation;" that is, I will bring all upon your heads, and will make the vengeance sore. For he that knew many to have sinned, and was not sobered, but himself hath committed the same sins again, and not the same only, but also far more grievous, would justly deserve to suffer a far more grievous punishment than they. For like as, if he had been minded, he would have gained greatly, had he grown better by their exam-

ples, even so, since he continued without amendment, he is liable to a heavier vengeance, as having had the benefit of more warning by them who had sinned before and been punished, and having reaped no advantage.

3. Then He directs His speech unto the city, in this way too being minded to correct His hearers, and saith, "O Jerusalem, Jerusalem!" [4] What meaneth the repetition? this is the manner of one pitying her, and bemoaning her, and greatly loving her. For, like as unto a woman beloved, herself indeed ever loved, but who had despised Him that loved her, and therefore on the point of being punished, He pleads, being now about to inflict the punishment. Which He doth in the prophets also, using these words, "I said, Turn thou unto me, and she returned not." [5]

Then having called her, He tells also her blood-stained deeds, "Thou that killest [6] the prophets, and stonest them that are sent unto thee, how often would I have gathered thy children together, and ye would not," in this way also pleading for His own dealings; not even with these things hast thou turned me aside, nor withdrawn me from my great affection toward thee, but it was my desire even so, not once or twice, but often to draw thee unto me. "For how often would I have gathered your children together, even as a hen gathereth her chickens, and ye would not." [7] And this He saith, to show that they were ever scattering themselves by their sins. And His affection He indicates by the similitude; for indeed the creature is warm in its love towards its brood. And everywhere in the prophets is this same image of the wings, and in the song of Moses and in the Psalms, indicating His great protection and care.

"But ye would not," He saith. "Behold your house is left desolate," [8] stripped of the succor which cometh from me. Surely it was the same, who also was before protecting them, and holding them together, and preserving them; surely it was He who was ever chastening them. And He appoints a punishment, which they had ever dreaded exceedingly; for it declared the entire overthrow of their polity. "For I say unto you, Ye shall not see me henceforth, till ye shall say, Blessed is He that cometh in the name of the Lord." [9] And this is the language of one that loves earnestly, earnestly drawing them unto Him by the things to come, not merely

---

[1] [That is, "His disciples."]   [2] Hosea iv. 2, LXX.
[3] Gen. ix. 5.

[4] Matt. xxiii. 37.   [5] Jer. iii. 7.
[6] [The form of the Greek participle varies in the MSS. of the Homily, as in those of the New Testament.—R.]
[7] [This citation is accurate ; compare the previous abridgement of the sentence.—R.]
[8] Matt. xxiii. 38.   [9] Matt. xxiii. 39.

warning them by the past; for of the future day of His second coming doth He here speak.

What then? Did they not see Him from that time? But it is not that hour which He meaneth in saying, Henceforth, but the time up to His crucifixion.

For since they were forever accusing Him of this, that He was a kind of rival God, and a foe to God, He moves them to love Him by this, namely, by showing Himself to be of one accord with His Father; and He indicates Himself to be the same that was in the prophets. Wherefore also He uses the same words as did the prophets.

And by these He intimated both His resurrection, and His second coming, and made it plain even to the utterly unbelieving, that then most surely they should worship Him. And how did He make this plain? By speaking of many things that were first to be, that He should send prophets, that they should kill them; that it should be in the synagogues; that they should suffer the utmost extremities; that their house should be left desolate; that they should undergo things more grievous than any, and such as never were undergone before. For all these things are enough to furnish even to the most senseless and contentious a clear proof of that which should come to pass at His coming.

For I will ask them, Did He send the prophets and wise men? Did they slay them in their synagogue? Was their house left desolate? Did all the vengeance come upon that generation? It is quite plain that it was so, and no man gainsays it. As then all these things came to pass, so shall those also come to pass, and most surely they shall submit then.

But they shall derive thence no advantage in the way of defense, as neither will they who repent of their course of life then.

Wherefore let us, while it is time, practise what is good. For like as they henceforth derived no advantage from their knowledge, even so neither shall we ourselves from our repentance for our wickedness. For neither to the pilot, when the bark is sunk in the sea from his remissness, will there remain anything more; nor to the physician, when the sick man is gone; but each of these must before the end devise, and execute all things, so as to be involved in no danger, nor shame; but after this, all is unprofitable.

Let us also then, while in sickness, send for physicians, and lay out money, and exert unceasing diligence, that having risen up from our affliction, we may depart hence in health.

And as much care as we exert about our servants, when their bodies are sick, so much let us show forth upon ourselves, when our soul is diseased. And indeed we are nearer to ourselves than our servants, and our souls are more necessary than those bodies, but nevertheless it were well if we exert at least an equal diligence. For if we do not this now, when gone, thenceforth we may obtain nothing more in the way of plea.

4. Who is so wretched, one may say, as not to show even as much thought as this? Why this is the marvellous thing, that we are held in so little esteem with our ownselves, that we despise ourselves more than our servants. For when our servants are sick of a fever, we send for physicians, and make a separation in the house, and compel them to obey the laws of that art; and if these are neglected, we are displeased with them, and set persons to watch them, who will not, even should they wish them, suffer them to satiate their desire; and if they who have the care of these persons should say, that medicines must be procured at great cost, we yield; and whatsoever they may enjoin, we obey, and we pay them hire for these injunctions.

But when we are sick (or rather there is no time when we are not sick), we do not so much as call in the physician, we do not lay out money, but as though some ruffian,[1] and enemy, and foe, were concerned, so do we disregard our soul. And these things I say, not finding fault with our attention towards our servants, but thinking it meet to take at least as much care of our souls. And how should we do? one may say. Show it to Paul when ill; call in Matthew; let John sit by it. Hear from them, what we ought to do that is thus ill, they will surely tell, and will not conceal. For they are not dead, but live and speak. But doth the soul take no heed to them, being weighed down by the fever? Do thou compel it, and awaken its reasoning power. Call in the prophets. There is no need to pay money to these physicians, for neither do they themselves demand hire for themselves, nor for the medicines which they prepare do they drive thee to the necessity of expense, except for almsgiving; but in everything else they even add to thy possessions; as, for instance, when they require thee to be temperate, they deliver thee from unseasonable and wrong expenses; when they tell thee to abstain from drunkenness, they make thee wealthier. Seest thou the skill of physicians, who besides health, are supplying thee also with riches? Sit down therefore by

---

[1] Lit., "executioner."

them, and learn of them the nature of thy disease. For instance, dost thou love wealth, and greedy gain, like as the fevered love water? Listen at any rate to their admonitions. For like as the physician saith to thee, If thou wilt gratify thy desire, thou wilt perish, and undergo this or that; even so also Paul: " They that will be rich, fall into temptation, and a snare of the devil, and into foolish and hurtful lusts, which drown men in destruction and perdition." [1]

But art thou impatient? Hear him saying, " Yet a little while, and He that cometh will come, and will not tarry. [2] The Lord is at hand, be careful for nothing;" [3] and again, " The fashion of this world passeth away." [4]

For neither doth he command only, but also soothes, as a physician should. And like as they devise some other things in the place of cold things, so doth this man draw off [5] the desire another way. Dost thou wish to be rich, saith he; let it be " in good works." Dost thou desire to lay up treasure? I forbid it not at all; only let it be in Heaven.

And like as the physician saith, that what is cold is hurtful to teeth, to nerves, to bones; so he too, more briefly indeed, as heedful of brevity, yet far more, clearly and more powerfully, saith, " For the love of money is the root of all evils." [6]

Of what then should one make use? He tells this also: of contentedness instead of covetousness. " For contentment," he saith, " with godliness is great gain." [7] But if thou art dissatisfied, and desirest more, and art not yet equal to cast away all superfluous things, he tells also him that is thus diseased, how he ought to handle these things too. " That they that rejoice in wealth, be as though they rejoiced not; and they that have, as though they possessed not; and they that use this world, as not abusing it." [8]

Seest thou what manner of things he enjoins? Wilt thou thou call in also another physician besides? To me at least it seems well. For neither are these physicians like those of the body, who often, while vying one with another, overwhelm the sick man. But not so these, for they have regard to the health of the sick, not to their own vainglory. Be not then afraid of the number of them; one Master speaks in all, that is, Christ.

5. See, for instance, another again entering in, and saying severe things concerning this disease, or rather it is the Master by him; [9] " For ye cannot serve God and mammon." [10]

Yea, saith he, and how will these things be? how shall we cease from the desire? Hence may we learn this also. And how shall we know? Hear him saying this too: " Lay not up for yourselves treasures upon the earth, where moth and rust doth corrupt, and where thieves break through and steal." [11]

Seest thou how by the place, by the things that waste there, He draws men off from this desire that is here, and rivets them to Heaven, where all things are impregnable? For if ye transfer your wealth there where neither rust nor moth corrupts, nor thieves break through and steal, ye will both expel this disease, and establish your soul in the greatest abundance.

And together with what we have said, He brings forward an example also to teach thee moderation. And like as the physician, to alarm the sick man saith, that such a one died from the use of cold water; so doth He also bring in the rich man, [12] laboring indeed, and longing for life and health, but not able to attain thereto, because of having set his heart on covetousness, but going away empty. And besides this man, another is shown to thee again by another evangelist, he that was in torment, [13] and was not master so much as of a drop of water. Then showing that His injunctions are easy, He saith, " Behold the fowls of the air." [14] But being compassionate, He suffers not even the rich to despair. " For the things which are impossible with men, are possible with God," [15] saith He. For though thou be rich, the physician is able to cure thee. For neither was it wealth that He took away, but to be slave of riches, and a lover of greedy gain.

How then is it possible for the rich man to be saved. By possessing his goods in common with them that are in need, being such as Job was, and exterminating out of his soul the desire of more, and in no points going beyond real need.

He shows thee together with these this self-same publican also, that was grievously oppressed by the fever of covetousness, quickly set free from it. For what more sordid than a publican? Nevertheless, the man became indifferent to wealth from obeying the laws of the physician. For indeed He hath for His disciples such persons as these, that were sick of the same diseases as we are, and have recovered their health quickly. And He shows us each, in order we may not despair. See at least this publican. Mark again another, a chief of the publicans, who promised fourfold indeed for all that he had extorted, and

1 1 Tim. vi. 9.   2 Heb. x. 37.   3 Phil. iv. 5, 6.
4 1 Cor. vii. 31.   5 μετοχετεύει.   6 1 Tim. vi. 10.
7 1 Tim. v. 6.   8 1 Cor. vii. 30, 31.
9 i. e., by Matthew.   10 Matt. vi. 24.

11 Matt. vi. 19.   12 Matt. xix. 16.   13 Luke xvi. 24–26.
14 Matt. vi. 26.   15 Luke xviii. 27.

the half of all that he possessed, that he might receive Jesus.

But art thou on fire with exceeding desire for riches. Have the possessions of all men instead of thine own. For indeed I give thee, He saith, more than thou seekest, in opening to thee the houses of the wealthy throughout the world. "For whosoever hath forsaken father or mother, or lands, or house, shall receive an hundredfold."[1] Thus wilt thou not enjoy more abundant possessions only, but thou wilt even remove this grievous thirst altogether, and wilt endure all things easily, so far from desiring more, not *seeking* often even necessary things. Thus doth Paul suffer hunger, and is held in honor more than when he ate. Forasmuch as a wrestler

also, when striving, and winning crowns, would not choose to give up and to be in repose; and a merchant who hath entered on sea voyages would not desire to be afterwards in idleness.

And we therefore, if we should taste as we ought of spiritual fruits, shall thenceforth not even account the things present to be anything, being seized by the desire of the things to come as with some most noble intoxication.

Let us taste of them, therefore, that we may both be delivered from the turmoil of the things present, and may attain the good things to come, by the grace and love towards man of our Lord Jesus Christ, to whom be the glory and the might, now and ever, and world without end. Amen.

[1] Matt. xix. 29.

HOMILY LXXV.

MATT. XXIV. 1, 2.

"And Jesus went out from the temple, and departed.[1] And His disciples came to Him to show Him the buildings of the temple. And He answered and said unto them, See ye not all these things? Verily I say unto you, there shall not be left here one stone upon another, that shall not be thrown down."

FOR inasmuch as He said, "Your house is left desolate," and had previously forewarned them of many grievous things; therefore the disciples having heard these things, as though marvelling at it, came unto Him, showing the beauty of the temple, and wondering, if so much beauty was to be destroyed, and materials so costly, and variety of workmanship past utterance; He no longer thenceforth talks to them of desolation merely, but foretells an entire destruction. "See ye not all these things," saith He, and do ye marvel, and are ye amazed? "There shall not remain one stone upon another." How then did it remain? one may say. But what is this? For neither so hath the prediction fallen to the ground. For He said these things either indicating its entire desolation, or at that spot where He was. For there are parts of it destroyed unto the foundations.

And together with its we would say another thing also, that from what hath been

done, even the most contentious ought to believe concerning the remains, that they are utterly to be destroyed.

"And as He sat upon the mount of Olives, the disciples came unto Him privately, saying, Tell us when shall these things be? and what shall be the sign of Thy coming, and of the end of the world?"[2]

Therefore did they come unto Him privately, as it was of such matters they meant to inquire. For they were in travail to know the day of His coming, because of their eager desire to behold that glory, which is the cause of countless blessings. And these two things do they ask him, when shall these things be? that is, the overthrow of the temple; and, what is the sign of thy coming? But Luke saith,[3] the question was one concerning Jerusalem, as though they were supposing that then is His coming. And Mark saith, that neither did all of them ask concerning the end of Jerusalem, but Peter and John,[4] as having greater freedom of speech.

[1] [R. V., "and was going on his way," to bring out the force of the imperfect tense.—R.]

[2] Matt. xxiv. 3.   [3] Luke xxi. 6, 7.   [4] See Mark xiii. 3.

What then saith He? "Take heed that no man deceive you. For many shall come in my name, saying, I am Christ, and shall deceive many.[1] And ye shall hear of wars and rumors of wars. See that ye be not troubled; for all these things must come to pass, but the end is not yet."[2]

For since they felt as being told of vengeance falling on others when hearing of that which was to be brought upon Jerusalem, and as though they were to be out of the turmoils, and were dreaming of good things only, and looked for these to befall them quite immediately; for this cause He again foretells to them grievous things, making them earnest, and commanding them on two grounds to watch, so as neither to be seduced by the deceit of them that would beguile them, nor to be overpowered by the violence of ills that should overtake them.

For the war, saith He, shall be twofold, that of the deceivers, and that of the enemies, but the former far more grievous, as coming upon them in the confusion and turmoils, and when men were terrified and troubled. For indeed great was the storm then, when the Roman power was beginning to flourish, and cities were taken, and camps and weapons were set in motion, and many were readily believed.

But of wars in Jerusalem is He speaking; for it is not surely of those without, and everywhere in the world; for what did they care for these? And besides, He would thus say nothing new, if He were speaking of the calamities of the world at large, which are happening always. For before this, were wars, and tumults, and fightings; but He speaks of the Jewish wars coming upon them at no great distance, for henceforth the Roman arms were a matter of anxiety. Since then these things also were sufficient to confound them, He foretells them all.

Then to show that He Himself also will assail the Jews with them, and war on them, He speaks not of battles only, but also of plagues sent from God, famines, and pestilences, and earthquakes. showing that the wars also He Himself permitted to come upon them, and that these things do not happen for no purpose according to what has been before the accustomed course of things amongst men, but proceed from the wrath on high.

Therefore He saith, they shall come not by themselves or at once, but with signs. For that the Jews may not say, that they who then believed were the authors of these evils,

therefore hath He told them also of the cause of their coming upon them. "For verily I say unto you," He said before, "all these things shall come upon this generation," having made mention of the stain of blood on them.

Then lest on hearing of the showers of evils, they should suppose the gospel to be broken through, He added, "See,[3] be not troubled, for all things must come to pass," i.e. which I foretold, and the approach of the temptations will set aside none of the things which I have said; but there shall indeed be tumults and confusion, but nothing shall shake my predictions.

Then since He had said to the Jews, "Ye shall not see me, till ye shall say, Blessed is He that cometh in the name of the Lord;" and the disciples supposed that together with the destruction would be the end also; to set right this secret thought of theirs, He said, "But the end is not yet." For that they did suspect even as I said, you may learn from their question. For, what did they ask? When shall these things be? i.e. when shall Jerusalem be destroyed? And what is the sign of Thy coming, and of the end of the world?

But He answered nothing directly to this question, but first speaks of those other things that are urgent, and which it was needful for them to learn first. For neither concerning Jerusalem straightway, nor of His own second coming, did He speak, but touching the ills that were to meet them at the doors. Wherefore also He makes them earnest in their exertions, by saying, "Take heed that no man deceive you;[4] for many shall come in my name, saying, I am Christ."

Afterwards, when He hath roused them to listen about these things (for, "take heed," saith He, "that no man deceive you");[4] and having made them energetic, and prepared them to be watchful, and hath spoken first of the false Christs, then He speaks of the ills of Jerusalem, assuring them ever by the things already past, foolish and contentious though they were, of those which were yet to come.

2. But by "wars and rumors of wars," He meaneth, what I before said, the troubles coming upon them. After this, because, as I have already said, they supposed after that war the end would come, see how He warns them, saying, "But the end is not yet. For nation," He saith, "shall rise against nation, and kingdom against kingdom."[5] Of the

---

[1] [R. V., "lead you astray," and "shall lead many astray."]
[2] Matt. xxiv. 4–6.

[3] [The Oxford translator renders "Take heed," but ὁρᾶτε is rendered "See" above; so A. V. and R. V.—R.]
[4] [R. V., "lead you astray."]   [5] Matt. xxiv. 7.

preludes to the ills of the Jews doth He speak. "All these are the beginning of sorrows,"[1] that is, of those that befall them. "Then shall they deliver you up to be afflicted, and shall kill you."[2]

In good season did He introduce their ills, having a consolation from the common miseries; and not in this way only, but also by His adding, that it is "for my name's sake. For ye shall be hated," He saith, "of all men for my name's sake. Then shall many be offended, and shall betray one another, and many false Christs and false prophets shall arise, and shall deceive many. And because iniquity shall abound, the love of many shall wax cold; but he that shall endure unto the end, the same shall be saved."[3]

This is the greater evil, when the war is intestine too, for there were many false brethren. Seest thou the war to be threefold? from the deceivers, from the enemies, from the false brethren. See Paul too lamenting over the same things, and saying, "Without were fightings, within were fears;"[4] and, "perils among false brethren,"[5] and again, "For such are false apostles, deceitful workers, transforming themselves into the apostles of Christ."[6]

After this again, what is more grievous than all, they shall not have so much as the consolation from love. Then indicating, that these things will in no degree harm the noble and the firm, He saith, Fear not, neither be troubled. For if ye show forth the patience that becomes you, the dangers will not prevail over you. And it is a plain proof of this, that the word shall surely be preached everywhere in the world, so much shall ye be above the things that alarm you. For, that they may not say, how then shall we live? He said more, Ye shall both live and preach everywhere. Therefore He added moreover, "And this gospel shall be preached in the whole world for a witness to all nations, and then shall the end come,"[7] of the downfall of Jerusalem.

For in proof that He meant this, and that before the taking of Jerusalem the gospel was preached, hear what Paul saith, "Their sound went into all the earth;"[8] and again, "The gospel which was preached to every creature which is under Heaven."[9] And seest thou him running from Jerusalem unto

Spain? And if one took so large a portion, consider what the rest also wrought. For writing to others also, Paul again saith concerning the gospel, that "it is bringing forth fruit, and growing up in every creature which is under Heaven."[10]

But what meaneth, "For a witness to all nations?" Forasmuch as though it was everywhere preached, yet it was not everywhere believed. It was for a witness, He saith, to them that were disbelieving, that is, for conviction, for accusation, for a testimony; for they that believed will bear witness against them that believed not, and will condemn them. And for this cause, after the gospel is preached in every part of the world, Jerusalem is destroyed, that they may not have so much as a shadow of an excuse for their perverseness. For they that saw His power shine throughout every place, and in an instant take the world captive, what excuse could they then have for continuing in the same perverseness? For in proof that it was everywhere preached at that time, hear what Paul saith, "of the gospel which was preached to every creature which is under Heaven."[11]

Which also is a very great sign of Christ's power, that in twenty or at most thirty years the word had reached the ends of the world. "After this therefore," saith He, "shall come the end of Jerusalem." For that He intimates this was manifested by what follows.

For He brought in also a prophecy, to confirm their desolation, saying, "But when ye shall see the abomination of desolation, spoken of by Daniel the prophet, standing in the holy place, let him that readeth understand."[12] He referred them to Daniel. And by "abomination" He meaneth the statue of him who then took the city, which he who desolated the city and the temple placed within the temple, wherefore Christ calleth it, "of desolation." Moreover, in order that they might learn that these things will be while some of them are alive, therefore He said, "When ye see the abomination of desolation."

3. Whence one may most marvel at Christ's power, and their courage, for that they preached in such times, in which most especially the Jewish state was warred against, in which most especially men regarded them as movers of sedition, when Cæsar commanded all of them to be driven away.[13] And the result was the same as if any one (when the sea was stirred up on every side, and darkness was filling all the air, and successive shipwrecks taking place, and when all their

1 Matt. xxiv. 8. [R. V., "travail," birth pangs.—R.]
2 Matt. xxiv. 9. [R. V., "unto tribulation."]
3 Matt. xxiv. 9-13. [In verse 9, "all *men*" is substituted for "all the nations" (τῶν ἐθνῶν omitted); in verse 11 "many false Christs and" occurs (taken from verse 24). The R. V. represents, in other details, the Greek text of the Homily. In verse 12, "the many" is the necessary rendering.—R.]
4 2 Cor. vii. 5.   5 2 Cor. xi. 26.   6 2 Cor. xi. 13.
7 Matt. xxiv. 14. [" Of the kingdom " omitted.]
8 Rom. x. 18.   9 Col. i. 23.

10 Col. i. 6. [Combined with Col. i. 23.]   11 Col. i. 23.
12 Matt. xxiv. 15. [Instead of οὖν the particle δέ (as in Mark and Luke) is found here.]
13 Acts xviii. 2.

fellow-sailors were at strife above, and monsters were rising up from beneath, and with the waves devouring the mariners, and thunderbolts falling, and their being pirates, and those in the vessel plotting one against another), were to command men inexperienced in sailing, and who had not so much as seen the sea to sit at the rudder, and to guide and fight the vessel, and when an immense fleet was coming against them with a great array, making use of a single bark, with her crew in this disturbed state, to sink and subdue the fleet. For indeed by the heathens they were hated as Jews, and by the Jews were stoned, as waging war against their laws; and nowhere could they stand.

Thus were all things, precipices, and reefs, and rocks, the things in the cities, the things in the fields, the things in the houses, and every single person was at war with them; generals and rulers, and private persons, and all nations, and all people, and a turmoil which cannot be set forth by words. For the Jewish race was exceedingly detestable to the government of the Romans, as having occasioned them endless trouble; and not even from this did the preaching of the word take hurt; but the city was stormed and set on fire, and involved its inhabitants in countless evils; but the apostles that came from thence, introducing new laws, prevailed even over the Romans.

O strange and wonderful facts! Countless myriads of Jews did the Romans then subdue, and they did not prevail over twelve men fighting against them naked and unarmed. What language can set forth this miracle? For they that teach need to have these two things, to be worthy of credit, and to be beloved by them whom they are instructing; and together with these, and besides them, that their sayings should be easy of reception, and the time should be free from trouble and tumults.

But then were all the contraries to these. For while they did not seem worthy of credit, they were withdrawing from such as did seem worthy of it, those who had been deceived by them. So far from being loved, they were even hated, and were taking men away from what they loved, both habits, and hereditary customs, and laws.

Again, their injunctions had great difficulty; but the things, from which they were withdrawing men, much pleasure. And many were the perils, many the deaths, both themselves and they that obeyed them underwent, and together with all this, the time also occasioned them much difficulty, teeming with wars, tumults, disturbance, so that, even if

there had been none of the things we have mentioned, it would have quite thrown all things into confusion.

We have good occasion to say, "Who shall tell the mighty works of the Lord, and make all His praises to be heard."[1] For if his own people amid signs hearkened not to Moses, because of the clay only, and the bricks; who persuaded these that every day were beaten and slain, and were suffering incurable evils, to leave a quiet life, and to prefer thereto this which was teeming with blood and death, and that when they who preached it were strangers to them, and very hostile in every way? For I say not unto nations and cities and people, but into a small house let one bring in him that is hated of all that are in the house, and by him endeavor to bring them away from those whom they love, from father, and wife, and child, will he not surely be seen torn in pieces, before he hath opened his mouth? And if there be added moreover a tumult and strife of husband and wife in the house, will they not stone him to death before he steps on the threshold? And if he also be one whom they may readily despise, and who enjoins galling things, and commands them who are living in luxury to practise self restraint, and together with this the conflict be against those who are far more in numbers and who excel him, is it not quite manifest that he will be utterly destroyed? Yet nevertheless, this, which is impossible to be done in one house, this hath Christ accomplished in all the world, through precipices and furnaces, and ravines, and rocks, and land and sea at war with Him, bringing in the healers of the world.

And if thou art minded to learn these things more distinctly, I mean, the famines, the pestilences, the earthquakes, the other calamities, peruse the history about these things composed by Josephus, and thou wilt know all accurately. Therefore Himself too said, "Be not troubled, for all must be;" and, "He that endureth to the end, the same shall be saved;" and, "The gospel shall surely be preached in all the world." For when weakened and faint at the fear of what had been said, He braces them up by saying, Though ten thousand things be done, the gospel must be preached in every part of the world, and then shall the end come.

4. Seest thou in what a state things were then, and how manifold was the war? And this is the beginning, when each of the things to be effected most required quiet. In what state then were they? for nothing hinders us

---

[1] Ps. cvi. 2.

from resuming the same things again. The first war was that of the deceivers; "For there shall come," He saith, "false Christs and false prophets:" the second, that of the Romans, "For ye shall hear," He saith, "of wars:" the third, that which bringeth on the "famines:" the fourth, "the pestilences" and "the earthquakes:" the fifth, "they shall deliver you into afflictions:" the sixth, "ye shall be hated of all men:" the seventh, "They shall betray one another, and hate one another" (an intestine war doth He here make known); then, "false Christs," and false brethren; then, "the love of the most[1] shall wax cold," which is the cause of all the ills.

Seest thou numberless kinds of war, new and strange? Yet nevertheless in the midst of these things, and much more (for with the intestine wars was mingled also that of kinsmen), the gospel prevailed over the whole earth. "For the gospel," He saith, "shall be preached in the whole world."

Where then are they who set up the power of a nativity and the cycle of times against the doctrines of the church? For who has ever recorded that another Christ appeared; that such a thing took place? Although they falsely affirm other things, that ten myriads of years passed, yet this they cannot even feign. Of what kind of cycle then would ye speak? For there was never another Sodom, nor another Gomorrah, nor another flood. How long do ye trifle, talking of a cycle and nativity?

How then, it is said, do many of the things they say come to pass? Because thou hast bereaved thyself of the help God bestows, and didst betray thyself, and didst place thyself without His providence; therefore doth the evil spirit turn and twist about thy matters as he will.

But not so among the saints, or rather not even amongst us sinners, who utterly despise it. For although our practice is beyond endurance, yet because by God's grace we cling with much exactness to the doctrines of the truth, we are above the malice of the evil spirits.

And altogether, what is a nativity? nothing else than injustice, and confusion, and that all things are borne along at random; or rather not at random only; but more than this, with folly.

"And if there is not any nativity, whence is such a one rich? whence is such a one poor?"

I know not: for in this way I will for a time reason with thee, instructing thee not to be curious about all things; neither in consequence of this to go on at random and rashly. For neither because thou art ignorant of this, oughtest thou to feign the things that are not. It is better to be ignorant well, than to learn ill. For he that knoweth not the cause, will come soon to the right one; but he who because he does not know the real cause, feigns one that is untrue, will not be able easily to receive the real; but he needs more both of labors and toil, in order to take away the former. For indeed on a tablet, if it have been wiped smooth, any one may easily write what he will, but when it is written upon, no longer in the same way, for we must first wipe out what has been ill written. And amongst physicians again, he that applies nothing, is far better than he that applies hurtful things; and he who builds unsoundly, is worse than he who doth not so much as build at all; like as the land is far better that bears nothing, than that which bears thorns.

Let us not then be impatient to learn all things, but let us endure to be even ignorant of some things, that when we have found a teacher, we may not afford him double toil. Or rather many oftentimes have remained even incurably diseased, by carelessly entangling themselves in evil opinions. For neither is the toil the same to pluck up first what hath taken root amiss, and then to sow, as to plant a clear ground. For in that case, he must overthrow first, and then put in other things; but in this, the hearing is ready.

Whence then is such a one rich? I will say, now; many acquire wealth, by God's gift; and many by His permission. For this is the short and simple account.

What then? it is said, doth He make the whoremongers to be rich, and the adulterers, and him that hath abused himself with mankind, and him that hath made a bad use of his possessions? He doth not make them, but permits them to be rich; and great is the difference, and quite infinite between making and permitting. But wherefore doth He suffer it at all? Because it is not yet the time for judgment, that every one may receive according to his merits.

For what more worthless than that rich man, who giveth not to Lazarus so much as of his crumbs? Nevertheless, he was more wretched than all, for he came to be possessed not even of a drop of water, and for this very cause most especially, that being rich he was cruel. For if there are two

---

[1] [Only one MS. inserts τῶν πολλῶν here. Field rejects it. If accepted, it should be rendered "of the many," as in the R. V. But internal reasons are against it. It would naturally be supplied from the New Testament passage. Moreover, the briefer reading yields a better sense : "Love shall wax cold, the cause of all these ills."—R.]

wicked men, who have not had the same portion here, but one in wealth, the other in poverty, they will not be similarly punished there, but the wealthier more grievously.

5. Dost thou not see at least even this man, suffering more fearfully because he had " received his good things ?" Do thou also therefore, when thou seest in prosperity one who is become rich by injustice, groan, weep; for indeed this wealth is to him an addition of punishment. For like as they who sin much, and are not minded to repent, treasure up to themselves a treasure of wrath; even so they, who, besides not being punished, are even enjoying prosperity, will undergo the greater punishment.

And the proof of this, if thou wilt, I will show thee, not from the things to come only, but also from the present life. For the blessed David, when he sinned that sin of Bathsheba, and was convicted by the prophet, for this cause most of all was he more severely reproved, that even when he had enjoyed such security, he was like this. Hear at least God upbraiding him with this especially. " Did not I anoint thee for a king, and delivered thee from the hand of Saul, and give thee all that pertained to thy master, and all the house of Israel and Judah, and if it had been little for thee, I would have added thus and thus; and wherefore hast thou done that which was evil in my sight?"[1] For not for all sins are there the same punishments, but many and diverse, according to the times, according to the persons, according to their rank, according to their understanding, according to other things besides. And that what I say may be more clear, let one sin be set forth, fornication; and mark how many different punishments I find not from myself, but from the divine Scriptures. Did any one commit fornication before the law, he is differently punished; and this Paul showeth, " For as many as have sinned without law, shall also perish without law."[2] Did any one commit fornication after the law? He shall suffer more grievous things. " For as many as have sinned in the law shall be judged by the law."[3] Did any one commit fornication being a priest, he receives from his dignity a very great addition to his punishment. So for this cause, whereas the other women were slain for fornication, the daughters of the priests were burnt; the lawgiver showing more amply, how great punishment await the priest if he commits this sin. For if on the

daughter he inflicts a greater punishment, because of her being a priest's daughter, much more on the man himself who bears the priest's office. Was fornication committed with any violence ? she is even freed from punishment. Did one play the harlot being rich, and another being poor? Here again also is a difference. And this is evident from what we have said before concerning David. as any one guilty of fornication after Christ's coming? Should he depart uninitiated, he will suffer a punishment more sore than all those. Was any guilty of fornication after the laver ? in this case not even a consolation is left for the sin any more. And this selfsame thing Paul declared when he said, " He that despised Moses' law dieth without mercy, under two or three witnesses: of how much sorer punishment suppose ye shall he be counted worthy, who hath trodden underfoot the Son of God, and hath counted the blood of the covenant an unholy thing, and hath done despite to the grace of the Spirit ?"[4] Hath any been guilty of fornication, bearing the priest's office now? this above all is the crown of the evil deeds.

Seest thou of one sin how many different forms ? one that before the law, another that after the law, another that of him who bears the priest's office; that of the rich woman, and that of the poor woman, of her that is a catechumen. and of the believing woman, of the daughter of the priest.

And from the knowledge again great is the difference; " For he which knew his Lord's will, and did it not, shall be beaten with many stripes."[5] And to sin after examples bringeth greater vengeance. Therefore He saith, " But ye, when ye had seen it, repented not afterwards,"[6] though ye had had the advantage of much care. Therefore He upbraids Jerusalem likewise with this saying, " How often would I have gathered thy children together, and ye would not !"[7]

And to sin being in luxury, this is shown by the history of Lazarus. And from the place also the sin becomes more grievous, which He Himself indicated when He said, " Between the temple and the altar."[8]

And from the equality of the offenses themselves, " It is not marvellous if one be taken stealing;"[9] and again, " Thou didst slay thy sons and thy daughters; this is beyond all thy whoredoms, and thine abominations."[10]

And from the persons again: " If one

---

[1] 2 Sam. xii. 7-9.   [2] Rom. ii. 12.
[3] Rom. ii. 12. [The article does not occur, either here or in the text of the New Testament. R. V., " under law " and " by law."—R.]

[4] Heb. x. 28, 29. [The last phrase is altered, as indicated in the above rendering.—R.]
[5] Luke xii. 47.   [6] Matt. xxi. 32.
[7] Luke xiii. 34.   [8] Matt. xxiii. 35.
[9] Prov. vi. 30. [Most editors supply the remainder of the verse.—R.]
[10] Ezek. xvi. 20, 21. LXX.

man sin against another, they shall pray for him; but if he sin against God, who shall entreat for him?"[1]

And when any one surpasses in negligence those who are far inferior; wherewith in Ezekiel He doth charge them, saying, "Not even according to the judgments of the nations hast thou done."[2]

And when one is not sobered even by the examples of others, "She saw her sister," it is said, "and justified her."[3]

And when one has had the advantage of more abundant care; "For if," He saith, "these mighty works had been done in Tyre and Sidon, they would have repented long ago; but it shall be more tolerable for Tyre and Sidon than for that city."[4]

Seest thou perfect exactness, and that all for the same sins are not paying the same penalty? For moreover when we have had the benefit of long-suffering, and profit nothing, we shall endure worse things. And this Paul shows, where he says, "But after thy hardness and impenitent heart, thou treasurest up for thyself wrath."[5]

Knowing then these things, let us not be offended, neither let us be confounded at any of the things that happen, nor bring in upon us the storm of thought, but giving place to God's providence, let us give heed to virtue, and flee vice, that we may also attain to the good things to come, by the grace and love towards man of our Lord Jesus Christ, by whom and with whom be glory unto the Father together with the Holy Spirit, now and always, and world without end. Amen.

---

[1] 1 Sam. ii. 25. [LXX. The Hebrew differs: for the clause "they shall pray for him," the R. V. has, "God shall judge him."—R.]
[2] Ezek. v. 7.   [3] Ezek. xvi. 51. [First half freely cited.]
[4] Matt. xi. 21, 22.

[5] Rom. ii. 5.

HOMILY LXXVI.

Matt. XXIV. 16—18.

" Then let them which be in Judæa flee into the mountains. And let him that is on the housetop not come down to take anything out of his house. Neither let him which is in his field return back to take his clothes."[1]

Having spoken of the ills that were to overtake the city, and of the trials of the apostles, and that they should remain unsubdued, and should overrun the whole world, He mentions again the Jews' calamities, showing that when the one should be glorious, having taught the whole world, the others should be in calamity.

And see how He relates the war, by the things that seem to be small setting forth how intolerable it was to be. For, "Then," saith He, "let them which be in Judæa flee into the mountains." Then. When? When these things should be, "when the abomination of desolation should stand in the holy place." Whence he seems to me to be speaking of the armies. Flee therefore then, saith He, for thenceforth there is no hope of safety for you.

For since it had fallen out, that they often had recovered themselves in grievous wars, as under Sennacherib, under Antiochus again (for when at that time also, armies had come in upon them, and the temple had been seized beforehand, the Maccabees rallying gave their affairs an opposite turn); in order then that they might not now also suspect this, that there would be any such change, He forbids them all thought of the kind. For it were well, saith He, to escape henceforth with one's naked body. Therefore them also that are on the housetop, He suffers not to enter into the house to take their clothes, indicating the evils to be inevitable, and the calamity without end, and that it must needs be that he that was involved therein should surely perish. Therefore He adds also, him that is in the field, saying, neither let this man turn back to take his clothes. For if they that are in doors flee, much more they that are out of doors ought not to take refuge within.

---

[1] [In minor details the Greek text agrees with the received against that of our oldest MSS. authorities.—R.]

"Woe unto them that are with child, and to them that give suck,"[1] to the one because of their greater inertness, and because they cannot flee easily, being weighed down by the burden of their pregnancy; to the other, because they are held by the tie of feeling for their children, and cannot save their sucklings. For money it is a light thing to despise, and an easy thing to provide, and clothes; but the bonds of nature how could any one escape? how could the pregnant woman become active? how could she that gives suck be able to overlook that which she had borne?

Then, to show again the greatness of the calamity, He saith, "Pray ye that your flight be not in the winter, neither on the Sabbath day. For then shall be great tribulation, such as was not since the beginning of the world until now, neither shall be."[2]

Seest thou that His discourse is addressed to the Jews, and that He is speaking of the ills that should overtake them? For the apostles surely were not to keep the Sabbath day, neither to be there, when Vespasian did those things. For indeed the most part of them were already departed this life. And if any was left, he was dwelling then in other parts of the world.

But wherefore neither "in the winter, nor on the Sabbath day?"[3] Not in the winter, because of the difficulty arising from the season; not on the Sabbath day, because of the absolute authority exercised by the law. For since they had need of flight, and of the swiftest flight, but neither would the Jews dare to flee on the Sabbath day, because of the law, neither in winter was such a thing easy; therefore, "Pray ye," saith He; "for then shall be tribulation, such as never was, neither shall be."

And let not any man suppose this to have been spoken hyperbolically; but let him study the writings of Josephus, and learn the truth of the sayings. For neither can any one say, that the man being a believer, in order to establish Christ's words, hath exaggerated the tragical history. For indeed He was both a Jew, and a determined Jew, and very zealous, and among them that lived after Christ's coming.

What then saith this man? That those terrors surpassed all tragedy, and that no such had ever overtaken the nation. For so great was the famine, that the very mothers fought about the devouring of their children,

and that there were wars about this; and he saith that many when they were dead had their bellies ripped up.

I should therefore be glad to inquire of the Jews. Whence came there thus upon them wrath from God intolerable, and more sore than all that had befallen aforetime, not in Judæa only, but in any part of the world? Is it not quite clear, that it was for the deed of the cross, and for this rejection? All would say it, and with all and before all the truth of the facts itself.

But mark, I pray thee, the exceeding greatness of the ills, when not only compared with the time before, they appear more grievous, but also with all the time to come. For not in all the world, neither in all time that is past, and that is to come, shall any one be able to say such ills have been. And very naturally; for neither had any man perpetrated, not of those that ever have been, nor of those to come hereafter, a deed so wicked and horrible. Therefore He saith, "there shall be tribulation such as never was, nor shall be."

"And except those days should be shortened, there should no flesh be saved; but for the elect's sake those days shall be shortened."[4] By these things He shows them to be deserving of a more grievous punishment than had been mentioned, speaking now of the days of the war and of that siege. But what He saith is like this. If, saith He, the war of the Romans against the city had prevailed further, all the Jews had perished (for by "no flesh" here, He meaneth no Jewish flesh), both those abroad, and those at home. For not only against those in Judæa did they war, but also those that were dispersed everywhere they outlawed and banished, because of their hatred against the former.

2. But whom doth He here mean by the elect? The believers that were shut up in the midst of them. For that Jews may not say that because of the gospel, and the worship of Christ, these ills took place, He showeth, that so far from the believers being the cause, if it had not been for them, all had perished utterly. For if God had permitted the war to be protracted, not so much as a remnant of the Jews had remained, but lest those of them who had become believers should perish together with the unbelieving Jews, He quickly put down the fighting, and gave an end to the war. Therefore He saith, "But for the elect's sake they shall be shortened." But these things He said to leave an encouragement to those of them who were

---

[1] Matt. xxiv. 19.   [2] Matt. xxiv. 20, 21.
[3] [There is a curious variation in the Greek text here. Our best New Testament MSS. reads σαββάτῳ; above the Homily has ἐν σαββάτῳ, but here σαββάτου, without any preposition.—R.]

[4] Matt. xxiv. 22. [R. V., "And except those days had been shortened, no flesh would have been saved: but," etc.]

shut up in the midst of them, and to allow them to take breath, that they might not be in fear, as though they were to perish with them. And if here so great is His care for them, that for their sakes others also are saved, and that for the sake of Christians remnants were left of the Jews, how great will be their honor in the time for their crowns?

By this He also encouraged them not to be distressed at their own dangers, since these others are suffering such things, and for no profit, but for evil upon their own head.

But He not only encouraged them, but also led them off secretly and unsuspectedly from the customs of the Jews. For if there is not to be a change afterwards, and the temple is not to stand, it is quite evident that the law also shall be made to cease.

However, He spake not this openly, but by their entire destruction He darkly intimated it. But He spake it not openly, lest He should startle them before the time. Wherefore neither at the beginning did He of Himself fall into discourse touching these things; but having first lamented over the city, He constrained them to show Him the stones, and question Him, in order that as it were in answering them their question, He might declare to them beforehand all the things to come.

But mark thou, I pray thee, the dispensation of the Spirit, that John wrote none of these things, lest he should seem to write from the very history of the things done (for indeed he lived a long time after the taking of the city), but they, who died before the taking, and had seen none of these things, they write it, in order that every way the power of the prediction should clearly shine forth.

"Then, if any man shall say unto you, Lo, here is Christ, or there; believe it not: for there shall arise false Christs, and false prophets, and shall show signs and wonders, so as to deceive, if possible, the very elect. Behold, I have told you before.[1] Wherefore if they shall say unto you, Behold, He is in the desert, go not forth; behold, He is in the secret chambers, believe it not. For as the lightning cometh out of the east, and shineth even unto the west, so shall also the coming of the Son of Man be. For wheresoever the carcase is, there shall the eagles be gathered together."[2]

Having finished what concerned Jerusalem,

He passes on to His own coming, and tells the signs of it, not for their use only, but for us also, and for all that shall come after us.

"Then." When? Here, as I have often said, the word, "then," relates not to the connection in order of time with the things before mentioned. At least, when He was minded to express the connection of time, He added, "Immediately after the tribulation of those days,"[3] but here not so, but, "then," not meaning what should follow straightway after these things, but what should be in the time, when these things were to be done, of which He was about to speak. So also when it is said, "In those days cometh John the Baptist,"[4] he is not speaking of the time that should straightway follow, but that many years after, and that in which these things were done, of which He was about to speak. For, in fact, having spoken of the birth of Jesus, and of the coming of the magi, and of the death of Herod, He at once saith, "In those days cometh John the Baptist;" although thirty years had intervened. But this is customary in the Scripture, I mean, to use this manner of narration. So then here also, having passed over all the intermediate time from the taking of Jerusalem unto the preludes of the consummation, He speaketh of the time just before the consummation. "Then," He saith therefore, "if any man shall say unto you, Lo, here is Christ, or there, believe it not."

Awhile He secures them by the place, mentioning the distinguishing marks of His second coming, and the indications of the deceivers. For not, as when at His former coming He appeared in Bethlehem, and in a small corner of the world, and no one knew Him at the beginning, so doth He say it shall be then too; but openly and with all circumstance, and so as not to need one to tell these things. And this is no small sign that He will not come secretly.

But mark how here He saith nothing of war (for He is interpreting the doctrine concerning His advent), but of them that attempt to deceive. For some in the days of the apostles deceived the multitude, "for they shall come," saith He, "and shall deceive many;"[5] and others shall do so before His second coming, who shall also be more grievous than the former. "For they shall show," He saith, "signs and wonders, so as to deceive if possible the very elect:"[6] here He is speaking of Antichrist, and indicates that some also shall minister to him. Of him

---

1 [R. V., "to lead astray, if possible, even the elect. Behold, I have told you beforehand."]
2 Matt. xxiv. 23-28. [The citation is in verbal agreement with the received text.—R.]
3 Matt. xxiv. 29.
4 Matt. iii. 1. See the comment on that place.
5 Matt. xxiv. 11.
6 Matt. xxiv. 24.

Paul too speaks on this wise. Having called him " man of sin," and " son of perdition," He added, " Whose coming is after the working of Satan, with all power and signs and lying wonders; and with all deceivableness of unrighteousness in them that perish." [1]

And see how He secures them; " Go not forth into the deserts, enter not into the secret chambers." He did not say, " Go, and do not believe;" but, " Go not forth, neither depart thither." For great then will be the deceiving, because that even deceiving miracles are wrought.

3. Having told them how Antichrist cometh, as, for instance, that it will be in a place; He saith how Himself also cometh. How then doth He Himself come? "As the lightning cometh out of the east, and shineth even unto the west, so shall also the coming of the Son of Man be. For wheresoever the carcase is, there also will the eagles be gathered together." [2]

How then shineth the lightning? It needs not one to talk of it, it needs not a herald, but even to them that sit in houses, and to them in chambers it shows itself in an instant of time throughout the whole world. So shall that coming be, showing itself at once everywhere by reason of the shining forth of His glory. But He mentions also another sign, " where the carcase is, there also shall the eagles be;" meaning the multitude of the angels, of the martyrs, of all the saints.

Then He tells of fearful prodigies. What are these prodigies? " Immediately after the tribulation of those days," saith He, " the sun shall be darkened." [3] Of the tribulation of what days doth He speak? Of those of Antichrist and of the false prophets? For there shall be great tribulation, there being so many deceivers. But it is not protracted to a length of time. For if the Jewish war was shortened for the elect's sake, much more shall this temptation be limited for these same's sake. Therefore, He said not, " after the tribulation," but IMMEDIATELY " after the tribulation of those days shall the sun be darkened," for almost at the same time all things come to pass. For the false prophets and false Christs shall come and cause confusion, and immediately He Himself will be here. Because no small turmoil is then to prevail over the world.

But how doth He come? The very creation being then transfigured, for " the sun shall be darkened," not destroyed, but overcome by the light of His presence; and the stars shall fall, for what shall be the need of

them thenceforth, there being no night? and " the powers of Heaven shall be shaken," and in all likelihood, seeing so great a change come to pass. For if when the stars were made, they trembled and marvelled (" for when the stars were made, all angels," it is said, " praised Me with a loud voice ") ; [4] much more seeing all things in course of change, and their fellow servants giving account, and the whole world standing by that awful judgment-seat, and those who have lived from Adam unto His coming, having an account demanded of them of all that they did, how shall they but tremble, and be shaken?

" Then shall appear the sign of the Son of Man in Heaven;" [5] that is, the cross being brighter than the sun, since this last will be darkened, and hide himself, and that will appear when it would not appear, unless it were far brighter than the beams of the sun. But wherefore doth the sign appear? In order that the shamelessness of the Jews may be more abundantly silenced. For having the cross as the greatest plea, Christ thus cometh to that judgment-seat, showing not His wounds only, but also the death of reproach. " Then shall the tribes mourn," for there shall be no need of an accusation, when they see the cross; and they shall mourn, that by His death they are nothing benefited; because they crucified Him whom they ought to have adored.

Seest thou how fearfully He has pictured His coming? how He has stirred up the spirits of His disciples? For this reason, let me add, He puts the mournful things first, and then the good things, that in this way also He may comfort and refresh them. And of His passion He suggests to them the remembrance, and of His resurrection, and with a display of glory, [6] He mentions His cross, so that they may not be ashamed nor grieve, whereas indeed He cometh then setting it forth for His sign. And another saith, " They shall look on Him whom they pierced." Therefore it is that they shall mourn, when they see that this is He.

And forasmuch as He had made mention of the cross, He added, " They shall see the Son of Man coming," no longer on the cross, but " in the clouds of Heaven, with power and great glory." [7]

For think not, He meaneth, because thou hearest of the cross, that it is again anything

---

[4] Job xxxviii. 7, LXX. [The LXX. is accurately cited. At this point there is a great variation in the readings of the MSS. of the Homilies, which may be due to the variation from the Hebrew. —R.]
[5] Matt. xxiv. 30.   [6] μετὰ λαμπροῦ τοῦ σχήματος.
[7] Matt. xxiv. 30.

[1] 2 Thess. ii. 9, 10.   [2] Matt. xxiv. 27, 28.   [3] Matt. xxiv. 29.

mournful, for He shall come with power and great glory. But He bringeth it, that their sin may be self-condemned, as if any one who had been struck by a stone, were to show the stone itself, or his garments stained with blood. And He cometh in a cloud as He was taken up, and the tribes seeing these things mourn. Not however that the terrors shall with them proceed no further than mournings; but the mourning shall be, that they may bring forth their sentence from within, and condemn themselves.

And then again, " He will send His angels with a great trumpet,[1] and they shall gather the elect from the four winds, from one end of Heaven to the other." [2]

But when thou hast heard of this, consider the punishment of them that remain. For neither shall they suffer that former penalty only, but this too. And as above He said, that they should say, " Blessed is He that cometh in the name of the Lord," [3] so here, that they shall mourn. For since He had spoken unto them of grievous wars, that they might learn, that together with the fearful things here, the torments there also await them, He brings them in mourning and separated from the elect, and consigned to hell; by this again rousing the disciples, and indicating from how many evils they should be delivered, and how many good things they shall enjoy.

5. And why now doth He call them by angels, if He comes thus openly? ' To honor them in this way also. But Paul saith, that they " shall be caught up in clouds." And He said this also, when He was speaking concerning a resurrection. " For [4] the Lord Himself," it is said, " shall descend from Heaven with a shout, with the voice of an archangel." So that when risen again, the angels shall gather them together, when gathered together the clouds shall catch them up; and all these things are done in a moment, in an instant. For it is not that He abiding above calleth them, but He Himself cometh with the sound of a trumpet. And what mean the trumpets and the sound? They are for arousing, for gladness, to set forth the amazing nature of the things then doing, for grief to them that are left.

Woe is me for that fearful day ! For though we ought to rejoice when we hear these things, we feel pain, and are dejected, and our countenance is sad. Or is it I only that feel thus, and do ye rejoice at hearing of these things ? For upon me at least there comes a kind of shudder when these things

are said, and I lament bitterly, and groan from the very depth of my heart. For I have no part in these things, but in those that are spoken afterwards, that are said unto the virgins, unto him that buried the talents he had received, unto the wicked servant. For this cause I weep, to think from what glory we are to be cast out, from what hope of blessings, and this perpetually, and forever, to spare ourselves a little labor. For if indeed this were a great toil, and a grievous law, we ought even so to do all things; nevertheless many of the remiss would seem to have at least some pretext, a poor pretext indeed, yet would they seem to have some, that the toil was great, and the time endless, and the burden intolerable; but now we can put forward no such objection; which circumstance most of all will gnaw [5] us no less than hell at that time, when for want of a slight endeavor, and a little toil, we shall have lost Heaven, and the unspeakable blessings. For both the time is short, and the labor small, and yet we faint and are supine. Thou strivest on earth, and the crown is in Heaven; thou art punished of men, and art honored of God; the race is for two days, and the reward for endless ages; the struggle is a corruptible body, and the rewards in an incorruptible.

And apart from these things, we should consider another point also, that even if we do not choose to suffer any of the things that are painful for Christ's sake, we must in other ways most assuredly endure them. For neither, though thou shouldest not have died for Christ, wilt thou be immortal; neither though thou shouldest not have cast away thy riches for Christ, wilt thou go away hence with them. These things He requires of thee, which although He should not require them, thou wilt have to give up, because thou art mortal; He willeth thee to do these by thy choice, which thou must do by necessity. So much only He requires to be added, that it be done for His sake; since that these things befall men and pass away, cometh to pass of natural necessity. Seest thou how easy the conflict ? What it is altogether necessary for thee to suffer, that choose to suffer for my sake; let this only be added, and I have sufficient obedience. The gold which thou intendest to lend to another, this lend to me, both at more profit, and in greater security. Thy body, wherewith thou art going to warfare for another, make it to war for me, for indeed I surpass thy toils with recompenses in the most abundant excess. Yet thou in all other matters preferrest him

---

[1] [So Tischendorf, and R. V. margin.—R.]
[2] Matt. xxiv. 31.　　　[3] Matt. xxii. 39.　　　[4] 1 Thess. iv. 16.　　　[5] διατρώγειν.

that giveth thee more as well in loans, as in marketing and in warfare; but Christ alone, when giving more, and infinitely more than all, thou dost not receive. And what is this so great hostility? Wnat is this so great enmity? Where will there be any excuse or defense left for thee, when the reasons for which thou preferrest man to man avail not to induce thee to prefer God to man?

Why dost thou commit thy treasure to the earth? "Give it into my hand," He saith. Doth not the earth's Lord seem to thee more worthy of trust than the earth? This indeed restoreth that which thou laidest in it, though oftentimes not even this, but He gives thee also recompense for His keeping of it? For indeed He doth exceedingly love us. Therefore if thou shouldest wish to lend, He stands ready; or to sow, He receives it; or if thou shouldest wish to build, He draws thee unto Himself, saying, Build in my regions. Why runnest thou unto poor, unto beggarly men, who also for little gains occasion thee great trouble? Nevertheless, not even on hearing these things, do we make up our minds to it, but where are fightings and wars, and wild struggles,[1] and trials and suits of law, and false accusations, thither do we hasten.

5. Doth He not justly turn away from us, and punish us, when He is giving up Himself unto us for all things, and we are resisting Him? It is surely plain to all. For whether thou art desirous to adorn thyself, "Let it, He saith, be with my ornaments;" or to arm thyself, "with my arms," or to clothe thyself, "with my raiment;" or to feed thyself, "at my table;" or to journey, "on my way;" or to inherit, "my inheritance;" or to enter into a country, "the city of which I am builder and maker;" or to build a house, "amongst my tabernacles." "For I, so far from asking thee for a recompense of the things that I give thee, to even make myself owe thee a recompense for this very thing, if thou be willing to use all I have." What can be equal to this munificence, "I am Father, I am brother, I am bridegroom, I am dwelling place, I am food, I am raiment, I am root, I am foundation, all whatsoever thou willest, I am." "Be thou in need of nothing, I will be even a servant, for I came to minister, not to be ministered unto; I am friend, and member, and head, and brother, and sister, and mother; I am all; only cling thou closely[2] to me. I was poor for thee, and a wanderer for thee, on the cross for thee, in the tomb for thee, above I intercede for thee to the Father; on earth I am come for

thy sake am ambassador from my Father. Thou art all things to me, brother, and joint heir, and friend, and member." What wouldest thou more? Why dost thou turn away from Him, who loveth thee? Why dost thou labor for the world? Why dost thou draw water into a broken cistern? For it is this to labor for the present life. Why dost thou comb wool into the fire? Why dost thou "beat the air?"[3] Why dost thou "run in vain?"[4]

Hath not every art an end? It is surely plain to every one. Do thou also show the end of thy worldly eagerness. But thou canst not; for, "yanity of vanities, all is vanity."[5] Let us go to the tombs; show me thy father; show me thy wife. Where is he that was clad in raiment of gold? he that rode in the chariot? he that had armies, that had the girdle,[6] that had the heralds? he that was slaying these, and casting those into prison? he that put to death whom he would, and set free whom he was minded? I see nothing but bones, and a worm, and a spider's web; all those things are earth, all those a fable, all a dream, and a shadow, and a bare relation, and a picture, or rather not so much as a picture. For the picture we see at least in a likeness, but here not so much as a likeness.

And would that the evils stop with this. For now the honor, and the luxury, and the distinction, end with a shadow, with words; but the consequences of them, are no longer limited to a shadow and to words, but continue, and will pass over with us elsewhere, and will be manifest to all, the rapine, the covetousness, the fornications, the adulteries, the dreadful things beyond number; these not in similitude, neither in ashes, but written above, both words and deeds.

With what eyes then shall we behold Christ? For if any one could not bear to see his father, when conscious to himself that he had sinned against him, upon Him who infinitely exceeds a father in forbearance how shall we then look? how shall we bear it? For indeed we shall stand at Christ's judgment-seat, and there will be a strict inquiry into all things.

But if any man disbelieve the judgments to come, let him look at the things here, at those in the prisons, those in the mines, those on the dunghills, the possessed, the frantic, them that are struggling with incurable diseases, those that are fighting against continual poverty, them that live in famine, them that are pierced with irremediable woes, those in captivity. For these persons would not suffer these things here, unless vengeance and

---

[1] παγκράτια.　　[2] οἰκείως ἔχε.

[3] 1 Cor. ix. 26.　　[4] Gal. ii. 2.　　[5] Eccl. i. 2.
[6] See On Stat. Hom. III. p. 59, a badge of military rank.

punishments were to await all the others also that have committed such sins. And if the rest have undergone nothing here, you ought to regard this very fact as a sign that there is surely something to follow after our departure here. For the self-same God of all would not take vengeance on some, and leave others unpunished, who have committed the same or more grievous offenses, unless He designed to bring some punishments upon them there.

By these arguments then and these examples let us also humble ourselves; and let them who are obstinate unbelievers of the judgment believe it henceforth, and become better men; that having lived here in a manner worthy of the kingdom, we may attain unto the good things to come, by the grace and love towards man of our Lord Jesus Christ, to whom be glory forever and ever. Amen.

HOMILY LXXVII.

Matt. XXIV. 32, 33.

"Now learn a parable of the fig tree; when his branch is yet tender, and putteth forth leaves, ye know that summer is nigh: so likewise ye, when ye shall see all these things, know that it is near, even at the doors." [1]

Forasmuch as He had said, "Immediately after the tribulation of those days;" but they sought of this, after how long a time it should be, and desired to know in particular the very day, therefore He puts also the similitude of the fig tree, indicating that the interval was not great, but that in quick succession would occur His advent also. And this He declared not by the parable alone, but by the words that follow, saying, "know that it is near, even at the doors." [2]

Whereby He foretells another thing also, a spiritual summer, and a calm that should be on that day (after the present tempest) for the righteous; but to the sinners the contrary, winter after summer, which He declares in what follows, saying, that the day shall come upon them, when they are living in luxury

But not for this intent only did He put forward this about the fig tree, in order to declare the interval; for it was possible to have set this before them in other ways as well; but that he might hereby also confirm His saying, as assuredly thus to come to pass. For as this *of the fig tree* is of necessity, so that too. For thus, wherever He is minded to speak of that which will assuredly come to pass, He brings forward the neces-

sary courses of nature, both Himself, and the blessed Paul imitating Him. Therefore also when speaking of His resurrection, He saith, "When the corn of wheat hath fallen into the earth, except it die, it abideth alone; but if it die, it bringeth forth much fruit." [3] Whereby also the blessed Paul being instructed uses the same similitude, [4] "Thou fool," he saith, "that which thou sowest is not quickened, except it die." [5]

After this, that they might not straightway return to it again, and say, "When?" he brings to their remembrance the things that had been said, saying, "Verily I say unto you, This generation shall not pass, till all these things be fulfilled!" [6] All these things. What things? I pray thee. Those about Jerusalem, those about the wars, about the famines, about the pestilences, about the earthquakes, about the false Christs, about the false prophets, about the sowing of the gospel everywhere, the seditions, the tumults, all the other things, which we said were to occur until His coming. How then, one may ask, did He say, "This generation?" Speaking not of the generation then living, but of that of the believers. For He is wont to distinguish a generation not by times only,

---

[1] [R. V., "Now from the fig-tree learn her parable : when her branch is now become tender, and putteth forth its leaves, ye know that the summer is nigh ; even so ye also, when ye see all these things, know ye that he (or, it) is nigh, *even* at the doors "]

[2] [The comment seems to imply a preference for the interpretation : "it is nigh," *i. e.*, the day of the Lord's coming.—R.]

[3] John xii. 24.

[4] [A clause is omitted here : "reasoning with the Corinthians about the resurrection.—R."]

[5] 1 Cor. xv. 36.

[6] Matt. xxiv. 34. [R. V., "pass away" and "accomplished."]

but also by the mode of religious service, and practice; as when He saith, "This is the generation of them that seek the Lord."[1]

For what He said above, "All these must come to pass,"[2] and again, "the gospel shall be preached,"[3] this He declares here also, saying, All these things shall surely come to pass, and the generation of the faithful shall remain, cut off by none of the things that have been mentioned. For both Jerusalem shall perish, and the more part of the Jews shall be destroyed, but over this generation shall nothing prevail, not famine, not pestilence, not earthquake, nor the tumults of wars, not false Christs, not false prophets, not deceivers, not traitors, not those that cause to offend, not the false brethren, nor any other such like temptation whatever.

Then to lead them on more in faith, He saith, "Heaven and earth shall pass away, but my words shall not pass away;"[4] that is, it were more easy for these firm, fixed, and immoveable bodies to be blotted out, than for ought of my words to fall to the ground. And he who gainsays these things, let him test His sayings, and when he hath found them true (for so he surely will find them) from what is past, let him believe also the things to come, and let him search out all things with diligence, and he will see the actual events bearing witness to the truth of the prophecy. And the elements He hath brought forward, at once to declare, that the church is of more honor than Heaven and earth, and at the same time to indicate Himself by this also to be maker of all. For since He was speaking of the end, a thing disbelieved by many, He brought forward Heaven and earth, indicating His unspeakable power, and showing with great authority, that He is Lord of all, and by these things rendering His sayings deserving of credit, even with those who are much given to doubt.

"But of that day and hour knoweth no man, no, not the angels of Heaven,[5] neither the Son,[6] but the Father." By saying, not the angels, He stopped their mouths, that they should not seek to learn what these angels know not; and by saying, "neither the Son," forbids them not only to learn, but even to inquire. For in proof that therefore He said this, see after His resurrection, when He saw they were become over curious,

how He stopped their mouths more decidedly. For now indeed He hath mentioned infallible signs, many and endless; but then He saith merely, "It is not for you to know times or seasons." And then that they might not say, we are driven to perplexity, we are utterly scorned, we are not held worthy so much as of this, He says, "which the Father hath put in His own power."[7] And this, because He was exceedingly careful to honor them, and to conceal nothing from them. Therefore He refers it to His Father, both to make the thing awful, and to exclude that of which He had spoken from their inquiry. Since if it be not this, but He is ignorant of it, when will He know it? Will it be together with us? But who would say this? And the Father He knoweth clearly, even as clearly as He knoweth the Son; and of the day is He ignorant? Moreover, "the Spirit indeed searcheth even the deep things of God,"[8] and doth not He know so much as the time of the judgment? But how He ought to judge He knoweth, and of the secrets of each He hath a full perception; and what is far more common than that, of this could He be ignorant? And how, if "all things were made by Him, and without Him was not even one thing made,"[9] was He ignorant of the day? For He who made the worlds,[10] it is quite plain that He made the times also; and if the times, even that day. How then is He ignorant of that which He made?

2. And ye indeed say that ye know even His substance,[11] but that the Son not even the day, the Son, who is always in the bosom of the Father; and yet His substance is much greater than the days, even infinitely greater. How then, while assigning to yourselves the greater things, do you not allow even the less to the Son, "in whom are hid all the treasures of wisdom and knowledge."[12] But neither do you know what God is in His substance, though ten thousand times ye talk thus madly, neither is the Son ignorant of the day, but is even in full certainty thereof.

For this cause, I say, when He had told all things, both the times and the seasons, and had brought it to the very doors ("for it is near," He saith, "even at the doors"), He was silent as to the day. For if thou seek after the day and hour, thou shalt not hear them of me, saith He; but if of times and preludes, without hiding anything, I will tell thee all exactly.

---

[1] Ps. xxiv. 6.
[2] Matt. xxiv. 6.
[3] Matt. xxiv. 14.
[4] Matt. xxiv. 35.
[5] [R. V., "no man, not even the angels of heaven."]
[6] Matt. xxiv. 36. Comp. Mark xiii. 32. [The received text (and A. V.) omit " neither the Son " in Matthew, but not in Mark. The R. V., with our best MSS., inserts the phrase in Matthew. The Fathers vary, but Chrysostom accepts it and comments upon it. Still the last clause, as given above, agrees exactly with Mark xiii. 32, and differs from Matt. xxiv. 36.—R.]

[7] Acts i. 7. [R. V., "set within his own authority."]
[8] 1 Cor. ii. 10.
[9] John i. 3. [Literally rendered.]
[10] αἰῶνας.
[11] Arians [The word οὐσίαν, here used, was the current term in the Arian controversy.—R.]
[12] Col. ii. 3.

For that indeed I am not ignorant of it, I have shown by many things; having mentioned intervals, and all the things that are to occur, and how short from this present time until the day itself (for this did the parable of the fig tree indicate), and I lead thee to the very vestibule; and if I do not open unto thee the doors, this also I do for your good.

And that thou mayest learn by another thing also, that the silence is not a mark of ignorance on His part, see, together with what we have mentioned, how He sets forth another sign also. "But as in the days of Noe they were eating and drinking, marrying and giving in marriage, until the day that the flood came, and took all away; so shall also the coming of the Son of Man be."[1] And these things He spake, showing that He should come on a sudden, and unexpectedly, and when the more part were living luxuriously. For Paul too saith this, writing on this wise, "When they shall speak of peace and safety, then sudden destruction cometh upon them;" and to show how unexpected, He said, "as travail upon a woman with child."[2] How then doth He say, "after the tribulation of those days?" For if there be luxury then, and peace, and safety, as Paul saith, how doth He say, "after the tribulation of those days?" If there be luxury, how is there tribulation? Luxury for them that are in a state of insensibility and peace. Therefore He said not, when there is peace, but "when they speak of peace and safety," indicating their insensibility to be such as of those in Noah's time, for that amid such evils they lived in luxury.

But not so the righteous, but they were passing their time in tribulation and dejection. Whereby He shows, that when Antichrist is come, the pursuit of unlawful pleasures shall be more eager among the transgressors, and those that have learnt to despair of their own salvation. Then shall be gluttony, then revellings, and drunkenness. Wherefore also most of all He puts forth an example corresponding to the thing For like as when the ark was making, they believed not, saith He; but while it was set in the midst of them, proclaiming beforehand the evils that are to come, they, when they saw it, lived in pleasure, just as though nothing dreadful were about to take place; so also now, Antichrist indeed shall appear, after whom is the end, and the punishments at the end, and vengeance intolerable; but they that are held by the intoxication of wicked-

ness shall not so much as perceive the dreadful nature of the things that are on the point of being done. Wherefore also Paul saith, "as travail upon a woman with child," even so shall those fearful and incurable evils come upon them.

And wherefore did He not speak of the ills in Sodom? It was His will to introduce an example embracing all men,[3] and disbelieved after it was foretold. So therefore, as for the more part the things to come are disbelieved, He confirms those things by the past, terrifying their minds. And together with the points I have mentioned, He shows this also, that of the former things also He was the doer. Then again He sets another sign, by all which things He makes it evident, that He is not ignorant of the day. And what is the sign? "Then shall two be in the field; one shall be taken, and one left. Two women shall be grinding at the mill, one shall be taken, and one left. Watch therefore, for ye know not what hour your Lord doth come."[4] And all these things are both proofs that He knew, and calculated to turn them from their inquiry. So for this cause He spake also of the days of Noe, for this cause He said too, "Two shall be on the bed," signifying this, that He should come upon them thus unexpectedly, when they were thus without thought, and "two women grinding at the mill," which also of itself is not the employment of them that are taking thought.

And together with this, He declares that as well servants as masters should be both taken and left, both those who are at ease, and those in toil, as well from the one rank as from the other; even as in the Old Testament He saith, "From him that sitteth upon the throne to the captive woman that is at the mill."[5] For since He had said, that hardly are the rich saved, He shows that not even these are altogether lost, neither are the poor saved all of them, but both out of these and out of those are men saved, and lost.

And to me He seems to declare, that at night will be the advent. For this Luke too saith.[6] Seest thou how accurately He knows all things?

After this again, that they may not ask about it, He added, "Watch therefore, for ye know not what hour your Lord doth come."[7] He said not, "I know not," but, "ye know not." For when He had brought

---

[1] Matt. xxiv. 38, 39. [The passage is abridged.]
[2] 1 Thess. v. 3.

[3] καθολικόν.
[4] Matt. xxiv. 40–42. [The citation agrees with the received text, except in the omission of the articles in verse 40. R. V., "is taken," " is left," in verses 40, 41.—R.]
[5] Exod. xi. 5. [LXX., both altered and abridged.]
[6] Luke xvii. 34.   [7] Matt. xxiv. 42.

them well nigh to the very hour, and had placed them there, again He deters them from the inquiry, from a desire that they should be striving always. Therefore He saith, "Watch," showing that for the sake of this, He did not tell it.

"But know this, that if the good man of the house had known in what watch the thief would come, he would have watched, and would not have suffered his house to be broken up. Therefore be ye also ready, for in such an hour as ye think not the Son of Man cometh." [1]

For this intent He tells them not, in order that they may watch, that they may be always ready; therefore He saith, When ye look not for it, then He will come, desiring that they should be anxiously waiting, and continually in virtuous action.

But His meaning is like this: if the common sort of men knew when they were to die, they would surely strive earnestly at that hour.

3. In order therefore that they may strive, not at that hour only, therefore He tells them not either the common hour, or the hour of each, desiring them to be ever looking for this, that they may be always striving. Wherefore He made the end of each man's life also uncertain.

After this, He openly calls Himself Lord, having nowhere spoken so distinctly. But here He seems to me also to put to shame the careless, that not even as much care as they that expect a thief have taken for their money, not even this much do these take for their own soul. For they indeed, when they expect it, watch, and suffer none of the things in their house to be carried off; but ye, although knowing that He will come, and come assuredly, continue not watching, saith He, and ready so as not to be carried away hence unprepared. So that the day cometh unto destruction for them that sleep. For as that man, if he had known, would have escaped, so also ye, if ye be ready, escape free.

Then, as He had fallen upon the mention of the judgment, He directs His discourse to the teachers next, speaking of punishment and honors; and having put first them that do right, He ends with them that continue in sin, making His discourse to close with that which is alarming.

Wherefore He first saith this, "Who then is the faithful and wise servant, whom his Lord shall set over [2] His household to give

them their meat in their [3] due season? Blessed is that servant, whom his Lord when He cometh shall find so doing. Verily I say unto you, that He shall make him ruler over all His goods." [4]

Tell me, is this too the language of one who is in ignorance? For if because He said, "neither doth the Son know," thou sayest He is ignorant of it; as He saith, "who then?" what wilt thou say? Wilt thou say He is ignorant of this too? Away with the thought. For not even one of them that are frantic would say this. And yet in the former case one might assign a cause; but here not even this. And what when He said, "Peter, lovest thou me?" [5] asking it, knew He not so much as this? nor when He said, "Where have ye laid Him?" [6]

And the Father too will be found to be saying such things. For He Himself likewise saith, "Adam, where art thou?" [7] and, "The cry of Sodom and Gomorrah is waxed great before me. I will go down therefore, and see whether their doings be according to their cry which cometh unto me, and if not, I will know." [8] And elsewhere He saith, "Whether they will hear, whether they will understand." [9] And in the gospel too, "It may be they will reverence my Son:" [10] all which are expressions of ignorance. But not in ignorance did He say these things, but as compassing objects such as became Him: in the case of Adam, that He might drive him to make an excuse for his sin: in that of the Sodomites, that He might teach us never to be positive, till we are present at the very deeds; in that of the prophet, that the prediction might not appear in the judgment of the foolish a kind of compulsion to disobedience; and in the parable in the gospel, that He might show that they ought to have done this, and to have reverenced the Son: but here, as well that they may not be curious, nor over busy again, as that He might indicate that this was a rare and precious thing. And see of what great ignorance this saying is indicative, if at least He know not even him that is set over. For He blesses him indeed, "For blessed," saith He, "is that servant;" but He saith not who this is. "For who is he," He saith, "whom His Lord shall set over?" and, "Blessed is he whom He shall find so doing."

But these things are spoken not of money

[1] Matt. xxiv. 43, 44. [R. V., "if the master of the house had known in what watch the thief was coming, . . . to be broken through . . . . in an hour ye think not," etc.]

[2] [The future tense is peculiar to this citation, also the addition of "their."—R.]

30

[3] See last note.

[4] Matt. xxiv. 45-47. [R. V., "that he will set him over all that he hath." The translator has made a similar change in verse 45. —R.]

[5] John xxi. 16.   [6] John xi. 34.   [7] Gen. iii. 9.

[8] Gen. xviii. 20, 21.   [9] Ezek. ii. 5.

[10] Luke xx. 13. [In Homily LXVIII. this form of the saying is cited as occurring in Matthew (xxi. 37).—R.]

only, but also of speech, and of power, and of gifts, and of every stewardship, wherewith each is entrusted. This parable would suit rulers in the state also, for every one is bound to make full use of what he hath for the common advantage. If it be wisdom thou hast, if power, if wealth, if what it may, let it not be for the hurt of thy fellow-servants, neither for thine own ruin. For this cause, therefore, He requires both things of him, wisdom, and fidelity: for sin arises from folly also. He calls him faithful then, because he hath purloined nothing, neither mispent his Lord's goods without aim or fruit; and wise, because he knew how to dispense the things given him, according as was fit. For indeed we have need of both things, as well not to purloin the goods of our Master, as also to dispense them as is fit. But if the one be wanting, the other halteth. For if he be faithful and steal not, yet were to waste and to spend upon that which concerned him not, great were the blame; and if he should know how to dispense it well, yet were to purloin, again there is no common charge against him.

And let us also that have money listen to these things. For not unto teachers only doth He discourse, but also unto the rich. For either sort were entrusted with riches; those that teach with the more necessary wealth, ye with what is inferior. When then at the time that the teachers are scattering abroad the greater, ye are not willing to show forth your liberality even in the less, or rather not liberality but honesty (for ye give the things of another), what excuse will you have? But now, before the punishment of them that do the contrary things, let us hear the honor of him that approveth himself. "For verily I say unto you, He will set him over all His goods."

What can be equal to this honor? what manner of speech will be able to set forth the dignity, the blessedness, when the King of Heaven, He that possesseth all things, is about to set a man over "all His goods?" Wherefore also He calleth him wise, because he knew, not to give up great things for small, but having been temperate here, hath attained to Heaven.

4. After this, as He ever doth, not by the honor only laid up for the good, but also by the punishment threatened against the wicked, doth He correct the hearers. Wherefore also He added, "But and if the evil servant say in his heart, my Lord delayeth His coming; and shall begin to smite his fellow-servants, and shall eat and drink with the drunken: the Lord of that servant shall come in a day when he looketh not for Him, and in an hour that

he is not aware of,[1] and shall cut him asunder,[2] and shall appoint him his portion with the hypocrites: there shall be weeping and gnashing of teeth."[3]

But if any one should say, "Seest thou what a thought hath entered into his mind, because of the day's not being known, "my Lord," he saith, "delayeth His coming?" we should affirm, that it was not because the day is not known, but because the servant is evil. Else wherefore came not this thought into the heart of the faithful and wise servant. For what, even though the Lord tarry, O wretched man, surely thou lookest that He will come. Why then dost thou not take care?

Hence then we learn, that He doth not so much as tarry. For this judgment is not the Lord's, but that of the evil servant's mind, wherefore also he is blamed for this. For in proof that He doth not tarry, hear Paul saying, "The Lord is at hand, be careful for nothing;"[4] and, "He that cometh will come, and will not tarry."[5]

But do thou hear also what followeth, and learn how continually He reminds them of their ignorance of the day, showing that this is profitable to the servants, and fitted to waken and thoroughly to rouse them. For what though some gained nothing hereby? For neither by other things profitable for them were some profited, but nevertheless He ceaseth not to do His part.

What then is the purport of that which followeth? "For He shall come in a day when he looketh not for Him, and in an hour that he is not aware of;"[6] and shall inflict upon him extreme punishment. Seest thou how even everywhere He puts this, the fact of their ignorance, indicating that it was profitable, and by this making them always earnest minded? For this is the point at which He labors, that we should be always on the watch; and since it is always in luxury that we are supine, but in afflictions we are braced up, therefore everywhere He saith this, that when there is relaxation, then come the terrors. And as further back He showed this by the example of Noah, even so here He saith it is, when that servant is drunken, when he is beating, and that his punishment shall be intolerable.

But let us not regard only the punishment appointed for him, but let us look to this other point too, lest we ourselves also be un-

---

[1] [R. V., "when he expecteth not, and in an hour when he knoweth not."]
[2] [R. V. margin, " severely scourge him."]
[3] Matt. xxiv. 48-51. [The textual variations are slight, and are indicated in the emendations of the A. V. appearing in the above rendering.—R.]
[4] Phil. iv. 5, 6.　　　[5] Heb. x. 37.　　　[6] Matt. xxiv. 50.

awares to ourselves doing the same things. For to this servant are they like, who have money, and give not to the needy. For thou too art steward of thine own possessions, not less than he who dispenses the alms of the church. As then he has not a right to squander at random and at hazard the things given by you for the poor, since they were given for the maintenance of the poor; even so neither mayest thou squander thine own. For even though thou hast received an inheritance from thy father, and hast in this way all thou possessest: even thus all are God's. And then thou for thy part desirest that what thou hast given should be thus carefully dispensed, and thinkest thou not that God will require His own of us with greater strictness, or that He suffers them to be wasted at random? These things are not, they are not so. Because for this end, He left these things in thine hand, in order " to give them their meat in due season." But what meaneth, " in due season?" To the needy, to the hungry. For like as thou gavest to thy fellow-servant to dispense, even so doth the Lord will thee too to spend these things on what is needful. Therefore though He was able to take them away from thee, He left them, that thou mightest have opportunity to show forth virtue; that bringing us into need one of another, He might make our love for one another more fervent.

But thou, when thou hast received, so far from giving, dost even beat. And yet if not to give be blame, what excuse is there for beating? But this, it seems to me, He speaks, hinting at the insolent, and the covetous, and indicating the charge to be heavy, when they beat them, whom they were commanded to feed.

5. But He seemeth to be here hinting also at those that live in luxury, since for luxury too there is laid up a great punishment. " For He eateth and drinketh, it is said, " with the drunken, pointing at gluttony. For not for this purpose didst thou receive, that thou should spend it on luxury, but that thou shouldest lay it out on alms. What! are they thine own things which thou hast? With the goods of the poor hast thou been entrusted, though thou be possessed of them by honest labor, or though it be by inheritance from thy father. What, could not God have taken away these things from thee? But He doth not this, to give thee power to be liberal to the poor.

But mark thou, I pray thee, how throughout all the parables He punishes them that lay not out their money upon the needy. For neither had the virgins robbed other men's goods, but they had not given their own; neither had he that buried the one talent embezzled, but he had not doubled; neither are they that overlooked the hungry punished, because they seized the possessions of others, but because they did not lay out their own, like as also this servant.

Let us hearken, as many as please the belly, as many as lay out on costly banquets the riches that pertain not at all to us, but belong to the needy. For do not, because out of great love to man thou art commanded to give as of thine, therefore suppose these things to be indeed thine own. He lent them to thee, that thou mightest be able to approve thyself. Do not then suppose them to be thine, when giving Him His own. For neither, if thou hadst lent to any one, that he might go and be able to find means of gain, wouldest thou say the money was his. To thee then also hath God given, that thou mightest traffic for Heaven. Make not then the exceeding greatness of His love to man a cause of ingratitude.

Consider of what prayer it were a worthy object, to be able to find after baptism a way to do away one's sins. If He had not said this, Give alms, how many would have said, Would it were possible to give money, and so be freed from the ills to come! But since this hath become possible, again are they become supine.

" But I give," thou sayest. And what is this? Thou hast not yet given as much as she, who cast in the two mites; or rather not so much as the half, nor a very small part of what she gave, but thou layest out the greater part on useless expenses, on banquets, and drunkenness, and extreme extravagance; now bidding, now bidden; now spending, now constraining others to spend; so that the punishment is even rendered twofold for thee, both from what thyself doest, and what thou movest others to do. See at any rate how He Himself blames His servant for this. " For he eateth," He saith, "and drinketh with the drunken." For not the drunken only, but those that are with them, doth He punish, and very fitly, because (together with corrupting their own selves) they make light also of the salvation of others. But nothing does so much provoke God, as for us to be inclined to overlook the things that concern our neighbor. Wherefore showing His anger, He commands him to be cut asunder. Therefore He also affirmed love to be a distinguishing mark of His disciples, since it is altogether necessary that he who loveth should take thought for the things of his beloved.

To this way then let us hold, for this is especially the way that leads up to Heaven, which renders men followers of Christ, which makes them, as far as possible, like God. See at any rate how these virtues are more needful, which have their dwelling by this way. And, if ye will, let us make an inquiry into them, and let us bring forth the sentences from the judgment of God.

Let there be then two ways of most holy life, and let the one secure the goodness of him that practises it, but the other of his neighbor also. Let us see whether is the more approved and leads us to the summit of virtue. Surely he, who seeks his own things only, will receive even from Paul endless blame, and when I say from Paul, I mean from Christ, but the other commendations and crowns. Whence is this evident? Hear what His language is to one, what to the other. "Let no man seek his own, but every man another's wealth." [1] Seest thou he rejects the one, and brings in the other? Again, "Let every one of you please his neighbor for good to edification." Then comes also the praise beyond words with an admonition, "For even Christ pleased not Himself." [2]

Even these judgments then are sufficient to show the victory; but that this may be done even superabundantly, let us see amongst good works, which are confined to ourselves, and which pass over from us to others also. Fasting then, and lying on the bare ground, and keeping virginity, and a self-denying life, these things bring their advantage to the persons themselves who do them; but those that pass from ourselves to our neighbors are almsgiving, teaching, charity. Hear then Paul in this matter also saying, "Though I bestow all my goods to feed the poor, and though I give my body to be burned, and have not charity, I am nothing profited." [3]

6. Seest thou it in itself gloriously celebrated, and crowned?

But if ye be willing, from a third point also let us compare them; and let the one fast, and deny himself, and be a martyr, and be burnt to death, but let another delay his martyrdom for his neighbor's edification; and let him not only delay it, but let him even depart without martyrdom; who will be the more approved after his removal hence? We need not have many words, nor a long circumlocution. For the blessed Paul is at hand, giving his judgment, and saying, "To depart and to be with Christ is better, nevertheless to abide in the flesh is more needful for you;" [4] even

to his removal unto Christ did he prefer his neighbor's edification. For this is in the highest sense to be with Christ, even to be doing His will, but nothing is so much His will, as that which is for one's neighbor's good.

Wilt thou that I tell thee a fourth proof also of these things? "Peter, lovest thou me," saith He; "Feed my sheep:" [5] and having asked him a third time, declared this to be an infallible proof of love. But not to priests only is this said, but to every one of us also, who are also entrusted with a little flock. For do not despise it, because it is a little flock: For "my Father," He saith, "hath pleasure in them." [6] Each of us hath a sheep, let him lead that to the proper pastures. And let the man, as soon as he has risen from his bed, seek after nothing else, but how He may do and say something whereby he may render his whole house more reverent. The woman again, let her be indeed a good housekeeper; but before attending to this, let her have another more needful care, that the whole household may work the works of Heaven. For if in worldly matters, before attending to the affairs of our household, we labor diligently to pay public dues, that we may not for our undutifulness in these matters be beaten and dragged to the market places, and suffer ten thousand unseemly things; much more ought we to do this in things spiritual, and to render what is due to God, the King of all, first, that we may not come to that place, "where is gnashing of teeth."

And after these virtues let us seek, which together with our own salvation will be able in the greatest degree to profit our neighbor. Such is almsgiving, such is prayer, or rather even this latter is by the former made efficacious, and furnished with wings. "For thy prayers," it is said, "and thine alms are come up for a memorial before God." [7] But not prayers only, but fasting also hath its strength from hence. Shouldest thou fast without almsgiving; the act is not so much as counted for fasting; but such a one is worse than a gluttonous man and a drunkard; and so much worse, as cruelty is a more grievous thing than luxury. And why do I speak of fasting? Though thou practise self-denial, though thou practise virginity, thou art set without the bridechamber, if thou hast not almsgiving. And yet what is equal to virginity, which not even in the new dispensation hath come under the compulsion of law, on account of its high excellence? but nevertheless it is cast

---

[1] 1 Cor. x. 24.　　　　　　　　[2] Rom. xv. 2, 3.
[3] 1 Cor. xiii. 3.　　　　　　　　[4] Philip. i. 23, 24.

[5] John xxi. 15-17.　　　[6] Luke xii. 32.　　　[7] Acts x. 4.

out, when it hath not almsgiving. But if virgins are cast out, because they have not this in due abundance, who will be able without this to obtain pardon? There is no man, but he must quite of necessity perish, who hath not this.

For, if in worldly matters no man lives for himself, but artisan, and soldier, and husbandman, and merchant, all of them contribute to the common good, and to their neighbor's advantage; much more ought we to do this in things spiritual. For this is most properly to live: since he at least who is living for himself only, and overlooking all others, is useless, and is not so much as a human being, nor of our race.

What then, thou wouldest say, if I neglect my own interests, while seeking after the good of the rest? It is not possible, for one who seeks after the good of the rest to overlook his own; for he who seeks after the good of the rest pains no man, but pities all, helps them to the utmost of his powers; will rob no man, will covet the goods of no man, will not steal, will not bear false witness; will abstain from all wickedness, will apply himself to all virtue, and will pray for his enemies, and do good to them that plot against him, and will neither revile any, nor speak ill of them, though he hear from them ten thousand evil things; but will speak the words of the apostle: "Who is weak, and I am not weak? who is offended, and I burn not?"[1] But when looking to our own good, it is not quite sure that the good of the rest will follow.

By all which things being persuaded that it is not possible for one to be saved, who hath not looked to the common good, and seeing this man that was cut asunder, and him that buried his talent, let us choose this way, that we may also attain unto eternal life, unto which God grant we may all attain, by the grace and love towards man of our Lord Jesus Christ, to whom be glory, world without end. Amen.

[1] 2 Cor. xi. 29.

HOMILY LXXVIII.

Matt. XXV. 1—30.[1]

"Then shall the kingdom of Heaven," He saith, "be likened unto ten virgins, which took their lamps, and went forth to meet the bridegroom. But five of them were wise, and the other five foolish, which took not," He saith, "oil."

"Then, while the bridegroom tarried, they all slumbered and slept. And at midnight there was a cry made, Behold, the bridegroom cometh, go ye out to meet Him. And the five arose, and being in perplexity, said to the wise, Give us of your oil. But they consented not, saying, Not so, lest there be not enough for us and you; go to them that sell, and buy."

"And while they were gone for this, the bridegroom came, and those went in; but these came afterwards, saying, Lord, Lord, open to us. But He answered and said, Verily I say unto you, I know you not. Watch therefore, for ye know not the day, nor the hour."

"Then He spake again another parable. A man travelling into a far country, called his own servants, and delivered unto them his goods; to one five talents, to another two, to another one, to every man according to his several ability, and took his journey. Then, when the two had brought him the double, he that had been entrusted with the one talent brought it alone, and being blamed saith, I knew that thou art a hard man, reaping where thou hast not sown, and gathering where thou hast not strawed; and I

---

[1] [The passage, as here given, corresponds with that prefixed to the Homily in Field's text. There are some omissions, and some variations from the received text. It seemed unnecessary to annotate it to any extent, since the variations appear in the rendering. In Migne's edition, the citation ends with the words, "while the bridegroom tarried."—R.]

was afraid, and hid thy talent; lo! there thou hast that is thine. His Lord answered and said, Thou wicked servant, thou knewest that I reap where I have not sown, and gather where I have not strawed: thou oughtest therefore to have put my money to the exchangers, and then at my coming I might have received mine own with usury. Take therefore the talent from him, and give it to him that hath ten talents. For to him that hath shall be given, and he shall have more abundantly; but from him that hath not, shall be taken away even that which he hath. And cast ye the unprofitable servant into outer darkness, there shall be weeping and gnashing of teeth."

These parables are like the former parable of the faithful servant, and of him that was ungrateful and devoured his Lord's goods. For there are four in all, in different ways admonishing us about the same things, I mean about diligence in almsgiving, and about helping our neighbor by all means which we are able to use, since it is not possible to be saved in another way. But there He speaks more generally of all assistance which should be rendered to one's neighbor; but as to the virgins, he speaketh particularly of mercifulness in alms, and more strongly than in the former parable. For there He punishes him that beats, and is drunken, and scatters and wastes his lord's goods, but here even him that doth not help, nor spends abundantly his goods upon the needy. For they had oil indeed, but not in abundance, wherefore also they are punished.

But wherefore doth He set forth this parable in the person of the virgins, and doth not merely suppose any person whatever? Great things had He spoken of virginity, saying, "There are eunuchs, who have made themselves eunuchs for the kingdom of Heaven's sake;" and, "He that is able to receive, let him receive it."[1] He knew also that the generality of men would have a great opinion of it. For indeed the work is by nature great, and is shown so by this, that neither under the old dispensation was it fulfilled by these ancient and holy men, nor under the new was it brought under the compulsion of the law. For He did not command this, but left it to the choice of his hearers. Wherefore Paul also said "Now, concerning virgins I have no commandment of the Lord."[2] "For though I praise him that attains thereto, yet I constrain not him that is not willing, neither do I make the thing an injunction." Since then the thing is both great in itself and hath great honor with the multitude, lest any one attaining to this should feel as though he had attained to all, and should be careless about the rest, He putteth forth this parable sufficient to persuade them, that virginity, though it should have everything else,

if destitute of the good things arising out of almsgiving, is cast out with the harlots, and He sets the inhuman and merciless with them. And most reasonably, for the one was overcome by the love of carnal pleasure, but these[3] of money. But the love of carnal pleasure and of money are not equal, but that of carnal pleasure is far keener and more tyrannical. And the weaker the antagonist, the less excusable are these[4] that are overcome thereby. Therefore also He calls them foolish, for that having undergone the greater labor, they have betrayed all for want of the less. But by lamps here, He meaneth the gift itself of virginity, the purity of holiness; and by oil, humanity, almsgiving, succor to them that are in need.

"Then, while the bridegroom tarried, they all slumbered and slept." He shows that the time intervening will not be short, leading His disciples away from the expectation that His kingdom was quite immediately to appear. For this indeed they hoped, therefore He is continually holding them back from this hope. And at the same time He intimates this too, that death is a sleep. For they slept, He saith.

"And about midnight there was a cry made." Either He was continuing the parable, or again He shows that the resurrection will be at night. But the cry Paul also indicates, saying, "With a shout, with a voice of an archangel, with the last trump, He shall come down from Heaven."[5] And what mean the trumpets, and what saith the cry? "The bridegroom cometh." When therefore they had trimmed their lamps, the foolish say unto the wise, "Give us of your oil." Again He calls them foolish, showing that nothing can be more foolish than they who are wealthy here, and depart naked thither, where most of all we have need of humanity, where we want much oil. But not in this respect only were they foolish, but also because they looked to receive it there, and sought it out of season; and yet nothing could be more humane than those virgins,

---

[1] Matt. xix. 12.   [2] 1 Cor. vii. 25.   [3] αἱ δέ.   [4] αἱ νικηθεῖσαι.
[5] 1 Thess. iv. 16 (comp. 1 Cor. xv. 52).

who for this especially were approved. Neither do they seek for it all, for, "Give us," they say, "of your oil;" and the urgency of their need is indicated; "for our lamps," they say, "are going out." But even so they failed, and neither the humanity of those whom they asked, nor the easiness of their request, nor their necessity and want, made them obtain.

But what now do we learn from hence? That no man can protect us there, if we are betrayed by our works, not because he will not, but because he cannot. For these too take refuge in the impossibility. This the blessed Abraham also indicated, saying, "Between us and you there is a great gulf,"[1] so that not even when willing is it permitted them to pass it.

"But go to them that sell, and buy." And who are they that sell? The poor. And where are these? Here, and then should they have sought them, not at that time.

2. Seest thou what great profit arises to us from the poor? shouldest thou take them away, thou wouldest take away the great hope of our salvation. Wherefore here must we get together the oil, that it may be useful to us there, when the time calls us. For that is not the time of collecting it, but this. Spend not then your goods for nought in luxury and vainglory. For thou wilt have need of much oil there.

Having heard these things, those virgins went their way; but they profited nothing. And this He saith, either pursuing the parable, and working it up; or also by these things showing, that though we should become humane after our departure, we shall gain nothing from thence towards our escape. Therefore neither did their forwardness avail these virgins, because they went to them that sell not here, but there; nor the rich man, when he became so charitable, as even to be anxious about his relations. For he that was passing by him that was laid at the gate, is eager to rescue from perils and from hell them whom he did not so much as see, and entreats that some be sent to tell them these things. But nevertheless, he derived no benefit from thence, as neither did these virgins. For when they having heard these things went their way, the bridegroom came, and they that were ready went in with Him, but the others were shut out. After their many labors, after their innumerable toils, and that intolerable fight, and those trophies which they had set up over the madness of natural appetite, disgraced, and with their lamps

gone out, they withdrew, bending down their faces to the earth. For nothing is more sullied than virginity not having mercy; so that even the multitude are wont to call the unmerciful dark. Where then was the profit of virginity, when they saw not the bridegroom? and not even when they had knocked did they obtain, but they heard that fearful saying, "Depart, I know you not."[2] And when He hath said this, nothing else but hell is left, and that intolerable punishment; or rather, this word is more grievous even than hell. This word He speaks to them also that work iniquity.[3]

"Watch therefore, for ye know not the day nor the hour."[4] Seest thou how continually He adds this, showing how awful our ignorance concerning our departure hence? Where now are they, who throughout all their life are remiss, but when they are blamed by us, are saying, At the time of my death, I shall leave money to the poor. Let them listen to these words, and be amended. For indeed at that time many have failed of this, having been snatched away at once, and not permitted so much as to give charge to their relations touching what they wished to be done.

This parable was spoken with respect to mercy in alms; but the one that comes after this, to them that neither in money, nor in word, nor in protection, nor in any other things whatever, are willing to assist their neighbors, but withhold all.

And wherefore can it be that this parable brings forward a king, but that a bridegroom? That thou mightest learn how close Christ is joined unto the virgins that strip themselves of their possessions; for this indeed is virginity. Wherefore Paul also makes this as a definition of the thing. "The unmarried woman careth for the things of the Lord;"[5] such are his words: and, "For that which is comely, and that ye may attend upon the Lord without distraction. These things we advise," he saith.

And if in Luke the parable of the talents is otherwise put, this is to be said, that the one is really different from the other. For in that, from the one capital different degrees of increase were made, for from one pound one brought five, another ten; wherefore neither did they obtain the same recompense; but here, it is the contrary, and the crown is accordingly equal. For he that received two gave two, and he that had received the five again in like manner; but there since from the same beginning one made the greater,

[1] Luke xvi. 26.   [2] Matt. xxv. 12.   [3] See Matt. vii. 23.
[4] Matt. xxv. 13.   [5] 1 Cor. vii. 34, 35.

one the less, increase; as might be expected, in the rewards also, they do not enjoy the same.

But see Him everywhere, not requiring it again immediately. For in the case of the vineyard, He let it out to husbandmen, and went into a far country; and here He committed to them the talents, and took His journey, that thou mightest learn His long-suffering. And to me He seems to say these things, to intimate the resurrection. But here it is no more a vineyard and husbandmen, but all servants. For not to rulers only, nor to Jews, but to all, doth He address His discourse. And they who bring a return unto Him confess frankly, both what is their own, and what their Master's. And the one saith, Lord, "Thou gavest me five talents;" and the other saith, "two," indicating that from Him they received the source of their gain, and they are very thankful, and reckon all to Him.

What then saith the Master? "Well done, thou good" (for this is goodness to look to one's neighbor) "and faithful servant; thou wast faithful over few things, I will set thee over many things: enter thou into the joy of thy Lord,"[1] meaning by this expression all blessedness.

But not so that other one, but how? "I knew that thou art a hard man, reaping where thou sowedst not, and gathering where thou strawedst not: and I was afraid, and hid thy talent: lo, there thou hast that is thine."[2] What then the Master? "Thou oughtest to have put my money to the exchangers,"[3] that is, "that oughtest to have spoken, to have admonished, to have advised." But are they disobedient? Yet this is nought to thee.

What could be more gentle than this? For men indeed do not so, but him that hath put out the money at usury, even him do they make also responsible to require it again. But He not so; but, Thou oughtest, He saith, to have put it out, and to have committed the requiring of it again to me. And I should have required it with increase; by increase upon the hearing, meaning the showing forth of the works. Thou oughtest to have done that which is easier, and to have left to me what is more difficult. Forasmuch then as he did not this, "Take," saith He, "the talent from him, and give it to him that hath ten talents.[4] For unto every one that hath shall be given, and he shall have abundance; but from him that hath not shall be taken away even that which he hath."[5] What then

is this? He that hath a gift of word and teaching to profit thereby, and useth it not, will lose the gift also; but he that giveth diligence, will gain to himself the gift in more abundance; even as the other loseth what he had received. But not to this is the penalty limited for him that is slothful, but even intolerable is the punishment, and with the punishment the sentence, which is full of a heavy accusation. For "cast ye," saith He, "the unprofitable servant into outer darkness: there shall be weeping and gnashing of teeth."[6] Seest thou how not only the spoiler, and the covetous, nor only the doer of evil things, but also he that doeth not good things, is punished with extreme punishment.

Let us hearken then to these words. As we have opportunity, let us help on our salvation, let us get oil for our lamps, let us labor to add to our talent. For if we be backward, and spend our time in sloth here, no one will pity us any more hereafter, though we should wail ten thousand times. He also that had on the filthy garments condemned himself, and profited nothing. He also that had the one talent restored that which was committed to his charge, and yet was condemned. The virgins again entreated, and came unto Him and knocked, and all in vain, and without effect.

Knowing then these things, let us contribute alike wealth, and diligence, and protection,[7] and all things for our neighbor's advantage. For the talents here are each person's ability, whether in the way of protection, or in money, or in teaching, or in what thing soever of the kind. Let no man say, I have but one talent, and can do nothing; for thou canst even by one approve thyself. For thou art not poorer than that widow; thou art not more uninstructed than Peter and John, who were both "unlearned and ignorant men;"[8] but nevertheless, since they showed forth a zeal, and did all things for the common good, they attained to Heaven. For nothing is so pleasing to God, as to live for the common advantage.

For this end God gave us speech, and hands, and feet, and strength of body, and mind, and understanding, that we might use all these things, both for our own salvation, and for our neighbor's advantage. For not for hymns only and thanksgivings is our speech serviceable to us, but it is profitable also for instruction and admonition. And if indeed we used it to this end, we should be imitating our Master; but if for the opposite ends, the devil. Since Peter also, when he

---

[1] Matt. xxv. 23.   [2] Matt. xxv. 24, 25.
[3] Matt. xxv. 27. [R. V., "bankers."]
[4] [R. V., "the ten talents."]   [5] Matt. xxv. 28, 29.

[6] Matt. xxv. 30. [R. V., "cast ye out," etc.]
[7] προστασίαν.   [8] Acts iv. 13.

confessed the Christ, was blessed, as having spoken the words of the Father; but when he refused the cross, and dissuaded it, he was severely reproved, as savoring the things of the devil. But if where the saying was of ignorance, so heavy is the blame, when we of our own will commit many sins, what favor shall we have?

Such things then let us speak, that of themselves they may be evidently the words of Christ. For not only if I should say, "Arise, and walk;"[1] neither if I should say, "Tabitha, arise,"[2] then only do I speak Christ's words, but much more if being reviled I bless, if being despitefully used I pray for him that doeth despite to me. Lately indeed I said, that our tongue is a hand laying hold on the feet of God; but now much more do I say, that our tongue is a tongue imitating the tongue of Christ, if it show forth the strictness that becometh us, if we speak those things which He wills. But what are the things which He wills us to speak? Words full of gentleness and meekness, even as also He Himself used to speak, saying to them that were insulting Him, "I have not a devil;"[3] and again, "If I have spoken evil, bear witness of the evil."[4] If thou also speak in this way; if thou speak for thy neighbor's amendment, thou wilt obtain a tongue like that tongue. And these things God Himself saith; "For he that bringeth out the precious from the vile, shall be as my mouth;"[5] such are His words.

When therefore thy tongue is as Christ's tongue, and thy mouth is become the mouth of the Father, and thou art a temple of the Holy Ghost, then what kind of honor could be equal to this? For not even if thy mouth were made of gold, no nor even of precious stones, would it shine like as now, when lit up with the ornament of meekness. For what is more lovely than a mouth that knoweth not how to insult, but is used to bless *and give good words?* But if thou canst not bear to bless him that curses thee, hold thy peace, and accomplish but this for the time; and proceeding in order, and striving as thou oughtest, thou wilt attain to that other point also, and wilt acquire such a mouth, as we have spoken of.

4. And do not account the saying to be rash. For the Lord is loving to man, and the gift cometh of His goodness. It is rash to have a mouth like the devil, to have a tongue resembling that of an evil demon, especially for him that partakes of such mys-teries, and communicates of the very flesh of the Lord. Reflecting then on these things, become like Him, to the utmost of thy power. No longer then will the devil be able so much as to look thee in the face, when thou art become such a one as this. For indeed he recognizes the image of the King, he knows the weapons of Christ, whereby he was worsted. And what are these? Gentleness and meekness. For when on the mountain Christ overthrew and laid low the devil who was assaulting him, it was not by making it known that He was Christ, but He entrapped him by these sayings, He took him by gentleness, he turned him to flight by meekness. Thou also must do this; shouldest thou see a man become a devil, and coming against thee, even so do thou likewise overcome. Christ gave thee also power to become like Him, so far as thy ability extends. Be not afraid at hearing this. The fear is not to be like Him. Speak then after His manner, and thou art become in this respect such as He, so far as it is possible for one who is a man to become so.

Wherefore greater is he that thus speaks, than he that prophecies. For this is entirely a gift, but in the other is also thy labor and toil. Teach thy soul to frame thee a mouth like to Christ's mouth. For it can create such things, if it will; it knows the art, if it be not remiss. And how is such a mouth made? one may ask. By what kind of colorings? by what kind of material? By no colorings, indeed, or material; but by virtue only, and meekness, and humility.

Let us see also how a devil's mouth is made; that we may never frame that. How then is it made? By curses, by insults, by envy, by perjury. For when any one speaks his words, he takes his tongue. What kind of excuse then shall we have; or rather, what manner of punishment shall we not undergo; when this our tongue, wherewith we are allowed to taste of the Lord's flesh, when this, I say, we overlook, speaking the devil's words?

Let us not overlook it, but let us use all diligence, in order to train it to imitate its Lord. For if we train it to this, it will place us with great confidence at Christ's judgment seat. Unless any one know how to speak thus, the judge will not so much as hear him. For like as when the judge chances to be a Roman, he will not hear the defense of one who knows not how to speak thus; so likewise Christ, unless thou speak after His fashion, will not hear thee, nor give heed.

Let us learn therefore to speak in such wise as our Judge is wont to hear; let it be

---

[1] Matt. ix. 5.   [2] Acts ix. 40.
[3] John viii. 49.   [Greek, " demon."]
[4] John xviii. 23.   [5] Jer. xv. 19.

our endeavor to imitate that tongue. And shouldest thou fall into grief, take heed lest the tyranny of despondency pervert thy tongue, but that thou speak like Christ. For He too mourned for Lazarus and Judas. Shouldest thou fall into fear, seek again to speak even as He. For He Himself fell into fear for thy sake, with regard to His manhood.[1] Do thou also say, "Nevertheless, not as I will, but as Thou wilt."[2]

And if thou shouldest lament, weep calmly as He. Shouldest thou fall into plots and sorrows, treat these too as Christ. For indeed He had plots laid against Him, and was in sorrow, and saith, "My soul is exceeding sorrowful, even unto death."[3] And all the examples He presented to thee, in order that thou shouldest continually observe the same measures, and not destroy the rules that have been given thee. So shalt thou be able to have a mouth like His mouth, so while treading on the earth, thou wilt show forth a tongue like to that of Him who sits on high; thou wilt maintain the limits He observed in despondency, in anger, in suffering, in agony.

How many are they of you that desire to see His form? Behold, it is possible, not to see Him only, but also to become like Him; if we are in earnest.

Let us not delay then. He doth not so readily accept prophets' lips, as those of meek and forbearing men. "For many will say unto me," He saith, "Have we not prophesied in Thy name? And I will say unto them, I know you not."[4]

But the lips of Moses, because he was exceeding gentle and meek ("for Moses," it is said, "was a meek man above all the men which were upon the face of the earth"[5]), He so accepted and loved, as to say, "Face to face, mouth to mouth, did He speak, as a man speaketh unto his friend."[6]

Thou wilt not command devils now, but thou shalt then command the fire of hell, if thou keep thy mouth like to Christ's mouth. Thou shalt command the abyss of fire, and shalt say unto it, "Peace, be still,"[7] and with great confidence shalt set foot in the Heavens, and enjoy the kingdom; unto which God grant all of us to attain, by the grace and love towards man of our Lord Jesus Christ, with whom, be unto the Father, together with the Holy Ghost, glory, might, honor, now and always, and world without end. Amen.

---

[1] κατὰ τὸν τῆς οἰκονομίας λόγον.   [2] Luke xxii. 42.
[3] Matt. xxvi. 38.

[4] Matt. vii. 22, 23.
[6] Exod. xxxiii. 11 ; Numb. xii. 8.

[5] Numb. xii. 3.
[7] Mark iv. 39.

HOMILY LXXIX.

MATT. XXV. 31—41.

"When the Son of Man shall come in the glory of His Father, and all the holy angels with Him, then shall He sit," saith He, "upon the throne of His glory, and He shall divide the sheep from the kids;"[1] [and the one He will accept, because they fed Him, when an hungered, and gave Him drink when thirsty, and took Him in when a stranger, and clothed Him when naked, and visited Him when sick, and came to see Him when in prison: and He will give the kingdom to them. But the others, accusing them for the opposite things, He will send into the eternal fire, prepared for the devil and his angels.][2]

UNTO this most delightful portion of Scripture, which we do not cease continually revolving, let us now listen with all earnestness and compunction, this wherewith His

---

[1] [So R. V. margin.]
[2] [The Greek text condenses the narrative of the Gospel, altering the form in some places, as appears from the rendering given above.—R.]

discourse ended, even as the last thing, reasonably; for great indeed was His regard for philanthropy and mercy. Wherefore in what precedes He had discoursed concerning this in a different way; and here now in some respects more clearly, and more earnestly, not setting forth two nor three nor five persons, but the whole world; although most assuredly the former places, which speak of two persons, meant not two persons, but two portions of mankind, one of them that disobey, the other of the obedient. But here He handleth the word more fearfully, and with fuller light. Wherefore neither doth He say, " The kingdom is likened," any more, but openly shows Himself, saying, "When the Son of Man shall come in His glory." For now is He come in dishonor, now in affronts and reproaches; but then shall He sit upon the throne of His glory.

And continually doth He make mention of glory. For since the cross was near, a thing that seemed to be matter of reproach, for this cause He raises up the hearer; and brings before his sight the judgment seat, and setteth round him all the world.

And not in this way only doth He make His discourse awful, but also by showing the Heavens opened. For all the angels will be present with Him, He saith, themselves also to bear witness, in how many things they had ministered, when sent by the Lord for the salvation of men.

And everything will help to render that day fearful. Then, " shall be gathered together," He saith, "all nations," that is, the whole race of men. "And He shall separate them one from another, as the shepherd his sheep." For now they are not separated, but all mingled together, but the division then shall be made with all exactness. And for a while it is by their place that He divides them, and makes them manifest; afterwards by the names He indicates the dispositions of each, calling the one kids,[1] the other sheep, that He might indicate the unfruitfulness of the one, for no fruit will come from kids; and the great profit from the other, for indeed from sheep great is the profit, as well from the milk, as from the wool, and from the young, of all which things the kid[2] is destitute.

But while the brutes have from nature their unfruitfulness, and fruitfulness, these have it from choice, wherefore some are punished, and the others crowned. And He doth not punish them, until He hath pleaded with them; wherefore also, when He hath put them in their place, He mentions the charges against them. And they speak with meekness, but they have no advantage from it now; and very reasonably, because they passed by a work so much to be desired. For indeed the prophets are everywhere saying this, " I will have mercy and not sacrifice,"[3] and the lawgiver by all means urged

them to this, both by words, and by works; and nature herself taught it.

But mark them, how they are destitute not of one or two things only, but of all. For not only did they fail to feed the hungry, or clothe the naked; but not even did they visit the sick, which was an easier thing.

And mark how easy are His injunctions. He said not, " I was in prison, and ye set me free; I was sick, and ye raised me up again;" but, " ye visited me," and, " ye came unto me." And neither in hunger is the thing commanded grievous. For no costly table did He seek, but what is needful only, and His necessary food, and He sought in a suppliant's garb, so that all things were enough to bring punishment on them; the easiness of the request, for it was bread; the pitiable character of Him that requesteth, for He was poor; the sympathy of nature, for He was a man; the desirableness of the promise, for He promised a kingdom; the fearfulness of the punishment, for He threatened hell. The dignity of the one receiving, for it was God, who was receiving by the poor; the surpassing nature of the honor, that He vouchsafed to condescend so far; His just claim for what they bestowed, for of His own was He receiving. But against all these things covetousness once for all blinded them that were seized by it; and this though so great a threat was set against it.

For further back also He saith, that they who receive not such as these shall suffer more grievous things than Sodom; and here He saith, " Inasmuch as ye did it not unto one of the least of these my brethren, ye did it not unto me."[4] What sayest Thou? they are Thy brethren; and how dost Thou call them least. Why, for this reason they are brethren, because they are lowly, because they are poor, because they are outcast. For such doth He most invite to brotherhood, the unknown, the contemptible, not meaning by these the monks only, and them that have occupied the mountains, but every believer; though he be a secular person, yet if he be hungry, and famishing, and naked, and a stranger, His will is he should have the benefit of all this care. For baptism renders a man a brother, and the partaking of the divine mysteries.

2. Then, in order that thou mayest see in another way also the justice of the sentence, He first praises them that have done right, and saith, " Come, ye blessed of my Father, inherit the kingdom prepared for you before

---

1 ἐρίφια, *hædos*, not *capras*; St. Jerome.   2 ἔριφος.
3 Hosea vi. 6.

4 Matt. xxv. 45; comp. verse 40. [" My brethren " is added here from verse 40. The order of words varies from that found in that verse.—R.]

the foundation of the world. For I was an hungered, and ye gave me meat," and all that follows.[1] For that they may not say, we had it not, He condemns them by their fellow-servants; like as the virgins by the virgins, and the servant that was drunken and gluttonous by the faithful servant, and him that buried his talent, by them that brought the two, and each one of them that continue in sin, by them that have done right.

And this comparison is sometimes made in the case of an equal, as here, and in the instance of the virgins, sometimes of him that hath advantage, as when he said, "The men of Nineveh shall rise up and shall condemn this generation, because they believed at the preaching of Jonas; and, behold, a greater than Jonas is here;" and, "The queen of the south shall condemn this generation, because she came to hear the wisdom of Solomon;"[2] and of an equal again, "They shall be your judges;"[3] and again of one at advantage, "Know ye not, that we shall judge angels, how much more things that pertain to this life?"[4]

And here, however, it is of an equal; for he compares rich with rich, and poor with poor. And not in this way only doth He show the sentence justly passed, by their fellow-servants having done what was right when in the same circumstances, but also by their not being obedient so much as in these things in which poverty was no hindrance; as, for instance, in giving drink to the thirsty, in looking upon him that is in bonds, in visiting the sick. And when He had commended them that had done right, He shows how great was originally His bond of love towards them. For, "Come," saith He, "ye blessed of my Father, inherit the kingdom prepared for you from the foundation of the world." To how many good things is this same equivalent, to be blessed, and blessed of the Father? And wherefore were they counted worthy of such great honors? What is the cause? "I was an hungered, and ye gave me meat; I was thirsty, and ye gave me drink;" and what follows.

Of what honor, of what blessedness are these words? And He said not, Take, but, "Inherit," as one's own, as your Father's, as yours, as due to you from the first. For, before you were, saith He, these things had been prepared, and made ready for you, forasmuch as I knew you would be such as you are.

And in return for what do they receive such things? For the covering of a roof, for a garment, for bread, for cold water, for visiting, for going into the prison. For indeed in every case it is for what is needed; and sometimes not even for that. For surely, as I have said, the sick and he that is in bonds seeks not for this only, but the one to be loosed, the other to be delivered from his infirmity. But He, being gracious, requires only what is within our power, or rather even less than what is within our power, leaving to us to exert our generosity in doing more.

But to the others He saith, "Depart from me, ye cursed," (no longer of the Father; for not He laid the curse upon them, but their own works), "into the everlasting fire, prepared," not for you, but "for the devil and his angels." For concerning the kingdom indeed, when He had said, "Come, inherit the kingdom," He added, "prepared for you before the foundation of the world;" but concerning the fire, no longer so, but, "prepared for the devil." I, saith He, prepared the kingdom for you, but the fire no more for you, but "for the devil and his angels;" but since ye cast yourselves therein, impute it to yourselves. And not in this way only, but by what follows also, like as though He were excusing Himself to them, He sets forth the causes.

"For I was an hungered, and ye gave me no meat." For though He that came to thee had been thine enemy, were not His sufferings enough to have overcome and subdued even the merciless? hunger, and cold, and bonds, and nakedness, and sickness, and to wander everywhere houseless? These things are sufficient even to destroy enmity. But ye did not these things even to a friend, being at once friend, and benefactor, and Lord. Though it be a dog we see hungry, often we are overcome; and though we behold a wild beast, we are subdued; but seeing the Lord, art thou not subdued? And wherein are these things worthy of defense?

For if it were this only, were it not sufficient for a recompense? (I speak not of hearing such a voice, in the presence of the world, from Him that sitteth on the Father's throne, and of obtaining the kingdom), but were not the very doing it sufficient for a reward? But now even in the presence of the world, and at the appearing of that unspeakable glory, He proclaims and crowns thee, and acknowledges thee as His sustainer and host, and is not ashamed of saying such things, that He may make the crown brighter for thee.

So for this cause, while the one are punished justly, the others are crowned by grace. For though they had done ten thousand

---

[1] Matt. xxv. 34-40.   [2] Matt. xii. 41, 42.
[3] Matt. xii. 27.   [4] 1 Cor. vi. 3.

things, the munificence were of grace, that in return for services so small and cheap, such a heaven, and a kingdom, and so great honor, should be given them.

"And it came to pass, when Jesus had finished these sayings,[1] He said unto His disciples, Ye know that after two days is the passover, and the Son of Man is betrayed to be crucified."[2] In good season again doth He speak of the passion, when He had reminded them of the kingdom, and of the recompense there, and of the deathless punishment; as though He had said, Why are ye afraid at the dangers that are for a season, when such good things await you?

3. But mark thou, I pray thee, how He hath in all His first sayings after a new manner worked up and thrown into the shade what was most painful to them. For He said not, Ye know that after two days I am betrayed, but, "Ye know that after two days is the passover,"[3] to show that what is done is a mystery, and that a feast and celebration is being kept for the salvation of the world, and that with foreknowledge He suffered all. So then, as though this were sufficient consolation for them, He did not even say anything to them now about a resurrection; for it was superfluous, after having discoursed so much about it, to speak of it again. And moreover, as I said, He shows that even His very passion is a deliverance from countless evils, having by the passover reminded them of the ancient benefits in Egypt.

"Then were assembled together the chief priests, and the scribes, and the elders of the people, in the palace of the high priest, who was called Caiaphas, and consulted that they might take Jesus by subtlety, and kill Him. But they said, Not on the feast day, lest there be an uproar among the people."[4]

Seest thou the unspeakable corruption of the Jewish state? Attempting unlawful acts, they come to the high priest, desiring to obtain their authority from that quarter, whence they ought to have found hindrance.

And how many high priests were there? For the law wills there should be one, but then there were many. Whence it is manifest, that the Jewish constitution had begun to dissolve. For Moses, as I said, commanded there should be one, and that when he was dead there should be another, and by the life of this person He measured the banishment of them that had involuntarily committed manslaughter. How then were there at that time many high priests? They were afterwards made for a year. And this the evangelist declared, when he was speaking of Zacharias, saying, that he was of the course of Abia. Those therefore doth he here call high priests, who had been high priests.

What did they consult together? That they might seize Him secretly, or that they might put Him to death? Both; for they feared the people. Wherefore also they waited for the feast to be past; for "they said, Not on the feast day."[5] For the devil, lest he should make the passion conspicuous, was not willing it should take place at the passover; but they, lest there should be an uproar. Mark them then ever fearing, not the ills from God, neither lest any greater pollution should arise to them from the season, but in every case the ills from men.

Yet for all this, boiling with anger, they changed their purpose again. For though they had said, "Not at the feast time;" when they found the traitor, they waited not for the time, but slew Him at the feast. But why did they take Him then? They were boiling with rage, as I said; and they expected then to find Him, and all things they did as blinded. For though He Himself made the greatest use of their wickedness for His own dispensation, they were not surely for this guiltless, but deserving of inflictions without number for their temper of mind. At least when all should be set free, even the guilty, then these men slew the guiltless, Him that had conferred on them countless benefits, and who for a time had neglected the Gentiles for their sake. But O lovingkindness! them that were thus depraved, them that were *thus froward, and*[6] full of countless evils, He again saves, and sends the apostles to be slain in their behalf, and by the apostles makes entreaty. "For we are ambassadors for Christ."[7]

Having then such patterns as these, I say not, let us die for our enemies, for we ought to do even this; but since we are too feeble for this, I say for the present, at least let us not look with an evil eye upon our friends, let us not envy our benefactors. I say not for the present, let us do good to them that evil entreat us, for I desire even this; but

---

[1] [R. V., "words;" the word "all" is omitted.—R.]

[2] Matt. xxvi. 1, 2.

[3] [A clause is omitted here: "and then He brings in 'is delivered up to be crucified.'" But some editors read: "'And the Son of Man is delivered up,' and then He brings in 'to be crucified.'" For the latter reading there is no good authority.—R.]

[4] Matt. xxvi. 3-5. [This passage contains some peculiar variations: in verse 3, "in the palace" (court) is substituted for "unto;" in verse 4, the more probable reading should be rendered, "were consulting" (or, taking counsel together). Verse 5 shows no variations, but should be rendered as in the R. V., "Not during the feast, lest a tumult arise among the people." The comments show that Chrysostom understood the verse as referring to the entire festival.—R.]

[5] ["Not during the feast."]

[6] [The words in italics are not sustained by the MSS. collated by Field.—R.]

[7] 2 Cor. v. 20. [R. V., "on behalf of Christ."]

since you are too gross for this, at least avenge not yourselves. What is our condition, a scene, and acting? Wherefore can it be that ye set yourselves directly against the acts enjoined? It is not for nought that all else hath been written and how many things He did at the very cross sufficient to recall them to Him; but that thou mightest imitate His goodness, that thou mightest emulate His lovingkindness. For indeed He cast them to the ground, and restored the servant's ear, and discoursed with forbearance; and great miracles did He show forth, when lifted up, turning aside the sunbeams, bursting the rocks, raising the dead, frightening by dreams the wife of him that was judging Him, at the very judgment showing forth all meekness (which was of power not less than miracles to gain them over), forewarning them of countless things in the judgment hall; on the very cross crying aloud, " Father, forgive them their sin."[1] And when buried, how many things did He show forth for their salvation? And having risen again, did he not straightway call the Jews? did He not give them remission of sins? did He not set before them countless blessings? What can be more strange than this? They that crucified Him, and were breathing murder, after they crucified Him, became sons of God.

What can be equal to this tenderness? On hearing these things let us hide our faces, to think that we are so far removed from Him whom we are commanded to imitate. Let us at least see how great the distance, that we may at any rate condemn ourselves, for warring with these, in behalf of whom Christ gave His life, and not being willing to be reconciled to them, whom that He might reconcile He refused not even to be slain; unless this too be some expense, and outlay of money, which ye object in almsgiving.

4. Consider of how many things thou art guilty; and so far from being backward to forgive them that have injured thee, thou wilt even run unto them that have grieved thee, in order that thou mayest have a ground for pardon, that thou mayest find a remedy for thine own evil deeds.

The sons of the Greeks, who look for nothing great, have often shown self-command toward these: and thou who art to depart hence with such hopes, shrinkest, and art slow to act; and that which time effects, this thou endurest not to do before the time for God's law, but willest this passion to be quenched without reward, rather than for a reward? For neither, if this should have

arisen from the time, wilt thou have any advantage, but rather great will be the punishment, because, what time hath effected, this the law of God persuaded thee not to do.

But if thou sayest that thou burnest with the memory of the insult; call to mind if any good hath been done thee by him that hath offended thee, and how many ills thou hast occasioned to others.

Hath he spoken ill of thee, and disgraced thee? Consider also that thou hast spoken thus of others. How then wilt thou obtain pardon, which thou bestowest not on others? But hast thou spoken ill of no one? But thou hast heard men so speaking, and allowed it. Neither is this guiltless.

Wilt thou learn how good a thing it is not to remember injuries, and how this more than anything pleases God? Them that exult over persons, justly chastised by Himself, He punishes. And yet they are justly chastised; but thou shouldest not rejoice over them. So the prophet having brought many accusations, added this also, saying, " They felt nothing for the affliction of Joseph;"[2] and again, " She that inhabiteth Enan, came not forth to lament for the place near her."[3] And yet both Joseph (that is, the tribes that were sprung from him), and the neighbors of these others, were punished according to the purpose of God; nevertheless, it is His will that we sympathize even with these. For if we, being evil, when we are punishing a servant, if we should see one of his fellow slaves laughing, we at the same time are provoked the more, and turn our anger against him; much more will God punish them that exult over those whom He chastises. But if upon them that are chastised by God it is not right to trample, but to grieve with them, much more with them that have sinned against us. For this is love's sign; love God prefers to all things. For as in the royal purple, those are precious amongst the flowers and dyes, which make up this robing; so here too, these virtues are the precious ones, which preserve love. But nothing maintains love so much as the not remembering them that have sinned against us.

" Why? did not God guard the other side also? Why? did He not drive him that hath done the wrong to him that is wronged? Doth He not send him from the altar to the other, and so after the reconciliation invite him to the table?" But do not therefore wait for the other to come, since thus thou hast lost all. For to this intent most especially doth He appoint unto thee an unspeaka-

---

[1] Luke xxiii. 34. [Freely cited.]　　　　[2] Amos vi. 6.　　　　[3] Micah i. 11, LXX.

ble reward, that thou mayest prevent the other, since, if thou art reconciled by his entreaties, the amity is no longer the result of the divine command, but of the other party's diligence. Wherefore also thou goest away uncrowned, while he receives the rewards.

What sayest thou? Hast thou an enemy, and art thou not ashamed? Why is not the devil enough for us, that we bring upon ourselves those of our own race also? Would that not even he had been minded to war against us; would that not even he were a devil!

Knowest thou not how great the pleasure after reconciliation? For what, though in our enmity it appear not great? For that it is sweeter to love him that doth us wrong than to hate him, after the enmity is done away thou shalt be able to learn full well.

5. Why then do we imitate the mad, devouring one another, warring against our own flesh?

Hear even under the Old Testament, how great regard there was for this, "The ways of revengeful men are unto death.[1] One man keepeth anger against another, and doth he seek healing of God?"[2] "And yet He allowed, ' eye for eye,' and ' tooth for tooth,' how then doth He find fault?" Because He allowed even those things, not that we should do them one to another, but that through the fear of suffering, we might abstain from the commission of crime. And besides, those acts are the fruits of a short-lived anger, but to remember injuries is the part of a soul that practises itself in evil.

But hast thou suffered evil? yet nothing so great, as thou wilt do to thyself by remembering injuries. And besides, it is not so much as possible for a good man to suffer any evil. For suppose there to be any man, having both children and a wife, and let him practise virtue, and let him have moreover many occasions of being injured, as well abundance of possessions, as sovereign power, and many friends, and let him enjoy honor; only let him practise virtue, for this must be added, and let us in supposition lay plagues upon him. And let some wicked man come unto him, and involve him in losses. What

then is that to him who accounts money nothing? Let him kill his children. What this to him, who learns to be wise touching the resurrection? Let him slay his wife; what is this to him who is instructed not to sorrow for them that are fallen asleep? let him cast him into dishonor. What this to him who accounts the things present, the flower of the grass? If thou wilt, let him also torture his body, and cast him into prison, what this to him that hath learnt, "Though our outward man perish, yet the inward man is renewed;"[3] and that "tribulation worketh approval?"[4]

Now I had undertaken that he should receive no harm; but the account as it proceeded hath shown that he is even advantaged, being renewed, and becoming approved.

Let us not then vex ourselves with others, injuring ourselves, and rendering our soul weak. For the vexation is not so much from our neighbors' wickedness, as from our weakness. Because of this, should any one insult us, we weep, and frown; should any one rob us, we suffer the same like those little children, which the more clever of their companions provoke for nothing, grieving them for small causes; but nevertheless these too, if they should see them vexed, continue to tease them, but if laughing, they on the contrary leave off. But we are more foolish even than these, lamenting for these things, about which we ought to laugh.

Wherefore I entreat, let us let go this childish mind, and lay hold of Heaven. For indeed, Christ willeth us to be men, perfect men. On this wise did Paul also command, "Brethren, be not children in understanding," he saith, "howbeit in malice be ye children."[5]

Let us therefore be children[6] in malice, and flee wickedness, and lay hold on virtue, that we may attain also to the good things eternal, by the grace and love towards man of our Lord Jesus Christ, to whom be glory and might, world without end. Amen.

---

[1] Prov. xii. 28, LXX.   [2] Ecclus. xxviii. 3.

[3] 2 Cor. iv. 16. [R. V., "our outward man is decaying.']
[4] Rom. v. 4. [R. V., "probation;" δοκιμήν cannot be accurately rendered by any single English term.—R.]
[5] 1 Cor. xiv. 20. [R. V., "be not children in mind; howbeit in malice be ye babes."]
[6] ["babes."]

HOMILY LXXX.

MATT. XXVI. 6, 7.

"Now when Jesus was in Bethany, in the house of Simon the leper, there came unto Him a woman having an alabaster box of very precious ointment, and poured it on His head, as He sat at meat."

THIS woman seems indeed to be one and the same with all the evangelists, yet she is not so; but though with the three she doth seem to me to be one and the same,[1] yet not so with John, but another person, one much to be admired, the sister of Lazarus.

But not without purpose did the evangelist mention the leprosy of Simon, but in order that He might show whence the woman took confidence, and came unto Him. For inasmuch as the leprosy seemed a most unclean disease, and to be abhorred, and yet she saw Jesus had both healed the man (for else He would not have chosen to have tarried with a leper), and had gone into his house; she grew confident, that He would also easily wipe off the uncleanness of her soul. And not for nought doth He name the city also, Bethany, but that thou mightest learn, that of His own will He cometh to His passion. For He who before this was fleeing through the midst of them; then, at the time when their envy was most kindled, comes near within about fifteen furlongs; so completely was His former withdrawing Himself a part of a dispensation.[2]

The woman therefore having seen Him, and having taken confidence from thence, came unto Him. For if she that had the issue of blood, although conscious to herself of nothing like this, yet because of that natural seeming uncleanness, approached Him trembling and in fear; much more was it likely this woman should be slow, and shrink back because of her evil conscience.

Wherefore also it is after many women, the Samaritan, the Canaanite, her that had the issue of blood, and other besides, that she cometh unto Him, being conscious to herself of much impurity; and then not publicly but in a house. And whereas all the others were coming unto Him for the healing of the body alone, she came unto Him by way of honor only, and for the amendment of the soul. For neither was she at all afflicted in body, so that for this most especially one might marvel at her.

And not as to a mere man did she come unto Him; for then she would not have wiped *His feet* with her hair, but as to one greater than man can be. Therefore that which is the most honorable member of the whole body, this she laid at Christ's feet, even her own head.

"But when His disciples saw it, they had indignation," such are the words, "saying, To what purpose is this waste? For this ointment might have been sold for much, and given to the poor. But when Jesus understood it, He said, Why trouble ye the woman? for she hath wrought a good work upon me? For ye have the poor always with you, but me ye have not always. For in that she hath poured this ointment on my body, she did it for my burial. Verily I say unto you, Wheresoever this gospel shall be preached in the whole world, there shall also this, that this woman hath done, be told for a memorial of her."[3]

And whence had they this thought? They used to hear their Master saying, "I will have mercy, and not sacrifice,"[4] and blaming the Jews, because they omitted the weightier matters, judgment, and mercy, and faith, and discoursing much on the mount concerning almsgiving, and from these things they inferred with themselves, and reasoned, that if He accepts not whole burnt offerings, neither

---

[1] St. Augustin, on St. John, Hom. XLIX. sec. 3, speaks of the identity as doubtful. See also Greswell, vol. ii., Diss. XVII., and vol. iii. Diss. III. It seems that the *occasion* recorded in Luke vii. 37 must have been different, whether the person were the same or not. St. Chrysostom supposes *two* unctions *at Bethany*. See note at the end of " Sermons preached at St. Saviour's Church, Leeds." [Augustin discusses the question more fully in his *Harmony of the Gospels*, see *Nicene Fathers*, vol. vi. pp. 173, 174; He holds that there were two occasions, one named by Luke, and the other by Matthew, Mark and John, but that Mary was the person anointing on both occasions. This leads to the identification of Mary, the sister of Lazarus, with Mary Magdalene. But there is no proof that Luke refers to the latter. The opinion of Chrysostom seems to be that Matthew, Mark and Luke refer to the same person, and John to another on a different occasion. But to this there are insuperable objections.—R.]

[2] Lit., an economy.

[3] Matt. xxvi. 8-13. [The Greek text agrees with the received with the exception of a change of order in the first clause of verse 11. In verse 12, the R. V. renders, "to prepare me for burial," and in verse 12, "be spoken of" for "be told."—R.]

[4] See ix. 13, and xii. 7.

the ancient worship, much more will He not accept the anointing of oil.

But though they thus thought, He knowing her intention suffers her. For indeed great was her reverence, and unspeakable her zeal; wherefore of this exceeding condescension, He permitted the oil to be poured even on His head.

For if He refused not to become man, and to be borne in the womb, and to be fed at the breast, why marvellest thou, if He doth not utterly reject this? For like as the Father suffered a savor of meat, and smoke, even so did He the harlot, accepting, as I have already said, her intention. For Jacob too anointed a pillar to God, and oil was offered in the sacrifices, and the priests were anointed with ointment.

But the disciples not knowing her purpose found fault unseasonably, and by the things they laid to her charge, they show the woman's munificence. For saying, that it might have been sold for three hundred pence, they showed how much this woman had spent on the ointment, and how great generosity she had manifested. Wherefore He also rebuked them, saying, "Why trouble ye the woman?" And He adds a reason, as it was His will again to put them in mind of His passion, "For she did it," He said, "for my burial." And another reason, "For ye have the poor always with you, but me ye have not always;" and, "Wheresoever the gospel shall be preached, that shall be told also which this woman hath done."

Seest thou how again He declares beforehand the going forth unto the Gentiles, in this way also consoling them for His death, if after the cross His power was so to shine forth, that the gospel should be spread abroad in every part of the earth.

Who then is so wretched as to set his face against so much truth? For lo! what He said is come to pass, and to whatever part of the earth thou mayest go, thou wilt see her celebrated.

And yet neither was the person that did it distinguished, nor had what was done many witnesses, neither was it in a theatre, but in a house, that it took place, and this a house of some leper, the disciples only being present.

2. Who then proclaimed it, and caused it to be spread abroad? It was the power of Him who is speaking these words. And while of countless kings and generals the noble exploits even of those whose memorials remain have sunk into silence; and having overthrown cities, and encompassed them with walls,[1] and set up trophies, and enslaved many nations, they are not known so much as by hearsay, nor by name, though they have both set up statues, and established laws; yet that a woman who was a harlot poured out oil in the house of some leper, in the presence of ten men, this all men celebrate throughout the world; and so great a time has passed, and yet the memory of that which was done hath not faded away, but alike Persians and Indians, Scythians and Thracians, and Sarmatians, and the race of the Moors, and they that dwell in the British Islands, spread abroad that which was done secretly in a house by a woman that had been a harlot.[2]

Great is the loving-kindness of the Lord. He endureth an harlot, an harlot kissing his feet, and moistening them with oil, and wiping them with her hair, and He receives her, and reproves them that blame her. For neither was it right that for so much zeal the woman should be driven to despair.

But mark thou this too, how far they were now raised up above the world, and forward in almsgiving. And why was it He did not merely say, "She hath wrought a good work," but before this, "Why trouble ye the woman?" That they might learn not at the beginning to require too high principles of the weaker sort. Therefore neither doth He examine the act merely itself by itself, but taking into account the person of the woman. And indeed if He had been making a law, He would not have brought in the woman, but that thou mightest learn that for her sake these things were said, that they might not mar her budding faith, but rather cherish it, therefore He saith it, teaching us whatever good thing may be done by any man, though it be not quite perfect, to receive it, and encourage it, and advance it, and not to seek all perfection at the beginning. For, that at least He Himself would rather have desired this, is manifest from the fact, that He required a bag to be borne, who had not where to lay His head. But then the time demanded not this, that He should correct the deed, but that He should accept it only. For even as, if any one asked Him, without the woman's having done it, He would not have approved this; so, after she had done it, He looks to one thing only, that she be not driven to perplexity by the reproof of the disciples, but that she should go from His care, having been made more cheerful and better. For indeed after the oil had been

[1] [A clause is omitted here: "and conquered in wars."—R.]

[2] [This accords with the assumed identity with the woman spoken of in Luke vii. But there seems to be no proof that Chrysostom identified the woman with Mary Magdalene. Compare p. 41, Homily VI. 8.—R.]

31

poured out, their rebuke had no seasonableness.

Do thou then likewise, if thou shouldest see any one provide sacred vessels and offer them, and loving to labor upon any other ornament of the church, about its walls or floor; do not command what has been made to be sold, or overthrown, lest thou spoil his zeal. But if, before he had provided them, he were to tell thee of it, command it to be given to the poor; forasmuch as He also did this not to spoil the spirit of the woman, and as many things as He says, He speaks for her comfort.

Then because He had said, ' She hath done it for my burial;'' that He might not seem to perplex the woman, by making mention of such a thing as this, His burial and death, I mean; see how by that which follows He recovers her, saying, ''What she hath done shall be spoken of in the whole world.''

And this was at once consolation to His disciples, and comfort and praise to her. For all men, He saith, shall celebrate her hereafter; and now too hath she announced beforehand my passion, by bringing unto me what was needed for a funeral, let not therefore any man reprove her. For I am so far from condemning her as having done amiss, or from blaming her as having not acted rightly, that I will not suffer what hath been done to lie hid, but the world shall know that which has been done in a house, and in secret. For in truth the deed came of a reverential mind, and fervent faith, and a contrite soul.

And wherefore did He promise the woman nothing spiritual; but the perpetual memory? From this He is causing her to feel a confidence about the other things also. For if she hath wrought a good work, it is quite evident she shall receive a due reward.

'' Then went one of the twelve, he that was called Judas Iscariot, unto the chief priests, and said unto them, What will ye give me, and I will deliver Him unto you?''[1] Then. When? When these things were spoken, when He had said, it is for my burial, and not even thereby was he moved to compunction, neither when he heard that the Gospel should be preached everywhere did he fear (and yet it was the language of unspeakable power), but when women showed so much honor, and women that had been harlots, then he wrought the devil's works.

But what can be the reason they mention his surname? Because there was also another

Judas. And they do not shrink from saying, He was of the twelve; so entirely do they hide none of those things which seem to be matters of reproach. And yet they might have said merely this, that he was one of the disciples, for there were others besides. But now they add, of the twelve, as though they had said, of the first company of those selected as the best, of them with Peter and John. Because for one thing did they care, for truth alone, not for concealing what things were done.

For this cause many of the signs they pass by, but of the things that appear to be matters of reproach they conceal nothing; but though it be word, though it be deed, though it be what you will of this kind, they proclaim it with confidence.

3. And not these only, but even John himself, who utters the higher doctrines. For he most of all tells us of the affronts and the reproachful things that were done unto Him.

And see how great is the wickedness of Judas, in that he comes unto them of his own accord, in that he does this for money, and for such a sum of money.

But Luke saith, that he conferred with the chief captains.[2] For after that the Jews became seditious, the Romans set over them those that should provide for their good order   For their government had now undergone a change according to the prophecy.

To these then he went and said, '' What will ye give me, and I will deliver him unto you. And they covenanted with him for thirty pieces of silver. And from that time he sought opportunity to betray Him.''[3] For indeed he was afraid of the multitude, and desired to seize him alone.

Oh madness! how did covetousness altogether blind him! For he that had often seen Him when He went through the midst, and was not seized, and when He afforded many demonstrations of His Godhead and power, looked to lay hold on Him; and this while He was using like a charm for him so many, both awful and soothing words, to put an end to this evil thought. For not even at the supper did He forbear from this care of him, but unto the last day discoursed to him of these things. But he profited nothing. Yet not for that did the Lord cease to do His part.

Knowing this, then, let us also not intermit

---

[1] Matt. xxvi. 14, 15. [R. V., '' Then one of the twelve, who was called Judas Iscariot, went unto the chief priests, and said, What are ye willing to give me,'' etc.]

[2] Luke xxii. 4. [The explanation is untenable. The '' captains'' (στρατηγοῖς) were not '' chiliarchs,'' but the officers of the temple guard; comp. Luke xxii. 52, where the same word occurs.—R.]

[3] Matt. xxvi. 15, 16. [R. V., '' And they weighed unto him thirty,'' etc. . . . '' to deliver Him *unto them*.'' The same word as in verse 15.—R.]

to do all things unto them that sin and are remiss, warning, teaching, exhorting, admonishing, advising, though we profit nothing. For Christ indeed foreknew that the traitor was incorrigible, yet nevertheless He ceased not to supply what could be done by Himself, as well admonishing as threatening and bewailing over him, and nowhere plainly, nor openly, but in a concealed way. And at the very time of the betrayal, He allowed him even to kiss Him, but this benefited him nothing. So great an evil is covetousness, this made him both a traitor, and a sacrilegious robber.

Hearken, all ye covetous, ye that have the disease of Judas; hearken, and beware of the calamity. For if he that was with Christ, and wrought signs, and had the benefit of so much instruction, because he was not freed from the disease, was sunk into such a gulf; how much more shall ye, who do not so much as listen to the Scripture, who are constantly riveted to the things present, become an easy prey to this calamity, unless ye have the advantage of constant care. Every day was that man with Him, who had not where to lay His head, and every day was he instructed by deeds, and by words, not to have gold, nor silver, nor two coats; and yet he was not taught self restraint; and how dost thou expect to escape the disease, if thou hast not the benefit of earnest attention, and dost not use much diligence? For terrible, terrible is the monster, yet nevertheless, if thou be willing, thou wilt easily get the better of him. For the desire is not natural; and this is manifest from them that are free from it. For natural things are common to all; but this desire has its origin from remissness alone; hence it takes its birth, hence it derives its increase, and when it has seized upon those who look greedily after it, it makes them live contrary to nature. For when they regard not their fellow countrymen, their friends, their brethren,[1] in a word all men, and with these even themselves, this is to live against nature. Whence it is evident that the vice and disease of covetousness, wherein Judas, being entangled, became a traitor, is contrary to nature. And how did he become such a one, you may say, having been called by Christ? Because God's call is not compulsory, neither does it force the will of them who are not minded to choose virtue, but admonishes indeed, and advises, and does and manages all things, so as to persuade men to become good; but if some endure not, it does not compel. But if thou wouldest learn from what cause he became such as he was, thou wilt find him to have been ruined by covetousness.

And how was he taken by this calamity? one may say. Because he grew remiss. For hence arise such changes, as on the other hand, those for the better from diligence. How many for instance that were violent, are now more gentle than lambs? how many lascivious persons have become afterwards continent? how many, heretofore covetous, yet now have cast away even their own possessions? And the contrary again has been the result of remissness. For Gehazi also lived with a holy man, and he too became depraved from the same disease. For this calamity is the most grievous of all. Hence come robbers of tombs, hence menslayers, hence wars and fightings, and whatsoever evil thou mayest mention, it cometh hence. And in every respect is such a one useless, whether it be requisite to lead an army or to guide a people: or rather not in public matters only, but also in private. If he is to marry a wife, he will not take the virtuous woman, but the vilest of all; if he have to buy a house, not that which becomes a free man, but what can bring much rent; if he is to buy slaves, or what else it may be, he will take the worst.

And why do I speak of leading an army, and guiding a people, and managing households; for should he be a king, he is the most wretched of all men, and a pest to the world, and the poorest of all men. For he will feel like one of the common sort, not accounting all men's possessions to be his, but himself to be one of all; and when spoiling all men's goods, thinks himself to have less than any. For measuring the things present by his desire for those whereof he is not yet possessed, he will account the former nothing compared to the latter. Wherefore also one saith, "There is not a more wicked thing than a covetous man."[2]

4. For such a one both setteth himself to sale, and goeth about, a common enemy of the world, grieving that the earth doth not bear gold instead of the corn, and the fountains instead of streams, and the mountains instead of stones; vexed at the fruitfulness of the seasons, troubled at common benefits; shunning every means whence one cannot obtain money; undergoing all things whence one can scrape together so much as two farthings; hating all men, the poor and the rich; the poor, lest they should come and beg of him; the rich, because he hath not their possessions. All men he accounts to be possessed

---

[1] [The words "their kinsmen" should be inserted here.—R.]   [2] Ecclus. x. 9.

of what is his, and as though he had been injured by all, so is he displeased with all. He knows not plenty, he has no experience of satiety, he is more wretched than any, even as, on the other hand, he that is freed from these things, and practises self-restraint, is the most enviable. For the virtuous man, though he be a servant, though a prisoner, is the most happy of all men. For no one shall do him ill, no not though all men should come together out of the world, setting in motion arms and camps, and warring with him. But he that is depraved and vile, and such as we have described, though he be a king, though he have on a thousand diadems, will suffer the utmost extremities, even from a common hand. So feeble is vice, so strong is virtue.

Why then dost thou mourn, being in a state of poverty. Why wailest thou keeping a feast, for indeed it is an occasion of feasting. Why weepest thou, for poverty is a festival, if thou be wise. Why lamentest thou, thou little child; for such a one we should call a little child. Did such a person strike thee? What is this, he made thee more able to endure? But did he take away thy money? He hath removed the greater part of thy burden. But hath he cut off thine honor? Again thou tellest me of another kind of freedom. Hear even those without teaching wisdom touching these things, and saying, "Thou hast suffered no ill, if thou show no regard to it." But hath he taken away that great house of thine, which hath enclosures about it? But behold the whole earth is before thee, the public buildings, whether thou wouldest have them for delight, or for use. And what is more pleasing or more beautiful than the firmament of Heaven.

How long are ye poor and needy? It is not possible for him to be rich, who is not wealthy in his soul; like as it is not possible for him to be poor, who hath not the poverty in his mind. For if the soul is a nobler thing than the body, the less noble parts have not power to affect it after themselves; but the noble part draws over unto herself, and changes those that are not so noble. For so the heart, when it has received any hurt, affects the whole body accordingly; if its temperament be disordered, it mars all, if it be rightly tempered, it profits all. And if any of the remaining parts should have become corrupt, while this remains sound, it easily shakes off what is evil in them also.

And that I may further make what I say more plain, what is the use, I pray thee, of verdant branches, when the root is withering? and what is the harm of the leaves being withered above, while this is sound? So also here there is no use of money, while the soul is poor; neither harm from poverty, when the soul is rich. And how can a soul, one may say, be rich, being in want of money? Then above all times might this be; for then also is it wont to be rich.

For if, as we have often shown, this is a sure proof of being rich, to despise wealth, and to want nothing; and of poverty again, to want, and any one would more easily despise money in poverty than in wealth, it is quite evident that to be in poverty rather makes one to be rich. For indeed that the rich man sets his heart on money more than the poor man, is surely plain to every one; like as the drunken man is thirsty, rather than he that hath partaken of drink sufficiently. For neither is his desire such as to be quenched by too much; but, on the contrary, it is its nature to be inflamed by this. For fire likewise, when it has received more food, then most of all waxes fierce; and the tyranny of wealth, when thou hast cast into it more gold, then most especially is increased.

If then the desiring more be a mark of poverty; and he that is in the possession of riches is like this; he is especially in poverty. Seest thou that the soul then most of all is poor, when it is rich; and then is rich, when it is in poverty?

And if thou wilt, let us exercise our reasoning in persons also, and let there be two, the one having ten thousand talents, the other ten, and from both let us take away these things. Who then will grieve the most? He that hath lost the ten thousand. But he would not have grieved more, unless he had loved it more; but if he loves more, he desires more; but if he desires more, he is more in poverty. For this do we most desire, of which we are most in want, for desire is from want. For where there is satiety, there cannot be desire. For then are we most thirsty, when we have most need of drink.

And all these things have I said, to show that if we be vigilant, no one shall harm us; and that the harm arises not from poverty but from ourselves. Wherefore I beseech you with all diligence to put away the pest of covetousness, that we may both be wealthy here, and enjoy the good things eternal, unto which God grant we may all attain, by the grace and love towards man of our Lord Jesus Christ, to whom be glory world without end. Amen.

HOMILY LXXXI.

Matt. XXVI. 17, 18.

"Now the first day of the feast of unleavened bread the disciples came to Jesus, saying, Where wilt Thou that we prepare for Thee to eat the Passover? And He said, Go into the city to such a man, and say unto him, The Master saith, My time is at hand; I will keep the Passover at thy house with My disciples."

By the first day of the feast of unleavened bread, he means the day before that feast; for they are accustomed always to reckon the day from the evening, and he makes mention of this in which in the evening the passover must be killed;[1] for on the fifth day of the week they came unto Him. And this one[2] calls the day before the feast of unleavened bread,[3] speaking of the time when they came to Him, and another saith on this wise, "Then came the day of unleavened bread, when the passover must be killed;"[4] by the word "came," meaning this, it was nigh, it was at the doors, making mention plainly of that evening. For they began with the evening, wherefore also each adds, when the passover was killed.

And they say, "Where wilt Thou that we prepare for Thee to eat the passover?" So even from this it is manifest, that He had no house, no place of sojourning; and I suppose neither had they. For surely they would have entreated him to come there. But neither had they any, having now parted with all things.

But wherefore did He keep the passover? To indicate by all things unto the last day, that He is not opposed to the law.

And for what possible reason doth He send them to an unknown person? To show by this also that He might have avoided suffering. For He who prevailed over this man's mind, so that he received them, and that by words; what would He not have done with them that crucified Him, if it had been His will not to suffer? And what He did about the ass, this He did here also. For there

too He saith, "If any man say aught unto you, ye shall say, that the Lord hath need of them;"[5] and so likewise here, "The Master saith, I will keep the passover at thy house." But I marvel not at this only, that he received Him, being unknown, but that expecting to bring upon himself such enmity and implacable hostility, he despised the enmity of the multitude.

After this, because they knew him not, He gave them a sign, like as the prophet touching Saul, saying, "Thou shalt find one going up and carrying a bottle;"[6] and here, "carrying a pitcher." And see again the display of his power. For He did not only say, "I will keep the passover," but He adds another thing also, "My time is at hand." And this He did, at once continually reminding His disciples of the passion, so that exercised by the frequency of the prediction, they should be prepared for what was to take place; and at the same time to show to themselves, and to him that was receiving Him, and to all the Jews, which I have often mentioned, that not involuntarily doth He come to His passion. And He adds, "with my disciples," in order that both the preparation should be sufficient, and that the man should not suppose that He was concealing Himself.

"Now when the even was come, He sat down with the twelve disciples."[7] Oh the shamelessness of Judas! For he too was present there, and came to partake both of the mysteries, and of the meal,[8] and is convicted at the very table, when although he had been a wild beast, he would have become tame.

For this cause the evangelist also signifies, that while they are eating, Christ speaks of His betrayal, that both by the time and by the table he might show the wickedness of the traitor.

[1] John xiii. 1.
[2] [But John does not call it the day before.—R.]
[3] Luke xxii. 7.
[4] [The language is somewhat obscure. But it would seem from this passage that Chrysostom believed our Lord ate the passover at the regular time. In Homily LXXXIV., he speaks of the chief priests as neglecting to eat it in their hate against our Lord, explaining in this way the difficulty arising from the statement in John xviii. 28. But in Homily LXXXIII. 3, on the Gospel of John, he presents both views, either that the whole feast is meant, or that our Lord had anticipated the observance of the Paschal supper.—R.]

[5] Matt. xxi. 3.
[6] 1 Sam. x. 3.
[7] Matt. xxvi. 20. [R. V., " was sitting at meat with the twelve disciples." The rec. text omits " disciples," as does one MS. of the Homilies here. Comp. R. V. margin. Below it is omitted by Chrysostom also.—R.]
[8] Lit., salt.

For when the disciples had done, as Jesus had appointed them, "when the even was come, He sat down with the twelve.[1] And as they did eat, He said," we are told, " Verily, I say unto you, that one of you shall betray me."[2] And before the supper, He had even washed his feet. And see how He spares the traitor. For He said not, such a one shall betray me; but, " one of you," so as again to give him power of repentance by concealment. And He chooseth to alarm all, for the sake of saving this man. Of you, the twelve, saith He, that are everywhere present with me, whose feet I washed, to whom I promised so many things.

Intolerable sorrow thereupon seized that holy company. And John indeed saith, they " were in doubt, and looked one upon another,"[3] and each of them asked in fear concerning himself, although conscious to themselves of no such thing. But this evangelist saith, that " being exceeding sorrowful, they began every one of them to say unto Him, Is it I, Lord?[4] And He answered and said, He it is, to whom I shall give a sop, when I have dipped it."[5]

Mark at what time He discovered him. It was when it was His will to deliver the rest from this trouble, for they were even dead with the fear, wherefore also they were instant with their questions. But not only as desiring to deliver them from their distress He did this, but also as willing to amend the traitor. For since after having often heard it generally, he continued incorrigible, being past feeling, He being minded to make him feel more, takes off his mask.

For when being sorrowful they began to say, " Is it I, Lord? He answered and said, He that dippeth[6] with me in the dish, the same shall betray me. The Son of Man goeth, as it is written of Him, but woe to the man by[7] whom the Son of Man is betrayed. It had been good for that man if he had not been born."[8]

Now some say that he was so bold as not to honor his Master, but to dip with Him: but to me Christ seems to have done this too, to shame him the more, and bring him over to a better disposition. For this act again has something more in it.

2. But these things we ought not to pass by at random, but they should be infixed in our minds, and wrath would find no place at any time.

For who, bearing in mind that supper, and the traitor sitting at meat with the Saviour of all, and Him who was to be betrayed thus meekly reasoning, would not put away all venom of wrath and anger? See at any rate how meekly He conducts Himself towards him, " The Son of Man goeth, as it is written of Him."

And these things again He said, both to restore the disciples, that they might not think the thing was a sign of weakness, and to amend the traitor.

" But woe unto that[9] man by whom the Son of Man is betrayed! it had been good for that man if he had not been born." See again in His rebukes His unspeakable meekness. For not even here with invective, but more in the way of compassion, doth He apply what He saith, but in a disguised way again; and yet not his former senselessness only, but his subsequent shamelessness was deserving of the utmost indignation. For after this conviction he saith, " Is it I, Lord?"[10] Oh insensibility! He inquires, when conscious to himself of such things. For the evangelist too, marvelling at his boldness, saith this. What then saith the most mild and gentle Jesus? "Thou sayest." And yet He might have said, O thou unholy, thou all unholy one; accursed, and profane; so long a time in travail with mischief, who hast gone thy way, and made satanical compacts, and hast agreed to receive money, and hast been convicted by me too, dost thou yet dare to ask? But none of these things did He say; but how? " Thou sayest?" fixing for us bounds and rules of long suffering.

But some one will say, Yet if it was written that He was to suffer these things, wherefore is Judas blamed, for he did the things that were written? But not with this intent, but from wickedness. For if thou inquire not concerning the motive, thou wilt deliver even the devil from the charges against him. But these things are not, they are not so. For both the one and the other are deserving of countless punishments, although the world was saved. For neither did the treason of Judas work out salvation for us, but the wisdom of Christ, and the good contrivance of His fair skill, using the wickednesses of others for our advantage.

" What then," one may say, " though Judas had not betrayed Him, would not another have betrayed Him?" And what has this to

---

[1] [See note 7, p. 485.]
[2] Matt. xxvi. 21. [R. V., " were eating."]
[3] John xiii. 22. [Freely cited.]   [4] Matt. xxvi. 22.
[5] John xiii. 26. [This verse is abridged in the Homily. " To whom, having dipped the sop, I will give it," is an exact rendering. " He it is " is supplied above.—R.]
[6] [The words " his hand " are omitted.]
[7] [R. V., " through ;" " that " is omitted.]
[8] Matt. xxvi. 23, 24. [R. V., " good were it," etc.]

[9] [Here " that " is given, as in the received text.—R.]
[10] Matt. xxvi. 25. [R. V., " Rabbi ;" but this change of title is first noticed below.—R.]

do with the question? "Because if Christ must needs be crucified, it must be by the means of some one, and if by some one, surely by such a person as this. But if all had been good, the dispensation in our behalf had been impeded." Not so. For the Allwise knows how He shall bring about our benefits, even had this happened. For His wisdom is rich in contrivance, and incomprehensible. So for this reason, that no one might suppose that Judas had become a minister of the dispensation, He declares the wretchedness of the man. But some one will say again, "And if it had been good if he had never been born, wherefore did He suffer both this man, and all the wicked, to come into the world?" When thou oughtest to blame the wicked, for that having the power not to become such as they are, they have become wicked, thou leavest this, and busiest thyself, and art curious about the things of God; although knowing that it is not by necessity that any one is wicked.

"But the good only should be born," he would say, "and there were no need of hell, nor punishment, nor vengeance, nor trace of vice, but the wicked should either not be born at all, or being born should straightway depart."

First then, it were well to repeat to thee the saying of the apostle, "Nay but, O man, who art thou that repliest against God? Shall the thing formed say to Him that formed it, Why hast Thou made me thus?"[1]

But if thou still demandest reasons, we would say this, that the good are more admired for being among the bad; because their long-suffering and great self-command is then most shown. But thou takest away the occasion of their wrestlings, and conflicts, by saying these things. "What then, in order that these may appear good, are others punished?" saith he. God forbid, but for their own wickedness. For neither because they were brought into the world did they become wicked, but on account of their own wickedness; wherefore also they are punished. For how should they fail to be deserving of punishment, seeing they have so many teachers of virtue, and gain nothing therefrom. For like as the noble and good are worthy of double honor, because they both became good, and took no hurt from the wicked; so also the worthless deserve twofold punishment, both because they became wicked, when they might have become good (they show it who have become such), and because they gained nothing from the good.

But let us see what saith this wretched man, when convicted by his Master. What then saith he? "Is it I, Rabbi?"[2] And why did he not ask this from the beginning? He thought to escape knowledge by its being said, "one of you;" but when He had made him manifest, he ventured again to ask, confiding in the clemency of his Master, that He would not convict him.[3]

3. O blindness! Whereunto hath it led him? Such is covetousness, it renders men fools and senseless, yea reckless, and dogs instead of men, or rather even more fierce than dogs, and devils after being dogs. This man at least received unto him the devil even when plotting against him, but Jesus, even when doing him good, he betrayed, having already become a devil in will. For such doth the insatiable desire of gain make men, out of their mind, frenzy-smitten, altogether given up to gain, as was the case even with Judas.

But how do Matthew and the other evangelists say, that, when he made the agreement touching the treason, then the devil seized him; but John, that "after the sop Satan entered into him."[4] And John himself knew this, for further back he saith, "The devil having now put into the heart of Judas, that he should betray Him."[5] How then doth he say, "After the sop Satan entered into him?" Because he enters not in suddenly, nor at once, but makes much trial first, which accordingly was done here also. For after having tried him in the beginning, and assailed him quietly, after that he saw him prepared to receive him, he thenceforth wholly breathed himself into him, and completely got the better of him.

But how, if they were eating the passover, did they eat it contrary to the law? For they should not have eaten it, sitting down to their meat.[6] What then can be said? That after eating it, they then sat down to the banquet.

But another evangelist saith, that on that evening He not only ate the passover, but also said, "With desire I have desired to eat this passover with you,"[7] that is, on that year. For what reason? Because then the salvation of the world was to be brought about, and the mysteries to be delivered, and the subjects of sorrow to be done away with by His death; so welcome was the cross to Him. But nothing softened the savage monster, nor

---

[1] Rom. ix. 20. [R. V., " Why didst thou make me thus?"]

[2] Matt. xxvi. 25.
[3] [A sentence is omitted here: " On this account, therefore, he also calls Him ' Rabbi ' "—R.]
[4] John xiii. 27.
[5] John xiii. 2. [The Greek text of the citations begins with the words, δείπνου γενομένου, "supper being ended" (A.V.). But the better attested text reads γινομένου, "during supper," (R. V.). The clause is omitted by the translator, for what reason does not appear.— R]
[6] Exod. xii. 11.   [7] Luke xxii. 15.

moved, nor shamed him. He pronounced him wretched, saying, "Woe to that man." He alarmed him again, saying, "It were good for him if he had not been born." He put him to shame, saying, "To whom I shall give a sop, when I have dipped it." And none of these things checked him, but he was seized by covetousness, as by some madness, or rather by a more grievous disease. For indeed this is the more grievous madness.

For what would the madman do like this? He poured not forth foam out of his mouth, but he poured forth the murder of his Lord. He distorted not his hands, but stretched them out for the price of precious blood. Wherefore his madness was greater, because he was mad being in health.

But he doth not utter *sayest thou*, sounds without meaning. And what is more without meaning than this language. "What will ye give me, and I will deliver Him unto you?"[1] "I will deliver," the devil spake by that mouth. But he did not smite the ground with his feet struggling? Nay, how much better so to struggle, than thus to stand upright. But sayest thou, he did not cut himself with stones? Yet how much better, than to do such things as these!

Will ye, that we bring forward the possessed and the covetous, and make a comparison between the two. But let no one account what is done a reproach to himself. For we do not reproach the nature, but we lament the act. The possessed was never clad with garments, cutting himself with stones, and running, he rushes over rough paths, driven headlong of the devil. Do not these things seem to be dreadful? What then, if I shall show the covetous doing more grievous things than these to their own soul, and to such a degree more grievous, that these are considered child's play compared with those. Will you indeed shun the pest? Come then, let us see if they are in any respect in a more tolerable state than they. In none, but even in a more grievous condition; for indeed they are more objects of shame than ten thousand naked persons. For it were far better to be naked as to clothing, than being clad with the fruits of covetousness, to go about like them that celebrate the orgies for Bacchus. For like as they have on madmen's masks and clothes, so have these also. And much as the nakedness of the possessed is caused by madness, so doth madness produce this clothing, and the clothing is more miserable than the nakedness.

And this I will hereby endeavor to prove.

For whom should we say was more mad, amongst madmen themselves; one who should cut himself, or one who together with himself should hurt those who met him? It is quite clear that it is this last. The madmen then strip themselves of their clothing, but these all that meet them. "But these tear their clothes to pieces." And how readily would every one of those that are injured consent that his garment should be torn, rather than be stripped of all his substance?

"But those do not aim blows at the face." In the first place, the covetous do even this, and if not all, yet do all inflict by famine and penury more grievous pains on the belly.

"But those bite not with the teeth." Would that it were with teeth, and not with the darts of covetousness fiercer than teeth. "For their teeth are weapons and darts."[2] For who will feel most pained, he that was bitten once, and straightway healed, or he that is for ever eaten up by the teeth of penury? For penury when involuntary is more grievous than furnace or wild beast.

"But those rush not into the deserts like the possessed of devils." Would it were the deserts, and not the cities, that they overran, and so all in the cities enjoyed security. For now in this respect again, they are more intolerable than all the insane, because they do in the cities these things which the others do in the deserts, making the cities deserts, and like as in a desert, where there is none to hinder, so plundering the goods of all men.

"But they do not pelt with stones them that meet them." And what is this? Of stones it were easy to beware; but of the wounds which by paper and ink they work to the wretched poor (framing writings full of blows without number), who, out of those that fall in with them, can ever easily beware?

4. And let us see also what they do to themselves. They walk naked up and down the city, for they have no garment of virtue. But if this doth not seem to them to be a disgrace, this again is of their exceeding madness, for that they have no feeling of the unseemliness, but while they are ashamed of having their body naked, they bear about the soul naked, and glory in it. And if you wish, I will tell you also the cause of their insensibility. What then is the cause? They are naked amongst many that are thus naked, wherefore neither are they ashamed, like as neither are we in the baths. So that if indeed there were many clothed with virtue, then would their shame appear more. But

---

[1] Matt. xxvi. 15.

[2] Ps. lvii. 4.

now this above all is a worthy subject for many tears, that because the bad are many, bad things are not even esteemed as a disgrace. For besides the rest, the devil hath brought about this too, not to allow them to obtain even a sense of their evil deeds, but by the multitude of them that practise wickedness, to throw a shade over their disgrace; since if it came to pass that he was in the midst of a multitude of persons practising self-restraint, such a one would see his nakedness more.

That they are more naked than the possessed is evident from these things; and that they go into the deserts, neither this again could any one gainsay. For the wide and broad way is more desert than any desert. For though it have many that journey on it, yet none from amongst men, but serpents, scorpions, wolves, adders, and asps. Such are they that. practise wickedness. And this way is not only desert, but much more rugged than that *of the mad*. And this is hereby evident. For stones and ravines and crags do not so wound those that mount them, as robbery and covetousness the souls that practise them.

And that they live by the tombs, like the possessed, or rather that they themselves are tombs, is plain by this. What is a tomb? A stone having a dead body lying in it. Wherein then do these men's bodies differ from those stones? or rather, they are more miserable even than they. For it is not a stone containing a dead body, but a body more insensible than stones, bearing about a dead soul. Wherefore one would not be wrong in calling them tombs. For so did our Lord too call the Jews, for this reason most especially; He went on at least to say, "Their inward parts are full of ravening and covetousness."[1]

Would ye that I show next, how they also cut their heads with stones? Whence then first, I pray thee, wilt thou learn this? From the things here, or from the things to come? But of the things to come they have not much regard; we must speak then of the things here. For are not anxieties more grievous than many stones, not wounding heads, but consuming a soul. For they are afraid, lest those things should justly go forth out of their house, which have come unto them unjustly; they tremble in fear of the utmost ills, are angry, are provoked, against those of their own house, against strangers; and now despondency, now fear, now wrath, comes upon them in succession, and they are as if

they were crossing precipice after precipice, and they are earnestly looking day by day for what they have not yet acquired. Wherefore neither do they feel pleasure in the things they have, both by reason of not feeling confidence about the security of them, and because with their whole mind they are intent upon what they have not yet seized. And like as one continually thirsting, though he should drink up ten thousand fountains, feeleth not the pleasure, because he is not satisfied; so also these, so far from feeling pleasure, are even tormented, the more they heap around themselves; from their not feeling any limit to such desire.

And things here are like this; but let us speak also of the day to come. For though they give not heed, yet it is necessary for us to speak. In the day to come then, one will see everywhere such men as these undergoing punishment. For when He saith, "I was an hungered, and ye gave me no meat; I was thirsty, and ye gave me no drink;"[2] He is punishing these; and when He saith, "Depart into the eternal fire prepared for the devil," He is sending thither them that make a bad use of riches. And the wicked servant, who gives not to his fellow-servants the goods of his Lord, is of the number of these men, and he that buried his talent, and the five virgins.

And whithersoever thou shalt go, thou wilt see the covetous punished. And now they will hear, "There is a void between us and you;"[3] now, "Depart from me into the fire that is prepared."[4] And now being cut asunder, they will go away, where there is gnashing of teeth, and from every place one may see them driven, and finding a place nowhere, but gathered in hell alone.

5. What then is the use of the right faith to us for salvation, when we hear these things? There, gnashing of teeth, and outer darkness, and the fire prepared for the devil, and to be cut asunder, and to be driven away; here, enmities, evil speakings, slanders, perils, cares, plots, to be hated of all, to be abhorred of all, even of the very persons that seem to flatter us. For as good men are admired not by the good only but even by the wicked; so bad men, not the good only, but also the worthless, hate. And in proof that this is true, I would gladly ask of the covetous, whether they do not feel painfully one toward another; and account such more their enemies than those that have done them the greatest wrong; whether they do not also accuse themselves, whether they do not account the thing

---

[1] Matt. xxiii. 25, and comp. verse 27.

[2] Matt. xxv. 42.   [3] Luke xvi. 26. [Freely cited.]
[4] Matt. xxv. 41.

an affront, if any one brings this reproach upon them. For indeed this is an extreme reproach, and a sure proof of much wickedness; for if thou dost not endure to despise wealth, of what wilt thou ever get the better? of lust, or of the mad desire of glory, or anger, or of wrath? And how would any be persuaded of it? For as to lust, and anger, and wrath, many impute it even to the temperament of the flesh, and to this do students of medicine refer the excesses thereof; and him that is of a more hot and languid temperament, they affirm to be more lustful; but him that runs out into a drier kind of ill temperament, eager, and irritable, and wrathful. But with respect to covetousness, no one ever heard of their having said any such thing. So entirely is the pest the effect of mere remissness, and of a soul past feeling.

Therefore, I beseech you, let us give diligence to amend all such things, and to give an opposite direction to the passions that come upon us in every age. But if in every part of our life we sail past the labors of virtue, everywhere undergoing shipwrecks; when we have arrived at the harbor destitute of spiritual freight, we shall undergo extreme punishment. For our present life is an out stretched ocean. And as in the sea here, there are different bays exposed to different tempests, and the Ægean is difficult because of the winds, the Tyrrhenian strait because of the confined space, the Charybdis that is by Africa because of the shallows, the Propontis, which is without the Euxine sea, on account of its violence and currents, the parts without Cadiz because of the desolation, and tracklessness, and unexplored places therein, and other portions for other causes; so also is it in our life.

And the first sea to view is that of our childish days, having much tempestuousness, because of its folly, its facility, because it is not steadfast. Therefore also we set over it guides and teachers, by our diligence adding what is wanting to nature, even as there by the pilot's skill.

After this age succeeds the sea of the youth, where the winds are violent as in the Ægean, lust increasing upon us. And this age especially is destitute of correction; not only because he is beset more fiercely, but also because his faults are not reproved, for both teacher and guide after that withdraw. When therefore the winds blow more fiercely, and the pilot is more feeble, and there is no helper, consider the greatness of the tempest.

After this there is again another period of life, that of men, in which the cares of the household press upon us, when there is a wife, and marriage, and begetting of children, and ruling of a house, and thick falling showers of cares. Then especially both covetousness flourishes and envy.

When then we pass each part of our life with shipwrecks, how shall we suffice for the present life? how shall we escape future punishment. For when first in the earliest age we learn nothing healthful, and then in youth we do not practise sobriety, and when grown to manhood do not get the better of covetousness, coming to old age as to a hold full of bilgewater, and as having made the barque of the soul weak by all these shocks, the planks being separated, we shall arrive at that harbor, bearing much filth instead of spiritual merchandise, and to the devil we shall furnish laughter, but lamentation to ourselves, and bring upon ourselves the intolerable punishments.

That these things may not be, let us brace ourselves up on every side, and, withstanding all our passions, let us cast out the lust of wealth, that we may also attain unto the good things to come, by the grace and love towards man of our Lord Jesus Christ, to whom be glory forever and ever. Amen.

HOMILY LXXXII.

Matt. XXVI. 26—28.

"And as they were eating, Jesus took bread, and gave thanks, and brake it, and gave [1] it to the disciples, and said, Take, eat; This is my body."

"And He took a cup, and gave thanks, and gave it to them, saying, Drink ye all of it; This is my blood of the New Testament, Which is shed for many, for the remission of sins." [2]

Ah! how great is the blindness of the traitor! Even partaking of the mysteries, he remained the same; and admitted to the most holy [3] table, he changed not. And this Luke shows by saying, that after this Satan entered [4] into him, not as despising the Lord's body, but thenceforth laughing to scorn the traitor's shamelessness. For indeed his sin became greater from both causes, as well in that he came to the mysteries with such a disposition, as that having approached them, he did not become better, either from fear, or from the benefit, or from the honor. But Christ forbad him not, although He knew all things, that thou mightest learn that He omits none of the things that pertain to correction. Wherefore both before this, and after this, He continually admonished him, and checked him, both by deeds, and by words; both by fear, and by kindness; both by threatening, and by honor. But none of these things withdrew him from that grievous pest.

Wherefore thenceforth He leaves him, and by the mysteries again reminds the disciples of His being slain, and in the midst of the meal His discourse is of the cross, by the continual repeating of the prediction, making His passion easy to receive. For if, when so many things had been done and foretold, they were troubled; if they had heard none of these things, what would they not have felt?

"And as they were eating, He took bread, and brake it." Why can it have been that He ordained this sacrament then, at the time of the passover? That thou mightest learn

from everything, both that He is the lawgiver of the Old Testament, and that the things therein are foreshadowed because of these things. Therefore, I say, where the type is, there He puts the truth.

But the evening is a sure sign of the fullness of times, and that the things were now come to the very end.

And He gives thanks, to teach us how we ought to celebrate this sacrament, and to show that not unwillingly doth He come to the passion, and to teach us whatever we may suffer to bear it thankfully, thence also suggesting good hopes. For if the type was a deliverance from such bondage, how much more will the truth set free the world, and will He be delivered up for the benefit of our race. Wherefore, I would add, neither did He appoint the sacrament before this, but when henceforth the rites of the law were to cease. And thus the very chief of the feasts He brings to an end, removing them to another most awful table, and He saith, "Take, eat, This is my body, Which is broken for many."

And how were they not confounded at hearing this? Because He had before told unto them many and great things touching this. Wherefore that He establishes no more, for they had heard it sufficiently, but he speaks of the cause of His passion, namely, the taking away of sins. And He calls it blood of a New Testament, that of the undertaking, the promise, the new law. For this He undertook also of old, and this comprises the Testament that is in the new law. And like as the Old Testament had sheep and bullocks, so this has the Lord's blood. Hence also He shows that He is soon to die, wherefore also He made mention of a Testament, and He reminds them also of the former Testament, for that also was dedicated with blood. And again He tells the cause of His death, "which is shed for many for the remission of

---

[1] [εὐχαριστήσας (from verse 27) is substituted for εὐλογήσας; and ἔδωκεν (from the same verse) for ἐδίδου (rec. text) or δούς, of the more ancient authorities.—R.]

[2] [The text agrees exactly with the received; except in the substitution of ὑπέρ for περί. The R. V. following the older authorities, omits "new," also rendering διαθήκης "covenant" in the text.—R.]

[3] [φρικωδεστάτης, "most awful;" literally, "most terrifying," but applied to religious awe.—R.]

[4] Luke xxii. 3; see also John xiii. 27.

sins;" and He saith, "Do this in remembrance of me." Seest thou how He removes and draws them off from Jewish customs. For like as ye did that, He saith, in remembrance of the miracles in Egypt, so do this likewise in remembrance of me. That was shed for the preservation of the firstborn, this for the remission of the sins of the whole world. For, "This," saith He, "is my blood, which is shed for the remission of sins."

But this He said, indicating thereby, that His passion and His cross are a mystery, by this too again comforting His disciples. And like as Moses saith, "This shall be to you for an everlasting memorial,"[1] so He too, "in remembrance of me," until I come.[2] Therefore also He saith, "With desire I have desired to eat this passover,"[3] that is, to deliver you the new rites, and to give a passover, by which I am to make you spiritual.

And He Himself drank of it. For lest on hearing this, they should say, What then? do we drink blood, and eat flesh? and then be perplexed (for when He began to discourse concerning these things, even at the very sayings many were offended),[4] therefore lest they should be troubled then likewise, He first did this Himself, leading them to the calm participation of the mysteries. Therefore He Himself drank His own blood. What then must we observe that other ancient rite also? some one may say. By no means. For on this account He said, "Do this," that He might withdraw them from the other. For if this worketh remission of sins, as it surely doth work it, the other is now superfluous.

As then in the case of the Jews, so here also He hath bound up the memorial of the benefit with the mystery, by this again stopping the mouths of heretics. For when they say, Whence is it manifest that Christ was sacrificed? together with the other arguments we stop their mouths from the mysteries also. For if Jesus did not die, of what are the rites the symbols?

2. Seest thou how much diligence hath been used, that it should be ever borne in mind that He died for us? For since the Marcionists, and Valentinians, and Manichæans were to arise, denying this dispensation, He continually reminds us of the passion even by the mysteries, (so that no man should be deceived); at once saving, and at the same time teaching by means of that sacred table. For this is the chief of the blessings; wherefore Paul also is in every way pressing this.

Then, when He had delivered it, He saith, "I will not drink of the fruit of this wine, until that day when I drink it new with you in my Father's kingdom."[5] For because He had discoursed with them concerning passion and cross, He again introduces what He has to say of His resurrection, having made mention of a kingdom before them,[6] and so calling His own resurrection.

And wherefore did He drink after He was risen again? Lest the grosser sort might suppose the resurrection was an appearance. For the common sort made this an infallible test of His having risen again. Wherefore also the apostles also persuading them concerning the resurrection say this, "We who did eat and drink with Him."[7]

To show therefore that they should see Him manifestly risen, again, and that He should be with them once more, and that they themselves shall be witnesses to the things that are done, both by sight, and by act, He saith, "Until I drink it new with you," you bearing witness. For you shall see me risen again.

But what is "new." In a new, that is, a strange manner, not having a passible body, but now immortal and incorruptible, and not needing food.

It was not then for want that He both ate and drank after the resurrection, for neither did His body need these things any more, but for the full assurance of His resurrection.

And wherefore did He not drink water after He was risen again, but wine. To pluck up by the roots another wicked heresy. For since there are certain who use water in the mysteries; to show that both when He delivered the mysteries He had given wine, and that when He had risen and was setting before them a mere meal without mysteries, He used wine, "of the fruit," He saith, "of the vine." But a vine produces wine, not water.

"And when they had sung an hymn, they went out unto the Mount of Olives."[8] Let them hear this, as many as, like swine eating at random, rudely spurn the natural[9] table, and rise up in drunkenness, whereas it were meet to give thanks, and end with an hymn.

Hear this, as many as wait not again for the last prayer of the mysteries, for this is a

---

[1] Exod. xii. 14.

[2] See 1 Cor. xi. 26, and St. Chrys. on the place, Hom. XXVII. on 1 Cor., where he attributes the words "until He come," expressly to St. Paul. Various early writers attribute them to our Lord.

[3] Luke xxii. 15.   [4] John vi. 60, 61, 66.

[5] Matt. xxvi. 29. [The word "henceforth" is omitted; "this" is joined with "vine," and "new" is in a different position in the Greek. All these are variations from the received text, which is also followed in the R. V.—R.]

[6] εἰς μέσον.

[7] Acts x. 41.

[8] Matt. xxvi. 30.   [9] αἰσθητήν.

symbol of that. He gave thanks before He gave it to His disciples, that we also may give thanks. He gave thanks, and sang an hymn after the giving, that we also may do this self-same thing.

But for what reason doth He go forth unto the mountain? Making Himself manifest, that He may be taken, in order not to seem to hide himself. For He hastened to go to the place which was also known to Judas.

Then "He saith unto them, All ye shall be offended in me."[1] After this He mentions also a prophecy, "For it is written, I will smite the shepherd, and the sheep shall be scattered abroad:"[2] at once persuading them ever to give heed to the things that are written, and at same time making it plain that He was crucified, according to God's purpose; and by everything showing He was no alien from the old covenant, nor from the God preached therein, but that what is done is a dispensation,[3] and that the prophets all proclaimed all things beforehand from the beginning that are comprised in the matter, so that they be quite confident about the better things also.

And He teaches us to know what the disciples were before the crucifixion, what after the crucifixion. For indeed they who, when He was crucified, were not able so much as to stand their ground, these after His death were mighty, and stronger than adamant.

And this self-same thing is a demonstration of His death, the fright and cowardice, I mean, of His disciples. For if when so many things have been both done and said, still some are shameless, and say that He was not crucified; if none of these things had come to pass, to what pitch of wickedness would they not have proceeded? So for this reason, not by His own sufferings only, but by what took place with respect to the disciples, He confirms the word concerning His death, and by the mysteries also, in every way confounding those that are diseased with the pest of Marcion. For this reason He suffers even the chief apostle to deny Him. But if He was not bound nor crucified, whence sprung the fear to Peter, and to the rest of the apostles.

He suffers them not however, on the other hand, to wait until the sorrows, but what saith He? "But after I am risen again, I will go before you into Galilee."[4] For not from Heaven doth He appear at once, neither will He depart into any distant country, but in the same nation, in which He had also been crucified, nearly in the same place, so as hereby again to assure them that He that was crucified was the very same that rose again, and in this way to comfort them more abundantly when in sorrow. Therefore also He said "in Galilee," that being freed from the fears of the Jews they might believe His saying. For which cause indeed He appeared there.

"But Peter answered and said, Though all men should be offended because of Thee, yet will I never be offended."[5]

3. What sayest thou, O Peter? the prophet said, "The sheep shall be scattered;" Christ hath confirmed the saying, and sayest thou, No? Is not what passed before enough, when Thou saidst, "Far be it from Thee,"[6] and thy mouth was stopped? For this then He suffers him to fall, teaching him thereby to believe Christ in all things, and to account His declaration more trustworthy than one's own conscience. And the rest too reaped no small benefit from his denial, having come to know man's weakness, and God's truth. For when He foretells anything, we must no longer be subtle, nor lift up ourselves above the common sort. For, "thy rejoicing," it is said, "thou shalt have in thyself, and not in another."[7] For where he should have prayed, and have said, Help us, that we be not cut off, he is confident in himself, and saith, "Though all men should be offended in Thee, yet will I never;" though all should undergo this, I shall not undergo it, which led him on by little and little to self-confidence. Christ then, out of a desire to put down this, permitted his denial. For since he neither submitted to Him nor the prophet (and yet for this intent He brought in the prophet beside, that they may not gainsay), but nevertheless since he submitted not to His words, he is instructed by deeds.

For in proof that for this intent He permitted it, that He might amend this in him, hear what He saith, "I have prayed for thee, that thy faith fail not."[8] For this He said sharply reproving him, and showing that his fall was more grievous than the rest, and needed more help. For the matters of blame were two; both that he gainsaid; and, that he set himself before the other; or rather a third too, namely, that he attributed all to himself.

To cure these things then, He suffered the fall to take place, and for this cause also

---

[1] Matt. xxvi. 31.
[2] See Zech. xiii. 7. [The words "of the flock" are omitted, as in Mark xiv. 27. They do not occur in the passage in Zechariah. —R.]
[3] οἰκονομία.   [4] Matt. xxvi. 32. [R. V., "am raised up."]

[5] Matt. xxvi. 33. [The word ἀλλά is inserted, as in Mark xiv. 29.—R.]
[6] Matt. xvi. 22.   [7] Gal. vi. 4. [R. V., "glorying."]
[8] Luke xxii. 32. [R. V., "made supplication."]

leaves the others, and addresses Himself earnestly to him. For, "Simon," [1] saith He, "Simon, behold Satan hath desired to have you that he may sift you as wheat;" that is, that he may trouble, confound, tempt you; but "I have prayed for thee, that thy faith fail not."

And why, if Satan desired all, did He not say concerning all, I have prayed for you? Is it not quite plain that it is this, which I have mentioned before, that it is as reproving him, and showing that his fall was more grievous than the rest, that He directs His words to him?

And wherefore said He not, But I did not suffer it, rather than, "I have prayed?" He speaks from this time lowly things, on His way to His passion, that He may show His humanity. For He that has built His church upon Peter's confession, and has so fortified it, that ten thousand dangers and deaths are not to prevail over it; He that hath given him the keys of Heaven, and hath put him in possession of so much authority, and in no manner needed a prayer for these ends (for neither did He say, I have prayed, but with His own authority, "I will build my church, and I will give thee the keys of Heaven"), how should He need to pray, that He might brace up the shaken soul of a single man? Wherefore then did He speak in this way? For the cause which I mentioned, and because of their weakness, for they had not as yet the becoming view of Him.

How then was it that He denied? he said not, that thou mayest not deny, but that thy faith fail not, that thou perish not utterly. For this came from His care.

For indeed fear had driven out all else, for it was beyond measure, and it became beyond measure, since God had to an exceeding degree deprived him of His help, and He did exceedingly deprive him thereof, because there was to an exceeding degree in him the passion of self-will and contradiction. In order then that He might pluck it up by the roots, therefore He suffered the terror to overtake him.

For in proof that this passion was grievous in him, he was not content with his former words, gainsaying both prophet and Christ, but also after these things when Christ had said unto him, "Verily I say unto thee, that this night, [2] before the cock crow, thou shalt deny me thrice," he replieth, "Though I should die with Thee, I will not deny Thee

in any wise." [3] And Luke signifies moreover, that the more Christ warned him, so much the more did Peter exceedingly oppose Him.

What mean these things, O Peter? When He was saying, "One of you shall betray me," thou didst fear lest thou shouldest be the traitor, and didst constrain the disciple to ask, although conscious to thyself of no such thing; but now, when He is plainly crying out, and saying, "All shall be offended," art thou gainsaying it, and not once only, but twice and often? For this is what Luke saith.

Whence then did this come to him? From much love, from much pleasure. I mean, that after that he was delivered from that distressing fear about the betrayal, and knew the traitor, he then spoke confidently, and lifted himself up over the rest, saying, "Though all men shall be offended, yet will I not be offended." [4] And in some degree too his conduct sprung from jealousy, for at supper they reasoned "which of them is the greater," [5] to such a degree did this passion trouble them. Therefore He checked him, not compelling him to the denial, God forbid! but leaving him destitute of His help, and convicting human nature.

See at any rate after these things how he was subdued. For after the resurrection, when he had said, "And what shall this man do?" [6] and was silenced, he ventured no more to gainsay as here, but held his peace. Again, towards the assumption, [7] when he heard, "It is not for you to know times or seasons," [8] again he holds his peace, and contradicts not. After these things, on the house, and by the sheet, when he heard a voice saying to him, "What God hath cleansed, call not thou common," [9] even though he knew not for the time what the saying could be, he is quiet, and strives not.

4. All these things did that fall effect, and whereas before that he attributes all to himself, saying, "Though all men shall be offended, yet will I not be offended;" and, "If I should die, I will not deny Thee" (when he should have said, If I receive the assistance from Thee);—yet after these things altogether the contrary, "Why do ye give heed to us, as though by our own power or holiness we had made him to walk?" [10]

Hence we learn a great doctrine, that a man's willingness is not sufficient, unless any one receive the succor from above; and that again we shall gain nothing by the succor

---

[1] Luke xxii. 31. [R. V., "Satan asked;" margin, "Or, obtained you by asking."]
[2] [The preposition ἐν is omitted from the Greek text.—R.]

[3] Matt. xxvi. 34, 35. [R. V., "If I must die with thee, *yet* will I not deny thee."]
[4] Matt. xxvi. 33. [Slightly changed.]
[5] Luke xxii. 24.   [6] John xxi. 21.   [7] *i. e.*, the Ascension.
[8] Acts i. 7.   [9] Acts x. 15.
[10] Acts iii. 12. [Slightly altered.]

from above, if there be not a willingness. And both these things do Judas and Peter show; for the one, though he had received much help, was profited nothing, because he was not willing, neither contributed his part; but this one, though he was ready in mind, because he received no assistance, fell. For indeed of these two things is virtue's web woven.

Wherefore I entreat you neither (when you have cast all upon God) to sleep yourselves, nor, when laboring earnestly, to think to accomplish all by your own toils. For neither is it God's will that we should be supine ourselves, therefore He worketh it not all Himself; nor yet boasters, therefore He did not give all to us; but having removed what was hurtful in either way, left that which is useful for us. Therefore He suffered even the chief apostle to fall, both rendering him more humbled in mind, and training him thenceforth to greater love. "For to whom more is forgiven," it is said, "he loveth more."[1]

Let us then in everything believe God, and gainsay Him in nothing, though what is said seem to be contrary to our thoughts and senses, but let His word be of higher authority than both reasonings and sight. Thus let us do in the mysteries also, not looking at the things set before us, but keeping in mind His sayings.

For His word cannot deceive, but our senses are easily beguiled. That hath never failed, but this in most things goeth wrong. Since then the word saith, "This is my body," let us both be persuaded and believe, and look at it with the eyes of the mind.

For Christ hath given nothing sensible, but though in things sensible yet all to be perceived by the mind. So also in baptism, the gift is bestowed by a sensible thing, that is, by water; but that which is done is perceived by the mind, the birth, I mean, and the renewal. For if thou hadst been incorporeal, He would have delivered thee the incorporeal gifts bare; but because the soul hath been locked up in a body, He delivers thee the things that the mind perceives, in things sensible.

How many now say, I would wish to see His form, the mark, His clothes, His shoes. Lo! thou seest Him, Thou touchest Him, thou eatest Him. And thou indeed desirest to see His clothes, but He giveth Himself to thee not to see only, but also to touch and eat and receive within thee.

Let then no one approach it with indifference, no one faint-hearted, but all with burn-ing hearts, all fervent, all aroused. For if Jews standing, and having on their shoes and their staves in their hands, ate with haste, much more oughtest thou to be watchful. For they indeed were to go forth to Palestine, wherefore also they had the garb of pilgrims, but thou art about to remove unto Heaven.

5. Wherefore it is needful in all respects to be vigilant, for indeed no small punishment is appointed to them that partake unworthily.

Consider how indignant thou art against the traitor, against them that crucified Him. Look therefore, lest thou also thyself become guilty of the body and blood of Christ. They slaughtered the all-holy body, but thou receivest it in a filthy soul after such great benefits. For neither was it enough for Him to be made man, to be smitten and slaughtered, but He also commingleth Himself with us, and not by faith only, but also in very deed maketh us His body. What then ought not he to exceed in purity that hath the benefit of this sacrifice, than what sunbeam should not that hand be more pure which is to sever this flesh, the mouth that is filled with spiritual fire, the tongue that is reddened by that most awful blood? Consider with what sort of honor thou wast honored, of what sort of table thou art partaking. That which when angels behold, they tremble, and dare not so much as look up at it without awe on account of the brightness that cometh thence, with this we are fed with this we are commingled, and we are made one body and one flesh with Christ. "Who shall declare the mighty works of the Lord,' and cause all His praises to be heard?"[2] What shepherd feeds his sheep with his own limbs? And why do I say, shepherd? There are often mothers that after the travail of birth send out their children to other women as nurses; but He endureth not to do this, but Himself feeds us with His own blood, and by all means entwines us with Himself.

Mark it, He was born of our substance. But, you say, this is nothing to all men; though it does concern all. For if He came unto our nature, it is quite plain that it was to all; but if to all, then to each one. And how was it, you say, that all did not reap the profit therefrom. This was not of His doing, whose choice it was to do this in behalf of all, but the fault of them that were not willing.

With each one of the faithful doth He mingle Himself in the mysteries, and whom He begat, He nourishes by Himself, and

---

[1] Luke vii. 47.　　[2] Ps. cvi. 2.

putteth not out to another; by this also persuading thee again, that He had taken thy flesh. Let us not then be remiss, having been counted worthy of so much both of love and honor. See ye not the infants with how much eagerness they lay hold of the breast? with what earnest desire they fix their lips upon the nipple? With the like let us also approach this table, and the nipple of the spiritual cup. Or rather, with much more eagerness let us, as infants at the breast, draw out the grace of the spirit, let it be our one sorrow, not to partake of this food. The works set before us are not of man's power. He that then did these things at that supper, this same now also works them. We occupy the place of servants. He who sanctifieth and changeth them is the same. Let then no Judas be present, no covetous man. If any one be not a disciple, let him withdraw, the table receives not such. For "I keep the passover," He saith, "with my disciples."[1]

This table is the same as that, and hath nothing less. For it is not so that Christ wrought that, and man this, but He doth this too. This is that upper chamber, where they were then; and hence they went forth unto the mount of Olives.

Let us also go out unto the hands of the poor, for this spot is the mount of Olives. For the multitude of the poor are olive-trees planted in the house of God, dropping the oil, which is profitable for us there, which the five virgins had, and the others that had not received perished thereby. Having received this, let us enter in that with bright lamps we may meet the bridegroom; having received this, let us go forth hence.

Let no inhuman person be present, no one that is cruel and merciless, no one at all that is unclean.

6. These things I say to you that receive, and to you that minister. For it is necessary to address myself to you also, that you may with much care distribute the gifts there. There is no small punishment for you, if being conscious of any wickedness in any man, you allow him to partake of this table. "His blood shall be required at your hands."[2] Though any one be a general, though a deputy, though it be he himself who is invested with the diadem, and come unworthily, forbid him, the authority thou hast is greater than his. Thou, if thou wert entrusted to keep a spring of water clean for a flock, and then wert to see a sheep having much mire on its mouth, thou wouldest not suffer it to stoop down unto it and foul the stream: but

now being entrusted with a spring not of water, but of blood and of spirit, if thou seest any having on them sin, which is more grievous than earth and mire, coming unto it, art thou not displeased? dost thou not drive them off? and what excuse canst thou have?

For this end God hath honored you with this honor, that ye should discern these things. This is your office, this your safety, this your whole crown, not that ye should go about clothed in a white and shining vestment.

And whence know I, you may say, this person, and that person? I speak not of the unknown, but of the notorious.

Shall I say something more fearful. It is not so grievous a thing for the energumens[3] to be within, as for such as these, whom Paul affirms to trample Christ under foot, and to "account the blood of the covenant unclean, and to do despite to the grace of the Spirit."[4] For he that hath fallen into sin and draws nigh, is worse than one possessed with a devil. For they, because they are possessed are not punished, but those, when they draw nigh unworthily, are delivered over to undying punishment. Let us not therefore drive away these only, but all without exception, whomsoever we may see coming unworthily.

Let no one communicate who is not of the disciples. Let no Judas receive, lest he suffer the fate of Judas. This multitude also is Christ's body. Take heed, therefore, thou that ministerest at the mysteries, lest thou provoke the Lord, not purging this body. Give not a sword instead of meat.

Nay, though it be from ignorance that he come to communicate, forbid him, be not afraid. Fear God, not man. If thou shouldest fear man, thou wilt be laughed to scorn even by him, but if God, thou wilt be an object of respect even to men.

But if thou darest not to do it thyself, bring him to me; I will not allow any to dare do these things. I would give up my life rather than impart of the Lord's blood to the unworthy; and will shed my own blood rather than impart of such awful blood contrary to what is meet.

But if any hath not known the bad man, after much inquiry, it is no blame. For these things have been said about the open sinners. For if we amend these, God will speedily discover to us the unknown also; but if we let these alone, wherefore should He then make manifest those that are hidden.

But these things I say, not that we repel

---

[1] Matt. xxvi. 18.   [2] Ezek. xxxiii. 8.

[3] *i. e.*, vexed with devils.
[4] Heb. x. 29. [Slightly altered, as in Homily LXXV. 5, p. 455.—R.]

them only, nor cut them off, but in order that we may amend them, and bring them back, that we may take care of them. For thus shall we both have God propitious, and shall find many to receive worthily; and for our own diligence, and for our care for others, receive great reward; unto which God grant we may all attain by the grace and love towards man of our Lord Jesus Christ, to whom be glory world without end. Amen.

HOMILY LXXXIII.

Matt. XXVI. 36—38.

" Then cometh Jesus with them unto a place called Gethsemane, and saith unto the disciples, Sit ye here, while I go and pray yonder. And He took with Him Peter and the two sons of Zebedee, and began to be sorrowful and very heavy: and He saith unto them, My soul is exceeding sorrowful, even unto death; tarry ye here, and watch with me." [1]

BECAUSE they clung to Him inseparably, therefore He saith, " Tarry ye here, while I go away and pray." For it was usual with Him to pray apart from them. And this He did teaching us in our prayers, to prepare silence for ourselves and great retirement.

And He takes with Him the three, and saith unto them, " my soul is exceeding sorrowful, even unto death." Wherefore doth He not take all with Him? That they might not be cast down; but these He taketh that had been spectators of His glory. However, even these He dismisses: " And He went on a little farther, and prayeth, saying, Father, if it be possible, let this cup pass from me; nevertheless not as I will, but as Thou wilt. And He cometh unto them, and findeth them sleeping, and saith unto Peter, What, could ye not watch with me one hour? Watch and pray, that ye enter not into temptation; the spirit indeed is willing, but the flesh is weak." [2]

Not without reason doth He inveigh against Peter most, although the others also had slept; but to make him feel by this also, for the cause which I mentioned before. Then because the others also said the same thing (for when Peter had said (these are the words), " Though I must die with Thee, I will not deny Thee; likewise also," it is added, " said all the disciples "); [3] He addresses Himself to all, convicting their weakness. For they who are desiring to die with Him, were not then able so much as to sorrow with Him wakefully, but sleep overcame them.

And He prays with earnestness, in order that the thing might not seem to be acting. And sweats flow over him for the same cause again, even that the heretics might not say this, that He acts the agony. Therefore there is a sweat like drops of blood, and an angel appeared strengthening Him, and a thousand sure signs of fear, lest any one should affirm the words to be feigned. For this cause also was this prayer. By saying then, " If it be possible, let it pass from me," He showed His humanity; but by saying, " Nevertheless not as I will, but as Thou wilt," He showed His virtue and self-command, teaching us even when nature pulls us back, to follow God. For since it was not enough for the foolish to show His face only, He uses words also. Again, words sufficed not alone, but deeds likewise were needed; these also He joins with the words, that even they who are in a high degree contentious may believe, that He both became man and died. For if, even when these things are so, this be still disbelieved by some, much more, if these had not been. See by how many things He shows the reality of the incarnation: by what He speaks, by what He suffers. After that He cometh and saith to Peter, as it is said, " What, couldest thou not watch one hour with me?" [4] All were sleeping, and He re-

---

[1] [The only variation of text is the substitution of καί for τότε at the beginning of verse 38. The R. V. renders, "sorrowful and sore troubled," and "abide" instead of " tarry."—R.]
[2] Matt. xxvi. 39-41. [The first part of verse 39 is abridged, and in 40 " them " is substituted for "the disciples." The remainder of the passage is in verbal agreement with the received text.—R.]
[3] Matt. xxvi. 36.

[4] Comp. Mark xiv. 37.

bukes Peter, hinting at him, in what He spake. And the words, "with me," are not employed without reason; it is as though He had said, Thou couldest not watch with me one hour, and wilt thou lay down thy life for me? and what follows also, intimates this self-same thing. For "Watch," saith He, "and pray not to enter into temptation." See how He is again instructing them not to be self-confident, but contrite in mind, and to be humble, and to refer all to God.

And at one time He addresses Himself to Peter, at another to all in common. And to him He saith, "Simon, Simon, Satan hath desired to have you, that he may sift you as wheat; but I have prayed for thee;" and to all in common, "Pray that ye enter not into temptation;" every way plucking up their self-will, and making them earnest-minded. Then, that He might not seem to make His language altogether condemnatory, He saith, "The spirit indeed is ready, but the flesh is weak." For even although thou dost desire to despise death, yet thou wilt not be able, until God stretch forth His hand, for the carnal mind draws down.

And again He prayed in the same way, saying, "Father, if this cannot pass from me except I drink it, Thy will be done,"[1] showing here, that He fully harmonizes with God's will, and that we must always follow this, and seek after it.

"And He came and found them asleep."[2] For besides that it was late at night, their eyes also were weighed down by their despondency. And the third time He went and spake the same thing, establishing the fact, that He was become man. For the second and third time is in the Scriptures especially indicative of truth; like as Joseph also said to Pharaoh, "Did the dream appear to thee the second time? For truth was this done, and that thou mightest be assured that this shall surely be."[3] Therefore He too once, and twice, and three times spake the same thing, for the sake of proving the incarnation.[4]

And wherefore came He the second time? In order to reprove them, for that they were so drowned in despondency, as not to have any sense even of His presence. He did not however reprove them, but stood apart from them a little, showing their unspeakable weakness, that not even when they had been rebuked, were they able to endure. But He doth not awake and rebuke them again, lest He should smite them that were already smitten,

but He went away and prayed, and when He is come back again, He saith, "Sleep on now, and take your rest." And yet then there was need to be wakeful, but to show that they will not bear so much as the sight of the dangers, but will be put to flight and desert Him from their terror, and that He hath no need of their succor, and that He must by all means be delivered up, "Sleep on now," He saith, "and take your rest; behold the hour is at hand, and the Son of Man is betrayed into the hands of sinners."[5]

He shows again that what is done belongs to a divine dispensation.

2. But He doth not this only, but also, by saying, "into the hands of sinners," He cheers up their minds, showing it was the effect of their wickedness, not of His being liable to any charge.

"Rise, let us be going; behold, he is at hand that doth betray me."[6] For by all means He taught them, that the matter was not of necessity, nor of weakness, but of some secret dispensation. For, as we see, He foreknew that Judas would come, and so far from flying, He even went to meet him. At any rate, "While He yet spake, lo, Judas, one of the twelve, came, and with him a great multitude with swords and staves, from the chief priests and elders of the people."[7] Seemly surely are the instruments of the priests! "with swords and staves" do they come against Him! And Judas, it is said, with them, one of the twelve. Again he calleth him "of the twelve," and is not ashamed. Now he that betrayed Him gave them a sign, saying, "Whomsoever I shall kiss, that same is He, hold Him fast."[8] Oh! what depravity had the traitor's soul received. For with what kind of eyes did he then look at his Master? with what mouth did he kiss Him? Oh! accursed purpose; what did he devise? What did he dare? What sort of sign of betrayal did he give? Whomsoever I shall kiss, he saith. He was emboldened by his Master's gentleness, which more than all was sufficient to shame him, and to deprive him of all excuse for that he was betraying one so meek.

But wherefore doth He say this? Because often when seized by them He had gone out through the midst, without their knowing it. Nevertheless, then also this would have been done, if it had not been His own will that He should be taken. It was at least with a view to teach them this, that He then blinded their eyes, and Himself asked, "Whom seek ye?"[9] And they knew Him not, though being with

[1] Matt. xxvi. 42. [The word "cup" is omitted as in R. V., but "from me" is retained, as in the received text.—R.]
[2] Matt. xxvi. 43. [R. V., "sleeping;" "again" is omitted. —R.]
[3] Gen. xli. 32.   [4] οἰκονομία.

[5] Matt. xxvi. 45.   [6] Matt. xxvi. 46.   [7] Matt. xxvi. 47.
[8] Matt. xxvi. 48. [R. V., "take him."]   [9] John xviii. 4.

lanterns and torches, and having Judas with them. Afterwards, as they had said, "Jesus;" He saith, "I am He" whom ye seek: and here again, "Friend, wherefore art thou come?"[1]

For after having shown His own strength, then at once He yielded Himself. But John saith, that even to the very moment He continued to reprove him, saying, "Judas, betrayest thou the Son of Man with a kiss?"[2] Art thou not ashamed even of the form of the betrayal? saith He. Nevertheless, forasmuch as not even this checked him, He submitted to be kissed, and gave Himself up willingly; and they laid their hands on Him, and seized Him that night on which they ate the passover, to such a degree did they boil with rage, and were mad. However, they would have had no strength, unless He had Himself suffered it. Yet this delivers not Judas from intolerable punishment, but even more exceedingly condemns him, for that though he had received such proof of His power, and lenity, and meekness, and gentleness, he became fiercer than any wild beast.

Knowing then these things, let us flee from covetousness. For that, that it was, which then drove him to madness; that exercises them who are taken thereby in the most extreme cruelty and inhumanity. For, when it makes them to despair of their own salvation, much more doth it cause them to overlook that of the rest of mankind. And so tyrannical is the passing, as sometimes to prevail over the keenest lust. Wherefore indeed I am exceedingly ashamed, that to spare their money, may indeed have bridled their unchastity, but for the fear of Christ they were not willing to live chastely and with gravity.

Wherefore I say, let us flee from it; for I will not cease for ever saying this. For why, O man, dost thou gather gold? Why dost thou make thy bondage more bitter? Why thy watching more grievous? Why thy anxiety more painful? Account for thine own the metals buried in the mines, those in the kings' courts. For indeed if thou hadst all that heap, thou wouldest keep it only, and wouldest not use it. For if now thou hast not used the things thou possessest, but abstainest from them as though they belonged to others, much more would this be the case with thee, if thou hadst more. For it is the way of the covetous, the more they heap up around them, the more to be sparing of it. "But I know," sayest thou, "that these

things are mine." The possession then is in supposition only, not in enjoyment. But I should be an object of fear to men, sayest thou. Nay, but thou wouldest by this become a more easy prey both to rich and poor, to robbers, and false accusers, and servants, and in general to all that are minded to plot against thee. For if thou art desirous to be an object of fear, cut off the occasions by which they are able to lay hold of thee and pain thee, whoever have set their hearts thereon. Hearest thou not the parable that saith, that the poor and naked man, not even a hundred men gathered together are ever able to strip? For he hath his poverty as his greatest protection, which not even the king shall ever be able to subdue and take.

3. The covetous man indeed all join in vexing. And why do I say men, when moths and worms war against such a man? And why do I speak of moths? Length of time is enough alone, even when no one troubles him, to do the greatest injury to such a man.

What then is the pleasure of wealth? For I see its discomforts, but do thou tell me the pleasure of it. And what are its discomforts? sayest thou: anxieties, plots, enmities, hatred, fear; to be ever thirsting and in pain.

For if any one were to embrace a damsel he loves, but were not able to satisfy his desire, he undergoes the utmost torment. Even so also doth the rich man. For he hath plenty, and is with her, but cannot satisfy all his desire; but the same result takes place as some wise man mentions; "The lust of an eunuch to deflower a virgin;" and, "Like an eunuch embracing a virgin and groaning;"[3] so are all the rich.

Why should one speak of the other things? how such a one is displeasing to all, to his servants, his laborers, his neighbors, to them that handle public affairs, to them that are injured, to them that are not injured, to his wife most of all, and to his children more than to any. For not as men does he bring them up, but more miserably than menials and purchased slaves.

And countless occasions for anger, and vexation, and insult, and ridicule against himself, doth he bring about, being set forth as a common laughing stock to all. So the discomforts are these, and perhaps more than these; before one could never go through them all in discourse, but experience will be able to set them before us.

But tell me the pleasure from hence. "I appear to be rich," he saith, "and am reputed to be rich." And what kind of pleas-

---

[1] Matt. xxvi. 50. [The Greek text in the Homily is ἐφ' ᾧ πάρει; but there is some authority for ἐφ' ὃ πάρει; which is abundantly attested in the New Testament passage. The latter reading is accepted in the R. V., "Friend, *do* that for which thou art come."—R.]   [2] Luke xxii. 48.

[3] Ecclus. xx. 4, xxx. 20.

ure to be so reputed? It is a very great name for envy. I say a name, for wealth is a name only void of reality.

"Yet he that is rich," saith he, "indulges and delights himself with this notion." He delights himself in those things about which he ought to grieve. "To grieve? wherefore?" asks he. Because this renders him useless for all purposes, and cowardly and unmanly both with regard to banishment and to death, for he holds this double, longing more for money than for light. Such a one not even Heaven delights, because it beareth not gold; nor the sun, forasmuch as it puts not forth golden beams.

But there are some, saith he, who do enjoy what they possess, living in luxury, in gluttony, in drunkenness, spending sumptuously. You are telling me of persons worse than the first. For the last above all are the men, who have no enjoyment. For the first at least abstains from other evils, being bound to one love; but the others are worse than these, besides what we have said, bringing in upon themselves a crowd of cruel masters, and doing service every day to the belly, to lust, to drunkenness, to other kinds of intemperance, as to so many cruel tyrants, keeping harlots, preparing expensive feasts, purchasing parasites, flatterers, turning aside after unnatural lusts, involving their body and their soul in a thousand diseases springing therefrom.

For neither is it on what they want they spend their goods, but on ruining the body, and on ruining also the soul therewith; and they do the same, as if any one, when adorning his person, were to think he was spending his money on his own wants.

So that he alone enjoys pleasure and is master of his goods, who uses his wealth for a proper object; but these are slaves and captives, for they aggravate both the passions of the body and the diseases of the soul. What manner of enjoyment is this, where is siege and war, and a storm worse than all the raging of the sea? For if wealth find men fools, it renders them more foolish; if wanton, more wanton.

And what is the use of understanding, thou wilt say, to the poor man? As might be expected thou art ignorant; for neither doth the blind man know what is the advantage of light. Listen to Solomon, saying, "As far as light excelleth darkness, so doth wisdom excel folly."[1]

But how shall we instruct him that is in darkness? For the love of money is dark-

ness, permitting nothing that is to appear as it is, but otherwise. For much as one in darkness, though he should see a golden vessel, though a precious stone, though purple garments, supposes them to be nothing, for he sees not their beauty; so also he that is in covetousness, knows not as he ought the beauty of those things that are worthy of our care. Disperse then I pray thee the mist that arises from this passion, and then wilt thou see the nature of things.

But nowhere do these things so plainly appear as in poverty, nowhere are those things so disproved which seem to be, and are not, as in self-denial.

4. But oh! foolish men; who do even curse the poor, and say that both houses and living are disgraced by poverty, confounding all things. For what is a disgrace to a house? I pray thee. It hath no couch of ivory, nor silver vessels, but all of earthenware and wood. Nay, this is the greatest glory and distinction to a house. For to be indifferent about worldly things, often occasions all a man's leisure to be spent in the care of his soul.

When therefore thou seest great care about outward things, then be ashamed at the great unseemliness. For the houses of them that are rich most of all want seemliness. For when thou seest tables covered with hangings, and couches inlaid with silver, much as in the theatre, much as in the display of the stage, what can be equal to this unseemliness? For what kind of house is most like the stage, and the things on the stage? The rich man's or the poor man's? Is it not quite plain that it is the rich man's? This therefore is full of unseemliness. What kind of house is most like Paul's, or Abraham's? It is quite evident that it is the poor man's. This therefore is most adorned, and to be approved. And that thou mayest learn that this is, above all, a house's adorning, enter into the house of Zacchæus, and learn, when Christ was on the point of entering therein, how Zacchæus adored it. For he did not run to his neighbors begging curtains, and seats, and chairs made of ivory, neither did he bring forth from his closets Laconian hangings; but he adorned it with an adorning suitable to Christ. What was this? "The half of my goods I will give, he saith, "to the poor; and whomsoever I have robbed, I will restore fourfold."[2] On this wise let us too adorn our houses, that Christ may enter in unto us also. These are the fair curtains, these are wrought in Heaven, they are woven there. Where these are, there is also the King of Heaven. But if thou

---

adorn it in another way, thou art inviting the devil and his company.

He came also into the house of the publican Matthew. What then did this man also do? He first adorned himself by his readiness, and by his leaving all, and following Christ.

So also Cornelius adorned his house with prayers and alms; wherefore even unto this day it shines above the very palace. For the vile state of a house is not in vessels lying in disorder, nor in an untidy bed, nor in walls covered with smoke, but in the wickedness of them that dwell therein. And Christ showeth it, for into such a house, if the inhabitant be virtuous, He is not ashamed to enter; but into that other, though it have a golden roof, He will never enter. So that while this one is more gorgeous than the palace, receiving the Lord of all, that with its golden roof and columns is like filthy drains and sewers, for it contains the vessels of the devil.

But these things we have spoken not of those who are rich for a useful purpose, but of the grasping, and the covetous. For neither is there amongst these, diligence nor care about the things needful, but about pampering the belly, and drunkenness, and other like unseemliness; but with the others about self-restraint. Therefore nowhere did Christ enter into a gorgeous house, but into that of the publican and chief publican, and fisherman, leaving the kings' palaces, and them that are clothed with soft raiment.

If then thou also desirest to invite Him, deck thy house with alms, with prayers, with supplications, with vigils. These are the decorations of Christ the King, but those of mammon, the enemy of Christ. Let no one be ashamed then of a humble house, if it hath this furniture; let no rich man pride himself on having a costly house, but let him rather hide his face, and seek after this other, forsaking that, that both here he may receive Christ, and there enjoy the eternal tabernacles, by the grace and love towards man of our Lord Jesus Christ, to whom be glory and might world without end. Amen.

HOMILY LXXXIV.

MATT. XXVI. 51—54.

" And, behold, one of them which were with Jesus stretched forth his hand, and drew his sword, and struck a servant of the high priest's, and smote off his ear."

" Then said Jesus unto him, Put up again thy sword unto his place, for all they that take the sword, shall perish by the sword. Thinkest [1] thou that I cannot pray to the Father, and He shall presently [2] give me more than twelve legions of angels? How then should the Scriptures be fulfilled that thus it must be?" [3]

WHO was this " one," who cut off the ear? John saith that it was Peter. [4] For the act was of his fervor.

But this other point is worth inquiry, wherefore they were bearing swords? For that they bore them is evident not hence only, but from their saying when asked, " here are two." But wherefore did Christ even permit them to have swords? For Luke affirms this too, that He said unto them, " When I sent you without purse, and scrip, and shoes, lacked ye anything?" And when they said, " Nothing," He said unto them, " But now, he that hath a purse, let him take it, and a scrip, and he that hath no sword, let him sell his garment, and buy one." And when they said, " Here are two swords," He said unto them, " It is enough." [5]

Wherefore then did He suffer them to have them? To assure them that He was to be betrayed. Therefore He saith unto them, " Let him buy a sword," not that they should

---

[1] [R. V., " Or thinkest."]   [2] [R. V., " even now."]
[3] [The citation is very accurate; the only variation is the omission of μου after πατέρα.—R.]
[4] John xviii. 10.

[5] Luke xxii. 35-38. [On the renderings of verse 36, see R. V. The text of the Homily admits of either interpretation, but the comment favors the rendering given in the text of the R. V.—R.]

arm themselves, far from it; but by this, indicating His being betrayed.

And wherefore doth He mention a scrip also? He was teaching them henceforth to be sober, and wakeful, and to use much diligence on their own part. For at the beginning He cherished them (as being inexperienced) with much putting forth of His power but afterwards bringing them forth as young birds out of the nest, He commands them to use their own wings. Then, that they might not suppose that it was for weakness He is letting them alone, in commanding them also to work their part, He reminds them of the former things, saying, "When I sent you without purse, lacked ye anything?" that by both they might learn His power, both wherein He protected them, and wherein He now leaveth them to themselves by degrees.

But whence were the swords there? They were come forth from the supper, and from the table. It was likely also there should be swords because of the lamb, and that the disciples, hearing that certain were coming forth against Him, took them for defense, as meaning to fight in behalf of their Master, which was of their thought only. Wherefore also Peter is rebuked for using it, and with a severe threat. For he was resisting the servant who came, warmly indeed, yet not defending himself, but doing this in behalf of his Master.

Christ however suffered not any harm to ensue. For He healed him, and showed forth a great miracle, enough to indicate at once both His forbearance and His power, and the affection and meekness of His disciple. For then he acted from affection, now with dutifulness. For when he heard, "Put up thy sword into its sheath,"[1] he obeyed straightway, and afterwards nowhere doeth this.

But another saith, that they moreover asked, "Shall we smite?"[2] but that He forbad it, and healed the man, and rebuked His disciple, and threatened, that He might move him to obedience. "For all they that take the sword," He said, "shall die with the sword."

And he adds a reason, saying, "Think ye that I cannot pray to my Father, and He shall presently give me more than twelve legions of angels? But that the Scriptures might be fulfilled."[3] By these words He quenched their anger, indicating that to the Scriptures also, this seemed good. Wherefore there too He prayed, that they might take meekly what befell Him, when they had learnt that this again is done according to God's will.

And by these two things, He comforted them, both by the punishment of them that are plotting against Him, "For all they," He saith, "that take the sword shall perish with the sword;" and by His not undergoing these things against His will, "For I can pray, He saith, "to my Father."

And wherefore did He not say, "Think ye that I cannot destroy them all?" Because He was more likely to be believed in saying what He did say; for not yet had they the right belief concerning Him. And a little while before He had said, "My soul is exceeding sorrowful even unto death," and, "Father, let the cup pass from me;"[4] and He had appeared in an agony and sweating, and strengthened by an angel.

Since then He had shown forth many tokens of human nature, He did not seem likely to speak so as to be believed, if He had said, "Think ye that I cannot destroy them." Therefore He saith, "What, think ye that I cannot pray to my Father?" And again He speaks it humbly, in saying, "He will presently give me twelve legions of angels." For if one angel slew one hundred and eighty-five armed thousands,[5] what need of twelve legions against a thousand men? But He frames His language with a view to their terror and weakness, for indeed they were dead with fear. Wherefore also He brings against them the Scriptures, saying, "How then shall the Scriptures be fulfilled?" alarming them by this also. For if this be approved by the Scriptures, do ye oppose and fight against them?

2. And to His disciples He saith these things; but to the others, "Are ye come out as against a thief with swords and staves for to take me? I sat daily teaching in the temple, and ye laid no hold on me."[6]

See how many things He doeth that might awaken them. He cast them to the ground, He healed the servant's ear, He threatened them with being slain; "For they shall perish with the sword," He saith, "who take the sword." By the healing of the ear, He gave assurance of these things also; from every quarter, both from the things present, and from the things to come, manifesting His power, and showing that it was not a work of their strength to seize Him. Wherefore He also adds, "I was daily with you, and sat teaching, and ye laid no hold on me;" by this also making it manifest, that the seizure

[1] John xviii. 11.   [2] Luke xxii. 49.   [3] Matt. xxvi. 53, 54.

[4] Matt. xxvi. 38, 39.   [5] 2 Kings xix. 35.
[6] Matt. xxvi. 55. [R. V., "robber" . . . "to seize me" . . . "ye took me not."]

was of His permission. He passed over the miracles, and mentions the teaching, that He might not seem to boast.

When I taught, ye laid no hold on me; when I held my peace, did ye come against me? I was in the temple, and no one seized me, and now do ye come upon me late and at midnight with swords and staves? What need was there of these weapons against Him, who was with you always? by these things teaching them, that unless He had voluntarily yielded, not even then would they have succeeded. For neither could they (who were not able to hold Him when in their hands, and who, when they had got Him in the midst of them, had not prevailed) even then have succeeded, unless He had been willing.

After this, He solves also the difficulty why He willed it then. For, "this was done," He saith, "that the Scriptures of the prophets might be fulfilled."[1] See how even up to the last hour, and in the very act of being betrayed, He did all things for their amendment, healing, prophesying, threatening. "For," He saith, "they shall perish by the sword." To show that He is suffering voluntarily, He saith, "I was daily with you teaching;" to manifest His accordance with the Father, He adds, "That the Scriptures of the prophets might be fulfilled."

But wherefore did they not lay hold on Him in the temple? Because they would not have dared in the temple, on account of the people. Wherefore also He went forth without, both by the place and by the time giving them security, and even to the last hour taking away their excuse. For He who, in order that He might obey the prophets, gave up even Himself, how did He teach things contrary to them?

"Then all His disciples," it is said, "forsook Him, and fled." For when He was seized, they remained; but when He had said these things to the multitudes, they fled. For thenceforth they saw that escape was no longer possible, when He was giving Himself up to them voluntarily, and saying, that this was done according to the Scriptures.

And when these were fled, "they lead Him away to Caiaphas; but Peter followed, and entered in to see what the end should be."[2]

Great was the fervor of the disciple; neither did he fly when he saw them flying, but stood his ground, and went in with Him. And if John did so too, yet he was "known to the high priest."[3]

And why did they lead Him away there,

where they were all assembled? That they might do all things with consent of the chief priests. For he was then high priest, and all were waiting for Christ there, to such a degree did they spend the whole night, and give up their sleep for this object. For neither did they then eat the passover, but watched for this other purpose. For John, when he had said that "it was early," added, "they entered into the judgment hall, lest they should be defiled, but that they might eat the passover."[4]

What must we say then? That they ate it on another day, and broke the law, on account of their eager desire about this murder. For Christ would not have transgressed as to the time of the passover, but they who were daring all things, and trampling under foot a thousand laws. For since they were exceedingly boiling with rage, and having often attempted to seize Him, had not been able; having then taken Him unexpectedly, they chose even to pass by the passover, for the sake of satiating their murderous lust.

Wherefore also they were all assembled together, and it was a council of pestilent men,[5] and they ask some questions, wishing to invest this plot with the appearance of a court of justice. For "neither did their testimonies agree together;"[6] so feigned was the court of justice, and all things full of confusion and disorder.

"But false witnesses came, and said, This fellow said, I will destroy this temple, and in three days I will raise it."[7] And indeed He had said, "In three days," but He said not, "I will destroy," but, "Destroy," and not about that temple but about His own body.[8]

What then doth the high priest? Willing to press Him to a defense, that by that he might take Him, he saith, "Hearest Thou not what these witness against Thee? But He held His peace."[9]

For the attempts at defense were unprofitable, no man hearing. For this was a show only of a court of justice, but in truth an onset of robbers, assailing Him without cause, as in a cave, or on a road.

Wherefore "He held His peace," but the other continued, saying, "I adjure Thee by the living God, that Thou tell us whether Thou be the Christ, the Son of the living God.

---

[1] Matt. xxvi. 56.
[2] Matt. xxvi. 57, 58. [Abridged and altered.]
[3] John xviii. 15.

[4] John xviii. 28. [Compare Homily LXXVI. 1, and the note there.—R.]
[5] συνέδριον λοιμῶν ; cf. Ps. i. 1.
[6] Mark xiv. 56, 59. [The passages are combined.—R.]
[7] Matt. xxvi. 60, 61. [The citation is very free, not agreeing with any one of the evangelists, according to our authorities ; but it seems to combine terms from several passages.—R.]
[8] See John ii. 19–21.
[9] Matt. xxvi. 62, 63. [Freely cited ; the beginning is from the language of Pilate ; chap. xxvii. 13—R.]

But He said, Thou hast said. Nevertheless I say unto you, Hereafter shall ye see the Son of Man sitting at the right hand of power, and coming in the clouds. Then the high priest rent his clothes, saying, He hath spoken blasphemy."[1] And this he did to add force to the accusation, and to aggravate what He said, by the act. For since what had been said moved the hearers to fear, what they did about Stephen,[2] stopping their ears, this high priest doth here also.

3. And yet what kind of blasphemy was this? For indeed before He had said, when they were gathered together, "The Lord said unto my Lord, Sit Thou on my right hand,"[3] and interpreted the saying, and they dared say nothing, but held their peace, and from that time forth gainsaid Him no more. Why then did they now call the saying a blasphemy? And wherefore also did Christ thus answer them? To take away all their excuse, because unto the last day He taught that He was Christ, and that He sitteth at the right hand of the Father, and that He will come again to judge the world, which was the language of one manifesting His full accordance with the Father.

Having rent therefore his clothes, he saith, "What think ye?"[4] He gives not the sentence from himself, but invites it from them, as in a case of confessed sins, and manifest blasphemy. For, inasmuch as they knew that if the thing came to be inquired into, and carefully decided, it would free Him from all blame, they condemn Him amongst themselves, and anticipate the hearers by saying, "Ye have heard the blasphemy;" all but necessitating and forcing them to deliver the sentence. What then say they? "He is guilty of death;" that having taken Him as condemned, they should thus work upon Pilate thereupon to pass sentence. In which matter those others also being accomplices say, "He is guilty of death;" themselves accusing, themselves judging, themselves passing sentence, themselves being everything then.

But wherefore did they not bring forward the Sabbaths? Because He had often stopped their mouths; and moreover they wanted to take Him, and condemn Him by the things then said. And *the high priest* anticipated them, and gave the sentence as from them, and drew them all on by rending his vestments, and having led Him away as now condemned unto Pilate, thus did all.

Before Pilate at any rate they said nothing of this kind, but what? "If[5] this Man were not a malefactor, we would not have delivered Him up unto thee;" attempting to put Him to death by political accusations. And wherefore did they not slay Him secretly? They were desirous also to bring up an evil report against His fame. For since many had now heard Him, and were admiring Him, and amazed at Him, therefore they endeavored that He should be put to death publicly, and in the presence of all.

But Christ hindered it not, but made full use of their wickedness for the establishment of the truth, so that His death should be manifest. And the result was the contrary to what they wished. For they wished to make a show of it, as in this way disgracing Him, but He even by these very things shone forth the more. And much as they said, "Let us put Him to death, lest the Romans come and take away our place and nation;"[6] and after they had put Him to death, this came to pass; so also here; their object was to crucify Him publicly, that they might injure His fame, and the contrary result took place.

For in proof that indeed they had power to have put Him to death, even amongst themselves, hear what Pilate saith: "Take ye Him, and judge Him according to your law."[7] But they would not, that He might seem to have been put to death as a transgressor, as an usurper, as a mover of sedition. Therefore also they crucified thieves with Him; therefore also they said, "Write not that this man is King of the Jews; but that He said it."[8]

But all these things are done for the truth, so that they might not have so much as any shadow of a defense that is surely shameless. And at the sepulchre too, in the like manner, the seals and the watches made the truth to be the more conspicuous; and the mockings, and the jeerings, and the revilings, wrought again this self-same effect.

For such is the nature of error: it is destroyed by those things whereby it plots; thus at least it fell out even here, for they that seemed to have conquered, these most of all were put to shame, and defeated, and ruined; but He that seemed to be defeated, this man above all hath both shone forth, and conquered mightily.

Let us not then everywhere seek victory, nor everywhere shun defeat. There is an occasion when victory brings hurt, but defeat

---

[1] Matt. xxvi. 63-65. [In verse 63, "the living God" occurs twice, peculiar to this Homily : in verse 64 "of heaven" is omitted. In other details the citation agrees with the received text.—R.]
[2] Acts vii. 59. [3] Matt. xxii. 43-46. [4] Matt. xxvi. 66.

[5] John xviii. 30. [R. V., "an evil-doer."]
[6] John xi. 48. [Freely paraphrased.] [7] John xviii. 31.
[8] John xix. 21. [The citation is accurate ; "it" is supplied by the translator to complete the sense.—R.]

profit. For, for instance, in the case of them that are angry; he that hath been very outrageous seems to have prevailed; but this man above all is the one subdued and hurt by the most grievous passion; but he that hath endured nobly, this man hath got the better and conquered. And while the one hath not had strength to overcome so much as his own disease; the other hath removed another man's; this hath been subdued by his own, that hath got the better even of another's passion; and so far from being burnt up, he quenched the flame of another when raised to a height. But if he had minded to gain what seems to be victory, both he himself would have been overcome; and having inflamed the other, he would have occasioned him to have suffered this more grievously; and, like women, both the one and the other would have been disgracefully and miserably overthrown by their anger. But now he that hath exercised self-control is both freed from this disgrace, and hath erected a glorious trophy over anger both in himself and in his neighbor, through his honorable defeat.

4. Let us not then everywhere seek victory. For he that hath overreached hath conquered the person wronged, but with an evil victory, and one that brings destruction to him that has won it; but he that is wronged, and seems to have been conquered, if he have borne it with self-command, this above all is the one that hath the crown. For often to be defeated is better, and this is the best mode of victory. For whether one overreaches, or smites, or envies, he that is defeated, and enters not into the conflict, this is he who hath the victory.

And why do I speak of overreaching and envy? For he also that is dragged to martyrdom, thus conquers by being bound, and beaten, and maimed, and slain. And what is in wars defeat, namely, for the combatant to fall; this with us is victory. For nowhere do we overcome by doing wrongfully, but everywhere by suffering wrongfully. Thus also doth the victory become more glorious, when we sufferers get the better of the doers. Hereby it is shown that the victory is of God. For indeed it hath an opposite nature to outward conquest, which fact is again above all an infallible sign of strength. Thus also the rocks in the sea, by being struck, break the waves; thus also all the saints were proclaimed, and crowned, and set up their glorious trophies, winning this tranquil victory. "For stir not thyself," He saith, "neither weary thyself. God hath given thee this might, to conquer not by conflict, but by endurance alone. Do not oppose thyself also

as he does, and thou hast conquered; conflict not, and thou hast gained the crown.[1] Why dost thou disgrace thyself? Allow him not to say that by conflicting thou hast got the better, but suffer him to be amazed and to marvel at thy invincible power; and to say to all, that even without entering into conflict thou hast conquered."

Thus also the blessed Joseph obtained a good report, everywhere by suffering wrong getting the better of them who were doing it. For his brethren and the Egyptian woman were amongst those that were plotting against him, but over all did this man prevail. For tell me not of the prison, wherein this man dwelt, nor of the kings' courts where she abode, but show me who it is that is conquered, who it is that is defeated, who that is in despondency, who that is in pleasure. For she, so far from being able to prevail over the righteous man, could not master so much as her own passion; but this man prevailed both over her and over that grievous disease. But if thou wilt, hear her very words, and thou shalt see the trophy. "Thou broughtest in unto us here an Hebrew servant to mock us."[2] It was not this man that mocked thee, O wretched and unhappy woman, but the devil that told thee that thou couldest break down the adamant. This *thy husband* brought not in unto thee an Hebrew servant to plot against thee, but the wicked spirit brought in that unclean lasciviousness; he it was that mocked thee.

What then did Joseph? He held his peace, and thus is condemned, even as Christ is also.

For all those things are types of these. And he indeed was in bonds, and she in royal courts. Yet what is this? For he was more glorious than any crowned victor, even while continuing in his bonds, but she was in a more wretched condition than any prisoner, while abiding in royal chambers.

But not hence alone may one see the victory, and the defeat, but by the end itself. For which accomplished his desired object? The prisoner, not the high born lady? For he strove to keep his chastity, but she to destroy it. Which then accomplished what he desired? he who suffered wrong, or she who did the wrong. It is quite plain, that it is he who suffered. Surely then this is the one who hath conquered.

Knowing then these things, let us follow after this victory, which is obtained by suffering wrong, let us flee from that which is got

---

[1] [The following clause is omitted in the translation : " Much better and stronger art thou than thine antagonist."—R.]
[2] Gen. xxxix. 17.

by doing wrong. For so shall we both live this present life in all tranquility, and great quietness, and shall attain unto the good things to come, by the grace and love towards man of our Lord Jesus Christ, to whom be glory and might world without end. Amen.

HOMILY LXXXV.

MATT. XXVI. 67, 68.

" Then did they spit in His face, and buffeted Him, and others smote Him with the palms of their hands,[1] saying, Prophesy unto us, thou Christ, who is he that smote[2] thee ? "[2]

WHEREFORE did they these things, when they were to put Him to death? What need of this mockery? That thou mightest learn their intemperate spirit by all things, and that having taken Him like a prey, they thus showed forth their intoxication, and gave full swing to their madness; making this a festival, and assaulting Him with pleasure, and showing forth their murderous disposition.

But admire, I pray thee, the self command of the disciples, with what exactness they relate these things. Hereby is clearly shown their disposition to love the truth, because they relate with all truthfulness the things that seem to be opprobrious, disguising nothing, nor being ashamed thereof, but rather accounting it very great glory, as indeed it was, that the Lord of the universe should endure to suffer such things for us. This shows both His unutterable tenderness, and the inexcusable wickedness of those men, who had the heart to do such things to Him that was so mild and meek, and was charming them with such words, as were enough to change a lion into a lamb. For neither did He fail in any things of gentleness, nor they of insolence and cruelty, in what they did, in what they said. All which things the prophet Isaiah foretold, thus proclaiming beforehand, and by one word intimating all this insolence. For " like as many were astonished at thee," he saith, " so shall thy form be held inglorious of men, and thy glory of the sons of men." [3]

For what could be equal to this insolence ? On that face which the sea, when it saw it, had reverenced, from which the sun, when it beheld it on the cross, turned away his rays, they did spit, and struck it with the palms of their hands, and some upon the head; giving full swing in every way to their own madness. For indeed they inflicted the blows that are most insulting of all, buffeting, smiting with the palms of their hands, and to these blows adding the insult of spitting at Him. And words again teeming with much derision did they speak, saying, " prophesy unto us, thou Christ, who is he that smote thee ?" because the multitude called Him a prophet.

But another[4] saith, that they covered His face with His own garment, and did these things, as though they had got in the midst of them some vile and worthless fellow. And not freemen only, but slaves[5] also were intemperate with this intemperance towards Him at that time.

These things let us read continually, these things let us hear aright, these things let us write in our minds, for these are our honors. In these things do I take a pride, not only in the thousands of dead which He raised, but also in the sufferings which He endured. These things Paul puts forward in every way, the cross, the death, the sufferings, the revilings, the insults, the scoffs. And now he saith, " let us go forth unto Him bearing His reproach;" [6] and now, " who for the joy that was set before Him endured the cross, despising the shame." [7]

" Now Peter sat in the court without; [8] and a damsel came unto him, saying, thou also wast with Jesus of Galilee. But he denied before them all,[9] saying, I know not what

---

[1] [R. V. margin, " Or, with rods."]
[2] [R. V., "struck thee." The variety of Greek terms used to express the maltreatment is remarkable, and is indicated in the R. V.—R.]
[3] Isa. lii. 14 [LXX.].
[4] Luke xxii. 64.
[5] Mark xiv. 65. [In this passage δοῦλοι does not occur, but ὑπηρέται, which has a wider sense.—R.]
[6] Heb. xiii. 13.
[7] Heb. xii. 2.
[8] [The order here is peculiar to this Homily.—R.]
[9] [αὐτῶν is inserted here.—R.]

thou sayest.   And when he was gone out into the porch, another maid saw him, and saith, this man also was there[1] with Jesus of Nazareth.   And again he denied with an oath. And after a while came unto him they that stood by, and said unto Peter, surely thou also art one of them, 'for thy speech bewrayeth thee.   Then began he to curse and to swear, I know not the man.   And immediately the cock crew.   And Peter remembered the words of Jesus, which said, before the cock crow, thou shalt deny me thrice.   And he went out, and wept bitterly."[2]

Oh strange and wonderful acts!   When indeed he saw his master seized only, he was so fervent as both to draw his sword, and to cut off the man's ear; but when it was natural for him to be more indignant, and to be inflamed and to burn, hearing such revilings, then he becomes a denier.   For who would not have been inflamed to madness by the things that were then done? yet the disciple, overcome by fears, so far from showing indignation, even denies, and endures not the threat of a miserable and mean girl, and not once only, but a second and third time doth he deny Him; and in a short period, and not so much as before judges, for it was without; for " when he had gone out into the porch," they asked him, and he did not even readily come to a sense of his fall.   And this Luke saith,[3] namely, that Christ looked on him, showing that he not only denied Him, but was not even brought to remembrance from within, and this though the cock had crowed; but he needed a further remembrance from his master, and His look was to him instead of a voice; so exceedingly was he full of fear.

But Mark saith,[4] that when he had once denied, then first the cock crew, but when thrice, then for the second time; for he declares more particularly the weakness of the disciple, and that he was utterly dead with fear; having learnt these things of his master[5] himself, for he was a follower of Peter.   In which respect one would most marvel at him, that so far from hiding his teacher's faults, he declared it more distinctly than the rest, on this very account, that he was his disciple.

2. How then is what is said true, .when Matthew affirms that Christ said, " Verily I say unto thee, that before the cock crow thou

shalt deny me thrice;"[6] and Mark declares after the third denial, that " The cock crew the second time?"[7]   Nay, most certainly is it both true and in harmony.   For because at each crowing the cock is wont to crow both a third and a fourth time, Mark, to show that not even the sound checked him, and brought him to recollection saith this.   So that both things are true.   For before the cock had finished the one crowing, he had denied a third time.   And not even when reminded of his sin by Christ did he dare to weep openly, lest he should be betrayed by his tears, but " he went out, and wept bitterly."

" And when it was day, they led away Jesus from Caiaphas to Pilate."[8]   For because they were desirous to put Him to death, but were not able themselves because of the feast, they lead Him to the governor.

But mark, I pray thee, how the act was forced on, so as to take place at the feast. For so was it typified from the first.

" Then Judas, which had betrayed him, when he saw that He was condemned, repented, and brought again the thirty pieces of silver."[9]

This was a charge both against him, and against these men; against him, not because he repented, but because he did so, late, and slowly, and became self-condemned (for that he delivered Him up, he himself confessed); and against them, for that having the power to reverse it, they repented not.

But mark, when it is that he feels remorse. When his sin was completed, and had received an accomplishment.   For the devil is like this; he suffers not those that are not watchful to see the evil before this, lest he whom he has taken, should repent.   At least, when Jesus was saying so many things, he was not influenced, but when his offense was completed, then repentance came upon him; and not then profitably.   For to condemn it, and to throw down the pieces of silver, and not to regard the Jewish people, were all acceptable things; but to hang himself, this again was unpardonable, and a work of an evil spirit. For the devil led him out of his repentance too soon, so that he should reap no fruit from thence; and carries him off, by a most disgraceful death, and one manifest to all, having persuaded him to destroy himself.

But mark, I pray thee, the truth shining forth on every side, even by what the adversaries both do and suffer.   For indeed even the very end of the traitor stops the mouths

---

[1] [The reading is peculiar (λέγει· Ἐκεῖ καὶ οὗτος), as indicated in the rendering.—R.]
[2] Matt. xxvi. 69-75. [In verse 74, καταθεματίζειν is read; in verse 75, αὐτῷ is omitted. These variations and those noted above are the only peculiarities.—R.]
[3] Luke xxii. 61.
[4] Mark xiv. 68, 72. [In both passages in Mark there are textual variations in the MSS. The clause in verse 68, telling of the first cock-crowing, is omitted in three of the best MSS. But the absence of any parallel statement would account for the omission.—R.]
[5] 1 Pet. v. 13.

[6] Matt. xxvi. 34.   [7] Mark xiv. 72.
[8] Chap. xxvii. 1, 2. [This is not a citation, but a combination of terms occurring in all four accounts.—R.]
[9] Matt. xxvi. 3. [R. V. omits " had," and reads " repented himself," " brought back."—R.]

of them that had condemned Him, and suffers them not to have so much as any shadow of an excuse, that is surely shameless. For what could they have to say, when the traitor is shown to pass such a sentence on himself.

But let us see also the words, what is said; " He brought again the thirty pieces of silver to the chief priests,[1] and saith, I have sinned in that I have betrayed innocent blood. And they said, what is that to us? see thou to that. And he cast down the pieces of silver in the temple,[2] and departed, and went and hanged himself.[3]

For neither could he bear his conscience scourging him. But mark, I pray thee, the Jews too suffering the same things. For these men also, when they ought to have been amended by what they suffered, do not stop, until they have completed their sin. For his sin had been completed, for it was a betrayal; but theirs not yet. But when they too had accomplished theirs, and had nailed Him to the cross then they also are troubled; at one time saying, " Write not, this is the king of the Jews "[4] (and yet why are ye afraid? why are ye troubled at a dead body that is nailed upon the cross?); at another time they guard over Him, saying, " Lest His disciples steal Him away, and say that He is risen again; so the last error shall be worse than the first."[5] And yet if they do it, the thing is refuted, if it be not true. But how should they say so, which did not dare so much as to stand their ground, when He was seized; and the chief[6] of them even thrice denied Him, not bearing a damsel's threat. But, as I said, the chief priests were now troubled; for that they knew the act was a transgression of the law is manifest, from their saying, " See thou to that."

Hear, ye covetous, consider what befell him; how he at the same time lost the money, and committed the sin, and destroyed his own soul. Such is the tyranny of covetousness. He enjoyed not the money. neither the present life, nor that to come, but lost all at once, and having got a bad character even with those very men, so hanged himself.

But, as I said, after the act, then some see clearly. See at any rate these men too for a time not willing to have a clear perception of the fact, but saying, " See thou to that:" which thing of itself is a most heavy charge against them. For this is the language of men bearing witness to their daring and their

transgression, but intoxicated by their passion, and not willing to forbear their satanical attempts, but senselessly wrapping themselves up in a veil of feigned ignorance.

For if indeed these things had been said after the crucifixion, and His being slain, of a truth even then the saying would have had no reasonable meaning, nevertheless it would not have condemned them so much; but now having Him yet in your own hands, and having power to release Him, how could ye be able to say these things? For this defense would be a most heavy accusation against you. How? and in what way? Because while throwing the whole blame upon the traitor (for they say, " See thou to that "), being able to have set themselves free from this murder of Christ, they left the traitor, and even pressed the crime further, adding the cross to the betrayal. For what hindered them, when they said to him, " See thou to that," tnemselves to forbear the criminal act? But now they even do the contrary, adding to it the murder and in every thing, both by what they do, and by what they say, entangling themselves in inevitable ills. For indeed after these things, when Pilate left it to them, they choose the robber to be released rather than Jesus; but Him that had done no wrong, but had even conferred on them so many benefits, they slew.

3. What then did that man? When he saw that he was laboring to no profit, and that they would not consent to receive the pieces of silver, " he cast them down in the temple, and went and hanged himself.[7] And the chief priests took the pieces of silver, and said, it is not lawful for to put them into the treasury, because it is the price of blood. And they took counsel, and bought with them the potter's field to bury strangers in. Wherefore that field was called, the field of blood, unto this day. Then was fulfilled that which was spoken by Jeremy the prophet, saying, and they took the thirty pieces of silver, the price of Him that was valued, and gave them for the potter's field, as the Lord appointed me."[8]

Seest thou them again self-condemned by their conscience? For because they knew that they had been buying the murder, they put them not into the treasury, but bought a field to bury strangers in. And this also became a witness against them, and a proof of their treason. For the name of the place more clearly than a trumpet proclaimed their blood-

---

[1] [The words " and elders " are omitted, though Tischendorf cites Chrysostom otherwise."—R.]
[2] [R. V., " into the sanctuary," accepting the reading given in the Homily.—R.]
[3] Matt. xxvii. 3-5. [R. V., " and he went away," etc.]
[4] John xix. 21.　　　[5] Matt. xxvii. 64. [Abridged.]
[6] ὁ κορυφαῖος.

[7] Matt. xxvii. 5. [See notes on the previous citation of this verse.—R.]
[8] Matt. xxvii. 6-10. [The only textual peculiarities are, the substitution of καί for δέ, at the beginning of verse 7 ; and the omission of a clause in verse 9, as indicated above.—R.]

guiltiness. Neither did they it at random, but having taking counsel, and in every case in like manner, so that no one should be clear of the deed, but all guilty. But these things the prophecy foretold from of old. Seest thou not the apostles only, but the prophets also declaring exactly those things which were matters of reproach, and every way proclaiming the passion, and indicating it beforehand?

This was the case with the Jews without their being conscious of it. For if they had cast it into the treasury, the thing would not have been so clearly discovered; but now having bought a piece of ground, they made it all manifest even to subsequent generations.

Hear ye as many as think to do good works out of murders, and take a reward for the lives of men. These almsgiving are Judaical, or rather they are Satanical. For there are, there are now also they, that take by violence countless things belonging to others, and think that an excuse is made for all if they cast in some ten or a hundred gold pieces.

Touching whom also the prophet saith, "Ye covered my altar with tears."[1] Christ is not willing to be fed by covetousness, He accepts not this food. Why dost thou insult thy Lord, offering Him unclean things? It is better to leave men to pine with hunger, than to feed them from these sources. That was the conduct of a cruel man, this of one both cruel and insolent. It is better to give nothing, than to give the things of one set of persons to others. For tell me, if you saw any two persons, one naked, one having a garment, and then having stripped the one that had the garment, thou wert to clothe the naked, wouldest thou not have committed an injustice? It is surely plain to every one. But if when thou hast given all that thou hast taken to another, thou hast committed an injustice, and not shown mercy; when thou givest not even a small portion of what thou robbest, and callest the deed alms, what manner of punishment wilt thou not undergo? For if men offering lame brutes were blamed, what favor wilt thou obtain doing things more grievous? For if the chief, making restitution to the owner himself, still doeth an injustice, and so doeth an injustice, as by adding fourfold scarcely to do away the charge against himself, and this under the old covenant;[2] he that is not stealing, but taking by violence, and not even giving to him that is robbed, but instead of him to another; nor yet giving fourfold, but not so much as the half; and moreover not living under the old dispensa-

tion, but under the new; consider how much fire he is heaping together upon his own head. And if he do not as yet suffer his punishment, for this self-same thing I say bewail him, for he is treasuring up against himself a greater wrath, unless he repent. For what? "Think ye," saith He, "that they alone were sinners upon whom the tower fell down? Nay, I say unto you, but except ye repent, ye also shall suffer the same things.[3]

Let us repent then, and give alms pure from covetousness, and in great abundance. Consider that the Jews used to feed eight thousand Levites, and together with the Levites, widows also and orphans, and they bore many other public charges, and together with these things also served as soldiers; but now there are fields, and houses, and hirings of lodgings, and carriages, and muleteers, and mules, and a great array of this kind in the church on account of you, and your hardness of heart. For this store of the church ought to be with you, and your readiness of mind ought to be a revenue to her; but now two wrong things come to pass, both you continue unfruitful, and God's priests do not practise their proper duties.

Was it not possible for the houses and the lands to have remained in the time of the apostles? Wherefore then did they sell them and give away? Because this was a better thing.

4. But now a fear seized our fathers (when you were so mad after worldly things, and because of your gatherings, and not dispersing abroad), lest the companies of the widows and orphans, and of the virgins, should perish of famine; therefore were they constrained to provide these things. For it was not their wish to thrust themselves unto what was so unbecoming; but their desire was that your good will should have been a supply for them, and that they should gather their fruits from thence, and that they themselves should give heed to prayers only.

But now ye have constrained them to imitate the houses of them that manage public affairs; whereby all things are turned upside down. For when both you and we are entangled in the same things, who is there to propitiate God? Therefore it is not possible for us to open our mouths, when the state of the church is no better than that of worldly men. Have ye not heard that the apostles would not consent so much as to distribute the money that was collected without any trouble? But now our bishops have gone beyond agents, and stewards, and hucksters

---

[1] Mal. ii. 13.　　　　[2] Exod. xxii. 1.　　　　[3] Luke xiii. 4, 5. [Freely cited.]

in their care about these things; and when they ought to be careful and thoughtful about your souls, they are vexing themselves every day about these things, for which the inn-keepers, and tax-gatherers, and accountants, and stewards are careful.

These things I do not mention for nought in the way of complaint, but in order that there may be some amendment and change, in order that we may be pitied for serving a grievous servitude, in order that you may become a revenue and store for the church.

But if ye are not willing, behold the poor before your eyes; as many as it is possible for us to suffice, we will not cease to feed; but those, whom it is not possible, we will leave to you, that ye may not hear those words on the awful day, which shall be spoken to the unmerciful and cruel. "Ye saw me an hungered, and fed me not."[1]

For together with you this inhumanity makes us laughing-stocks, because leaving our prayers, and our teaching, and the other parts of holiness, we are fighting all our time, some with wine merchants, some with corn-factors, others with them that retail other provisions.

Hence come battles, and strifes, and daily revilings, and reproaches, and jeers, and on each of the priests names are imposed more suitable for houses of secular men; when it would have been fit to take other names in the place of these, and to be named from those things, from which also the apostles ordained, from the feeding of the hungry, from the protection of the injured, from the care of strangers, from succoring them that are de-spitefully used, from providing for the orphans, from taking part with the widows, from presiding over the virgins; and these offices should be distributed amongst us in-stead of the care of the lands and houses.

These are the stores of the church, these the treasures that become her, and that afford in great degree both ease to us and profit to you; or rather to you ease with the profit. For I suppose that by the grace of God they that assemble themselves here amount to the number of one hundred thousand;[2] and if each bestowed one loaf to some one of the poor, all would be in plenty; but if one farthing only, no one would be poor; and we should not undergo so many revilings and jeers, in consequence of our care about the money. For indeed the saying, "Sell thy goods, and give to the poor, and come and follow me,"[3] might be seasonably addressed to the prelates of the church with respect to the property of the church. For in any other way it is not possible to follow Him as we ought, not being freed from all grosser and more worldly care.

But now the priests of God attend at the vintage and harvest, and at the sale and purchase of the produce; and whereas they that served the shadow had an entire immu-nity from such matters, although entrusted with a more carnal service; we, who are in-vited to the very inmost shrines of the heavens, and who enter into the true holy of holies, take upon ourselves the cares of tradesmen and retail dealers.

Hence great neglect of the Scriptures, and remissness in prayers, and indifference about all the other duties; for it is not possible to be split into the two things with due zeal. Where I pray and beseech you that many fountains may spring up to us from all quarters, and that your forwardness may be to us the threshing floor and the wine press.

For in this way both the poor will more easily be supported, and God will be glorified, and ye will advance unto a greater degree of love to mankind, and will enjoy the good things eternal; unto which God grant we may all attain, by the grace and love towards man of our Lord Jesus Christ, to whom be glory world without end.   Amen.

---

[1] Matt. xxv. 42.

[2] i. e., the sum of all the congregations in Antioch.
[3] Matt. xix. 21. [Abridged.]

HOMILY LXXXVI.

Matt. XXVII. 11, 12.

" And Jesus stood before the governor; and the governor asked Him, saying, Art thou the king of the Jews? And Jesus said unto him, Thou sayest. And when He was accused of the chief priests and elders, He answered nothing." [1]

Seest thou what He is first asked? which thing most of all they were continually bringing forward in every way? For since they saw Pilate making no account of the matters of the law, they direct their accusation to the state charges. So likewise did they in the case of the apostles, ever bringing forward these things, and saying that they were going about proclaiming king one Jesus,[2] speaking as of a mere man, and investing them with a suspicion of usurpation.

Whence it is manifest, that both the rending the garment and the amazement were a pretense. But all things they got up, and plied, in order to bring Him to death.

This at any rate Pilate then asked. What then said Christ? "Thou sayest." He confessed that He was a king, but a heavenly king, which elsewhere also He spake more clearly, replying to Pilate, "My kingdom is not of this world;"[3] that neither they nor this man should have an excuse for accusing Him of such things. And He gives a reason that cannot be gainsaid, saying, "If I were of this world, my servants would fight, that I should not be delivered." For this purpose I say, in order to refute this suspicion, He both paid tribute,[4] and commanded others to pay it, and when they would make Him a king, He fled.[5]

Wherefore then did he not bring forward these things, it may be said, at that time, when accused of usurpation? Because having the proofs from His acts, of His power, His meekness, His gentleness, beyond number, they were willfully blind, and dealt unfairly, and the tribunal was corrupt. For these reasons then He replies to nothing, but holds His peace, yet answering briefly (so as not to get the reputation of arrogance from continual silence) when the high priest adjured Him, when the governor asked, but in reply to their accusations He no longer saith anything; for He was not now likely to persuade them.

Even as the prophet declaring this self-same thing from of old, said, "In His humiliation His judgment was taken away."[6]

At these things the governor marvelled, and indeed it was worthy of admiration to see Him showing such great forbearance, and holding His peace, Him that had countless things to say. For neither did they accuse Him from knowing of any evil thing in Him, but from jealousy and envy only. At least when they had set false witness, wherefore, having nothing to say, did they still urge their point? and when they saw Judas was dead, and that Pilate had washed his hands of it, why were they not pricked with remorse. For indeed He did many things even at the very time, that they might recover themselves, but by none were they amended.

What then saith Pilate? "Hearest thou not how many things these witness against thee?"[7] He wished that He should defend Himself and be acquitted, wherefore also he said these things; but since He answered nothing, he devises another thing again.

Of what nature was this? It was a custom for them to release one of the condemned, and by this means he attempted to deliver Him. For if you are not willing to release Him as innocent, yet as guilty pardon Him for the feast's sake.

Seest thou order reversed? For the petition in behalf of the condemned it was customary to be with the people, and the granting it with the rulers; but now the contrary hath come to pass, and the ruler petitions the people; and not even so do they become gentle, but grow more savage and bloodthirsty, driven to frenzy by the passion of envy. For neither had they whereof they should accuse Him, and this though He was silent, but they were refuted even then by reason of the abundance of His righteous deeds, and being silent He overcame them that say ten thousand things, and are maddened.

---

[1] [The article is omitted before "elders," as in the best New Testament mss. In all other details the agreement with the received text is exact.—R.]

[2] Acts xvii. 7.
[4] Matt. xxii. 17.
[3] John xviii. 36.
[5] John vi. 15.

[6] Isa. liii. 8, lxx., see margin of our version.
[7] Matt. xxvii. 13. [The word "these" is peculiar to this citation.—R.]

" And when he was set down on the judgment seat, his wife sent unto him, saying, have thou nothing to do with this just man, for I have suffered many things this day in a dream because of Him." [1] See what a thing takes place again, sufficient to recall them all. For together with the proof from the things done, the dream too was no small thing. And wherefore doth he not see it himself? Either because she was more worthy, or because he, if he had seen it, would not have been equally believed; or would not so much as have told it. Therefore it was ordered that the wife should see it, so that it might be manifest to all. And she doth not merely see it, but also suffers many things, that from his feeling towards his wife, the man may be made more reluctant to the murder. And the time too contributed not a little, for on the very night she saw it.

But it was not safe, it may be said, for him to let Him go, because they said He made Himself a king. He ought then to have sought for proofs, and a conviction, and for all the things that are infallible signs of an usurpation, as, for instance, whether He levied forces, whether He collected money, whether he forged arms, whether He attempted any other such thing. But he is led away at random, therefore neither doth Christ acquit him of the blame, in saying, " He that betrayeth me unto thee hath greater sin." [2] So that it was from weakness that he yielded and scourged Him, and delivered Him up.

He then was unmanly and weak; but the chief priests wicked and criminal. For since he had found out a device, namely, the law of the feast requiring him to release a condemned person, what do they contrive in opposition to that? " They persuaded the multitude," it is said, " that they should ask Barabbas." [3]

2. See how much care he taketh for them to relieve them from blame, and how much diligence they employed, so as not to leave to themselves so much as a shadow of an excuse. For which was right? to let go the acknowledged criminal, or Him about whose guilt there was a question? For, if in the case of acknowledged offenders it was fit there should be a liberation, much more in those of whom there was a doubt. For surely this man did not seem to them worse than acknowledged murderers. For on this account,

it is not merely said they had a robber; but one noted, that is, who was infamous in wickedness, who had perpetrated countless murders. But nevertheless even him did they prefer to the Saviour of the world, and neither did they reverence the season because it was holy, nor the laws of humanity, nor any other thing of the kind, but envy had once for all blinded them. And besides their own wickedness, they corrupt the people also, that for deceiving them too they might suffer the most extreme punishment.

Since therefore they ask for the other, He saith, " What shall I do then with the Christ," [4] in this way desiring to put them to the blush, by giving them the power to choose, that at least out of shame they might ask for Him, and the whole should be of their bountifulness. For though to say, He had not done wrong, made them more contentious, yet to require that He should be saved out of humanity, carries with it persuasion and entreaty that cannot be gainsaid.

But even then they said, " Crucify Him. But he said, why, what evil hath He done? but they cried out exceedingly,[5] let Him be crucified. But he, when he saw that he profited nothing, washed his hands, saying, I am innocent." Why then didst thou deliver Him up? Why didst thou not rescue Him, as the centurion did Paul.[6] For that man too was aware that he would please the Jews; and a sedition had taken place on his account, and a tumult, nevertheless he stood firm against all. But not so this man, but he was extremely unmanly and weak, and all were corrupt together. For neither did this man stand firm against the multitude, nor the multitude against the Jews,[7] and in in every way their excuse was taken away. For they " cried out exceedingly," that is, cried out the more, " Let Him be crucified." For they desired not only to put Him to death, but also that it should be on a charge of wickedness, and though the judge was contradicting them, they continued to cry out the same thing.

Seest thou how many things Christ did in order to recover them? For like as He often times checked Judas, so likewise did He restrain these men too, both throughout all His Gospel, and at the very time of His condemnation. For surely when they saw the ruler and the judge washing his hands of it,

---

[1] Matt. xxvii. 19. [The readings ἔπεμψε for ἀπέστειλεν, and τούτῳ for ἐκείνῳ, are peculiar. R. V., " And while he was sitting on the," etc.—R.]
[2] John xix. 11. [" delivereth " is preferable, since the reference is not necessarily to Judas. Similarly in R. V.—R.]
[3] Matt. xxvii. 20. [R. V., " ask for ;" but the form of the verb in the Homily is peculiar.—R.]

[4] Matt. xxvii. 22. [Abridged, but given in full in some editions of the Homily.—R.]
[5] Matt. xxvii. 22–24. [Abridged. R. V., " prevailed nothing." —R.]
[6] Acts xxi.
[7] i. e., the Jewish rulers ; Mr. Field has observed in his note on this passage, that οἱ Ἰουδαῖοι is thus used, especially in St. John's Gospel.

and saying, "I am innocent of this blood," they should have been moved to compunction both by what was said, and by what was done, as well when they saw Judas had hanged himself, as when they saw Pilate himself entreating them to take another in the place of Him. For when the accuser and traitor condemns himself, and he who gives sentence puts off from himself the guilt, and such a vision appears the very night, and even as condemned he begs Him off, what kind of plea will they have? For if they were not willing that He should be innocent, yet they should not have preferred to him even a robber, one that was acknowledged to be such, and very notorious.

What then did they? When they saw the judge washing his hands, and saying, "I am innocent," they cried out "His blood be on us, and on our children."[1] Then at length when they had given sentence against themselves, he yielded that all should be done.

See here too their great madness. For passion and wicked desire are like this. They suffer not men to see anything of what is right. For be it that ye curse yourselves; why do you draw down the curse upon your children also?

Nevertheless, the lover of man, though they acted with so much madness, both against themselves, and against their children, so far from confirming their sentence upon their children, confirmed it not even on them, but from the one and from the other received those that repented, and counts them worthy of good things beyond number. For indeed even Paul was of them, and the thousands that believed in Jerusalem; for, "thou seest it is said, brother, how many thousands of Jews there are which believe."[2] And if some continued *in their sin*, to themselves let them impute their punishment.

"Then released he Barabbas unto them, but Jesus, when he had scourged Him, he delivered to be crucified."[3]

And wherefore did he scourge Him. Either as one condemned, or willing to invest the judgment with due form, or to please them. And yet he ought to have resisted them. For indeed even before this he had said, "Take ye Him, and judge Him according to your law."[4] And there were many things that might have held back him and those men, the signs and the miracles, and the great patience

of Him, who was suffering these things, and above all His untold silence. For since both by His defense of Himself, and by His prayers, He had shown His humanity, again He showeth His exaltedness and the greatness of His nature, both by His silence, and by His contemning what is said; by all leading them on to marvel at Himself.[5] But to none of these things did they give way.

3. For when once the reasoning powers are overwhelmed as it were by intoxication or some wild insanity, it would be hard for the sinking soul to rise again, if it be not very noble.

For it is fearful, it is fearful to give place to these wicked passions, wherefore it were fit in every way to ward off and repel their entering in. For when they have laid hold of the soul, and got the dominion over it, like as fire lighting upon a wood, so do they kindle the flame to a blaze.

Wherefore I entreat you to do all things so as to fence off their entrance; and not by comforting yourselves with this heartless reasoning to bring in upon yourselves all wickedness, saying, what of this? What of that? For countless ills have their birth from hence. For the devil, being depraved, makes use of much craft, and exertion, and self-abasement for the ruin of men, and begins his attack on them with things of a more trifling nature.

And mark it, he desired to bring Saul into superstition of witchcraft. But if he had counselled this at the beginning, the other would not have given heed; for how should he, who was even driving them out? Therefore gently and by little and little he leads him on to it. For when he had disobeyed Samuel, and had caused the burnt-offering to be offered, when he was not present, being blamed for it, he says, "The compulsion from the enemy was too great,"[6] and when he ought to have bewailed, he felt as though he had done nothing.

Again God gave him the commands about the Amalekites, but he transgressed these too. Thence he proceeded to his crimes about David, and thus slipping easily and by little and little he stayed not, until he came unto the very pit of destruction, and cast himself in. So likewise in the case of Cain, he did not at once urge him to slay his brother, since he would not have persuaded him, but first wrought upon him to offer things more or less vile, saying, "This is no sin:" in the second place he kindled envy and jealousy, saying, neither is there anything in this;

[1] Matt. xxvii. 25.
[2] Acts xxi. 20. [The R. V. accepts a different reading; but "which have believed" is the more accurate rendering of the received text.—R.]
[3] Matt. xxvii. 26. [R. V., "he scourged and delivered to be crucified."—R.]
[4] John xviii. 31.

[5] πρὸς τὸ οἰκεῖον θαῦμα.
[6] Cf. 1 Sam. xiii. 12; and xxviii. 15.

thirdly, he persuaded him to slay and to deny his murder; and did not leave him before he had put on him the crowning act of evil.

Wherefore it is necessary for us to resist the beginning. For at any rate, even if the first sins stopped at themselves, not even so were it right to despise the first sins; but now they go on also to what is greater, when the mind is careless. Wherefore we ought to do all things to remove the beginnings of them.

For look not now at the nature of the sin, that it is little, but that it becomes a root of great sin when neglected. For if one may say something marvellous, great sins need not so much earnestness, as such as are little, and of small account. For the former the very nature of the sin causes us to abhor, but the little sins by this very thing cast us into remissness; and allow us not to rouse ourselves heartily for their removal. Wherefore also they quickly become great, while we sleep. This one may see happening in bodies also.

So likewise in the instance of Judas, that great wickedness had its birth. For if it had not seemed to him a little thing to steal the money of the poor, he would not have been led on to this treachery. Unless it had seemed to the Jews a little thing to be taken captive by vainglory, they would not have run on the rock of becoming Christ's murderers. And indeed all evils we may see arise from this.

For no one quickly and at once rusheth out into vices. For the soul hath, yea it hath a shame implanted in us, and a reverence for right things; and it would not at once become so shameless as in one act to cast away everything, but slowly, and by little and little doth it perish, when it is careless. Thus also did idolatry enter in, men being honored beyond measure, both the living and the departed; thus also were idols worshipped; thus too did whoredom prevail, and the other evils.

And see. One man laughed unseasonably; another blamed him; a third took away the fear, by saying, nothing comes of this. "For what is laughing? What can come of it?" Of this is bred foolish jesting; from that filthy talking; then filthy doings.

Again, another being blamed for slandering his neighbors, and reviling, and calumniating, despised it, saying, evil-speaking is nothing. By this he begets hatred unspeakable, revilings without end; by the revilings blows, and by the blows oftentimes murder.

4. From these little things then that wicked spirit thus brings in the great sins; and from the great despair; having invented this other while not less mischievous than the former. For to sin destroys not so much as to despair.

For he that hath offended, if he be vigilant, speedily by repentance amends what hath been done; but he that hath learnt to despond, and doth not repent, by reason thereof fails of this amendment by not applying the remedies from repentance.

And he hath a third grievous snare; as when he invests the sin with a show of devotion. And where hath the devil so far prevailed as to deceive to this degree? Hear, and beware of his devices. Christ by Paul commanded "that a woman depart not from her husband,[1] and not to defraud one another, except by consent;"[2] but some from a love of continence forsooth, having withdrawn from their own husbands, as though they were doing something devout, have driven them to adultery. Consider now what an evil it is that they, undergoing so much toil, should be blamed as having committed the greatest injustice, and should suffer extreme punishment, and drive their husbands into the pit of destruction.

Others again, abstaining from meats by a rule of fasting, have by degrees gone so far as to abhor them; which even of itself brings a very great punishment.

But this comes to pass, when any hold fast their own prejudices contrary to what is approved by the Scriptures. Those also among the Corinthians thought it was a part of perfection to eat of all things without distinction, even of things forbidden, but nevertheless this was not of perfection, but of the utmost lawlessness. Wherefore also Paul earnestly reproves them, and pronounces them to be worthy of extreme punishment. Others again think it a sign of piety to wear long hair. And yet this is amongst the things forbidden, and carries with it much disgrace.

Again, others follow after excessive sorrow for their sins as a profitable thing; yet it also comes of the devil's wiles, and Judas showed it; at least in consequence thereof he even hanged himself. Therefore Paul again was in fear about him that had committed fornication, lest any such thing should befall him, and persuaded the Corinthians speedily to deliver him, "lest perhaps such a one should be swallowed up with overmuch sorrow."[3] Then, indicating that such a result cometh of the snares of that *wicked* one, he saith, "Lest Satan should get an advantage over us, for we are not ignorant of his devices,"[4] meaning that he assails us with much craft. Since if he fought against us plainly and openly, the victory would be ready and easy; or rather even now, if we be vigilant, victory

---

[1] 1 Cor. vii. 10.   [2] 1 Cor. vii. 5.
[3] 2 Cor. ii. 7.   [4] 2 Cor. ii. 10, 11.

will be ready. For indeed against each one of those ways God hath armed us.

For to persuade us not to despise even these little things, hear what warning He gives us, saying, "He that saith to his brother, thou fool, shall be in danger of hell;"[1] and he that hath looked with unchaste eyes is a complete adulterer.[2] And on them that laugh he pronounces a woe, and everywhere He removes the beginning and the seeds of evil, and saith we have to give an account of an idle word.[3] Therefore also Job applied a remedy even for the thoughts of his children.[4]

But about not despairing, it is said, "Doth he fall, and not arise? Doth he turn away, and not return?"[5] and, "I do not will the death of the sinner, so much as that he should turn and live:"[6] and, "To-day if ye will hear His voice:"[7] and many other such things, both sayings and examples are set in the Scripture. And in order not to be ruined under the guise of godly fear, hear Paul saying, "Lest perhaps such a one be swallowed up by overmuch sorrow."

Knowing therefore these things, let us set for a barrier in all the ways that pervert the unwary the wisdom which is drawn from the Scriptures. Neither say, why, what is it, if I gaze curiously at a beautiful woman? For if thou shouldest commit the adultery in the heart, soon thou wilt venture on that in flesh. Say not, why, what is it if I should pass by this poor man? For if thou pass this man by, thou wilt also the next; if him, then the third.

Neither again say, why, what is it, if I should desire my neighbor's goods. For this, this caused Ahab's ruin; although he would have paid a price, yet he took it from one unwilling. For a man ought not to buy by force, but on persuasion. But if he, who would have paid the fair price, was so punished, because he took from one unwilling, he who doeth not so much as this, and taketh by violence from the unwilling, and that when living under grace, of what punishment will he not be worthy?

In order therefore that we be not punished, keeping ourselves quite pure from all violence and rapine, and guarding against the sources of sins together with the sins themselves, let us with much diligence give heed to virtue; for thus shall we also enjoy the good things eternal by the grace and love towards man of our Lord Jesus Christ, to whom be glory world without end. Amen.

---

[1] Matt. v. 22.   [2] Matt. v. 28.   [3] Matt. xii. 36.
[4] Job i. 5.   [5] Jer. viii. 4.
[6] Ezek. xviii. 23. [Abridged from the LXX.]
[7] Ps. xcv. 7.

HOMILY LXXXVII.

Matt. XXVII. 27—29.

"Then the soldiers of the governor took Jesus into the common hall,[1] and gathered unto him the whole band of soldiers; and they stripped Him, and put on Him a purple robe; and when they had platted a crown of thorns, they put it on His head, and a reed in His right hand; and they bowed the knee before Him, and mocked Him, saying, Hail, king of the Jews."[2]

As though on some signal the devil then was entering in triumph[3] into all. For, be it that Jews pining with envy and jealousy were mad against Him, as to the soldiers, whence was it, and from what sort of cause? Is it not clear that it was the devil who was then entering in fury into the hearts of all? For indeed they made a pleasure of their insults against Him, being a savage and ruthless set. I mean that, when they ought to have been awestruck, when they ought to have wept, which even the people did, this they did not, but, on the contrary, were despiteful, and insolent; perhaps themselves also seeking to please the Jews, or it may be doing all in conformity to their own evil nature.

---

[1] [Greek, "Prætorium;" comp. Mark xv. 16, A. V.—R.]
[2] [The Greek text, as given by Field, agrees throughout with the received.—R.]
[3] ἐχόρευεν.

And the insults were different, and varied. For that Divine Head at one time they buffeted, at another they insulted with the crown of thorns, at another they smote with the reed, men unholy and accursed !

What plea shall we have after this for being moved by injuries, after Christ suffered these things ? For what was done was the utmost limit of insolence. For not one member, but the whole entire body throughout was made an object of insolence; the head through the crown, and the reed, and the buffeting; the face, being spit upon; the cheeks, being smitten with the palms of the hands; the whole body by the stripes, by being wrapped in the robe, and by the pretended worship; the hand by the reed, which they gave him to hold instead of a sceptre; the mouth again by the offering of the vinegar. What could be more grievous than these things ? What more insulting ?

For the things that were done go beyond all language. For as though they were afraid lest they should seem to fall short at all in the crime, having killed the prophets with their own hands, but this man with the sentence of a judge, so they do in every deed; and make it the work of their own hands, and condemn and sentence both among themselves and before Pilate, saying, "His blood be on us and on our children,"[1] and insult Him, and do despite unto Him themselves, binding Him, leading Him away, and render themselves authors of the spiteful acts done by the soldiers, and nail Him to the cross, and revile Him, and spit at Him, and deride Him. For Pilate contributed nothing in this matter, but they themselves did every thing, becoming accusers, and judges, and executioners, and all.

And these things are read amongst us, when all meet together. For that the heathens may not say, that ye display to people and nations the things that are glorious and illustrious, such as the signs and the miracles, but that ye hide these which are matters of reproach; the grace of the Spirit hath brought it to pass, that in the full festival, when men in multitude and women are present, and all, as one may say, at the great eve of the passover, then all these things should be read; when the whole world is present, then are all these acts proclaimed with a clear voice. And these being read, and made known to all, Christ is believed to be God, and, besides all the rest, is worshipped, even because of this, that He vouchsafed to stoop so much for us as actually to suffer these things, and to teach us all virtue.

These things then let us read continually; for indeed great is the gain, great the advantage to be thence obtained. For when thou seest Him, both by gestures and by deeds, mocked and worshipped with so much derision, and beaten and suffering the utmost insults, though thou be very stone, thou wilt become softer than any wax, and wilt cast out of thy soul all haughtiness.

Hear therefore also what follows. For after "they had mocked Him, they led Him to crucify Him," it is said, and when they had stripped Him, they took His garments, and sat down and watched Him, when He should die. And they divide His garments amongst them, which sort of thing is done in the case of very vile and abject criminals, and such as have no one belonging to them, and are in utter desolation.

They parted the garments, by which such great miracles were done. But they wrought none now, Christ restraining His unspeakable power. And this was no small addition of insult. For as to one base and abject, as I said, and the vilest of all men; so do they dare to do all things. To the thieves at any rate they did nothing of the kind, but to Christ they dare it all. And they crucified Him in the midst of them, that He might share in their reputation.

And they gave Him gall to drink, and this to insult Him, but He would not. But another saith, that having tasted it, He said, "It is finished."[2] And what meaneth, "It is finished?" The prophecy was fulfilled concerning Him. "For they gave me," it is said, "gall for my meat, and for my thirst they gave me vinegar to drink."[3] But neither doth that evangelist indicate that He drank, for merely to taste differs not from not drinking, but hath one and the same signification.

But nevertheless not even here doth their contumely stop, but after having stripped and crucified Him, and offered Him vinegar, they proceeded still further, and beholding Him impaled upon the cross, they revile Him, both they themselves and the passers by; and this was more grievous than all, that on the charge of being an impostor and deceiver He suffered these things, and as a boaster, and vainly pretending what He said. Therefore they both crucified Him publicly, that they might make a show of it in the sight of all; and therefore also they did it by the hands of the soldiers, that these things being perpetrated even by a public tribunal, the insult might be the greater.

---

[1] Matt. xxvii. 25.

[2] Matt. xxvii. 31. [ἤγαγον for ἀπήγαγον.]
[3] John xix. 30.   3 Ps. lxix. 21.

2. And yet who would not have been moved by the multitude that was following Him, and.lamenting Him? Nay, not these wild beasts. Wherefore also He to the multitude vouchsafes an answer, but to these men not so. For after having done what they would, they endeavor also to injure His honor, fearing His resurrection. Therefore they say these things publicly, and crucified thieves with Him, and wishing to prove Him a deceiver, they say, "Thou that destroyest the temple, and buildest it in three days come down from the cross." [1] For since on telling Pilate to remove the accusation (this was the writing, "The king of the Jews"), they prevailed not, but he persevered in saying, "What I have written, I have written," [2] they then endeavor by their derision of Him to show that He is not a king.

Wherefore they said those things, and also these. If "He is the king of Israel, let Him come down now from the cross. He saved others, Himself He cannot save," [3] aiming hereby to bring discredit even on His former miracles. And again, "If He be Son of God, and He will have Him, let Him save Him." [4]

O execrable; most execrable! What, were not the prophets prophets, nor the righteous men righteous, because God rescued them not out of their dangers. Nay surely they were, though suffering these things. What then could be equal to your folly? For if the coming of the dangers upon them did not injure their honor with you, how much more in the case of this man, was it wrong for you to be offended, when both by what He did, by what He said, He was ever correcting beforehand this suspicion of yours.

Yet nevertheless, even when these things were said and done, they prevailed nothing, not even at the very time. At any rate, he, who was depraved in such great wickedness, and who had spent his whole life in murders and house-breakings, when these things were being said, then confessed Him, and made mention of a kingdom, and the people bewailed Him. And yet the things that were done seemed to testify the contrary in the eyes of those who knew not the mysterious dispensations, that He was weak and of no power, nevertheless truth prevailed even by the contrary things.

Hearing then these things, let us arm ourselves against all rage, against all anger. Shouldest thou perceive thy heart swelling, seal thy breast setting upon it the cross. Call to mind some one of the things that then took place, and thou wilt cast out as dust all rage by the recollection of the things that were done. Consider the words, the actions; consider that He is Lord, and thou servant. He is suffering for thee, thou for thyself; He in behalf of them who had been benefited by Him and had crucified Him, thou in behalf of thyself; He in behalf of them who had used Him despitefully, thou oftentimes at the hands of them who have been injured. He in the sight of the whole city, or rather of the whole people of the Jews, both strangers, and those of the country, before whom He spake those merciful words, but thou in the presence of few; and what was more insulting to Him, that even His disciples forsook Him. For those, who before paid Him attention, had deserted Him, but His enemies and foes, having got Him in the midst of themselves on the cross, insulted, reviled, mocked, derided, scoffed at Him, Jews and soldiers from below, from above thieves on either side: for indeed the thieves insulted, and upbraided Him both of them. How then saith Luke that one "rebuked?" [5] Both things were done, for at first both upbraided Him, but afterwards one did so no more. For that thou mightest not think the thing had been done by any agreement, or that the thief was not a thief, by his insolence he showeth thee, that up on the cross he was a thief and an enemy, and at once was changed.

Considering then all these things, control thyself. For what sufferest thou like what thy Lord suffered? Wast thou publicly insulted? But not like these things. Art thou mocked? yet not thy whole body, not being thus scourged, and stripped. And even if thou wast buffeted, yet not like this.

3. And add to this, I pray thee, by whom, and wherefore, and when, and who it was; and (the most grievous matter) that these things being done, no one found fault, no one blamed what was done, but on the contrary all rather approved, and joined in mocking Him and in jeering at Him; and as a boaster, impostor, and deceiver, and not able to prove in His works the things that He said, so did they revile Him. But He held His peace to all, preparing for us the most powerful incentives to long suffering.

But we, though hearing such things, are not patient so much as to servants, but we rush and kick worse than wild asses, with respect to injuries against ourselves, being savage and inhuman; but of those against God not making much account. And with

---

[1] Matt. xxvii. 40.   3 John xix. 22.   3 Matt. xxvii. 42.
[4] Matt. xxvii. 43. [In the citations from verses 40–43, the exact order is not preserved, but the only textual variation is in the clause, "let Him save Him," which does not occur in the Gospels. "If" is read, with the received text, in verse 42.—R.]

[5] Luke xxiii. 40.

respect to friends too we have the same disposition; should any one vex us, we bear it not; should he insult us, we are savage more than wild beasts, we who are reading these things every day. A disciple betrayed Him, the rest forsook Him and fled, they that had been benefited by Him spat at Him, the servants of the high priest smote Him with the palm of the hand, the soldiers buffeted Him; they that passed by jeered Him and reviled Him, the thieves accused Him; and to no man did He utter a word, but by silence overcame all; instructing thee by His actions, that the more meekly thou shalt endure, the more wilt thou prevail over them that do thee evil, and wilt be an object of admiration before all. For who will not admire him that endures with forbearance the insults he receives from them that are using him despitefully? For even as, though any man suffer justly, yet enduring the evil meekly, he is considered by the more part to suffer unjustly; so though one suffer unjustly, yet if he be violent, he will get the suspicion of suffering justly, and will be an object of ridicule, as being dragged captive by his anger, and losing his own nobility. For such a one, we must not call so much as a freeman, though he be lord over ten thousand servants.

But did some person exceedingly provoke thee? And what of that? For then should self-control be shown, since when there is no one to vex, we see even the wild beasts gentle; for neither are they always savage, but when any one rouses them. And we therefore, if we are only then quiet, when there is no one provoking us, what advantage have we over them. For they are both oftentimes justly indignant, and have much excuse, for by being stirred and goaded are they roused, and besides these things they are devoid of reason, and have savageness in their nature.

But whence, I pray thee, canst thou find a plea for being savage and fierce? What hardship hast thou suffered? Hast thou been robbed? For this self-same reason shouldest thou endure it, so as to gain more amply. But wast thou deprived of character? And what is this? Thy condition is in no way worsened by this, if thou practise self-command. But if thou sufferest no grievance, whence art thou angry with him that hath done thee no harm, but hath even benefited thee? For they who honor, make them that are not watchful the more vain; but they who insult and despise render those that take heed to themselves more steadfast. For the careless are more injured by being honored than by being insulted. And the one set of persons, if we be sober, become to us authors

of self-control, but the others excite our pride, they fill us with boastfulness, vainglory, folly, they make our soul the feebler.

And to this fathers bear witness, who do not flatter their own children so much as they chide them, fearing lest from the praise they should receive any harm, and their teachers use the same remedy to them. So that if we are to avoid any one, it should be those that flatter us rather than those that insult us; for this bait brings greater mischief than insult to them, who do not take heed, and it is more difficult to control this feeling than that. And the reward too is far more abundant from thence, and the admiration greater. For indeed it is more worthy of admiration to see a man insulted, and not moved, than beaten and smitten, and not falling.

And how is it possible not to be moved? one may say. Hath any one insulted thee? Place the sign upon thy breast, call to mind all the things that were then done; and all is quenched. Consider not the insults only, but if also any good hath been ever done unto thee, by him that hath insulted thee, and straightway thou wilt become meek, or rather consider before all things the fear of God, and soon thou wilt be mild and gentle.

4. Together with these things even from thine own servants take a lesson concerning these matters; and when thou seest thyself insulting, but thy servant holding his peace, consider that it is possible to practise self-control, and condemn thyself for being violent; and in the very time of offering insults learn not to insult; and thus not even when insulted, wilt thou be vexed. Consider that he who is insolent is beside himself and mad, and thou wilt not feel indignant, when insulted, since the possessed strike us, and we, so far from being provoked, do rather pity them. This do thou also; pity him that is insolent to thee, for he is held in subjection by a dreadful monster, rage, by a grievous demon, anger. Set him free as he is wrought upon by a grievous demon, and going quickly to ruin. For so great is this disease as not to need even time for the destruction of him that is seized with it. Wherefore also one said, "The sway of his fury shall be his fall;"[1] by this most of all showing its tyranny, that in a short time it works great ills, and needs not to continue long with us, so that if in addition to its strength it were apt to last, it would indeed be hard to strive against.

I should like to show what the man is who insulteth, what he that practises self-control, and to bring nakedly before you the soul of

[1] Ecclus. i. 22

the one and the other. For thou shouldest see the one like a sea tost with a tempest, but the other like a harbor free from disturbance. For it is not disturbed by these evil blasts, but puts them to rest easily. For indeed they who are insulting, do everything in order to make it sting. When then they fail of that hope, even they are thenceforth at peace, and go away amended. For it is impossible that a man, who is angry, should not utterly condemn himself, even as on the other hand it is impossible for one who is not angry to be self-condemned. For though it be necessary to retaliate, it is possible to do this without anger (and it were more easy and more wise than with anger) and to have no painful feeling. For if we be willing, the good things will be from ourselves, and we shall be with the grace of God sufficient for our own safety and honor.

For why seekest thou the glory that cometh from another? Do thou honor thyself, and no one will be able to insult thee; but if thou dishonor thyself, though all should honor thee, thou wilt not be honored. For like as, unless we put ourselves in an evil state, no one else puts us in such a state; even so unless we insult ourselves, no one else can put us to shame.

For let any man be great and worthy of admiration, and let all men call him an adulterer, a thief, a violater of tombs, a murderer, a robber, and let him be neither provoked or indignant, nor be conscious to himself of any of these crimes, what disgrace will he thence undergo? None. What then, you may say, if many have such an opinion of him? Not even so is he disgraced, but they bring shame upon themselves, by accounting one, who is not such, to be such. For tell me, if any one think the sun to be dark, doth he bring an ill name on that heavenly body, or on himself? Surely on himself, getting himself the character of being blind or mad. So also they that account wicked men good, and they that make the opposite error, disgrace themselves.

Wherefore we ought to give the greater diligence, to keep our conscience clear, and to give no handle against ourselves, nor matter for evil suspicion; but if others will be mad, even when this is our disposition, not to care very much, nor to grieve. For he that hath got the character of a wicked man, being a good man, is in no degree thereby hurt as regards his being such as he is; but he that hath been suspecting another vainly and causelessly, receives the utmost harm; as, on the other hand, the wicked man, if he be supposed to be the contrary, will gain nothing thence, but will both have a heavier judgment, and be led into greater carelessness. For he that is such and is suspected thereof, may perhaps be humbled, and acknowledge his sins; but when he escapes detection, he falls into a state past feeling. For if, while all are accusing them, offenders are hardly stirred up to compunction, when so far from accusing them, some even praise them, at what time will they who are living in vice be able to open their eyes? Hearest thou that Paul also blames for this, that the Corinthians (so far from permitting him that had been guilty of fornication, to acknowledge his own sin), applauding and honoring him, did on the contrary urge him on in vice thereby? Wherefore, I pray, let us leave the suspicions of the multitude, their insults and their honors, and let us be diligent about one thing only, that we be conscious to ourselves of no evil thing, nor insult our own selves. For so, both here, and in the world to come, we shall enjoy much glory, unto which God grant we all may attain, by the grace and love towards man of our Lord Jesus Christ, to whom be glory world without end. Amen.

HOMILY LXXXVIII.

MATT. XXVII. 45—48.

"Now from the sixth hour there was darkness over all the earth until the ninth hour. And
about the ninth hour Jesus cried with a loud voice, and said, Eli, Eli, lima sabachthani? that is to say, my God my God, why hast thou forsaken me? Some of them
that stood there, when they heard *that* said, this man calleth for Elias. And straightway one of them ran, and took a sponge, and filled it with vinegar, and put it on a
reed, and gave Him to drink."[1]

THIS is the sign which before He had promised to give them when they asked it, saying, "An evil and adulterous generation
seeketh after a sign, and there shall no sign
be given to it, but the sign of the prophet
Jonas;"[2] meaning His cross, and His death,
His burial, and His resurrection. And again,
declaring in another way the virtue of the
cross, He said, "When ye have lifted up the
Son of Man, then shall ye know that I am He."[3]
And what He saith is to this purport: "When
ye have crucified me, and think ye have overcome me, then, above all, shall ye know my
might."

For after the crucifixion, the city was destroyed, and the Jewish state came to an end,
they fell away from their polity and their
freedom, the gospel flourished, the word was
spread abroad to the ends of the world; both
sea and land, both the inhabited earth and
the desert perpetually proclaim its[4] power.
These things then He meaneth, and those
which took place at the very time of the crucifixion. For indeed it was much more marvellous that these things should be done,
when He was nailed to the cross, than when
He was walking on earth. And not in this
respect only was the wonder, but because
from heaven also was that done which they
had sought, and it was over all the world,
which had never before happened, but in
Egypt only, when the passover was to be
fulfilled. For indeed those events were a
type of these.

And observe when it took place. At mid-
day, that all that dwell on the earth may
know it, when it was day all over the world;
which was enough to convert them, not by
the greatness of the miracle only, but also by
its taking place in due season. For after all

their insulting, and their lawless derision, this
is done, when they had let go their anger,
when they had ceased mocking, when they
were satiated with their jeerings, and had
spoken all that they were minded; then He
shows the darkness, in order that at least so
(having vented their anger) they may profit
by the miracle. For this was more marvellous than to come down from the cross, that
being on the cross He should work these
things. For whether they thought He Himself had done it, they ought to have believed
and to have feared; or whether not He, but
the Father, yet thereby ought they to have
been moved to compunction, for that darkness was a token of His anger at their crime.
For that it was not an eclipse, but both wrath
and indignation, is not hence alone manifest,
but also by the time, for it continued three
hours, but an eclipse takes place in one
moment of time, and they know it, who have
seen this; and indeed it hath taken place even
in our generation.

And how, you may say, did not all marvel,
and account Him to be God? Because the
race of man was then held in a state of great
carelessness and vice. And this miracle was
but one, and when it had taken place, immediately passed away; and no one was concerned to inquire into the cause of it, and
great was the prejudice and the habit of ungodliness. And they knew not what was the
cause of that which took place, and they
thought perhaps this happened so, in the way
of an eclipse or some natural effect. And
why dost thou marvel about them that are
without, that knew nothing, neither inquired
by reason of great indifference, when even
those that were in Judæa itself, after so many
miracles, yet continued using Him despitefully, although He plainly showed them that
He Himself wrought this thing.

And for this reason, even after this He
speaks, that they might learn that He was

---

[1] [In verse 46, ἔκραξεν is substituted for ἀνεβόησεν, and καὶ
εἶπεν for λέγων; as indicated above, λιμά is the form given. In
other respects the agreement with the received text is exact.—R.]
[2] Matt. xii. 39.   [3] John viii. 28.   [4] Or, "His."

still alive, and that He Himself did this, and that they might become by this also more gentle, and He saith, " Eli, Eli, lima sabachthani?"[1] that unto His last breath they might see that He honors His Father, and is no adversary of God. Wherefore also He uttered a certain cry from the prophet,[2] even to His last hour bearing witness to the Old Testament, and not simply a cry from the prophet, but also in Hebrew, so as to be plain and intelligible to them, and by all things He shows how He is of one mind with Him that begat Him.

But mark herein also their wantonness, and intemperance, and folly. They thought (it is said) that it was Elias whom He called, and straightway they gave Him vinegar to drink.[3] But another came unto Him, and " pierced His side with a spear."[4] What could be more lawless, what more brutal, than these men; who carried their madness to so great a length, offering insult at last even to a dead body?

But mark thou, I pray thee, how He made use of their wickednesses for our salvation. For after the blow the fountains of our salvation gushed forth from thence.

"And Jesus, when He had cried with a loud voice, yielded up the Ghost."[5] This is what He said, " I have power to lay down my life, and I have power to take it again," and, " I lay it down of myself."[6] So for this cause He cried with the voice, that it might be shown that the act is done by power. Mark at any rate saith, that " Pilate marvelled if He were already dead:"[7] and that the centurion for this cause above all believed, because He died with power.[8]

This cry rent the veil, and opened the tombs, and made the house desolate. And He did this, not as offering insult to the temple (for how should He, who saith, " Make not my Father's house a house of merchandise "),[9] but declaring them to be unworthy even of His abiding there; like as also when He delivered it over to the Babylonians. But not for this only were these things done, but what took place was a prophecy of the coming desolation, and of the change into the greater and higher state; and a sign of His might.

And together with these things He showed Himself also by what followed after these things, by the raising of the dead. For in the instance of Elisha;[10] one on touching a dead body rose again, but now by a voice He raised them, His body continuing up there, on the cross. And besides, those things were a type of this. For that this might be believed, therefore is that all done. And they are not merely raised, but also rocks are rent, and the earth shaken, that they might learn, that He was able to strike themselves blind, and to rend them in pieces. For He that cleft rocks asunder, and darkened the world, much more could have done these things to them, had it been His will. But He would not, but having discharged His wrath upon the elements, them it was His will to save by clemency. But they abated not their madness. Such is envy, such is jealousy, it is not easily stayed. At that time then they were impudent in setting themselves against the actual appearances; and afterwards *even against the things themselves*,[11] when a seal being put upon Him, and soldiers watching Him, He rose again, and they heard these things from the very guards; they even gave money, in order both to corrupt others, and to steal away the history of the resurrection.

Marvel not therefore if at this time also they were perverse, being thus altogether prepared to set themselves impudently against all things; but observe this other point, how great signs He had wrought, some from Heaven, some on earth, some in the very temple, at once marking His indignation, and at the same time showing that what were unapproachable are now to be entered, and that Heaven shall be opened; and the work removed to the true Holy of Holies. And they indeed said, " If He be the King of Israel, let Him come down now from the cross,"[12] but He shows that He is King of all the world. And whereas those men said, " Thou that destroyest this temple, and buildest it in three days,"[13] He shows that it shall be made forever desolate. Again they said, " He saved others, Himself He cannot save,"[14] but He while abiding on the cross proved this most abundantly on the bodies of His servants. For if for Lazarus to rise on the fourth day was a great thing, how much more for all those who had long ago fallen asleep, at once to appear alive, which was a sign of the future resurrection. For, " many bodies of the saints which slept, arose," it is said, " and went into the holy city, and appeared to many."[15] For in order that what was done might not be accounted to be an imagination,

---

[1] Matt. xxvii. 46. [2] Ps. xxii. 1 [3] Matt. xxvii. 48.
[4] John xix. 34. [This occurred later, as the next sentence seems to suggest. But in some New Testament MSS., the incident is interpolated at this point in Matthew Chrysostom *may* have referred to it as belonging to this Gospel. See Tischendorf *in loco*, Westcott and Hort, vol. ii., Notes on Select Readings.—R.]
[5] Matt. xxvii. 50. [The word "again" is omitted. R. V., " yielded up His Spirit."—R.]
[6] John x. 18. [7] Mark xv. 44.
[8] Mark xv. 39. [9] John ii. 16.

[10] 2 Kings xiii. 21.
[11] [The words in italics have no equivalent in the Greek.—R.]
[12] Matt. xxvii. 42. [13] Matt. xxvii. 40. [14] Matt. xxvii. 42.
[15] Matt. xxvii. 52, 53. [Slightly abridged, and with a few minor variations, not appearing in our New Testament MSS.—R.]

they appear, even to many, in the city. And the Centurion too then glorified God, saying, "Truly this was a righteous man. And the multitudes that came together to that sight, returned beating their breasts."[1] So great was the power of the crucified, that after so many mockings, and scoffs, and jeers, both the centurion was moved to compunction, and the people. And some say that there is also a martyrdom of this centurion, who after these things grew to manhood in the faith.

"And many women were there beholding afar off, which had followed Him, ministering unto Him, Mary Magdalene, and Mary the mother of James, and Joses, and the mother of Zebedee's sons."[2]

These things the women see done, these who were most inclined to feel for Him, who were most of all bewailing Him. And mark how great their assiduity. They had followed Him ministering to Him, and were present even unto the time of the dangers. Wherefore also they saw all; how He cried, how He gave up the ghost, how the rocks were rent, and all the rest.

And these first see Jesus; and the sex that was most condemned, this first enjoys the sight of the blessings, this most shows its courage. And when the disciples had fled, these were present. But who were these? His mother, for she is called *mother* of James,[3] and the rest. But another evangelist[4] saith, that many also lamented over the things that were done, and smote their breasts, which above all shows the cruelty of the Jews, for that they gloried in things for which others were lamenting, and were neither moved by pity, nor checked by fear. For indeed the things that were done were of great wrath, and were not merely signs, but signs of anger all of them, the darkness, the cloven rocks, the veil rent in the midst, the shaking of the earth, and great was the excess of the indignation.

" But Joseph went, and begged the body."[5] This was Joseph, who was concealing his discipleship of late; now however he had become very bold after the death of Christ. For neither was he an obscure person, nor of the unnoticed; but one of the council, and highly distinguished; from which circumstance especially one may see his courage. For he exposed himself to death, taking upon him enmity with all, by his affection to Jesus, both having dared to beg the body, and not having desisted until he obtained it. But not by taking it only, nor by burying it in a costly manner, but also by laying it in his own new tomb, he showeth his love, and his courage. And this was not so ordered without purpose, but so there should not be any bare suspicion, that one had risen instead of another.

"And there was Mary Magdalene, and the other Mary, sitting over against the sepulchre."[6] For what purpose do these wait by it? As yet they knew nothing great, as was meet, and high about Him, wherefore also they had brought ointments, and were waiting at the tomb, so that if the madness of the Jews should relax, they might go and embrace the body. Seest thou women's courage? seest thou their affection? seest thou their noble spirit in money? their noble spirit even unto death?

Let us men imitate the women; let us not forsake Jesus in temptations. For they for Him even dead spent so much and exposed their lives, but we (for again I say the same things) neither feed Him when hungry, nor clothe Him when naked, but seeing Him begging, we pass Him by. And yet if ye saw Himself, every one would strip himself of all his goods. But even now it is the same. For He Himself has said, I am he. Wherefore then dost thou not strip thyself of all? For indeed even now thou hearest Him say, Thou doest it unto me; and there is no difference whether thou givest to this man or to Him; thou hast nothing less than these women that then fed Him, but even much more. But be not perplexed! For it is not so much to have fed Him appearing in His own person, which would be enough to prevail with a heart of stone, as (because of His mere word) to wait upon the poor, the maimed, him that is bent down. For in the former case, the look and the dignity of Him who appears divides with thee that which is done; but here the reward is entire for thy benevolence; and there is the proof of the greater reverence towards Him, when at His mere word waiting upon thy fellow-servant thou refreshest him in all things. Refresh him, and believe Him, who receiveth it, and saith, Thou givest to me. For unless thou hadst given to Him, He would not have counted thee worthy of a kingdom. If thou

---

[1] Luke xxiii. 47, 48.
[2] Matt. xxvii. 55, 56. [There are three omissions: ἀπό before μακρόθεν, τῷ Ἰησοῦ ἀπὸ τῆς Γαλιλαίας, and ἐν αἷς ἦν.—R.]
[3] In Homily V. 4, he maintains her perpetual virginity; "how then, you will say, are James and others called His brethren? In the same way as Joseph himself too was considered the Husband of Mary." This is at least consistent with the explanation given in the spurious Homilies "on the Annunciation," Ben. t. ii. p. 797. And "on the women bearing spices," t. ii. p. 159, Appendix, that she was the *step-mother* of James. Theodoret, on Gal. i. 19, rejects this view, and makes them sons of Cleopas by her sister.
[4] Luke xxii. 48.
[5] Matt. xxvii. 57, 58. [R. V., "asked for." The reading ᾔτει is peculiar here.—R.]
[6] Matt. xxvii. 61. [R. V., "And Mary Magdalene was there," etc.]

hadst not turned away from Him, He would not have sent thee to hell, if thou hadst overlooked a chance person; but because it is He Himself that is despised, therefore great is the blame.

Thus also Paul persecuted Him, in persecuting them that are His; wherefore too He said. "Why persecutest thou me?"[1] Thus therefore let us feel, as bestowing on Christ Himself when we bestow. For indeed His words are more sure than our sight. When therefore thou seest a poor man, remember His words, by which He declared, that it is He Himself who is fed. For though that which appears be not Christ, yet in this man's form Christ Himself receiveth and beggeth.

But art thou ashamed to hear that Christ beggeth? Rather be ashamed when thou dost not give to Him begging of thee. For this is shame, this. is vengeance and punishment. Since for Him to beg is of His goodness, wherefore we ought even to glory therein; but for thee not to give, is of thy inhumanity. But if thou believe not now, that in passing by a poor man that is a believer, thou passest by Him, thou wilt believe it then, when He will bring thee into the midst and say, "Inasmuch as ye did it not to these, ye did it not to me."[2] But God forbid that we should so learn it, and grant rather that we may believe now, and bring forth fruit, and hear that most blessed voice that bringeth us into the kingdom.

But perhaps some one will say, "Thou art every day discoursing to us of almsgiving and humanity." Neither will I cease to speak of this. For if ye had attained to it, in the first place, not even so ought I to desist, for fear of making you the more remiss; yet had ye attained, I might have relaxed a little; but if ye have not arrived even at the half; say not these things to me, but to yourselves. For indeed thou doest the same in blaming me, as if a little child, hearing often of the letter alpha, and not learning it, were to blame its teacher, because he is continually and for ever reminding him about it.

For who from these discourses has become more forward in the giving of alms? Who has cast down his money? Who has given the half of his substance? Who the third part? No one. How then should it be other than absurd, when ye do not learn, to require us to desist from teaching? Ye ought to do the contrary. Though we were minded to desist, ye ought to stop us and to say, we have not yet learnt these things, and how is it ye have desisted from reminding us of them?

If it befell any one to suffer from his eye, and I happened to be a physician, and then having covered it up and anointed it, and having applied other treatment, I had not benefited it much, and so had desisted; would he not have come to the doors of my surgery and cried out against me, accusing me of great remissness, for that I had of myself withdrawn, while the disease remained; and if, on being blamed, I had said in reply to these things, that I had covered it up, and anointed it, would he have endured it? By no means, but would immediately have said; "And what is the advantage, if I still suffer pain." Reason thus also with respect to thy soul. But what if after having often fomented a hand that was lifeless and shrunk, I had not succeeded in mollifying it? Should I not have heard the same thing? And even now a hand that is shrunk and withered we bathe, and for this reason, until we can stretch it out perfectly, we will not desist. Would that you too were to discourse of nothing else, at home and at market, at table and at night, and as a dream. For if we were always careful about these things by day, even in our dreams we should be engaged in them.

What sayest thou? Am I forever speaking of almsgiving? I would wish myself that there were not great need for me to address this advice to you, but that I were to speak of the battle against the Jews, and heathens, and heretics; but when ye are not yet sound, how can any one arm you for the fight? How should he lead you to the array, yet having wounds and gashes. Since if indeed I saw you thoroughly sound in health, I should lead you forth to that battle array, and ye would see by the grace of Christ ten thousands lying dead, and their heads cast one upon another. In other books at any rate, many discourses have been spoken by us touching these things, but not even so are we able thoroughly to triumph in the victory, because of the remissness of the multitude. For when we conquer them ten thousand times over in doctrines, they reproach us with the lives of the multitude of those who join our congregations, their wounds, their diseases in their soul.

How then shall we with confidence show you in the battle array, when ye rather do us mischief, being straightway wounded by our enemies, and made a mock of? For one man's hand is diseased, and shrunk so as not to be able to give away. How then should such a one hold a shield, and thrust it before him, and avoid being wounded by the jeers of cruelty. With others the feet halt, as

---

[1] Acts ix. 4.   [2] Matt. xxv. 45. [Abridged.]

many as go up to the theatres, and to the resorts of the harlot women. How shall these then be able to stand in the battle, and not to be wounded with the accusation of wantonness? Another suffers and is maimed in his eyes, not looking straight, but being full of lasciviousness, and assailing women's chastity, and overthrowing marriages. How then should this man be able to look in the face of the enemy, and brandish a spear, and throw his dart, being goaded on all sides with jeers. We may see also many suffering with the belly not less than the dropsical, when they are held in subjection by gluttony and drunkenness. How then shall I be able to lead forth these drunken men to war? With others the mouth is rotten; such are the passionate, and revilers, and blasphemers. How then shall this man ever shout in battle, and achieve anything great and noble, he too being drunk with another drunkenness, and affording much laughter to the enemy?

Therefore each day I go about this camp, dressing your wounds, healing your sores. But if ye ever rouse yourselves up, and become fit even to wound others, I will both teach you this art of war, and instruct you how to handle these weapons, or rather your works themselves will be weapons to you, and all men will immediately submit, if ye would become merciful, if forbearing, if mild and patient, if ye would show forth all other virtue. But if any gainsay, then we will also add the proof of what we can show on our part,[1] bringing you forward, since now we rather are hindered (at least as to your part) in this race.

And mark. We say that Christ hath done great things, having made angels of men; then, when we are called upon to give account, and required to furnish a proof out of this flock, our mouths are stopped. For I am afraid, lest in the place of angels, I bring forth swine as from a stye, and horses mad with lust.

I know ye are pained, but not against you all are these things spoken, but against the guilty, or rather not even against them if they awake, but for them. Since now indeed all is lost and ruined, and the church is become nothing better than a stable of oxen, and a fold for asses and camels, and I go round seeking for a sheep, and am not able to see it. So much are all kicking, like horses, and any wild asses, and they fill the place here with much dung, for like this is their discourse. And if indeed one could see the things spoken at each assemblage,[2] by men, by women, thou wouldest see their words more unclean than that dung.

Wherefore I entreat you to change this evil custom, that the church may smell of ointment. But now, while we lay up in it perfumes for the senses, the uncleanness of the mind we use no great diligence to purge out, and drive away. What then is the advantage? For we do not so much disgrace the church by bringing dung into it, as we disgrace it by speaking such things one to another, about gains, about merchandise, about petty tradings, about things that are nothing to us, when there ought to be choirs of angels here, and we ought to make the church a heaven, and to know nothing else but earnest prayers, and silence with listening.

This then let us do at any rate, from the present time, that we may both purify our lives, and attain unto the promised blessings, by the grace and love towards man of our Lord Jesus Christ, to whom be glory world without end. Amen.

---

[1] τὰ παρ' ἑαυτῶν.

[2] σύναξιν. [The word is usually applied to Christian assemblies, and in the edition of the Homilies it is sometimes rendered "communion." But this passage confirms the wider application defended in the notes to Homily V., p. 31.—R.]

HOMILY LXXXIX.

MATT. XXVII. 62—64.

" Now the next day,that followed the day of the preparation, the chief priests and Pharisees came together unto Pilate, saying, Sir, we remember that that deceiver said, while He was yet alive,[1] After three days I will[2] rise again. Command therefore that the sepulchre be made sure until the third day, lest His disciples come and steal Him away, and say to the people, He is risen from the dead: so the last error should be[3] worse than the first."

EVERYWHERE deceit recoils upon itself, and against its will supports the truth. And observe. It was necessary for it to be believed that He died, and that He rose again, and that He was buried, and all these things are brought to pass by His enemies. See, at any rate, these words bearing witness to every one of these facts. " We remember," these are the words, " that that deceiver said, when He was yet alive," (He was therefore now dead), "After three days I rise again. Command therefore that the sepulchre be sealed," (He was therefore buried), " lest His disciples come and steal Him away." So that if the sepulchre be sealed, there will be no unfair dealing. For there could not be. So then the proof of His resurrection has become incontrovertible by what ye have put forward. For because it was sealed, there was no unfair dealing. But if there was no unfair dealing, and the sepulchre was found empty, it is manifest that He is risen, plainly and incontrovertibly. Seest thou, how even against their will they contend for the proof of the truth ?

But mark thou, I pray thee, the disciples' love of truth, how they conceal from us none of the things that are said by His enemies, though they use opprobrious language. Behold, at any rate, they even call Him a deceiver, and these men are not silent about that.

But these things show also their savageness (that not even at His death did they let go their anger), and these men's simple and truthful disposition.

But it were worth while to inquire concerning that point also, where He said, " After three days I rise again ?" For one would not

find this thus distinctly stated,[4] but rather the example of Jonah. So that they understood His saying, and of their own will dealt unfairly.

What then saith Pilate? " Ye have a watch; make it as sure as ye can. And they made it sure, sealing the sepulchre, and setting the watch."[5] He suffers not the soldiers alone to seal, for as having learnt the things concerning Christ, he was no longer willing to co-operate with them. But in order to be rid of them, he endures this also, and saith, " Do ye seal it as ye will, that ye may not have it in your power to blame others." For if the soldiers only had sealed, they might have said (although the saying would have been improbable and false, yet nevertheless as in the rest they cast aside shame, so in this too they might have been able to say), that the soldiers, having given up the body to be stolen, gave His disciples opportunity to feign the history concerning His resurrection, but now having themselves made it sure, they are not able to say so much as this.

Seest thou how they labor for the truth against their will ? For they themselves came to Pilate, themselves asked, themselves sealed, setting the watch, so as to be accusers, and refuters one of another. And indeed when should they have stolen Him? on the Sabbath? And how? for it was not lawful so much as to go out.[6] And even if they transgressed the law, how should they have dared, who were so timid, to come forth? And how could they also have been able to persuade the multitude? By saying what? By doing what? And from what sort of zeal could they have stood in behalf of the dead? expecting

---

[1] [ὅτι is inserted at this point (but not in the subsequent citation). There are no other variations. R. V., " Now on the morrow, which is *the day* after the Preparation, the chief priests and the Pharisees were gathered together," etc.—R.]
[2] [R. V. omits " will."]   [3] [R. V., " will be."]

[4] Not to the Jews, for it was often plainly declared to the disciples, as St. Chrysostom himself observes a little further on.
[5] Matt. xxvii. 65, 66. [The only peculiarity is indicated in the above rendering ; for "made the sepulchre sure, sealing the stone." R. V., " guard " for " watch," and " the guard being with them."—R.]
[6] Exod. xvi. 29.

what recompense? what requital? Seeing Him yet alive and merely seized, they had fled; and after His death were they likely to speak boldly in His behalf, unless He had risen again? And how should these things be reasonable? For that they were neither willing nor able to feign a resurrection, that did not take place, is plain from hence. He discoursed to them much of a resurrection, and continually said, as indeed these very men have stated, "After three days I rise again." If therefore He rose not again, it is quite clear that these men (having been deceived and made enemies to an entire nation for His sake, and come to be without home and without city) would have abhorred Him, and would not have been willing to invest Him with such glory; as having been deceived, and having fallen into the utmost dangers on His account. For that they would not even have been able, unless the resurrection had been true, to feign it, this does not so much as need reasoning.

For in what were they confident? In the shrewdness of their reasonings? Nay of all men they were the most unlearned. But in the abundance of their possessions? Nay, they had neither staff nor shoes. But in the distinction of their race? Nay, they were mean, and of mean ancestors. But in the greatness of their country? Nay, they were of obscure places. But in their own numbers? Nay, they were not more than eleven, and they were scattered abroad. But in their Master's promises? What kind of promises? For if He were not risen again, neither would those be likely to be trusted by them. And how should they endure a frantic people. For if the chief of them endured not the speech of a woman, keeping the door, and if all the rest too, on seeing Him bound, were scattered abroad, how should they have thought to run to the ends of the earth, and plant a feigned tale of a resurrection? For if he stood not a woman's threat, and they not so much as the sight of bonds, how were they able to stand against kings, and rulers, and nations, where were swords, and gridirons, and furnaces, and ten thousand deaths day by day, unless they had the benefit of the power and grace[1] of Him who rose again? Such miracles and so many were done, and none of these things did the Jews regard, but crucified Him, who had done them, and were they likely to believe these men at their mere word about a resurrection? These things are not, they are not so, but the might of Him, who rose again, brought them to pass.

2. But mark, I pray thee, their craft, how ridiculous it is. "We remember," these are their words, "that that deceiver said, while He was yet alive, After three days I rise again." Yet if He were a deceiver, and boastfully uttered falsehoods, why are ye afraid and run to and fro, and use so much diligence? We are afraid, it is replied, lest perchance the disciples steal Him away, and deceive the multitude. And yet this has been proved to have no probability at all. Malice, however, is a thing contentious and shameless, and attempts what is unreasonable.

And they command it to be made sure for three days, as contending for doctrines, and being minded to prove that before that time also He was a deceiver, and they extend their malice even to His tomb. For this reason then He rose sooner, that they might not say that He spake falsely, and was stolen. For this, His rising sooner, was open to no charge, but to be later would have been full of suspicion. For indeed if He had not risen then, when they were sitting there, and watching, but when they had withdrawn after the three days, they would have had something to say, and to speak against it, although foolishly. For this reason then He anticipated the time. For it was meet the resurrection should take place, while they were sitting by and watching. Therefore also it was fit it should take place within the three days, since if it had been when they were passed, and the men had withdrawn, the matter would have been regarded with suspicion. Wherefore also He allowed them to seal it, as they were minded, and soldiers sat around it.

And they cared not about doing these things, and working on a Sabbath day, but they looked to one object only, their own wicked purpose, as though by that they were to succeed; which was a mark of extreme folly, and of fear now greatly dismaying them. For they who seized Him, when living, are afraid of Him when dead. And yet if He had been a mere man, they had reason to have taken courage. But that they might learn, that when living also He endured of His own will, what He did endure; behold, both a seal, a stone, and a watch, and they were not able to hold Him. But there was one result only, that the burial was published, and the resurrection thereby proved. For indeed soldiers sat by it, and Jews are on the watch.

"But in the end of the Sabbath,[2] as it began to dawn towards the first day of the week, came Mary Magdalene and the other Mary to see the sepulchre. And behold there was a

---

[1] ῥοπῆς.

[2] [R. V., "Now late on the Sabbath day."]

great earthquake. For an angel of the Lord descended from Heaven, and came and rolled back the stone from the door of the tomb,[1] and sat upon it. His countenance was like lightning, and his raiment white as snow."[2]

After the resurrection came the angel. Wherefore then came he, and took away the stone? Because of the women, for they themselves had seen Him then in the sepulchre.[3] Therefore that they might believe that He was risen again, they see the sepulchre void of the body. For this cause he removed the stone, for this cause also an earthquake took place, that they might be thoroughly aroused and awakened. For they were come to pour oil on Him, and these things were done at night, and it is likely that some also had become drowsy. And for what intent and cause doth he say, " Fear not ye ?"[4] First he delivers them from the dread, and then tells them of the resurrection. And the ye is of one showing them great honor, and indicating, that extreme punishment awaits them that had dared to do, what the others had dared, except they repented. For to be afraid is not for you, he means, but for them that crucified Him.

Having delivered them then from the fear both by his words, and by his appearance (for his form he showed bright, as bearing such good tidings), he went on to say, " I know that ye seek Jesus the Crucified."[5] And he is not ashamed to call Him " crucified;" for this is the chief of the blessings.

" He is risen."[6] Whence is it evident? " As He said." So that if ye refuse to believe me, he would say, remember His words, and neither will ye disbelieve me. Then also another proof, " Come and see the place where He lay."[7] For this he had lifted up the stone, in order that from this too they might receive the proof. "And tell His disciples, that ye shall see Him in Galilee."[8] And he prepares them to bear good tidings to others, which thing most of all made them believe. And He said well "in Galilee," freeing them from troubles and dangers, so that fear should not hinder their faith.

" And they departed from the sepulchre with fear and joy."[9] Why could this be? They had seen a thing amazing, and beyond expectation, a tomb empty, where they had before seen Him laid. Wherefore also He had led them to the sight, that they might become witnesses of both things, both of His tomb, and of His resurrection. For they considered that no man could have taken Him, when so many soldiers were sitting by Him, unless He raised up Himself. For this cause also they rejoice and wonder, and receive the reward of so much continuance with Him, that they should first see and gladly declare, not what had been said only, but also what they beheld.

3. Therefore after then they had departed with fear and joy, " Behold, Jesus met them, saying, All hail." But " they held Him by the feet,"[10] and with exceeding joy and gladness ran unto Him, and received by the touch also, an infallible proof, and full assurance of the resurrection. " And they worshipped Him." What then saith He? " Be not afraid." Again, He Himself casts out their fear, making way for faith, " But go, tell my brethren, that they go into Galilee, and there shall they see me."[11] Mark how He Himself sends good tidings to His disciples by these women, bringing to honor, as I have often said, that sex, which was most dishonored, and to good hopes; and healing that which was diseased.

Perchance some one of you would wish to be like them, to hold the feet of Jesus; ye can even now, and not His feet and His hands only, but even lay hold on that sacred head, receiving the awful mysteries with a pure conscience. But not here only, but also in that day ye shall see Him, coming with that unspeakable glory, and the multitude of the angels, if ye are disposed to be humane; and ye shall hear not these words only, " All hail !" but also those others, " Come ye blessed of my Father, inherit the kingdom prepared for you before the foundation of the world."[12]

Be ye therefore humane, that ye may hear these things; and ye women, that wear gold, who have looked on the running of these women, at last, though late, lay aside the disease of the desire for golden ornaments. So that if ye are emulous of these women, change the ornaments—which ye wear, and clothe yourselves instead with almsgiving. What is the use, I pray you, of these precious stones, and of the garments spangled with gold ? " My soul," you say, " is glad, and is pleased with these things." I asked thee the profit, but thou tellest me the hurt. For nothing is

---

1 [The only textual variation is the addition of τοῦ μνημείου. The R. V. omits "from the door of the tomb," and renders "rolled away," to distinguish from Mark xvi. 4.—R.]
2 Chap. xxviii. 1–3.
3 [εἶδον, " saw," i. e., when He was buried.—R.]
4 Matt. xxviii. 5. [The emphatic ὑμεῖς occurs in the Greek of the New Testament passage.—R.]
5 [τὸν ἐσταυρωμένον.]	6 Matt. xxviii. 6.
7 [This agrees with the reading of the two oldest New Testament MSS. So R. V. margin.—R.]
8 Matt. xxviii. 7. [Abridged.]
9 Matt. xxviii. 8. [The word " great " is omitted.—R.]

10 Matt. xxviii. 9. [R. V., "took hold of his feet."]
11 Matt. xxviii. 10. [R. V., " that they depart."]
12 Matt. xxv. 34.

worse than being taken up with these things, and delighting in them, and being riveted to them. For more bitter is this grievous slavery, when any one finds delight even in being a slave. For in what spiritual matter will she ever be diligent as she ought; when will she laugh to scorn, as she should, the things of this world, who thinks it a worthy matter for joy, that she hath been chained in gold? For he that continues in prison, and is pleased, will never desire to be set free; as indeed neither will this woman; but as having become a kind of captive to this wicked desire, she will not endure so much as to hear spiritual language with becoming desire and diligence, much less to engage in such work.

What then is the profit of these ornaments and this luxury? I pray thee. "I am pleased with them," thou sayest. Again thou hast told of the hurt and the ruin. "But I enjoy also," thou sayest, "much honor from the beholders." And what is this? This is the occasion of another destruction, when thou art lifted up to haughtiness, to arrogance. Come now, since thou hast not told me of the profit, bear with me while I tell thee of the mischiefs. What then are the mischiefs resulting therefrom? Anxiety, which is greater than the pleasure. Wherefore many of the beholders, these I mean of the grosser sort, derive more pleasure from it than she who wears the gold. For thou indeed deckest thyself with anxiety, but they, without this, feast their eyes.

Moreover, there are other things again, the debasing of the soul, the being looked upon with envy on all sides. For the neighboring women stung by it, arm themselves against their own husbands, and stir up against thee grievous wars. Together with these things, the fact that all one's leisure and anxiety are spent on this object, that one doth not apply one's self earnestly to spiritual achievements; that one is filled with haughtiness, arrogance, and vainglory; that one is riveted to the earth, and loses one's wings, and instead of an eagle, becometh a dog or a swine. For having given up looking up into Heaven, and flying thither, thou bendest down to the earth like the swine, being curious about mines and caverns, and having an unmanly and base soul. But dost thou, when thou appearest, turn towards thee the eyes of them at the market-place? Well then; for this very reason, thou shouldest not wear gold, that thou mayest not become a common gazing stock, and open the mouths of many accusers. For none of those whose eyes are toward thee admireth thee, but they jeer at thee, as fond of dress, as boastful, as a carnal woman. And

shouldest thou enter into a church, thou goest forth, without getting anything but countless jeers, and revilings, and curses, not from the beholders only, but also from the prophet. For straightway Isaiah,[1] that hath the fullest voice of all, as soon as he hath seen thee, will cry out, "These things saith the Lord against the princely daughters of Sion; because they walked with a lofty neck, and with winkings of the eyes, and in their walking, trailing their garments, and mincing at the same time with their feet; the Lord shall take off their bravery, and instead of a sweet smell there shall be dust, and instead of a stomacher, thou shalt gird thyself with a cord."[2]

These things for thy gorgeous array. For not to them only are these words addressed, but to every woman that doeth like them. And Paul again with him stands as an accuser, telling Timothy to charge the women, "not to adorn themselves with braided hair, or gold, or pearls, or costly array."[3] So that everywhere the wearing of gold is hurtful, but especially when thou art entering into a church, when thou passest through the poor. For if thou wert exceedingly anxious to bring an accusation against thyself, thou couldest not put on any other array than this visage of cruelty and inhumanity.

4. Consider at any rate how many hungry bellies thou passest by with this array, how many naked bodies with this satanical display. How much better to feed hungry souls, than to bore through the lobes of thy ears, and to hang from them the food of countless poor for no purpose or profit. What? is to be rich a commendation? What? is to wear gold a praise? Though it be from honest earnings that these things are put on you, even so what thou hast done is a very heavy charge against thee; but when it is moreover from dishonesty, consider the exceeding greatness of it.

But dost thou love praises and honor? Strip thyself therefore of this ridiculous clothing, and then all will admire thee; then shalt thou enjoy both honor and pure pleasure; since now at any rate thou art overwhelmed with jeers, working for thyself many causes of vexation arising out of these things. For should any of these things be missing, consider how many are the evils that have their birth therefrom, how many maidservants are beaten, how many men put to trouble, how many led to execution, how many cast into prison. And trials arise hence, and actions, and countless curses and accusations against the wife from the husband, against the hus-

---

[1] Isa. iii. 16, 24 [LXX.]   [2] 1 Tim. ii. 9.   [3] εἰσαγωγαί.

band from her friends, against the soul from itself. "But it will not be lost." In the first place, this is not easy to secure, but even if it be kept safe constantly, yet by being kept, it occasions much anxiety and care and discomfort, and no advantage.

For what kind of profit arises from hence to the house? What advantage to the woman herself who wears it? No advantage indeed, but much unseemliness, and accusation from every quarter? How wilt thou be able to kiss Christ's feet, and cling to them, when thus dressed? From this adorning He turneth away. For this cause He vouchsafed to be born in the house of the carpenter, or rather not even in that house, but in a shed, and a manger. How then wilt thou be able to behold Him, not having beauty that is desirable in His eyes, not wearing the array that is lovely before Him, but what is hateful. For he that cometh unto Him must not deck himself out with such garments, but be clothed with virtue.

Consider what after all these jewels are. Nothing else than earth and ashes. Mix water with them, and they are clay. Consider and be ashamed to make clay thy master, forsaking all, and abiding by it, and carrying and bearing it about, even when thou enterest into a church, when most of all thou oughtest to flee from it. For neither for this cause was the church built, that thou shouldest display therein these riches, but spiritual riches. But thou, as though thou wert entering into a pompous procession, thus deckest thyself out on every side, imitating the women on the stage, even so dost thou carry about in profusion that ridiculous mass.

Therefore, I tell thee, thou comest for mischief to many, and when the congregation is dismissed, in their houses, at their tables, one may hear the more part describing these things. For they have left off saying, thus and thus said the prophet and the apostle, and they describe the costliness of your garments, the size of your precious stones, and all the other unseemliness of them that wear these things.

This makes you backward in almsgiving, and your husbands. For one of you would not readily consent to break up one of these ornaments to feed a poor man. For when thou wouldest choose even thyself to be in distress rather than to behold these things broken to pieces, how shouldest thou feed another at the cost of them?

34

For most women feel towards these things, as to some living beings, and not less than towards their children. "God forbid," thou sayest. Prove me this then, prove it by your works, as now at least I see the contrary. For who ever of those that are completely taken captive, by melting down these things, would rescue a child's soul from death? And why do I say a child's? Who hath redeemed his own soul thereby, when perishing? Nay, on the contrary, the more part even set it to sale for these things every day. And should any bodily infirmity take place, they do everything, but if they see their soul depraved, they take no such pains, but are careless both about their children's soul, and their own soul, in order that these things may remain to rust with time.

And whilst thou art wearing jewels worth ten thousand talents, the member of Christ hath not the enjoyment so much as of necessary food. And whereas the common Lord of all hath imparted to all alike of heaven, and of the things in Heaven, and of the spiritual table, thou dost not impart to Him even of perishing things, on purpose that thou mayest continue perpetually bound with these grievous chains.

Hence the countless evils,[1] hence the fornications of the men, when ye prepare them to cast off self-restraint, when ye teach them to take delight in these things with which the harlot women deck themselves. For this cause they are so quickly taken captive. For if thou hadst instructed him to look down upon these things, and to take delight in chastity, godly fear and humility, he would not have been so easily taken by the shafts[2] of fornication. For the harlot is able to adorn herself in this way even to a greater degree than this, but with those other ornaments not so. Accustom him then to take delight in these ornaments, which he cannot see placed on the harlot. And how wilt thou bring him into this habit? If thou take off these, and put on those others, so shall both thy husband be in safety, and thou in honor, and God will be propitious to you, and all men will admire you, and ye will attain unto the good things to come, by the grace and love towards man of our Lord Jesus Christ, to whom be glory and might, world without end. Amen.

---

[1] [The Oxford translator inserts here "hence the jealousies," but there is no corresponding phrase in the Greek text.—R.]
[2] πτεροῖς.

HOMILY XC.

MATT. XXVIII. 11—14.

" Now when they were going, behold, some of the watch came into the city, and declared
unto the chief priests all the things that were done.[1]   And when they had assembled
with the elders, and had taken counsel, they gave large money unto the soldiers, saying, Say ye, His disciples came by night, and stole Him away while we slept.   And if
this come to the governor's ears, we will persuade him, and secure you."

FOR the sake of these soldiers that earthquake took place, in order to dismay them,
and that the testimony might come from
them, which accordingly was the result.   For
the report was thus free from suspicion, as
proceeding from the guards themselves.   For
of the signs some were displayed publicly to
the world, others privately to those present on
the spot; publicly for the world was the darkness, privately the appearance of the angel,
the earthquake.   When then they came and
showed it (for truth shines forth, being proclaimed by its adversaries), they again gave
money, that they might say, as it is expressed,
" that His disciples came and stole Him."

How did they steal Him?   O most foolish
of all men!   For because of the clearness and
conspicuousness of the truth, they are not
even able to make up a falsehood.   For indeed what they said was highly incredible,
and the falsehood had not even speciousness.
For how, I ask, did the disciples steal Him,
men poor and unlearned, and not venturing
so much as to show themselves?   What? was
not a seal put upon it?   What? were there not
so many watchmen, and soldiers, and Jews
stationed round it?   What? did not those men
suspect this very thing, and take thought,
and break their rest, and continue anxious
about it?   And wherefore moreover did they
steal it?   That they might feign the doctrine
of the resurrection?   And how should it enter
their minds to feign such a thing, men who
were well content to be hidden and to live?
And how could they remove the stone that
was made sure?   how could they have escaped
the observation of so many?   Nay, though
they had despised death, they would not have
attempted without purpose, and fruitlessly to
venture in defiance of so many who were on
the watch.   And that moreover they were
timorous, what they had done before showed

clearly, at least, when they saw Him seized,
all rushed away from Him.   If then at that
time they did not dare so much as to stand
their ground when they saw Him alive, how
when He was dead could they but have feared
such a number of soldiers?   What? was it to
burst open a door?   Was it that one should
escape notice?   A great stone lay upon it,
needing many hands to move it.

They were right in saying, " So the last
error shall be worse than the first,"[3] making
this declaration against themselves, for that,
when after so much mad conduct they ought
to have repented, they rather strive to outdo
their former acts, feigning absurd fictions,
and as, when He was alive, they purchased
His blood, so when He was dead and risen
again, they again by money were striving to
undermine the evidence of His resurrection.
But do thou mark, I pray thee, how by their
own doings they are caught everywhere.   For
if they had not come to Pilate, nor asked for
the guard, they would have been more able to
act thus impudently, but as it was, not so.
For indeed, as though they were laboring to
stop their own mouths, even so did they all
things.   For if the disciples had not strength
to watch with Him, and that, though upbraided
by Him, how could they have ventured upon
these things?   And wherefore did they not
steal Him before this, but when ye were
come?   For if they had been minded to do
this, they would have done it, when the tomb
was not yet guarded on the first night, when
it was to be done without danger, and in security.   For it was on the Sabbath that they
came and begged of Pilate to have the watch,
and kept guard, but during the first night
none of these was present by the sepulchre.

2.   And what mean also the napkins that
were stuck on with the myrrh; for Peter saw
these lying.   For if they had been disposed
to steal, they would not have stolen the body

---

[1] [R. V., " come to pass."]
[2] [R. V., " and rid you of care." The entire passage is in verbal agreement with the received text.—R.]

[3] Matt. xxvii. 64.

naked, not because of dishonoring it only, but in order not to delay and lose time in stripping it, and not to give them that were so disposed opportunity to awake and seize them. Especially when it was myrrh, a drug that adheres so to the body, and cleaves to the clothes, whence it was not easy to take the clothes off the body, but they that did this needed much time, so that from this again, the tale of the theft is improbable.

What? did they not know the rage of the Jews? and that they would vent their anger on them? And what profit was it at all to them, if He had not risen again?

So these men, being conscious that they had made up all this tale, gave money, and said, "Say ye these things, and we will persuade the governor." For they desire that the report should be published, fighting in vain against the truth; and by their endeavors to obscure it, by these even against their will they occasioned it to appear clearly. For indeed even this establishes the resurrection, the fact I mean of their saying, that the disciples stole Him. For this is the language of men confessing, that the body was not there. When therefore they confess the body was not there, but the stealing it is shown to be false and incredible, by their watching by it, and by the seals, and by the timidity of the disciples, the proof of the resurrection even hence appears incontrovertible.

Nevertheless, these shameless and audacious men, although there were so many things to stop their mouths, "Say ye," these are their words, "and we will persuade, and will secure you." Seest thou all depraved? Pilate, for he was persuaded? the soldiers? the Jewish people? But marvel not, if money prevailed over soldiers. For if with His disciple it showed its might to be so great, much more with these.

"And this saying is commonly reported," it is said, "until this day."[1] Seest thou again the disciples' love of truth, how they are not ashamed of saying even this, that such a report prevailed against them.

"Then the eleven disciples went away into Galilee, and some worshipped, and some when they saw Him doubted."[2]

This seems to me to be the last appearance in Galilee, when He sent them forth to baptize. And if "some doubted," herein again admire their truthfulness, how they conceal not even their shortcomings up to the last

day. Nevertheless, even these are assured by their sight.

What then saith He unto them, when He seeth them? "All power is given unto me in heaven and on earth."[3] Again He speaketh to them more after the manner of man, for they had not yet received the spirit, which was able to raise them on high. "Go ye, make disciples of all nations, baptizing them in the name of the Father, and of the Son, and of the Holy Ghost: teaching them to observe all things whatsoever I have commanded you;"[4] giving the one charge with a view to doctrine, the other concerning commandments. And of the Jews He makes no mention, neither brings forward what had been done, nor upbraids Peter with his denial, nor any one of the others with their flight, but having put into their hands a summary of the doctrine, that expressed by the form of baptism, commands them to pour forth over the whole world.

After that, because he had enjoined on them great things, to raise their courage, He says, "Lo! I am with you alway, even unto the end of the world."[5] Seest thou His own proper power again? Seest thou how those other things also were spoken for condescension? And not with those men only did He promise to be, but also with all that believe after them. For plainly the apostles were not to remain here unto "the end of the world;" but he speaks to the believers as to one body. For tell me not, saith He, of the difficulty of the things: for "I am with you," who make all things easy. This He said to the prophets also in the Old Testament continually, as well to Jeremiah objecting his youth,[6] as to Moses[7] and Ezekiel[8] shrinking from the office, "I am with you," this here also to these men. And mark, I pray thee, the excellence of these, for the others, when sent to one nation, often excused themselves, but these said nothing of the sort, though sent to the world. And He reminds them also of the consummation, that He may draw them on more, and that they may look not at the present dangers only, but also at the good things to come that are without end.

"For the irksome things, saith He, that ye will undergo are finished together with the present life, since at least even this world itself shall come to an end, but the good things which ye shall enjoy remain immortal, as I have often told you before." Thus having

[1] Matt. xxviii. 15. [R. V., "was spread abroad.' The phrase "among the Jews" is omitted, and ἡμέρας is added, as in the Vatican MS., and Vulgate.—R.]
[2] Matt. xxviii. 16, 17. [The citation is abridged and altered. —R.]

[3] Matt. xxviii. 18. [The citation is accurate. R. V., "All authority hath been given," etc.]
[4] Matt. xxviii. 18, 19. [οὖν is omitted, as in many MSS. R. V., "make disciples of all the nations, baptizing them into," etc. . . . "whatsoever I commanded you."—R.]   [5] Matt. xxviii. 20.
[6] Jer. i. 6, 8.   [7] Exod. iv. 10, 12.   [8] Ezek. ii. and iii.

invigorated and roused their minds, by the remembrance of that day, He sent them forth. For that day to them that live in good works is to be desired, even as on the other hand to those in sin, it is terrible as to the condemned.

But let us not fear only, and shudder, but let us change too, while there is opportunity, and let us rise out of our wickedness, for we can, if we be willing. For if before grace many did this, much more after grace.

3. For what grievous things are we enjoined? to cleave mountains asunder? to fly into the air? or to cross the Tuscan sea? By no means, but a way of life so easy, as not so much as to want any instruments, but a soul and purpose only. For what instruments had these apostles, who effected such things? Did they not go about with one vestment and unshod? and they got the better of all.

For what is difficult of the injunctions? Have no enemy. Hate no man. Speak ill of no man. Nay, the opposites of these things are the greater hardships. But He said, you reply, Throw away thy money. Is this then the grievous thing? In the first place, He did not command, but advised it. Yet even if it were a command, what is it grievous not to carry about burdens and unseasonable cares?

But oh covetousness! All things are become money; for this cause all things are turned upside down. If any one declares another happy, he mentions this; should he pronounce him wretched, hence is derived the description of wretchedness. And all reckonings are made on this account, how such an one gets rich, how such an one gets poor. Should it be military service, should it be marriage, should it be a trade, should it be what you will that any man takes in hand, he does not apply to what is proposed, until he see these riches are coming in rapidly upon him. After this shall we not meet together and consult how we shall drive away this pest? Shall we not regard with shame the good deeds of our fathers? of the three thousand, of the five thousand, who had all things common?

What is the profit of this present life, when we do not use it for our future gain? How long do ye not enslave the mammon that hath enslaved you? How long are ye slaves of money? How long have ye no love for liberty, and do not rend in pieces the bargains of covetousness? But while, if ye should have become slaves of men, you do all things, if any one should promise you liberty; yet being captives of covetousness, ye do not so much

as consider how ye may be delivered from this bitter bondage. And yet the one were nothing terrible, the other is the most bitter tyranny.

Consider how great a price Christ paid for us. He shed His own blood; He gave up Himself. But ye, even after all this, are grown supine; and the most grievous thing of all is, that ye even take delight in the slavery, ye luxuriate in the dishonor, and that, from which ye ought to flee, is become an object of desire to you.

But since it is right not only to lament and to blame, but also to correct, let us see from what cause this passion and this evil have become an object of desire to you. Whence then, whence hath this come to be an object of desire? Because, thou sayest, it makes me to be in honor and in security. In what kind of security, I pray thee? In the confidence, not to suffer hunger, nor cold, not to be harmed, not to be despised. Wilt thou then, if we promise thee this security, refrain from being rich? For if it is for this that riches are an object of desire, if it be in your power to have security without these, what need hast thou of these any more? "And how is it possible," thou sayest, "for one who is not rich to attain to this?" Nay, how is it possible (for I say the opposite thing) if one is rich? For it is necessary to flatter many, both rulers and subjects, and to entreat countless numbers, and to be a base slave, and to be in fear and trembling, and to regard with suspicion the eyes of the envious, and to fear the tongues of false accusers, and the desires of other covetous men. But poverty is not like this, but altogether the contrary. It is a place of refuge and security, a calm harbor, a wrestling ground, and school of exercise to learn self-command, an imitation of the life of angels.

Hear these things, as many as are poor; or rather also, as many as desire to be rich. It is not poverty that is the thing to be feared, but the not being willing to be poor. Account poverty to be nothing to fear, and it will not be to thee a matter for fear. For neither is this fear in the nature of the thing, but in the judgment of feeble-minded men. Or rather, I am even ashamed that I have occasion to say so much concerning poverty, to show that it is nothing to be feared. For if thou practise self-command, it is even a fountain to thee of countless blessings. And if any one were to offer thee sovereignty, and political power, and wealth, and luxury, and then having set against them poverty, were to give thee thy choice to take which thou wouldest, thou wouldest straightway seize upon poverty, if indeed thou knewest the beauty thereof.

4. And I know that many laugh, when these things are said; but we are not troubled; but we require you to stay, and soon ye will give judgment with us. For to me poverty seems like some comely, fair, and well-favored damsel, but covetousness like some monster shaped woman, some Scylla or Hydra, or some other like prodigies feigned by fabulous writers.

For bring not forward, I pray thee, them that accuse poverty, but them that have shone thereby. Nurtured in this, Elias was caught up in that blessed assumption. With this Eliseus shone; with this John; with this all the apostles; but with the other, Ahab, Jezebel, Gehazi, Judas, Nero, Caiaphas, were condemned.

But if it please you, let us not look to those only that have been glorious in poverty, but let us observe the beauty itself of this damsel. For indeed her eye is clear and piercing, having nothing turbid in it, like the eye of covetousness, which is at one time full of anger, at another sated with pleasure, at another troubled by incontinence. But the eye of poverty is not like this, but mild, calm, looking kindly on all, meek, gentle, hating no man, shunning no man. For where there are riches, there is matter for enmity, and for countless wars. The mouth again of the other is full of insults, of a certain haughtiness, of much boasting, cursing, deceit; but the mouth and the tongue of this are sound, filled with continual thanksgiving, blessing, words of gentleness, of affection, of courtesy, of praise, of commendation. And if thou wouldest see also the proportion of her members, she is of a goodly height, and far loftier than wealth. And if many flee from her, marvel not at it, for indeed so do fools from the rest of virtue.

But the poor man, thou wilt say, is insulted by him that is rich. Again thou art declaring to me the praise of poverty. For who, I pray thee, is blessed, the insulter, or the insulted? It is manifest that it is the insulted person. But then, the one, covetousness, urges to insult the other; poverty persuades to endure. "But the poor man suffers hunger," thou wilt say. Paul also suffered hunger, and was in famine.[1] "But he has no rest." Neither "had the Son of Man where to lay His head."[2]

Seest thou how far the praises of poverty have proceeded, and where it places thee, to what men it leads thee on, and how it makes thee a follower of the Lord? If it were good to have gold, Christ, who gave the unutterable blessings, would have given this to His disciples. But now so far from giving it them, He forbad them to have it. Wherefore Peter also, so far from being ashamed of poverty, even glories in it, saying, "Silver and gold have I none; but what I have give I thee."[3] And who of you would not have desired to utter this saying? Nay, we all would extremely, perhaps some one may say. Then throw away thy silver, throw away thy gold. "And if I throw it away, thou wilt say, shall I receive the power of Peter?" Why, what made Peter blessed, tell me? Was it indeed to have lifted up the lame man? By no means, but the not having these riches, this procured him Heaven. For of those that wrought these miracles, many fell into hell, but they, who did those good things, attained a kingdom. And this you may learn even of Peter himself. For there were two things that he said, "Silver and gold have I none;" and, "In the name of Jesus Christ rise up and walk."

Which sort of thing then made Him glorious and blessed, the raising up the lame man, or the casting away his money? And this you may learn from the Master of the conflicts Himself. What then doth He Himself say to the rich man seeking eternal life? He said not, "raise up the lame," but, "Sell thy goods, and give to the poor, and come and follow me, and thou shalt have treasure in Heaven."[4] And Peter again said not, "Behold, in Thy name we cast out devils;" although he was casting them out, but, "Behold, we have forsaken all and followed Thee what shall we have?"[5] And Christ again, in answering this apostle, said not, "If any man raise up the lame," but, "Whosoever hath forsaken houses or lands, shall receive an hundredfold in this world, and shall inherit everlasting life."[6]

Let us also then emulate this man, that we may not be confounded, but may with confidence stand at the judgment-seat of Christ; that we may win Him to be with us, even as He was with His disciples. For He will be with us, like as He was with them, if we are willing to follow them, and to be imitators of their life and conversation. For in consequence of these things God crowns, and commends men, not requiring of thee to raise the dead, or to cure the lame. For not these things make one to be like Peter, but the

---

[1] 1 Cor. iv. 11 ; 2 Cor. xi. 27 ; Phil. iv. 12.   [2] Matt. viii. 20.

[3] Acts iii. 6.   [4] Matt. xix. 21.
[5] Matt. xix. 27.   [6] Matt. xix. 29. [Abridged.]

casting away one's goods, for this was the apostles' achievement.

But dost thou not find it possible to cast them away? In the first place, I say, it is possible; but I compel thee not, if thou art not willing, nor constrain thee to it; but this I entreat, to spend at least a part on the needy, and to seek for thyself nothing more than is necessary. For thus shall we both live our life here without trouble, and in security, and enjoy eternal life; unto which God grant we all may attain, by the grace and love towards man of our Lord Jesus Christ, to whom be glory and might, together with the Father and the Holy Ghost, now and always, and world without end. Amen.

INDEXES

INDEX OF SUBJECTS

cil of, 33; destruction of, foretold, 422.

Jesus, mysteries in the name of, 25.

Jewels, shewn useless, 529.

Jews, the, account of their unbelief, 15, 76, 87, 119, 273, 406; their pride of birth, 16; gained nothing from Abraham, 59, 69; envious disposition of, 43 ; reproved by Heathens, 38; were first favored in the gospel, 45, 422; yet outrun by the Gentiles, 47; said, and did not, 167; confusion of, 170; unthankful, 175; convicted by their inconsistency, 246; punishment of, foretold, 275, 395, 415, 421 ; blindness of, proved wilful, 284 ; asked no right questions, 246, 286, 292 ; final conversion of, by Elijah, 353; how to be judged by the apostles, 392; craft of, 410; cowardice of, 411; how bidden, 421; their troubles from God, 451; hated by all, 452; why to flee, 457; how much and why punished, 457; madness of, against Christ, 477. 506, 516; government of, changed, 482 ; how broke the Passover, and why, 503, 512; perverted justice in the trial of Christ, 503, 511 ; resisted all warning, 508, 513, yet not all reprobated, 513; sole authors of the Passion, 516 ; used all cruelties, 516 ; how convicted themselves, 525. (See Pharisees.)

Job, patience of, 84; righteous, 107; bore all but reproach, 96; charitable interference of, 101; not a slave to wealth, 147, 225; virtues of, eminent, 224, under special disadvantages, 225, as compared with other saints, 225 ; prevailed by his piety, without miracle, 290; trials of, ordered by God, 192, 310.

John, the Baptist, humility of, 19; time of his preaching, 61; why sent, 62; how baptized for Remission, 62; how prepared for Christ, 63; effect of his preaching, 63, 65; austerity of, 64; great before grace, 65 ; why did no miracles, 87; disciples of, envious of Christ's, 201; message of, explained, 238; how predicted the Cross, 240; equalled the prophets in knowledge, 240 ; clear from charge of fickleness by Christ, 243; stood between the law and the gospel, 244; his system contrasted with Christ's, 246; murder of, how aggravated, 300; in what sense, Elias, 353.

John, the Evangelist, purpose of his Gospel, to establish the Godhead, 3 (note) ; not jealous of Peter after Pentecost, 401; why did not speak of the destruction of Jerusalem, 458 ; the most spiritual in doctrine, 482.

Joseph, an example of forgiveness, 381, of self-denial, 505; a type of Christ, 505.

Joseph, the husband of Mary, genealogy of, why traced, 6, 11, 14 ; his descent from David proved by his marriage, 11; his espousals were to shelter the Virgin, 15; his conduct proved the miraculous birth, 23 ; encouraged to adopt the Child, 25; referred to the prophets, 32 ; praised for self-restraint, 23, and for obedience, 33.

Joseph, of Arimathæa, emboldened by the Cross, 522.

Josephus, to be believed, because a zealous Jew, 457.

Judah, incest of, why mentioned in the Gospel, 15, 17.

Judas, ruined by avarice, 61, 193, 482, 488; irritated by reproach, 96 ; had received grace, 168; had been once elect, 392; hardness of, 482, 499; deaf to all warning, 482; not excused by predestination, 486; utter ruin of, 508; downward progress of, 514.

Judgment, of others blamed, 397; of our own soul, commended, 271.

Judgment, The, why compared to threshing, 72; certainty of, 86; day of, a theatre, 132; suddenness of, 146; will be equitable to all, 242; foreseen by Isaiah, 260 ; is partly present, partly future, 267; fairness of, 270; expectation of, in the early church, 342; why named in the Monks' Grace, 342 ; shewn in the Transfiguration, 349 ; how to be thought of, 460; how proved, 462 ; why hidden, 465 ; not really delayed, 466 ; justice of, shown, 476.

Julian, miracles in the time of, 21.

KINGDOM, the, rewards, guides, and wars of 6; glories of, 7; a New Polity, begun at the Baptism of Jesus, 44; shown to be distant, 458; is our inheritance, 476; yet of grace, 477.

LABOR, pleasantness of, 331.

Lamech, what the sin of, 446.

Landlords, oppressions of, 377.

Laughter, excess of, reproved, 26, 41.

Law, the, given in terrors, 2, 8; was typified in Phares, 16, 17; given in consequence of Gentile grossness, 38; ceased at the Baptism of Christ, 78 ; enlarged by Christ, 103; with new sanctions, 106 ; how fulfilled by Christ, 107, 108; not evil, though defective, 107 ; retaliation of, really merciful, 109, 123; how permitted evil, 120; an education for the gospel, 121; re-

spected by Christ in His charge to the leper, 173; abrogation of, hinted by Christ, 316, 329, 458; how hangs on love, 431 ; put for the whole Old Testament, 435 ; in morals confirmed, in ceremonials repealed, 436, 441; how measured punishments, 455; rites of, when ceased, 491.

Life, inequalities of, solved by the doctrine of a judgment, 86, 461; a prison, 90; full of joy as of sorrow, 330; different ages, and sins of, 490.

Lord's Day, the, how to be spent, 31; little improved, 73.

Luke, addresses heathens, 4 ; his genealogy fuller than Matthew's, 7 ; imitates the style of Paul, 20 ; added to Matthew's account, 24, 96, 178, 201, 205, 206, 471.

Lust, a possession of the Devil, 193; leads to cruelty, 300; how best cured, 371; comes of drunkenness, 429 ; invites Devils, 430; forbidden in thought, 515.

Luxury, why compared to thorns, 283; in feasting reproved, 301, and in dress, 307; pain of, 330; lust the cause of, 356; destructiveness of, 430; sin of, 467.

Lysias, compared with Pilate, 512.

MACCABEES, praise of the, 241.

Macedonians, heresy of the, 77.

Manichæans, heresy of the, 108, 181, 305, 317, 343. (See Creatures.)

Marcion, heresy of, 47, 252, 274, 492.

Marriage, Jewish law of, 11, 12, 22, 25, 428; a great mystery, 42; duties of, 49; protected by Christ, 119; law of, explained by Christ, 382; prudent, in youth, 371; abuse of, 443.

Martyrs, the, the real conquerors, 505.

Mary the Virgin, the parents of, not named by Matthew, 6, 11, 12; protected by her marriage, 15, 22; character of, considered in the Annunciation, 24; the perpetual virginity of, not contradicted by Matthew, 33; made illustrious by her stay in Egypt, 53; vanity of, reproved, 279.

Mary, of Bethany, promise to, 314; the faith of, 486; fame of, 481; an example of liberality in church offerings, 482.

Matthew, the humble condition and high graces of, 2; wrote in Hebrew for the Jews, 3; Christ spoke in, 6; difficulties of, 6; wrote before Mark, 20; call of, 198; how trained by Christ, 205; virtues of, 295; candor of, 345.

Meats, question of, indirectly settled, 317; Christ's law of, 318; Manichæan doctrine of, reproved, 343.

Pharisees, design of the, against John, 68; righteousness of, real, but defective, 107; ignorant of the scriptures, 201; how "wise and prudent," 251; enraged with the disciples, 255, with Christ's healing, 259, on account of envy, 265; false sons of Abraham, 269; why they asked, and were refused a sign, 273, 328–29; unbelief of, foreseen, 274; self-convicted of adding to the law, 350; of breaking it, by Christ, 350; by Isaiah, 351; why put questions often, 381; never abashed, 388; gave a third of their goods in charity; never repented, 412, 426; vainglory of, 433, 437, 441, 446; when in real authority, supported by Christ, 436; yet rebuked for hardness, 437; corrupters of youth, 440; whence ruined, 442; how worse than their fathers, 444. (See Jews.)

Pharisee, the proud, lost for want of humility and charity, 17, 92, 396, in spite of almsgiving, 396.

Philistines, the, taught the truth by the heifers, 39.

Philosophers, the Grecian, doctrines of, unnatural and devilish, 5; despised by Christians, 54; despised externals, 59, 100; contrasted with John the Baptist, 65; a shame to evil Christians, 100; contrasted with the apostles, 222.

Pilate, character of, compared to that of Lysias, 512.

Plato, the Republic of, censured, 5; and contrasted with Christ's, 6.

Pleasure, when innocent, 250; of labor, 331.

Plotinous, his doctrine of souls refuted, 191.

Poor, the, ill-treatment of, censured, 236; represented by the apostles, 391; only a tenth part of the population, 407; how Christ's brethren, and ours, 475.

Poverty, a furnace, 29; outward and inward care of, 30; of the rich man in torment, 60; praise of voluntary, 92; Christ's gradual training for, 150; real lightness of, 254; glory and reward of, 295–6; real dignity of, 500, 532.

Praise, danger of, 96; love of, a snare, 263.

Prayer, for others, not always effectual, 34, 374; requires perseverance, 67, 155; never unreasonable, 156; Christ's rule of, 132; forgiveness, the special moral of the Lord's, 137; enjoined after hard commands, 160; two conditions of, 161; a remedy for sin, 268; requires purity of tongue, and of heart, 319; Hezekiah's, 331; blessedness of concord in, 374.

Preaching, a school, 73; why necessary, 523.

Predestination, no excuse for Judas, 486; objections from, how answered, 487.

Profaneness, censure of, 74; sin of listening to, 248.

Promises, the, of Christ always conditional, 392.

Prophets, the, why appealed to personal revelations, 20; disregarded by the Jews, 38; of the Philistines, seconded by God, 39; maintained the doctrine of Providence, 57; the works of some lost, 58 (note); anticipated the history of John, 64; rebuked pride, 68; double sense of, 72; persecution of, 95; how fulfilled by Christ, 104; confirmed by miracle, 180; accuracy of, 260, 406; all had wives, 344.

Providence, doctrine of, maintained by the prophets, 57; urged by Christ to console the apostles, 228.

Psalms, study of, profitable, but neglected, 13; chanted in the church, 73.

Publican, the, saved by penitence, 198; a lesson not to despair, 449.

Publicans, the, virtue of, a shame to Christians, 128; trade of, mean, 199; why Christ sat with, 200; wickedness of, proved, 373; comparative obedience of, 422.

Punishment, scale of, under the gospel, 111; under the law, 455; two kinds of, 373.

Purification, the, waited for by Mary, 58; law of, enlarged by the Pharisees, 314–5; must be inward, 319.

Purity, blessing of, 94; required for prayer, 319; Christ's law of, 441.

RABBI, title of, why forbidden, 438.

Rahab, why mentioned in the genealogy, 17.

Reconciliation, religious duty of, 112, 478.

Regeneration, by the Spirit in baptism, asserted, 10, 41, 62, 78.

Relapse after baptism, dangerous, 276; how to be recovered, 467.

Repentance, blessed in Hannah, 41; good works, a great part of, 66; more needful than bodily cure, 89; why ought to be painful, 89; not be had after death, 90, 241; proved not in vain, by the example of David, 182; its power to avert wrath, shown in the Ninevites, 392; striking example of, at Antioch, 412; of Manasseh, Paul, and others, 413; its labor small, its gain great, 414; accepted in believing Jews, 513.

Repetitions, when forbidden in

prayer, 133; why used in Holy Scripture, 498.

Reproach, the greatest trial, 96; effect of, on Job and others, 96; when undeserved and for Christ's sake, alone glorious, 99; overcome by virtue, 99; endured by Christ, 380.

Reserve, examples of, in Christ's life and teaching: in the Nativity, 10; in the Incarnation, 14, 15, 44; in the Epiphany, 52; in His early life, 63; in John's report of Him, 71; in the temptation, 82; commanded in the Sermon, 159; in retiring from the Gergesenes, 193; from the Scribes, 198; in teaching the resurrection and other mysteries, 202; in doing miracles, 207; in delaying to heal, 210; after sending out the Twelve, 238; how long continued, 260, 345; before Pilate, 511.

Restitution, duty of, 326.

Resurrection, the, truth of, argued from reason, 85–6; shown in the raising of Jairus's daughter, and Lazarus, 206; proved real by the history of Jonah, 273; shown in the parable of the marriage feast, 421; why denied by the Sadducees, 428; how contained in the Old Testament, 429; foretasted by the monks, 429; should be rejoiced at by Christians, 460; natural emblems of, 462, 472; to be at night, 470; our best support in trouble, 479; how most commonly proved, 492.

Resurrection of Christ, proved by men's faith, 34; reserve in teaching the, 202; foretold by John, 240; signs of the, 521; how proved by the Jews' behavior, 525, and by that of the apostles, 526; why so early in the day, 526; witnessed by the guard, 530.

Revenge, sinfulness of, 271; reasons against, 478.

Reviling, the author of, suffers most, 320; may be borne, by the example of Christ, 380; brings to hell, 395.

Reward, of Christians certain, 85; is both spiritual, 95, and temporal, 96; partly given here, 169; accumulation of, in Isaiah, 337; will be given impartially, 402; of God's grace, not our merit, 476.

Riches, contempt of, the true wealth, 30, 35; taught gradually by Christ, 142; dependence on, unsafe, 60; disquiet of keeping, 142; peril of pursuing, 144; love of, unnatural, 144, 320; how overcome, 145; cast out of God's service, 146; compared with charity, 166; love of, condemned in the rich young man,

INDEX OF TEXTS

N.B. These passages in Matthew are quoted incidentally, *in addition* to the general Commentary.